HAWAIIAN ISLANDS

KEVIN WHITTON

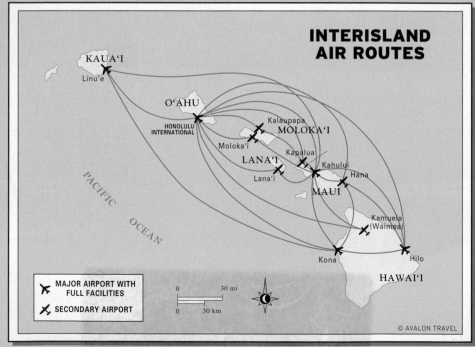

INTERISLAND
AIR ROUTES

KAUA'I
Linu'e

O'AHU
HONOLULU
INTERNATIONAL

Moloka'i

Kalaupapa
MOLOKA'I

LANA'I

Kapalua

Kahului

Lana'i

Hana

MAUI

PACIFIC

OCEAN

Kamuela
(Waimea)

Kona

Hilo

HAWAI'I

✈ **MAJOR AIRPORT WITH
FULL FACILITIES**

✕ **SECONDARY AIRPORT**

0   30 mi

0   30 km

© AVALON TRAVEL

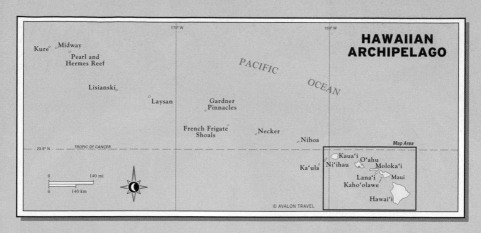

HAWAIIAN ARCHIPELAGO

Kure   Midway
Pearl and
Hermes Reef

Lisianski

PACIFIC
OCEAN

170° W   160° W

Laysan   Gardner
Pinnacles

French Frigate   Necker
Shoals   Nihoa

23.5° N   TROPIC OF CANCER

Ka'ula

0   140 mi
0   140 km

© AVALON TRAVEL

Map Area

Kaua'i   O'ahu
Ni'ihau   Moloka'i
Lana'i   Maui
Kaho'olawe
Hawai'i

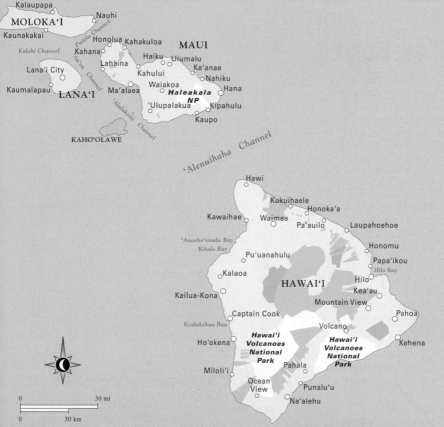

Kalaupapa

MOLOKA'I   Nauhi

Kaunakakai

Kalohi Channel

Pailolo Channel

Honolua   Kahakuloa   MAUI
Kahana
Lana'i City   Lahaina   Haiku   Ulumalu
Ke'anae
Kahului   Nahiku
Kaumalapau   Ma'alaea   Waiakoa   Hana
LANA'I   Haleakala
'Ulupalakua   NP   Kipahulu
Au'au Channel
Kaupo
'Alalakeiki Channel

KAHO'OLAWE

'Alenuihaha Channel

Hawi

Kukuihaele
Honoka'a
Kawaihae   Waimea
Pa'auilo   Laupahoehoe
'Anaeho'omalu Bay
Kiholo Bay   Honomu
Pu'uanahulu   Papa'ikou
Hilo Bay
Kalaoa   HAWAI'I   Hilo
Kea'au
Kailua-Kona   Mountain View
Captain Cook   Pahoa
Volcano
Kealakekua Bay   Kehena
Hawai'i   Hawai'i
Ho'okena   Volcanoes   Volcanoes
National   National
Park   Park
Miloli'i   Pahala
Ocean
View   Punalu'u
Na'alehu

0   30 mi
0   30 km

© AVALON TRAVEL

Contents

Hawaiian Islands

Escape the world you know in Hawaii. Wander beautiful stretches of white sand. Swim in warm, crystal-clear water. Explore colorful reefs teeming with marine life. Lose yourself under a canopy of tropical rainforest. Cool off in passing rain showers and enjoy the rainbows that follow them.

One source of Hawaii's appeal is the diversity of the islands. As the most isolated archipelago on the planet, Hawaii is a place of geologic and biological extremes and a living experiment in evolution. Active volcanoes and erosion continually redefine a land populated by myriad endemic and native plant species found nowhere else on earth. The islands are also a true cultural melting pot. Their rich agricultural promise has attracted immigrants from all over the globe, contributing to Hawaii's eclectic cultural heritage, cuisine, and lifestyle. At the heart of Hawaii's ambiance is aloha, a gift of hospitality from native Hawaiian tradition that resonates among all who live and travel here. Aloha brings with it a deeply ingrained reverence for nature: a respect for the land, the ocean, family, and friends.

Though tied together by statehood, each island offers a world of its own. O'ahu is the Gathering Place, where big-city pleasures overlap with tropical adventure. Maui is dominated by endless beaches. The Big Island of Hawai'i is a primal wonderland, with barren lava fields alongside fertile forests and farmland. Kaua'i is the Garden Isle, where verdant cliffsides plummet into the sea below. And secluded Moloka'i and Lana'i offer a journey back in time to Old Hawaii.

How can you choose just one? It's possible to explore each of these worlds, with all of their diverse charms—especially if you're the kind of traveler who can't stay put for too long. Island-hopping is an art, not a science: an opportunity to make your own way based on what you want to see and do. A strategically planned two-week itinerary offers you the chance to visit all of the main islands. With one week, it's possible to explore two islands at a slightly slower pace. Read on to discover the treasures of all of the islands for yourself.

Planning Your Trip

Where to Go

O'AHU

Home to world-famous Waikiki as well as 70 percent of the state's population, O'ahu is the marriage of big city and tropical paradise. Enjoy all the comforts of city life, including diverse culture and nightlife, alongside verdant mountains and crystal-clear water. State capital Honolulu is home to historical sites like 'Iolani Palace, the only royal residence in the United States, and World War II pilgrimage site Pearl Harbor. Legendary surf pounds the coast for much of the winter, while the summer offers magnificent diving. You can spend the morning sightseeing in downtown Honolulu, surrounded by crowds of people, but be on a secluded beach by noon, surrounded only by crashing waves.

MAUI, LANA'I, AND MOLOKA'I

The second largest island, Maui is lined with endless, accessible sandy beaches, especially along the south and west shores. With ample accommodations, Maui offers the complete resort experience, but much more spread out than the cluster of hotels in Waikiki. Maui is also the best island for whale watching and the windiest island— making it a mecca for windsurfers. The Road to Hana is Maui's most popular attraction: a winding drive to a sleepy town in a lush setting. A quick ferry ride or plane flight away, the islands of Moloka'i and Lana'i offer secluded getaways—and glimpses of the Hawaii of yesteryear.

BIG ISLAND OF HAWAI'I

Hawai'i, better known as the Big Island, is a raw and powerful place, the youngest island in geological time. It's the site of Hawai'i Volcanoes National Park, with its barren lava fields and emerging native forests. Snow-capped Mauna Kea is one of the best spots on earth for star gazing, while Mauna Loa remains active and Kilauea has been continuously erupting since 1983. Agriculture still permeates the lives of island residents. Hawaiian cowboys and coffee plantations mix with the spacious resorts that line the dry western coastline.

Set sail from Waikiki.

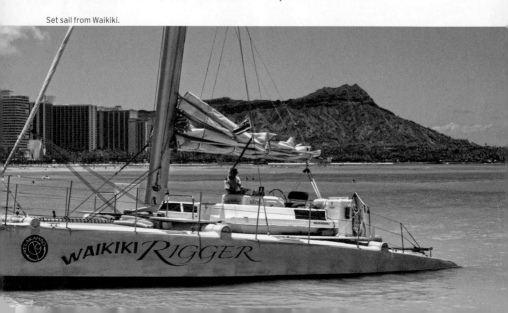

Waimea Canyon

KAUA'I

Kaua'i is known as the Garden Isle for good reason. Its Mount Wai'ale'ale is one of the wettest spots on earth, where waterfalls pour down its vertical walls almost daily. Botanical gardens abound, as does hiking, both along the famous Na Pali Coast and in Waimea Canyon. Accommodations are split between the green north and the sunny south, where resorts, vacation rentals, and golf courses are abundant. Expect romance, freedom, and a slower pace.

When to Go

Hawaii is beautiful all year long, with a comfortable tropical climate that sees ocean and air temperature dip by only a few degrees between summer and winter. While winter and spring are known for more rain, showers and squalls are possible at any time, in any season. Thank the frequent passing showers for the rainbows they leave behind. The predominant trade winds keep the islands fresh and cool. The biggest seasonal difference is the surf. North shores see higher waves in winter (October through March), which produce world-class surf breaks. During this period, the south shore waters are flat, with better conditions for snorkeling and diving. The opposite is true during the summer (May–September), when south shore surf rises, although it's still gentler for beginners.

Before You Go

No need to pack survival gear. No matter which island you're visiting, you'll find all the comforts of modern life. Pack light clothes for the warm, tropical weather. Shorts and slippers are the norm. Bring a hat for sun protection, as well as sunscreen and insect repellent. Binoculars are great for whale watching. A light jacket or cover is all that's necessary for cooler winter nights.

Foreign nationals must have a current passport and most must have a proper visa, an ongoing or return air ticket, and sufficient funds for the proposed stay. Visitors from many countries, including Canada, do not need a visa to enter the United States for 90 days or less. Check in your country of origin to determine your requirements for U.S. entry.

Everyone visiting Hawaii must fill out a Plants and Animals Declaration Form. Items targeted for inspection include fruits, vegetables, plants, seeds, and soil, as well as live insects, seafood, snakes, and amphibians. All pets are subject to 120 days' quarantine, which includes fees for boarding.

Which Island is for You?

If you're interested in...

- **beaches:** Maui
- **nature:** Kaua'i and the Big Island
- **sailing:** O'ahu
- **surfing:** O'ahu and Maui
- **whale-watching:** Maui
- **snorkeling or scuba:** O'ahu, Maui, and Kaua'i
- **hiking:** O'ahu and Kaua'i

- **beachside bars:** O'ahu
- **views:** Kaua'i
- **a family vacation:** Maui
- **romance:** Kaua'i
- **authentic island culture:** the Big Island
- **history:** O'ahu and the Big Island
- **getting away from it all:** Moloka'i and Lana'i

The Two-Week All-Island Trip

You can be forgiven for thinking that the islands are all the same. They're so close to each other and so isolated in the middle of the Pacific. How much could they differ? In fact, each island has its own unique personality, its own geography, plant and bird life, culture, activities, historical sites—and opportunities for new experiences. It's possible to see the best of all the islands in two weeks. If you have more time, follow the advice below to extend your stay to three weeks for full immersion in island living.

O'ahu, Maui, the Big Island, and Kaua'i all have airports servicing international, national, and interisland carriers. So with proper planning, you can begin a multi-week itinerary from any island. However, most national and international flights traffic through Honolulu International Airport, so O'ahu makes a great starting point. Whichever islands you're visiting, it's easy to spend an extra day or two on O'ahu at the beginning or end of your trip.

Getting between the islands is a quick flight: thirty minutes at most. Flight time across the entire state, tip to tip from the Big Island to Kaua'i, is about ninety minutes, although many flights stop for a quick layover on O'ahu. Car rental companies are located at all major airports and each island has ample accommodations. You'll have to pack up camp and get re-situated with each island hop, but it's a small price for enjoying the diversity of the islands.

O'ahu
DAY 1
After arriving on O'ahu, you'll most likely head straight to Waikiki, where most of the island's accommodations are located. Acclimate by swimming and relaxing on the beach. If you're ready for something more active, take surf lessons, go for an outrigger canoe ride, or hike the Diamond Head crater. Treat yourself to a delicious meal at Duke's Waikiki or Sansei Seafood Restaurant and Sushi Bar

surfing at Turtle Bay on O'ahu

and get a good night's rest to adjust for any time difference.

DAY 2

Venture out and explore. Head to the Pearl Harbor historic sites, getting there early to beat the crowd. Heading back into Downtown Honolulu, visit the Historic and Capitol District, where museums and historic buildings abound. End the afternoon with some relaxing beach time. That evening, walk to Chinatown, just a few blocks away, and take in the burgeoning art and food scene. Restaurants, bars, clubs, markets, shops, and art galleries line the streets. Sample the culinary diversity with pizza and beer at J.J. Dolan's, Chinese at Little Village Noodle House, or Cuban fare at Soul De Cuba Cafe.

DAY 3

After breakfast, hop on the freeway and over to the windward side for one of the prettiest drives on the island. Take the coast highway up the windward side to the North Shore. If it's winter, relax at the beach and check out the waves. If it's summer, get in the water and snorkel. Sharks Cove, Three Tables, and Waimea Bay have the most marine life, but will also be the most crowded. Head back through historic Hale'iwa town where you can shop, eat and drink. Hale'iwa Joe's is one of the best restaurants on the North Shore. And don't miss the legendary Matsumoto Shave Ice.

EXTEND YOUR STAY

If you have a few more days to spend on O'ahu, pack your bags and relocate to the North Shore. Consider a stay at Turtle Bay Resort or a vacation rental along the North Shore beaches, where you can really immerse yourself in the beauty of the area. Or stay put in your Waikiki hotel, using it as a base to visit the southeast corner of the island, from Hawai'i Kai to Kailua. Water activities abound in Maunalua Bay, with surf schools, fishing and dive charters, and recreational boating. Koko Crater is home to a dryland botanical garden, there are hikes from Makapu'u to Kailua. Yokohama Bay, at the end of the road on the leeward side, is one of the most pristine and uncrowded spots on the island. It's also the starting point of a hike to Ka'ena Point, where a natural preserve is home to monk seals and seabirds.

Big Island of Hawai'i

DAY 4

You're Big Island bound! If ocean recreation is your priority, fly into Kailua Kona and set up a home base on the leeward side. If the volcanoes are your focus, base yourself in Hilo. Long driving distances separate the coasts, so you'll need to relocate your accommodations from one side to the other and plan your time wisely to see the whole island. Get an early start by exploring the beautiful waters and town of Kailua-Kona. No trip to the area is complete without a visit to the Captain Cook Monument and Kealakekua Bay State Historical Park, which can also serve as a starting point for a kayaking. In the afternoon, visit Amy B.H. Greenwell Ethnobotanical Garden to learn how native Hawaiians farmed the land, then explore the coffee plantations and tasting rooms around Kona. Or relax near your hotel, taking advantage of the sunshine.

DAY 5

Drive north to the Kohala Coast, stopping to enjoy the white sands of Hapuna Beach or the Puako tide pools, one of the best snorkeling spots on the island. In the afternoon, head inland to the upcountry paniolo town of Waimea. Dine at Merriman's Market Café, one of the originators of Hawaii Regional Cuisine. Or head back to the coast to Kawaihae for dinner and dancing at Blue Dragon Coastal Cuisine & Musiquarium. Another option is a prearranged guided tour to the top of Mauna Kea for sunset and star gazing. Stay the night on the Kohala Coast.

DAY 6

Take a scenic drive to beautiful Waipi'o Valley.

Welcome to Hilo, on the Big Island.

Arrange for a scenic tour of the valley or hike down if you're adventurous. Drive along the Hamakua Coast, stopping at Onomea Bay, where a short trail leads down to a beautiful cove. Then drive into Hilo for the farmers market followed by dinner. Try delicious and popular Café Pesto. Stay the night in Hilo.

DAY 7

Today is all about Hawai'i Volcanoes National Park. After about an hour drive from Hilo, you'll enter the park, where you can explore the visitor's center, lava fields, drive around and view and active volcano, and hike through lava tubes and native Hawaiian forests. After a full day in the park, enjoy food and art in Volcano Village before heading back to your hotel in Hilo.

EXTEND YOUR STAY

It's easy to extend a stay on the big island. Just hang tight for more in-depth exploration in the region of your choice. Add a day trip over the Saddle Road between Mauna Kea and Mauna Loa. Or spend more time in Hawai'i Volcanoes National Park, staying overnight at

quaint lodgings in Volcano Village for a full two or more days of exploration.

Maui, Lana'i, and Moloka'i

DAY 8

A change of scenery is in store on Maui, where long stretches of beautiful sandy beaches are the main draw. Stay along in Kihei on the south side or around Ka'anapali on the west side. Greet Maui by soaking up the sun at D.T. Fleming Beach Park or Keawakapu Beach. Enjoy the refreshing water and take a long sunset stroll.

DAY 9

Head upcountry and visit Haleakala, a dormant volcano that dominates all of the views on the island. Drive to the top and hike around, or take a biking tour of the area. Guides can take you to the top to witness sunrise above the clouds, then cycle with you along the windy road down the mountain and through green pastures. Break up your ride with a stop in the upcountry town of Kula. Afterwards, check out Pa'ia, enjoying food and drink at Charley's or Mama's Fish

House. Or head to the old whaling town of Lahaina to explore island history and enjoy dinner at Cilantro or Kimo's.

DAY 10
Take a snorkeling, scuba diving, fishing, or whale-watching tour. Tour operators leave from Lahaina, Maʻalaea Harbor and Kaʻanapali. You can select snorkeling and diving tours to Molokini, Lanaʻi, Molokaʻi, and up and down Maui's coast. Molokini is a must see, but make sure to get the early boat to avoid the crowds. If a secluded beach day is more to your liking, take the ferry to Molokaʻi or Lanaʻi for the day.

DAY 11
Today is the day: Road to Hana. Start off as early as possible. The drive takes at least three hours (from the beginning, just past Hoʻokipa) and you'll want to make lots of stops along the way. Take your time. Hike to waterfalls, eat at a roadside fruit stand, and take lots of pictures. Visit a *heiau* and botanical gardens in Hana, grab lunch from the general store, and find a nook on Paʻiloa Beach to relax and take it all in.

EXTEND YOUR STAY
If you extend your stay on Maui, take the time to enjoy the island at a slower pace. Spend the night in Hana to break up the drive over two days. Or plan on longer side trips to Molokaʻi and Lanaʻi, which are easiest to do from Maui. Or enjoy more beach time at your resort or vacation rental.

Kauaʻi
DAY 12
On Kauaʻi, choose either the North Shore or South Shore as a home base. The South Shore is much sunnier, while the North Shore is lush due to frequent showers. Begin with a beach day at Poʻipu. The National Tropical Botanical Garden and Spouting Horn blowhole nearby are available for exploration. The quaint town of Koloa is a perfect place to grab lunch. After lunch, head into Lihue for a stop at the Kauaʻi Museum and dinner at Duke's on Kalapaki Beach or Gaylord's at the Kilohana Plantation.

spectacular scenery on Maui's Road to Hana

along the Na Pali Coast

DAY 13

Wake early and drive to Waimea Canyon, where amazing photo-ops await at the lookout. If you're the adventurous type, take a hike in forested Koke'e State Park. On the way back to your hotel, stop in historic Waimea town and Hanapepe, full of art galleries and curious shops and eateries.

DAY 14

Time to explore the North Shore, one of the most beautiful places in all the state. Take your beach gear. Stop at the lighthouse in Kilauea and see the wildlife refuge, where seabirds nest in the cliffs. Continue on to Hanalei Bay, filled with shops and eateries. The perfect half-moon beach is great for surfing or stand-up paddling. After lunch in Hanalei, head north to the end of the road at Ke'e Beach. Swim, relax, and head to mustsee Limahuli Botanical Garden when you need a break from the sun.

EXTEND YOUR STAY

Plan on splitting your time with a few days on both the North and South Shores to fully experience each region to its fullest. Spend an extra day taking a helicopter tour of Waimea Canyon and the inaccessible Na Pali Coast or a boat tour of the Na Pali Coast.

Limahuli Botanical Garden, on Kaua'i

One-Week Island Pairings

If you only have one week for your island getaway, you still have time to experience two islands. The following islands complement one another like fine wine added to a great meal. For specific suggestions on how to spend your time on each island, see the daily itineraries starting on page 13.

O'ahu and Maui

O'ahu and Maui are located in close physical proximity, yet offer two distinct versions of island living. O'ahu offers fast times due to the bustling pace of Honolulu, with dozens of attractions, both cosmopolitan (Honolulu Museum of Art) and historic (Pearl Harbor, Bishop Museum), as well as the deluxe resort experience of Waikiki. The North Shore on O'ahu is another hotbed of activity, whether you're into snorkeling or surfing. Slow things down on laid-back Maui, where swimming, sunbathing, and a long stroll down a sandy beach are considered a busy afternoon. Get away from it all at a B&B in Maui's sleepiest town, Hana. Tour beautiful farmland in

Haleakala National Park near Hana

the upcountry and add some physical exertion with hiking or biking on Haleakala.

Maui and the Big Island

Combining Maui and the Big Island makes the perfect getaway for nature lovers. Maui is the go-to for ocean sports, with ample snorkeling and diving sites both on Maui itself and its small neighbor islands, Moloka'i and Lana'i. Divers won't want to miss Molokini, a small half crater in the channel between the smaller islands. Moloka'i and Lana'i also offer off-the-map escapes from modern life and a glimpse of Old Hawaii. Jump over to the Big Island for hiking and mountain activities. Instead of seaside accommodations, stay in Volcano, the small village just outside Hawai'i Volcanoes National Park. You'll be minutes away from the raw origins of all the islands. Hike through a native Hawaiian forest, across barren lava fields, and along the caldera of an active volcano. Other hiking opportunities on the Big Island include the lush Waipi'o Valley.

O'ahu and Kaua'i

Island-hopping between O'ahu and Kaua'i gives you both a civilized vacation and a true backcountry getaway. On O'ahu, soak up the nightlife, award-winning cuisine, and high-rise hotels of the Waikiki enclave. Explore the art scene in Chinatown and the restaurant scene in Kaimuki. O'ahu also offers structured ocean activities, with guides to teach you surfing and stand-up paddling and charters and tours devoted to kayaking and whale-watching. Leave the tall buildings of O'ahu behind and get back to nature on Kaua'i. Trek along the gorgeous Kalalau Trail, hiking to remote beaches, magnificent waterfalls, and unparalleled views from sheer coastal cliffs. Hiking opportunities also abound in Waimea Canyon State Park. There's an art scene on Kaua'i as well, but it's much more grass roots. You'll find it in small towns like Waimea and Hanapepe.

Best Beaches

Tropical destinations are defined by the quality of their beaches. While all the beaches in Hawaii are beautiful, they vary from island to island and coast to coast. Different beaches have different types of sand; depending on what's on the ocean floor, the water color glistens from deep blue to sparkling turquoise. Whether you're looking for recreation, isolation, or convenience, there's a beach that's right for you.

O'ahu
WAIKIKI BEACH AND KUHIO BEACH PARK

Side by side in the middle of a legendary shoreline, these two beaches present the essence of Waikiki: white sand framed by Diamond Head, historic hotels, and the sparkling blue Pacific. Queen's and Canoes surf breaks are just off the shore, catamarans and outrigger canoes line the beach, and sunbathers stretch out in all directions.

WAIMEA BAY BEACH PARK

This protected marine area on O'ahu's North Shore, framed by rocks and boulders on both sides, sees pods of spinner dolphins gracing the bay in the summer. The water is calm and perfect for swimming and snorkeling. Don't forget to leap off Jump Rock.

SUNSET BEACH

This is the quintessential North Shore. The coarse sand made of tiny bits of coral and shells stretches out in both directions and is thick with tropical vegetation along the dunes. Walk north to the point for an unspoiled view of the Wai'anae Mountains.

SANDY BEACH PARK

Set along the dramatic volcanic southeast coast of O'ahu next to Halona Blowhole, Sandy Beach is a popular sunbathing locale. Its infamous pounding shorebreak offers the best bodysurfing on the island.

Waikiki Beach

KAILUA BEACH PARK
Fine white sand gently arcing up the coast for four miles. Crystal-clear water with a sandy bottom that's perfect for swimming, stand-up paddling, and kayaking. A grassy and shady park. Rental outfitters and dining across the street. What's not to love?

Maui
KA'ANAPALI BEACH
Whether you're looking for snorkeling, stand-up paddling, cliff jumping, or scuba diving, you'll find it here. This resort district is the see-and-be-seen shoreline for the island's West Side.

MOKULEI'A BAY
During summer, there are few better ways to start the day than by snorkeling at Mokulei'a. Tucked away at the base of the cliffs and hidden from the road, it's also a scenic and sandy spot for watching the large winter surf.

Hamoa Beach
Travelers from Michener to Twain have written of its beauty. The bodysurfing, surfing, and sandy shoreline make this the nicest beach in Hana. If your vision of paradise involves a book, a palm tree, and the sound of waves at your feet, you'll find it here.

D.T. FLEMING BEACH PARK
D.T. Fleming Beach Park has it all: surfing, beachcombing, and hiking. It's also a family-friendly beach with facilities.

MAKENA STATE PARK
There are three beaches within this state park; Big Beach is the best known. It's free of coastal development, a nice respite from nearby hotel-lined shores. The vibe is free and easy.

Lana'i
HULOPO'E BEACH PARK
This Lana'i marine reserve has a sandy cove, vibrant reef, and palm-fringed shoreline that continue to make it an island favorite. Summer months bring good surfing and bodysurfing, and there are coastal hiking trails on both ends of the beach. Public restrooms, showers, and picnic tables make this a family-friendly outing.

O'ahu's Sandy Beach Park

Maui's Ka'anapali Beach at sunset

Moloka'i

PAPOHAKU BEACH

This westward-facing shoreline offers the island's best sunsets. Even though Papohaku is one of the longest beaches in Hawaii, on most days you'll be putting the only set of footprints in the sand. It's the perfect beach escape.

The Big Island

WAIPI'O BEACH

You have to hike down a nearly vertical road before you arrive at the beach at Waipi'o Valley on the Big Island. Even with the black sand and a waterfall far below you, you can't really argue its appeal. Given the effort it takes to get here, you might as well stay the whole day to explore the valley.

RICHARDSON'S BEACH PARK

There are drive-up beaches galore on Kalaniana'ole Avenue in Hilo, all with something different to offer. In this case, you'll enjoy shade, full facilities, and clear blue water perfect for swimming and snorkeling.

HAPUNA BEACH STATE RECREATION AREA

Locals rank Hapuna Beach one of the top 20 beaches in the world. The smooth, wide white sand is welcoming to swimmers, body boarders, and snorkelers, drawing huge weekend crowds.

MAKALAWENA BEACH

It's a walk over a desolate lava field to this beach in Kekaha Kai State Park, but the payoff is worth it: a nearly uninhabited silky white beach, with truly nothing around you but sun and ocean.

MANINI'OWALI BEACH

If a sweltering walk isn't your idea of a vacation, no worries—Makalawena Beach has a sister beach in the Kua Bay section of Kekaha Kai State Park. When you've got it this good (a beautiful white-sand beach, great snorkeling and body boarding, close parking, bathrooms), expect to share the beach with a crowd.

the pier at Hanalei Bay

Kaua'i
MAHA'ULEPU BEACHES
Take the bumpy dirt road out to the Maha'ulepu Beaches for secluded beach time. You'll have your choice of Gillin's Beach and Kawailoa Bay for relaxation.

Po'ipu Beach is great for surfing or snoozing.

PO'IPU BEACH PARK
Home to a long strip of fluffy white sand, Po'ipu Beach is great for surfing, both for beginners and experienced surfers, and safe swimming. Restrooms and showers add to the convenience of the easily accessible location.

SEALODGE BEACH
Nestled below Princeville's cliffs, this small paradise cove is accessible via a roughly 15-minute hike. The small crescent of sand is backed by shade-giving trees. The water offers good swimming and great snorkeling.

HANALEI BAY
The long, crescent-moon-shaped beach offers fine white sand to stroll on, calm waters to swim in, and popular surf breaks for all levels.

HA'ENA BEACH PARK
Nestled in front of a backdrop of lush green mountains at the end of the road, this beach has full amenities and a lifeguard. It's great for beachcombing and watching surfers.

Best Snorkeling and Diving

Hawaii's reefs teem with marine life: fish, sea turtles, rays, sharks, octopus, and many other sea creatures only found in these waters. Diving the wrecks, ledges, lava tubes, and deep-water rock formations only add to the diversity. Snorkeling and diving are contingent on calm, clear water. If one side of the island has waves or is windy, the other side might be calm and flat: just right for underwater exploration.

O'ahu

THREE TABLES

Part of the Pupukea-Waimea Marine Life Conservation District, this area consists of three flat reef outcroppings that barely break the water's surface just 50 feet off the beach. The area teems with endemic marine life like puffer fish and reef squid.

SHARKS COVE

The premier shore diving area has interesting underwater topography like lava tubes, caverns, and walls. Marine life is abundant. You're sure to see creatures like the spotted eagle ray, wrasse, and unicorn fish.

WAIMEA BAY

During summer when the waves are flat on O'ahu's North Shore, Waimea Bay has perfect conditions for snorkeling. Pods of spinner dolphins frequent these waters and rock outcroppings at both ends of the bay attract diverse marine life.

HANAUMA BAY NATURE PRESERVE

This popular marine conservation area is set in an arid cinder cone, creating a protected environment where hundreds of marine species thrive. Snorkel beyond the inner fingers of the reef to escape the crowd.

Kaua'i

NA PALI COAST

You'll find the island's most spectacular snorkeling along Kaua'i's Na Pali Coast, accessible only by boat tour. A snorkel cruise will take you through jaw-dropping underwater terrain with an array of sea life from dolphins to sea turtles.

KE'E BEACH

At the very end of the road on the north

snorkeling at Tunnels, off Makua Beach

shore of Kaua'i lies this semi-protected pool great for beginners. Experts will find the truly spectacular snorkeling in the open ocean beyond it.

TUNNELS/MAKUA BEACH
The most renowned snorkeling spot on Kaua'i offers beginners good snorkeling not far from shore. Experts can explore beyond the ledge that drops off into the deep ocean.

PK'S
Across from Prince Kuhio Park, this tiny strip of beach offers wonderful underwater shows. Fish like to snack on the seaweed that grows in abundance on the rocks.

Maui
HONOLUA BAY
A world-renowned surf spot during winter, Honolua Bay has the island's best snorkeling during the calmer summer. Hawaiian green sea turtles are a common sight, as are parrotfish, octopus, and the rare spinner dolphin.

PU'U KEKA'A (BLACK ROCK)
Maui's most famous snorkeling spot is also one if its best. This rocky promontory on the Ka'anapali strip is a magnet for sea turtles and reef fish. Keep an eye out for the dozens of cliff jumpers who throw themselves off the rock.

NAHUNA (MAKENA LANDING/5 CAVES)
Known as Turtle Town, the volcanic Makena coastline is pockmarked with caves, which provide the perfect shelter for sea turtles. During the winter months, everyone from scuba divers to kayakers frequents this rugged shoreline.

MOLOKINI CRATER
This crescent-shaped volcanic caldera offers 100-foot visibility most days of the year. Over a dozen snorkeling tours make the early morning pilgrimage to the crater. The crystal clear waters are home to over 250 species of fish. Expert scuba divers explore the famous Back Wall, which drops straight down for nearly 300 feet.

Lana'i
HULOPO'E BEACH PARK
This marine reserve has one of the healthiest reefs in Maui County and fronts a beach ranked as the nation's best. Come face-to-face with multihued parrotfish as they snack on colorful coral, or search the shallows for the Hawaii state fish, the *humuhumunukunukuapua'a*.

The Big Island
KEALAKEKUA BAY
An organized kayak trip to Kealakekua Bay not only gets you to the best snorkel location on the island but gives you a tour of this undeveloped and inaccessible coast.

KEAUHOU BAY
One of the most exhilarating things you can do on the Big Island is night diving with the manta rays in Keauhou Bay.

PAWAI BAY
This is one of the best snorkeling spots on the Kona Coast. A small beach offers easy access to the water along this otherwise rocky coastline.

a *humuhumunukunukuapua'a*, Hawaii's state fish

Best Surfing

Legendary Olympic gold medalist swimmer, original beachboy, and ambassador of aloha Duke Kahanamoku introduced surfing to the world. Be part of that legacy by getting on a board during your stay. Whether you're a first-timer or a lifer, year-round surf means you'll find the perfect wave for you.

Beginners
O'AHU
POPULARS AND PARADISE
Once you're comfortable with your feet in the wax, paddle out to Populars and Paradise for longer rides on Waikiki's outer reefs.

CANOES
No stay in Waikiki is complete without surfing this famous break. The slow-rolling wave is fun whether it's your first time or you can hang ten.

CHUN'S REEF
A beautiful right breaking point on the North Shore, this slow-breaking wave is

sculpture of Duke Kahanamoku

perfect for beginners and even has small waves occasionally during the summertime.

KAUA'I
KALAPAKI BEACH
Much like the friendly waves in Waikiki, Kalapaki Beach has soft waves that break just offshore. It's perfect for surf lessons.

PO'IPU BEACH PARK
On the west end of Po'ipu Beach Park, in front of the rock outcropping, is Lemon Drops, a great wave for beginners. It breaks right and left and washes into deeper water, so you don't have to worry about hitting bottom.

MAUI
LAUNIUPOKO BEACH PARK
Lahaina locals learn to ride their first waves at this happening beach park. There are multiple peaks for longboarders to choose from.

LAHAINA BREAKWALL
Crowded, shallow, and always sunny, this breakwall is dominated by surf schools on the inside reef, while advanced surfers hang on the outside. While most days are calm with gentle surf, this becomes an advanced spot on the large south swells of summer.

THE COVE
This is the epicenter of the Kihei surf scene. The shallow, protected cove is home to the south side's numerous surf schools.

POHAKU BEACH PARK (S-TURNS)
A longboarder's dream, S-Turns is Maui's most user-friendly winter break. The long paddle out means a long ride in. This rolling, forgiving wave is the perfect spot for honing your skills.

surfing off Lahaina, Maui

Experts

O'AHU
ALA MOANA BOWLS AND KAISERS

Some of the best waves on the south shore are along a strip of reef in front of the Ala Moana Small Boat Harbor. Kaisers is a barreling right that breaks in extremely shallow water over sharp reef and Ala Moana Bowls is a long, fast left that local surfers keep under lock and key, coveting every barrel.

SUNSET BEACH

This powerful and unforgiving wave on the North Shore is famous for separating the experts from the herd. The right boards, the right frame of mind, and stamina are a must to surf the heaving walls of water that break along Sunset Beach.

MAKAHA

Makaha is a predominant right-hand point break on the leeward side of O'ahu, famous for its powerful surf, the characters in the lineup, and its backwash close to shore.

Makaha breaks nearly all year long, on south, west, and north swells, and sees gigantic waves during the winter.

KAUA'I
HANALEI BAY

This right hand point break is a long, beautiful wave that attracts surfers from all over the island. Shortboarders prefer to surf further up the point, while longboarders and stand-up paddlers like the end section that breaks into the channel. Hanalei is generally a wintertime break.

MAUI
HONOLUA BAY

Honolua Bay is a place of local legend. During winter, this can be one of the best right-hand waves in the world. If you respect local surfers and wait your turn in the lineup, there's a chance you could snag a wave that makes your entire vacation worth it.

HO'OKIPA BEACH PARK

This popular break is the center of the Pa'ia surf scene. During the large swells of winter this becomes an experts-only amphitheater of towering 20-foot surf.

PA'IA BAY

Walking distance from the center of town is one of Maui's only real beach breaks, best for shortboarding and bodyboarding.

THE BIG ISLAND
HONOLI'I BEACH PARK

Located just outside of Hilo, Honoli'i offers the best waves in the region. There are several different breaks depending on the swell direction. Since it sits at a river mouth, the water is cold compared to most beaches.

PINE TREES

One of the most famous surf breaks on Kona Coast, Pine Trees is one of the best high-performance waves in the region.

Best Hikes

Hawaii's majestic mountains and forests hold verdant treasures that can only be seen by foot. There is a rich diversity of trails, from shaded valleys leading to waterfalls to ridges overlooking coastline and valleys with views of neighbor islands. As you gain elevation, you'll see more of Hawaii's endangered and native trees and shrubs and hear the calls of the forest birds.

O'ahu

DIAMOND HEAD SUMMIT TRAIL

This hike inside a volcanic cinder cone offers a unique perspective of O'ahu's geology and its military past. The summit offers sweeping views of the south shore.

LYON ARBORETUM TRAILS

Shaded, damp, and devoid of crowds, the vast network of trails at Lyon Arboretum introduces hikers to hundreds of different tropical plants and trees. The fragrant and bright blossoms of ginger and heliconia are everywhere, palms and canopy trees reign, and

vines and epiphytes grow in the trees. A small waterfall is the prize in the back of the valley.

KULI'OU'OU TRAILS

These valley and ridge trails reach a summit just above 2,000 feet and offer stunning views of Waimanalo and the windward coast, panning all the way to Diamond Head across Maunalua Bay.

MAUNAWILI FALLS

A popular, short hike just outside of Kailua in the shadow of Olomana, the trail follows Maunawili Stream to cascading Maunawili Falls, where there's a deep swimming pool. There are also great views of the Ko'olau Mountains and Kane'ohe Bay.

KA'ENA POINT

This hot and dry hike to the western tip of O'ahu takes you along a rocky and rutted dirt road skirting a rugged volcanic coastline with surf pummeling the cliffs. Whether you come from the North Shore

the view from the Kalalau Trail, O'ahu

the Alaka'i Swamp Trail

or Yokohama Bay side, this natural preserve, home to nesting seabirds, native plants, and Hawaiian monk seals, will wow you.

Kaua'i
KALALAU TRAIL
Kaua'i's Kalalau Trail is a strenuous 11-mile hike one way, with unmatched views of the Na Pali Coast through switchbacks, mud, hills, and stream crossings. You'll pass Hanakapi'ai Beach and end on the secluded Kalalau Beach.

HANAKAPI'AI BEACH AND HANAKAPI'AI FALLS
Beginning at Ke'e Beach, this section of the Kalalau Trail, which is roughly four hours round-trip, features beautiful views of the Na Pali Coast and ends with a dip in the cool freshwater pool at Hanakapi'ai Falls.

KUILAU TRAIL
Taking about two or three hours to complete, this moderately strenuous trail offers wonderful rewards, including including an amazing view of Mount Wai'ale'ale and sweeping vistas from Kapa'a to Lihu'e.

ILIAU NATURE LOOP AND KUKUI TRAIL
The family-friendly Iliau Nature Loop in Waimea Canyon State Park wanders through native forest for about 20 minutes of walking time. From here you can connect to the Kukui Trail, which will take you down to the Waimea River in the canyon (roughly four hours round-trip).

PIHEA TRAIL AND ALAKA'I SWAMP TRAIL
These trails take you through otherworldly terrain: dwarf forests, vine-covered trees, and the world's highest swamp. Amazing sweeping views to the north shore can be seen at the Kilohana Overlook.

Maui
KEONEHE'EHE'E TO HALEMAU'U
Otherwise known as the Sliding Sands to Switchback Loop, this 12.2-mile sojourn crosses the floor of Haleakala Crater, weaving past cinder cones bursting with color. Keep

an eye out for *nene* and glistening silversword plants. For a real thrill, hike by the light of the full moon.

POLIPOLI SPRING RECREATION AREA

Tucked in one of the least-visited corners of Maui, Polipoli looks more like Northern California than a Pacific island. A network of trails weaves through towering redwoods. The silence is broken only by passing pheasants.

PIPIWAI TRAIL

If expansive banyan trees, dark bamboo forests, and numerous waterfalls aren't enough of a thrill, this four-mile trail reaches a dramatic terminus at the base of 400-foot Waimoku Falls. This hike, Maui's best, should be on every itinerary for a day in Hana.

Moloka'i

HALAWA VALLEY

Halawa Valley is one of the oldest settlements in the Hawaiian Islands, so sacred it can only be explored with a guide. More than just a hike to a waterfall, a guided trek in Halawa Valley is an educational and powerful journey to the heart of Hawaiian culture.

The Big Island

MAUNA LOA OBSERVATORY TRAIL

Brace altitude and weather on the most extreme hike on the Big Island: the summit of Mauna Loa. This hike has two access points; it's a closer hike if you begin from near the Mauna Loa observatory on the Saddle Road.

CRATER RIM TRAIL

Hike from the Thomas A. Jaggar Museum along the crater rim toward the visitor center for unparalleled views of the vast Kilauea Caldera. Pass through desert-like conditions as well as lush native tropical forest.

KILAUEA IKI TRAIL

The Kilauea Iki Trail takes you from the top of the Kilauea crater, with lush tropical rainforests, to the bottom of the crater floor, which is devoid of vegetation and filled with volcanic steam. It is a moderate four-hour loop.

The Mauna Loa Observatory Trail on the Big Island is considered the most technically difficult hike in the state.

Best Historical and Cultural Sites

To truly experience Hawaii, you need to understand its people and place in the modern world. Hawaii's relatively short history has been tumultuous and prosperous, war-torn yet rich. Its museums, historic sites, and artifacts all have compelling stories to tell.

O'ahu

'IOLANI PALACE

The only royal residence in the United States, this grand and regal palace was the official home of the monarch of the Hawaiian kingdom. Tours cover the lavishly furnished basement and the first and second floors.

HISTORIC CHINATOWN

Chinatown's historic buildings are home to a vibrant mix of cuisine, culture, art, and nightlife. The only way to experience it all is to park the car and set out on foot, block by block.

HONOLULU MUSEUM OF ART

O'ahu's premier fine art museum has amassed a collection including 50,000 pieces spanning 5,000 years and featuring Asian, African, American, European, and Oceanic artifacts. There is also a theater, and its sister museum Spalding House in Makiki Heights holds a modern art collection. The entry fee is good for both museums on a same-day visit.

BISHOP MUSEUM

Bishop Museum is the premier natural history museum in the Pacific and the largest museum in the state of Hawaii. It has seasonal rotating exhibits and an extensive collection of cultural artifacts from peoples across the Pacific.

PEARL HARBOR HISTORIC SITES

One of the most heavily visited areas in Hawaii, this historic site includes free tours of the USS *Arizona* Memorial and paid tours of the USS *Bowfin* Submarine Museum and Park, the Battleship *Missouri*, and the Pacific Aviation

The royal crest decorates 'Iolani Palace, on O'ahu.

the USS *Arizona* Memorial at Pearl Harbor, O'ahu

Museum. All are part of the World War II Valor in the Pacific National Monument.

Kaua'i
KILAUEA LIGHTHOUSE
Stop for both educational and photo opportunities at the Kilauea Lighthouse and the Kilauea Point National Wildlife Refuge on Kaua'i's north shore.

LIMAHULI BOTANICAL GARDEN
Check out the preserved wetland taro terraces and native plants at Limahuli Botanical Garden. A self-guided tour weaves through the gorgeous, vibrant green grounds.

KILOHANA PLANTATION
This sprawling sugar plantation is home to a perfectly preserved mansion built in the 1930s. Browse the home and its many original pieces of decor, explore the beautiful grounds, and enjoy a historical train ride.

WAILUA RIVER SACRED SITES
Along the banks of the Wailua River are many cultural sites, including the *heiau* where the Hawaiian royalty were born and a site that may have witnessed human sacrifice. Wander the Kamokila Hawaiian Village, which showcases traditional Hawaiian life.

Maui
PI'ILANIHALE HEIAU
Inside of Hana's Kahanu Garden, this towering, 50-foot tall *heiau* is the largest remaining in the state of Hawaii. The stone platforms encompass an area the size of two professional football fields.

BAILEY HOUSE MUSEUM
Step inside this one-time missionary home to get a glimpse into 19th-century Maui. This museum houses ancient Hawaiian artifacts, a surfboard ridden by Duke Kahanamoku, and one of the best bookstores for Hawaiian-themed literature.

Moloka'i
KALAUPAPA PENINSULA
At one time, a visit to Kalaupapa was a death sentence. Today, go to this remote peninsula to learn about the struggles of Hawaii's

the memorial to Father Damien, Moloka'i

leprosy patients and Father Damien, the man who gave everything to save them.

Lana'i

LANA'I CULTURE AND HERITAGE CENTER
This small, informative cultural center in the heart of Lana'i City traces Lana'i's history from its original inhabitants through its era as the world's largest pineapple plantation.

The Big Island

KEALAKEKUA BAY STATE HISTORICAL PARK
Kealakekua Bay was the site of the first significant and sustained contact between Hawaiians and Europeans. While it started off well, the relationship deteriorated, ending in the death of many Hawaiians, Captain James Cook, and several of his crewmembers. A white obelisk memorial marks the spot where Cook fell.

PU'UKOHOLA HEIAU NATIONAL HISTORIC SITE
As part of a prophecy, Kamehameha I was told to build a temple to the war god Ku. Sitting high on the hill overlooking Kawaihae Harbor, this commanding stone structure was the last large *heiau* built before the dissolution of the Hawaiian religious system.

KOHALA HISTORICAL SITES STATE MONUMENT
Two remarkable sites are drawn together in this state monument. The Kamehameha 'Akahi 'Aina Hanau marks the spot where Hawaii's most well known historical figure was born. Much, much older is Mo'okini Luakini Heiau, a sacrificial temple, one of the oldest *heiau* on the island.

LAUPAHOEHOE TRAIN MUSEUM
You can't miss this Big Island museum—there is a full-size train car on the side of the road. The museum houses an impressive photo archive of the Big Island in the early 20th century.

HISTORICAL KAILUA
King Kamehameha lived his last years at Kamakahonu Beach, using Ahu'ena Heiau for governing purposes. Later rulers built Hulihe'e Palace, an escape from the affairs of state in Honolulu. Land was given to the first missionaries to put up Moku'aikaua Church across the street from the palace.

O'AHU

O'ahu is the heartbeat of the Hawaiian Islands. The island is home to almost one million residents, about 70 percent of the state's total population, and is, by far, the most culturally and socially diverse of the eight main Hawaiian Islands. Here you can experience the comforts and convenience of city life within reach of verdant mountains and sparkling blue ocean.

O'ahu is home to Honolulu, the state's economic and political center, where historic buildings and art museums pepper the city's historic district, Chinatown is the epicenter of the art scene, and pulsing nightlife captures your immediate attention. With no ethnic majority, O'ahu best exemplifies its east-meets-west melting pot culture through its exceptional regional cuisine. From the Polynesian roots of its first settlers to O'ahu's strategic role for the United States during World War II and its importance as an international agricultural hub, the breadth of the Hawaii's history and evolution is also tangible here.

Pull back the curtain of O'ahu's urban landscape and there is a natural backdrop that makes up the ebb and flow of island style and tropical living. Thanks to its 112 miles of coastline, beaches and ocean activities are the cornerstone of daily life. The powerful waves of the North Shore draw the world's best surfers. The ledges off the leeward coast attract big game fish. Waikiki's calm water is the ultimate playground for the outrigger

canoe. Kailua's fine, white sand rivals the most beautiful beaches in the world. And with two mountain ranges that span the island from north to south, valleys, ridges, and cliffs offer ample hiking and lush open space.

For every budget and every taste, for every tourist, visitor, backpacker, traveler, and globe-trotter seeking adventure or leisure, town or country, fine dining or food truck, mountains or beaches – O'ahu has it all.

Planning Your Trip

WHERE TO GO
Waikiki
The quintessential O'ahu destination, Waikiki has beaches with **gentle surf** and **warm water,** great weather year-round, ocean activities, shopping, and dining, and is home to the majority of the hotels on the island. Waikiki's 2.5-mile strip of coastline is the stuff of legends. Not too far away is iconic landmark **Diamond Head.** The **Honolulu Zoo** and the **Waikiki Aquarium** exhibit local flora and fauna, while **Kapi'olani Park** is a beautiful green space in the city. Waikiki's bars and restaurants offer cuisine from around the world and a **lively bar scene** once the sun sets.

Honolulu
The **economic and political center** of the state, Honolulu is also the capital of . Best known for its **historic district** and Chinatown, Honolulu stretches from Honolulu International Airport to the ridges and valleys of the Ko'olau Mountains. Here you'll find **stately government buildings** like the **Hawaii State Capitol** and historic sites such as **Washington Place** and **'Iolani Palace.** For museum enthusiasts, there's the **Hawai'i State Art Museum** and the **Honolulu Museum of Art.** Chinatown offers both **fine art galleries** and **Pacific Rim cuisine.**

North Shore
O'ahu's rural North Shore is all about **beautiful beaches, diving, surfing,** and **snorkeling.** The coastline is natural and unspoiled, and the beaches are the hallmark of **tropical bliss.** During winter, the North Shore attracts surfers from around the world to ride the **powerful, barreling waves** that break all along the coast. During summer, the ocean surface remains calm and flat, the perfect conditions for diving and snorkeling at **Three Tables** and **Sharks Cove.** Relax at **Waimea Bay,** take a walk through a botanical garden and historical cultural site at **Waimea Valley,** or drive up to Pupukea to visit the **Pu'u O Mahuka Heiau,** an ancient Hawaiian temple site.

Southeast and Windward
The southeast shore spans affluent Kahala to Makapu'u. **Maunalua Bay** offers a variety of **water activities,** from Jet Skiing and wakeboarding to surfing and diving. **Sandy Beach** is the best bodysurfing beach on the island. From Makapu'u north to La'ie is the windward coast, hugging the spectacular **verdant cliffs** of the Ko'olau Mountains. The windward side is known for its numerous **white sand beaches. Kailua** has a beautiful crescent beach with fine sand and calm water, and the town is full of boutiques and restaurants. Hike up to **Maunawili Falls,** or along the **Kawainui Marsh** to see **native Hawaiian waterfowl.** Take the leisurely drive up the coast to the quiet town of La'ie, home of the **Polynesian Cultural Center.**

Pearl Harbor and the Leeward Coast
The **Pearl Harbor Historic Sites** are a must to grasp the history of Hawaii and O'ahu and their role during World War II. The arid leeward side runs from the **Ko Olina Resort** to **Yokohama Bay** and **Ka'ena Point.** Ko Olina has fine dining,

O'AHU

Kuilima Point

Kahuk
Poir

Turtle Bay

TURTLE BA
RESORT

KAMEHAMEHA HWY

Sunset
Beach

'Ehukai Beach
BANZAI PIPELINE

Waimea
Bay

Waimea

Pupukea-
Paumalu
Forest
Reserve

Waimea Beach

WAIMEA VALLEY
AUDUBON CENTER

83

Hale'iwa Beach
County Park

Mokule'ia Beach
County Park

Hale'iwa

Pu'u Ka'inapua'a
2,360ft

930

FARRINGTON HWY

Waialua

99

Kaua'i Channel

Ka'ena
Point

Pu'u Pueo
768ft

DILLINGHAM
AIRFIELD

803

KAMEHAMEHA

Ka'ena Point
State Park

Kuaokala
Forest Reserve

Wai'anae Range

KAUKONAHUA HWY

Whitmore
Village

Yokohama Bay

Mokuleia
Forest Reserve

Mt Ka'ala
4,020ft

KUKANILOKO
BIRTHING STONES

Wahiawa

WAHIAWA
BOTANICAL
GARDEN

93

Makua
Keaau
Forest
Reserve

Schofield
Barracks

Kea'au Beach
County Park

KANE'AKI
HEIAU

Waianae Kai
Forest Reserve

Puu Kalena
3,504ft

WHEELER
AIR FORCE
BASE

Makaha Beach

Makaha

LUALUALEI

750

Mililani

H2

Wai'anae
Harbor

Wai'anae

NAVAL

KUNIA RD

99

Poka'i Bay Beach
County Park

RESERVATION

Palikea
3,098ft

Patsy T. Mink
Central Oahu
Regional Park

Pearl
City

Ma'ili

PACIFIC

Lualualei

Nanakuli
Forest
Reserve

Waipahu

93

Nanakuli

OCEAN

Nanakuli Beach
County Park

H1

Makakilo

FORT WEAVER RD

Pearl
Harbor

USS MISSOUR

Kahe Point Beach
County Park

FARRINGTON HWY

KO'OLINA
RESORT

Kapolei

'Ewa

US NAVAL
RESERVATION

'Ewa Beach

BARBERS POINT
NAVAL AIR
STATION

Barbers Point

Mamala Bay

0   5 mi

0   5 km

JAMES CAMPBELL
WILDLIFE REFUGE

○ Kahuku

La'ie Bay

▲ *Malaekahana State*
Recreation Area

■ La'ie
RMON ★
MPLE   ★ POLYNESIAN
             CULTURAL CENTER

▲ *Hau'ula Beach*
  County Park

▲ Hau'ula

Kaliuwa'a
Sacred Falls

○ Punalu'u

Kahana Bay

○ PACIFIC

▲ *Swanzy Beach*
  County Park

Ka'a'awa

'u Pauao
2,565ft   ▲

Kahana Valley
State Park

OCEAN

83

▲ *Kualoa*
  Park

Pu'u Ka'aumakua ▲
2,681ft

Waikane

Waiahole
Forest
Reserve

Waiahole

Kahalu'u

He'eia Kea
Harbor

KANE'OHE MARINE
CORPS AIR STATION

Mokapu Point

83

830

Kane'ohe
Bay

Mokolea Rock

Ewa Forest
Reserve

BYODO-IN
TEMPLE ★

Keaiwa Heiau
ate Recreation Area

Kane'ohe

KAWAINUI
MARSH

Kailua
Bay

H3

▲ *Kailua Beach*
  County Park

Mokulua
Islands

Aiea

H3

HO'OMALUHIA
BOTANICAL
GARDEN ★

ULUPO
HEIAU

Kailua

ALOHA
STADIUM

63

Lanikai
Beach

SS ARIZONA MEMORIAL

Honolulu
Forest Reserve

▲ *Bellows Field Beach*
  County Park

78

PALI
TUNNELS

Waimanalo

CKAM
AFB

FORT
SHAFTER

BISHOP
MUSEUM

PALI
LOOKOUT

Manoa
Falls

Waimanalo
Beach

72

▲ *Waimanalo Beach*
  County Park

H1

61

Round Top
Forest Reserve

▲ *Makapu'u Beach*
  County Park

HONOLULU INT'L
AIRPORT

HONOLULU

UNIVERSITY OF
HAWAII AT MANOA

Koko
Crater

Makapu'u
Point

Sand Island State
Recreation Area

IOLANI PALACE/
STATE CAPITOL

'Aina
Haina

Hawaii
Kai

▲ *Sandy Beach*
  County Park

H1

Waikiki

Le'ahi
▲ 761ft

Maunalua
Bay

72

Koko Head
642ft ▲

Hanauma
Bay

Kaiwi Channel

Diamond
Head

Diamond Head
State Monument

Kaua'i

Ni'ihau

O'ahu

Moloka'i

Lana'i   Maui

Kaho'olawe

Hawai'i

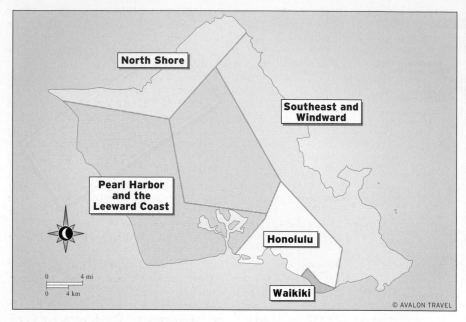

a golf course, and four artificial **seaside lagoons.** The predominantly calm conditions of the leeward beaches result in **great visibility** for snorkeling and diving. Hike out to **Ka'ena Point State Park,** the westernmost tip of the island, and look for **Hawaiian monk seals, spinner dolphins,** and **seabirds** nesting in the **sand dunes.**

PLANNING YOUR TIME ON O'AHU

Taking full advantage of a few days on O'ahu requires strategic daily planning. Try to narrow down exactly what you'd like to see in a particular region, and if possible, find a way to combine that activity with other sights and stops on the way to or from your main daily destination. Time your activities to avoid the daily **morning and afternoon rush hour traffic** on the freeways and highways.

Where you stay on O'ahu depends on your interests. If you want all the choices of dining, beaches, and recreation without setting foot in the car, stay in **Waikiki.** If you prefer quaint bed-and-breakfasts and long walks along uncrowded white-sand beaches, stay in **Kailua.** For a true escape from city life in paradise, spend at least one night on the **North Shore.** Stay at Turtle Bay Resort, the only high occupancy hotel in the region, or a vacation rental.

For a day taking in the history and culture of the islands, start out at **Pearl Harbor** as early as possible to beat the morning traffic. Spend a half day visiting the **Pearl Harbor Historic Sites** and then return to **Honolulu Historic District,** where you'll find the **state capitol,** '**Iolani Palace,** the **Hawai'i State Art Museum,** and other historic churches and buildings. A quick drive over to Chinatown will help you miss the afternoon traffic. Enjoy dinner at one of the many restaurants and bars, peruse myriad art galleries and possibly catch a performance at the historic Hawai'i Theatre.

If the beaches and surfing are more your style, your route will most likely be season dependent. During the winter, heavy surf pounds the **North Shore.** Drive up to see the big waves, but don't get in the water, as ocean conditions are extremely dangerous—diving and snorkeling are out. If you'd like to snorkel or dive, try south shore locales during winter, like the extremely popular and beautiful **Hanauma Bay** or the **Waikiki Marine Life Conservation District.** During the summer, waves roll over south shore reefs, but don't get as big as the winter surf. Famous for its user-friendly surf, Waikiki is perfect for beginners. Head up north for pristine ocean conditions perfect for snorkeling and diving, especially from **Waimea Bay** to **Sharks Cove.** The North Shore is one of the most beautiful stretches of rural tropical scenery in the islands. No matter what the season, make the one-hour drive and take in its grandeur. When venturing to the North Shore, stop in **Hale'iwa Town** for meals and shopping. When you return to Town, take a leisurely drive down the **windward side.** Pull over for a swim, hike along the majestic Ko'olau mountains, and enjoy the views of offshore islets that dot the windward side.

No matter the direction your path on O'ahu takes you, always make sure to have a back-up plan. Unpredictable weather, such as a sudden afternoon downpour, can force you to change your beach plans quickly.

GETTING TO O'AHU

All interisland, national, and international commercial flights to O'ahu are routed to the

Honolulu International Airport (300 Rodgers Blvd., 808/836-6411, http://hawaii.gov/hnl). The Honolulu International Airport has three terminals: the Overseas Terminal accommodates international and mainland flights, the Interisland Terminal handles Hawaiian Airlines flights, and the Commuter Terminal handles the small interisland carriers. There is a free intra-airport shuttle service for getting around the airport, and ground transportation is available just outside the baggage claim areas on the lower level, along the center median, where you can get a taxi, catch a shuttle to a rental car agency office, board TheBus, or pick up one of the private shuttle buses that ferry visitors to Honolulu, Waikiki, and beyond. The airport is 10 miles from Waikiki, and six miles from downtown Honolulu.

If you're island hopping, **Hawaiian Airlines** (800/367-5320, hawaiianairlines.com) is the leading commercial carrier, with the largest selection of flights between the main Hawaiian Islands. **Mokulele Airlines** (866/260-7070, mokuleleairlines.com) utilizes a prop caravan service to ferry passengers to and from Moloka'i and Lana'i. With their small prop planes they also service the smaller airports in Hana and Kapalua, Maui. **Island Air** (800/652-6541, islandair.com) has a fleet of turboprop planes that service routes from Kaua'i, Maui, Moloka'i, and Lana'i to O'ahu.

© KEVIN WHITTON

A Hawaiian Airlines jet waits at Honolulu International Airport.

WAIKIKI

White sandy beaches, swaying palm trees, and outrigger canoes share the lineup at the famous Canoes and Queen's surfing breaks. Swimmers and sunbathers grace the shoreline for a refreshing dip. The average daytime high temperature is in the low 80s and water temperature is in the mid-70s. It's no wonder Waikiki has long been a coveted destination for world travelers

© KEVIN WHITTON

HIGHLIGHTS

LOOK FOR **C** TO FIND RECOMMENDED SIGHTS, ACTIVITIES, DINING, AND LODGING.

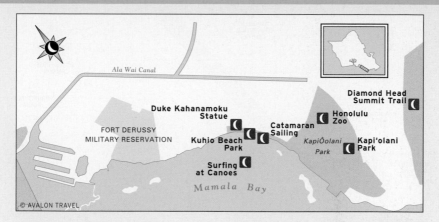

C Kuhio Beach Park: Visit the famous Duke Kahanamoku Statue, rent a surfboard, take a catamaran ride—or just relax under a palm tree (page 50).

C Surfing at Canoes: Whether it's your first time with your feet on the wax or you've been surfing your entire life, this is the place to participate in Hawaii's surf legacy (page 52).

C Catamaran Sailing: Take a break from the beach and get out on the open water. The sunset sails on the bigger boats offer a particularly good time (page 57).

C Diamond Head Summit Trail: This short hike will get your heart pumping and take you to the best views in Waikiki (page 58).

C Honolulu Zoo: The Honolulu Zoo showcases wildlife from the African savannah, the Asian and American tropical forest, and the Pacific Islands, for a great family outing (page 61).

C Kapi'olani Park: It's Waikiki's outdoor gym. Play tennis, go for a run, or stretch out with beachside yoga (page 63).

C Duke Kahanamoku Statue: Pay homage to the original ambassador of aloha, who shared the sport of surfing with the world (page 65).

seeking the enchantment of a tropical oasis. But make no mistake, while the surf and sun rarely disappoint, you'll be hard pressed to find peace, solitude, or tranquility on Waikiki's narrow beaches, busy avenues, or in its packed restaurants.

A scant 2.5 miles of shoreline on the South Shore between Diamond Head and the Ala Wai Small Boat Harbor, Waikiki pulses year-round with the footsteps of visitors from all over the world marching up and down Kalakaua and Kuhio Avenues and sinking

their toes in the sand. Lined with high-rise hotels, condominiums, and apartment buildings, Waikiki is a complete destination, a beachside hamlet with all the amenities of city life within its mesmerizing embrace: shopping, dining, nightlife, health, fitness, spas, and, of course, ocean sports and activities. The Honolulu Zoo and the Waikiki Aquarium are a must for families. Kapi'olani Park is a runner's delight, and tai chi and yoga are commonplace under the park's flowering canopy trees.

O'AHU

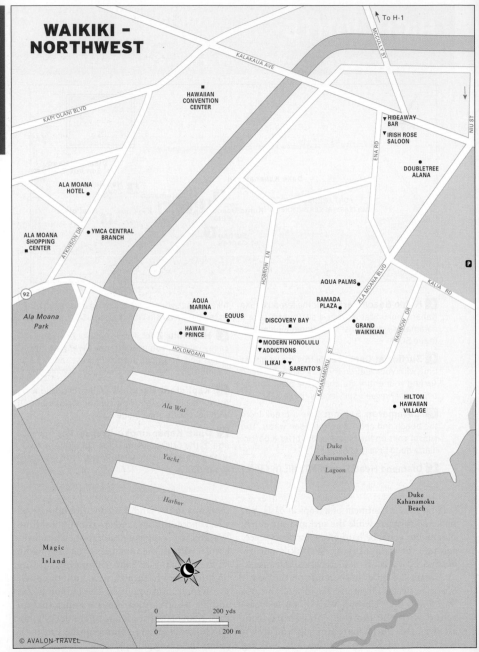

WAIKIKI - NORTHWEST

To H-1

MCCULLY ST

KALAKAUA AVE

HAWAIIAN
CONVENTION
CENTER

KAPI'OLANI BLVD

HIDEAWAY
BAR

IRISH ROSE
SALOON

ENA RD

NIU ST

DOUBLETREE
ALANA

ALA MOANA
HOTEL

ATKINSON DR

ALA MOANA
SHOPPING
CENTER

YMCA CENTRAL
BRANCH

HOBRON LN

92

AQUA PALMS

ALA MOANA BLVD

KALIA RD

P

Ala Moana
Park

AQUA
MARINA

EQUUS

RAMADA
PLAZA

DISCOVERY BAY

GRAND
WAIKIKIAN

RAINBOW DR

HAWAII
PRINCE

HOLOMOANA

MODERN HONOLULU
ADDICTIONS

ILIKAI

SARENTO'S

KAHANAMOKU ST

ST

HILTON
HAWAIIAN
VILLAGE

Ala Wai

Duke
Kahanamoku
Lagoon

Yacht

Duke
Kahanamoku
Beach

Harbor

Magic
Island

0   200 yds

0   200 m

© AVALON TRAVEL

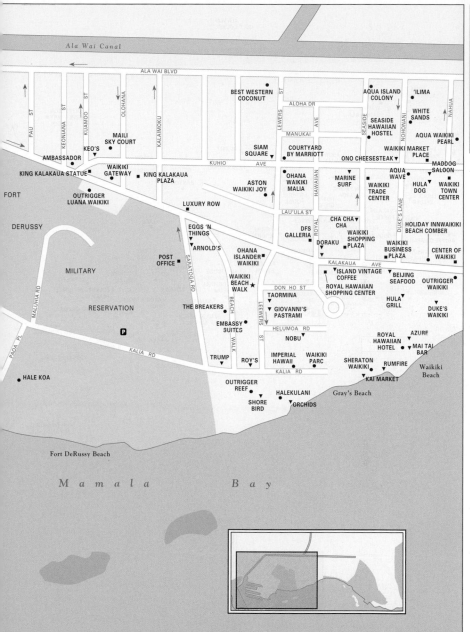

O'AHU

Ala Wai Canal

ALA WAI BLVD

PAU ST
KEONIANA ST
KUAMOO ST
OLOHANA
KALAIMOKU
LEWERS ST
ALOHA DR
AVE
SEASIDE
NOHONANI
NAHUA

BEST WESTERN
COCONUT

AQUA ISLAND
COLONY

'ILIMA

WHITE
SANDS

MAILI
SKY COURT

MANUKAI

SEASIDE
HAWAIIAN
HOSTEL

AQUA WAIKIKI
PEARL

KEO'S

SIAM
SQUARE

COURTYARD
BY MARRIOTT

WAIKIKI MARKET
PLACE

AMBASSADOR

KUHIO
AVE

ONO CHEESESTEAK

MADDOG
SALOON

KING KALAKAUA STATUE

WAIKIKI
GATEWAY

KING KALAKAUA
PLAZA

OHANA
WAIKIKI
MALIA

HAWAIIAN

MARINE
SURF

AQUA
WAVE

HULA
DOG

WAIKIKI
TOWN
CENTER

FORT

OUTRIGGER
LUANA WAIKIKI

ASTON
WAIKIKI JOY

WAIKIKI
TRADE
CENTER

DERUSSY

LUXURY ROW

LAU'ULA ST

DUKE'S LANE

LUXURY ROW

EGGS 'N
THINGS

DFS
GALLERIA

ROYAL

CHA CHA
CHA

WAIKIKI
SHOPPING
PLAZA

HOLIDAY INN WAIKIKI
BEACH COMBER

ARNOLD'S

DORAKU

WAIKIKI
BUSINESS
PLAZA

CENTER OF
WAIKIKI

POST
OFFICE

SARATOGA RD

OHANA
ISLANDER
WAIKIKI

KALAKAUA
AVE

MILITARY

ISLAND VINTAGE
COFFEE

BEIJING
SEAFOOD

OUTRIGGER
WAIKIKI

RESERVATION

WAIKIKI
BEACH
WALK

BEACH WALK

THE BREAKERS

DON HO ST

TAORMINA

ROYAL HAWAIIAN
SHOPPING CENTER

HULA
GRILL

DUKE'S
WAIKIKI

GIOVANNI'S
PASTRAMI

LEWERS ST

EMBASSY
SUITES

HELUMOA RD

NOBU

ROYAL
HAWAIIAN
HOTEL

AZURE

MAI TAI
BAR

KALIA RD

TRUMP

ROY'S

IMPERIAL
HAWAII

WAIKIKI
PARC

SHERATON
WAIKIKI

RUMFIRE

Waikiki
Beach

KALIA RD

KAI MARKET

HALE KOA

MALUHIA RD

PAOA PL

OUTRIGGER
REEF

HALEKULANI

Gray's Beach

SHORE
BIRD

ORCHIDS

Fort DeRussy Beach

M a m a l a   B a y

O'AHU

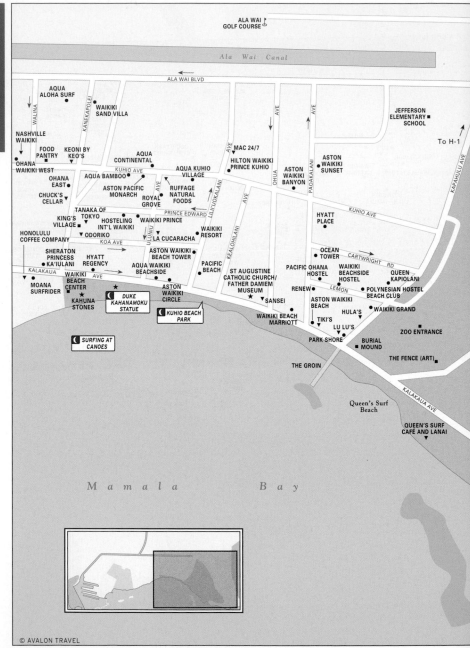

ALA WAI
GOLF COURSE

Ala Wai Canal

ALA WAI BLVD

AQUA
ALOHA SURF

WALINA

KANEKAPOLEI

WAIKIKI
SAND VILLA

AVE

AVE

JEFFERSON
ELEMENTARY ■
SCHOOL

NASHVILLE
WAIKIKI

To H-1

KAPAHULU AVE

FOOD
PANTRY

KEONI BY
KEO'S

AQUA
CONTINENTAL

AVE

MAC 24/7

HILTON WAIKIKI
PRINCE KUHIO

ASTON
WAIKIKI
SUNSET

OHANA
WAIKIKI WEST

KUHIO AVE

AQUA KUHIO
VILLAGE

OHUA

ASTON
WAIKIKI
BANYON

PAOAKALANI

OHANA
EAST

AQUA BAMBOO

AVE

KUHIO AVE

CHUCK'S
CELLAR

ASTON PACIFIC
MONARCH

ROYAL
GROVE

RUFFAGE
NATURAL
FOODS

LILIUOKALANI

HYATT
PLACE

TANAKA OF
TOKYO

PRINCE EDWARD

KING'S
VILLAGE ■

HOSTELING
INT'L WAIKIKI

WAIKIKI PRINCE

ULUNIU

AVE

HONOLULU
COFFEE COMPANY

ODORIKO

WAIKIKI
RESORT

KEALOHILANI

OCEAN
TOWER

CARTWRIGHT RD

KOA AVE

LA CUCARACHA

SHERATON
PRINCESS
KA'IULANI

HYATT
REGENCY

ASTON WAIKIKI
BEACH TOWER

PACIFIC
BEACH

PACIFIC OHANA
HOSTEL

WAIKIKI
BEACHSIDE
HOSTEL

QUEEN
KAPIOLANI

KALAKAUA

WAIKIKI
BEACH
CENTER

AVE

AQUA WAIKIKI
BEACHSIDE

ST AUGUSTINE
CATHOLIC CHURCH/
FATHER DAMIEM
MUSEUM

LEMON

POLYNESIAN HOSTEL
BEACH CLUB

MOANA
SURFRIDER

ASTON
WAIKIKI
CIRCLE

RENEW

ASTON WAIKIKI
BEACH

SANSEI

WAIKIKI GRAND

★
KAHUNA
STONES

★
DUKE
KAHANAMOKU
STATUE

HULA'S

TIKI'S

WAIKIKI BEACH
MARRIOTT

LU LU'S

ZOO ENTRANCE

KUHIO BEACH
PARK

PARK SHORE

BURIAL
■ MOUND

THE FENCE (ART)■

SURFING AT
CANOES

THE GROIN

KALAKAUA AVE

Queen's Surf
Beach

QUEEN'S SURF
CAFÉ AND LANAI
▼

Mamala   Bay

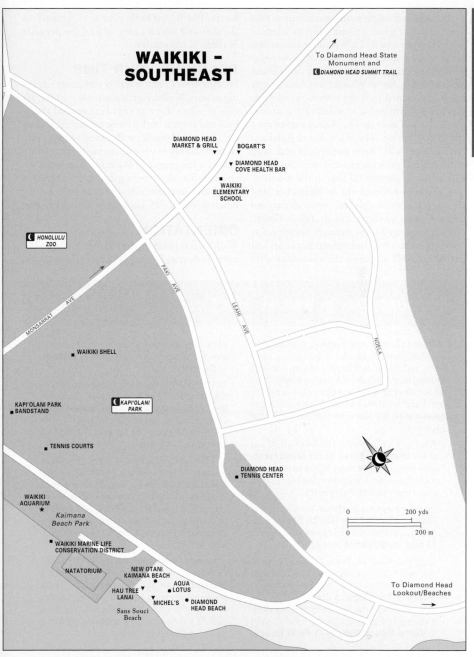

WAIKIKI – SOUTHEAST

To Diamond Head State
Monument and
☾ *DIAMOND HEAD SUMMIT TRAIL*

DIAMOND HEAD
MARKET & GRILL ▼   BOGART'S
                    ▼

                    ▼ DIAMOND HEAD
                       COVE HEALTH BAR

                    ■ WAIKIKI
                       ELEMENTARY
                       SCHOOL

☾ HONOLULU
    ZOO

PAKI AVE

LEAHI AVE

NOELA

MONSARRAT AVE

■ WAIKIKI SHELL

KAPI'OLANI PARK
■ BANDSTAND   ☾ KAPI'OLANI
                        PARK

■ TENNIS COURTS

WAIKIKI
AQUARIUM
★   DIAMOND HEAD
    Kaimana   ■ TENNIS CENTER
    Beach Park

■ WAIKIKI MARINE LIFE
   CONSERVATION DISTRICT

NATATORIUM   NEW OTANI
                    KAIMANA BEACH
                    ●   ● AQUA
HAU TREE ▼   LOTUS
LANAI   ● MICHEL'S ● DIAMOND
                          HEAD BEACH
Sans Souci
Beach

To Diamond Head
Lookout/Beaches
→

0   200 yds
0   200 m

As cliché as it might sound, make sure to take a surf lesson or go on a canoe ride with a beachboy to become a part of a Waikiki tradition that harks back a century to the father of modern-day surfing and original ambassador of aloha Duke Kahanamoku. Across Waikiki, *pau hana* (happy hour) is celebrated every day with food and drink specials and live music to welcome the sunset. Once the sun goes down, Waikiki takes on a whole new tempo. The sidewalks of Kalakaua Avenue teem with street performers and swell with curious onlookers, and the clubs and bars welcome patrons till four in the morning.

Waikiki is not without its blemishes, and the town can get rough and rowdy in the cool hours of early morning. Prostitution is illegal, but tolerated on Kuhio Avenue; homelessness is ever-present; theft and muggings occur; and bar fights spill out onto the sidewalks after hours. But if you keep your eyes focused on the surf and sun, it's easy to find the paradise Waikiki is famous for.

PLANNING YOUR TIME

For first-time O'ahu travelers and many returning visitors, Waikiki is the perfect home base. It's easy to take a day trip anywhere around the island and make it back in time for dinner. It's also the ideal locale to relax at the water's edge in very close proximity to your accommodations. To experience the gamut of Waikiki's sights and activities, set aside a day to spend in the Diamond Head area in addition to the time you plan for beach activities and shopping in Waikiki proper.

ORIENTATION

Waikiki is framed by the Ala Wai Canal to the north and west, Diamond Head to the east, and

Your Best Day in Waikiki

There is so much to do in Waikiki, from outdoor activities like surfing, stand-up paddling, snorkeling, and hiking, to shopping, dining, or simply relaxing on the beach under an umbrella. Of all the activities on offer, some tap into the history and character of Waikiki, which have evolved to make Waikiki the iconic and unique place that it is today.

- Wake up early and walk, run, bike, taxi, or bus to the **Diamond Head State Monument.** Hike through the extinct Diamond Head crater to the summit and take in the entire south shore from your morning perch.

- On your way back to Waikiki proper, stop at **Diamond Head Cove Health Bar** for a delicious acai bowl. If you'd rather have eggs or a bagel, try **Bogart's** next door.

- After refueling, you'll want to head back to the beach and partake in Waikiki's ample ocean activities. If you snorkel, post up at **Queen's Surf Beach** and check out the fish and reef in the marine protected area. If you surf or stand-up paddle, head straight to **Kuhio Beach Park** or **Waikiki Beach,** where you can rent a board and paddle out into the legendary Waikiki surf at **Canoes** or **Queen's.**

- As afternoon rolls around, freshen up back at the hotel and head back outside and cruise the shops on Kalakaua Avenue while being entertained by the street performers. Pick up Hawaiiana goodies for your friends and loved ones back home.

- Is it five yet? Happy hour, better known as *pau hana* in the islands, beckons you into one of Waikiki's many dining establishments. Your best bet is to choose one with an ocean view—think oceanfront hotel. If you'd rather be on the water for sunset, hop on one of the **catamaran cruises** along the beach for a 1.5-hour sail.

- For dinner, immerse yourself in the beach culture of Waikiki and head to **Duke's Waikiki** for an amazing beachfront steak and seafood meal with the best sunset views. Make sure to order a Hula Pie after dinner. If sushi is your game, try **Doraku** in the Royal Hawaiian Shopping Center.

the beautiful Pacific Ocean to the south. Most streets in Waikiki are one-way thoroughfares: **Kalakaua Avenue,** the main drag, runs east to Diamond Head, **Ala Wai Boulevard** runs west, and in between them, **Kuhio Avenue** has two-way traffic east and west. Residents generally define directionality in relation to towns or major landmarks.

Beaches

Waikiki's narrow beaches are generally packed shoulder to shoulder with people, or umbrella to umbrella, for most of the day. In the heart of Waikiki, the towering hotels have been built right to the water's edge, leaving anywhere from 20 to 50 feet of beach for public use. If a leisurely walk along the beach is your fancy, the feat is best accomplished during the first few hours after sunrise or after 6pm, when most people have made their way back to their hotel to prepare for dinner. It's not uncommon for the moon to rise over Diamond Head while the sun is still setting in the west. To get away from the crowds altogether, find a patch of sand along Diamond Head's seaside cliffs and revel in the fact that a short, steep walk down a gravelly path will deter most visitors.

DUKE KAHANAMOKU BEACH

At the west end, or 'Ewa (EH-va) side of Waikiki, is **Duke Kahanamoku Beach,** one of the wider beaches in Waikiki. Fronting the Hilton Hawaiian Village and Beach Resort, it stretches from the Ala Wai Small Boat Harbor to the Hilton's catamaran pier. A shallow outer reef with great waves keeps the inner waters calm and very kid friendly. There's even an artificial ocean-fed lagoon between the beach and the hotel, the perfect spot to try out stand-up paddle surfing without having to worry about ocean chop or currents. The lagoon does have a synthetic feel to it though, especially apparent in its coarse compacted shoreline that makes sand play an all-out construction job. Kahanamoku Beach was recognized in 2012 as Number 3 on Dr. Beach's Best Beaches in America list.

There is a beach path that runs the length of Waikiki, but if you're coming from Kalakaua Avenue, you'll have to trek down Lewers Street,

Beach Walk, or Saratoga Road to reach the sand. There is public beach access on the west side of the Outrigger Reef. Once you hit the beach path, keep walking west till you pass the catamaran pier. If you're coming by car, there is free parking in the Ala Wai Small Boat Harbor.

FORT DERUSSY BEACH

Just east of the catamaran pier, **Fort DeRussy Beach** runs all the way to the Outrigger Reef. Now a clean and tidy public beach and manicured park shaded by canopy trees, this military reservation was one of several shore batteries on O'ahu during WWII and served as an R&R locale for soldiers during the Vietnam War. The beach fronts the Hale Koa hotel, which caters strictly to armed forces personnel and their families, and the U.S. Army Museum, and has a distinct military presence and vibe. It's also known for its calm inner waters, perfect for swimming or snorkeling. An open-air parking lot across from Fort DeRussy Beach Park on Kalia Road is a relatively safe place to park for access to the beach. The rates are average for Waikiki standards at $3 per half hour, and they offer military discounts.

GRAY'S BEACH

Continuing east, the beach ends, and a raised cement walking path on top of the armored shoreline provides transport to **Gray's Beach,** a nook of coarse, imported sand in between the Halekulani and Sheraton Waikiki Hotel. There is also beach access from Kalia Road between the two hotels.

WAIKIKI BEACH

Widened in the spring of 2012, **Waikiki Beach** is half of the heart of Waikiki. Stretching from the Royal Hawaiian to the Moana Surfrider, the first two hotels in Waikiki, this is prime real estate for visitors and the sand fills up quickly with beachgoers. This strip is lined with beach service providers and beachside bars and dining. Because of the sand bottom off Waikiki Beach, the water is a translucent aqua-green and perfect for swimming, stand-up paddling, or just floating on a fluorescent blow-up mat. There is a sandbar just offshore from the Royal Hawaiian that people wade or float out to in order to play in the knee-deep water and small surf. For snorkeling, there's not much to see in the way of marine life, save for the occasional green sea turtle. The famous surf spot Canoes breaks quite a ways offshore, and while this part of the beach does have small shorebreak—quite exciting for the kids—the inner waters are calm and sheltered from the prevailing trade winds.

The easiest way to get to Waikiki Beach is to walk down the shore from Kuhio Beach to the east. Otherwise, make your way through one of the big hotels on the beach to access the world-famous sand, sparkling waters, and iconic view of Diamond Head. Parking in Waikiki is very expensive, whether you valet or self-park at one of the hotel parking garages. Your best bet is to park in the Waikiki Shell parking lot, which is free, and walk down Kalakaua Avenue. There is also free parking on the *makai* side (ocean side) of Kalakaua Avenue from Kapahulu Avenue all the way down to Diamond Head. Since landing one of the coveted free parking spots is hard to do, there is also metered parking on the *mauka* side (mountain side) of Kalakaua Avenue along Kapi'olani Park for a reasonable $0.25 per half hour.

◖ KUHIO BEACH PARK

Stretching from the east side of the Moana Surfrider to the concrete pier where Kapahulu Avenue intersects Kalakaua Avenue, **Kuhio Beach Park** is the other half to the thumping heart of Waikiki. It has a snack bar, restrooms and showers at the west end, two lagoons for sheltered swimming, grassy knolls for

relaxing in the shade under a palm tree, ample beach services, and one of the best waves in Waikiki—Queen's. Just as on Waikiki Beach, you'll want to arrive early to stake a claim in the sand with a beach towel or chair.

Kuhio Beach Park is the hub of surfing in Waikiki, with the forgiving waves of Queen's and Canoes breaking fairly close to shore by Hawaii standards. You'll find a host of beach-boys in red shorts stoked to rent surfboards, stand-up paddle surfboards, bodyboards, and floating mats. They also offer surf lessons and outrigger canoe rides. Along the beach park you'll also find the iconic statue of Duke Kahanamoku adorned in lei and the statue of Prince Kuhio, as well. Once again, it's best to find parking around Kapi'olani Park and walk to Kuhio Beach Park. The beach park is closed 2am-5am.

QUEEN'S SURF BEACH

On the east side of the concrete pier, **Queen's Surf Beach** offers two things you won't find anywhere else in Waikiki: a No Surfboard zone and the Waikiki Marine Life Conservation District. Demarcated by buoys on the east side of the concrete pier, just off the shoreline, the No Surfboard zone sees small waves roll across the shallow waters and up the beach. The ocean floor is a sharp, flat reef with the odd coral head, so swimming and body surfing are not a good idea.

On the east side of the jetty, the Waikiki Marine Life Conservation District stretches to the Waikiki War Memorial Natatorium's crumbling western wall. With fishing forbidden in this 76-acre marine conservation area and calm, shallow inner waters, this healthy reef ecosystem offers the best snorkeling in Waikiki.

Kapi'olani Park, with its wide-stretching banyan trees, runs the length of the beach. There are restrooms, showers, and a hip shoreline café open for breakfast, lunch, and dinner. The Waikiki Aquarium is at the Diamond Head end of the park. Publics is the main surfing wave along the beach, a dangerous left that

© KEVIN WHITTON

Kuhio Beach Park, in the heart of Waikiki

breaks along a shallow reef of odd-shaped coral heads that rise above sea level on an extremely low tide. The beach and park area at Publics, where the beach ends, is a favorite for LGBT visitors. The park is also home to many of Waikiki's homeless population. Parking is available along Kalakaua Avenue and around Kapiʻolani Park.

SANS SOUCI BEACH

A small patch of sand between the eroding Waikiki War Memorial Natatorium and the New Otani Kaimana Beach Hotel, **Sans Souci Beach,** also known as **Kaimana Beach,** is a favorite spot for residents seeking easy access to a family-friendly beach and park without the hassle of getting in and out of Waikiki. There's limited free parking, restrooms, an outdoor shower at the beach, and indoor showers at the natatorium. In front of the natatorium is great for snorkeling, and swimmers take advantage of a wide, deep channel through the reef out to a wind sock fixed on its outer corner. Four laps from the beach to the wind sock is roughly

a mile. The water is very calm, making it the perfect locale for children of all ages.

MAKALEI BEACH PARK

If you're in the mood to escape Waikiki and find solace on your own slice of beach, **Makalei Beach Park** is the best option within Waikiki. Only the quaint park is visible from Diamond Head Road. Tucked back behind some houses in the southwest corner of the park, the beach is a quiet, small strip of sand no more than 100 feet long favored by residents and surfers attracted to Suicides surf break. It's also best to visit on a low tide, when more sand is exposed. Once you are in the water, the seafloor is entirely reef, so ocean life abounds, but choppy conditions and strong currents are prevalent in this area. There are no lifeguards, so exercise caution when snorkeling and swimming off the beach. There are a shower and picnic tables in the beach park. To get there, park around Kapiʻolani Park and walk east up Diamond Head Road. The entrance to the beach park is signed.

O'AHU

DIAMOND HEAD BEACH PARK

At the base of Diamond Head's seaside cliffs are some of the best beaches on the South Shore for escaping the crowds and enjoying the island's natural scenery. There's parking on both sides of Diamond Head Road and a paved footpath that cuts down the cliff. At the bottom of the path, **Diamond Head Beach Park** stretches out in both directions. The shoreline is lined with shells and sea glass, and there are tidepools on the west end of the beach. There are several surf breaks along the reef, but the pervasive trade winds, strong ocean currents, wind chop, and extremely shallow patches of reef make snorkeling and swimming dangerous. The beach below Diamond Head is a great spot for a romantic winter season stroll as the sun sets straight off Waikiki. Diamond Head Beach Park is closed 10pm-5am.

Surfing

Surfing is synonymous with Waikiki. Not only did Hawaiians invent the sport of surfing, but the legendary Duke Kahanamoku—original beachboy, Olympic gold-medalist swimmer, and the father of modern-day surfing who hailed from Waikiki—introduced the fluid sport to the world. The surf breaks that Duke made famous riding on heavy wooden boards are the same spots that surfers seek out today. While the waves are biggest, best, and most consistent during summer, June till September, Waikiki has the potential to see surf at any time during the year. Whether you are a longboarder, shortboarder, experienced, novice, or first-timer, Waikiki has a number of breaks that suit all abilities. Just remember that proper surfing etiquette applies at all breaks, and with so many people in the water, safety and respect for others are of the utmost importance. When in doubt, don't go out.

ALA MOANA BOWLS TO KAISER'S

Ala Moana Bowls is a fast, hollow left that is heavily guarded by a seasoned crew of local surfers. The wave breaks into the mouth of the Ala Wai Small Boat Harbor and is best viewed from across the channel on Magic Island. **Kaiser's** is a predominant right that breaks over a very shallow reef shelf. With a tight take-off zone and a pack of hungry locals, it's also best left to the residents. If you plan on surfing in this area, it's best to surf the stretch of reef between the two spots, known as **Rockpile.** Good for both shortboarding and longboarding, the fast lefts break over sharp, shallow reef and allow for a quick cover up if you're lucky. Paddle out from the small swatch of beach fronting the parking lot (with designated free and paid parking), but avoid the areas of very shallow reef straight out from the beach. There are some slow whitewater rollers on the inside perfect for beginner surfers.

FOURS TO POPULARS

Straight out from the U.S. Army Museum, on the east side of a deep channel, is **Fours,** a wave that only comes alive when the surf gets big. Just to the east of Fours, way out over the outer reef, is **Threes,** a perfect right that breaks best on a low tide and holds it shape at all sizes. Threes is a favorite with local surfers and gets very crowded. To the east of Threes is **Paradise,** a surf zone with big, rolling, shifty peaks. It's a favorite for longboarders and stand-up paddle surfers. Continuing east, the next break is a favorite for all board riders—**Populars.** Locally referred to as Pops, this long right breaks over a sand-covered reef and can handle big surf. When the trade winds are stiff, Pops does get choppy.

C CANOES

Canoes is straight out from the west end of Kuhio Beach Park. It breaks both right and left and has several takeoff zones. A slow

Waikiki Beachboys

If there's something about Waikiki that sets it apart from other tropical sea destinations, it's the Waikiki beachboys. Hailing back a century, the beachboy culture has evolved with the changing face of tourism in Hawaii, but the gentlemen in the red shorts still practice the same core values of sharing the sports of surfing, outrigger canoe riding, and aloha with visitors.

After Calvinist missionaries decimated the Hawaiian culture in the 19th century, the sport of surfing, a purely Hawaiian endeavor, was nearly extinguished. It was seen as sinful because of how much skin was shown while surfing. Only a few surfers remained at the end of the century, namely legendary waterman and three-time Olympic gold medalist Duke Kahanamoku and a few of his friends. As the first wave of wealthy American tourists arrived on steamers in the early decades of the 20th century, these few surfers took it upon themselves to entertain the visitors, teaching them how to surf, ride canoes, and have a good time. In essence, they created a way to earn a living surfing year-round on the beach at Waikiki. These first visitors came to Hawaii for extended stays and were able to develop relationships with the beachboys, who became their tour guides and a bridge to the Hawaiian culture and a different lifestyle. After giving surfing lessons during the day, the beachboys entertained their guests with ukulele, song, and libations at night, a hedonistic lifestyle by all accounts.

The fun was curtailed by WWII, and as travel and tourism have changed since then, so too have the beachboys. With the ease and affordability of flying across the Pacific, a vacation to Waikiki is accessible for so many more people, not just the wealthy elite. Today, with thousands of visitors flocking to the beach daily, the beachboys focus on surfing and outrigger canoe surfing and have shifted roles from entertainers and tour guides to beach services. While only a few of Waikiki's beachboys can still trace their ties back to the original beachboys, any beachboy can still show you how to have the time of your life in Waikiki's gentle surf.

rolling longboard wave, Canoes is perfect for beginners. Start off slow on the inside, catching the whitewater till you learn to stand up and balance on the board. Once you're more confident and comfortable, sit out the back with a mix of locals, beachboys, and people from all around the world sharing in this Hawaiian tradition. Canoes is very crowded with all types of watercraft, from 12-foot longboards to canoes and catamarans. Stay aware and by all means, if something large is coming your way, don't be a deer in the headlights; paddle out of the way.

QUEEN'S

Queen's, also called Queen's Surf, is one of the best waves in Waikiki. Straight off the beach from the east end of Kuhio Beach Park, before the lagoon, it's best for longboarding. Professional and amateur contests are often held here. The perfect turquoise rights draw a host of the best longboarders in Hawaii, who hang ten down the line with style and ease. Queen's is usually very crowded, and if there's any swell in the water, Queen's is breaking. Because of the tight takeoff zone and thick crowd, beginners should stick to Canoes.

PUBLICS TO TONGG'S

Just on the east side of the rock jetty off Queen's Surf Beach, way off the beach on the outer reef, **Publics** is a long left that breaks over shallow, sharp, and irregularly shaped coral heads. Sound inviting? For longboarders, the long, sloping wave offers a chance to get out of the thick crowds in the heart of Waikiki. The wave is best ridden at high tide when the coral heads are submerged. On low tide, the coral heads go dry, and the wave breaks right over them. The break can get choppy from its exposure to the trade winds, and on big south swells, the waves can get quite big and the currents very strong.

A lifeguard in the tower on the beach can assist you with ocean conditions.

To the east of Kaimana are two breaks best for longboarding on the outer reef: **Old Man's** is on the left side of the channel and **Tongg's** just up the reef. These soft, sloping waves offer respite from the Waikiki crowds, but keep an eye peeled for coral heads.

DIAMOND HEAD

On the west end of Diamond Head, off Makalei Beach Park, is a left for experts only called **Suicides**. It's windy, quite a ways off-shore, and subject to strong currents. Below the Diamond Head Lookout parking lots are several good breaks, the two most popular being **Lighthouse** and **Cliffs**. At the bottom of the trail down the cliff is a deep channel through the reef. From the beach, to the right of the channel is Lighthouse, a fast and powerful right for experts only. On the left of the channel is Cliffs, several peaks along the reef that break both right and left and are suited for all types of board riders. Diamond Head can get very windy, as the trade winds blow right across the break. It's a favorite for kite-boarders and sailboarders during the extreme conditions.

OUTFITTERS

Koa Board Sports (2420 Koa Ave., 808/923-0189, www.koaboardsports.com, 10am-6pm daily) has a huge selection of longboards and shortboards available for rent. Rates go from $20 for a half day, $25 for one day (overnight), to $50 for two days. You can also change the board anytime the shop is open.

Hans Hedemann Surf Adventures (2586 Kalakaua Ave., 808/924-7778, www.hhsurf.com, 8am-5pm daily) is located in the Park Shore Hotel between Starbucks and the hotel lobby. The surf school specializes in surf lessons out at Publics. You will have to carry a soft-top longboard from the retail outlet to the break, about a 10-minute walk. They also

offer stand-up paddle lessons, guided surf adventures, and surfboard rentals.

If you prefer to rent your board right on the beach or take a lesson with one of Waikiki's famous beachboys, then you'll want to check out some of Waikiki's vetted beach services. **Faith Surf School** (www.faithsurfschool.com), operated by the legendary Moniz family, offers their expertise at several beach locations: the Outrigger Reef (2169 Kalia Rd., 808/924-6084), the Outrigger Waikiki (2335 Kalakaua Ave., 808/926-9889), and the Sheraton (2255 Kalakaua Ave., 808/922-4422). They rent longboards starting at $20 per hour and offer 1.5-hour group lessons for $60 and private lessons for $125.

Aloha Beach Services (808/922-3111, http://alohabeachservices.com, 8am-4pm daily), serving guests since 1932, has a small palapa, but a lot of boards, in between the Outrigger Waikiki and the Moana Surfrider. They rent longboards for $15 per hour and $5 each additional hour and have one-hour group lessons for $40 and private lessons for $80. They also have a photo package with the group lesson and rent beach umbrellas, chairs, and air mats and rings. Aloha Beach Services accepts cash only.

You'll find **Star Beachboys** (no phone, 8am-4pm daily) at the west end of Kuhio Beach Park, by the concession stand and the bathrooms. They rent 8- to 10-foot longboards for $10 per hour and 11- to 12-foot boards for $15 per hour with a $5 charge for each additional hour. They also have one-hour group lessons for $40 and private lessons for $75. On the sand just to the east of the Duke Kahanamoku statue and at the far eastern end of Kuhio Beach Park are the **Hawaiian Ocean Waikiki** (808/721-5443) beachboys. They have one-hour group lessons for $40 and two-hour private lessons for $100. They also rent longboards starting at $10 per hour and shortboards for $15 per hour, with $5 each additional hour or $35 for a half day. You can rent beach chairs and umbrellas, as well.

Other Water Sports

SNORKELING

The snorkeling in Waikiki is decent at best any time of year. Overuse and overfishing for decades have led to the decline in the number of species and fish in the nearshore waters. All that fine white sand over the reef, which gives the water its light, crystal color, leaves little shelter for reef dwellers. However, patience and luck can yield some great underwater exploring.

Duke Kahanamoku and Fort DeRussy Beach

Since the near-shore waters off **Duke Kahanamoku Beach** and **Fort DeRussy Beach** are not heavily used, the potential to encounter marine life is definitely heightened. The water is shallow, waist- to chest-deep, all the way out to the waves breaking at Threes and Fours, and the bottom is a mix of reef and sand. As an added bonus, you won't have to keep your eye out for surfers, swimmers, canoes, or catamarans, so you can stay focused on what fish you can find.

Waikiki Marine Life Conservation District

The **Waikiki Marine Life Conservation District,** located along Queen's Surf Beach from the jetty to the Waikiki War Memorial Natatorium's western wall, is hands down the best snorkeling in Waikiki. The 76-acre marine conservation area is a regulated and patrolled no-take zone, where fishing or removing of any sea creature is illegal. The protection has allowed a plethora of reef-dwelling vertebrates and invertebrates to thrive. The shallow inner waters are generally calm, but heavy trade winds can texture the surface. Look for bonefish, funny face fish, wrasse, puffer fish, eel, and yellow tang. Chances are you'll even catch a glimpse of the sleek *humuhumunukunukuapuaʻa*.

Diamond Head

The near-shore waters off the beaches of Diamond Head are great for snorkeling, but more suited for experienced snorkelers and swimmers. The reefs at Diamond Head attract all sorts of marine life, including sharks and the endangered Hawaiian monk seal. Shallow water and lots of nooks and crannies in the sharp reef make for great habitat, but beware of extremely shallow areas of reef, strong currents, and wind chop. Snorkeling is best in winter when the waves are small to nonexistent.

Outfitters

Whether you purchase your own snorkel gear or rent equipment is for you to decide. Renting allows you to travel without lugging around cumbersome snorkel gear, while owning gives you the luxury of a custom fit only your mouth knows. **Aqua Zone Scuba Diving & Snorkeling** (2552 Kalakaua Ave., 866/923-3483, www.aquazonescuba.com, 8am-5pm daily), in the Waikiki Beach Marriott, rents and sells gear and is a short walk from the Waikiki Marine Life Conservation District. They rent complete snorkel sets starting at $10 for 24 hours, $20 for three days, and $25 for five days.

    Snorkel Bob's (702 Kapahulu Ave., 808/735-7944, www.snorkelbob.com, 8am-5pm daily), just outside of Waikiki on Kapahulu Avenue, sells equipment and rents complete sets, snorkels, fins, flotation, and wetsuits. They rent several different sets of snorkeling gear. The most basic starts at $2.50 per day and $9 per week.

    Nearly all the beach services at the beachfront hotels rent and sell snorkel gear and most **ABC Stores** sell complete sets as well.

SCUBA DIVING

Once you get offshore from Waikiki, the seafloor slowly sinks away and the water becomes a rich, deep blue. At these greater depths are a few great dive sites, from reefs to shipwrecks. Offshore, the water teems with life, and turtles, eels, triggerfish, octopus, and a host of other reef fish abound. Diving off Waikiki is a year-round pursuit, weather and wave permitting.

In the heart of Waikiki you'll find two PADI diver centers. **Waikiki Diving Center** (424 Nahua St., 808/922-2121, www.waikikidiving.com) dives two wrecks and 10 different sights right off Waikiki. With 32 years of experience, they offer dives for every type of diver, rent and sell equipment, and offer PADI certification. Two-tank beginner dives start at $109, wreck dives start at $99, and PADI certification courses start at $250. **Aqua Zone Scuba Diving & Snorkeling** (2552 Kalakaua Ave., 866/923-3483, www.aquazonescuba.com) is in the Waikiki Beach Marriott. They offer free pool lessons for beginners and rusty divers and daily boat dives for all levels. They offer two levels of PADI certification and provide daily snorkel tours, equipment rental and sales. Two-tank boat dives with rental equipment start at $129. Both Waikiki Diving Center and Aqua Zone dive numerous locations outside of Waikiki as well.

STAND-UP PADDLING

Long before stand-up paddling became a full-fledged sport, a few of the Waikiki beachboys were known to cruise around the lineups kneeling or standing up on longboards and paddling with their canoe paddles. Now the equipment has been refined and stand-up paddling is popular both for surfing and flat-water paddling, each a full-body workout. **Paradise, Populars,** and **Canoes** are the go-to surf breaks for stand-up paddle surfing in Waikiki. If you prefer to just paddle and check out the water from a different perspective, get away from the crowds by paddling out beyond Canoes and **Queen's** and explore. Make your way to **Publics** and paddle in with the wind at your back. You'll be amazed that even at 10-15 feet deep, you'll still be able to see the bottom.

Faith Surf School (www.faithsurfschool.com) rents stand-up paddle boards from the Outrigger Reef (2169 Kalia Rd., 808/924-6084), Outrigger Waikiki (2335 Kalakaua

---

Stand-Up Paddle Surfing

Stand-up paddle surfing, also known as SUP, is a relatively new sport in the surfing world. Originally, Waikiki beachboys rested on their knees on their big longboards and used a canoe paddle to get around. Today's stand-up paddle boards are high-tech, light, and very stable. Stand-up paddle boards range 9-12 feet long, are thick and wide, and made from epoxy resin. Surfers stand with their feet parallel, like a skier, in the center of the board and use a long paddle to accelerate forward. With a little practice, it's easy to pick up the technique rather quickly. Stand-up paddle boards are great for flat-water paddling (distance paddling) and for surfing. Stand-up paddle surfing is a great workout, from your core to your legs and arms, and it affords a great perspective looking down over the reef. Because the boards are so big, though, only experienced stand-up paddlers should try surfing waves, as the boards are hard to maneuver and can be very dangerous for others in the water.

Ave., 808/926-9889), and Sheraton (2255 Kalakaua Ave., 808/922-4422) starting at $25 for one hour and going up to $70 for all day. They also have stand-up paddle lessons starting at $65 up to $125 for a 1.5-hour private lesson.

Aloha Beach Services (808/922-3111, http://alohabeachservices.com, 8am-4pm daily), between the Outrigger Waikiki and the Moana Surfrider, rents stand-up paddle boards for $30 for the first hour and $10 each additional hour. Their lessons start at $60 and go to $80 for a private one-hour lesson. In Kuhio Beach Park, **Star Beachboys** (no phone, 8am-4pm daily) rents boards for $20 for the first hour and $10 for the second. Nearby, **Hawaiian Ocean Waikiki** (808/721-5443, 8am-4pm daily) rents stand-up paddle boards for $25 for the first hour and $10 for each additional hour.

BODYBOARDING

While you can bodyboard any of the waves around Waikiki, bodyboarders congregate in two areas. Just off the cement pier at the east end of Kuhio Beach Park is a break called Walls, where warbley waves break over very shallow reef and wash over the lagoon wall. To the east of the pier, along Queen's Surf Beach, is a specially marked No Surfboard zone. The waves here break over some shallow coral heads along the fringe reef and roll all the way to the shore.

Aloha Beach Services (808/922-3111, http://alohabeachservices.com, 8am-4pm daily), **Star Beachboys** (Kuhio Beach Park, no phone, 8am-4pm daily), and **Hawaiian Ocean Waikiki** (Kuhio Beach Park, 808/721-5443, 8am-4pm daily) rent bodyboards for $5 per hour or $20 per day.

OUTRIGGER CANOEING

The outrigger canoe is one of the defining facets of Hawaiian culture. After all, it is how early Polynesian voyagers first arrived in these islands. Before surfboards came along, native Hawaiian fishers would stand up and "surf" their canoes back to shore. Outrigger canoe paddling and surfing have remained popular in Hawaii to this day, and Waikiki offers the only place on O'ahu you'll be able to hop into a real six-person outrigger canoe with a professional rudder operator to guide you through the surf.

Faith Surf School (www.faithsurfschool. com) runs six-person canoes at $25 each for three waves, with locations at the Outrigger Reef (2169 Kalia Rd., 808/924-6084), the Outrigger Waikiki (2335 Kalakaua Ave., 808/926-9889), and the Sheraton (2255 Kalakaua Ave., 808/922-4422). **Aloha Beach Services** (808/922-3111, http://alohabeachservices.com, 8am-4pm daily) runs eight-person canoes for $15 each for two waves. In Kuhio Beach Park **Star Beachboys** (no phone, 8am-4pm daily) canoe rides are $15 per person for three waves, and **Hawaiian Ocean Waikiki** (808/721-5443, 8am-4pm daily) runs a four-person canoe at $15 each for two waves.

⟨ CATAMARAN SAILING

There are seven catamaran cruises that launch from the beach and sail the waters off Waikiki

almost every day, weather dependent, from Ala Moana to Diamond Head. The boats are different sizes and cater to different interests (some of the catamaran tours are known locally as the "booze cruise"), but the tours all offer a beautiful perspective of Waikiki, the city skyline, and the verdant Ko'olau Mountains from out at sea. **Waikiki Cruises** (no phone, 2-passenger min., 6-passenger max., $20 per person) operates a 24-foot catamaran from the beach fronting the Outrigger Reef. Known for its fluorescent pink sail, the cat sails for one hour Monday-Saturday. First sail launches at 10:30am and the last sail departs around 3pm. You'll need to bring your own refreshments on board and make reservations from the beach.

Waikiki Rigger (808/922-2210, www. waikikirigger.com, $30 pp), a championship racing catamaran, also launches from the beach fronting the Outrigger Reef. Their High Speed Tradewind Sail departs at 11am, 1pm, and 3pm on Tuesday, Thursday, Saturday, and Sunday, and 1pm and 3pm on Monday, Wednesday, and Friday. Nonalcoholic beverages are $1, cocktails

© KEVIN WHITTON

a Waikiki Cruises catamaran

are $3. The daily Sunset Sail ($42 pp) departs at 5pm and offers complimentary beverages. Waikiki Rigger also has a 2.5-hour Aquatic Eco Tour ($51 pp) combining sailing and snorkeling. The 44-foot **Maita'i Catamaran** (808/922-5665, www.leahi.com) seats 47 people comfortably and departs from the beach between the Sheraton Waikiki and the Halekulani hotels. The 90-minute Tradewind Sail ($28 adults, $14 children) leaves the beach at 11am, 1pm, and 3pm. Beverages start at $3. There is a two-hour Underwater Adventure Sail ($45 adults, $27 children) at 10:30am on Monday, Wednesday, and Friday. The Sunset Mai Tai Sail ($39 adults, $19 children) is aptly named for its stocked bar and free beverages. It departs at 5pm. On selected nights the Maita'i offers a Mahina Moonlight Sail ($39 adults, $19 children); times may vary. Children three and under are free on all trips.

On Waikiki Beach you'll find three catamaran operators. In front of the Royal Hawaiian is the **Kepoikai II** (no phone, http://kepokai. com), a 42-foot cat operating in Waikiki for more than 35 years. Their one-hour sail begins at 10:30am daily for $20 per person. Last sail is at 6pm during the summer. On board they sell $1 mai tais, $2 beer, juice, soda, and water. You'll need to make reservations or bookings from the beach.

The **Manu Kai** (808/554-5990) beaches in front of the Outrigger Waikiki and offers one-hour trips ($25 pp with alcoholic beverages, $20 pp without). The 43-foot catamaran's last sail ($30 pp) is at 5:30pm and is a 1.5-hour trip. Right next to the Manu Kai you'll find the famous yellow and red **Na Hoku II** (no phone, www.nahokuii.com, $30 pp with alcoholic beverages, $25 pp without). They offer 1.5-hour trips, and the first leaves the beach at 11:30am. They also have a sunset sail that departs at 5:30pm. Both of these boats have a 49-person maximum capacity and fill up quickly. If you're planning a weekend sunset sail, it's best to make a reservation at least a few days in advance.

At Kuhio Beach Park you'll find the **Mana Kai** (no phone, $20 pp), which holds up to 27 passengers, but will sail with just six. The crew does not serve any beverages, but you are welcome to bring your own. The first one-hour sail departs at 9:30am, and the last sail is around 6pm, depending on the season.

PARASAILING

Parasailing offers the thrill of hang gliding while affixed by a prescribed length of line to a boat motoring across the warm Pacific Ocean. The parachute can soar up to 1,000 feet above the ocean, and as you can imagine, it really is a bird's-eye view. **Hawaii Active** (808/871-8884 or 866/766-6284, www.hawaiiactive.com) is an easy way to book a parasailing trip. There are four options for line length and time in the air, starting with the 300-foot line for 5-7 minutes for $44 per person, up to a 1,000-foot line for 10-12 minutes for $77.

Hiking, Biking, and Bird-Watching

HIKING

You won't need a pair of hiking boots during your stay in Waikiki, even if you do plan on trekking the two "trails" on offer: the Diamond Head Summit Trail inside the Diamond Head crater, or the Waikiki Historic Trail that encircles the region.

Diamond Head Summit Trail

The **Diamond Head Summit Trail** is inside the Diamond Head crater, an extinct tuff cone volcano that erupted about 300,000 years ago, and is part of the **Diamond Head State Monument** (www.hawaiistateparks.org, 6am-6pm daily, $5 per vehicle, $1 walk-in visitor).

A Day At Diamond Head

© KEVIN WHITTON

the Diamond Head Lighthouse

Diamond Head, named Leʻahi in Hawaiian, is the tuff cone of an extinct volcano that erupted approximately 300,000 years ago. Today, the profile of Diamond Head as seen from Waikiki has become an iconic image that conjures up all the beauty and lore of Hawaii. However, there's more to do at this natural wonder than just take a picture for posterity. Here are a few great ways to explore Diamond Head:

- The **Diamond Head Summit Trail** is the most heart-pumping trail in Waikiki. The summit hike climbs 560 feet inside the volcano, from the crater floor to the rim. It is as much a walk through a natural museum as it is a window to Oʻahu's military role in the 20th century: Diamond Head's panoramic view made it the perfect site for coastal defense; five artillery batteries were installed in the crater. The views at the summit lookout are breathtaking and span the entire South Shore.

- Whether you walk, run, or drive to the **Diamond Head Lookout** on Diamond Head Road, it's a great place to relax for a spell and take in the scenery. Mansions line the beach to the east out to rugged Black Point, surfers and windsurfers ride the waves below and sailboats and barges cruise the Pacific in the distance. From December through May, humpback whales can be seen breaching, spouting, and playing off the coast from this vantage point. There's even a working lighthouse on the edge of the cliff.

- Located on Diamond Head Road in between the lookout and Kapiʻolani Park, **Leʻahi Beach Park** is a quiet seaside spot that is a great retreat for a picnic or simply to unwind and gaze out at the ocean. There is no beach at this park, as the surf rushes up against a rock wall protecting the oceanside estates, but there is a nice shaded area, and the park is seldom used.

- To experience Diamond Head in its entirety, take the short paved path down the cliff and take a walk on the beach. There are tidepools at both ends of the beach and straight out from lookout up above is the surf spot called **Cliffs.** It's a great wave for longboarding, and the view from the water, looking back up at magnificent Diamond Head, is something most people don't get to see.

- The **Diamond Head Tennis Center,** a 10-court tennis complex, is nestled up against the west side of the outer crater wall. There's nothing like hitting the ball back and forth with the ever-present Diamond Head as your teammate.

The historic trail, built in 1908, climbs 560 feet from the crater floor to the summit in just 0.8 miles. The steep trail up the inner southwestern rim of the crater is a combination of concrete walkway, switchbacks, stairs, uneven natural terrain, and lighted tunnels. Inside the semiarid crater is hot and rather dry, so bring plenty of water and sun protection. Along the hike you'll see remnants of O'ahu's natural and military history, punctuated by the breathtaking views of the entire South Shore from the observation station at the summit. Plan on 1.5-2 hours round-trip. The entrance to the Diamond Head State Monument is off Diamond Head Road between Makapu'u Avenue and 18th Avenue. The last entrance to hike the trail is 4:30pm. Visitors must exit the park by 6pm. To get there by bus, use route 22, 23, or 24.

Waikiki Historic Trail

The self-guided **Waikiki Historic Trail** (www.waikikihistorictrail.com) takes you throughout Waikiki, covering fascinating historical, geological, and cultural sights with tidbits about Waikiki past and present. Informative surfboard markers at viewing areas correspond to a prescribed map and program available online. Print out a copy of the map and guide to take with you or use a personal electronic device while on the go. You can follow the order of sights in the program or just visit those areas you prefer. The trail begins at Queen's Surf Beach, hugs the coast to the west (the most scenic section of the trail), rounds up to the Ala Wai Canal and follows Kalakaua Avenue back into the heart of Waikiki. At a normal walking pace, the trail takes about two hours to complete.

BIKING

Since bicycles are prohibited on Waikiki sidewalks and the busy avenues of Waikiki, sans bike lanes, are not exactly bike-friendly for those wishing to get around on two wheels, biking is best suited to near and around **Diamond Head** where traffic is lighter and moves a bit slower. Biking to the Diamond Head lookout and beaches will also alleviate the task of finding parking and allow more time for exploring and enjoying your surroundings. You can circumnavigate Diamond Head easily by traveling from Diamond Head Road to Monsarrat Avenue (a great place to stop for a beverage and a bite to eat) to Paki Avenue and then back to Diamond Head Road.

Hawaiian Style Rentals (2556 Lemon Rd., 808/946-6733, www.hawaiianstylerentals.com, 8:30am-5:30pm daily) rents bicycles with helmet, lock, map, front pouch, and rear rack starting at $20 per day and $10 per day for three days or more. You'll also find bicycle rentals at **Adventure Rentals** (159 Kaiulani Ave., 808/924-2700, 8am-5:30pm daily) and **Big Kahuna Motorcycle Tours and Rentals** (407 Seaside Ave., 808/924-2736 or 888/451-5544, www.bigkahunarentals.com, 8am-5pm daily).

BIRD-WATCHING

On the east end of Waikiki, on the Diamond Head-side of where Kapahulu and Kalakaua Avenues intersect, **Kapi'olani Park** (www.kapiolanipark.net) is the place to spot birds in Waikiki. Look up in the trees for green parrots, several types of waxbills, northern and red-crested cardinals, spotted and zebra doves, and the yellow-fronted canary. Look in the grass for the cute Java sparrow, Pacific golden plovers, cattle egrets, and the sassy common myna.

Spas

Several high-end hotels offer spa services. **SpaHalekulani** (2199 Kalia Rd., 808/931-5322, www.halekulani.com/living/spahalekulani, 9am-8pm daily) in the luxurious Halekulani hotel incorporates Polynesian therapeutic rituals into their award-winning services. They offer a full range of custom massage treatments, and their services include professional salon staff. One-hour experiences start at $140; facials start at $140. They have special spa offerings for teenagers 11-15, and their complete packages start at $390.

The **Abhasa Waikiki Spa** (2259 Kalakaua Ave., 808/922-8200, www.abhasa.com, 9am-9pm daily) offers private garden cabanas nestled in the secluded Royal Grove Courtyard of the Royal Hawaiian. The outdoor tropical garden setting is a one-of-a-kind spa experience in Waikiki. Massages and facials start at $135 for 50 minutes, and packages begin at $260.

Next door at the Outrigger Waikiki on the Beach you'll find the **Waikiki Plantation Spa** (2335 Kalakaua Ave., 808/926-2880, www.waikikiplantationspa.com, 9am-7pm daily) in the hotel's penthouse on the 17th floor offering a different, expansive perspective with views of Waikiki Beach and the Pacific Ocean. Stylized with elements of a traditional Zen rock garden, the full service spa also offers private fitness programs to highlight the spa experience. Massages start at $115 for 50 minutes, facials begin at $120 for 50 minutes, packages start at $250, and the spa also features a host of body polishes and wraps, like the popular Papa'ala, which uses cooling aids to help heal sunburns—$100 for the 50-minute treatment.

Set in the historic Moana Surfrider, Waikiki's first hotel, **Moanalani Spa** (2365 Kalakaua Ave., 808/237-2543, www.moanalanispa.com, 8am-8pm daily) combines traditional Hawaiian healing with steam rooms, dry saunas, and water therapy areas with ocean views, along with all the other standard spa services. Moanalani also caters to couples treatments, with two private ocean front lanai. Massage and facials start at $145 for 50-minute sessions, and spa packages begin at $245.

The **Na Ho'ola Spa** (2424 Kalakaua Ave., 808/923-1234, http://waikiki.hyatt.com/hyatt/pure/spas, 7:30am-9pm daily) is located on the fifth floor of the Hyatt Regency Waikiki. The two-story, 10,000 square-foot spa has 16 treatment rooms that evoke the sense of Waikiki, a dry sauna, and steam showers. Massages and body treatments start at $140 for 50 minutes, 50-minute facials begin at $145, and spa packages start at $275.

Sights

◖ HONOLULU ZOO

Only a mere 2,392 miles from the nearest zoo, the **Honolulu Zoo** (151 Kapahulu Ave., 808/971-7171, www.honoluluzoo.org, 9am-4:30pm daily, $14 adults, $8 military adults, $6 children 3-12 with an adult, $4 military children with an adult, children 2 and under free) is a must-see in Waikiki. The plant and animal collections emphasize Pacific tropical ecosystems and are organized into three ecological zones: the African savannah, the Asian and American tropical forest, and the Pacific Islands. Mammals and birds are the spotlight here, with just a few reptiles on display, including a handful of Galapagos tortoises, a Komodo dragon, and dangerous-looking gharials. There's an Indian elephant enclosure with two playful inhabitants. The baboons are quite interactive as well. Zebras, giraffes, hippos, and rhinoceroses are also major draws. The kids

OʻAHU

© KEVIN WHITTON

giraffe at the Honolulu Zoo

will love the massive jungle gym by the snack bar and the Sumatran tiger area. Right next door is the Keiki Zoo, with a crawl-through circular koi fish tank, lizards, farm animals, and a goat petting area.

Art on the Zoo Fence

Fancy yourself an art aficionado? Maybe you'd like to take home a piece of art to remember Hawaii. **Art on the Zoo Fence** (www.arton-thezoofence.com, Sat.-Sun. 9am-4pm) is a great outdoor venue where you can check out a range of art, from photography to postcards to paintings, and speak with the artists, as well. A tradition in Waikiki for over 50 years, artists hang their works from the exterior of the zoo fence along Monsarrat Avenue. Stroll under the towering banyan trees, peruse the art, and engage the artists. It's not uncommon for the artists to be painting on-site.

There are several after-hours events at the zoo, as well. Twilight Tours are on Friday and Saturday evenings. The guided, two-hour walk is a great chance to see who wakes up after everyone has left, and the Dinner Safari is a buffet and a two-hour guided night tour. Every Wednesday during the summer, The Wildest Show Summer Concert Series is a fun family event featuring local musicians. Check the website for the schedule. If you plan on returning to the zoo more than once during your stay or visit Oʻahu several times a year, consider an annual pass. There are several levels of membership, but the average family can take advantage of the Chimpanzee Family membership: unlimited entrance and benefits for one year for two adults and up to four children under 18. There is a pay parking lot for the zoo on Kapahulu Avenue, $1 per hour and the kiosks accept credit cards or coins only, no bills. Free parking is located at the Waikiki Shell parking lots across Monsarrat Avenue on the *makai* side (ocean side) of the zoo.

© KEVIN WHITTON

the Waikiki Aquarium

WAIKIKI AQUARIUM

Situated on 2.35 acres right on the shoreline in Kapi'olani Park, the **Waikiki Aquarium** (2777 Kalakaua Ave., 808/923-9741, www.waquarium.org, 9am-4:30pm daily, $9 adults, $6 military, students, seniors, $4 youth 13-17, $2 children 5-12, children 4 and under free) has a number of beautiful collections focusing on the South Pacific and Hawaiian marine communities. With your paid admission you receive a free audio tour wand, which gives insight and information for all the different collections. The aquarium has both indoor and outdoor viewing areas. Inside you'll find displays showcasing the marine life around the different islands and the creatures living in different marine ecosystems, from the intertidal zone to the open ocean. Corals, giant clams, colorful reef-dwelling fish, predators like sharks, trevally, and groupers, jellyfish, chambered nautilus, and even a gold American lobster (only one in 30 million American lobsters show this genetic disposition) are some of the curious residents at the aquarium. Outside you'll find the monk seal, a tidal pool with fish that reflect the marine life around Waikiki, an interactive area where people can hold hermit crabs and other little creatures, and a serene grassy open space under palm trees right next to the ocean for the kids to run around on and get some energy out or to sit and enjoy a snack.

The Waikiki Aquarium also has a signature summer concert series on the lawn that draws a more mature crowd than the zoo's summer concert series. Ke Kani O Ke Kai: The Sound of the Ocean starts in June and runs through August. Check the website for the latest schedule and information. Parking at the aquarium is very limited. Park along Kalakaua Avenue, the ocean side is free and the mountain side is metered parking, $0.25 per half hour.

◖ KAPI'OLANI PARK

Kapi'olani Park (intersection of Kapahulu and Kalakaua Avenues, www.kapiolanipark.net) is the oldest public park in Hawaii, established in 1877 by King David Kalakaua, monarch of Hawaii. What was once marshland and lagoons

© KEVIN WHITTON

Kapiʻolani Park

is now a 300-acre expanse of grass, sports fields, canopy trees, and running trail. The park attracts all types of sports, from rugby and cricket to soccer and softball and has four lit tennis courts. It's a hub for picnics, birthdays, large family gatherings, and barbecues. The park also draws runners and walkers who circle it on the 3-mile running path. The park is the best spot for bird-watching on the South Shore, and birders set up binoculars and cameras to spy on the avian parkgoers in the mature shower trees, mesquite, and banyans.

The Waikiki Shell, an outdoor concert venue, and the Victorian-style **Kapiʻolani Bandstand,** built in the late 1890s, are in close proximity, just across from the zoo. The park hosts festivals all year long to celebrate culture, food, and community, such as the Korean Festival and the Ukulele Festival. The park extends across Kalakaua Avenue, all the way to the beach. There is free parking along Monsarrat Avenue by the Waikiki Shell and the bandstand, along Paki Avenue, and on the ocean side of Kalakaua Avenue. There are parking meters (10am-6pm daily, $0.25/30 min., 4-hour limit) on the mountain side of Kalakaua Avenue.

DIAMOND HEAD LOOKOUT

Where Kalakaua Avenue and Paki Avenue meet at the east end of Kapiʻolani Park, Diamond Head Road begins its easy climb to the **Diamond Head Lookout.** At the apex, there are two designated areas to pull off the road and park right at the edge of the cliff for spectacular views up and down the coast. Keep in mind that the Waikiki Trolley and tour buses of all sizes also stop at the lookouts, so sometimes they are tranquil and uncrowded, while at other times they are infiltrated by mobs of visitors, taking pictures shoulder to shoulder. The tour buses will block any parked cars from leaving, but on the bright side, they usually don't stay long. From the lookout you can see the waves crashing on shallow reefs to the west, the surfers at Diamond Head's popular surf spots, and

Black Point to the east, its rugged coastline fringed by palm trees and mansions.

Just before the first parking area on the ocean side of Diamond Head Road, coming from Waikiki, is the **Diamond Head Lighthouse** (3399 Diamond Head Rd.). First constructed in 1899, then rebuilt in 1917, the lighthouse still uses its original Fresnell lens, and its beacon can be seen more than 18 miles out to sea. The Lighthouse Keeper's dwelling, where the lighthouse is situated, is a private residence, the quarters of the commander of the Fourteenth Coast Guard district. A gate restricts access to the lighthouse, but its close proximity to the gate, approximately 30 feet, still makes for a Kodak moment.

◖ DUKE KAHANAMOKU STATUE

"The Father of Modern Surfing," Duke Paoa Kahanamoku, is immortalized in a larger than life bronze statue on the sidewalk fronting Kuhio Beach. Hang lei from his outstretched arms, pose with a loved one in front of Duke, and have someone snap a picture—a stop at the Duke statue is a must in Waikiki. Duke is the embodiment of Waikiki, of ocean recreation, and of aloha. Mornings are best to avoid the crowd and to catch the sunlight illuminating the statue. Duke grew up near the Hilton Hawaiian Village and was an accomplished surfer, canoe paddler, and Olympic gold-medalist swimmer. As Hawaii's first

Duke's Legacy

© KEVIN WHITTON

the original ambassador of aloha, Duke Kahanamoku

Born Duke Paoa Kahinu Mokoe Hulikohola Kahanamoku on August 24, 1890, Duke grew up in Waikiki near what is now the Hilton Hawaiian Village. In the course of his childhood on the beach, Duke quickly became a skilled waterman, mastering surfing, outrigger canoe paddling, and swimming. As one of the original Waikiki beachboys, Duke shared his passions with wealthy, upper-class tourists from the U.S. mainland, and by doing so saved the sport of surfing from near extinction. A champion swimmer, Duke won his first gold medal at the 1912 Olympics in Stockholm, Sweden. In 1912 he also traveled to Southern California to give swimming and surfing exhibitions, introducing surfing to America. In 1914, he traveled to Sydney, Australia, for more exhibitions and turned the Aussies on to surfing as well. In the 1920 Olympics in Antwerp, Belgium, he won two more gold medals in swimming. Duke's success and early relationships as a beachboy opened doors for him in the Hollywood film industry, where he played in nearly 20 films from 1925 until 1967. He also served as the sheriff of Honolulu from 1932 to 1961. Known as the original ambassador of aloha, Duke is immortalized in Hawaii for sharing the sport of surfing with the world and embodying the aloha spirit throughout his life.

OAHU

ambassador of aloha, Duke spread the sport of surfing around the world, traveling to the U.S. mainland and Australia for surfing exhibitions. Later in life he became a Hollywood star and held elected office in Honolulu for 29 years.

U.S. ARMY MUSEUM OF HAWAI'I

Located on Fort DeRussy Beach, the **U.S. Army Museum of Hawai'i** (808/955-9552, http://hiarmymuseumsoc.org, 9am-5pm Tues.-Sat., free) highlights O'ahu's military history. The museum is actually inside Battery Randolph, a massive concrete coastal defense structure with reinforced walls up to 12 feet thick. The battery was constructed in 1911 to house two 14-inch guns, part of a system set up to protect Honolulu Harbor from invasion. The battery was rendered obsolete by the rise of the aircraft carrier in WWII. Audio tours are available for $5. The museum validates parking tickets for the Fort DeRussy Parking Facility directly across the street.

DAMIEN MUSEUM

Across from Kuhio Beach is St. Augustine Catholic Church, a David among the high-rise Goliaths. Look for its angular, oxidized green roof resembling a series of A-frames. The **Damien Museum** (130 Ohua Ave., 808/923-2690, 9am-3pm Mon.-Fri., free) is housed in a separate building to the rear, displaying photos and other artifacts of Father Damien, the Belgian priest who humanely cared for the lepers of Kalaupapa, Moloka'i, until his own death from complications of leprosy. Although entrance is free, donations are gratefully accepted because they are the museum's only source of revenue.

Shopping

ROYAL HAWAIIAN CENTER

The **Royal Hawaiian Center** (2201 Kalakaua Ave., 808/922-2299, www.royalhawaiian-center.com, 10am-10pm daily), in the heart of Waikiki on Kalakaua Avenue, stretches from Lewers Street to the Outrigger Waikiki hotel. Here you'll find a mix of high-end retailers—clothing, accessories, and jewelry—surf shops and aloha wear, boutiques, beauty products, and food and drink from coffee to cocktails. If you're looking for local-style luggage and backpacks, check out **DaKine** (808/921-0373) on the second floor of building B. For women's swimwear, **Allure Swimwear** (808/926-1174) is located on the first level of building C. For those visiting Waikiki for romance, visit **Princesse Tam-Tam Lingerie** (808/922-3330) on the third level of building A for fine to moderate French lingerie. For glam accessories and premium denim and leather, find **Remix Hawaii** (808/922-3119) on the first level of building C. With more than 110 shops and restaurants, there's even an **Apple Store** (808/931-2480) for your tech needs. Big-name stores front Kalakaua Avenue, but there is a parallel walkway through the mall with a host of other stores, a great way to get out of the sun. A small outdoor performance area with hewn stone seats under a banyan tree leads to a beautifully landscaped Hawaiian botanical garden and into the Royal Hawaiian hotel courtyard.

LUXURY ROW

Just to the west of the Royal Hawaiian Center on Kalakaua Avenue, on the mountain side of the street, is **Luxury Row** (2100 Kalakaua Ave., 808/541-5136, www.luxury-row.com, 10am-10pm daily). The name says it all. At Luxury Row you'll find high-end international brands like **Coach** (808/924-1677), **Chanel** (808/971-9011), **Tiffany & Co.** (808/926-2600), **Yves Saint Laurent** (808/924-6900), **Bottega Veneta** (808/923-0800), and **Gucci** (808/921-1000).

ART GALLERIES

Art abounds in Waikiki, with Hawaiian, ocean, and nature themes being the most prevalent. **Wyland Galleries Waikiki** (270 Lewers St., 808/924-1322, www.wyland. com, 10am-10pm daily) features Wyland's signature ocean art and is the most comprehensive Wyland source in Hawaii. Also on Lewers Street in the Waikiki Beach Walk shops is the **Peter Lik Gallery** (226 Lewers St., 808/926-5656, www.lik.com/galleries/waikiki.html, 10am-11pm daily), featuring bold prints from landscape photographer Peter Lik. Inside the Outrigger Waikiki on the Beach (2335 Kalakaua Ave.) you'll find **Tabora Gallery** (808/922-5400, 8am-11pm daily) with originals from seascape painter Roy Tabora. **Sand People** (2369 Kalakaua Ave., 808/924-6773, www.sandpeople.com, 9:30am-9:30pm daily), next door to the Outrigger in the Moana Surfrider, is a quaint gift shop with ocean-themed trinkets, art, and clever gift ideas like vintage signs and surf art.

Entertainment and Events

NIGHTLIFE

Lu Lu's (2586 Kalakaua Ave., 808/926-5222, www.luluswaikiki.com, 7am-2am daily) serves breakfast, lunch, and dinner, but is more widely known as a place to hang out, have a beer, and enjoy their second-story view. Right on the corner of Kalakaua and Kapahulu Avenues, it's the spot for people-watching.

Maddog Saloon (2301 Kuhio Ave., 808/924-3400, www.MaddogSaloonWaikiki.com, 10am-4am daily) is a great after-hours bar (after 2am) with dartboards and pool tables.

The Hideaway Bar (1913 Dudoit Ln., 808/949-9885, 6am-2am daily) is a famous little dive that prides itself on being the first establishment in Waikiki to start serving alcohol fresh and early at 6am. It's also notorious for interesting characters.

For a more upscale experience, check out **Rum Fire** (2255 Kalakaua Ave., 808/922-4422, www.rumfirewaikiki.com, 11am-12:30am Fri.-Sat., 11am-midnight Sun.-Thurs.) in the Sheraton Waikiki. Set by the infinity pool, the food is globally influenced to complement the cocktails.

Next door at the Royal Hawaiian is the **Mai Tai Bar** (2259 Kalakaua Ave., 866/716-8109, www.royal-hawaiian.com/dining/maitaibar, 10am-midnight daily). Right on the beach, the views are exquisite, and there are a couple of cabanas to lounge under. The food and drink are on the expensive side.

The **Irish Rose Saloon** (478 Ena Rd., 808/947-3414, www.irishrosesaloon.com, 6am-2am daily) is a great Irish pub with live and loud rock and roll and a great selection of Irish whiskey, of course. Smoking is still allowed in the Irish Rose, which you'll either love or hate.

Nashville Waikiki (2330 Kuhio Ave., 808/926-7911, www.nashvillewaikiki.com, 4pm-4am daily) is Waikiki's only country-and-western bar, complete with line dancing. Open till early morning, a military favorite, and located along the more seedy part of Kuhio Avenue, it is notorious for fights and skirmishes.

Arnold's Beach Bar & Grill (339 Saratoga Rd., 808/924-6887, 10am-2am daily) is a kitschy throwback to the 1950s. It's warm and cozy, the service is friendly, and the drinks are priced just right.

One of the only true nightclubs in Waikiki, **Addiction Nightclub** (1775 Ala Moana Blvd., 808/943-5800, http://addictionnightclub.com, 10:30pm-3am Thurs.-Sat.) is in the chic Modern Honolulu hotel. DJs, dancing, bottle service—check the website for who's spinning while you're in town.

On the second floor of the Waikiki Grand hotel, **Hula's Bar & Lei Stand** (134 Kapahulu Ave., 808/923-0669, www.hulas.com,

10am-2am daily) is Waikiki's premier gay and lesbian bar. Famous for its open-air lanai and beautiful views from the rail, they have DJs and dancing, daily drink specials, and a limited menu of entrées and appetizers. Check their website for a complete monthly events calendar.

LUAU AND REVUES

There are two traditional luau in Waikiki. The Hilton Hawaiian Village's (2005 Kalia Rd., 808/949-4321, www.hiltonhawaiianvillage.com) **Waikiki Starlight Luau** is an outdoor luau featuring traditional Hawaiian, Tahitian, and Samoan live music and dance, as well as traditional luau fare with accompanying dishes for the less adventurous like huli huli chicken and Hawaiian fried rice. Held Sunday through Thursday (weather permitting) on the rooftop of the Mid-Pacific Conference Center, the two-hour show begins at 5:30pm with general seating for $102 adult, $51 children 4-11, and premier seating for $125 adult, $62.50 children 4-11. Children under 3 are free. The premier seating includes a fresh orchid lei greeting, preferred table seating closest to the stage, and first dibs at the buffet. All prices include two complimentary beverages.

The Sheraton Princess Kaiulani (120 Kaiulani Ave., 808/922-5811, www.princess-kaiulani.com) hosts **Creation: A Polynesian Journey,** a lavish and dramatic luau and show featuring Hawaiian legend, Samoan and New Zealand dance, and modern hula. Creation shows five nights a week (closed Monday and Wednesday) starting at $110 adult, $82.50 for children 5-12, for the basic dinner show package. There is also a deluxe dinner show package for a higher rate, as well as a cocktail show package for $65 adult and $48.75 children 5-12.

The Royal Hawaiian (2259 Kalakaua Ave., 808/923-7311, www.royal-hawaiian.com) has a plated luau dinner and show held on the Ocean Lawn called **'Aha'aina,** a cultural journey through time. The special dinner is served Monday evenings 5:30pm-9pm for $175 adult, $97 for children 5-12. There is a nominal charge for children under 5 years.

If you're in the mood for an evening revue with cocktails, check out **Society of Seven** (2335 Kalakaua Ave., 808/923-7469, www.societyofseven.com) on the second floor of the Outrigger Waikiki on the Beach. The show presents Broadway hits, pop music favorites with artists in full costume, and skits and original pieces as well. The show runs Tuesday through Saturday with two seatings: a show and dinner option at Hula Grill starting at 5:30pm or simply the show and cocktails at 7:30pm.

LIVE MUSIC AND CONCERT VENUES

The Waikiki Shell (2805 Monsarrat Ave., www.blaisdellcenter.com/venues/waikikishell.html) in Kapi'olani Park is Waikiki's premier concert venue and draws all sorts of performers and musicians. The outdoor, shell-shaped amphitheater has an acoustically sophisticated stage to help amplify music and sound, which reaches all the way to the Pacific Ocean with remarkable clarity. With seating and an expansive lawn area, the Shell is the perfect venue for twilight concerts. There is a free parking lot at the Shell and ample free and paid parking

Street Performers

Once the sun sets over Waikiki, the streets teem with people shopping, walking to dinner (or just waiting for a table), and strolling the main drag, simply enjoying the warm tropical night. Taking advantage of this makeshift nightly audience, Waikiki's street performers line the mountain side of the 2300 block of Kalakaua Avenue, wrapping around Kaiulani Avenue and up to King's Village. Break-dancers, spray paint artists, portrait artists, musicians, and gold- and silver-painted mimes entertain for a drop in the hat. Some of the acts draw quite a crowd, so if you're on the move and don't want to get caught up in the melee, it's best to walk on the other side of the street.

around the park. The Waikiki Shell events schedule is posted online.

A good portion of the restaurants and bars in Waikiki, especially the ocean-front establishments, have live music during *pau hana* and at night, usually a solo guitarist and singer or duo playing a mix of island-style classic rock peppered with a few island lounge classics. By far, the most popular free concert in Waikiki is **Duke's on Sunday.** From 4pm-6pm every Sunday at Duke's Waikiki (2335 Kalakaua Ave., 808/922-2268, www. dukeswaikiki.com) in the Outrigger Waikiki hotel, Hawaiian rock legend Henry Kapono plays a lively 2-hour rock-and-roll set of his own hits and classic rock covers done in his own style. Known as the "Wild Hawaiian," he draws residents and visitors alike to Duke's lower lanai, right on the sand, to catch the show, dance, and enjoy a few beverages in the afternoon sun. Kapono plays every Sunday unless he's on tour, in which case there are several other noteworthy bands in the lineup that put on a great show.

Food

COFFEE

Honolulu Coffee Company (2365 Kalakaua Ave., 808/533-1500, ext. 4, www.honolulucoffee.com, 6am-10pm daily) can be found at the Moana Surfrider, but is right on the sidewalk of Kalakaua Avenue, so you don't need to enter the hotel to find it. They have a wide variety of bagels, breads, and pastries and several tables, even sidewalk window seats.

Upstairs in the Royal Hawaiian Shopping Center, on the second floor, you'll find **Island Vintage Coffee** (2201 Kalakaua Ave., 808/922-2299, www.islandvintagecoffee.com, 6am-11pm daily), serving 100 percent Kona coffee, prepared foods, bakery treats, and aìai bowls. They also have a nice lanai where you can enjoy your coffee and snack.

QUICK BITES AND CAFÉS

Giovanni's Pastrami (227 Lewers St., 808/923-2100, www.giovannipastrami.com, 10am-10pm daily, $9-23) is a great New York-style deli and sports bar. With choice ingredients to nosh, 17 TVs, breakfast served till midnight, and a weekday happy hour 3pm-6pm, it's a great place to watch the game and have a sandwich and beer in style.

At **Ono Cheesesteak** (2280 Kuhio Ave., 808/923-8080, www.onocheesesteak.com, open 24 hours daily, $4-10) you know what you're getting—a Philly cheesesteak. They have chicken, beef, and vegetarian sandwiches with steak fries, curly fries, or onion rings anytime you can handle.

A toasted hole in the bun, tropical relishes, and one-of-a-kind garlic lemon sauces on a polish sausage make **Hula Dog** (2301 Kuhio Ave., 808/924-7887, www.huladoghawaii.com, 8am-midnight daily, $7) a snack, or meal, to experience. Doubling as a sports bar, during football season they open at 6am.

Mac 24/7 (2500 Kuhio Ave., 808/921-5564, www.mac247waikiki.com, open 24 hours daily, $14-28) serves so many different purposes in Waikiki. It's a bar, it's a club, it's a restaurant, and it's a breakfast joint. Find it inside the Hilton Waikiki Beach Hotel and see if you're up to the pancake challenge—eat three 14-inch pancakes topped with a slew of fixings in under 90 minutes for free breakfast, prizes, and bragging rights.

What's the perfect meal in Waikiki? How about an afternoon surf at Publics and then dinner at **Queen's Surf Café & Lanai** (2701 Kalakaua Ave., 808/924-2233, 7am-7pm Mon.-Wed., 7am-9pm Thurs.-Sat., 7am-8pm Sun., $9-15) overlooking Queen's Surf Beach and the beautiful waves that peel along the reef. Open-air seating right on the beach and good food—what could be better? Live music Thursday through Sunday and beach barbecue Friday and Saturday starting at 5:30pm—that's what.

Bogart's Café (3045 Monsarrat Ave., 808/739-0999, 6am-6:30pm Mon.-Fri., 6am-6pm Sat.-Sun., $6-21) is a great little breakfast spot for escaping the bustle of Waikiki proper. The eggs, bagels, pancakes, waffles, and coffee are the perfect breakfast options after a walk or run across Kapi'olani Park.

From homemade cakes, salads, and dips to cold sandwiches, local food, and burgers right off the grill, **Diamond Head Market & Grill** (3575 Campbell Ave., 808/732-0077, www.diamondheadmarket.com, 6:30am-9pm daily, $5-17) has a little bit of everything on offer. The grill has a walk-up window on the exterior of the building. Be prepared for a bit of a wait at lunch, as the food is popular with locals and visitors alike. And check out all the bakery delights inside. The scones are beyond delicious, if there are any left.

BREAKFAST

Eggs 'n Things (343 Saratoga Rd., 808/923-3447, www.eggsnthings.com, 6am-2pm, 5pm-10pm daily, $8-17) is an extremely popular breakfast joint serving American-style breakfast with a few local style variations. Meat, eggs, pancakes, waffles, and even crepes are the crux of the menu. They serve dinner as well. There is also a location on Kalakaua Avenue, called the **Waikiki Beach Eggspress** (2464 Kalakaua Ave., 808/926-3447, 6am-2pm, 5pm-10pm daily, $8-17), which has an interesting seating method. First you'll have to wait in line to order, then you wait in line to get seated, and then sometimes you'll have to wait a little longer for your food to arrive. With an average wait of 30-40 minutes from the moment it opens, it's apparent Eggs 'n Things has developed quite a following.

STEAK AND SEAFOOD

The **Hau Tree Lanai** (2863 Kalakaua Ave., 808/921-7066, http://kaimana.com/hautree-lanai.htm, 7am-2pm, 5:30pm-9pm daily, $30-52) is a quaint open-air restaurant right on Sans Souci Beach, nestled under the canopy of a distinctive hau tree growing on the property for more than a century. In fact, American author Robert Louis Stevenson enjoyed its shade in the early 1900s as a place where he could relax and put pen to paper. Serving breakfast, lunch, and dinner, they offer traditional American and Asian-influenced cuisine.

Azure (2259 Kalakaua Ave., 808/923-7311, www.azurewaikiki.com, 5:30pm-9pm daily, $26-52) is the pinnacle of fine seafood dining. Set inside the Royal Hawaiian, it serves the freshest seafood there is, hand selected from the Honolulu fish auction every morning. The focus is on high-heat aromatic herb-roasted and Hawaii regional preparations with bright tropical flavors. Sommeliers can assist in selecting the perfect wine for your dinner. Azure has beachfront dining cabanas in addition to the dining room and a traditional six-course degustation menu with samplings of the chef's signature dishes and wine pairings.

Tired of ordering a steak and finding it not done to your liking? Then the **Shore Bird** (2169 Kalia Rd., 808/922-2887, http://shorebirdwaikiki.com, 7am-2am daily, $16-30), a beachfront restaurant in the Outrigger Reef, is your calling. At the Shore Bird's Famous Grill, you can cook your own steak, chicken, or fish. They also serve breakfast and lunch, and have a late night menu with classic bar food.

Roy's (226 Lewers St., 808/923-7697, http://royshawaii.com, 11am-9:30pm Mon.-Thurs., 11am-10pm Fri.-Sun., $15-45) has Hawaiian fusion wired, and the quality of ingredients, consistency, and service are exceptional. They are open for appetizer service 11am-5pm and offer a prix fixe menu with a sampling of all the favorites in addition to a well-balanced offering of meat and fish entrées, as well as sushi.

Orchids (2199 Kalia Rd., 808/923-2311, www.halekulani.com/living/dining/orchids, 7:30am-10pm daily, $28-60) is located inside the Halekulani hotel. As the name suggests, colorful orchids abound, and the restaurant opens out to a breathtaking view of the Pacific Ocean unencumbered by beach umbrellas or sunbathers. Their Sunday brunch is punctuated by a three-meat carving station, something you won't find at most Waikiki breakfast buffets, and their signature dinner entrée is a light onaga (snapper) Orchids-style, with sesame oil, shoyu, and ginger. They also offer a lunch menu.

Kai Market (2255 Kalakaua Ave., 808/921-4600, www.sheraton-waikiki.com/dining/kai, 6am-11am, 5:30pm-9:30pm daily, breakfast $22-29, dinner $55-58) prides itself on locally sourcing all its products and ingredients, from the baked goods to the meat and produce. Kai Market is inside the Sheraton Waikiki, and both breakfast and dinner are buffet style. Kids 5 and under eat free anytime, and children 6-12 eat for half price.

Top of Waikiki (2270 Kalakaua Ave., 808/923-3877, http://topofwaikiki.com, 5pm-9:30pm daily, starting at $37) is truly a unique dining experience. On the top floor of the Waikiki Business Plaza, the three-tiered round restaurant slowly revolves 360 degrees per hour, offering guests a complete view of O'ahu's glowing South Shore. An open sit-down bar provides an additional level for viewing the sights. Great Pacific Rim cuisine and nightly happy hour specials—5pm-7pm and 9pm-11pm—complete the experience.

Duke's Waikiki (2335 Kalakaua Ave., 808/922-2268, www.dukeswaikiki.com, 7am-12:30am daily, $15-33) is a must, whether its for the breakfast buffet, lunch, dinner, or just cruising in the Barefoot Bar and watching the surfers out at Canoes and Queen's. Decorated with historic and recent pictures of the Waikiki beachboys and surf nostalgia, the relaxed, beachside atmosphere complements the excellent food and service. They have live music Monday through Thursday in the bar 4pm-6pm, and Friday through Sunday the show moves out to their lower lanai under the sun, the highlight being Duke's on Sunday, featuring Henry Kapono (unless he's on tour). For dinner, make a reservation or be prepared to wait up to an hour during busy times, which isn't that bad if you retire to the bar and relax till your table is ready.

Hula Grill (2335 Kalakaua Ave., 808/923-4852, www.hulagrillwaikiki.com, 6:30am-10pm daily, $20-34), in the Outrigger Waikiki and just upstairs from Duke's, is a great steak and seafood option if you don't have the time to wait for a table downstairs. With comfortable, Hawaiiana home decor and live music nightly 7-9pm, they provide a comfortable ambience in which to savor several fish specialties including the popular Macadamia Nut Crusted, as well as the succulent Filet Steak Kiana, their take on the steak Diane. Hula Grill has a great Aloha Hour 4pm-6pm with half-off selected menu and drink items.

Chuck's Cellar (150 Kaiulani Ave., 808/923-4488, www.chuckshawaii.com/cellar.html, 5:30pm-10pm daily, starting at $20) offers an all-you-can-eat salad bar with every entrée, but the real draw for Chuck's Cellar is live jazz Thursday through Sunday. The decor, and a little jazz flute, will take you back in time.

In the Aston Waikiki Beach Hotel on the second floor overlooking Kuhio Beach Park, **Tiki's Grill & Bar** (2570 Kalakaua Ave., 808/923-8454, http://tikisgrill.com, 10:30am-2am daily, $24-29) is a locally owned and operated establishment with tasty lunch and dinner menus serving regional and Pacific Rim cuisine. Their ingredients are locally sourced, and they partner with local farmers for the freshest produce, as well as following a Green Program in all aspects of their business. Catch Hawaiian Hula Nights every Thursday 5pm-11pm featuring traditional and contemporary Hawaiian music, hula, and food and drink specials on their open lanai.

Michel's (2895 Kalakaua Ave., 808/923-6552, http://michelshawaii.com, 5:30pm-9pm Mon.-Thurs. and Sun., 5:30pm-10pm Fri.-Sat., $40-75) is the pinnacle of French haute cuisine in Waikiki and has been recognized as the "Best Restaurant for Romance" since 1985. Overlooking a beautiful stretch of reef and ocean closer to Diamond Head and away from the Waikiki crowds, their stunning setting, live music, and delectable menu are worth the price for a truly special occasion. They also offer a chef's choice six-course tasting menu.

MEXICAN

Cha Cha Cha (342 Seaside Ave., 808/923-7797, 11am-midnight Mon., Wed.-Sun., 11am-2am

Tues., $10-16) is a great change of pace for your palate. A cross between Mexican and Caribbean, with jerk side by side on the menu with nachos and fish tacos, they also have a few great homemade salsas to accompany their meals. Doubling as a tequileria, try 'em all and get your name on the wall.

ITALIAN

Perched at the top of the Ilikai hotel, **Sarento's** (1777 Ala Moana Blvd., 808/955-5559, www.sarentoswaikiki.com, 5pm-10:30pm Sun.-Thurs., 5pm-midnight Fri.-Sat., $24-42) has magnificent views of Waikiki and Honolulu's skyline. Fine Italian dining with a Mediterranean flair is accompanied with live piano music and great service.

Taormina (227 Lewers St., 808/926-5050, http://taorminarestaurant.com, 11am-10pm Sun.-Thurs., 11am-11pm Fri.-Sat., $17-49) serves Sicilian cuisine in a fine dining setting. With fresh fish and homemade breads and pastas for their specials, they offer over 125 wines for the perfect pairing. A favorite is the Fresh Pasta Nero "Frutti Di Mare."

JAPANESE

No detail has been left unexplored at **Nobu** (2233 Helumoa Rd., 808/237-6999, www.noburestaurants.com, 5:30pm-10pm Mon.-Thurs. and Sun., 5:30pm-10:30pm Fri.-Sat., $48), where the architecture and interior help create an intimate and elegant setting, and the innovative and award-winning "New Style" Japanese cuisine is unmatched. A sophisticated seafood-centric menu covers a range of hot and cold dishes, sushi and sashimi, complete dinners, and kushiyaki and tempura. Their happy hour (5pm-7pm Sun.-Thurs.) has drink and food specials that could suffice for a meal by themselves, though it's only available in the bar and lounge area.

Serving contemporary, inventive sushi and Asian-influenced dishes, (**Sansei Seafood Restaurant and Sushi Bar** (2552 Kalakaua Ave., 808/931-6286, www.sansei-hawaii.com, 5:30pm-10pm Mon.-Thurs. and Sun., 5:30pm-1am Fri.-Sat., starting at $8) is one of the most popular sushi restaurants in Waikiki. With its handful of award-winning sushi creations, the à la carte menu is perfect for sampling the gamut. They have a popular early bird special 5:30pm-6pm Sunday and Monday with half-off most of the menu (people line up early at the door) and half-off drink specials 10pm-1am Friday and Saturday.

Odoriko (2400 Koa Ave., 808/923-7368, http://odorikohawaii.com, 6am-midnight daily, $4-50) serves up traditional Japanese cuisine for breakfast, lunch, and dinner, as well as offering an assortment of fresh seafood and sushi—even live Maine lobster. If you're not feeling like fish, they also have hot pot entrées like shabu-shabu or sukiyaki. Odoriko has private party and karaoke rooms for rent by the hour starting at $30.

Tanaka of Tokyo (131 Kaiulani Ave., 808/922-4233, www.tanakaoftokyo.com, 5:30pm-11pm daily, $19-95) is a Japanese seafood and steak house teppanyaki restaurant where the food is prepared by master chefs on tabletop grills. It's a fun and relaxed atmosphere with excellent food and service. The Shogun Special, with tenderloin, lobster tail, and sea scallops, is a house favorite. Find them on the third floor of King's Village.

Doraku Sushi (2233 Kalakaua Ave., 808/922-3323, http://dorakusushi.com, 11:30am-11pm Mon.-Thurs., 11:30am-2am Fri.-Sat., 11:30-midnight Sun., $4-44) features izakaya dining, where dishes are brought to the table throughout the meal to share. On the menu you'll find hot and cold dishes as well as a beautiful assortment of specialty sushi rolls, sashimi, and soups and salads. A relaxing and enjoyable experience.

CHINESE

For fine Chinese seafood dining check out **Beijing Chinese Seafood Restaurant** (2301 Kalakaua Ave., 808/971-8833, www.beijing-hawaii.com, 11:30am-2:30pm, 5pm-9:30pm daily, $35-92). Specializing in set dinner menus with a variety of delectable seafood creations paired with entrées including duck, chicken, and beef, this place won't let you leave hungry. Their lunch menu features a range of steamed dumplings.

THAI

Keo's Thai Cuisine (2028 Kuhio Ave., 808/951-9355, www.keosthaicuisine.com, 7am-10pm daily, $13-20) is an internationally known and award-winning restaurant that has great prices for the quality of the food, the chic atmosphere, and a colorful tropical garden interior. The owner sources many of his ingredients from his two North Shore farms.

Keoni by Keo's (2375 Kuhio Ave., 808/922-9888, www.keonibykeos.com, 4pm-10:30pm daily, $11-18) is Keo's sister restaurant and has Thai and Western cuisine on the menu.

Siam Square (408 Lewers, 808/923-5320, www.siamsquaredining.com, 11am-10:30pm daily, $10-15) is a great little Thai place located upstairs from the ABC Store on the corner—look for the small sign. It's clean and comfortable with good food, as well.

HEALTH FOOD

◖ Diamond Head Cove Health Bar (3045 Monsarrat Ave., 808/732-8744, www.diamondheadcove.com, 10am-8pm Mon. and Fri.-Sat., 10am-11pm Tues.-Thurs., and Sun., $5-13) is a small juice and kava bar that's also famous for hearty and healthy aìai bowls. The staff is friendly, the food is fresh and delicious, and surf art, posters, and decorations fill every space on the walls and ceiling, creating a cool hangout to beat the midday heat. The Cove, as it's known by local patrons, stays open late for Kava Nights, Tuesday through Thursday, when they turn the lights low and let the live musicians set the mood.

One of the few places in Waikiki that caters to vegetarians and vegans, **Ruffage Natural Foods** (2443 Kuhio Ave., 808/922-2042, 9am-6pm daily, $5-10) has simple but great sandwiches, salads, burritos, and other prepared foods (they do have meat options, too). They also sell health foods as well as blend great smoothies.

Getting There and Around

CAR

If you didn't pick up a rental car at the airport and find you would like to make use of a vehicle during your stay, there are national big-brand companies in Waikiki as well as several smaller independent firms that rent vehicles including sedans, four-wheel drives, SUVs, and convertibles. **Thrifty** (2002 Kalakaua Ave., 808/971-2660, www.thrifty.com, 7am-8pm daily) and **Dollar** (2002 Kalakaua Ave., 808/952-4264, www.dollar.com, 7am-8pm daily) share a lot at the west end of Waikiki. Among the independent companies are **VIP (Very Inexpensive Prices) Car Rentals** (234 Beach Walk, 808/922-4605, www.vipcarrentalhawaii.com, 7am-5pm daily) and **Paradise Rent-A-Car** (1837 Ala Moana Blvd., 808/946-7777; 151 Uluniu Ave., 808/926-7777; http://paradiserentacarhawaii.com, 8am-5pm daily).

The most distinctive cars in Waikiki are the sports cars and luxury imports available from **Hawaii Luxury Car Rentals** (2025 Kalakaua Ave., 808/222-2277, www.hiluxurycarrentals.com, 8am-5pm daily). This company has a fleet of American and European classic cars, like the Viper, Corvette, Porsche, Cadillac Escalade, H2 Hummer, BMW, and the only Prowler for rent in Hawaii, all at the Aloha Gas Station. Rates start at $250 per day for the Prowler. They offer multiple day discounts and welcome customers 21 and over.

BUS

Many popular island destinations and attractions are reachable via the Honolulu public bus system, called **TheBus** (www.thebus.org), either directly from Waikiki or from the Ala Moana Shopping Center bus depot after a short ride from Waikiki. Routes 19 and 20 will get travelers to the airport in Honolulu; Diamond

Head can be reached via buses running on Routes 22, 23, and 24.

TAXI AND LIMOUSINE

There are several taxicab companies that service Waikiki. **Star Discount Taxi Service** (808/942-7827, www.startaxihawaii.com) offers a $30-or-less flat rate to or from the Honolulu International Airport from any Waikiki hotel and has discount flat-rate fares for a variety of O'ahu destinations; **TheCAB** (808/422-2222, www.thecabhawaii.com) operates 24 hours a day, 365 days a year; **Honolulu Taxi Service** (808/699-9999, http://honolulu-taxi.com) has door-to-door service; and for **Honolulu Taxi Cab** (808/741-7545), call one hour ahead for best service.

Limos are a great way to get around in style and are popular for wedding parties and transfer to and from the airport. **Duke's Limousine** (808/738-1878, www.dukeslimo.com) has a fleet of limos with varying carrying capacity and rates starting at $60 per hour with a two-hour minimum. **Hawaii Limo** (808/294-1124, http://hawaiilimo.org) has rates that start at $75 per hour for six passengers, flat rates for airport service, and offers a five-hour circle island tour for $300. **Platinum Limousine Hawaii** (808/739-0007, www.platinumlimousinehawaii.com) operates 24 hours a day, seven days a week, and with award-winning service and high-end, showy luxurious vehicles, they've built quite a star-studded clientele. Rates start at $85 per hour for the eight-passenger Lincoln Towncar limo with a two-hour minimum, or a three-hour minimum on Sunday.

MOTORCYCLE AND MOPED

For rentals, try **Big Kahuna Motorcycle Tours and Rentals** (407 Seaside Ave., 808/924-2736 or 888/451-5544, www.bigkahunarentals.com, 8am-5pm daily), where rentals run $50-180 for four hours, with full-day and weekly rentals available. **Cruzin Hawaii** (1980 Kalakaua Ave., 808/945-9595 or 877/945-9595, www.cruzinhawaii.com, 8am-6pm daily) rents Harley-Davidsons at its shop near the Ambassador Hotel, $79-99 for three hours, $99-149 all day, with 24-hour, three-day, and weekly rates available. **Paradise Rent-A-Car** (1837 Ala Moana Blvd., 808/946-7777; 151 Uluniu Ave., 808/926-7777; http://paradiserentacarhawaii.com, 8am-5pm daily) also rents Harleys. And **Chase Hawaii Rentals** (355 Royal Hawaiian Ave., 808/942-4273, www.chasehawaiirentals.com; 138 Uluniu Ave., 808/348-6070; 8am-6pm daily) has over 30 models of Harley-Davidsons for rent, as well as sport bikes and cruisers.

Mopeds and motor scooters are common across the island and a great way to get around, but accident statistics prove they are quite dangerous. Even though there is no helmet law in Hawaii, motorcycle and moped riders should always wear one. **Big Kahuna Motorcycle Tours and Rentals** (407 Seaside Ave., 808/924-2736 or 888/451-5544, www.bigkahunarentals.com, 8am-5pm daily) rents mopeds starting at $25 for four hours and larger scooters starting at $65 for four hours, with full-day and weekly rentals available. **Chase Hawaii Rentals** (355 Royal Hawaiian Ave., 808/942-4273; 138 Uluniu Ave., 808/348-6070; www.chasehawaiirentals.com, 8am-6pm daily) rents Vespas starting at $79 for 10 hours and $99 for 24 hours. **Paradise Cruisers** (2413 Kuhio Ave., 808/926-2847, http://paradisecruisershawaii.com, 8am-8pm daily) rents mopeds and scoot cars, and you can also find mopeds and scooters at **Adventure on 2 Wheels** (1946 Ala Moana Ave., 808/944-3131, 8am-4pm daily; 2552 Lemon Rd., 808/921-8111, 8am-5pm daily).

HONOLULU

The capital of the Hawaiian Islands since 1845, Honolulu means "sheltered bay" in the Hawaiian language. Honolulu is the political, cultural, and economic center of O'ahu and the state of Hawaii, thanks largely to Honolulu Harbor's commercial port and the Honolulu International Airport. Its over 400 high-rises create a skyline in stark contrast to the verdant backdrop of

HIGHLIGHTS

LOOK FOR ◖ TO FIND RECOMMENDED SIGHTS, ACTIVITIES, DINING, AND LODGING.

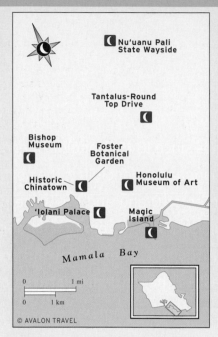
© AVALON TRAVEL

◖ **'Iolani Palace:** This grand and stately palace is the only royal residence in the United States (page 90).

◖ **Historic Chinatown:** It's a hub for international dining, art, nightlife–and for Chinese food and goods, of course (page 94).

◖ **Honolulu Museum of Art:** Hawaii's most prestigious museum has over 50,000 pieces spanning 5,000 years, with Asian, European, American, and African works of art (page 94).

◖ **Foster Botanical Garden:** Along with the palms, orchids, and cycads, you'll find curious leafy plants that date back to prehistoric times (page 95).

◖ **Nu'uanu Pali State Wayside:** Partake in the grandeur of the Ko'olau Mountains, the tropical beauty of Kane'ohe Bay, and the majesty of the vertical cliffs of the Pali (page 96).

◖ **Tantalus-Round Top Drive:** This leisurely, scenic drive winds up the Tantalus Crater to beautiful Pu'u 'Ualaka'a Park at the top of the cone. The view scans Diamond Head, Punchbowl Crater, and greater Honolulu (page 96).

◖ **Magic Island:** Beautiful coastal views and shade trees make this manicured park perfect for a seaside picnic. There's also a protected beach and lagoon where *keiki* can safely play. (page 83).

◖ **Bishop Museum:** The premier museum in the Pacific explores Hawaiian culture and history, the peoples of other Polynesian and Pacific cultures, and the natural history of the islands (page 98).

forested ridges and valleys. Honolulu combines the hustle, convenience, and abundance of a major city and an ethnically diverse population of 350,000 people with a history made unique by its architecture and thriving neighborhoods.

Just east of Pearl Harbor, Honolulu is defined by its city center, the economic heart of the county and state. Containing the Hawaii state capitol building and the neighboring 'Iolani Palace, the historic district is surrounded by towering skyscrapers. It gives way to Chinatown, a relic of O'ahu's whaling, migrant worker, and war-torn past. Today, Chinatown is chock-full of art galleries, nightclubs, bars, and some of O'ahu's best restaurants.

Honolulu's neighborhoods spread out in all directions and are as dynamic as the rainbows that hang over the mountains. Manoa Valley is home to the University of Hawai'i and Lyon

Arboretum at the back of the valley. Kaimuki is known for its shopping and restaurants. Kakaʻako's industrial spaces have become the bastion for a burgeoning urban art scene, and Ala Moana Beach Park affords expansive grassy space, great waves, and a calm swimming area on the inside of the reef.

PLANNING YOUR TIME

Many of the activities in Honolulu, whether sightseeing in the Historic District or hiking in the Koʻolau Mountains, require at least a half day's time. Mix in a meal or two and you have a packed day.

When heading downtown to see the Historic District, leave early to beat the hot midday sun, since the best option is walking to the different buildings and museums. Downtown metered street parking has a two-hour time limit, so when its time to get back to the car, head over to Chinatown, park in one of the municipal lots, and explore the small, historic city blocks. Plan on saving your appetite for eating in Chinatown, as the diversity of cuisine here will make your head spin.

For an art day, start out at the Honolulu Museum of Art. With your paid admission you'll also get entry at the Honolulu Museum of Art Spalding House in Makiki Heights, featuring contemporary art and a botanical garden. Stop by the Hawaiʻi State Art Museum, which is free to the public, to check out the finest work from top local artists, then hop over to Chinatown for a walking tour of art galleries and dinner on Bethel Street and Nuʻuanu Avenue.

After a day in the city center, you might enjoy a little peace and quiet. To attain such solace in nature, go for a hike in Manoa Valley or at Waʻahila Ridge State Park, then grab a bite to eat at one of the casual BYOBs in Kaimuki. If you need to expand your horizons, take the windy drive up Tantalus or Round Top Drives to Puʻu ʻUalakaʻa Park and relax with views of Honolulu and Diamond Head. If you feel like walking, there are several trailheads in the vicinity.

Honolulu might be urban, but it still has beaches. Spend the morning swimming, surfing, or stand-up paddling at Ala Moana Beach Park, then head across the street to Ala Moana Center for shopping and dining.

ORIENTATION
Downtown

Downtown is the epicenter of Honolulu, and the financial and political center of the island and the state. Within downtown are the Historic District, comprised of the state capitol, ʻIolani Palace, government buildings and offices, as well as other historical and cultural buildings. To the immediate west of the historic district is the financial district, where high-rise office buildings perch along one-way streets.

Chinatown

Just west of the financial district is the historic Chinatown neighborhood, which stretches from Vineyard Boulevard to the north, to Aloha Tower along the harbor, with the Nuʻuanu Stream as its western border. Chinatown is home to a curious mix of bars, hip ethnic restaurants, Chinese and Pacific Rim cuisine, Chinese grocery stores, small local eateries, art galleries, and chic coffee shops.

Kakaʻako

At the forefront of the urban art scene, much of Kakaʻako is industrial, especially the streets southeast of downtown. Young artists have transformed the area into an explosion of color and art, and drab building walls are now radiant and expressive. In addition to colorful building exteriors, art galleries, coffee shops, and restaurants, Kakaʻako also has a green waterfront park. Kakaʻako stretches toward the mountains all the way to the H-1 freeway.

Ala Moana

Dominated by Ala Moana Beach Park, Magic Island, and Ala Moana Center, the Ala Moana neighborhood straddles the gap between Kakaʻako, Waikiki, and the McCully residential neighborhoods to the east. This

O'AHU

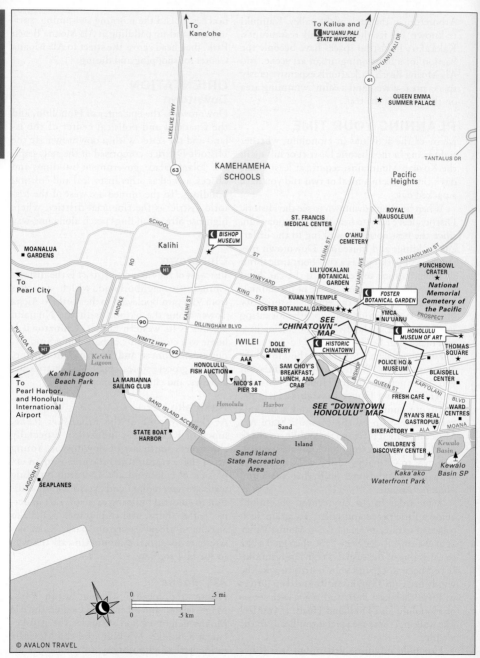

To
Kane'ohe

To Kailua and
NU'UANU PALI
STATE WAYSIDE

QUEEN EMMA
SUMMER PALACE

TANTALUS DR

KAMEHAMEHA
SCHOOLS

Pacific
Heights

ROYAL
MAUSOLEUM

ST. FRANCIS
MEDICAL CENTER

O'AHU
CEMETERY

MOANALUA
GARDENS

Kalihi

BISHOP
MUSEUM

SCHOOL ST

'ANUAIOLIMU ST

PUNCHBOWL
CRATER

National
Memorial
Cemetery of
the Pacific

LILI'UOKALANI
BOTANICAL
GARDEN

VINEYARD

KING ST

To
Pearl City

KUAN YIN TEMPLE

FOSTER
BOTANICAL GARDEN

FOSTER BOTANICAL GARDEN

PROSPECT

YMCA
NU'UANU

SEE
"CHINATOWN"
MAP

HONOLULU
MUSEUM OF ART

DILLINGHAM BLVD

THOMAS
SQUARE

NIMITZ HWY

IWILEI

DOLE
CANNERY

HISTORIC
CHINATOWN

POLICE HQ &
MUSEUM

BLAISDELL
CENTER

KAPI'OLANI

To
Pearl Harbor,
and Honolulu
International
Airport

Ke'ehi
Lagoon

Ke'ehi Lagoon
Beach Park

LA MARIANNA
SAILING CLUB

AAA

HONOLULU
FISH AUCTION

NICO'S AT
PIER 38

SAM CHOY'S
BREAKFAST,
LUNCH, AND
CRAB

QUEEN ST

FRESH CAFÉ

SEE "DOWNTOWN
HONOLULU" MAP

RYAN'S REAL
GASTROPUB

WARD
CENTRES

MOANA

Honolulu Harbor

BIKEFACTORY

ALA

STATE BOAT
HARBOR

Sand

Island

CHILDREN'S
DISCOVERY CENTER

Kewalo
Basin

SAND ISLAND ACCESS RD

Sand Island
State Recreation
Area

Kewalo
Basin SP

Kaka'ako
Waterfront Park

LAGOON DR

SEAPLANES

0   .5 mi

0   .5 km

© AVALON TRAVEL

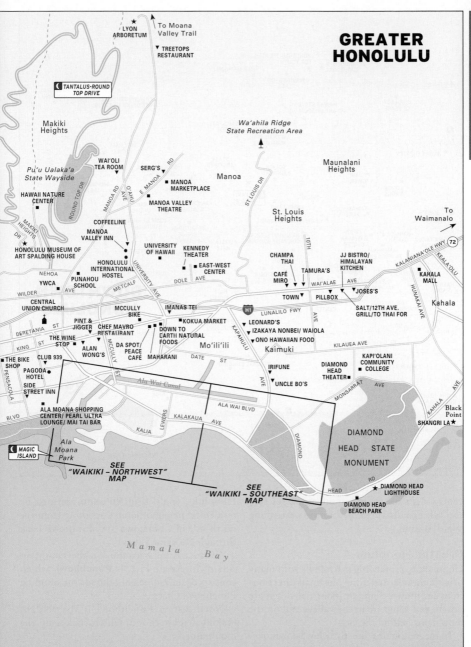

GREATER HONOLULU

To Moana Valley Trail

LYON ARBORETUM

▼ TREETOPS RESTAURANT

☾ TANTALUS-ROUND TOP DRIVE

Makiki Heights

Wa'ahila Ridge State Recreation Area

Maunalani Heights

Pu'u Ualaka'a State Wayside

WAI'OLI TEA ROOM ▼

SERG'S ■

Manoa

To Waimanalo

72

HAWAII NATURE CENTER ■

■ MANOA MARKETPLACE

■ MANOA VALLEY THEATRE

St. Louis Heights

COFFEELINE ■

MANOA VALLEY INN

UNIVERSITY OF HAWAII ■

KENNEDY THEATER ■

CHAMPA THAI ■

JJ BISTRO/ HIMALAYAN KITCHEN

HONOLULU MUSEUM OF ART SPALDING HOUSE ■

HONOLULU INTERNATIONAL HOSTEL ■

■ EAST-WEST CENTER

CAFÉ MIRO ▼

TAMURA'S ▼

KAHALA MALL

NEHOA

PUNAHOU SCHOOL ■

DOLE AVE

TOWN ▼

PILLBOX ▼

JOSES'S ▼

Kahala

YWCA ■

METCALF

WILDER AVE

H1 LUNALILO FWY

SALT/12TH AVE. GRILL/TO THAI FOR

CENTRAL UNION CHURCH ✝

MCCULLY BIKE ■

IMANAS TEI ■

DERETANIA ST

PINT & JIGGER ■

CHEF MAVRO RESTAURANT ■

■ KOKUA MARKET

LEONARD'S ▼

DIAMOND HEAD THEATER ■

KAPI'OLANI COMMUNITY ● COLLEGE

THE WINE STOP ▼

KING ST

DOWN TO EARTH NATURAL FOODS

IZAKAYA NONBEI/ WAIOLA ▼

ONO HAWAIIAN FOOD ▼

ALAN WONG'S ▼

DA SPOT/ PEACE CAFÉ ▼

Mo'ili'ili

Kaimuki

KILAUEA AVE

THE BIKE SHOP ■

CLUB 939 ■

MAHARANI ▼

DATE ST

PAGODA HOTEL ■

IRIFUNE ▼

SIDE STREET INN ■

Ala Wai Canal

UNCLE BO'S ▼

MONSARRAT AVE

ALA MOANA SHOPPING CENTER/ PEARL ULTRA LOUNGE/ MAI TAI BAR ■

ALA WAI BLVD

BLVD

KALAKAUA AVE

Black Point

KALIA

DIAMOND

SHANGRI LA ★

☾ MAGIC ISLAND

Ala Moana Park

SEE "WAIKIKI – NORTHWEST" MAP

DIAMOND HEAD STATE MONUMENT

SEE "WAIKIKI – SOUTHEAST" MAP

HEAD RD

★ DIAMOND HEAD LIGHTHOUSE

DIAMOND HEAD BEACH PARK

M a m a l a   B a y

O'AHU

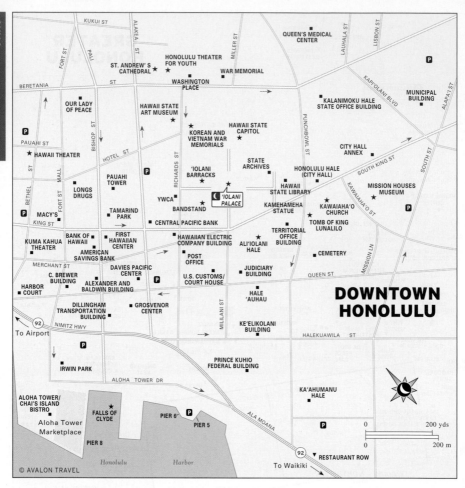

central area for shopping encompasses several other malls are located to the west, along Ward Avenue.

Greater Honolulu

Honolulu is a sprawling metropolis with many neighborhoods stretching out in all directions from downtown. Some are industrial, others are urban, and some are in the valleys and on the mountains behind the city.

In the mountains directly behind downtown Honolulu, you'll find **Nu'uanu,** defined by residential neighborhoods stretching from the north side of Chinatown and downtown back through Nu'uanu Valley.

To the east of Nu'uanu, on the mountain side of Interstate H-1, is **Punchbowl,** which consists of the old neighborhoods surrounding Punchbowl Crater.

Northeast of Punchbowl is the verdant **Makiki** neighborhood, which snakes up the mountains.

Your Best Day in Honolulu

© KEVIN WHITTON

Lyon Arboretum

While there are many neighborhoods that comprise Greater Honolulu, most of what appeals to visitors is centrally located in the downtown vicinity. Plan your Honolulu day around avoiding the daily rush-hour traffic to maximize your time.

· Instead of rushing immediately into the historic district in the morning and getting caught in traffic, head to **Lyon Arboretum** in Manoa Valley and explore the extensive trail system, bird watch, and learn about native Hawaiian plants. If you'd like to be closer to downtown, try **Foster Botanical Garden** just outside of Chinatown.

· Next, visit the historic district and take in the **Hawaii State Capitol** and **'Iolani Palace,** the only royal residence in the United States.

· For lunch, head to the **Ala Moana Center,**

where you can grab lunch in the comfortable, open-air **Mai Tai Bar** on the upper lanai of the mall. Or, head into Kaka'ako, where you can find hip and unique shops and restaurants.

· A visit to the **Honolulu Museum of Art** is a must in the afternoon. If you have your own transportation, take advantage of the free same-day admission to the Spalding House in Makiki Heights, a museum of contemporary art.

· For dinner, head back into Chinatown and peruse the many restaurants and bars. Whether you're after Chinese food from **Little Village Noodle House,** French cuisine at **Brasserie Du Vin,** or pizza from Irish pub **J.J. Dolan's,** Chinatown has you covered.

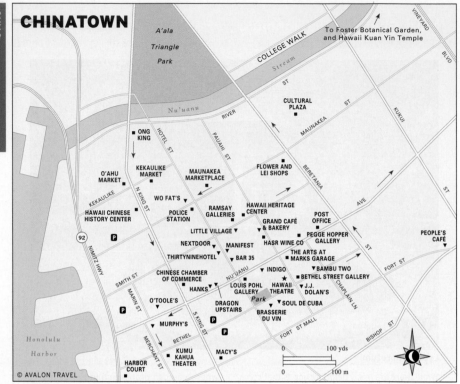

CHINATOWN

Heading east takes you to the upscale neighborhood of **Manoa,** which stretches from deep in Manoa Valley to the University of Hawai'i at Manoa.

To the east and south are the old, congested neighborhoods of **Kaimuki,** where you'll find ample shopping and dining on Waialae and Kapahulu Avenues.

Just to the west of Kaimuki is **Moili'ili,** another predominantly residential area with some shops and dining along King and Beretania Streets.

To the west of downtown Honolulu and Nu'uanu lie the local communities of **Kalihi** and Kalihi Valley. There is also a small area to the south of Kalihi called **Iwilei,** known for its seafood restaurants on Pier 38 in Honolulu Harbor.

Sand Island, south of downtown Honolulu across the harbor, is an industrial port with an oceanfront state recreation area.

To the west is the airport, and inland from the airport are the **Salt Lake** and **Moanalua** communities.

Beaches

Bustling Honolulu Harbor stretches along much of Honolulu's coastline, and only a few beaches fall within its borders. Not to mention, the beach parks in Honolulu are more park than actual sandy beach. The beach parks draw big crowds all summer long when there's surf along the south shore, while the weekends seem to be crowded all year long. The city beaches and parks are also the stomping grounds of many of Honolulu's pervasive homeless population.

ALA MOANA
◖ Magic Island

Magic Island is an artificially constructed peninsula that creates the western flank of the Ala Wai Canal and Small Boat Harbor. This grassy park with shade trees, walking paths, restrooms, and outdoor showers also includes a tranquil *keiki* beach at the end of the point. It's blocked from the waves by towering rock jetties and framed in all around by beach, making it a perfect place for the kids to play and swim safely. The jetties are constructed so that fresh ocean water can flow in and out of the lagoon without creating currents or waves. During the summer months, a wave known as Bomburas breaks beyond the jetty at the end of the point.

There is ample parking, but it does fill up during the summer and on weekends when people turn out en masse with barbecue grills and tents to take advantage of the beautiful weather. To get to Magic Island, turn onto Ala Moana Park Drive from Ala Moana Boulevard where it intersects Atkinson Drive. After you pass the first right bend in the road, the parking lot is on the left, and it's free. The lot and park are closed 10pm-4am daily.

© KEVIN WHITTON

Magic Island has a protected beach perfect for families.

O'AHU

Ala Moana Beach Park

Connected to Magic Island, but on the west side of the peninsula, is **Ala Moana Beach Park.** Ala Moana Beach is a 4,000-foot-long, rather straight strip of sand falling into an artificial channel that runs along the entire beach. Buoys demarcate a swimming lane and one for stand-up paddling. Across the channel is a very shallow reef that stretches way out to the waves washing up on the sharp coral. There are many surf breaks along the outer reef, all the way across the beach park. A rectangular park, with busy Ala Moana Boulevard on one side and the beach on the other, has a tide-fed stream meandering through it with a pond at each end. There are many shade trees, lots of picnic tables and barbecue areas, facilities, a snack bar, tennis courts, a community center, and lots of parking along Ala Moana Park Drive, which intersects Ala Moana Boulevard at both ends of the park. Parking can get crazy during the summer when the surf is up and on the weekends when the park is packed with families. Be sure you don't use one of the designated lifeguard parking spots. Parking is free, but the park is closed 10pm-4am daily.

SAND ISLAND
Sand Island State Recreation Area

Wedged between the Honolulu International Airport's reef runway and Honolulu Harbor is Sand Island. The expansive, but aesthetically challenged **Sand Island State Recreation Area** (808/832-3781, www.hawaiistateparks. org, sunrise-sunset daily) is on its south shore. There is a camping area, park, picnic areas, restrooms and outdoor showers, and a steep sandy beach that stretches from the island's western point, nearly to the harbor channel entrance. Since the beach and park are in an industrial zone and the park is littered with bits of rubbish, paradise isn't the first thing that comes to mind here. Planes zoom overhead on a regular basis. The large, rectangular sand trappers exposed on both ends of the beach could be a safety hazard for small children. Still, there are a few decent surf breaks off the beach if you're looking to get away from the crowds at Ala Moana Beach, and the area is popular with local families on the weekends. To get to the beach, turn onto Sand Island Access Road from North Nimitz Highway and follow this to the end. Parking is free. The gated parking lot is locked when the recreation area is closed.

Water Sports

SURFING, BODYSURFING, AND STAND-UP PADDLING

The surf breaks in Honolulu come alive during the summer months, when south swells generated by storms in the southern hemisphere travel thousands of miles to Hawaiian waters. And the breaks are usually crowded with bodyboarders, shortboarders, and longboarders.

Bomburas is a predominant left that breaks at the top of Magic Island, with the white water pushing right into the jetty. When the surf is big enough, the waves break far enough out to round the point and swing into the bay on the Ala Moana side. The wave breaks best on a low tide. You'll have to paddle out and in through a gap in the jetty across the *keiki* pool, timing

the white water on the way in so you don't get pushed into the rocks.

The reef that stretches across Ala Moana Beach has a handful of waves that break on different conditions. Some of the more shallow breaks are preferred by bodyboarders, and some waves don't start breaking until the surf is breaking above head high. Two of the more popular waves that are easy to pick out from shore are **Concessions** and **Big Rights.** Toward the west side of the beach, in front of the concession stand, there is a sandy path in the reef that leads straight out in between the two breaks. You'll see surfers walking in and out in knee-deep water along the channel. The break to the east is Concessions, a right and left breaking wave that gets pretty shallow if you go right. To the west of the channel in the reef is Big Rights, a predominant right that gets pretty hollow, and surfers will try to nab one of the fast barrels. Park along Ala Moana Park Drive.

The channel running parallel to Ala Moana Beach is designated as a swimming and stand-up paddling zone. Buoys demarcate lanes. The water is flat and calm, even when it's windy, because the reef protects it from the surf. It's a great place to learn how to paddle or to paddle for exercise.

There are a couple of breaks along Kewalo Basin Park as well, the most popular being a left and right peak called **Kewalo's.** The left breaks into the Kewalo Basin channel that the boats use to access the harbor. The right breaks into shallow and sharp reef. Kewalo's is often crowded since it's a favorite break for school-age kids when class is out. There are a few more breaks along the reef to the east that are usually less crowded. Access the water by carefully climbing down the seawall and paddling out over the reef. Keep in mind you'll have to come in by climbing up the seawall, which can be a challenge when the surf is big and the surges are pushing up and pulling away from it with force.

There are two small parking lots, showers, and restrooms in Kewalo Basin Park. To get to Kewalo Basin, you'll need to be driving east on Ala Moana Boulevard. Once you pass Ward Avenue, take the second right turn into the harbor. If you come to the signal at Ala Moana Park Road, you've missed it. Follow the road past all the boats and tour operators. It bends right at the park, and the two parking lots are just ahead on the right.

Across the Kewalo Basin Harbor channel, fronting Kaka'ako Waterfront Park and the Kewalo Marine Laboratory, is O'ahu's only strictly bodysurfing wave, **Point Panic.** It is against the law and punishable by a fine to surf the break with a board. Point Panic is a beautiful, barreling right off the rocky point. There is no beach in this area. However, there are restrooms, showers, and a small parking lot at the end of Ahui Street.

Flies is a lumpy, soft wave that breaks in front of the seawall along Kaka'ako Waterfront Park. There are several right and left breaking peaks that break best on a low tide, as the backwash can be a bit much on a higher tide. It is a good break for novice surfers intimidated by the crowds at other spots. Watch how the local surfers enter and exit the water. To get to the waterfront, park at the end of Ahui Street.

Outfitters

Hawaiian South Shore (320 Ward Ave., #112, 808/597-9055, www.hawaiiansouthshore.com, 10:30am-7pm Mon.-Sat.) is a complete surf shop in the Ala Moana/Kaka'ako area, right by Ala Moana Beach. They sell surf-related apparel, accessories, shortboards, and longboards. Board rentals run $25 per day. **Blue Planet** (540 Ward Ave., 808/596-7755, www.blueplanetsurf.com, 10am-6pm daily) is just up the street and still conveniently close to Ala Moana Beach. They sell new and used longboards, shortboards, stand-up paddle boards, and accessories. They also offer long-term surfboard rentals (two or more days) starting at $40, long-term stand-up paddle rental starting at $75, and 90-minute private stand-up paddle lessons for $90.

Surf Garage (2716 S. King St., 808/951-1173, www.surfgarage.com, 10am-7pm Mon.-Sat., 11am-5pm Sun.) and **Aloha Boardshop** (2600 S. King St., 808/955-6030, www.alohaboardshop.com, 10am-6:30pm Mon.-Sat., 11am-5pm Sun.) are right next to each other at the intersection of University Avenue and King Street. Check out Surf Garage for longboards, stand-up paddle boards, and accessories. Aloha Boardshop has a ton of shortboards, new and used, as well as longboards and surf accessories for sale.

Closer to Waikiki and Diamond Head in the Kapahulu area, **RV's Ocean Sport** (3348 Campbell Ave., 808/732-7137, http://rvsocean.com, 11am-5:30pm daily) is the place for used longboards and shortboards. The small shop is wall-to-wall boards, and they also specialize in ding repair.

Hawaiian WaterSports (415 Kapahulu Ave., 808/739-5483, www.hawaiianwatersports.com,

9am-5pm daily) specializes in the sale and rental of strong and light epoxy boards. They offer shortboards, longboards, and stand-up paddle boards. Surfboards rent for $29 for 24 hours, $149 for seven days, and stand-up paddle boards go for $69 for 24 hours and $350 for seven days. Group surfing lessons start at $99 for two hours, and private lessons are $179 for two hours. They surf breaks around Diamond Head. Stand-up paddle lessons start at $99 for two-hour group lessons and $179 for two-hour private lessons.

DIVING

Diving Honolulu waters is all about exploring shipwrecks and finger reefs. The YO-257 and San Pedro wrecks are home to whitetip reef sharks, eels, and green sea turtles with deep-water reef fish on the surrounding reefs. The Sea Tiger wreck, rumored to be a forcibly retired smuggling vessel, rests in a protected area. Look for white-spotted eagle rays, large puffer fish, and filefish. There is also an area of finger reefs called Turtle Canyons that is home to a number of eel species, reef fish, and turtles. Most of the dive charters leave from Kewalo Basin.

Two-tank boat charters with **Kaimana Divers** (1051 Ala Moana Blvd., 808/772-1795, www.waikikiscuba.com, 7am-8pm daily) start at $89, including tanks and weights. Gear rental is $5 per piece or $10 full set. They also have a 10-dive package with everything included for $495. In addition to charters, they offer intro dive, private, standard, and advanced open-water courses starting at $125.

Dive Oahu (1085 Ala Moana Blvd., 808/922-3483, http://diveoahu.com, 8am-3pm daily) offers two-tank charters with Waikiki hotel pickup and drop-off, gear, tanks, and weights included in the rate: $129 standard, $385 five-day unlimited package. They also offer PADI online scuba courses and have a full dive shop.

Also in Kewalo Basin is **Rainbow Scuba** (1086 Ala Moana Blvd., 808/224-7857, http://rainbowscuba.com, 7am-5pm daily). Their rates include Waikiki hotel transportation, light snacks and water on the charter, two tanks, and full gear rental. They offer two-site

beginner dives for $100 for first-time divers, certified divers charter to one wreck site and one reef site for $110, and PADI certification courses starting at $275.

Breeze Hawaii Diving Adventures (3014 Kaimuki Ave., 808/735-1857, http://breeze-hawaiidiving.com, 7am-5pm daily) has a retail shop in the Kapahulu area and offers two-tank boat charters for $115, three-tank charters for $172, one-tank night dives $149, and two-tank sunset/night dives for $200. They also have three levels of PADI beginner dive courses.

While **Pearl Harbor Divers** (725 Auahi St., 808/589-2177, http://pearlharbordivers.com, 9am-6pm Mon.-Fri., 8am-5pm Sat.-Sun.) has dive charters available only on the leeward side, they do have scuba courses in Honolulu. They offer NAUI certification starting at $379 group and $449 private.

FISHING

The bulk of the fishing charters are found in Kewalo Basin, where they can easily access the deeper south shore waters. If you're interested in shoreline fishing, you can cast from anywhere along the seawall at Kaka'ako Waterfront Park or from the beach at Sand Island.

Magic Sport Fishing (1125 Ala Moana Blvd., 808/596-2998, www.magicsportfishing.com) runs a 50-foot Pacifica sportfishing yacht out of Kewalo Basin and provides everything except lunch and beverages. The captain has over 20 years of experience commercial fishing in Hawaiian waters, and they will divvy up a small portion of fish per person on shared trips and larger portions for private charters. With up to six passengers, eight-hour full-day shared trips run $200 per person, private trips $975. There are also half-day private charters for $775.

Sea Verse Sport Fishing (1125 Ala Moana Blvd., 808/262-5587, http://seaversesportfishing.com), with a 44-foot twin-engine vessel equipped for angling and trolling, runs private half-day trips for $700, three-quarter-day trips for $750, and full-day private charters for $900. Full-day shared charters are $200 per person. They also offer bottom fishing trips.

Operating since 1985, **Tradewind Charters** (1125 Ala Moana Blvd., 808/973-0311, www.tradewindcharters.com) has a variety of vessels for different types of fishing expeditions, from 40-foot sailing yachts to a 65-foot sportfishing yacht, and they offer two different fishing expeditions: catch-and-release reef fishing and deep-sea sportfishing. Their private reef fishing charter includes snorkeling and sightseeing and for one to six people, starts at $595 for three hours, $795 for four-and-a-half hours, $995 for six hours, and $1,195 for eight hours. Their private deep-sea charters for one to six people start at $895 for four hours, $1,095 for six hours, and $1,295 for eight hours.

Aikane Sport Fishing (866/920-0979, www.aikanesportfishing.com) has shallow-water fishing charters for trevally and snappers or deep-sea fishing charters for big game fish like wahoo, mahimahi, blue marlin, and yellowfin tuna. They have a 42-foot Ocean Yacht and 38-foot Bertram Sportfisher. The shallow-water charters start at $500 for four hours and go to $625 for eight hours; the deep-sea big game fishing charters start at $650 for four hours and go to $990 for 10 hours.

Established in 1950, **Maggie Joe Sport Fishing** (1025 Ala Moana Blvd., 808/591-8888, www.maggiejoe.com) has a fleet of boats designed to catch big game fish like blue marlin, yellowfin tuna, mahimahi, and skipjack tuna. They have half-day to full-day private and shared trips as well as night shark fishing for $550. Their biggest boat, a 53-foot custom sportfishing yacht, starts at $890 for a three-quarter day and $933 for a private, full-day charter. Full-day shared charters are $179 per person, and half-day shared charters are $150 per person. Bananas are not permitted onboard due to superstition.

Hiking, Biking, and Bird-Watching

HIKING
Makiki
The **Makiki-Tantalus** hike is an eight-mile loop that circles Tantalus Peak and is a great way to see a few different valleys and Ko'olau peaks up close. The trail is known for songbirds and some native Hawaiian flora. Look for the native white hibiscus and *'ohi'a 'ahihi,* with clusters of delicate red flowers. The hike takes advantage of the Kanealole Trail at the trailhead, then connects in succession to the Makiki Valley Trail, the Nahuina Trail, the Kalawahine Trail, the Pauoa Flats Trail, the Manoa Cliff Trail, the Moleka Trail, and back to the Makiki Valley Trail as it rounds Tantalus. The junctions are marked well. To get to the trailhead, from Makiki Street heading north, bear left on Makiki Heights Drive. As the road switches back to the left, continue straight on an unnamed paved road into the Makiki Forest Recreation Area and past the Hawai'i Nature Center. Park on the side of the road by the gate. There is a native plant identification guide available in the nature center office for a small fee.

Manoa
In the back of rainy Manoa Valley are a myriad of trails all within **Lyon Arboretum** (3860 Manoa Rd., 808/988-0456, www.hawaii.edu/lyonarboretum, 8am-4pm Mon.-Fri., 9am-3pm Sat.). These trails are designed to take you through the different sections of the arboretum, so there's a wealth of interesting and colorful exotic, tropical, and native Hawaiian plants and trees everywhere you look. There's so much area to cover that you could hike for a half day and not walk the same trail twice. The trails range from wide and dry to narrow, muddy, and graded. They are marked with numbers on wooden stakes that correspond to a trail map, which you can pick up in the visitor center. The main trail through the arboretum terminates at a small waterfall. Be prepared for mud, rain, and mosquitoes. Lyon Arboretum has its own free parking lot by the visitor center.

© KEVIN WHITTON

Manoa Falls

Follow Manoa Road all the way to the back of the valley, past the houses, past Paradise Park, and turn onto the arboretum's private drive before the end of the road.

Also in the rear of Manoa Valley are several of the 18 trails that comprise the Honolulu *mauka* trail system. **Manoa Falls** is a great introduction to the area, a short 0.8-mile hike with a gradual grade under canopy and through lush foliage, up to a small waterfall and pool. Manoa is famous for its pervasive mist, so the trail can be muddy and crossed with roots in some sections. This is a popular hike, so it is well used, especially on the weekends. To get to the trailhead, either park on Manoa Road just before it narrows at the intersection with Wa'akaua Street, or continue driving on Manoa Road till you reach Paradise Park, where $5 flat-rate parking is available. If you prefer to park for free in the nearby neighborhood, tack on a quarter-mile walk just to reach the trailhead. From the paid parking lot, continue on

foot on the gravel road until it becomes the Manoa Falls Trail. The trail follows Waihi Stream to the falls and pool.

Kaimuki
At the top of Saint Louis Heights, in Kaimuki, you'll find a hike with views of Manoa Valley and Palolo Valley, terminating on top of Mount Olympus, a massive peak at the back of Manoa Valley. The **Wa'ahila Ridge Trail** begins in a stand of Cook pines—a misnomer since they are actually columnar araucaria, native to New Caledonia. The hike along the ridgeline is perfect for novices, but once you find the narrow trail that ascends to the summit, the route is more suited for intermediate hikers. At the 2,486-foot summit, in addition to breathtaking views, you'll find a thicket of native vegetation, including slow-growing *hapu'u* ferns. The hike is 6 miles round-trip. To get to the trailhead, park in the **Wa'ahila Ridge State Recreation Area** (www.hawaiistateparks.org, 7am-7:45pm daily Apr-early Sept., 7am-6:45pm daily early Sept.-Mar.) by following Saint Louis Drive to nearly the top of the rise and turning left on Ruth Place. There are restrooms, drinking fountains, and picnic tables by the parking lot. Parking is free, but the gate is locked when the recreation area is closed.

MOUNTAIN BIKING
While there are a plethora of trails all around O'ahu, mountain biking is prohibited on most of them. Fortunately for those looking to go off road on two wheels, there are a handful of mountain biking trails on the North Shore and the southeast and windward sides. Mountain biking is prohibited on all Honolulu area trails, but the big name local bicycle shops are all in town.

Outfitters
The Bike Shop (1149 S. King St., 808/596-0588, www.bikeshophawaii.com, 9am-8pm Mon.-Fri., 9am-5pm Sat., 10am-5pm Sun.) is a full-service rental, retail, and repair shop in

the Kaka'ako neighborhood. They rent mountain bikes for $85 per day, road bikes starting at $40 per day, and seven-speed city bikes for $20 day. If you need racks for your rental car, they charge $5 per day.

The **BikeFactory** (740 Ala Moana Blvd., 808/596-8844, http://bikefactoryhawaii.com, 10am-7pm Mon.-Fri., 9am-5pm Sat., 11am-5pm Sun.), also in Kaka'ako, sells bicycles and

accessories, but does not rent equipment. And in Moili'ili, **McCully Bicycle and Sporting Goods** (2124 S. King Street, 808/955-6329, http://mccullybike.com, 9am-8pm Mon.-Fri., 9am-6pm Sat., 10am-5pm Sun.) sells bicycles of all shapes and sizes, as well as other sporting goods like fishing gear, tennis rackets, and athletic shoes. They do not rent bicycles, however.

BIRD-WATCHING
Bird-watching in Honolulu is all about finding the forest birds along the **Ko'olau Range trails,** including the **Lyon Arboretum trails.** Most of the birds are introduced species, like the shama thrush and the red-billed leiothrix, but beautiful nonetheless. The shama thrush is black on top with a chestnut-colored chest and a long, black and white tail and is able to mimic other birds' songs. There are few native forest birds remaining on O'ahu in accessible places, but this region is a great place to look for the red *'apapane,* which likes to feed on nectar from *'ohi'a lehua* blossoms, and *'amakihi,* a yellow Hawaiian honeycreeper with a black, curved beak.

Golf

KAIMUKI
The **Ala Wai Golf Course** (404 Kapahulu Ave., 808/296-2000, www1.honolulu.gov/des/golf/alawai.htm), on the mountain side of the Ala Wai Canal, is the closest golf course to Waikiki and a local favorite for a quick round of golf. The 18-hole course is flat and has views of Diamond Head and the Ko'olau Range. Greens fees are $52 daily for 18 holes and $26 daily for twilight or nine holes. Golf cart fees are $20 for 18 holes, $10 for nine holes.

MOANALUA
Even though Hawaii's oldest golf course, **Moanalua Golf Club** (1250 Ala Aolani St., 808/839-2311, www.mgchawaii.com), is a private club with membership benefits, access is open to the public. Built in 1898, the nine-hole course can be played as an 18-hole course by utilizing different sets of tees. The Moanalua Stream winds through the challenging course, set along the slopes of Moanalua, creating natural hazards. There are views of Diamond Head and the Honolulu skyline. Greens fees start at $45.

Spas

DOWNTOWN

Heaven on Earth Salon & Day Spa (1050 Alakea St., 808/599-5501, www.heavenonearthhawaii.com, 9am-7pm Mon.-Fri., 8am-5pm Sat., 10am-4pm Sun.) is a full-service salon and spa located in the heart of downtown Honolulu. In addition to their complete set of services, they offer signature spa packages of skin and body treatments, or you can create your own. Massages start at $88 for 50 minutes and $118 for 80 minutes, facials start at $80 for 50 minutes, and 50-minute body treatments are $95. The spa packages range from 80 minutes to four hours and start at $210. They also have gentlemen's spa services like facials, manicures, pedicures, and waxing.

ALA MOANA

On the third floor in the Ala Moana Center is **Ho'ala Salon and Spa** (1450 Ala Moana Blvd., 808/947-6141, http://hoalasalonspa.com, 9am-9pm Mon.-Sat., 10am-7pm Sun.), a full-service salon and spa using natural and eco-sensitive products from Aveda. The award-winning spa is a quiet respite from the bustle of the mall

and town. Their signature massage care ranges 25-90 minutes; 50-minute therapies start at $100; 75 minutes start at $150. They have an extensive menu of facials: 25 minutes start at $65 and 60 minutes start at $125. Ho'ala Spa also offers nail, hand, and foot care, spa body treatments, and hair care, as well as a 50- or 75-minute pregnancy massage.

Elements Spa and Salon (1726 Kapiolani Blvd., #206, 808/942-0033, www.elementshawaii.com, 10am-8pm Mon.-Fri., 9am-6pm Sat., 10am-6pm Sun.) is right across from the Hawaii Convention Center and specializes in custom offerings, including tea service, foot treatment, mini facials, and scalp massages with their full-service salon and spa treatments. They provide three basic massages and several specialty massages like shiatsu, hot stone, and deep tissue. The basic massages are $50 for 30 minutes, $85 for 60 minutes, and $110 for 90 minutes. Their specialty massages start at $100 for 60 minutes. Couples massages start at $165 for 60 minutes. Facials start at $85 for 60 minutes, and they offer series rates for both facials and massages. Elements provides salon, nail, waxing, and bridal services.

Sights

DOWNTOWN

◖ 'Iolani Palace

Set on a grassy 11 acres, shaded by canopy trees in the heart of the Capitol District, **'Iolani Palace** (364 S. King St., 808/522-0822, www.iolanipalace.org, 9am-5pm Mon.-Sat.) is the second royal palace to grace the grounds. The building, with its glass and ironwork imported from San Francisco and its Corinthian columns, is the only true royal palace in America. 'Iolani Palace, begun in late 1879 under orders of King Kalakaua, was completed in December 1882 at a cost of $350,000. It was

the first electrified building in Honolulu, having electricity and telephones even before the White House in Washington, D.C. The palace served as the official residence of the monarch of Hawaii until the overthrow of the Hawaiian kingdom in 1893. It then became the main executive building for the provisional government, with the House of Representatives meeting in the throne room and the Senate in the dining room, until 1968. It has since been elevated to a state monument and National Historic Landmark.

Through the first floor of this palace runs

© KEVIN WHITTON

'Iolani Palace is the only royal residence in the United States.

a broad hallway with a grand stairway that leads to the second story. On the east side of the building is the large and opulent Throne Room, the scene of formal meetings and major royal functions. On the west side are the smaller Blue Room, an informal reception area, and the dining room. The upstairs level was the private residence of the king and his family. It also has a wide hallway, and on each side are bedrooms, sitting rooms, a music room, and office. The basement held servants' quarters, the kitchen, and offices of certain government officials. On the palace grounds you'll find the Coronation Pavilion, which originally stood directly in front of the palace, but was later moved to where it stands today as a bandstand for the Royal Hawaiian Band, and a raised earthen platform, the original site of the royal mausoleum, which was later moved out along the Pali Highway.

'Iolani Palace has docent-guided tours and self-guided tours of the first and second floors, both with self-guided exploration of the basement gallery. One-hour tours enter the palace every 15 minutes. Reservations are required for the **guided tour** (808/522-0832, palacetickets@ iolanipalace.org, Tues. and Thurs. 9am-10am, Wed., Fri.-Sat. 9am-11:15am, $20 adults, $6 children ages 5-12), but not for the **self-guided audio tour** (9am-5pm Mon., 10:30am-5pm Tues. and Thurs., noon-5pm Wed. and Fri.-Sat., $12 adults, $5 children ages 5-12, $1 fee for the audio recording). The **Basement Gallery exhibits** (9:30am-5pm Mon.-Sat., $7 adults, $3 children) are another option for touring. Tickets are also sold at the 'Iolani Barracks (9am-4pm Tues.-Sat.), behind the palace. Also in the barracks is the palace gift shop and bookstore (8:30am-4pm Mon.-Sat.).

There is limited metered parking on the palace grounds. From South King Street, turn left onto Likelike Street, a one-way drive, just before the major Punchbowl Street intersection. Turn left through the decorated gate onto palace grounds.

Hawaii State Capitol
Directly behind 'Iolani Palace sits the unique

© KEVIN WHITTON

sculpture of Saint Damien of Moloka'i, in front of the Hawaii State Capitol

Hawaii State Capitol (415 S. Beretania St., 808/587-0478, www.capitol.hawaii.gov), built in 1969. The structure is a metaphor for Hawaii: the pillars surrounding it are palms, the reflecting pool is the sea, and the cone-shaped rooms of the Legislature represent the volcanoes of Hawaii. The walls are lined with rich *koa* wood from the Big Island and further graced with woven hangings, murals, and two gigantic, four-ton replicas of the State Seal hanging at both entrances. The inner courtyard has a 600,000-tile mosaic and standing at the *mauka* entrance to the building is a poignant sculpture of Saint Damien of Moloka'i, while the statue *The Spirit of Lili'uokalani* fronts the building on the ocean side. The State Legislature is in session for 60 working days starting on the third Wednesday in January. The legislative session opens with dancing, music, and festivities, and the public is invited. Peek inside, then take the elevator to the fifth floor for outstanding views of the city. There is also a Korean-Vietnam War Memorial paying tribute to those that died in the two wars.

Washington Place
Begun in 1841 by Captain John Dominis, **Washington Place** (320 S. Beretania St., 808/536-8040, www.washingtonplacefoundation.org) is best known as the home of Queen Lili'uokalani and her husband, John Owen Dominis, son of Captain Dominis. The Greek revival mansion was both Queen Lili'uokalani's home and also her prison beginning in 1893, when the Hawaiian kingdom was overthrown. She resided at Washington Place till her death in 1917. In 1918 the home became the official residence of governors of Hawaii. The mansion was converted into a museum in 2001, and a new governor's mansion was built behind it. Washington Place is still used for state dinners and official functions and remains the official residence of the governor. The mansion is on the mountain side of Beretania Street, directly across from the Hawaii State Capitol.

St. Andrew's Cathedral
Just to the west of Washington Place is **St. Andrew's Cathedral** (229 Queen Emma Sq., 808/524-2822, www.thecathedralofstandrew. org). Construction started in 1867, but wasn't really finished until 1958. Many of its stones and ornaments were shipped from England, and its stained-glass windows, especially the large contemporary-style window on the narthex end, the bell tower, and its pipe organ, touted as the largest pipe organ in the Pacific, are of particular interest. Hawaii's monarchs worshiped here, and the church is still active. There is a free guided tour following the 10:30am Sunday service. After the service, simply wait below the pulpit for a docent. There is limited public parking on church grounds during the week.

Hawai'i State Art Museum
The **Hawai'i State Art Museum** (250 S. Hotel St., #2, 808/586-0900, http://hawaii.gov/sfca/ HiSAM.html, 10am-4pm Tues.-Sat.) is on the second floor of the No. 1 Capitol District

Building and has four galleries: the Diamond Head Gallery, the Ewa Gallery, the Sculpture Lobby, and the Sculpture Garden. The exhibitions highlight the finest collection of work by Hawaii artists and the gallery displays rotate regularly. The museum gift shop is on the first floor.

King Kamehameha I Statue

The statue of King Kamehameha I is centered in a roundabout near the junction of King and Mililani Streets. Running off at an angle is Merchant Street, the oldest thoroughfare in Honolulu. This statue is much more symbolic of Kamehameha's strength as a ruler and unifier of the Hawaiian Islands than as a replica of the man himself. It is one of three. The original, lost at sea near the Falkland Islands en route from Paris where it was bronzed, was later recovered, but not before the insurance money was used to cast this second one. The original now stands in the tiny town of Kapa'au, in the Kohala District of the Big Island, not far from where Kamehameha was born. The Honolulu statue was dedicated in 1883, as part of King David Kalakaua's coronation ceremony. Its black and gold colors are striking, but it is most magnificent on June 11, King Kamehameha Day, when 18-foot lei are draped around the neck and the outstretched arms. The third stands in Washington, D.C., dedicated when Hawaii became a state.

Kawaiaha'o Church

The **Kawaiaha'o Church** (957 Punchbowl St., 808/522-1333, www.kawaiahao.org) was built between 1836 and 1842. The first Christian church in Hawaii, its New England-style architecture was crafted from 14,000 coral slabs, quarried by hand from local reefs. King Liholiho and his wife Queen Emma, who bore the last child born to a Hawaiian monarch, wed at the church, and on June 19, 1856, Lunalilo, the first king elected to the throne, took his oath of office in the church. Lunalilo is buried in a tomb at the front of the church, along with his father, Charles Kana'ina, and nearby lies the grave of his mother, Miriam Kekauluohi.

© KEVIN WHITTON

Kawaiaha'o Church is constructed of coral blocks hewn from nearby reefs.

In the graveyard at the rear of the church rest many members of the Parker, Green, Brown, and Cooke families, early missionaries to the islands. Most are recognizable as important and influential people in 19th-century Hawaiian history. Hidden away in a corner of the grounds is an unobtrusive adobe building, the remains of a schoolhouse built in 1835 to educate Hawaiian children. Kawaiaha'o holds beautiful Christmas services with a strong Polynesian and Hawaiian flavor, and Hawaiian-language services are given here every Sunday, along with English-language services.

Mission Houses Museum

The days when tall ships with tattered sails bore in God-fearing missionary families dedicated to Christianizing the savage islands are alive in the halls and buildings of the **Mission Houses Museum** (553 S. King St., 808/447-3910, www.missionhouses.org, Tues.-Sat. 10am-4pm), now a registered National Historic Landmark. Set behind Kawaiaha'o Church, the complex includes

O'AHU

two main houses, a printing house annex, a research library, and a gift shop. The printing office was the first in the islands just as the Frame House is the oldest wooden structure in Hawaii. One-hour guided tours are offered every hour 11am-3pm; admission is $10 adults, $6 students.

CHINATOWN
◖ Historic Chinatown
Chinese immigrants came to Hawaii in the 1800s as the first contract laborers for the burgeoning sugar industry. They established a vibrant community with herb shops, restaurants, temples, and retail outlets in what is now **historic Chinatown**. Today, Chinatown is a vibrant mix of art galleries, coffeehouses, upscale restaurants, bars and clubs, outdoor markets, and quick and delicious ethnic food restaurants. It also has a seedy side of homeless sleeping in doorways, prostitution, and fights spilling out of dive bars onto the sidewalk, which gives the historic neighborhood depth and character.

The best way to see Chinatown is to park the car and explore the streets on foot. Chinatown is relatively small, and the square grid of streets makes it easy to get around quickly. There are six municipal parking lots across Chinatown, which have the best rates. There is one on River Street, one on Maunakea Street, two on Smith Street, and two on Bethel Street.

On the east side of Chinatown, Fort Street Mall is a pedestrian area dominated by take-out restaurants and mingling students from Hawaii Pacific University as they wait for classes. The art galleries are generally on the east end of Chinatown, on Smith Street, Nu'uanu Avenue, and Bethel Street. The cuisine on offer in Chinatown is truly international, from Irish and Cuban to French and Mediterranean, much of which is found on Bethel Street. But the main draw, traditional Chinese fare, is also easily found. The wealth of Chinese establishments are on Smith and Maunakea Streets. Noodle shops and Chinese restaurants merely complement the variety of Asian food found in the **Maunakea Marketplace Food Court,** on the corner of Maunakea and Hotel Streets. Chinese, Thai, Korean, Vietnamese, and Filipino plates are served from small market stalls with family-style seating available for enjoying the myriad flavors. Just across Beretania Street, on the outskirts of Chinatown, is the **Chinatown Cultural Plaza Center,** a small indoor mall with gift and herb shops, as well as a host of small eateries. There is paid parking at the plaza, as well.

Chinatown has an abundance of historical buildings dating back to the early 20th century, like the **Hawaii Theatre** on Bethel Street, which opened in 1922. The upper-story facades of the buildings along Hotel Street, between Bethel and Maunakea Streets, still retain vestiges from the World War II era. There is also the **Hawaii Kuan Yin Temple** on the mountain side of Vineyard Boulevard at the entrance to Foster Botanical Garden. The temple is dedicated to the Chinese deity of compassion.

KAKA'AKO
◖ Honolulu Museum of Art
With a rich history dating back to its opening in 1927, the **Honolulu Museum of Art** (900 S. Beretania St., 808/532-8700, http://honolulumuseum.org, 10am-4:30pm Tues.-Sat., 1pm-3pm Sun.) has a collection of 50,000 pieces spanning 5,000 years of Asian art and textiles, American and European painting and decorative art, works on paper, and traditional works from Africa, Oceania, and the Americas. Within its earthy, revival mission-style architecture, the museum also houses a library, an education wing, a contemporary gallery, a café, and a 280-seat theater. Admission is $10 adult, $5 children 4-17, children 3 and under free. The fee also covers the Honolulu Museum of Art Spalding House for same day entry.

Parking can be a bit tricky. There is metered street parking on the blocks around the museum, but make sure to check for time restrictions. The museum maintains two parking lots: the Honolulu Museum of Art School lot behind the Honolulu Museum of Art School with entrances on Beretania Street and Young Street ($3 with validation for four hours), and the Kinau Street Lot (1035 Kinau St., 4:30pm-11pm Mon.-Fri., 10am-11pm Sat.-Sun., free).

There are five spaces at the museum for visitors with disabilities.

Kaka'ako Waterfront Park and Kewalo Basin Park

Kaka'ako Waterfront Park is a 35-acre expanse of grassy rolling hills that runs to the water's edge on the west side of Kewalo Basin. There are restrooms, picnic tables, and a paved jogging path, but no sandy beach. If you want to jump in the water, there are cement steps that scale down the rocky jetty wall.

On the eastern flank of Kewalo Basin is **Kewalo Basin Park,** a small coastal refuge with shade trees, restrooms, picnic tables, great views of the ocean, and a couple of popular surf breaks. If you've chartered a boat out of Kewalo Basin for diving or fishing, the park is the perfect place to kill some time before or after your tour. There are two small parking lots, which often fill up on the weekends.

Children's Discovery Center

The **Children's Discovery Center** (111 Ohe St., 808/524-5437, www.discoverycenter-hawaii.org, 9am-1pm Tues.-Fri., 10am-3pm Sat.-Sun.) at Kaka'ako Waterfront Park is an interactive, hands-on children's museum and activity center focused on learning and discovering through play. The center has six exhibits, one for visitors five years and younger and five for older children. They can learn about their bodies, role play to discover how a community functions, find out about Hawaiian history and culture, as well as cultures beyond Hawaiian shores, and explore and understand the importance of rainforests. Admission is $10 general, $6 senior citizen, children under one year are free.

NU'UANU
(Foster Botanical Garden

Wedged between the H-1 freeway and downtown's skyscrapers, **Foster Botanical Garden** (50 N. Vineyard Blvd., 808/522-7066, www1.honolulu.gov/parks/hbg/fbg.htm, 9am-4pm daily, adult $5, children 6-12 $1, under 5 free) finds itself in an unlikely area for abundant

© KEVIN WHITTON

Foster Botanical Garden features many of Honolulu's Exceptional Trees.

Exceptional Trees

In 1975, the Hawaii state legislature passed Act 105, The Exceptional Tree Act. The law recognizes the ecological and cultural significance and value of trees deemed exceptional and establishes the protection of designated trees. What is an exceptional tree? Exceptional trees on O'ahu must have historic or cultural value or meet certain criteria of age, rarity, location, size, aesthetic quality, and endemic status. Exceptional trees are marked with a gold or silver plaque that identifies their scientific and common name and county of origin. There are over 150 exceptional trees on O'ahu. Find the complete list of exceptional trees and their location at www.honolulu.gov.

greenery. But once you set foot into the garden, you'll be mesmerized by the lush foliage and incredibly tall trees and all things urban will melt away. Since some of the trees in the collection were planted back in 1853, when the grounds were the residence of German physicist and botanist William Hillebrand, the enormity of the trees on the main lawn are a wonder of nature. There are 26 "Exceptional Trees" on the 13.5-acre property, and the garden boasts indoor and outdoor orchid sections, a palm section, and a cycad garden. Cycads are curious leafy plants that date back 200 million years to the Jurassic period. The garden has ample parking.

Queen Emma Summer Palace

Hanaiakamalama, today known as the **Queen Emma Summer Palace** (2913 Pali Hwy., 808/595-3167, http://daughtersofhawaii.org, 9am-4pm daily), was King Kamehameha IV and Queen Emma's summer retreat from 1857 to 1885. Today the historic landmark is a museum set on beautifully landscaped grounds. Admission is $6 per adult and $1 per child. They also offer docent-led tours of the 19th-century home. To get to the palace, take the Pali Highway exit from the H-1 freeway. The palace is on the east side of the highway.

Nu'uanu Pali State Wayside

Better known as the Pali Lookout, the **Nu'uanu Pali State Wayside** is on the Honolulu side of the tunnels on the Pali Highway. The lookout has amazing views of Kane'ohe Bay, Kailua, and the Ko'olau Range. The lookout is often windy. If you're feeling adventurous, there is a ramp that leads down to the Old Pali Road, which you can walk along till it is literally swallowed up by vegetation and decay.

PUNCHBOWL
National Memorial Cemetery of the Pacific

The **National Memorial Cemetery of the Pacific** (2177 Puowaina Dr., 808/532-3720, 8am-6:30pm daily Mar.-Sept., 8am-5:30pm daily Oct.-Feb.) is inside Punchbowl Crater. Established in 1949, the cemetery is a memorial to those who served in the U.S. Armed Forces and is listed on the National Register of Historic Places. Spreading across 112 acres, the beautiful, solemn grounds are a quiet place good for reflection. A small office and restrooms are located at the entrance (8am-4:30pm Mon.-Fri.). At the back of the cemetery, behind the main memorial, a pathway leads to a magnificent viewing area on the crater rim overlooking Honolulu.

There are several ways to reach the cemetery and many signs around the crater indicating the way. From the H-1 freeway eastbound, take the Pali Highway exit, turn right on Iolani Avenue immediately after crossing the bridge, then take the next left onto Lusitana Street. Bear right onto Puowaina Drive and follow the signs. One-lane roads curve through the cemetery.

MAKIKI
Tantalus-Round Top Drive

One of only two roadways in Hawaii listed on the National Register of Historic Places, **Tantalus Drive** and **Round Top Drive** meet at the **Pu'u 'Ualaka'a State Wayside** on top of a cinder cone with amazing views of Honolulu, from Diamond Head to Pearl Harbor, including Manoa Valley. Tantalus Drive approaches

Sailor Jerry

Hawaii is socially and culturally accepting of tattoos on the whole. After all, tattooing is engrained in Polynesian, and Hawaiian, culture. So it comes as no surprise that the father of the traditional Americana tattoo style, Sailor Jerry, practiced his art and gained his international acclaim working from a small shop on Smith Street in Chinatown.

Born Norman Keith Collins in 1911, Sailor Jerry joined the Navy at age 19 and, after his time at sea and abroad, fell in love with the imagery of Southeast Asia and the Hawaiian Islands. He settled in Hawaii in the 1930s and cemented his reputation as the best tattoo artist in Chinatown during World War II, when

sailors docking at Aloha Tower were flocking to Chinatown for booze, hookers, and tattoos. Sailor Jerry established paradigms in tattooing for cleanliness and sterilization, pigments producing bright colors, and a technique and style that is still mimicked to this day.

Sailor Jerry passed away in 1973 and is buried in the National Memorial Cemetery of the Pacific in Punchbowl Crater. Most important, Sailor Jerry passed on an appreciation for the tattoo as a legitimate form of art to be cultivated and collected. And as for his small shop on Smith Street, it's still a tattoo studio to this day.

the wayside park from the west, while Round Top Drive comes in from the east. A round-trip on the winding roads is about 20 miles. The leisurely drive passes hillside homes, is thick with vegetation, and often quite narrow. If you're easily carsick, this is a drive you'll probably want to avoid. Reach Tantalus Drive from Auwaiolimu Street via Nehoa Street. Reach Round Top Drive from Makiki Street via Nehoa Street. You can also take Makiki Street to Makiki Heights Drive, then to Tantalus Drive. The wayside park is also the trailhead for several forest hiking trails and known for auto theft, so be sure not to leave any valuables in your vehicle, even if you're just stopping for a few minutes to take in the view.

Honolulu Museum of Art Spalding House

Formerly the Contemporary Museum, the **Honolulu Museum of Art Spalding House** (2411 Makiki Heights Dr., 808/526-0232, http://honolulumuseum.org, 10am-4pm Tues.-Sat., noon-3pm Sun., $10 adults, $5 children 4-17, children 3 and under free) was gifted the entire contemporary art collection, covering from the 1940s to present, in 2011. The museum is set on three and a half acres of terraced,

sculpture, and botanical gardens. Admission also covers entry to the Honolulu Museum of Art for same-day entry. There is a one-hour docent-led walking tour at 1:30pm Tuesday through Sunday, and the museum is free to the public the first Wednesday of each month. Parking is also free. From Nehoa Street, turn onto Makiki Street, then take Makiki Heights Drive at the fork.

MANOA
University of Hawai'i at Manoa

On University Avenue, just off the H-1 freeway, the **University of Hawai'i at Manoa** is a beautiful, compact campus with mature landscaping and fascinating architecture spanning decades. Founded in 1907, UII Manoa holds the distinction of being a land-, sea-, and space-grant research institution, with nine colleges rounding out their academic programs. Of particular interest on campus are the trees planted across its 320 acres. Stop by the botany department and pick up their *Campus Plants* pamphlet. It has a map of the campus and identifies the myriad unique and unusual plants, making for a lovely walk. Also noteworthy is the art department's two free art galleries. The **University of Hawai'i Art Gallery,** off the main foyer, features local and international artists and thematic exhibitions in many different media. The **Commons Gallery,** upstairs, rotates exhibitions on a weekly basis and allows students to experiment with exhibition design and display. And don't miss the giant baobab tree on the west side of the art building—a natural work of art.

To get to UH Manoa, take the University Avenue exit from the H-1 freeway from either direction. There is free parking in the neighborhoods surrounding campus, requiring a bit of a walk, or there is paid meter parking on campus. You can access on-campus parking lots from East West Road, from Dole Street, or on Maile Way from University Avenue. A great time to visit is mid-May to mid-July, when the Summer Session is in, but the campus is rather empty.

Lyon Arboretum
Nestled in the back of verdant and often misty Manoa Valley, **Lyon Arboretum** (3860 Manoa Rd., 808/988-0456, www.hawaii.edu/lyonarboretum, 8am-4pm Mon.-Fri., 9am-3pm Sat.) is a 194-acre botanical garden in a tropical rainforest setting. With over 5,000 tropical plants and a vast network of trails, you'll have the opportunity to see heliconias, gingers, aroids, native Hawaiian plants, and one of the largest collections of palms in Hawaii. Initially established as a watershed restoration project in 1918, the garden is shaded with a variety of far-reaching canopy trees, their trunks laden with bromeliads, moss, and ferns. With the arboretum receiving an average of 165 inches of precipitation annually, you should be prepared for long periods of rain, mud, and mosquitoes. Bring binoculars for spotting birds. Pick up a trail map at the Visitor Center and take the time to explore the smaller trails off the main artery that winds back up the valley.

To get to Lyon Arboretum, follow Manoa Road all the way back into the valley, past Paradise Park, and turn left onto the arboretum's private drive before the end of the road. There's a parking lot after a couple switchbacks. The Visitor Center also has a very nice

bookstore focusing on conservation, biology, and botany.

KALIHI
◖ Bishop Museum
The premier natural and cultural history institution in the Pacific and the largest museum in the state, **Bishop Museum** (1525 Bernice St., 808/847-3511, www.bishopmuseum.org, 9am-5pm Wed.-Mon.), the Hawai'i State Museum of Culture and Natural History, was founded in 1889 by Charles Reed Bishop in honor of his late wife, Princess Bernice Pauahi Bishop. It was erected as a bastion for her extensive collection of Hawaiian artifacts and royal family heirlooms as the last descendant of the royal Kamehameha family. The museum also has an extensive library and archives for research purposes.

Bishop Museum has both rotating and mainstay exhibits. Hawaiian Hall utilizes its three floors to explore the different realms of Hawaiian culture from the gods and legends to the customs of daily life. Polynesian Hall, which opened in 2013, represents the peoples of Pacific cultures across Polynesia, Micronesia, and Melanesia. And the Abigail Kinoiki Kekaulike Kahili Room honors the kings of the Hawaiian monarchy and displays their *kahili,* feather standards, and other heirlooms. The Science Adventure Center has interactive exhibits focusing on Hawaii's volcanic origins and environment. It's a great installation to let the kids get hands-on and explore every nook and cranny. From the amazing collection of Pacific seashells to the planetarium, Bishop Museum explores Hawaii's culture through many different disciplines.

Admission is $17.95 adult, $14.95 senior and children age 4-12, children 3 and under are free. To get there from the H-1 freeway, take the Likelike Highway and turn right on Bernice Street.

MOANALUA
Moanalua Gardens
A large grassy park shaded by famous monkeypod trees with canopies creating beautiful,

© KEVIN WHITTON

Bishop Museum

cooling shade, **Moanalua Gardens** (1352 Pineapple Pl., 808/839-5334, www.mgf-hawaii. org, 7:30am-sunset daily) is a 24-acre privately owned reserve open to the public during daylight hours. It is also the site of the home of Prince Lot Kapuaiwa, who later became King Kamehameha V. The Prince Lot Hula Festival is held at Moanalua Gardens every summer. From the Moanalua Freeway H-201, take the Puuloa Road exit toward Tripler Hospital. Turn right immediately after the exit sign into the gardens. The exit is from the off-ramp.

Shopping

DOWNTOWN
Aloha Tower Marketplace
Aloha Tower, a lighthouse that has welcomed ships into Honolulu Harbor since 1926, is the backdrop of the **Aloha Tower Marketplace** (1 Aloha Tower Dr., 808/566-2337, www.aloha-tower.com, 9am-9pm Mon.-Sat., 9am-6pm Sun.). Here you'll find dining, shopping, and a festive atmosphere at one of Honolulu's iconic landmarks.

Check out **Ann's Fashion** (808/545-1017), which sells aloha wear, sarongs, sundresses and other relaxing beachwear. **Imperial Galley** (808/529-8866) specializes in Asian-inspired art, apparel, accessories, and home decor. Or for unique gifts, stop by the **Aloha Candles** kiosk. It's full of colorful and intricately hand-carved candles and other Hawaiiana gift ideas.

ALA MOANA AND KAKA'AKO
Ala Moana Center
Ala Moana Center (1450 Ala Moana Blvd., 808/955-9517, www.alamoanacenter.com, 9:30am-9pm Mon.-Sat., 10am-7pm Sun.) is the world's largest open-air shopping center with over 290 stores and restaurants. The mall is conveniently located near Waikiki and features high-end international clothiers

Farm to Table

KCC Farmers' Market

Honolulu has a rich farm-to-table restaurant culture. With the popularity of farmers' markets, anyone can get on board and find fresh local produce and prepared foods. Check out these farmers' markets in Honolulu:

- **KCC Farmers' Market:** 4303 Diamond Head Rd., Kapi'olani Community College Parking Lot C, 4pm-7pm Tuesday, 7:30am-11am Saturday

- **Ala Moana Farmers' Market:** 1450 Ala Moana Blvd., Ala Moana Center upper deck by Sears, 4pm-7pm Tuesday, 8am-noon Saturday

- **Honolulu @ Night:** 777 Ward Ave., Neal Blaisdell Concert Hall, 4pm-7pm Wednesday

- **Kaka'ako Makai Community Cultural Marketplace:** corner of Ilalo and Ahui Sts., 4:30pm-8pm Friday, 9am-2pm Saturday

- **Manoa Marketplace:** 2752 Woodlawn Dr., 7pm-11pm Sunday, Tuesday, and Thursday

and jewelers, alongside popular brand-name stores. Department stores **Macy's** (808/941-2345), **Neiman Marcus** (808/951-8887), and **Nordstrom** (808/953-6100) surround the open-air central mall area. At the heart of the mall is an auditorium with seating on multiple mall levels where daily hula performances and other shows are put on.

For technical athletic wear for yoga, running, dancing, and other aerobic pursuits, check out **Lululemon Athletica** (808/946-7220, www.lululemon.com/honolulu/alamoanacenter) on the second floor, Nordstrom wing. Also on the second level, right by Sears, is **Na Hoku** (808/946-2100, www.nahoku.com), a local jewelry store featuring island-themed jewelry, stones, and pearls. **Shirokiya** (808/973-9111, www.shirokiya.com), next to Macy's on the second floor, is like a Japanese

mall within the mall. There are food and confections, a beer garden, Japanese goods, toys, trinkets, and other wares.

If you're in need of a bikini, on the first level is **San Lorenzo Bikinis** (808/946-3200, www.sanlorenzobikinis.com) with all the best in Brazilian bikini fashion. For local surfwear, head to **Hawaiian Island Creations** (808/973-6780, www.hicsurf.com) is on the first floor by Sears, and **Town and Country Surf Design** (808/973-5199, www.tcsurf.com) on the third floor, Sears wing. And for authentic Hawaiian quilts and accessories, head up to the Ho'okipa Terrace and check out **Hawaiian Quilt Collection** (808/946-2233, www.hawaiian-quilts.com).

If you're looking for a great used bookstore in the Kaka'ako area, check out **Jelly's** (670 Auahi St., 808/587-7001, www.jellyshawaii.

com, 10am-7pm Mon.-Sat., 10am-6pm Sun.). Not only do they have a great selection of fiction, nonfiction, and children's books, but you'll also find used LPs, CDs, and videos.

Ward Warehouse

Just a couple blocks west of Ala Moana Center is a small, two-story open-air mall called **Ward Warehouse** (1050 Ala Moana Blvd., 808/591-8411, www.wardcenters.com, 10am-9pm Mon.-Sat., 10am-6pm Sun.), part of a conglomerate of five open-air malls in the immediate vicinity.

Island Guitars (808/591-2910, www.islandguitars.com) is a one-stop shop for new, used, and vintage fretted instruments. **Native Books/Na Mea Hawaii** (808/596-8885, www.nativebookshawaii.com) has locally made gifts, clothing, food, and art, as well as a complete collection of books about Hawaii and the Pacific. If you're looking for surf apparel or wetsuits, check out **Xcel Wetsuits** (808/596-7441, www.xcelwetsuits.com). And if you're in the mood for a specialty beer, wine, or liquor, the **Liquor Collection** (808/524-8808, http://liquorcollection.com) is a must.

CHINATOWN

If you're interested in picking up a bottle of wine, stop by **HASR Wine Co.** (31 N. Pauahi St., 808/535-9463, www.hasrwineco.com, 10am-8pm Mon.-Fri., 10am-5pm Sat.-Sun.). They have a very knowledgeable staff and offer wine tastings Tuesday and Friday (5pm-7pm).

KAIMUKI

Kapahulu Avenue is a hub for dining and shopping. The mile-long stretch, running from Leahi Avenue by the fire station nearly up to the H-1 freeway, has plenty of places to grab a quick bite, sit-down restaurants, clothing stores, sporting goods stores, coffee shops, and a supermarket. There are even two tattoo parlors on the strip.

The Clothes Chick (415 Kapahulu Ave., 808/739-2442, http://theclotheschick.com, 10am-9pm daily) is a designer resale and consignment shop with chic clothes and accessories

located next to a gas station. Parking is in the rear of the building. **Glam Rok** (449 Kapahulu Ave., 808/732-6278, http://glamrokhawaii.com, 10:30am-6pm daily) is a consignment boutique specializing in designer jeans, handbags, and trendy clothes in Hee Hing Plaza next to the bank. Free parking is available under the two-story center. **Bailey's Antiques and Aloha Shirts** (517 Kapahulu Ave., 808/734-7628, http://alohashirts.com, 10am-9pm daily), next to another gas station up the street, is a score if you're looking for Hawaiiana wear and decoration. Along with over 15,000 aloha shirts in stock—new, used, and vintage—they also sell antiques like figurines, jewelry, postcards, and Hawaiian music LPs. **Peggy's Picks** (732 Kapahulu Ave. Ste. 1, 808/737-3297, Mon.-Sat. 11am-7pm) is an eclectic shop with Hawaiiana and other collectibles from around the world, furniture, jewelry, and curious odds and ends. Limited street parking is available.

Waialae Avenue also has retail outlets worth a stop. **Drift Boutique** (3434 Waialae Ave., #4, 808/284-1177, 1pm-6pm Mon.-Sat.) between 8th and 9th Avenues is a beach girl boutique selling unique locally handmade jewelry, bathing suits, and specialty accessories. If you're crafty, check out **Bead It** (1152 Koko Head Ave., 808/734-1182, http://ibeads.com/kaimuki.htm, 10am-6pm Mon.-Sat., noon-4pm Sun.). They have a full range of beads, gemstones, books, chains, and tools, and also offer classes. **Gecko Books & Comics** (1151 12th Ave., 808/732-1292, 11am-7pm Sun.-Tues., 10am-9pm Wed.-Sat.) is right off Waialae Avenue and packed with books and comics. The owner is extremely knowledgeable and helpful.

MOILI'ILI

If you're just in the mood for a nice bottle of wine, stop by **The Wine Stop** (1809 S. King St., 808/946-3707, www.thewinestophawaii.com, 10am-9pm Mon.-Thurs., 10am-10pm Fri.-Sat., 11am-7pm Sun.). This quaint beer and wine boutique has an in-store sommelier to help with your wine selection or pairings.

Entertainment and Events

NIGHTLIFE
Chinatown
On Nuuanu Avenue, **The Dragon Upstairs** (1038 Nuuanu Ave., 808/526-1411, www.thedragonupstairs.com, 7pm-2am) is a warm and classy jazz club located above Hank's Café. They also feature world music. For a different beat, check out **O'Toole's Irish Pub** (902 Nuuanu Ave., 808/536-4138, http://otoolesirishpub.com, 10am-2am daily). The pub has live Irish, folk, and reggae music and is also a cigar bar where smoking is allowed inside.

On Bethel Street you'll find **Bambu Two Cafe** (1144 Bethel St., 808/528-1144, www.bambutwo.com, 2pm-2am Mon.-Sat.), a café and martini bar with indoor and outdoor seating. They serve $3.50 martinis all day, every day.

On Hotel Street, check out **Thirtyninehotel** (39 N. Hotel St., 808/599-2552, www.thirtyninehotel.com, 4pm-2am Tues.-Sat.). This upstairs art gallery and indoor/outdoor bar serves tapas and is a great place to relax outside and listen to live music or DJs. Right next door on the street level is the aptly named **Nextdoor** (43 N. Hotel St., 808/548-6398, http://nextdoorhnl.com, 8pm-2am Wed.-Sat.). A two-story combination nightclub and creative arts venue, Nextdoor is as versatile as its acts, ranging from a cinema house to a dance hall, but it's best known as a music venue. There are full-service bars upstairs and downstairs, with VIP bottle service and table reservations upstairs. Also on the same block is **Bar 35** (35 N. Hotel St., 808/537-3535, www.bar35.com, 4pm-2am Mon.-Fri., 6pm-2am Sat.), a warm and modern spot featuring hundreds of international beers, indoor and patio bars, daily happy hour specials, DJs, and live music. They also have table reservations and bottle service, and serve fusion-gourmet pizzas and simple tapas. **Manifest** (32 N. Hotel St., 808/523-7575, http://manifesthawaii.com, 8am-10pm Mon., 8am-2am Tues.-Fri., 10am-2am Sat.) also holds valuable real estate on Hotel Street. A coffee shop by day, Manifest is a sophisticated cocktail bar after dark and a venue for artists of all mediums. Live music includes hip-hop, bluegrass, punk, and everything in between.

Kaka'ako
Pint + Jigger (1936 S. King St., 808/744-9593, www.pintandjigger.com, 4:30pm-midnight Sun. and Tues.-Thurs., 9am-1:30am Fri.-Sat.) is a modern public house offering creative pairings of cuisine, beer, and cocktails within a relaxed atmosphere. Along with 21 beers on tap and specialty cocktails, the menu changes to reflect the selection of libations.

Ala Moana
One of the premier night clubs on O'ahu is on the Ho'okipa Terrace at the top of Ala Moana Center. **Pearl Ultralounge** (1450 Ala Moana Blvd., 808/944-8000, www.pearlhawaii.com, Tues.-Fri. 11am-1am daily) offers a luxury lounge experience with cuisine, live music, and dancing. Reservations for VIP bottle service are taken at 10:30pm and held for 30 minutes. The dress code is strictly enforced.

Also on the Ho'okipa Terrace is a lively open-air bar called the **Mai Tai Bar** (1450 Ala Moana Blvd., 808/947-2900, www.maitaibar.com, 11am-1am daily). They offer daily *pau hana* specials (4pm-7pm), nightly happy hour pricing (9:30pm-12:30am), and beer specials all day during football season. The appetizers and entrées have local flair, and they also have island-style live music for happy hour every night (8pm-11pm).

Rumors (410 Atkinson Dr., 808/955-4811, 5pm-3am Fri.-Sat.), located in the Ala Moana Hotel, has a more relaxed atmosphere focusing on the music and dancing. They play everything from hip-hop to hits of the '70s, '80s, and '90s.

THE ARTS

Chinatown is the home of Honolulu's art scene, and there are nearly 20 art galleries that support and promote the local artists comprising Honolulu's art community. **The ARTS at Marks Garage** (1159 Nuuanu Ave., 808/521-2903, www.artsatmarks.com, 11am-6pm Tues.-Sat.) is the heartbeat of Chinatown's art scene. With 12 major exhibits and performances, lectures, screenings, and workshops, Marks has transformed the Chinatown community through the arts. **Ong King Art Center** (184 N. King St., http://ongking.com) has carved out a niche for performance art. Whether it be through spoken word, poetry, live music, or visual art, Ong King encourages creative risk taking. **Pegge Hopper** (1164 Nuuanu Ave., 808/524-1160, http://peggehopper.com, 11am-4pm Tues.-Fri., 11am-3pm Sat.) has been a mainstay in Chinatown since 1983. Her gallery features her own work, including her famous paintings and drawings of Hawaiian women, as well as that of guest artists. **Bethel Street Gallery** (1140 Bethel St., Ste. G-4, 808/524-3552, www.bethelstreetgallery.com, 11am-4pm Tues.-Fri., 11am-3pm Sat.) is Hawaii's largest artist owned and operated gallery, showcasing top artists in different media.

Food

DOWNTOWN

Hawaiian

On the outskirts of downtown Honolulu is a long-established Hawaiian food joint called the **People's Cafe** (1300 Pali Hwy., 808/536-5789, 10am-8pm Mon.-Sat., 10am-5pm Sun., $6-12). Just *makai* of the Pali Long's parking lot, look for the bright red neon sign for this small restaurant having all the favorite Hawaiian combos plus some extras like salted meat and kimchi.

American

For a delicious burger and seasonal brews overlooking Honolulu Harbor, check out **Gordon Biersch** (1 Aloha Tower Dr., 808/599-4877, www.gordonbiersch.com, 11am-midnight Sun.-Thurs., 11am-1am Fri.-Sat., $12-24). They have a wide variety of beers on tap and live music Wednesday through Saturday.

CHINATOWN

Honolulu's Chinatown is chock-full of restaurants providing regional cuisine from all over the globe. Just about every other storefront is a restaurant or serves food in some fashion.

Tea

For a quaint and quiet afternoon tea, stop at unpretentious **Tea at 1024** (1024 Nuuanu Ave., 808/521-9596, www.teaat1024.net, 11am-2pm Tues.-Fri., 11am-3pm Sat.). Relax in the charming teahouse, don a special hat from the hat stand, and choose your china for tea time.

Asian

Samplw the cuisine from China, Korea, Vietnam, Thailand, and the Philippines, at the **Maunakea Marketplace Food Court** (1120 Maunakea St., 808/524-3409). In the center of the shopping complex that spans the small city block are vendors with stalls lined up shoulder to shoulder and family-style seating in the middle. The air is thick with the sweet smells of seafood and spices from different countries mingling together. Most vendors offer their food bento or plate lunch style.

Chinese

In historic Chinatown, **Little Village Noodle House** (1113 Smith St., 808/545-3008, http://littlevillagehawaii.com, 10:30am-10:30pm Mon.-Fri., 10:30am-midnight Sat.-Sun., $7-13) is the quintessential Chinese restaurant for grabbing a bite. With over 100 menu items covering meat, poultry, seafood, rice, and noodle dishes, the family-friendly restaurant has every palate covered.

Irish Pubs

J.J. Dolan's (1147 Bethel St., 808/537-4992, www.jjdolans.com, 11am-2am Mon.-Sat., $16-19) is an Irish pub serving delicious New York pizza. With a full bar and a selection of Irish whiskey, this small pub can get pretty rowdy when there is a packed house.

Murphy's Bar & Grill (2 Merchant St., 808/531-0422, http://murphyshawaii.com, 11:30am-2am Mon.-Fri., opens at 4pm Sat.-Sun., $11-19) has a separate bar and dining room under one historic roof. The menu features a combination of bar food, burgers, and Irish food. The bar favors Irish whiskey and draught beer, with shuffleboard on offer.

Cuban

On Bethel Street you'll find **Soul De Cuba Cafe** (1121 Bethel St., 808/545-2822, http://souldecuba.com, 8am-8pm daily, $10-24). The authentic flavorful and rich Cuban fare is prepared from family recipes passed down through generations. The classic Cuban dish *ropa vieja* is a Honolulu favorite. If you stop by for lunch, the Cuban sandwiches are also extremely delicious.

French

Brasserie Du Vin (1115 Bethel St., 808/545-1115, brasserieduvin.com, 11:30am-10pm Sun.-Thurs., 11:30am-midnight Fri.-Sat., $11-26) is a French restaurant with a casual and rustic environment offering indoor and patio seating. The seasonal menu includes small dishes, entrées, artisan cheeses, charcuterie, and classic French desserts. They also have food and drink specials during happy hour (4pm-6pm Mon.-Sat.).

KAKAʻAKO
Quick Bites

For coffee, sandwiches, quick bites, breakfast foods, and Internet access, stop in at **Fresh Café** (831 Queen St., 808/688-8055, http://freshcafehi.com, 8am-11pm Mon.-Sat., 9am-6pm Sun., $5-9), where the ingredients are locally sourced. Fresh Café is the center of the

---

Public Art

At first glance, the industrial zone in Kakaʻako, between Ala Moana Boulevard and Kapiolani Boulevard, can be a mind-numbing experience. Auto repair Quonsets, warehouses, and homogeneous industrial edifices appear crushed together with little regard for open space. But young urban artists are gentrifying this industrial zone with imagery and color, free for all to see, sparking a renaissance of cafés, art studios, and galleries.

Artists are taking art outside and have created murals of varying sizes all over the exterior of buildings in parts of Kakaʻako, mostly in the urban graffiti style. Just drive slowly down Queen Street between Cooke Street and Ward Avenue and check out all the public art. Now that you know what to look for, go explore and find more.

Kakaʻako urban art scene revival, and hip art decorates the walls of the establishment as well as the walls of the buildings surrounding it. They also have a performance space in the back of the restaurant for live music and art shows. Check their website for the calendar of events.

Steak and Seafood

On the second floor of Ward Center you'll find a great steak and seafood restaurant. **Ryan's Grill** (1200 Ala Moana Blvd., 808/591-9132, www.ryansgrill.com, 11am-midnight daily, $13-21) has a varied menu with small and big salads, pasta and pizza, sandwiches, and steak and seafood options. They also have a relaxing bar area and beautiful views of Ala Moana Beach Park.

Gastropub

In the Ward Farmer's Market, **REAL a gastropub** (1020 Auahi St., 808/596-2526, www.realgastropub.com, 2pm-2am Mon.-Sat., $3-12) is spearheading the gastropub trend in Honolulu with smart combinations of flavors in their tapas-style menu items, designed for sampling. You can combine your choice with one of over 200 bottled beers, imported from all over the world, and 24 rotating taps. They also have a full bar and wine.

MANOA
Quick Bites
Find coffee, home-cooked quick bites, and lots of reading material at **Coffeeline Campus Coffeehouse** (1820 University Ave., 808/778-7909, 8am-2pm Mon.-Fri., 8am-noon Sat.-Sun.). In the back of the YWCA building on University Ave., across from UH Manoa, look for the stairs on the south side of the building leading up to Coffeeline's patio, complete with tables, couches, and more reading material than you can handle. There is free parking behind the building.

Tea
Wai'oli Tea Room (2950 Manoa Rd., 808/988-5800, www.thewaioliatearoom.net, 10:30am-8:30pm Mon.-Fri., 8am-3:30pm Sat.-Sun., $8-14) is a sophisticated restaurant and bakery set in a historic dwelling among beautiful landscaping. Enjoy breakfast, lunch, or dinner with sandwiches, salads, quiche, homemade soup, and of course, afternoon tea.

Hawaiian
Deep in the valley, by the Manoa Falls trailhead and Lyon Arboretum, is a restaurant set among the trees of Manoa's verdant rainforest. **Treetops Restaurant** (3737 Manoa Rd., 808/988-6838, www.thetreetopsrestaurant.com, 11am-2pm Mon.-Fri., opens at 10:30am Sat.-Sun., $7-16) serves both a weekday and a weekend buffet lunch, perfect for a post-hike meal.

Mexican
For authentic Mexican food, stop in at **Serg's Mexican Kitchen** (2740 E. Manoa Rd., 808/988-8118, 11am-9pm Mon.-Sat., 8am-8pm Sun., $4-16). With open-air, family-style seating and mariachi music, this BYOB joint

is the spot for a quick taco or a sit down meal with a big group.

KAIMUKI
Quick Bites
Rainbow Drive-In (3308 Kanaina Ave., 808/737-0177, www.rainbowdrivein.com, 7am-9pm daily, $6-8) has served choice plate lunches since 1961, always at a reasonable price. Protein, rice, and gravy never tasted so good.

Steak and Seafood
On Waialae Avenue are a handful of popular restaurants. **Town** (3435 Waialae Ave., 808/735-5900, www.townkaimuki.com, 7am-9:30pm Mon.-Thurs., 7am-10pm Fri.-Sat., $16-26) serves breakfast, lunch, and dinner. The hip spot, with modern art decor, is a mix between Hawaii regional and Italian cuisine, all with the focus of serving organic, fresh, and locally sourced ingredients. They have a full bar, or you can BYOB for a corkage fee of $15. Limited street parking is available, but there is a small parking lot behind the restaurant as well.

Café Miro (3446 Waialae Ave., 808/734-2737, www.cafemirohawaii.com, Tues.-Sun. 5:30pm-10:30pm, $43-54) is an exquisite steak and seafood restaurant with mostly French cuisine, serving a three-course prix fixe menu and a four-course Chef's Special menu. Think oysters, lamb, duck, scallop, abalone, and steak, each drizzled in an appropriate sauce.

12th Ave Grill (1120 12th Ave., 808/732-9469, www.12thavegrill.com, 5:30pm-9pm Mon.-Thurs., 5:30pm-10pm Fri.-Sat., $25-30) is just off Waialae Avenue and offers award-winning contemporary American cuisine and a commitment to locally sourced and seasonal ingredients. A well-selected wine list and scratch bar pair nicely with the flavorful fare. The small dining room is intimate, yet comfortable.

Salt (3605 Waialae Ave., 808/744-7567, http://salthonolulu.com, 5:30pm-midnight daily, $6-25) is another popular Waialae Avenue establishment. Salt Kitchen and Tasting Bar offers an extensive wine list from around the world, signature cocktails, and a variety of beers, paired with eccentric *pupu*-style dishes meant to be shared using locally sourced ingredients. You'll find local rabbit, oysters, salads, cheese boards, and salted, dried, and cured meats, or you can just get a burger.

On Kapahulu is a popular and often packed **Uncle Bo's** (559 Kapahulu Ave., 808/735-8311, www.unclebosrestaurant.com, 5pm-2am daily, $12-27). Combining American bistro with Pacific Rim cuisine, Uncle Bo's is a small, modern, but casual restaurant. They serve an extensive *pupu* menu, as well as steak, seafood, pasta, and pizza. Be prepared for a bit of wait on the weekends, and if the bar is full, that means you'll have to stand outside.

Award-winning chef Colin Nishida creates Hawaiian-style comfort food, served as complete meals or *pupu* style, inside the Prudential Locations building in an offshoot of the famous Side Street Inn in Kaka'ako called **Side Street Inn on Da Strip** (614 Kapahulu Ave., 808/739-3939, http://sidestreetinn.com, 3pm-midnight daily, $12-22). The restaurant has family-style seating with a touch of fine dining, and the portions are quite large and designed to be shared.

Hawaiian

For authentic Hawaiian food, check out **Ono Hawaiian Food** (726 Kapahulu Ave., 808/737-2275, 11am-8pm Mon.-Sat., $6-22). The family-run restaurant is small and cozy, with just a few tables. Be prepared to wait outside during peak hours.

Thai

On Waialae Avenue there are two consistent picks for Thai food. **Champa Thai** (3452 Waialae Ave., 808/732-0054, www.champathai.com, 11 am-2pm and 5:30pm-9:30pm Mon.-Sat., 5pm-9pm Sun., $7-13) is a BYOB restaurant that serves lunch and dinner and offers sit-down or take-out service. There is street parking available in the neighborhood and four parking spaces behind the restaurant. **To Thai For** (3571 Waialae Ave., 808/734-3443, www.itstothaifor.com, 10:30 am-9:30pm Mon.-Sat., 5pm-9pm Sun., $9-20)

has a basic Thai menu through which you can combine the dish with the protein of your liking.

Japanese

On Kapahulu Avenue are three noteworthy Japanese restaurants. **Irifune** (563 Kapahulu Ave., 808/737-1141, 11:30 am-1:30pm and 5:30pm-9:30pm Tues.-Sat., $10-15) is a curious hole-in-the-wall with some of the best ahi on O'ahu. The entire menu consists of some combination of garlic and ahi, served with local-style sides. This restaurant is very popular, and on the weekends you can expect a wait. They do have a bench outside. Park across the street in the pay parking lot, or there is street parking in the neighborhood behind the restaurant.

Tokkuri Tei (611 Kapahulu Ave., 808/732-6480, http://tokkuri-tei.com, 11 am-2pm and 5:30pm-midnight Mon.-Fri., 5:30pm-midnight Sat., 5pm-10:30pm Sun., $4-50) is a popular izakaya restaurant offering traditional Japanese food with French and local influences. It takes several visits to sample the wealth of food on all 13 pages of the menu. It's located on the second floor of Hee Hing Plaza, and there is valet parking under the plaza. Reservations are necessary.

At the opposite end of Kapahulu Avenue, just off the main drag, is another top-notch izakaya establishment offering traditional Japanese fare. **Izakaya Nonbei** (3108 Olu St., 808/734-5573, 5pm-11:30pm Mon.-Thurs., 5pm-1:30am Fri.-Sat., 5pm-10:30pm Sun., $6-25) is a small restaurant with a sushi bar and shared and private seating. They have a vast selection of sake and beer, but they are known for their frozen sake.

Mexican

Jose's Mexican Cafe & Cantina (1134 Koko Head Ave., 808/732-1833, www.joseshonolulu.com, 11am-10pm Mon.-Sat., 11am-9pm Sun., $14-25) serves up simple Mexican food with seafood, beef, and pork specialties, and even a few egg dishes. They have happy hour weekdays 3pm-6pm and a selection of Mexican beers and different styles of margaritas, mixed either for a glass or a pitcher.

Indian

Himalayan Kitchen (1137 11th Ave., #205, 808/735-1122, 11am-2pm and 5:30pm-10pm Tues.-Fri., 5:30pm-10pm Sat.-Mon., $11-22) serves Nepali and Indian cuisine in a small restaurant with indoor and patio seating. This second-story BYOB is a local favorite and often packed with those seeking their variety of vegetarian and meat dishes. The entrance to the restaurant is in an alcove between a gift store, a barbecue joint, an Italian restaurant, and a salon. There is a paid parking lot with ample parking.

Sweets and Treats

You can grab a delicious pastry, dessert, or cup of coffee on Waialae Avenue at **JJ Bistro & French Pastry** (3447 Waialae Ave., 808/739-0993, 9am-9pm Mon.-Thurs., 9am-9:30pm Fri.-Sat., noon-8pm Sun., $5-19). They also have pizza, pasta, sandwiches, and à la carte entrées. If you're down for an old-fashioned ice cream cone, stop by the **Pill Box** (1133 11th Ave., 808/737-4966, 9am-9pm Mon.-Fri., 9am-5pm Sat., 9pm-11pm Sun.). This full-service neighborhood pharmacy has friendly staff, books, and the best ice cream in town. There are a couple spaces out front on 11th Avenue, or you can park in the paid parking lot behind the building. If you're quick and can get your ice cream within the 15-minute grace period, parking is free.

On Kapahulu Avenue, residents and visitors flock to **Leonard's Bakery** (933 Kapahulu Ave., 808/737-5591, www.leonardshawaii.com, 5am-11pm daily) in record numbers, often backing up traffic on Kapahulu while they wait for a parking stall in the small parking lot out front. Look for the neon sign and the line out the door. Leonard's is famous for its *malasadas* and doughnuts, but also has delicious pastries, cookies, bread, pies, and wraps. **Waiola Shave Ice** (3113 Mokihana St., 808/735-8886, 10:30am-7:30pm daily) is tucked away right off Kapahulu Avenue, across from Safeway.

MOILI'ILI
Health Food

Down To Earth (2525 S. King St., 808/947-7678, www.downtoearth.org, 7:30am-10pm daily) is an all-vegetarian, natural, and organic food store with a deli, salad bar, hot foods, and smoothies. Parking is on the roof behind the store. Take the alley right past the entrance and turn up the ramp.

Kokua Market (2643 S. King St., 808/941-1922, www.kokua.coop, 8am-9pm daily) is a natural food store co-op on the other side of University Avenue from Down To Earth. They have bulk foods and natural and organic groceries, but the real draw is the deli, with hot and cold items. The menu includes raw, vegan, macrobiotic, and natural meats options. There are also freshly baked desserts. Parking is behind the store from Kahuna Lane.

An oasis of charm and natural food on busy and urban King Street, **Peace Cafe** (2239 S. King St., 808/951-7555, www.peacecafehawaii.com, 11am-9pm Mon.-Sat., 11am-3pm Sun., $9-11) serves vegan home cooking in a comfortable setting. Within its eclectic decorating scheme, Peace Cafe has sandwiches, salads, stews, and prepared goods like granola for the taking.

Japanese

Sometimes the restaurants that are the hardest to find turn out to be the best. This is the case at **Imanas Tei** (2626 S. King St., 808/941-2626, 5pm-11:30pm Mon.-Sat., $6-10). Tucked away behind the 7-11, the traditional Japanese menu is a favorite with locals, as well as the chanko nabe, a hearty seafood stew. There are only a few designated parking stalls for Imanas Tei, so if they're full, you'll need to park at Puck's Alley around the corner off University Avenue; the plaza has a paid parking lot.

Indian

Cafe Maharani (2509 S. King St., 808/951-7447, http://cafemaharanihawaii.com, 5pm-10pm daily, $14-16) is an award-winning casual restaurant blending natural ingredients and a host of spices to create some of the most sought after Indian food in Honolulu.

Mediterranean

Da Spot (2469 S. King St., 808/941-1313, 10:30am-9:30pm Mon.-Sat., $6-10) is a roomy Mediterranean café that is completely open to King Street from the front. They offer vegetarian fare, including Thai and Egyptian cuisine and desserts, as well as rustic salads and prepared foods like mango salsa, imported cheeses, olives, and hummus. Take a seat and take advantage of Internet access with your meal.

Steak and Seafood

Chef Mavro (1969 S. King St., 808/944-4714, www.chefmavro.com, 6pm-9pm Tues.-Sun., $75-165) offers the quintessential modern dining experience. The French-influenced cuisine is award-winning and the ingredients are locally sourced. Seasonal menus are geared toward wine pairings. Children must be 5 years of age or older, and attire is aloha casual.

Renowned chef specializing in Hawaii regional cuisine Alan Wong pairs fine dining with fresh and local ingredients at his flagship restaurant **Alan Wong's** (1857 S. King St., 808/949-1939, www.alanwongs.com, 5pm-10pm daily, $30-50). Locally raised beef and sustainable seafood combined with O'ahu farm fresh produce are served up with a completely local flair. In addition to entrées, they offer two set multicourse tasting menus available with wine pairings.

In the same vein of Hawaii regional cuisine and locally sourced ingredients, **Side Street Inn** (1225 Hopaka St., 808/591-0253, http://sidestreetinn.com, 2 pm-2am daily, $12-22) has transformed over the years from a little hole-in-the-wall with exceptional food to a big-hole-in-the-wall with phenomenal cuisine where local and international chefs go to eat. With the full bar and large portions served *pupu* style, this is a great place to share the experience of food and drink with family and friends.

IWILEI
Seafood

In the Honolulu Harbor area, seafood is the main attraction. **Nico's at Pier 38** (808/540-1377, http://nicospier38.com, 10am-4pm and 5pm-9pm Mon.-Sat., 10am-4pm Sun., $13-17) is both a fish market and restaurant. They serve Hawaiian-style seafood with a French twist—gourmet food with plate lunch delivery. The open-air restaurant also has a full bar. From Nimitz Highway, access Pier 38 from Alakawa Avenue.

Sam Choy's Breakfast Lunch and Crab (580 N. Nimitz Hwy., #1, 808/545-7979, http://samchoyhawaii.com, 7am-9pm Mon.-Thurs., 7am-10pm Fri., 8am-10pm Sat., 8am-9pm Sun., $16-40) is a local favorite, serving up big portions of Hawaiian-style seafood with gourmet flair. They also have a local brewing company right next door for fresh, handcrafted beers to complement the seafood. Their Sunday brunch buffet, complete with carving and omelet stations, is also a big draw.

On the way out to Sand Island is one of the few real tiki bars still in operation. **La Mariana** (50 Sand Island Access Rd., 808/848-2800, www.lamarianasailingclub.com, 11am-9pm daily, $14-42) is a steak and seafood restaurant located in the La Mariana Sailing Club. Nestled at the edge of Ke'ehi Lagoon, the restaurant is a veritable museum of Hawaiiana treasures and collectibles, with an unmatched ambience from the warm glow of colorful lights, wood decor, and the grin of tikis all around.

Getting There and Around

AIR

All commercial flights to Oʻahu are routed to the **Honolulu International Airport** (300 Rodgers Blvd., 808/836-6411, http://hawaii. gov/hnl), as are most other flights with neighboring islands as their final destinations. The Honolulu International Airport has three terminals: the Overseas Terminal accommodates international and mainland flights, the Interisland Terminal handles Hawaiian Airlines flights, and the Commuter Terminal handles the small interisland carriers. There is a free intra-airport shuttle service for getting around the airport, and ground transportation is available just outside the baggage claim areas on the lower level, along the center median, where you can get a taxi, catch a shuttle to a rental car agency office, board TheBus, or pick up the other private shuttle buses that ferry visitors to Honolulu, Waikiki, and beyond. The airport is 10 miles from Waikiki and six miles from downtown Honolulu.

CAR

Urban community planning was not top of mind for state officials as Honolulu grew and expanded up and out. Two-way roads suddenly change to one way only, roads curve and bend with the geography, narrow neighborhood roads have street parking that blocks an entire lane, and it can be extremely frustrating to find a freeway on-ramp. Add to this confusion rush hour traffic and contra flow, and you're sitting in literally the worst traffic in the United States. Don't be too discouraged, though, because with proper planning and an up-to-date road map, the adventure of getting around Honolulu can be quite exciting.

The H-1 freeway runs east/west through Honolulu at the base of the Koʻolau Mountains.

Ala Moana Boulevard, which becomes Nimitz Highway, Route 92, parallels the H-1 along Honolulu Harbor. Beretania Street is a one-way, westbound thoroughfare that also parallels the H-1, and King Street, once you enter Chinatown, becomes an eastbound thoroughfare parallel to Beretania. Beretania and King Streets are a great way to get across town without using the freeway. From downtown, King Street forks after the Historic District. If you take the right fork, Kapiolani Boulevard, you'll go by Ala Moana Center and can turn right on Kalakaua Avenue to get into Waikiki. On the other side of the mall, Ala Moana Boulevard runs along the coast and will put you directly into Waikiki.

From the H-1 freeway westbound coming into downtown, take the Vineyard Boulevard exit and turn left at the first signal, Punchbowl Street. This will take you right into the Historic District. From the H-1 freeway eastbound, you can exit on Pali Highway and take a right, which will put you directly in downtown. Chinatown is a couple blocks to the west. You can also exit on Punchbowl Street, which puts you again in the Historic District.

Making the most of your time in Honolulu will mean working with the daily tide of traffic. Typical rush hour traffic is 5am-8am, when people flood into downtown from the east and west and the H-1 freeway slows to a crawl. Kapiolani Boulevard and Nimitz Highway are modified with an extra contra flow lane and there are turning restrictions. In the afternoon, rush hour starts up again for 3pm-6:30pm, contra flow lanes are added in the opposite direction for traffic to flow out of town, and the H-1 freeway again slows to a crawl. With limited freeway on-ramps, entire side streets will back up for blocks as cars jam onto the H-1.

Plan your meals during these periods, or activities where you'll be out of the car and off the road for an extended period of time.

Dealing with parking in Honolulu is another matter in itself. The historic district has metered street parking, which is free on Sundays and holidays, and downtown and Chinatown have ample structure parking. For the best rates, look for the Chinatown municipal parking lots. You can also park in the high-rises downtown, but the rates are much higher.

BUS

TheBus (808/848-4500, www.thebus.org) provides islandwide transportation, including transportation from the airport. If you're planning on riding the bus from the airport to your hotel, keep in mind that your bags have to be able to fit under the seat or on your lap without protruding into the aisle. There are several bus stops on the second level of the airport on the center median. Route Nos. 19, 20, and 31 access the airport, and Route No. 19 eastbound will take you to Waikiki.

There are nine transit centers on O'ahu. The major Honolulu transit centers are the Ala Moana Center Bus Stops, the Alapai Transit Center in downtown, and the Kalihi Transit Center. Fares are $2.50 for adults, $1.25 children ages 6-17, children 5 and under are free if they sit on an adult's lap. The Visitors Pass, a four consecutive day pass, is $25 with unlimited use. Call or visit their website for route information, maps, and timetables.

NORTH SHORE OF OʻAHU

Just 30 miles from Honolulu is the famed North Shore, the big city's polar opposite. Local surfers appropriately make the distinction and have coined the regions "town" and "country." With an average of 30 inches of rainfall annually, the North Shore is an escape to a natural haven and a simpler, almost hedonistic lifestyle. It's all about the beaches, diving, fishing, and, of course, surfing.

HIGHLIGHTS

LOOK FOR ◖ TO FIND RECOMMENDED SIGHTS, ACTIVITIES, DINING, AND LODGING.

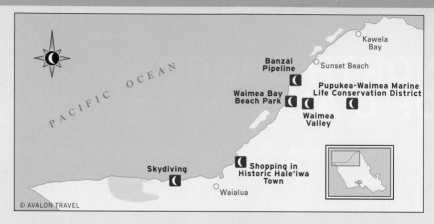

◖ **Waimea Bay Beach Park:** This expansive sandy shore yields to turquoise water that is home to reef fish, spinner dolphins, and green sea turtles (page 119).

◖ **Banzai Pipeline:** Watch expert surfers attempt to ride the barrel at one of the most dangerous breaks in the world (page 123).

◖ **Pupukea-Waimea Marine Life Conservation District:** Comprised of Waimea Bay, Three Tables, and Sharks Cove, this mile-long protected shoreline is the best area for snorkeling and shore diving on the North Shore (page 125).

◖ **Skydiving:** Skydiving operators in Mokule'ia offer a once-in-a-lifetime opportunity to tandem skydive on the North Shore, affording you a bird's-eye view of paradise (page 130).

◖ **Waimea Valley:** Both verdant garden and restored ancient cultural site, Waimea Valley is a bastion of beauty and education (page 132).

◖ **Shopping in Historic Hale'iwa Town:** The official gateway to the North Shore, quaint Hale'iwa is packed with boutiques, surf shops, and galleries (page 133).

From the northernmost tip of the island to Ka'ena Point to the west, the North Shore's coastline looks more like a backwards L, or even the open jaws of a shark, and captures the powerful open-ocean swells that track across the Pacific during the northern hemisphere's winter. That's the reason for the enormous, powerful surf that pounds the reefs from October through April. Save for the town of Hale'iwa, the gateway to the North Shore, and Turtle Bay Resort, this area has remained undeveloped, a mix between residential housing and farmland. Locals have taken great pride in their grassroots efforts to

establish a marine protected area along Waimea Bay, Three Tables, and Sharks Cove, and to preserve the bluff known as Pupukea-Paumalu that frames the quaint North Shore community.

Along the extreme northern stretch of the North Shore, you'll find world-class surf spots like Laniakea, Waimea Bay, the Banzai Pipeline, and Sunset Beach. Because of the quality and sheer number of surf breaks, this part of the North Shore is known as the "Seven Mile Miracle." Hale'iwa, sitting just off the Kamehameha Highway at the bottom of the pineapple fields, is where you'll find shopping,

OʻAHU

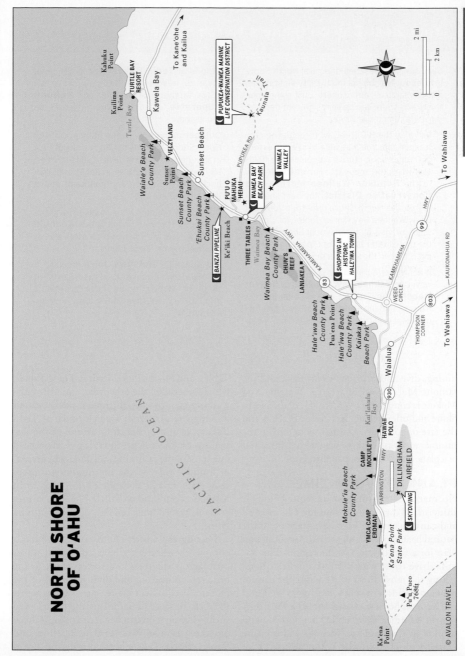

NORTH SHORE OF OʻAHU

Kaʻena Point

Puʻu Pueo 768ft

Kaʻena Point State Park

YMCA CAMP ERDMAN

Mokuleʻia Beach County Park

SKYDIVING

DILLINGHAM AIRFIELD

FARRINGTON HWY

CAMP MOKULEʻIA

HAWAII POLO

Kaiʻalahulu Bay

Waialua

930

803

THOMPSON CORNER

To Wahiawa

WEED CIRCLE

KAUKONAHUA RD

KAMEHAMEHA

99

To Wahiawa

KAMEHAMEHA HWY

SHOPPING IN HISTORIC HALEʻIWA TOWN

83

LANIAKEA

CHUN'S REEF

Haleʻiwa Beach County Park

Kaiaka Beach Park

Pua ena Point

Haleʻiwa Beach County Park

Waimea Bay Beach County Park

Waimea Bay

THREE TABLES

WAIMEA BAY BEACH PARK

WAIMEA VALLEY

PUPUKEA RD

PUʻU O MAHUKA HEIAU

PUPUKEA-WAIMEA MARINE LIFE CONSERVATION DISTRICT

Kaunala Trail

BANZAI PIPELINE

Keʻiki Beach

ʻEhukai Beach County Park

Sunset Beach County Park

Sunset Point

VELZYLAND

Waialeʻe Beach County Park

Sunset Beach

Kawela Bay

Turtle Bay

TURTLE BAY RESORT

Kuilima Point

Kahuku Point

To Kaneʻohe and Kailua

PACIFIC OCEAN

2 mi

2 km

© AVALON TRAVEL

Your Best Day on O'ahu's North Shore

Surf, sun, and beaches—the rural North Shore is all about leaving behind the city and tapping into the laidback atmosphere. Just remember, the North Shore can be very different depending if it's summer or winter.

• Drive up the H-2 freeway, through the central plateau. You'll be able to see the extent of O'ahu's agriculture base—pineapple fields as far as the eye can see. Head directly to the **Pupukea-Waimea Marine Life Conservation District,** the best snorkeling on the North Shore. Whether you post up at Waimea Bay, Three Tables, or Sharks Cove, or visit all three, you'll be amazed at the underwater beauty of the area. Snorkeling is best in the summertime.

• If it's winter during your stay, check out the waves at **Waimea Bay, Pipeline,** or **Sunset Beach.** They attract professional surfers from around the world. The action is spectacular, especially once the waves get really big.

• Stop in at **Ted's Bakery** for lunch, local style, or head out to Kahuku, just a few miles farther north, and visit **Kahuku Superette** for some of the best *poke* on the island.

• Outdoor activities are the hallmark of the North Shore. If you're daring, try **skydiving** in Mokule'ia. If staying on land suits you better, there are two outfitters that offer horseback rides in the verdant mountains above the North Shore beaches.

• During the summer, you can also spend the afternoon stand-up paddling the **'Anahulu River** in Hale'iwa Town or try a shore dive at Sharks Cove or Three Tables.

• For dinner, try **Hale'iwa Joe's** if you're in Hale'iwa town. If you're closer to the northern tip of the island, stop by Turtle Bay Resort and have a great meal at the local favorite, **Lei Lei's.**

dining, dive and surf rental outfitters, and the famous Matsumoto Shave Ice. Waialua and Mokule'ia comprise the western side of the North Shore and offer quieter, less visited beaches and the rare opportunity to watch polo during the summer months. To those who wish to jump out of a plane and skydive in paradise: Head this way.

PLANNING YOUR TIME

No matter if it's summer or winter, rain or shine, the North Shore shouldn't be missed and can't be rushed. Take advantage of all the natural beauty and ocean activities on offer and plan for a full-day trip to the region. The 33-mile drive from Waikiki to the North Shore, taking the most direct route across the central plateau, will last an hour if all goes well and traffic is light. If your stay on O'ahu is during the summer, drive up in the morning and snorkel in the Pupukea-Waimea Marine Life Conservation District at Waimea Bay, Three

Tables, and Sharks Cove. Park at Three Tables, which is between the other two, and utilize the walking trail to visit all three locales without moving the car. Grab a quick lunch at Ted's Bakery at Sunset Beach or at one of the numerous establishments in Hale'iwa, then head out to Mokule'ia for Hawaii Polo, skydiving, or a glider ride. If the mountains are more your style, take a trail ride on Pupukea or in Kahuku, then head to Turtle Bay for a sunset cocktail at the Hang Ten Bar, right on Kuilima Point.

During the winter the North Shore has a completely different vibe, as powerful waves push across the reefs and surfers flock to the beaches. Snorkeling and diving are out of the picture, as turbulent white water sweeps across the reefs, but watching the surf and the talented surfers taking it on can be mesmerizing. Check out the action at Waimea Bay, Pipeline, and Sunset Beach. Take a break during the day to

© KEVIN WHITTON

Welcome to Historic Haleʻiwa Town.

drive to Kahuku and visit Kahuku Superette for some fresh *poke* and rice, then head back to the beach to eat while wave-watching. Enjoy dinner in Haleʻiwa before setting out back to Honolulu.

For a longer, but more scenic trip to the North Shore from Waikiki, follow the Likelike Highway to Kaneʻohe and drive up the windward coast in the morning. The roughly 45-mile drive will take about an hour and a half as the sun rises over the east side. The mellow, gently meandering drive will put you in the right mood for a relaxing day on the North Shore.

If you want a rural, coastal setting far removed from the city, then a vacation rental along the North Shore Beaches or a room at Turtle Bay Resort are great options. Just be aware that it will take more time and planning for sightseeing and activities in most other island regions.

ORIENTATION
Haleʻiwa
As you descend from the pineapple and

coffee fields, the first town you'll come to is Historic Haleʻiwa Town, the official gateway to the North Shore. On either side of town, Kamehameha Highway makes a detour through Haleʻiwa. If you want to pass around Haleʻiwa and continue up the coast, stay on the Joseph P. Leong Highway bypass.

Haleʻiwa is full of places to eat, markets, and clothing, souvenir, and surf shops, as well as art galleries. Sportfishing, shark tour, and scuba operators are congregated in Haleʻiwa Harbor, which has lovely beaches on both sides, though they are better for surfing and stand-up paddling rather than swimming or snorkeling. The ʻAnahulu River empties out by the harbor and beaches, offering potential for stand-up paddling upriver.

Just to the west of Haleʻiwa, between the Waiʻanae Mountains and the coast as you head toward Kaʻena Point, are **Waialua** and **Mokuleʻia**. Both are sleepy rural agricultural communities. Farrington Highway rejoins the coast through Mokuleʻia, where if it's not too windy, the beaches are nice, the water is crystal

O'AHU

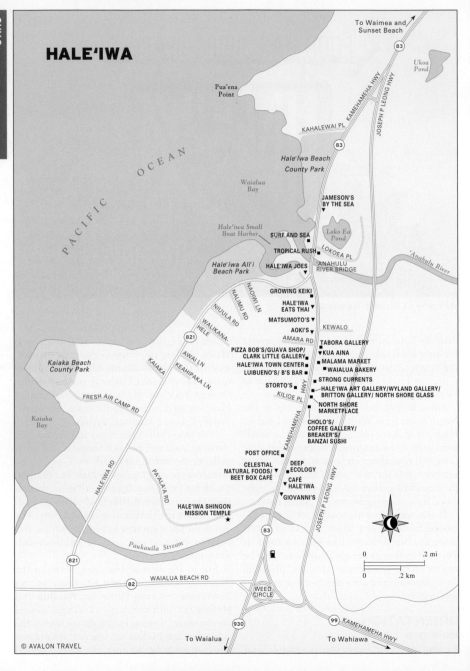

HALE'IWA

To Waimea and
Sunset Beach

83

Ukoa
Pond

Pua'ena
Point

KAMEHAMEHA HWY

JOSEPH P LEONG HWY

KAHALEWAI PL

83

*Hale'iwa Beach
County Park*

*Waialua
Bay*

JAMESON'S
BY THE SEA
▼

Loko Ea
Pond

'Anahulu River

*Hale'iwa Small
Boat Harbor*

SURF AND SEA ■

TROPICAL RUSH ■

LOKOEA PL

HALE'IWA JOES ■

'ANAHULU
RIVER BRIDGE

*Hale'iwa Ali'i
Beach Park*

GROWING KEIKI ■

HALE'IWA
EATS THAI ▼

MATSUMOTO'S ▼

KEWALO

NAOIWI LN

NALIMU RD

NIUULA RD

WALIKANA

HELE

AOKI'S ▼

AMARA RD

TABORA GALLERY

821

▼KUA AINA

AWAI LN

PIZZA BOB'S/GUAVA SHOP/
CLARK LITTLE GALLERY

■ MALAMA MARKET
■ WAIALUA BAKERY

*Kaiaka Beach
County Park*

KAIAKA

KEAHIPAKA LN

HALE'IWA TOWN CENTER ■
LUIBUENO'S/ B'S BAR ■

■ STRONG CURRENTS

STORTO'S ■

HALE'IWA ART GALLERY/WYLAND GALLERY/
BRITTON GALLERY/ NORTH SHORE GLASS

FRESH AIR CAMP RD

KILIOE PL

NORTH SHORE
MARKETPLACE

*Kaiaka
Bay*

KAMEHAMEHA HWY

CHOLO'S/
COFFEE GALLERY/
BREAKER'S/
BANZAI SUSHI

HALEIWA RD

PA'ALA'A RD

POST OFFICE ■

CELESTIAL
NATURAL FOODS/ ▼
BEET BOX CAFÉ

DEEP
ECOLOGY

CAFÉ
▼ HALE'IWA

JOSEPH P LEONG HWY

▼ GIOVANNI'S

HALE'IWA SHINGON
MISSION TEMPLE ★

Paukauila Stream

83

821

0   .2 mi

0   .2 km

82

WAIALUA BEACH RD

WEED
CIRCLE

930

99 KAMEHAMEHA HWY

To Waialua

To Wahiawa

clear, and solitude surrounds you. Mokule'ia offers polo matches on Sunday afternoons in the summer, skydiving throughout the year, and a seaside hike in a natural reserve at the end of the road to the western tip of the island.

North Shore Beaches

The North Shore Beaches comprise an immaculate stretch of coastline along Kamehameha Highway from **Laniakea,** just past Hale'iwa town, to the legendary **Sunset Beach** to the north. Spinner dolphins frolic in Waimea Bay, sea turtles feed off the shoreline rocks, and reef fish abound along the **Pupukea-Waimea Marine Life Conservation District,** which includes Three Tables and Sharks Cove just north of Waimea Bay, some of the best snorkeling and scuba diving on the island. In the summer, the calm water along this stretch of coast is perfect for swimming and snorkeling, but in the winter, powerful surf draws expert surfers from around the world in search of giant waves at Waimea Bay and Sunset Beach and the awe-inspiring barrels of the Banzai Pipeline. While the most popular beaches might be busy with tourists hopping off buses all year long, a short walk up or down the beach will easily remove you from the melee and most of your cares or worries. For meals you'll mostly find food trucks along the highway, and for accommodations, vacation rentals are the only way to go, save for the only hostel in the region at Three Tables. Sunsets are remarkable from this stretch of coast.

Turtle Bay

Turtle Bay is the area along Kamehameha Highway from **Kawela Bay** to **Kahuku,** the old sugar town. This region sits at the northern tip of the island and is prone to wind and rain throughout the year. The Turtle Bay Resort on **Kuilima Point** dominates the area, with surf and golf being the main attractions, along with the bars and restaurants that many residents and visitors along the North Shore Beaches make the short drive to indulge in.

Just to the east of Turtle Bay is Kahuku, with a nine-hole golf course of its own. Locals prefer the affordable fees and relaxed atmosphere at the Kahuku course to the resort's professional course. Kahuku is also home to a little market with some of the best *poke* on O'ahu. There is a working ranch here offering horseback trail rides for all levels of riders.

Beaches

The North Shore beaches are some of the finest on the island. With the natural backdrops of the Pupukea-Paumalu escarpment along the northern portion of the coast and the Wai'anae Range behind Hale'iwa stretching to Ka'ena Point, natural beauty catches your eye in every direction. Ample vegetation separates the sand from the beachfront property, and the coast is broken up by interesting rock and reef rock formations and sandy bays.

The North Shore also has two distinct personalities: benign and tranquil during the summer (May-September) and powerful and fierce in the winter (October-April). This duality is caused by powerful storms in the North Pacific that send swells thousands of miles across open ocean, straight to the Hawaiian Islands. The North Shore reefs absorb this energy as giant waves that pound the coast, breaking up to 50 feet from crest to trough. During high surf events in the winter, the water is closed to swimming, and lifeguards monitor the spectators on the beach, as well as the surfers in the water, to make sure everyone is safe. During the biggest swell events, the beaches are closed as well.

On the other hand, summer provides perfect conditions for swimming, snorkeling, and diving. The ocean remains generally calm and flat, and the beaches are at their widest. Sunsets are also better during this time as the sun tracks farther west on the horizon.

O'AHU

HALE'IWA
Ali'i Beach Park

Just to the west of the Hale'iwa Small Boat Harbor is **Ali'i Beach Park,** where the small beach is framed by rocks. It's a great place for the kids to jump around in the small shorebreak. Ali'i Beach Park also has a community center, restrooms, and a large, shaded grassy park with palm trees, picnic tables, and shrubs along the vegetation line that offer shade. If there are waves breaking along the outer reef, there is a strong and dangerous rip current that sweeps across the beach. From Kamehameha Highway, turn onto Haleiwa Road, and the beach park is past the entrance to the boat harbor. There is ample parking.

Hale'iwa Beach Park

On the other side of the harbor entrance and the 'Anahulu River, across the famous Rainbow Bridge, is **Hale'iwa Beach Park.** The water is a bit murky and the sand somewhat silty from the rivermouth, but the calm waters are a favorite for kayakers and stand-up paddlers. You can paddle in the ocean or forge up the 'Anahulu River. Park on the side of the road or in the designated parking area. To the north of the parking lot is a big grassy area and restrooms. The beach park is beside Kamehameha Highway. The parking lot and restrooms are closed 10pm-6am daily.

Pua'ena Point Beach Park

Pua'ena Point Beach Park has lots of shade and is a great place to explore in and out of the water. From Kamehameha Highway, turn onto Kahalewai Place and drive to the parking lot at the end. From there walk through the ironwood trees to the small cove. Snorkel the inner waters with their a mix of sand and reef bottom, or walk up the beach to the rocky outcropping of Pua'ena Point.

Mokule'ia Beach Park

Situated on the western flank of the North Shore, **Mokule'ia Beach Park** is a quiet, un-crowded beach across from the Dillingham Airfield. The sand is narrow, but stretches out in both directions with interesting nooks and crannies along the coast. There are shrubs along the beach and some trees for shade to the east. Mokule'ia Beach Park is great for a long walk on the beach or relaxing in the sun. It's in the path of the trade winds, so it can get blustery. If you plan on swimming or snorkeling, the conditions are best with light winds. There are showers and portable toilets at the beach park along Farrington Highway, close to the end of the road. The parking lot is closed 7pm-7am daily.

NORTH SHORE BEACHES
Laniakea

Famous for the turtles that rest in the sand and feed off of the rocky shelf at the water's edge, **Laniakea** is a beautiful stretch of beach once you get away from the hordes of people that jam onto the small pocket of sand where the majority of the turtles rest. Park in the dirt parking lot on the mountain side of Kamehameha Highway just north of a ranch with horses. Cross the road with extreme caution. Tour buses of all sizes stop here and direct people to the northern corner of the beach. The turtles, however, feed along the rocks that run the length of the beach, so walk to the south to escape the melee. Where the beachfront

Hawaii Polo

Enjoy the camaraderie and festive atmosphere of a polo match by the sea in beautiful Mokule'ia. **Hawaii Polo matches** (http://hawaii-polo.org, 2pm Sun. Apr.-Sept., $10 adults, children 12 and under free) are held on Sundays April through September. Game day feels like a giant tailgate party, as people pull their vehicles right up to the field and open blankets under the ironwood trees. Bring a cooler full of food and beverages and enjoy a few chuckers. It makes for a perfect summer afternoon. Gates open at noon.

Waimea Bay doesn't start breaking until the waves reach at least 20 feet.

properties begin at the southern end of the beach, the sand widens and there are beautiful views of the Wai'anae Mountains and the western side of the North Shore. If you plan on swimming or snorkeling, this is also the best place to enter and exit the water. The farther south you walk along the beach, the better the chance of finding seclusion.

Chun's Reef

A beautiful spot for a beach day, **Chun's Reef** is the next beach north of Laniakea, but without the tour buses and crowds. The wide sandy beach has tidepools in the southern corner up against the rocky point, and the water right off the beach is a bit deeper here and more suitable for swimming and snorkeling. The beach gets wider to north end of Chun's and is lined with tall ironwood trees, providing ample shade. Little waves break over the reef quite a distance offshore almost all year long, so it's a great place for beginners to surf in the summer. It's also a favorite area for stand-up paddle surfers. Park in the dirt on the mountain side of the road across from the beach. There are lifeguards, but no facilities at Chun's.

(Waimea Bay Beach Park

At the mouth of the Waimea River and Waimea Valley is the scenic **Waimea Bay Beach Park.** The tight bay is lined with beautiful white sand, and the water is crystal clear, perfect for swimming and snorkeling. There are rocky points on both sides of the bay, while the center is all sand, producing light blue water. Stand-up paddle across the bay, relax on the beach, or jump off the famous Jump Rock, a 20-foot-tall rock spire right off the beach. Spinner dolphins and green sea turtles are frequent visitors. Park in the designated parking area, but if it's full, there is paid parking in Waimea Valley, which is about a ten-minute walk to the beach. Use the white pedestrian bridge to cross the river and access the beach park, which has restrooms, showers, picnic areas, and a grassy park. The beach park is closed 10pm-5am daily.

Three Tables

Once you round Waimea Bay, the first beach you come to heading north is **Three Tables,** named after three flat reef platforms that rise above the ocean surface just off the beach. This is part of the Pupukea-Waimea Marine Life Conservation District, a protected area where fishing is illegal. The resulting copious amounts of reef fish in the water mean the main draw here is snorkeling. Three Tables has a quaint beach with shallow water stretching between rock outcroppings. Perfect for families, there are shade trees on the beach and picnic tables up by the bike path. There are a few parking spaces in front of the beach on the side of Kamehameha Highway, or you can park in the parking lot just to the north of Three Tables. Turn into the lot at the Pupukea Road traffic signal. There are restrooms here as well, though they are notoriously dingy.

Ke'iki Beach

On the north side of the prominent reef rock point that frames Sharks Cove, **Ke'iki Beach** is the place to go for solitude. The beach stretches out to the north, and even though the name might change every quarter mile,

it's still one beautiful ribbon of sand with aquamarine water pushing up against it. The water gets deep rather quickly here, so it's also great for swimming and snorkeling. From the highway, turn onto Keiki Road and look for parking. There is also intermittent parking along Kamehameha Highway on the ocean side. Follow one of the designated public access paths to the beach. There are no facilities and no shade here.

'Ehukai Beach Park

Across from Sunset Elementary School is a small parking lot for **'Ehukai Beach Park.** Walk through the small park toward the lifeguard tower and onto the sand. To the immediate left is the world-famous **Banzai Pipeline** surf break. If it's summer, the water is beautiful and clear, but there will be no waves. To the right is 'Ehukai Beach, which stretches north up to Rocky Point. Swimming is great up and down the beach, which is lined with palms and shrubs offering midday shade. During the summer, the snorkeling is better on the Pipeline side of the park where there is a wide shelf of reef, canyons, and caves to explore. 'Ehukai Beach Park has restrooms and showers, and there are additional public restrooms across the street in front of the school. The beach park is closed 10pm-5am daily.

Sunset Beach

To the north of Sunset Elementary School, homes line the ocean side of Kamehameha Highway, and the beach is hidden from view. But once you pass a gas station, **Sunset Beach** is all you see: a wide swath of sand from the highway to the water's edge. Sunset is famous for its big winter waves, but its natural beauty is splendid, waves or not. In the summer, it's perfect for swimming and snorkeling, or you can stand-up paddle up and down the coast from here for a good look at the shore. Take a walk up the point to the north for a great view back toward Hale'iwa. There is parking on the ocean side of the highway, along the bike

Jump In!

In the mid-1900s, sand mining at Waimea Bay unearthed a large rock in the sand. Today that rock is at the water's edge and stands about 20 feet high. People flock to the rock, aptly named **Jump Rock,** to take the plunge into the turquoise water below. The ascent is gradual, starting from the sand to Jump Rock's highest point. Most people jump off the east side. North Shore surfers actually practice a balled-up type of belly flop to better prepare themselves for any unfortunate wipeouts during the upcoming winter's extra-large surf. If the main jumping point is a bit too high for your liking, the very end of the rock, farthest out into the bay, is only about six feet high.

© KEVIN WHITTON

'Ehukai Beach

path. If you luck into one of these spots, it's pleasant enough to relax, have a snack or some coffee, and watch the ocean sparkle. During the winter, it's also a great vantage point for whale-watching. There is another parking lot on the mountain side of the highway where you'll find restrooms and showers.

TURTLE BAY
Kawela Bay

One of the most protected and secluded bays on the North Shore, **Kawela Bay** shelters a small strip of sand and a calm lagoon protected by an outer reef between Sunset Beach and Turtle Bay. It's great for snorkeling, swimming, and getting away from it all. Park on the side of the highway across from the fruit stand and walk through the trees to the beach.

Kuilima Point

Kuilima Point, today known as **Turtle Bay,** is the site of the Turtle Bay Resort, a dramatic coastline, and a sandy beach. To the west of the resort and rugged Kuilima Point is a sand and rock beach that stretches to the eastern point of Kawela Bay. Walk the beach at low tide when there is more sand or snorkel over rock and reef. On the immediate east side of the point and the main resort is a small protected cove great for families and for swimming, but you'll have to share it with the other hotel guests. Farther east of the small bay is a beach seldom visited even though it sits right next to the resort. Walk along the sand or relax under some trees. The reef is shallow right up to the shore, so this is not the best spot for swimming. Visit the beach when the winds are light, as the trade winds blow straight on shore and get quite blustery. Turtle Bay is a great stop if you're looking for a little beach time followed by lunch or dinner.

To get to Kuilima Point from the Kamehameha Highway, turn onto Kuilima Road and follow it to the main resort parking lot. There is beach access on both sides of the main resort tower.

Surfing

The North Shore is synonymous with surfing. Dubbed the "Seven Mile Miracle," this area has more high-quality surf breaks packed into the scenic coastline from Hale'iwa to Turtle Bay than in any other place in the world. The powerful waves draw surfers from around the world, and for over three decades professional surfing's elite world tour has wrapped up the title season at the infamous Banzai Pipeline.

The waves on the North Shore are also some of the most dangerous, and deadliest, in the world. With huge breaks, strong currents, and shallow reefs, even top athletes are not immune to severe injury or death. Because of these and other factors, only expert surfers should paddle out. There are lifeguards posted at most North Shore beaches; check with them for ocean conditions and safety. If you're having doubts about the waves and your ability, it's best to have a seat on the beach, enjoy the spectacle, and live to surf another day on a different wave.

HALE'IWA
Hale'iwa Break
Located in Hale'iwa town to the west of the harbor, **Hale'iwa** breaks off Ali'i Beach. A peak when it's small, the wave becomes exponentially more dangerous the larger it gets, breaking as a predominant right. The fast waves closeout over a very shallow inside reef ledge known as the Toilet Bowl. A strong rip current is a staple at Hale'iwa. Paddle out from the west side of the beach, to the left of the Toilet Bowl section.

Pua'ena Point
Pua'ena Point is one of smaller and softer waves on the North Shore, just to the north of the 'Anahulu River. It has both right and left breaking waves and is friendly for longboarders when it's small. The waves can still get big at Pua'ena, but it doesn't happen that often. Paddle straight out from the beach. The parking lot can be a bit suspect, so don't leave any valuables in plain sight.

NORTH SHORE BEACHES
Laniakea
Best on north swells, **Laniakea** is a right point break that breaks over flat reef and sand. Depending on the direction of the swell, the wave is one of the longest on the North Shore. Expert surfers tend to sit up at the point, while novice surfers and longboards prefer the inside section off the south end of the beach. Paddle out from the south end of the beach. Laniakea is to the immediate north of a ranch, and there is a long dirt parking lot on the mountain side of Kamehameha Highway.

Chun's Reef
Just north of Laniakea, the next beach and surf spot you can see from the highway is **Chun's Reef.** Chun's is a soft breaking right point, but also has a fast breaking left at the top of the sandy point that most often closes out. Chun's is a favorite wave for beginners, longboarders, and kids. It's one of the most user-friendly waves on the North Shore. Keep in mind that even though the wave itself is good for learning, the shallow bottom is still dangerous, since it's covered by a sharp, flat reef. Chun's is one

---

Surfing the Seven Mile Miracle

In the surf world, the stretch of coastline from Hale'iwa to Kuilima Point is known as the **Seven Mile Miracle.** Unlike anywhere else on planet, the North Shore has just the right combination of geography, geology, wind, weather, and swell to make it one of the most sought after surfing destinations in the world. The quality, consistency, size, and sheer number of surf breaks along the seven-mile stretch are unmatched. This is truly a surfer's paradise.

of the few breaks on the North Shore that also has very small waves in the summer.

Leftovers

At the next small break in homes along the highway where you can see the water you'll find a wave called **Leftovers.** The wave is a left that breaks into deep water, so there is a defined channel where you can paddle out. A right also breaks off the peak on the very outside. The inside section covers an extremely shallow and sharp reef. Getting in and out of the water can also be an obstacle, as the beach is covered with rocks and large boulders that stretch out into the water.

Waimea Bay

A big wave spot that only starts to break when the waves are 15 to 20 feet on the face, **Waimea Bay** is the only chance for many to see waves of this size, a feat of nature that should not be missed if the bay is breaking. The shorebreak is also something to see, as huge waves barrel and detonate in spectacular fashion in inches

of water. Parking at Waimea fills up quickly when the waves are big. There is limited additional parking along the highway on the west side of the bay heading west, or you can pay to park at Waimea Valley, just past the turn off to Waimea Bay. You could also park by Three Tables and Sharks Cove and walk back along the highway. Many spectators watch and snap photos from the railing above the rocks on the east side of the bay.

◖ Banzai Pipeline

The **Banzai Pipeline** is one of the most dangerous waves in the world. Guarded closely by a territorial crew of local surfers, Pipeline is one of those waves where visiting surfers will find it more to their advantage to sit on the beach and watch its grandeur rather than test their mettle. Breaking just 75 yards off the beach, Pipeline is a spectator's delight. Massive round and hollow lefts explode over a shallow reef, and brave surfers try to place themselves as deep as possible inside the barrel, hoping to emerge out the end on their feet. On the sand,

© MICHELLE WHITTON

A crowd of spectators witnesses the Banzai Pipeline.

The Eddie

Waimea Bay is home to the iconic **Quiksilver In Memory of Eddie Aikau,** an annual one-day event that honors the late North Shore waterman Eddie Aikau and the surfers who dedicate their lives to riding giant waves. Eddie was the first official lifeguard at Waimea Bay and a revered big wave surfer. In 1978, Eddie was selected to help crew a Polynesian voyaging canoe, a cultural expedition bound for Tahiti. When the canoe encountered treacherous seas outside the Hawaiian Islands and capsized, Eddie struck out fearlessly on a paddleboard back to Hawaii to save his stranded crew. He was never seen again.

Since 1985, The Eddie is staged every year to test the strongest and best big wave surfers in the spirit of Eddie's courageous selflessness. The invitational has some impressive criteria: the waves must be at least 20-feet for the entire day of competition. Because of this minimum wave height requirement, The Eddie has only run eight times in 27 years. The waiting period is from December through February and as the saying goes on the North Shore, "The Bay calls the day."

you can feel the waves break on the beach and sense the tension and emotion in the water. Park in the 'Ehukai Beach Park parking lot or along the highway. Pay attention to the sporadic No Parking signs.

'Ehukai

Also accessible from 'Ehukai Beach Park is the North Shore's only beach break, **'Ehukai**. Depending on the sand and the swells, the waves can break right or left and range from phenomenal shape to junky and lumpy surf.

Sunset Beach

Sunset Beach offers one of the most powerful and dangerous waves in the world, breaking from Sunset Point all the way into the bay. Strong currents and closeout sets are the hallmark of Sunset, along with a dredging inside section called **The West Bowl**, which breaks closest to the beach. A wave for experts only, when the water is gigantic, you'll find surfers attempting to ride the mountainous fluid walls. Bring binoculars to catch all the action way out to sea.

TURTLE BAY
Kuilima Point

Kuilima Point, known locally as **Turtle Bay,** is a funky, soft wave that breaks along a sharp reef outcropping into deep water. Since the break is just off Kuilima Point, where the Turtle Bay Resort is situated, you can literally watch the surfers from Turtle Bay's pool bar. The inside has soft rolling white water that is perfect for beginners. You can also rent longboards at the resort. The beach and water are open to the public. Paddle out from the rocky shore in front of the bungalows.

VANS TRIPLE CROWN OF SURFING

For six weeks every winter, from early November through late December, the **Vans Triple Crown of Surfing** (www.triplecrownofsurfing.com, Nov.-Dec.) takes over the North Shore. This professional surfing event is comprised of three contests, the first at Ali'i Beach Park in Hale'iwa, the second at Sunset Beach, and the final one at the Banzai Pipeline. An international field of hundreds of competitors, as well as a cadre of hungry locals, battle it out on the biggest and best days of surf during the holding period for each event. Spectators flock to the beach to watch the action, some of the best surfing in the world. There are food vendors, restrooms, drinking water, souvenirs, and giveaways at each event. With limited parking and an influx of people on the North Shore, expect driving delays and plan to either pay for parking or park and walk quite a distance, especially during the Pipeline event.

OUTFITTERS

Hale'iwa town is full of surf shops that sell apparel, boards, and surf accessories. **Hawaiian Island Creations** (66-224 Kamehameha Hwy., 808/637-0991, www.hicsurf.com, 10am-6pm Mon.-Sat., 9:30am-5pm Sun.) and **Wave Riding Vehicles** (66-451 Kamehameha Hwy., 808/637-2020, www.waveridingvehicles.com, 9am-7pm daily) are two local surf brands with retail shops, and **Xcel** (66-590 Kamehameha Hwy., 808/637-6239, www.xcelwetsuits.com, 9am-5pm daily) is a local wetsuit company where you can find all manner of wetsuits to stay warm and protect yourself from the sun. **Surf N Sea** (62-595 Kamehameha Hwy., 808/637-9887, http://surfnsea.com, 9am-7pm daily) not only has apparel and new and used boards for sale, but they also rent shortboards and longboards by the hour, day, and week. Shortboards are $5 the first hour, $3.50 each additional hour, $24 daily, and $120 weekly; longboards are $7 the first hour, $6 each additional hour, $30 daily, and $150 weekly. Right across the street is **Tropical Rush** (62-620 Kamehameha Hwy., 808/637-8886, 9am-7pm daily). They sell apparel, new surfboards, and gear, and rent boards by the hour, day, and week.

Hawaii Eco Divers (61-101 Iliohu Pl., 808/499-9177, www.hawaiiecodivers.com, 7:30am-9pm daily) offers surf tours for experienced surfers and lessons for beginners. The surf tours include personalized surf coaching and a video of the session, $150 for a morning session or $250 all day for a group of up to three surfers. Surfboards are not included. Their surf lessons run $100 for a three- to four-hour session focusing on catching and riding waves. The lesson rate includes boards and transportation. **Sunset Suratt Surf Academy** (808/783-8657, http://surfnorthshore.com) gives beginner surfing and stand-up paddling lessons. With an arsenal of boards and vans, they drive to where the surf is best suited for learning. Book online.

Located across from Sharks Cove, **North Shore Surf Shop** (59-053 Kamehameha Hwy., 808/638-0390, 10am-7:30pm daily) has a huge selection of shortboards, new and used, and carries a lot of the professional surfers' used boards. They rent shortboards for $25 daily, $60 for three days, $125 weekly, and $300 for a month; longboards are $30 daily, $75 for three days, $140 weekly, and $300 for a month. They also have a retail location in the town of Hale'iwa.

At Turtle Bay Resort you can rent boards at **Hans Hedemann Surf** (57-091 Kamehameha Hwy., 808/447-6755 or 808/293-7779, www.hhsurf.com, 8am-5pm daily). They rent shortboards and longboards for $15 per hour, $40 for four hours, $50 all day, $60 overnight, $35 each additional day, and $250 per week. Two-hour private lessons go for $150, semi-private lessons are $125, and group lessons, for up to four surfers, are $75. All equipment is included.

Snorkeling and Diving

NORTH SHORE BEACHES

During the summer, from May to September, when the ocean is flat, the North Shore Beaches are an amazing place to snorkel. With a mix of rocks, reef, sand, calm waters, and favorable winds, just about anywhere you jump in the water will have some interesting underwater topography, coral, and marine life.

◖ Pupukea-Waimea Marine Life Conservation District

The most abundant marine life is found at **Three Tables, Sharks Cove,** and **Waimea Bay,** which comprise the **Pupukea-Waimea Marine Life Conservation District.** Established in 1983 to conserve and replenish marine species at Three Tables and Sharks Cove, the reserve

Snorkel vs. Surf

While Hawaii's slight seasonal changes in temperature and precipitation might not be apparent to visitors who only stay a week or two at a time, there is one natural phenomenon that strikingly differentiates summer and winter on the North Shore—waves! During Hawaii's winter, October-April, and sometimes into spring, storms in the North Pacific create very large, open ocean swells that track toward the equator, passing by the state and expending the wave energy on the reefs and beaches. This is great news for surfers, who follow these swells closely and live to surf the powerful waves, which can break up to 60 feet on the face during the biggest surges on the outermost reefs. For snorkelers and divers, high surf is a worst-case scenario.

Once summer rolls around, the tables turn. From May to September, the North Shore becomes a tranquil swimmer's paradise. The waves usually remain flat the entire period, the sand settles, and the water becomes crystal clear. Snorkelers and divers revel in the conditions, and the focus on the North Shore shifts from the waves above the surface to the exploration of its underwater world.

was expanded in 2003 to include Waimea Bay, covering 100 acres of coastline about a mile long. Fishing or the taking of any marine species is strictly prohibited in the area. Look for wrasse, surgeonfish, reef squid, puffer fish, the spotted eagle ray, palani, unicorn fish, harlequin shrimp, and frogfish, just some of the creatures that inhabit the area. Waimea Bay is also known for pods of spinner dolphins that frolic in the middle of the bay.

There are boat dives and shore dives available on the North Shore. The shore dives explore Three Tables and Sharks Cove, where there are flourishing reefs teeming with endemic fish and lava tubes, caverns, and walls to explore. The boat dives provide access to the extraordinary underwater topography and pristine offshore reefs of the North Shore Beaches: Atlantis is an area full of trenches, valleys, walls, and lava tubes, and Cathedrals has rock formations, reefs, and caverns where turtles, eels, and whitetip reef sharks are common; Grand Canyon is a drift dive along the North Shore Beaches where you'll find sponges hanging from the ledges and trevallies and rays in the deep water; two reef sites, Nanny's Reef and Nautilus Reef, are 40-foot dives with a plethora of marine life. Diving the North Shore during the winter is contingent on the size of the surf.

OUTFITTERS

Surf N Sea (62-595 Kamehameha Hwy., 808/637-9887, http://surfnsea.com, 9am-7pm daily) in Haleʻiwa is the North Shore's most complete surf and dive shop. They sell new gear, rent beach and ocean-related gear and accessories, and even lead shore and boat dives. They rent dive equipment by the piece at a daily or weekly rate. For snorkel gear, they rent by the piece or in a set, the latter runs $6.50 for four hours, $9.50 daily, and $45 weekly. Their guided dives are operated by **Hawaii Scuba Diving,** which offers shore and boat dives as well as certification courses. Their morning dives are for certified divers, while the afternoon charters to shallow reef sites are open to any level diver. One-tank shore dives are $75 for certified divers and $95 for noncertified; two-tank shore dives are $100 certified, $125 noncertified; one-tank night dives are $100; two-tank boat dives are $140. PADI diving certification courses are $375 for Open Water Diver, $295 for Advanced Open Water Diver, and $650 for Divemaster.

Deep Ecology (66-456 Kamehameha Hwy., 808/637-7946 or 800/578-3992, www.oahuscubadive.com, 8am-6pm Mon.-Sat., 8am-5pm Sun.) also has a retail dive center in Haleʻiwa town. Their shop also has clothing and ocean art for sale, and they sell dive and snorkel equipment. They rent snorkel sets for $12 daily and $60 weekly, with 2 days free rental. They also rent complete two-tank scuba sets for $60 daily and $300 weekly with two days free rental. Boat dives and night boat dives are $145, shore dives are $109, night shore dives are $95, intro dives are $109, and boat intro dives are $159. Gear is included in the price, and they will give discounts if you have your own equipment. Deep Ecology also has a broad range of PADI certification courses.

Hawaii Eco Divers (61-101 Iliohu Pl., 808/499-9177, www.hawaiiecodivers.com, 7:30am-9pm daily), operating from Hale'iwa Harbor, specializes in personalized small group shore dives. Two-tank shore dives or one-tank night dives for certified divers are $89, and one-tank shore dives for noncertified divers are $99. All gear is included in the rate along with snacks, refreshments, and photos of the dives. They will also shoot a video of your dive for $75.

If you get to Sharks Cove and discover you really want to snorkel but don't have any gear, then you're in luck: Right across the street is **North Shore Surf Shop** (59-053 Kamehameha Hwy., 808/638-0390, 10am-7:30pm daily). They rent complete snorkel sets for $15 daily and $30 for three days. They also have rash guards for rent for $5, which are great for sun protection while you're snorkeling.

Other Water Sports

STAND-UP PADDLING AND FISHING

Hale'iwa is the hub of stand-up paddling and kayaking on the North Shore, largely because of the **'Anahulu River** and the protected and calm waters off **Hale'iwa Beach Park.** You can access the shoreline in the small parking lot next to Surf N Sea or along Hale'iwa Beach Park. From there, you can paddle around the shallow rivermouth, north to Pua'ena Point and beyond, or head upriver for a smooth and mellow ride.

On the North Shore, stand-up paddling is popular at **Waimea Bay, Laniakea,** and **Chun's Reef.** The conditions are best in the summer when the ocean surface is flat. Chun's and Laniakea often have very small waves in the summer, so you can even try surfing the stand-up board.

In Hale'iwa, **Surf N Sea** (62-595 Kamehameha Hwy., 808/637-9887, http://surfnsea.com, 9am-7pm daily) rents single kayaks for $7 the first hour, $5 for each additional hour, $20 for a half day, and $75 for a full day. Their weekly rate is $300. Stand-up paddle boards rent for $10 for the first hour, $8 for each additional hour, and $40 for a full day.

The weekly rate is $200. They also rent water bikes and pedal boats and have the distinction of being situated on the bank of the river mouth for easy ocean access.

Hawaii Eco Divers (61-101 Iliohu Pl., 808/499-9177, www.hawaiiecodivers.com, 7:30am-9pm daily) offers a two-hour Hale'iwa Beach and River Tour all year long for $79. In the summer they also have a three-hour Waimea Bay Tour for $109 and a four-mile drift Sunset Beach to Waimea Bay Tour for $125. Snorkeling gear is included for both summer tours.

At the Turtle Bay Resort, **Hans Heddeman Surf** (57-091 Kamehameha Hwy., 808/447-6755 or 808/293-7779, www.hhsurf.com, 8am-5pm daily) rents stand-up paddle boards for $25 per hour, $50 for three hours, $80 all day, $100 overnight, $50 each additional day, and $400 per week. Two-hour private lessons go for $150, semiprivate lessons are $125, and group lessons, up to four surfers, is $75. All equipment is included.

FISHING

During the summer, spearfishing is common along the North Shore, where reef fish and

O'AHU

© KEVIN WHITTON

paddling the 'Anahulu River in Hale'iwa

octopus are the desired take. The conditions are prime during this season with the calm, flat ocean surface. Shoreline fishing is also common from Mokule'ia out to Ka'ena Point and along the beach south of Laniakea. Remember that the area from the west side of Waimea Bay to the north side of Sharks Cove is a marine protected area and fishing or taking any marine species is strictly prohibited. Fishing gear is available in Hale'iwa at **Haleiwa Fishing Supply** (66-519 Kamehameha Hwy., 808/637-9876, 10am-8pm daily).

The North Shore is very favorable for sportfishing with deep water offshore and strong currents from the northwest that continually bring in bait and game fish. Several deepsea sportfishing operators are located in the Hale'iwa Small Boat Harbor if you're interested in fishing for big game fish like wahoo, mahimahi, tuna, and marlin.

Chupu Charters (66-105 Haleiwa Rd., Slip 312, 808/637-3474, www.chupu.com) operates a 53-foot Hatteras with amenities like air-conditioning, a custom Pompanetter fighting chair, and top-of-the-line rods and reels. Bait,

tackle, ice, and fish packaging supplies are provided. They offer full-day shared charters for $250, full-day private charters for $850, morning half-day private charters $700, afternoon half-day private charters $750. Private charters have a maximum of six passengers.

Sport Fishing Hawaii (808/721-8581 or 808/450-7601, www.sport-fishing-hawaii.com) operates a 47-foot Hatteras and charges for $650 for half-day charters and $825 for the full-day, 10-hour charter. They have a six-passenger limit.

Kuuloa Kai (66-195 Kaamooloa Rd., 808/637-5783, www.kuuloakai.com) has private charters for up to six anglers and lets you take home enough fish for a couple dinners. They offer full-day charters for $800 and half-day charters for $700.

H2O Adventures Hawaii (808/864-3102, www.h2oadventureshawaii.com) has five-hour deep-sea trolling charters for $500 and eighthour charters for $700, with a four-passenger maximum. They also offer four-hour bottom fishing charters for $400 and six-hour trips for $600 with a maximum of six passengers.

Hiking, Biking, and Bird-Watching

HIKING

You can hike to **Kaʻena Point,** the western tip of the island, from the North Shore. About five miles round-trip, the route follows an old dirt road to the point. It is a dry, windswept, but extremely beautiful hike with views of the North Shore the entire way out. Once you reach the nature reserve at the end of the point, cross through the special predator-proof fence to see seabird nesting grounds, monk seals, spinner dolphins, and possibly humpback whales if you're hiking from November to March. Drive to the end of Farrington Highway, past Mokuleʻia, park, and proceed on foot. Bring plenty of water. There are no facilities in the area.

At the very end of Pupukea Road is **Kaunala Trail** (6 mi loop), which runs through the verdant gulches and across the ridges of the Koʻolau foothills above Pupukea. The trail is wide and well graded with a slight elevation gain. There are great views of the North Shore on the return route. Drive to the end of Pupukea Road and park on the side of the road. Follow the dirt road past the Boy Scout camp and go around the locked gate. The trail is not far ahead to the left of the dirt road. This trail is open on weekends and holidays.

The **Kealia Trail** (7 mi round-trip) is an intermediate hike that climbs the cliff behind Mokuleʻia to a summit in the Waiʻanae Range. The prize is an overlook of beautiful Makua Valley. After hiking about 4 of the 19 switchbacks you'll find amazing views of the entire North Shore, as well as native trees and shrubs along the trail. To get to the trail, take Farrington Highway through Mokuleʻia. As you pass the end of the airport runway, look for an access gate in the fence and turn left. It's open 7am-6pm daily. Go past the runway and park in the lot in front of the control tower. Walk toward the mountain and go through the gate in the fence and immediately turn left.

BIKING

The **North Shore Bike Path** stretches from Waimea Bay to Sunset Beach. Much of the trail is shaded, and there are several ocean views along the way. Most of the trail is flat, great for a leisurely cruise or a more relaxing way to beach hop without having to worry about parking.

If you prefer going off-road, mountain bike out to Kaʻena Point on the **Kaʻena Point Trail,** an old railroad bed which is now a dirt road that hugs the coast around the point, a five-mile round-trip. The road is rough and rocky, there is no shade, and the surroundings are arid. Conversely, the scenery of the coastal dunes, the rugged shoreline, and the beautiful water is amazing. In the winter months, huge swells can wrap around the point, creating a cooling sea mist from the white water crashing against the rocks.

In Haleʻiwa you can rent bikes at **Surf N Sea** (62-595 Kamehameha Hwy., 808/637-9887, http://surfnsea.com, 9am-7pm daily) for $10 per hour, $20 daily, and $100 weekly.

Across from Sharks Cove, the **North Shore Surf Shop** (59-053 Kamehameha Hwy., 808/638-0390, 10am-7:30pm daily) rents cruisers for $15 per day. **Hele Huli Rental** (57-091 Kamehameha Hwy., 808/293-6024, www.turtlebayresort.com) at Turtle Bay Resort rents bikes for $10 for one hour, $20 for two hours, or $25 per day. **North Shore Bike Rentals** (888/948-5666, www.northshorebikerentals.com) is a bike rental and delivery service. They deliver cruisers to any location from Mokuleʻia to Velzyland. They rent cruisers for $19 a day, children's bikes for $10 a day, tandem bikes for $29 a day, pull carriers for $12 a day, and adult cruisers with a pull carrier for $28 a day. For three-day minimum rentals, they waive the $10 delivery charge. Free helmets and locks are included with rental.

BIRD-WATCHING

The **James Campbell National Wildlife Refuge** (66-590 Kamehameha Hwy., 808/637-6330, www.fws.gov/jamescampbell) is two separate sections of wetland habitat in between Turtle Bay and Kahuku, 164 acres in total. The wetlands are dedicated to the recovery of Hawaii's endemic waterfowl, primarily the endangered Hawaiian stilt, Hawaiian moorhen, Hawaiian coot, and the Hawaiian duck. The 126-acre Ki'i Unit is open to the public during the nonbreeding season, October to February. Also utilizing the wetlands is the bristle-thighed curlew. Guided tours are offered twice per week, on Thursday afternoons and Saturday mornings on the first two Saturdays of the month and in the afternoon on the last two Saturdays of the month. Reservations are required.

Adventure Sports

SHARK DIVING

There are two shark diving tour operators out of Hale'iwa Harbor. They travel three to four miles offshore and drop a metal shark cage in the water, where guests dive in to see Galapagos, tiger, hammerhead, and other sandbar sharks from a safe underwater vantage point. The tours are weather dependent, and no diving experience is required. If you're lucky, you'll see spinner dolphins, turtles, and even humpback whales during your time at sea. **North Shore Shark Adventures** (808/228-5900, www.hawaiisharkadventures.com) offers two-hour tours throughout the day for $120 adult, $60 children 3-13 years old. If you require transportation from Waikiki, they charge $55. **Hawaii Shark Encounters** (808/351-9373, www.hawaiisharkencounters.com) offers tours for $105 for adults and $75 for children under 12 years old.

HORSEBACK RIDING

The North Shore is a rural enclave from Kahuku to Mokule'ia, and farms and ranches are common along the coast. Up on Pupukea, overlooking Waimea Valley and the North Shore is **Happy Trails Hawaii** (59-231 Pupukea Rd., 808/638-7433, www.happytrailshawaii.com). Their trails meander through forest, ranch land, and tropical orchards, offering panoramic mountain and ocean views. Two-hour tours are $99, and one-hour tours are $79. Riders must be at least six years old. **Gunstock Ranch** (56-250 Kamehameha Hwy., 808/293-2026, http://gunstockranch.com), just outside of Kahuku, is a family owned and operated working ranch at the base of the Ko'olau Mountains. They have a network of trails and tours for all riding levels. The mountain terrain and beautiful ocean views stretch all the way down the windward coast to Kane'ohe Bay. Their Scenic Ride is a 90-minute guided ride suitable for all skill levels for $89; the Keiki Experience is a 30-minute horse experience and ride for children ages 2-7 years old for $39; the Advanced Trail Ride is a one-hour ride with trotting and cantering during the ride for $109, and previous riding experience is required. They also offer a Moonlight Ride, a Picnic Ride, a Sweetheart Ride, a Sunset Ride, and a Dinner Sunset Ride.

◖ SKYDIVING

What could be more exhilarating than seeing the entire island of O'ahu, all at once, from 20,000 feet? Jumping out of the plane that took you that high and parachuting back to earth. **Skydive Hawaii** (68-760 Farrington Hwy., 808/637-9700 or 808/945-0222, www.skydivehawaii.com) operates from Dillingham Airfield in Mokule'ia and specializes in tandem skydiving for first-time jumpers, but their services also extend to experienced skydivers and skydiving students. They make three jumps a day and offer a free shuttle service from several points in Honolulu. Tandem skydiving from 12,000 feet is $225, from 14,000 feet is $250, and from 20,000 feet (the highest tandem sky-dive in Hawaii) is $998. Skydivers must be at least 18 years old. You can also find similar rates and services literally right next door at **Pacific Skydiving Hawaii** (68-760 Farrington Hwy., 808/637-7472, www.pacificskydiving-hawaii.com).

GLIDER FLIGHTS

For those who would rather stay inside an air-craft, yet still partake of those North Shore views, **Hana Hou Air** (808/222-4235, www.hanahouair.com) offers 20-minute scenic glider flights above the Wai'anae Mountains along the North Shore for $100. Reservations are required. Also accessing the Dillingham Airfield is **Honolulu Soaring** (808/637-0207, www.honolulusoaring.com). They have several planes in their fleet and offer scenic as well as acrobatic glider flights. The average visibility is 30 to 40 miles. One-passenger scenic flights start at $79 for 10 minutes and go to $215 for 60 minutes. Two-passenger scenic flights start at $128 for 10 minutes and go to $390 for 60 minutes. One-passenger acrobatic flights start at $165 for 15 minutes and go to $285 for 60 minutes. Combination scenic and acrobatic flights are also available.

Golf

Turtle Bay Resort (57-091 Kamehameha Hwy., 808/293-6000 or 800/203-3650, www.turtlebayresort.com/hawaii_golf) is the premier golf destination on the North Shore, with two 18-hole championship courses, the **Palmer Course** and the **Fazio Course.** One of the best courses on O'ahu, the Palmer Course is set across natural wet-lands, with its signature 17th hole right on the coast. At 180 acres, there are no interruptions from homes or resort amenities. Rates for the Palmer Course are $174 till noon, $140 noon-2pm, $105 2pm-4pm, and $84 after 4pm, which include fees, golf cart, practice balls, and bottled water. The Fazio Course is more forgiving than the Palmer Course and has a walker-friendly layout set among na-tive Hawaiian palms along the coastline. It is designed for short game play. Rates includ-ing fees, golf cart, practice balls, and bottled water are $115 till noon, $95 noon-2pm, $75 2pm-4pm, and $50 after 4pm. Walking rates are $90 till noon, $70 noon-3pm, and $25 after 3pm. Add $35 to the rate for the course you play in the morning to create a 36-hole package. The resort also has complete prac-tice facilities including target greens, chip-ping area, bunkers, and putting greens. You can contact the pro shop to reserve tee times at 808/293-8574.

For a more relaxed and informal round of golf, visit the **Kahuku Golf Course** (56-501 Kamehameha Hwy., 808/293-5842, www1.honolulu.gov/des/golf/kahuku.htm). The nine-hole seaside course is a walking-only course that can be challenging due to predominantly windy conditions. The greens fee for two nine-hole rounds is $30, twilight or just nine holes is $15. Golf club rental is $12, and handcarts are available for $4.

Spas

Spa Luana (57-091 Kamehameha Hwy., 808/447-6868 or 808/293-6000, www.turtle-bayresort.com/oahu_spa, 8am-8pm daily) is Turtle Bay Resort's luxurious spa. Located in your choice of one of six treatment rooms or an outdoor oceanside cabana, their signature services use local fruit and plant ingredients to complement the spa's relaxing tropical atmosphere. Seaside single massages start at $165 for 50 minutes and $325 for couples. They have nine other types of massage on the menu, starting at $135 for 50 minutes; six body treatments starting at $135 for 50 minutes; facials and skin care enhancements starting at $135 for 50 minutes; spa treatment packages and salon services are also available.

At the **North Shore Wellness Retreat** (59-142 Kamehameha Hwy., 808/638-8137, http://surfintoyoga.com), the choice is yours whether to relax inside in the Spa Room or outdoors in their lush tropical garden. They offer three types of massage starting at $90 for 60 minutes and $130 for 90 minutes. They also offer light body energy work, acupuncture, polarity treatment, body scrubs for $75, and 60-minute facials starting at $80.

Sights

PU'U O MAHUKA HEIAU

Located on the Pupukea bluff right above Waimea Bay and covering two acres, **Pu'u O Mahuka Heiau** is the largest *heiau* on O'ahu. Three- to six-foot stacked stone walls are what remain of the original three enclosures thought to have been built in the 17th century. The structure was integral to the social, political, and religious systems for the once thriving Waimea Valley community. The *heiau* has views of Waimea Valley and the North Shore. There are dirt walking paths around the structure and interpretive signage, but no water or facilities. Follow the trail to the edge of the cliff for a unique view of Waimea Bay. To get there, drive up Pupukea Road and take the first right turn after the switchbacks. The paved road is rough and narrow, so drive slowly and be aware of oncoming vehicles.

◖ WAIMEA VALLEY

Waimea Valley (59-864 Kamehameha Hwy., 808/638-7766, www.waimeavalley.net, 9am-5pm daily) is one of O'ahu's last partially intact *ahupua'a* (land division stretching from the mountain to the sea), and is part botanical garden and part native Hawaiian cultural site. Once a thriving native Hawaiian community based around the river running down

Waimea Valley is both a botanical garden and a cultural heritage site.

© KEVIN WHITTON

the valley to the sea, it offered sustenance in many forms for native Hawaiians. Today, Waimea Valley is home to many collections of tropical plants, but it is most famous for the hybrid hibiscus collection at the front of the garden and the ginger and heliconia collection at the back of the valley. Peacocks run wild through the gardens, and native birds are common along the stream. There are several native Hawaiian historic living sites along the three-quarter-mile paved trail back to the waterfall and pool. General admission is $15 for adults and $7.50 for children ages 4-12 and seniors 60 and over. Golf cart transportation from the ticket booth to the waterfall is available for $4 one way and $6 round-trip. They also have several guided hikes led by staff on Thursday and Saturday. Reservations must be made at least three days in advance for these, and additional fees apply. Check the website for the detailed information about the guided hikes.

Shopping

HALE'IWA
◖ Historic Hale'iwa Town

Historic Hale'iwa Town is packed full of restaurants and shops, most within a comfortable walking distance. Art galleries, surf shops, souvenir shops, and clothing and swimwear boutiques line Kamehameha Highway through this old seaside town established at the turn of the 20th century.

In the **North Shore Marketplace** (66-250 Kamehameha Hwy.) on the south end of town you'll find **Wyland Galleries** (808/637-8729, www.wyland.com, 10am-8pm Mon.-Thurs., 10am-9pm Fri.-Sat., 10am-7pm Sun.), featuring a handful of acclaimed artists with works based on ocean and outdoor themes, **Britton Gallery** (808/637-6505, www.brittongallery.com, 10am-6pm daily), with prints, sculpture,

© KEVIN WHITTON

the North Shore Marketplace

jewelry, and Hawaiiana decor from 35 island artists, and **North Shore Glass** (808/780-1712, www.northshoreglass.com, 11am-4pm daily) where they blow glass on-site. For women's swimwear, check out **North Shore Swimwear** (808/637-7000, www.northshoreswimwear.com, 10am-6pm daily).

Directly north of the Marketplace is **Haleiwa Art Gallery** (66-252 Kamehameha Hwy., 808/637-3368, www.haleiwaartgallery.com, 10am-6pm daily), Hale'iwa's oldest gallery. They feature the work of 30 island artists in media from oil and watercolor to bronze and embroidery.

In the heart of Hale'iwa, in the **Hale'iwa Town Center,** you'll find **Clark Little Gallery** (66-165 Kamehameha Hwy., 808/626-5319, www.clarklittlephotography.com, 10am-6pm Mon.-Sat., 10am-5pm Sun.) featuring the underwater and wave photography of award-winning local photographer Clark Little. Next door is the boutique clothing and beach shop **Guava Shop** (66-165 Kamehameha Hwy.,

808/637-9670, 10am-6pm daily). And at the north end of town is a popular children's store, the **Growing Keiki** (66-051 Kamehameha Hwy., 808/637-4544, http://thegrowingkeiki.com, 10am-6pm daily). They have unique clothes, locally published children's book, and handmade wooden toys.

Hale'iwa Farmers Market (59-864 Kamehameha Hwy., 808/388-9696, http://haleiwafarmersmarket.com, 3pm-7pm Thurs.) is a grassroots community market held at Waimea Valley, rain or shine. They also have live music and free arts and crafts for the kids.

Waialua

If you're in Waialua, head to the old Waialua Sugar Mill, where the **North Shore Soap Factory** (67-106 Kealohanui St., 808/637-7627, www.hawaiianbathbody.com, 9am-6pm Mon.-Fri., 8:30am-6pm Sat., 10am-5pm Sun.) specializes in premier Hawaiian bath and body products, the cornerstone being their own handmade and natural soaps.

Entertainment

NIGHTLIFE

Hale'iwa has two popular bars that draw the crowds at night, but also double as restaurants by day. Located in the North Shore Marketplace, **Breakers** (66-250 Kamehameha Hwy., 808/637-9898, www.restauranteur.com/breakers, 8am-2am daily, $11-24) serves breakfast, lunch, and dinner, but the surf-themed restaurant is best known for its full bar and relaxed beach vibe. Packed with surf memorabilia and one of the few places in Hale'iwa that stays open late, it often hosts big parties and has live music. Next to Longs in the Hale'iwa Town Center, **B's Bar and Grinds** (66-197 Kamehameha Hwy., 808/744-4125, www.bsbarandgrinds.com, 11am-2am daily, $12-24) is a full bar that serves lunch and dinner, a mix of sandwiches, steak, seafood, and appetizers, with a late-night menu running till midnight.

Many people on the North Shore venture

to **Turtle Bay Resort** (57-091 Kamehameha Hwy., 808/293-6000 or 800/203-3650, www.turtlebayresort.com) to visit the only outdoor bar where you can grab a drink and watch the surf, the **Hang Ten Bar & Grill** (808/293-6000, 10am-10pm daily, $8-19), better known as the Pool Bar. Stiff mai tais and other tropical drink concoctions are their specialty. Situated right on the point, this is a great place for a sunset beverage. Inside the resort there is **Surfer, The Bar** (808/293-6000, 6pm-midnight daily, $12-24), a modern mixed-media bar centered around surfing and its legacy on the North Shore. Along with a light food menu, they offer tropical drinks, wine by the glass, and a bunch of local beers. Check out Talk Story Wednesday, where prominent figures in the surf industry share their stories for the crowd. Video and live music also add to the experience.

Food

HALEʻIWA
Coffee

In the North Shore Marketplace, the **Coffee Gallery** (66-250 Kamehameha Hwy., 808/637-5355, www.roastmaster.com, 6:30am-8pm daily) is a popular stop for coffee, both brewed and roasted beans. They have a great selection of bakery goods and sell local coffee by the pound. They also offer free wireless Internet for customers at the rustic covered patio seating or outdoor benches.

Quick Bites

Kua Aina (66-160 Kamehameha Hwy., 808/637-6067, www.kua-aina.com, 11am-8pm daily, $7-10) is great for the standard burger and fries combo.

Storto's (66-215 Kamehameha Hwy., 808/637-6633, 8am-6pm daily, $5-12) is the go-to sandwich deli in Haleʻiwa. The friendly staff makes big sandwiches for big appetites. For a normal serving, order a half sandwich. Don't forget the papaya seed dressing.

Cafe Haleiwa (66-460 Kamehameha Hwy., 808/637-5516, 7am-1:45pm daily, also 6pm-9:30pm Tues.-Sat., $4-10) is a delicious pancakes and eggs breakfast restaurant with Mexican specialties and a signature mahimahi plate.

In the mood for shrimp? Visit **Giovanni's** (66-472 Kamehameha Hwy., 808/293-1839, www.giovannisshrimptruck.com, 10:30am-5pm daily, $4-13) shrimp truck. The white truck is an icon on the North Shore, and they've been serving up shrimp plates since 1993. They have three shrimp plates to choose from and a hot dog for the *keiki*. They also have another truck in Kahuku by the old sugar mill that stays open till 6:30pm.

Steak and Seafood

Overlooking the Haleʻiwa Harbor, right by the Rainbow Bridge, is **Haleiwa Joes** (66-011 Kamehameha Hwy., 808/637-8005, http://haleiwajoes.com, 11:30am-9:30pm daily, $19-40). Joes serves up fresh and delicious seafood with Hawaiian-influenced Pacific Rim preparations. They also have meat selections and great salads. Indoor and patio seating are available. Sit in the bar for a more casual experience with the full benefits of the menu. Make reservations to avoid the wait.

Across from Haleʻiwa Beach Park and overlooking the Haleʻiwa Harbor as well, **Jameson's By The Sea** (62-540 Kamehameha Hwy., 808/637-6272, www.restauranteur.com/jamesonshawaii, 11am-9:30pm Mon.-Fri., opens at 9am Sat.-Sun., $20-37) offers fresh local seafood with indoor and patio seating. Though the decor is a bit outdated, it is a romantic spot to eat and watch the sunset.

Pacific Rim

◖ Haleʻiwa Eats Thai (66-079 Kamehameha Hwy., 808/637-4247, http://haleiwaeatsthai.com, noon-9pm Mon.-Thurs., noon-9:30pm Fri.-Sun., $12-18) is a BYOB that has a religious local following. Don't be in a rush though; every order is made fresh, and there can be a bit of a wait for a table in the compact one-room restaurant. The flavorful Thai cuisine is consistent and delicious. Try a refreshing Thai iced tea with your meal.

Banzai Sushi (66-246 Kamehameha Hwy., 808/637-4404, www.banzaisushibarhawaii.com, noon-9:30pm daily, $6-48) in the North Shore Marketplace is the go-to joint for sushi. Sit at a table or try the floor seating for an authentic Japanese experience on a finely decorated outdoor covered lanai. The fish is fresh, the rolls are inventive, and they have a list of premium sake. They have vegan options on the menu as well as large party sushi combinations. The tempura avocado is a treat, as is the live music often on hand.

O'AHU

© KEVIN WHITTON

Hale'iwa Eats Thai

Pizza

A staple in Hale'iwa town for nearly four decades, **Pizza Bob's** (66-145 Kamehameha Hwy., 808/637-5095, http://pizzabobshawaii.com, 7am-9pm Sun.-Thurs., 7am-10pm Fri.-Sat., $11-30) is a casual pizza parlor serving breakfast, lunch, and dinner. They have indoor and patio seating and nightly specials on food and drinks. They also have burgers and pasta in addition to signature and build-your-own pizzas.

Mexican

Luibueno's (66-165 Kamehameha Hwy., 808/637-7717, http://luibueno.com, 11am-10:30pm daily, $6-29) serves authentic Mexican and Latin seafood, something that's hard to find on O'ahu. The restaurant decor is modern and colorful, the atmosphere is lively, and they source their ingredients locally, including the fish that comes right off the boat at Hale'iwa Harbor.

Cholo's (66-250 Kamehameha Hwy.,

808/637-3059, www.cholosmexican.com, 9:30am-9pm Sun.-Thurs., 9:30am-9:30pm Fri.-Sat., $10-15), in the North Shore Marketplace, is a popular eatery, but more for the tequila bar rather than the food, which is the standard taco, burrito, chimichanga affair.

Health Food

Celestial Natural Foods (66-445 Kamehameha Hwy., 808/637-6729, 9am-6pm Mon.-Fri., 10am-6pm Sat.-Sun.) has been the premier health food grocer in Hale'iwa since 1974. They carry organic and natural foods, organic and local produce, vitamins, cosmetics, and other natural and healthy products.

In the back of the store, the **Beet Box Café** (66-443 Kamehameha Hwy., 808/637-3000, www.thebeetboxcafe.com, 9am-5pm Mon.-Sat., 9am-4pm Sun., $6-11) offers an extensive organic vegetarian menu for breakfast and lunch. Egg dishes served all day, and acai bowls, soup, sandwiches, salads, smoothies, and raw organic vegetable juice are all possibilities.

Sweets and Treats

Established in 1951, **Matsumoto Shave Ice** (66-087 Kamehameha Hwy., 808/637-4827, www.matsumotoshaveice.com, 9am-6pm daily) is an integral part of the history of quaint Hale'iwa town. They have developed a huge following for ices over the years. The result is a long line that snakes around the building just to get a cup of the Hawaiian treat. Be prepared to wait quite a while, especially on the weekends and during the summer. Originally a sundries store, they still have souvenirs, snacks, and items like sunscreen and sunglasses.

You'll also find a line at **Aoki's Shave Ice** (66-117 Kamehameha Hwy., 808/637-7017, http://aokishaveice.com, 11am-6:30pm daily). In addition to delicious shaved ice made with homemade syrups, Aoki's also serves ice cream, smoothies, shakes, and other snacks.

The **Waialua Bakery** (66-200 Kamehameha Hwy., 808/341-2838, 10am-5pm Mon.-Sat.) has much more than just baked goods. The locally owned bakery also has juices, a long list of smoothies, and fresh sandwiches. Much of their produce is from the family farm in Mokule'ia.

Markets

Malama Market (66-190 Kamehameha Hwy., 808/637-4520, 7am-8pm Mon., 1pm-8pm Tues., 8am-10pm Wed., 11am-9pm Thurs., 7am-10pm Fri., 10am-9pm Sat.-Sun.) is the big brand grocery store in the heart of Hale'iwa with alcohol, produce, dry goods, meats, and groceries.

NORTH SHORE BEACHES AND TURTLE BAY

Quick Bites

Sharks Cove Grill (59-712 Kamehameha Hwy., 808/638-8300, www.sharkscovegrill.com, 8:30am-8:30pm daily) is right across from Sharks Cove and enjoys great ocean views. Known for grilled skewer plates, the food truck serves breakfast, smoothies, and lunch all day. They have a few covered tables to take in the view while you eat.

Across from Sunset Beach, **Ted's Bakery** (59-024 Kamehameha Hwy., 808/638-5974, www.tedsbakery.com, 7am-8pm daily) provides homemade bakery goods, pies, salads, burgers, sandwiches, and plate lunches. Expect a wait of 30 minutes during the lunch rush if you order hot food.

Steak and Seafood

When North Shore locals celebrate a big occasion, they go to **Lei Lei's Bar and Grill** (57-049 Kuilima Dr., 808/293-2662, www.turtlebayresort.com/explore/restaurants/lei_leis_bar, 7am-10pm daily, $22-36). The open-air restaurant and bar has indoor and patio seating, just steps away from the Fazio Golf Course. They serve rich and savory fresh seafood cuisine with Hawaiian favorites like ahi *poke*. The prime rib is also a favorite, as is the escargot appetizer. Lei Lei's is open for breakfast, lunch, and dinner.

Markets

The Pupukea **Foodland** (59-720 Kamehameha Hwy., 808/638-8081, www.foodland.com, 6am-11pm daily) is the only grocery store on the North Shore. Luckily, the big brand grocery store has everything on premises: produce, meat, groceries, alcohol, and a deli with great made-to-order sandwiches. Expect higher prices, even by Hawaii standards.

Kahuku Superette (56-505 Kamehameha Hwy., 808/293-9878, 6am-10pm daily), across from Kahuku High School, is known and treasured for the fresh *poke*, Hawaiian favorites like lomi lomi salmon, and marinated raw meats. They also have alcohol and beverages, beach gear and fishing supplies, and a bare-bones assortment of snacks and groceries.

O'AHU

Getting There and Around

CAR

To get to the North Shore, you can either take Kamehamcha Highway, Route 83 on the windward coast, or travel the H-2 up the middle of the island. At Wahiawa the freeway ends and becomes Wilikina Drive through Schofield Barracks, which turns into Kaukonahua Road and then finally becomes Farrington Highway as you pass Waialua and drive out to Mokule'ia at the end of the road. Or, as the H-2 ends, you can take the Wahiawa off ramp, exit 8, which puts you on Kamehameha Highway through Wahiawa. Kamehameha Highway continues through the town of Hale'iwa, across the North Shore, and back down the windward side. You can bypass Hale'iwa on the Joseph P. Leong Highway, Route 83.

BUS

You can get to the North Shore from Honolulu via **TheBus** (808/848-5555, www.thebus.org) on Routes 55 and 88A, both of which traverse the windward coast. If you want to leave the car parked for a bit, Route 76 travels between Waialua and Hale'iwa.

TRAFFIC

During the Vans Triple Crown of Surfing and periods of high surf on the North Shore, traffic can slow to a crawl from Hale'iwa to Sunset Beach. There are several notorious choke points along this stretch. Traffic backs up at Laniakea, Chun's Reef, Waimea Bay, and Sunset Beach. Look out for pedestrians crossing the highway. The weekends are notorious for stop-and-go traffic from Hale'iwa through Chun's Reef.

If the waves are extremely large and Waimea Bay is breaking, traffic gets crazy around the bay as people try to pull off the road to get a view and take photos. Parking on the mountain side of the road is illegal, and there is only limited space on the ocean side shoulder of the highway. It's much safer to park around Sharks Cove and walk back to the bay for photos. Parking laws are strictly enforced in the area.

On the North Shore, parking along the highway is haphazard at best. Be sure not to block residential driveways and be aware of No Parking signs and bus stops. The No Parking signs have arrows pointing in the direction of the area where it is illegal to park, and No Parking areas are strictly enforced.

SOUTHEAST AND WINDWARD

The windward side of Oʻahu, the eastern shore of the island, spans the entire length of the Koʻolau Mountain Range. It's known for its ample rainfall, the lush and dramatic corduroy cliffs of the Koʻolaus, and the chance to pull off the winding Kamehameha Highway right to the water's edge. Windward towns, save for Kailua and Kaneʻohe, are primarily residential

HIGHLIGHTS

LOOK FOR  TO FIND RECOMMENDED SIGHTS, ACTIVITIES, DINING, AND LODGING.

for shade, calm water for swimming, and empty white sand: Waimanalo has everything you need (page 149).

◖ Kailua Beach Park: Kailua Beach Park is the destination for an endless list of ocean activities: fishing, kayaking, stand-up paddling, kiteboarding... (page 150).

◖ Hanauma Bay Nature Preserve: Live coral reef, 400 species of fish, and endangered sea turtles call this unique circular bay home (page 155).

◖ Mokulua Islands: Paddling out to the Mokulua Islands is invigorating, with a view of the mainland that can't be topped. (page 158).

◖ Koko Crater Botanical Garden: This garden nestled inside an extinct volcano is home to dryland species from around the world, with succulents, cycads, a native Hawaiian *wili-wili* tree stand, and a plumeria grove (page 165).

◖ Makapu'u Point State Wayside: Hike around the point to the lighthouse, watch for whales, swim and bodysurf, and explore the black lava tidepools (page 165).

◖ Sandy Beach Park: Test your mettle at this infamous break, which detonates right on the sand (page 148).

◖ Waimanalo Beach Park: Ironwood trees

◖ La'ie Point State Wayside: A dramatic wave-battered sea arch sits just off a rugged point jutting sharply out into the Pacific. Leap from the cliff on the south side—if you dare (page 168).

and historically rooted in agriculture and aquaculture: *kalo lo'i,* banana plantations, papaya, and fishponds. A drive up the windward coast is a trip back in time, with weathered wooden fruit stands offering family farm goods. It's a leisurely drive that should be enjoyed at every turn in the road.

Kailua and Kane'ohe have developed into major population centers and desirable destinations, each with its own draw. Kailua is full of hip shops, restaurants, and some of the best fine, white sand beaches on O'ahu.

It's also known for kitesurfing and kayaking, with several islets just offshore. Kane'ohe town definitely caters to locals with its dining and shopping services, but there are more than enough reasons for a visit with the Ho'omaluhia Botanical Garden and the famous Kane'ohe Bay Sandbar, perfect for a half-day kayaking adventure.

The southeast corner of O'ahu is one of the drier locales of the island. Makapu'u and Sandy Beach are O'ahu's premier bodysurfing beaches, and Makapu'u offers a short hike to its

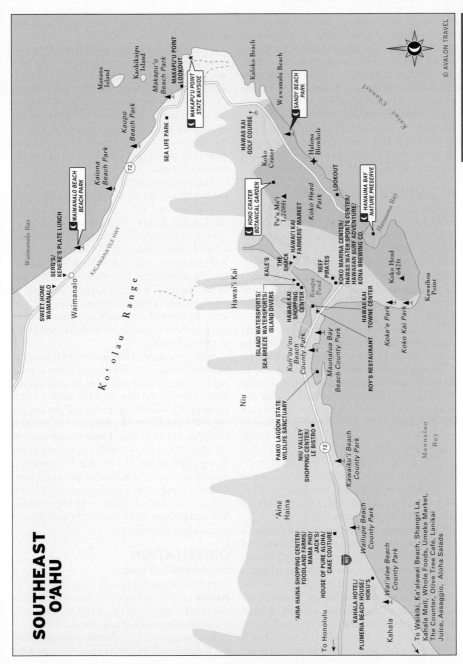

SOUTHEAST
O'AHU

© AVALON TRAVEL

lighthouse and prime whale-watching opportunities during the humpback whales' annual stay in the Hawaiian Islands from November to March. Constantly battered by wind and chop, the coastline is dramatic; the island seems to fall into the ocean here. Koko Crater is home to a dryland botanical garden with a plumeria grove. Across the highway is Hanauma Bay marine preserve and Koko Head, which gives way to Maunalua Bay, known for its ample water sports activities, from surf and stand-up paddle lessons to Jet Ski rentals and wakeboarding.

PLANNING YOUR TIME

The southeast stretch of Oʻahu, from Kahala to Makapuʻu, and north to Laʻie near the island's northern tip on the windward coast, is a lot of coastline to cover, about 50 miles. With a 35 mph speed limit on both the Kalanianaole Highway and Kamehameha Highway, it's not a drive you want to rush. Not to mention, some of the attractions can easily become a full-day activity.

If you're heading to a windward locale and want to extend your scenic drive, taking the Kalanianaole Highway at least one way is a great option. There are numerous lookouts to see the rugged, dry, and wave-pummeled coastline. But it will add at least an hour to your day just to get from Kahala to Kailua. Otherwise, a full day can easily be spent enjoying the unique southeast coast. Hiking the Koko Crater stairs, snorkeling at Hanauma Bay, taking surf lessons or diving in Maunalua Bay are all half-day activities at least. Or there's bodysurfing at Sandy Beach or hiking and watching whales at Makapuʻu. Round it out with a meal in Hawaiʻi Kai and you're ready for bed.

On the windward side, other than the ranch tours at Kualoa Ranch and the Polynesian Cultural Center, everything is centered around the ocean. Whether you're snorkeling, fishing, stand-up paddling, or walking along a deserted stretch of sand, the beaches are the main attractions. If you see a nice spot along your drive and feel the need to pull over and swim, do it! The closer you look, the more you'll find the hidden gems. Don't forget, there are a few good hikes, if you don't mind mud and mosquitoes.

The weather changes quickly on the windward side. A typical day might start out with sun in the morning, change to clouds by midday, and bring heavy showers by the afternoon. Or, depending on the wind, it could be raining all morning, with the sun finally poking through in the late afternoon. Either way, on the windward side, you have to get out and explore or you'll never know. Don't trust the weather report.

The predominant trade winds blow out of the northeast and push air heavy with moisture evaporated from the ocean up against the Koʻolau Range. As the warm, humid air rises, it cools, condenses, and forms clouds, which become saturated and dump their payload, freshwater raindrops, down on the coast and the mountains. The windward side is wet to say the least, with the highest amounts of precipitation falling between Kaneʻohe and Laʻie. In times of extremely heavy rainfall, the Kamehameha Highway often floods and closes to through traffic.

Still, typical rain showers are often fleeting, localized events. Just because a shower is passing by doesn't mean you need to pack up the beach gear for the day. And the farther south along the Koʻolau Range past Kaneʻohe you go, the less rainfall hits the ground. On the dry, southeast tip of Oʻahu, Koko Crater receives 12-20 inches of rain annually, compared to the average 100 inches of rain that Hoʻomaluhia Botanical Garden in Kaneʻohe gets every year. The best thing to do if you're planning a beach day on the windward side is to hope for the best and prepare for the worst. At least it's still warm when it rains.

ORIENTATION
Southeast Oʻahu

Stretching from the upscale neighborhood of **Kahala** on the east side of Diamond Head to the easternmost tip of the island at Makapuʻu, the southeast coast has two distinct zones.

Beginning with Kahala and spanning along the Kalanianaole Highway east, there are **Aina**

O'AHU

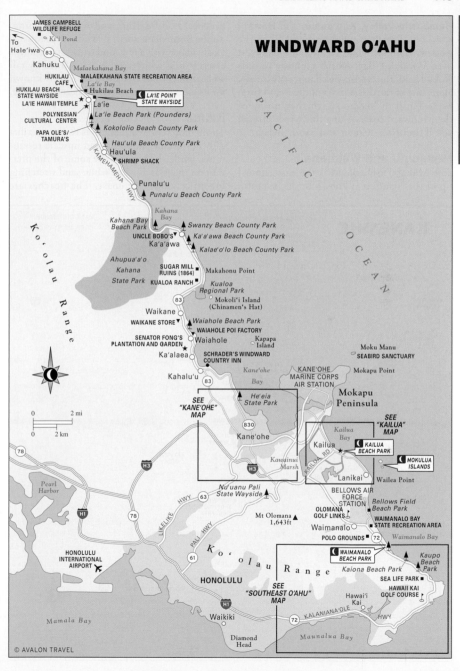

WINDWARD O'AHU

JAMES CAMPBELL
WILDLIFE REFUGE
Ki'i Pond
To
Hale'iwa 83
Kahuku
Malaekahana Bay
HUKILAU
CAFE MALAEKAHANA STATE RECREATION AREA
HUKILAU BEACH La'ie Bay
STATE WAYSIDE Hukilau Beach
LA'IE HAWAII TEMPLE La'ie LA'IE POINT
STATE WAYSIDE
POLYNESIAN
CULTURAL CENTER La'ie Beach Park (Pounders)
PAPA OLE'S/ Kokololio Beach County Park
TAMURA'S
Hau'ula Beach County Park
Hau'ula
SHRIMP SHACK

PACIFIC

Punalu'u
Punalu'u Beach County Park

Kahana
Bay
Kahana Bay
Beach Park Swanzy Beach County Park
UNCLE BOBO'S Ka'a'awa Beach County Park
Ka'a'awa
Kalae'o'lo Beach County Park

OCEAN

Ahupua'a'o
Kahana
State Park SUGAR MILL
RUINS (1864) Makahonu Point
KUALOA RANCH Kualoa
Regional Park
83 Mokoli'i Island
(Chinamen's Hat)
Waikane
WAIKANE STORE Waiahole Beach Park
WAIAHOLE POI FACTORY
SENATOR FONG'S Waiahole Kapapa
PLANTATION AND GARDEN Island
Ka'alaea SCHRADER'S WINDWARD
COUNTRY INN
Kahalu'u 83

Moku Manu
SEABIRD SANCTUARY

Kane'ohe
Bay KANE'OHE
MARINE CORPS
AIR STATION Mokapu Point

Mokapu
Peninsula

SEE
"KANE'OHE"
MAP He'eia
State Park

Kailua
Bay SEE
"KAILUA"
MAP

830
Kane'ohe KAILUA
Kailua BEACH PARK

0   2 mi
0   2 km

Kawainui
Marsh
H3 Lanikai MOKULUA
ISLANDS
Wailea Point

78 Nu'uanu Pali
State Wayside BELLOWS AIR
FORCE
STATION Bellows Field
Beach Park

Pearl
Harbor 63 OLOMANA
GOLF LINKS WAIMANALO BAY
STATE RECREATION AREA

H1 78 Mt Olomana ▲ Waimanalo
1,643ft
POLO GROUNDS 72 Waimanalo Bay

HONOLULU INTERNATIONAL AIRPORT 61 Ko'olau Range WAIMANALO
BEACH PARK Kaupo
Beach
Park
Kaiona Beach Park

HONOLULU SEA LIFE PARK
SEE
"SOUTHEAST O'AHU"
MAP Hawai'i
Kai HAWAII KAI
GOLF COURSE

H1 Waikiki 72 KALANIANA'OLE HWY

Mamala Bay Diamond
Head Maunalua Bay

© AVALON TRAVEL

KAMEHAMEHA HWY
Ko'olau Range
LIKELIKE HWY
PALI HWY

Haina, Niu Valley, Kuli'ou'ou, and **Hawai'i Kai.** The Portlock neighborhood lines the western flank of Koko Head and looks west over Maunalua Bay. As the highway rounds Koko Head, the landscape changes drastically along one of the driest parts of the island from Koko Head to Makapu'u, the beginning of the windward coast. Along this windy stretch you'll find Koko Crater and Sandy Beach.

Makapu'u and Waimanalo

The Makapu'u headland is the easternmost tip of the island. It is known for its beautiful beaches, bodysurfing, and whale-watching. To the immediate north is Waimanalo town, a local village with a few food trucks, plate lunch eateries, and white sand beaches lined by tall whispy ironwood trees. Waimanalo is known for its local farms, ranches, and beach camping.

Kailua

To the north of Waimanalo is Kailua. Kailua offers boutique shopping and upscale restaurants, while the beaches are some of the prettiest on the island—fine white sand stretching for miles along the coast. The beaches are

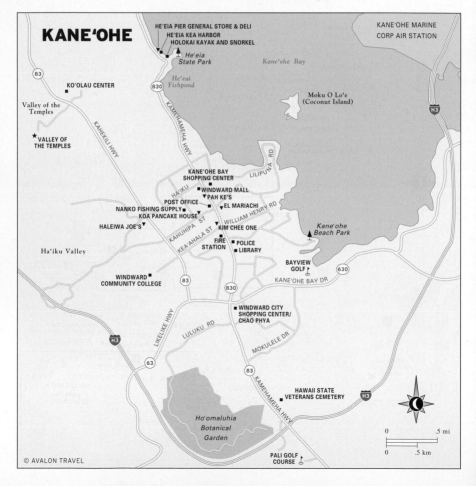

© AVALON TRAVEL

Your Best Day in Southeast and Windward O'ahu

The Southeast and Windward regions are a mix of suburban and rural communities and cover a lot of coastline. Framed by the Pacific Ocean and the Ko'olau mountain range, these regions are strikingly diverse and beautiful. To experience the area to its fullest, a rental car is a must to cover the distance and have the flexibility for a change of plans if the weather dictates.

- Start the day by snorkeling one of the best reef habitats on O'ahu, **Hanauma Bay Nature Preserve.** Keep in mind that if you arrive after 9:30am, you could be turned away if the parking lot is full. If you'd rather start your morning with a hike, walk the Makapu'u trail to the lighthouse. From November to April, this vantage point is one of the prime locations to view Pacific humpback whales.

- For lunch, pick up a sandwich at **Kalapawai**

Market and head to **Kailua Beach Park** or **Lanikai Beach** for a picnic on the beach. Lanikai has beautiful views of the Mokulua Islands; Kailua Beach is one of the most beautiful white sand beaches on O'ahu.

- After taking in all that beauty from the beach, you'll want to get in the water and cruise around. The best way to do that is to rent a kayak. Kailua town is the hub for kayak rentals. Either stick around in Kailua and paddle to **Flat Island** and the **Mokulua Islands,** or put the kayak on the roof and go exploring.

- After all that outdoor activity, you'll be in the mood for a delicious meal. Try **Buzz's,** just across the street from Kailua Beach Park, for a great steak. For a more relaxed atmosphere and great local beers on tap, try **Kona Brewing Co.** in Hawai'i Kai.

generally windy and known for kitesurfing and windsurfing. To the immediate south of Kailua is the quaint Lanikai neighborhood, where the Mokulua Islands sit right offshore.

Kane'ohe

Complete with a mall and ample fast food, Kane'ohe is one of the larger and more congested towns on the windward coast. Because of the bay there are no beaches, but the sheltered waters offer great potential for kayaking in the bay and out to the Kane'ohe Bay Sandbar. Fishing is also the draw here.

Kualoa to La'ie

Once you travel past the northern neighborhood of Kane'ohe, Kamehameha Highway hugs the coast from one beach town to the next. Most are quite small—maybe a food truck and convenience store—and others are strictly residential. But they all have beautiful beaches in common. Kualoa Regional Park and Kualoa Ranch are points of interest in the Kualoa area. To the north is Ka'a'awa, the last stop for fuel until La'ie, then the beautiful Kahana Bay with the remnants of an ancient Hawaiian fishpond and hiking in the valley. Farther north is Punalu'u, then Hau'ula, and finally La'ie, a town defined by its connection to the Church of Jesus Christ of Latter-day Saints and the home of the Polynesian Cultural Center, which is under the church's wing.

O'AHU

Beaches

Because of the natural geography of Maunalua Bay on the southeast shore, there are only a few beaches along this stretch of coast. Houses have been built to the water's edge along the peninsulas and what little beach is accessible at low tide is soon underwater as the tide rises. Fortunately, for those looking to escape the crowds of Honolulu and Waikiki beaches, Kahala is close by.

The beaches along O'ahu's windward coast, from Makapu'u to La'ie, are raw, natural, and often windswept, thanks to the pervasive trade winds blowing from northwest to southeast. The different ribbons of sand tend to be bastions of solitude, where you can pull off the highway and find a quiet nook under *naupaka* and palm trees. A barrier reef stretching the length of the windward coast keeps waves to most beaches to a minimum. You'll find driftwood, rocks, fine white sand, shells, and spectacular views of the verdant Ko'olau Mountains from the water's edge. Beachgoers should be

prepared for passing showers, as the trade winds also bring rain.

KAHALA
Ka'alawai Beach

Tucked away in the affluent Ka'alawai neighborhood, **Ka'alawai Beach** is a narrow strip of sand that runs from the end of Kulamanu Place to the Diamond Head cliffs. Framed by lavish beachfront properties beyond the vegetation line, the secluded spot draws a younger crowd and is a favorite for topless sunbathers. The shoreline is predominately rock and reef, so getting in the water can involve finding a sandy nook to take a dip. The view to the east of Black Point is picturesque, and the clear water is often choppy from the trade winds.

To access the beach, park on Kulamanu Street and walk down Kulamanu Place to the access point. Follow the sand to the right, west, and find your own spot.

There are also some great tidepools at

Disappearing Sands

It's no secret: O'ahu's beaches are its top attractions and best commodities, for recreational, social, and cultural reasons. But in some locales where urban development has marched right up to the high tide mark, the beaches are in serious danger of disappearing, if they're not gone already. There are natural processes in Hawaii, like large swell events, seasonal currents, and storms with heavy rainfall, that move sand up and down the beach, offshore, and then back again. This natural and transient process is called coastal erosion and has been going on for centuries and will continue to shape the beaches until the island erodes back into the Pacific altogether.

In the meantime, recent human alteration

of the shoreline has played a detrimental leading role in the disappearance of sand and entire beaches altogether. On O'ahu, when the ocean shoreline encroaches within 20 feet of a structure, the property owner can be granted a variance that allows them to build a seawall to protect the property. Once the natural beach dune system is stripped away and replaced with a seawall, the beach has no way to store or replenish sand for periods of natural coastal erosion, leading to a permanent state of beach erosion. You'll find this phenomenon in Kahala, Lanikai, and on other stretches of beach along the windward coast where dwellings have been built right up to sand. Where the shoreline is armored, the beaches have washed away.

Ka'alawai. Once through the access point, turn left instead of right and explore them. Be aware that the terrain is smooth and slippery in some spots as well as sharp and jagged in others. There are no services in the vicinity.

Waialae Beach Park

From Diamond Head Road, follow Kahala Avenue east toward the Kahala Hotel & Resort. Once you cross the Waialae Stream bridge, turn right into the **Waialae Beach Park** parking lot. Complete with free parking, showers, bathrooms, picnic benches, and a shaded arbor at the beach's edge, Waialae Beach Park is usually uncrowded and a favorite destination for kitesurfers and newlyweds taking wedding pictures. It's a fine place for a barbecue or picnic. The park is actually split in two by the stream, and a beautiful narrow beach unwinds to the west. This quiet stretch of sand, dotted with shells and bits of coral, is fringed by O'ahu's most magnificent homes and mansions. The shallow waters, with a flat sand and rock

bottom, are great for snorkeling and great for families looking to escape the Waikiki crowds, but are right in the path of the predominant trade winds, so be prepared to tie down umbrellas and keep your light and loose belongings secure. There are several access points along Kahala Avenue from the beach park to Hunakai Street. Park along Kahala Avenue. The beach park is closed 10pm-5am daily.

AINA HAINA
Kawaiku'i Beach Park

In Aina Haina you'll find that **Kawaiku'i Beach Park** is more of a park than a beach. At low tide there is a small strip of coarse sand fronting the park, which has mature shade trees, an expansive lawn, and bathrooms and showers. The inner waters are usually murky and not exactly inviting, but this park is still favored by surfers, windsurfers, kiteboarders and stand-up paddlers for the surf spots that break along the barrier reef quite a ways out and by anglers taking advantage of the shallow bay.. From Kalanianaole Highway heading east, turn right at Puuikena Drive (there is a traffic signal here) to access the parking lot. Parking is free.

KULI'OU'OU
Kuli'ou'ou Beach Park

Nestled up against the Paiko Lagoon Wildlife Sanctuary in the Kuli'ou'ou neighborhood, **Kuli'ou'ou Beach Park** is one of the few areas along the Maunalua Bay coastline offering a shallow bay beside a well-maintained park. The sandy seafloor of Maunalua Bay is very shallow and dotted with bits of rock, reef, and seaweed. At low tide the water is literally ankle deep, while at high tide, it's waist deep at best. In fact, take a walk all the way out to the barrier reef, roughly a quarter-mile out to sea, keeping an eye out for sea cucumbers, crabs, and fish, all within knee-deep water. The park has facilities, picnic benches, and a free parking lot. From Kalanianaole Highway, Bay Street will take you straight there. Kuli'ou'ou Beach Park is closed 10pm-5am daily.

© KEVIN WHITTON

the west end of Waialae Beach

O'AHU

HAWAI'I KAI
◖ Sandy Beach Park

A few minutes past the eastern side of Koko Head in Hawai'i Kai, along rugged and dramatic coastline, you'll find the infamous **Sandy Beach Park.** Sandy Beach is notorious for its high-impact shorebreak and draws bodysurfers, bodyboarders, and surfers to its challenging waves. The beach is rather wide by Hawaii standards and draws a host of locals and visitors who come to watch the aqua blue waves slam onto the shore. The ocean currents here are dangerous, the sand is studded with rocks, and the surf can get big and extremely powerful, detonating onto dry sand. The shorebreak has caused injuries and even fatalities, so only expert swimmers should enter the water. However, when the waves are pumping, it is quite a spectacle to watch. Parking in the dirt lot can get somewhat haphazard and choked on the weekends. And while parking is free, theft is common so take precautions.

Sandy Beach Park is just off Kalanianaole Highway. The turn is visible from both directions. At the beach park, a road runs the length of the beach, and Wawamalu Beach Park sits at the north end. There's no sand here, just jagged lava running into the ocean, but it is a great place to stop and stretch or have a bite while watching waves break just off the rocks. There are restrooms, and a long park frequented by kite-flying enthusiasts.

MAKAPU'U AND WAIMANALO
Makapu'u Beach Park

Makapu'u Point marks the arid southeast tip of O'ahu. Just to the north of the formidable headland, you'll find **Makapu'u Beach Park,** a beautiful crescent of white sand set against the deep blue ocean and dry, rugged cliffs. The scenery at Makapu'u is breathtaking, complete with Rabbit Island and Black Rock, two seabird sanctuaries, protruding from deep water just offshore. Makapu'u is also known for its pounding shorebreak, alluring to bodyboarders, bodysurfers, and locals and visitors alike. Because of the wave action, there are strong currents, and swimming should be done with

© KEVIN WHITTON

Sandy Beach Park

caution. Check with the lifeguard for current ocean conditions. On days when the surf is flat and the wind is light, the water becomes very clear. Snorkeling is best at the south end of the beach, where the rocks and cliff begin. There are restrooms and showers, but parking is very limited, so it's best to get there early. There is a small paved parking lot for the beach park, another dirt lot that is severely rutted and only safe for four-wheel-drive vehicles, or you can park up on the highway in the designated lookout area and walk down to the beach.

On the north side of the beach park are the **Makapu'u Tidepools.** The coast is fringed with black lava, creating some wonderful tidepools to explore. Be aware that the surf can wash up onto the tidepools, so its best explore the area when the surf is small to flat. To get to the tidepools, you can walk up the coast on dirt paths from Makapu'u Beach Park and meander across the lava as far as you'd like to go, or you can park right at the tidepools. Coming from Koko Head, turn just past Sea Life Park into the oceanside parking area.

Kaupo Beach Park

Just on the other side of the Makapu'u Tidepools you'll come to **Kaupo Beach Park**, a great beach for snorkeling, playing on the sand, fishing or learning to surf, with all the same great views as Makapu'u. Here, the lava opens up to offer sandy beaches among the rocks and coastal shrubs. It has character, is safe for kids, and is a favorite for local families on the weekends. It's the perfect spot to take a break from the road and have a dip or bite to eat while enjoying the scenery. As the beach arcs north toward the Makai Research Pier, there are small, gentle waves that break just off the shore. The parking lot for Kaupo Beach Park is at the same turn as the Makapu'u Tidepools, just stay to the left. There is also roadside parking for several vehicles right in front of where the waves break, or you can park down by the research pier. There are restroom and shower facilities in the beach park parking lot.

Kaiona Beach Park

About a mile north of the research pier on Kalanianaole Highway in Waimanalo is a small grassy park with restrooms and showers and a narrow but beautiful beach. **Kaiona Beach Park** is a favorite area for local families, with shallow, clean, and clear water great for swimming and snorkeling. The ocean floor, a combination or white sand and reef, gives the water a magnificent azure color. Just to the south of the beach access is Pahonu Pond, an ancient Hawaiian turtle pond. Today, it's perfect for the youngest of kids to get comfortable in a calm and sheltered setting. The beach is also called Shriners by the locals after the Shriners Beach Club at the water's edge. The free parking lot is small and fills up quickly. Use caution if you park along the road. The restroom at the beach park closes 7pm-7am daily.

◖ Waimanalo Beach Park

Right in the heart of Waimanalo town, **Waimanalo Beach Park** offers the same fine white sand, great snorkeling, swimming, and azure water as all along the Waimanalo coast. The beach park has free parking, showers, restrooms, and a grassy camping area, which is predominantly used by the homeless. While lean-tos and laundry lines don't sound like paradise, the camping area is just a small portion of the three-mile beach, one of the longest on O'ahu. The beach is also lined with ironwood trees, so it's easy to duck into the shade if the sun becomes too intense. Mostly uncrowded during the week, the beach shows a different face during the weekends as families post up, fish, relax, and have a good time. It can get pretty rowdy. The beach park is closed 9:30pm-7am daily.

Bellows Beach Park

At the north end of Waimanalo town, Bellow Air Force Station harbors **Bellows Beach Park.** It's open to the public every Friday, Saturday, and Sunday. Here you'll find more of Waimanalo's signature white sand, ironwood-lined beaches. Camping complete with facilities is also available at Bellows by permit. Take the well-marked Bellows AFB turnoff from Kalanianaole Highway and follow the road to the beach, where parking is free.

KAILUA
◖ Kailua Beach Park
This ocean activity hub of the windward coast offers everything—swimming, bodyboarding, kitesurfing, sailboarding, stand-up paddling, and kayaking. **Kailua Beach Park,** at the south end of Kailua, marks the start of the world-famous Kailua Beach, composed of fine grains of white sand and stretching 2.5 miles up the coast in a gentle arc. The water is shallow and often calm, perfect for families and swimming, but there can be small shore-breaking waves along parts of the beach.

Because the ocean floor is sand, ditch the snorkel mask and fins and get into a kayak. There are outfitters within walking distance to the beach and along Kaʻelepulu Stream. Popoiʻa Island, better known as Flat Island, is a quick paddle offshore. There is also a boat ramp where residents launch their watercraft.

Locals tend to gravitate to the small beach on the south side of the boat ramp, where they can park their trucks and anchor just off the beach.

Kailua Beach Park has restrooms, showers, and three free parking lots that fill to maximum capacity nearly every day. The park is clean with manicured landscaping, a walking path, and beautiful canopy trees. There is also a restaurant and market right across the street. Weekends are always more crowded than weekdays, but summer weekends see the crowds swell in both the park and along the beach. Police adamantly ticket illegally parked vehicles.

To get to Kailua Beach Park from Honolulu, the Pali Highway turns into Kalanianaole Highway, which becomes Kailua Road. From Waimanalo, turn right onto Kailua Road from Kalanianaole Highway. Continue straight on Kuulei Road as Kailua Road veers right and into Kailua's shopping district. Follow Kuulei Road until it dead-ends at South Kalaheo Avenue. Turn right, then make a left at Kailua Road to access the first parking lot, or continue

Kailua Beach Park is famous for its fine white sand.

© KEVIN WHITTON

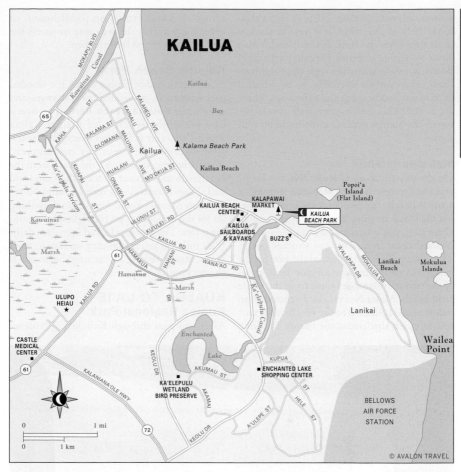

KAILUA

Kailua

Bay

65

KALAHEO AVE

KAINALU

KALAMA ST

OLOMANA

MALUNIU AVE

Kailua ⚓ Kalama Beach Park

Kailua Beach

Popoi'a
Island
(Flat Island)

KALAPAWAI
MARKET

KAILUA BEACH
CENTER

KAILUA
BEACH PARK

KAILUA
SAILBOARDS
& KAYAKS

BUZZ'S

'A'ALAPAPA DR

MOKULUA DR

Lanikai
Beach

Mokulua
Islands

Kawainui

Marsh

61

HAMAKUA

HAHANI ST

WANA'AO RD

Hamakua

Lanikai

Marsh

ULUPO
HEIAU

KAILUA RD

Enchanted

Wailea
Point

CASTLE
MEDICAL
CENTER

61

KEOLU DR

Lake

AKUMAU ST

KUPUA

ENCHANTED LAKE
SHOPPING CENTER

KALANIANA OLE HWY

KA'ELEPULU
WETLAND
BIRD PRESERVE

AKAMAI

HELE ST

ST

BELLOWS
AIR FORCE
STATION

0   1 mi

72

A'ULEPE ST

KEOLU DR

0   1 km

© AVALON TRAVEL

on Kalaheo Avenue and over the bridge as the road turns into Kawailoa Road. The next parking lot is on the left, just on the south side of the stream. At the stop sign, take a left onto Alala Road; the third parking lot is on the left side of the boat ramp. All three lots border Kailua Beach Park and are closed 10pm-5am daily. The restrooms are locked until 6am.

Lanikai Beach

Lanikai Beach fronts the affluent and quaint Lanikai neighborhood. The aesthetics of Lanikai Beach are the same as Kailua, except Lanikai Beach gets narrower as you head south, until it disappears altogether and a seawall and million-dollar homes take its place. The draw at Lanikai Beach, apart from the great swimming and calm, turquoise water, is the Mokulua Islets. A trip to "The Moks," as they are locally referred to, is the quintessential kayak destination on O'ahu. You can take a tour or paddle the 0.75 mile solo to the islands. Most people land on Moku Nui, the larger and more northerly of the two islets. It has a small beach that offers a postcard perfect view of the mainland and the Ko'olau Mountains, a perspective most visitors will never attain. There is also a trail to the back of the island. It is against the law to deviate from the trail, as the island is also home to nesting seabirds. Parking for Lanikai Beach is on the street through the neighborhood. There are no sidewalks, so be mindful of residents' landscaping and driveways. There are several public beach access walkways in between the homes, which are obvious and well signed.

Mokulua Islands

On the western shore of **Moku Nui,** the larger and more northern of the **Mokulua Islands,** is a small beach, the perfect respite after making the kayak crossing from Kailua or Lanikai. Once here, you'll find an amazing view of the leeward coast from a unique vantage point. The water is clear and blue, and the vibe on the beach is often festive. You can spot the burrows of the island's nesting sea birds from the white sand beach. Moku Nui is a bird sanctuary, so public access is limited to the beach and a narrow footpath that circles the island. Paddling across via kayak, stand-up paddleboard, or other watercraft is the only way to access the beach. There are no facilities here.

Kalama Beach Park

At the north end of Kailua Beach is a wooded park with a soft, manicured lawn, showers, and restrooms: **Kalama Beach Park**. The beach here is slightly less crowded than at Kailua Beach Park, and at Kalama Beach Park you'll avoid many of the kitesurfers and kayakers. Walk either way up or down the beach from the beach park to nab your own swath of sand and surf. From Kuulei Road, turn left onto North Kalaheo Avenue. You'll see the small parking lot for the beach park on the right where parking is free. The gate gets locked 6pm-7am daily. If it's full or if you're planning on staying after hours, street parking in the neighborhoods is the next option.

KUALOA TO LA'IE
Kualoa Regional Park

After you pass through Kahalu'u, Waikane,

a view of the two Mokulua Islands

and Waiahole on Kamehameha Highway, all set in Kaneʻohe Bay with nearshore mudflats instead of beaches, the next beautiful sandy beach you come to is at **Kualoa Regional Park** (49-479 Kamehameha Hwy., 808/237-8525, www1.honolulu.gov/parks/programs/beach/kualoa.htm). The water is clear and calm, and the ocean bottom is a mix of sand, rock, and reef, a good place to swim and snorkel. Kualoa Regional Park is also a kayaker's destination because of the Mokoliʻi Islet just offshore. Chinaman's Hat, as it's known, has a small beach on the north side. There are showers and restrooms, but no outfitters here, so you'll need to rent a kayak either in Kailua or in Honolulu. There is camping by permit in the park. The parking lot is free, and the entrance to the park is signed and visible from the highway. The park is closed and gated 8pm-7am daily.

Kaʻaʻawa Beaches

Just north of Kualoa you'll pass through Kaʻaʻawa. The Pacific Ocean pushes right up to Kamehameha Highway along much of Kaʻaʻawa, but there are a couple sandy nooks worth a stop. The first beach you'll come to is **Kalaeʻoʻio Beach Park.** Simply pull off the highway under the trees. There's a grassy area, picnic tables, and a clean beach with light blue water. The beach is usually empty.

Kaʻaʻawa Beach Park is just a skip to the north up the highway. You'll see the restrooms and showers from the road, and notice there are only three parking spaces. If they're full, just pull off the highway and park on the shoulder. This narrow beach is a local favorite for fishing and camping and can be packed on the weekends. The restrooms are closed 9pm-6:30am daily.

Beyond the beach park, across from the U.S. post office and gas station is **Swanzy Beach Park,** where camping is allowed with a permit. The beach is small and a mix of sand and rock, but it's a great zone for snorkeling when the winds are calm. The beach park has restrooms, showers, and an expansive grassy area with no shade. The views of the Koʻolaus from Swanzy are quite extraordinary. The parking lot is closed 10pm-6am daily.

Kahana Bay Beach Park

Kahana Bay Beach Park (52-222 Kamehameha Hwy., 808/237-7767, www.hawaiistateparks.org), found in dramatic Kahana Bay, offers camping by permit, a great area for a picnic, and calm, sheltered water for stand-up paddling. At the base of the bay, the Kahana Valley meets the sea and Kahana Stream spills into the Pacific, depositing fine silty sand along the beach and out into the bay. The water is often murky and a bit chilly, but remains shallow quite a ways out. The area is perfect for families with kids. Parking is right off Kamehameha Highway on the ocean side, and there are restrooms and showers. The remnants of the ancient Huilua fishpond are on the south side of the bay. The beach park and facilities are open during daylight hours.

Kokololio Beach Park

Kokololio Beach Park, at the north end of Hauʻula, offers a wide beach by Hawaii standards with a shoreline fringed with tropical almond canopy trees and *naupaka*. The ocean floor is sandy and the water is clear when the winds are light. During the winter months when the surf is up, the shorebreak can get quite powerful, and a surf break appears on the outer reef. Swimming becomes dangerous during periods of high surf due to strong currents. There are restrooms and showers in the park, as well as a large grassy area with a large parking lot. Camping is allowed with a permit, and on the weekends, especially during the summer, the park is filled with local residents and families. The beach is also a favorite for fishing. The gated parking lot is locked 8pm-6:45am daily.

Laʻie Beach Park

Just to the north, on the other side of an outcropping of limestone cliffs that marks the end of Kokololio Beach Park, is **Laʻie Beach Park**. The beach park is also known as Pounders, named after the bodysurfing area near the cliffs, where the shorebreak can get big and powerful during the winter months. The beach is relatively small and often lined with organic debris, but the park is beautiful and dotted with picnic benches. Swimming here is better in the summer months. Stroll to the north to find another small beach on the other side of the point. There are no facilities at this beach park, but a paved parking lot is right off the highway.

Hukilau Beach

On the north end of La'ie town sits the lovely **Hukilau Beach,** a long, crescent-shaped sandy beach with dunes covered in *naupaka*. During the summer months the water is great for swimming, but the surf and currents make for poor conditions during the winter months. Throughout the year, this area has the propensity for strong trade winds, which can also create unfavorable beach and swimming conditions. The park itself is beautiful, with shade from ironwood trees, grass, and picnic benches—beachgoers are always welcome. There are showers, but no restrooms, and a dirt parking lot off Kamehameha Highway, which is closed on Sunday.

Malaekahana State Recreation Area

Continuing up the same crescent of sand from Hukilau Beach, you'll come to the **Malaekahana State Recreation Area** (808/537-0800, www.hawaiistateparks.org), framed in by Kalanai Point and Goat Island to the north. When the wind is not whipping onshore from the northwest and the surf is flat, the sandy bottom makes for great swimming and crystal clear water. There is more rock and reef to the north end of the beach, which is better for snorkeling if all the other weather conditions are favorable. The beach is also a favorite for fishing. Malaekahana State Recreation Area has showers, restrooms, and picnic tables, and camping is allowed with a permit on the south side of Kalanai Point. On the north side, or Kahuku side of Kalanai Point is Malaekahana Park-Kahuku section, a private 37-acre camping area. The entrance to Malaekahana State Recreation Area is off Kamehameha Highway and well marked; the beach is not visible from the highway. Follow the road back to the parking lot, which is known as a high theft area. The entrance to the Malaekahana Park-Kahuku section is just north of the state recreation area. Look for a small faded blue sign on the side of the road. From Labor Day to March 31 the recreation area is open 7am-6:45pm daily. From April 1 to Labor Day it remains open till 7:45pm daily.

Snorkeling and Diving

This region has some great snorkeling locales, but it's up to you find the best spots. The windward side is heavily affected by the trade winds, which create chop on the ocean surface and stir up sediment in the water. Beaches with an outer reef that blocks the surf and shallow, protected inner waters with a mix of rock, reef, and sand are best. And unless you're heading to Kailua, where the snorkeling is subpar, you'll need to have your own gear ready at hand because there are no shops to rent equipment along the windward coast. Scuba diving is centered in Maunalua Bay, with charters leaving from Hawai'i Kai Marina.

SNORKELING

Beyond Makapu'u Point, most of the windward coast is fringed by an outer reef, which creates calm and shallow nearshore waters. Add an ocean floor covered in rock and reef to that equation and you have the perfect conditions for snorkeling. **Waimanalo, Kualoa, Ka'a'awa, Hau'ula,** and **La'ie** all have great beaches to explore in mask and fins, as long as weather conditions are also cooperating. Wind is always a factor on the windward side, as the trade winds barrel straight into the coastline, creating chop on the water surface—the stronger the trades, the choppier the ocean. The northern windward beaches, like Hau'ula and La'ie, are also prone to high surf in the winter months, which creates dangerous ocean currents and can stir up the usually crystal clear water. Because of the dips and bends in the coastline, ocean conditions can vary greatly from beach to beach, so it can be as much of an adventure to find the perfect spot to snorkel as it is to explore the water.

Most windward towns are small, residential communities without snorkeling or diving outfitters renting or selling gear, with the exception of a few options in Kailua. **Kailua Sailboards & Kayaks** (130 Kailua Rd., Ste. 101B, 808/262-2555 or 888/457-5737, www.kailuasailboards.com, 8:30am-5pm daily) rents mask, snorkel, and fins for $12 half day, $16 full day, and $48 per week. **Twogood Kayaks** (134B Hamakua Dr., 808/262-5656, www.twogoodkayaks.com, 9am-6pm Mon.-Fri., 8am-6pm Sat.-Sun.) has snorkel sets for $10 day, $35 per week. **Aaron's Dive Shop** (307 Hahani St., 808/262-2333 or 888/847-2822, www.hawaii-scuba.com, 7am-7pm Mon.-Fri., 7am-6pm Sat., 7am-5pm Sun.) also rents and sells snorkel gear.

◖ Hanauma Bay Nature Preserve

Hanauma Bay Nature Preserve (7455 Kalanianaole Hwy., 808/395-2211 or 808/396-4229, 6am-6:20pm Wed.-Mon., $7.50 admission, $1 parking) is the first Marine Life Conservation District in the state and the most popular snorkeling site on O'ahu. Located just to the east of Koko Head on the southeast shore, the bay lies within a volcanic cone with a semicircular beach and fingers of shallow reef that stretch from the edge of the bay all the way to the beach. After decades of preservation following rampant overuse, Hanauma Bay now boasts about 400 species of fish and an abundance of green sea turtles. Keep in mind that the water close to shore can get quite crowded with snorkelers and you'll have to swim a ways out to find some territory to yourself. If you're driving in, arrive as early as possible, as the parking lot usually fills to capacity by 10am and cars are turned away till others leave,

© TAKAYUKI NAKAMURA/123RF.COM

You might see a green sea turtle while snorkeling in Hanauma Bay Nature Preserve.

usually around 2pm. You can bring your own snorkel gear, or snorkel sets are available to rent for $12 per day. There are also food concessions at the beach. Visitors are required to view a short film and presentation about the preserve and proper etiquette while snorkeling. Admission is free for children under 13 and Hawaii residents.

DIVING

Island Divers (377 Keahole St., 808/423-8222 or 888/844-3483, www.oahuscubadiving.com, 6am-8pm daily) is a PADI 5-Star Dive Center that operates out of the Hawaii Ka'i Shopping Center. They cater to all levels of divers and offer PADI certification courses. They have pickup and drop-off services available from Waikiki hotels, or you can meet at their own private dock. Their two-tank boat charter dives start at $85. Island Divers is a complete dive center as well, with snorkel and scuba equipment available for rent and sale.

Reef Pirates Diving (7192 Kalanianaole

Hwy., 808/348-2700, www.reefpirates.com, 7am-6pm daily) also operates in Hawai'i Kai, but is based in the Koko Marina Shopping Center. They are a complete dive center with sales and rentals and offer PADI certification as well as dive charters. Their two-tank charters start at $120.

A complete dive shop based in Kailua, with scuba and diving sales and rentals, **Aaron's Dive Shop** (307 Hahani St., 808/262-2333 or 888/847-2822, www.hawaii-scuba.com, 7am-7pm Mon.-Fri., 7am-6pm Sat., 7am-5pm Sun.) offers certification and dive charters out of Hawai'i Kai Marina. They have pickup and drop-off service for Waikiki hotels, or you can meet at the shop or the dock. Two-tank charters start at $130.

China Walls

Maunalua Bay, which stretches from Kahala to Koko Head along the southeastern shore, has a wealth of dive sites and several operators that specifically service this region, with charters leaving from the Hawai'i Kai Marina. Special to the area is a dive site known as **China Walls.** This vertical wall drops off the south side of Koko Head and reaches down to depths of 75 feet. Its caves and ledges attract sharks, turtles, jacks, rays, eels, and the endangered Hawaiian monk seal. Whale songs can be heard in the area during the winter months. China Walls is located at the southernmost tip of Koko Head, the headland that frames the eastern side of Maunalua Bay.

Maunalua Bay is home to airplane- and shipwrecks, like the WWII-era Corsair plane, a barge, and a marine landing craft known as an LST. There are also caves, reefs, and overhangs where you'll find turtles, Galapagos sharks, whitetip reef sharks, eels, countless tropical fish, and rare black coral.

Diving in the Maunalua Bay is dependent on ocean and weather conditions, and high winds or high surf can cause diving conditions to deteriorate.

Surfing, Stand-Up Paddling, and Kitesurfing

The windward side is typically just that, windy, a weather condition that can adversely affect surfing conditions unless the winds are blowing offshore. Unfortunately, the windward side usually sees onshore winds, leaving little in the way of consistent, good quality waves for surfing. On the other hand, sports like sailboarding and kitesurfing that flourish in the windy conditions are popular in this region, centered around Kailua where most of the outfitters are located.

HAWAI'I KAI

The outer reefs of **Maunalua Bay** hold a wealth of surf spots for expert surfers who are comfortable with very long paddles to the breaking waves and surfing over shallow and sharp coral reefs. Because the waves break so far offshore mixed with a lack of shoreline access, it's nearly impossible for the visiting surfer to distinguish between the different breaks and know which break is surfable and which waves are breaking over dry reef.

There are some options, however, for those who would like to learn to surf, or charter a boat to surf in Maunalua Bay. **Hawaiian Surf Adventure** (7192 Kalanianaole Hwy., 808/396-2324, http://hawaiiansurfadventure. com, 9am-5pm Mon.-Sat.) accesses a secluded wave in Maunalua Bay by boat, which is a gentle surf break perfect for beginner surfers. There are no crowds to contend with, just you and the instructor. Group lessons are $89; private lessons are $149. Hawaiian Surf Adventure also offers stand-up paddle lessons and tours of Maunalua Bay starting at $99 as well as outrigger canoe tours. **Island Watersports Hawaii** (377 Keahole St., 808/224-0076, www.islandwatersportshawaii.com, 7am-7pm daily) also taps into the uncrowded waves of Maunalua Bay with two-hour group surf lessons for $99 and 1.5-hour private lessons starting at $125. If you'd rather stand-up paddle the bay, two-hour group lessons are $99 and 1.5-hour private lessons start at $125.

Sandy Beach

To the east of Koko Head is the infamous **Sandy Beach,** known for its powerful shorebreak. As a favorite of local bodyboarders and bodysurfers, the water's edge fills with heads bobbing up and down, waiting to drop into a heaving barrel, right onto the sand. If this sounds dangerous, that's because it is. Every year people are seriously injured at Sandy Beach, with everything from broken limbs to broken necks, even death. The waves can get big, especially in the summer months. If you're not a strong swimmer or comfortable in the surf zone, take solace in the fact that it's quite amusing to watch people get slammed from the safety of the beach. Check with lifeguards for current conditions. There are also two surfing breaks over a sharp and shallow coral reef, Full Point and Half Point, at the north end of the beach.

KAILUA

All along Kailua beaches, from Lanikai to Kalama Beach Park, the ocean conditions are usually just right for stand-up paddling. With a soft, sandy bottom, little to no shorebreak, and generally calm water, the area around **Kalama Beach Park** is perfect for distance paddling up and down the coast. If you paddle out from **Kailua Beach,** there is **Flat Island** to explore. And if you're paddling from **Lanikai Beach,** there is a bit more rock and reef off the beach, so you can explore the near-shore waters or paddle out to the **Mokulua Islands.** During the winter months, there are two surf breaks that reveal themselves on either side of Moku Nui, the larger of the two islands. Keep in mind that if the surf is big enough for waves to be breaking on the outer reefs, the ocean currents will be much stronger. Stand-up paddle surfing

should only be attempted by expert stand-up paddlers.

Stand-up paddling can become more of a chore than a pleasurable experience in extremely windy conditions. When the wind does pick up and the ocean surface becomes choppy and bumpy, sailboarders and kitesurfers take to the water in Kailua instead.

You can rent stand-up paddle boards at **Kailua Sailboards & Kayaks** (130 Kailua Rd., Ste. 101B, 808/262-2555 or 888/457-5737, www.kailuasailboards.com, 8:30am-5pm daily) for $49 half day and $59 full day, with multiday prices and free carts to walk the board to the beach. They rent beginner and advanced sailboard setups starting at $59 half day and $69 full day, and offer a Windsurf Tour for $99. They have kiteboards and gear for sale, but pre-ordering your gear is recommended. The retail outlet is within walking distance of Kailua Beach Park. **Windward Watersports** (33 Hoolai St., 808/261-7873, www.windward-watersports.com, 9am-5pm daily) is a complete water sports shop selling new and used boards and gear for many activities. They rent stand-up paddle boards starting at $49 half day and $59 full day, with two-hour lessons for $99. They rent kiteboards starting at $30. Actual rental of the kite is contingent upon your skill level, or beginners can take a one-hour course with a certified instructor. Located in Kailua town, they'll help you put racks and watercraft on your vehicle for the short drive to the beach. **Hawaiian WaterSports** (167 Hamakua Dr., 808/262-5483, www.hawaiianwatersports.com, 9am-5pm daily) also located in Kailua, rents stand-up paddle boards starting at $69 for a full day with multiday rentals. They have a wide range of boards 7-14 feet and boards for all skill levels, and you can exchange your board at any time during your rental period. Sailboard rentals start at $59 half day, $69 full day, and they also offer two-hour lessons—group lessons start at $99, private for $179. Kiteboards are also available for rent starting at $29 per day. Different lessons are offered depending on your skill level. Private lessons start at $179 for 1.5 hours of instruction.

O'AHU

Kayaking and Boating

KAILUA
Kailua Beach Park

The same reasons that make **Kailua Beach Park** an attractive destination for swimming, stand-up paddling—shallow and calm water, and beautiful views all around—make it the hub for kayaking on O'ahu. You can launch from Kailua Beach Park and paddle out to Flat Island, or paddle up and down the coast. Another popular place to launch from is Lanikai.

Those not comfortable with a little chop on the ocean surface can also kayak in Ka'elepulu Stream, which spills into the ocean at Kailua Beach Park. The stream opens up into Ka'elepulu Pond, a wetland area that was flooded to create the Enchanted Lake neighborhood. The water in the stream will contain urban runoff, and if the mouth of the stream has not opened in some time, it can be a bit stinky. On the other side of the coin, the water will be smooth, calm, and more protected from the wind. Just try not to get wet. For first-time kayakers, a group tour is a great way to get acquainted with the water.

🄲 Mokulua Islands

The **Mokulua Islands,** less than a mile offshore from Kailua Beach, are a popular draw. You can actually land on Moku Nui, the larger, more northern island. There's an inviting beach on the leeward side, just make sure to pull your kayak all the way up to the rocks to allow other people to land. Pack a lunch and put your camera in a dry sack because the view of mainland O'ahu from the island is breathtaking. There is trail that circles the island, but make sure to remain on the trail because the island is a seabird nesting sanctuary.

Outfitters

In Kailua, you can rent kayaks at **Hawaiian WaterSports** (167 Hamakua Dr., 808/262-5483, www.hawaiianwatersports.com,

9am-5pm daily). Single kayaks start at $49 half day, and double kayaks start at $59 half day. All rentals include life vests, paddles, seats, backrests, and dry bags. Add a snorkel set to a kayak rental for an extra $15. They also offer two- and four-hour group and private tours of Kane'ohe Bay and the Mokulua Islands. Rates start at $99 per person for the group tour and $179 for private tours.

Windward Watersports (33 Hoolai St., 808/261-7873, www.windwardwatersports. com, 9am-5pm daily) rents single kayaks starting at $49 half day, double kayaks for $55 half day, and triple kayaks for $79 half day. Kayaks can be picked up at their retail store or dropped off and ready for you at the beach. They offer a three-hour guided excursion to Flat Island and Lanikai Beach for $95, a four-hour guided adventure that includes a trip to

Whale-Watching

Humpback whales make an annual migration of 3,500 miles from the Gulf of Alaska to the warm waters of the main Hawaiian Islands every winter. While the greatest congregation of whales is found off the windward coast of Maui, humpback whales routinely frequent O'ahu waters during their Hawaii stay from October to March. Once in the shallow waters, they engage in mating behaviors and give birth to massive calves.

On the windward coast, whales can be seen breaching, tail slapping, and spitting plumes of spray from their blowhole as they cruise along the coast. Fortunately for whale-watchers, humpback whales like to congregate in the waters from Makapu'u to Koko Head, and swim very close to shore as they pass by. The lookouts at the Makapu'u Point State Wayside are a great vantage point for watching their exhibitions, as well as the several lookouts along the winding Kalanianaole Highway toward Hanauma Bay.

the Mokulua Islands and lunch for $125, and a six-hour guided fishing expedition starting at $175.

Twogood Kayaks (134B Hamakua Dr., 808/262-5656, www.twogoodkayaks.com, 9am-6pm Mon.-Fri., 8am-6pm Sat.-Sun.) rents single kayaks for $45 half day and tandem kayaks for $55 half day. Rentals come with a paddle, but there is an additional charge for a dry bag and backrest. They offer free delivery of kayaks to Ka'elepulu Stream at Kailua Beach Park and basic instruction. They will deliver kayaks to other Kailua areas for $15. Twogood Kayaks has two packages that run 9am-3pm: an Adventure Package for $75 per person with kayak rental, life jacket, paddle, lunch, and round-trip transportation from Waikiki and a Guided Tour for $125 per person with extras like a guide, snorkel gear, dry bag, and backrest.

Just across the street from Kailua Beach Park you'll find **Kailua Sailboards & Kayaks** (130 Kailua Rd., Ste. 101B, 808/262-2555 or 888/457-5737, www.kailuasailboards.com, 8:30am-5pm daily). They rent single kayaks for $59 half day, and high-performance single kayaks and double kayaks for $69 half day. Dry bag, cooler, and backrest are an additional fee. They have a four-hour guided tour for beginners that includes snorkeling, transportation from your hotel, and lunch for $129 adults and $114 children 8-12; a two-hour guided kayak tour with a one-hour massage after your paddle for $229; a four-hour guided adventure of Kailua Bay, Flat Island, and the Mokulua Islands with snorkeling, lunch, and hotel transportation for $179; and a six-hour exploration tour for experienced kayakers with snorkeling, lunch, and hotel pickup for $249.

HAWAI'I KAI

Hawaii Ka'i Marina and Maunalua Bay are home to all the aquatic thrill rides available in this region for adventure seekers. Wakeboard, water ski, and ride a Bumper Tube and Banana Boat at high speeds in the marina, or Jet Ski, parasail, and drive a sub scooter in the bay.

New to the lineup is Jetlev flight, using a controlled, water-propelled jet pack that can send you soaring 30 feet into the air.

Sea Breeze Watersports (377 Keahole St., #E-103, 808/396-0100, www.seabreezewatersports.com, opens 8:30am daily), based in the Hawaii Ka'i Shopping Center, has a wide range of activities on offer. Bumper Tubes and Banana Boat rides are $49 per person, Jet Ski rentals are $49 per person for a two-seater and $69 for a single rider. Jet Ski rates are based on half-hour rides. Parasail flights are $49 per person for a 7- to 10-minute ride, with two people sailing at a time, and Sea Breeze is the only outfitter offering the Jetlev flight, starting at $169 for 15 minutes. They also offer snorkeling, scuba, speed sailing, and surfing lessons, and have discounts for multiple activity reservations.

Island Watersports Hawaii (377 Keahole St., 808/224-0076, www.islandwatersportshawaii.com, 7am-7pm daily), also based in the Hawaii Ka'i Shopping Center, has the sub scooter, an electric submersible scooters that allow you to explore underwater without diving or scuba gear; $99 for a 20-minute ride. They have kayak tours starting at $99 per person, two-hour whale-watching cruises from November to May for $99, two-hour turtle watching and sunset cruises also for $99 per person. In addition they offer snorkeling, scuba, fishing, and hiking adventure packages.

Based in the Koko Marina Shopping Center, behind Kona Brewing Company, **Hawaii Water Sports Center** (7192 Kalanianaole Hwy., 808/395-3773, http://hawaiiwatersportscenter.com, 8:30am-4pm daily) is another operator offering a slew of activities. Bumper tube and Banana Boat rides run $29 per person, wakeboarding and water skiing run $49 per person, and parasailing is $59 per person and they flight side-by-side riders. Jet Skis are also available for $49 per person for two riders, and $69 for a single-person craft. They also offer scuba and snorkeling packages and multiple activity discounts.

Fishing

Shoreline fishing and spearfishing are popular activities on the windward coast, whether for hobby, sport, or sustenance. Between Sandy Beach and La'ie, there are miles of accessible coastline where you can pull out the rod and reel, or hold your breath, and fish. You can shoreline fish from the beaches of **Waimanalo, Kailua, Ka'a'awa, Kahana, Punalu'u, Hau'ula, La'ie Point State Wayside,** and **Malaekahana State Recreation Area.** In Kane'ohe Bay, people often fish from **He'eia Pier.** In some areas, especially from Kualoa to Kahana, where the ocean pushes right up again the highway, you can find a place to pull off on the shoulder, pop up a tent, and cast a line. Spearfishing is also popular along the shallow nearshore waters where rock and reef make up the ocean bottom. Waimanalo, Kualoa, Ka'a'awa, and Malaekahana State Recreation Area are all good spots to spearfish, and octopus, locally known as *tako,* is abundant in these areas—if you can find them.

If you're inclined to get out on the open water to fish, kayak fishing is the easiest way to go. Waimanalo, Kailua, and Kane'ohe Bay are more protected from the wind and better for fishing from a kayak. Ka'a'awa also has nice long stretches of nearshore water to troll as well, but is more prone to the trade winds.

The deep waters off the southeast and windward coast can be rough, so deep-sea fishing charters stick to the south and west shores. But the dark blue deep also holds the bigger fish like wahoo, yellowfin tuna, and marlin. **Island Watersports Hawaii** (377 Keahole St., 808/224-0076, www.islandwatersportshawaii.com, 7am-7pm daily) is the only fishing charter operating out of the Hawaii Ka'i Marina. Depending on ocean and weather conditions, they troll for big game fish or fish the ledges off of Maunalua Bay. The charter is $300 per hour, with a four-hour minimum and six-passenger maximum. Fishing gear and a captain are included in the price, and they will let you keep some of your catch, something a lot of charters don't offer. Call the office, located in the Hawaii Ka'i Shopping Center, to inquire about discounted rates.

Fishponds

Ancient Hawaiians communities were organized by *ahupua'a,* land divisions that stretched in giant swaths from the mountains all the way into the sea. Fishing was just as important as farming, and pre-contact Hawaiians were expert at both. Fishponds were constructed in shallow, nearshore waters by the people of the *ahupua'a* to store fish for food, because high surf and adverse ocean conditions often kept them onshore. This way they could guarantee a catch. Even more important, the fishponds were constructed as spawning grounds to ensure sustainability of certain species. In fact, Hawaiian fishponds were the first marine protected areas in Hawaii, and the people were not allowed to catch the fish that were spawning and considered *kapu,* off limits.

The fishponds were made by building a wall of stone on the reef that would enclose a body of water. The remnants of these fishponds are visible up and down the windward coast, and some are being restored and put into practice. There is the Moli'i fishpond at Kualoa Ranch, the Huilua fishpond in Kahana Bay, the Kahalu'u fishpond, the Pahonu Pond at Kaiona Beach Park in Waimanalo, which was also used to keep turtles, and He'eia fishpond on the north end of Kane'ohe Bay. Friends of He'eia Fishpond is a nonprofit organization dedicated to maintaining the working fishpond for the community.

If you're coming from Honolulu and forget your fishing gear, you'll need to stop at **Nanko Fishing Supply** (46-003 Alaloa St., 808/247-0938, 8am-6pm Mon., 8am-8pm Tues.-Sat., 9am-2pm Sun.), the hub of fishing gear for the windward side. Also, **Longs** (46-047 Kamehameha Hwy., 808/235-4511, 7am-midnight daily) in the Kaneohe Bay Shopping Center sells basic fishing supplies and three-prong spears.

Hiking, Biking, and Bird-Watching

HIKING
Hawai'i Kai
For a great cardio workout and 360-degree views of the southeast shore, the **Koko Crater Trail** is a daunting 1,048 steps up the south side of Koko Crater. The stairs, actually railroad ties, follow the track of an old World War II military tramway that took supplies to the top of Koko Crater more than 1,000 feet to the summit. At the top you'll find several cement military installations and amazing views all around. From Kalanianaole Highway, turn *mauka* onto Koko Head Park Road and park in the Koko Head District Park parking lot. It's about a 0.25-mile walk to the base of the stairs.

Kailua
There is a popular walking trail along **Kawainui Marsh,** one of the few wetland ecosystems on O'ahu and home to several species of native waterbirds like the Hawaiian coot, Hawaiian moorhen, and the Hawaiian stilt along with a host of other feathered inhabitants. The mile-long path is a raised, paved trail that crosses the marsh from Kailua Road to Kaha Street, off Oneawa Street on the north end of the Kailua neighborhood known as Coconut Grove.

© KEVIN WHITTON

Follow 1,048 stairs to the top of Koko Crater, in Hawai'i Kai.

Maunawili Falls is a short hike in the shadow of Olomana that follows Maunawili Stream and terminates at the falls. From Kalanianaole Highway, turn into A'uola Road in the Maunawili neighborhood. Immediately fork left onto Maunawili Road and follow it

Riding the Thermals

The drastic, verdant and corduroy cliffs of the **Ko'olau Range** are not actually mountains in the traditional sense, but the remnants of the western half of the Ko'olau Volcano, which erupted nearly two million years ago. The caldera and eastern portion are thought to have slid cataclysmically into the ocean in prehistoric times. As erosion has chipped away at the peaks over hundreds of thousands of years, the tallest peak, Pu'u Konahuanui, now measures only 3,100 feet, but was once thought to be about three times that height. Spanning the entire windward coast, the smaller and more recent volcanoes we refer to today as Diamond Head, Punchbowl Crater, Hanauma Bay, Koko Crater, Koko Head, and Tantalus were all created by eruptions from the Ko'olau Volcano.

The pervasive, fresh trade winds blowing up against the Ko'olau Range, combined with the splendid beauty of clear, tropical waters and verdant cliffs, create the perfect amphitheater for **hang gliding** and **paragliding.** Makapu'u is the premier ridge-soaring site with five launch zones and one landing zone on the beach. Pilots also fly in the Kahana area. These are not recreational activities where you can merely rent a hang glider and jump off a cliff, but regulated endeavors for trained pilots who must register with one of the accredited associations on O'ahu to fly from specific sites.

Visiting paragliding pilots with their own gear should contact the **Hawaii Paragliding Association** (53-040 Pokiwai Pl., www.windlines.net). Contact any board member to become a member and get in the air. Visiting hang gliding pilots with gear need to contact the **Hawaiian Hang Gliding Association** (45-015 Likeke Pl., http://files.windlines.net/hha/index.htm).

through the subdivision and a forested area to the end at Kelewina Street. Park near the intersection and continue on foot on the one-lane private road. A sign indicates the way to the falls, which in part is on private land, so stay on the trail. Along the stream look for *'ape,* a plant with huge, elephant-ear-shaped leaves. A ridgeline section offers views of Ko'olau Range, Olomana and Kane'ohe Bay. Regain the stream and follow it to a large, deep pool and Maunawili Falls. On the hike you'll cross the stream several times and the trail can be quite muddy. It is also very popular and heavily used on the weekends. There is a second smaller pool at the top of the falls and the trail continues back from there if you wish to continue exploring the forest.

BIKING
Kailua

Kailua is the most bike-friendly town on O'ahu. The beaches and neighborhoods are in relatively close proximity to the town center, where all the di ning, shopping, and services are located. The town is flat, the weather is exceptional, and the traffic is usually so congested that it's faster to get around on two wheels. In addition to riding around town, bikes are allowed on the trail that crosses the Kawainui Marsh.

Because of these factors, Kailua is home to the first bike share program in the state. There are two **Hawaii B-cycle** kiosks in the town center: 767 Hamakua Drive (near the intersection of Hamakua Dr. and Kailua Rd.), and 515 Kailua Road (near the intersection of Hahani St. and Kailua Rd.). Simply swipe your credit card at the kiosk, grab a bike, and go. When you park the bike at either location, your card is charged for the time you used it. The cruisers come equipped with a lock, comfy seat, and baskets.

Or you can rent a bike the traditional way, from an outfitter. **The Bike Shop** (270 Kuulei Rd., 808/261-1553, www.bikeshophawaii.com/kailua, 10am-7pm Mon.-Fri., 9am-5pm Sat., 10am-5pm Sun.) is a full-service bicycle shop. They rent 21-speed cruisers for $20 per day and road bikes for $40 per day. **Kailua Sailboards & Kayaks** (130 Kailua Rd., Ste. 101B, 808/262-2555 or 888/457-5737, www.kailuasailboards.com, 8:30am-5pm daily) rents bikes for $25 a full day and $85 for seven days.

BIRD-WATCHING
Kuli'ou'ou

Just to the west of Kuli'ou'ou Beach Park, the **Paiko Lagoon Wildlife Sanctuary** was established in 1981 to protect native Hawaiian waterbirds, migratory species, and their habitat. Hawaiian stilts, plovers, ducks, and other fowl grace the shallow lagoon, which is naturally separated from Maunalua Bay by a small strip of earth complete with plants and trees. It is illegal to remove anything from the area.

Kailua

There are several areas perfect for bird-watching in Kailua. The 800-acre **Kawainui Marsh** is the largest wetland area in the state. A paved trail traverses it from Kailua Road to Kaha Street, about a mile long. Look for native Hawaiian waterbirds, migrant waterfowl, and other curious residents, like the black-crowned night heron with its large black beak and piercing red eyes. Binoculars are a must for this area.

If you don't have binoculars and want to get an up-close look at a Hawaiian moorhen or a Hawaiian stilt, check out the **Hamakua Marsh,** which parallels Hamakua Drive. In the parking lot behind Down To Earth market is a viewing area with informative signs about the residents of the marsh. Though the parking lot leaves much to be desired for a natural setting for

A coot is spotted in Kailua.

© KEVIN WHITTON

bird-watching, many of the native Hawaiian waterbirds congregate here in large numbers.

Another area close by to view waterbirds is in the Enchanted Lake neighborhood. The **Ka'elepulu Wetland Bird Preserve** is a small wetland area bordered by homes, and this little nook is a favorite for waterbirds. In addition to the Hawaiian duck, stilt, moorhen, and coot, look for red-footed boobies and great frigatebirds. From Keolu Drive, turn into Kiukee Place, a short dead-end road. Park and watch the birds from the sidewalk.

Golf

HAWAI'I KAI

With beautiful views of Koko Crater, the Makapu'u cliffs, and the Pacific Ocean, the **Hawaii Kai Golf Course** (8902 Kalanianaole Hwy., 808/395-2358, www.hawaiikaigolf.com) is both enjoyable and challenging. The Championship Course has the largest greens in the state with deep bunkers, and the Executive Coarse, a much shorter layout with undulating, sloping greens, focuses on putting and chipping for the most advanced golfers. The wind is always a factor as well, blowing straight off the ocean and creating another factor to consider on these courses. Greens fees for the Championship Course are $110, $70 twilight (after 1pm) and for Executive Course are $38.50 weekday, $43.50 weekend. The entrance to the golf course is right off Kalanianaole Highway, between Sandy Beach Park and Makapuʻu.

WAIMANALO

Just outside of Waimanalo town, on the Kailua side, is **Olomana Golf Links** (41-1801 Kalanianaole Hwy., 808/259-7926, www.olomanagolflinks.com), an 18-hole, par-72 course. The front nine has level fairways and water hazards at every hole, while the back nine features rolling hills and sand bunkers. The course also has stunning views of the Koʻolau Mountains. Play 18 holes with a cart for $95, $80 second

visit, and $60 each additional visit. Twilight greens fees are $80 after 1:30pm.

KANEʻOHE

Bay View Golf Park (45-285 Kaneohe Bay Dr., 808/247-0451, www.bayviewgolfcourse.com) is an affordable 18-hole course in Kaneʻohe that has a double-decker range facility and is open for night play during the week. Visitor rates are $18 weekday, $26 weekend, $10 cart fee for 9 holes, and $26 weekday, $34 weekend, $14 cart fee for 18 holes.

For a more scenic and lush experience, visit the 18-hole **Pali Golf Course** (45-050 Kamehameha Hwy., 808/233-7499). This challenging, hillside course has three sets of tees for different skill levels. Greens fees are $50 daily.

Spas

KAHALA

Based in the ritzy Kahala Hotel & Resort, **Kahala Spa** (5000 Kahala Ave., 808/739-8938, www.kahalaresort.com/spa, 8am-9pm daily) has 10 lavish, tropically decorated treatment rooms with shower, deep-soak tub, changing area, and wardrobe closet. Known for their award-winning exceptional service, the staff combines the latest trends in spa therapy with organically grown, natural, and locally sourced ingredients from Hawaii to produce the finest results in healing, relaxing, detoxifying, and rejuvenation. One-hour massages start at $170, with four different styles; 30-minute poolside massages and treatments start at $60; one-hour facials start at $160; and 75-minute signature massages begin at $230. They offer teeth whitening, waxing, and nail care service, as well as 90-minute massage and body treatment packages starting at $250.

KAILUA

Honu You Hawaiian Spa (122 Oneawa St., 808/261-1268, www.honuyou.com) focuses on balance and simplicity. They have

treatments on par with the major hotel spas and, in addition, employ an educated staff focused on providing the individual with designer treatments. They offer three levels of service experience: Junior Therapists, Senior Therapists, and Master Therapists. Facials with a Master Therapist start at $48 for 30 minutes, lomi lomi and body treatments with a Master Therapist start at $35 for 30 minutes, and they have a two-hour couples package for $340. Honu You provides waxing services as well. There is also a location next to the Kailua Wellness Center on the other side of the Kailua town center (320 Ulumiu St., 808/261-5200, 9am-5pm Tues.-Sat.).

Located near many of the other wellness providers in downtown Kailua, **Maluhia Face & Body** (408 Uluniu St., 808/262-2100, www.maluhiafaceandbody.com, 9am-5pm Tues.-Fri., 9am-3pm Sat.) is a boutique day spa offering massage, skin care, and waxing. Facials start at $85 for 55 minutes, or they have an express facial, $45 for a 30-minute treatment. Massages start at $75 for 55 minutes, and they offer a signature massage, lomi lomi, and deep tissue massage.

Sights

HAWAI'I KAI
Haunama Bay Nature Preserve Park

The first marine protected area in the state of Hawaii, **Hanauma Bay Nature Preserve Park** (7455 Kalanianaole Hwy., 808/395-2211 or 808/396-4229, 6am-6:20pm Wed.-Mon.) is the most popular snorkeling site on O'ahu. Located just to the east of Koko Head on the southeast shore, the nearly circular bay lies within a volcanic cone with a semicircular beach and fingers of shallow reef that stretch from the edge of the bay all the way to the beach. If you're driving in, arrive as early as possible, as the parking lot usually fills to capacity by 10am and cars are turned away till others leave, usually around 2pm. There is a $1 parking fee per car and a $7.50 entry fee. Children under 13 are free. You can bring your own snorkel gear or rent snorkel sets for $12 per day. There are also food concessions at the beach. Visitors are required to view a short film and presentation about the preserve and proper etiquette while snorkeling.

Halona Blowhole

Formed by molten lava tubes meeting with the ocean, the **Halona Blowhole** funnels ocean surges through a narrow opening in the rock to create a geyser that can send a plume of spray 30 feet into the air. The blowhole isn't always active; it takes a windy day, a high tide, and high surf on the windward side to get the blast really shooting high. However, if you're there on an off day, the view toward Sandy Beach is still worth the stop.

The Halona Blowhole is located along the Kalanianaole Highway, in between Sandy Beach and Makapu'u. There is a good-sized parking lot located on the cliff side of Kalanianaole Highway, and several designated viewing areas along the cliff, right above the blowhole.

◖ Koko Crater Botanical Garden

Sited inside arid Koko Crater, **Koko Crater Botanical Garden** (end of Kokonani St., 808/522-7060, www1.honolulu.gov/parks/hbg/kcbg.htm, closed Christmas Day and New Year's Day) takes advantage of the sheltered spot for plantings of rare and endangered dryland plant species from around the world. Koko Crater is actually two craters in one, an inner and outer crater, of which 60 acres of the basin have been cultivated. A two-mile loop trail takes you from the fragrant and magnificent hybrid plumeria grove in the inner crater, to a stand of native Hawaiian *wiliwili* trees in the back of the outer crater. In between are succulents, cycads, and over 200 species of trees. The plumeria grove is in full bloom April to June. There are no facilities on-site, except for a lone portable toilet, so it's best to use those at nearby Sandy Beach Park. To get here from Kalanianaole Highway, turn onto Kealahou Street, then turn left onto Kokonani Street. The paved road becomes a dirt road and ends at the garden parking lot. The gardens are open from sunrise to sunset, and there are trail maps at the entrance gate.

MAKAPU'U TO WAIMANALO
◖ Makapu'u Point State Wayside

Makapu'u, which translates to "bulging eye" in Hawaiian, marks the rugged and dry eastern tip of O'ahu. The rough black rock is dotted with cacti and small flowering shrubs, like the native Hawaiian *'ilima* with its cute yellow and orange blossoms. The **Makapu'u Point State Wayside** holds several areas of interest. There are two parking lots at Makapu'u. Coming from Hawai'i Kai on Kalanianaole Highway, the first parking lot offers direct access to the trail that rounds Makapu'u Point and leads to the Makapu'u Point Lighthouse. Roughly a 3-mile round-trip walk, the wide, paved road gains elevation gradually as you circle the point from the south to face the

O'AHU

© KEVIN WHITTON

Koko Crater Botanical Garden is dedicated to dryland species.

Pacific Ocean. On a clear day you can see the islands of Moloka'i and Maui in the far distance. The hike has an added bonus of being one of the premier whale-watching venues while the humpback whales breed and rear their young in Hawaiian waters from November to March. It is also cooler during this period as well, as the shadeless hike can get rather hot in the midday, summer sun. There are informational signs along the trail about humpback whale activity and behavior.

At the end of the hike are a couple lookout platforms and the **Makapu'u Point Lighthouse,** a 46-foot-tall active lighthouse constructed in 1909. The lighthouse itself is off limits to the public, but you can get close enough to get a nice picture with the blue Pacific as the backdrop. Feel free to scamper around the rocks and explore the summit at 647 feet, but be careful as the area is scattered with sharp rocks, boulders, and cactus.

At the second parking lot, just to the north of the first, is a magnificent lookout area with views of the Waimanalo Coast, the rugged southern end of the Ko'olau Range, and two nearby offshore islands, **Manana Island and Koahikaipu Island State Seabird Sanctuary.** The islands are home to nesting wedge-tailed shearwaters, sooty terns, brown noodies, and several other species. It is illegal to set foot on the islands. Manana Island is commonly referred to as Rabbit Island, because a rancher actually tried to raise rabbits here prior to its designation as a seabird sanctuary.

If you consider yourself an avid hiker, from the lookout you can scramble up the back side of the point to the summit, regain the trail near the lighthouse, and follow the paved path back to the lookout for a nice loop.

KAILUA
Ulupo Heiau State Historic Site

The massive stone platform of the **Ulupo Heiau State Historic Site** was supposedly built by the legendary *menehune* and shows remarkable skill with stone, measuring 140 feet wide by 180 feet long by 30 feet high at its tallest edge, although the stepped front wall has partially

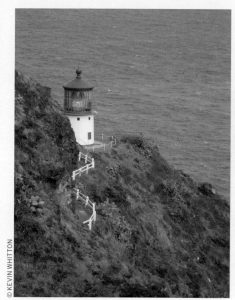
© KEVIN WHITTON

Makapu'u Point Lighthouse

collapsed under a rockfall. The *heiau* overlooks Kawainui Marsh, and below the *heiau,* you can see traditional *kalo lo'i,* taro growing in small ponds. Ulupo Heiau was one of three *heiau* that once overlooked the former fishpond. The other two, located on the west side of the marsh, are Pahukini and Holomakani Heiau. Some restoration has been done to Pahukini Heiau, but both remain largely untouched and inaccessible.

To get to Ulupo Heiau as you approach Kailua on the Pali Highway, turn left at the Castle Medical Center onto Uluoa Street, following it one block to Manu Aloha Street, where you turn right. Turn right again onto Manu O'o and park in the Windward YMCA parking lot. The *heiau* is directly behind the YMCA building.

KANE'OHE
Ho'omaluhia Botanical Garden
Ho'omaluhia Botanical Garden (45-680 Luluku Rd., 808/233-7323, www1.honolulu.gov/parks/hbg/hmbg.htm, 9am-4pm daily, closed Christmas Day and New Year's Day) is a botanical gem nestled at the base of the verdant corduroy of the Ko'olau Range. With 400 acres of geographically organized gardens—covering the Philippines, Hawaii, Africa, Sri Lanka, India, Polynesia, Melanesia, Malaysia, and Tropical America—and a network of trails interconnecting the plantings, one could spend an entire day in the garden. The Visitor Center is staffed with extremely knowledgeable docents who can help identify birds and interesting plants in flower during your visit. You can also grab a trail map there, too. A paved road links all the plantings and there are separate parking lots for each, so you can pick and choose where you'd like to spend your time. Drive slowly on the road, as the path is a lovely, popular walk for residents and garden guests. Ho'omaluhia also boasts its own lake, Lake Waimaluhia. Catch-and-release fishing is permitted on the weekends 10am-2pm. The garden is serene, quiet, lush, and often wet, so be prepared for the passing shower, mud, and mosquitoes. Rustic camping is also permitted from Friday afternoon till Monday morning. Check in at the Visitor Center for a pass. The garden is located in a residential area on Luluku Road, which you can access from both Kamehameha Highway and the Likelike Highway.

KUALOA TO LA'IE
Chinaman's Hat
Just offshore from Kualoa Regional Beach Park (49-479 Kamehameha Hwy.) is the curious islet known as **Chinaman's Hat.** Mokoli'i Island is its Hawaiian name. The island is a quick kayak trip from the beach and has a tiny private alcove of sand on the back side. You can hike, or rather scramble, up to its 213-foot summit.

Kualoa Ranch
Kualoa Ranch (49-560 Kamehameha Hwy., 808/237-7321, www.kualoa.com) is both a 4,000-acre working cattle ranch, activity, and cultural center and the site for many of the Hollywood blockbuster movies filmed in Hawaii. They offer historical and cultural

OAHU

© KEVIN WHITTON

Chinaman's Hat sits just offshore from Kualoa Regional Beach Park.

tours like their Movie Sites and Ranch Tour, Jungle Expeditions Tour, Ancient Fishing Grounds and Tropical Garden Tour, or Kahiko Hula Lessons starting at $24 adult, $15 children. They provide one- and two-hour ATV or horseback packages, starting at $69. They also have venues for weddings and corporate events, and even have tours that include lunch or dinner. Cultural/historic tour package tours start at $59, adventure tour packages start at $99.

La'ie Point State Wayside

The **La'ie Point State Wayside** is a hidden marvel, the perfect place to pull up to the edge of the rugged point, relax, have a snack, and watch waves crash against a small seabird sanctuary just offshore, a little island noteworthy for its sea arch. There are trash cans, but no services in the area. It is also a popular spot for cliff jumping. On the south face of the cliff is a small area where jumpers plunge roughly 30 feet to the warm water below. There is a nook in the cliff to climb

out of the water and up an extremely sharp and rocky gorge to the top of the cliff. It's best to watch a few others jump and get back up before you try. There are no lifeguards, and you're on your own, quite far from a sandy beach.

Tucked away at the back of a neighborhood and out of view from the highway, turn off of Kamehameha Highway onto Anemoku Street, then hang a right onto Naupaka Street and follow it to the end of the point. Anemoku Street is across the highway from the Laie Village Center.

Laie Hawaii Temple

Built in 1919, the **Laie Hawaii Temple** (55-600 Naniloa Loop, 808/293-2427, www.ldschurch-temples.com/laie, 9am-8pm daily) was the first temple erected by the Church of Jesus Christ of Latter-day Saints outside the state of Utah, and also the first in Polynesia. You can tour the grounds and gardens of this stark white, grand edifice, and there's an accompanying visitors' center free to the public.

© KEVIN WHITTON

La'ie Point State Wayside

Shopping

KAHALA

The small and airy, two-story **Kahala Mall** (4211 Waialae Ave., 808/732-7736, www.kahalamallcenter.com, 10am-9pm Mon.-Sat., 10am-5pm Sun.) is conveniently located right off the H-1 freeway. From Honolulu, take the Waialae Avenue exit and the mall is on your right. Some of the boutique stores are worth a look. **Super Citizen** (808/599-4333) offers a new look and style that combines sustainable living with modern fashion. Their original jewelry, art, and clothing are all sourced locally and made with earth-friendly materials. **In My Closet** (808/734-5999) is a small, hip boutique with eclectic and fashionable clothing and accessories. **Island Sole** (808/738-8430) is a one-stop shop for slippers, or what you might call flip-flops or sandals. Check out the plethora of shells and beachy knickknacks at **SoHa Living** (808/591-9777).

KAILUA

In downtown Kailua, park the car, get outside, and walk around the busy town center, where most of Kailua businesses are located. There are definitely some great finds in Kailua town.

Haute couture has made its mark on the seaside hamlet of Kailua thanks to **Mu'umu'u Heaven** (767 Kailua Rd., 808/263-3366, www.muumuuheaven.com, 10am-6pm Mon.-Sat., 11am-4pm Sun.), a fashionable and stylish boutique that sells island-style dresses made from vintage mu'umu'u and aloha wear. The store is warm and inviting, the staff is extremely friendly, and the outfits are in high demand. The one-of-a-kind pieces are handmade right in Hawaii. They also sell art, handmade and unique jewelry and accessories, vintage home decor, recycled T-shirts, and collared shirts for the guys.

Get your fill of reading material at **Book**

Ends (600 Kailua Rd., 808/261-1996, 9am-8pm Mon.-Sat., 9am-11pm Sun.), a great independent bookstore (one of the few left) with volumes stacked ceiling to floor. The knowledgeable staff can get you into the perfect book for your stay. For records, CDs, and other music paraphernalia, check out **Hungry Ear Records** (418 Kuulei Rd., 808/262-2175, http://hungryear.com, 10:30am-6pm Mon.-Sat.), a classic independent record store with a great selection of new and used music. Hungry Ear is a must for record collectors. If you'd rather play than listen to music, next door is Kailua's famous **Coconut Grove Music** (418 Kuulei Rd., 808/262-9977, www.coconutgrovemusic.com, 10am-6pm Mon.-Sat., 11am-4pm Sun.), a complete music store selling new, used, and vintage instruments. There's nothing like strumming a ukulele while you're relaxing on Kailua Beach. And if by chance you need a new swimsuit for said beach, **Pualani** (111 Hekili St., Ste. 102, 808/262-3830, http://pualanikailua.com, 10am-7pm Mon.-Sat., 10am-5pm Sun.) is a smart bikini boutique with functional mix-and-match suits and women's activewear.

For local farm-fresh produce and prepared foods, hit up the **Kailua at Night** farmers market (609 Kailua Rd., 5pm-7:30pm Thurs.). The market sets up in the covered parking lot by Longs.

There is also a Sunday market featuring all local farmers and vendors: **Kailua Town Farmers' Market** (315 Kuulei Rd., 808/388-9696, http://haleiwafarmersmarket.com, 9am-1pm Sun.) sets up in the Kailua Elementary School parking lot. Just look for the rows of white tents.

Entertainment

NIGHTLIFE
Hawai'i Kai
The Shack (377 Keahole St., 808/396-1919, 11am-2am daily, $7-24) is the quintessential pub and sports bar, with dark wood furniture, darts, pool, and TVs all around. The curious decorations make this bar come alive. It's located right on the water in the Hawaii Ka'i Shopping Center, with outside seating as well. The happy hour and daily specials will make you extra happy.

Kailua
Located at the intersection of Hamakua Drive and Hahani Street, **Boardriders Bar & Grill** (201 Hamakua Dr., 808/261-4600, www.boardridersbarandgrill.com, noon-2am daily, $9-15) is better known as a bar than a grill, but they do serve pizza, salad, steak, stir-fry, and classic bar munchies. Boardriders has a couple pool tables and is the best venue for catching live music on the windward side. The bar sees local, national, and international artists and favors reggae and jawaiian music. *Pau hana* is 4pm-6pm daily.

Nestled next to the Hamakua Marsh is the friendly blue-collar bar called **The Creekside Lounge** (153 Hamakua Dr., 808/262-6466, http://creeksidelounge.com, 8am-2am daily). Established in 1982, the Creekside is a biker bar with a cadre of friendly female bartenders. The bar shows live sporting events and is no frills, but they have a huge local following. Smoking is allowed on the patio overlooking the marsh, where most patrons regularly spill out to.

CULTURAL TOURS AND LUAU
The windward side has two venues for cultural tours and luau. **Kualoa Ranch** (49-560 Kamehameha Hwy., 808/237-7321, www.kualoa.com) offers hikes and historical and cultural tours of the working ranch, bordering valleys, and coastline. Established in 1850, the ranch is steeped in tradition and has a unique perspective and story to tell. Tours are $24 adult and

$15 child; the hike is $15 adult and includes one child.

On the northern end of the windward side, in La'ie, the **Polynesian Cultural Center** (55-370 Kamehameha Hwy., www.polynesiancul-turalcenter.com, 800/367-7060, 11:30am-9pm Mon.-Sat.) introduces visitors to the people and cultures of Hawaii, Samoa, Maori New Zealand, Fiji, Tahiti, Marquesas, and Tonga as you walk through and visit the different villages and interact with the people demonstrating their specific arts and crafts. There is also a canoe ride that explores the villages as well. Dining is paramount to the experience, and you can choose between the Island Buffet with a mix of local Hawaiian fare, Prime Dining with prime rib, crab legs, and sushi in a secluded setting, or the famous Ali'i Luau, with authentic Hawaiian food including traditional *imu* pork, a large pig cooked in an earthen oven. There is also an evening show called "Ha: Breath of Life," which is a culmination of story, dance, Polynesian music, and fire. General admission, which is for the day experience only, is $49.95 adult, $39.95 child. Admission, buffet, and evening show will run $69.95 adult, $54.95 child, and packages for admission, the luau, and show start at $91.95 adult, $67.95 child.

Food

The gastronomic landscape of this vast region changes just as much as the climate as you make your way from Kahala to La'ie. In the more affluent areas, health food is king, while in others, fast food and Hawaiian food reign.

KAHALA
Steak and Seafood
Located in The Kahala Hotel & Resort is **Hoku's** (5000 Kahala Ave., 808/739-8760, www.kahalaresort.com, 5:30pm-10pm Wed.-Sun., $28-69), an award-winning fine dining restaurant. The food is a fusion of Hawaiian, Asian, and European cuisine with steak, duck, lamb, chicken, and fish entrées as well as a sushi menu. An artisan cheese menu makes for a delightful appetizer, and their Sunday brunch, 10am-2pm, features a wide variety of seafood and a prime rib and lamb cutting station.

Italian
Assaggio Bistro (4346 Waialae Ave., 808/732-1011, 11:30am-2:30pm and 5pm-9:30pm Sun.-Thurs., 5pm-10pm Fri.-Sat., $16-36) has a huge menu of classic Italian dishes. Their portions come in two sizes, small and large, with the small portion more than enough for a complete meal. Each main dish has the choice of pasta, potatoes, rice, or vegetables for the side. Reservations are recommended. To get to Assaggio from Hawai'i Kai, take the Waialae Avenue off-ramp and turn right into the parking lot from the ramp. From Waialae Avenue eastbound, turn left onto Kilauea Avenue and then make an immediate right into the parking lot.

Mediterranean
Located on the corner of Kilauea Avenue and Pahoa Avenue is a popular BYOB called the **Olive Tree Café** (4614 Kilauea Ave., Ste. 107, 808/737-0303, 5pm-10pm daily, $11-15). Offering Mediterranean and Greek fare, the menu has plenty of vegetarian, as well as meat, options. The environment is warm, friendly, and casual with both indoor and outdoor seating. The café has open seating and there is no waiter service. It is a popular joint, so it's best to arrive either early or late to avoid a long wait. Luckily, there is a wine shop just next door.

Health Food
Not only is **Whole Foods** (4211 Waialae Ave., 808/738-0820, www.wholefoodsmarket.com/stores/honolulu, 7am-10pm daily, $3.50 and up) a market where you can pick up organic

and locally grown produce and vegetables, but they also make to order sushi, Chinese food, burgers, Mexican food, and sandwiches. Sample the hot food bar, salad bar, and dessert and coffee bar. Known to be on the high side of the price point, they do have $1 street tacos on Tuesday and $2 off per pound from the hot food bar on Wednesday. They are located in the Kahala Mall, ground level, right off Waialae Avenue.

☾ Aloha Salads (4211 Waialae Ave., 808/735-8334, www.alohasalads.com, 10am-9pm daily, $6-10) is another locally owned and operated establishment dedicated to using locally sourced products and produce and gourmet meats and cheese. Their menu is simple yet sophisticated, and they have a nice selection of island-inspired soups, sandwiches, and salads. With greens from the North Shore, tomatoes from the windward side, papayas from Moloka'i, and ahi tuna from Hawaii waters, the food is fresh, delicious, and eco-conscious. The Aloha Passion with grilled steak and the Ono Island Ahi salads are the most popular. They are located inside Kahala Mall on the ground level right next to Whole Foods.

Across the street from Kahala Mall is a small strip mall on the mountain side of Waialae Avenue and the freeway overpass. Facing the Kalanianaole Highway off-ramp is **Lanikai Juice** (4346 Waialae Ave., 808/732/7200, www.lanikaijuice.com, 7am-8pm Mon.-Sat., 7am-7pm Sun., $5-8), a locally owned and operated smoothie shop that uses organic and locally sourced products.

AINA HAINA
Sweets and Treats

If you're looking to satisfy your sweet tooth, the Aina Haina Shopping Center has two delicious options. **Cake Couture** (808/373-9750, http://cakecouture.com, 10:30am-6:30pm Mon.-Fri., 10:30am-5:30pm Sat., $3-4) has ridiculously delicious cupcakes in nearly 40 distinctive flavors that rotate throughout the week. Check their website for the flavor schedule.

☾ Uncle Clay's House of Pure Aloha (808/373-5111, www.houseofpurealoha.com, 11am-6pm Mon.-Thurs., 10:30am-8pm Fri.-Sun., $4-9) indulges in the local favorite shave ice. Rising above the competition with handmade syrups actually produced from locally sourced ingredients and friendly, family-style service, Uncle Clay's takes shave ice to a new culinary level. The small shop also has healthy grab-bag snacks for sale.

HAWAI'I KAI
Steak and Seafood

At the water's edge in the Koko Marina Center in Hawai'i Kai is the **☾ Kona Brewing Co.** (7192 Kalanianaole Hwy., 808/396-5662, http://konabrewingco.com, 11am-10pm daily, $12-26), a local brewpub serving fresh steak and seafood, all with a twist—their signature brew is incorporated in some way into most of the recipes. They have a huge signature pizza menu, specialty beers on tap you can't find in the stores, and brews to go. They also have a great weekday happy hour 3pm-6pm: half off draft beers and select appetizer specials.

For fine dining in Hawai'i Kai, **☾ Roy's** (6600 Kalanianaole Hwy., 808/396-7697, 5:30pm-9pm Mon.-Thurs., 5:30pm-9:30pm Fri., 5pm-9:30pm Sat., 5pm-9pm Sun., $15-45) is a must. They serve signature Hawaiian fusion cuisine with exemplary service and attention to detail, and their sushi creations pair wonderfully with the entrées. They also have indoor and lanai bar seating that is first-come, first-served, accompanied by soft, live music, a much more casual option than the main, second floor dining room with beautiful views of Maunalua Bay.

Health Food

In the Hawai'i Kai Shopping Center is **Kale's Natural Foods** (377 Keahole St., 808/396-6993, www.kalesnaturalfoods.com, 8am-8pm Mon.-Thurs., 8am-5pm Fri.-Sat., $6-10), a market and deli serving natural products and organic produce. The small kitchen specializes in vegetarian, vegan, macrobiotic foods, and free-range meat options. The food is fresh, homemade, and surprisingly creative.

For produce direct from local farmers, the **Hawaii Kai Farmers Market** (511 Lunalilo Home Rd., 808/388-9696, http://haleiwafarmersmarket.com/hawaii-kai.html, 9am-1pm Sat.) has you covered. At the Kaiser High School parking lot location, you'll find the freshest fruits and vegetables, prepared foods like honey and jelly, baked goods, and best of all, hot food from a handful of health-conscious establishments. From Kalanianaole Highway, turn north onto Lunalilo Home Road. The market is open rain or shine.

MAKAPU'U TO WAIMANALO
Quick Bites
Waimanalo has a few places to stop and grab a quick bite as you make your way along the Kalanianaole Highway. **Keneke's Plate Lunch & BBQ** (41-857 Kalanianaole Hwy., 808/259-9811, 9:30am-5:30pm daily, $2-7) serves up the typical Hawaiian plate lunch and is very popular. **Serg's** (41-865 Kalanianaole Hwy., 808/259-7374, 11am-8pm Mon.-Sat., opens at 8am Sun., $3-12) brings Mexican food to Waimanalo with carnitas, carne asada, carne al pastor, and their famous flauta. **Sweet Home Waimanalo** (41-1025 Kalanianaole Hwy., 808/259-5737, http://sweethomewaimanalo.com, 9:30am-7pm Thurs.-Mon., 9:30am-3pm Tues.-Wed., $6-10) mixes Hawaiian-style cooking with the principles of sourcing their ingredients locally and using organic when possible.

KAILUA
Steak and Seafood
◀ **Buzz's Lanikai** (413 Kawailoa Rd., 808/261-4661, http://buzzssteakhouse.com/lanikai.htm, 11am-9:30pm daily, $17-33) is famous for its kiawe charcoal broiled burgers and steaks as well as its salads. The small, popular restaurant is quirky and fun, complete with a tree right in the middle of the lanai seating. It's right across from Kailua Beach Park, so it's usually packed with a wait. Buzz's is also known for its signature mai tai, a mix of rum with a

cherry on top. If you'd like a juice mixer with it, order the B.F.R.D. Don't forget to ask what that stands for.

Formaggio Grill (305 Hahani St., 808/263-2633, www.formaggio808.com, 11:30am-11pm Mon.-Thurs., 11:30am-1am Fri.-Sat., 11am-11pm Sun., $12-69) blends Italian dishes with favorites from the grill like prime rib, lamb chops, barbecued ribs, and filet mignon. Thin crust pizzas and rich lobster bisque complement the dishes, as does the wine-by-the-glass selection, over 50 bottles. Parking is extremely limited in front of the restaurant. Try the lot across the street by Macy's.

Quick Bites
Kalapawai Market (306 S. Kalaheo Ave., 808/262-4359, www.kalapawaimarket.com, 6am-9pm daily, $8-24) is right at Kailua Beach Park, with another location in downtown Kailua (750 Kailua Rd., 808/262-3354, 6am-9pm Mon.-Thurs., 6am-9:30pm Fri., 7am-9:30pm Sat., 7am-9pm Sun., $8-24). The beach park location has a small sandwich deli and a limited grocery store that also sells beer and wine. The downtown location is strictly a café and deli with a coffee and wine bar and bakery. Open for breakfast, lunch, and dinner with indoor and outdoor seating, they have made-to-order sandwiches and a selection of prepared gourmet foods.

Boots and Kimo's Homestyle Kitchen (151 Hekili St., 808/263-7929, 7:30am-2pm Mon.-Fri., 7am-2:30pm Sat.-Sun., $4-14) is all about pancakes, and people line up for them—macadamia nut pancakes to be exact. They also serve other traditional breakfast items and Hawaiian-style favorites all day long with a few lunch items as well. The restaurant is awash in sports memorabilia.

◀ **Morning Brew** (600 Kailua Rd., 808/262-7770, http://morningbrewhawaii.com, 6am-9pm Sun.-Thurs., 6am-10pm Fri.-Sat., $1-9) is the go-to coffeehouse and bistro in Kailua. With good coffee, a great assortment of bakery goods, sandwiches, snacks, free Internet, and two-stories of seating, plus outdoor seating, it's an easy all-day hangout if you have some work to do.

Mexican

Cactus (767 Kailua Rd., 808/261-1000, http://cactusbistro.com, 11am-10pm daily, $6-24) offers a blend of locally sourced ingredients and Central and South American cuisine, including influences from Cuba, Puerto Rico, and Mexico. The restaurant has a modern style, complete with regional wines and premium rums, tequilas, and liquors. They serve lunch and dinner.

Japanese

Noboru (201 Hamakua Dr., A-102, 808/261-3033, http://noborukailua.com, 11:30am-3pm Mon.-Sat., 5pm-9pm daily, $4-29) is the premier sushi restaurant in Kailua. They also serve teishoku, shabu-shabu, and chanko nabe. The modern bar offers over 25 different kinds of sake.

Thai

Check out **Champa Thai** (306 Kuulei Rd., 808/263-8281, www.champathai.com, 11am-2pm and 5:30pm-9:30pm Mon.-Sat., 5pm-9pm Sun., $7-11). Once you pick from the nearly 100 options of sauce, noodle, meat, and vegetable combinations, all that's left for you to decide is how spicy to make it.

Health Food

Down To Earth (201 Hamakua Dr., 808/262-3838, www.downtoearth.org, 7:30am-10pm daily) is an all-vegetarian organic and natural food store. In addition to groceries, vitamins, cosmetics, bulk items, and produce, they also have a hot food bar and bakery. There are a few tables in front of the store where you can enjoy your meal. Hamakua Marsh is just across the parking lot.

Whole Foods (629 Kailua Rd., #100, 808/263-6800, www.wholefoodsmarket.com/stores/kailua, 7am-10pm daily) has a hot food

bar, sandwiches, cold prepared foods, fresh pizza, Chinese food, burgers, burritos, even a few beers on tap, and a comfortable outdoor lanai for sitting down and enjoying your grub.

KANEʻOHE

Kaneʻohe has not been largely altered by tourism, the proof being that you won't find any fine dining restaurants or chic clothing boutiques. Instead, Kaneʻohe is littered with local and national fast-food chains and small and simple ethnic eateries.

Hawaiian

Once you pass into Kaneʻohe, it's all about mom-and-pop places where you can grab a quick bite. At the top of the list is the **Waiahole Poi Factory** (49-140 Kamehameha Hwy., 808/239-2222, http://waiaholepoifactory.com, 11am-6pm daily, $5-11), serving up real Hawaiian food like squid and beef luau, kalua pig, lomi salmon, lau lau, and chicken long rice. They have mini plates that come with rice and lomi salmon and combo plates for larger appetites. They also sell hand-pounded poi, which has a firmer texture and lighter flavor than milled poi.

Breakfast

Local favorite **Koa Pancake House** (46-126 Kahuhipa St., 808/235-5772, 6:30am-2pm daily, $2-8) is a popular breakfast spot on the weekends and is usually packed all morning, so expect a wait. The parking lot is very small, and if it's full, park on Kawa Street.

Korean

Kim Chee Restaurant (46-010 Kamehameha Hwy., 808/235-5560, 9am-9pm Mon.-Sat., 7am-9pm Sun., $8-27) is revered as the best local-style Korean food eatery on the windward side. The big potions come with different styles of kimchi. The menu is full of choices, but the kalbi is a must. One downside: there are only a couple parking spots in front of the restaurant.

Delis

⟨ He'eia Pier General Store & Deli (46-499 Kamehameha Hwy., 808/235-2192, www.heeiapier.com, 7am-4pm Tues.-Sun., $9-13) is a breath of fresh air in terms of high-quality fresh local food. Whether you order guava chicken, fresh fish, or burgers, the deli is known for sourcing organic and local produce and meats. They also have a few old-time dishes on offer.

Steak and Seafood

For a true steak and seafood dining experience, **⟨ Haleiwa Joes** (46-336 Haiku Rd., 808/247-6671, http://haleiwajoes.com, 4:30pm-9:30pm Mon.-Thurs., 4:30pm-10:30pm Fri., 4:30pm-10pm Sat., 7am-9pm Sun., $24-33) is Kane'ohe's answer. Nestled in a lush garden setting, Joes serves up prime rib, fresh fish, and a handful of local favorites like poke, sashimi, sizzling mushrooms, and sticky ribs. They also have a Sunday brunch.

KUALOA TO LA'IE
Quick Bites

In Hau'ula you'll find the **Shrimp Shack** (58-360 Kamehameha Hwy., 808/256-5589 http://shrimpshackoahu.com, 10am-5pm daily, $2-24), a big yellow food truck serving up garlic and coconut shrimp, mahi, crab, mussels, calamari, and even steak.

Papa Ole's Kitchen (54-316 Kamehameha Hwy., 808/293-2292, www.papaoles.com, 7am-9pm Thurs.-Mon., 7am-3pm Tues., $3-12) is a Hawaiian food family restaurant open for breakfast, lunch, and dinner with loco moco, plate lunches, and fresh baked desserts.

In La'ie, stop by **Hukilau Cafe** (55-662 Wahinepee St., 808/293-8616, 6am-2pm Tues.-Fri., 6am-11:30am Sat., $5-13) for

Hawaiian breakfast and lunch plates. Think burgers with egg or kalua pork with two scoops of white rice. The food is delicious, and the portions are ample. Cash only.

Markets

Tamura's (54-316 Kamehameha Hwy., 808/232-2332, 8am-9pm daily) is a small, fully stocked grocery store—and the last place you'll be able to buy alcoholic beverages until you get to the North Shore.

You can also pick up groceries in La'ie at **Foodland** (55-510 Kamehameha Hwy., 808/293-4443, 5am-midnight Mon.-Sat.). This location does not sell alcohol and is closed on Sundays.

La'ie Town

If you drive through La'ie town on a Sunday, it might take a few minutes to notice that there's something different here that you won't find anywhere else on O'ahu–or in Hawaii, for that matter. Everything is closed. Everything, that is, except for the places of worship of the Church of Jesus Christ of Latter-day Saints. Mormons first came to La'ie in the mid-1800s and purchased a 6,000-acre parcel in 1865. By 1919, the first Mormon temple outside of Utah had been built, the Hawaii Temple.

The town of La'ie, O'ahu's only "dry" town, has developed in concert with the growth of the church in Hawaii and reflects the values of the religious institution. The Latter-day Saints erected their signature, private Brigham Young University next door, and built the Polynesian Cultural Center, providing jobs for the students and capitalizing on tourism to spread their message to the masses.

O'AHU

Getting There and Around

CAR

Getting around the southeast and windward coasts is very simple, because for the most part, the highway is hemmed in by the Pacific Ocean on one side and the Ko'olau Mountains on the other. On the southeast shore, the H-1 becomes Kalanianaole Highway (Highway 72) as it merges with Waialae Avenue. Kalanianaole Highway circles the southeastern tip of O'ahu and runs through Waimanalo before pulling away from the coast and intersecting the Pali Highway (Highway 61) at the Kamehameha Highway (Highway 83) junction in the Maunawili area. Kamehameha Highway runs north/south through the town of Kane'ohe, regaining the coast for the rest of the way to the North Shore. There is a parallel highway in Kane'ohe, the Kahekili Highway (Highway 83), which mirrors Kamehameha Highway, but bypasses the town closer to the mountains and with much fewer traffic signals.

There are three basic ways to go to get to the windward side from Honolulu or Waikiki: the Kalanianaole Highway takes you along the southeast shore, from Kahala to Kailua; the Pali Highway puts you directly into Kailua; and the Likelike Highway puts you directly into Kane'ohe. From Kane'ohe to the North Shore, the Kamehameha Highway unfolds with the Pacific Ocean on one side and the dramatic Ko'olau Mountains on the other.

To get to Kailua directly from Honolulu without going around the southeastern tip of O'ahu, simply take the H-1 to the Pali Highway. Once you are descending the Pali on the windward side, the Pali Highway becomes Kalanianaole Highway for a short way until you reach Castle Medical Center, where Kalanianaole Highway takes a right turn toward Waimanalo. Kailua-bound traffic continues straight ahead on Kailua Road and straight into Kailua town.

To get to Kane'ohe directly from Honolulu, take the H-1 to Likelike Highway (Highway 63). Once you are descending on the Likelike, you can either take the Kahekili Highway turn off and continue heading north toward the North Shore, bypassing Kane'ohe town, or continue to the Kamehameha Highway intersection. Turning left, or north, takes you toward the North Shore. Turning right, south, takes you to the Pali Highway and Kalanianaole Highway junction.

BUS

TheBus (808/848-5555, www.thebus.org) has several routes accessing southeast and windward locales. If you're traveling from Waikiki, get to Kahala, Hanauma Bay, and Sea Life Park by using Routes 22 or 23.

From Honolulu, get to Hawai'i Kai via Routes 80, 80A, or 82; travel onward to Kane'ohe via Route 65, or to Kailua and Waimanalo via Route 89. Routes 56, 57, and 57A travel to Kailua, departing from the Ala Moana Shopping Center (1450 Ala Moana Blvd.), with Route 56 continuing to Kane'ohe.

PEARL HARBOR AND THE LEEWARD COAST

Pearl Harbor, a placid, deep-water harbor, still evokes a military presence and sense of reverence for the people who lost their lives during the attack on December 7, 1941. The World War II Valor in the Pacific National Monument is part of the National Park Service and is comprised of the Pearl Harbor Visitor Center and four historic sites. It is the most heavily visited sight on O'ahu.

O'AHU

HIGHLIGHTS

LOOK FOR ◖ TO FIND RECOMMENDED SIGHTS, ACTIVITIES, DINING, AND LODGING.

◖ **Makaha Beach Park:** Steeped in surfing history, this dramatic point offers one of the best waves on O'ahu, which breaks nearly year-round. The wide, sandy beach forms a small bay where trees provide shade for picnicking and surf-gazing (page 182).

◖ **Ko Olina Lagoons:** Four ocean-fed lagoons offer a safe and beautiful environment for a family day at the beach (page 183).

◖ **Pearl Harbor Historic Sites:** The most visited place in the state pays homage to the lives lost during the Pearl Harbor attack on December 7, 1941 (page 191).

◖ **Kane'aki Heiau:** This restored stone structure is a historic and spiritual window into Hawaiian culture and perseverance (page 192).

◖ **Ka'ena Point State Park:** Stretching from breathtaking Yokohama Bay to the western tip of the island, Ka'ena Point State Park includes verdant valleys, a secluded beach, and a dramatic volcanic coast (page 193).

Less visited is the leeward side of O'ahu, also known as the Wai'anae Coast. It's arid and rugged, receiving only sporadic rainfall throughout the year. The dry, red dirt ridgelines extend to the coast, where reef, rocks, and cliffs often take the place of sandy beaches. Undesirable land in other communities becomes home to the most economically depressed segment of society; the leeward coast is no different and has historically been a refuge for O'ahu's displaced native Hawaiian population. At times, generally after dark, the vibe can be unwelcoming, if not unfavorable for outsiders, and theft is common in beach parks and roadside parking areas.

Warnings aside, the leeward coast also has some of the most beautiful beaches on the island and an unobstructed view for every day's precious sunset, where green flashes occur on a regular basis. The deep waters off the coast are prime grounds for sportfishing and a few surf spots break year-round, the most famed being Makaha, home to the first world championship professional surfing event. Spinner dolphins, humpback whales, and sea turtles frequent the waters, and the conditions are usually perfect for diving. Don't forget to look inland, where the verdant valleys of the Wai'anae Range lie in stark contrast to the parched land along the coast.

If luxury, pampering, golf, and fine dining better suit your taste, then Ko Olina, at the southwestern tip of the island, is a prime destination. A sprawling community of condos, timeshares, hotels, dining, golf, and four artificial lagoons on private land, Ko Olina is an oasis in the desert. Geared to be the next

Waikiki, the area offers full-service amenities, but the price is definitely on the high side.

PLANNING YOUR TIME

A visit to Pearl Harbor can take anywhere from a couple of hours to a full day, depending on how many memorials you plan to visit and how early you arrive. If you'd like to see all the memorials, it's best to arrive first thing in the morning to reserve your place on the tours throughout the day. Arriving early is also the best way to beat rush hour traffic if you're coming from Waikiki or Honolulu.

If you're planning on any activity in the Ka'ena Point State Park, whether it be hiking to the natural reserve at the tip of the point, mountain biking the dirt road to the point, or kayaking in Yokohama Bay, then head there first, as early as possible, to beat the heat of the midday sun. After a half day in the state park, head back south and take in the sights and snap some pictures along the way. The beaches and valleys will be perfectly lit by the afternoon sun. Finish up with dinner in Ko Olina at one of their premier restaurants.

On a beach day on the west side, it is absolutely essential to bring an umbrella, plenty of water, and sunscreen. Shade is sparse in the region. If you're heading west just for the sunset, don't wait too late in the afternoon, as rush hour traffic heading west could spoil your sunset plans. Check out Pearl Harbor in the morning, then make your way to the west side. Lounge in one of the Ko Olina Lagoons all afternoon or post up at one of the leeward beaches, where you'll be in a prime sunset-viewing location. Keep in mind that Ko Olina is a busy resort, so there will be many people with the same sunset ideas. You'll need to keep heading west if you're in the market for your own piece of private beach real estate to watch the sun go down on another day.

If golfing is your main reason for heading to the leeward side, you can choose from two courses. The course in Wai'anae Valley is very affordable while the Ko Olina resort community offers a world-class golf experience and a shorter drive.

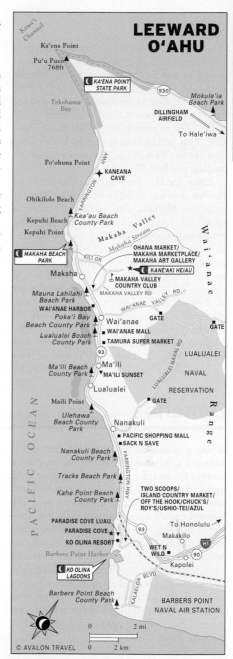

ORIENTATION
Pearl Harbor

Pearl Harbor dominates this region, both geographically and psychologically. Three lochs comprise the harbor—East Loch, Middle Loch, and West Loch—and most of the area, save for the West Loch Shoreline Park and the Pearl Harbor Historic Sites, is off limits to the public. The communities of Waipahu, Pearl City, 'Aiea, and Halawa border the harbor from west to east. Waikele and Waipio are to the immediate north of Waipahu.

Along the H-2 freeway, north of the Pearl Harbor district, is the master-planned community of **Mililani.** The residential enclave is known for tract homes, golf courses, and parks. **Wahiawa** is north of Mililani on O'ahu's central plateau. It is surrounded by Lake Wilson, military installations, and agriculture. To the west of Pearl Harbor, on O'ahu's arid southwestern plain, is the residential community of **'Ewa**—miles and miles of apartment complexes, condominiums, and homes. 'Ewa Beach stretches out west to Kalaeloa and the Kalaeloa Airport, an old military operation now used for light, local air traffic. To the west of 'Ewa on the 'Ewa Plain is **Kapolei,** a brand-new planned community on the south side of the H-1 freeway.

Ko Olina

Ko Olina is a private resort and lifestyle community located on the coast in between Barbers Point and Nanakuli, right where the highway meets the coast after crossing the 'Ewa Plain. Ko Olina has its own exit off Farrington Highway and a gated entrance manned by resort staff. This high-end community is home to three major resort hotels and four artificial lagoons for both resort guests and the public.

Leeward Coast

The leeward coast stretches about 20 miles from Barbers Point to Yokohama Bay in Ka'ena Point State Park, and is connected by one thoroughfare, Farrington Highway. The majority of the commercial property is along the highway, as the neighborhoods snake back into the dry valleys between the massive ridges that extend to the coast. The main communities from south to north are **Nanakuli, Ma'ili, Wai'anae,** and **Makaha.** The highway dead-ends at Ka'ena Point State Park, the westernmost tip of the island.

Beaches

If you're feeling adventurous and don't mind an hour's drive across the island, the beaches of leeward O'ahu offer wide swaths of white sand under clear, sunny skies. As the trade winds blow across the island from east to west, the leeward coast's waters remain calm and protected, offering beautiful conditions for swimming, surfing, fishing, snorkeling, diving, or just soaking up the sun. Waves are common along leeward beaches all year long, but generally get the biggest in the winter, from October to March. Make sure to exercise caution and assess the ocean conditions before entering the water. Check with a lifeguard for the safest place to swim.

MA'ILI
Ma'ili Beach Park

Marking the beginning of Ma'ili town and its long stretch of beach, **Ma'ili Point** is one of the more dynamic and picturesque settings along the leeward coast. There is a small park with picnic tables and grass on the southern side of the point. The shoreline rocks extend out into the water and meet up with the shallow reef here, creating a lot of whitewater and surf action to watch while relaxing or having a snack. On the north side of the point, **Ma'ili Beach Park** runs the length of Ma'ili town. Situated between two streams that run down from the mountains, the sandy beach is widest during

Your Best Day in Pearl Harbor and the Leeward Coast

© KEVIN WHITTON

the USS *Arizona* Memorial

Pearl Harbor is a bastion of reverence and reflection, while the Leeward Coast is rough, rugged, and beautiful in its own right. This side of O'ahu tends to be hot and dry, so be prepared with sunscreen, hats, and plenty of water.

- Wake up early and head directly to the **Pearl Harbor Historic Sites.** Getting there early helps to cut down on the wait time for the tour package you choose. If visiting Pearl Harbor becomes an all-day affair, you'll want to plan for dinner back at your hotel. After half-day Pearl Harbor excursions, continue on to Ko Olina or the leeward side for beach time and dining.

- If you're more interested in nature than history, plan on hiking to **Ka'ena Point** instead. Mitigate the heat by arriving as early as possible, preferably as the sun is coming up. Explore the **Ka'ena Point Natural Area Reserve.** You'll most likely see Hawaiian monk seals and nesting seabirds.

- On your return to your vehicle, take a refreshing dip in the ocean at **Yokohama Bay.**

- Head south down the Leeward Coast. Grab a quick snack at **Ohana Market** in Makaha. Continue south until you get **Ko Olina.** Have a sit-down lunch at one of the poolside restaurants at the three resort properties.

- Families should spend a playful afternoon in one of the four sheltered lagoons in Ko Olina. Couples can schedule a treatment at **Ihilani Spa.**

- For dinner, try **Roy's** for Hawaiian fusion cuisine, **Ushio-Tei** for traditional Japanese fare, or **Azul,** an award-winning Italian restaurant.

the summer when the waves are smaller, and the gently arcing beach is great for swimming and snorkeling. During the winter, however, the sand tends to migrate elsewhere with the more frequent high surf, revealing a rock shelf along the shore. There are restrooms, picnic areas, and camping on the weekends by permit only. Ma'ili Beach Park is closed 10pm-5am daily.

WAI'ANAE
Poka'i Bay Beach Park
Between the small boat harbor and Kane'ilio Point sits a beautiful sheltered bay and wide sandy beach called **Poka'i Bay Beach Park.** There is a breakwater offshore and a reef in the middle of the bay that keep the water calm along the shoreline year-round, making this a perfect spot for swimming and families. Small waves break over the reef during the winter, which attracts novice surfers. In addition to the beautiful beach, the **Ku'ilioloa Heiau** is also out on the point and has three terraced platforms. The *heiau* is thought to have been a place for learning the arts of fishing, navigation, and ocean-related skills. The beach park is closed 10pm-5am daily.

MAKAHA
◖ Makaha Beach Park
A world-class surf break with a recent history entwined with the birth of international professional surfing, **Makaha Beach Park** is the hub of surfing on the leeward coast. The beautiful beach is framed at both ends by rocky headlands, the north end being the site of the surf break and the sharp reef that absorbs the ocean's energy. The surf here breaks all year, but is biggest in the winter months, when waves can reach 40 to 50 feet high on the face during the biggest swell episodes. In the summer, swimming is best in the middle of the beach, or if the waves are completely flat, you can snorkel over the reef shelf. There are restrooms, showers, and a few shade trees and hau bushes along the road where everyone parks. If there is surf during your stop at Makaha, check with the lifeguards for the best place to enjoy the water.

Makua Beach
At the north end of Makua Valley, the only valley in the area fenced off and privately held by the U.S. Army, is a small parking area on the ocean side of the road under some trees with access to **Makua Beach.** This undeveloped, secluded white sand beach is a great place to find solitude. When the waves are flat, it's also fine for swimming and snorkeling, but during high surf the ocean is dangerous at Makua Beach.

Yokohama Bay
Referred to on maps and by many as **Yokohama Bay,** Keawa'ula Bay is by far the most picturesque beach on the leeward coast. Part of **Ka'ena Point State Park,** the white sand beach curves to the northwest and points the way toward the western tip of the island, Ka'ena Point. The turquoise water sees waves throughout the year and is extremely dangerous for swimming during times of high surf. The surf breaks in the area are for expert surfers only. When the water is calm, the ocean is ideal for swimming. There is no shade on the beach, so be prepared with an umbrella or tent to mitigate the piercing sun. To complete the stunning views, behind the bay are several valleys that change from a dry, reddish hue to verdant green the farther back your eye takes you. There are public restrooms and lifeguards on duty.

KO OLINA
Paradise Cove
Just past the entrance gate to Ko Olina and next to Paradise Cove Luau is a small, yet beautiful sandy cove and lagoon called **Paradise Cove.** In the past it has been called Lanikauka'a and then Lanikuhonua Beach. Paradise Cove is one of three sacred lagoons in the immediate area where Queen Ka'ahumanu was said to have bathed and performed religious ceremonies. The shallow lagoon is protected from ocean swells by a raised reef rock shelf on its ocean side. There are trees on the beach for shade and tidepools. All in all, it's a great out-of-the-way nook to take the kids and explore. Parking is a little tricky. Take a right into the third driveway past the entrance gate. On the right is a small,

© KEVIN WHITTON

Ko Olina has four manmade lagoons.

free public parking area for about 10 cars. The sidewalk leads to a sandy pathway between two tall fences down to the beach.

Ko Olina Lagoons

Ko Olina has four lagoons open to the public from sunrise to sunset. The **Ko Olina Lagoons** are numbered one through four, heading from west to east, and also have the Hawaiian names Kohola, Honu, Napa, and Ulua, respectively. They are more widely known and referred to by their number. The lagoons are artificially constructed semicircles cut from the sharp and rugged reef rock shelf that creates the shoreline. Channels were cut into the shelf to allow ocean water to flow in and out of the lagoons while blocking any surf from entering. With sandy beaches, grassy parks, a fair bit of shade from palms and trees, and a meandering pathway connecting all four lagoons, this oasis provides a sheltered, manufactured, resort-style of beach experience, completely opposite to the rest of the leeward beaches. Each lagoon has its own access road from Aliinui Drive, the main road through Ko Olina. Turn right on Kamoana Place to reach Lagoon 1. The next three consecutive streets will lead to a lagoon and its parking area. There are no lifeguards on duty, but there is plenty of security known as the Aloha Patrol monitoring the lagoons from golf carts. Ever vigilant, they will be sure to let you know if you're breaking any rules from the long list of prohibited actions and items. Parking is free, but very limited at each lagoon, with Lagoon 4 having the most.

Surfing

Much of the surf on the leeward side breaks over sharp and shallow reef, making it best suited for expert surfers. Scaling rocks and reef to enter and exit the water can be a challenge for newcomers, and the locals are quite territorial when it comes to their surf breaks. Still, with the right attitude, there's definitely a wave to be had on the leeward coast.

The leeward coast basically faces west, so it is prone to waves all year long. Southerly summer swells and the northwesterly winter swells both offer opportunities for great quality surf. Winter swells can get quite big—scary big actually. When a high surf advisory is called for the coast and waves are above the 20-foot mark, it's best to leave the surfboard at home and watch the locals who are familiar with the challenging breaks.

Master-Planned Paradise

If you notice that there's something too good to be true about Ko Olina's four clamshell-shaped lagoons on the southwest tip of O'ahu, that's because the coastline has been severely altered to created Lagoons 1-4, part of the master-planned resort and lifestyle community. Before Ko Olina and the lagoons were developed, the rugged shoreline was quite inhospitable. Four- to six-foot cliffs of extremely sharp fossil reef rock protruded from the land into the sea, dropping straight into the surging waves. The area was devoid of sandy beaches. To create safe and desirable shoreline access for resort guests, they cut channels in the reef rock shelf to allow the flow of natural ocean water into half-moon lagoons, while keeping the surf and ocean currents at bay. Add sand, grass, and a few tall palm trees, and you have an artificial tropical paradise in a safe and controlled setting—not for everyone, but the ideal vacation for many.

MA'ILI
Ma'ili Point

Ma'ili Point is one of the best waves on this stretch of coastline. A predominantly left breaking point break, the wave breaks over a shallow coral shelf, which can be a nearly dry reef at low tide. On south swells, the wave is a bit slopey and sometimes rights will break off the main peak. On northwesterly swells, Ma'ili Point is a freight train wave, with fast breaking and barreling lefts suited for experts only. Park in the parking lot on the north side of the point. Getting in and out of the water can be tricky because of the rocky shelf along the beach, so watch or ask one of the local surfers the best way to get in without getting hurt.

WAI'ANAE
Poka'i Bay

Inside the breakwater in Poka'i Bay in Wai'anae is a rolling wave perfect for beginners. Longboarders, stand-up paddlers, and first-time surfers can get the feel of a board under their feet at this soft break. The wave breaks over a wide reef and is small and calm, even when the surf is larger elsewhere.

MAKAHA
Makaha Beach Park

Makaha is a righthand point break steeped in surf history. The site of the Makaha International Surfing Championships from 1954 to 1971, the waves at Makaha can range from fun and playful to massive and life threatening. Makaha breaks in summer and winter, with the largest waves occurring during the wintertime high surf advisories. The wave breaks over shallow reef at the top of the point and runs into deeper water with a sandy bottom near the beach, famous for its backwash. Makaha gets crowded and has a well-established pack of locals of all ages. If you paddle out at Makaha, smile, say hello, and don't hassle anyone for a wave, or you'll be on the

Makaha Beach is a legendary surf break.

beach before you know it. At Makaha, you'll find people pursuing ocean sports of all kinds: surfing, bodyboarding, stand-up paddling, and bodysurfing. Parking along the road is the safest so you can keep an eye on your car.

Yokohama Bay

About eight miles past Makaha, in the Ka'ena Point State Park at the end of the road, are several challenging, barreling surf breaks. Nestled in the beautiful and secluded Keawa'ula Bay, better known as **Yokohama Bay,** swells approach out of deep water from the north and the south and detonate along the bay's shallow reefs. The waves are very dangerous as they break on extremely shallow reef shelves close to shore. This is a favorite spot for expert surfers and bodyboarders.

Outfitters

Hale Nalu (85-876 Farrington Hwy., #A2, 808/696-5897, http://halenalu.com, 10am-5pm daily) has new and used boards and rents bodyboards starting at $14 per day, shortboards starting at $20 per day, longboards starting at $30 per day, and stand-up paddle boards starting at $50 per day. They also have discounts for three-day and week rentals.

West Oahu SUP (84-1170 Farrington Hwy., 808/954-2091, http://westoahusup.com, 9am-5pm daily) rents bodyboards for $20 per day, $60 per five-day week; shortboards $25 per day, $85 per week; longboards $15 hourly, $25 full day, and $95 per week; and stand-up paddle boards with paddle for $25 hourly, $60 full day, and $215 per week.

Snorkeling and Diving

SNORKELING

When the surf is flat and the ocean is calm, generally during the summer, the leeward coast is a snorkeler's dream come true. Crystal clear turquoise water, ample rock outcroppings and patches of reef beside white sandy beaches, and calm nearshore waters protected from the trade winds make for excellent snorkeling all along the coast. Look for areas where a sandy beach connects to rock and reef for the best opportunities to see marine life with safe and easy passage in and out of the water. While there are many places to just pull off the road and jump in the water, it's always safer to swim or snorkel by lifeguards and first check with them about the current ocean conditions. And remember that strong currents accompany high surf, even if there are no waves breaking in your immediate aquatic locale. Green sea turtles and spinner dolphins are common sights on the leeward side.

The best bet is to bring your snorkel gear with you from your point of origin, because if you find yourself on the west side in need of snorkel gear, you'll have to drive to Wai'anae or Makaha to rent or purchase equipment. **Hale Nalu** (85-876 Farrington Hwy., #A2, 808/696-5897, http://halenalu.com, 10am-5pm daily) is a sporting goods store located in Wai'anae across from Poka'i Bay renting snorkel gear for $10 per day, $20 for three days, and $35 per week. In Makaha, **West Oahu SUP** (84-1170 Farrington Hwy., 808/954-2091, http://westoahusup.com, 9pm-5am daily) rents snorkel sets for $15 full day and $50 five days. Inside the same retail space you'll also find **Paradise Isle** (84-1170 Farrington Hwy., #AE, 808/695-8866), a fish and dive shop where you can purchase new gear.

DIVING

Nestled in the lee of the trade winds, the west side has some of the best conditions for diving on a consistent basis. The underwater world has shallow reef diving with lava tubes and arches, the Makaha caverns and rock formations—a favorite for turtles and monk seals—and several wrecks including a plane fuselage, a landing craft unit, an airplane, and a minesweeping vessel. Look for octopus, whitemouth morays, porcupine puffer fish, whitetip reef sharks, Hawaiian stingrays, and spinner dolphins.

Outfitters

Captain Bruce's (86-222 Moeha St., 808/373-3590, www.captainbruce.com) operates a Pro-42 Jet Boat built for 28 passengers, yet only takes a maximum of 16 divers with one guide per six divers. They dive all the wrecks and reefs along the leeward coast and can accommodate all skill levels. The boat is decked out for ultra comfort with hot water showers, complimentary snacks and beverages, and restrooms. They even set up all your gear for you. A two-tank certified dive is $150; two-tank introductory dive, $135. They have snorkel ride-alongs for $79 adult and $59 child. They also offer a three-day open water certification course for $550 and PADI and NAUI two-day referral dive courses for $325.

Ocean Concepts (85-371 Farrington Hwy., 808/696-7200, www.oceanconcepts.com) is based in Pearl Harbor yet operates primarily out of the Wai'anae Small Boat Harbor. They offer daily two-tank boat dives for $115. They also have multiday rates: two two-tank dives for $210 and three two-tank dives for $300. All equipment can be rented as a set for $25 or by the piece. Ocean Concepts has photo options and will burn you a CD of your scuba trip or they can use your SD card when taking pictures.

Pearl Harbor Divers (725 Auahi St., 808/589-2177, http://pearlharbordivers.com), also based in Honolulu, dives the west side in addition to the south and southern coasts. Their two-tank boat dives from the Wai'anae Small Boat Harbor are $99 per person. They also offer a special three-tank Ka'ena Point drift dive once or twice a month for $109.

Kayaking and Sailing

KAYAKING

From the water, the leeward coast is nothing less than spectacularly beautiful. Its rugged coastline, a combination of white sand beaches, rock and reef outcroppings, and jagged cliffs, is only complemented by the deep valleys lying in succession all the way up the coast. Sea kayaking affords a perspective unmatched and unobtainable by land, far from the spiderweb of power lines over the neighborhoods and the bustle of Farrington Highway. In addition, the crystal clear water runs from turquoise to deep blue, and humpback whale-watching is at its best on this side of the island during their annual stay from November to March.

As the trade winds rise over the Wai'anae Range, they create pristine conditions for ocean activities. Calm nearshore waters afford easy paddling and more abundant ocean life. You can enter the water from Tracks, at the south end of the leeward coast, but be prepared to deal with small waves along the shore. From here, you can explore the jagged cliffs and find small pockets of sand only accessible from the water. Sheltered Poka'i Bay in Wai'anae is perfect for launching the kayaks. For the best views of the valleys, put in at Makaha, Makua Beach, or Yokohama Bay, but only if the surf is flat, which is more likely to occur in summer.

West Oahu SUP (84-1170 Farrington Hwy., 808/954-2091, http://westoahusup.com, 9am-5pm daily) rents single-rider kayaks for $25 hourly, $50 full day, and $175 per five-day week. They rent two-person kayaks for $25 hourly, $60 full day, and $215 per week. They also rent roof racks or tie-downs for $10.

SAILING

If you prefer to charter a catamaran and let someone else do the navigating for you so you can focus on taking in the sights, **Wild Side Hawaii** (87-1286 Farrington Hwy., 808/306-7273, http://sailhawaii.com) has three tours that leave from Wai'anae Small Boat Harbor: Morning Wildlife Cruise is a three-hour nearshore cruise with snorkeling, spinner dolphin swims, and seasonal whale-watching for $115; Best of the West is a 3.5-hour tour with dolphin swims, whale-watching, and tropical reef snorkeling with a maximum of six guests for $195 per person; the Deluxe Family Charter is a midmorning three-hour cruise focusing on hands-on learning about Hawaii's marine creatures with dolphin swims, snorkeling instruction, and whale-watching for $175 adult, $145 child. They also have a full-day cruise departing from Honolulu to the leeward coast for $335.

Eo Waianae Tours (2101 Nuuanu Ave., 808/538-9091, www.eowaianaetours.com) has morning and afternoon west side catamaran tours with snorkeling and kayaking. Adults $115, children ages 5-12 $95, children ages 4 or younger $45. They also offer transportation from Waikiki.

Fishing

While shoreline fishing is common from the cliffs and beaches in the region—papio, kumu, and moana being the sought-after take—fishing charters also run out of the area and take advantage of the frequently calm ocean conditions and the steep ledges offshore attracting pelagic fish. There is a 3,000-foot ledge just three miles from Wai'anae Harbor and another 6,000-foot ledge just seven miles out. It's also not uncommon to see people fishing from kayaks just offshore along the coast.

In the Ko Olina Marina, **Kahuna Sportfishing Hawaii** (92-100 Waipahe Pl., 808/227-3305, http://hawaiioffshoresportfishing.com) offers deep-sea excursion off Ko Olina and the west coast on their 43-foot fishing yacht. Their private charters are for a maximum of six passengers: the four-hour charter is $550, six hours go for $700, and eight hours will run you $800. Shared charters for two people start at $275 for the four-hour charter. The rate drops per additional passenger up to four passengers on the shared charter.

In the Wai'anae Small Boat Harbor you'll find **Boom Boom Sportfishing** (85-371 Farrington Hwy., Pier A, 808/306-4162, www.boomboomsportfishing.com). They offer private and shared charters for a maximum of six passengers with two departure times daily. Four-hour private charters are $595, six hours $695, 8-10 hours $875, and 12 hours $1,250. They offer shared charters starting at $150 for four hours and free round-trip transportation or a 10 percent discount for Ko Olina Resort guests.

Live Bait Sportfishing (808/696-1604, www.live-bait.com) also operates out of the Wai'anae Harbor from slip B-2 and provides all equipment and tackle. You are responsible for bringing food and drinks. They primarily fish for marlin, wahoo, tuna, and mahimahi, and give a meal-sized portion of the catch to passengers. They offer half-day trips for $550 and full-day trips for $750 with a four-passenger maximum.

For fishing gear and tackle retailers, check out **Westside Tackle and Sports Shop** (87-701 Manuaihue St., 808/696-7229) in Wai'anae or **Paradise Isle** (84-1170 Farrington Hwy., #AE, 808/695-8866) in Makaha.

Hiking, Biking, and Bird-Watching

HIKING
Leeward
The leeward side is notoriously dry, sunny, and hot, so hiking is best done early in the morning or late in the day. No matter when you go, bring plenty of water, a hat, and sunscreen.

In **Ka'ena Point State Park** (www.hawaiistateparks.org), hiking out to **Ka'ena Point** is a special experience. The rough and rocky trail, a little over five miles round-trip, follows a well-worn dirt road along the cliff out to the point. The volcanic coast is breathtaking, with tidepools, natural stone arches, and surf surging onto rock outcroppings. The road has washed away not far from the point, so follow the narrow side trail around the cliff. You'll reach a formidable fence designed to keep out invasive species; enter through the double doors. Once you are inside the **Ka'ena Point Natural Area Reserve** (www.state.hi.us/dlnr/dofaw/kaena/index.htm), an ecosystem restoration project, it is of the utmost importance to stay on the marked trails as not to disturb the seabird nesting grounds. The dunes are covered with native Hawaiian plants and home a handful of Hawaiian and migratory seabirds. Continue down to the shoreline past some old cement installments and look for Hawaiian monk seals basking in the sun. There are no facilities along the hike and no water, so bring plenty of fluids. To get to the trail, follow Farrington Highway to Yokohama Bay. Drive along the beach till the paved road ends. Park in the dirt parking area and proceed down the dirt road on foot. The state park is open from sunup to sundown.

Explore the deep valley behind Wai'anae, in the shadow of O'ahu's tallest peak, Mount Ka'ala. The six-mile **Wai'anae Kai** loop trail is full of ups and downs with a final climb to an overlook. It then follows an ancient Hawaiian trail back to the main route. You'll find native Hawaiian trees, shrubs, and herbs along the hike and the likes of the Japanese bush warbler. There are views of Wai'anae, Lualualei, and Makaha Valleys. The trail is unimproved and rough, so proper footwear is essential. To get there, follow Waianae Valley Road to the back of the valley. Continue on it after it turns

Predator-Proof Fence

Kaʻena Point has long been home to a variety of Hawaii's wildlife, a chorus of flora and fauna on land and in the sea. In years past, human impact took a devastating toll on the fragile ecosystem: off-road vehicles tore up the dunes, destroying native vegetation and disturbing seabird nesting sites, and feral cats, dogs, rats, and mongooses decimated seabird populations, namely the wedge-tailed shearwater and Laysan albatross that nest in the dunes, by eating eggs and killing juvenile birds.

Today, because of the Kaʻena Point Natural Area Reserve Ecosystem Restoration Project, Kaʻena Point is a natural restoration success story. Integral to the return of native plant species, native insects, and nesting seabirds is the predator-proof fence. Completed in 2011, the 6.5-foot-high fence uses a fine mesh technology to protect the 59-acre reserve from predation by invasive species. Spanning 700 yards and following an old railroad track roadbed around the point, the fence is also buried underground with the ability to keep two-day-old mice from entering. A double-gated entry system ensures unwanted pests cannot sneak in, as only one door can open at a time. The fence is unobtrusive and colored to blend in with the natural vegetation and geography. Since its completion, native vegetation has returned and nesting seabird populations are steadily increasing.

into a one-lane dirt road. Park in the dirt lot across from the last house at the locked gate. Continue past the locked gate and follow the dirt road on foot.

BIKING

The leeward coast does have a gem of a mountain biking trail, the road to **Kaʻena Point.** Part of **Kaʻena Point State Park** (www.hawaiistateparks.org), the trail is flat, so there's no climbing or downhill involved, but the rocky, rutted, and curving cliffside dirt road is a challenging ride none the less. At 2.7 miles one way from the parking area to the point, the ride is extremely scenic, passing rocky coves, sea arches, and crashing waves. Once at the fence to keep out invasive species from the natural reserve portion of the park, you can bike around the point along the perimeter of the fence to the Mokuleʻia side and continue up the North Shore, or you can walk your bike through the double doors in the fence. However, the trails inside the reserve are narrow and sandy. The sun is intense, and there is no shade in the area, so bring plenty of water and wear sunscreen.

To get to the trail, follow Farrington Highway to Yokohama Bay. Drive along the beach until the paved road ends. Park in the dirt parking area and proceed down the dirt road on foot. The state park is open from sunup to sundown.

Hale Nalu (85-876 Farrington Hwy., #A2, 808/696-5897, http://halenalu.com, 10am-5pm daily), in Waiʻanae, rents mountain bikes for $30 per day, $60 for three days, or $90 for one week.

BIRD-WATCHING

The **Pearl Harbor National Wildlife Refuge** (808/637-6330, www.fws.gov/pearlharbor) is a sanctuary for native Hawaiian waterbirds and migratory waterfowl. There are two small conservation areas, which are not open to the public, but you can view the refuge from the Pearl Harbor Bike Path as it rounds Middle Loch. Since you can't physically enter the refuge, bring binoculars.

The **Kaʻena Point Natural Area Reserve** (www.state.hi.us/dlnr/dofaw/kaena/index.htm) inside the Kaʻena Point State Park is the premier bird-watching area on the leeward coast. The 59-acre reserve is an active ecosystem restoration project designed to restore the native ecosystem on the point and bolster the number of endangered species, both flora and fauna, that call the area home. Look for Laysan albatross, wedge-tailed shearwater, and white-tailed tropicbird that nest in dunes. Nesting begins in November, with the adults departing in late spring and juveniles leaving the nests by late June. The area is also home to several species of native Hawaiian birds including the great frigatebird, red-footed, brown, and masked boobies, sooty and white terns, and the Hawaiian short-eared owl. Other migratory birds like the wandering tattler and the Pacific golden plover also frequent the area.

Golf

In the master-planned communities of central and suburban O'ahu, golf courses take center stage, and there are a plethora of public courses, especially on the 'Ewa Plain.

PEARL HARBOR

Overlooking Pearl Harbor, the USS *Arizona* Memorial, and the USS *Missouri,* the **Pearl County Club** (98-535 Kaonohi St., 808/487-3802, www.pearlcc.com) combines scenery and engaging golf with challenging course conditions and speedy downhill putts. The mature course also has a driving range, practice putting green, and a short game area. Rates for 18 holes are $130, twilight (after 3:30pm) $50.

With views of Pearl Harbor, downtown Honolulu, and Diamond Head, the **Royal Kunia Country Club** (94-1509 Anonui St., 808/688-9222, www.royalkuniacc.com) in Waipahu is a Robin Nelson-designed course situated across an undulating landscape with abundant water features and 101 bunkers. Greens fees for 18 holes are $150, twilight rates (after 2pm) are $80.

Makaha

In Makaha you'll find the **Makaha Valley Country Club** (84-627 Makaha Valley Rd., 808/695-9578, www.makahavalleycc.com) surrounded by the ridges of the Wai'anae Mountains in the expansive Makaha Valley. Opening out to the Pacific Ocean, the 18-hole, par-71 course has a rolling topography known for its challenging par-3 holes. Greens fees start at $65 weekdays and $75 weekends.

Ko Olina

The manicured **Ko Olina Golf Club** (92-1220 Aliinui Dr., 808/676-5300, www.koolina. com) is the region's premier golf destination. The beautiful, Ted Robinson layout features views of the Wai'anae Mountains and the Pacific Ocean. The 18-hole course has expansive landing areas and multitiered greens for golfers of all skill levels. They also have an internationally recognized golf shop and offer private, group, and corporate classes at the Ko Olina Golf Academy, with a PGA Professional teaching staff. Greens fees start at $189 with discounted rates for Ko Olina Resort guests.

Spas

KO OLINA

Inside the **JW Marriott Ihilani Resort** (92-1001 Olani St.) in Ko Olina you'll find the **Ihilani Spa** (808/679-3321, www.ihilanispa. com). In addition to standard spa services like massage, facials, and body treatments, they offer full salon and nail services, as well as spa fitness. The spa is situated by the ocean, and the ocean theme is represented throughout. Fifty-minute massages start at $130, 50-minute facials start at $140, and 50-minute body treatments start at $65 for a cool *ti* leaf wrap. For men, the spa offers a 25-minute salt scrub and water massage for $65. Couples can get side-by-side massages by choosing from any of the services offered. Prices are per person. Ihilani Spa also has several complimentary fitness group classes like a guided lagoon walk, aqua job, beach workout, and Zumba. They offer 60-minute yoga sessions for $15. Contact the spa for the current schedule of classes.

Sights

PEARL HARBOR
C Pearl Harbor Historic Sites

The USS *Arizona* Memorial, USS *Bowfin* Submarine Museum and Park, USS *Oklahoma* Memorial, and the Battleship *Missouri* Memorial comprise the **Pearl Harbor Historic Sites.** Over 1.7 million people visit the USS *Arizona* Memorial and the historic sites each year, making this one of the most heavily toured areas in the state. The four sites together tell the story of Hawaii's and the United States' involvement in World War II, from the surprise attack on Pearl Harbor to the surrender of the Japanese. Pearl Harbor also serves as the central point of the **World War II Valor in the Pacific National Monument.**

Once you arrive and find free parking in one of several designated lots, enter the 17-acre park where you'll first see the **visitor center** (808/454-1434, www.pearlharborhistoric-sites.org, 7am-5pm daily) and the USS *Bowfin* Submarine Museum. If you're planning on touring any of the historic sites, especially the USS *Arizona,* arrive as early as possible and head directly to the Visitor Center to get in line to receive a stamped ticket for a tour time.

© KEVIN WHITTON

The Pearl Harbor Historic Sites see over 1.7 million visitors a year.

O'AHU

Admission to the monument is free and the 1.25-hour program includes a 23-minute documentary and a short boat ride to the memorial. Tickets are issued on a first-come, first-served basis. On a busy day, be prepared to wait several hours for your tour.

A better option is to reserve tickets online at www.recreation.gov. You can select the date, time, tour, or tour package you'd like to take. When you arrive at the Visitor Center, a separate line awaits for those who have reserved tickets.

If you do have a long wait ahead of you, check out the other historical sites, like the USS *Bowfin* Museum, or take the shuttle bus, which departs every 15 minutes, to the Battleship *Missouri* Memorial and the **Pacific Aviation Museum.** Other than the USS *Arizona* Memorial, which is free, all sites charge admission for adults and children ages 4-12. There are also package tours, half-day tours, and one- or two-day passes available. Alleviate the wait time by taking advantage of the online ticket reservations to streamline your visit to Pearl Harbor.

The Pearl Harbor Historic Sites park is located off Kamehameha Highway, Route 99, just south of Aloha Stadium. There is ample signage coming from both directions. If you're on the H-1 freeway west, take exit 15A and follow the signs. You can also take TheBus, nos. 20 or 42 from Kuhio Avenue in Waikiki, or nos. 20, 42, or 52 from Ala Moana Center or downtown and be dropped off within a minute's walk of the entrance. Depending on stops and traffic, this ride could take over an hour. Also, The Arizona Memorial Bus Shuttle (808/839-0911), a private operation from Waikiki run by VIP Transportation, takes about half an hour and will pick you up at any Waikiki hotel. It charges $11 round-trip; reservations are necessary, so call a day in advance. Because the park is on an active military base, there are no bags allowed inside the area. There is a $3 bag storage fee.

MAKAHA
◖ Kane'aki Heiau

Located deep in Makaha Valley is one of the best preserved *heiau* on O'ahu, the **Kane'aki Heiau.** Begun in 1545, the final structure was

The Military on O'ahu

O'ahu differs from the other main Hawaiian Islands in that there is a strong military presence here. All four branches of the military have installations on the island, and men and women in uniform are a common sight from the windward to the leeward side.

A few military strategists realized the importance of Hawaii early in the 19th century, but most didn't recognize the advantages until the Spanish-American War. It was clearly an unsinkable platform in the middle of the Pacific from which the United States could launch military operations. General Schofield first surveyed Pearl Harbor in 1872, and this world-class anchorage was given to the U.S. Navy for its use in 1887 as part of the Sugar Reciprocity Treaty. In August 1898, four days after the United States annexed Hawaii, U.S. Army troops created Camp McKinley at the foot of Diamond Head, and American troops were stationed there until

it became obsolete in 1907. Named in General Schofield's honor, Schofield Barracks in central O'ahu became (and remains) the largest military installation in the state. It first housed the U.S. 5th Cavalry in 1909 and was heavily bombed by the Japanese at the outset of World War II. Pearl Harbor, first dredged in 1908, was officially opened on December 11, 1911. The first warship to enter was the cruiser *California*.

The Japanese navy attacked Pearl Harbor and other military installations on December 7, 1941. The flames of Pearl Harbor ignited World War II's Pacific theater operations, and there has been no looking back. Ever since that war, the military has been a mainstay of the island economy. Following the war, the number of men, women, and installations decreased; today there is a force of more than 55,000 active duty personnel, with all branches of the military represented.

only completed by 1812, during the reign of King Kamehameha. Two restoration phases of construction occurred to preserve the physical, spiritual, and historic aspects of the *heiau*. Originally dedicated to Lono, the Hawaiian god of harvest and fertility, it was later converted to a *luakini heiau* for human sacrifice. The thatched huts used as prayer and meditation chambers, along with a spirit tower and carved images, have all been replicated. Because the *heiau* is within a private gated community, access is limited to 10am-2pm Tuesday through Sunday. It may be closed even during those times when it's too rainy or muddy. Stop at the guardhouse and let them know where you're heading. They will ask to see your identification and car registration or car rental agreement before they sign you in.

Kaneana Cave

Spelunkers rejoice, just off Farrington Highway on the edge of Makua Valley is the **Kaneana Cave,** a sacred ancient Hawaiian site. At 100 feet high and about 450 feet deep, this cave, *ana,* is spoken of in Hawaiian legend as the womb of the earth, where mankind emerged and spread throughout the Wai'anae coast. It is named after Kane, the god of creation. In Hawaiian lore it is also thought to be the home of Nanaue, the shark man. The cave is dark and often slippery, so bring a flashlight. It is also unmaintained, and there are several side tunnels off the main cavern that should be avoided for your own safety. Look for the painted cement road barrier that marks the entrance.

◖ Ka'ena Point State Park

Ka'ena Point State Park (www.hawaiistate-parks.org/parks/oahu) is the most scenic, raw, and naturally breathtaking area on the leeward side. It is also an embodiment of all things found on the leeward coast. Located at the end of Farrington Highway and stretching all the way out to the western tip of O'ahu, Ka'ena Point State Park provides outdoor and ocean recreational activities, wildlife viewing, native plantlife, verdant valleys, a secluded white sand beach with turquoise water, and a dramatic volcanic coast all under the hot west side sun. It is truly about as far removed from Honolulu and Waikiki as you can get on O'ahu.

© KEVIN WHITTON

rugged Ka'ena Point

Soul's Leap

Ka'ena Point is a sacred place, and not just for its natural beauty. Ancient Hawaiians thought Ka'ena Point to be a jumping-off point for the spirits of the dead to enter the afterlife. Legend has it that humankind emerged from the depths of Kaneana Cave, the womb of the Earth goddess, and spread across the Wai'anae coast. The souls of the deceased would find their way to Ka'ena Point by following the sun past the sunset, to the eternal night. Their leap would take them to Po, the realm of ancestral spirits, a spiritual place akin to heaven and described as being a sea of eternity. Once in Po, the soul is thought to have completed the cycle of life.

As you round the last bend in the road with a slight elevation, the gentle arcing white sand of Yokohama Bay, also known as Keawa'ula Bay, stretches out in front of you to the west. Pristine and uncrowded, it begs for you to pull the car over and take in the serenity. Look back into the valley to catch a glimpse of the unspoiled, verdant mountains of the Wai'anae Range. As you come to the end of the paved road, a rutted, rocky dirt track completes the way to Ka'ena Point. You can walk or mountain bike out to the western tip of the island, where you'll find the **Ka'ena Point Natural Area Reserve.** This is prime territory for wildlife viewing. Look for spinner dolphins and green sea turtles in the water; on the beach you'll probably see Hawaiian monk seals basking in the sun; and the sand dunes are a protected site for nesting seabirds.

Entertainment

KO OLINA

Paradise Cove Luau (92-1089 Aliinui Dr., 808/842-5911 or 800/775-2683, www.paradisecovehawaii.com) is located just inside the Ko Olina main entry gate. Set on 12 oceanfront acres, the luau probably has one of the best sunset views on O'ahu. An evening at Paradise Cove actually begins before sunset. For about two hours, guests can explore the beautiful property, trying traditional arts and crafts, playing traditional Hawaiian games, shopping, or sipping mai tais. Guests can even partake in a *hukilau,* pulling fishing nets up onto the shore. After a sunset ceremony, the feast starts with traditional luau favorites, then begins the Paradise Cove Hawaiian Revue. Packages start at $88 adult, $78 youth, and $68 children. Two packages with higher rates offer better seats. Reservations are available online.

Food

PEARL HARBOR

Overlooking Pearl Harbor, **Buzz's Pearl City** (98-751 Kuahao Pl., 808/487-6465, 5pm-9pm daily, $17-33) is Buzz's original steak house; the sister location is in Lanikai. Famous for their kiawe broiled steaks, seafood, and no-nonsense cocktails, Buzz's is the perfect finish to a day at Pearl Harbor. Call at 4pm and make reservations.

Local favorite **Taniokas** (94-903 Farrington Hwy., 808/671-3779, www.taniokas.com, 8am-5pm Mon.-Fri., 9am-5pm Sat., 9am-3pm Sun., $5-15) specializes in Hawaiian food, bentos, and *poke.* The extensive menu covers the wide range of flavors found in local food from teriyaki and musubi to stews and kimchi, but seafood, in many preparations, is definitely the cornerstone of the menu.

MA'ILI
Steak and Seafood

For a sit-down meal overlooking the ocean,

check out **Maili Sunset Bar & Grill** (87-064 Farrington Hwy., 808/679-9080, www.mailisunsetbarandgrill.com, 4pm-2am daily, $8-24). Open for dinner and late-night shenanigans, it's just about the only restaurant on the west side with a great location, modern decor, full bar, and a sit-down menu. The cuisine is a combination of steak, seafood, and bar food prepared local-style. They also have live music and entertainment on occasion.

Expressly Pineapple

© KEVIN WHITTON

The Dole Plantation was originally opened as a fruit stand in 1950.

Ananas comosus of the family Bromeliaceae is a tropical fruit that originated in southern South America. During the 1500s and 1600s, voyaging ships' captains took this unusual and intriguingly sweet fruit around the world on their journeys. Pineapples seem to have been brought to Hawaii from somewhere in the Caribbean in the early 1800s, but it wasn't until the mid-1880s that any agricultural experimentation was done with them. James Dole planted the first commercial pineapple plots for production on the Leilehua Plateau at Wahiawa just after the turn of the 20th century. To preserve the fruit, he built an on-site cannery in 1903 and later a second in Iwilei in Honolulu. Expanding his operation, Dole bought the island of Lana'i in 1922 and proceeded to turn the Palawai Basin into one huge pineapple plantation–some 18,000 acres at its greatest extent. The Lana'i plantation produced a million pineapples a day during peak harvest. Relying heavily on canning, Dole made the "king of fruits" a well-known and ordinary food to the American public.

Pineapple production is a lengthy process. First the ground must be tilled and harrowed to ready the soil for planting. The crowns of the pineapple fruit (which themselves look like miniature pineapple plants) or slips from the stem are planted by hand into long rows–some 30,000 plants per acre. A drip-irrigation system is then installed and the soil covered with ground cloth to help control pests and weeds. Fertilizers and pesticides are sprayed as needed, and the plants grow in the warm tropical sun. After 11-13 months these plants fruit. Generally each plant yields one fruit, which grows on a center stalk surrounded by sharp and spiky curved leaves. The plant sprouts again and, about 13 months later, a second crop is taken. Sometimes a third crop is also harvested from these same plants, before the remainders are tilled into the soil and the process begins again. Pineapples are picked by hand–a hot, dusty, and prickly job–and then placed on a boom conveyor that dumps them into trucks for transportation to the cannery. There, all are pressure-washed and sorted by size and quality before being canned or fresh-packed into boxes and shipped to market. Generally about two-thirds are sold as fresh fruit; the remainder is canned. All aspects of production are rotated to keep pineapples available for market throughout the year. There are no longer any pineapple canneries on O'ahu.

MAKAHA

Markets

In the Makaha Marketplace on the corner of Farrington Highway and Makaha Valley Road, you'll come to **Ohana Market** (84-1170 Farrington Hwy.), your last chance for snacks, local sundries, and beverages if you're headed to Ka'ena Point.

KO OLINA

If you're looking for a traditional sit-down, white tablecloth meal on the west side, then drop into Ko Olina, where top chefs have set up shop to cater to the resort guests.

Quick Bites

Off the Hook (92-1185 Aliinui Dr., 808/674-6200, http://resorts.disney.go.com/aulani-hawaii-resort, 9am-11pm daily, $9-15) is an open-air, beachside lounge in the Aulani Resort, resembling a seaside fishing shack with Hawaiiana-inspired decor. The appetizer menu features Asian-influenced fare with the option to build your own seafood platter priced per piece. The full bar specializes in tropical cocktails.

Island Country Market (92-1048 Olani St., 808/671-2231, 6:30am-11pm daily) and **Two Scoops Ice Cream** (92-1048 Olani St., 808/600-9888, www.twoscoopsicp.com, 11am-9pm daily, $3-9) are both located in the Ko Olina Center & Station, near the Ko Olina entrance on the mountain side of the golf course and train tracks. The market has a full deli with hot and cold prepared foods, groceries, produce, raw foods, and alcohol. They also have tourist garb like towels, shirts, and souvenirs. Two Scoops is a locally owned ice cream parlor with sundaes, frozen drinks, smoothies, and coffee drinks. In addition to supreme ice cream, they also have a jumbo hot dog and Philly cheesesteak on the menu.

Steak and Seafood

Inside the Marriott Beach Club, **Chuck's Steak & Seafood** (92-161 Waipahe Pl., 808/678-8822, www.chuckshawaii.com/steakseafood.html, 4:45pm-9:30pm Mon.-Thurs., 4:45pm-10pm Fri.-Sun., $20-45) serves classic, no frills steak and seafood dishes. Enjoy indoor or outdoor seating and a full bar with two nightly happy hours.

A Hawaii staple, **Roy's** (92-1220 Aliinui Dr., 808/676-7697, www.roysrestaurant.com, 11am-2pm and 5:30pm-9:30pm Mon.-Fri., 11am-2pm and 5pm-9pm Sat.-Sun., $15-45) offers lunch and dinner in the Ko Olina Golf Club. Known for its signature Hawaiian fusion cuisine, Roy's blends fresh ingredients with European sauces and Asian spices. A prix fixe menu includes wine pairings and the exceptional desserts are made fresh to order. Indoor and outdoor seating overlooks the golf course.

Japanese

Located in the JW Marriott Ihilani, **Ushio-Tei** (92-1001 Olani St., 808/679-0079, www.ihilani.com, 5:30pm-9pm daily, $5-52) brings traditional Japanese fare to Hawaii along with sushi and sashimi selections in an authentic Japanese garden setting. They have steak and seafood complete dinners, as well their Tabehodai all-you-can-eat buffet (Fri.-Sun., $43 adult, $21.50 children 5-12) featuring cold items, hot fare, and maki sushi.

Italian

Azul (92-1001 Olani St., 808/679-0079, www.ihilani.com, 6pm-9pm daily, $20-42) is also located in the JW Marriott Ihilani. This award-winning, fine dining Italian restaurant blends Italian cuisine with island ingredients. Reservations are recommended, and resort evening attire is required.

Getting There and Around

CAR

To get to the leeward coast from Waikiki or Honolulu, take the H-1 freeway west. Right before Ko Olina the H-1 turns into Farrington Highway, Route 93. Farrington Highway runs the entire length of the leeward coast. The drive from Honolulu to Ko Olina takes about 45 minutes if traffic is flowing. If Ko Olina is your destination, take the Ko Olina exit, which puts you right onto Aliinui Drive, Ko Olina's main road. If you have questions about where to go once inside the community, ask the attendant at the gate as you enter Ko Olina.

Getting around the leeward side is simple; there is only one major road running north and south along the coast—Farrington Highway. Farrington Highway loops past Ko Olina and shoots up the west side, parallel to the coast, all the way to the Ka'ena Point State Park where it ends. Farrington Highway has two lanes in

each direction. From Nanakuli to Makaha, there are a lot of traffic signals, so the short distance drive can take upwards of 45 minutes. Road construction, which is quite common, will bring the highway down to one lane in each direction and cause immediate traffic delays. Even though the west side is still rugged and underdeveloped compared to most other communities on O'ahu, there are still frequent gas stations, several grocery stores, and places to stop and eat if you don't mind fast food.

BUS

TheBus (808/848-4500, www.thebus.org) routes C, 40, 401, 402, and 403 service the leeward side, and there is a transfer station in Wai'anae. Route C is an express route from Ala Moana Center in Honolulu to Makaha. Route 40 runs from Ala Moana Center to Makua, while routes 401, 402, and 403 service the leeward valleys and neighborhoods.

WHERE TO STAY ON O'AHU

Waikiki

With over sixty hotels and resorts packed in between the Ala Wai Canal and the Pacific Ocean, Waikiki's options for accommodations to suit your needs, and your budget, can seem daunting. Selecting a hotel here is all about setting your priorities during your stay. Are you after a beachfront hotel with sand and ocean activities just steps from your room, or is location not a factor because you plan on spending little time in Waikiki? Are you on a romantic getaway where ocean views are a must, or are you traveling with the family and looking for an affordable two-bedroom suite? For business or leisure, Waikiki has it all, including the beautiful beaches, weather, and water it's famous for.

UNDER $100

Pacific Ohana Hostel (2552 Lemon Rd., 808/921-8111, www.hawaiihostelwaikiki. com, $28-85) has female dorms, coed dorms, semiprivate single and double rooms, and private rooms. They have private rooms available with air-conditioning for an additional $10 per night. All rooms have private bathrooms and some units have full kitchens. There is a community kitchen open 8am-8pm. There is

a small charge for linens and towels, and there's coin-operated laundry on-site.

Also on Lemon Road on the east end of Waikiki, **Waikiki Beachside Hostel** (2556 Lemon Rd., 808/923-9566, www.waikiki-beachsidehostel.com, $22-218) is the largest hostel on O'ahu. They offer small and large coed and female dorms. Their semiprivate rooms have two beds, air-conditioning, lockers, private lanai, and a shared kitchen, while the small and large private suites sleep from two to four people and include full kitchen, bathroom, lockers, closet, and electronic door locks. The facility has free wireless Internet access, coffee and toast in the morning, and free local calls from every room. They also have a storage room for $5 per day if you need to leave personal items for an extended period of time.

The **Waikiki Sand Villa** (2375 Ala Wai Blvd., 808/922-4744, www.sandvillahotel.com, $98) is a traditional high-rise hotel for budget travelers. Located on Ala Wai Boulevard, the tower has city views and premium rooms have golf course views for a slightly higher rate. Their suites have kitchenettes.

On the beautiful stretch of coast closer to Diamond Head and away from the bustle of Waikiki, **Diamond Head Beach Hotel** (2947 Kalakaua Ave., 808/922-1928, www.obrhi.com/hawaii/diamond-head-beach-hotel, $95-99) offers discount vacation rentals in a 15-floor pyramid-shaped tower. The studio, one- and two-bedroom condos are fully furnished, with the best views toward the top of the building. There is also a private oceanfront lounge and private beach access from the property.

$100-250

For families or large parties looking for multiple-room accommodations, the **Aston at the Waikiki Banyan** (201 Ohua Ave., 808/922-0555, www.astonwaikikibanyan.com, $191-207) is a condo resort where every suite has separate bedrooms, full kitchens, private lanai, and free wireless Internet. There is also a focus on recreation with a swimming pool, jet spas, sauna, tennis, basketball court, putting green, and playground.

The **Waikiki Gateway Hotel** (2070 Kalakaua Ave., 808/942-6006, www.waikikigateway.com, $118), located in Gateway Park, has stylish and modern standard rooms, while premium rooms have a private lanai. Most of the rooms in the tower offer unobstructed views of the ocean, city, and Fort DeRussy Beach Park. The hotel also has larger rooms with kitchenettes designed for extended stays.

The Equus (1696 Ala Moana Blvd., 808/949-0061, www.equushotel.com, $149-169) is on the western outskirts of Waikiki, near the Ala Wai Harbor and Ala Moana Center. The contemporary, equestrian-themed decor is a departure from most hotel island-style furnishings. All 67 rooms have a midsize refrigerator and wireless Internet access. There is a small plunge pool as well.

Boasting beautiful views of Fort DeRussy Beach Park, **Outrigger Luana** (2045 Kalakaua Ave., 808/955-6000, www.outriggerluanawaikikihotel.com, $159-169) is decorated in contemporary island style with standard rooms, studios with kitchenettes, and suites with full kitchens starting at $219. There is a swimming pool, sundeck, and fitness center at the hotel.

For accommodations closer to Diamond Head and outside the pulse of Waikiki in this price range, check out the **New Otani Kaimana Beach Hotel** (2863 Kalakaua Ave., 808/923-1555, www.kaimana.com, $164-256). With beachfront at Kaimana Beach and right across from Kapi'olani Park, the well-appointed modern rooms have ocean or park views, free Wi-Fi or broadband Internet, private lanai, and refrigerators. Rooms in the Diamond Head Wing also have a microwave and kitchen sink. With Kaimana Beach right out front and the zoo nearby, it's the perfect family location.

Known for award-winning service, the **Aqua Waikiki Pearl** (415 Nahua St., 866/970-4162, www.aquawaikikipearl.com, $177) is a good choice for families looking for affordable multi-bedroom accommodations. The one-, two-, and three-bedroom suites are simply decorated with an island theme and have full kitchens complete with dinnerware and cookware and

Where to Stay in Waikiki

Name	Type	Price
Aqua Bamboo	boutique hotel	$219
Aqua Waikiki Pearl	condo hotel	$177
Aston at the Waikiki Banyan	condo resort	$191-207
Aston Pacific Monarch	condo resort	$196-229
Aston Waikiki Beach Tower	hotel	$607-707
Courtyard by Marriott	hotel	$269-316
Diamond Head Beach Hotel	vacation rental	$95-99
DoubleTree Alana	hotel	$209-229
Embassy Suites	hotel	$399
The Equus	hotel	$149-169
◖ Halekulani	historic hotel	$490-675
Hawaii Prince Hotel Waikiki	hotel	$219-279
Hilton Hawaiian Village	resort	$339-369
Holiday Inn Waikiki Beachcomber	hotel	$217-235
Hotel Renew	boutique hotel	$229-239
Hyatt Regency Waikiki Beach	hotel	$345-395
Ilikai	hotel	$299-319
◖ Moana Surfrider	historic hotel	$415-515
◖ The Modern Honolulu	boutique hotel	$329-379
New Otani Kaimana Beach Hotel	hotel	$164-256
Outrigger Luana	hotel	$159-169
Outrigger Reef on the Beach	hotel	$265-279
◖ Outrigger Waikiki on the Beach	hotel	$319-389
Pacific Beach Hotel	hotel	$205-220

O'AHU

Features	Why Stay Here?	Best Fit For
studios and suites with kitchens	luxury suites with outdoor lanai	couples, honeymooners
full kitchens, private lanai	affordable suites	families
free Wi-Fi, full kitchen, private lanai, pool, jet spa	family focus	families, large groups
studios and suites with kitchens, rooftop pool	location, affordable	families, couples
all suites, gourmet kitchens	location, spacious suites	families, groups
high-speed Internet, business center	open spaces for business	business travelers
studio and multi-room condos, private beach	oceanfront, near Diamond Head	couples, budget travelers
pool, 24-hour fitness center	modern rooms, high-tech	business travelers, couples
all suites, mini-kitchens, fitness center	condo experience in Waikiki	couples, families
in-room Wi-Fi	location	business travelers, budget travelers
deep soak tubs, spa, fine dining	elegant, oceanfront	couples, honeymooners
oceanfront, day spa, fitness center	luxury oceanfront resort	golfers, luxury lovers
oceanfront, pools, saltwater lagoon	self-contained resort	couples, families, honeymooners
sundeck, swimming pool	location	families, couples
Wi-Fi	emphasis on nature	couples
spa, mall	location	beach lovers, couples, families
full kitchens	affordable ocean views	couples, families
oceanfront pool, spa, dining	historic hotel, great location	couples, honeymooners
pool, sundeck, plush furnishings	luxury experience	couples, honeymooners
ocean and park views, free Wi-Fi, private lanai	oceanfront, near Diamond Head	families, couples
pool, sundeck, fitness center, full kitchens	affordable suites	families, budget travelers
free high-speed Internet, restaurants, shops, pool	beachfront location	groups, families, couples
pool, oceanfront location	beachfront location	beach lovers, couples, families
almost 1,000 rooms in two towers	affordable, ocean views	families, couples

(continued)

Where to Stay in Waikiki (continued)

Name	Type	Price
Pacific Ohana Hostel	hostel	$28-85
Queen Kapiolani Hotel	hotel	$199-239
☾ Royal Hawaiian	historic hotel	$455-580
Sheraton Princess Kaiulani	hotel	$250-285
☾ Sheraton Waikiki	hotel	$375-465
Trump Hotel	hotel	$509
Waikiki Beach Marriott	hotel	$279-319
Waikiki Beachside Hostel	hostel	$22-218
Waikiki Gateway Hotel	hotel	$118
Waikiki Parc	hotel	$238-269
Waikiki Sand Villa	hotel	$98

a private lanai with city views. Two-bedroom suites are 986 square-feet for $407 a night, and three-bedroom suites are 1,157 square-feet for $477 a night.

The **Aston Pacific Monarch** (2427 Kuhio Ave., 808/923-9805, www.astonpacificmonarch.com, $196-229) is a small condominium resort just a couple blocks from famous Kuhio Beach Park. They have studios with kitchenettes and one-bedroom suites with full kitchens. One-bedroom suites start at $252 with partial ocean views. Their suites have floor to ceiling glass doors that open up to the trades. There is also a rooftop pool.

Queen Kapiolani Hotel (150 Kapahulu Ave., 808/954-7418, www.queenkapiolani.com, $199-239) is all about location. With great views of Kapi'olani Park and the ocean looking toward Diamond Head, the beach is right across the street, as is the park and the Honolulu Zoo.

Across from Kuhio Beach is the **Pacific Beach Hotel** (2490 Kalakaua Ave., 808/922-1233, www.pacificbeachhotel.com, $205-220). With 839 rooms in two towers, they are able to offer very reasonable rates for ocean view rooms, starting at $228.

On the west end of Waikiki with mountain, ocean, and park views is the contemporary **DoubleTree Alana** (1956 Ala Moana Blvd., 808/941-7275, http://doubletree3.hilton.com, $209-229). The smart design with Hawaiian accents complements the chic and modern rooms with the latest in technology and amenities. There is a small heated outdoor pool and 24-hour fitness center. They offer smoking and nonsmoking rooms, and their high-end suites have private outdoor decks.

The **Holiday Inn Waikiki Beachcomber** (2300 Kalakaua Ave., 808/922-4646, www.waikikibeachcomberresort.com, $217-235) has a central location, and the rooms are bright with light tropical accents. There is a swimming pool on the sundeck and a large workout center. Oceanview one-bedroom suites start around $700.

Decked out in cool, tropical, and Asian-influenced decor from the pool and lobby to the guest rooms, **Aqua Bamboo** (2425 Kuhio Ave., 808/922-7777, www.aquabamboo.com,

Features	Why Stay Here?	Best Fit For
private bathrooms, full kitchens	affordable	budget travelers, backpackers
ocean and park views	location	families, couples
authentic decor, tropical gardens, spa, fine dining	historic, beachfront location	couples, honeymooners
private lanai, pool	location	families, couples
infinity pool, bars, restaurants	oceanfront location	couples, families, honeymooners
studios and suites, marble bathrooms, business service	luxury and service	couples, honeymooners
pool, spa, private lanai	location	couples, families
lockers, free Wi-Fi	affordable, location	budget travelers, backpackers
ocean, city, and park views; studios	affordable, extended stay	business travelers, budget travelers
contemporary, urban luxury	luxury and services	couples, honeymooners
suites, kitchenettes	affordable, private	budget travelers

$219) has standard rooms, studio kitchenettes, and one- and two-bedroom suites. The boutique hotel's sky-high luxury bedroom has an outdoor lanai with a gas grill and patio furniture.

The **Hawaii Prince Hotel Waikiki** (100 Holomoana St., 888/977-4623, www.princeresortshawaii.com/hawaii-prince-hotel-waikiki, $219-279) is an all-oceanfront accommodation, meaning that its design affords every room a floor-to-ceiling ocean view, overlooking Ala Moana Harbor and Ala Moana Beach and Park. Located on the western edge of Waikiki near Ala Moana Center, the sophisticated hotel has 57 luxury suites, restaurants, a day spa, and a fitness center, and caters to golfers with packages for play at the Hawaii Prince Golf Club in 'Ewa. One-bedroom suites start at $379, and two-bedroom suites start at $599.

Hotel Renew (129 Paoakalani Ave., 808/687-7700, www.hotelrenew.com, $229-239) is a small, modern boutique hotel with a sophisticated interior focused on balance and harmony. Wireless Internet, use of beach gear, and morning coffee or tea are complimentary in all 72 rooms, themed to echo the natural environment. Their oceanview rooms start at $289 a night.

The **Waikiki Parc** (2233 Helumoa Rd., 808/921-7272, www.waikikiparc.com, $238-269) offers contemporary urban style and luxury. It's modern, the guest rooms are plush, and it's billed as the chicest boutique hotel in Waikiki. Guests also have access to services at their sister hotel, Halekulani, right across the street.

$250-400

Located on one of the busiest corners in Waikiki, the **Sheraton Princess Kaiulani** (120 Kaiulani Ave., 808/922-5811, www.princess-kaiulani.com, $250-285) has three distinct buildings that comprise the hotel. All rooms in the Kaiulani Wing and Ainahau Tower have a private lanai. There is a pool in the center courtyard, and the hotel has suites and family rooms. The rooms have a simple and clean feel with light colors and wood furnishings.

A beachfront hotel on the western end of Waikiki, the **Outrigger Reef on the Beach**

(2169 Kalia Rd., 808/923-3111, www.outrigerreef-onthebeach.com, $265-279) offers restaurants, shops, and renewed accommodations in an elegant modern style. Their moderate-rate rooms have no view, but there is free high-speed Internet access throughout the hotel. For families and large groups, the hotel has one-bedroom ocean and city-view suites, and two-, three-, and four-bedroom oceanview suites.

The **Courtyard by Marriott** (400 Royal Hawaiian Ave., 808/954-4000, www.marriott. com/hotels/travel/hnlow-courtyard-waikiki-beach, $269-316), just behind the Duty Free Shopping Galleria on Kuhio Avenue, has comfortable rooms with soft colors and wood decor. With high-speed Internet throughout the hotel, business center, and flexible open spaces in the lobby, the hotel is geared toward business travel.

The **Waikiki Beach Marriott** (2552 Kalakaua Ave., 808/922-6611, www.marriott. com/hotels/travel/hnlmc-waikiki-beach-marriott-resort-and-spa, $279-319) is a resort right across the street from Kuhio Beach Park. There are shops and restaurants on the 5.2-acre property, swimming pool and spa, and the rooms are stylish with wood accents and private lanai.

Located on the west side of the Hilton Hawaiian Village, fronting the Ala Wai Boat Harbor, the **Ilikai** (1777 Ala Moana Blvd., 808/949-0892, www.ilikaihotel.com, $299-319) has 30 stories of ocean views. They also have mountain-view and oceanview full kitchen rooms starting at $339, as well as mountain- and oceanview two-bedroom suites starting at $399.

For accommodations right in the heart of Waikiki on Waikiki Beach, check out the ❰ **Outrigger Waikiki on the Beach** (2335 Kalakaua Ave., 808/923-0711, www.outrigger.com/hotels-resorts/hawaiian-islands, $319-389). Perfect for visitors interested in taking advantage of all of Waikiki's ocean activities, the hotel also has one of the best, and most famous, restaurants in Waikiki, Duke's Waikiki. The guest rooms are Hawaiian themed with dark wood furnishings.

Overlooking the Ala Moana Small Boat Harbor, ❰ **The Modern Honolulu** (1775 Ala Moana Blvd., 808/954-7427, www.themodern-honolulu.com, $329-379) mixes sophistication and smart modern design with a laid-back surf culture vibe. The Sunrise Pool has a warm, wood deck with potted shade trees, and the Sunset Pool, an adults-only blue-tiled pool, is surrounded by sand imported from neighboring islands. The luxurious rooms have innovative design features and plush furnishings. One-bedroom suites are available.

The **Hilton Hawaiian Village** (2005 Kalia Rd., 808/949-4321, www.hiltonhawaiianvillage.com, $339-369), a 22-acre oceanfront mega-resort on the west end of Waikiki, is practically its own town. Nestled right up to the sand on Duke Kahanamoku Beach, the widest beach in Waikiki with calm water perfect for the family, the resort has swimming pools, waterslides, and waterfalls, a saltwater lagoon, its own luau, 18 restaurants, retail shops, and a Friday night fireworks show. For accommodations, there are five towers: the Rainbow Tower is right on the beach with amazing views, the Ali'i Tower focuses on luxury, with separate check-in, a private pool, whirlpool, and fitness center, and three Village Towers offer lower-rate rooms.

The **Hyatt Regency Waikiki Beach** (2424 Kalakaua Ave., 808/923-1234, http://waikiki. hyatt.com, $345-395) holds prime real estate across from Waikiki Beach and is the perfect hub for travelers looking to take advantage of all the beach activities Waikiki has to offer. Within its central location, it also has a spa, a mall on ground level, and several well-known restaurants. The rooms are simple but classy with a light tropical feel. The suites are modern and sophisticated.

Another beachfront resort that towers over the Pacific, the ❰ **Sheraton Waikiki** (2255 Kalakaua Ave., 808/922-4422, www.sheraton-waikiki.com, $375-465) has stylish and comfortable accommodations, two pools, and on-site dining and shopping. The Infinity Edge pool is a treat for guests 16 and older. There is no beach in front of the hotel, but there is a pathway that runs along the edge of the water and offers beach access in both directions.

Situated in the Waikiki Beach Walk outdoor mall, a hub for Waikiki shopping and dining, **Embassy Suites** (201 Beach Walk St., 808/921-2345, http://embassysuiteswaikiki. com, $399) is an all-suite hotel that offers a condo-like experience. One- and two-bedroom suites have complimentary high-speed Internet, made-to-order breakfasts, and mini-kitchens. There is also a fitness center.

$400-650

The **(Halekulani** (2199 Kalia Rd., 808/923-2311, www.halekulani.com, $490-675) has a long history of hospitality in Waikiki going back nearly 100 years. Today, the Halekulani is a mark of elegance and sophistication. The rooms and suites are light and bright with marble vanities, deep soaking tubs, and glassed-in showers. The oceanfront hotel has a full-service spa and several fine dining restaurants.

Just steps from Kuhio Beach, the **Aston Waikiki Beach Tower** (2470 Kalakaua Ave., 808/926-6400, www.astonwaikikibeachtower. com, $607-707) is an all-suites hotel specializing in spacious two-bedroom suites with fully equipped gourmet kitchens and in-room washer and dryer. Perfect for families that want to be close to the beach for ocean activities.

The first hotel in Waikiki, opening in 1901, the **(Moana Surfrider** (2365 Kalakaua Ave., 808/922-3111, www.moana-surfrider.com, $415-515) is a historic icon along the Waikiki shoreline. Situated in the heart of Waikiki on Waikiki Beach, the original, stately building remains with additional wings and towers to offer over 800 rooms. The hotel also offers an oceanfront spa, a pool, and dining on the veranda under the historic banyan tree. The room decor is modern, yet captures the legacy of the hotel.

Opening in 1927, the **(Royal Hawaiian** (2259 Kalakaua Ave., 808/923-7311, www. royal-hawaiian.com, $455-580) is a landmark hotel also known as "The Pink Palace of the Pacific." The classic elegance of the guest rooms have been preserved, down to the hand-carved wooden doors in the main building. There is also a tower in addition to the historic original hotel. There are garden-view rooms of the tropical gardens and coconut grove, and a range of oceanview rooms and suites on the beachfront on hopping Waikiki Beach. Spa, fine dining, shopping, and a pool and hot tub round out the services.

The **Trump Hotel** (223 Saratoga Rd., 877/683-7401, www.trumphotelcollection. com/waikiki, $509) is all about luxury and service. They offer large studios to three-bedroom suites with fully equipped kitchens with brand-name appliances, Italian marble bathrooms with deep soaking tubs, and sophisticated furnishings. Studios range from 400 to 500 square feet, while the three-bedrooms have over 2,000 square feet of living space. They also offer business services, beach gear, nanny services, a 24-hour fitness center, a spa, and complimentary wireless Internet access.

Honolulu

Even though it is the biggest metropolis in the middle of the Pacific, there aren't many places to stay in Honolulu, most likely because Waikiki is practically next door. There are a few hotels near the airport for those who have an overnight layover and don't wish to take a taxi into Waikiki, one hotel downtown serving a strictly business clientele, and a two more hotels near Ala Moana Center.

ALA MOANA
Under $100
The **YMCA Central Branch** (401 Atkinson Dr., 808/941-3344, www.ymcahonolulu.org, $45-75), next to the Hawai'i Convention Center and across from Ala Moana Center, is the largest YMCA facility on O'ahu. They have partially furnished single and double rooms for men, women, and couples. They also offer rooms with a private shower and bathroom for an additional $10 a day. The double rooms with private baths have a minifridge and microwave, and all guests can use the laundry and fitness facilities. There is no smoking or alcohol permitted on the premises. Weekly and monthly rates are available.

The **YMCA Nu'uanu Branch** (1441 Pali Hwy., 808/536-3556, www.ymcahonolulu.org, $42) is a male-only facility just north of downtown and Chinatown and has 70 single rooms for $42 per night. For women, the **YWCA Fernhurst** (1566 Wilder Ave., 808/941-2231, www.ywca.org, $45) offers a secure residence with 24-hour electronic access located in the downtown Historic District. Double occupancy rooms are $45 per night and singles are $65 per night. The rooms are equipped with telephones and free Internet access. They also have a free computer lab.

$100-250
The **Pagoda Hotel** (1525 Rycroft St., 808/948-8356, www.pagodahotel.com, $128-192), near the Ala Moana Center, is a great option for travelers on a budget who won't be spending a lot of time at their hotel and don't feel

Where to Stay in Honolulu

Name	Type	Price
Airport Honolulu Hotel	budget hotel	$169
Ala Moana Hotel	hotel	$169-219
Best Western the Plaza Hotel	budget hotel	$199-209
Manoa Valley Inn	bed and breakfast	$125-195
Pagoda Hotel	hotel	$128-192
Sand Island State Recreation Area	camping	$18
YMCA Central Branch	hostel	$45-75
YMCA Nu'uanu Branch	hostel	$42
YWCA Fernhurst	hostel	$45

the necessity to stay in Waikiki. The Asian-influenced design and decor is complete with Japanese gardens, koi ponds, and waterfalls. The 359-room hotel has standard guest rooms in the main tower and studios, one-, and two-bedroom units with kitchenettes in the five-story terrace wing.

Just on the outskirts of Waikiki and situated between the Ala Moana Center and the Hawai'i Convention Center is the **Ala Moana Hotel** (410 Atkinson Dr., 808/955-4811, www.alamoanahotelhonolulu.com, $169-219). A bargain compared to some of the beachfront hotels in Waikiki, the location lends itself to those attending a convention or visitors wanting the flexibility of getting out the door and on the road without worrying about the congestion of Waikiki. The two towers offer ocean and city skyline views, and the rooms have free Internet access. They also have one-bedroom suites. And with Ala Moana Center next door, there are plenty of dining options a quick walk from the hotel.

GREATER HONOLULU
$100-250
Built in 1912 in lush Manoa Valley and listed in the National Register of Historic Places,

the **Manoa Valley Inn** (2001 Vancouver Dr., 808/947-6019, www.manoavalleyinn.com, $125-195) is a bed-and-breakfast set in a luxurious Victorian inn filled with European antiques. Nestled in verdant Manoa Valley, the intimate retreat is peaceful and unique, with six rooms and a country cottage available. The residence is surrounded by a tropical garden and has a heated saltwater swimming pool with a meandering waterfall. There are four friendly dogs and a cat on the premises.

The **Airport Honolulu Hotel** (3401 N. Nimitz Hwy., 808/836-0661, www.outrigger.com/hotels-resorts/hawaiian-islands/oahu-waikiki/airport-honolulu-hotel, $169) has basic 300-square-foot rooms with free wireless high-speed Internet, microwave, refrigerator, and free 24-hour airport shuttle service to the hotel.

Clean and scenic for a hotel near the airport, the **Best Western the Plaza Hotel** (3253 N. Nimitz Hwy., 808/836-3636, http://bestwesternhawaii.com/hotels/best-western-the-plaza-hotel, $199-209) offers 274 rooms with microwaves, refrigerator, and free high-speed Internet. They also have free airport shuttle service. There's even a pool if you need to take a quick dip and can't make it to the beach.

Features	Why Stay Here?	Best Fit For
Wi-Fi, microwave, 24-hour airport shuttle	close to airport	business and budget travelers
Internet access	location for business	business and budget travelers
Wi-Fi, microwave, 24-hour airport shuttle, pool	close to airport	business and budget travelers
saltwater pool	peaceful garden setting	couples, honeymooners
Japanese gardens, multi-room suites	location	families, budget travelers
basic facilities	only camping in Honolulu	budget travelers, backpackers
rooms for men, women, and couples; monthly rates	affordable for extended stay	budget travelers, backpackers
men only	Chinatown location	budget travelers, backpackers
women only, free Internet, computer lab	downtown location	budget travelers, backpackers

O'AHU

North Shore

Keeping true to the North Shore's rural and relaxed atmosphere, you won't find the high-rise hotels that identify Waikiki, though many visitors would love to spend their entire vacation in this beautiful region. Turtle Bay Resort has the distinction of being the only high-occupancy accommodation on the North Shore, a designation reflected in its room rates. Luckily for travelers enamored by the North Shore, the community is full of vacation rentals. The North Shore is more family-friendly in the summer when the surf is flat and the conditions for swimming and snorkeling are perfect.

NORTH SHORE BEACHES
Under $100

Hawaii Backpackers (59-788 Kamehameha Hwy., 808/638-7838, http://backpackers-hawaii.com, $27-62) is the North Shore's only hostel and is a collection of several properties around the Three Tables area. They have three location choices for hostel beds and four locations for private rooms and studios as well. Their hostel beds start at $27 per night; they have private rooms with shared kitchen and bath starting at $62 per night; their private studio apartments have ocean views and a patio overlooking the beach with a full bath and start at $120 per night; and their private cabins sleep four to eight people and have full kitchens starting at $160 per night. They also offer a 10 percent discount off weekly rates.

$100-250

◖ **Ke Iki Beach Bungalows** (59-579 Ke Iki Rd., 808/638-8829, http://keikibeach.com, $160-230) is located on Ke Iki Beach, just to the north of Sharks Cove and not far from Pipeline. The studio, one-, and two-bedroom bungalows are clean, stylishly appointed in tropical décor, and could not be in a more beautiful location, fronted by the Pacific Ocean and surrounded by tropical foliage. The five beach-front bungalows sleep between three and five people and start at $195 per night. Six garden-view bungalows sleep between two and eight people and start at $160 per night. Extra cleaning fees apply.

TURTLE BAY
$250-400

◖ **Turtle Bay Resort** (57-091 Kamehameha Hwy., 808/293-6000, www.turtlebayresort.com, $251-315) is the North Shore's premier

Where to Stay on O'ahu's North Shore

Name	Type	Price
Hawaii Backpackers	hostel	$27-62
Kaiaka Bay Beach Park	camping	$50
◖ **Ke Iki Beach Bungalows**	cottages	$160-230
◖ **Turtle Bay Resort**	resort	$251-315

OʻAHU

Turtle Bay Resort is the North Shore's only high-occupancy hotel.

hotel and resort. The property is spread across almost five miles of beachfront and the family-friendly, surf-friendly, and golf-friendly resort has a wide range of accommodations including 375 guest rooms and 25 suites ($330-660) in their six-story main hotel, 42 beach cottages ($500), and luxury ocean villas with beachfront locations along Kuilima Cove. The pool and waterslide will keep the kids busy all day. There is a surf break right off Kuilima Point where the hotel sits, and the resort is home to two championship golf courses. Package rates for golf and accommodations are also available.

Features	Why Stay Here?	Best Fit For
private rooms, ocean views	accommodates large groups	backpackers, budget travelers
beach camping	natural setting	nature lovers, budget travelers
bungalows, five beachfront	affordable, natural setting	nature lovers, couples, honeymooners
suites, beach cottages, villas	only resort on the North Shore	nature lovers, couples, honeymooners, families

OʻAHU

Southeast and Windward

On the southeast shore you'll find the only resort in this region, the high-class Kahala Hotel & Resort, and vacation rentals in Hawai'i Kai. On the windward coast, camping is prevalent in the beach parks, just be prepared for rain and wind, common weather conditions on this side of the island. Kailua boasts an array of bed-and-breakfast accommodations and vacation rentals to service the seaside hamlet, a great option for escaping from the Waikiki scene to one of the prettiest white sand beaches on the island.

SOUTHEAST OʻAHU
$400-650

At the end of Kahala Avenue in the affluent

Kahala neighborhood is the luxurious ◖ **Kahala Hotel & Resort** (5000 Kahala Ave., 808/739-8888, www.kahalaresort.com, $495-675). The rooms and suites are decorated in a light tropical palette with island accents, and guests can enjoy the secluded white sand beach just steps away. The hotel has its own private lagoon where guests can interact with dolphins and other sea creatures. A swimming pool, high-end spa with 10 private treatment suites, and a beachfront fitness center are a few of the amenities.

KAILUA
Under $100

Set on the Kaʻelepulu Stream, four blocks from

Where to Stay on the Southeast and Windward Coast

Name	Type	Price
Ahupuaʻa O Kahana	camping	$18
Bellow Field Beach Park	camping	$30
Hauʻula Beach Park	camping	$50
Hawaii's Hidden Hideaway Bed and Breakfast	B&B	$145-195
Hoʻomaluhia Botanical Garden	camping	$30
◖ Kahala Hotel and Resort	resort	$495-675
Kokololio Beach Park	camping	$50
Kualoa Regional Park	camping	$30-50
◖ Lanikai Bed and Breakfast	B&B	$160-175
Papaya Paradise	bed and breakfast	$100
Pillows in Paradise	bed and breakfast	$99-119
Sharon's Kailua Serenity Bed & Breakfast	B&B	$80-95
Sheffield House Bed & Breakfast	bed and breakfast	$129-169
Waimanalo Bay Beach Park	camping	$50

Kailua Beach, **Sharon's Kailua Serenity Bed & Breakfast** (127 Kakahiaka St., 808/262-5621, www.sharonsserenity.com, $80-95) has two rooms and one suite available with a continental breakfast. Casual and homey, the Blue Room has one queen-size bed, and the Poolside Room has a king and a twin bed. The suite is designed for a family of three to four. There are no cleaning fees. There is also a dog on the premises.

$100-250

Just a few blocks away from Kailua Beach, **Pillows in Paradise** (336 Awakea Rd., 808/262-8540, www.pillowsinparadise.com, $99-119) offers two units: a private one-bedroom unit and a spacious studio suite with king- and queen-size beds, perfect for families. Both units have private bathrooms and

entrances, coffeemaker, refrigerator, microwave, and other kitchen items. A swimming pool graces the tropical garden.

The **Sheffield House Bed & Breakfast** (131 Kuulei Rd., 808/262-0721, www.hawaiisheffieldhouse.com, $129-169) is just steps away from Kailua Beach and has two suites with private entrances, Mexican tile floors, wireless Internet, kitchenettes, and off-street parking. The Ginger Studio with Secret Garden sleeps two to three and has a tropical garden and fountain outside the entrance. The Garden Suite sleeps two to four and can be combined with the Ginger Studio to form a two-bedroom, two-bath rental. There are cleaning fees in addition to the rate and a complimentary breakfast on the first morning of the stay.

Located a half-mile from the beach, **Papaya**

Features	Why Stay Here?	Best Fit For
beachfront camping	close to valley hiking	couples, nature lovers, budget travelers
lifeguards, gated campground	campsite on active military base	families, budget travelers, couples
pavilion, convenient store	location	budget travelers
private bathrooms, kitchenettes, laundry	location	couples, honeymooners
basic facilities	fishing, bird-watching	groups, families, nature lovers
beachfront, private lagoon, spa	luxury, beach location	luxury lovers, couples, honeymooners
beachfront	fishing	budget travelers
basic facilities	fishing and recreation	couples, families, nature lovers
suites, king-size bed, kitchenettes	beautiful setting	couples, honeymooners
pool, Wi-Fi, mountain views	family-oriented	couples, families
private bathrooms, pool, kitchen	location, privacy	couples, families
pool, Wi-Fi	family-oriented	families
private entrance, Wi-Fi, kitchenettes	beach location, privacy	couples, families
shaded beach, basic facilities	beautiful beach	budget travelers, nature lovers, couples

Paradise (395 Auwinala Rd., 808/261-0316, www.kailuaoahuhawaii.com/papaya.htm, $100) has a large swimming pool, great views of the Ko'olau Mountains, and a covered lanai for relaxing, reading, and enjoying the daily complimentary continental breakfast on. The rooms have wireless Internet, private entrances, private baths, two beds, and tropical furnishings. They also have beach accessories on hand to borrow.

Just south of Kailua in the Lanikai enclave, **Hawaii's Hidden Hideaway Bed and Breakfast** (1369 Mokolea Dr., 808/262-6560, www.ahawaiibnb.com, $145-195) has several suites surrounded by tropical foliage with private entrances, private bathrooms, kitchenettes, dining areas, lanai, wireless Internet, and laundry facilities. The Deluxe Studios each sleep two and offer a choice of king, queen, or twin beds. The Peacock Suite sleeps two to three and has a large lanai with an outdoor spa. The units can be interconnected, and there are additional cleaning fees of $55 per unit.

❰ **Lanikai Bed and Breakfast** (1277 Mokulua Dr., 808/261-7895, http://lanikaibedandbreakfast.com, $160-175) is 100 yards from Lanikai Beach. The Garden Studio has teak and bamboo furnishings, an outdoor dining area, and a king-size bed. The Tree House is a spacious upstairs two-bedroom suite surrounded by mature trees. Both units have high-speed Internet and kitchenettes.

Pearl Harbor and the Leeward Coast

Only two hotels service the Pearl Harbor area, both geared toward long-term guests. Ko Olina is a great family destination for those seeking a controlled and manicured resort atmosphere without the crowds and nightlife of Waikiki. Inside Ko Olina you'll find the amenities of

Where to Stay near Pearl Harbor and on the Leeward Coast

Name	Type	Price
❰ Aulani	resort	$505-650
Harbor Arms	apartment hotel	$113-125
Harbor Shores	apartment hotel	$120
Hawaiian Princess	condominium	$149-209
❰ JW Marriott Ihilani	hotel	$369-419
Kea'au Beach Park	camping	$50
Ko Olina Beach Villas Resort	luxury villas	$832
Ma'ili Beach Park	camping	$30
Makaha Shores	apartments	$525/week
Marriott's Ko Olina Beach Club	villas and suites	$295-600
Nanakuli Beach Park	camping	$50

luxury resorts, hotels, and vacation rentals, but you'll also sacrifice Waikiki's selection of restaurants, ocean activities, and nearby sights, as Ko Olina is very isolated on the southwestern tip of the island. Makaha has vacation rentals in condominium towers right on the beach. There is also camping at westside beach parks.

PEARL HARBOR
$100-250

The **Harbor Shores** (98-145 Lipoa Pl., 808/488-5742, www.harborshoreshi.com, $120) is an apartment hotel located on the shore of Pearl Harbor. They have basic, no frills two-bedroom units with full-size kitchens, private lanai, microwave, refrigerator, toaster oven, wireless Internet access, and a swimming pool. They cater to military families, budget travelers, and business travelers. Rates depend on the number of guests per room, and they offer weekly rates as well.

In similar fashion, the **Harbor Arms** (98-145 Lipoa Pl., 808/488-5556, www.harborarms.com, $113-125) apartment hotel has one- and two-bedroom suites with partial or full kitchens, private lanai, and free cable TV and wireless Internet. They also have a swimming pool and offer weekly rates.

LEEWARD COAST
$100-250

You'll only find visitor accommodations at Makaha. The **Hawaiian Princess** (84-1021 Lahilahi St., 800/776-2541, www.hawaiianprincessmakaha.com, $149-209) is one of the more stylish and well-maintained condominium buildings along Makaha Beach. Their one- and two-bedroom units have 180-degree views of the Pacific, full kitchens, washer/dryer, and private lanai. There is also a pool, hot tub, barbecue area, tennis court, and recreation room. One-bedroom units start at $149, and two-bedrooms rent for $209.

Makaha Shores (84-265 Farrington Hwy., 808/696-4186, www.makahashores.com) rents simple studio apartments with full-size kitchens and private lanai. There is a barbecue area by the swimming pool, and beautiful

Features	Why Stay Here?	Best Fit For
aquatic park, spa, fine dining, suites	family-oriented Disney resort	families
suites, pool, Wi-Fi, cable	long-term stay	military families, business travelers
two-bedroom units, full kitchen, private lanai	long-term stay	military families, business travelers
full kitchens, laundry, private lanai, ocean views	slow pace	couples, families
spacious suites, spa, fine dining, pools	luxury golf resort	luxury lovers, couples, honeymooners, families
grassy campsites	affordable	budget travelers
two- and three-bedroom villas, ocean views	private, long-term stay	luxury-loving families, couples, honeymooners
basic facilitres	fishing	budget travelers
studios with full kitchens, pool	slow pace	couples, families
full kitchens, lanai, washer/dryer	family-oriented	couples, families
shaded campsites	fishing	budget travelers

Makaha Beach is steps away. Other than ocean activities, there's not much to do in the area, or places to eat out, so guests should be comfortable with being self-sufficient on this quiet nook of coastline. Rates start at $525 per week and discounts are offered for longer stays.

KO OLINA
$250-400

Three swimming pools, seven whirlpool spas, and a beautiful seaside lagoon make the **Marriott's Ko Olina Beach Club** (92-161 Waipahe Pl., 808/679-4700, www.marriott.com/hotels/travel/hnlko-marriotts-ko-olina-beach-club, $295-600) the ultimate kid-friendly resort. Their one-, two-, and three-bedroom villas with fully equipped kitchens and tableware provide for a family vacation that is much more comfortable, and their master suites with oversize soaking tubs and king-size beds are the ultimate in relaxation for couples. The villas also have private lanai, washer/dryer, and wireless high-speed Internet.

the JW Marriott Ihilani, Ko Olina

© JW MARRIOTT IHILANI RESORT AND SPA

$400-650

The **⚜ JW Marriott Ihilani** (92-1001 Olani St., 808/679-0079, www.ihilani.com, $369-419) is a bastion of luxury with marble bathrooms, dual vanities, and balconies for all their 640-square-foot rooms and spacious suites. The resort is complete with award-winning Ihilani Spa, two pools, tennis, golf, fine dining, and informal all-day restaurants and lounges. The resort also has direct access to one of Ko Olina's seaside lagoons.

⚜ Aulani (92-1185 Aliinui Dr., 808/674-6200 or 714/520-7001, http://resorts.disney.go.com/aulani-hawaii-resort, $505-650), A Disney Resort & Spa, is set on one of the trademark Ko Olina lagoons, and its Hawaiian theme is everything you'd expect from Disney. At the center of this family-oriented resort is Waikolohe Valley. The aquatic adventure park has a winding river with two tubing adventures, one with rapids and caverns, an enormous swimming pool with waterslides, a private snorkeling lagoon with tropical fish, and an interactive play area for the littlest ones. There are also a separate pool and spas away from the main pool for parents wanting to enjoy some peace and quiet. During the day, Disney characters make appearances, and after the sun goes down there are age-specific theme parties for the kids. The rooms are modern and luxurious, and there are several types of views that dictate the room rate. The suites are designed for large families. They also have a spa, fine dining, and casual dining at the resort.

For families or couples after a romantic getaway, the **Ko Olina Beach Villas Resort** (92-106 Waialii Pl., 808/679-4088 or 877/333-3808, http://koolinabeachvillasresort.com) features private villa suites, each with a unique floor plan and an elegant and sophisticated interior design. The two- and three-bedroom villas feature separate living and dining areas, private lanai, and partial to full ocean views. One-bedroom villas are only available during the low season for $405 per night. All rooms have a seven-night minimum stay.

MAUI, LANA'I, AND MOLOKA'I

There is a prominent Hawaiian saying about Maui: *Maui no ka oi*. "Maui is the best." Residents and visitors alike can agree that there is something special—even magical—about Hawaii's second largest island. Yet it's hard to pinpoint exactly one thing that places Maui among the most dreamed-of vacation locations in the world.

The endless stretches of golden sand are an obvious and noteworthy draw, but that alone doesn't entice millions of visitors to flock to a 727-square-mile dot in the middle of the Pacific. Perhaps it's more than just the image of yourself in a lounge chair on the sand with a mai tai in hand and the soft breeze rustling the palm trees overhead. Maybe it's also the way the trade winds blow across a beach of black sand at Wai'anapanapa State Park, stirring up waves on the sparkling blue waters. Or it's the hope of a close encounter with a giant green sea turtle while snorkeling off the coast of Napili Bay. Or maybe it's the way the setting sun reflects in the waters off Makena, creating an atmosphere that's both fiery and calm in the same fleeting moment.

There's a good chance the secret to Maui's allure lies in the many moments that stick with you long after you've left the island behind. Hiking through a bamboo forest so thick it nearly obscures the sun and

finding yourself at the base of a 400-foot waterfall cascading down a rocky cliff. Riding your first wave and feeling the thrill of the surf as you glide across a silky blue break. Waking at 3am to drive up a dark mountainside in the freezing cold to see the first rays of light illuminate the rich colors of Haleakala Crater.

These are the moments that make a trip to Maui truly *no ka oi*.

Planning Your Trip

WHERE TO GO
West Maui
West Maui pulses with a unique coastal vibe. The historic town of **Lahaina** was once the capital of the Hawaiian kingdom, and it retains a port town atmosphere. Warm weather and mostly dry conditions make this region a spectacular place for outdoor adventure. Snorkel with sea turtles at **Napili Bay,** lounge on the beach in **Kapalua,** ride the zipline above **Ka'anapali,** or hike to **Nakalele Blowhole.**

Central Maui
Central Maui is the island's population center and the seat of county government. Most visitors blow through town en route to their beachfront resort, but Central Maui has its own set of sights off the regularly worn trail. The twisting road into **'Iao Valley** is the region's most popular attraction. **Kepaniwai Heritage Garden** exhibits Maui's multicultural heritage, and down on the shoreline at **Kanaha Beach Park,** windsurfers and kitesurfers take to the waves along the stretch of Maui's north shore.

South Maui
From the celebrity-laden resorts of **Wailea** to the condo-dwelling snowbirds of **Kihei,** South Maui is all about worshipping the sun and enjoying the procession of beaches. **Makena** remains South Maui's most adventurous venue with snorkeling, scuba diving, hiking trails, kayaking, and some of the island's most photoworthy beaches. Just offshore, **Molokini Crater** offers 100-foot visibility and the chance to snorkel with up to 250 species of fish.

Upcountry
Rural, laid-back, and refreshingly cool, Upcountry is Maui's most underrated zone. Agriculture and produce dominate **Kula,** and everything from vegetables to vineyards, coffee, and goat cheese can be found in this rural and relaxing enclave. **Polipoli** is the island's little-known adventure zone, where mountain biking, paragliding, and hiking take place in a forest shrouded in mist. Watch the dramatic sunrise from the frosty peak of towering **Haleakala,** the sacred volcano from which the demigod Maui famously snared the sun.

East Maui: the Road to Hana
The New Age town of **Pa'ia** is as trendy as it is jovial. Surfers ride waves along undeveloped beaches, patrons shop in locally owned boutiques, and the town is home to some of the island's best restaurants. Along the famous, twisting **Road to Hana,** tumbling waterfalls and rugged hiking trails await. The **Pools of 'Ohe'o** spill down cliffs to the sea. The hike through a bamboo forest to the base of **Waimoku Falls** is considered the island's best trek.

Lana'i
Home to 3,300 residents and two large resorts, this island is a playground of outdoor adventure. Whether you are staying here or making a day trip from Maui, everything from **hiking** to **scuba diving, golfing,** and **surfing** can be enjoyed readily without the crowds. Learn about the island's history at the **Lana'i Culture and Heritage Center,** and make the journey down

Honokohau
Bay
Honolua
Bay
Po'elua
Bay

Pailolo Channel

Kapalua

West Maui

Kahakuloa

Kahana

Napili-Honokowai

KAPALUA-WEST
MAUI AIRPORT

340

30

Kaanapali

West
Maui
Mountains

Waihee-Waiehu

KANAHA POND
STATE WILDLIFE
SANCTUARY

KAHULUI
AIRPORT

36

Paia

Pu'u Kukui
5,788ft

Wailuku

KAHULUI

37

Lahaina

'Iao Needle

Puunene

370

Waikapu

SUGAR
MILL

30

Olowalu

311

3

Ma'alaea

Kealia Pond
Natural Wildlife
Refuge

30

Ma'alaea
Bay

31

Keo

'Au'au Channel

37

Ulupalaku
Ranch

Molokini
Island

MAUI'S LAST
LAVA FLOW

'Ahihi-kina'u Natural
Area Reserve

La Perouse
Bay

'Alalakeiki Channel

Kaho'olawe
Island

1,477ft

MAUI

Makilo Bay

Waipi'o Bay

Haiku

(36)

Ulumalu

Haliimaile

Makawao

Pukalani

(390)

Olinda

(37)

(394)

(377)

Kula

Waiakoa

(378)

East Maui

Keanae

Wailua

Nahiku

(360)

HANA AIRPORT

Wai'anapanapa State Park

Hana

Haleakala

National

Park

(31)

Hamoa Beach

Pu'u 'Ula'ula 10,023ft

Waimoku Falls

Polipoli Spring State Recreation Area

'Ohe'o Gulch

Kipahulu Ohana

Kaupo

(31)

'Alenuihaha

Channel

Inset map

Kaua'i

Ni'ihau

Lihu'e

Ka'ula

O'ahu

Honalulu

Moloka'i

Lana'i

Kahului

Lahaina

Maui

Kaho'olawe

Waimea

Hawai'i

Hilo

0   100 mi

0   100 km

0   5 mi

0   5 km

© AVALON TRAVEL

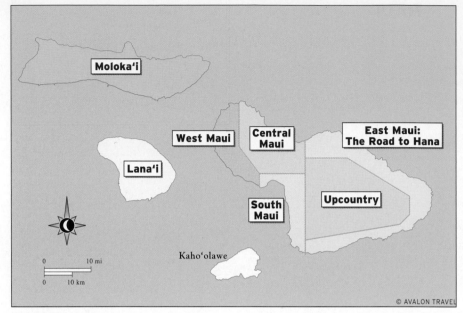

© AVALON TRAVEL

to **Kaunalu** to see an ancient village settlement frozen in time.

Moloka'i

Taking time to explore this island offers a chance to experience the roots of native Hawaiian culture. Take a guided tour into historic **Halawa Valley,** one of the oldest settlements in Hawaii, or ride on the back of a friendly mule as you visit the former leper colony of **Kalaupapa.** Watch the sunset from **Papohaku Beach,** one of the state's longest most deserted stretches of sand, or climb your way high into the mists of the **Moloka'i Forest Reserve.**

PLANNING YOUR TIME ON MAUI

With so many activities and distinct regions on Maui proper, along with the chance to island hop to its neighbor islands of Lana'i and Moloka'i, Maui Nui is a destination where any amount of time spent will never seem enough. The best way to take full advantage of all there

is to do and see is to find accommodations that suite your taste and stay put for the duration of your stay, creating a home base from which you can trek out and explore. Since most of the visitor accommodations on Maui are either on the south shore or the west side of the island, both having similar resort-lined beach scenes with dry, sunny weather, your biggest decision will probably be whether you're after a vacation rental or a hotel room. Not to mention that staying along the south shore, you're about a half-hour drive closer to many of Maui's destinations.

From these areas it's simple to plan activities, many of which on Maui turn out to be day trips. Leave early for journeys to Hana or Haleakala and upcountry Maui. On the way back, stop in funky Pa'ia town for dinner. Conversely, both locales, the sourth and west shores, are great for just staying put. You'll find myriad ocean activities, restaurants and plenty of sandy beach to relax and enjoy the sun and surf. Most of the island's fishing, diving and

Waimoku Falls

tour operators are also located in these two areas.

Moloka'i and Lana'i present opportunities for day trips on land, in the water, or even an overnight getaway from your Maui getaway. Diving operators service the reefs fringing the islands for day trips that explore the beautiful ocean life. Or take the ferry across the channel to experience these small communities set back in time. If the extremely laidback vibe captures your interest, there are accommodations on both islands for overnight stays. If you're interested in touring Kalaupapa, you must acquire permits prior to making travel reservations.

GETTING TO MAUI

In Maui County, the **Kahului Airport** (1 Kahului Airpot Rd., 808/872-3830, hawaii. gov/ogg) is the primary airport on Maui, a hub for overseas and interisland flights. The main interisland carrier flies directly to Maui from all the other major islands. With the smaller carriers, flights from Kaua'i are routed through O'ahu. There are two other small airports on the island serviced only by commuter airlines: Hana Airport (808/248-4861, hawaii.gov/hnm) on the northeast coast, and the Kapalua Airport (808/665-6108, hawaii.gov/jhm) on the west side of Maui, a quick drive to Ka'anapali and Lahaina.

Once on Maui, you can fly or ferry to Moloka'i and Lana'i. On Moloka'i, the **Moloka'i Airport** (808/567-9660, hawaii.gov/mkk) is located about seven miles northwest of Kaunakakai and is serviced by interisland and commuter planes. **Lana'i Airport** (808/565-7942, hawaii.gov/lny) is serviced by interisland and commuter planes. It is located three miles southwest of Lanai City.

Travelers on Maui also have the option of taking a ferry to Moloka'i and Lana'i. **Discover Moloka'i** (658 Front St. #101, 808/667-9266, 877/500-6284, www.molokaiferry.com) provides interisland ferry service from Maui to Moloka'i twice daily with two boats, the *Maui Princess* and the *Molokai Princess*. One-way rates for adults are $68.53, children are $34.27, and infants three years and under are free. Rates include taxes and fuel surcharge. The ferries depart from Lahaina Harbor on Maui and Kaunakakai Harbor on Moloka'i. The company also offers ferry and car rental packages. One-way travel time aboard the high-speed ferry is about 90 minutes. **Expeditions** (658 Front St., 808/661-3756, 800/695-2624, www.go-lanai.com) operates the Maui-Lana'i Ferry. Ferries depart five times daily from Lahaina Harbor and Manele Bay, Lana'i. One-way rates for adults are $30 and $20 for children.

WEST MAUI

The slopes and shores of West Maui are what many visitors picture when they close their eyes and envision paradise: white sandy beaches, rocky coves, lush valleys, and oceanfront restaurants where the clinking glasses of mai tais and the smooth sounds of a slack key guitar complement the setting sun. The beaches are some of the best on the island. In winter, Honolua

© KYLE ELLISON

HIGHLIGHTS

LOOK FOR (TO FIND RECOMMENDED SIGHTS, ACTIVITIES, DINING, AND LODGING.

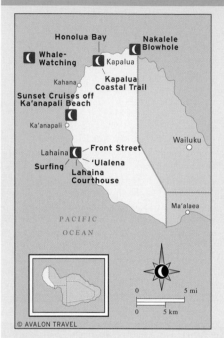

© AVALON TRAVEL

(**Honolua Bay:** In summer, snorkel with sea turtles in this legendary protected bay. In winter, watch as the island's best surfers drop into waves over 20 feet high (page 234).

(**Surfing Lahaina:** This ancient capital is one of the island's best places for learning the Hawaiian sport of kings (page 248).

(**Sunset Cruises off Ka'anapali Beach:** Feel the trade winds in your hair as you literally sail into the sunset off West Maui's most iconic beach (page 252).

(**Whale-Watching:** During December through April, the waters off Maui are home to the highest concentration of humpback whales on the planet. Head out for an up-close encounter with these 50-ton creatures (page 253).

(**Kapalua Coastal Trail:** Spend an hour scouring the coastline along this luxuriant yet rugged 1.75-mile trail. Along the way you will pass some of the country's most beautiful beaches (page 257).

(**Nakalele Blowhole:** At this thunderous blowhole, pressure transforms incoming waves into a 100-foot geyser (page 263).

(**Lahaina Courthouse:** With an art gallery in the basement, old photos on the ground level, and a museum on the third story, this is the best way to learn the unique history of Lahaina (page 266).

(**Front Street:** Get your shopping, people-watching, and dining fixes by walking the length of the island's most famous thoroughfare (page 270).

(**'Ulalena:** The history of Hawaii is told through rhythms, dance, and creative special effects inside the impressive Maui Theatre (page 274).

Bay shapes the kind of legendary right-hand point breaks that attract surfers from across the globe. In summer, this same bay offers some of the island's finest snorkeling, where bright parrotfish, shy octopuses, and curious sea turtles occupy an expansive reef.

Hot, busy, and incomparably historic, Lahaina was once the whaling capital of the Pacific as well as the capital of the Hawaiian kingdom. Today,

it's Maui's quintessential tourist town. The name "Lahaina" translates as "cruel, merciless sun." Almost every day is sunny in Lahaina. As a result, it buzzes with an energetic fervor that draws pedestrians to the streets, fishers to the harbor, and surfers to the breaks offshore. Some critics say that Lahaina is little more than a tourist trap. While there is some truth in that gripe, when you look past the T-shirt stands, you will notice

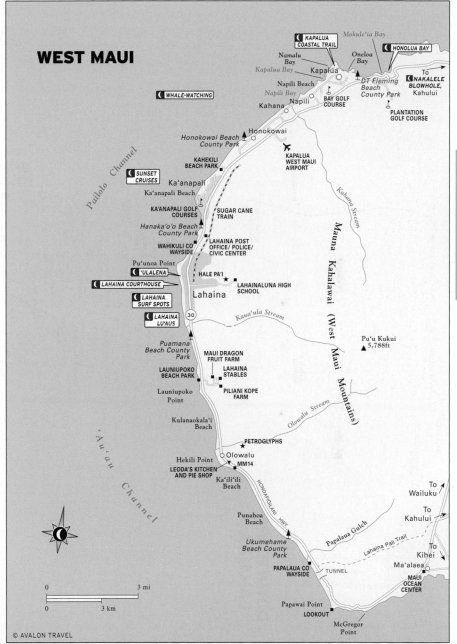

WEST MAUI

(((KAPALUA COASTAL TRAIL

Mokule'ia Bay

(((HONOLUA BAY

Namalu Bay

Oneloa Bay

Kapalua Bay   Kapalua

To NAKALELE BLOWHOLE, Kahului

Napili Beach

DT Fleming Beach County Park

Napili Bay   Napili

(((WHALE-WATCHING

BAY GOLF COURSE

Kahana

PLANTATION GOLF COURSE

Honokowai

Honokowai Beach County Park

KAPALUA WEST MAUI AIRPORT

Paitolo Channel

KAHEKILI BEACH PARK

(((SUNSET CRUISES

Ka'anapali

Ka'anapali Beach

Kahana Stream

KA'ANAPALI GOLF COURSES

SUGAR CANE TRAIN

Mauna Kahalawai (West Maui Mountains)

Hanaka'o'o Beach County Park

WAHIKULI CO. WAYSIDE

LAHAINA POST OFFICE/ POLICE/ CIVIC CENTER

Pu'unoa Point

((('ULALENA

HALE PA'I

LAHAINALUNA HIGH SCHOOL

(((LAHAINA COURTHOUSE

Lahaina

Pu'u Kukui ▲ 5,788ft

(((LAHAINA SURF SPOTS

Kaua'ula Stream

(((LAHAINA LU'AUS

30

Puamana Beach County Park

MAUI DRAGON FRUIT FARM

LAHAINA STABLES

LAUNIUPOKO BEACH PARK

PILIANI KOPE FARM

Launiupoko Point

Olowalu Stream

Kulanaokala'i Beach

PETROGLYPHS

'Au'au Channel

Hekili Point   Olowalu

LEODA'S KITCHEN AND PIE SHOP   MM14

To Wailuku

Ka'ili'ili Beach

To Kahului

Punahoa Beach

HONOAPI'ILANI HWY

Papalaua Gulch

To Kihei

Ukumehame Beach County Park

Lahaina Pali Trail

Ma'alaea

PAPALAUA CO. WAYSIDE

TUNNEL

MAUI OCEAN CENTER

Papawai Point   LOOKOUT

McGregor Point

0   3 mi

0   3 km

MAUI

MAUI

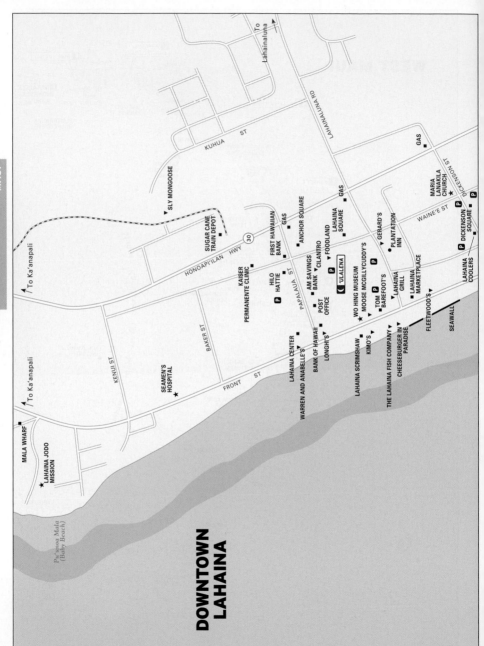

DOWNTOWN LAHAINA

To Lahainaluna

LAHAINALUNA RD

KUHUA ST

SLY MONGOOSE

SUGAR CANE TRAIN DEPOT

GAS

DICKENSON ST

MARIA LANAKILA CHURCH ★

HONOAPI'ILAN HWY 30

To Ka'anapali

To Ka'anapali

WAINE'E ST

FIRST HAWAIIAN BANK

ANCHOR SQUARE

GAS

LAHAINA SQUARE

FOODLAND

GERARD'S

PLANTATION INN

P

P

KAISER PERMANENTE CLINIC

HILO HATTIE

PAPALAUA ST

AM SAVINGS BANK

CILANTRO

'ULALENA

WO HING MUSEUM ★

MOOSE MCGILLYCUDDY'S

P

TOM BAREFOOT'S

LAHAINA GRILL

LAHAINA MARKETPLACE

LAHAINA COOLERS

BAKER ST

POST OFFICE

KENUI ST

LAHAINA CENTER

BANK OF HAWAII

LONGHI'S

WARREN AND ANABELLE'S

LAHAINA SCRIMSHAW

KIMO'S

THE LAHAINA FISH COMPANY

CHEESEBURGER IN PARADISE

FLEETWOOD'S

SEAWALL

SEAMEN'S HOSPITAL ★

FRONT ST

MALA WHARF

LAHAINA JODO MISSION ★

Pu'unoa Mala (Baby Beach)

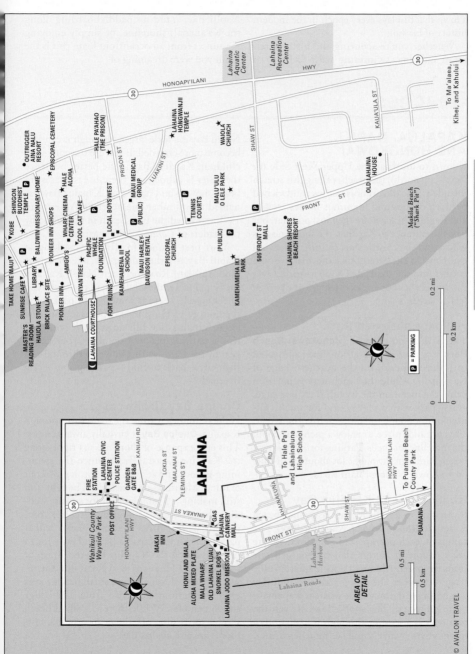

MAUI

© AVALON TRAVEL

a town that displays every epoch in the modern history of Hawaii.

Whether you're scouring the historic relics of Lahaina, swimming with reef fish at Napili Bay, stand-up paddleboarding along the Ka'anapali shoreline, or simply enjoying the sunset from an oceanfront luau, this is the Maui you were dreaming of.

Beaches

KAPALUA, NAPILI, AND HONOKOWAI

Known to locals as the Upper West Side (or simply, up north), the beaches along this stretch include tropical, turquoise coves sandwiched between condos and luxurious homes. Napili and Kapalua beaches are the most popular, but past the entrance to Kapalua, the shoreline gets wilder and the crowds start to thin. The wind can howl in the afternoons and massive surf crashes into the coastline October-April. Over the winter the shorebreak often grows up to 10 feet or larger.

Honokowai Beach Park

The farthest point south, **Honokowai Beach Park** is a narrow stretch of sand connected to Kahekili Beach on the northern edge of Ka'anapali. While the beach here is far from being the nicest on the island, there is a large, grassy park with a playground for small children and a couple of shops across the street. This is a nice place to enjoy a picnic or comb the shoreline for shells. Parking for Honokowai Beach Park is in the public lot about a half-mile down Lower Honoapi'ilani Road.

Napili Bay and Kapalua Bay

If you want to see a hot debate, ask which beach is better: **Napili Bay** or **Kapalua Bay.** The camps on each side are staunchly loyal. There are a couple of factors that distinguish one from the other. Although a mere quarter-mile from each other, the shorebreak at Napili Bay can be larger in the winter whereas Kapalua is more protected. The snorkeling between the two reefs is a tossup, although Kapalua often has more fish while Napili has more sea turtles.

Napili Bay is a little larger, although it can also become more crowded. If you are traveling with children, Kapalua Bay is the better bet since the water is calmer and there is easy access to beach showers and restrooms. Kapalua Bay was named the number one beach in America in 1991 and voted the Best Beach in the World by the readers of *Condé Nast* magazine.

Your best chance for finding parking at Napili Bay is either along the side of Lower Honoapi'ilani Road between Napili Kai and the Kapalua Tennis Club, or, on the south end of the beach, there is some beach parking at the bottom of Hui Drive. The beach parking lot at Kapalua Bay fills up early. If you can't find a parking place, drop all of your beach gear by the stairs leading down to the sand and then circle back to find a parking spot along the road.

Oneloa Bay (Ironwoods)

Hidden from view from the main road through Kapalua, **Oneloa Bay** is virtually always empty. This epic expanse of shoreline sits right along the Kapalua Coastal Trail. Since the swimming is poor and it's out of sight, it's also out of mind. Mornings on Oneloa can be calm and still, making it a popular spot for sunrise wedding shoots. Oneloa is a great beach for communing with nature. To reach Oneloa, either park at the lot for Kapalua Bay and walk for 15 minutes along the Kapalua Coastal Trail, or follow Lower Honoapi'ilani Road into the resort complex of Kapalua to a small beach access path and parking lot across from The Ridge condo complex. While there is a small beach shower for rinsing off, the nearest public restrooms are at Kapalua Bay.

the empty expanse of Ironwoods Beach, on Oneloa Bay

© KYLE ELLISON

MAUI

D.T. Fleming Beach Park

D.T. Fleming Beach Park was the most recent of Maui's beaches to be named number one beach in the United States, garnering the title in 2006. Fleming's is a hybrid stretch of sand where the southern half is dominated by Ritz-Carlton resort guests and the northern half is popular with locals. This is one of the best beaches on the island for bodysurfing and bodyboarding, although the surf here can get rough and dangerous in the winter. Luckily, this is one of the only beaches on the west side with lifeguards. Other amenities include restrooms and showers on the northern section. Out at the point on the southern end of the beach, jagged rocks shape a coastal formation known as **Dragon's Teeth.** Walk parallel to the golf course to reach the end of the point. Once you reach the rocky outcropping, you're greeted with thunderous surf crashing onto the rocks and glimpses of sea turtles poking their heads above the surface. There is a large labyrinth here if you'd like to take a reflective stroll, and

this is also a good vantage point for snapping a photo looking back toward the beach. To access D.T. Fleming Beach Park, take Honoapiʻilani Highway (Hwy. 30) 0.9 miles past the main entrance to Kapalua and turn once you've reached the bottom of the hill for the largest parking area. The road will dead-end in the lot.

Mokuleiʻa Bay (Slaughterhouse)

Mokuleiʻa Bay is another beach where the crowds are thin since you can't see it from the road. Tucked at the base of dramatic cliffs, Mokuleiʻa offers some of the best snorkeling on the west side. It's known to locals as Slaughterhouse Beach, but the name is less sinister than it sounds: a slaughterhouse was once located here but is now long gone. The bay is part of the Honolua Bay Marine Life Conservation District, so no fishing or spearfishing—or any other kind of slaughter—is allowed. This is also a popular beach for bodysurfing, although the surf can be treacherous during the large swells of winter.

This beach is nearly always deserted in the early morning hours. To reach Mokulei'a, travel 2.5 miles past the entrance to Kapalua and park on the left side of the road, where you will then notice a paved stairway leading down to the beach, as well as a sign that details the rules of the marine reserve.

Punalau Beach (Windmills)

Only a handful of visitors will ever make it to **Punalau Beach** at mile marker 34 of Highway 30 since is hidden from the road. The local name of Windmills derives from an old windmill which once stood here but has long since been destroyed. This is now a popular place for advanced surfers and ambitious beachcombers who scour the shoreline for flotsam and shells. The road down to the shoreline can often be rough, so unless you have a high clearance vehicle, it's best to leave your car parked by the highway and make the five-minute trek on foot. Bring all of your valuables with you, and also pack a blanket or towel for lying in the sun and soaking up the silence. Rarely are there crowds at Punalau. Since the reef is shallow and can be razor sharp, don't snorkel or swim here. This is also one of Maui's best spots to watch large winter surf, and the left break at the far southern end has been referred to as Maui's version of Pipeline.

Honokohau Beach

Finally, 5.8 miles past the entrance of Kapalua is the rocky beach of **Honokohau Bay.** The best thing about this beach is the scenery, both of the rural valley and the coast. Unfortunately, despite the scenic conditions, car break-ins have been known to occur, so take your valuables with you. The swimming here is marginal and the waves can be dangerous in the winter.

KA'ANAPALI

The beaches in Ka'anapali are long, wide, and lined by resorts. Much like Kapalua, however, the wind can often be a factor here in the afternoon, so it's best to get your water activities in early before the trade winds start blowing.

Ka'anapali Beach

Few stretches of Maui shoreline are more iconic than famous **Ka'anapali Beach.** This long, uninterrupted expanse of sand is lined from end to end with world-class resorts, it was voted as the number one beach in the United States in 2003, and it's the pulsing epicenter of the West Side's see-and-be-seen crowd. It should come as no surprise that the area is a constant hotbed of activity. Pick any island beach activity: surfing, snorkeling, scuba, snuba, paddleboarding, volleyball, parasailing (summer), or whale-watching (winter), and you'll find it on Ka'anapali Beach. A paved pathway runs the length of the beach and is popular with joggers in the morning.

The best snorkeling is found at Pu'u Keka'a (Black Rock) in front of the Sheraton at the far northern end of the beach. Most of the water sports such as surf lessons take place at KP Point in front of the Ka'anapali Ali'i, and the beach volleyball court is in front of the Sheraton on the north end of the beach. For bodyboarding, the best area is between Whalers Village and Pu'u Keka'a. Since the beach faces directly west, it can pick up waves any time of the year. Be careful on days with big shorebreak, however, and use common sense.

Another favorite activity at Ka'anapali Beach is cliff jumping off Pu'u Keka'a. While this 20-foot jump is popular with visitors and locals, the rock is one of the most sacred places on the island for native Hawaiians who believe it's an entry point for a person's soul passing from this world into the next. To jump off Pu'u Keka'a is to mimic the soul at the moment of death, a legend still told during the evening torch lighting ceremony that takes place before each sunset.

Since Ka'anapali Beach is exposed to the afternoon trade winds, the weather can often be wetter and windier than down the road in Lahaina. The morning hours are best for paddleboarding or snorkeling, and if the wind is blowing too hard by the Sheraton, you can find a pocket of calm at the southern end of the beach by the Hyatt. Also, if you plan on going for a morning swim, realize that there are

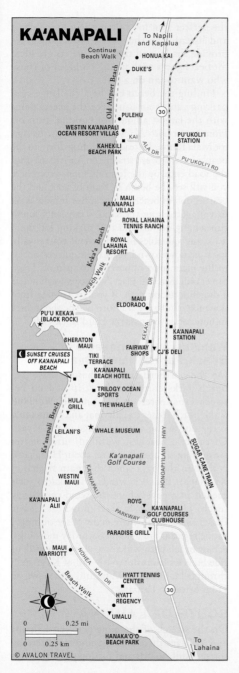

KA'ANAPALI

To Napili
and Kapalua

Continue
Beach Walk

HONUA KAI

DUKE'S

Old Airport Beach

PULEHU

30

WESTIN KA'ANAPALI
OCEAN RESORT VILLAS

KAI

ALA DR

PU'UKOLI'I
STATION

KAHEKILI
BEACH PARK

PU'UKOLI'I RD

Keka'a Beach

MAUI
KA'ANAPALI
VILLAS

ROYAL LAHAINA
TENNIS RANCH

ROYAL
LAHAINA
RESORT

Beach Walk

DR

KEKA'A

MAUI
ELDORADO

PU'U KEKA'A
(BLACK ROCK)

KA'ANAPALI
STATION

SHERATON
MAUI

FAIRWAY
SHOPS

CJ'S DELI

SUNSET CRUISES
OFF KA'ANAPALI
BEACH

TIKI
TERRACE

KA'ANAPALI
BEACH HOTEL

TRILOGY OCEAN
SPORTS

Ka'anapali Beach

HULA
GRILL

THE WHALER

LEILANI'S

WHALE MUSEUM

HONOAPI'ILANI HWY

SUGAR CANE TRAIN

Ka'anapali
Golf Course

WESTIN
MAUI

KA'ANAPALI

KA'ANAPALI
ALII

ROYS

KA'ANAPALI
GOLF COURSES
CLUBHOUSE

PARKWAY

PARADISE GRILL

MAUI
MARRIOTT

NOHEA KAI DR

Beach Walk

HYATT TENNIS
CENTER

30

HYATT
REGENCY

UMALU

0   0.25 mi

0   0.25 km

HANAKA'O'O
BEACH PARK

To
Lahaina

© AVALON TRAVEL

two areas where large catamarans come ashore to pick up passengers, so keep a keen lookout when in the water in front of Ka'anapali Beach Hotel or Whalers Village.

Unless you're staying at one of the resorts along the Ka'anapali strip, parking is going to be a challenge. Free public parking can be tough to come by, since most public spots are taken by 9am. There is one small public garage between the Sheraton and the Ka'anapali Beach Hotel, a lot between Whalers Village and the Westin, a handful of beach parking stalls in the front lot of the Ka'anapali Beach Hotel, and a small public lot on Nohea Kai Drive that leads down to the Hyatt. While there's always a chance that you'll luck out and snag a spot, more often than not you'll end up having to pay to park in the garage of Whalers Village. Remember, however, that if you end up shopping at a store or eating at a restaurant in Whalers Village you can validate the parking ticket.

MAUI

Kahekili Beach Park

There was a time not too long ago when **Kahekili Beach Park,** named after the great king of Maui, was an undeveloped scrubland of kiawe trees and coastal dunes that existed as an afterthought when compared to Ka'anapali Beach. Over time, there has been so much development at Airport Beach (also known as Ka'anapali North Beach) that it's almost as busy as neighboring Ka'anapali. Yet Kahekili still has a family-friendly atmosphere where locals lounge on the grassy area in front of the beach pavilion or snorkel the offshore reef. The beach here is just as long as Ka'anapali Beach, although the steep grade of the shoreline makes it difficult for jogging. Most visitors use the boardwalk along the shoreline, and if you're up for a stroll you can follow this as it weaves through the Royal Lahaina and Sheraton parking areas to meet up with the Ka'anapali beach path. There are easily accessible public restrooms, and there is a large public parking lot at the Kai Ala entrance from the highway. If the lot is full, there's more parking on the north end of the beach, accessible from Lower

Honoapiʻilani Road. The swimming here is much better than at Kaʻanapali since there isn't as much catamaran traffic. If Kaʻanapali Beach is just a little too busy for you, you'll enjoy how Kahekili offers a world-class beach atmosphere but slinks by at a slower pace.

LAHAINA

The beaches of Lahaina are the most underrated on the island. The swimming is poor due to the offshore reef, but they are sunnier, less crowded, and more protected from the wind than most other beaches on Maui. If it's raining in Kapalua or Napili, or windy on Kaʻanapali Beach, 90 percent of the time it's going to be sunny and calm on the beaches of Lahaina.

Makila Beach

Also known as **Breakwall, 505,** or **Shark Pit,** this is the most happening stretch of sand in Lahaina. Most visitors access the beach from Kamehameha Iki Park, and there is beach parking in a small lot or in the back of the Front Street tennis courts. This is the area where most of the surf schools set out from. There is also a beach volleyball court, which can get busy during the afternoons. Visitors are encouraged to marvel at the Polynesian voyaging canoes on display as part of the **Hui O Waʻa Kaulua Canoe Club.** Visitors rarely wander to the south end of the beach where palm trees hang out over a secluded cove. Locals call this area Shark Pit, referencing the harmless reef sharks which hang around the offshore ledge. The swimming here is poor due to the offshore reef, although it provides calm water for wading with small children. There is one shower but no restroom at this beach.

Puʻunoa (Baby Beach)

On the northern end of Front Street, the beach that runs along Puʻunoa Point (and known to locals as **Baby Beach**) is an oasis of tranquility where you have to ask yourself if you're still in Lahaina. Shielded from visitors by its residential location—and protected from big surf by the offshore reef—the sand running along this lazy promontory is

the perfect spot for a sitting in a beach chair and listening to the waves. Numerous trees provide shade, and the calm waters are ideal for beachgoers with young children or those who want to tan on a raft.

Finding the beach can be a challenge, and parking can be an issue. For the access point with the largest amount of parking, turn off Front Street onto Ala Moana Street by the sign for Mala Ramp. Instead of heading down to the boat launch, proceed straight on Ala Moana until the road ends by the Jodo mission. From here you will see the beach in front of you, and the best section of beach will be a five-minute walk to your left along the sand. Transients sometimes hang out around this parking lot; don't leave any valuables in your car. If you're walking from downtown Lahaina, the quickest access to the nicest part of beach is to turn off Front Street onto Kai Pali Place, where you will notice a shoreline access path. If you are coming from downtown Lahaina, this turn will be about three minutes after you pass the Hard Rock Café.

Wahikuli and Hanakaoʻo Beach Parks (Canoe Beach)

On the northern tip of Lahaina, these two beach parks comprise the strip of land between Front Street and Kaʻanapali. **Wahikuli** is the beach closer to Lahaina, and **Hanakaoʻo** is the one at the southern edge of the Hyatt. Of the two beaches, Wahikuli offers better swimming, although a secret about Hanakaoʻo is that on the days when the main stretch of Kaʻanapali Beach is windy, Hanakaoʻo stays tucked in a cove where the wind can barely reach. Hanakaoʻo is also known as Canoe Beach since this is where many of the outrigger canoe regattas are held on Saturday mornings. A new beach path will allow visitors to walk or ride bicycles from the south end of Kaʻanapali through Hanakaoʻo, Wahikuli, and down to Front Street in Lahaina.

SOUTH OF LAHAINA

On the stretch of shoreline between Lahaina and Maʻalaea there are a grand total of zero resorts. Paddleboards and fishing poles rule this section of coast, and even though the swimming is poor, there is one spot that offers good snorkeling. Most visitors choose to pass these beaches by without giving them another thought, but if you do decide to pull over to watch the whales, visit the beach, or photograph the sunset, don't stop in the middle of the road. If you're headed in the Lahaina direction, it's easiest to pull off on the right side of the road and wait for traffic to clear before crossing.

Olowalu

Known to visitors as Mile Marker 14, the real name of this beach is **Olowalu,** after the village that stretches far back into the valley. The snorkeling here is the best south of Lahaina, although plenty of beachgoers—particularly those with young children—come here simply to wade in the calm waters. While the water may be calm, however, it's also shallow, and the swimming area is nonexistent during low tide. Parking is along the side of the highway, although it's easy to get stuck in the sand.

Launiupoko Beach Park

Located at the only stoplight between Ma'alaea and Lahaina, **Launiupoko** is the most family-friendly beach park on the west side of Maui. It has a protected wading area for small *keiki,* a decent sandy beach on the south end of the park, a wide, grassy picnic area, and numerous surf breaks that cater to beginner surfers and stand-up paddle surfers. This park is so popular with the weekend barbecue crowd that local families arrive before dawn to stake their claim for a birthday party with a bouncy house. There is a large parking lot as well as restrooms and showers, and since most of the parking spots are taken by 8am, there is an overflow lot on the *mauka* (mountain side) of the highway. The water here is too shallow for swimming and the snorkeling is poor, but this is a good place for putting your finger on the local pulse and striking up a good conversation.

Puamana Beach Park

There's a decent chance that during your time on the island you'll hear a famous Hawaiian song by the name of "Puamana." This light-hearted, gently flowing melody was written about this section of shoreline that serves as the entry to Lahaina. While there is a private, gated community that goes by the same name, the general public can only visit the small **Puamana Beach Park** one mile north of Launiupoko. As at other beaches in the area, the swimming is poor, although the tables provide a nice setting for a picnic. If you're looking to take a stroll down the beach, the sandy shoreline fronting the condos is public property, so at low tide you can walk from the beach park to the other end of the private, gated section (although the grassy area is still private and should be treated as such). There aren't any restrooms at the beach park, but there's a refreshing shower in the north end of the parking lot.

Puamana Beach Park

Snorkeling

Snorkeling is the most popular activity in West Maui. Hundreds of people ply the waters of the island's western shoreline, flipping their fins as they chase after schools of yellow and black *manini* (convict tang). But there is always room to find your own section of reef, and the waters of West Maui teem with everything from graceful green sea turtles to the playfully named *humuhumunukunukuapua'a*—the Hawaiian state fish (the name is translated as "big lips with a nose like a pig").

Mornings are the best time of day for snorkeling. Different times of year also mean different snorkeling conditions. During the winter, places such as Honolua Bay and Napili can be dangerous due to the huge surf, so summer is the best time for exploring these reefs. Similarly, snorkeling spots on the south shore such as Olowalu can be prone to large surf during summer, although with much less frequency than the northern beaches in winter. If the surf is too big or the conditions too poor, there is probably another place that is calm and beautiful just a 20-minute drive away.

KAPALUA, NAPILI, AND HONOKOWAI
(Honolua Bay

When it comes to snorkeling along Maui's shoreline, **Honolua Bay** is the gold standard. This wide, scenic cleft in the coastline is not only a bio-diverse marine reserve, but it's also protected from the afternoon trade winds. Honolua Bay is one of the most sacred and revered spots on the West Side of the island, and there has been a herculean movement over the last decade to "Save Honolua" and spare the area from development. The valley, bay, and shoreline exude a supernatural beauty. Somewhere between the lush green foliage of the valley and the shimmering, turquoise waters, there is a palpable magic unlike anywhere else.

As the highway morphs into a rural county road, the first glimpse you will get of Honolua is from the paved overlook 1.8 miles past the entrance to Kapalua. This is a nice place to pull over for a picture, but there are better lookouts a mile later. Toward the bottom of the hill, parking for the shoreline is in a lush and shaded valley where you might encounter some merchants selling their crafts. To reach the water, find a parking spot wherever you can (all the trails in a 0.5-mile stretch eventually lead to the shoreline), grab all of your snorkeling gear, and make a short, five-minute trek through a dense green understory which chirps with activity and drips with vines.

The "beach" is more a collection of boulders. If you are facing the water, the right side has a much larger snorkeling area and a greater concentration of marine life. The center of the bay has a sandy bottom and is mostly devoid of marine life, so it's best to trace the shoreline and snorkel around to the right. If it's between the hours of 9am and noon and there aren't any charter boats tied up on the right side of the bay, it means that the conditions aren't acceptable enough to bring paying snorkelers here. Also, if you see breaking waves out toward the point and there are over 20 surfers in the water, it means that the visibility is going to be less than stellar and conditions will be dangerous if you venture in too shallow. If it isn't raining on the shoreline but the stream on the left side of the bay is gushing with brown water, it means that it's raining farther up the mountain and all of the runoff is emptying into the bay. This, of course, will also make for subpar conditions.

If, however, the sun is shining brilliantly, here's your guide to the best snorkeling area: When you enter the water from the rocky shoreline, swim straight out for about 20 yards and then turn right toward the shoreline. You'll want to hug the shoreline in 5-10 feet of water and follow it in a ring around the right side of the bay. If you're on a mission to find Hawaiian green sea turtles, the best spot to check out is

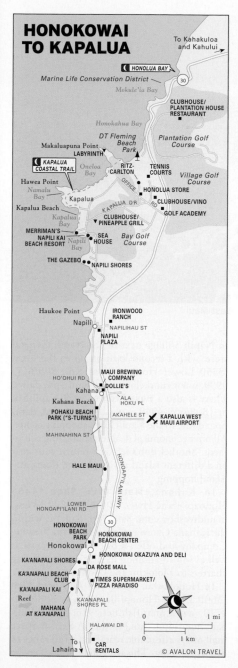

MAUI

the **turtle cleaning station** on the right/center of the bay. It's about 200 yards out from the boat ramp, in line with the bend in the cliff on the right side of the bay, and in about 15-20 feet of water. If you're fortunate enough to snorkel Honolua Bay during winter, dive a few feet underwater to listen for the distant song of humpback whales. Keep a keen eye out for boat traffic as a number of catamarans make their approach through the middle of the bay.

Mokulei'a Bay

Parking for **Mokulei'a Bay** is along the highway 1.5 miles past the entrance to Kapalua, and the best snorkeling is in the cove on the right side of the bay. Even though Mokulei'a is still a part of the Honolua Marine Life Conservation District, the reef here is completely different than at Honolua Bay, so you're likely to see different species than you would right around the corner. Although there's still the likelihood of seeing a sea turtle, there's also a chance for some spotted eagle rays swimming over the sand by the end of the point or perhaps an octopus clinging to the wall at the far end of the cove. Mokulei'a is a little more exposed to the afternoon trade winds, so morning hours during flat, calm days are the best time for snorkeling.

Kapalua Bay

Kapalua Bay is a sandy cove that is a favorite for those who are snorkeling with small children. The relatively small size means it's easy to scour the entire bay, and you can expect to see colorful parrotfish, lots of goatfish, and even the occasional green sea turtle. Although depths rarely exceed 20 feet, the best snorkeling is found along the right side of the bay where the rocks extend out to the distant point. If you're a super-snorkeler and the conditions are calm, you can even snorkel around the northern point into neighboring Namalu Bay.

Napili Bay

A short walk from Kapalua Bay is neighboring **Napili Bay,** and you could easily snorkel at both bays without even reparking your car. Whereas Napili Bay doesn't have quite as many

MAUI

© KYLE ELLISON

Turtles are a common sight when snorkeling in West Maui.

fish as Kapalua Bay, there is a higher likelihood of finding a green sea turtle. While many snorkelers hug the wall on the right side of the bay, there is another reef in the center of the bay that's almost exposed during low tide. About 20 yards farther out from here is a second, lesser-visited reef, and although it's deeper at about 15-20 feet, this is the area with the highest concentration of fish. This outer reef is far from shore, so if you're uncomfortable in the water, stay on the inside reefs and enjoy the shallower waters.

Rental Shops

In Kapalua, the most comprehensive shop is **Kapalua Dive Company** (1 Bay Dr., 808/669-3448, www.kapaluadive.com, 8am-5pm daily) on the northern edge of Kapalua Bay. This is a full-service dive and snorkel operation that also offers guided snorkeling tours, just a short stroll down the Kapalua beach path.

In Napili, **Snorkel Bob's** (5425 Lower Honoapi'ilani Rd., 808/669-9603, www.snorkelbob.com, 8am-5pm daily) and has a shop in Napili Village next to the Napili General store, with a second location down the street (3350 Lower Honoapi'ilani Rd., 808/667-9999, www.snorkelbob.com, 8am-5pm daily). There is also a **Boss Frog's** (5059 Napilihau St., 808/669-4949, www.bossfrog.com, 8am-6pm daily) in the Napili Plaza shopping center. All offer economical deals on snorkeling equipment. Snorkel Bob's lets you return your gear on a different island if you plan on doing any island hopping.

In Kahana, **Maui Dive Shop** (4405 Honoapi'ilani Hwy., 808/669-3800, www.mauidiveshop.com, 8am-9pm daily) is within the Kahana Gateway Center by Maui Brewing Company and offers a full range of rentals as well as information on its dive and snorkeling charters to Molokini and Olowalu.

In Honokowai, locally run **All About Fish** (3600 Lower Honapi'ilani Hwy., 808/669-1710, www.mauifish.net, 9am-5pm Mon.-Sat., noon-4pm Sun.) in the 5A Rent A Space mall offers affordable rentals on a full range of dive equipment. This is a good option if you're staying in a condo in Honokowai and looking for local advice on snorkeling conditions. You can relax knowing you can walk in here to rent some snorkeling gear without somebody trying to sell you a helicopter tour.

KA'ANAPALI
Kahekili Beach Park
In the northern part of Ka'anapali, **Kahekili Beach Park** offers decent snorkeling off the beach park and at the far southern end of the beach. The reef on the northern edge isn't quite as nice as the area in front of the beach park. The reef extends from the shoreline out to about 25 feet of water. Expect to see a healthy amount of herbivorous reef fish here. The moderate depth and easy entry make this a user-friendly snorkeling spot during the early morning hours. At the far southern end of the beach is a rock jetty that also offers good snorkeling, and the rocky promontory here is the "back" of Pu'u Keka'a (Black Rock).

Pu'u Keka'a (Black Rock)
The best snorkeling in Ka'anapali is at **Pu'u Keka'a,** better known as **Black Rock.** At the far northern end of Ka'anapali Beach in front of the Sheraton, this area offers the most consistently beautiful snorkeling conditions and a relatively easy entry. The morning hours are going to be best, and the best chance for seeing sea turtles here is during high tide, when the water comes up on the side of the rock and all of the *limu* (seaweed) falls into the water. Since this is a favorite delicacy of the green sea turtles, there can occasionally be three or four different turtles all congregating in the shallow cove in only 5-10 feet of water. Since the cliff here is also a favorite place for cliff jumping, steer clear of the immediate landing zone, and if you see the wind whipping up whitecaps out by the point, stay in the cove where it's protected and the current isn't as strong.

Ka'anapali Point
On the other end of Ka'anapali Beach is the reef at **Ka'anapali Point.** While it's not nearly as popular as the reef at Pu'u Keka'a, this reef

in front of the Marriott covers a larger area and isn't nearly as crowded. If Pu'u Keka'a is a flotilla of fins, take a 10-minute stroll to the southern end of the beach and try your luck at this lesser-visited spot.

Rental Shops
Every major resort along the strip of Ka'anapali is going to have a rental shack by the sand. Prices vary slightly between all of the operators, although expect to pay the more expensive resort prices rather than what they ask at a snorkeling store off the resort strip. A rental of a couple of hours is commonly $12, although the best deal on Ka'anapali Beach is at the **Maui Dive and Surf** (808/270-9846) kiosk just south of Leilani's at Whalers Village. Snorkeling sets are either $15 for the day or $25 for the week; combine them with a boogie board rental for $35/week.

Snorkeling Charters
A number of catamarans depart directly from Ka'anapali Beach on half-day excursions sailing along the West Maui coastline. For excursions to either Lana'i or Molokini Crater you will still need to go to the Lahaina or Ma'alaea harbors. For all boats departing from Ka'anapali Beach, the preferred snorkeling destination is Honolua Bay. Since the surf at Honolua Bay during the winter can get large, the alternate snorkeling destination is Olowalu on the south shore. During most days of the year these sleek sailing yachts are able to pull their bows right up on the sand and load passengers directly from the beach, although during days with large surf the shorebreak can be too rough and there's a slight chance the trip might be moved to Lahaina Harbor. If a member of your party has restricted mobility, then trips out of Lahaina Harbor will prove a safer option.

Of the crews departing from Ka'anapali Beach, **Trilogy** (808/874-5649, www.sailtrilogy.com) loads in front of the Ka'anapali Beach Hotel and offers 8am snorkeling charters, thereby making them the first boat to Honolua Bay. Trilogy tours from Ka'anapali are usually aboard *Trilogy IV,* a few feet smaller than other

© MARK DRIESSEN

Snorkeling excursions to Molokini Crater depart from Lahaina or Ma'laea harbors.

boats along the beach. The maximum capacity on these trips is only about 35 people. All of the food is made fresh on board. Both the Trilogy crew and the level of customer service are widely regarded as the best in the industry. You shouldn't need to raise a finger since everything is served to you. Due to its slightly smaller size and its lightweight makeup, the *Trilogy IV* is the fastest of the Ka'anapali sailboats. Half-day charters are $119 for adults, include all food and equipment, and usually return to the beach around 1:30pm.

On the stretch of sand in front of Whalers Village, **Teralani** (808/661-7245, www.teralani.net) has two boats that regularly make excursions along the West Maui coastline. The Teralani boats are larger than Trilogy's and cap their trips at 49 people. The primary snorkeling tour departs at 9:30am and returns to the beach around 2:30pm. An abridged trip departs at 11am and returns to the beach at 3pm. All food and equipment are included in the price. There's also an open bar (once you've finished snorkeling, of course), whereas Trilogy charges $5 a drink. With the open bar, however, the price also increases. The adult price of the longer sail is $139 while the four-hour cruise is $112.

Other catamarans departing from Ka'anapali Beach include **Gemini** (808/669-0508, www.geminicharters.com) and **Hula Girl** (808/665-0344, www.sailingmaui.com), both of which load on the stretch of beach in front of Leilani's restaurant. *Gemini* is just as large as Teralani's boats and offers much the same trip, with a difference being that the primary snorkeling charter departs at 11am and returns to the beach between 3 and 3:30pm. Equipment, food, and open bar are included in the tour, and the adult price is $115. *Hula Girl,* on the other hand, is an ornately painted boat that takes a different approach from the others. At first glance the adult price of only $98 for the five-hour tour (9:30-2:30) appears to be cheap, but that's because it doesn't include the cost of food. *Hula Girl* has a kitchen on board where chefs make the food to order. There is also free Wi-Fi for anyone who wants to immediately upload the

GoPro footage of an encounter with a sea turtle. Scuba diving is offered as an additional upgrade for both certified ($65) and introductory ($75) divers.

LAHAINA
Wahikuli Beach Park
Since the majority of Lahaina is ringed by a barrier reef, there are surprisingly few options for decent snorkeling. The few exceptions should only be snorkeled if they're your only choice. Of the two places to snorkel in Lahaina, the one with the easiest entry is **Wahikuli Beach Park** between Ka'anapali and Lahaina. While much of the bottom here is boring old sand, on the far southern end of the beach is a rocky point that can have a large number of reef fish.

Mala Wharf
In the actual town of Lahaina, the best snorkeling spot is **Mala Wharf,** and since this is a functioning small boat harbor, you need to keep an eye out for boat traffic. The reward, however, is a snorkeling site where legions of sea turtles and numerous reef sharks live under the pilings littering the ocean floor. This is a site most often accessed by boat, but the easiest way to reach it from shore is to park in the public parking area and cross over to where the pier meets the sand. From here, it's a kick out to where the pier drops into the water. While conditions are nice most times of the year, the only period you wouldn't want to snorkel here is if the river draining into the bay is a rushing torrent of runoff. To find the parking for Mala Wharf, turn off Front Street onto Ala Moana Street, following the signs for Mala Ramp (which is just on the south side of the bridge from the Lahaina Cannery Mall). Once you turn, you will make an immediate right down toward the boat ramp where there are restrooms, showers, and a moderate amount of parking.

Rental Shops
The most comprehensive shop in Lahaina with the largest selection of gear is **Maui Dive and Surf** (315 Keawe St., 808/661-5388, www.mauidiveshop.com, 7am-6pm daily) in the Lahaina Gateway Center. Although when you first walk in it appears to be a massive retail and surf store, the staff here will help you with everything you need from a set of fins to a new dive watch. While short-term rentals are available, this is also a good shop for purchasing your own gear. You can find something of quality that will last longer than a three-day rental period.

Smaller but just as credible, **Lahaina Divers** (143 Dickenson St., 808/667-7496, www.lahainadivers.com, 8am-8pm daily) will have everything you need for snorkeling, despite the fact it's a full-service dive shop. This is another place you would come if you were looking to own gear for an extended period of time, and since the staff are all divers themselves, they can give you up-to-date information on the current conditions around the West Side.

If, on the other hand, you're just looking for cheap rental gear to get you through your vacation, both **Boss Frog's** (150 Lahainaluna Rd., 808/661-3333, www.bossfrog.com, 8am-5pm daily) and **Snorkel Bob's** (1217 Front St., 808/661-4421, www.snorkelbob.com, 8am-5pm daily) provide economical rentals which can be as low as $2/day. Remember, however, that not only do you get what you pay for, but the main impetus for getting you through the door is to sell activities or upsell you to a fancier mask and snorkel package. If you aren't picky about a mask fitting perfectly or are on a budget, all of the offerings here are completely fine and will get you through a couple of sessions at the beach.

For a similar operation in the center of Lahaina you can also check out **The Snorkel Store** (840 Waine'e St., 808/669-1077, www.thesnorkelstore.com, 8:30am-5pm daily), a small but friendly shop squirreled away in the Lahaina Square Center a block inland from Front Street. There are often 2 for 1 specials on snorkeling gear. There are also masks with built-in cameras that can potentially take some good videos while you snorkel. The prices here are fair, and the staff won't try to upsell you too hard. This is a good option for renting gear

© MARK DRIESSEN

white spotted moray

if you're willing to walk a block into a lesser-visited portion of town.

Snorkeling Charters

Before sunrise, Lahaina Harbor teems with activity as fishers fuel their boats and charter captains prepare for the day ahead. The harbor basin is a whirlwind of activity with lines forming and reforming, food coolers being slung across the docks, and fresh fish being laid on ice. Most snorkeling charters depart from behind the banyan tree on Front Street; a few set out from Mala Ramp on the northern edge of town. Snorkeling charters in Lahaina run the gamut from small inflatable rafts to massive two-tiered catamarans. It's important to match the tour company to the type of experience you want.

SAILBOATS

The company with the largest number of snorkeling charters out of Lahaina Harbor is **Trilogy** (808/874-5649, www.sailtrilogy.com), which offers all-day cruises to Lana'i as well as a four-hour snorkel along the West Maui coastline. While a couple of other boat companies also travel to Lana'i to snorkel for the day, Trilogy is the only one with a commercial permit to have crew and facilities based on the island. The all-day experience is truly in a class of its own.

Departing from Lahaina Harbor at 10am (during busier times of the year there can also be a 6:30am departure), the 60-foot sailing catamarans travel to Manele Harbor on Lana'i where passengers will disembark to snorkel at Hulopo'e Bay. Since Hulopo'e faces south, during summer there is the potential for large surf, so the snorkeling can be subpar. While this is only during a handful of days in summer, winter is nearly guaranteed to have pristine conditions. On the beach itself, Trilogy has exclusive access to the left side of Hulopo'e Bay and it is the only company with lifeguards, beach mats, beach chairs, refreshments, beach volleyball, and all of the snorkeling gear right on the beach. Also included with the price is an optional guided van tour of Lana'i City.

The other sailing catamaran departing out of Lahaina Harbor and heading to the island of Lana'i is **Paragon** (808/244-2087, www.sail-maui.com), a 47-foot boat that only takes 24 passengers and is the island's fastest catamaran under sail. The seven-hour, $159-trip departs at 8:30am and docks at Manele Harbor on Lana'i. You're unsupervised while you snorkel (since the crew doesn't have permission to operate on shore), and you're given a picnic lunch to the enjoy while at the beach. The trip returns to Lahaina around 3:30pm, and on lucky days the crew might even hook up with an *ono* or mahimahi while trolling the fishing lures under sail.

While it mostly focuses on sunset sails and sailing charters, **Scotch Mist II** (808/661-0386, www.scotchmistsailingcharters.com) is a 50-foot Santa Cruz monohull that also operates four-hour sailing and snorkeling charters along the western shoreline of the island for $109.

POWERBOATS
Of the larger diesel boats that operate out of Lahaina Harbor, **Pacific Whale Foundation** (612 Front St., 808/942-5311, www.pacific-whale.org) offers the most options. Its large boats can fit upward of 149 people, and while that's a crowd, there's simply no arguing with the price. Its five-hour tour to Lana'i departs at 9am. It's only $80 for adults; each paying adult is allotted one child free of charge. Unlike other boats that dock at Manele Harbor, the Pacific Whale Foundation cruises snorkel off the boat, with the two preferred destinations being either Kaunolu (Shark Fin Cove) or the Manele reef outside of the small boat harbor. The level of customer service on a boat this size isn't quite the same as on the more intimate vessels, but for families who are on a budget and want to go snorkeling for the day, it's tough to argue with the affordability.

During summer, a smaller adventure rafting tour departs Lahaina for Lana'i at 7:30am. The price is significantly higher ($119 adult, $75 child), but you get a much more personalized experience than on the larger boat and you're able to hug the shore for a better view of the undeveloped coastline. Another summer rafting excursion ($55) departs at 10:30am to snorkel along the West Maui coastline instead of going all the way to Lana'i. All trips for Pacific Whale Foundation check in at the storefront across the street from the famous banyan tree, and loading is by the main loading dock of the harbor where you will wait for one of the crew to escort you down to the boat.

Also during summer (many of these boats defer to whale watches in the winter), **Lahaina Cruise Company** (877/500-6284, www.lahainacruisecompany.com) has a fleet of aging but functional diesel boats that offer snorkeling charters to Lana'i and along the coastline of West Maui. While much of the focus for these boats is on whale-watching during the winter and cocktail cruises in the evening, there are still snorkeling charters available for those who are on a budget. The cost of the snorkeling tour is an affordable $79 for adults, and trips are offered Monday-Saturday on vessels that can accommodate up to 149 people.

Captain Woody's (808/667-2290, www.captainwoody.nct) operates charters of only six people for private excursions. Fishing, snorkeling, and seasonal whale-watching can all be included in these small group tours, and six-hour tours usually depart from Mala Ramp at 7:30am.

RAFTS
For those who don't like crowds, there are a number of rafts that have small group sizes and place you closer to the water than any other type of vessel. Due to their bouncy nature, however, rafts aren't recommended for women who are pregnant or anyone with back problems, and if you're prone to seasickness, they won't be the best option since the waters can often become rough during the afternoon. Some companies will swap their snorkeling charters for whale watches during winter, however, so check ahead of time that snorkeling tours are available for the date of your excursion.

Of all the rafts, **Ultimate Snorkel Adventure** (808/667-5678, www.ultimate-whalewatch.com) is the best option. It operates out of slip 17 of Lahaina Harbor. Group sizes are kept to a minimum at only 16 passengers, and this rigid inflatable is the fastest boat in Lahaina Harbor at speeds in excess of 35 mph. Snorkeling locations are chosen off the island of Lana'i based on the best conditions, and unlike some of the other options which head ashore on Lana'i, this excursion takes place from off the raft. Due to its small size, the raft can navigate close to the shoreline of Lana'i to find blowholes or follow pods of spinner dolphins hanging out by the rocks. Five-hour snorkeling trips are offered at $139, and there is also a two-hour option available along the West Maui shoreline for only $49. Snorkel gear, drinks, and snacks are included in the price of the excursion. This is a great option for those wanting a semiprivate tour with relaxed but professional captain and crew.

Hawaii Ocean Rafting (808/661-7238, www.islandstarexcursions.com) operates out of slip 8 in Lahaina Harbor. Group sizes are kept low on these charters, which are offered as either full-day tours to Lana'i for $115 or half-day tours for $73. Full-day tours depart at 6:30am and return at 2:30pm, whereas the half-day option departs at 7:30am and is back in Lahaina by 12:30pm. Snorkeling gear, snacks, and beverages are included.

For a raft that docks at Manele Harbor and spends time on the island of Lana'i, **Maui Adventure Cruises** (808/661-5550, www.mauiadventurecruises.com) operates two trips from Lahaina Harbor, one of which allows passengers to spend three hours of beach time at Lana'i's Hulopo'e Bay. This $115 excursion operates on Monday, Wednesday, and Friday, docks in Manele Harbor, and allows its guests to walk Hulopo'e Bay unsupervised. Breakfast, snacks, and a deli lunch are included in the cost of the trip. Excursions depart at both 7am and 9pm

from slip #11 in Lahaina Harbor. On Tuesday, Thursday, and Saturday, an abridged 4.5-hour trip is offered for $87 where you will still have the opportunity to snorkel off Lana'i from the boat, rather than docking at Manele Harbor.

Departing from Mala Ramp at 6:30am, **Maui Ocean Riders** (808/661-3586, www.mauioceanriders.com) is the only boat to circumnavigate the island of Lana'i. Covering an astounding 70 miles over the course of the trip, this excursion features multiple snorkeling spots and the opportunity to witness little-seen areas of Lana'i, such as the waters off Shipwreck Beach, Polihua Beach, and the snorkeling area known as Three Stone. On calm days this excursion is the best of all the rafting options. On days when the trade winds are blowing early in the morning, the ride can get rough.

SOUTH OF LAHAINA

The best snorkeling south of Lahaina is at **Olowalu,** otherwise known as "mile marker 14." The reef here is a wide expanse of coral heads. The outer reef is popular with tour and dive boats, and the inside sections can teem with large parrotfish and Hawaiian green sea turtles. Directly out from the mileage marker is a sand channel that leads through the shallow reef and allows you access to deeper water. If, on the other hand, you venture out from a random spot along the coastline, there is a good chance you will get trapped in a maze of shallow coral heads where the water is often murky and the snorkeling is poor. Morning hours are best at Olowalu. **Kayak Olowalu** (808/661-0606, www.kayakolowalu.com) rents gear for only $5 and can be found at the Camp Olowalu location. To reach Camp Olowalu, turn toward the water across from Olowalu General Store and follow the road for a half-mile until it ends at the shoreline.

Scuba Diving

Scuba diving from the west side of the island involves one of two options: Departing from a west side harbor for an excursion to Lana'i or diving along the West Maui shoreline. While certified divers should seek out a dive charter, there are also a number of shore operators who offer introductory dives. Or, if you're a certified diver renting gear and planning on diving independently, ask at the rental shop about current conditions and use a dive flag. Dive spots along the northern section of the island are inaccessible during winter due to large surf. Summer is the best time for diving up north.

KAPALUA, NAPILI, AND HONOKOWAI
Dive Sites
The best shore dive in West Maui is **Honolua Bay,** although slogging all of your gear down to the water can be an exhausting undertaking. If diving from shore, you will want to launch from the center of the beach and hug the right side of the bay where the reef drops off into the sand channel. Maximum depth here can reach about 40 feet, and you can expect to see green sea turtles, a wide variety of reef fish, or even have rare encounters with spinner dolphins. Of the boats offering dive trips to Honolua Bay, **Hula Girl** (808/665-0344, www.sailingmaui. com) offers scuba diving as an add-on to the regular snorkel charter, although most dive charters head elsewhere along the West Side.

For a beginner-friendly introductory dive, **Kapalua Bay** can offer everything from a shallow dive of 25 feet to a more advanced dive of 40 feet rounding the corner toward neighboring Namalu Bay. There are showers and facilities here, as well as an easy, sandy beach entry.

Dive Operators
The largest dive operation on the Upper West Side of the island is **Kapalua Dive Company** (1 Bay Dr., 808/669-3448, www.kapaluadive. com, 8am-5pm daily) at the northern end of Kapalua Bay. Introductory beach dives are offered at 10:30am for $85, or you can increase your dive area by taking a scooter dive into neighboring Namalu Bay for $125. To get to areas usually inaccessible from shore, there are also guided kayak dives which depart at 7:30am for turtle-laden areas such as Hawea Point, although inquire at the shop about availability. Those wanting to get certified on vacation can also work with the PADI-certified instructors. Occasional night dives are also offered.

Down in Honokowai, **Tiny Bubbles Scuba** (3350 Lower Honoapi'ilani Rd., 808/870-0878, www.tinybubblesscuba.com, 8am-5pm daily) operates shore dives along the West Maui coast. Under the lead of the vivacious and knowledgeable instructor "Timmerz," all of the instructors for Tiny Bubbles have been diving the Maui shoreline for over a decade and are acquainted with the nuances of Maui diving. Introductory courses are $109, and certified divers can partake in a private, guided beach dive for $89. Night dives and scooter dives are also offered. Depths on these shore dives rarely exceed 35 feet. All gear is included, and as an added convenience, Tiny Bubbles will pick you up from wherever you're staying on the West Side.

Also operating out of Honokowai, **Scorpion Scuba** (3600 Lower Honoapi'ilani Rd., 808/669-1710, www.mauifish.net) is another trusted operator with years of experience on the shorelines of West Maui. The dives here are an exceptional value: Introductory dives are offered for as low as $89 and certified beach dives for as low as $70. All gear is included. Inquire about their certification classes, night dives, and scooter dives. The scuba operation is run out of the All About Fish store in Honokowai where you can pick up any gear you need or ask about conditions and dive sites.

MAUI

KA'ANAPALI
Dive Sites

The northernmost dive site in Ka'anapali and the one most preferred by independent instructors is **Kahekili Beach Park.** The depth here is shallow and rarely exceeds 35 feet, and the coral begins immediately the moment you get in the water. The reef here parallels the shoreline, with the greatest diversity of life found at 15-25 feet. While the beach itself is long, the healthiest amount of coral is found right off the beach park and is uncrowded compared to neighboring Ka'anapali Beach. There is also easier parking here for lugging all of your gear from the car, and showers and restrooms are conveniently located in the middle of the beach park.

The best dive in Ka'anapali, however, continues to be **Pu'u Keka'a,** otherwise known as Black Rock. Despite the relative ease of the dive and the fairly shallow depths, the rocky promontory has an inexplicable way of drawing in all sorts of marine life. Although not always a guarantee, dives here can frequently involve sightings of sea turtles, reef fish, eels, octopuses, or perhaps something strange such as squid or cowrie. The best way to dive Pu'u Keka'a is either to do a drift dive from the southern end of Kahekili Beach Park and swim around to the front of the rock, or enter the water in front of the Sheraton, swim partway around the rock, and then double back the way you came. This is a great dive for those who have just been certified. For a real treat, consider a night dive.

To dive away from the crowds, head to the large reef at **Ka'anapali Point,** stretching from the Marriott down toward the Hyatt. The depth here ranges 10-30 feet. You'll likely see a large number of turtles, corals, and technicolor parrotfish.

Dive Operators

The Ka'anapali resort diving scene is dominated by **Five Star Scuba** (www.5starscuba. com), which has operations at many of the Ka'anapali resorts. Options include pool sessions and one-tank dives to certification and night dives. A single one-tank dive for certified divers will usually be $89 with the exact dive location determined by what resort you're staying in and where conditions are best.

In front of Ka'anapali Beach Hotel, **Trilogy Ocean Sports** (808/661-7789) also offers one-tank dives, pool classes, and certification courses. Introductory dives are offered at $95, and certified dives are only $69, which is the best deal you'll find along the resort strip.

LAHAINA
Dive Sites

Within walking distance of southern Ka'anapali, **Hanakao'o Beach Park** is the northernmost beach in Lahaina and the site of many introductory classes. This is a good dive if you're practicing your skills over sand. The shallow area is also good for spotting turtles and colorful reef fish.

The best dive in Lahaina is **Mala Wharf,** although it's most often accessed as a boat dive. When Hurricane Iniki came storming through in 1992, the 30-foot waves it created were strong enough to destroy the outer half of Mala Ramp. Over 20 years later the collapsed pilings are still lying in 25 feet of water, and the result has been two decades of live coral development on what is now one of the island's best artificial reefs. The caverns of the pilings are home to numerous turtles and whitetip reef sharks, some of which can reach up to about six feet. Even though the depth never exceeds 35 feet, this is still a favorite of island dive charters due to its proximity to the harbors and wealth of marine life.

The *Carthaginian* is an old whaling ship which was scuttled in 100 feet of water by Atlantis Submarines about a half mile offshore from Puamana. A couple of West Side dive charters include this deep-water dive in their weekly schedule, with a maximum depth of about 100 feet. While the *Carthaginian* hasn't yet developed the same amount of live coral as at neighboring Mala Ramp, it's the deepest dive in the area. Winter dives are punctuated by whale song.

Dive Operators

Lahaina Divers (143 Dickenson St., 808/998-3483, www.lahainadivers.com) has the largest number of dive options available. Their two, custom-built, 46-foot dive boats departing out of Lahaina Harbor are the largest dive boats on Maui. Two-tank dives range from $139 for dives off Lana'i to $199 for a dive off Moku Ho'oniki (Moloka'i), famous for scalloped hammerhead sharks. There are also trips to the Back Wall of Molokini Crater as well as four-tank dive trips for those who just can't get enough of the water. The full-service dive shop in Lahaina has everything from equipment sales to rentals. Since certain dives are only available on certain days, inquire ahead of time.

On the north end of Lahaina at Mala Ramp, **Extended Horizons** (94 Kupuohi St., 808/667-0611, www.extendedhorizons.com) is another reputable operation that offers tours to Lana'i and the west shore of Maui. Extended Horizons only takes six passengers, and it's the only charter boat on the island to run completely on 100 percent biodiesel. Morning tours check in at 6:30am at the Mala boat ramp for two-tank dives to Lana'i, the cost of which is $149. Other dive options available include trips along the Maui shoreline as well as night dives, beach dives, and certification classes.

A smaller operation offering scuba tours of Lana'i, **Dive Maui** (1223 Front St., 808/661-7333, www.hawaiianrafting.com) departs from Mala Ramp aboard a rigid aluminum inflatable vessel. The group sizes are small and a deli lunch is included with the two-tank dive. The shop is conveniently located within walking distance from Mala Ramp.

SOUTH OF LAHAINA
Dive Sites

Known to some operators as Turtle Reef or Turtle Point, **Olowalu** is an offshore, turtle-laden area popular with charter boats on the offshore reefs. Maximum depths are about 30 feet, and on nice days the visibility is close to 100 feet. This area is also popular with independent dive operators as a "confined water" area for practicing dive skills. If you are shore diving independently, the easiest way to get to deeper water is to enter around the mile marker 14 sign and swim in a straight line until you reach depths of 20-25 feet. When navigating your way through the coral heads, it's imperative to make sure that your gear doesn't drag across the reef, and bring a dive flag with you so that boats know you're below.

Ukumehame is a special spot only accessible by boat charter. Huge manta rays congregate here to be "cleaned" by reef fish who nibble algae off their wings, and the depths here are a moderately deep 30-60 feet. Don't even think about trying to do this dive as a shore dive because the manta ray area is about a 25-minute surface swim from shore and it takes trained dive instructors to determine if the water clarity is good enough for diving.

Surfing

Surfing is more than a hobby in West Maui—it's a way of life. In Lahaina, legions of long-boarders begin each morning by watching the sunrise from the water, and flotillas of surf schools operate throughout the day. Up north, Honolua is the proving ground of the island's burgeoning surfers, and whenever "The Bay" starts breaking, a palpable buzz goes out through the community. Granted, not all breaks are suitable for beginners. Out of respect for island surfers only a handful of breaks are included in this guide. Practice common etiquette, and enjoy the serenity that comes with surfing one of the most beautiful spots in the world.

KAPALUA, NAPILI, AND HONOKOWAI

Winter is the best time for surfing "up north" and the waves get larger the farther north that you head. With the exception of S-Turns, however, most of the breaks on the Upper West Side are for experienced surfers. Beginners will have better luck at the breaks south of Lahaina.

Surf Spots

Beginning in Honokowai, **Rainbows** is a fickle break that is best for intermediate surfers. The wave is in front of the Ka'anapali Beach Club. Parking can be found by taking the first left on Lower Honoapi'ilani Road across from the Times Supermarket. There can often be some strong currents here, and Rainbows will only break on the largest of northwest swells or any swell which is north or northeasterly.

Pohaku Beach Park in Kahana is the epicenter of the West Side's longboard community. The break, commonly known as **S-Turns,** is perfect for beginners. Travel on Honoapi'ilani Highway until you reach the intersection with

Summer offers the best surf in Lahaina.

© MARK DRIESSEN

MAUI

Ho'ohui Street with the McDonald's on the corner. Turn toward the ocean, and make a left once you reach the bottom of the hill. Drive for a quarter mile and you will see the parking lot for S-Turns on your right. When standing in the parking lot, you will notice two distinct breaks: one to the left and one to the right. The break to the left is S-Turns, and the one to the right is Mushrooms. While Mushrooms can be a fun wave, it's shallow on the inside section. Over at S-Turns, you'll notice a couple of A-frame peaks a long paddle offshore. Surfing at S-Turns is as much of a paddle workout as a surfing workout, and you can be forgiven if you need to stop a couple of times to catch your breath on the way out. Beginners stay on the inside section, while more experienced surfers favor the outer peaks. Also, there have been some shark issues at S-Turns in the past, so if the water is murky and no one else is out, there's probably a reason for that. S-Turns starts breaking on a moderate northwest swell, and on the largest of days can reach a few feet overhead.

The surf break at **D.T. Fleming Beach Park** is at the far northern end of the beach. The wave here is a combination of a beach break and a point break, and it can get crowded with bodyboarders during weekends. This is one of the few places on the West Side that picks up windswell, so if it's windy and there aren't waves anywhere else, check Fleming's.

If you're an avid surfer, **Honolua Bay** needs no introduction. The wave here is truly one of the best in the world, holding almost religious significance for the locals. Honolua is reserved for experienced surfers, but even non-surfers should come here during a large swell to watch the island's best pull into the gaping, barreling perfection. Also, Honolua can become crowded, and if you paddle out and nobody recognizes you, your chances of getting a wave decrease significantly. Granted, on days when the surf is only about head high and the crowd isn't too thick, there can still be enough waves for everyone—provided you know what you're doing.

Even through **Windmills** is a surf break

beyond the ability level of most visitors, it's an epic spot for watching the island's best surfers. The massive left tube barrels with such ferocity it's been called Maui's Pipeline. Many professional surf films have been shot here. The best vantage point is on the side of the road at the edge of a dramatic cliff. If you see cars parked on the side of the road a mile past Honolua Bay, large surf is breaking.

Rental Shops

Experienced surfers will get the best selection of boards with **808 Boards** (808/283-1384, www.808boards.com), who will pick up and drop off the board at no additional charge.

Two places you can rent a board up north are at the **Boss Frog's** locations in Napili (5095 Napilihau St., 808/669-4949, www.bossfrog.com, 8am-6pm daily) and Kahana (4310 Lower Honoapi'ilani Rd., 808/669-6700, www.bossfrog.com, 8am-5pm daily). Rates are around $20/day for soft top longboards or $25/day for fiberglass boards.

For the cheapest boards you'll find on this side of the island, little-known **A&B Ocean Rentals** (3481 Lower Honoapi'ilani Rd., 808/669-0027, 9am-4pm daily) is hidden in Da Rose mall in Honokowai on the ocean side of the highway. Surfboards are only $15/day or $70 for the whole week.

KA'ANAPALI
Surf Spots

The only surf break in Ka'anapali is **Ka'anapali Point,** in front of the Marriott on Ka'anapali Beach. This is where the Ka'anapali surf lessons take place, although the wave here is tricky because it bends at a weird angle. Also, the inside section can get shallow and rocky, so surf school students are given booties. Ka'anapali Point can pick up both southwesterly and northeasterly swells, which means there can be surf any month of the year.

Rental Shops and Schools

While the waves in Lahaina are more amenable to learning, there are still a number of operators along Ka'anapali Beach for those who would prefer to walk directly from the resort to the lesson. Since Ka'anapali gets windier than Lahaina, it's important to book the first lesson of the day for the best conditions.

For the most affordable lessons, the **Trilogy** beach shack in front of the Ka'anapali Beach Hotel offers two hours for $70. On the other side of Whalers Village, lessons can be booked with **Island Style** (808/244-6858) in front of the Westin or with **Royal Hawaiian** (808/357-8988, www.royalhawaiiansurfacademy.com) at the kiosk at the Marriott. Both places offer two hours for $75. For rentals down by Ka'anapali Point, expect to pay in the $20-40 range depending on the length of rental. Booties are included in the price of all lessons and rentals.

LAHAINA

Lahaina and the areas south of Lahaina have small waves breaking during most of the year, while summer has the most consistent surf. Most days will only have waves in the waist-high range, but on the best swells of summer the surf can reach overhead.

◖ Surf Spots

The most popular surf break in Lahaina is **Lahaina Breakwall,** located between the 505 shopping center and Lahaina Harbor. This is where most of the Lahaina surf schools operate. All of the surf schools hang out in the shallow inside section, whereas the more experienced surfers sit farther outside. The outside section at small levels can be either a left or a right, although when it gets big on a large summer swell it can turn into a huge left that can grow to 10 feet or larger. During low tide it can get shallow enough here that you need to paddle with your fingertips and your skeg can scrape the bottom, so high tide is the optimal time for those who are concerned about falling. It shouldn't come as a surprise that this spot can get crowded, a fact of life which has earned it the moniker of Snakewall. If you're a beginning surfer who has rented a board you're better off going a few miles south to Puamana Beach Park or Guardrails.

Rental Shops and Schools

Inside the 505 shopping center, **Goofy Foot** (505 Front St., 808/244-9283, www.goofy-footsurfschool.com, 7am-9pm daily, no lessons Sun.) has helped over 100,000 students ride their first wave since opening in 1994. Two-hour lessons are $65/person, and the owner, Tim, often enjoys time on the water as the private surf coach for Jimmy Buffett. For board rentals, expect to pay $20 for two hours or $25 for three hours.

One block away on Prison Street are **Royal Hawaiian** (117 Prison St., 808/276-7873, www.royalhawaiiansurfacademy.com, 7am-7pm Mon.-Fri., 7am-3:30pm weekends) and **Maui Wave Riders** (133 Prison St., 808/875-4761, www.mauiwaveriders.com, 7am-9pm daily). Royal Hawaiian has been operating since 1996 and Maui Wave Riders since 1997, and all of the instructors are competent and patient professionals who are guaranteed to get you up and riding. Group rates at Royal Hawaiian are $65/person, whereas Maui Wave Riders is cheaper at $60/person and $50 for kids ages 8-12. For rentals, expect to pay $20 for three hours or $30 for the whole day.

Maui Surfer Girls (808/214-0606, www.mauisurfergirls.com) is the island's premier female-only surf camp operator, although they also offer coed group lessons for $75/person. Even though it's a few dollars more than in town, the lessons take place a few miles south of town along a mellow stretch of beach that isn't as crowded as Breakwall. All-inclusive one- and two-week classes are offered during select months of the year to empower teenaged girls through the sport of surfing.

To surf in a secluded location in a private group, try **Hawaiian Paddle Sports** (808/660-4228, www.hawaiianpaddlesports.com), which offers completely private lessons. The lessons usually take place along the shoreline south of Lahaina. Since these two-hour lessons are completely private, they are understandably more expensive at $159 for a single person or $109/person for private groups of five or more.

If you're just looking to rent a board in downtown Lahaina and prefer to teach yourself, you'll get a better deal if you move a few blocks away from the busy surf schools. The **Boss Frog's** (150 Lahainaluna Rd., 808/661-3333, www.bossfrog.com, 8am-5pm daily) in the center of town has soft top boards for either $25/day or $75/week, and fiberglass boards are $35/day. Of course, you can't walk to the surf break from here, so rent or purchase straps for your vehicle.

SOUTH OF LAHAINA

For beginning surfers and longboard riders, the mile-long stretch of coastline between **Puamana Beach Park** and **Launiupoko Beach Park** has numerous breaks with mellow waves for beginners. In between the two parks are peaks which are known as **Guardrails, Woody's,** and **Corner Pockets.** While the beach parks and Guardrails have parking on the ocean side of the road, parking for Woody's is in a dirt lot on the inland side of the highway. There can be small waves here most times of the year, although summer sees the most consistent surf. If you're a slightly more advanced surfer, park in the lot for Puamana Beach Park and walk the length of shoreline all the way to the right along the Puamana condominium complex. At the far northern end of the beach is another break known as **Beaches** that offers a fun right point welcoming to visiting surfers.

Or, if you're an experienced surfer who prefers to ride a shortboard, the wave at **Olowalu** offers two A-frame peaks that are popular with locals and can get crowded. In a different spot than the snorkeling spot by the same name, the Olowalu surf break is by mile marker 15.5.

At mile marker 12, **Ukumehame Beach Park** is another break that caters to beginners and longboarders but requires a much longer paddle than places such as Guardrails or Puamana. However, a longer effort means a longer ride. This is a favorite of the island longboarding community. While the beach itself is fairly long, the best waves are found directly in front of the small parking lot.

Tucked right at the base of the cliffs by mile marker 11, **Grandma's** is the name of the break on the far southern end of Papalaua Beach Park. This is a playful wave that caters to beginners and longboarders.

Stand-Up Paddling

KAPALUA, NAPILI, AND HONOKOWAI

One of the best stretches of coast for paddling is the section between Kapalua Bay and Hawea Point. The sandy entry at Kapalua Bay makes it easy to launch a board into the water. Napili Bay is another popular spot for morning paddles. But never bring a stand-up paddleboard into Honolua Bay.

Rental Shops

In Napili, **Boss Frog's** (5095 Napilihau St., 808/669-4949, www.bossfrog.com, 8am-6pm daily) has paddleboard rentals for $40/day. You can find the same rates down the road at the store in the Kahana Manor (4310 Lower Honoapi'ilani Rd., 808/669-6700, www.bossfrog.com, 8am-5pm daily).

For the cheapest boards on this side of the island, go to **A&B Ocean Rentals** (3481 Lower Honoapi'ilani Rd., 808/669-0027, 9am-4pm daily) in Da Rose mall in Honokowai. It has paddleboards for $35/day or $140 for the whole week.

KA'ANAPALI

Sandy Ka'anapali is the perfect spot for stand-up paddling, but only during the morning hours before the wind picks up. On winter days, the water can be as smooth as glass with dozens of whales breaching around you. While being out on the water during whale season can be an exciting adventure, the same laws apply to stand-up paddlers as to boats: Paddlers are required to maintain a 100-yard distance from humpback whales—unless, of course, they swim over to you.

MAUI

Rental Shops

Almost every hotel along the main strip has activity huts offering paddleboard rentals. At **Trilogy Ocean Sports** (808/661-7789) in front of the Ka'anapali Beach Hotel, boards are $25 for the first hour and $15/hour after that. In front of the Westin Maui on the south side of Whalers Village, boards are $30 for the first hour and $10 for each additional hour. The cheapest rate is offered by the **Maui Dive and Surf** (808/270-9846, www.mauidiveshop.com) kiosk just south of Leilani's restaurant in Whalers Village, where board rentals are $26 for the first hour or $41 for a four-hour rental.

LAHAINA

Lahaina is ringed by a barrier reef, which can make it shallow and dangerous for paddling. The trained instructors, however, know all of the *pukas* (holes) in the reef, and by allowing them to lead the way, you'll be awarded with sweeping views of the island's West Side. When you are over the Shark Pit, there's a decent chance you'll encounter an endangered Hawaiian monk seal or a harmless whitetip reef shark. While the 505 area can be a little difficult to navigate, it has the added benefit of being protected from the wind and will usually have calm, flat conditions when Ka'anapali is rough and blustery. If you've rented your own board, the best place in the immediate area for stand-up paddling is the stretch of shoreline between Puamana and Launiupoko Beach Parks, where the water isn't nearly as shallow and it's still protected from the afternoon trade winds.

Rental Shops and Schools

Stand-up paddling lessons are offered in the Lahaina Breakwall area by **Royal Hawaiian** (117 Prison St., 808/276-7873, www.royalhawaiiansurfacademy.com, 7am-7pm Mon.-Fri., 7am-3:30pm weekends), **Goofy Foot** (505 Front St., 808/244-9283, www.goofyfootsurfschool.

com, 7am-9pm daily, no lessons Sun.), and **Maui Wave Riders** (133 Prison St., 808/875-4761, www.mauiwaveriders.com, 7am-9pm daily). Rather than mingling with all the surf school students, the stand-up paddling tours go the other direction from the Lahaina Breakwall down to the section of beach known as Shark Pit. Also in front of the 505 Front Street area, **Maui Paddle Sports** (808/283-9344, www.mauipaddlesports.com, 8am and 10am) offers lessons for $95/person and has personalized ratios of three paddlers per instructor. For rentals, expect to pay in the $35 range for three hours to $45 for all day.

For more personalized service in an area that isn't as crowded, **Maria Souza Stand Up Paddle School** (808/579-9231, www.standuppaddlesurfschool.com) and **Hawaiian Paddle Sports** (808/660-4228, www.hawaiianpaddlesports.com) both offer lessons on beaches south of Lahaina. These operations are run by instructors who have a deep-rooted respect for the island, the environment, and Hawaiian cultural history. While they're more expensive, these tours will leave you with a deeper appreciation for all things surrounding the ocean. Lessons with Maria Souza's are $159/person and are offered Monday to Friday at 9 and 11am, and lessons with Hawaiian Paddle Sports are $159 for a private lesson or $109/person for private groups of five or more.

SOUTH OF LAHAINA
Rental Shops

For a laid-back rental experience in a unique location, **Kayak Olowalu** (808/661-0606, www.kayakolowalu.com) has stand-up boards available from a campground location for either $20/hr or $30 for a three-hour session. To reach the campground, turn toward the water at Olowalu General Store and follow the signs for Camp Olowalu for half a mile until you reach the shoreline.

Kayaking and Canoeing

West Maui has numerous options for both kayaking and outrigger canoeing. While kayaking isn't as hard on the shoulder muscles and allows you to hug the coastline a little closer, outrigger canoeing comes with a culturally rich experience unique to Polynesia. The morning hours are the best time to paddle, with most operators offering an early morning tour followed by another one during the mid to late morning.

KAPALUA, NAPILI, AND HONOKOWAI

The most popular kayak trip on the Upper West Side of the island is the paddle from D.T. Fleming Beach Park to Honolua Bay. Along this stretch of coastline you will pass rugged rock formations inaccessible from the road, and you'll hug this dramatic coast past Mokulei'a Bay and into Honolua. Because of the high surf during winter, these tours are only offered during the summer, and all trips depart D.T. Fleming Beach Park in the early morning hours before the afternoon trade winds pick up. Snorkeling in Honolua Bay is included in the excursions, and you have a high likelihood of encountering Hawaiian green sea turtles or potentially even Hawaiian spinner dolphins.

Of the companies offering tours up here, **Hawaiian Paddle Sports** (808/660-4228, www.hawaiianpaddlesports.com) operates completely private excursions for $159 for a private tour, $129/person for tours of 2-4 people,

and $109/person for tours of five or more. **Maui Kayaks** (808/874-4000, www.mauikayaks.com) offers a three-hour trip for $78/person with a 7am check-in at D.T. Fleming Beach Park.

KA'ANAPALI

Off Kahekili Beach Park in front of the Westin Villas, **Maui Paddle Sports** (808/283-9344, www.mauipaddlesports.com) offers two-hour outrigger canoe rides in a six-man outrigger for $85/person. All canoe tours take place during the morning, but on days with light winds tours can go as late as 1pm.

SOUTH OF LAHAINA

The main areas for kayaking south of Lahaina are either Olowalu (mile marker 14) or Coral Gardens, off Papalaua Beach Park (mile marker 11). This is a popular area for kayaking in winter since the large surf on the northern shores makes kayaking there impossible. These are fantastic reefs for spotting Hawaiian green sea turtles. While **Maui Kayaks** (808/874-4000, www.mauikayaks.com, $69) and **Hawaiian Paddle Sports** (808/660-4228, www.hawaiianpaddlesports.com, private tours from $109-159/person) both offer tours in this area, one tour company which is area-specific is **Kayak Olowalu** (808/661-0606, www.kayakolowalu.com), which either offers tours for $65/adult or unguided rentals for $30-40 for two hours.

Boating

❰ SUNSET CRUISES

Few Maui activities are more iconic than a sunset sail off the West Maui coastline. The feeling of the trade winds in your hair as you glide along the ocean is a sensation of freedom you can't experience on land. Watch as the setting sun paints the sky every shade of orange and pink, while on most days you can also make out a rainbow hovering over the lush valleys of Mauna Kahalawai.

Ka'anapali

While a **sunset sail off Ka'anapali Beach** can be the most magical moment of your vacation, there are a few things to understand for making the most of the magic. To begin with, make sure to ask when you need to check in, because departure times for sunset sails are 30 minutes different during summer and winter. Secondly, while it's always nice to get a little bit dressed up, remember that you're still going on a moving boat and should be outfitted accordingly. The Ka'anapali boats are all sailing catamarans, which load from the sand, and since some days can have moderate shorebreak, there's a good chance you'll end up wet from the shins down. Also, your shoes will be collected prior to boarding (to keep from tracking sand on the boat), so don't put too much time into matching them with your outfit. There's even a chance that the departure could be moved to Lahaina Harbor due to large surf on the beach. Since this isn't possible to predict until the day before the sail, it's a good idea to double check on the morning of your sail to confirm where the boat will be loading from. The northerly trade winds can often be chilly, so it's a good idea to bring a light jacket. Finally, remember that you'll be sailing. Even though the vessels are wide, stable catamarans, it may be difficult to move around and spray may come over the sides. If your idea of a sunset sail is a stable platform that putts along at three knots, the dinner cruises from Lahaina are probably a better bet.

Trilogy (808/874-5649, www.sailtrilogy.com) offers sunset sails on Tuesday, Thursday, and Saturday, as well as an Aloha Friday sunset sail that features lives music and Pacific Rim *pupus*. Trilogy's sail isn't marketed as a booze cruise. Three alcoholic beverages are included in the price, with a three-drink maximum. Unless the surf is high and they need to load from Lahaina Harbor, all Trilogy tours check-in in front of the Ka'anapali Beach Hotel. Regular sunset sails are $69, and the Aloha Friday sail is $79.

In front of Whalers Village, **Teralani** (808/661-7245, www.teralani.net) offers two different sails departing nightly during the busier parts of the year. The original sunset sail is $71/adult and includes a *pupu* menu as well as a full open bar of various beers and mixed drinks. For those who would rather dine on board, the full dinner sail is $94/adult, 30 minutes longer, and includes a filling menu.

© KYLE ELLISON

heading out for a sunset cruise on the *Trilogy VI*

Gemini (808/669-0508, www.geminicharters.com) similarly offers sunset sails for $70/adult which feature a *pupu* menu as well as Bikini Blonde beer and mai tais.

The most "yacht-like" experience departing from the beach is on **Hula Girl** (808/665-0344, www.sailingmaui.com), which not only offers the newest boat, but also luxurious upgrades like throw pillows, free Wi-Fi, panoramic viewing from the fly-bridge, and high-tech sailing. Regular sunset sails are offered on Monday, Wednesday, and Friday, and while the $68 price looks in-line with the rest of the options, all food and drink are available for purchase from the kitchen and full-service bar, and such luxury and convenience come at an added price. For a full-service dinner cruise, *Hula Girl* also offers cruises on Tuesday, Thursday, and Saturday for $80/adult featuring upscale Pacific Rim dining options made fresh in the onboard kitchen. It's more of a floating restaurant with an $80 cover charge. Menu items range $5-23 and a full-service bar slings top-shelf cocktails.

Lahaina
DINNER CRUISES
A sailboat is a better venue for a sunset cruise than a powerboat. But for those who would rather be on a large, stable diesel vessel instead of a catamaran, the best dinner cruise from Lahaina is offered by **Pacific Whale Foundation** (612 Front St., 808/942-5311, www.pacificwhale.org). The power catamaran used for this charter is the nicest of the large diesel boats, and the menu includes locally sourced produce and sustainably harvested seafood. Regular seats are $80, but if you don't want to share a table with another party, upgrade to the premium seating for $100/adult. A maximum of three alcoholic beverages is included in the cruise, as is live music.

Also out of Lahaina Harbor, **Lahaina Cruise Company** (877/500-6284, www.mauiprincess.com) offers two different dinner cruises aboard vessels which are a generation older than others. The 2.5-hour dinner cruise aboard *Maui Princess* stays out well past dark (usually until 8pm) and offers rooftop seating aboard a 120-foot vessel. Waiters in gray tuxedos serve meals of prime rib, roasted chicken, or island fish, and the string of white lights illuminating the upper deck aims to create a romantic atmosphere. Dancing is offered in the downstairs portion of the boat. Prices for the cruise are $75/adult, three alcoholic drinks are included, and additional drinks are available for purchase at the bar. A similar cruise is offered aboard *Kaulana*, where dinner consists of a small amount of *pupus* and two drinks are included with the price of the sail. There is a live musician on the aft deck. This is the closest thing to a "booze cruise" that you'll find anywhere on the West Side. Prices for this tour are $47/adult, and the cruise spends two hours motoring along the West Maui shoreline.

SAILBOATS
If you know what it means to "shake a reef," you'll be much happier watching the sunset aboard a small sailboat than on a large, motorized platform.

The only sailing catamaran offering sunset sails from Lahaina is **Paragon** (808/244-2087, www.sailmaui.com), which provides sailing, *pupus,* beer, wine, and mai tais for only $59/adult. Trips depart on Monday, Wednesday, and Friday. The maximum capacity of the cruise is only 24 people.

Or, if you're a monohull sailor, **Scotch Mist II** (808/661-0386, www.scotchmistsailingcharters.com) offers evening sunset sails for $69 aboard a Santa Cruz 50-foot racing boat, which departs from Slip #2.

◖ WHALE-WATCHING
Any single vessel that floats is going to be offering whale watching between December 15 and April 15. Even though whale season officially lasts until May 15, the whales aren't encountered with enough regularity after mid-April to guarantee sightings. The peak of the season for whale watching is January through March, and whether you're on a sailboat, powerboat, raft, fishing boat, kayak, or ferry, simply being out on the water turns the experience into whale-watching. Most snorkeling and sailing

Whale-Watching FAQ

© AWAPUHI DANCIL

Whale watching season is December to April.

The waters off Maui have the highest concentration of humpback whales anywhere on the planet. Here are answers to commonly asked whale-watching questions:

Q: What kind of whales are in Maui?

A: Although there are rarely seen species such as pilot whales and false-killer whales that inhabit the waters off Maui year-round, 99 percent of the time you will be watching North Pacific humpback whales.

Q: Where are these whales from?

A: These whales were born here in the warm, protected waters of Hawaii. The humpbacks will then migrate 3,000 miles to their summer feeding grounds in Alaska where they gorge themselves on small fish and krill, and return again in the winter to mate and give birth.

Q: Why don't the whales mate in Alaska?

A: Since baby humpbacks are born with minimal amounts of fat, the water is too cold in Alaska.

Q: Do the whales eat at all in Hawaii?

A: No. While there's no evidence to suggest that whales wouldn't eat if given the opportunity, the waters off Maui don't contain the same degree of zooplankton and marine organisms that humpback whales feed on. Adults go for months at a time without eating, losing up to one-third of their body weight.

Q: How much do humpback whales weigh?

A: At birth, humpback whales are 10-12 feet long and weigh about a ton. Full-grown adults weight about one ton per foot, which means that a 45-foot humpback will weigh about 90,000 lbs!

Q: Are males or females bigger?

A: Females are a little bit larger than males, which is known as "reverse sexual dimorphism," a fancy way of saying "I need to give birth to a 2,000 lb. animal so I need to be bigger than you."

Q: How quickly do whales swim?

A: Although they can sprint up to about 20 mph, on average humpback whales travel at a steady rate of 3-5 mph.

Q: How long does it take them to get to Alaska?

A: Whales spend 6-8 weeks migrating between Alaska and the Hawaiian Islands.

Q: Are whales more active in the morning?

A: No. Since whales only take short "cat naps," there isn't a set time of day when they are asleep. Mornings are often best for whale-watching because the water is calmer and the whales are easier to spot.

Q: What is "getting mugged?"

A: "Getting mugged" refers to the fact that all boats are required to maintain a 100-yard radius from humpback whales. Should the whales decide to approach the boat it is out of your hands. You need to wait until the whale loses interest. This can be 45 minutes or more.

operators also offer whale watching during winter, with most boats carrying whale naturalists well-versed in the study of these gentle giants. Since most prices are about the same, the choice ultimately comes down to what sort of vessel best suits your comfort level. Small rafts from Lahaina Harbor will place you the closest to the water. All sailboats also offer whale-watching trips from both Lahaina Harbor and Ka'anapali Beach. The large, 149-passenger diesel boats in Lahaina provide the most affordable rates, but you'll be sharing the vessel with over 100 other people and won't get 360° views. Pacific Whale Foundation has the largest presence for whale-watching in Lahaina.

SUBMARINE

If riding a submarine has always been on your bucket list, **Atlantis Submarines** (Slip 18, 808/667-2224, www.atlantisadventures.com/maui, 9am-2pm daily) operates regular charters from Lahaina Harbor to the *Carthaginian,* a sunken whaling ship sitting in 100 feet of water. Rates for the submarine tour are $109/adult and $35/child.

For those who are a little nervous about descending completely underwater and want to see fish without snorkeling, **Reef Dancer** (Slip 6, 808/667-2133, www.mauiglassbottomboat.com) is a yellow "semi-sub" that remains partially submerged for its journey along the coastline. While there is an above deck portion of the sub that never plunges underwater, passengers are seated in an underwater cabin that offers 360° views of the underwater world. All of the boat staff double as scuba divers who can point out anything that might be living along the reef such as eels, octopuses, turtles, or urchins. This is a great way for young children, elderly visitors, or those who aren't comfortable swimming to enjoy Maui's reef system without ever having to get their hair wet. Sixty-minute tours take place three times each morning ($35/adult, $20/child), with a longer 90-minute tour departing Lahaina Harbor at 2:15pm ($45/adult, $25/child).

FISHING

In no place is Lahaina's port town heritage more evident than at dingy yet lovable Lahaina Harbor. The smell of fish carcasses still wafts on the breeze and shirtless, tanned, sweat-covered sailors casually sip beers as they lay the fresh catch on ice. On some days you can buy fresh mahimahi or ono straight from the folks who caught it, or, if you'd rather take your shot at reeling the big one in yourself, there are a slew of sportfishing boats ready to get you on the water. The charters that have the best chance of catching fish are those that leave early and stay out for a full day. These are more expensive, but during a full-day charter you're able to troll around the buoys on the far side of Lana'i or Kaho'olawe, whereas on half-day charters you're confined to shallower water where the fish aren't biting as much (particularly during the winter). On virtually all charters you need to provide your own food and drinks. Although it sounds silly, don't bring bananas on board since it's considered bad luck. Most boats will let you keep what you catch so you can cook it the same night.

Of all the boats in the harbor, one of the companies with the best reputation is **Start Me Up** (808/667-2774, www.sportfishingmaui.com), where prices range from $99/person for a quarter-day charter to $199/person for a full day on the water.

A boat with a sterling reputation is **Die Hard** (808/344-5051, www.diehardsportfishing.com), run by the legendary Captain Fuzzy. Rates for these charters vary, but expect to pay $200/person for six-hour charters and $220/person for full-day, eight-hour charters.

Down at the south end of the harbor away from many of the other boats, **Luckey Strike** (808/661-4606, www.luckeystrike.com) has two different boats and operates on the premise that using live bait for smaller fish is better. Captain Tad Luckey has been fishing these waters for well over 30 years, and as with most captains in the harbor, he has an enviable and well-earned amount of local knowledge to put into every trip.

MAUI

One of the nicest yachts in the harbor, **Jayhawk** (808/870-6994, www.jayhawkyacht. com), offers private charters for $700/hour on a swanky 48-foot Cabo with all the amenities. It's more than just a fancy ride, however. Captain Steve has been fishing these waters for over two decades and can hook up fish as well as anyone else in the harbor.

PARASAILING

Parasailing isn't available December 15-May 15. Since the waters off West Maui are part of the Hawaiian Islands Humpback Whale National Marine Sanctuary, all "thrillcraft," such as high-speed parasailing boats, are outlawed during the time of year when the whales are nursing their calves. All parasailing operations go dormant during the winter and open up promptly on the morning of May 16. Should you happen to be visiting Maui during the summer or fall, however, parasailing is a peaceful adventure option for gazing at West Maui from hundreds of feet above the turquoise waters. It's one of the best views you'll find anywhere on the island.

Ka'anapali
UFO Parasail (800/359-4836, www.ufopara-sail.net) departs off Ka'anapali Beach in front of Leilani's restaurant and is one of the two operators departing from the beach. Only eight people are on a boat at a time, which means that your overall time on the water is only a little over an hour. Of that hour, your own personal flight time will last 10-12 minutes depending on the length of your line (you'll end up being 400-500 feet off the water). The staff and captains who run these tours do hundreds of trips over the course of the season, and from a safety and efficiency standpoint, the crew has it down to a science. Taking off and landing on the boat is a dry entry and exit, and you will be blown away by the serenity experienced up in the air. Prices range $75-85 depending on the height; you must weigh at least 130 pounds to fly alone.

Down in front of the Hyatt, **West Maui Parasail** (808/661-4060, www.westmauipa-rasail.com) offers similar tours with the same length of lines at a slightly discounted rate of $70 for 800 feet or $80 for 1,200 feet. If you aren't staying in the Ka'anapali resort area, a perk of going with West Maui Parasail is that free, convenient parking can be had in the Hanakao'o Beach Park area just a three-minute walk from the Hyatt.

Lahaina
The only parasailing operation in Lahaina is **West Maui Parasail** (808/661-4060, www. westmauiparasail.com) out of slip #15. The prices here are the same as at the Ka'anapali operation, but a benefit of parasailing from Lahaina is that the water is consistently calmer and glassier than in neighboring Ka'anapali.

JET SKIING

Just like parasailing, Jet Skiing is only available May 16-December 14. During summer the island's only Jet Ski operation is **Maui Watersports** (808/667-2001, www.mauiwatersports.com), in Ka'anapali just south of the Hyatt. Even though the area south of the Hyatt is relatively protected from the wind, morning hours are still the best to guarantee the calmest conditions. Also, the Jet Skiing here is fairly regulated and isn't just a free-for-all. Riders are required to ski in a relatively organized pattern, stay inside the mandated buoys, and maintain a healthy distance from other Jet Skis at any given time. Prices are $70 for a 30-minute ride and $98 for a full hour.

WAKEBOARDING

Captain Ryan at **Wake Maui** (808/269-5645, www.wakemaui.com) now offers wakeboarding trips in the flat water between Lahaina and Ka'anapali. Wake Maui provides the only service of its kind where a six-passenger ski boat is equipped with all the wake toys for a fun day on the water. Since Maui's winds can often be extreme, however, wakeboarding charters usually depart around sunrise to capitalize on glassy conditions. Prices for these dawn patrol wakeboarding sessions are $109/person for trips of three hours, or, if you'd prefer to charter the boat as a private group, two-hour charters can be arranged for $480 or four-hour charters for $739.

Hiking and Biking

HIKING

There aren't nearly as many hiking trails on the West Side of the island as you might expect. Much of the access in West Maui is blocked by private land or lack of proper trails. Also, since much of West Maui sits in the lee of Mauna Kahalawai, there aren't any accessible waterfalls as in East Maui. Nevertheless, the hiking options in West Maui offer their own sort of beauty, from stunning coastal treks to grueling ridgeline hikes.

Kapalua, Napili, and Honokowai
◖ KAPALUA COASTAL TRAIL

Even though it's only 1.75 miles long, the **Kapalua Coastal Trail** might just be the best coastal walk in Hawaii. The trail is bookended on each side by beaches that have each been voted as the #1 beach in the United States: Kapalua Bay and D.T. Fleming Beach Park.

While most walkers, joggers, and hikers begin the trail at Kapalua Bay, you can also access the trail from other junctions at the Kapalua Bay Villas, Oneloa Bay, the Ritz-Carlton, and D.T. Fleming Beach Park.

What makes the Kapalua Coastal Trail legendary are the various environments it passes through. Should you begin at Kapalua Bay, the trail starts as a paved walkway paralleling the beach and weaves its way through ultra-luxurious residences. At the top of a short hill the paved walkway reaches a junction by the Kapalua Bay Villas, where the path suddenly switches to dirt. While signs point to the continuation of the trail, a spur trail leads straight out toward Hawea Point, a protected reserve home to the island's largest colony of *u'au kani*, or wedge-tailed shearwaters. If you follow the grass trail to the left of the three-way junction, it will connect with the trail to Namalu

© KYLE ELLISON

Take a morning walk on the Kapalua Coastal Trail.

MAUI

Bay—the rocky, Mediterranean cove hidden in the craggy recesses.

Continuing along the main Kapalua Coastal Trail will take you over a short rocky section before emerging at a smooth boardwalk along Oneloa Bay. The boardwalk here was constructed as a means of protecting the sensitive dunes native to Kapalua, and Oneloa in the mornings is one of the most gloriously empty beaches you'll find on Maui. At the end of the boardwalk the trail will change into stairs and eventually connect with Lower Honoapiʻilani Road. From here you will take a left and follow the sidewalk as it connects with the trail running in front of the Ritz-Carlton before finishing at the water's edge at D.T. Fleming Beach Park. For a side trip, hike out parallel to the golf course to the point on the left side of the beach known as Dragon's Teeth, and there is a massive labyrinth where you can walk in circles and try to make sense of the beauty around you.

VILLAGE WALKING TRAILS

The **village walking trails** are the next most popular hikes in the Kapalua resort area. Weaving their way up the mountainside through the cool and forested uplands, hikers can choose from either the 1.25-mile Cardio Loop or the 3.6-mile Lake Loop, an uphill, butt-burning workout popular with local joggers. More than just a great morning workout, there are also sections of the trail that offer sweeping views looking out toward Molokaʻi and the area around Honolua Bay. To find the access point for the trails, park in the lot for the Kapalua Village Center (between Sansei Restaurant and the Kapalua Golf Academy), and follow a paved cart path winding its way down toward an underpass where you will find the trailhead for both loops.

MAUNALEI ARBORETUM TRAIL

To climb even farther up the mountainside, follow the **Maunalei Arboretum Trail** as it winds its way through a forest planted by the great D.T. Fleming. The manager of Honolua Ranch during the 1920s, Fleming forested the mountainside with numerous plant species from across the globe in an effort to preserve the watershed. Today, over 85 years after the arboretum was established, hikers can still climb the ridges of this historic upland and be immersed in the serenity of a global forest. Trails in the arboretum range from short, 0.5-mile loops to a moderate, 2.5-mile round-trip, which winds its way up Honolua Ridge. Reaching the trails, however, is strange: You need to take a shuttle to the trailhead since access crosses over expensive private property. Shuttles depart from the Kapalua Village building at 9:30am and 11:30am, and there are pickups at the trailhead at 9:50am, 11:50am, and 1:50pm. For more information on the shuttle or to arrange a ride call 808/665-9110. The other—albeit longer—option, is to catch a ride on the shuttle up to the Maunalei Arboretum and then hike your way back down the Mahana Ridge Trail for a grand total of around seven miles.

MAHANA RIDGE TRAIL

The **Mahana Ridge Trail** is the longest continuous trail in the Kapalua resort area and the best option for serious hikers. Although you can access the Mahana Ridge Trail from the village trails, a less confusing and more scenic trailhead may be found in the parking lot of D.T. Fleming Beach Park along the access road from the highway. This trail climbs up the ridge for nearly six miles and offers dramatic ocean and gulch views. The Mahana Ridge Trail is a proper hiking trail with narrow areas, moderate uphills, and exposed tree roots. The trail can either be hiked as an out and back trip, or if you are connecting the trail with the Maunalei Arboretum Trail, you can arrange to catch the 1:50pm shuttle for a sticky and sweaty shuttle ride down. A better option is to catch the 9:30am shuttle ride up to the Maunalei Arboretum trailhead in the morning and then hike the Mahana Ridge Trail all the way down to D.T. Fleming Beach Park for a refreshing dip in the ocean. Maps are posted at the Kapalua Adventure Center and are also available online at www.kapalua.com.

OHAI TRAIL

The 1.2-mile **Ohai Trail** awards hikers with panoramic vistas of the island's North Shore. This area is often windy, and the way in which the wind drowns out all other sounds makes it a peaceful respite on the northern coast. The Ohai trailhead is 10 miles past the entrance to Kapalua by mile marker 41 between the Nakalele Blowhole and Olivine Pools. Along the moderate, winding trail there are a few placards with information on the island's native coastal plants. This is also a great perch to watch for tropical seabirds soaring on the afternoon breeze. There isn't any readily available water on this stretch of coastline.

Ka'anapali

KA'ANAPALI BOARDWALK

The **Ka'anapali Boardwalk** is about three miles long from end to end. There are various historical placards scattered along the beach path. The southern terminus of the boardwalk is in front of the Hyatt resort, and the easiest public beach parking is at Hanakao'o Beach Park along the highway between Ka'anapali and Lahaina. From here the boardwalk runs north all the way to the Sheraton about a mile and half later, although if you follow the paved walkway through the lower level of the Sheraton and through the parking lot you will notice the trail reforms and starts skirting the golf course. The walkway then wraps its way through the Royal Lahaina resort and the parking lot of adjoining hotels. By following the Beach Walk signs you will eventually join with another boardwalk which runs all the way down to the Honua Kai resort.

South of Lahaina

LAHAINA PALI TRAIL

Hot, dry, and with incomparable views, the **Lahaina Pali Trail** is a literal walk back in time to days when reaching Lahaina wasn't quite so easy. This five-mile, three-hour (one-way) hike is the most strenuous trek in West Maui, as the zigzagging trail climbs for 1,600 feet before reaching a crest by the Kaheawa Wind Farm. While torturous on both your legs and

your thirst, the reward for the uphill slog is panoramic views over the central valley and dozens of humpback whales off the coast during the winter. Tracing its way over a part of the island that receives less than 10 inches of rainfall annually, this trail was originally constructed about 400 years ago during the reign of Pi'ilani, who envisioned a footpath wrapping around the island. When a dirt road was constructed along the coast in 1911, the trail fell into disrepair. Nevertheless, hikers will still encounter evidence of ancient activity such as stone shelters and rock walls. It's surreal to imagine that only 100 years ago this was the preferred route for reaching Lahaina. To get the most out of this hike, pick up the hiking guide the Na Ala Hele trail system has published entitled "Tales from the Trail," which provides an interactive historical tour aligned with markers along the trail. Copies are available at the Department of Land and Natural Resources building in Wailuku (54 High St.), or, if you have a smartphone, download it as a PDF (www.mauiguidebook.com/hikes/lahaina-pali-trail) you can carry with you on the trip.

The downside of this trail is that since it's a one-way hike it can take some logistical planning. The Ukumehame trailhead on the Lahaina-side is at mile marker 10.5 about a half-mile after the tunnel in a small dirt parking lot on the inland side of the highway. If you depart from the Ukumehame trailhead, the path ascends moderately and offers pristine views of the coral reefs below. After the trail levels out at 1,600 feet and you reach the crest by the wind farm, it will descend steeply and sharply to the opposite trailhead between Ma'alaea and the junction of Honoapi'ilani Highway (Hwy. 30) and North Kihei Road. Your four options for the return route are to either leave a car at the opposite trailhead, hike back the way you came, hitchhike back to the original trailhead, or turn back the way you came once you reach the wind farm (which is the shortest and most practical option). If you plan on only hiking half the trail, setting out from the Ma'alaea trailhead offers better views of the valley and Kealia Pond, whereas departing from the Ukumehame trailhead offers better views of the coastline and whale-watching opportunities. For the intrepid and those equipped with headlamps, the Ukumehame side is the best sunset perch on the West Side. Since there is absolutely no shade on this hike and it can get brutally hot, it's imperative to avoid the middle of the day and to pack more water than you would normally need. Also, since this area is so dry, it's a tinderbox ready to ignite at any moment, so don't smoke or use a lighter at any point on your hike. You'll be passing over rocky, rugged terrain, so wear closed-toe shoes.

BIKING

Whether you're going for a 60-mile cycle around the West Maui Mountains or a leisurely ride down Front Street on a beach cruiser, all of the biking on the West Side of the island consists of cycling on island roadways. For serious cyclists looking to rent a proper road bike, **West Maui Cycles** (1087 Limahana Pl., 808/661-9005, www.westmauicycles.com, 9am-5pm Mon.-Sat., 10am-4pm Sun.) in the industrial park of Lahaina is the best bike shop on the West Side. Rentals of mountain bikes and high-performance road bikes range from $50/day to $285/week, or you can also get basic beach cruisers for $15/day. This is also the only shop on the island where you can rent a tandem bicycle.

Closer to the center of Lahaina, **Boss Frog's Cycles** (156 Lahainaluna Rd., 808/661-1344, www.mauiroadbikerentals.com, 8am-5pm daily) also offers beach cruisers for $15/day, $50/week, and high-performance road bikes for $50/day. While this location is closer to town and more convenient, die-hard cyclists will appreciate the passion for the sport found at West Maui Cycles.

Adventure Sports

Even though water sports dominate the recreation options on the island's West Side, there are still a number of places where you can get a thrill either on the land or cruising over the water.

ATV RIDES

The best ATV ride on the West Side of the island is with **Kahoma Ranch** (808/667-1978, www.kahomaranch.com), a company with whom you not only have the ability to get dirty and rip across private dirt roads on your own ATV, but at the end when you're all hot and sweaty you can also take a plunge down one of three different waterslides. Tour participants are awarded with views looking out at the island of Lana'i and back into Kahoma Valley. The area you tour is closed to the public, so this is the only way you will see these views. The waterslides themselves aren't at all what you'd expect. When you first see them, you might be skeptical in that they look like little more than tarps stretched over a hole in the ground. When it comes to slides, however, it isn't a beauty contest, and the speeds you can get while careening down one are better than average. The cost for adults riding their own vehicle is $199, whereas a shared ATV is $129. Children are $65, and those as young as five years old can accompany a driver of legal age. Tours take place at 8am, 11am, and 2pm, although the 8am tour doesn't involve the waterslide.

ZIPLINING

Despite the explosion in zipline operators on the island, the only zipline tour in West Maui is **Skyline Eco-Adventures** (2580 Keka'a Dr., 808/878-8400, www.zipline.com, 7am-6pm daily), a company that was the first zipline operator on Maui and continues to be a leader in the industry. When Skyline opened an Upcountry course in 2002, it was in fact the first zipline company in the United States. Seizing upon the initial success, it opened up a second course in the hills above Ka'anapali offering greater views and longer lines than the sister course. Aside from there being eight ziplines crisscrossing the canyons, each one has an historical, environmental, or cultural connection explained to you by the affable guides. The main draw of this trip—nearly more so than the ziplines themselves—is the view looking out toward Lana'i and Moloka'i that incorporates 180° of horizon. From an elevation inaccessible to the public visitors are also afforded glimpses into the island's valleys as well as of small waterfalls during the wetter months of the year. These tours are so popular they run seven times a day, with the earliest setting out from the Fairway Shops office at 7am. The benefit of an early tour is that the temperature is still cool and the wind hasn't picked up yet, although there can sometimes be some lingering morning rain showers and the dirt roads can be muddy from this moisture. Try to get on the 8am or 9am tour, although there is never a *bad* time to be zipping over a rugged ravine and gazing out at the wide-open Pacific. Children must be 10 years of age for the Ka'anapali course, closed-toe shoes are required, and the maximum weight is 260 pounds.

Golf

KAPALUA, NAPILI, AND HONOKOWAI

For serious golfers, the name Kapalua should be synonymous with the **Kapalua Plantation Course** (2000 Plantation Club Dr., 877/527-2582, www.golfatkapalua.com), a windy, challenging, and scenic course that spreads out across the mountainside above D.T. Fleming Beach Park. This par-73, 7,411-yard course is the most famous course on the island and the site of the Hyundai Tournament of Champions. With the course's fame and prestige, however, come greens fees toward the upper end of the spectrum. Regular golfers will need to shell out $278 for a chance at tackling the Plantation, but those staying in the Kapalua resort receive a discount that knocks the price down to $228. Greens fees decrease as the day wears on, so those opting to play in the late afternoon can squeak in a round for only $128 (although expect the wind to be howling). Club rentals are $65 (including two sleeves of balls), and shoe rental is $14. To the find the clubhouse for the Plantation Course, travel along Honoapi'ilani Highway (Hwy. 30) for one mile past the main entrance to Kapalua resort and make a right onto Plantation Club Drive. You will wind your way up the hillside and eventually see the clubhouse on your right.

The **Kapalua Bay Course** (300 Kapalua Dr., 877/527-2582, www.golfatkapalua.com) along the Kapalua shoreline is a touch more forgiving at par 72 and 6,600 yards. While all of the holes offer resort-quality play, the highlight is hole #5, where the green is sandwiched between Oneloa Bay and D.T. Fleming Beach Park. While putting here you are surrounded by 270 degrees of brilliant blue ocean. The Bay Course is windy in the afternoon, so early morning hours are best for calm conditions. Greens fees here are still expensive at $208 for regular guests and $188 for those staying in Kapalua resort. The fees decrease throughout the day; you can pick up a late afternoon round for as low as $98. To find the clubhouse for the Bay Course, turn on Kapalua Drive from Lower Honoapi'ilani Road across the street from Oneloa Bay (Ironwoods Beach). Travel up the road by the tennis center and you will see the clubhouse on your right.

The **Kapalua Golf Academy** (1000 Office Rd., 808/662-7740, www.golfatkapalua.com/golf-academy) has been voted as one of the best golf schools in the country, with 23 acres devoted to bettering your game. Everything you could possibly need to improve your golf game is available here from private instruction and video analysis to on-course lessons and custom

MAUI

club fitting. Though the golf instruction is by no means cheap, seasonal packages and specials can sometimes offer surprisingly affordable deals.

KA'ANAPALI

There are a number of benefits about playing the courses in Ka'anapali. They're cheaper than Kapalua and closer to the majority of resorts. Perhaps most important, however, they're less prone to wind and rain, and it takes the trade winds about two hours longer to reach Ka'anapali than Kapalua. What this means is that an 8am tee time at Kapalua on most days will begin getting blustery around the 6th hole, whereas at Ka'anapali you could be well into the back nine before the wind becomes a factor. The sacrifice in Ka'anapali is that the views aren't quite as nice (though they are still spectacular by normal standards), and the greens are just *slightly* less manicured when compared to Kapalua.

Of the two courses in Ka'anapali, the **Royal**

Ka'anapali (2290 Ka'anapali Pkwy., 808/661-3691, www.kaanapaligolfcourses.com) has the best views and is the nicer course. In addition to paralleling the Pacific Ocean, this par-71, 6,700-yard course is also historic as the island's original course, having opened in 1962. Rates for the Royal course are $249 for non-resort guests, and those staying in Ka'anapali can play for $189. For those willing to tee off after 1pm, the price drops down to $149.

The **Ka'anapali Kai** (2290 Ka'anapali Pkwy., 808/661-3691, www.kaanapaligolfcourses. com) course has most of its holes on the inland side of the highway. The fairways here aren't as nicely maintained as the Royal, although since you're playing at a slight elevation there are still the kind of ocean views you would expect from a resort course in Hawaii. Rates for the Kai course are $205 for non-resort guests and $149 for those staying in Ka'anapali. Rates drop to $119 after 1pm, club rental is $49, and shoes are available for $10. Both Ka'anapali courses check in at the same clubhouse.

Spas

While the following spa and massage services are broken down by their geographic location, if you would rather enjoy an in-room, mobile massage service regardless of where you're staying, **Na Ali'i Massage** (808/250-7170, www.mymauimassage.com) will meet you anywhere on the West Side and offers rates which are much lower than the resorts or local massage parlors. A 60-minute massage is $85, and they also offer a full range of other services such as body scrubs, reflexology, and hand and foot treatments.

KAPALUA, NAPILI, AND HONOKOWAI

Just like its workout facility, the **Kapalua Spa** (100 Bay Dr., 808/665-8282, www.kapaluaspa. com, 9am-7pm daily) has the best spa services on the northwestern side of the island. This spa has been voted as the best luxury destination

spa in the United States. This truly is a luxurious wellness retreat unlike any other, incorporating elements of native Hawaiian culture into the treatments for an experience you won't find at smaller, more affordable spas. When your treatment is through, you can use the spa facilities or sit by the edgeless pool. Fees at the spa reflect higher resort prices; 50-minute massages—the shortest option—are $160.

For a spa experience outside a resort, **Zensations Spa** (3600 Lower Honoapi'ilani Rd., 808/669-0100, www.zensationsspa.com, 10am-5pm Mon.-Sat., 9am-7pm Sun.) in the 5A mall in Honokowai offers 60-minute massages for $99 as well as a full range of aromatherapy, facial, and body treatment options. The spa is within walking distance of many Honokowai condos.

Maui Massage and Wellness (3636 Lower Honoapi'ilani Rd., 808/669-4500, www.

mauimassageandwellness.com, 9am-6pm Mon.-Fri., 10am-5pm weekends) by the Honokowai Farmers Market offers massage and spa services for cheaper than the resort rates. Sixty-minute massages range $105-115, and there are also facials, foot scrubs, and various packages.

KA'ANAPALI
While nearly every resort in the Ka'anapali complex is going to offer a spa or beauty center, there are a couple which stand out.

At the Westin Maui next to Whalers Village, **Heavenly Spa** (2365 Ka'anapal Pkwy., 808/661-2588, www.westinmaui.com/spa, 8am-7pm daily) has been lauded as one of the top spas in the United States and has 50-minute massages beginning at $145.

For slightly more affordable rates, the **Spa at Black Rock** (2605 Ka'anapali Pkwy., 808/667-9577, www.blackrockspa.com, 8:30am-7pm

daily) offers 60-minute massages beginning at $125 in addition to a complete menu of spa packages.

LAHAINA
Although there aren't any fancy resort spas in the middle of Lahaina, the upside is that you can get relaxing spa sessions from seasoned professionals at prices that are a fraction of those at the resorts. If you tweaked your neck during a surf lesson at Breakwall or pulled a muscle while jumping off Black Rock, one of the most popular massage centers in town is **Maui Zen Day Spa** (181 Lahainaluna Rd., 808/661-7200, www.mauizen.com, 10am-6pm daily), smack in the middle of Lahaina about one block inland from Cheeseburger in Paradise. Massage sessions range between $99 and $115 depending on the treatment. For an additional $15 the therapists will come and meet you at your resort or condo.

Sights

KAPALUA, NAPILI, AND HONOKOWAI
Despite the prevalence of beaches here, there are still a few sights worth exploring, located along the remote northwestern corner of the island, which is like a miniature Road to Hana without the waterfalls. If you continue all the way around the back of West Maui past the town of Kahakuloa (the road isn't four-wheel drive like your rental car map might say, but it *is* far narrower, curvier, and scarier than the Road to Hana), you can combine the drive with the waterfalls of Makamaka'ole Valley in Central Maui for a full-day experience. This journey is not for the timid. Most turn back toward Kapalua once they reach Kahakuloa.

◖ Nakalele Blowhole
Eight miles past the entrance to Kapalua by mile marker 38 is the famous **Nakalele Blowhole.** Outside of Honolua Bay this is the most popular stop along this stretch of coast.

It's about a fifteen-minute drive past the entrance to Kapalua if you go straight through without stopping. On the right days, the Nakalele Blowhole can jettison water upward of 100 feet into the air. The best conditions for witnessing Nakalele are when the trade winds are blowing and during the hours around the high tide. To check the current tide tables for the highest time of day, look at www.hawaiitides.com. In the full throes of its performance, Nakalele Blowhole is a natural, saltwater geyser erupting on a windswept outcropping, and it's one of the most powerful forces of the sea you can witness on the island. Visitors in the past have been killed by standing too close to the blowhole.

Finding the blowhole can be a challenge for those who don't know where to look. At mile marker 38 there is dirt pullout on the ocean-side of the highway, although the trail from here that leads down toward the water will only take you as far as the decrepit old lighthouse

© MARK DRIESSEN

Nakalele Blowhole

and a marginal view of the blowhole. A better access point is a half a mile farther down the road where a second dirt pullout serves as the trailhead for the path leading to the blowhole. Between the two parking areas are dozens of dirtbike tracks which serve as red herrings and don't lead anywhere, so the best thing to do is park by mile marker 38.5 (although there isn't an actual sign) and make your way down from there. The trail to the blowhole is just over a half-mile long, and the last half of the trail becomes a scramble down a moderate scree slope, which is best left to those who are steady on their feet.

The Olivine Pools

A little over four miles past the Nakalele Blowhole by mile marker 16, the Olivine Pools are one of the more controversial sights on the northwestern side of the island. The coastal panoramas from here are breathtaking, and even if you never walk down to the pools, the views alone are reason enough to stop. For most visitors, the whole point of coming here is to swim and bathe in the shallow tidepools perfectly perched on a lava rock outcropping. On calm days when the wind is light and the ocean is mellow and smooth, this can be one of the most serene perches you'll find anywhere on the island. However, the ocean is rarely calm along this stretch of shoreline, and winter can see 20-foot surf cascading over the rocky pinnacle. That makes swimming in the pools exceptionally dangerous. A good rule of thumb is to sit and watch them for a while and wait to see if any waves are crashing into them. If the ocean is calm and isn't reaching the pools, then this is the safest time for swimming or wading. If waves are washing into the pools—even small ones—keep out. Visitors have been swept to their deaths here.

KA'ANAPALI
Pu'u Keka'a

Known to most visitors as Black Rock, **Pu'u Keka'a** is the correct name for this volcanic outcropping at the northern end of Ka'anapali Beach. Today the rock is a popular spot for snorkeling, scuba diving, and cliff jumping, although the most popular time of day is about 20 minutes prior to sunset when a torch-wielding, shirtless member of the Sheraton staff scrambles onto the rock and lights a row of carefully placed tiki torches. Once all of the torches are lit, his flaming staff is ceremoniously chucked into the water moments before he performs a swan dive off the rock. More than just a creative marketing plan, the ceremony is a reenactment of the sacred belief that this is one of the spots on the island where a person's soul leaps from this world to the next immediately following death.

Whalers Village Museum

There's actually more to Whalers Village than high-end luxury shopping and beachfront, barefoot bars. On the third story high above the fancy stores and bustling courtyard, the **Whalers Village Museum** (2435 Kaʻanapali Pkwy., 808/661-5992, www.whalersmuseum. com, 10am-6pm daily, $3 adults, $2 seniors, $1 children) is the best resource for whale education on the island's West Side. Visitors can wander through the museum to learn everything from *why* whales were hunted in the first place to what life was like aboard a 19th-century whaling ship. There is a large display of scrimshaw art (drawings carved on whale's teeth), and there are also movies playing throughout the day that explore the dismal yet fascinating world of 19th-century whaling. During winter, a visit to the museum is the perfect way to fortify the knowledge gained on a whale-watching excursion. Despite the fact the museum discusses whaling, the focus has shifted toward protecting our winter companions today.

LAHAINA

From 1820-1845, this seaside town—which was originally called *Lele*—was the capital of the Hawaiian kingdom. At about the same time that the *aliʻi* and royalty were establishing their capital, fleets of New England whaling ships began anchoring in the Lahaina Roads. From 1820-1860, thousands of crusty

whalers paddled ashore in wooden rowboats to reprovision their ships, soak their livers, and soothe their rusty loins. Answering the call to save these poor souls, Christian missionaries from New England began to arrive in the early 1820s, bolstered by the support of Queen Kaʻahumanu who had embraced the values of Christianity. Lahaina became a literal and metaphorical battleground between drunken whalers and pious missionaries to win the native Hawaiian populace. Lahaina truly was the Wild West of the Pacific. Today, scores of historic sites pertaining to this era are scattered about town.

Thanks to the tireless work of the Lahaina Restoration Foundation, many of the town's historical sites are well marked and accessible. Pick up a walking tour map from the Lahaina Visitor Center in the Courthouse next to Lahaina Harbor or a *Moʻolelo O Lahaina* historical and cultural walking tour map from the offices of the Lahaina Restoration Foundation on the grounds of the Baldwin Missionary home.

The Banyan Tree

This magnificent tree is the most recognizable landmark in West Maui. You can't miss it at the corner of Hotel and Front Streets, because it spreads its shading boughs over almost an acre. This tree is the **largest banyan in the state,** planted in April 1873 by Sheriff Bill Smith in commemoration of the Congregationalist Missions' golden anniversary. Every year during the month of April a birthday party is held for the tree which draws hundreds of people to its shady confines. During most days you can find old-timers sitting here chatting, and artists gather here on weekends to display their artwork under the tree's broad branches.

Fort

On the southwestern edge of the park are the restored coral remnants of the historic Lahaina fort. By 1825 the missionaries had convinced Hawaiian royalty that drunken sailors running amok in town was morally lamentable, so strict laws forbade native women from visiting the ships and whalers from coming ashore after nightfall. These rules, as you can imagine, proved a severe hindrance to any lascivious pursuits, and riots frequently broke out between angry whalers and the missionaries. In 1827, whalers anchored offshore went so far as to lob cannonballs into the lawn of missionary William Richards' house, and it was decided by Hoapili—the governor of Maui—that a fort needed to be built to protect the town from the pent-up whalers. Hence, in 1832, a fort was constructed out of coral blocks with walls 20 feet high and laden with cannons, the restored remnants of which are still visible today. One of the cannons from the fort is across the street at Lahaina Harbor, facing out toward the water to serve as a reminder of the "tensions" which once gripped this town.

◖ Lahaina Courthouse

The old **Lahaina Courthouse** contains the most informative museum in downtown Lahaina. During its tenure as the town's political center, it also served as governor's office, post office, customs office, and police station, complete with a jail in the underground basement. The jail is now home to the Lahaina Arts Society's **Old Jail Gallery,** and the society has its main **Banyan Tree Gallery** on the first floor. Since renovation in 1998, the **Lahaina Visitor Center** (808/667-9193, 9am-5pm daily) has also occupied a room on the main floor. Here anyone can come for gifts and tourist information and brochures about the town, and there are also numerous coupon books that can help save you a few dollars. In the old courtroom on the second floor, the **Lahaina Heritage Museum** (9am-5pm daily, suggested $3 donation) displays historical objects and old photographs, and there is even the original Hawaiian flag which was lowered from the courthouse on the day it was replaced in 1898 by the American stars and stripes. On the lower level there is also a small theater with informative documentaries about life in the islands, and this is a must-stop venue for anyone with an interest in the history of Lahaina.

Lighthouse

A tall, white lighthouse stands on the northern edge of the main loading dock. During summer months you will also notice local surfers launching themselves into the water by the breakwall here, and it's the perfect spot for soaking up some sun and people-watching. What makes this lighthouse historic, however, is that it's the oldest one in the state of Hawaii, constructed in 1840 as an aid to whaling ships navigating offshore.

Baldwin Missionary House

On the inland side of Front Street on the corner with Dickenson Street, you will notice the sprawling green lawn and whitewashed front of the historic **Baldwin Missionary House** (10am-4pm daily, $7 adults, $5 seniors). Established in 1834, this restored and peaceful property has stood since the days of the earliest missionaries, and was the home of Doctor/Reverend Dwight Baldwin, his wife Charlotte, and their eight children. Baldwin was the first modern doctor and dentist in Hawaii (having studied at Harvard), and in the back of the museum are his tools of the trade. This building also served until 1868 as a dispensary, meeting room, and boardinghouse, and Rev. Baldwin was instrumental in not only educating scores of Hawaiian citizens, but also in helping to fight the smallpox epidemic which struck the island in 1853. Various rooms contain period furniture and artifacts indicative of missionary life in Lahaina, and coin collectors will appreciate the array of historic coins that were used as legal tender in early Hawaii, including silver bullion which was minted in Bolivia as early as the 1500s. Entrance to the museum also covers the Wo Hing Museum up the street, and if you purchase a $10 Passport to the Past, admission to the A&B Sugar Museum in Kahului and the Bailey House Museum in Wailuku are also included. While visiting in the daytime is educational enough, for a true experience of missionary life, take part in a candlelit tour 6pm-8:30pm every Friday evening.

Plantation Museum

For a look at a period of Lahaina's history that didn't have to do with whalers, missionaries, or Hawaiian royalty, idle on over to the Wharf

Cinema Center and climb the stairs to the third story for a glimpse inside the informative **Plantation Museum** (9am-6pm daily, free). Although it isn't much larger than a closet, there are dozens of old photos showing life during plantation times as well as a video detailing harvesting sugarcane. The Pioneer Mill was the social and economic engine of the West Side for the better part of 100 years, and the plantation days are just as much a part of Lahaina's heritage as harpoons, grog, and Bibles. A visit here only takes a couple of minutes, but you'll be glad you stopped in.

Wo Hing Museum

The **Wo Hing Museum** (858 Front St., 10am-4pm daily, $7) is a small Chinese museum sandwiched between the modern commercial ventures of Front Street. Built in 1912 as a social and religious hall for Chinese workers, it's been placed on the National Register of Historic Places. Downstairs are displays, and upstairs is the temple altar. In the cookhouse next door, you can see film clips of Hawaii taken by Thomas Edison in 1898 and 1906. On the Chinese New Year, the Wo Hing Museum is the center of the activities that play out on Front Street. The entrance fee is also good for entrance to the Baldwin House.

Hale Pa'ahao

When Luakini crosses Prison Street, turn left and walk a few yards to **Hale Pa'ahao** (10am-4pm daily, free), better known as Lahaina's old prison. This is one of the more historically informative sights in Lahaina. Now the peaceful courtyard inside the prison walls is a place of serenity and calm where benches rest beneath the shade of a mango tree, but there was once a time when this compound housed dozens of sailors and Hawaiians who had violated the laws set forth by the royalty and their missionary advisors. To get an idea of an offense that would land you in the Lahaina slammer read the list from the 1850s posted on the wall of one of the whitewashed, wooden cells.

Sugar Cane Train

The historic **Sugar Cane Train** (975 Limahana Pl., 808/661-0080, www.sugarcanetrain.com,

MAUI

© CHRISTOPHE TESTI/123RF.COM

the Sugar Cane Train

$23 adults, $16 children) continues to be the island's only train ride and as such remains a novelty. It's a misnomer, since there hasn't been any sugarcane since Pioneer Mill shuttered its operations in 1999 and the six-mile route now wraps its way through residential backyards and industrial construction sites. Nevertheless, the old-fashioned trestle is still the highlight of the trip and provides a few views looking out toward the water. The train ride is popular with young children and those with a love for trains, and the narration provides a decent history about the plantation era of Lahaina. Round-trip trains depart Lahaina three times daily at 11:05am, 1pm, and 2pm, and this is also an alternative (albeit expensive) way of transporting yourself to the resort area of Ka'anapali.

SOUTH OF LAHAINA
Olowalu Petroglyphs

For every 1,000 people who snorkel at Olowalu, probably only one makes it back to the *ki'i pohaku,* or petroglyphs behind the Olowalu General Store. Hidden a half-mile back in the recesses of Olowalu valley, the 70 rock carvings on the face of Pu'u Kilea date to a time nearly 300 years ago when there was no written language and drawings were one of the only ways of communicating other than storytelling, song, or dance. The Olowalu valley is an area that is heavily steeped in Hawaiian history, and though a century of sugar cultivation and the encroachment of modern development has eroded the traditional village sites, there are still a number of families living back in the valley who aim to perpetuate the lifestyle of their ancestors. To find the petroglyphs, drive on the road behind the Olowalu fruit stand at mile marker 15 and proceed on the paved segment, which runs back toward the valley. After half a mile you will see signs for the Olowalu Cultural Reserve, and when the road turns to dirt, the petroglyphs will be on the rock face about 200 yards down. Unfortunately, some of the petroglyphs have been vandalized, so visitors are kindly asked to keep a respectful distance from the rock face.

Piliani Kope Coffee Farm

The **Piliani Kope Coffee Farm** (15 Wailau Pl., 808/661-5479, www.pilianikopefarm.com), high on the hill in the Launiupoko subdivision, offers tours that will walk you through every step of the coffee process. Hawaii is the only U.S. state where coffee is commercially harvested. Aside from having a stunning ocean view, this working coffee farm produces some of the island's best coffee and is an educational experience. Ninety-minute tours are held regularly on Tuesday and Thursday during the cooler morning hours at $10/person. The farm just requests that you call a couple of days ahead to confirm the exact timing. During September through December when the farm is processing coffee, there is an in-depth, three-hour, $90/person processing tour covering every single aspect of the growing and roasting process. This tour also includes lunch and offers the island's best insight into what has become the fastest-growing and most successful crop on Maui.

Maui Dragon Fruit Farm

The **Maui Dragon Fruit Farm** (833 Punakea Lp., 808/264-6127, www.mauidragonfruit. com), also in the Launiupoko subdivision, makes for a curious combination of agriculture and adventure. Dragon fruit is a tropical fruit native to Central and South America, although it's most often seen in markets throughout Southeast Asia. With the consistency of an apple but the look of an exotic poppy seed muffin, dragon fruit is one of the most colorfully named as well as colorful produce species on the island. In addition to the dragon fruit, various other crops are grown on this certified organic farm. Daily walking tours take place 1pm-2pm daily for $25/adult. Additional adventure activities are available throughout the farm such as a 450-foot-long zipline and an enormous, plastic "Aquaball," which is filled with water and then rolled 450 feet downhill (with you inside, of course). The zipline inclusion is $80/adult or $50/child, and the Aquaball is $100/adult and $70/child. Zipline tours of the farm take place at 10am, 2pm, and 5pm, and the Aquaball tour is at either 11:30am or 3:30pm. Combine the farm tour, the zipline, and the Aquaball into a zany package for $140/adult or $100/child.

Shopping

KAPALUA, NAPILI, AND HONOKOWAI

Shopping in the northwestern corner of the island is utilitarian, paling in comparison to the shops of Ka'anapali and Lahaina. Nevertheless, there are still a few stores worthy of a mention of you're staying in the area and need some emergency retail therapy.

In Kapalua, the **Honolua Store** (502 Office Rd., 808/665-9105, 6am-6:30pm daily) has a small apparel and souvenir section to accompany the food market, and if you save your receipt from any purchase, you will receive a free gift on your next time shopping there.

For Polynesian jewelry, **La Perle** (700 Office Rd., 808/669-8466, 10am-7pm Mon.-Sat., 10am-6pm Sun.) is a small shop next to Sansei restaurant that specializes in black pearls and gold jewelry.

Down the road in Kahana, both **HIM** (808/281-1418, www.himmaui.com) as well as **Women Who Run With Wolves** (808/665-0786, www.womenwhorunwithwolves.com, 10am-6pm daily) are in the downstairs portion of the Kahana Manor (4310 Honoapi'ilani Rd.) and offer the best apparel and accessory shopping for men and women that you'll find on the northwest side.

KA'ANAPALI
Whalers Village

Without a doubt, the undisputed epicenter of the Ka'anapali shopping scene is **Whalers Village** (2435 Ka'anapali Pkwy., 808/661-4567, www.whalersvillage.com, 9:30am-10pm daily), smack in the middle of Ka'anapali Beach between the Whaler hotel and the Westin Resort. Three levels of restaurants, clothing boutiques, jewelry galleries, and kiosks, Whalers Village is the see-and-be-seen spot for all of your island souvenir shopping. While many of the stores are name-brand outlets you're already familiar with, there are still a handful of locally run stores. Get your parking validated since the garage rates are expensive.

If you park in the Whalers Village garage, you can't help but walk directly past **Totally Hawaiian** (808/667-4070, www.totallyhawaiian.com), a gift gallery featuring the wares of over 100 local artists. Works of craftsmanship such as hand-painted Hawaiian gourds are on display, as is an impressive collection of Ni'ihau shell jewelry. There's also a fascinating array of ancient Hawaiian weapons handcrafted from shark's teeth and wood.

Sand People (808/662-8785, www.sandpeople.com) is a "coastal lifestyle emporium" featuring home decor and furnishings inspired by the ocean. This is a good place to find that whitewashed, driftwood picture frame you've been searching for.

Other popular apparel favorites range from **Blue Ginger** (808/667-5793, www.blueginger.com), a store specializing in women's and children's resort wear, to **Maggie Coulombe** (808/344-6672, www.maggiecoulombe.com), a world-renowned dress fashionista who has clothed some of the world's top celebrities. A wide variety of pearl shops, jewelry stores, and surf outlets round out the popular mall.

Shops at the Hyatt Regency
While nearly all of the Ka'anapali shopping takes place at Whalers Village, there are enough stores in the lobby of the Hyatt at the far southern end of the Ka'anapali strip that it's at least

MAUI

craft shopping in Lahaina

worth a mention. A handful of galleries, souvenir stores, clothing boutiques, and jewelry outlets populate the recesses of the lobby.

LAHAINA

Frenetic and fast-paced, Lahaina is the shopping capital of Maui. The section of Front Street between the Old Lahaina Center and the 505 shopping center is where you'll find the majority of shops.

⟨ Front Street

Front Street is a sight unto itself that centers around commerce and a voracious love of shopping. Front Street has been listed as one of the "Great Streets in America" by the American Planning Association. Walking the length of this vivacious thoroughfare is one of the West Side's most popular activities. Along this flat, oceanfront stretch you'll find everything from art galleries to surf shops all compressed together in a nonstop string of merchandise. Most shops are open 9am-10pm.

The **Wyland Gallery** (711 Front St., 808/667-2285, www.wyland.com) offers the artist's trademark array of marine life scenes in a perfect oceanfront location. On the opposite side of the street, acclaimed photographer **Peter Lik** (712 Front St., 808/661-6623, www.peterlik.com) has a popular showroom of his oversize art with the ability to transport you directly into the photograph. Other galleries of note are **Sargent's Fine Art** (802 Front St., 808/667-4030, www.sargentsfineart.com) on the corner of Lahainaluna Road, the **Village Gallery** (120 Dickenson St., 808/661-5199, www.villagegalleriesmaui.com), and **Martin Lawrence** (808/661-1788, www.martinlawrence.com). Those with a passion for art should also remember that every Friday night is art night in Lahaina, when many galleries put on their finest show, featuring artist appearances or live jazz, 7pm-10pm.

Bella Lulu (626 Front St., 808/667-5657) and **Serendipity** (752 Front St., 808/667-7070, www.serendipitymaui.com) offer unique female apparel. **Hale Zen** (180 Dickenson St., 808/661-4802, www.halezen.com)—a two-minute walk up Dickenson Street—is a local favorite for everything from homewares to candles, lotions, and crafts from local artists. For jewelry, stop into **Glass Mango Designs** (858 Front St., 808.662-8500, www.glassmango.com) for a colorful selection of "wearable art."

Classic retail outpost **Lahaina Scrimshaw** (845 Front St., 808/667-9232, www.lahainascrimshawmaui.com) showcases the seafarers' craft of carving scenes on ivory.

505 Front Street

Down at the southern end of Front Street, most shops are open 9am-9pm, including several art shops, clothing shops, and a **Whalers General Store** for sundries.

Banyan Tree Market

While the Friday art nights are always a festive event, those who prefer smaller artists are encouraged to visit the fair beneath the banyan tree, held on various weekends throughout the year 9am-5pm. For a full schedule on when the art fair is on, visit www.lahaina-arts/events.

Lahaina Cannery Mall

Enough visitors who still frequent **Lahaina Cannery Mall** (1221 Honoapi'ilani Hwy., www.lahainacannery.com, 9:30am-9pm Mon.-Sat., 9:30am-7pm Sun.) to keep a few stores open. Stores of note include **Honolua Surf Co.** (808/661-5777, www.honoluasurf.com) which

has the same apparel as you would find in Whalers Village or on Front Street for slightly reduced rates, and **Maui Toy Works** (808/661-4766), the de facto stop for picking up children's gifts.

Lahaina Gateway Center

On the inland side of the highway across from the Lahaina Cannery Mall is the **Lahaina Gateway Center** (305 Keawe St., www.lahainagateway.com, 9:30am-9pm daily) where you'll find **Local Motion** (808/661-7873, www.localmotionhawaii.com) surf shop, **Mahina** (808/661-0383, www.mahinamaui.com) women's clothing boutique, and **Maui Dive and Surf** (808/661-5388, www.mauidiveshop.com) for ocean-related merchandise. Walking distance along the highway back toward the center of Lahaina, **West Side Vibes** (1087 Limahana Pl., 808/667-1900, www.westsidevibes.com, 10am-7pm Mon.-Sat., noon-6pm Sun.), stocks reggae-inspired clothing and smoking-related accessories.

SOUTH OF LAHAINA
Olowalu General Store

The only shopping to be found south of Lahaina is at **Olowalu General Store** (820 Olowalu Village Rd., 808/667-2883, 5am-7pm daily) where you can pick up refreshingly cheap clothing. This is a good place for finding a shirt that no one else will have.

Entertainment

West Maui is the island's entertainment hot spot. Here you'll find the island's best luaus and most happening bars. You can't walk more than 10 yards in Lahaina without tripping over an evening drink special. More than just booze, West Maui is also home to family entertainment options ranging from free hula performances and whale lectures to evening magic performances. Despite the happening surroundings, however, if you're the clubbing type who likes to party into

the wee hours of the morning, you're out of luck since most bars close by 11pm, and only a handful stay open later than 1am. Also, even though almost all of the nightlife options involve bars and pubs that have lively atmospheres, the options for dancing are woefully inadequate. For the most up-to-date info on the latest evening scene, pick up a free copy of *Maui Time* newspaper, or, check out The Grid section on the website at www.mauitime.com.

MAUI

KAPALUA, NAPILI, AND HONOKOWAI

Evening Shows

Can't get enough of *ki ho'alu* (slack key guitar)? The **Masters of Slack Key** (5900 Lower Honoapi'ilani Rd., www.slackkeyshow.com, 7:30pm Wed.) performance at the Aloha Pavilion of the Napili Kai Beach Resort is the best show you'll find on the island. Tickets can either be purchased online or at 6:45pm when the doors first open. Prices for the show are normally $38, although you can also book a package dinner combo for $79 which includes a sunset dinner at the Sea House restaurant immediately before the show.

Bars, Live Music, and Nightlife

The late-night karaoke sessions at **Sansei** (600 Office Rd., 808/669-6286, www.sanseihawaii. com, 5:30pm-10pm Mon.-Thurs., 5:30pm-1am Fri.-Sat.) restaurant in the Kapalua resort are the most happening evenings on the northwestern side. This popular sushi and sake bar stays open until 1am on Thursday and Friday during karaoke night, and more so than the drinks and the singing, the main draw is the award-winning late-night menu (10pm-1am) that offers dozens of sushi plates at heavily discounted rates.

A short walk away at the Ritz-Carlton hotel you can find live music in the **Alaloa Lounge** Thursday-Monday evenings. It has the most consistent live music in the Kapalua resort.

In the Kahana Gateway Center, **Maui Brewing Company** (4405 Honoapi'ilani Hwy., 808/669-3474, www.mauibrewingco. com, open until midnight) is the island's only brewery. Sit at the bar so you can keep your beer cold on the slab of ice that's inside the bar. Over a dozen beers are only available on draft at the brewery.

Dollie's (4310 Lower Honoapi'ilani Rd., 808/669-0266, www.dolliespizzakahana. com, open until midnight) is the West Side's de facto sports bar where cheap beer and good pizza are served throughout the night. This is where island locals come to catch the Monday Night Football game or Sunday NFL. Fifteen different televisions also show NBA, hockey, college sports, and whichever game you're hoping to catch.

In the strip mall by Times Supermarket in Honokowai **Soup Nutz/Java Jazz** (3350 Lower Honoapi'ilani Rd., 808/667-0787, www.javajazz.net, open until 10pm) has live music seven nights a week 7pm-10pm in an eccentric, artsy, and dimly lit interior. Coffee shop by day and trendy parlor by night, this establishment has a decor that includes a bear rug, a disco ball, and a chandelier made up of dozens of different wine bottles. This is a good place to sit and listen to some underground acoustic artists.

KA'ANAPALI

Whalers Village

The center stage area at Whalers Village constantly teems with free events. Stalwarts of the entertainment schedule include lei making classes, hula classes, arts and crafts sessions, and live music on most weekend nights. While the schedule of events is constantly shifting, you can visit www.whalersvillage.com for an up-to-date calendar of the current month's activities. Any time of the afternoon you can find a band or ukulele musician strumming live tunes along the Ka'anapali strip.

Luaus

There is no shortage of luaus to be found along the Ka'anapali strip. While the best luau on the island (Old Lahaina Luau) is in nearby Lahaina, there are four luaus in Ka'anapali for those who would prefer to simply stroll from their resort down to the luau grounds. Also, if the only reason you want to go to a luau is for the fire dancing, you'll want to choose one of the luaus here in Ka'anapali for your fire twirling fix. All will feature buffet food mass produced for over 100 people, all will feature local craft artisans, and all will offer some sort of premium seating for an added price. Most shows begin at either 5 or 5:30pm. Ka'anapali can experience higher winds and a greater likelihood of rain than nearby Lahaina, so the chances of the luau needing to be moved inside or cancelled are higher. Most nights are gorgeous, but if you want to guarantee calm conditions, you'll have better luck in Lahaina.

Of the numerous luaus in Ka'anapali the best show is the **Wailele Polynesian Luau** (2365 Ka'anapali Pkwy., 808/667-2525, www.westinmaui.com) at the Westin Maui resort. The fire dancers here are the best, and the food is above average when compared to the other options. Also, the backdrop for the show faces out toward the ocean as opposed to being hunkered in the corner of a resort. The fast-paced performance weaves a storyline of tales from various corners of Polynesia. Shows take place Tuesday and Thursday evenings (as well as Sunday during busier times of the year), and prices range between $110 and $135 for adults and $65-80 for kids. If you're coming from elsewhere and will be driving to Ka'anapali, the one downside of this show is that parking can be a little challenging. Your best bet is to try and find a free beach parking spot in the lot between Whalers Village and the entrance to the Westin. If you can't find any free spots, your most economical option is going to be parking in the Whalers Village garage and then buying something small (such as an ice cream or a quick beer after the show) to get your parking validated for three hours of parking.

Ka'anapali Sunset Luau at Black Rock (2605 Ka'anapali Pkwy., 808/877-4852, www.sheratonmauiluau.com) is at the Sheraton resort. The crowds here aren't quite as large as other shows, and the grassy luau grounds are more spacious. While the food is fine and the dancers are entertaining, the best part about this show is the atmosphere of looking out at Pu'u Keka'a and experiencing the torch lighting ceremony. While children are welcome to enjoy the show, it mainly caters to couples and adults. The luau takes place Monday and Wednesday evenings. Prices range $105-115 for adults and $57-67 for children.

At the far end of the beach at the southern tip of Ka'anapali, the **Drums of the Pacific** (200 Nohea Kai, 808/667-4727) at the Hyatt resort is managed by the same production company (Tihati) as the show at the Sheraton, so you can expect something similar. The luau at the Hyatt is larger than the one at the Sheraton. While the fire dancing and the performance are on par with other Ka'anapali shows, the food portion of the evening leaves much to be desired. Prices are $105-115 for adults, $49-61 for kids, and shows take place every evening except Sunday.

On the northern side of Pu'u Keka'a facing out toward the ocean, the **Royal Lahaina Luau** (2780 Keka'a Dr., 808/661-9119, www.royallahaina.com) is a Ka'anapali original and the best option for those traveling with children. This is the island's longest running luau (although don't confuse it with *Old* Lahaina Luau, which is better), and while there's no shaking the tourist trap kitsch, there's a palpable charm that goes along with the old-school venue. Everything over on this side of "the rock" is more laid-back than along the main Ka'anapali strip. A nice bonus right away is that parking for the show is ample, easy, and only $5. Although the show doesn't face the beach, it's nevertheless set along a wide stretch of sand, and guests are encouraged to watch the sun go down while sipping a drink from the luau grounds. The show features a fire dance finale, and the entertainers will bring children on stage for an impromptu hula lesson. The food is average. Mai tais and Blue Hawaiians are included in the price of the ticket, but premium drinks will cost extra at the bar. During summer the luau takes place daily 6pm-8:30pm, while September through May there aren't any shows on Saturday or Monday and the festivities begin at 5:30pm.

Bars, Live Music, and Nightlife

Most of the bar scene in Ka'anapali plays out at the pool bars within the resorts. My favorite is the **Grotto Bar at the Hyatt** which is tucked beneath two different waterfalls. While the happy hour and dinner scene can be fun, if you're looking for anything later than 10pm, you're going to have to get a cab down to Lahaina. **Hula Grill** in Whalers Village has live

MAUI

music every afternoon and evening, and neighboring **Leilani's** occasionally has live music during happy hour. There is also live music on the center stage of **Whalers Village** on Friday and Sunday evenings, and most restaurants and lobbies inside the resorts will also provide it during the later afternoons, sunset, and peak dinner hours.

The only place in Ka'anapali with anything that resembles proper nightlife is **Paradise Grill** (2291 Ka'anapali Pkwy., 808/662-3700, www. paradisegrillkb.com, open until 2am) featuring live entertainment every night 10pm-1:30am. Paradise Grill and the associated Mello's Bar are on the corner of Ka'anapali Parkway and Honoapi'ilani Highway. It's the first building you see at the main entrance to the Ka'anapali resort. Most of the late-night entertainment takes place downstairs in Mello's, while the upstairs section of the restaurant usually has live music during the dinner hours 6pm-9pm. Expect to find acoustic music upstairs during dinner, and rock, reggae, and karaoke later hours downstairs.

LAHAINA
Hula Shows
The **free hula shows** at the **Lahaina Cannery Mall** (1221 Honoapi'ilani Highway by Safeway) take place in the center of the mall at 1pm on weekends, and evening shows begin at 7pm on Tuesday and Thursday.

◖ 'Ulalena
'Ulalena (Maui Theatre, 808/856-7900, www. mauitheatre.com, 6:30pm Mon.-Fri., $40-80) is a captivating show that details the history of the Hawaiian Islands. Told through chant, dance, and visual effects, the show takes place in the 680-seat Maui Theatre. The show is musical, performed without words. Because of the use of creative audience participation, words aren't necessary. Ticket prices vary depending on seats and packages; the most expensive tickets will allow you to spend 20 minutes with the cast. If you're a fan of shows or have an interest in Hawaiian history, this isn't an evening to be missed.

Art Night
Friday night is **Art Night in Lahaina.** In keeping with its status as the cultural center of Maui, Lahaina opens the doors of its three dozen galleries 7pm-10pm, throws out the welcome mat, sets out food and drink, provides entertainment, and usually hosts a well-known artist or two for this weekly party. Take your time and stroll Front Street from one gallery to the next. Stop and chat with shopkeepers, munch the goodies, sip the wine, look at the pieces on display, corner the featured artist for a comment on his or her work, soak in the music of the strolling musicians, and strike up a conversation with the person next to you who is eyeing that same piece. People dress up, but don't be afraid to come casually.

Luaus
Lahaina is the best place on the island for taking part in a luau. It's drier and calmer than in nearby Ka'anapali. The luaus in Lahaina are arguably the two best on the island, and you can't go wrong with either show since they're in oceanfront locations and feature some of the best performers.

Of all the island's luaus, **Old Lahaina Luau** (1251 Front St., 808/667-1998, www.oldlahainaluau.com, $99 adults, $69 children) is regarded as the best. The food is the best, the luau grounds are immaculate, and everything from the show to the service runs like a well-oiled machine. Despite the fact that the luau seats 440 people, it still manages to retain an intimate atmosphere. You are greeted with a lei made of fragrant fresh flowers. Premium bar selections are included in the price. There is a large *imu* for unearthing the pig (although it gets insanely crowded, so hang by the *imu* early if you want to get a good view), and the private oceanfront setting provides the perfect perch for watching the sun go down. There is ample free parking, or if you plan on having more than a couple of drinks, it's a short cab ride from the resorts in Ka'anapali.

The evening mimics an authentic experience in the surroundings of a Hawaiian fishing village. There is a cultural integrity and commitment to historical accuracy often lost on other shows. However, this means there is no fire dancing, which is a craft that is native to Samoa as opposed to Hawaii. The show at Old Lahaina Luau traces the history of the original Hawaiians as they migrated across oceans from French Polynesia to establish a unique culture here in Hawaii.

For seating arrangements, you can either choose between traditional seating on lauhala mats (which are the closest to the stage), or you can sit at tables with chairs which still provide a good view. The only vantage point where it's tough to see the show is from the seats in the far corners. Seating preference is given to those who book the earliest. Check-in for the luau is either 5:15pm or 5:45pm, depending on the time of year. When you consider all that you're getting—an all you can eat buffet of good food, an open bar of premium drinks, and a professional cultural performance in an oceanfront setting—the tickets are obscenely affordable. Remarkably, shows are offered seven days a week.

The **Feast at Lele** (505 Front St., 808/667-5353, www.feastatlele.com, $115 adults, $85 children) is a luau on the oceanfront in the 505 shopping center. "Lele" is the ancient Hawaiian name for the town of Lahaina, and this show begins with a look at the dance which is native to Hawaiian culture. The Feast at Lele then migrates its way through various Polynesian cultures, including those of Aotearoa (New Zealand), Tahiti, and Samoa. The combination of cultures makes for a fast-paced, fiery, and heart-pumping performance that is capped off by everyone's favorite, the Samoan fire and knife dancing. Shows take place nightly; check-in begins at 6:30pm and the show begins at 7pm.

Bars and Live Music

Rooted in the grog shop days of its boisterous port town past, Lahaina is Maui's nightlife capital. There are only a handful of places where you can actually dance. Just because places don't stay open late, however, doesn't mean that you can't find live music and a genuinely good time.

For free, family-friendly live music in a historic outdoor setting, the Lahaina Restoration Foundation hosts a **Hawaiian Music Series** 6pm-7:30pm on the last Thursday of every month. Shows take place on the lawn of the Baldwin House, a preserved missionary site on the corner of Dickenson and Front Streets right in the center of town. Musical artists vary from month to month, but most sessions involve live music and *kanikapila* storytelling. Seating is limited at this popular event, although attendees are encouraged to bring a blanket or beach chair for enjoying the show.

The family-friendly **Friday Town Party** (www.mauifridays.com/lahaina) takes place on the second Friday of every month between the Baldwin House and Wharf Cinema Center. Part of the Maui Fridays series, the free event runs 6pm-9pm and features everything from live music and *keiki* competitions to silent auctions and dance performances. Various bars and restaurants feature live music, and most restaurants offer specials valid for that night only.

One of the best spots for live entertainment in Lahaina is **Fleetwood's** (744 Front St., 808/669-6425, www.fleetwoodsonfrontst.com), a two-story bar and restaurant that offers the only rooftop perch in Lahaina. This bar was opened by legendary rock musician Mick Fleetwood, and Mick himself has been known to jump in with the band for some impromptu percussion. Live music is offered most frequently on the rooftop bar.

For the closest thing on Front Street that you'll find to a club atmosphere, **Moose Mcgillicuddy's** (844 Front St., 808/667-7758, www.moosemcgillicuddys.com, open until 2am) is the DJ and dancing hot spot for dollar drinks on Tuesday and Saturday nights. While it's tough to turn down dollar drinks ($5 cover), the place will get insanely crowded with groups of locals looking to start a fight—especially late at night. General sloppiness tends to reign on most evenings.

Off Front Street in the Lahaina Cannery

Mall, **Lulu's Lahaina Surf Club** (1221 Honoapi'ilani Hwy., 808/661-0808, www.lu-luslahaina.com, open until 2am) is the town's other dance club. Saturday night is the big night at Lulu's, so there is usually a $5 cover. Live music can sporadically be found on the other nights of the week. While the dance floor is large and there are a couple of pool tables in the back, the mall location detracts from the vintage Lahaina experience. Another problem here seems to have plagued Maui nightlife since the invention of the subwoofer: late nights and loud music can lead to fights.

Also, while the schedule is highly irregular, **Longhi's** (888 Front St., 808/667-2288, www.longhis.com) will occasionally have late-night music until 1am, which can feature jazz, rock bands, or visiting DJs. This is the classiest venue in Lahaina, and as of the time of research, Thursday is the best night for late-night dancing.

Both **Cool Cat Café** (658 Front. St., 808/667-0908, www.coolcatcafe.com) and **Kimo's** (845 Front St., 808/661-4811, www.kimosmaui.com) provide live music during the dinner hour seven nights a week. There isn't an official dance floor so the atmosphere is relegated to drinks and mingling.

For **karaoke,** the most happening place in Lahaina for late-night sake and singing is **Kobe** (136 Dickenson St., 808/667-5555, www.kobemaui.com, open until 1am) steak house on Friday and Saturday nights from 9:30pm until well after midnight.

A couple of classic watering holes stay open until 2am. On Front Street, **Spanky's Riptide** (505 Front St., 808/667-2337, www.spankys-ripstide.com) in the 505 shopping center on the far southern end is a good place to grab a cheap goblet of PBR, play pool, and engage in conversation with a colorful cast of characters.

Legendary dive bar **Sly Mongoose** (1036 Limahana Pl., 808/661-8097) is in a nondescript location in the Lahaina industrial park, on the inland side of the highway behind Pizza Hut. This is a no-nonsense dive where the beer is cold, the drinks are cheap, and the patrons are regular. This bar isn't walking distance from Front Street so you'll have to take a cab here.

Food

The number of dining options on the west side is overwhelming. In most places, it isn't only the food you're paying for, but also the location. That sunset view doesn't come cheap. It's still possible to get a meal for under $10 per person—just look outside of the main visitor areas.

KAPALUA, NAPILI, KAHANA, AND HONOKOWAI
Continental
There are three facts about Maui you can take home with you: Haleakala is 10,023 feet tall, the island of Maui is 727 square miles, and **◖ The Gazebo** (5315 Lower Honoapi'ilani Rd., 808/669-5621, 7:30am-2pm daily, $9-13) restaurant has the island's best breakfast. This isn't exactly a secret, however, and there is a line out the door by 6:45am. What makes

this spot so popular is not only the oceanfront location gazing out toward Moloka'i, but also the famous macadamia nut pancakes and heaping three-egg omelets. Lunch is offered until closing at 2pm. Finding parking can be a little challenging. You can try for a spot along the side of the road along Napili Place, or if everything is full, you can park by the Napili Bay beach access on Hui Drive and walk to the restaurant across the sand of Napili Bay. If standing on the beach looking out toward the water, the Gazebo is on the point to your left.

Local Style
From the outside, you might wonder what's so special about the hole-in-the-wall **◖ Honokowai Okazuya and Deli** (3600 Lower Honoapi'ilani Rd., 808/665-0512,

11am-2:30pm and 4:30pm-8:30pm Mon.-Sat., $9-15). You might not notice the restaurant, since the front door is often closed behind a colorfully decorated exterior of bamboo and surfing photos, although once inside you'll find huge portions, great local food, and budget-friendly prices that leave you wondering why you would ever eat anywhere else. Even though it's inside a strip mall next to the 5A Rent A Space, what this restaurant lacks in atmosphere it makes up for in practicality and taste. Although there are a few seats inside for dining, most visitors use this as a takeaway window for enjoying a meal back at the condo. The food here can rival any on the island, and the prices can be half as much as when the same food is served with an oceanfront view. Try the lemon caper mahimahi if you're looking for fresh fish at an affordable price.

Mexican

In Honokowai, **Ohana Tacos** (3600 Lower Honoapiʻilani Rd., 808/283-7768, 11am-9pm Sun.-Thurs., 11am-8pm Fri.-Sat., $7-11) is a family-run restaurant with a badge of its authenticity: it's frequented by the local Spanish-speaking community. This is one of the few places on the island where you can order *sopes* or choose *lengua* as a meat option. Cash only, and only a few outdoor tables.

Italian and Mediterranean

Cornering the casual Italian market, **Pizza Paradiso** (3350 Lower Honoapiʻilani Rd., 808/667-2929, 10am-9pm daily, $19-27) also features cuisine from the greater Mediterranean region. Fresh produce is sourced on the island, the beef is from Maui Cattle Company, and passion goes into the preparation. Try the Big Fat Greek pizza with gyro meat! Organic and gluten-free options are available. Pasta options grace the dinner menu while gyros are the budget-friendly lunch option.

American

On the Kapalua Bay golf course, **Pineapple Grill** (200 Kapalua Dr., 808/669-9600, www. cohnrestaurants.com, 8am-10pm daily, bar

$7-12, lunch $12-19, dinner $22-48) is one of the most popular restaurants in Kapalua. Breakfast is a local secret (try the Benedicts or Belgian waffles). The bar menu has affordable island classics such as ahi poke tacos or kalua pork quesadillas topped with Maui onions. Lunch includes burgers and fish tacos and dinner has fine entrées such as Kona kampachi fish plates and shiitake-accented filet mignon.

On the Plantation course, the **Plantation House** (200 Kapalua Dr., 808/669-9600, www. theplantationhouse.com, 8am-9pm daily, $10-22) offers expansive views from the hillside. Considering the luxurious venue, the affordable breakfast and lunch menu makes you feel like you're getting away with something. Enjoy breakfast items like omelets and eggs Benedict while overlooking the Honolua coastline. Lunch offers fresh green salads, teriyaki pineapple burgers, and barbecue pork sandwiches. For dinner, choose fish such as ahi and monchong or meat selections like braised short ribs and chicken stroganoff. The popular bar has an extensive wine list.

For good old-fashioned Southern barbecue, check out the **Iron Imu BBQ** (5315 Lower Honoapiʻilani Rd., 808/298-4575, www.ironimubbqmaui.com, 5pm-9pm daily, $11-14), a food cart in the parking lot of the Napili Shores. Brisket, rib, sausage, and chicken plates are all there, and you get to choose from a selection of three home-style sides.

Japanese

If you ask West Side locals where to get sushi, they'll say **■ Sansei** (600 Office Rd., 808/669-6286, www.sanseihawaii.com, 5:30pm-10pm Sat.-Wed., 5:30pm-1am Thurs.-Fri., $8-30), a legendary sushi outpost on the main entrance road to Kapalua resort. If you want to maximize your Sansei experience, here's what you do: Call ahead for reservations on Thursday or Friday evening and make them for 5:30pm. This is when the restaurant opens, and they'll usually run an "early bird" special for the first 30 minutes. If you miss the early bird wave and would rather wait a few hours, the same specials are often offered 10pm-1am.

Hawaiian Regional

◖ **Merriman's** (1 Bay Club Pl., 808/669-6400, www.merrimanshawaii.com, 3pm-9pm daily, dinner menu begins at 5:30pm, $25-49) is the "nicest" restaurant on the island's northwestern side, and this venue on Kapalua Bay is one of the most scenic dining spots on the island. Arrive early to enjoy a glass of wine while watching the sunset from the oceanfront fire pit. Then enjoy a menu of farm to table fare where over 90 percent of the ingredients are sourced from local farmers, fishers, and ranchers. Acclaimed chef Peter Merriman is one of the founders of the Hawaiian Regional movement, and his genius is evident is everything from the avocado ahi poke salads to citrus ponzu-flavored mahimahi. Five spice roasted Jidori chicken is masterfully paired with Moloka'i sweet potato ravioli, and there are probably nations with constitutions shorter than the wine list (which features over 40 different varietals). Reservations are highly recommended.

Brewpub

A visit to ◖ **Maui Brewing Company** (4405 Honoapi'ilani Hwy., 808/669-3474, www.mauibrewingco.com, 11am-midnight daily, $12-15) should be at the top of every beer lover's island to-do list. This is the island's only brewery, and while you can find a number of their beers in local supermarkets, at least a dozen more can only be found on tap in the brewhouse. The interior is basic, but this isn't a place you come to for the decor. Even though the beer is the main draw, the Hawaiian beef burger, sliders, and coconut porter beef stew are all hearty accompaniments to a rich pint of stout. There are also filling and affordable pizzas and vegan or gluten-free options.

Coffee Shops

In the Napili Plaza, **The Coffee Store** (5095 Napilihau Rd., 808/669-4170, www.mauicoffee.com, 6am-6pm daily) is the northernmost place on the island completely dedicated to the wonders of the coffee bean. If you're heading out for an early morning stroll on the Kapalua Coastal Trail, this small shop has the usual selection of caffeinated options in addition to selling locally grown beans. Beyond just coffee, food options include health-conscious fare such as acai bowls and zucchini muffins you can enjoy in the comfortable atmosphere.

At the Kahana Gateway Center, **Hawaiian Village Coffee** (4405 Honoapi'ilani Hwy., 808/665-1114, www.hawaiianvillagecoffee.com, 5:30am-6pm daily) is another classic coffee shop with a strong local following and good community vibe. This is the earliest place to open on the northwest side, and the sunrise hours are a collection of late-shift police officers refueling after a long night and sleepy-eyed locals stopping in on their way to work. Although small, the shop has a welcoming atmosphere for reading the morning paper or checking your email on the free Wi-Fi.

KA'ANAPALI

When it comes to dining in Ka'anapali, there are only three options: restaurants in Whalers Village, restaurants in the resorts, and a handful of restaurants a block off the strip.

Italian

The best Italian in Ka'anapali is at **Pulehu** (808/667-3200, www.westinkaanapali.com, 5:30pm-9:30pm Thurs.-Mon., $23-39), inside the Westin Ka'anapali Villas. The antipasti menu features locally-sourced bruschetta and Caprese *insalata*. and Pacific Italian fusion takes over on the main menu where selections of risotto-crusted, pan-seared fish are offered alongside chianti-braised short ribs. Considering the venue and level of cuisine, dishes are surprisingly affordable.

American

In front of the Honua Kai resort, **Duke's** (130 Kai Malina Pkwy., 808/662-2900, www.dukesmaui.com, 7:30am-9:30pm daily, $10-25) is in the same family of moderately priced restaurants as Kimo's, Leilani's, and Hula Grill. Affordable breakfasts include banana, macadamia nut pancakes, while lunches tend toward sandwiches, burgers, and fish tacos. Dinner entrées are a touch more expensive. Duke's sources ingredients from over 20 different local farms. Afternoon trade winds can make the outdoor dining frustrating, so go for breakfast before 10am, or for dinner after sundown.

Hawaiian Regional

Even though every resort in Ka'anapali has some sort of Hawaiian Regional option, none can hold a candle to world-famous **【 Roy's** (2290 Ka'anapali Pkwy., 808/669-6999, www.roysrestaurant.com, 11am-9:30pm daily, $15-45). The location inside the golf clubhouse would be nicer if it had an ocean view, but for what the restaurant lacks in decor, it makes up for in flavor. Chef Roy Yamaguchi was one of the founders of the Hawaiian Regional movement, and his mastery is evident in the misoyaki butterfish and honey mustard-braised short ribs. Even though there are over 30 Roy's locations around the country, every restaurant has a menu and a style unique to the venue. Dinner entrées are pricey; ordering sandwiches, salads, and appetizers off the lunch menu is more affordable. The chocolate soufflé will change your life; order it half-way through your meal since it takes 20 minutes to prepare.

【 Hula Grill (2435 Ka'anapali Pkwy., 808/667-6636, www.hulagrillkaanapali.com, 11am-11pm, $13) in Whalers Village is my favorite for oceanfront dining. The barefoot bar has a better atmosphere than the dining room, and it's the only place on the island where you walk through sand to get to your table. There's live music in the afternoons. The Kapulu Joe pork sandwich and the wood-fired, goat cheese and roasted pumpkin pizza are two affordable options along an otherwise expensive shoreline.

Across the Whalers Village walkway, **Leilani's On The Beach** (2435 Ka'anapali Pkwy., 808/661-4495, www.leilanis.com, 11am-11pm daily, $15) serves the best fish tacos on the island. The tacos are enormous, served Cajun style, and accompanied by a special sauce that brings it all together. Take advantage of discounts Tuesday 3pm-5pm. Whether you dine on the casual patio or the upstairs in the dining room, save room for a world-famous

Hula Pie with macadamia nut ice cream and chocolate cookie crust; it's big enough to share.

At the far southern end of the Ka'anapali strip, **Japengo** (200 Nohea Kai Dr., 808/667-4796, 5pm-10pm daily, $20) has enormous and affordable sushi rolls which rival even Sansei. You'll be amazed that by ordering a big roll and blackened ahi hand rolls, you can dine at a fancy resort and completely stuff two people on fresh sushi. At sushi school (2nd and 4th Sat. each month, 3pm-4:30pm, $35/person), you can learn to make hand rolls from one of the restaurant's master chefs.

Natural Foods

The best gourmet natural foods market on the West Side, **'Aina Gourmet Market** (130 Kai Malina Pkwy., 808/662-2832, www.ainagourmet.com, 7am-9pm daily) is tucked away in the lobby of Honua Kai Beach Resort. 'Aina is in the same restaurant group as Pacifico, I'o, and O'o Farms, and this is a great place for grabbing a cup of 100 percent Maui coffee, organically raised produce, or a healthy panini made from locally sourced ingredients. There are a few tables, or enjoy your meal on the beach.

Coffee Shops

The only local coffee shop in Ka'anapali is **Island Press Coffee** (2580 Keka'a Dr., 808/667-2003, 6am-7pm Mon.-Sat., 7am-4pm Sun.) in the Fairway Shops. The location isn't exactly prime for anyone staying in an oceanfront resort, but if you're up early from jet lag and want to go for an early morning stroll, it's nice that the doors open at 6am most days.

LAHAINA
Local Style

There's a place in Lahaina where you can eat good food by the water and the bill won't give you a heart attack. At the northern end of Lahaina next to the Old Lahaina Luau (with which it's affiliated), **【 Aloha Mixed Plate** (1285 Front St., 808/661-3322, www.alohamixedplate.com, 8am-10pm daily, $8-12) offers affordable plate lunches in a casual oceanfront setting. The private setting is up there with some of the most scenic in Lahaina, the food is the best local food you'll find outside of a luau, and it's cheap. For lunch and dinner you can sample luau items such as lomi lomi salmon or poi. For the main course, get a kalua pig plate lunch (with two scoop rice and macaroni salad) or spring for the Aloha Mixed Plate of shoyu chicken, teriyaki beef, and fresh fish served with rice and mac salad. Breakfast is just as affordable with omelets and loco moco dishes. There's also a full service bar, although alcohol isn't served at the oceanfront tables.

Mexican

The freshest, healthiest, and best Mexican food in Lahaina is **Cilantro** (170 Papalaua St., 808/667-5444, www.cilantrogrill.com, 11am-9pm Mon.-Sat., 11am-8pm Sun., $9-13), in the Old Lahaina Center next to Jamba Juice and Foodland. The atmosphere here is unassuming, and there is an open-air kitchen where you can watch your food being made. Being set a block off Front Street makes for affordable prices, and the portions are huge. The $10 Mother Clucker Flautas are the tastiest item on the menu (how can you go wrong with chicken drizzled in spicy-sweet roasted jalapeño sauce?). All meals are made from scratch using old-world recipes, and there are even a few gluten-free options. Pair your meal with a creamy horchata drink to round things out.

French

If you take your fine dining seriously, then you're going to love **Gerard's** (174 Lahainaluna Rd., 808/661-8939, www.gerardsmaui.com, 6pm-8:30pm daily, $50) in the Plantation Inn. Chef Gerard Reversade has been serving French food with an island twist for over 30 years and was one of the pioneers of Hawaiian Regional cuisine. Classics such as foie gras and escargot punctuate the appetizer menu, and favorites include the roasted lamb in lemon/peppermint jelly accompanied by potato au gratin, as well as the fresh fish that changes with the day's selection. Gerard's has received the *Wine Spectator*'s Award of Excellence 19 times for its extensive collection of French and American

labels. Ignore the cost and let your taste buds take over. Reservations are imperative.

American

Lahaina Grill (127 Lahainaluna Rd., 808/667-5177, www.lahainagrill.com, 6pm-10pm daily, $25-49) is the best restaurant in Lahaina, which is quite an accolade considering the competition. Opened on Valentine's Day of 1990, this restaurant continues to be one of Lahaina's most romantic evenings. Everything from the ambience to the service to the extensive wine list is what you would expect of a fine dining experience. The only thing missing is an ocean view, but for what the restaurant lacks in views it makes up for in a classy bistro setting. The food is a combination of new American cuisine infused with Pacific Rim favorites, where meat dishes include the coveted Kona coffee-roasted rack of lamb, and seafood selections range from sesame-crusted ahi filets to Maine lobster crab cakes. Much of the produce is sourced locally from independent farmers. Reservations are recommended.

The best burger in Lahaina is at **Cool Cat Café** (658 Front St., 808/667-0908, www.coolcatcafe.com, 10:30am-10:30pm daily, $10-25). Overlooking the banyan tree, the inside portion of the restaurant is decorated in 1950s decor, while the outdoor patio is livelier. Cool Cat is consistently voted as the island's best burger, and the live music here is better than down the street. All of the meat is massaged with a secret seasoning, and specialty burgers like the Don Ho (teriyaki and pineapple burger), Luna (covered in avocado), and Frisco (served on sourdough bread with grilled onions and jack cheese) are what make it such a legendary choice. There are also fish sandwiches, blackened fish tacos, salads (get the Buddy Holly with chicken strips on top), and a popular bar. It's extra to add fries to your meal (and cheaper to get a basket for the table than to add to each burger separately). This is where you'll find Lahaina Harbor boat crew spending their tips at the bar.

Right next door, sister restaurant **Captain Jack's Island Grill** (672 Front St.,

808/667-0988, 8am-midnight daily, $10-25) does for fish what Cool Cat does for burgers. Whether it's fish tacos, fish-and-chips, or fish salad, this casual bar and grill overlooking Front Street has tasty dishes at moderate prices and is always running some sort of special. This is a good family lunch option. Young kids will enjoy the pirate theme that goes hand in hand with the town's nautical history (though whalers weren't exactly pirates…).

One of Lahaina's best-kept secrets is **Lahaina Coolers** (180 Dickenson St., 808/661-7082, www.lahainacoolers.com, 8am-midnight daily, $27), a laid-back, local favorite that can rival anywhere in town. All three meals provide reason for visiting (particularly breakfast). The dinner menu is just as good as the fancier names in town. There are also pizzas, pastas, and an affordable bar menu (think kalua pig tacos).

Japanese

If there were an award for best cuisine in the most unlikely of locations, **(Star Noodle** (285 Kupuohi St., 808/667-5400, www.star-noodle.com, 10:30am-10pm daily, $12) would take the competition by storm. This popular noodle establishment on an obscure corner at the top of the Lahaina Gateway industrial area has been sculpted by Sheldon Simeon, a local chef who made it to the final three contestants on the reality show *Top Chef.* The Asian-infused menu is spectacularly affordable, with bowls of udon, plates of pad thai, and dishes such as miso salmon or chicken in ponzu sauce. If the wait is too long, sit at the bar and order from the main menu.

Hawaiian Regional

In the 505 shopping area, **(Pacific'O** (505 Front St., 808/667-4341, www.pacificomaui.com, 11:30am-10pm daily, $29-46) is one of the best venues in Lahaina for enjoying an oceanfront meal. Many of the ingredients are grown at the organic O'o Farm in Kula. The seaside patio is the perfect lunch spot for pairing a sesame fish salad with a crisp glass of white wine, and the fish tacos are affordable

at $14 when you consider the oceanfront setting. Reservations are necessary for dinner, where you can feast on entrées such as Pasta 'ele'ele (blackened fresh fish over whole wheat spaghetti in a cilantro pesto) and Hapa/Hapa Tempura (sashimi-grade fish and caviar wrapped in nori). The wine list is one of the most comprehensive on the West Side.

On the far northern end of Lahaina, **(Honu** (1295 Front St., 808/667-9390, www.honumaui.com, 11am-9:30pm Mon.-Sat., 4:30pm-9pm Sun., $18-45) offers locally sourced food in an oceanfront setting. *Honu* is the Hawaiian name for sea turtle, and there's a high likelihood that you'll spot a turtle coming up for a breath at some point during your meal. Chef Mark Ellman (one of the original founders of the Hawaiian Regional movement) has crafted a masterpiece where butternut squash coconut soup complements main courses ranging from lentil quinoa burgers to pork osso bucco. The pizzas are similarly delicious. The extensive craft beer selection features over 50 different microbrews—a rarity among island restaurants. If there's a wait, try sister restaurant **Mala,** next door.

In the heart of Front Street, **Kimo's** (845 Front St., 808/661-4811, www.kimosmaui.com, 11am-10pm daily, $25-32) has a deck looking out over the waters of the Lahaina Roadstead and moderately priced lunch items such as coconut crusted fish sandwiches or koloa pork ribs for $12-16. The dinner entrées in the dining room are pricier, but the signature Molokini Cut, 14-ounce prime rib is served with an au jus that will leave you sopping up the juices however you can. The staff at Kimo's is phenomenal.

Natural Foods

To the delight of those who care about what they put in their body, **(Choice** (1087 Limahana Pl., 808/661-7711, www.choicemaui.com, 8am-4pm Mon.-Sat., $8) is devoted to the benefits of a healthy, active lifestyle. When you walk in the door (where a sign informs you this is a "bummer free zone"), you can sense the antioxidants and free radicals in the air. The

MAUI

smoothies use all-natural superfood ingredients (spirulina, acai, coconut meat, and almond milk), so your body will thank you. Make your smoothie "epic" by adding superfoods such as kale and blue green algae. A large selection of freshly made kale salads are available after 11:30am each day.

Thai

The best Thai food on the West Side—if not the entire island—is at **Thai Chef** (878 Front St., 808/667-2814, www.thaichefrestaurant-maui.com, 11am-2pm, 5pm-9pm Mon.-Fri., 5pm-9pm Sat., $14), a small, hole-in-the-wall restaurant squirreled away in the parking lot between Longhi's and the Maui Theatre. The family-run restaurant is BYOB if you'd like to accompany your chicken pad thai with a Singha beer, but beer and wine are available at Foodland across the parking lot. Vegetarians are also well taken care of with plenty of spicy tofu and vegetable dishes. While it's not fancy, you won't be disappointed. Takeout is available; reservations are recommended.

Coffee Shops

For a quick coffee on the run, **Sir Wilfred's** (707 Front St., 808/661-0202, www.sirwil-freds.com, 8:30am-9pm daily) is the island's original coffee shop, having opened its doors in 1976. In 1979 Sir Wilfred's introduced the island's first espresso machine, and the Front Street store is still one of the best spots in Lahaina to stop in and buy some locally grown beans or inquire about fine cigars. Those in need of an early wakeup, however, will unfortunately have to wait until the 8:30am opening time to sip the classic roasts.

If, on the other hand, you're looking for a place you can linger, grab breakfast, get free Internet access, and sip on a proper espresso, try **Café Café** (129 Lahainaluna Rd., 808/661-0006, www.cafecafelahaina.com, 7am-7pm Mon.-Sat.) on Lahainaluna Road next to Mr. Sub sandwich shop. There are a few outdoor tables for sipping your macchiato, and you can also pick up organic, locally sourced, open-faced bagel sandwiches for $5-6.

Shave Ice

There are few things better than a cold shave ice on a hot Lahaina day, and the best shave ice in Lahaina is at **Local Boys West** (624 Front St., 808/344-9779, www.localboyshaveice.com, 10am-9pm daily) across the street from the banyan tree. In addition to the copious array of flavors, what makes Local Boys great is the way they offer free Roselani (made on Maui) ice cream, Kaua'i cream, and azuki beans at the bottom of the shave ice, which any island local knows is the only way to enjoy shave ice.

SOUTH OF LAHAINA
American

The only restaurant between Lahaina and Ma'alaea is 【 **Leoda's Kitchen and Pie Shop** (820 Olowalu Village Rd., 808/662-3600, www.leodas.com, 10am-8pm daily, $8-12), in the Olowalu store building. Using many sustainable ingredients from local farms, this sandwich and pie shop has quickly become a favorite. The deli sandwiches, potpies, and baked goods are so good, however, that you'll often find a line stretching out the front door. All of the food here is made fresh, so don't expect to get a quick sandwich.

Getting There and Around

AIR

Above Kahana is the small **Kapalua-West Maui Airport,** which is a convenient option for those commuting to Honolulu. The interisland fares are often a little higher than at the larger Kahului Airport ($70-80 one way), but when you factor in the hour of driving you save, it's worth the few extra dollars. This small airport is used principally by Island Air and Mokulele Airlines, but it's also used by small commercial tour companies such as Volcano Air Tours. Surrounded by former pineapple fields, the single airstrip is short and used by small propeller aircraft only. The check-in counters, inspection station, boarding gate, and baggage claim are only a few steps from each other.

Island Air operates two flights daily between Kapalua Airport and Honolulu, and Mokulele Airlines has either five or seven flights a day depending on the date. The earliest flight departs for Honolulu at 8:27am, and the last flight of the day is at 6:12pm. It's also possible to connect from here with airports on Moloka'i and Lana'i; although you will need to stop in Honolulu first, so it's largely impractical over taking the ferry or a direct flight out of Kahului Airport.

CAR

Car Rentals

The largest car rental providers on the West Side are in Honokowai, equidistant between Lahaina Harbor and Kapalua Airport. Here you'll find both **Avis** (11 Halawai Dr., 808/661-4588, 7am-5pm daily) and **Budget** (11 Halawai Dr., 808/661-8721, 7am-5pm daily). Provided you arrive at the harbor or Kapalua Airport during business hours, they have a shuttle that will pick you up.

In the Sheraton resort in Ka'anapali, **Enterprise** (2605 Ka'anapali Pkwy., 808/661-8804, 7am-5pm daily) has a service counter and will pick you up anywhere from Lahaina Harbor to Kapalua.

For car rental in downtown Lahaina, **Hertz** (256 Papalaua St., 808/661-7735, 8am-4pm daily) has a desk in the strip mall on the inland side of the highway by the Subway sandwich shop.

Taxi

In West Maui, taxi options include **West Maui Taxi** (808/661-1122) **AB Taxi** (808/667-7575), and **Paradise Taxi** (808/661-4455). A ride from Lahaina to Ka'anapali is about $15, and from Ka'anapali to Kapalua about $25. Going rates for a cab ride to Kahului Airport from Ka'anapali are about $100, so you might want to think twice about that plan to take a cab to the hotel.

Shuttle

Both Kapalua and Ka'anapali offer resort shuttles within the resort and to select areas of West Maui. The free **Kapalua Shuttle** (808/665-9110) runs throughout the resort for guests on an on-demand basis between 6am and 11pm. There's even complimentary transportation to the Kapalua Airport five times daily.

In Ka'anapali, the **resort shuttle** offers free transportation across the resort and runs on a set schedule 9am-9pm.

Motorcycle and Moped

If you want the wind whipping through your hair, there are a number of different motorcycle, Harley, and moped rentals scattered across the West Side. The place with the largest selection of bikes is **Aloha Motorsports** (30 Halawai Dr., 808/667-7000, www.alohamotorsports.com, 8am-5pm daily), in Honokowai across the highway from the Honua Kai resort. It doesn't matter where they're located, however, since the company offers free pickup and drop-off on the West Side. Minimum time for rentals is four hours, although most people opt for 24 hours. Rates for mopeds can be as low as $49 for four hours or $59 for 24 hours, and

Harley rentals average around $109 for four hours and $149 for 24 hours. During slower times of the year there can be better specials advertised.

In downtown Lahaina, the best option for hopping on a Harley is at **Cycle City Lahaina** (602 Front St., 667-2800, www.cyclecitymaui.com, 8:30am-6pm daily), which is steps from the banyan tree. This is a satellite operation of a larger store in Kahului. Rates here are usually around $140 for 24 hours, although lower specials are often advertised.

If you don't need a full-on hog and just want a moped for the day, check out **Motoroshi** (129 Lahainaluna Rd., 808/661-0006, 7am-7pm Mon.-Sat.) moped rentals on Lahainaluna Road. Only a few steps off Front Street in the parking lot of the Café Café coffee shop, its mopeds are available from $40 for three hours to $55 to for the whole day. There are also a number of Vespa scooters which range from $65-95/daily depending on the size of the bike.

BUS

The cheapest way to get about West Maui (albeit much slower), is the **Maui Bus** (808/871-4838, www.co.maui.hi.us/bus). There are four different routes servicing the West Maui area, departures are once per hour, all routes are $2.00/person per boarding, and you can buy a day pass for $4. The bus stations in Lahaina are in the back of the Wharf Cinema Center across the street from the banyan tree, and on the intersection of Front Street and Papalaua Street across the road from the Hard Rock Café. For getting from one side of Lahaina to the other, Bus #23 makes various stops around town from 8am until 11pm. For those traveling from Napili or Kahana to Whalers Village in Ka'anapali (where you can connect with buses to Lahaina and beyond), Bus #30 begins service at 5:30am at the Napili Kai Beach Resort and makes various stops along Lower Honoapi'ilani

Road until 9pm. Bus #25 connects Whalers Village in Ka'anapali with the Wharf Cinema Center in Lahaina from 6am until 9pm, and Bus #20 connects the Wharf Cinema Center with Queen Ka'ahumanu Mall in Kahului, making a stop in Ma'alaea for anyone who wants to transfer on a bus down to Kihei.

Since a taxi from Napili to Kahului Airport will cost about $120, if you need to get from Napili to the airport and don't have a car, the cheapest way is to buy a $4 day pass and take Bus #30 to Whalers Village, change to #25 to the Wharf Cinema Center, hop on #20 the Queen Ka'ahumanu Center, and then take #40 to the Kahului Airport. Total transit time for this sojourn is two hours and 10 minutes, but hey, for $4, who's complaining? You aren't allowed to have more luggage than you can place on your lap or under your seat.

SEA

Though not many visitors access West Maui from the water, those traveling from the islands of Lana'i or Moloka'i will arrive at Lahaina Harbor by interisland ferry. **Expeditions** (808/661-3756, www.go-lanai.com) ferry runs five times daily between Manele and Lahaina Harbors, and the **Moloka'i Princess** (877/500-6284, www.molokaiferry.com) ferry runs twice daily between Kaunakakai and Lahaina. If coming from Lana'i, the earliest arrival time in Lahaina is 9am, and the latest is 7:45pm. If traveling from Moloka'i, the earliest arrival in Lahaina is 6:45am, and the latest is 4:30pm. Only the afternoon boat is offered on Sundays. When arriving in Lahaina by ferry you'll find there are a large number of taxis to get you to your resort, or, if you plan on renting a car, call ahead to the rental car offices listed above and they'll pick you up. If you are traveling from Lana'i, the rental car offices will be closed if you are on the last ferry of the day.

CENTRAL MAUI

The site of Kahului International Airport, Central Maui is the first part of the island most visitors will encounter. Kahului is the island's largest town, with about 26,000 residents. Neighboring Wailuku is the location of most government offices. More than just the island's business and commercial hub, Central Maui has an underlying charm and a lot of history that stretches

HIGHLIGHTS

LOOK FOR ◖ TO FIND RECOMMENDED SIGHTS, ACTIVITIES, DINING, AND LODGING.

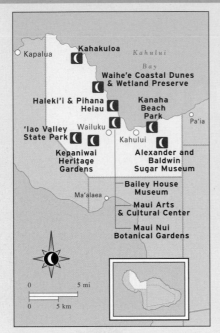

a movie or live performance in this state-of-the-art facility is one of the best nights out on Maui (page 301).

◖ **Maui Nui Botanical Gardens:** More than 70 species of taro and dozens of native plants are preserved in this urban garden (page 302).

◖ **Alexander and Baldwin Sugar Museum:** Peer into the daily lives of plantation laborers and read about the herculean undertakings that went into building the island's sugar industry (page 302).

◖ **Bailey House Museum:** See authentic Hawaiian artifacts, a surfboard ridden by Duke Kahanamoku, and the best compilation of Hawaiiana literature found on the island (page 303).

◖ **Kepaniwai Heritage Gardens:** This small riverside park is dedicated to Maui's immigrant communities. Sample the traditional architecture of the island's "mixed plate" community (page 304).

◖ **'Iao Valley State Park:** Learn about King Kamehameha's decisive victory at the Battle of Kepaniwai and snap a photo of the iconic 'Iao Needle (page 304).

◖ **Haleki'i and Pihana Heiau:** These two stone *heiau* were once the religious center of the island—and the site of the last human sacrifice on Maui (page 305).

◖ **Kahakuloa:** Kahakuloa is window into old Hawaii, where taro is still farmed in the valleys and fish are gathered from the sea. Be sure to buy some banana bread when passing through town (page 306).

◖ **Kanaha Beach Park:** Watch the world's best windsurfers and kitesurfers zip through the air at this unheralded beach park (page 288).

◖ **Waihe'e Coastal Dunes and Wetlands Preserve:** Hike the trail of this undeveloped preserve as it passes by the ruins of Kapoho fishing village and its associated *heiau* (page 294).

◖ **Maui Arts and Cultural Center:** Seeing

beyond the big-box stores and dozens of traffic lights.

Although the backdrop of the verdant mountains and the turquoise water along the shoreline creates a tranquil scene, Central Maui is anything but passive. Kahului's Kanaha Beach Park is home to some of the world's best windsurfing and is one of the beaches where kitesurfing was born. If you want to put your finger on the pulse of the local water sports scene and are looking to step outside of "resort Maui," this is the place.

MAUI

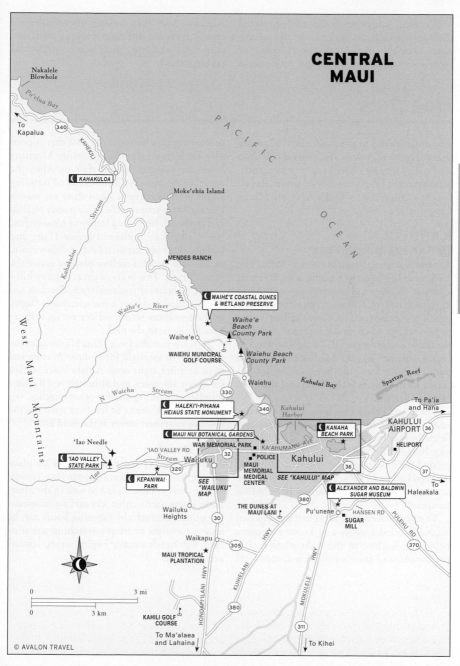

CENTRAL MAUI

Nakalele Blowhole

Po'elua Bay

PACIFIC

To Kapalua

(340)

KAHEKILI HWY

KAHAKULOA

Moke'ehia Island

OCEAN

West Maui Mountains

Kahakuloa Stream

MENDES RANCH

Waihe'e River

WAIHE'E COASTAL DUNES & WETLAND PRESERVE

Waihe'e Beach County Park

Waihe'e

Waiehu Beach County Park

WAIEHU MUNICIPAL GOLF COURSE

N Waiehu Stream

Waiehu

Kahului Bay

Spartan Reef

'Iao Needle

HALEKI'I-PIHANA HEIAUS STATE MONUMENT

(330)

(340)

Kahului Harbor

KANAHA BEACH PARK

To Pa'ia and Hana

KAHULUI AIRPORT

(36)

'IAO VALLEY STATE PARK

'IAO VALLEY RD

'Iao Stream

MAUI NUI BOTANICAL GARDENS

WAR MEMORIAL PARK

Wailuku

(320)

(32)

KA'AHUMANU AVE

POLICE

MAUI MEMORIAL MEDICAL CENTER

Kahului

(36)

SEE "KAHULUI" MAP

HELIPORT

(37)

To Haleakala

KEPANIWAI PARK

SEE "WAILUKU" MAP

ALEXANDER AND BALDWIN SUGAR MUSEUM

(380)

Wailuku Heights

(30)

THE DUNES AT MAUI LANI

Pu'unene

HANSEN RD

SUGAR MILL

(370)

Waikapu

(305)

MAUI TROPICAL PLANTATION

KUIHELANI HWY

HONOAPIILANI HWY

MOKULELE HWY

PULEHU RD

0   3 mi

0   3 km

(380)

KAHILI GOLF COURSE

To Ma'alaea and Lahaina

(311)

To Kihei

© AVALON TRAVEL

Wailuku, just beneath the mist-shrouded cliffs of 'Iao Valley, is in the midst of a renaissance. The culinary scene takes its influence from everything from Filipino to German sources. And even among the residential sprawl, there are still rugged hiking trails, ancient *heiau,* and long, sandy beaches perfect for taking a stroll.

Beaches

The undeveloped beaches of Central Maui are defined by wind, waves, and water sports. You won't find any tiki bars or activities stands, but there are long stretches of undeveloped beaches where the world's best watermen hang out.

KAHULUI
◖ Kanaha Beach Park

Kanaha is the best beach in Central Maui. The early morning hours at Kanaha offer dramatic views of the mountains before the midmorning clouds roll in. There are a number of sandy beaches interspersed among various rocky points, which, when strung together, make for the perfect morning stroll. Those who want to go for a longer jog can head out on a paved path running from the last parking lot entrance all the way to Stable Road and the town of Sprecklesville.

The large, grassy beach park has showers, restrooms, and lifeguards, and there are also fields for playing Frisbee and one of the island's best beach volleyball courts. There's a campground on western end of the park, although it's been known to attract more unsavory characters and feral cats than actual law-abiding campers.

The beach area itself is broken up into two sections called Uppers and Lowers (Uppers being the farthest to the right when facing the ocean), and there's a protected, roped-off swimming area between the two that is popular with those wanting to wade. Morning hours are popular for spearfishing when the water is calm and with longboard and stand-up paddle surfers on days when there are waves. During the afternoon the trade winds pick up and the beach becomes a frenzy of windsurfers. No windsurfing is allowed before 11am, and by 5pm the wind has usually died down again, making the beach a mellow place to spend the sunset hours. This is also a great place to kill a couple of hours if you've already checked out of your hotel and have a late-afternoon flight, as the rental car return offices are only about a half-mile from the park.

To reach Kanaha from Hana Highway, make a right at the stoplight for Hobron Avenue and then another right onto Amala Place. Drive for about 1.5 miles, and although you'll pass a number of parking lots for other beaches, the best ones for Kanaha Beach Park itself are the last two entrances down at the dead end.

Kite Beach

As the name implies, **Kite Beach** is *the* place on the island for Maui's kitesurfing crowd. While there is little reason to visit in the afternoon if you aren't either kitesurfing or watching others kitesurf, the morning hours can be nice for a stroll or simply watching the sunrise. The beach usually begins seeing lessons around 9am.

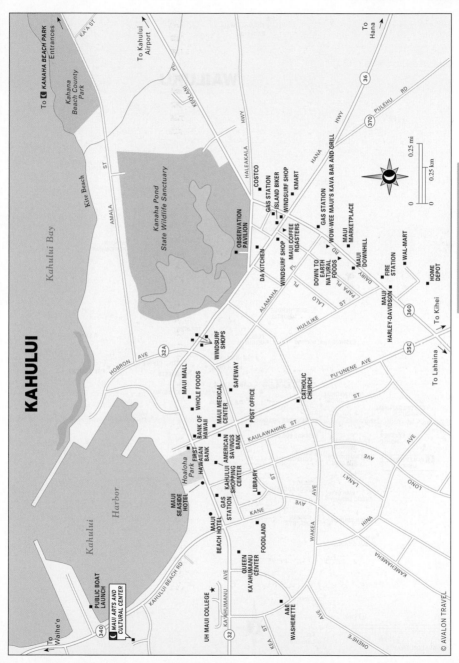

KAHULUI

MAUI

To Waihe'e

To KANAHA BEACH PARK Entrances

To Kahului Airport

To Hana

Kahului Bay

Kite Beach

Kahana Beach County Park

Kanaha Pond State Wildlife Sanctuary

OBSERVATION PAVILION

COSTCO
GAS STATION
ISLAND BIKER
WINDSURF SHOP
KMART

GAS STATION
WOW-WEE MAUI'S KAVA BAR AND GRILL
MAUI MARKETPLACE
WAL-MART

DA KITCHEN
WINDSURF SHOP
MAUI COFFEE ROASTERS

DOWN TO EARTH NATURAL FOODS
MAUI DOWNHILL
FIRE STATION
HOME DEPOT

MAUI HARLEY-DAVIDSON

To Kihei

To Lahaina

Kahului Harbor

Kahului

Harbor

PUBLIC BOAT LAUNCH

MAUI ARTS AND CULTURAL CENTER

MAUI SEASIDE HOTEL

Hoaloha Park

WINDSURF SHOPS

MAUI MALL
WHOLE FOODS
SAFEWAY

MAUI MEDICAL CENTER
POST OFFICE

BANK OF HAWAII
FIRST HAWAIIAN BANK
AMERICAN SAVINGS BANK
KAHULUI SHOPPING CENTER
LIBRARY

GAS STATION
MAUI BEACH HOTEL
FOODLAND

QUEEN KA'AHUMANU CENTER

UH MAUI COLLEGE

A&E WASHERETTE

CATHOLIC CHURCH

0   0.25 mi
0   0.25 km

© AVALON TRAVEL

MAUI

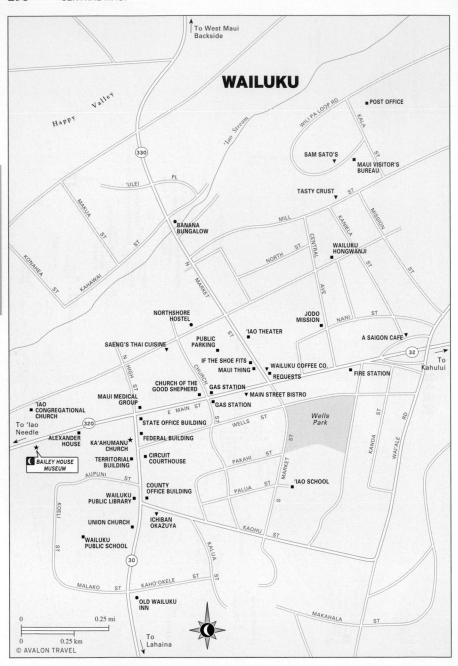

WAILUKU

To West Maui
Backside

Happy   Valley

'Iao Stream

330

'ULEI   PL

■ POST OFFICE

WILI PA LOOP RD

KALA   ST

● BANANA
BUNGALOW

SAM SATO'S
▼

MAUI VISITOR'S
BUREAU
■

TASTY CRUST
▼

MILL   ST

NORTH   ST

MAKUA   ST

KAHAWAI   ST

KONAHEA   ST

N   MARKET   ST

CENTRAL   AVE

KANIELA   ST

MISSION   ST

WAILUKU
HONGWANJI
■

NORTHSHORE
HOSTEL
●

SAENG'S THAI CUISINE
■

PUBLIC
PARKING
▼

'IAO THEATER
▼

JODO
MISSION
■

NANI   ST

A SAIGON CAFE
▼

N   HIGH   ST

CHURCH   ST

IF THE SHOE FITS
MAUI THING ■

WAILUKU COFFEE CO.
■

REQUESTS ▼

32

To
Kahului

FIRE STATION
■

CHURCH OF THE
GOOD SHEPHERD
■

GAS STATION
▼

'IAO
CONGREGATIONAL
CHURCH
■

MAUI MEDICAL
GROUP
■

GAS STATION
■

MAIN STREET BISTRO
▼

To 'Iao
Needle

320

E MAIN ST

WELLS   ST

Wells
Park

ALEXANDER
HOUSE
■

STATE OFFICE BUILDING
■

★ BAILEY HOUSE
MUSEUM

KA'AHUMANU
CHURCH
★

FEDERAL BUILDING
■

TERRITORIAL
BUILDING
■

CIRCUIT
COURTHOUSE
■

PAKAHI   ST

KANOA   ST

WAI'ALE   RD

AUPUNI   ST

COUNTY
OFFICE BUILDING
■

PALUA   ST

S   MARKET   ST

'IAO SCHOOL
■

KOELI   ST

WAILUKU
PUBLIC LIBRARY
■

UNION CHURCH
■

ICHIBAN
OKAZUYA
▼

KAOHU   ST

WAILUKU
PUBLIC SCHOOL
■

30

KALUA   ST

MALAKO   ST

KAHO'OKELE   ST

● OLD WAILUKU
INN

MAKAHALA   ST

0   0.25 mi

0   0.25 km

© AVALON TRAVEL

To
Lahaina

Surfing

Since the beaches of Central Maui face north and east, the majority of the surfing on this side of the island takes place October-April. Some eastward-facing locations can pick up windswell during summer, but often it's choppy, and sloppy. No surf schools operate along this stretch of coast; anyone opting to surf around here needs to be at least an intermediate. Since part of this stretch runs along Maui's fabled North Shore, only the spots that are accessible to the average surfer are mentioned.

SURF SPOTS
Kahului
The most popular surf break in Kahului is **Lowers** at **Kanaha Beach Park.** If you're an intermediate to advanced longboarder, then this is the place to come on any sort of northerly swell. To reach the surfing section of the park, travel down Amala Place all the way to the end of the road and park in one of the last two parking lots. Grab your board and wear your slippers as you walk down to the shoreline to avoid kiawe thorns and burrs. Once you're standing on the sand, look for the lifeguard tower you'll paddle out from. The wave at Kanaha breaks on an offshore reef. Given the length of the paddle (usually about 15 minutes), Kanaha is frequented by longboarders and stand-up paddle surfers. When standing in front of the lifeguard tower, you'll notice a defined channel for reaching the lineup, and the surf usually won't close it out until the faces reach 10 feet or higher. Mornings are best before the wind picks up (usually around 11am).

Wailuku
Looking for a mellow longboarding wave? There's a break in front of **Waiehu Beach Park** that usually has fewer people than neighboring Paukukalo. The wave quality isn't as good, but this is still a good wave in the early morning during any sort of north swell. As at the other breaks in the area, localism can be an issue, so share the waves. To reach Waiehu Beach Park, travel along Waiehu Beach Road before taking a right-hand turn on Lower Waiehu Beach Road, where you will follow it to the parking lot at the end.

WINDSURFING
Maui is one of world's top windsurfing destinations. The summer trade winds are consistent, arriving like clockwork around 11am to offer 5-6 hours of steady, flat water. During winter, the trade winds aren't nearly as consistent and waves reach 15 feet or higher.

There's strictly no windsurfing before 11am, and Kanaha is split into two main launching areas conveniently named Uppers and Lowers. Many of the windsurfing schools operate by Uppers at a cove known as Kook's Beach. Lowers is in the area by the lifeguard

windsurfing

© KYLE ELLISON

MAUI

MAUI

tower and is the preferred launching point for most Maui visitors. In between the two areas is a roped-off swimming zone off limits to all windsurfers even if you're swimming your board. If there are waves breaking on the reef, you'll notice a channel off the lifeguard stand where you can get past the break and out beyond the surf.

For more information on Maui windsurfing go to www.mauiwindsurfing.net for photos, rental operators, and descriptions of the various launching sites. Or, for a live cam of the conditions at Kanaha, check out www.maui-windcam.com.

KITESURFING

The best place for kitesurfing on Maui is at the aptly named **Kite Beach,** a place of hallowed ground where the sport was born. This is the beach where all kitesurfing schools operate. Even if you aren't a kitesurfer yourself, this is a fantastic spot to sit and watch as hundreds of colorful kites zip through the gusty trade winds. To reach Kite Beach from Hana Highway follow Hobron Avenue toward the Port of Kahului and make a right on Amala Place. Kanaha Kai rental shop will be on your right, then follow the road for a mile until just before a cement bridge. A dirt parking lot on the left side of the road will have a number of vans offering lessons and information. Since Kite Beach is so close to Kanaha, the unwritten rule is that kitesurfers are supposed to stay downwind (closer to Kahului Harbor) of the windsurfers to avoid a high-speed entanglement. Even though this is one of the premier spots on the planet for kitesurfing, the winds can be strong and gusty during the summer (particularly on an east wind), and the waves can be big during winter. Unless you're an advanced kitesurfer, take a lesson to learn the local conditions and ensure you have the safest, most enjoyable kitesurfing experience possible.

For information relating to Maui kitesurfing, safety, and maps of which areas are prohibited, check out www.kitesurfmaui.org. For a webcam of current wind and weather conditions, go to www.kitebeachcam.com.

Stand-Up Paddling

There aren't any stand-up paddleboard lessons offered along the island's central coast. If you have your own board (or have rented one), the best bet for flat-water paddling is **Kanaha Beach Park** on the inside of the reef. Since the reef is a couple of hundred yards offshore, it forms a nice lagoon on the inside, and the water is often calm during the morning before the trade winds pick up. If you're a competent paddle surfer and want to get into the waves, paddle through the channel off the lifeguard stand at Lowers, where you will find waves perfectly suited for stand-up paddle surfing. These are only for advanced paddlers who can handle themselves in large surf.

RENTAL SHOPS

Kahului boasts a large number of rental shops where you can pick up anything from surfboards to stand-up paddleboards and kitesurfing to windsurfing gear. Of all the shops, **HI Tech Surf Sports** (425 Koloa St., 808/877-2111,www.surfmaui.com, 9am-6pm daily) has the largest selection of surf and stand-up paddleboards, which are $25 and $35 per day respectively. **Hawaiian Island Surf and Sport** (415 Dairy Rd., 808/871-4981, www.hawaiianisland.com, 8:30am-6pm daily) has surfboards start at $20/day or $110/week, and you can save 10 percent by prebooking your board online. There are also stand-up boards for $35/day or $199/week, and the same early booking discounts apply.

If you're a fan of Naish equipment, **Naish** (111 Hana Hwy., 808/871-1503, www.naish-maui.com, 9am-5pm daily) also has a store in Kahului offering a full range of rentals. For windsurfing, **Second Wind** (111 Hana Hwy.,

808/877-7467, www.secondwindmaui.com, 9am-6pm daily) offers full packages with all the gear you'll need from $55/day to $575 for a 14-day package.

The shop closest to the beach itself is **Kanaha Kai** (96 Amala Pl., 808/877-7778, www.kanahakai.com, 9am-5pm daily), which offers a 20 percent prebooking special on windsurf bookings of seven days or more. Regular rates without the discount are $50/day for a windsurfing rig to $560 for a 14-day package. You can also get a surfboard for only $90/week, although the selection is smaller than at the stores back in town.

SCHOOLS AND LESSONS

Since Maui can offer some of the most exhilarating, yet challenging, conditions for windsurfing and kitesurfing, those who want to pick up the sports can save themselves hours of frustration by taking lessons from a pro. When it comes to both, one class isn't going to be enough, so ideally you want to book at least a five-hour package to maximize your investment. Then again, every school offers a single-session option.

One of the largest schools is **Action Sports Maui** (96 Amala Pl., 808/871-5857, www.actionsportsmaui.com), a company that runs its North Shore operation out of Kanaha Kai surf shop on the road toward Kite Beach. Kiting lessons range from $199 for a 2.5-hour intro class to $2,050 for a 10-day, 30-hour intensive training package. Windsurfing lessons range from $89 for 2.5 hours to $395-575 (group/private) for a five-day course. Action Sports Maui also offers classes that focus on honing individual skills such as jibing, waterstarting, and shortboard basics.

Kitesurfing School of Maui (808/873-0015, www.ksmaui.com) is a school which focuses, as the name suggests, specifically on kitesurfing. The operation is inside the NeilPryde shop in Kahului. A three-hour, one-day class to teach you the basics will cost $270, and a six-hour, two-day class is $495. If you want to delve into the sport, you can spring for the 18-hour, five-day class for $1,295.

Another operation with multisport instruction is **Hawaiian Sailboard Techniques** (425 Koloa St., 808/871-5423, www.hstwindsurfing.com), inside HI Tech Surf Sports. Founder Alan Cadiz has been teaching windsurfing on Maui since 1985, making this the longest-running outfit on the island's North Shore. When kitesurfing came into existence, Cadiz was among some of the first instructors to teach the sport to others, and what's nice about Cadiz's lessons is that an instructor will accompany you on a stand-up paddleboard to talk you through the finer points. Three-hour kitesurfing lessons are $255, and private windsurfing lessons run from $127.50 for 1.5 hours to $459 for a six-hour package.

Aqua Sports (Kite Beach, 808/242-8015, www.mauikiteboardinglessons.com) is right on Kite Beach and offers a $99 two-hour rate for beginners who want to give kiteboarding a try. The classes start at 9am so the beach isn't crowded with other kiters. Even though you don't get in the water, you're able to learn how to control the kite and see if this is a sport you could take up. Additional courses are offered at competitive rates, and online booking specials frequently lower the cost to some of the island's best rates.

MAUI

MAUI

Hiking and Biking

HIKING
'Iao Valley

Even though the drive into **'Iao Valley** goes deep into Mauna Kahalawai, the valley itself doesn't have very good public hiking. The only part of 'Iao Valley which could be considered a hike is the 10-minute, paved walking trail leading up to a lookout peering out at 'Iao Needle. If you go out there, you'll notice a railing that keeps visitors from walking into the bush, and on the other side of the railing you'll notice a thin trail, which disappears back into the trees. This trail snakes its way through the forest for a couple of miles, although this area is officially off-limits due to the fact that it's easy to get lost—especially if the clouds roll in.

If you want to swim in 'Iao Stream, the best place for accessing the swimming holes is from Kepaniwai Heritage Gardens where short trails lead down to the refreshing—and cold—water.

◖ Waihe'e Coastal Dunes and Wetlands Preserve

Set on land protected by the Hawaiian Islands Land Trust, this hike passing for two miles along the undeveloped shoreline of Waihe'e has only recently been opened to visitors. Within the 277-acre preserve are the remains of the Kapoho fishing village as well as two different ancient *heiau*. Scholars estimate that the Waihe'e area was populated as early as AD 300-600, which is not surprising, as the freshwater streams, fertile valleys, and lush uplands provide all the natural resources for sustaining life. The lonesome shoreline is covered in driftwood and is a great place for beachcombing. This is one of the few places on the island where you can walk down a sandy beach and be the only person around.

The trail itself parallels the shoreline and passes by a couple of abandoned houses before

© KYLE ELLISON

'Iao Needle is an iconic symbol of Central Maui.

© KYLE ELLISON

Hike back through time at the Waiheʻe Coastal Dunes and Wetland Preserve.

reaching the cultural relics at Kapoho. Expect the round-trip journey to take a little over an hour; add on 30 minutes to explore the coastline or ruins. To reach the trailhead, make a right on Halewaiu Place off Kahekili Highway (Hwy. 340) and follow the signs for Waiehu Golf Course. When the road makes a sharp turn to the right and starts heading toward the golf course, you'll notice an unmarked dirt road going to the left. From this turnoff it's 0.25 mile to the parking area and trailhead, although the unpaved road and small stream crossing are unsuitable for rental cars. You can either park your car here at the turnoff or on the access road, which leads down to Waiheʻe Beach Park just before the golf course. It's best to park away from the fairway since golfers sometimes drive balls into the parking lot.

Waiheʻe Ridge Trail

Driving the Kahekili Highway from Wailuku, the parking area for the **Waiheʻe Ridge Trail** is immediately across the road from Mendes Ranch, at the seven-mile marker. This 2.5-mile trail starts innocently enough but does become a switchback farther up. It also crosses some areas that become boggy after a rain. The trail rises to over 2,560 feet with spectacular views into Waiheʻe and Makamakaʻole Valleys. The trail continues to Lanilili summit where on clear days you can see the northern slope of the mountain. This area can get cloudy, blocking the views, although if you start hiking before 9am you'll finish the trail before the clouds start rolling in. This trail takes some energy, so count on three hours for the five-mile trip.

Makamakaʻole Valley

If you're on the hunt for waterfalls, head to the *makai* (ocean-side) section of **Makamakaʻole Valley** where a couple of small waterfalls are hidden in the jungle. Although it's a short, user-friendly hike, the trail can be slippery and requires climbing over a couple of boulders. Be respectful of No Trespassing signs and leave the area as you found it.

If approaching from Wailuku, the discreet trailhead is 7.8 miles after making the turn onto Waiehu Beach Road, or 0.8 miles after the Mendes Ranch. At this point the road has climbed in elevation and narrowed at parts to only a single lane. You'll pass a sharp turn in the valley, and when the road starts pointing back toward the ocean, you'll notice a small, dirt pullout, which can accommodate four or five vehicles. The trailhead is a narrow, well-defined dirt pathway that heads downhill into the brush. There's also a false trailhead that departs from the same parking area but only goes for about five yards. If the trail suddenly ends after 10 seconds, turn around and look for the other one. Once you are on the correct trail, it will wind its way downhill for about 10 minutes before arriving at a small swimming hole where you'll find a rushing waterfall and a rope swing. Along the way you're rewarded with a dramatic view of Makamakaʻole Valley as it wends its way to the ocean below.

The trail continues deeper into the valley toward a waterfall more dramatic than the first. You'll have to climb over a large boulder to keep on the trail, which will then parallel the river over some slippery rocks. The mosquitoes can be vicious in this shaded section, so be sure you've applied repellent or have covered yourself. After tracing the river for 10 minutes, the trail will end at a large banyan tree whose serpentine roots snake down a near-vertical cliff face. In order to reach the pool below, climb down using the roots of the banyan tree as handholds as if it were a natural ladder. This maneuver requires some athletic ability and skill, so it should only be attempted by those who are agile and accepting of the risks. The reward, however, is a small swimming hole where you can bathe beneath a waterfall in a hidden tropical setting. This spot is popular with many professionally guided hiking tours.

HIKING TOURS

Hike Maui (808/879-5270 or 866/324-6284, www.hikemaui.com, 6am-8pm daily) offers knowledgeable guides who will take you to some of the island's most scenic locations. Group sizes are usually fairly small, and again, what makes these hikes worthwhile is not only being taken directly to the trailhead, but also learning about the island's flora, fauna, history, and mythology from local guides who love what they do. Hike Maui meets guests in a large community parking lot in Kahului near the intersection of Kuihelani Highway (Hwy. 380) and Puʻunene Avenue and offers waterfall hikes, trips into Haleakala Crater, and options that combine kayaking with an afternoon hike through the rainforest.

BIKING

Despite the steep grade of the West Maui Mountains there aren't any official mountain biking trails. The most popular road cycling ride is heading from Kahului to the fishing village of **Kahakuloa** and back. Distances will vary depending on where you start, but along the way cyclists will be treated to quad-burning ascents, hairpin turns through rainforest surroundings, and sweeping views of the entire North Shore. Sharing the road with cars can be tough considering how narrow it gets, but most cars are traveling so slowly around the tight turns that altercations are rare. If you would prefer to be on a designated bike path that stays on level ground, the **North Shore Greenway** runs from the last parking lot at Kanaha Beach Park all the way to the town of Paʻia, and along the route of the seven-mile bike path only 0.25 mile passes along the shoulder of the main highway. To reach the Kahului terminus of the bike path, follow Amala Place all the way to the end and park in the last parking lot of Kanaha Beach Park. Parts of the bike path go directly behind the airport runway, and this ride is best in the morning due to the strong trade winds which can create momentum-destroying headwinds during the afternoon (the wind normally blows from Paʻia toward Kahului).

Rental Shops

Across the street from K-Mart by the Tesoro Gas Station, **Island Biker Maui** (415 Dairy Rd., 808/877-7744, www.islandbikermaui.com, 9am-5pm weekdays, 9am-3pm Sat.) offers rentals which range from $60/day to $250/week. All bike rentals come with flat repair tools, water bottles, one spare tube, and local insights from staff members who ride these roads on a regular basis. Both mountain bikes and road bikes are available.

At **Crater Cycles** (358 Papa Pl., 808/893-2020, www.cratercycleshawaii.com, 9am-5pm Mon.-Sat.), rentals range $65-85/day depending on which ride you're going to be doing. The focus here is mainly on mountain biking. If you're looking for information on trail conditions in Polipoli, Skyline Drive, or Makawao Forest Reserve, these are the folks to call.

Horseback Riding and Bird-Watching

HORSEBACK RIDING

The most well-known horseback riding outfit on this side of the island is **Mendes Ranch** (3530 Kahekili Hwy., 808/871-5222, www.mendesranch.com), a family-run operation on the road to Kahakuloa. Just before the seven-mile marker on Kahekili Highway, often you will smell Mendes Ranch before you see it. That's what happens when you have a fully operational ranch with more than 300 head of cattle, but it's all part of the *paniolo* experience. While group sizes can be large and the 1.5-hour rides run $110/person, what separates Mendes from all the other ranches is that you can actually run the horses. You can gallop at Mendes, so there's no nose-to-tail riding here. The ride itself goes from the family ranch house down the bluffs to the windswept shoreline, and lunch can be included with some of the tours. Expect afternoon rides to be windy and the morning rides to be clearer and calm. The coastal views here aren't accessible by any other means, and Mendes Ranch is a fabulous option to see them.

Much closer to the main resort areas is the central **Makani Olu Ranch** (363 W. Waiko Rd., 808/870-0663, www.makanioluranch.com), another working cattle ranch set back in the Waikapu Valley. Only 25 minutes from Wailea and 35 minutes from Ka'anapali, Makani Olu maintains a herd of 100 longhorn cattle and caps the trail rides at only four riders. The two-hour, $125 ride takes guests across Waikapu Stream into the forest behind the Maui Tropical Plantation and eventually turns inland and works its way up the valley.

The views from this part of the trail look back at Haleakala and the green central isthmus, and this is the only way you can gain access to this remote part of the island. All tours are at walking pace only, which makes them a better option for novice riders. A lunch option is available with the ride, and experienced riders can opt for a $150, private or semiprivate ride that includes 45 minutes in a round pen working on skills. While this is a nice option for families, all riders must be over 10 years old and under 220 pounds.

the Makani Olu Ranch

© KYLE ELLISON

MAUI

MAUI

BIRD-WATCHING
Kahului
The best bird-watching in Central Maui is at the **Kanaha Pond State Wildlife Sanctuary,** five minutes from the Kahului airport along Hana Highway. This royal fishpond used to provide island *ali'i* with a consistent supply of mullet, although the dredging of Kahului Harbor in 1910 altered the natural flow of water. Today this pond is on the migratory route of various birds and serves as a temporary home to dozens of vagrant bird species. Most important, it's also home to the endangered Hawaiian stilt (*ae'o*), a slender, 16-inch bird with a black back, white belly, and sticklike pink legs. The Hawaiian coot (*'alae ke'oke'o*), a gray-black, duck-like bird that builds large floating nests, may also be seen here. An observation pavilion is maintained on the pond's south edge, accessible through a gate by a short walkway from the parking area. This pavilion is always open and free of charge. Entry to the walking trails within the sanctuary is free, but only by permit on weekdays from the first day of September to the last day of March. Apply 8am-3:30pm Monday-Friday at the **Department of Natural Resources, Division of Forestry and Wildlife** (54 S. High St., Rm. 101, Wailuku, 808/984-8100) and supply the exact dates and times of your intended visit.

Wailuku
The best place for bird-watching in Wailuku is the **Waihe'e Coastal Dunes and Wetlands Preserve,** an expanse of low grassland where various seabirds and native species can be observed.

Adventure Sports

ZIPLINE TOURS
The most beginner-friendly zipline in the central valley is the **Maui Zipline** (1670 Honoapi'ilani Hwy., 808/633-2464, www.mauizipline.com), within the grounds of the Maui Tropical Plantation. This five-line zipline course is affordable at only $90, and children as young as five years old and as light as 50 pounds can take part in the adventure. As you might expect, a course that caters to such young children won't have the same element of extremism as some of the other courses, but the fact that the guides also introduce educational elements into the program (such as the weather patterns of the area and lessons on the surrounding plant species) makes this a great option for families traveling with children. Cable lengths range 300-900 feet, and there are two cables running parallel to each other so you can go at the same time as a friend or loved one.

For those who want to go big or go home, the eight-line **Flyin Hawaiian Zipline** (1670 Honoapi'ilani Hwy., 808/463-4786, www.flyinhawaiianzipline.com, $185) covers 2.5 miles of West Maui mountainside and finishes in a different town. Guests meet at the Maui Tropical Plantation for a 4-by-4 ride back into Waikapu Valley where you will suit up for your midair journey across the mountain. Reservations are highly recommended.

In addition to views toward Haleakala, this zipline ecotour incorporates elements of habitat restoration for Hawaii's native plants and works to remove nonnative species. The company champions sustainable, educational tourism, and the ecological element of the organization isn't just something done to appear green—it's the real deal.

The most enticing reason to book this tour is the ultra-long, cheek-clenching, three-screamer zipline that runs for more than 3,600 feet—the longest on the island. The lines aren't parallel to each other (so you can't watch your friend's cheeks flap at 50 mph), and the elevation isn't as high as the final, fifth line at Pi'iholo, but you also get a short ATV ride at the end of the tour as they shuttle you from the town of Ma'alaea back to Waikapu. Expect the tour to take 4-5 hours. Small snacks are included. The age limit is 10 years old and weight limit is 75-250 pounds.

ATV TOURS

The only ATV tours in Central Maui are at **Mendes Ranch** (3530 Kahekili Hwy., 808/871-5222, www.mendesranch.com, $79). Trails run from the riding corral down to the shoreline, and the views extend out over the Pacific. Riders must be at least 16 years old to drive one of the ATVs. Over the course of the one-hour ride, guides tell you about the history of Maui, the ranch, and the lineage of the Mendes family. This is one of the only ATV opportunities still available on the island and the only way besides riding a horse that you're going to get to experience the remote stretch of coastline.

HELICOPTER RIDES

Much of Maui is only accessible by helicopter. Helicopter tours are expensive, but if you treat yourself to one splurge, make it a helicopter tour. Eroded valleys, sheer ridgelines, and inaccessible waterfalls are all parts of most Maui helicopter tours. All pilots flying for the major tour operators have logged thousands of flying hours and put an emphasis on safety. Most pilots also double as geologists, biologists, historians, and naturalists as they narrate tours above the island's interior. Morning hours are best because they offer the clear conditions necessary for visiting spots such as 1,100-foot Honokohau Falls. As an added bonus, during winter, you're able to spot humpback whales as they lounge in the waters below.

All helicopter flights depart from the Kahului Heliport (located 0.5 mile from the junction of Hana Highway and Haleakala Highway), and the two most popular tour options are those combining the West Maui Mountains with Moloka'i and East Maui (Hana) with Haleakala. Regardless of which operator you choose, inquire about getting the two front seats next to the pilot since it's much easier to take photos. Also, if you plan on booking a helicopter tour, remember that you cannot have been scuba diving within a 24-hour period before the flight (snuba, due to the shallow depth, is still permitted). All prices listed below are for online specials given for advance reservations.

Blue Hawaiian Helicopters (1 Kahului Airport Rd., #105, 808/871-8844 or 800/745-2583, www.bluehawaiian.com, 7am-10pm daily) is the largest tour operator and accommodates the largest number of island visitors. With offices on all of the major islands, these guys have been leaders in the Maui helicopter industry since their founding in 1985. They offer tours on two different types of 6-seat helicopters: the A-Star and the Eco-Star. The difference is that the Eco-Star provides individual bucket seats, has larger viewing windows, and can accommodate a greater amount of weight than the A-Star. As you might expect, flights on the Eco-Star are a little more expensive. Packages run $149/person for a 30-minute tour of the West Maui Mountains to $440/person for a two hour tour of Maui and the Big Island (Hawai'i Volcanoes National Park not included). There's also a tour that touches down at an exclusive landing zone within Ulupalakua Ranch during a stopover of a full-island tour, offering access to a part of the island you would never visit otherwise. DVDs of your experience can be purchased for an additional $25.

The only other tour operator with Eco-Star (referred to as Whisper-Star) helicopters in their fleet is **Sunshine Helicopters** (1 Kahului Airport Rd., #107, 808/270-3999 or 866/501-7738, www.sunshinehelicopters.com), and the seats in the front will cost you more than those in the back. Prices range from $170/person for a 30-minute West Maui flight to $350/person for a 55-65 minute West Maui and Moloka'i package. If Mendes Ranch horseback riding or the Atlantis Submarine are also on your list of activities, you can book them as a combo package through Sunshine Helicopters and save a little bit on both of the excursions.

A smaller yet reputable operation is **Air Maui** (1 Kahului Airport Rd, Hangar 110, 808/877-7005 or 877/238-4942, www.airmaui.com), a company with prices that are slightly higher but proudly boasting a perfect safety record. Fees range from $175/person for a 30-minute tour to

$307/person for a 60-minute tour of West Maui and Moloka'i (which is 15 minutes longer than the same, albeit cheaper Blue Hawaiian Tour).

If you want to be *that* much closer to the scenery, **Alex Air** (108 Kahului Heliport, 808/877-4354, www.helitour.com, 8am-4pm daily) is the only company that offers flights with the doors off. Tours with the doors on range from $168/person for a 30-minute West Maui Mountains tour to $229 for a 50-minute tour of West Maui and Moloka'i. Doors-off tours cost a little bit more but are well worth it for the added adventure. If you would rather have a private tour, there are R44 helicopters, which can accommodate 1-3 people and range from $450 for a 30-minute tour to $1,200 for a 90-minute East Maui tour combined with a private beach landing.

FLIGHTSEEING TOURS

While helicopters are the best choice for seeing the waterfalls of West Maui and the northern shore of Moloka'i, the only way that you're going to experience Kilauea Volcano on the Big Island is by taking a flightseeing tour with **Maui Air** (808/877-5500, www.volcanoair-tours.com) out of either Kahului or Kapalua Airport. The two-hour flight from Kahului Airport passes by the North Shore of Maui and the waterfalls of Kohala on the Big Island's northwestern tip, and circles over Hawai'i Volcanoes National Park looking for active lava flows. The plane can accommodate 10 passengers, and you're likely to be sharing the ride with other guests. Those who sit toward the back won't have as much of the wing obstructing the view. At $385/person it isn't a cheap trip, and since weather is a highly variable factor, it can be a gamble. Also, as the eruption at Kilauea is constantly shifting, there's no guarantee of seeing red lava, although on those clear, lava-filled days when everything comes together, this is the best way to experience both islands from the air.

Golf

KAHULUI

The only golf course in Kahului is **The Dunes at Maui Lani** (1333 Maui Lani Pkwy., 808/873-0422, www.dunesatmauilani.com, 6:30am-6pm daily), a Scottish-style links course that weaves its way through natural sand dunes. Course designer Robert Nelson utilized the natural topography of the dunes in creating this 6,841-yard course, so it includes a healthy number of bunkers. On the par-5 18th, two pot bunkers short of the green famously challenge even those with the lowest of handicaps. The afternoon trade winds can make this course difficult, and the greens fees are priced accordingly: $112 for visitors, $99 after 11am, and $79 after 2pm. Rates are substantially cheaper for resident golfers. The central location makes it easy to sneak in a round before heading to the airport.

WAILUKU

Set on the hillside in Waikapu, the 6,554-yard **Kahili Golf Course** (2500 Honoap'ilani Hwy., 808/242-4653, www.kahiligolf.com, 6am-6pm daily) is one of the island's best values. Greens fees for visitors are $99, although those teeing off after 2:30pm can squeeze in 18 holes for only $59. The bicoastal views are better than at Maui Lani, although instead of links-style golf, the course is set on a gently sloping hillside. It's a 30-minute drive from the resort complexes.

Intermediate golfers who don't want to shell out too much for a round can head to the **Waiehu Golf Course** (200 Halewaiu Rd., 808/243-7400, 6:45am-5pm weekdays, 6am-5pm weekends). This par-72, 6,330-yard municipal course is popular with locals because of the $25 resident's rate, although visitors can expect to pay $55 plus a $20 cart fee. The front

MAUI

© KYLE ELLISON

Tee off along the water at the municipal Waiehu Golf Course.

nine are fairly straightforward with little elevation gain, and three of the holes go right along the shoreline. The back nine gain a little in elevation and offer views looking out over Waiheʻe Reef where humpback whales can often be seen jumping during winter.

Sights

KAHULUI
☾ Maui Arts and Cultural Center

One of the reasons that Maui is *no ka oi* (the best) is that it truly does have a little of everything: tropical weather, world-class beaches, multicultural cuisine, hidden waterfalls, and live entertainment and cultural exhibitions on par with any metropolitan urban center. Though concerts and events are regularly held at various locations around the island, none offer the big-city professionalism of the $32-million-dollar **Maui Arts and Cultural Center** (1 Cameron Way, 808/242-7469, www.mauiarts.org), a figure that doesn't take into account the massive renovation undertaken in 2012.

Although it doesn't look like much from the highway, when you first step inside the Castle Theater or wander through the museum-quality Schaefer Gallery, you quickly realize that this is a place you would expect to find in New York, Chicago, or San Francisco. The 1,200-seat Castle Theater boasts three levels of seating, and the acoustics are designed in such a way that an unamplified guitar can be heard throughout the venue. The 250-seat **McCoy Studio** is a classic black-box theater which hosts smaller plays and theatrical events. The

MAUI

sprawling, 5,000-person A&B amphitheater has drawn some of the world's biggest musical talents from Elton John to Prince and Jimmy Buffett to The Eagles. The Maui Film Festival is partially held here on a screen inside the Castle Theater, and movies regularly show throughout the year. The constantly changing schedule of performances is listed on the website.

(Maui Nui Botanical Gardens

For anyone with an interest in Polynesian flora or sustainable farming techniques, the **Maui Nui Botanical Gardens** (150 Kanaloa Ave., 808/249-2798, www.mnbg. org, 8am-4pm Mon.-Sat., free) is an absolute must-stop. From the moment you walk in the entranceway, native trees and their informational placards are displayed in a shaded walkway, and small signs warn you to watch out for falling *ulu,* or breadfruit, which populate the treetops above. As you meander along the self-guided walking tour, various signs discuss the differences between

endemic, indigenous, and introduced plant species. A central theme of the garden is the way in which traditional irrigation techniques maximize the ability to farm in a semiarid climate. Freshwater was considered to be among the most precious of resources to Polynesian farmers, and more than 70 species of dryland *kalo,* or taro, are successfully growing in what is otherwise a dry coastal dunes system. Although not as expansive as the botanical gardens in Kula, the way in which the gardens espouse the Polynesian view that humans are but stewards of the land offers reason enough to visit.

(Alexander and Baldwin Sugar Museum

There's no place on the island where you can gain a better understanding of Maui's plantation heritage than at the **Alexander and Baldwin Sugar Museum** (3957 Hansen Rd., 808/871-8058, www.sugarmuseum.com, 9:30am-4pm daily, $10), a small, worn-down building in the Central Maui near-ghost town

Alexander and Baldwin Sugar Museum

© KYLE ELLISON

of Puʻunene. This town, which was once the beating heart of Maui's sugar industry, has been reduced to a faint pulse: a post office, a bookstore, the museum, and the stinky sugar mill are all that remain.

While the admission fee is steep, it's worth it for the historical components alone. Exhibits discuss everything from how the sugar plant moved across Polynesia in traditional voyaging canoes to historical profiles of the island's first sugar barons. In addition to educating visitors about the growth of the sugar industry, what makes the museum a must-see attraction is the window it provides into the daily lives of the plantation workers who came from around the globe and endured long days in the fields. The cultural exhibits within the museum include everything from the hand-sewn Japanese clothing used to protect workers from centipedes to Portuguese bread ovens used by immigrants from the Azores to make their famous staple. There's even an exhibit relating to Filipino cockfighting.

WAILUKU
◖ Bailey House Museum

Regardless of whether or not you're a "museum person," every visitor to Maui should see the **Bailey House Museum** (2375-A Main St., 10am-4pm Mon.-Sat., $7 adults, $2 children 7-12) on the road to ʻIao Valley. The Bailey House was built between 1833 and 1850, and from 1837 to 1849 this whitewashed, missionary-style building housed the Wailuku Female Seminary, of which Edward Bailey was principal. With the opening of Lahainaluna High School in 1831 (which is as the oldest public high school in the United States west of the Rocky Mountains), it was decided that the young, educated graduates of Lahainaluna would need refined, educated women whom they could eventually take as wives, hence the need for the seminary. After the closing of the institution the Baileys bought the property, began to raise sugarcane, and lived here until 1888. During this time, Edward Bailey became the manager of the Wailuku Sugar Company, and more important for posterity, he became

MAUI

the Bailey House Museum

a prolific landscape painter of various areas around the island. Most of his paintings record the period 1866-1896 and are now displayed in the Bailey Gallery, which was once the sitting room of the house. In 1973 it was placed on the National Register of Historic Places.

Inside the museum, the Hawaiian Room houses artifacts of precontact Hawaii such as wooden spears, stone tools, knives made from conch shells, and daggers made from shark's teeth. In the same room there are also stone *ki'i*, or statues, depicting the Hawaiian war god Ku, expertly crafted wooden calabashes, and an exhibit of artifacts found on the island of Kaho'olawe from both the pre- and post-bombing eras. Upstairs are two bedrooms which feature detailed information about the lineage of the Hawaiian royalty as well as missionary-era furniture, jewelry boxes, clothing, and handmade quilts. Back downstairs is the room full of Bailey's paintings. The bookstore ranks as the best educational, cultural resource on the island where you can find many of the best titles ever written on Hawaiian history.

Tropical Gardens of Maui

As you make your way up the road toward 'Iao Valley, you'll notice the **Tropical Gardens of Maui** (200 'Iao Valley Rd., 808/244-2085, www.tropicalgardensofmaui.com, 9am-4:30pm daily, $5) on the right side of the road. What separates this garden from the Maui Nui Botanical Gardens in Kahului is that not only is the foliage incredibly lush, but there is also a nursery which is authorized to export plants. What this means is that not only can you spend 30-40 minutes taking a self-guided tour through the tropical surroundings, but if you have a garden at home and would like to import some tropical species, you can speak with the nursery staff about bringing a piece of the surroundings home with you.

◖ Kepaniwai Heritage Gardens

Tucked away on the banks of 'Iao Stream is **Kepaniwai Heritage Gardens** (870 'Iao Valley Rd., 7am-7pm daily, free), a simple, run-down, but culturally informative park that details Maui's "mixed plate" culture. In addition to numerous pavilions that make great picnic spots (and sometimes double as a great *drinking* spots for locals), the park features a small monument devoted to each of the island's plantation-era immigrant communities. From Japanese to Chinese and Puerto Rican to Portuguese, each monument has an informational placard about the respective culture and a typical dwelling constructed in the traditional style. Along the stream are a few places where you can bathe in the shallow (and cold!) waters, although use some caution scrambling down to it as there aren't any official trails. A visit of 30 minutes will usually suffice.

◖ 'Iao Valley State Park

What makes **'Iao Valley State Park** (end of 'Iao Valley Rd., 7am-7pm daily) such a popular attraction is that it's the easiest, most accessible way to delve into the valleys of Mauna Kahalawai. Every other valley in the mountains requires some hiking, some bushwhacking, or some illicit private property crossing, so the park draws its fame from the convenience offered by the three-mile road back into the valley. 'Iao is not a one-stop destination, but an outing in which the journey is the highlight of the trip. The thin ribbon of asphalt which snakes its way up the valley floor is flanked on both sides by towering mountain ridges that get more dramatic as you move your way up the valley.

When you finally reach 'Iao Valley State Park, return visitors will be shocked to find a parking lot attendant collecting fees. Instituted in 2010, parking is now $5/vehicle for nonresidents. Once inside, the "trail" within the park is a paved, semi-crowded walkway which winds its way up 133 steps to a lookout for 2,250-foot Kuka'emoku, better known as the 'Iao Needle. This erosional structure erupts 1,200 feet from the valley floor below and was once used as a lookout point by native Hawaiian settlers. While the Needle itself is worthy of a photo, the towering cliff faces that form the photo's backdrop are even more dramatic. The center of the West Maui Mountains is virtually

© KYLE ELLISON

Kepaniwai Heritage Gardens

untouched by modern culture, and it's believed that the bones of Hawaiian royalty are buried in caves back here, which are so remote they will never be disturbed.

On the walk back down to the parking lot there are a few short spur trails worthy of a look. One leads down toward the waters of 'Iao Stream, whereas the trail right next to the bridge leads to an ethnobotanical garden highlighting plant species introduced by Polynesian settlers. This loop trail will only take about 10 minutes to explore thoroughly, and there's a nice example of taro irrigation.

Maui Tropical Plantation

The **Maui Tropical Plantation** (1670 Honoapi'ilani Hwy., 808/242-8983, www.mauitropicalplantation.com, 9am-5pm daily, free admission) is a 60-acre working plantation that grows everything from coconuts to star fruit and apple bananas to coffee. Although it mainly caters to the old and the young, the plantation remains an informative stop for anyone interested in Hawaii's agriculture. Some

additions have recently been put in as a way to attract a more active crowd, so the **Maui Zipline** (808/633-2464, www.mauizipline.com) and **Maui Paddler** (808/281-2826, www.mauipaddler.net, 9am-3:30pm daily) outfits both operate on the plantation grounds. While the zipline is a popular tour that caters to small children and beginners, the paddle tour navigates a small lake and teaches you the basics of outrigger canoe work. Both excursions are tame, although they do offer an educational experience for families who just might want their children to learn something on vacation.

The longtime draw is the **Tropical Express Tram Tour** ($15 adults, $5 children), otherwise known as "the train." This 40-minute train ride makes a large loop through the agricultural fields narrated by a driver who is well versed in the crops. Trams run eight times per day 10am-4pm, and while children will be excited to be on a train, adults will learn something about the crops growing around them.

You can purchase crops grown right on the property at **Kumu Farms** (167 Honoapi'ilani Hwy., 808/244-4800, 10am-5pm Tues.-Fri., 10am-3pm weekends), a certified-organic market. There isn't anywhere else in Central Maui where you can buy organic produce that's going to be this fresh. The farm features everything from cilantro to peppers to chard and carrots, as well as the famous sunrise papayas which are grown at the sister store on Moloka'i. You can also purchase bags of their homemade macadamia nut and basil pesto. If you're staying on the west side of the island and plan on doing some cooking in your condo, there is no better place to pick up your produce on your drive back from Central Maui.

◖ Haleki'i and Pihana Heiau

Few island visitors ever stop at the **Haleki'i and Pihana Heiau,** which is a shame considering their historical importance. This site is officially classified as a Hawaii State Park, but the gate to the *heiau* is no longer open for vehicular access and its condition has fallen into disrepair. It's still easy to park on the residential street in front of the *heiau* and make the

MAUI

five-minute walk to the top of the hill. The 360-degree view stretches from 'Iao Valley to the waters of Kahului Bay. It's one of the best vistas of Central Maui and a powerful, dramatic, and empty place to watch the sunrise.

In ancient Hawaii these two *heiau* served as the religious center of the entire Wailuku *ahupua'a,* or land division. Many of Maui's ruling *ali'i* came here to either honor their deceased or commune with religious deities. It's believed that Keopuolani, the woman who would become queen, was born here at Pihana *heiau,* a site which is also believed to have been a *luakini heiau* occasionally used for human sacrifice. Hawaiian scholars believe that one of the last human sacrifices on the island was performed right here at Pihana in 1790 by King Kamehameha after his victory at the Battle of Kepaniwai. Much of Pihana *heiau* was destroyed during the 19th century when the Hawaiian monarchy converted to Christianity, but numerous walls and terraces from Haleki'i still remain.

To reach the *heiau,* travel along Waiehu Beach Road until you cross the bridge over 'Iao Stream. On the other side you'll make your first left onto Kuhio Place, and then the first left again onto Hea Place. Since the access gate to the *heiau* will most likely be locked, park your car on the street and walk up the access road.

Kahakuloa

Though technically Kahakuloa is part of Wailuku, this old fishing village is an entity all to itself. Lonely and remote, there are few places left in all of Hawaii that are quite like Kahakuloa. Many choose to get to Kahakuloa from the west side of the island by following the road past Kapalua, Honolua Bay, and Nakalele Blowhole, but because this road is a loop, Kahakuloa can similarly be accessed from Wailuku. It will take you 30-45 minutes to reach Kahakuloa from Wailuku—and there aren't any gas stations—so be sure you have at

least a half a tank of gas before venturing out into the wilderness.

Following Kahekili Highway (Hwy. 340) past Mendes Ranch and Makamaka'ole Valley, the road becomes narrow and the foliage dense. The first stop you'll happen upon is **Turnbull Studios** (5030 Kahekili Hwy., 808/244-0101, www.turnbullstudios.org, 10am-5pm Mon.-Fri.), an eclectic sculpture garden that also features paintings and handmade crafts by local Hawaiian artists. The artist has been making sculptures at this mountainside garden for over 25 years. There are only a few parking spaces, and if it's been raining heavily, think twice before going down the short but steep driveway in a low-clearance rental car.

Farther down the road you'll reach the **Kaukini Gallery** (808/244-3371, www.kaukini-gallery.com, 10am-5pm daily), which is inside a mountaintop home overlooking Kahakuloa Valley. The gallery features more than 120 local artists and their associated paintings, jewelry, ceramics, and handmade crafts, and the views from the parking lot looking up the valley easily make it the most scenic gallery on the island.

Finally, after a few hairpin turns on a narrow one-lane road, you reach the village of Kahakuloa. This place truly is unlike anywhere else on the island, and all sorts of clichés abound: "Old Hawaii," "turn back time," and "a place that time has forgotten." No matter which one you like, they're all true. Stop just before you drop into town to pick up banana bread from **Julia's Banana Bread** (www.juliasbananabread.com, 9am-5:30pm) stand in the bright green, wooden building.

Driving through this town of 200 residents takes no more than two minutes, and before you know it, you'll be climbing around another hairpin turn and leaving the fishing village behind. At the overlook on the Kapalua side of the village is **Kauikeolani Lunchwagon** (9:30am-4pm daily), a yellow food truck that sells mouthwatering fish-and-chips and where every item on the menu is gloriously deep fried.

Shopping

KAHULUI

Kahului has the most shopping on the island. The two-story **Queen Ka'ahumanu Shopping Center** (www.queenkaahumanucenter.com, 9:30am-9pm Mon.-Sat., 10am-5pm Sun.) along Ka'ahumanu Avenue is Kahului's largest mall, with the widest selection of stores, many of which are large corporate chains. The open-air **Maui Mall** (www.mauimall.com, 10am-6pm daily, until 8pm Fri. and 4pm Sun.) is more pedestrian, yet it has a pleasant ambience as its buildings are set around a central T-shaped courtyard.

Kahului also has the greatest concentration of water sports shops on the island, many of them at or near the corner of Hana Highway and Dairy Road. Stop here for surf clothing, accessories, boardshorts, or equipment sales. Favorites include **Hawaiian Island Surf and Sport** (415 Dairy Rd., 808/871-4981, www.hawaiianisland.com, 8:30am-6pm daily), **HI Tech Surf Sports** (425 Koloa St., 808/877-2111, www.surfmaui.com, 9am-6pm daily), **Neilpryde Maui** (400 Hana Hwy., 808/877-7443, www.neilprydemaui.com, 9am-6pm daily), and **Maui Tropix** (261 Dairy Rd., 808/871-8726, 9am-8pm Mon.-Sat., 9am-6pm Sun.), which sells the ubiquitous Maui Built wear.

WAILUKU

Wailuku has woefully little to offer in way of the retail sector. What shopping does occur, however, takes place on Market Street.

Near the corner of Market Street and Main Street you'll find **If The Shoe Fits** (21 N. Market St., 808/249-9710, www.hotbiskitshoes.com, 10am-5pm Mon.-Fri., 10am-2pm Sat.), which is Maui's only shoe-repair shop and also specializes in specialty footwear.

Also near the corner of Market and Main is **Maui Thing** (7 N. Market St., 808/249-0215, www.mauithing.com, 10am-5pm Mon.-Fri., 10am-4pm Sat.), a clothing store that focuses on Maui-themed clothing and accessories. This is a great store if you're looking for a unique Maui clothing gift you aren't going to find anywhere else on the island.

Across the street is a longtime Wailuku institution, **Requests** (10 N. Market St., 808/244-9315, www.requestshawaii.com, 10am-6pm Mon.-Sat.), the last holdout of true island record shops. It's been kept alive by a loyal customer fan base of music lovers who still want to feel the vinyl, admire the album covers, and talk with people who *really* love music. Most of the merchandise caters to the reggae and roots lifestyle, but the basement is filled with music that goes back decades.

At the far end of Market Street are two local water sports stores, **TriPaddle Maui** (54 N. Market St., 808/243-7235, www.tripaddlemaui.com, 10am-5pm Mon.-Fri., 10am-3pm Sat.) specializing in everything having to do with outrigger paddle sports and **Maui Sporting Goods** (92 N. Market St., 808/244-0011, 9am-6pm Mon.-Fri., 9am-5pm Sat.), the de facto fishing headquarters for most of Maui's anglers.

Intriguing antiques and pawn shops run the length of Market Street. At **Kama'aina Loan** (98 N. Market St., 808/242-5555, www.kamaainaloan.com, 9am-5pm Mon.-Fri., 10am-4pm Sat.-Sun.), you'll find everything from surfboards to ukuleles to ritual drums used by the shamans of Nepalese tribes.

MAUI

Entertainment

KAHULUI

Daytime Entertainment

On Saturday (1pm) and Sunday (11am) there are free hula shows and live performances at the **Maui Mall** (70 E. Ka'ahumanu Ave., 808/877-8952, www.mauimall.com), and a monthly calendar of events can be found on the website. Across town, the **Queen Ka'ahumanu Shopping Center** (275 W. Ka'ahumanu Ave., 808/877-3369, www.queenkaahumanucenter.com) offers free hula shows on Monday mornings at 10:30am as well as a rotating schedule of other free performances. A calendar of events can be found online.

Evening Shows

The best option for evening entertainment in Kahului is the **Maui Arts and Cultural Center** (1 Cameron Way, 808/242-7469, www.mauiarts.org) where a constantly changing schedule of live concerts, movies, exhibits, comedy shows, and family events takes place many nights of the week. Multiple events often happen on the same evening. It's best to check the website for a list of upcoming events.

Bars

The most popular nightlife option in Kahului is the **Kahului Ale House** (355 E. Ka'ahumanu Ave., 808/877-9001, www.alehouse.net, 11am-12:30am Mon.-Thurs., 11am-2am Fri.-Sun.) in the parking lot of the Maui Mall. On Friday and Saturday nights there are either live performances by local artists (mostly reggae) or DJs spinning nightclub tunes.

If you would rather shoulder up to a bar without the fanfare of a full-on nightclub, **Koho's Grill and Bar** (275 W. Ka'ahumanu Ave., 808/877-5588, 7am-10pm Sun.-Thurs., 7am-11:30pm weekends) inside the Queen Ka'ahumanu Shopping Center offers happy hour and evening drink specials.

WAILUKU

Sleepy Wailuku isn't the island's entertainment hub, although there is the monthly **First Friday** event. Market Street in the historic downtown is closed to vehicular traffic 5:30pm-9pm, and the area becomes a festive pedestrian thoroughfare. There's live music in Banyan Tree Park, street performers, food concessions from local restaurants, activities for children, and a beer garden for the adults. This is the original and most popular of the "Maui Friday Town Parties," and more information can be found on the website at www.mauifridays.com/wailuku.

Shows

The only shows which take place in Wailuku are sporadic stage performances at the historic **'Iao Theater** (68 N. Market Street), a Spanish mission-style theater that was opened in 1928 and is listed on the National Register of Historic Places. The 'Iao is the oldest theater building in the Hawaiian Islands and has hosted performers such as Bob Hope and Frank Sinatra over the course of its lengthy history. You can find more information about showtimes at the MauiOnStage website, www.mauionstage.com.

Bars

Every town needs a good dive bar, and the **Steel Horse Saloon** (1234 Lower Main St., 808/243-2200, 10am-2am daily) has got Wailuku covered. This Lower Main Street dive specializes in cheap drinks, rowdy bikers, loud music, and an old-fashioned good time. Set inside a 1930s-era building, the Steel Horse is questionable from the outside and lovable from the moment you walk in the door. On the fringe of the Wailuku Industrial Park this isn't your typical tourist bar, but live music on Friday and Saturday nights cranks the atmosphere up another decibel.

Just down the street, **Tiffany's Bar and Grill**

(1424 Lower Main St., 808/249-0052, www. tiffanysmaui.com, 10:30am-12am Mon.-Sat., 10:30am-11pm Sun.) is another longtime Lower Main Street institution that caters to a heavily local crowd. Karaoke is the name of the game here. Since it's also a full restaurant you can pick up some more substantial food than at the Steel Horse.

Food

KAHULUI
Local Style
When it comes to plate lunch **(Da Kitchen** (425 Koloa St., 808/871-7782, www.da-kitchen.com, 11am-9pm Mon.-Sat., $10-17) has the most *ono-kine, broke da mouth grinds* anywhere in town. The restaurant is tucked away in a small strip mall off Ka'ahumanu Avenue; the same mall as HI Tech Surf Sports and Denny's—look for the huge sign that says "Restaurant." Despite the obscure location, it's always packed. Some of the items on the "Moco Madness" are big enough to split between two people (lunch for under $20). For a tasty albeit artery-clogging meal, go all-in with fried spam musubi followed by a Polynesian Paralysis Moco of fish tempura, kalua pork, two eggs, onion, mushrooms, and gravy over fried rice.

Mexican
For quick and authentic Mexican food, visit **Las Piñatas** (395 Dairy Rd., 808/877-8707, www.pinatasmaui.com, 8am-8pm Mon.-Sat., 9am-8pm Sun., $7-10), next to Kinko's off Dairy Road. The "Kitchen Sink" burrito is so big that a growing teenager will have trouble cleaning the plate. Bottled beer and *horchata* are available to drink. As the name suggests, over a dozen piñatas dangle from the ceiling. It's a great lunch option if you're heading to or from the airport.

Italian
The finest restaurant in Kahului, **Bistro Casanova** (33 Lono Ave., 808/873-3850, www.bistrocasanova.com, 11am-9:30pm Mon.-Sat., $14-38) livens up downtown with a fusion of Mediterranean and Italian cuisine. The tapas menu served after 3pm has affordable crostinis,

gnocchi, and grilled calamari. A swanky bar attracts the after-work cocktail crowd. The wine list features over 20 selections from various global wine regions. The dinner menu features meat entrées such as lamb chops and New York steak and pasta dishes like ravioli al tartufo and linguini al funghi.

Pizza in Paradise (60 E. Wakea Ave., 808/871-8188, www.pizza-maui.com, 11am-9pm Mon.-Thurs., 11am-10pm Fri.-Sat., $13-26) puts out arguably the best pizza on the island in one of its most unassuming locations. This family-run joint makes its own dough and sauce. Whole pies are available, but the "by the slice" option is nice for lunch on the go. The menu also features subs and pasta, but it's the pizza that keeps locals walking through the door. It's best to not be in a rush; the food can take some time. Parking can be a challenge.

Natural Foods
If you're a vegetarian, vegan, or just care about what you put in your body, you will love the salad bar and deli inside the **(Down to Earth** (305 Dairy Rd., 808/877-2661, www.downtoearth.org, 7am-9pm Mon.-Sat., 8am-8pm Sun.) grocery store. There's a wide selection of bottled juices, all-natural snack options, and vitamins and supplements.

Japanese
The best Japanese in Kahului is at **Ichiban Restaurant** (65 W. Ka'ahumanu Ave., 808/871-6977, www.ichibanrestaurantandsushimaui.com, 7am-2pm, 5pm-9pm Mon.-Fri., 1:30pm-2pm, 5pm-9pm Sat., $8-12), squirreled away in the Kahului Shopping Center. The building appears to be closed, but once you step inside, the traditional Japanese decor will

MAUI

make you forget you're in an industrial section of Kahului. Rainbow rolls and heaping bowls of udon punctuate the menu. Cap it all off with a Kirin beer or a cup of sake.

At the Ka'ahumanu Shopping Center, **Ramen-Ya** (275 W. Ka'ahumanu Ave., 808/873-9688, 10:30am-9:30pm Mon.-Sat., 10:30am-8:30pm Sun., $7-9) is a hole-in-the-wall that is always packed. It's that good. While the decor isn't quite as authentic as Ichiban, the prices for huge bowls of ramen and udon are tough to beat.

Chinese

The most well-known Chinese restaurant in Kahului is **Dragon Dragon** (70 E. Ka'ahumanu Ave., 808/893-1628, 10:30am-2pm, 5pm-9pm Sun.-Thurs., 10:30am-2pm, 5pm-9:30pm Fri.-Sat., $10-19), inside the Maui Mall. Traditional Chinese options such as moo shu shrimp and vegetables or chow fun Singapore-style dominate the menu. Dim sum options are available during lunch. It isn't the same cuisine you'd find in a Hong Kong back alley, but it's a decent place for Chinese food with moderate prices.

Thai

Thailand Cuisine II (70 E. Ka'ahumanu Ave., 808/873-0225, www.thailandcuisinemaui.net, 10:30am-3:30pm, 5pm-9:30pm daily, $11-16) has been awarded the honor of "Best Ethnic Restaurant on Maui" four separate times. The food is authentic and tasty, but the location at Maui Mall isn't anything special. Menu items feature a classic selection of Thai curries, pad thai noodles, and tom yum soup.

Filipino

Considering the island's sizable Filipino community, you would expect more Filipino restaurants around town, but the only one with any prominence is **Bistro Manila** (230 Hana Hwy., 808/871-6934, 5pm-8:30pm Mon.-Sat.). The local favorite serves dishes so authentic you would think you were in Manila. The restaurant is near some car dealerships in a warehouse off Hana Highway. While there is no liquor

license, you are free to pair your pancit, sisig, or pan-fried bangus with beer or wine that you bring in yourself.

German

Industrial Kahului is the last place you would expect to find a Bavarian aprés-ski lodge, but **Brigit and Bernard's Garden Café** (335 Ho'ohana, 808/877-6000, 11am-2:30pm Mon., 11am-2:30pm, 5pm-9:30pm Tues.-Fri., 5pm-9:30pm Sat., $16-32) pumps out stick-to-your-bones German fare that could easily be in the Black Forest. The vaulted A-frame ceiling is hung with colorful steins, cross-country skis, and posters of alpine ski resorts. Order a massive plate of bratwurst or schnitzel served with a huge potato rosti and wash it down with a Bitburger brew. The garden area outside makes for a nice *biergarten*.

Coffee Shops

For local coffee beans, head to 🄲 **Maui Coffee Roasters** (444 Hana Hwy., 808/877-2877, www.mauicoffeeroasters.com, 7am-6pm Mon.-Fri., 8am-5pm Sat., 8am-2:30pm Sun., $9), the best little coffee shop in all of Kahului. In the same shopping complex as Marco's Grill and Deli, Maui Coffee Roasters has an assortment of brews made from Maui, Kona, Kaua'i, and Moloka'i beans. The full breakfast and lunch menu features bagels, breakfast wraps, sandwiches, and salads. There are a number of tables, free Wi-Fi, and a full range of coffee accessories for sale as well.

Food Truck

Plate lunch stands occasionally line the harbor. The one with the greatest staying power is the **Geste Shrimp Truck** (Kahului Beach Rd., 808/298-7109, 10:45am-5pm Tues.-Sat., $12, cash only) that parks on Kahului Beach Road, a quarter mile past the turnoff for the Maui Arts and Cultural Center. $12 gets you 12 pieces of shrimp served with crab macaroni salad and two scoops of rice. Based on the aroma of shrimp emanating from the white truck, it's no surprise that it often runs out of food before 5pm.

WAILUKU
Local Style

When—and if—you finally find **(Sam Sato's** (1750 Wili Pa Loop, 808/244-7124, 7am-2pm Mon.-Sat., bakery open until 4pm, $6, cash only), you'll probably say to yourself, *Really? This is the famous restaurant?* Hidden deep with the Wailuku mill yard in a building you can't even see from the road, this family-run institution has been providing Wailuku with dry noodles, plate lunch, and famous *manju* pastries since the 1930s. It's the dry noodles that make Sam Sato's legendary. Served with a side of homemade broth and topped with char siu pork and sprouts, they make an affordable and addictive meal. Despite its fame, Sam Sato's has never lost its local roots.

To help you find Sam Sato's: When traveling toward the mountains on Lower Main Street, you will make a right onto Mill Street, and then another right on Imi Kala Street into a baseyard with a number of blue roofs. One final left on to Wili Pa Loop, and you'll see a sign for the restaurant parking lot on your right.

Italian

Family-owned **(Giannotto's Pizza** (2050 Main. St., 808/244-5979, www.giannottospizza.com, 11am-9pm Mon.-Sat., 11am-8pm Sun., $7) serves up homemade Italian recipes "just like Mama used to make." Squirreled away into a small corner unit next to the hopelessly mediocre Main Street Food Court, this place is as authentic as the "Joisey" accents emanating from the kitchen, the mafioso photos on the wall, and the cheese pizza sold by the slice.

American

For good old-fashioned American barbecue, pop into **Bruddah Willy's Sticky Ribs** (1670 Honoapiʻilani Hwy., 808/243-7427, 11am-6pm Thurs.-Sat., $8-12) at the Maui Tropical Plantation. The biggest problem with this finger-lickin' take-out stand is that it's only open three days a week. The meat is soft, juicy, and falls off the bone.

Japanese

If there were an award for most popular restaurant in the ugliest location, then **Tokyo Tei** (1063 Lower Main St., 808/242-9630, 10:30am-1:30pm, 5pm-8:30pm Mon.-Sat., 5pm-8:30pm Sun., $10-17) would win it. Hidden deep within a dark parking garage in an industrial part of Wailuku, this family-run Japanese restaurant has been serving famous shrimp tempura dishes since 1935. It's consistently voted as the best Japanese cuisine on the island. Dishes include teriyaki steak, yakitori, and teishoku combination platters.

Thai

In Wailuku's funkiest corner, **(Saeng's Thai Cuisine** (2119 W. Vineyard St., 808/244-1567, 11am-2:30pm, 5pm-9:30pm Mon.-Fri., $9-12) offers surprisingly good food in a peaceful garden setting. The pad thai and curries are as authentic as they come. Pair your meal with a Singha beer or wine. The friendly service, peaceful setting, and authentic flavors make it a top pick.

Vietnamese

Sandwiched between a bridge and a low-income housing unit is one of Maui's most popular Vietnamese venues, **(A Saigon Café** (1792 Main St., 808/243-9560, 10am-9:30pm Mon.-Sat., 10am-8pm Sun., $9-15). The affordable clay pot dishes, with heaping mounds of rice, chicken, peas, and vegetables, have made this a Wailuku culinary staple. There are plenty of com dia rice plates, as well as pho, banh hoi, and Vietnamese soup. The portions are enormous, the place is always packed, and there's a full bar. If locals recommend eating at "Jennifer's," this is the place they mean. Parking can be a challenge.

Coffee Shops

Set in the heart of historic Market Street, **Wailuku Coffee Company** (26 N. Market St., 808/495-0259, 7am-5pm Mon.-Fri., 8am-3pm weekends, $5-8), is where—as the website claims—"the hip come to sip." The lounge atmosphere, free Wi-Fi (for an hour), and funky

MAUI

location contribute to the vibe. Breakfast includes ham, egg, and cheese bagels; lunch features "pitzas" served on pita bread.

Tours

Tour da Food (www.tourdafood.com) takes guests to tucked away mom-and-pop restaurants and introduces them to how "the other side of Maui" eats. Groups are capped at four people. Tours meet at the Kepaniwai Heritage Gardens up 'Iao Valley Road, where the guide, Bonnie, introduces you to the island's immigrant communities via the architectural monuments dedicated to each group's heritage. This is a fantastic outing if you're a fan of food tours and have a desire to delve deeper into the culture than booking a two-for-one luau.

Getting There and Around

CAR
Rental Cars
At the Kahului Airport, **Hertz** (808/893-5200), **Avis** (808/871-7575), **Budget** (808/871-8811), **Enterprise** (808/871-6982), **Alamo** (888/826-6893), and **Thrifty** (808/847-4389) all offer the standard corporate options for island rental cars. Other options in Kahului (which are usually cheaper) include **Maui Car Rentals** (181 Dairy Rd., 808/877-3300 or 800/567-4659, www.mauicarrentals.net), **Aloha Rent A Car** (190 Papa Pl., 808/877-2436 or 800/533-5929, www.mauirentacar.com), **Kimo's Rent A Car** (440 Alamaha St., 808/280-6327, www.kimosrentacar.com), and the budget service **Discount Hawaii Car Rental** (800/292-1930, www.discounthawaiicarrental.com).

The only reason you need a 4WD vehicle on Maui is if you decide to go hunting in Polipoli, fishing at some remote location, or venture onto soft sand. Many visitors spend a lot of money on 4WD (often double the price of a 2WD) and never end up using it. Rent a 4WD vehicle just for the day you need it.

MOTORCYCLE
If the idea of zipping oceanside on a massive Harley is your preferred method of getting from A to B, **Maui Harley Davidson** (150 Dairy Rd., 808/831-2614, www.hawaiiharleyrental.com, 9am-5pm daily) offers rentals from the Kahului shop only five minutes from Kahului Airport.

BUS
The Queen Ka'ahumanu Shopping Center is the central hub of the **Maui Bus,** and if you are connecting from one bus to another, there is a good chance that you'll end up making a stop at the mall. All segments on the bus cost $2/person (or $4/person for a day pass), and this is the terminus and starting point for routes heading up-country as well as to Kihei and Lahaina.

If you're just trying to get across town, buses on the Wailuku Loop (Route #1) make various stops around Wailuku and run hourly 6:30am-9:30pm. Similarly, buses on the Kahului Loop (Route #5) make various stops around Kahului and run hourly 6:30am-9pm. If you're trying to get to the Kahului Airport from Queen Ka'ahumanu, you have to get on the Upcountry Islander bus (Route #40) which runs every 90 minutes 6:10am-9:10pm. For more information, a full schedule, or to see routes to other parts of the island, you can visit www.mauicounty.gov and navigate to "For Residents" and then "Maui Bus."

SOUTH MAUI

If one word defines South Maui, it's "beaches." South Maui is graced with dozens of sandy stretches waiting for your footprints, including the island's longest beach, Sugar Beach, and one of its smallest, Pa'ako Cove. You could visit a different beach every day of a weeks-long vacation and still leave some areas untouched. Best of all, because much of South Maui faces

HIGHLIGHTS

LOOK FOR ◖ TO FIND RECOMMENDED SIGHTS, ACTIVITIES, DINING, AND LODGING.

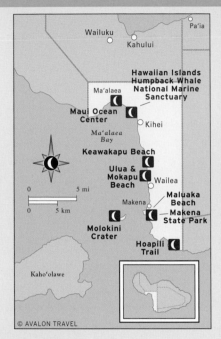

© AVALON TRAVEL

◖ **Maluaka Beach:** Maluaka Beach is the perfect place for a morning stand-up paddle along Makena's historic coastline (page 322).

◖ **Makena State Park:** There are actually three beaches within the state park, known to most locals simply as "Big Beach." The sunsets are legendary (page 322).

◖ **Molokini Crater:** The water inside this offshore caldera is some of the clearest in the world. The snorkeling ranks as some of the best in the state and the scuba diving is some of the best in the world (page 324).

◖ **Ulua Beach and Mokapu Beach:** These protected, sandy beaches offer friendly snorkeling conditions and an abundance of marine life (page 329).

◖ **Hoapili Trail:** This ancient footpath of kings meanders through the island's most recent lava flows. Wander deserted Hawaiian fishing villages whose stone foundations stand frozen in time (page 343).

◖ **Maui Ocean Center:** Surround yourself with sharks, eagle rays, and dozens of fish, all without getting your hair wet (page 348).

◖ **Hawaiian Islands Humpback Whale National Marine Sanctuary:** Learn about Maui's most exciting winter visitors with free educational displays in an oceanfront setting (page 350).

◖ **Keawakapu Beach:** While the northern end of Keawakapu Beach teems with activity, the southern expanse is a peaceful getaway for a blanket and a book (page 319).

west, the end of each day comes with a sunset that somehow surpasses the day before. It's the picture of paradise.

It's also one of the driest and hottest areas in the state. Mornings in South Maui are perfect for snorkeling or stand-up paddling, while the Maui Ocean Center in Ma'alaea provides the opportunity to explore Maui's underwater world regardless of the conditions outside.

Here the mega-resorts of West Maui give way to rows of condos, making South Maui one

of the fastest growing zip codes in the United States. The beaches of Kihei and Wailea are full of amenities. In the luxurious enclave of Wailea in particular, names such as Fairmont and The Four Seasons are paired with high-end shopping and dining.

Yet South Maui still has a wild side waiting to be explored. The far southern coastline is still rugged, with semi-nudist drum circles at Little Beach and walking trails that were once the footpaths of kings.

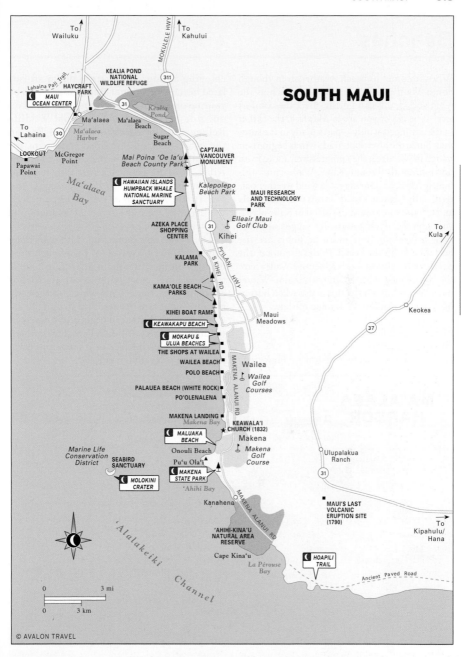

SOUTH MAUI

To Wailuku

To Kahului

MOKULELE HWY

311

KEALIA POND NATIONAL WILDLIFE REFUGE

Lahaina Pali Trail

HAYCRAFT PARK

MAUI OCEAN CENTER

31

Ma'alaea

Kealia Pond

Ma'alaea Beach

To Lahaina

30

Ma'alaea Harbor

Sugar Beach

CAPTAIN VANCOUVER MONUMENT

LOOKOUT

McGregor Point

Papawai Point

Mai Poina 'Oe Ia'u Beach County Park

To Kula

Ma'alaea Bay

HAWAIIAN ISLANDS HUMPBACK WHALE NATIONAL MARINE SANCTUARY

Kalepolepo Beach Park

MAUI RESEARCH AND TECHNOLOGY PARK

AZEKA PLACE SHOPPING CENTER

31

Kihei

Elleair Maui Golf Club

KALAMA PARK

S KIHEI RD

PIILANI HWY

KAMA'OLE BEACH PARKS

KIHEI BOAT RAMP

Maui Meadows

KEAWAKAPU BEACH

Keokea

37

MOKAPU & ULUA BEACHES

THE SHOPS AT WAILEA

WAILEA BEACH

Wailea

POLO BEACH

MAKENA ALANUI RD

Wailea Golf Courses

PALAUEA BEACH (WHITE ROCK)

PO'OLENALENA

MAKENA LANDING

Makena Bay

KEAWALA'I CHURCH (1832)

Marine Life Conservation District

MALUAKA BEACH

Makena

Makena Golf Course

Ulupalakua Ranch

SEABIRD SANCTUARY

Onouli Beach

Pu'u Ola'i

31

MOLOKINI CRATER

MAKENA STATE PARK

'Ahihi Bay

Kanahena

MAUI'S LAST VOLCANIC ERUPTION SITE (1790)

To Kipahulu/ Hana

'Alalakeiki

'AHIHI-KINA'U NATURAL AREA RESERVE

MAKENA ALANUI RD

Cape Kina'u

La Pérouse Bay

HOAPILI TRAIL

Ancient Paved Road

Channel

0   3 mi

0   3 km

MAUI

© AVALON TRAVEL

Beaches

When it comes to beach weather, even though South Maui is dry, other elements such as the wind and clouds can greatly affect the comfort level. The closer you are to Ma'alaea, the earlier in the day it gets windy—particularly in the summer. Since the afternoon trade winds begin their march in Ma'alaea, they progressively move from north to south through Kihei, Wailea, and ultimately Makena. During trade wind weather patterns, "the Makena cloud" forms over Haleakala and extends out toward the island of Kaho'olawe, although this doesn't normally happen until the early afternoon. The morning hours are the best time to hit the beach. In the afternoon, the pocket of beaches in south Kihei and Wailea have the best chance of being sunny and calm. Winter months aren't as windy; this is also when humpback whales can be seen leaping offshore.

MA'ALAEA
Sugar Beach
If your picture-perfect vision of Hawaii is enjoying a long, lonely stroll down an isolated beach, then **Sugar Beach** is going to be your favorite spot on the island. Bordered on one side by Kealia Pond National Wildlife Refuge and the waters of Ma'alaea Bay on the other, this undeveloped strip runs for five miles all the way to the condos of North Kihei. Nesting green sea turtles often haul out on the sand here to lay their eggs, and the Turtle X-ing signs which once graced the highway were the target of memorabilia thieves for years.

There isn't any snorkeling. Although there can sometimes be waves for boogie boarding during summer, the main attraction here is taking a long, quiet stroll. Most afternoons are marked by fierce trade winds, so the early morning hours are the best time to visit. To access Sugar Beach you can begin at the northern terminus at Haycraft Beach Park, the southern terminus in North Kihei, or at numerous entry points along North Kihei Road.

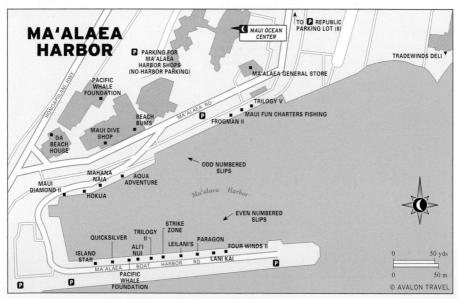

KIHEI
Mai Poina 'Oe la'u Beach Park

This beach is known as the "Kanaha of Kihei," due to the windsurfers who gather along the shoreline. In the morning this is a nice beach for a stroll, as it's much more tranquil than the fast pace of South Kihei. There isn't any swimming or snorkeling, though there are picnic tables and pavilions if you're thinking of having a picnic. This is also a nice place for stand-up paddling in the morning.

Kalepolepo Beach Park

Set on the northern edge of the headquarters for the Hawaiian Islands Humpback Whale National Marine Sanctuary (say that 10 times fast), **Kalepolepo Beach Park** is—from a historical perspective—Kihei's most underrated beach. What makes this little-visited enclave so special are the ancient Hawaiian fishponds. Masterfully restored in recent years by local volunteers, the fishponds were once reserved for royalty and the site of a native Hawaiian settlement. Historical placards within the park detail the area's rich cultural history. The fishponds also create a protected swimming area nice for small children. The snorkeling is murky and it isn't a great beach for swimming, but it's worth a stop while driving down South Kihei Road to look at the fishponds and get a feel for this unheralded part of town.

Waiohuli Beach

Even in ultra-crowded Kihei it's nice to know there are still some places you can stop and hear yourself think. Small, hidden, and forgotten, **Waiohuli Beach** is one of those spots. Not only is this beach rarely frequented by visitors, but locals hardly make it here either. There isn't any snorkeling and the water is too shallow for swimming, so what makes this beach great is the ability to sit on a sandy shoreline and hear nothing but the lapping of waves and intermittent gusts of wind. At the end of Waiohuli Road—a residential street next to the Kihei Veterinary Clinic—there is room to park next to the public beach access sign labeled number "117." *Limu* (seaweed) will often wash onto the

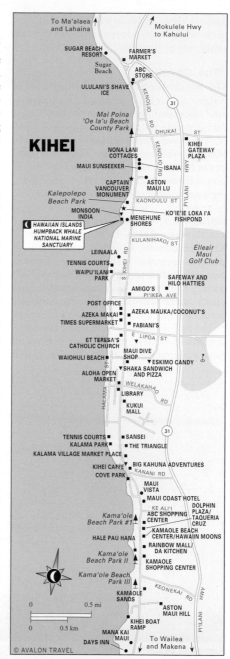

© AVALON TRAVEL

beach at high tide. If you walk to the north end of the beach at low tide you can follow the sand all the way to Waipuilani Beach Park.

"The Cove"

This popular surf spot at the far south end of Kalama Beach Park has a small horseshoe of sand where you can lay out in the sun. This is a great people-watching spot full of volleyball players, canoers, stand-up paddlers, and surfers. While it isn't the nicest beach in Kihei, if you're in the Kalama Village area and want to kill time at the beach while a family member shops, this small stretch of sand will do the trick.

Kamaole I, II, and III

The **Kamaole Beach Parks** form the core of Kihei's beach scene. Grassy areas run parallel to the roadway, and all of the parks have showers, restrooms, picnic tables, and barbecue grills for putting together a relaxing sunset meal. Kam I has a beach volleyball court on the north side of the park.

The best way to experience these beaches is to take a stroll along the coastline and link all three parks together. The lava rock headlands can be rough on your feet and kiawe trees drop thorns; wear footwear if you plan on walking all three beaches. The tidepools between Kam II and Kam III are a particularly nice place to explore. When you reach the southern end of Kam III, there's a walking trail that runs for 0.75 mile to the Kihei Boat Ramp.

Calm mornings are the best time for stand-up paddling and snorkeling; by noon the wind can pick up and turn the surface to whitecaps. Summers often have some shorebreak. Parking for Kam I and Kam II is at free spots curbside. Larger Kam III has its own parking lot dedicated exclusively for beachgoers. There is also overflow parking between Kam III and the boat ramp.

Sometimes you will hear locals say they enjoy spending time at **Charley Young Beach;** this is just another name for the northern end of Kam I. What's nice about this beach is that it's protected from the wind when the southern section of the beach is choppy. Parking for Charley Young is along Kaiau Place, which is a small offshoot of South Kihei Road not far from the Cove Park.

© KYLE ELLISON

Kamaole I beach

© KYLE ELLISON

sunset from Keawakapu Beach

◖ Keawakapu Beach

Outside of Kam III, **Keawakapu** is Kihei's most popular beach. This long, sandy stretch is more protected from the wind than the beaches farther north, and water sports are the name of the game. A small rental shop on the north end of the beach rents out stand-up paddleboards, kayaks, and snorkeling gear, and during the calm morning hours this beach is a bustle of activity. Snorkeling is best around the north and south headlands, while the sandy, gentle entry in the middle section of the beach is an enjoyable place to go for a quick swim. There is ample parking on the north end of the beach, and there is a lot off South Kihei Road on the north side of the Days Inn.

Compared to the north end of the beach, the south end is an oasis of calm. To reach the south end of Keawakapu you can either take a stroll down the length of the beach, or if you would rather drive, when South Kihei Road begins to head uphill toward the resorts of Wailea, continue driving straight until the road dead-ends in a small parking lot. There

aren't many spaces here, but there is a small shower for hosing off. As if two entrances weren't enough, there's also a central entrance to Keawakapu that's known as Sidewalks with public parking on the corner of Kilohana Drive and South Kihei Road.

WAILEA
Ulua Beach and Mokapu Beach

Ulua and Mokapu are the northernmost of Wailea's beaches, separated by a small, grassy headland. Mokapu is on the north side of the hill, Ulua is on the south, and the point that separates the two is one of the best spots for snorkeling in Wailea. Ulua is slightly larger than Mokapu and more protected from the surf. Mokapu Beach is also the northern terminus of the Wailea Coastal Walk, although the trail technically crosses the sand dune on Mokapu and continues down the beach to the southern end of Keawakapu. Restrooms and showers are available. A large public parking lot is at the bottom of Ulua Beach Road, just north of the Shops at Wailea.

Wailea Beach

Home to Maui's "see and be seen" crowd, **Wailea Beach** epitomizes Wailea. Fronted by the Grand Wailea and the Four Seasons Maui, this is a beach where corporate CEOs and professional athletes mingle with regular travelers. Beyond luxury, however, this beach is also characterized by fun. Wailea Beach buzzes with activity, and there's a trampoline for the kids, snorkeling around Wailea Point, stand-up paddleboard rentals, outrigger canoe tours, and dozens of visitors playing in the surf who are happy to just be spending a day on Maui. Despite the private nature of the resorts, public access to the beach is quite easy, as there is a large public parking lot just past the entrance for the Four Seasons. In the parking lot there are public restrooms and showers.

Polo Beach

Polo Beach is the southernmost of Wailea's resort beaches, and is the southern terminus of the Wailea Coastal Walk. The cloud-white Fairmont Kea Lani dominates the shoreline, its Arabian spires providing a unique backdrop to the shimmering blue waters. Of all of Wailea's beaches, Polo Beach is the most popular with locals due to the large public parking area being

Wailea Beach

© KYLE ELLISON

a convenient place for launching stand-up paddleboards and kayaks. There are public restrooms, showers, and one small barbecue grill. Polo Beach can also be good for boogie boarding in summer, and there is a small activity booth on the north side of the beach if you want to rent a paddleboard or kayak. To reach Polo Beach, travel south along Wailea Alanui Road before making a right on Kaukahi Street and following it to the end.

MAKENA AND BEYOND
Palauea Beach (White Rock)

If there were an official border between Wailea and Makena, then **Palauea Beach** would probably straddle it. Known to locals as White Rock, for decades this was a lesser-visited stretch of shoreline in an otherwise heavily developed area. Compared to a spot like Wailea Beach, however, Palauea is still mellow and empty. Similar in appearance to Keawakapu Beach in Kihei, this long stretch of sand is lined with private luxury homes. Parking for Palauea is along the side of Makena Road. Public access

paths scattered along the roadway lead through the kiawe trees and down to the beach. There's good snorkeling along both the north and south ends of the beach. If the nearby beaches of Wailea are too crowded and you want to find your own corner to relax in, Palauea is off the radar of most South Maui visitors. Since there aren't any facilities or showers, expect to track a lot of sand into your car on the drive home.

Po'olenalena Beach

Once frequented only by locals, **Po'olenalena Beach** can now get so busy it's tough to find a space in the potholed parking lot. Despite the lack of parking, however, the beach itself is big enough that it never feels too crowded. Volleyball enthusiasts will enjoy the pickup games on Sunday afternoons. Po'olenalena is also a local favorite for watching the sunset. The south end of the beach has more rocks than the north. There are public restrooms on the north side by the gravel parking lot.

To find Po'olenalena, travel on Wailea Alanui Road until you see Wailea Golf Club

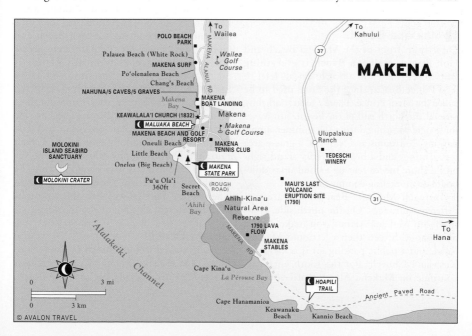

Drive on your left. Continue straight for one more minute and you will see the parking area for the beach on your right. To access the small public parking lot on the south side of the beach, look for the lot just before the Makena Surf on the right side of the road. Barely visible and only 10 spots large, it's next to the yellow fire hydrant numbered 614.

Chang's Beach

If you're looking for a tiny pocket of sand with exceptional snorkeling and not many people, then **Chang's Beach** will be your favorite spot in Makena. Not many make it to this beach because it's hidden from the road. Chang's Beach is about a mile and half past the Fairmont Kea Lani on Makena Alanui Road. Just look for the small parking lot immediately past the Makena Surf. If you find a spot in the parking lot *before* the Makena Surf building (the one by the fire hydrant 614), walk south for 100 yards past the gated entrance, and another small parking lot will be on your right. From here there is a small trail that leads down to the shore and the fingernail of sand.

◖ Maluaka Beach

Directly in front of the Makena Beach and Golf Resort, **Maluaka Beach** is everything you've ever wanted in a beach. Locals refer to it as Prince Beach, since the hotel used to be called the Maui Prince. There's good snorkeling around the north end of the beach, fun waves for boogie boarding during the summer, ample parking, restrooms and showers, a grassy area for relaxing, and a beach activity stand right on the shoreline for renting a stand-up paddleboard or snorkeling equipment.

To reach Maluaka Beach there are two different entrances. On the north side, coming in on Makena Alanui, you make a right on Honoiki Street, then a left onto Makena Road, and a public parking lot is across from Keawala'i Church. For the south entrance, continue on Makena Alanui until you pass the entrance for the Makena Beach and Golf Resort, continue past the turnoff for the golf and tennis club. As the road bends around to the right, you'll see another sign for Makena Road on your right. Make a right, and follow it all the way to the parking area.

◖ Makena State Park

Makena isn't short on shore. Despite the number of sandy getaways, however, one beach in particular will forever define the rugged beauty carefree spirit of Makena: **Big Beach,** also known by its Hawaiian name, Oneloa. Big Beach is one of the island's last beaches free of development. In addition to the undeveloped beauty, one of the biggest reasons locals visit Big Beach is for a shorebreak unlike anywhere else on the island. This is the most popular beach on the island for local bodyboarders. This is not the place for casual boogie boarding unless you are a professional. During times of big surf the rip currents can be strong, so unless it's completely flat, think twice before entering the water.

To reach Big Beach and Makena State Park, travel on Makena Alanui road for a mile past the entrance to the Makena Beach and Golf Resort. There are three different access points to the beach, conveniently known as First Entrance, Second Entrance, and Third Entrance. The first two have large parking areas, but Third Entrance (0.5 mile south of First Entrance) is just a dirt area on the side of the road. If you plan on going to Little Beach, the closest parking spot will be at First Entrance. Don't leave any valuables in your vehicle, as car break-ins have been known to be a problem. There are no showers at Big Beach. The nearest place to wash off the sand is at Maluaka Beach, a half a mile to the north.

Oneuli Beach

Sparsely visited **Oneuli Beach** is also part of Makena State Park, although it's nowhere near as scenic as neighboring Big or Little Beach.

© KYLE ELLISON

MAUI

Big Beach at Makena State Park

Although it is often referred to as the "black sand beach," the sand is more of a dark brown and nowhere near the deep black of the sand at Waiʻanapanapa Beach on the outskirts of Hana. This beach sits at the base of Puʻu Olai, the volcanic red hill towering over Makena, and there is good snorkeling off the left side of the beach on the calmest of days. This spot is popular with locals and a good place to get away from it all. To reach Oneuli Beach make a right turn off Makena Alanui Road 0.2 mile past the turnoff for Maluaka Beach and 0.2 mile before the first entrance to Big Beach. The entrance road is dirt and poorly paved.

Paʻako Beach (Secret Cove)
If you want to go back home and tell your friends you found the "secret beach" on Maui, then take the time to sniff out this gem. The problem, however, is that even though this is called **Secret Cove,** the tiny inlet of sand is anything but a secret. Weddings take place here on a daily basis, and the chances of having it all to yourself are slim. To access this beach, you need to walk through a hole in a lava rock wall just south of the Third Entrance for Big Beach. You need to pay attention to find the tiny opening. As you climb up and over a little hill where Big Beach ends, you will notice a lava rock wall running along the right side of the road. You will also notice raised speed tables on the road itself. Next to the second speed table you will see a blue Beach Access sign and a shoulder-width opening in the lava rock wall. If you're not sure if you're at the right spot, a telephone pole on the other side of the street has the code "E2 3" written on it. Parking is only along the ocean side of the road, but on many occasions (due to the popularity of the "secret" beach), it's easier to just park at the Third Entrance for Big Beach and walk the rest of the way.

Snorkeling

MA'ALAEA

Although you will often see little red dive flags fluttering in the wind off the harbor at **Ma'alaea Bay,** these are local spearfishers who are diving for *tako* (octopus). Don't mistake this for a nice snorkeling spot. Although Ma'alaea Bay once had a teeming reef prior to the 1990s, nearly 100 percent of it has died due to invasive algae species overcrowding the reef. It has been a case study for what will happen to all the island's reefs if environmental dangers go unmitigated.

C Molokini Crater

When it comes to snorkeling, what Ma'alaea is known for is the harbor that serves as the starting point for boats to **Molokini Crater,** a half-submerged volcanic caldera that rises from 300 feet of water. The reason Molokini is such a world-renowned dive destination is the fact that the visibility can stretch more than 100 feet on any day of the year. There isn't anywhere else in Hawaii where you can find water this clear. The deep crater isn't affected by breaking surf in the same way that the beaches along the coastline can be. Since only a tiny bit of Molokini rises out of the water, the amount of runoff after a period of rain isn't enough to affect water quality. Whereas the back of Molokini Crater drops off to almost 300 feet, the inside bowl where snorkel boats tie up is only about 40 feet deep, and the best snorkeling is along the rim of the crater in 15 feet of water. At Molokini you have a great chance of finding colorful parrotfish, endemic reef species, octopuses, eels, and—if you're lucky—maybe a harmless whitetip reef shark. One species notably absent from Molokini, however, are Hawaiian green sea turtles, although most tour operators combine a trip to Molokini with a second snorkeling spot along the coast of Maui so that you can check turtles off the list.

Snorkeling at Molokini is such a popular activity that it seems there are more humans in the water than fish. One of the best ways to avoid the mass of humanity is to get on the earliest boat you can. If you visited Molokini 20 years ago and are returning for another trip, you might notice there are fewer fish than the last time you were at the crater. The fish feeding that was a popular activity during the 1980s completely disrupted the area's natural food chain. The larger fish drove out the smaller fish, and a handful of species began to take over the entire reef. In an effort to return the crater to its former health, Molokini is now a tightly controlled marine preserve, and you will be required to fill out a form which outlines the rules for visiting. Boat trips from Ma'alaea take about an hour to reach the crater.

Boats to Molokini fall into three categories: small, medium, and large. The cheaper the ticket to Molokini, the more people there are going to be on the boat, which also means the more people there are going to be in the water snorkeling with you. The larger boats can have upward of 100 people on board during the busier months of the year. All of these large boats are diesel catamarans, but if you would prefer to sail on your excursion to Molokini, there are three sailboat companies that travel with 20-50 people on board.

Tree raft companies offer group sizes of no more than 24, which get you to Molokini quickly and easily. These trips can be economical, and the small groups ensure personalized service. However, the food won't be as good as on larger boats, and the bathroom situation can often be tight.

There are three departure points for reaching Molokini: Ma'alaea Harbor, Kihei Boat Ramp, and Maluaka Beach in Makena. Of the three departure points, nearly all boats leave from Ma'alaea Harbor. The only boats starting from Kihei Boat Ramp are the three rafts—Blue Water Rafting, Seafire, and Redline Rafting—as well as most scuba diving boats. In Makena, the sailing catamaran *Kai Kanani*

© HARRY HU/123RF.COM

snorkeling at Molokini

departs directly in front of the Makena Beach and Golf Resort, and its early trip is one of the first boats to arrive at Molokini.

Rental Shops

The best place for renting snorkel gear in Ma'alaea is at **Maui Dive Shop** (300 Ma'alaea Harbor Rd., 808/244-5514 www.mauidive-shop.com, 6am-6pm daily) in the Ma'alaea Harbor Shops. There is a wide range of snorkeling equipment for rent or purchase, and you can pick up an optical mask if you normally wear prescription glasses. Maui Dive Shop is affiliated with the *Ali'i Nui* sailing catamaran in the harbor just across the street, so you can often secure discounts on your rental gear if you end up combining it with a snorkeling charter (although snorkeling gear is provided on the boat free of charge).

Snorkeling Charters

Trilogy Excursions (Slip 62 and Slip 99, 808/874-5649, www.sailtrilogy.com) has been setting the gold standard for charter boats in

Maui for 40 years. At $120/adult their Molokini trip is pricier than the budget options, but you always get what you pay for. Trilogy boats only have 40-50 passengers, snuba is available as an upgrade, and since Trilogy has two catamarans in Ma'alaea Harbor, if you show up for your trip and the boat is empty, there's a good chance you just need to get the other side of the harbor. Trips depart at 8am, make stops at two snorkeling spots, and return to the harbor six hours later.

Paragon (Slip 72, 808/244-2087, www.sail-maui.com) offers a great trip for anyone whose priority is sailing, making only one snorkeling stop (almost always Molokini). The emphasis on the trip back toward Ma'alaea is racing at top speeds on their high-performance 47-foot catamaran. The boat can reach upward of 20 knots. There are only 20 or 30 people on the boat. Trips depart at 7:30am, are five hours long, and cost $100/adult.

Along with *Trilogy II* and *Kai Kanani* down in Makena, *Ali'i Nui* (Slip 56, 808/875-0333, www.aliinuimaui.com) is a sailing catamaran

What Every Molokini Visitor Needs to Know

Time of day is important. Molokini Crater is rarely accessible in the afternoon due to the trade winds blowing out of the north or the east. During about 80 percent of the year the trade winds are so strong that Molokini Crater is filled with four-foot wind waves by noon. This is why all of the boats leave early in the morning. So when you are presented with a discount tour to Molokini and you see it departs at 2pm (conditions permitting), understand that the conditions will only rarely be permitting. You might get lucky, but chances are you'll end up snorkeling at a spot named Coral Gardens along the Maui shoreline.

The ride back to Ma'alaea is going to be rough. For 80 percent of the year (and almost 100 percent of summer), the ride back to Ma'alaea Harbor is *very* rough. It's not dangerous; it's just that it's blowing 30 knots and sheets of sea spray coming over the bow. Some people love the ride; others are terrified. It's best to grab a protected seat toward the back of the boat and brace yourself.

Do you *really* need that wet suit? The water temperature in Maui fluctuates between 73 degrees in the winter to 79 degrees in the summer—colder than the Gulf of Mexico, but still warmer than most oceans around the world. If you go on one of the large diesel boats, you will be asked if you want to rent a wet suit. The crew receives a commission on wet suit rentals, so expect a sales pitch. Only spend extra money on a wet suit if you think you will actually need it.

There aren't any turtles at Molokini. Molokini Crater offers dozens of species of fish, impossibly clear water, and healthy, vibrant corals, but the one thing missing is green sea turtles. All of the turtles are found along the southern shoreline, so if you want to see some turtles, book a charter that stops along the shoreline.

Large surf means green turtles. Wait. Aren't turtles always green? This means that if there is large surf along the southern shoreline (more frequent in summer than winter), then the water color at Turtle Town will be closer to green than blue. If the visibility along the shoreline isn't what you expected, it's due to increased surf.

Molokini isn't always accessible. Molokini is inaccessible most afternoons due to the trade winds; if the wind is blowing out of the north then the crater isn't accessible in the morning either. Often this wind switch can occur within a matter of minutes, so there is a slight chance you might end up snorkeling at a Plan B spot, which usually still ends up being a good trip.

Don't feed the fish! Molokini Crater is a tightly controlled marine reserve. Feeding fish or stepping on coral can carry heavy penalties. Don't show up with a bag of frozen peas and expect to get away with it.

---

that edges closer to yacht than regular charter boat. With sleekly black and white trim, this 65-foot catamaran is also one of the island's widest at 36 feet, thereby ensuring a stable platform. *Ali'i Nui* is affiliated with Maui Dive Shop. While their snorkeling excursion is more expensive than the other excursions ($147/adult), they also include complimentary transportation to and from your hotel if you're staying on the west or south side of Maui. *Ali'i Nui* still offers scuba diving whereas other companies have switched to snuba. *Ali'i Nui*

visits Molokini three times per week (Tues., Thurs., and Sat.), opting on the other days to sail to Olowalu (or as they call it, "Turtle Point").

The company with the largest presence in Ma'alaea Harbor is **Pacific Whale Foundation** (300 Ma'alaea Boat Harbor Rd., 808/249-8811, www.pacificwhale.org), a nonprofit organization that has its headquarters in the Ma'alaea Harbor Shops. Instead of checking in down at the harbor, check in at their shop. These cruises are more economical than some of the higher-priced excursions, although on busier days you could potentially be sharing the boat with more than 100 fellow passengers.

There are four different options for trips to Molokini. The "standard" itinerary departs at 7am, features two snorkeling spots, and is currently listed at $85/adult. If you would rather sleep in a little bit and only want to see Molokini, the 9am Molokini Eco Express only lasts 3.5 hours at $55/adult. An 8:30am trip makes stops at both Molokini *and* at a bay off Lanaʻi ($95/adult), although this means spending *a lot* of time crossing the channel, which can often be rough on the way home. If you would prefer to be on a smaller vessel, the 7:30am Molokini Wild Side excursion costs $110/adult and spends a greater amount of time focusing on the marine and bird species found in the waters of South Maui.

The **Pride of Maui** (101 Maʻalaea Boat Harbor Rd., 808/242-0955, www.prideofmaui.com) offers a five-hour excursion aboard a large power catamaran for $96/adult. Trips depart at 8am from an area next to the U.S. Coast Guard station, although this is another popular boat that can frequently load over 100 passengers. During the summer and fall months (when it isn't whale season), there's also an afternoon snorkel trip to a location along the West Maui shoreline, which runs for 3.5 hours and is only $48/adult.

The **Four Winds II** (Slip 80, 808/879-8188, www.fourwindsmaui.com) catamaran offers both morning and afternoon excursions. Despite the fact that *Four Winds II* has a mast, often it's so windy in Maʻalaea Bay that the boat isn't able to sail. Small children will love the glass bottom part of the boat when stopped at Molokini, and unlike other boats which also make a stop along the shoreline, *Four Winds* makes Molokini its only stop so you have plenty of time to relax and explore the crater at your own pace. The downside of this, however, is that you won't get the chance to snorkel with turtles. The trip departs at 7am and costs $98/adult. There's also an afternoon charter at a much reduced price of $45, which

goes to a spot named Coral Gardens tucked out of the wind.

One of the cheapest trips to Molokini is on **Frogman II** (Slip 87, 888/700-3764, www.frogman-maui.com). *Frogman* offers excursions often tied in with a promotion at Boss Frog's charters, and as long as your expectations aren't too high, you can still have an enjoyable day on the water. The price for the morning trip is only $60/adult. *Frogman* also offers an afternoon trip at the cheap rate of only $30/adult, although it can only make it to Molokini on the rarest and calmest of afternoons. On most occasions *Frogman* ends up tying up next to *Four Winds II* at Coral Gardens, and while it might not be the same as Molokini, for that price you can't complain. If you want to upgrade to the next level of quality (but also upgrade the number of people on the boat), the sister boat is **Quicksilver** (Slip 44, 888/700-3764, www.frogman-maui.com), whose Molokini snorkeling trip visits two spots for $85/adult. While this trip is similar to those offered by the other large powerboats, what *Quicksilver* is known for is the semi-formal dinner cruise, which features live music. Rates for the dinner cruise are $70/adult, and the boat often tucks around the corner of West Maui to get a good angle on the sunset and hide from the wind.

If you want to visit Molokini from Maʻalaea but don't want to spend a lot of time getting there, **Aqua Adventure** (Slip 51, 808/573-2104, www.mauisnorkelsnuba.com) leaves at 7:30am and cruises at speeds much faster than the larger boats. The small passenger numbers are also a plus on this boat (they cap the number at 40), and snuba is the name of the game when it comes to getting people in the water. You can of course just choose to snorkel, but if your main priority is getting to Molokini quickly and snuba diving once you're there, this trip costs $105/adult for two snorkeling spots and is an additional upgrade for snuba.

A similar operation that features snuba and small crowds is **Lani Kai** (Slip 76,

808/244-1879, www.mauisnorkeling.com), a trip that departs at 7am and visits two snorkeling locations for $98. Lani Kai also has an afternoon charter, and for $44 you can cruise the cliffs over to Coral Gardens and tie up next to *Four Winds* and *Frogman,* with the difference being there are far fewer people on your boat than theirs.

The 58-foot **Mahana Nai'a** (Slip 47, 808/871-8636, www.maui-snorkeling-adventures.com) looks a little funny now that the mast from its sleek sailing days has been removed, but the family-run boat still chugs along, offering $90/adult snorkeling cruises to Molokini and the South Maui coastline.

KIHEI

Mornings are the best time of day for snorkeling in Kihei, and summer can have consistent winds and periods of surf, which affect visibility. Although the snorkeling in summer can still be enjoyable, winter mornings are the best bet for light winds and clear visibility, and as an added bonus, if you dive down a few feet while snorkeling, you're guaranteed to hear whale song reverberating in the distance.

Snorkeling Spots

North Kihei doesn't offer anything in the way of snorkeling because the water is too shallow and murky. The northernmost beach in Kihei where you would want to snorkel is **Charley Young** beach, which is also known as the north end of Kamaole I. There's a rocky point here on the right side of the beach that offers good snorkeling, although during periods of high surf it can become popular with boogie boarders. Down at the other end of the beach, the rocky point between **Kamaole I** and **Kamaole II** is another area where you can find reef fish, a few eels, and maybe even a Hawaiian green sea turtle. Similarly, the rocky point that separates Kamaole II from **Kamaole III** is another nice place for a morning snorkel.

A half-mile to the south of Kamaole III is **Keawakapu** beach, where there is good snorkeling on both the north and south side of the

bay. The north end can get crowded due to the large public parking lot and bustling activity stand, and during busier periods of the year you have a better chance of being kicked in the face than finding a turtle. Not many people follow the outer edge of this reef in front of the hotel, however, so if you want to escape the crowd, either get here early before everyone arrives or just snorkel to the far side where the crowds thin out. To combine a morning snorkel with a leisurely morning stroll, park at the northern end of Keawakapu Beach and walk to the southern point. There are fewer crowds, it's a larger area for snorkeling, and the walk back to your car is one of the best beach walks on the island.

Rental Shops

The streets of Kihei are covered in snorkel shops. Since choosing a shop can be overwhelming, it's important to understand the nature of the snorkel rental business on Maui. Most snorkel shops and activity stands in Kihei are fronts for activity sales and timeshare presentations, so you may hear a sales pitch for a helicopter ride or vacation rental when your intention is just to go snorkeling.

Top picks for rental shops in the South Maui area are the **Maui Dive Shop** locations sprinkled from Ma'alaea to Wailea. There are two different venues in Kihei (2463 S. Kihei Rd., 808/879-1533, www.mauidiveshop.com, 7am-9pm daily; 1455 S. Kihei Rd., 808/879-3388, 6am-9pm daily), and the corporate store in central Kihei opens at 6am. Maui Dive Shop also operates the *Ali'i Nui* catamaran, so there will be a sell on that particular activity, but *Ali'i Nui* is a beautiful boat that puts on a good trip, and you can frequently get discounts with a snorkel gear and snorkeling trip combo.

The other snorkel shop you'll see with just as much frequency is **Boss Frog's** (main office 1770 S. Kihei Rd., 808/874-5225, www.bossfrog.com, 8am-5pm daily), which has three locations scattered across Kihei. Boss Frog's offers the cheapest deals on snorkel rentals on the island, but the company is heavily embedded in the activities sales market, often timeshare-related. If you rent snorkeling gear for a week (which can be as low as $9), you will also get a discounted snorkeling trip on their boat out of Ma'alaea, the *Frogman II.*

Snorkel Bob's has multiple stores across Kihei, with one in the Kamaole Beach Center (2411 S. Kihei Rd., 808/878-7449, www.snorkelbob.com, 8am-5pm daily), and another in the Azeka II shopping area in Central Kihei (1279 S. Kihei Rd., 808/875-6188, 8am-5pm daily). Snorkel Bob's is a statewide chain that also incorporates activity sales, and you're sure to see their quirky ads if you flip through any island visitor magazines. Snorkel Bob's is known for selling gear that they design themselves, and a nice feature of the operation is that you can rent gear on one island and return it on another island completely free of charge. Packages range from $2/day for a basic mask and snorkel rental to $44/week for a package that includes prescription lenses and fins.

Snorkeling Boats

While most of the boats leaving from Kihei Boat Ramp are scuba diving charters, there are still a few rafting boats that focus on sightseeing and snorkeling. They only carry about 24 people, so if you don't like crowds and just want a mellow, informative day on the water, these are going to be the trips for you.

Of all the rafting options, the top pick is **Blue Water Rafting** (808/879-7238, www.bluewaterrafting.com), which meets at the boat ramp at 6:30am. If you've already been to Molokini once before and are looking for an adventure snorkel, Blue Water Rafting has a trip to the Kanaio Coast where you can snorkel along a rugged volcanic coastline most visitors will never get to see. This forgotten southwestern coastline is pockmarked with thundering sea caves and jagged lava formations, and there are multiple places where you can see the remnants of ancient fishing villages. The captains are geologists, historians, and marine naturalists all rolled into one. They're skilled enough to hug the coast so closely you could almost reach out and touch it. The waters in this area

can often be rough, however, so this isn't the best trip if you're prone to motion sickness. You can either book the four-hour Kanaio Coastline tour from $100/adult and $79/child, or you can combine it with an 11am excursion to Molokini for $125/adult and $100/child. If you only want to book a two-hour tour to Molokini, the cost is $50/adult and $39/child and it departs at 11:30am. This is one of the most affordable options for visiting the crater if all you're looking for is a ride there and back. There is no breakfast, coffee, or bathroom on board.

The other primary snorkeling option from Kihei Boat Ramp is **Redline Rafting** (808/757-9211, www.redlinerafting.com), which also offers tours to Molokini and the Kanaio Coast. Tours meet at 6:30am, and at $140/adult and $100/child the cost is a little higher than Blue Water Rafting, but they also include breakfast and coffee and have a (small) bathroom on board. Although they are still one of the only boats that traverses the Kanaio Coast, they don't go as far down the coast as Blue Water, spending more time in Makena and Molokini.

If you've always wanted to look like you're in the U.S. Coast Guard, **Seafire** (808/879-2201, www.molokinisnorkeling.com) offers a trip at 7:30am on its orange and silver jet-drive raft that not only looks like a Coast Guard boat, but is driven by a member of the Coast Guard Reserve. Trips last for three hours. At $55 it's one of the best budget options for reaching Molokini Crater.

WAILEA
🄲 Ulua Beach and Mokapu Beach

The best two locations for snorkeling in Wailea are **Ulua Beach** and **Mokapu Beach,** which are listed together because the rocky point that separates them is where you'll find the most marine life and coral. Ulua (the southernmost of the two) is more protected and offers a gentle, sandy entry. This is the perfect spot for beginning snorkelers. Morning hours are calm and the best time for finding turtles. As at neighboring Kihei, winter is guaranteed to offer the best visibility. If you're staying at one of the Wailea resorts, you can reach the beaches by strolling along the Wailea Coastal Walk. If you are driving, there are two small public parking lots which can fill up early; arrive before 9am. To reach the parking area, turn on Ulua Beach Road off Wailea Alanui Drive just north of the Shops at Wailea, and follow the road down until the parking lots at the end.

Wailea Point

The second most popular spot for snorkeling in Wailea is **Wailea Point,** a rocky promontory rife with green sea turtles that separates the Four Seasons and Fairmont Kea Lani. The easiest point of entry is from the south side of Wailea Beach in front of the Four Seasons. You'll notice some people trying to enter and exit the water by launching off the point itself, and while this can be efficient, it's also a great way to slip on the rocks or have a wave wash you into some sea urchins. Entering from the beach is the safest bet, although be prepared for a five-minute swim over sand.

Rental Shops

Inside the Shops at Wailea there's a **Maui Dive Shop** (3750 Wailea Alanui Rd., 808/875-9904, www.mauidiveshop.com, 8am-9pm daily) which is similar to the other stores throughout South Maui. The staff can offer good advice on snorkeling locations, it's within walking distance of many of the hotels, and the rental prices will be cheaper than what the activity booth stands will charge inside the resorts.

MAKENA AND BEYOND

As you move south from Wailea to Makena, you'll notice that the terrain becomes just a little more raw. While Makena offers some of the south side's best snorkeling, the entry and exit points can be a little more challenging than at Kihei or Wailea beaches. Makena is a little more exposed to southerly swell than the beaches to the north are, so not only is visibility affected, but the waves can sometimes crash into the lava rocks with such a fury it's the last place you would want to find yourself. High surf is most typical in summer. During winter, nearly every day will be flat and calm.

Snorkeling Spots

The best place for beginner-level snorkeling in Makena is **Maluaka Beach** in front of the Makena Beach and Golf Resort. There's a rocky point that wraps around the north end of the beach, and the entry from the sand into the water is gentle and forgiving.

While Maluaka might be the *easiest* place to snorkel in Makena, the best snorkeling overall can be found at **Makena Landing.** Getting in the water can be a little challenging here, but once you make it out past the shallow areas, you'll be glad you made the effort. There are multiple entry and exit points for Makena Landing, the most common of which is the public parking area off Makena Road. To reach the parking area, drive along Makena Alanui until you reach Honoiki Street and the turn for Keawala'i Church. When you reach the bottom of Honoiki, turn right, and follow the road for a quarter of a mile until you see a parking area on your left. Once in the water, hug the coastline as it wends its way around the rocky point to the north, and when you have rounded the tip, you'll notice there is a long finger of lava underwater that extends out toward Molokini. This is what's known as the South Finger, and there's a sea cave here that houses green sea turtles. This area is often referred to as Turtle Town by many of the snorkel boat operators, and unless you want to share the water with 200 other snorkelers, try to be out here before 10am when all of the Molokini charter boats begin mooring offshore. If you swim north from the South Finger, you will pass over lime green coral heads. Keep an eye out for moray eels or the strange-looking flying gurnard. Eventually, you'll come to the North Finger, another underwater lava formation that houses many turtles. This finger is often covered in bright red slate-pencil urchins that the ancient Hawaiians would use for red dye, and eagle rays and manta rays are sometimes seen off the deeper end of the finger.

An alternate entry point for Makena Landing is via the north side at a spot known as **Five Graves.** Parking is scarce here, and the entry can be challenging, but it's a much shorter swim to reach the fingers. The beach access is tough to find, however, so you need to pay close attention. Instead of turning into the parking lot on Makena Road, continue driving up and over the hill. When the road drops back down to the shoreline, you'll notice a dirt area on the right that can fit about five cars. Park here. On the other side of the street you'll notice a small trail. You'll know this is the right path if you see five graves in a small graveyard on the left. Follow this trail to the shoreline. The easiest place to get in and out of the water is a protected nook in the rocks on your right. Although the beach area to the left of the trail looks like it would be the easiest, it's shallow for a long way out, and you don't want to contend with the breaking waves. On calm days this is the quickest means of reaching the fingers.

Moving south, there are a few places that offer decent snorkeling inside **Makena State Park,** the best of which is the point that separates Big Beach from Little Beach. The best thing to do is to park in the first entrance to Big Beach and turn right when you hit the sand. This will bring you to the far northern end of the beach where you can enter the water to snorkel around the point. The surf can get big here in the summer, so this is only possible on a flat day. For more direct access to the reef, clamber up and over the hill to Little Beach and snorkel in the cove off the left side of the bay. If there are waves in the bay, however, it's best to go elsewhere because this will put you right in the path of oncoming boogie boarders.

Some say that the best snorkeling in South Maui is at **Ahihi Kinau.** But once popular spots such as the Fishbowl and the Aquarium are closed to the general public until 2014—and potentially longer. The only place where you can still snorkel in the Ahihi Kinau Natural Area Reserve is a small cove a mile past Pa'ako Beach (Secret Cove). Even though the parking situation here can be abysmal, the snorkeling warrants the effort. If you're not sure if you're at the right place, the house number of the large estate just past the cove is 7750 and it has a large lava rock wall in front of it. While this cove is not within the dramatic lava flow like the other Ahihi spots, it is still a scenic area for finding reef fish and green sea turtles. Entry into the water can be difficult since you need to go over lava rocks, so on days when there are waves breaking all the way into the cove, find somewhere else to snorkel.

On the other side of the hill from the Ahihi Kinau snorkeling area is a cove that's referred to simply as **Dumps.** There's a small gravel parking lot here just before the road begins its trek across the lava flow, and a short five-minute trail leads down to a rocky beach. While the snorkeling here can be good at times, there isn't that much more to find here that you can't see at any other South Maui snorkeling spot. The waves can get *very* large in summer, and you only want to snorkel here if the conditions are completely calm. To reach Dumps, travel 1.6 miles past the first entrance for Big Beach. Don't leave valuables in your car; break-ins are an ongoing problem.

Finally, just when you think that the road will never end, the asphalt gives way to a gravel parking lot in a spot known as **La Perouse Bay.** The lava field that you drive over en route to La Perouse is the remnants of Haleakala's last eruption. The bay is named for the French explorer Jean Francois de Galaup Compte de La Pérouse, who in 1786 was the first European to set foot on the island of Maui in this very spot. As you enter the parking area, there's a stone structure memorializing this event.

The snorkeling in La Perouse Bay can be phenomenal, although there are also times when it can be a total bust. Early mornings are best before the trade winds fill the bay with whitecaps, and summer can bring large surf, which turns the shoreline into a cauldron of white water. On calm days, however, the best snorkeling is found to the right of the parking lot where you must scramble across a lava rock point to reach the protected inlet. The water here is an enchanting color of turquoise against the young black lava rock.

Rental Shops

If you make it all the way down to Makena and realize that you left your mask back in your hotel, you can still rent equipment for the day at the beach activities center in front of the Makena Beach and Golf Resort.

Snorkeling Boats

Kai Kanani (808/879-7218, www.kaikanani. com) is the only option for snorkeling boats leaving from Makena. Only a few years old and still sparkling, it has all the added amenities you would expect from a luxury yacht with top-notch captains. *Kai Kanani* departs directly from Maluaka Beach in front of the Makena Beach and Golf Resort, which, if you're staying in Makena, makes it a far more convenient option for sailing to Molokini than driving all the way to Ma'alaea Harbor. If Molokini was too crowded the last time you visited, *Kai Kanani*'s early-morning Molokini express charter ($63/ adult) departs the beach at 6:30am and guarantees you're the first boat at the crater. This trip is just over two hours long, and while its second trip of the day ($138/adult) visits the crater when it's far more crowded, the fact that it's four hours long as opposed to two allows for twice the amount of snorkeling time. If you're concerned about getting seasick, the journey time from Maluaka Beach to Molokini is much shorter than the journey between Molokini and Ma'alaea.

Scuba Diving

South Maui has some of the island's best shore diving. With so many locations and so many different operators, planning your dives can be overwhelming. The following information should help you match your ability level with the operations and locations that suit you the best.

MA'ALAEA
Dive Sites

While **Molokini Crater** can be a great place to snorkel, to truly tap into the magic of the crater you need to put a tank on your back and go and see what's down there. For experienced divers, Molokini ranks in the upper echelon of dive locations around the world. For novice divers who have just been certified, it's a window into a new aquatic universe. Only certified divers are allowed to dive at Molokini Crater. If you aren't certified but still want to experience Molokini from below, sign up for a 20-minute snuba dive to depths of up to 10 feet.

What makes the crater such an exceptional dive spot is the combination of two different factors: Its pelagic location means there is the possibility of seeing anything, and there are multiple dive spots within the crater that cater to a wide range of ability levels. Novice divers will want to inquire about trips that go to either Middle Reef or Reef's End, as depths on these dives don't usually exceed 70 feet. Middle Reef is home to large schools of pelagic species such as jacks and reef sharks, and the sand channel houses curious-looking garden eels. There's also a huge drop-off at the Middle Reef section where it can be easy to exceed your dive profile, so keep an eye on your depth gauge when swimming over the ledge. Similarly, at Reef's End, the dive traces the wall of the underwater caldera to the point where it drops off into the abyss. Since this underwater promontory sits on the fringe of the crater, this is the area with the best chance of sightings of bottlenose dolphins, manta rays, humpback whales, and even the occasional whale shark. While Middle Reef and Reef's End are both fantastic dives, the best and most advanced dive in Molokini Crater is a drift dive of the legendary Back Wall. Beginning at Reef's End, divers will follow the current along the back of Molokini, where a vertical wall drops over 250 feet to the ocean floor below. If you're the type of diver who dabbles in nitrox or mixed gases, this is the deepest dive available anywhere in Maui County, although you should still stay within the recreational dive limit of 145 feet.

Even though diving at Molokini offers

a chance of seeing sharks, if you want a 100 percent guarantee of diving with sharks, the most unique dive on the island is offered at the **Maui Ocean Center** where you can go diving *inside the shark tank.* As part of its Shark Dive Maui program, certified divers are able to spend 30-40 minutes surrounded by various species of sharks, some of which can include hammerhead and tiger sharks. The dive has a maximum limit of four divers, costs $199, and is only offered on Monday, Wednesday, and Friday mornings. The cost includes the tank and the weight, although divers will need to provide the rest of their gear. Although diving at an aquarium might seem like cheating, even some of Maui's most seasoned divers claim it's a great dive. More than just a novelty, this is your best opportunity to be completely surrounded by the ocean's most feared and misrepresented creatures.

One of the island's newest wreck dives is a **Helldiver** WWII airplane which was abandoned by a pilot on a training run off Sugar Beach. When the pilot ejected, his plane sank in 50 feet of water, and for the better part of 60 years this plane sat forgotten in the mudflats off Ma'alaea. When a local fisher tipped off a Kihei dive instructor that there was probably something down there, the exploratory dive mission yielded a historical discovery which is now property of the U.S. military; divers aren't allowed to touch or enter the aircraft. While there isn't an overwhelming amount of marine life here, this is a unique dive you won't find in many people's logbooks. There aren't any regularly scheduled trips to the Helldiver, but many South Maui operators periodically plan excursions to the site, so inquire about when the next outing might be.

Rental Operators

The only retail operator in Ma'alaea that rents out dive gear is **Maui Dive Shop** (300 Ma'alaea Harbor Rd., 808/244-5514, www.mauidive-shop.com, 6am-6pm daily) in the Ma'alaea Harbor Shops. Although most dive operations will furnish their own gear, this is a good place to pick up equipment if you're diving at the

Maui Ocean Center, are planning a dive off a nearby shoreline, or need some accessories such as a flashlight or a knife.

Dive Boats

Although most Molokini dive boats depart from the Kihei Boat Ramp, two that depart from Ma'alaea Harbor are the 48-foot **Maka Koa,** which is operated by Maui Dive Shop (808/875-1775, www.mauidiveshop.com), as well as the 40-foot **Maui Diamond II** (Slip 23, 808/879-9119, www.mauidiamond.com). Maui Dive Shop offers two-tank trips to Molokini Crater three times per week, and the second dive is either along the shoreline of Maui or at the St. Anthony wreck off Kihei. Rates for a two-tank dive are $139, and BC and regulator rental is an additional $20. Snorkelers are allowed to accompany divers for a reduced rate of only $80, and this is a good option for the novice to intermediate diver who wants to explore in the 65-70 feet range. In addition to providing a good trip, an added perk of booking with Maui Dive Shop is that they provide complimentary transportation from your hotel to Ma'alaea Harbor. If you're driving yourself to the harbor, check-in is at 6:30am at the store in the Ma'alaea Harbor Shops.

For a few dollars less, *Maui Diamond II* offers 2-tank trips to Molokini and the South Maui shoreline for $129, and BC and regulator rental is an additional $15. If you aren't a certified diver, you have the option of partaking in a Discover Scuba Diving introductory class in which you will snorkel at Molokini and then dive with an instructor at the second spot along the shoreline. The rate for the snorkel and introductory dive combo is $145, although the price is inclusive of all your equipment.

KIHEI
Dive Sites

The only real dive site in Kihei is the **St. Anthony Wreck** off the south end of Keawakapu Beach. Maui Dive Shop offers dives to this part of a massive artificial reef system twice weekly as part of a two-tank excursion combined with Molokini.

MAUI

Rental and Shore Dive Operators

If you're a certified diver who needs to rent some gear, get some gear serviced, pick up some tanks for a shore dive, or book a guided shore dive with an instructor, there are a number of different retail operators throughout Kihei. My top pick in Kihei is **Maui Dreams** (1993 S. Kihei Rd., 808/874-5332, www.mauidreamsdiveco.com, 7am-6pm daily) in the shop across from the southern end of Kalama Park. These guys *love* to dive, and they offer a full range of excursions from scooter dives ($99) to night dives ($79) to regular introductory dives if it's your first time trying the sport ($89). Guided shore dives for certified divers are $69. Maui Dreams is also the only PADI 5-Star Instructor Development Center in South Maui. At $399 the certification courses are more expensive than others, and it's $499 if you haven't already completed the academic portion online (PADI E-learning).

Inside the Azeka Makai shopping center on the ocean side of the highway, **B&B Scuba** (1280 S. Kihei Rd., 808/875-2861, www.bbscuba.com, 8am-6pm Mon.-Fri., 8am-5pm weekends) offers guided shore dives for only $59, and they can also arrange a guided kayak dive to some of the spots which would normally only be accessible by boat. They also offer night dives ($65) as well as scooter dives ($119) along the South Maui shoreline. Whereas some other operators in town focus strictly on recreational diving, these guys are a little more hardcore. In addition to offering PADI certification classes ($349), they also offer IANTD tech diving classes such as trimix, nitrox, and rebreather training. They provide basic gear rental and tank pumping.

Check out **Scuba Shack** (2349 S. Kihei Rd., 808/891-0500, www.scubashack.com), which is tucked behind the gas station across from Kamaole I Beach. Guided dives are pricier here. Certified divers can book a guided shore dive for $85, whereas introductory divers will need to shell out $105. Certification classes last three days and are $350, and the shop also offers a full range of gear and equipment rentals.

Dive Boats

All dive boats in Kihei leave from Kihei Boat Ramp, which is just south of Kamaole III Beach. Parking is tight in the main lot, so it's best to head to the overflow lot on the right. The scene at the boat ramp in the morning can be kind of hectic—especially in the dark. Most boats offer coffee aboard their trips if you still need a wakeup, and most boats also offer private bathrooms if the coffee just goes right through you. Since a number of boats that leave from Kihei Boat Ramp don't have offices, bring a credit card or cash so you can process payment on board. If you plan on diving during your time in Maui, bring your certification card.

Of all the choices in Kihei, the unanimous top pick among island locals is always **Mike Severn's** (808/879-6596, www.mikesevernsdiving.com), Kihei's original dive boat operation. Although a number of the other operators in Kihei all provide exceptional service, it's impossible to beat Mike Severn's. Since Mike Severn's caters to seasoned divers, the instructors don't mandate an underwater game of "follow the leader." They give you the freedom to enjoy the dive at your own pace. Two-tank dives are $130 (plus $15 BC, regulator, and computer rental), and dives meet at 6am at the Kihei Boat Ramp aboard the 38-foot *Pilikai*.

Pro Diver (808/875-4004, www.prodiver-maui.com) is one of the last dive boats to cap its trips at only six divers (whereas other boats will usually max at 12 divers with two instructors). The small group size guarantees a personal experience, and their 34-foot boat meets at 6am at Kihei Boat Ramp. Two-tank dives are offered at $139, and it's an additional $15 for gear rental in the event you don't have your own.

Also ranking among the South Maui elite, **Ed Robinson's** (808/879-3584, www.mauiscuba.com) caters to advanced divers and underwater photographers. If you're afraid you're going to get stuck with a group of greenhorns, you can confidently sign on with Ed Robinson's and know that everyone aboard is relatively skilled. Meet at 6:30am at the Kihei Boat Ramp. Regular two-tank dives are offered Monday, Thursday, and Saturday for $129. More advanced two-tank drift dives are offered Sunday and Friday for the same price. A three-tank dive on Tuesday departs on a different boat. Experienced divers can join an Adventure X dive on Wednesday for $149. Ed Robinson's has a shop in central Kihei in an industrial yard at 165 Halekuai Street that also serves as a dive museum.

In addition to offering shore dives and rental options, **B&B Scuba** (1280 S. Kihei Rd., 808/875-2861, www.bbscuba.com) also has a dive boat, which does two-tank dives out of Kihei Boat Ramp aboard the 40-foot *Kilikina II*. When it comes to diving, these guys don't screw around; they're out on the water by 5:45am, and since the goal is to beat all of the crowds and get an early start, it's frowned upon to show up late. The payoff for the early wakeup, however, is that you reach your first dive site before any other boats are around, and if that first dive site is Molokini, there is a certain magic to having the solitude most visitors will never get to experience. You're usually back to the dock by 10am. The wallet-friendly price of $119 is also a strong selling point.

Two outfits focusing primarily on recreational divers are **Makena Coast Dive Charters** (808/874-1273, www.mauiunderwater.com) and **Scuba Shack** (808/891-0500, www.scubashack.com). Both have boats leaving from Kihei Boat Ramp, offering one dive at Molokini and one dive along the South Maui shoreline.

WAILEA
Dive Sites
Unlike Ma'alaea or Kihei, which only serve as departure points for diving elsewhere, Wailea offers shore dives with shallow depths perfect for novices. The entry points in Wailea are sandy and easy. Of all the beaches in Wailea, the best for a morning shore dive is the point at **Ulua Beach.** This is where most dive operators bring students during their certification courses, as the maximum depth is about 35 feet. There is ample parking at the bottom of Ulua Beach Road, and the concrete walkway down to the shoreline is convenient for hauling tanks and gear. Although the dive wraps around the point toward Mokapu Beach, it's best to enter and exit the water from the Ulua side since it's more protected from wind and waves. Expect to see a number of Hawaiian green sea turtles along with healthy coral formations, endemic reef fish, and perhaps a rare spotted eagle ray or spiny lobster.

Although most dive operations operate off Ulua Beach, if you're renting your own gear, you can dive at **Wailea Point.** Entry for the dive is off the south side of Wailea Beach. This is a great place for seeing turtles on days with clear visibility (which are more common in winter than summer). The nearest public access and parking lot are on the south end of the Four Seasons resort.

Rental Operators
The only dive shop in Wailea is **Maui Dive Shop** (3750 Wailea Alanui Rd., 808/875-9904, www.mauidiveshop.com, 8am-9pm daily) within the Shops at Wailea. You can pick up dive-related accessories and inquire about current conditions. If you're in need of gear and tank rental, you're better off visiting one of the larger outlets in Kihei.

MAKENA AND BEYOND
Dive Sites
In addition to being one of the best shore dives in Makena, **Nahuna/Makena Landing/5 Caves/5 Graves** also takes the cake as the spot with the greatest number of names. As if four names weren't enough already, this general area is also referred to as Turtle Town by many charter boat operators, which was concocted to sell snorkeling tours. Each of the many monikers is accurate for different reasons: Geographically, the dive lies within the Makena Landing area and is close to Makena Landing park. There are multiple caves here where sea turtles and whitetip reef sharks often hang out, all accessible to divers. You walk right past five tombstones if you choose to use the northern beach access. Nahuna is the Hawaiian name for this area.

MAUI

What makes this dive so fantastic is not only the turtles, but also pelagic species such as manta rays, spotted eagle rays, bottlenose dolphins, and large ʻawa. Throughout the winter, divers are surrounded by whale song. There can also be nudibranchs, harlequin shrimp, flying gurnards, slate pencil urchins, and a wide range of eels. On calm days the visibility can often reach 100 feet, although on days where there is a south swell (usually in the summer), visibility can be reduced to 20 feet at best.

While many dive boats frequent this area, the easiest place to enter from shore is the parking lot by Makena Landing park. Once in the water, turn to the right and follow the coastline until you reach a long finger of lava. This is what's known as the South Finger, and the depth here is only about 15 feet. Follow the South Finger away from the shoreline, and halfway to the end you will notice a large cave, which you can swim through from below. There are numerous turtles that hang out in here, and there is almost always a whitetip reef shark under a ledge. Emerging on the other side of the cave, you can kick your way parallel to the shoreline across a field of peculiar coral formations, whereby you will eventually reach the North Finger after three minutes of swimming. If you somehow haven't seen a turtle yet, there is another large cave on the north side of this finger where turtles are known to hang out.

Since this area is popular with charter boats, arrive early before the crowds and always dive with a dive flag. For an alternate entry on calm days, park at the small beach access on Makena Road on the north side of the hill past Makena Landing park. There will be a few dirt parking spaces on the right, and the small beach access trail that leads past the five graves.

Another nice shore dive is the **Ahihi Kinau** cove 1.5 miles past the first entrance for Big Beach. The depth here goes to about 40 feet. Since this cove is protected from the wind, it offers pristine diving conditions as long as the surf isn't up. Expect to find green sea turtles and the rare spinner dolphin if you're on the outer edge of the reef. The entry into the water can be tricky since you have to navigate your way over slippery rocks, but you don't need to worry about boats in this cove, although it can often be packed with snorkelers as the morning wears on, making parking an issue.

Surfing

If you look at a map of South Maui, you'll notice that much of it actually faces west. This means that South Maui can get waves at any time of year. It's the southwest swells of summer that bring the best waves, but large northwest winter swells can also wrap into select areas to provide the occasional out of season surf. If you're a complete beginner, the only spot in South Maui you should attempt to surf is The Cove in South Kihei, but if you're an intermediate or advanced surfer, there are other spots to check out.

MAʻALAEA
Realistically, the chances of you surfing in Maʻalaea during your time on Maui are slim, because most of the breaks are either way too fickle or way too advanced. Maʻalaea is one of the few spots on Maui that actually faces almost due south, which means that summer is the only time there will be waves.

Surf Spots
The most consistent wave in Maʻalaea is a spot known as **Off the Wall.** This is an A-frame, shifty peak that breaks directly in front of the harbor wall, and you can usually only surf here in the morning hours before the afternoon trade winds start howling. To access Off the Wall, park in the dirt parking area between Buzz's Wharf restaurant and the beginning of the harbor breakwall. From this little corner of harbor the paddle out to the peak is easy, and it beats jumping off the breakwall

and clambering over the slippery rocks. Expect short but fun rides, and while it isn't the best break in all of South Maui, it's at least a nice place to get wet.

Half a mile up the highway when you're headed toward Lahaina is **McGregor Point,** a right-hand point break that's a poor man's Honolua Bay. Although McGregor's rarely gets bigger than head-high, the spot can offer a long wave and is best surfed in the morning before the wind comes up. Parking for McGregor's is in a dirt lot on the road heading toward the lighthouse. Be careful when pulling off the highway because it can be a sketchy turn. To get down to the shoreline you have to clamber down a thin, steep trail, which can be tough if you're surfing with a longboard.

Rental Shops

The only rental shop for surfboards in Ma'alaea is **Da Beach House** (300 Ma'alaea Rd., 808/986-8279, www.dabeachhousemaui. com, 10am-5:30pm daily) inside the Ma'alaea Harbor Shops. Surfboards rent for $25/day or $75/week, and there are stand-up paddleboards for $40/day or $125/week. There are also boogie boards and beach chairs, and this is a good place to pick up a board if you're planning on surfing some of the beginner breaks on the road toward Lahaina. Since most of the boards are of the "soft top" variety which caters to beginner surfers, however, there isn't anywhere within Ma'alaea itself that you could ever hope to use one.

KIHEI
Surf Spots

The surf epicenter for all of Kihei is **The Cove** park, at the southern end of Kalama Park. This is where all of the surf schools give lessons, and while the waves are gentle, the downside is that it can get ultra-crowded. On some days you'll swear you could walk on water across all of the longboards crammed into the small area, but in the early morning hours before all the surf schools show up, there is still a fun (albeit small) wave. If your goal in Hawaii is to try surfing for the first time, then this is where you'd come.

If the Cove gets too crowded and you've progressed past the beginner stage, just to the north is a peak known as **Kalama Bowls** that you could almost reach by paddling from the Cove. Some people just paddle out from the rocks in front of Kalama Park, and while the wave is better here (and less crowded), the water can get murky and it's more exposed to the wind.

For intermediate or advanced level surfers, the best wave in Kihei is an A-frame that breaks next to the **Kihei Boat Ramp.** This is a fickle wave that needs a big southwest or west swell to start working, and you need to be careful of the boat traffic coming in and out of the harbor area. Access can be a little tricky since you're asked to not walk in the sand dune area that runs along the shoreline. If you're on a longboard and are up for a paddle, you could always paddle from the far southern tip of Kamaole III Beach.

Shortboarding in Kihei can be found at **Sidewalks** on the south-central end of Keawakapu Beach. This is a beach break that offers a fast wave, and the vibe here isn't nearly as strong as at the boat ramp or farther south. Nevertheless, it's still an intermediate wave that isn't suitable for longboards or beginners. Parking for Sidewalks is at the public lot on the corner of Kilohana Drive and South Kihei Road, or all the way at the southern end of South Kihei Road where it comes to a dead end in the parking lot.

Rental Shops and Schools

When it comes to surf lessons in Kihei, there's only one place to go, and that's The Cove. This is the best place on the island for lessons because the water is just the right depth, it's a gentle wave, and rarely is it completely flat. Although heading here for a lesson is the obvious choice, finding out exactly *who* to go with is more of an undertaking. In the area surrounding The Cove there are no fewer than five or six operators all crammed into the same city block. Even with the wide selection it's best to make a reservation. Nearly all lessons take place in the morning hours between 8am and noon before the trade winds have filled in, and all operations offer a standard length of two hours for every lesson. If you've moved past the phase of learning how to pop up and ride straight, most operations also offer "surf safaris" where they will act as your personal surf guides for the day and take you out to different breaks where the current conditions suit your ability level. The rates for something like this are higher than taking a two-hour lesson.

One of the few places in The Cove area that has an actual shop (as opposed to just a van stacked with boards) is **Big Kahuna Adventures** (1913 S. Kihei Rd., 808/875-6395, www.bigkahunaadventures.com, 7:30am-7pm Mon.-Sat., 7:30am-5pm Sun.) inside Kihei Kalama Village. Lessons are the standard $60/person for a two-hour lesson and take place at two different times in the morning. Meet at the surf truck parked across the street from the shop.

Surf Shack (1993 S. Kihei Rd., 808/875-0006, www.surfshackmaui.com, 7:30am-3pm daily) is across the street from The Cove. Park inside the Island Surf building. Lessons are $59 to be in a group of up to six people, or private lessons begin at $125 for a single student and go all the way up to $350 for a private group of 4 ($87.50/person).

When it comes to the "van shops," one of the largest operations in the area is **Maui Wave Riders** (1975 S. Kihei Rd., 808/875-4761, www.mauiwaveriders.com), a company that also has a Lahaina location and has helped thousands of visitors stand up on their first wave. Lesson rates are $60/person to be included in a group of up to six people, $85/person for a semiprivate lesson, and $140 if you're looking for some one-on-one instruction.

Although they function on a smaller scale, another operation providing lessons in both Kihei as well as on the west side is **Maui Beach Boys** (808/283-7114, www.mauibeachboys.com), a company that offers the same prices of $60/person for a group lesson and $85 for a semiprivate lesson, although private instruction

is a few dollars cheaper at only $129 for a two-hour session.

Surf Yoga Maui (808/264-9136, www.surfyoga.com) combines surf lessons with a yoga workout. Lessons are offered on an individualized scale ($90/person semiprivate, $140 private instruction). If you're worried about integrating downward dog while you're sitting out in the lineup, instructors can also provide surfing lessons separate from yoga classes.

If you're just looking to rent a surfboard for the day and only need a basic longboard, head to any of the **Boss Frog's** (www.bossfrog.com) locations around town. Not only are they cheaper than renting from the surf schools ($20/day as opposed to $25), but the surf school rentals often cap your time limit at four hours whereas Boss Frog's is open until 5pm. There are three locations in Kihei, including the stores in Dolphin Plaza (2395 S. Kihei Rd., 808/875-4477), across from Kukui Mall (1770 S. Kihei Rd., 808/874-5225), and in the Long's Shopping Center (1215 S. Kihei Rd., 808/891-0077). All Boss Frog's are open 8am-5pm.

On the other hand, while the Boss Frog's stores and similar rental agencies are great if you only need a beginner board for the day, the best service for intermediate surfers who want to rent a board for the duration of their trip is **808 Boards** (808/283-1384, www.808boards.com, 7am-5:30pm), who will not only match you up with a board that will suit your ability, but will also drop off and pick up the board where you're staying for no extra charge. You can get a beginner board from $25/day to $100/week, or a premium, fiberglass board from $35/day to $140/week.

Island Surfboard Rentals (808/281-9835, www.islandsurfboardrentals.com) rents for longboards from $56 for two days to $180 for the week. Shortboards will only cost $40 for two days and $130 for the week. The selection of funboards, fishes, and shortboards is superior to that at other rental agencies. They'll even include a leash, some wax, and some inside knowledge of the current swell conditions at no extra cost.

WAILEA
Surf Spots
On the north side of Mokapu Beach, **Stouffer's** is a local spot for shortboarding. This is an A-frame peak for intermediate surfers. It can pick up southwest swells in the summer and large west swells in the winter. Parking is either at the south lot of Keawakapu Beach or in the public parking at the bottom of Ulua Beach Road.

MAKENA AND BEYOND
Surf Spots
Not many visitors surf in Makena, although it isn't because there isn't any surf in Makena. There simply aren't any surf breaks that are suitable for visitors. If you're an intermediate to advanced surfer, your best bet is on the north end of the park at **Little Beach.** To reach the wave you need to carry your board up and over the hill that separates Little Beach from Big Beach.

STAND-UP PADDLING
Kihei
Kihei is one of the best spots on the island for stand-up paddling, and all of the major surf schools will also offer paddleboard services. Getting out on the water in the morning is imperative with stand-up paddling because once the trade winds pick up it can become impossible to paddle upwind. For a truly meditative experience, rent a board the evening before and get up early the next morning for a sunrise paddle. One of the best runs in Kihei is to go from Sugar Beach to the Menehune Shores condominium and back, or you can always just putt around the coastline by Kamaole and stop at whichever beach is calling your name.

Rental Shops and Schools
Learning to stand-up paddle can often consist of a single lesson. Professional instructors can give you all the pointers you need—such as where to stand on the board, how far apart to keep your feet, and the correct side of the paddle to use—and after the one lesson you should be solid enough to rent a board on your own.

Of all the schools in Kihei, **Maui Wave Riders** (1975 S. Kihei Rd., 808/875-4761,

MAUI

© KYLE ELLISON

Stand-up paddling is the perfect start to a day in South Maui.

www.mauiwaveriders.com) offers 90-minute lessons which run $60 if you're part of a group, and $85 if it's a semiprivate lesson. For $140, you can get a one-on-one session with an instructor guaranteed to get you up and paddling.

Maui Beach Boys (808/283-7114, www.mauibeachboys.com) offers slightly longer classes (two hours) at a slightly higher price ($79).

You can also try out a multisport operator such as **South Pacific Kayaks and Outfitters** (808/875-4848, www.southpacifickayaks.com), which offers two-hour lessons for $75 as part of a group, $99 semiprivate, or $139 for the private experience.

If you don't feel like being packed in with the rest of the students around The Cove, you can opt for a multisport operator such as **Blue Soul** (3414 Akala Dr., 808/269-1038, www.bluesoul.com) that will arrange for a custom experience suited to your location and ability level. Rates with Blue Soul are $80 for a semiprivate lesson, $120 for private lessons.

If you want to rent a board and paddle on your own, one of the cheapest options is **Auntie Snorkel** (2439 S. Kihei Rd., 808/879-6263, www.auntiesnorkel.com, 8:30am-8pm daily) in the Rainbow Mall in South Kihei. Boards will only cost you $35 (versus $40/hr at some high-end resort stands), and since stand-up boards can be a pain to strap to your car, this location is best if you are staying by Kamaole Beach I or II so that your condo, the store, and the beach are all within walking distance of each other.

Wailea

If you're staying in Wailea, there are stand-up operators along Wailea Beach. Situated in the thick of the action is the **Maui Beach Club** in front of the Grand Wailea, which is an activities company that provides stand-up paddleboard rentals and guided tours. The rates for a single hour can be steep, so the best deal if you plan on putting in a lot of beach time is to buy a four-day membership to the beach club, which gets you unlimited paddleboard, kayak, and boogie board rental for $103/person.

If you would prefer to take part in a guided tour, **Paddle On** (888/663-0808, www.paddleonmaui.com) offers early morning tours from Polo Beach in front of the Fairmont Kea Lani. These tours have a flexible itinerary. The main focus is simply on being out on the water and communing with the tranquil calm of morning. Inquire about meditative sunrise tours.

Makena and Beyond

The only place in Makena for stand-up paddleboard rentals and lessons is at the stand in front of the **Makena Beach and Golf Resort** (5400 Makena Alanui, 808/874-1111, www.makenaresortmaui.com), steps from the sand. Lessons are available from $60/hr, or you can rent a board and go on your own for $40/hr. Advance reservations are required for a lesson. During summer it takes the wind longer to reach here than at areas such as Kihei, which means that your window for paddling lasts an hour or two longer.

For a lengthier, guided stand-up paddling tour, the crew at **Hawaiian Paddle Sports** (808/660-4228, www.hawaiianpaddlesports.com) can meet you at Makena Landing where you can take part in a two-hour lesson and tour of the historic Makena coastline. These are private tours. Rates vary between $159 for a solo person to $109/person for private groups over five.

WINDSURFING

While the north shore of the island is the windsurfing center of Maui, occasionally there are days when the wind direction makes Kihei a better option. This usually happens when the wind is out of the due north or there is a strong *kona* wind blowing out of the south. If it happens to be one of the days when Kihei is better than Kanaha, the most popular area for launching is **Mai Poina 'Oe Ia'u Beach Park** in North Kihei toward the intersection of Ohukai and South Kihei Road. There's a large grassy area here for rigging your equipment. Despite the fact that this is the second most popular part of the island for windsurfing after the north shore, all of the rental shops for windsurfing gear are in Kahului.

Kayaking and Canoe Paddling

When all factors are considered, Makena is the best area for kayaking and paddling. Not only is the area far more culturally rich, but it takes the wind about an hour longer to reach down here than in neighboring Kihei or Wailea.

When it comes to a paddling tour, don't let the food be a deciding factor. Most tours are only a few hours long, and you can only do so much when it comes to paddling with food. Since many companies will charge substantially more for a tour with food, you're better off having a hearty breakfast or bringing a few snacks for a tour, which is only 2-3 hours long.

My top pick for paddling activities is **Hawaiian Paddle Sports** (808/600-4228, www.hawaiianpaddlesports.net), a private tour operator that offers excursions on both the west side as well as the south side of the island. Every single tour is geared to the individual's specific ability level, and owner and head guide Tim Lara perfectly fuses adventure and sustainability with a deep-rooted respect for Hawaiian culture and surroundings. The guides are all accomplished watermen and women who are active in volunteering in the local community. The company was awarded the silver level of certification by the Hawai'i Ecotourism Association. While the private component can be pricier than a group tour, it's guaranteed to be a cultural, historical, environmental, and thoroughly enjoyable tour which will exceed your expectations. For South Maui, Hawaiian Paddle Sports offers three-hour excursions in both outrigger canoes and kayaks, which depart from Makena and incorporate snorkeling, paddling, and storytelling. Trips cost $149 per person for the outrigger canoes and $109-159 per person for kayaking depending on the size of your group. If you're an Ironman triathlete on vacation, tackle the Molokini Challenge where you leave at the break of dawn and make the 3.5-mile channel crossing to Molokini Crater (conditions permitting).

KIHEI

Though the actual location of your kayak tour is variable, **Big Kahuna Adventures** (1913 S. Kihei Rd., 808/875-6395, www.bigkahunaadventures.com, 7:30am-7pm Mon.-Sat., 7:30am-5pm Sun.) in Kihei Kalama Village can arrange a half-day kayaking excursion if you enquire at the office.

Down the street in the Island Surf building, ask **Surf Shack** (1993 S. Kihei Rd., 808/875-0006, www.surfshackmaui.com, 7:30pm-3pm daily) about its combination packages of surf lessons and kayak excursions if you want to spend a full day out on the water. There is a second location at the north end of Keawakapu Beach (2960 S. Kihei Rd.) open 8am-5pm daily.

WAILEA

While there are a number of options for paddling tours in Wailea, the one that focuses the most on Hawaiian culture is **Hawaiian Outrigger Experience** (808/633-3547, www.hoemaui.com) operating from Wailea Beach. A play on words, the acronym, *HOE,* translates as "paddle!" in the Hawaiian language. From the moment you begin this tour, you will realize this is as much a cultural experience as it is about spending a morning on the water. In addition to the time you'll spend snorkeling with Hawaiian green sea turtles, you'll gain authentic cultural insight from instructors who are not only richly ingrained in the Hawaiian community, but also exude the genuine spirit of aloha.

If a full-on paddling tour is too much exertion for you, another activity with cultural roots is the family-operated **Maui Sailing Canoe** (808/281-9301, www.mauisailingcanoe.com), which departs off Polo Beach. The distinctly red sail of the sailing canoe *Hina* is visible off the shoreline of Wailea on most mornings, and this is the only tour where you can harness the light breeze to slowly sail along the coastline similar to the Polynesians who voyaged here

MAUI

centuries ago. Snorkeling time is also included in the tour, and this is a nice combination of snorkeling, paddling, sailing, learning, and relaxing in the sun. Rates for the tour are $99/ adult and $79 for children. With a maximum of only six people, this is perfect adventure for families wanting to do something different.

Wailea Watersports (808/875-2011, www.waileawatersports.com) also meets at Polo Beach for traditional kayak tours along the Wailea coastline. Tours depart at 8am and cruise the rocky shore between Wailea and Makena. One of the unique features of this tour is the opportunity to go bottom fishing directly off your kayak. Regular tours cost $75/ person or $120 if going by yourself, and if you want to try catch your own dinner, you'll have to get up a little bit earlier (6am tour) and fork out a little more cash ($150/person).

MAKENA

Only two main places in Makena feature canoe paddling or kayaking: **Maluaka Beach** in front of the Makena Beach and Golf Resort

and **Makena Landing** beach park on Makena Road. Unless you book with the operators through the Makena Beach and Golf Resort, more likely than not you're going to be departing from Makena Landing.

The only options with land-based facilities are the tours that depart from the **Makena Beach and Golf Resort** (5400 Makena Alanui, 808/874-1111, www.makenaresortmaui.com). Rent your own kayak for $25-30/hour or take part in a two-hour guided snorkeling tour for $75 with one of the knowledgeable guides. If you want to take part in a paddling experience that's far more culturally oriented (and will give you a better workout), there are also **outrigger canoe tours** that depart from in front of the hotel and cost the same as the kayaks at $75 for a two-hour trip. Snorkeling time is included with both tours. The beach parking area is half a mile past the main entrance to the resort.

The rocky shoreline of Makena Landing is the preferred spot of all other kayak operators, most of whom also have operations elsewhere on the island. My top pick from

© KYLE ELLISON

Makena's historic shoreline is one of the best places for kayaking.

MAUI

Makena Landing is **Hawaiian Paddle Sports** (808/600-4228, www.hawaiianpaddlesports. net), but other operators you can choose from include **Kelii's Kayaks** (808/874-7652, www.keliiskayaks.com), **Aloha Kayaks Maui** (808/270-3318, www.alohakayaksmaui. com), as well as **Makena Kayak and Tours** (808/879-8426, www.makenakayaks.net), whose prices are usually the cheapest among many of the competitors. Most tours are about $55-70 for a 2.5-hour tour and $85 for a four-hour tour. There are usually two tours offered per day. If you plan on kayaking from Makena Landing, do yourself a favor and book the early tour, because not only will you beat the wind, but you'll beat the crowds of snorkel boats that converge on the area later on in the morning.

Hiking and Biking

HIKING
Kihei
Kihei isn't exactly a place for hiking. The closest thing to hiking in Kihei is taking long walks down the beach, like five-mile-long **Sugar Beach,** which runs between North Kihei and Ma'alaea. You can access the beach from Haycraft Park on the Ma'alaea side, from Kenolio Park on the Kihei side, or at any of the access points along North Kihei Road.

Another popular **coastal walk** in Kihei connects the trio of Kamaole Beaches by following the trails around their respective headlands. Starting at Charley Young Beach on the north end of Kamaole I (parking is in a public lot on Kaiau Place), you can walk to the south end of Kamaole III by going along the shoreline and around the rocky points. Although it's always nice to feel the sand between your toes, the rocks around the headlands can be sharp, so if you have sensitive feet, it might be best to bring footwear.

If you want to extend the coastal walk just a little bit farther, there is a short, 0.5-mile **walking path** that parallels the coastline from the southern end of Kamaole III Beach and finishes at the Kihei Boat Ramp. Along the way you will pass signs educating you about the coastal dune system and the *u'au kani* seabirds that come to shore to nest in the dunes. There are a few benches sprinkled along the walking path that make either a good resting point or, in winter, a place to sit down and watch for whales.

Wailea
WAILEA COASTAL WALK
If your idea of a hike means throwing on some Lululemon, talking on your iPhone, and stopping to pick up some Starbucks, then the **Wailea Coastal Walk** is going to be your favorite hike on the island. This paved pathway running from Ulua Beach to Polo Beach is undeniably gorgeous. The round-trip walk covers a distance of 3.5 miles, and along the way you'll pass a host of native coastal plants which have been put in in an effort to revitalize the area's natural foliage. You'll also pass the Grand Wailea, Four Seasons, Kea Lani, Marriott, and Wailea Beach Villas. To reach the "trailhead" for the walkway, you can either park in the public lot at Ulua Beach (at the bottom of Ulua Beach Road) or in the public lot on the southern end of the trail at Polo Beach (at the bottom of Kaukahi Street).

Makena and Beyond
◖ HOAPILI TRAIL
Anyone who heads out on the **Hoapili Trail** will realize right away that this isn't your average hike. Hot and barren and set in the middle of nowhere, the Hoapili Trail isn't as much about hiking as it is about taking a literal step back in time. Although walking the full length of the 5.5-mile trail (round-trip) takes most visitors about four hours, even spending an hour on the coastal section introduces you to a side of the island most visitors never see.

The trail was once an ancient Hawaiian

walking path reserved for royalty. In 1824, sections of the trail were reconstructed and the road took on a structure that remains untouched to this day. The trailhead for Hoapili (also known as the "King's Highway") is located in the parking lot of the La Perouse Bay snorkeling area at the end of Makena Alanui Road, 3.1 miles past the first entrance to Big Beach. If you're still confused on how to get here, just drive south on Makena Alanui Road until the road dead-ends in a lava field and you can't drive any farther.

From the La Perouse Bay parking lot you'll notice a trail that parallels the shoreline and weaves its way along the coast toward the south. Before you set out on the trail, however, understand that this place is hot, barren, mostly devoid of shade, and traverses jagged *a'a* lava that's so sharp you'll want some proper hiking boots. Since much of this hike is outside of cell phone range, it's important to be prepared with plenty of food and water. Reduce the chance of overheating by starting this hike early in the morning.

After you've followed the shoreline for 15 minutes, you'll notice a small cross on the ocean side of the trail that denotes a popular surfing spot known as Laps (short for La Perouse). After the surf spot the trail will climb in elevation for 10 minutes before arriving at a junction and veering off to the left. There will be a sign informing you that you're entering the King's Highway and to respect the historic sites. The sign will also indicate that Kanaio Beach is two miles ahead.

When on the inland section of trail where the path deviates from the coastline, there's a short spur trail that leads down to the lighthouse at Cape Hanamanioa, although there isn't much to see down here except for the old weathered light. A better side trip is to take the short spur trail found 20 minutes later that leads down to Keawanaku Beach, where you're almost guaranteed to have the beach to yourself. After the turnoff for Keawanaku the trail continues for another 20 minutes until you finally reach the coast again at Kanaio Beach, a salt and pepper-colored shoreline that's composed of equal parts black lava rock and sun-bleached coral. You'll notice the remnants of multiple structures, which were once a part of an ancient fishing village.

Although Kanaio Beach is the turn-around point for the majority of hikers, the King's Highway continues all the way until it joins with Highway 31 on the "back road to Hana." To reach the highway, however, would require an overnight stay along the trail; camping is permitted along the shoreline from points east of Kanaio Beach. For the average hiker who wants to travel just a *little* farther, however, a sandy road continues from Kanaio Beach and winds its way along the coast. Another 20 minutes of walking from Kanaio will bring you to a shoreline that's completely bathed in bleached white coral, and on the southern end of the "white beach" is an ancient Hawaiian *heiau* set out on the point that looks much the same now as it must have when it was built.

BIKING

Despite the flat terrain and sunny weather, South Maui doesn't have the same number of biking options that you might find upcountry or on the road to Hana. The most scenic ride in all of South Maui is the one between Wailea and the end of the road at La Perouse Bay. Early mornings are the best time for cycling, as the road can get narrow and congested with visitor traffic. On the far northern end of Kihei, a bike path parallels Mokulele Highway, running almost all the way toward Kahului. The wind can be brutal in the afternoons and the scenery is nothing but cane fields and the highway. South Maui is best for a leisurely ride on a beach cruiser, swapping spandex for a bikini or boardshorts and pedaling the flat shoreline with the sun on your face.

Kihei

If you're looking for proper cycling during your stay in South Maui, your best bet is going to be at **South Maui Cycles** (1992 S. Kihei Rd., 808/874-0068, www.southmauibicycles.com, 10am-6pm Mon.-Sat.) across the street from the south end of Kalama Park. Rental prices on road bikes range $22-60/day depending on the caliber of bike, and there are also weekly rates which range $99-250/week. This is a full-service bicycle shop that also offers sales and repairs.

Or, for those who just want a rental for beach-hopping throughout the day, basic beach cruisers are available from **Boss Frog's Bike Shop** (1770 S. Kihei Rd., 808/661-3333, www.bossfrog.com, 8am-5pm daily) for $15/day or $50 week. There are also mountain bikes, hybrid bikes, and proper road bikes to accompany the cruisers, and you can also pick up a cruiser at another location in the Dolphin Plaza across from the southern end of Kamaole II Beach Park.

Makena and Beyond
Although it isn't an actual shop, if you are staying at the **Makena Beach and Golf Resort** (5400 Makena Alanui Rd., 808/874-1111, www.makenaresortmaui.com), the hotel offers free bicycles for guests to use anywhere in the Makena and Wailea area.

Golf

KIHEI
If you just want to go out and play a relaxing round without shelling out resort prices, **Elleair Golf Course** (1345 Pi'ilani Hwy., 808/874-0777, www.elleairmauigolfclub.com) is one of the island's best golf values. It offers views looking out toward Molokini Crater and the West Maui Mountains. This par-71 course isn't as challenging as the Wailea Gold course, but it still provides an enjoyable round for the everyday golfer. Club and equipment rentals are available from the pro shop, and there's a driving range for working on your stroke before your round. The afternoon trade winds can have a major effect on the play here. Rounds can usually be found in the $85-115 range. To save a few dollars, check the website for online specials. They also offer an affordable nine-hole twilight special if you want to sneak in a few holes after a morning excursion to Molokini.

WAILEA
The **Wailea Gold** (100 Wailea Golf Club Dr., 808/875-7450, www.waileagolf.com) course is the best course in all of South Maui. This is where the pros play when they come to town, and the 7,000+-yard course and 93 bunkers will challenge even those with the lowest of handicaps. Guests staying in the Wailea resort complex can play a morning round for $190, whereas guests from other resorts will have to shell out $209. May 1-December 20 the rates are only $179 for all visitors regardless of where they're staying. Afternoon rounds are heavily discounted. Club rental and practice facilities are located at the main Wailea clubhouse.

If the length and level of difficulty of the Gold course are intimidating, the **Wailea Emerald** (100 Wailea Golf Club Dr., 808/875-7450, www.waileagolf.com) course has been called the "pretty sister" of the Gold course and is reputed to be easier for shorter hitters. Although the course isn't quite as long, this is still a proper resort course with all of the technical challenges and amenities, so you still need to bring your A-game to get any birdies. Greens fees will run the same as at the Gold course.

The **Wailea "Old Blue"** (100 Wailea Golf Club Dr., 808/875-7450, www.waileagolf.com) course constructed in 1972 is the South Maui original and the second course to be built on Maui (behind Ka'anapali). More forgiving than the other two courses, rates for "Old Blue" are more affordable and usually hover around the $90-170 range depending on what time of day you play and what time of year it is. After you card your best round of your vacation, head down to Manoli's to celebrate at the bar.

MAKENA AND BEYOND
When everything is factored in—design, price, views, and location—my favorite

South Maui golf course is the **Makena Golf Course** (5415 Makena Alanui Rd., 808/879-3344, www.makenaresortmaui.com/golf), also known as the Makena North course. The course is a 10-minute drive south from Wailea, and the wind down here isn't as much of a factor. The natural design of the course forces you to weave your way around kiawe trees and drive over ravines, which are laden with jagged lava rocks, so you can forget about playing from out of bounds. In addition to being challenging, the views afforded from the back nine look out over four different islands. The prices are more affordable than at neighboring Wailea. Unfortunately, the course is closed through the first quarter of 2014 for a major renovation, although look for it to be nicer than ever when it eventually does reopen. Although a regular morning round will run $185, guests of certain resorts can play for $169, it's only $119 after 12pm, and only $90 if you tee off after 3pm.

Spas

KIHEI

Despite the fact that **Valley Isle Day Spa** (1847 S. Kihei Rd., 808/298-9246, www.valleyisle-dayspa.homestead.com, 8am-8pm daily) is in a Central Kihei strip mall, the services inside could still be exactly what you're looking for. The rates here are far more affordable than the fancy resorts ($95 for 60-minute massage), and like other spas, they also offer aromatherapy, reflexology, facials, body treatments, couples packages, and a decent range of beauty products.

If you're staying in Ma'alaea or North Kihei and don't want to travel all the way down to South Kihei or Wailea, **Massage Maui** (145 N. Kihei Rd., 808/357-7317, www.massage-maui.com) is another low-key massage option where you can either meet the masseuse in the Sugar Beach location or arrange for an outcall massage where the therapist visits you in your condo. A 60-minute massage will cost $95, and outcall services will usually run about $20 higher than the in-spa price.

WAILEA

When it comes to choosing the best spa in South Maui, it is tough to argue with a 50,000-square-foot luxury arena that has been voted not only as the best spa in the Hawaiian Islands, but also among the top 10 spas in all of the United States. Such is the case with **Spa Grande** (3850 Wailea Alanui Dr., 800/772-1933, www.spagrande.com), the palatial spa inside the Grand Wailea, which completely redefines the concept of pampering. All guests are advised to arrive an hour early so as to enjoy a casual—and complimentary—soak in the termé hydrotherapy baths before moving on to your scheduled treatment. Can't decide between the Roman hot tub, Japanese Furo baths, or honey-mango loofah exfoliation? Do them all. They're included with your package! Of course, you're ultimately paying for all of the extravagance (a 50-minute massage treatment will be $155-175 on average). Along with an enormous selection of facials and treatment options, there's also a beauty salon and fitness center.

The Spa at Four Seasons (808/874-8000, www.fourseasons.com/maui/spa, 8am-9pm daily) is just as lavish and over the top, and a nice perk here is the option of getting a massage in an oceanfront cabana. The prices are often a touch higher than at Spa Grande, but the offerings of wellness options, facials, body treatments, and massage are no less impressive.

Other Wailea resort spas include those at the **Fairmont Kea Lani** (4100 Wailea Alanui Dr., 808/875-2229, www.fairmont.com) and the **Mandara Spa** (3700 Wailea Alanui Dr., 808/891-8774, www.mandaraspa.com, 8am-8pm daily) at the Wailea Marriott.

If the high prices of the resorts are too much to stomach, but you don't want to travel far, then the **Maui Zen Day Spa** (Wailea Gateway Center, 808/874-6000, www.mauizen.com, 10am-6pm daily) is just up the road at the Wailea Gateway Center and offers much of the same services at a moderately discounted rate. It's in the upstairs section of an upscale strip mall, but if the only thing that matters is relieving that stress in your neck, you can come up here to work it out and still have some money left over for dinner. A 60-minute massage will cost $99, and they also offer facials, acupuncture, aromatherapy, and even botox injections.

Aroma Stone Wailea Healing Center (161 Wailea Ike Pl., 808/264-9999, www.aromastonewailea.com) is another "out of resort" option that only requires a five-minute drive, yet saves you enough money you could almost come back for a second round. Close to the Wailea Tennis Center in between the Shops at Wailea and the Wailea Gateway Center, this healing zone offers 60-minute massage treatments for $90 that focus on the use of hot stones and aromatherapy.

MAKENA

The best option for a spa treatment this far south is at the oceanfront **Makena Kai Day Spa** (5400 Makena Alanui Rd., 808/875-5858, 9am-6pm daily) on the beautiful shores of Maluaka Beach. Value is the name of the game: the $115 50-minute massage treatment beats the resort prices just 10 minutes up the road. If you're looking for an oceanfront massage at a comparatively affordable price, then your best bet is going to be found at the end of the road.

Horseback Riding and Bird-Watching

HORSEBACK RIDING
Makena and Beyond

The only horseback riding in South Maui is found *way* down south at the end of the road at **Makena Stables** (8299 South Makena Rd., 808/879-0244, www.makenastables.com), a family-run outfit that has been leading horseback riding tours since 1983. The trails here meander over Ulupalakua Ranch land only accessible via a private tour. Along the way there's a good chance of spotting axis deer or wild goats that clamber across the jagged *a'a* lava. This is one of the few horseback riding operations on the island with the possibility of riding your horse directly along the shoreline. The only other way you can access this stretch of coastline on horseback is if you take a tour from Triple L Ranch beginning in Upper Kanaio. Since Triple L is 40 miles from Wailea, however, and Makena Stables is only seven, this is the obvious choice if your vacation is based in South Maui. Not only do the views stretch out over the waters of La Perouse Bay to the island of Kaho'olawe in the distance, but you ride directly through the island's most recent lava flow, taking time to stop at Kalua O Lapa, the volcanic vent from which Madame Pele leaked her fiery liquid only a few centuries ago. Group sizes are capped at six, and riders must be under 205 pounds. To escape the brutal South Maui sun, take a sunset ride during the coastline's most artistic and romantic hour.

BIRD-WATCHING
Kihei

If there were a bird to be associated with South Maui it would be the Pacific golden plover, or *kolea*. Like many of the condo dwellers that occupy the beaches of Kihei during the winter, the *kolea* leaves its summer home in the Arctic in favor of warm, tropical Maui winters.

One of the best places to see *real* birds in South Maui is at the **Kealia Pond National Wildlife Refuge** (www.fws.gov/kealiapond) between Ma'alaea and North Kihei. This 700-acre reserve is home to over 30 species of birds, the most notable of which are the *a'eo* (Hawaiian stilt), *'alae ke'oke'o* (Hawaiian coot), and *koloa maoli* (Hawaiian duck). The greatest number of species can be found here during winter. There are short walking trails that leave from the visitor center (mile marker 6 on Mokulele Hwy.) into the Kealia Pond area. There's also a short boardwalk from Ma'alaea to North Kihei that parallels the shoreline and offers a number of informative placards about the island's native wildlife. The boardwalk takes about 30 minutes to walk to the end and back, and if you plan on visiting it's best to approach from the Ma'alaea side of the road because there's no left turn allowed into the parking lot off North Kihei Road.

Although there's a good chance you won't see any birds at all, another place to try your luck is on the beachwalk running between the Kihei Boat Ramp and the south end of Kamaole III Beach. The coastal dune system here is home to *'ua'u kani* (wedge-tailed shearwaters), and the fledgling season is usually October-December.

Although **Molokini Crater** is best known as a marine reserve and world-class snorkel and dive destination, few people know that the 161-foot tall islet is also a seabird sanctuary above water. Molokini Crater is home to a healthy population of *'ua'u kani*. If you're an avid birder and are planning a trip to Molokini, bring a pair of binoculars to check out what's happening *above* water.

Those with an interest in Maui County's seabirds should check out the **Maui Nui Seabird Recovery Project** (www.mauinuiseabirds.org).

Makena and Beyond

The best place for bird-watching in Makena is at **Oneuli Beach** by Makena State Park. Although the chances of seeing many species of birds are slim, this coastal wetland area is home to avians such as the *'auku'u* (black-crowned night heron), *'alae ke'oke'o* (Hawaiian coot), and *ulili* (wandering tattler).

Sights

MA'ALAEA
(Maui Ocean Center

There isn't a snorkeling spot on the island where you're going to see as wide a range of marine life as at the **Maui Ocean Center** (192 Ma'alaea Rd., 808/270-7000, www.mauioceancenter.com, 9am-5pm daily, until 6pm in July and Aug., $25.50/adult, $18.50/child). This three-acre marine park has the nation's largest collection of live tropical coral. Children will enjoy the tidepool exhibits and the green sea turtle lagoon, but everyone comes here to experience the 54-foot-long acrylic tunnel that runs beneath a 750,000-gallon aquarium filled with dozens of rays and sharks.

The center educates visitors on our unique marine ecosystem and as well as native Hawaiian culture, with exhibits on everything from Polynesian wayfaring to ancient Hawaiian fishponds. The center is committed to providing animals with a realistic, natural environment. This is one of the island's best family attractions and its best rainy day activity. With over 400,000 visitors every year, it gets crowded. To avoid the crowds, visit in the morning right as the facility opens. A self-guided tour meanders through the various exhibits; head directly to the last exhibit and work your way toward the front. Allow at least two hours. Lunch is available at the Seascape Restaurant (11am-2:30pm) or the Reef Café (10am-4pm).

KIHEI

Kihei doesn't have a defined city center or any real historical sites. Historically, however, Kihei was known for being empty as opposed to full. During the days of the ancient Hawaiians the Kihei area was referred to as "Kamaole," a word that loosely translates as "barren." Nevertheless, there are still a few places in Kihei to either get back to nature or catch a glimpse of the past.

© KYLE ELLISON

Explore the sea at the Maui Ocean Center.

MAUI

Kealia Pond National Wildlife Refuge

If you drive the road between Maʻalaea and North Kihei, you'll notice that it passes through a large mudflat that parallels the shoreline. Although most of this area is dry during summer, on the inland side of the highway is 200-acre **Kealia Pond National Wildlife Refuge** (www.fws.gov/kealiapond). The main reason for visiting is to catch a glimpse of native bird species such as the *aʻeo* (Hawaiian stilt) and *ʻalae keʻokeʻo* (Hawaiian coot). Even if you aren't an avid birder, the boardwalk off North Kihei Road makes for an informative place to stretch your legs and learn about the threats facing the island's native species.

The main visitor center for the wildlife refuge is off Mokulele Highway (Highway 311) near the six-mile marker, and there are short hiking trails which lead from here into the flats of the preserve. If you plan on visiting Kealia Pond, morning hours are best before the wind comes up, and during the driest periods of the year (August-November) the area can sometimes reek of the fish that have died from the water level receding.

Koiʻeiʻe Loko Iʻa Fishpond

Inside Kalepolepo Beach Park in North Kihei, the **Koiʻeiʻe Loko Iʻa fishpond** is the most prominent example of ancient Hawaiian existence from Maʻalaea to Wailea. Estimated to be around 500 years old, this ancient fishpond was formed by rocks passed by hand from the *mauka* (uplands) of Haleakala all the way *makai* toward the sea in Kihei. Thanks to the hard work of the **Maui Fishpond Association** (726 S. Kihei Rd., 808/359-1172, www.maui-fishpond.com), however, a dedicated group of volunteers has been working since 1996 to restore the fishpond to its former glory using the same—now submerged—rocks which were placed there by their ancestors many centuries before. The fishpond is available for viewing

© JENNA STRUBHAR

the boardwalk at Kealia Pond National Wildlife Refuge

at any time by visiting Kalepolepo Beach Park. Or, for a unique experience, the organization offers guided cultural canoe trips on Monday, Wednesday, and Friday mornings at 8am for those who prearrange a visit.

(Hawaiian Islands Humpback Whale National Marine Sanctuary

Right next door to Kalepolepo Beach Park is the headquarters for the **Hawaiian Islands Humpback Whale National Marine Sanctuary** (726 S. Kihei Rd., 808/879-2818, www.hawaiihumpbackwhale.noaa.gov, 10am-3pm Mon.-Fri., 10am-1pm Sat., free), a phenomenal educational resource for anyone with an interest in humpback whales. It's out of the way when compared to the rest of the action in Kihei, but everything about this compound is historic or educational in one way or another. Aside from offering exhibits about both the humpback whales as well as the sanctuary itself, the center also boasts some unique architecture, as evidenced by the 1940s-era, coastal, clapboard structure that seems better suited for Nantucket than North Kihei; its distinct blue color makes it easy to notice from offshore. Parts of the Koi'ei'e fishpond also run in front of the compound, and informative displays discuss not only the fishponds, but the ways in which ancient Hawaiians acted in concert with the island's marine species.

Shopping

MA'ALAEA
Ma'alaea Harbor Shops

The **Ma'alaea Harbor Shops** (300 Ma'alaea Rd.) are the only place in Ma'alaea with any shopping at all. The best shopping in Ma'alaea is found at the large **arts and crafts fair** (9am-5pm daily) overlooking the harbor. Dozens of local artists cycle through here, so every time you visit there's sure to be something new springing up. Much of the artwork is ocean-themed.

The only surf shop is **Da Beach House** (808/986-8279, 10am-5:30pm daily), which has a surprisingly decent assortment of beach and surf wear to accompany a wide range of accessories.

KIHEI
North End

At the far northern end of Kihei is the **Sugar Beach General Store** (145 N. Kihei Rd., 808/879-9899) within the Sugar Beach Resort. It can accommodate your basic sundry needs if you're staying at a condo in the area.

Up on Pi'ilani Highway the **Kihei Gateway Plaza** is a sprawling semi-industrial compound with a smattering of clothing shops that might interest visitors. Of the main stores in the plaza, the largest is **Maui Clothing Outlet** (362 Huku Li'i Pl., 808/875-0308, 9am-8pm Mon.-Sat., 10am-6pm Sun.) with an enormous selection of resort wear and island-themed clothing at discount prices. One of the sister stores in the same area is **Pretty Wahine** (362 Huku Li'i Pl., 808/879-1199, 10am-6pm daily) which focuses primarily on women's boutique clothing options.

While the **Azeka shopping centers** on South Kihei Road are mostly full of chain stores, **Paradise Sandal Company** (808/879-4884) is the exception in the Azeka Mauka Center, and across the street at the Azeka Makai shopping complex, the **Maui Quilt Shop** (808/874-8050) can provide anything you need for relaxing mornings of quilting in paradise.

If you turn up Pi'ikea Avenue between the Azeka Mauka Center and the Long's Shopping Center, you'll quickly come to the **Pi'ilani Village Shopping Center** (291 Pi'ikea Ave.), which has the most relevant shopping options for visitors to North Kihei. A big draw is the **Hilo Hattie's** (808/875-4545, 9am-9pm daily) clothing store where there's a wide range of men's and women's apparel, and if you forgot your swimsuit at home (or want another one), **Maui Waterwear** (808/891-8319, 9am-9pm Mon.-Sat., 9am-7pm Sun.) specializes in women's bikinis and beach accessories.

Central Kihei

Central Kihei is the land of the roadside shopping stall. Although most stores have gone this direction, an exception is the **Local Motion** (1819 S. Kihei Rd., 808/879-7873, www.localmotionhawaii.com, 9am-8pm Mon.-Sat., 9am-5pm Sun.) surf shop inside the Kukui Mall. This is one of longest-running surf shops in Kihei and an undisputed local favorite, carrying a large collection of surf and bodyboard accessories. Across the parking lot, **The Bikini Market** (1819 S. Kihei Rd., 808/891-8700, www.thebikinimarket.com, 8am-6pm daily) not only caters to a female clientele, but prides itself on promoting high-end swimwear and pieces designed by local artists.

On the other side of the road from Kukui Mall is the **Aloha Open Market** (1794 S. Kihei Rd., 9am-7pm daily), which has grown over the years from some random tents and roadside crafts to a legitimate retail outlet. The most popular shop inside the marketplace is **Maui Mana** (808/875-7881), probably because it's a headshop in a laid-back, warm-weather, island destination.

The largest concentration of shopping in Kihei is in the **Kihei Kalama Village** (1941 S. Kihei Rd., 10am-7pm daily), where serious shoppers could lose themselves for hours, if not days. This shopping complex houses over 40 businesses, the most notable being **Da Beach House** (808/891-1234, www.dabeach-housemaui.com) for surf-themed apparel, **Mahina** (808/879-3453, www.mahinam-aui.com) for women's apparel, **Serendipity** (808/874-8471, www.serendipitymaui.com) for fine women's clothing, and **The Love Shack Maui** (808/875-0303, www.loveshack-maui.com) for your intimate moments back at the hotel. In addition to the brick and mortar stores, there are myriad kiosks and stands where you can do anything from get henna tattoos to play with a dijeridoo. This shopping area is within walking distance of the Cove Park where most of the surf rentals take place, so if part of your group is out surfing, you can wander down here for some souvenir browsing while they finish their time on the water.

South End

As you move south from the Kalama Village area down into the Kamaole area, the strip malls get smaller but also more frequent. In the **Dolphin Plaza** you'll find **Maui Gifts and Crafts** (2395 S. Kihei Rd., 808/874-9310, 9am-9pm Mon.-Thurs., 9am-6pm Fri.-Sun.), a store which has everything from carved wood turtles and elephants to exotic imports from Indonesia and beyond.

The next shopping complex is small **Kamaole Beach Center** where the main retail outlet is **Honolua Surf Company** (2411 S. Kihei Rd., 808/874-0999). This is another surf store that focuses on high-quality surf-themed clothing and is named after Maui's legendary north shore surfing spot. What's nice about this store is that you can occasionally get the exact same Honolua brand clothing here for cheaper than you will find it at places such as Whalers Village in Ka'anapali or at the nearby Shops at Wailea.

Rainbow Mall is home to **Maui Fine Art & Frame** (2439 S. Kihei Rd., 808/222-3055, www.mauiartframe.com, 11am-8pm daily), one of the few art galleries found anywhere in Kihei. In addition to having numerous island-themed paintings and ceramics, the frames that

encompass the artwork are a separate art form unto themselves.

WAILEA
Shops at Wailea

Any longtime visitor to Maui will remember when the **Shops at Wailea** (3750 Wailea Alanui Dr., 808/891-6770, www.theshop-satwailea.com, 9:30am-9pm daily) were a plantation-style shopping complex with wide open grassy areas and free hula shows from local *halau*. These days, words such as "discount" and "affordable" rarely exist inside these walls, although there are still a few locally run stores where you can find items at a reasonable price. Once inside, you'll notice art galleries such as **Ki'i Gallery** (808/874-1181) and **Dolphin Galleries** (808/891-8000) accompanying surf shops like **Billabong** (808/879-8330) and **Honolua Surf Company** (808/891-8229). You can often spot celebrities hanging out in luxury stalwarts such as **Tiffany and Co.** (808/891-9226), **Gucci** (808/879-1060), or **Louis Vuitton** (808/875-6980).

Aside from the high-end corporate stores, you can also find a few island-themed shops offering unique and boutique souvenirs. At **Sand People** (808/891-8801, www.sandpeo-ple.com) you can pick up coastal-inspired gifts and home decor, and **Martin & MacArthur** (808/891-8844, www.martinandmacarthur.com) showcases Hawaiian-made crafts and an assortment of koa woods. If you're in town for a wedding but you're missing something from your cosmetics kit, **Cos Bar** (808/891-9448, www.cosbar.com) carries makeup lines such as Bobbi Brown that you can't find anywhere else on the island. If you're in need of a fancy gift, **Na Hoku** (808/891-8040) offers unique Hawaiian-inspired jewelry.

Wailea Gateway Plaza

Although it doesn't have anywhere near the glitz and glamour of the Shops at Wailea, the awkwardly placed little **Wailea Gateway Center** (10 Wailea Ike Dr.) still has a couple of boutique shops worth paying a visit. There are two clothing boutiques on the lower level, one of which, **Maui Memories** (808/298-0261, www.mauiislandmemories.com, 10am-9pm daily), features locally made jewelry, fashions, and artwork. Among the two standout items in the store are Nina Kuna jewelry, which has been featured on the cover of *Sports Illustrated,* and artwork from local photographer Randy Jay Braun. Right next door, **Otaheite Hawaii** (808/419-6179, www.otaheitehawaii.com, 10am-9pm Mon.-Sat., 10am-6pm Sun.) specializes in chic beach clothing centered around the island lifestyle, which means lots of swimwear and sundresses to accompany the gifts and accessories.

With the clothing shopping taken care of, move next door to **Jeré Diamonds and Fine Jewelry** (808/879-1967, www.jerediamonds.com, 10:30am-8pm Mon.-Sat., noon-6pm Sun.), which features an impressive range of not only diamonds, but also pearls, gemstones, and local paintings. This store holds its own with Tiffany's or Baron and Leeds down the street. The prices are more reasonable as well.

If your sweet tooth is aching after shopping, **Sweet Paradise Chocolatier** (808/344-1040, www.sweetparadisechocolate.com, 10am-8pm daily) will lure you with the scent of richly made chocolate. In addition to having an ornate spread of fine chocolates, all of the items are made right here on the island, and some of the cacao is even grown in Hawaii—the only state which currently grows cacao.

The **Aloha Shirt Museum and Boutique** (808/875-1308, www.the-aloha-shirt-museum.com, 11am-9pm daily) above Pita Paradise is a fascinating stop if you're looking for an aloha shirt. They carry styles that haven't been seen in decades (particularly the long sleeves), and some of the collection even dates back to the 1940s. If you've ever wondered what a $2,000 aloha shirt looks like, this is the place to find out.

Wailea Town Center

Although this is mostly an office complex, there's one retail outlet worth a mention. **Wailea Wine** (161 Wailea Ike Pl., 808/879-0555, www.waileawine.com, 10am-6pm Mon.-Fri., 10am-5pm Sat.) has an exceptional selection of wines from all across the globe (and one of the largest selections on the island), and the gourmet culinary options are on par with any other fine foods mart you'll find across the state.

Entertainment

MA'ALAEA
Live Music
In the downstairs section of the Ma'alaea Harbor Shops, **Beach Bums** (300 Ma'alaea Rd., 808/243-2286, open until 9pm) occasionally has live music during the late afternoon and evening to accompany periodic drink specials and a jovial sports bar atmosphere. If you're staying in one of the condos at Ma'alaea, this is your best bet for finding a happening atmosphere and the chance to mingle with local fishers and boat crews who are drinking their way through that morning's tips.

KIHEI
Live Music and Dancing
INSIDE THE TRIANGLE
The majority of Kihei's nightlife takes place at The Triangle, as in, The *Barmuda* Triangle, where you could end up getting lost for days. This collection of bars within the Kihei Kalama Village can almost seem like a tropical frat row where each house on the street is having a different sort of theme party.

If you're starting your night off early, check out **Haui's Life's A Beach** (1913 S. Kihei Rd., 808/891-8010, www.mauibars.com, open until 2am), aka The Lab. This rockin' beach bar has an outdoor patio that looks out toward South Kihei Road and is a great place for people-watching. There is live music on most nights, or you could just shoot some pool, watch some sports, and eavesdrop on some local happenings.

The best venue within the Triangle for live music is **Three's Bar and Grill** (1945 S. Kihei Rd., 808/879-3133, www.threesbarandgrill. com, open until 1:30am), a semi-formal dining establishment that also has a VIP Surf Lounge with a built-in stage area and lighting. While there can occasionally be music earlier in the evening on weekdays, late-night shows usually begin at 10pm and run until closing time.

The most popular club in the traditional sense of the word is the **South Shore Tiki Lounge** (1913 S. Kihei Rd., 808/874-6444, www.southshoretikilounge.com, open until 2am) where resident DJs play for a small but crowded dance floor. This place gets popular on the weekends with its thumping house beats and young singles.

Swap your draft beer for some cutting-edge mixology at **Ambrosia** (1913 S. Kihei Rd., 808/891-1011, www.ambrosiamaui.com, open until 2am), a small martini bar that specializes in "upscale drinking." DJs spin on many nights of the week here, and the vibe is decidedly classier and more refined than at some of the neighboring venues.

One of less refined venues is **Kahale's Beach Club** (36 Keala Pl., 808/875-7711, open until 2am), a working-class dive bar that has live music, cheap drinks, and a legitimately local atmosphere. This is your classic neighborhood hangout, and you won't find any grass skirts, rented convertibles, or timeshare resales within a respectable radius.

Dog and Duck Irish Pub (1913 S. Kihei Rd., 808/875-9669, www.theworldfamousdoganduck.com, open until 2am) offers a good old-fashioned touch of the *craic*. Throw darts, eat bangers and mash, drink Guinness, rock out to live music, or take part in one of their popular quiz nights.

OUTSIDE THE TRIANGLE

There are some scattered places outside the Triangle where you can catch some live music. In the Azeka Mauka shopping area, **Stella Blues Café** (1279 S. Kihei Rd., 808/879-3779, www.stellablues.com, open until 11pm) caters to the baby boomer generation, occasionally bringing in big names to perform. Although live performances on some evenings come without a cover, other acts such as Hapa or John Cruz can carry a $30 cover charge, or be combined with a dinner menu for $60/person.

Down at the other end of the parking lot of the Azeka Mauka is **Diamonds Ice Bar** (1279 S. Kihei Rd., 808/874-9299, www.diamondsicebar.com, open until 2am), a smaller establishment tucked in the end unit that offers live music on most nights of the week. If you have a large group or party there's a private VIP room. While it doesn't see the same amount of crowds as down at the Triangle, it can still be a happening place if the right band happens to be playing.

Moose McGillicuddy's (2511 S. Kihei Rd., 808/891-8644, www.moosemcgillicuddys.com, open until 2am) harnesses the late-night crowd in South Kihei who are looking for cheap drink specials and an old-fashioned good time. This sports bar cranks up the music at 9pm, and the radio ads they run championing their late-night *pupu* menu as being your best bet for staving off the munchies should give you a general idea of the clientele.

WAILEA
Shows

While there surprisingly aren't that many dinner shows on Maui, if you're looking for one that will completely wow you, there's no better option than the **Willie K Dinner Show** held at Mulligan's On The Blue (100 Kaukahi St., 808/874-1131, www.mulligansontheblue.com, open until 1am). Even if you've never heard of Uncle Willie K, once you see him play live you'll never forget him. An insanely talented local Hawaiian musician who grew up on Maui, Willie K's prowess stretches across a wide range of genres from blues to Hawaiian to rock and roll and opera. Tickets are $30/person, or if you want to combine it with the dinner buffet option (and thereby get a better seat), the price rises to $65/person. The show goes on several times throughout the month, but since the schedule is highly variable, the best thing to do is to check the website at www.mulligansontheblue.com.

If you're on a budget and looking for a free public show, head to **Wailea on Wednesdays** (6:30pm-8pm), held at the **Shops at Wailea** (3750 Wailea Alanui Dr.). Local Hawaiian artists perform live music in the lower courtyard section, and all of the surrounding art galleries and restaurants get in on the action with varying specials and festivities of their own.

All of the resorts feature a rotating schedule of live performances within the hotel grounds, so if you just take a wander through the area around sunset, you're sure to find a couple of slack key guitar players picking sweet melodies as the sun goes down or live hula performances taking place around the hotel lobbies.

Luau

The best luau on the island is Old Lahaina Luau in Lahaina, but if you're staying on the south end of the island and don't want to drive that far, there are two luau options in South Maui from which you can choose.

Of the two luaus in Wailea, my top pick is **The Grand Luau at Honua'ula** (3850 Wailea Alanui Dr., 808/875-7710, www.honuaula-luau.com, 4pm, $105/adult, $57/child) because the show focuses more on Hawaiian history as opposed to the general South Pacific. The luau takes place on the grounds of the Grand Wailea, and Honua'ula is a name given to this section of the island by the original Polynesians who migrated here centuries ago. The food and drinks are par for the luau course, although the main stage has a rock wall backdrop as opposed to facing out toward the ocean. Shows run on Monday, Thursday, Friday, and Saturday

evenings, although call in advance to double check since the schedule can sometimes be variable.

Just a few steps down the coastal walkway is the other luau in Wailea, **Te Au Moana** (3700 Wailea Alanui, 877/827-2740, www.teaumoana.com, 4:30pm, $104/adult, $57/child), at the Wailea Beach Marriott. The show times overlap exactly with neighboring Grand Wailea, and take place on Monday, Thursday, Friday, and Saturday evenings. While this show focuses more on the dance and mythology of greater Polynesia than specifically on Hawaii, it's still a highly entertaining performance—particularly if it's your first luau. The stage backs up to the coastline in front of the hotel. The backdrop of the setting sun creates a panorama you would expect from a luau in paradise.

Live Music

For live entertainment after the sun goes down, the most popular place in Wailea is **Mulligan's On The Blue** (100 Kaukahi St., 808/874-1131, www.mulligansontheblue.com, open until 1am). This Irish pub is owned by a real Irishman, and aside from the Willie K dinner show, the next most popular evening is on Sunday when the Celtic Tigers Irish folk band takes to the stage. There are also periodic performances by award-winning local artists, so pick up a copy of a local entertainment catalog to see what the happenings are.

Although the live music here is only for happy hour, **Monkeypod** (10 Wailea Ike Dr., 808/891-2322, www.monkeypodkitchen.com, open until 10:30pm) restaurant in the Wailea Gateway Center has the best craft beer list in Wailea.

Bars

For a traditional bar scene, head to **Manoli's Pizza Company** (100 Wailea Ike Dr., 808/874-7499, www.manolispizzacompany.com, open until midnight), where, in addition to draft and bottled beers, there are 20 wines which are either organic or grown on sustainable vineyards.

Late-night happy hour is 9pm-midnight. It's within walking distance of many of the resorts.

Inside the Shops at Wailea the best bar scene is at **Longhi's** (3750 Wailea Alanui, 808/891-8883, www.longhis.com, open until 10pm), and you can also find cold beers and tropical drinks inside **Tommy Bahama's** (808/875-9983, open until 10pm) and **Cheeseburger Island Style** (808/874-8990, open until 10pm).

The Red Bar at **Gannon's** (100 Wailea Golf Club Dr., 808/875-8080, www.gannonsrestaurant.com, open until 9:30pm) pairs the sexiest and sleekest drinks in Wailea with a stunning ocean view. Choose from affordable draft beers, an extensive list of over 100 wines, and enticing cocktails made with everything from sweet tea vodka to acai liqueur. There's also occasional live entertainment, usually paired with happy hour.

Food

MA'ALAEA
American
If your idea of the perfect lunch is clutching a pint of PBR with barbecue-covered fingers, **Beach Bums Bar and Grill** (300 Ma'alaea Boat Harbor Rd., 808/243-2286, 8am-9pm daily, $8-25), downstairs in the Harbor Shops, is the perfect spot. It's a festive open-air sports den of pulled pork sandwiches, barbecue ribs, and sweet potato fries.

Hawaiian Regional
Surrounded by boats in various stages of dry dock **Buzz's Wharf** (Ma'alaea Harbor, 808/244-5426, www.buzzswharf.com, 11am-9pm daily, $14-18 lunch, $18-46 dinner) is the oldest restaurant in Ma'alaea. Don't let the outward appearance fool you. The atmosphere inside classy and the menu is laden with Pacific Rim classics. Start off with an appetizer of Tahitian *poisson cru,* and either continue with the Tahitian theme or switch directions to a wasabi crusted ahi steak or their signature shrimp scampi.

KIHEI
Local Style
The only true local style plate lunch in Kihei is at **⟨ Da Kitchen** (2439 S. Kihei Rd., 808/875-7782, www.da-kitchen.com, 9am-9pm daily, $8-15), toward the back of the Rainbow Mall in South Kihei. Although the restaurant itself isn't as large as its Kahului counterpart, the portions are enormous, most

large enough that you could split them and still walk away full. This hole-in-the-wall, strip-mall special is one of the best deals in town. If you're looking for a place where locals eat, this is it.

Mexican
An authentic option is **Taqueria Cruz** (2395 S. Kihei Rd., 808/875-2910, 11am-8pm Mon.-Sat., $9-10), tucked in the back of South Kihei's Dolphin Plaza. It's reminiscent of a roadside *taqueria* on the back roads of Baja. Mexican music emanates from the kitchen before it even opens. The BYOB option is a nice perk: Enjoy your fish tacos with a Pacifico from your cooler. There's live music 6:30pm-8:30pm on Tuesday and Saturday nights.

Seafood
Hidden back in the central Kihei industrial yard is **⟨ Eskimo Candy** (2665 Wai Wai Pl., 808/879-5686, www.eskimocandy.com, 10:30am-7pm Mon.-Fri., $10-17), Kihei's best local secret for fresh seafood and *poke.* The ocean-themed decorations show that this place means business when it comes to seafood. Try the seafood chowder, fish-and-chips, and *poke,* featuring four different styles of seasoned ahi tuna. There are only a few tables outside for dining. To find it, make the turn off South Kihei Road by Maui Dive Shop and the Avis car rental outlet, continuing on toward the end of the road; the restaurant will be on your right.

Pizza

Locals say the best pizza in Kihei is at the **South Shore Tiki Lounge** (1913 S. Kihei Rd., 808/874-6444, 11am-2am daily, $6-9), ensconced in the Kihei Kalama Village. Pies are handcrafted with local ingredients and wheat flour. Sit outside on the garden-view deck.

Another favorite for south shore pizza is **⟨ Fabiani's Bakery and Pizza** (95 Lipoa St., 808/874-0888, www.fabianis.com, 7am-10pm daily, $10-12) in central Kihei. Located in a strip mall, it's tough to find, but once you get there, you'll realize why it's a local hangout. Lunch and dinner are dominated by fresh, tasty pizzas and paninis crafted by a chef from Italy. There's also a decent wine selection and the atmosphere inside is much nicer than the exterior suggests. The fresh breakfast pastries are a local secret.

Irish

Kihei is sunnier than Dublin, but when you order bangers and mash and a cold Guinness at the dimly lit **Dog and Duck Irish Pub** (1913 S. Kihei Rd., 808/875-9669, www.theworldfamousdogandduck.com, 10am-1am daily, $8-20), you feel like you're dining at the famous Temple Bar. This lively pub is one of the few places you can catch that international game Americans insist on calling soccer. Located at the back of the Kihei Kalama Village, this is a great spot if you want some stick-to-your-ribs meat and potatoes washed down with good conversation and a bit of the *craic*.

American

One of the best breakfast finds on the south side is **⟨ Kihei Caffe** (1945 S. Kihei Rd., 808/879-2230, www.kiheicaffe.net, 5am-3pm daily, $7-10). It's also the earliest, perfect for a meal before an early-morning boat trip. The portions are enormous; try a generous omelet or gargantuan breakfast burrito. Breakfast is served all day. The atmosphere can be hectic; get here early before the traffic (both human and vehicular) picks up.

Named after a Grateful Dead song, local favorite **Stella Blues Café** (1279 S. Kihei Rd., 808/874-3779, www.stellablues.com, 7:30am-10pm daily, $12-14 lunch, $15-29 dinner) serves American comfort food. It's a nice option for families looking for a mellow, quiet meal. Lunch offers sandwiches and burgers while dinner focuses on pastas, pork chops, and fish plates.

Japanese

⟨ Sansei (1881 S. Kihei Rd., 808/879-0004, www.sanseihawaii.com, 5pm-10pm Sun.-Mon., 5:30pm-10pm Tues.-Wed., 5:30pm-1am Thurs.-Sat., $16) has been a South Maui favorite since 2002. Award-winning dishes such as the panko-crusted ahi rolls and signature shrimp dynamite keep locals flocking to this nondescript spot. The half-priced sushi menu (Thurs.-Sat. after 10pm), with options like *unagi* and rainbow rolls, will leave sushi-lovers feeling like kids in a candy store. Late nights can be noisy, with karaoke in full swing.

Hawaiian Regional

Since most of Kihei's restaurants are in strip malls, there isn't an overabundance of fine dining. The exception, however, is **⟨ Sarento's On The Beach** (2980 S. Kihei Rd., 808/875-7555, www.sarentosonthebeach.com, 7am-11pm and 5:30pm-10pm daily, $28-49), on the water at the north end of Keawakapu Beach. You won't find a more romantic or relaxing spot in Kihei. Start off with the seared ahi or beef carpaccio before moving on to the pan-roasted island snapper or rack of lamb Placourakis. Valet parking is free.

Another local favorite is **Three's Bar and Grill** (1945 S. Kihei Rd., 808/879-3133, www.threesbarandgrill.com, 8:30am-9:30pm Wed.-Sun., 11am-9:30pm Mon.-Tues., $10-15 lunch, $20-25 dinner), inside the Kihei Kalama Village. Opened by three chefs who each boast their own culinary specialty—Hawaiian, Southwestern, and Pacific Rim—the menu at Three's can pull your palate in a direction unique even to the Hawaiian fusion scene. The lunch and appetizer items such as Hawaiian style ribs and kalua pig quesadilla are tasty and affordable. The dinner menu features entrées such as chicken roulade and a raw bar of sushi, oysters, sashimi, and *poke*. Stick around for the live performance in the Surf Lounge.

Natural Foods
The only natural foods store in town is **Hawaiian Moons** (2411 S. Kihei Rd., 808/875-4356, www.hawaiianmoons.com, 8am-9pm daily), within the Kamaole Beach Center across from Kamaole I. The food will make you feel just like home if your diet tends toward the organic, raw, or gluten-free. The hot bar serves up filling lunches.

Coffee Shops
The most modern coffee shop in Kihei is **Java Café** (1279 S. Kihei Rd., 808/214-6095, www.javacafemaui.com, 6am-9pm daily, $7-9) in the Azeka Mauka shopping center. Seventy-five percent of the coffee served is grown in Hawaii. You can also buy bags of unground beans from coffee farms on Maui, Kaua'i, Moloka'i, and the Big Island. Flatbreads and paninis are available for lunch; there's also a large selection of breakfast bagels.

Farmers Market
In North Kihei, right across from Kenolio Park and the Kihei Canoe Club area, the **farmers market** (61 South Kihei Rd., 8am-4pm Mon.-Thurs., 8am-5pm Fri.) is a great way to support local island farmers. On weekends, there's another **farmers market** (95 E. Lipoa Street, 8:30am-11am Sat.-Sun.) between South Kihei Road and the main highway.

WAILEA
Prices in Wailea are much higher than in other parts of the island. You're often paying for master chefs, exceptional service, and unparalleled ambience in world-class resorts. Prices for most meals in Wailea will be double what a similar meal might cost in Kihei. If you venture outside of the resort areas, there are numerous places for a filling and affordable meal.

Italian
The best pizza in Wailea can be found walking distance from many of the hotels at **Manoli's Pizza Company** (100 Wailea Ike Dr., 808/874-7499, www.manolispizzacompany.com, 11:30am-10pm daily, $16-22), across from the Shops at Wailea. Expect 14-inch thin crusts (with both organic wheat and gluten-free options), with toppings like shrimp, pesto, kalamata olives, artichoke hearts, and feta cheese. There are also salads and a few pasta options.

At the luxurious Four Seasons Resort, **Ferraro's Bar e Ristorante** (3900 Wailea Alanui Dr., 808/874-8000, 11:30am-8pm daily, $30-50) has tables close enough to the ocean that you can hear the waves. Clink glasses beneath the stars and savor the aromas of authentic *cucina rustica* cuisine: classic dishes like tagliatelle and chicken involtini, complemented by wine selections like sangiovese and chianti. Lunch is more casual, with wood-fired pizzas.

American
The first restaurant you'll encounter in Wailea approaching from Pi'ilani Highway is **Monkeypod Kitchen** (10 Wailea Ike Dr., 808/891-2322, www.monkeypodkitchen.com, 11:30am-10:30pm daily, $13-35), the brainchild of renowned Maui chef Peter Merriman. Ingredients are all sourced locally, supporting sustainable farming and ensuring fresh, healthy meals. Dinner options range from sesame-crusted mahimahi to bulgogi pork tacos in an Asian pear aioli, or an organic spinach and quinoa salad big enough to share. Garlic truffle oil fries are one of the most popular items on the menu. Lunch options like burgers and sandwiches are less expensive. Enjoy the best craft beer selection in Wailea along with your meal.

Irish
Mulligan's On The Blue (100 Kaukahi St., 808/874-1131, www.mulligansontheblue.com, 11am-midnight Mon-Fri, 8:30am-midnight Sat.-Sun., $10-15) is Wailea's only legitimate sports bar: one of the few places to catch international events such as soccer or rugby. The ocean views, happy hour menu, Willie K dinner show, and Celtic Tigers bagpiping draw

people up the hill above the Fairmont Kea Lani. Fish-and-chips and shepherd's pie, burgers and sandwiches are all economical.

Hawaiian Regional

The Hawaiian regional restaurants in Wailea are utterly fantastic, romantic, and expensive.

At the Four Seasons, **Duo** (3900 Wailea Alanui, 808/874-8000, 6:30am-11am Mon.-Sat., 6:30am-noon Sun., $30-50) ranks in the upper echelon of fine island cuisine. The dinner menu is dominated by steak and seafood options such as Brandt True filet mignon and shiso panko-crusted ahi. For something light, try the lobster bisque. The breakfast buffet is lauded as the best in Wailea.

Humuhumunukunukuapua'a (3850 Wailea Alaui Dr., 808/875-1234, www.wailearesort-dining.com, 5:30pm-9pm nightly, $30-49), at the Grand Wailea, is not only one of the hardest restaurants to pronounce, it's also one of the most popular. Named after the state fish, "Humu" sits in a thatched-roof Polynesian structure afloat on its own million-gallon saltwater lagoon. Large plates include the famous Hawaiian spiny lobster as well as hoisin and pear-braised short ribs.

Seafood

In the Fairmont Kea Lani, **Nick's Fishmarket** (4100 Wailea Alanui Dr., 808/879-7224, www.nicksfishmarktmaui.com, 5:30pm-9:45pm daily, $30-50) focuses on the bounty of the sea. Whitewashed walls and vine-covered trellises give the open-air restaurant a Mediterranean ambience. Selections include opah, mahimahi Kona kampachi, and Moroccan spiced salmon, along with creative sides like wasabi mashed potatoes and mango peppercorn chutney. Reservations are recommended.

MAKENA AND BEYOND

When it comes to finding food this far south, there are three options: Grab lunch at one of the food trucks on the side of the road, eat at one of the Makena Beach and Golf Resort restaurants, or turn back around and head to Kihei or Wailea.

MAUI

Getting There and Around

South Maui is easily navigable by car, although there are a number of parking challenges. First, anyone staying at a Wailea resort is likely to incur a daily parking fee, some of which can be upward of $20/day. Inquire if your resort has a parking fee and factor this into the cost of the rental. One perk of the Makena Beach and Golf Resort is that there isn't any parking fee. Second, when it comes to parking in Kihei, spots along the street in the Kamaole II area can be tough to come by during the middle of the day, so either arrive at the beach early or be prepared to do a little walking. Third, the only public parking lot where you will encounter a fee in South Maui is in Ma'alaea where spaces are charged at a rate of $5 for the day. While having a car is a necessity for anyone wanting to do a lot of exploring, those who just want to relax on the beach and make sporadic ventures elsewhere can get by with a combination of walking, shuttles, public buses, and taxis.

CAR
Rental Cars

If you've already made your way to Kihei and decide you need a rental car, there are a number of local options to get you out on the road. One of the most popular services is family-owned **Kihei Rent a Car** (96 Kio Loop, 808/879-7257 or 800/251-5288, www.kiheirentacar.com). They will even arrange a free pickup or drop-off at the Kahului Airport for any rentals longer than five days. The rates are competitive and often beat out the major corporate competitors.

If you would rather get corporate rewards points, **Avis** (1455 S. Kihei Rd., 808/874-4077, 8am-5pm Mon.-Fri., 8am-4pm weekends) has an outlet in central Kihei right next to Maui Dive Shop and Pizza Madness.

Taxi

To have someone do the driving for you and not worry about pesky details such as parking, directions, or being sober, the best taxi service in Kihei is **MJ Taxi Service** (808/280-9309, mauijimtaxi@hotmail.com).

Shuttle

For those who are staying at the Makena Beach and Golf Resort, a **complimentary shuttle** (808/875-5833, 6am-9:30pm) runs on a first-come, first-served time schedule between the areas of Wailea and Makena Resort. Although the shuttle can't take you any farther than the Shops at Wailea, you can then hop on the Maui Bus if you need to connect to another location.

Anyone needing a ride to the airport can contact **Roberts Hawaii** (866/293-1782, www.robertshawaii.com/mauiexpress). Expect fares to run $13-41 per person, one-way, depending on where you're staying.

Motorcycles and Mopeds

If you just want to cruise around town on a small moped or feel the wind through your hair on a steel horse, there are a number of different operators in town to choose from.

In the Azeka Makai shopping center in North Kihei, **Hawaiian Island Cruisers** (1280 S. Kihei Rd., 808/446-1111, www.hawaiian-cruisers.com, 9am-5pm Mon.-Sat., 10am-2pm Sun.) offers mopeds which range from $35/day to $300/week.

In the Kukui Mall in central Kihei, **Maui Boy Mopeds** (1819 S. Kihei Rd., 808/874-8811, www.mauiboymopeds.com, 8am-5pm daily) has rentals from $15 for two hours to $300/week, and they usually offer the most competitive rates around town.

In the Kamaole Shopping Center beneath Denny's, **Aloha Motorsports** (2463 S. Kihei Rd., 808/667-7000, www.alohamotorsports.com, 8am-5pm daily) rents out everything from Harleys ($119 for four hours) to mopeds ($343/week). They sometimes offer free hotel pickup.

Bus

Maui Bus operates a number of lines throughout South Maui. All sections are $2/boarding, or you can also buy a $4/day pass if you know you'll be hopping on and off a lot. The Kihei Villager Route #15 runs between Ma'alaea Harbor Village and Pi'ilani Shopping Center 6:05am-8:30pm with various stops in between. The Kihei Islander Route #10 runs between Wailea Ike Drive by the Shops at Wailea and Queen Ka'ahumanu Center in Kahului 5:30am-9:30pm, and if you are trying to get to North Kihei or Ma'alaea, you can transfer at Pi'ilani Shopping Center to the Kihei Villager Route #15. A commuter bus leaves from the corner of Kilohana Street and South Kihei Road at 6:15am and reaches the Ritz-Carlton in Kapalua at 7:45am, making various stops along the way. This is convenient if you have a morning boat charter out of Lahaina Harbor or need to get to Ka'anapali.

UPCOUNTRY

Upcountry is Maui's little secret. Occupying the slopes of the towering 10,023-foot Haleakala Volcano, it's a far cry from the postcard-perfect beaches and resort-lined shores so often equated with the island—although the sunsets are equally as spectacular. Here the smell of eucalyptus trees replaces the rustle of palms and ranching and farming still dominate the

MAUI

HIGHLIGHTS

LOOK FOR ◖ TO FIND RECOMMENDED SIGHTS, ACTIVITIES, DINING, AND LODGING.

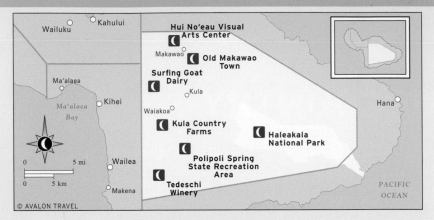

◖ **Polipoli Spring State Recreation Area:** Hidden in the least-visited corner of the island, Polipoli is the only place on Maui where you can walk through a redwood forest up in the clouds (page 367).

◖ **Hui No'eau Visual Arts Center:** This old Baldwin family mansion now houses one of the island's largest art centers (page 376).

◖ **Kula Country Farms:** Kula Country Farms not only offers fresh local produce, it also provides a sweeping view over most of the island (page 377).

◖ **Surfing Goat Dairy:** Take the only tour on Maui where you can both snack on gourmet cheeses and hand-milk a goat (page 378).

◖ **Tedeschi Winery:** Sip on either pineapple or grape wine and enjoy an elk burger at the neighboring grill (page 380).

◖ **Haleakala National Park:** While sunrise gets all of the attention, watching the sunset atop Haleakala is just as spectacular—and doesn't involve waking up at 3am (page 381).

◖ **Old Makawao Town:** Linger for a while in a town that manages to be New Age and rustic all at the same time (page 385).

local lifestyle. Upcountry is where you throw on a light flannel and take a morning drive through the crisp mountain air, perhaps stopping to relax on the porch of a family-run coffeehouse where the patrons and staff all know one another by name. It's a place to hike on the forested trails of Polipoli or Hosmer's Grove, take in the view from the summit of Haleakala, or gaze all the way to the shoreline from 2,000 feet while tasting wine

at Maui's only vineyard. It's also Maui's most artistic community. In the ranching town turned New Age outpost of Makawao, it's just as easy to buy a saddle as it is to purchase freshly blown glass or boutique clothing. Whether you're catching a Sunday morning polo match, eating freshly baked, homemade doughnuts, or buying farm-fresh vegetables straight from the source, you'll see a side of Maui you never expected.

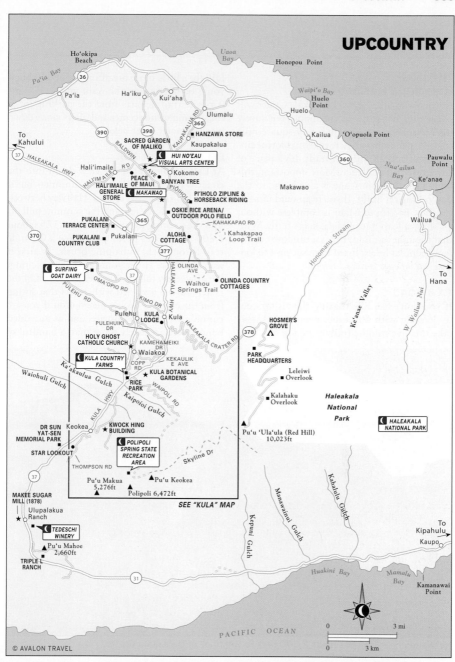

UPCOUNTRY

Ho'okipa Beach
Pa'ia Bay
Pa'ia
36
Ha'iku
Kui'aha
Uaoa Bay
Honopou Point
Waipi'o Bay
Huelo Point
Huelo
Kailua
'O'opuola Point
Ulumalu
390
398
365
KAUPAKALUA RD
BALDWIN RD
SACRED GARDEN OF MALIKO
HANZAWA STORE
Kaupakalua
360
Pauwalu Point
Nua'ailua Bay
Ke'anae
To Kahului
37
HALEAKALA HWY
HUI NO'EAU VISUAL ARTS CENTER
Hali'imaile
HALI'IMAILE RD
Kokomo
PEACE OF MAUI
BANYAN TREE
PI'IHOL RD
Makawao
HALI'IMAILE GENERAL STORE
MAKAWAO
PI'IHOLO ZIPLINE & HORSEBACK RIDING
Wailua
OSKIE RICE ARENA/ OUTDOOR POLO FIELD
370
PUKALANI TERRACE CENTER
365
KAHAKAPAO RD
Kahakapao Loop Trail
Honomanu Stream
PUKALANI COUNTRY CLUB
Pukalani
ALOHA COTTAGE
377
MAUI
SURFING GOAT DAIRY
OMA'OPIO RD
OLINDA AVE
HALEAKALA HWY
Waihou Springs Trail
OLINDA COUNTRY COTTAGES
To Hana
Ke'anae Valley
W Wailua Nui
PULEHU RD
KIMO DR
Pulehu
KULA LODGE
Kula
HOSMER'S GROVE
PULEHUIKI DR
HOLY GHOST CATHOLIC CHURCH
KAMEHAMEIKI DR
Waiakoa
HALEAKALA CRATER RD
378
PARK HEADQUARTERS
KULA COUNTRY FARMS
KEKAULIK E AVE
COPP RD
KULA BOTANICAL GARDENS
Leleiwi Overlook
Ka'akaulua Gulch
RICE PARK
WAIPOLI RD
Kalahaku Overlook
Haleakala National Park
HALEAKALA NATIONAL PARK
Waiohuli Gulch
KULA HWY
Kaipoioi Gulch
DR SUN YAT-SEN MEMORIAL PARK
Keokea
KWOCK HING BUILDING
POLIPOLI SPRING STATE RECREATION AREA
Pu'u 'Ula'ula (Red Hill) 10,023ft
STAR LOOKOUT
THOMPSON RD
Skyline Dr
37
Pu'u Makua 5,276ft
Pu'u Keokea
MAKEE SUGAR MILL (1878)
Polipoli 6,472ft
SEE "KULA" MAP
Ulupalakua Ranch
Kepuni Gulch
Manawainui Gulch
Kahalulu Gulch
To Kipahulu
TEDESCHI WINERY
Pu'u Mahoe 2,660ft
Kaupo
TRIPLE L RANCH
31
Huakini Bay
Mamalu Bay
Kamanawai Point
PACIFIC OCEAN
0   3 mi
0   3 km

© AVALON TRAVEL

MAUI

Hiking and Biking

HIKING
Haleakala National Park
Anyone who hikes across Haleakala Crater will swear they could be on the moon, but surely not Maui. The crater basin is a 19-square-mile volcanic panorama crisscrossed by colorful cinder cones and 28 miles of trails. It's a place of adventure and of silence. More important, this high-altitude moonscape is also home to the best hiking on Maui. If you're an outdoors enthusiast, no trip to Maui is complete without tackling at least one of Haleakala's trails. With that thought in mind, here's a rundown of the most popular hikes, listed from shortest to longest (*all mileage is round-trip*).

PA KA'OAO
If you don't feel like sharing the visitor center lookout with 400 other people at sunrise, take this five-minute trail to the top of White Hill for a little more breathing room (although you'll be huffing on the walk up there). This 0.4-mile trail departs from the parking lot at the summit visitor center and offers views down into the crater floor below.

LELEIWI OVERLOOK
At **Leleiwi Overlook,** the view down into the crater is the same as from the summit—but it isn't as far, and it isn't as cold. Halfway between the park headquarters and the summit, pull off into the parking lot at mile marker 17.5 (about 8,800 feet in elevation) and follow a 0.5-mile trail through the subalpine brush. At first it won't look like you're going anywhere exciting, but after a few minutes you reach the rim of the crater and are awarded with colors that spring from the earth. This is a nice option if you are running late for the sunrise, and as an added bonus there are rarely more than a handful of

© MARK DRIESSEN

Keonehe'ehe'e Trail descends 2,500 feet to the floor of Haleakala Crater.

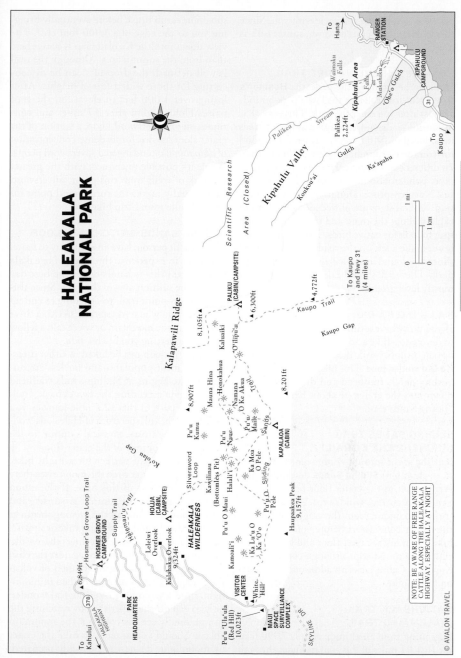

HALEAKALA NATIONAL PARK

MAUI

To Hana

RANGER STATION

Waimoku Falls

Makahiku Falls

'Ohe'o Gulch

Kipahulu Area

KIPAHULU CAMPGROUND

31

To Kaupo

Palikea Stream

Palikea 2,224ft

Kipahulu Valley

Koukou'ai

Gulch

Ka'apahu

Scientific Research Area (Closed)

1 mi

1 km

0

0

PALIKU (CABIN/CAMPSITE)

6,300ft

To Kaupo and Hwy 31 (4 miles)

4,772ft

Kaupo Trail

Kaupo Gap

Kalapawili Ridge

8,105ft

Kaluaiki

'O'ilipu'u

Mauna Hina

Honokahua

8,907ft

Pu'u Kumu

Pu'u Naue

Namana O Ke Akua

Pu'u Maile

Maile Trail

8,201ft

Ko'olau Gap

Silversword Loop

Kawilinau (Bottomless Pit)

Halali'i

Ka Moa O Pele

Pu'u O Pele

Sliding Sands

KAPALAOA (CABIN)

HOLUA (CABIN, CAMPSITE)

HALEAKALA WILDERNESS

Pu'u O Maui

Ka Lu'u O Ka 'O'o

Haupaakea Peak 9,157ft

Kamoali'i

Supply Trail

Halemau'u Trail

Hosmer's Grove Loop Trail

HOSMER GROVE CAMPGROUND

Leleiwi Overlook

Kalahaku Overlook 9,324ft

6,849ft

378

To Kahului

HALEAKALA HIGHWAY

PARK HEADQUARTERS

VISITOR CENTER

White Hill

MAUI SPACE SURVEILLANCE COMPLEX

Pu'u 'Ula'ula (Red Hill) 10,023ft

SKYLINE DR

NOTE: BE AWARE OF FREE RANGE CATTLE ALONG THE HALEAKALA HIGHWAY, ESPECIALLY AT NIGHT

© AVALON TRAVEL

MAUI

people watching the spectacle with you. Since this lookout faces east, however, sunset isn't as nice.

HOSMER'S GROVE NATURE TRAIL
Unlike other trails in the park, the **Hosmer's Grove Nature Trail** is at the lower park boundary just after you enter the park. This easy, 0.5-mile trail leads you through a stand of trees introduced in 1910 to see if any would be good for commercial lumber. There are more than 20 different species here. Here you'll see Jeffrey pine, ponderosa pine, incense cedar, eucalyptus, Norway spruce, Douglas fir, and Japanese sugi. Several signs are posted along the trail to explain about the trees, and this is also a good spot to look for native birds. To reach the trailhead, make a left on the road pointing toward the campground immediately after entering the park. The walk should take a half hour over mostly level ground.

KA LU'U O KA O'O
If you don't have a full day (or couple of days) to devote to a hike across the crater floor, a nice option is the 5.5-mile descent to the **Ka Lu'u O Ka O'o** cinder cone. This hike departs from the Sliding Sands trailhead and drops two miles down into the crater, or about halfway down Sliding Sands trail.

SLIDING SANDS TRAIL (KEONEHE'EHE'E TRAIL)
Starting at the summit visitors center (at 9,800 ft. in elevation) **Sliding Sands** descends 2,500 vertical feet to the crater floor below. Sliding Sands is a barren, windswept, shadeless, and stunning conduit from the craggy summit to the cinder cone desert before you. If you just hike down to the crater floor and back, it's an eight-mile round-trip, although continuing to Kapalaoa Cabin tacks an additional 3.5 miles on to the hike.

SWITCHBACK TRAIL (HALEMAU'U TRAIL)
Beginning from an altitude of only 7,990 feet, the first 1.1 miles of this trail meander through subalpine scrub brush before eventually bringing you to the edge of a 1,000-foot cliff. The view down into the Ko'olau Gap is better here than from the summit area. Although the trail is well-defined, the drop-offs can be disconcerting for those with a fear of heights. After losing over 1,000 feet in elevation, the trail passes Holua Cabin after 3.7 miles and continues on to Silversword Loop, a section of the crater floor known for its dense concentration of *ahinahina,* or endangered silversword plants. While it's possible to connect with the greater network of trails from this point, Silversword Loop usually marks the turnaround point for this 9.2-mile round-trip hike.

SLIDING SANDS-SWITCHBACK LOOP
If you're a fit person, have an entire day to spare, and want to experience the best of Haleakala Crater, then this is hands-down the best day hike in the summit area of the park. Since this is a point-to-point trail, you're going to end up six miles from where you started, so either drive two cars up the mountain or sweet-talk a fellow visitor into letting you hitch a ride.

While the loop can be hiked in either direction, the most popular—and far less strenuous—route begins at Sliding Sands trailhead and exits via ascending the Switchback Trail. Along the path of this 12.2 mile-journey you experience the full spectrum of Haleakala wonders, from the frosty, mystical summit, to the otherworldly solitude of the crater floor.

The trail is also perfect for a night hike. Depending on what time the moon rises there are two variations of this hike: If the moon rises early, depart the summit at sunset, and if the moon rises later in the evening, begin at about midnight and finish your hike at sunrise. There are few more surreal feelings than walking completely alone, bundled against the chill of the night air, hearing the crunch of volcanic cinder beneath your feet, bathed in moonlight amid a panorama of geological wonder, only to cap off the experience by watching the sun gradually set the colors of the mountain ablaze. Should you attempt to hike the crater by moonlight, it's best to be overly prepared.

MAUI

the open expanse of Haleakala Crater

Bring a backpack full of extra clothing, carry extra water, pack an extra flashlight. You'll be exposed to windchills that can dip below freezing at any time of the year.

KAUPO GAP

"Shooting the gap" is the most extreme hike on the island. It takes two days, covers 17.5 miles, and has an elevation drop of 9,500 feet. In order to complete the hike you need to be in prime physical condition and comfortable in the backcountry. The majority of hikers spend the night at Paliku Cabin, which at a distance of 9.2 miles from Sliding Sands trailhead is the remotest—and lushest—of the crater's three backcountry cabins. For those without a cabin reservation, there is a primitive campsite at Paliku; free permits can be arranged at the park headquarters. On the second day of the hike you'll make a steep descent from Paliku, pass through a gate that marks the park boundary, and continue across private land (which is allowed) from here until Kaupo Store. Once outside of the park boundary, keep a lookout

for axis deer and feral goats as they will occasionally leap across the trail. You finish the hike in the semi-deserted outpost of Kaupo at a distance of 53 road miles from where you started, so if you ever want to make it back to civilization, you either have to arrange a ride or convince the rare passerby to shuttle your sweaty, backcountry body all the way to the other side of the island. If you're up for the challenge, however, pack accordingly, be prepared, let someone know where you're going, and take lots of pictures. There aren't many places in America as pristine as what you'll find out here.

◖ Polipoli Spring State Recreation Area

Polipoli is an out-of-the-way, rarely visited destination offering some of the best hiking on the island. The trails at Polipoli pass through stands of old-growth redwoods, eucalyptus, ash, and pines. To reach Polipoli, drive on Highway 37 (Kula Highway) as if you were heading to Ulupalakua Ranch and the Tedeschi Winery. At the second junction of Highways 37

© IOFOTO/123RF.COM

Polipoli Spring State Recreation Area

and 377 (just past Kula Country Farms), make a left on Highway 377 and travel for 0.3 mile until you reach Waipoli Road, where you will take a right. Follow Waipoli Road for about a mile until it crosses a cattle guard, and continue on the switchbacking road through the pastures. This is the scenic—and only—entranceway for vehicles to reach the hiking trails above.

The first hike you'll encounter in Polipoli is the **Waiakoa Loop Trail,** which begins just after the hut at the hunter's check-in station. The trailhead technically doesn't begin for 0.75 mile down the hunter access road, but unless you have a four-wheel-drive vehicle, it's better to park at the hunter's station and walk down to the trailhead. Once you are there, a three-mile loop with a moderate elevation change of 400 feet passes through lowland brush and pines. The area around Waiakoa is also popular with hunters, so stay on the trail and wear bright clothing.

Farther up the switchbacking road, just past the cattle guard (where the road turns to dirt) is the trailhead for the **Boundary Trail,** a 4.4-mile one-way trail that descends down to the lower fence line of Polipoli before connecting with other trails. This trail offers sweeping views of South Maui and—since it's about 1,000 vertical feet lower than some of the other trails—won't leave you quite as winded. This can either be done as an out-and-back hike or combined with other trails as a loop. The shortest loop is to go up the **Lower Waiohuli Trail,** which intersects the Boundary Trail at the 2.6-mile mark. Turning left on the Lower Waiohuli Trail, it's 1.4 miles back uphill to the main road, and then a 2.5-mile trek back along the dirt road to your car.

If seven miles seems too far, most of the shorter walks in Polipoli begin and end at the campground at the end of the road. While some are only a mile long, the best hike in the park for first-time visitors is the 5.3-mile loop trail formed by connecting the **Haleakala Ridge Trail, Polipoli Trail, Redwood Trail,** and **Plum Trail.** This loop departs from the parking lot by the campground and winds its way through redwoods, pines, and plum trees, which occasionally bear fruit during the summer. Bring water on the trail and pack a light jacket in case the mists roll in. Hunters sometimes patrol these same areas so stick to the well-signed and established trails.

It's possible to hike all the way from Polipoli to the summit of Haleakala by following the 6.8-mile dirt road known as **Skyline Drive.** This road provides a "back entrance" into Haleakala National Park. If it has snowed recently on top of Haleakala and the rangers have the main road closed down, this is an alternative way to hike into the park and be the only person in a tropical snowstorm. Even on regular days, however, Skyline is a strenuous hike providing panoramic views down the southwest rift zone of Haleakala. Though Haleakala has been dormant for more than 220 years, volcanologists claim that if (and when) the mountain erupts again, magma would seep from the earth in the barren landscape that's visible from this trail. To reach the Skyline Drive trailhead, turn left at the fork that leads down to the campground from the main dirt road. From here the road keeps climbing and begins to double back toward the north, along the way passing the trailhead for the 1.8-mile **Mamane Trail.** Eventually you'll reach a locked gate at an area known as The Ballpark; from this 7,000-foot elevation it's a 3,000-foot vertical switchback to the summit. Pack plenty of water and warm clothing. Be aware of the challenges of hiking at altitude.

Makawao

While much of the land behind Makawao is either privately owned ranchland or part of the state watershed system, two well-maintained trails provide Makawao hikers with a couple of options for getting back into the forest.

In the heart of the Makawao Forest Reserve, the **Kahakapao Loop Trail** is popular with hikers, bikers, and families taking their dogs for a walk. This 5.7-mile loop trail climbs its way through the sweet smell of eucalyptus, Cook pines, tropical ash, and a handful of other native plant species in the cool air at 3,000 feet. You would expect to find a trail like this in

New England or Oregon, but not in Maui. This trail is a favorite of Upcountry locals. To reach the trailhead from Makawao, follow Makawao Avenue toward Ha'iku for 0.3 mile before making a right on Pi'iholo Road. After 1.5 miles (just past the Pi'iholo zipline tours) take a left where the road forks and follow it for 0.5 mile. Here you'll make a right onto Kahakapao Road and drive 1.5 miles on a narrow uphill until you reach a metal gate, open 7am-7pm. From the gate, a steep asphalt road continues for another 0.5 mile until it reaches a gravel parking lot in front of the trailhead. As this is a multiuse trail network, keep an eye out for bikers.

If you don't feel like dealing with bikers on your relaxing morning stroll, you're better off heading to the two-mile-long **Waihou Spring Trail** toward the top of Olinda Road. This trail is only open to hikers and doesn't have as steep of an elevation gain as the one at Kahakapao. It's uniquely situated among a pine tree experiment so that all the pines appear like towering rows of corn. While the wooded trail is nice enough for walking, the treat is at the end where a brief, steep switchback descends down into an old irrigation gulch. In the 30-foot rock face at the end of the trail you can make out tunnels bored through the rock. You can climb into the tunnels and follow them back for a bit, although it's tough to do without a light. To reach the Waihou Springs trailhead, go to the only intersection in Makawao and follow Olinda Road uphill for five miles before you see the pine-needle parking lot on the right.

BIKING

With miles of open road and some of the best trails on Maui, Upcountry is the most popular part of the island for both road bikers and mountain bikers. The air up here is nice and cool, the views stretch all the way to the ocean below, and the traffic levels are lower than on many of the island's other main roads. The only rental operator Upcountry is in downtown Makawao: **Krank Cycles** (1120 Makawao Ave., 808/572-2299, www.krankmaui.com, 8am-6pm daily) specializes in mountain bike rentals ($60/day, $220/week). For road cycles, the

Biking the Volcano

Riding a bike down Haleakala can be one of the best days of your vacation. Here are some tips to ensure that your ride is smooth.

- If you go with a rental company, you can no longer ride from the summit, and instead must begin biking at the 6,500-foot level. If you want to bike from the summit, you need to provide your own bicycle and transport.

- Seeing the sunrise isn't guaranteed. 15 percent of the time, the crater will be socked in with clouds. The variations aren't even seasonal, so all you can do is hope for the best.

- If you're planning on joining a sunrise tour, be prepared to wake up *really* early. Companies collect guests from the farthest hotels first, so if you're staying in Makena or Kapalua, you can expect to meet your driver as early as 1:45am.Try to book this excursion early in your trip, when you're still jet-lagged and waking up early. Maui is 2-6 hours behind the continental U.S., so jet lag works in your favor.

- If you're on a budget, opt for a midmorning tour. It isn't as cold, you don't have to wake up as early, it isn't as crowded, and the trips are

substantially cheaper. Companies charge more for the sunrise tours because they're popular.

- Pack closed-toe shoes, long pants, a rain jacket, and warm clothing. Early morning temperatures can often dip below freezing at the summit. Although many tour companies provide rain gear, the more protection you have against the elements, the better.

- Don't expect to get any sleep in the van ride up. The road switchbacks so many times you can never get in a rhythm, and drivers entertain the crowd with island history and jokes. It's best to just get a good night's sleep.

- If you're skittish, go with a guided group. If you're an independent person, choose an independent company where you can ride without a guide. The only option for watching the sunrise and riding independently is with Haleakala Bike Company. With this company, you can't ride all the way to the beach without paying an extra fee.

- To avoid decompression sickness, don't fly or travel to higher altitudes for 24 hours after diving. That means you shouldn't schedule a ride down Haleakala on a day after scuba diving.

closest options are **Haleakala Bike Company** (810 Haʻiku Rd., #120, 808/575-9575 or 888/922-2452, www.bikemaui.com, 8:30am-5pm Mon.-Sat., 9am-4pm Sun.) in Haʻiku and **Maui Cyclery** (99 Hana Hwy., 808/579-9009, www.gocyclingmaui.com, 8am-6pm Mon.-Fri., 8am-4pm Sat., 8am-noon Sun.) in Paʻia.

Road Cycling

For avid cyclists there are few better climbs in the United States than the 10,000-foot ascent up Haleakala Volcano. If biking for 36 miles straight *uphill* sounds like something only crazy people would do, consider that over 140 people took part in the 2013 Cycle to the Sun race, which goes from the warm beaches of Paʻia to the frigid air of the summit.

If, however, you want to enjoy the Haleakala panorama without having to aggressively strain your quads, a better choice is to **bike down Haleakala,** where the most strenuous thing you'll have to do is flex your fingers as you pump the brakes. One of the most popular visitor activities on the island, the "ride down the volcano" has become tamer in recent years due to the fact you can only bike from the summit on your own personal bike. Anyone on a rental is now only allowed to bike from the 6,500-foot level outside of the park boundaries.

For those who employ basic safety, however, this ride is a great way to tour Upcountry. Since you can no longer ride down from the summit on a rental—but nearly all people want to see Haleakala Crater—tour companies will

© KYLE ELLISON

Bike 6,500 feet down the side of a dormant volcano.

drive cyclists to the top of the mountain to view the sunrise (or simply peer into the crater if it's a later trip), and then everyone climbs back into the van to head down to 6,500 feet. While this largely detracts from what the ride used to be, the ride from the boundary of the park down to sea level still takes you through the scenic pasturelands of Kula, the cowboy town of Makawao, and finishes on the beach at Pa'ia where sea salt blows on the afternoon trade winds. Even though all companies must start at the same location, there are still a number of differences between tour groups as to where the ride finishes and how they're set up.

If you're the type of person who doesn't move with a herd, yet you still want to see the sunrise, your best bet is going to be **Haleakala Bike Company** (810 Ha'iku Rd., #120, 808/575-9575 or 888/922-2452, www.bikemaui.com, 8:30am-5pm Mon.-Sat., 9am-4pm Sun.), giving you the freedom to descend without a guide. This is the only company that has this option for a sunrise tour. The benefit is that once you're dropped off at the top you're free to make as many stops on the ride down as you'd like. If you chose to catch the shuttle from your hotel, however, you can't linger forever because you need to be back by 11am. Alternately, you can drive yourself to the Ha'iku office in the morning. The downside of the Haleakala Bike Company tour is that since the office is in Ha'iku (at around the 1,000 feet), you don't get the opportunity to ride all the way down to the beach. If you "make a wrong turn" and decide to end up at the beach in Pa'ia anyway, they'll still come and pick you up, but it's going to cost you an extra fee. Tours available are the sunrise tour ($120), a 9am tour ($85), and an express tour that doesn't include the trip into Haleakala National Park ($70). If you're set on biking from the summit, Haleakala Bike Company also provides rentals if you can find someone to drop you at the top.

If you would feel more comfortable biking down with a guide, companies such as **Maui Downhill** (199 Dairy Rd., 808/871-2155, www.mauidownhill.com) provide guided services down the volcano with well-trained guides who stick with you every step of the way. The sunrise tours will cost more ($149), although you can shave a few dollars off the price by driving yourself to the Kahului baseyard and opting to reach the summit after sunrise ($119). They do provide warm clothing and gloves, but the lunch in Pukalani isn't included, and you finish the last 1,500 feet of the journey on a van ride back to Kahului headquarters. Other trips available are the express excursion, which goes directly to the 6,500-foot starting point (and doesn't include hotel pickup) for $109 or a trip which combines the descent with a van tour out to the Tedeschi Winery ($129).

If finishing the ride next to the ocean is a must, **Cruiser Phil's** (58 A Amala Pl., 808/893-2332 or 877/764-2453, www.cruiserphil.com, 7am-7pm daily) offers riders the ability to bike from 6,500 feet all the way down to the beach in Pa'ia ($150). The section of road between Makawao and Pa'ia passes pineapple fields and historic churches, and it's a much better option than finishing in Pukalani or Ha'iku. Day trips that don't view the sunrise are also available ($135), or if you would like to ride independently with Cruiser Phil's ($99), on select days of the week you can meet a guide at 8:15am in Pa'ia and be driven up the mountain from there. Tours eat breakfast/lunch in either Kula or Pa'ia, although the cost of the meal isn't included in the trip. This is a good tour if you want to ride independently all the way to Pa'ia and don't care if you see the sunrise. Companies offering similar itineraries

and services are **Maui Mountain Cruisers** (381 Baldwin Ave., 808/871-6014, www.mauimountaincruisers.com, 9am-5pm weekdays, 10am-4pm weekends), **Mountain Riders** (15 South Wakea Ave., 808/877-4944, www.mountainriders.com), and **Bike It Maui** (808/878-3364, www.bikeitmaui.com), all of which finish in the town of Pa'ia.

For regular road cyclists who aren't looking to ride down the volcano, one of the best Upcountry rides is the stretch of highway from Kula to Kanaio. Starting at Rice Park off Kula Highway (Hwy. 37), the 30-mile round-trip takes you south through the communities of Keokea, Ulupalakua, and finally to Kanaio, a dry ranching outpost on the "back road" to Hana. There's a 500-foot elevation drop from Kula to Kanaio, and the views along this ride span from the north shore all the way to Makena and Lahaina. This is a popular weekend ride where cyclists often take halftime at Grandma's Coffee House in Keokea.

Mountain Biking

Many people are surprised to learn that on an island best known for its ocean activities there is decent mountain biking. While it doesn't compare to places such as Tahoe or Moab, there are still downhill rides and single-track trails where even the most hard-core mountain biker can still have a good time.

The area with the most trails is the **Polipoli** section of mountainside high above the pastures of Kula. While a number of the trails in Polipoli are rated as pedestrian only, the **Waiakoa Loop Trail** is a three-mile loop with a 400-foot elevation gain which is open to both hikers and bikers. To reach Waiakoa, travel up Waipoli Road off Highway 377, go past the lavender farm, and park your car off the side of the road just past the hunter's check-in station. The trailhead is 0.75 mile down a four-wheel-drive access road. Since this is also a hunting area, wear bright clothing. Toward the top of Waipoli Road the pavement changes to dirt, and a good ride is to park your car where the Upper Waiohuli Trail and Mamane Trail intersect the dirt road. From here you can ride a loop trail where you climb the dirt road, turn left where the road forks, and continue climbing until you reach the trailhead for the Mamane Trail, which offers a two-mile, single-track descent back down to your car. If you want to tack on a few more miles before bombing down the Mamane Trail, ride Kahua Road out to the hunting shelter and back before heading back down to your car.

While the Waiakoa Loop Trail and Mamane Trail are fine rides, the best ride in Polipoli (and the entire island) is the dirt road known as **Skyline Drive.** From the trailhead of the Mamane Trail it's about six more miles up the southwestern ridge of the mountain to the summit of Haleakala, and the switchbacking ascent is so steep in places that you'll occasionally need to get off and walk your bike. If you park your car at the Polipoli campground, it's about 8.5 miles to the summit, or, if you have four-wheel drive, you can take your car all the way up to a locked gate at area known as The Ballpark. Even if you start at The Ballpark, however, it's a 3,000-foot climb before you reach the summit of Haleakala, with the reward, of course, being the screamer of a descent you're awarded on the way down.

Begin by having someone drop you off at the summit of Haleakala and start Skyline Drive at the top! To reach the start of Skyline Drive, when approaching from the summit, drive as if you're going to the observation platform in the upper parking lot, but before you get there take a left on the service road that leads toward Science City. On the left-hand side of this service road you'll see a locked gate, and the dirt road that's on the other side is the start of the Skyline Trail. Beginning from this point, you'll switchback down Skyline Drive for six miles before linking up with the Mamane Trail, at which point you will enjoy the two miles of single-track down to the dirt portion of Waipoli Road. Take a right and begin riding down Waipoli Road until it turns to pavement. If you're feeling like an extra workout, you can branch off and tackle the Waiakoa Loop Trail on your way down. Ascend from the loop trail back to the main road, and then continue down Waipoli Road all the way to Highway 377. From here, go left, down to Highway 37, then left again, and finish your epic ride with a two-mile gradual descent on pavement to Grandma's Coffee House in Keokea for a celebratory lunch. Along the ride you will have dropped more than 7,000 vertical feet. Arrange to have someone pick you up here to cap off what is the best mountain descent on the island.

If you don't have a day to devote to a downhill epic, however, and are just looking to squeeze in a couple of hours on the trail, the **Kahakapao Loop Trail** in the Makawao Forest Reserve offers a 5.7-mile loop that climbs its way through eucalyptus, pine, and a handful of native plants. At 3,000 feet, the cool mountain air combined with the dense forest gives the feeling of riding in British Columbia or the foothills of Vermont. From the gravel parking lot, a 0.5-mile entry trail leads to a junction where bikers can choose between the east and west loops. In planning for the descent, note that the west loop has more jumps, but the east loop is a smoother ride.

Horseback Riding and Bird-Watching

HORSEBACK RIDING
Makawao

Sprawling across 800 acres, **Pi'iholo Ranch** (808/270-8750, www.piiholo.com, 8:30am-1pm Mon.-Sat.) is a working cattle operation set back in the pastures above Makawao. One-hour ($75), two-hour ($120), and private rides are available for journeys across open ranchland 2,000 feet up on the mountainside. Groups are capped at six people and the one-hour and two-hour rides go at a mellow pace. Coffee is provided for the early morning rides (8:30 and 9am), and every Tuesday and Thursday at 4pm there are free roping sessions open to the public to come and enjoy. To reach Pi'iholo Ranch go 1.5 miles up Pi'iholo Road before branching left on to Waiahiwi Road. Follow this for 0.5 mile, and the sign for the ranch will be on the left.

Kula

In addition to offering rides across the pastureland of Haleakala Ranch ($95-110), **Pony Express** (18303 Haleakala Hwy., 808/667-2200, www.ponyexpresstour.com) is the only operation on the island that takes you down inside the crater on horseback. Saddling up from the 9,800-foot level near the summit, riders depart down Sliding Sands Trail before eventually reaching the crater floor over 2,500 vertical feet below ($182). Over the course of this 7.5-mile, four-hour excursion, you're able to descend into the backcountry of Haleakala National Park and a realm accessible only by trail. It can be cold and breezy up here, but riding in the saddle as you crunch your way across an otherworldly panorama of cinder is a riding experience unlike any other on the island.

Keokea and Ulupalakua

If you want the feeling that you're riding with a genuine ranching family in their scenic backyard, then book an excursion with the folks at **Thompson Ranch** (Middle Rd., 808/878-1910, www.thompsonranchmaui.com). The rides take place in the pastures of a working cattle ranch, and there isn't one thing about this ride that feels "touristy" in any way. You meet Jerry and Toni Thompson at their ranch house and then hitch a ride with them up to the horse stables where you are introduced to your steed for the next two hours ($100). Once saddled up, you climb up toward the uppermost edge of the ranch where the pasture bumps into the edge of the Polipoli forest. Since this is all private land—and there is no other way to access this section of the mountain—riding across these pastures provides a glimpse into one of the only places in the United States where you can ride near forests of native koa and sandalwood trees and gaze down on the clear blue Pacific. This is

a fantastic ride for couples or families looking for an off the beaten path riding experience.

To ride across the back of a dormant volcano on horseback, head to **Triple L Ranch** (15900 Pi'ilani Hwy., 808/280-7070, www.triple-l-ranchmaui.com, 8am-6pm daily). While one-hour and two-hour rides are offered for $125 and $150 (and include a voucher for a free Bully's Burger), the real reason to choose this ranch over any other is the chance to book either a half-day ($285) or full-day ($375) ride down to a rocky beach completely inaccessible from anywhere else on the island. Centuries ago this section of mountain sported a large native Hawaiian population, and along the way the guides will point out archaeological sites dating to the days of ancient Hawaii. Furthermore, if you are an advanced rider and want to trot, canter, or gallop your horse, there isn't anyone who's going to stop you. Four miles past the Tedeschi Winery in Ulupalakua, this is truly the "last frontier" out here, a place of rugged beauty, relentless sun, and genuine guides who have been ranching this land for more than 50 years.

BIRD-WATCHING
Haleakala National Park

The forests of **Haleakala National Park** offer the best opportunity for spotting endangered and endemic forest birds. Given the extreme isolation of the Hawaiian archipelago, 71 species of birds have been classified as being endemic to the islands, a distinction meaning they are found nowhere else on earth. Unfortunately, of those initial 71 species, 23 have already become extinct, and dozens of others are critically endangered. Due to rodents, feral cats, and mongooses, as well as the removal of the native bird's habitat, species such as the 'i'wi, 'apapane, 'amakihi, Maui creeper, and 'akohekohe now find themselves clinging to existence on the remote slopes of Haleakala.

One of the best places for amateur bird-watchers to catch a glimpse of Hawaii's native species is at **Hosmer's Grove** on the moderate, half-mile loop trail. Even if you don't see

MAUI

© DENIS DORE/123RF.COM

a *nene* in Haleakala National Park

treetops of Hosmer's Grove chirp with a bird-song different than anywhere else on the planet. While casual hikers have a good chance of spotting an *'i'wi* or *'apapane,* the best way of spotting a rare species is to take a guided walk into the **Waikamoi Preserve** with a national park ranger. Every Monday and Thursday at 8:45am rangers lead three-mile guided walks into the preserve monitored by The Nature Conservancy, which focus on the area's native flora and fauna. For more information call park staff at 808/572-4400. Reservations are essential. Although operating on a less frequent basis, hikes into the preserve are also occasionally arranged by the **Maui Forest Bird Recovery Project** (808/573-0280).

Higher on the slopes of the park, bird-watchers should keep an eye out for two endangered species, the *'u'au* (Hawaiian petrel), which burrows in areas near the summit visitor center, and the *nene* (Hawaiian goose), which can be spotted along roadways as well as the valley floor. The *nene* is also the official state bird. One of the best places for spotting the rare goose is in the wet grasslands and pastures surrounding Paliku Cabin on the eastern edge of the crater floor.

any of the native species of honeycreepers—birds whose bills have been specially adapted to extract nectar out of native plant species—the

Adventure Sports

PARAGLIDING

Anyone driving up the slopes of Polipoli might look out and see a lot of grass, but to the trained eye of a paraglider, this misty green hillside offers perfect conditions for throwing yourself off a ledge and getting a bird's-eye view of Maui. **Proflyght Hawaii Paragliding** (1598 Waipoli Rd., 808/874-5433, www.paraglidemaui.com, 7am-7pm daily) is the oldest—and only—full-fledged paragliding school in all of Hawaii. Because of the island's optimal conditions, tandem instructors are able to help people soar above the pasturelands 330 days out of the year, and the launching and landing sites are perfectly suited to learning the sport of paragliding. Nearly all of the flights take place in the

still morning hours before the clouds fill in. Tandem flights cost $95 for a 1,000-foot descent, or $185 for a 3,000-foot drop over the forest treetops and down to the landing site below.

ZIPLINE TOURS
Makawao

The largest zipline on the island with two lines that run parallel to each other is at **Pi'iholo Zipline Tours** (799 Pi'iholo Rd., 808/572-1717 or 800/374-7050, www.piiholozipline.com, 7am-9pm daily) in the forested uplands above Makawao. There is a 4-line course that is more economical at $140, but if you're going to spend the money and make the drive up here, you may as well spend the little bit extra to do the 5-line course ($190) where the last two lines offer a different thrill. The second to last line of the 5-line course zips for 1,420 feet to the base of Pi'iholo Hill, where you are then driven to the top for a 360° view of the surrounding Makawao and Ha'iku area. As if the view weren't enough, the final pièce de résistance is a 2,800-foot zip that leaves your feet dangling over 600 feet above the forested ravine below. This is the longest side-by-side zipline in the state and well worth the experience. In order to be eligible to zip you need to be at least eight years old and between 75 and 275 pounds. Closed-toe shoes are required. Bring a jacket for the cool early morning hours. Complimentary coffee is provided at the site, and helmets equipped with GoPro cameras are available for an additional charge. Makawao is on the windward side of the island and receives considerably more rain than Lahaina and Wailea. Trips continue to run rain or shine (and there are even small waterfalls in the ravine when it rains), so all you can do is cross your fingers and hope for the best. More than just ziplines, Pi'iholo also offers

canopy tours (808/270/8750) where you zip from tree stand to tree stand on either a 3-line ($90), 6-line ($135), or 9-line ($165) course through the treetops. For the ultimate test of strength and agility, combine a 3-line zipline course with a climb up the 42-foot military-style **Tango Tower.**

Kula

Farther up the mountainside on the road to Haleakala, **Skyline Eco-Adventures** (12 Kiopa'a Pl., 808/878-8400, www.zipline.com, 7am-7pm daily) holds the distinction of not only being the original zipline course on Maui, but also the first one found anywhere in the United States. Here's the good news when compared to Pi'iholo: At $95 it's much cheaper. Although there are five lines, they are much tamer than the ones at Pi'iholo, the age limit is 10 years old (as compared to eight at Pi'iholo), you can't ride side by side, and seeing as it's located at 4,000 feet, you can't have been scuba diving the day before. The weight limit for this course is 80-260 pounds. Still, this is a good option if you're on a budget or it's your first time ziplining.

Sights

MAKAWAO
◖ Hui No'eau Visual Arts Center
About one mile downhill from Makawao is the **Hui No'eau Visual Arts Center** (2841 Baldwin Ave., 808/572-6560, www.huinoeau.com, 10am-4pm Mon.-Sat., $2 donation suggested), located on the Baldwin family's 10-acre estate. Matriarch Ethel Baldwin is described as "a child of privilege who used every gift she possessed for the creation of a more beautiful, more intelligent, and more just world." Given her commitment to education and the arts, it came as no surprise that in 1934 the resplendent neo-Spanish mansion was transformed into a sprawling arts center. Today, artisans here produce everything from ceramics to *lau hala* weaving and drawings to sculptures. The

old house is home to the center office, gift gallery, periodic shows, and an informative historical museum about the estate, while the former stable and carriage house have been changed into working studios. Classes are available for both visitors and locals. A full class schedule of everything from ceramics to felting can be found on the website.

KULA
Gentle Kula is rural and rustic, and most of the sights have agricultural ties. Occupying a swath of mountainside at 2,000-4,000 feet, Kula's bicoastal views are reason enough to visit. There's just something calming about driving a backcountry road while shopping for local produce. This is a side of Maui most

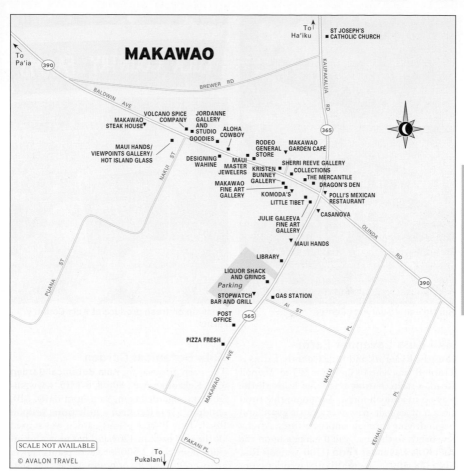

MAKAWAO

To Ha'iku

ST JOSEPH'S
■ CATHOLIC CHURCH

To
Pa'ia
390

KAUPAKALUA RD

BALDWIN AVE

BREWER RD

365

VOLCANO SPICE
COMPANY

JORDANNE
GALLERY
AND
■ STUDIO

MAKAWAO
STEAK HOUSE▼

ALOHA
COWBOY

GOODIES ■

MAUI HANDS/
VIEWPOINTS GALLERY/
HOT ISLAND GLASS

RODEO
GENERAL
STORE

MAKAWAO
GARDEN CAFÉ

DESIGNING
WAHINE

MAUI
MASTER
JEWELERS

SHERRI REEVE GALLERY

KRISTEN
BUNNEY
GALLERY

COLLECTIONS
■ THE MERCANTILE
■ DRAGON'S DEN

MAKAWAO
FINE ART
GALLERY

KOMODA'S
LITTLE TIBET

POLLI'S MEXICAN
RESTAURANT

NAKUI ST

JULIE GALEEVA
FINE ART
GALLERY

CASANOVA

OLINDA RD

▼ MAUI HANDS

PUANA ST

LIBRARY

LIQUOR SHACK
AND GRINDS

Parking

STOPWATCH▼
BAR AND GRILL

■ GAS STATION

AI ST

390

POST
OFFICE

365

PIZZA FRESH
■

MAKAWAO AVE

MAUI PL

KEHAU PL

PAKANI PL

SCALE NOT AVAILABLE

© AVALON TRAVEL

To
Pukalani↓

MAUI

visitors never see, and the infrequency with which tourists properly explore the area has inspired the country's largest travel outlets to label it as "the secret Maui." Although Kula is not intentionally secret, if you take even half a day to explore the area, you might find yourself chuckling about how you scored this place all to yourself.

◖ Kula Country Farms

The **Kula Country Farms** (Kula Hwy. past mile marker 13, 808/878-8381, www.kula-countryfarmsmaui.com, 10am-5pm Tues.-Fri.,

8am-4pm Sat.-Sun.) genuinely captures the agricultural spirit of Kula. This roadside farmer's market also has one of the best views on the island. Everything is locally grown, and the colors of the vegetables explode off the shelves. You can eat a box of fresh strawberries at a picnic table overlooking the southern coastline or visit the pumpkin patch and canoodle in the hay. At the end of the day, however, two of the best reasons for visiting here are that you're supporting local farmers and the prices are a fraction of what they would be at the major supermarkets.

MAUI

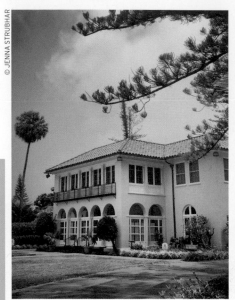
© JENNA STRUBHAR

© KYLE ELLISON

Hui No'eau Visual Arts Center

Stock up on fresh produce at Kula Country Farms.

Ali'i Kula Lavender Farm

Just past Rice Park and Kula Country Farms is a turnoff which heads up Route 377 to Waipoli Road, a steep, narrow track that leads all the way up to Polipoli forest. Turn onto this rural ribbon of asphalt, pass over a cattle guard and begin driving through empty pastures. After a few bends in the road you'll happen upon the **Ali'i Kula Lavender Farm** (1100 Waipoli Rd., 808/878-3004, www.aliikulalavender.com, 9am-4pm daily), a relaxing outpost of serenity. The views from 4,000 feet stretch all the way down to the ocean, the air is crisp, and the calls of ring-necked pheasants sing out over the eucalyptus and pine. The farm itself sprawls across 13.5 acres. While the general admission is only $3, the farm offers guided walking tours ($12) five times daily, 9:30am-2:30pm. A small café serves scones and tea, and the gift shop is a great place to pick up anything from organic lavender body butter to a soft lavender eye mask. Check the event calendar on the website for special events like lavender treasure hunts or gourmet picnic lunches.

Kula Botanical Garden

The steep driveway for **Kula Botanical Garden** (638 Kekaulike Ave., 808/878-1715, www.kulabotanicalgarden.com, 9am-4pm daily, $10, children $3) is less than a mile from Waipoli Road. This 19-acre private garden was started all the way back in 1969 and has grown to include more than 2,500 species of plants. There are over 90 varieties of protea alone. The self-guided walking tour will take about 45 minutes to drink it all in. If you are on your way down from Haleakala and didn't get the chance to see a *nene,* there are two that make a permanent home in the botanical garden—which means you can at least get your photos of Hawaii's endangered state bird. There is also a Jackson chameleon exhibit for kids, a Christmas tree farm, three carved wooden tiki gods, and five acres of coffee trees producing beans you can buy right from the farm.

☾ Surfing Goat Dairy

While out of the way, the eccentric **Surfing**

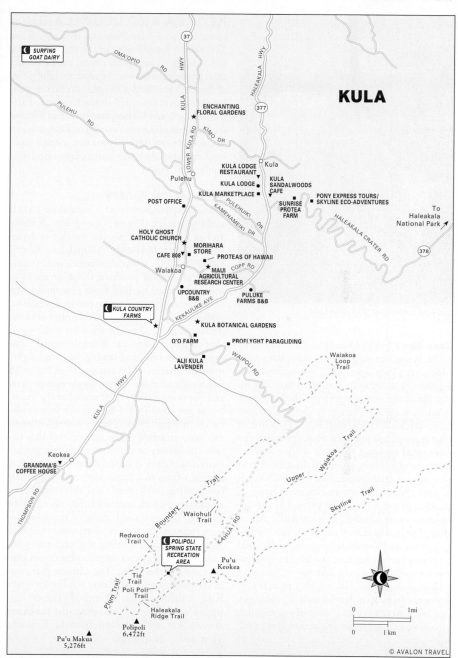

MAUI

KULA

SURFING
GOAT DAIRY

OMA'OPIO RD

KULA HWY

HALEAKALA HWY

37

PULEHU RD

ENCHANTING
FLORAL GARDENS

377

KULA RD

LOWER KULA RD

KIMO DR

KULA LODGE
RESTAURANT

Kula

Pulehu

KULA LODGE

KULA SANDALWOODS
CAFE

KULA MARKETPLACE

PULEHUIKI

PONY EXPRESS TOURS/
SKYLINE ECO-ADVENTURES

POST OFFICE

KAMEHAMEIKI DR

SUNRISE
PROTEA
FARM

To
Haleakala
National Park

HOLY GHOST
CATHOLIC CHURCH

MORIHARA
STORE

CAFE 808

PROTEAS OF HAWAII

HALEAKALA CRATER RD

378

Waiakoa

MAUI
AGRICULTURAL
RESEARCH CENTER

COPP RD

UPCOUNTRY
B&B

PULUKE
FARMS B&B

KEKAULIKE AVE

KULA COUNTRY
FARMS

KULA BOTANICAL GARDENS

O'O FARM

PROFLYGHT PARAGLIDING

ALII KULA
LAVENDER

WAIPOLI RD

Waiakoa
Loop
Trail

KULA HWY

Trail

Keokea

GRANDMA'S
COFFEE HOUSE

Upper

Waiakoa

Trail

THOMPSON RD

Trail

Skyline

Trail

Boundary

Waiohuli
Trail

KAHUA I RD

Redwood
Trail

POLIPOLI
SPRING STATE
RECREATION
AREA

Pu'u
Keokea

Tie
Trail

Plum Trail

Poli Poli
Trail

Haleakala
Ridge Trail

Pu'u Makua
5,276ft

Polipoli
6,472ft

0   1mi

0   1 km

© AVALON TRAVEL

MAUI

Surfing Goat Dairy's namesake

© KYLE ELLISON

Goat Dairy (3651 Omaopio Rd., 808/878-2870, www.surfinggoatdairy.com, 9am-5pm Mon.-Sat., 9am-2pm Sun.) is a must-see attraction because, quite frankly, where else on the island are you going to get the chance to hand-milk a goat? Three miles down Omaopio Road off Kula Highway (Hwy. 37), a line of enormous palms provides what's probably the most regal entrance to a goat dairy anywhere in the world. There are more than 30 flavors of gourmet goat cheese, more than 25 types of goat cheese truffles, and an ever-changing number of goats on the property. For the up-to-the-minute number, check out the side of the red barn where it's written in chalk. While the errant surfboards, baby goats, and cheese sampling station are nice and all, the real reason for coming here is to take the 3:15pm tour. There are tours for $10, which run every 30 minutes 10am-3pm, but for only $5 more you can take part in the only tour of the day that allows you to get in on the action and hand-milk a goat.

KEOKEA AND ULUPALAKUA

Once you pass Rice Park and the turnoff for 377, the highway begins to take on a different feel. The elevation slowly drops, the jacaranda trees provide shade over the road, and the views of South Maui begin to open up before you. Life is slow up here. This is the hangout of artists, farmers, and lifelong ranchers. You'll know you've reached the community of Keokea when you see **Keokea Park** to your left, a small, one-field opening that also has a playground and public restrooms.

◖ Tedeschi Winery

The expansive beauty of Ulupalakua Ranch and the winery that goes along with it alone makes a trip to this winery worth the drive. While **Tedeschi Winery** (Ulupalakua Ranch, 808/878-6058, www.mauiwine.com, 10am-5pm daily) does produce three varieties of wine which are derived from pineapples, the Ulupalakua grape vines also produce grenache, malbec, syrah, viognier, and chenin blanc varietals. What makes the winery a must-see is that in addition to the complimentary tastings, the grounds and tasting room are sights unto themselves. The tasting room bar is 18 feet long and made from a single mango tree, and the tasting room itself served as the guesthouse for King David Kalakaua's visit to the ranch in April 1874. There's a small historical room attached to the tasting area that details the history of the ranch, and free guided tours discuss how this land has gone from being a potato farm to a sugar plantation to a fully functioning cattle ranch and vineyard. Many of the trees which surround the tasting room are over 100 years old, most of them having been imported by former ranch owner Captain James Mackee—a whaling ship captain—who collected them as specimens on his ocean voyages around the globe. The cannon that rests in the yard outside the winery was fired to greet King Kalakaua upon his arrival. The combination of the history, the wine, the ranching atmosphere, and the scenery make Tedeschi Vineyards a must-stop.

© KYLE ELLISON

Keokea Park

MAUI

◖ HALEAKALA NATIONAL PARK

Hale-a-ka-la: House of the Sun. Few places are more aptly named in the Hawaiian language than this 10,023-foot volcano. Dormant since its last eruption in 1790 (the summit area has been inactive for 600 years), Haleakala has been the site of grandiose experiences since before the arrival of humans. Bubbling over 30,000 feet from the seafloor below, only one-third of the mountain's mass exists above water. Along with neighboring Mauna Kea and Mauna Loa—two peaks on the Big Island visible from the summit—Haleakala ranks as one of the largest mountains on earth.

Stoic and spellbinding, its lofty summit was where the Polynesian demigod Maui captured the sun in mythology. Legend states that since the sun would race across the sky far too quickly to allow any crops to grow or any daily tasks to be accomplished, Maui snared the sun with his great net and only agreed to let him go if he promised to slow his path, thereby providing enough warmth for farmers to grow their crops and for life on the island to continue. Today, scores of visitors make the predawn sojourn to the summit to watch the sun illuminate the eastern horizon, squinting in excitement as it crests the clouds and bathes the crater in a brilliant orange light.

When to Visit

The biggest question surrounding Haleakala is not *if* you should visit, but when. Sunrise is the most popular option, and although everyone should experience a Haleakala sunrise at least once in their lifetime, by no means does that mean that it's the *only* time to visit. While the sunrise can indeed be spectacular, it's also crowded, tough to find parking, requires waking up at 3am, and is often near or below freezing. To see a light display nearly as colorful but without all the crowds, visit for sunset. Although you don't get the benefit of watching the sun emerge from the horizon, there are often only 20 people instead of 400 and it isn't as cold. Visit in the middle of the day to give yourself with time to hike

BRRRR...

On any given morning at the top of Haleakala there always seems to be at least one unfortunate person shivering away in a tank top and boardshorts. People forget that Haleakala tops out at over 10,000 feet, which means that even though this is the tropics, the temperature can often be 30° colder than at sea level. Even though Haleakala is "The House of the Sun," the early morning windchill—particularly in the winter—will often be below freezing, and about every five years or so Haleakala will get a dump of snow (2-5 inches) that sticks around for a couple of days. Whenever it snows on Haleakala the road to the top is usually closed due to ice, and when it reopens, hundreds of locals rush to the summit to build snowmen and take pictures with their children.

During most mornings, however, the temperature will only be in the lower 40s, but when combined with 30 mph wind gusts, that can warrant the use of gloves, a beanie, a windbreaker, and a couple of jackets. Pack accordingly, lest you be the person sitting in the parking lot with the heater on while everyone else is getting pictures of the sunrise. By midmorning the temperature is usually into the mid 60s, but any sunrise or sunset visitors should be prepared to bundle up.

down into the crater or explore the forests of Hosmer's Grove.

The largest factor, however, is working around the weather. Unfortunately, since Haleakala is a windward-facing mountain, the weather can be fairly unpredictable. Though rain (or even snow) can fall at any time of year, summer is usually a safer bet than winter, when there is the chance of a big storm rolling through. Statistically the sunrise is visible on 85 percent of days, with the other 15 percent being socked in with clouds, so at least the odds are with you. If, on the other hand, you're planning on heading up during the day or for sunset, a good rule of thumb is that if you can't see the *mountain itself,* then you probably shouldn't bother. On the other hand, if you can see the mountain itself, but just not the top, then you know you're going to be in for a fabulous sunset. During the midmorning to afternoon hours, a cloud layer known as the *mauna lei* creeps its way across the mountain between 5,000 and 8,000 feet. Although you will be driving through the clouds on your way up to the top, on most occasions you will pop out above the clouds to watch the sunset from your own floating island, awash in a sea of white. Or, to take the guesswork out of the equation, simply call the National Weather Service hotline for Haleakala summit (866/944-5025, ext. 4) for an up-to-date weather forecast, or check out the website (www.ifa.hawaii.edu) for up-to-the-minute weather data (including windchill, wind speed, visibility, and rainfall) before taking off for the summit.

Headquarters and Hosmer's Grove

Admission to Haleakala National Park (www.nps.gov/hale) is $10 per car and $5 for bikers, hikers, and motorcycles, but it is good for three days. If you're driving up here for sunrise, you're going to want to drive straight to the summit to catch the show. If you're meandering up the mountain during the middle of the day (or are on your way up for sunset), take a side trip to **Hosmer's Grove,** a densely forested swath of hillside where an early 20th-century forester by the name of Ralph Hosmer experimented with over 80 species of nonnative timber in hopes of kick-starting the island's lumber industry. There is an enjoyable 0.5-mile nature hike and a campground for visitors who are just passing through. To reach Hosmer's Grove make a left on a short access road just after entering the park.

Continuing straight past the Hosmer's Grove turnoff you'll soon arrive at **park headquarters**

MAUI

Haleakala sunrise

(808/572-4400, daily 7am-3:45pm) at an elevation of 6,800 feet. Campers can get their permits here, and others can stop for information concerning the park, gifts, water, or to use the toilet or pay phone. There are some *'ahinahina* (silversword) plants outside, and a few *nene* can occasionally be seen wandering the area.

After you pass the park headquarters and zig and zag a couple more times, there's parking for another hiking option: Halemau'u Trail. Following that are two overlooks, **Leleiwi** and **Kalahaku,** both offering tremendous views and different perspectives looking down into the crater basin.

Visitors Center

Near road's end is the visitors center at an elevation of 9,740 feet. It's approximately 10 miles up the mountain from headquarters or about a 30-minute drive. This is where all of the bike tour companies bring you for sunrise because you get one of the best views into the basin from here. It's open from sunrise to 3pm and contains a clear and concise display on

the geology of Haleakala. Maps and books are available, and ranger talks are particularly informative. A 20-minute ranger talk takes place daily at 9:30am, 10:30am, and 11:30am at the summit observation center above the visitors center, and various ranger-led hikes are also given (Tues. and Fri. 9am for a two-mile hike on Sliding Sands Trail). By 10am, there will be lots of people at the top, so enjoy the time between when the bikers leave and the buses arrive.

Bikes going down the mountain travel about 20-25 miles per hour, sometimes faster. If you're caught behind a string of bikes on your way down, just slow up and wait for them to pull over and let you pass. On your way down, shift into a low gear to control your speed to prevent riding the brakes.

Summit Observation Building

At the road's end is **Pu'u 'Ula'ula** (Red Hill), the highest point on Maui at 10,023 feet, where a glass-sided observation area is open 24 hours. From here, you have more expansive vistas than from the visitors center below, but the view into the crater isn't quite as good. This is where many people come to see the sunset. To add some perspective to size and distance, it's 100 miles from the top of Haleakala to the volcanic peak of Mauna Loa on the Big Island to the southeast.

Behind you on the slope below is **Maui Space Surveillance Complex** (www.ifa.hawaii. edu/haleakala), aka Science City, a research facility with telescopes used by the University of Hawai'i, a satellite tracking station that's staffed by the U.S. Air Force, and the largest telescope controlled by the Department of Defense. This complex is closed to the public.

Camping and Cabins

While watching the sunrise, hiking the crater floor, or looking up at the stars as they come out are great introductions to the crater, spending a night in the backcountry is the absolute best way to commune with nature on this mountain. The most accessible campground is the one at **Hosmer's Grove** where you don't even need a permit. There are only tent sites and no open fires are allowed, but there is a pit toilet and running water, and you can drive right up to the campsite. At an elevation of 6,800 feet, the nights can still get chilly (and can drop close to freezing in the winter), but the camping area is largely protected from the wind. This is a great place to camp if you're looking to make an early assault to see the sunrise, are planning to hike into the crater basin from here (a 2.3-mile supply trail connects the campground with the Halemau'u trailhead), or want to sleep among the eucalyptus for the evening.

Two **wilderness campsites** are located at Holua (elevation: 6,940 ft.) and Paliku (6,380 ft) campgrounds. Anyone planning on spending a night in the backcountry needs to secure a permit from the park headquarters, which is free, but requires that you watch an 8-minute orientation video and pick up the permit before 3pm. Pit toilets and non-potable water are available at both campsites, and although the sites are officially first-come, first-served, they

can accommodate 25 people and are rarely full. Maximum length of stay is three nights total in a 30-day period, and no more than two nights in a row at the same site. Holua is accessible by a 3.7-mile hike down Halemau'u Trail and is set amid subalpine scrub brush looking over the Ko'olau Gap. Paliku, on the other hand, requires a 9.2-mile hike on Sliding Sands Trail (or a 10.3-mile hike on Halemau'u Trail), and is wet, lush, and surrounded by foliage. In addition to being a great place to spot *nene,* Paliku is also the preferred camping area for hikers opting to walk out the Kaupo Gap.

There are three **backcountry cabins** available at Holua, Kapalaoa (elevation: 7,250 ft.), and Paliku, although due to their popularity, securing a reservation can be a little difficult. Cabin reservations can only be made up to 90 days in advance either by calling the park headquarters at 808/572-4400, or online at https://fhnp.org/wcr. Local people are usually waiting on the 91st day to secure the reservation first thing in the morning, so if this is something you want to include on your Maui trip, plan ahead and be flexible. If you manage to reserve a cabin, however, the cost is $75/night and includes 12 padded berths, a wood-burning stove, and basic kitchen utilities. Pit toilets and non-potable water are available, and all trash must be packed out.

TOURS

If you still think that pineapples grow underground or on a tree, then you will learn a lot by going out on the **Maui Pineapple Tour** (875 Hali'imaile Rd., 808/665-5491, www. mauipineappletours.com, tours 9:30am and 11:45am Mon.-Fri.). Not only do you get a free pineapple with every tour, but you also learn all about the current state of an agricultural industry fighting to stay alive. Find out about all the other uses of pineapple you never knew about such as pineapple jam, pineapple lemonade, and even pineapple wine. Tours run $65/person or $75/person if you include lunch. Seeing as the food is from the acclaimed Hali'imaile General Store, the extra $10 charge is a good deal.

Pono of **Open Eye Private Tours**

(808/572-3483, www.openeyetours.com) is a private tour guide who delivers a cultural connection to the island. He has been a private tour guide on Maui since 1983, and communicates with the clients before the tour to get an assessment of what sort of activities might suit them best. For visitors with an interest in music or dance, he might arrange a tour on which hula dancers from a local *halau* offer a private performance with chants that relate to the land around you. If you're interested in the spirituality of the islands, Pono can plan an itinerary of places steeped in Hawaiian mythology and spirit. As a former teacher, Pono also specializes in tours with children and offers activities for kids such as making fish out of coconut leaves. Pono takes you places few other people get to go. He's built up contacts over the years that enable him to bring guests to the properties of local people who regard him as a friend. For example, a large tour bus of 45 people won't be able to stop at a taro field on the way to Hana and pull taro with the owners. You won't be disappointed.

Shopping

◖ OLD MAKAWAO TOWN

There's no faster way to make an Upcountry local cringe than by referring to Old Makawao Town as another Lahaina. The galleries and boutiques here are on par—if not better—than the shops and galleries lining Lahaina's Front Street, but you don't have the tourist kitsch, swarms of cruise ship passengers, and drum machine musicians that would mold it into "just another tourist town." Instead Makawao prefers to stay off the radar, yet accessible enough so as to attract art patrons and fashionistas who are passionate about what they're purchasing. Add in the *paniolo* ranching heritage of the town (there are still hitching posts lining the storefronts), and walking the shops of Old Makawao Town becomes a sight unto itself.

Art Galleries

Those interested in fine Polynesian jewelry will enjoy stepping inside **Maui Master Jewelers** (3655 Baldwin Ave., 808/573-5400, www.mauimasterjewelers.com, 10am-5pm Mon.-Fri., 10am-4pm Sat.) where works by over 30 local artists are consistently on display. They are the island's leading source for New Zealand bone and jade carvings and also offer Tahitian pearl jewelry and colored gemstones.

Sherri Reeve Gallery (3669 Baldwin Ave., 808/572-8931, www.sreeve.com, 9am-5pm Mon.-Fri., 10am-4pm Sat.) showcases this ebullient Makawao artist whose distinctive floral designs have graced shirts, cards, paintings, and prints for years. Despite the large number of galleries in town, no visit to Makawao would be complete without at least popping in and having a look around.

Jordanne Gallery and Studio (3625 Baldwin Ave., 808/563-0088, www.jordannefineart.com, 10:30am-5pm daily) is toward the bottom of the shops on Baldwin Avenue. This plein-air painter landed in Hawaii when she decided at the airport during a family trip to Lana'i that she wasn't getting back on the plane. With little money and no plan she let her painting talents pave what was once an unforeseen path.

The first store you'll notice in the Courtyard shopping area is **Viewpoints Gallery** (3620 Baldwin Ave., 808/572-5979, www.viewpointsgallerymaui.com, 10am-6pm daily), a large, clean gallery which features a rotating array of artists focusing predominantly on paintings.

Back behind the gallery next to Market Fresh Bistro is **Hot Island Glass** (3620 Baldwin Ave., 808/572-4527, www.hotislandglass.com, 9am-5pm daily), the island's most well-known glass studio where you can watch artists blow glass right before your eyes. Although the gallery is open every day, live glass blowing demonstrations only take place Monday-Saturday 10:30am-4pm.

The **Kristen Bunney Gallery** (3660 Baldwin Ave., 808/573-1516, www.kristenbunney.com, 11am-5pm daily) provides passersby with playful, animated, and inspiring artwork.

In the building right next door you will find the **Makawao Fine Art Gallery** (3660 Baldwin Ave., 808/573-5972, www.makawaofineartgallery.com, 11am-5pm Mon.-Sat., noon-5pm Sun.), a gallery with a collection of over a dozen featured artists. Among the highlights of the works on display are watercolors of wine by Eric Christensen, familial portraits by Bob Byerley, and the perception-altering visual art of Andreas Nottebohm.

Right on the corner of the center of town, **Julie Galeeva Fine Art** (3682 Baldwin Ave., 808/573-4772, www.juliegaleeva.com, 10am-5pm Mon.-Sat.) showcases the highly textured paintings of this talented Russian-born artist and Maui resident.

Clothing and Gifts

Trendy boutiques and global fashions seem to pop up at every other storefront. Working your way down Baldwin Avenue from the center of town, you'll hit a number of standouts. **Collections** (3677 Baldwin Ave., 808/572-0781, www.collectionsmauiinc.com, 9am-6pm Mon.-Sat., 11am-5pm Sun.) has been providing men's and women's clothing and boutique home furnishings since opening its doors in 1975.

The Mercantile (3673 Baldwin Ave., 808/572-1401, 10am-6pm daily) specializes in boutique women's clothing. Past Rodeo General Store you'll find **Aloha Cowboy** (3643 Baldwin Ave., 808/573-8190, www.alohacowboy.net, 9:30am-6pm Mon.-Sat., 10am-5pm Sun.), one of the best stores in Makawao and a place that captures the combined Hawaiian and *paniolo* spirit. Inside this old building you'll find western-themed clothing, Makawao-centric items, saddles, horse tack, a cowhide-colored surfboard, and a train going around the ceiling above the wares. If you're walking down the street and looking for the store, you don't even have to spot the sign—the smell of leather is noticeable from two storefronts down.

The collection of clanging wind chimes will announce your arrival at **Goodies** (3633 Baldwin Ave., 808/572-0288, 10am-6pm daily), an eccentric but genuinely artsy clothing boutique that caters to the female crowd.

Check out the **Volcano Spice Company** (3623 Baldwin Ave., 808/575-7729, www.volcanospicecompany.com, 10am-5pm Mon.-Sat., 11am-3pm Sun.), a small shop run by the owner and head chef who creates handmade rubs and spices out of a kitchen right on the property. There are a few crafts in the store, such as hand-turned wood bowls, but the real stars of the show are the bottles of coffee barbecue rub and the original volcano spice blend, which goes great on seared ahi.

Designing Wahine Emporium (3640 Baldwin Ave., 808/573-0990, 10am-6pm Mon.-Sat., 11am-5pm Sun.) offers everything from locally made crafts to children's clothing to a few pieces of menswear—something rare here in Makawao.

Around the corner at Komoda Bakery is the tiny little enclave of **Little Tibet** (3682 Baldwin Ave., 808/573-2275, 10am-5pm Mon.-Sat.), where an array of ancient gemstones and crystals from all across the world warrant a peek.

At the far end of the same building is **Jewels of the White Tara** (3682 Makawao Ave., 808/573-5774, 10am-6pm Mon.-Sat., 11am-5pm Sun.), an obscure-sounding import store that features home decor and clothing items from India, Indonesia, Laos, Vietnam, and a handful of other international venues.

Adding to an array of already existing shops in Pa'ia, Lahaina, and Ka'anapali, **Maui Hands** (1169 Makawao Ave., 808/572-2008, www.mauihands.com, 10am-6pm Mon.-Sat., 11am-5pm Sun.) took over an old health food market and has transformed it into a spacious gallery of consignment craft work.

KULA
Art Galleries

It isn't possible to talk about Upcountry art without mentioning the **Curtis Wilson Cost Gallery** (15200 Haleakala Hwy., 808/874-6544, www.costgallery.com, 8:30am-5pm daily). Tucked neatly beneath the Kula Lodge Restaurant, the gallery has the feeling of a fine wine cellar, though the wine is swapped for exceptionally fine art. It's fair to say that nobody paints rural Maui better. Cost's love for the island is apparent in his innate ability to capture its fleeting magic. A recent addition to the collection are pieces by Cost's daughter, Julia Cost. This gallery is a must stop for anyone with an appreciation for fine art.

If you thought the only place you could find locally made blown glass was in Makawao, then you haven't stumbled upon **Worcester Glassworks** (4626 Lower Kula Rd., 808/878-4000, www.worcesterglassworks.com, 10am-5pm Mon.-Sat., by appointment Sun.), a studio you would never know was there unless you accidentally ran into the kiln. Just twenty yards up the road from Kula Bistro and Morihara Store, the clean and well-lit gallery only occupies a small corner of the rustic studio, with the

Protea

© IDREAMPHOTO/123RF.COM

Protea blooms in Upcountry.

Protea are large flowers that grow in a variety of colors from dark brown to brilliant orange, bright yellow, and pale pink. Natural or hybridized, some have pincushion-like heads, others have tops that resemble a bunch of wispy feathers, while others look like bottlebrushes. Originally from South Africa, these beautiful flowers have been grown on Maui since the mid-1960s and are now big business as the state's showiest of flowers. Dozens of hybrids have been created for their long stems, colors, or size and shape of petals. Kula and its environs at about 3,000-foot elevation make a perfect place to grow protea as they need sunny days, cool crisp nights, and moderate, even temperatures that don't usually go above 80°F. Upcountry boasts numerous protea growers, some with shops, many of whom ship.

MAUI

remaining space taken up by numerous heavy-industrial machines instrumental in the glass-blowing process. This gallery is worth a wander in conjunction with a meal at Kula Bistro.

Gifts and Flowers

Right next to the Kula Lodge is the **Proteas of Hawaii Gift Shop** (15200 Healakala Hwy., 808/878-2533, www.proteasofhawaii.com, 8am-4pm daily) where you can pick up a bouquet of freshly cut protea ($75-140) grown only a half mile away. In addition to the flowers this small store also sells a number of other locally made crafts, artwork, and gifts.

Down the driveway and between the Kula Lodge and the Proteas of Hawaii Gift Shop, tucked just out of sight, is the larger **Kula Marketplace** (808/878-2135, www.kulamarketplace.com, 8am-7pm daily) where you could easily spend half an hour browsing all the various local offerings. Everything from locally made jam to clothing to Hawaiian music to photography and bamboo cutting boards is on display in this store. It's a great place to wander through while digesting a Kula Lodge breakfast or making your way down from the crater.

Pick up baskets of locally grown protea at the **Upcountry Harvest Gift Shop** (638 Kekaulike Ave., 808/878-2824, www.upcountryharvest.com, 9am-4pm daily) inside the Kula Botanical Garden. The gift shop offers a full range of floral arrangements at $59-250, as well as bags of coffee beans grown right on the property ($22).

Food

MAKAWAO
Mexican

Mix some mango margaritas, a seafood burrito, and a great community atmosphere, and it will be obvious why **☾ Polli's Mexican Restaurant** (1202 Makawao Ave., 808/572-7808, www.pollismexicanrestaurant.com, 11am-10pm daily, $11-22) has been a Makawao classic since its founding in 1981. The portions are enormous: whether you order a seafood enchilada, a chicken burrito supreme, a sizzling beef fajita, or even a "Makawowie" nachos appetizer, you'll be be hard-pressed to finish. More than just Mexican, Polli's also offers Maui Cattle Company cheeseburgers, barbecue pork sandwiches, a heaping array of vegetarian options, and baby back ribs that fall off the bone. The festive interior is decorated with photographs from Mexico, surf photography from Hawaii, and authentic souvenirs from all corners of the Latin American world.

Italian

Holding down the other corner of Makawao's only intersection since 1986, **Casanova** (1188 Makawao Ave., 808/572-0220, www.casanovamaui.com, 7:30am-9:30pm Sun.-Tues., 7:30am-2am Wed.-Sat., $18-34) restaurant is a three-part establishment where you can either grab a quick deli sandwich for lunch, have a fine meal of pizza and pasta for dinner, or dance to the wee hours of the morning at Upcountry's only nightclub. While the restaurant is also open for lunch, most diners come here for the fine Italian dinner menu where authentic selections such as *linguine pescatore* and *filetto di manzo* punctuate an affordable menu. Pair Upcountry's best wine list with wood-fired pizzas baked in an Italian oven, and Casanova has all the makings of a romantic date night you might find in a big city in a town that doesn't even have stoplights.

If you're looking for Italian that's a lot more casual, **Pizza Fresh** (1043 Makawao Ave., 808/572-2000, 4pm-9pm daily, $13-29) is just a half mile down the road. Specialty pizzas such as pesto chicken or eggplant gouda are available either whole or by the slice and can be accompanied by fresh salads. There's limited seating, but ordering pizza to go is always an option.

American

The two best things about **Market Fresh**

© KYLE ELLISON

Come in and eat at Polli's Mexican Restaurant.

Bistro (3620 Baldwin Ave., 808/572-4877, www.marketfreshbistro.com, 9am-3:30pm Tues.-Sat., 9am-2pm Sun., dinner 6pm-8:30pm Thurs.-Fri., $12) are the courtyard setting and the salmon and tomato Benedict. Although this place is also open for lunch (and dinner two nights of the week), breakfast, served until 11am, is the meal of choice.

A true hole-in-the-wall favorite, the **Makawao Garden Café** (3669 Baldwin Ave., 808/573-9065, www.makawaogardencafe.com, 11am-3pm Mon.-Sat., $6-9) is hidden in an alcove next to the Sherri Reeve art gallery. The café only offers outdoor seating, which means that when it rains, the restaurant closes. Laidback and only open for lunch, its options include a baby brie and bacon sandwich or quinoa salad with goat cheese.

If you're in the mood for a turkey or club sandwich paired with freshly squeezed juices, the deli counter inside **Rodeo General Store** (3661 Baldwin Ave., 808/572-1868, 6:30am-10pm Mon.-Sat., 6:30am-9pm Sun., $8-10) serves filling and affordable deli sandwiches which are great for anyone on the run. Spend the extra money for a "Green Machine," an all-natural collection straight from the juicer, with celery, apple, parsley, kale, and cucumber blended into a healthy dose of energy.

If you're looking to catch the big game or craving a local draft beer, the local hangout **Stopwatch Bar and Grill** (1127 Makawao Ave., 808/572-1380, www.stopwatchmaui.com, 11am-10pm Mon.-Sat., 8am-10pm Sun., $8-10) is Makawao's token sports bar. Flat screen TVs circle the bar, and burger and sandwich offerings round out the lunchtime menu.

Of course an authentic ranching town has its own steak house, the dimly lit, dark wood **Makawao Steak House** (3612 Baldwin Ave., 808/572-8711, 5pm-9pm Tues.-Sun., $25-30). There are few things better than hunkering down behind this old-western-style storefront with a warm bowl of Maui onion soup. The steak fillets are expertly prepared (though curiously served with a side of beans). This is a longtime local date-night venue where the price is steeper than other places around town.

MAUI

© KYLE ELLISON

Stick doughnuts from Komoda's are an Upcountry classic.

Hawaiian Regional

The 【 **Hali'imaile General Store** (900 Hali'imaile Rd., 808/572-2666, www.bevgannonrestaurants.com/haliimaile, lunch 11am-2:30pm Mon.-Fri., dinner 5:30pm-9pm daily, $22-42), serves elegant gourmet food to anyone lucky enough to find this Upcountry roadhouse. In Hali'imaile village along Hali'imaile Road between Baldwin Avenue and the Haleakala Highway, the restaurant is housed in what was this pineapple town's general store. Master chef Beverly Gannon presents creative "Hawaiian regional cuisine with an American and international twist," and while the menu changes seasonally, a sampling of what you might expect includes appetizers such as the brie and grape quesadilla, sashimi Napoleon, and Bev's crab pizza. Entrées include *paniolo* barbecue ribs, coconut seafood curry, rib eye steak, rack of lamb Hunan-style, or pan-seared scallops. The food is always healthy and fresh, and the portions plentiful. The setting is casual, but because of the elevation, long sleeves and pants might be in order.

Coffee Shops

The best coffee bar is inside the **Rodeo General Store** (3661 Baldwin Ave., 808/572-1868, 6:30am-10pm Mon.-Sat., 6:30am-9pm Sun.). It's one of the few places on the island that serves organically roasted coffee with organic milk.

Bakery

You haven't officially visited Upcountry until you've stood on the corner of Makawao's only intersection and treated yourself to the doughy perfection served at 【 **Komoda Store and Bakery** (3674 Baldwin Ave., 808/572-7261, 7am-5pm Mon.-Tues. and Thurs.-Fri., Sat. 7am-2pm). Komoda's *defines* Upcountry. The unmistakable aroma of its "stick" doughnuts and cream puffs wafts on the predawn air each morning. Lines still form outside before the 7am opening, and popular items such as the baked butter rolls will often sell out within hours. The store continues to operate without computers, so expect to pay with cash.

Tours

Even laid-back Makawao town has managed to get in on the recent explosion in food tours. **Local Tastes of Maui** (1079 Maohu St., 808/446-1190, www.localtastesofmaui.com, 9:30am-11:30am weekdays) offers tours of both Makawao and Pa'ia where participants hit a number of eateries across town and learn about the history and lore behind the culinary establishments. Makawao tours run Tuesday and Thursday and Pa'ia tours are on Monday, Wednesday, and Friday.

KULA
American

The **Kula Lodge** (15200 Haleakala Hwy., 808/878-1535, www.kulalodge.com, 7am-9pm daily, breakfast until 10:45am, $12-34) has been welcoming hungry patrons into its rustic interior for so long it's become synonymous with Kula dining. Set inside a private home constructed in the 1940s, this panoramic, mountainside perch hasn't changed much. At 3,200 feet in elevation it's little bit cooler up here, and the Lodge's dark-wood interior seems a perfect fit with the low temperatures and low-hanging clouds. The entranceway is adorned with Curtis Wilson Cost paintings (his gallery is located beneath the restaurant), and the warm, welcoming atmosphere is the biggest draw for dining at the Lodge. The service can be hit-or-miss, but you'll be too full from a huge breakfast of *paniolo* steak and eggs or a dinner of kiawe-roasted prime rib to care about anything else.

Kula Sandalwoods Café (15427 Haleakala Hwy., 808/878-3523, www.kulasandalwoods. com, 7am-3pm daily, $9-11) is a laid-back venue where the owners will chat you up like an old friend. Breakfast is served until 11am, although if you're a few minutes late and hankering for an omelet, they'll probably be nice enough to let it slide. While the outdoor lanai is still a nice place to enjoy your meal, the cozy interior features a fireplace in the corner and country music on the radio. For breakfast, try the Keokea omelet; at lunch, go for the kalua pig sandwich.

Italian

▶ **Kula Bistro** (4556 Lower Kula Rd., 808/871-2960, www.kulabistro.com, 7:30am-8:30pm daily, $12-20) has infused the Kula culinary scene with new life. Upon first bite of the pesto chicken flatbread or grilled vegetable panini, it's apparent that head chef Luciano Zanon has been perfecting this cuisine since his childhood spent in Venice. The barbecue chicken and Maui onion pizza and creamy vodka pomodoro only further prove his success. Kula Bistro mainly uses locally sourced ingredients, bakes fresh desserts daily, and allows patrons to bring their own beer or wine without charging a corkage fee. Forgot the bottle of wine? Morihara Store sells some right across the street.

French

To call **La Provence** (3158 Lower Kula Rd., 808/878-1313, www.laprovencekula.com, 7am-9pm Wed.-Fri., 8:45am-1:45pm weekends, $1, cash only) a hidden gem might read like a cliché, but in the case of this boutique French restaurant, it's hidden so well you could drive by without even noticing it. On Lower Kula Road just past the True Value hardware store, La Provence offers everything from flaky croissants and café au lait for breakfast to affordable and filling crepes. Order a mushroom and spinach or vegetable and goat cheese crepe accompanied by Kula greens and roasted potatoes. It's cash only; there's an ATM at the True Value.

Food Cart

Inside the gate of the **Kula Country Farms** (Kula Hwy. past mile marker 13, 808/878-8381, www.kulacountryfarmsmaui.com, 10am-3pm Tues.-Fri., 8am-3pm Sat.-Sun.) is a food truck serving $6 fish tacos and $8 Papa Rice Burgers made from beef sourced straight from Kula's Ka'ono'ulu Ranch. Lunch items can sell out early since the price is a steal for what you're getting.

Markets

If Kula were to have anything resembling a town center, the argument could be made for

MAUI

it being **Morihara Store** (4581 Lower Kula Rd., 808/878-2578, 6:30am-8pm Mon.-Sat., 7:30am-8pm Sun.), the main general store that services most of Kula's basic culinary needs. Pick up anything from condiments for a picnic in Rice Park, cheap to-go items for lunch, or a beer or bottle of wine for the BYOB restaurant across the street. Morihara is a throwback to antiquity where the fast pace of modern life can be checked at the door.

Coffee Shops

Although the best coffee shop in all of Upcountry is out in Keokea, those in need of a quick— and early—cuppa joe can find it at the **Crater Coffee** (15200 Haleakala Hwy., 808/757-1342, 3am-7am Mon.-Sat.) truck sitting right in front of the Kula Lodge and opening at a REM-shattering 3am. The main customers here are visitors heading up to catch the sunrise at Haleakala in the morning, and seeing as it's the only place open this early that serves coffee and bagels, this is going to be a life-saver if you find yourself struggling through the early sunrise wakeup.

Getting There and Around

BUS

Select parts of Upcountry are serviced by the **Maui Bus** (808/871-4838, www.co.maui.hi.us/bus), although no routes extend into Kula. The three bus stop locations which link Upcountry with Kahului are in front of the Pukalani Community Center, in front of the Makawao Library, and in the center of town at Hali'imaile. Rates are $2/person, and the bus makes stops at the Kahului Airport as well as at Queen Ka'ahumanu Mall where you can link up with other lines. The earliest bus leaves from Pukalani Community Center at 6:30am, and later buses run every 90 minutes until 9:30pm, although the last service of the day only goes as far as Kahului Airport. For buses heading farther Upcountry, the earliest departure from Kahului is 6am and the latest is 9pm. For a detailed schedule, check online at www.mauicounty.gov.

EAST MAUI: THE ROAD TO HANA

East Maui is more than just a destination—it's a completely different mind-set. Lush, tropical, and laden in waterfalls, East Maui is home to the famous Road to Hana. From the windswept taro patches of the Ke'anae Peninsula to the empty pastures of Kaupo, time in East Maui ticks by at a slower place. By no means, however, does that make East Maui lazy. It's also the

© HEATHER ELLISON

Locally Grown
Avocados
$1.75 lb.

Organic
Cucumber
$2.30 lb.

Organic
Zucchini
$2.50 lb.

Organic
Carrotts
$3.50 lb.

MAUI

on the Road to Hana

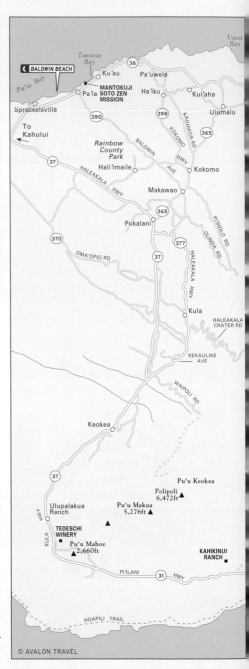

island's adventure center, where an average day could consist of trekking to remote waterfalls, cliff jumping in a bamboo rainforest, spelunking hidden caves on a black sand beach, or bodysurfing off sandy shores.

Many who drive the legendary Road to Hana end up confused when they pull into town. Perhaps the two most commonly asked questions are *"This is it?"* and *"Where is the rest of town?"* Understand that Hana is not a destination unto itself; it's more famous for what it *isn't* than for what it is. Hana is *not* like the rest of the island. This sleepy little fishing hamlet is content to drift along at its own pace. You don't come to Hana to reach something; you come out here to leave everything else behind.

Hana was already a plantation town in 1849 when a hard-boiled sea captain named George Wilfong started producing sugar on 60 acres. Later, Danish brothers August and Oscar Unna came to run the plantation. Through the years, the laborers were a mixture of Hawaiian, Japanese, Chinese, Portuguese,

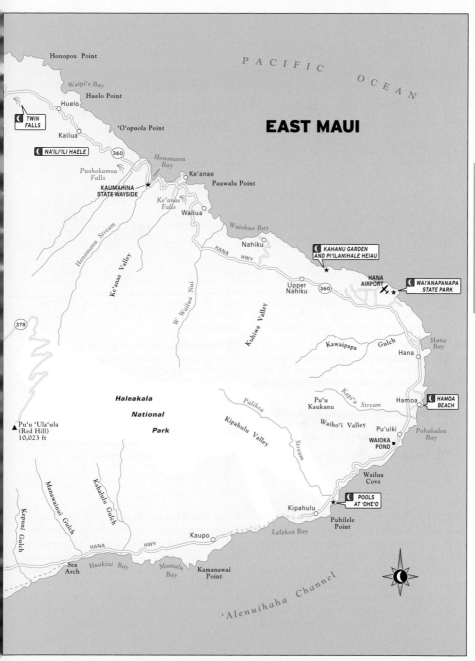

PACIFIC OCEAN

Honopou Point

Waipi'o Bay

Huelo Point

Huelo

TWIN FALLS

Kailua

'O'opuola Point

NA'ILI'ILI HAELE   360

Puohokamoa Falls

Honomanu Bay

KAUMAHINA STATE WAYSIDE

Ke'anae

Pauwalu Point

Ke'anae Falls

Wailua

Waiohue Bay

EAST MAUI

MAUI

Nahiku

HANA HWY

KAHANU GARDEN AND PI'ILANIHALE HEIAU

Upper Nahiku

360

HANA AIRPORT

WAI'ANAPANAPA STATE PARK

Honomanu Stream

Ke'anae Valley

W. Wailua Nui

Koliwa Valley

Kawaipapa Gulch

Hana Bay

Hana

378

Haleakala

National

Park

Palikea

Kipahulu Valley

Pu'u Kaukanu

Kapi'a Stream

Waiho'i Valley

Hamoa

HAMOA BEACH

Pu'uiki

WAIOKA POND

Pohakuloa Bay

Pu'u 'Ula'ula (Red Hill) 10,023 ft

Stream

Wailua Cove

Kipahulu

POOLS AT 'OHE'O

Manawainui Gulch

Kahalulu Gulch

Puhilele Point

Kaupo

Lelekea Bay

HANA   HWY

Sea Arch

Huakini Bay

Mamalu Bay

Kamanawai Point

Kepuni Gulch

'Alenuihaha Channel

HIGHLIGHTS

LOOK FOR ☾ TO FIND RECOMMENDED SIGHTS, ACTIVITIES, DINING, AND LODGING.

☾ **Kahanu Garden and Pi'ilanihale Heiau:** Take a journey back to ancient Hawaii and gaze upon the largest *heiau* anywhere in the state (page 402).

☾ **Wai'anapanapa State Park:** Swim inside hidden caves, bask on the shores of a black sand beach, and walk in the footsteps of kings (page 402).

☾ **Pools of 'Ohe'o:** At Maui's iconic **"Seven Sacred Pools,"** you can swim beneath waterfalls that tumble down to the ocean (page 405).

☾ **Baldwin Beach:** Start your journey to

Hana on the right foot with an early morning stroll down this undeveloped expanse of shoreline (page 408).

☾ **Hamoa Beach:** Surf or snorkel at a beach that Mark Twain and James Michener both recognized as one of the most beautiful they'd ever seen (page 410).

☾ **Twin Falls:** Swim beneath waterfalls in an accessible, family-friendly setting (page 414).

☾ **Na'ili'ili haele:** Trek through a bamboo forest punctuated by waterfalls, guava trees, and natural swimming holes (page 415).

Filipino, and even Puerto Rican stock. The *luna* were Scottish, German, or American. All have combined to become the people of Hana. After sugar production faded out by the 1940s, Paul Fagan founded Hana Ranch, which still raises more than 1,200 head of cattle on about 4,500 acres today.

A worthwhile stopover on the Road to Hana is trendy, funky, and undeniably sexy

Pa'ia (Pa-EE-ah). Nominated by *Coastal Living* magazine as one of the "happiest seaside towns in America," it's unlike anywhere else on the island. It only takes 10 minutes in town to realize that the residents of Pa'ia are stoked on life in every sense of the word. Laid-back and worry-free, Pa'ia is a town that skanks along to the beat of its own bongo. Pa'ia is Maui's token hippie outpost.

MAUI

Driving the Road to Hana

Ah yes, the "Road to Hana." The most loved and loathed section of the island divides visitors into two distinct camps: those who swear it's heaven on earth and those who would rather pull their teeth out than ever drive it again. Most people who don't enjoy their excursion to Hana didn't know what they were getting themselves into. Three little words will make or break your trip:

Don't rush Hana.

Devote a full day to the experience. *Minimum.* You're visiting arguably the most beautiful place on earth; allocate at least an entire day. Two or three days are even better. Don't expect to breeze through and just see it quickly and don't expect to be back on the other side of the island to make dinner reservations. If you're staying in Ka'anapali or Wailea, it will take you 3.5 hours just to reach the Pools of 'Ohe'o (aka Seven Sacred Pools). That's not including any stops—and stops are what make the journey worthwhile.

No one should ever have to endure a journey to Hana without knowing exactly where the next waterfall, hiking trail, ATM, food cart, or restroom is going to be. Since sights can spring up in an instant—and making a U-turn just isn't possible— be prepared. A mile-by-mile rundown of what you'll see along the side of the road follows, with specific sights and places worth stopping to linger described in greater detail.

- **Mile Marker 7:** Start in the town of Pa'ia, located around mile marker 7 on the Hana Highway (Hwy. 36).

- **Mile Marker 8.8:** Ho'okipa Beach Park

- **Mile Marker 10.3:** Maliko Gulch

- **Mile Marker 13.5:** Turnoff for Jaws, quite possibly the most famous surf break on the planet.

- **Mile Marker 14.5:** Maui Grown Market and Deli advertises that it's the last stop for food before Hana. Don't worry. It isn't.

- **Begin Highway 360.**

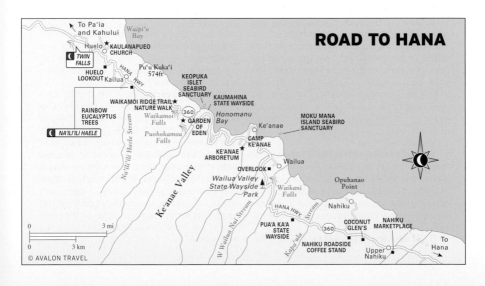

10 Tips for Driving the Road to Hana

Perhaps one of the most beautiful activities on Maui is driving the Road to Hana. Weaving its way for 52 miles around 600 curves and over 56 one-lane bridges, it's the most loved and loathed stretch of road on the entire island. Here's how to plan a visit to Hana that will leave you poring over a photo album instead of searching for a divorce lawyer.

1. Hana is not a destination, but a journey. Visitors race all the way to the sleepy village of Hana and are left saying only one thing: "This is it?" With a population of around 1,800, Hana is not big. Hana is not a destination; it's a place to get away from it all.

2. The Road to Hana doesn't actually end at Hana. Technically the famous Road to Hana is only 52 miles long and stretches between Kahului Airport and the town of Hana itself. But the actual road doesn't end in Hana. Many of Hana's natural treasures lie in the 10 miles beyond Hana town. Hamoa Beach, consistently voted as one of the top beaches in the country, is a couple of miles past Hana. So is Waioka Pond, a hidden pool on the rocky coastline. Thirty minutes beyond Hana town are the pools of 'Ohe'o (also known as the Seven Sacred Pools), with a series of cascading waterfalls and pools falling directly into the blue Pacific.

3. Don't drive back the same way you came in. Your rental car contract tells you the road around the back of the island is for four-wheel-drive vehicles only, but that's just not true. Parts are bumpy, and a few miles are dirt road, but unless there's torrential rain, the road is passable with a regular vehicle. Following the back road all the way around the island, you are graced with all new views as your surroundings change from lush, tropical rainforest to wind-swept, arid lava flows.

4. Don't make dinner reservations. Too many people try to squeeze Hana into half a day or end up feeling rushed. Hana is a place to escape from the rush, not add to it. If you're planning a day trip to Hana, block off the entire day, leave early (7am), and see where the day takes you.

5. Stop early, stop often. Take a break for a morning stroll or for breakfast at a tucked-away café. Pick up some snacks and then watch the waves. Stop and swim in waterfalls, hike through bamboo forests, pull off at roadside stands for banana bread or locally grown fruit. If the guy behind you is on your tail, pull over and let him pass. Who cares? This is Hana, and there isn't any rush.

6. Think hard before taking a van tour. If you question your ability to drive narrow, mountainous roads, then take a guided van tour. Local guides can provide insights into Hawaiian history, culture, and personal anecdotes, which add humor to the lengthy drive. The problem is that you're on someone else's schedule. If you decide you want to go body-surfing, you can't. If you see a waterfall that you want to go swim under, you can't. You're going to be called back to the van.

7. Bring a bathing suit and hiking shoes. Hana is a land of adventure. Pack the necessary wardrobe and equipment for your activity of choice.

8. *Kapu* means keep out. If you see a sign which says *kapu,* it translates to "No Trespassing" or "Keep Out." Move along and enjoy a spot more accessible to the public.

9. Don't stay too long. While Hana can be tough to leave, don't drive home in the dark—particularly if going the back way. If you think driving on narrow, one-lane roads with precipitous drop-offs is difficult during the day, try doing it at night. Leave by 4pm to ensure a well-lit journey home.

10. Stay overnight. A day trip to Hana makes for a long day. Most locals stay overnight, either camping at the Pools of 'Ohe'o or staying in a bed-and-breakfast or the Travaasa Hana hotel. When you wake up, you'll have beaches and swimming holes all to yourself before throngs of day-trippers arrive—usually around 11am. If you've already booked a hotel stay for the entirety of your trip, but you don't want to rush Hana, stay at a bed-and-breakfast and forget about your hotel room on the other side of the island. It will be the best $200 you ever spend.

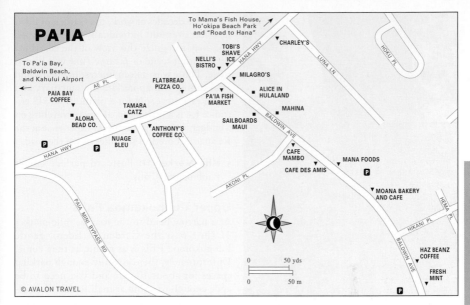

- **Mile Marker 0:** Note the change in mile markers at the junction of Hana Highway and Kaupakalua Road.

- **Mile Marker 0.3:** Congratulations, your first waterfall! Just joking. They get much better than this.

- **Mile Marker 2:** Twin Falls

- **Mile Marker 2.8:** Your first taste of the turns that you're going to experience for the next 20 miles.

- **Mile Marker 4.5:** Huelo Lookout fruit stand

- **Mile Marker 4.9:** Your first narrow bridge crossing!

- **Mile Marker 6.5:** Naʻiliʻili haele hike (aka Bamboo Forest)

- **Mile Marker 6.7:** Rainbow eucalyptus trees

Rainbow Eucalyptus Trees

Just past the trailhead for the Naʻiliʻili haele hike is a grove of rainbow eucalyptus trees, silently springing from the green pasturelands.

One of the most-photographed sights on the Road to Hana, these trees have bark which drips with pastel hues of red, pink, orange, green, and gray, as if a painter had taken a brush directly to the bark, with deliberate strokes running the length of each narrow tree. Unlike trees which have a cork-like bark, rainbow eucalyptus have a smooth, hard exterior, which is constantly going through stages of regrowth. As a section of tree undergoes exfoliation and sheds a section of bark, the young wood exposed has a deep green hue. As the new bark ages in the sun, the wood morphs from green to blue and from purple to orange, eventually dying off once again to reveal the green growth below, starting the cycle anew. Parking can be found either at the trailhead for the Naʻiliʻili haele hike (mile marker 6.5) or at a small pullout for a hunting road a hundred yards past the trees.

- **Mile Marker 8.1:** First scenic view of a valley gazing out toward the ocean

- **Mile Marker 8.5:** Sweeping view of dense swaths of bamboo crawling their way up the eastern flank of the mountain

© JENNA STRUBHAR

Rainbow Eucalyptus provide colorful foliage along the winding drive.

- **Mile Marker 9.5:** Waikamoi Ridge Trail. This small picnic area provides a relaxing place to stretch your legs or enjoy a roadside snack (although there are no restrooms or other facilities). There's a short loop trail here that gains 200 feet of elevation in the surrounding forest.

- **Mile Marker 10:** Waikamoi Falls, the first roadside waterfall and swimming hole

- **Mile Marker 10.5:** The Garden of Eden Botanical Garden and Garden Gourmet food cart

Garden of Eden
Half a mile up the road from Waikamoi Falls is the enticing **Garden of Eden** (808/572-9899, www.mauigardenofeden.com, 8am-3pm daily, $15/person), an ornately manicured 26-acre rainforest utopia. In 1991, Alan Bradbury, the state's first I.S.A. certified arborist, slowly but surely began clearing the hillside and replanting native trees. It was truly a labor of love:

After two decades of work, the Garden of Eden now has over 600 individually labeled plants. You may recognize this view of the coastline: the opening scene of *Jurassic Park* was filmed there. Those with a keen interest in botany and landscaping will appreciate the sanctuary and it makes a great spot for a picnic. The $15 entrance fee is a little steep. If you're traveling on a budget, you can get a similar experience at the Ke'anae Arboretum six miles down the road.

- **Mile Marker 11:** Postcard-perfect Upper Puohokamoa Falls

Upper Puohokamoa Falls
At a narrow bend in the road at mile marker 11 (just past the Garden of Eden), gentle Puohokomoa Falls is as scenic as they come. Unfortunately, there are only enough parking spaces for about 10 cars and you need to be agile enough to climb a small rock wall to access the trail. If you're lucky enough to find a parking spot and are fit enough, the reward is a swimming hole of tropical simplicity.

- **Mile Marker 11.5:** Haipua'ena Falls is half a mile past Upper Puohokamoa Falls. Parking here can also be limited. The falls aren't nearly as nice as at Puohokamoa, but that may mean it will be less crowded.

- **Mile Marker 12.2:** Kaumahina State Wayside Park. Public restrooms and a picnic area with a sweeping view of Ke'anae coastline.

- **Mile Marker 14:** Honomanu Bay

- **Mile Marker 16.5:** Ke'anae Arboretum

Ke'anae Arboretum
Myriad species of trees, from rainbow eucalyptus to guava and sugarcane, are spread throughout the free Ke'anae Arboretum. A 30-minute, paved, wheelchair-accessible trail winds back into the lush surroundings. After 10 minutes of walking, the paved portion of the trail comes to an end and changes to dirt as you make your way past a fence. If you make a left once inside the boundary and head toward Pi'ina'au

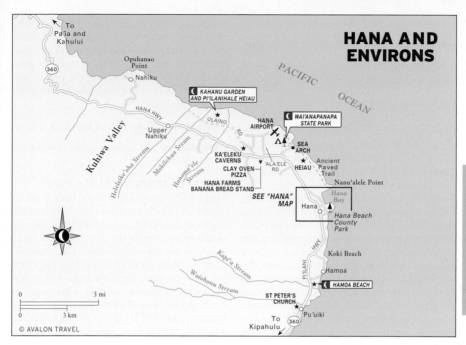

HANA AND ENVIRONS

Stream, you'll find a small hidden swimming hole. Reaching it requires a scramble down the rocks.

- **Mile Marker 16.6:** Turnoff for Keʻanae village

- **Mile Marker 17:** Keʻanae Overlook

- **Mile Marker 17.3:** Halfway to Hana store and ATM

- **Mile Marker 18:** Turnoff for Wailua village and Uncle Harry's food stand

- **Mile Marker 18.5:** Taro *loʻi* (fields) and small waterfalls coming down the road

- **Mile Marker 18.7:** Wailua Valley Wayside Park offers a panoramic vista from the **Keʻanae Overlook.** It's a good place to stretch your legs and get a photo that not too many others will have. Once in the designated parking area, look to your right for a hidden set of stairs to access the lookout.

- **Mile Marker 19.6:** Upper Waikani Falls is also referred to as Three Bears Falls. This is a great place to stop for a swim.

- **Mile Marker 22.6:** Puaʻa Kaʻa State Wayside Park has restrooms and a small picnic pavilion on the *mauka* side of the highway looking out over the stream. A short, three-minute walk leads from the road up the stream to an underrated swimming pool and waterfall.

- **Mile Marker 24.1:** Painted Little Green Shack

- **Mile Marker 25:** Turnoff for Lower Nahiku Road and pullout for Makapipi Falls

- **Mile Marker 26.5:** Nahiku Roadside Coffee Stand

- **Mile Marker 27.5:** Coconut Glen's Ice Cream Stand

- **Mile Marker 28.3:** Banana bread stand

- **Mile Marker 28.7:** Nahiku Marketplace

- **Mile Marker 29.7:** View of the Hana Airport

- **Mile Marker 31:** Turnoff for Kaʻeleku Caverns and Kahanu Garden

Kaʻeleku Caverns

As you make your way from Nahiku Marketplace, the first sights you'll encounter are a few miles before "downtown" Hana. At mile marker 31 you'll see the signs for **Kaʻeleku Caverns** (808/248-7307, www.mauicave.com, 10:30am-4pm daily, $12.50/person). Turn down ʻUlaʻino Road to visit this subterranean, 2-mile network of lava tubes, the 18th largest in the world and the only lava tubes on Maui that are navigable and open to the public. Cave explorers are given a flashlight to examine the stalactite-encrusted surroundings. On your way out, navigate your way through the maze of red *ti* leaves which create the only such maze found anywhere on the planet. Walking the caverns at an average pace will take about 30 minutes. There are no garbage cans or restrooms, so pack out your trash.

- **Mile Marker 31.2:** Hana Farms banana bread stand and clay-oven pizza

◖ Kahanu Garden and Piʻilanihale Heiau

On ʻUlaʻino Road, the pavement gradually gives way to dirt road leading to **Kahanu Garden** (808/248-8912, www.ntbg.org, 9am-2pm Mon.-Sat., $10). This 464-acre property is in Honomaʻele, an area ceded in 1848 to Chief Kahanu by King Kamehameha III. The land has remained largely unchanged since the days of ancient Hawaii. The sprawling gardens focuses on plant species that are integral parts of Polynesian culture. You're greeted by a massive grove of *ulu* (breadfruit). There are also groves of bananas, coconuts, taro, sweet potato, sugarcane, and *ʻawa*. A self-guided tour details the history of these plants and the uses they had for native Polynesians.

Towering **Piʻilanihale Heiau,** a massive, multi-tiered stone structure, is the largest remaining *heiau* in the state of Hawaii. The walls stretch over 50 feet high in some places and the stone platforms are the size of two professional football fields. Multiple archaeological surveys have determined that the temple was most likely built in stages and dates back as far as the 14th century.

- **Mile Marker 31.4:** Turnoff for Hana Airport

- **Mile Marker 32:** Turnoff for Waiʻanapanapa State Park

◖ Waiʻanapanapa State Park

Rugged Waiʻanapanapa State Park is often known as "black sand beach." At the beach overlook, you'll be greeted with one of the most iconic vistas on the drive to Hana. Take it slow on the 0.5-mile road down to the park; there are often small children playing. Once you reach the park, turn left at the parking lot and follow the road to the end, where you can access the black sand of Paʻiloa Beach and its freshwater caves. Comprised of crushed black lava rock, the sand is as black as Hana's gaping night sky. Lush green foliage clings to the surrounding coastline, and dramatic sea arches and volcanic promontories jut into the frothy white sea. Since it faces nearly directly east, this is a popular venue for sunrise weddings.

On the main paved trail by the parking lot overlook, you'll see a trail that runs in the opposite direction of the beach; this is the beginning of a popular coastal hike. One of the more popular stops along this trail is a blowhole that erupts on days with large surf. Maintain a safe distance; visitors have been swept into the ocean here.

The other main draw of Waiʻanapanapa is the system of freshwater caves hidden in a grotto not far from the parking area. Following the cave trail from the parking lot, you'll be met with a sign that details the legend of the caves. Go left at the sign and travel downhill on a short loop trail. After a three-minute walk you'll reach the cave entrance. The clear, fresh water is crisp and cold.

- **Mile Marker 32.7:** Hana school

© HEATHER ELLISON

the black sand beach at Wai'anapanapa State Park

- **Mile Marker 34:** Fork in the road; stay left. Road will rejoin with main highway in 1.5 miles via a right turn at the softball field in Hana town.

HANA TOWN

Hana has deep ties to its history. Before the arrival of Western explorers, it was a stronghold that was conquered and reconquered by the kings of Maui and those of the Big Island. The most strategic and historically rich spot is Ka'uiki Hill, the remnant of a cinder cone that dominates Hana Bay. It's said that the demigod Maui transformed his daughter's lover into Ka'uiki Hill and turned her into the gentle rains that bathe it to this day.

Hana was already a plantation town in 1849 when sea captain George Wilfong started producing sugar on 60 acres here. After sugar production faded out in the 1940s, San Francisco industrialist Paul Fagan bought 14,000 acres of what was to become the **Hana Ranch.** Today, Hana's population, at 1,200, continues to be predominantly Hawaiian. Visitors will enjoy a host of sights scattered throughout the community.

Fagan Memorial

Once you finally roll in to Hana town, one of the most prominent sights is a massive cross presiding above the village. Set on the 545-foot summit of Pu'u O Kahaula (Lyon's Hill), the **Fagan Memorial** was constructed to honor the town's modern founder—Paul Fagan—after he passed away in 1960. The memorial is accessible by following a steep walking path departing from the parking lot of the Travaasa Hana hotel. Atop the summit you're treated to the best view in Hana, with a panoramic vista out over historic Hana Bay and 'Alau Island in the distance.

Hana Cultural Center

While it might not look like much from the outside, the humble yet informative **Hana Cultural Center** (4974 Uakea Rd., 808/248-8622, www.hanaculturalcenter.org, 10am-4pm Mon.-Thurs., $3) provides a historical

MAUI

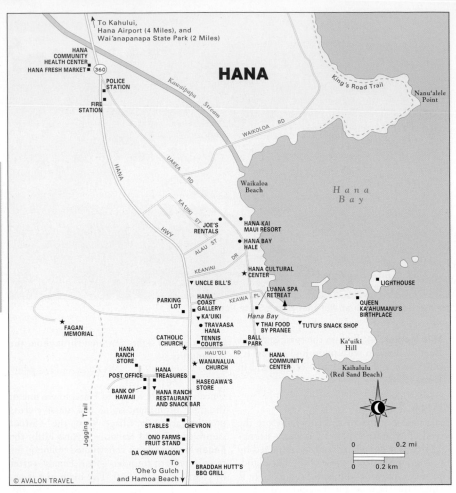

To Kahului,
Hana Airport (4 Miles), and
Wai'anapanapa State Park (2 Miles)

HANA

HANA COMMUNITY HEALTH CENTER
HANA FRESH MARKET
360
POLICE STATION

FIRE STATION

Kawaipapa Stream

King's Road Trail

Nanu'alele Point

WAIKOLOA RD

UAKEA RD

HANA HWY

KA'UIKI ST

Waikaloa Beach

Hana Bay

JOE'S RENTALS
HANA KAI MAUI RESORT
ALAU ST
HANA BAY HALE
DR
KEANINI
HANA CULTURAL CENTER
UNCLE BILL'S
LUANA SPA RETREAT
LIGHTHOUSE
PARKING LOT
HANA COAST GALLERY
KEAWA PL
QUEEN KA'AHUMANU'S BIRTHPLACE
KA'UIKI
Hana Bay
FAGAN MEMORIAL
TRAVAASA HANA
THAI FOOD BY PRANEE
TUTU'S SNACK SHOP
CATHOLIC CHURCH
TENNIS COURTS
BALL PARK
Ka'uiki Hill
HAU'OLI RD
HANA RANCH STORE
WANANALUA CHURCH
HANA COMMUNITY CENTER
Kaihalulu (Red Sand Beach)
POST OFFICE
HANA TREASURES
HASEGAWA'S STORE
BANK OF HAWAII
HANA RANCH RESTAURANT AND SNACK BAR
Jogging Trail
STABLES
CHEVRON
ONO FARMS FRUIT STAND
DA CHOW WAGON
To 'Ohe'o Gulch and Hamoa Beach
BRADDAH HUTT'S BBQ GRILL

0   0.2 mi
0   0.2 km

© AVALON TRAVEL

backbone for the town. Over the course of Maui's history, Hana has been a unique eastern outpost, with one foot on Maui and one foot on the Big Island. Visitors to the Hana Cultural Center can not only see ancient Hawaiian artifacts excavated from the Hana region (such as stone adzes and hand-woven fishnets), but they'll also get a chance to walk around the Hana courthouse listed on the National Register of Historic Places in 1991. Like something out of an old Western movie, the one-room courthouse still holds sessions on the first Tuesday of each month, and in a testament to the island's multicultural heritage, the proceedings can take place in no fewer than 24 languages. During the rest of the month when court isn't in session, the courthouse serves as a somber museum where Hana residents recount the morning of the 1946 tsunami, which devastated the eastern end of the island. If you have an interest in the history of Hana, there's no finer place to stop along your journey.

• **Highway 330:** Technically, Highway 360

ended at Hana Bay and Highway 330 started back at the fork in the road by the fire station. Once you drive past the center of Hana town (i.e., Hasegawa General Store and the gas station), you are now traveling on Highway 330, although the mileage markers don't start again for a couple of miles, and when they do, they are now counting down as opposed to up. The turnoff for Hamoa Beach and Koki Beach is at the first turnoff for Haneo'o Road about 1.5 miles past the center of Hana town, which is before the mileage markers begin again. There are two turnoffs for Haneo'o Road, and you want to make sure you take the first one because this is the direction that local traffic naturally travels.

HANA TO KIPAHULU

- **Mile Marker 51:** The mileage markers restart
- **Mile Marker 48:** Waioka Pond
- **Mile Marker 47.5:** Fruit and flower stand popular with tour buses
- **Mile Marker 46.3:** Karen Davidson Fine Art

- **Mile Marker 45.3:** The road becomes *narrow* and offers dramatic views of coast
- **Mile Marker 44.8:** On the right side of the road is 80-foot Wailua Falls, a wispy cascade that could be the most photographed waterfall on Maui. The best way to experience these falls is to take the short trail down to the base and take a dip in the swimming pools, away from the crowds.
- **Mile Marker 43.2, 42.9:** Old bridges from 1910
- **Mile Marker 42.2:** Start of Haleakala National Park, Kipahulu section
- **Mile Marker 42.1:** 'Ohe'o Stream and bridge looking over the incorrectly named Seven Sacred Pools

◖ Pools of 'Ohe'o

The fabled **Pools of 'Ohe'o** inside Haleakala National Park (808/248-7375, www.nps.gov/hale) are one of the island's most popular attractions. The name Seven Sacred Pools is the largest misnomer on the island. There are far more than seven pools and there's no record in

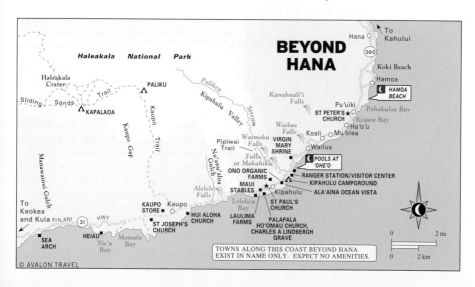

Hawaiian history of these pools being sacred. The name likely began as a marketing ploy by the staff at a nearby hotel (now the Travaasa Hana) in the 1940s. But the name stuck and continues to be used to this day. The real name is 'Ohe'o (pronounced oh-HEY-oh); locals will appreciate you using it.

This part of the island is truly stunning. The first taste you'll get of the park is crossing over 'Ohe'o Gulch on a bridge at mile marker 42.1. There's a breathtaking view of the pools here. Try not to linger too long as you'll stop traffic. The entrance to the park is 0.4 mile down the road. The entrance fee is $10/vehicle (if you have visited Haleakala National Park within the last three days, your paperwork will still allow you entry).

Once inside the park you'll notice a large parking lot next to an informative visitor center. Take time to explore the visitor center because it's the best place on this side of the island to gain an understanding of the history, culture, and unique environment of the Kipahulu region. Rangers here are the best sources of information on current conditions of trails and waterfalls throughout the park.

The visitor center is also where you begin the Kuloa Point Loop Trail leading down to the famous pools. Along the 10-minute walk, you'll go through groves of *hala* trees and past a number of historic sites. Eventually the trail emerges at a staircase down to the pools and one of the most iconic vistas in Hawaii.

On most days the three main pools are open for exploring and swimming, although they're closed during heavy rains and flash floods. Reaching the uppermost pools requires some rock scaling; it's well worth the effort if you're physically fit.

- **Mile Marker 41.9:** Trailhead for Pipiwai Trail (parking for trailhead is inside park)

- **Mile Marker 41.7:** Entry to Haleakala National Park

- **Mile Marker 41.2:** Ono Organic Farms

Ono Organic Farms

The granddaddy of all the organic farms is **Ono Organic Farms** (808/248-7779, www.ono-farms.com, tours $35 adult, children under 10 free), half a mile past the entrance to Haleakala National Park. If you're a fan of exotic produce, you'll be absolutely blown away by the selection at this 50-acre farm. In addition to growing over 3,000 pounds of bananas *every week,* this farm also cultivates durian, cacao, coffee, tea, star fruit, Surinam cherries, and 60 other types of tropical and exotic fruits. Tours run Monday-Friday at 1:30pm and last two hours. The cost of the tour more than pays for itself in food, local knowledge, and genuine island experience, offering a culinary journey of certified organic and GMO-free produce plucked directly from the land. A genuine spirit of aloha permeates the compound. It's easiest to take the tour if you're staying overnight in Hana. The driveway up to the farm is part of the adventure.

- **Mile Marker 40.9:** Ho'onanea Farms fruit and coffee stand

© JENNA STRUBHAR
the unparalleled beauty of 'Ohe'o

- **Mile Marker 40.8:** Turnoff for Palapala Ho'omau Church, the final resting place of historic aviator Charles Lindbergh.

- **Mile Marker 40.6:** Laulima Farm fruit stand and kitchen, a sprawling compound growing a wealth of organic produce and a roadside kitchen.

- **Mile Marker 39.2:** Lelekea Bay

- **Mile Marker 39:** Road begins to deteriorate and becomes narrow with precipitous drop-offs. This is where you should turn back if you don't want to drive around the "back" of the island. As a point of reference, from this point it's 50 miles to Kahului Airport going around the back side, and it will take about two hours without stopping. If you choose to return the way you came, it's 60 miles, and it will take about 2.5 hours without stopping. While bumpier, the back road is much straighter and has less traffic.

- **Mile Marker 38.8:** Alelele Falls is a 60-foot waterfall requiring a short 10-minute hike to reach it.

- **Mile Marker 38.5:** Highway 31 begins.

- **Mile Marker 38.4:** The scariest section of road you'll encounter. If you make it past this without a heart attack, you'll be fine the rest of the way.

- **Mile Marker 37.8:** Road turns to dirt.

- **Mile Marker 36:** Surroundings morph from tropical and lush to windswept and arid. Welcome to Kaupo!

- **Mile Marker 34.6:** Kaupo Store

Kaupo Store

No other store on the island will amaze you quite like **Kaupo Store** (mile marker 34.6, 10am-5pm Mon.-Sat.). The area surrounding Kaupo Store feels like the end of the earth. It's squirreled away inside a building constructed in 1925. Inside, visitors will be happy to find cold drinks and Haagen-Dazs ice-cream bars.

© HEATHER ELLISON

MAUI

the remote outpost of Kaupo

It won't come as a surprise that transactions are cash only. Stock up on water and snacks because it's a long, winding, beautiful drive from here to the next place that sells anything.

- **Mile Marker 33.5:** Kaupo Gap warrants a stop for the sweeping view. At the upper rim of the gap is the 6,800-foot floor of Haleakala Crater.

- **Mile Marker 31.8:** The most amazing view of Haleakala you will ever see

- **Mile Marker 31.1:** The gate which leads to Nu'u Bay

Nu'u Bay, Huakini Bay, and the Rugged "Back Side"

If you thought the stretch of road between Kipahulu and Kaupo was desolate, you're in for a real treat. The southeastern flank of Haleakala opens up into the most dramatic panorama you'll find on the island—a pristine expanse of wide-open country. You can be excused for wanting to pull over every 5-10 minutes simply to gawk at the desolate beauty. The road on this section of coast is exceptionally bumpy, so give the car in front of you plenty of space. After Manawainui Gulch (with a bridge in the middle of nowhere), the road begins its gradual climb away from the coast and up to the 3,000-foot elevation of Keokea.

- **Mile Marker 30.1:** Huakini Bay

- **Mile Marker 29:** You survived the worst part of the road! Smooth pavement begins.

- **Mile Marker 28.7:** Beautiful view of a lava rock sea arch

- **Mile Marker 27.3:** Manawainui Bridge and gulch

From this point the road climbs in elevation through the rural communities of Kahikinui and Kanaio before wrapping around to the Tedeschi Winery in Ulupalakua 13 miles later. If it's before 5pm, you can toast to your success at the winery, although you won't find any real restaurants or gasoline until you get to Grandma's Coffee House in Keokea another 5.2 miles past Ulupalakua.

Congratulations! You've just survived the drive around the "back" of the island. When you make it back to your hotel at night, it will truly feel as if you've journeyed to the end of the earth and back.

Beaches

There isn't a single stretch of sand in all of East Maui that is home to a condo or resort. Beaches remain windswept, undeveloped, and rural. Due to the easterly trade winds, there isn't much snorkeling along east shore beaches. The water can be rough due to exposed and choppy ocean conditions. Bodysurfing replaces scuba diving, windsurfing replaces kayaking. Mornings offer the calmest conditions, perfect for a jog, a quick dip, or a chance to simply to quiet your head and commune with nature.

PA'IA
⬛ Baldwin Beach
Not enough visitors spend time at long, wide, and mostly empty **Baldwin Beach**. This is a popular local bodysurfing spot, although the waves can get large during winter. The best way to kick off a trip to Hana is to arrive in Pa'ia around 7am, grab a coffee in town from Anthony's, and spend 30 minutes walking the length of Baldwin, the turquoise water and white sand creating a reflective amphitheater of calm.

At the far western end of the beach (the side farthest from Pa'ia) is a small cove known as **Baby Beach,** where a fringing reef creates a natural pool perfect for wading with young ones. Instead of walking the length of Baldwin, you can also access Baby Beach by turning on Nonohe Place off Hana Highway, followed by a right on Pa'ani Place, and a quick left onto Kealakai Place. On the far eastern end of Baldwin (the side closest to Pa'ia), a small trail leads around the point and connects with a hidden beach that's next to Pa'ia Bay. This little-known stretch of sand is often occupied by sun-worshipping nudists, affable hippies, and locals passing around the *pakalolo*. If you visit during the afternoon and the wind is howling, the cove on the far eastern end of Baldwin is protected from the wind and offers calm swimming during most of the year.

Not everything here is idyllic. The parking lot can attract unsavory characters. Respect the warning signs that lifeguards have posted. Green port-a-potties are the lone facilities.

Pa'ia Bay
The closest beach to the center of town, **Pa'ia Bay** is as active as Baldwin is calm, with a basketball court in a small park area and overflow parking for the town. The skate park at the Pa'ia Youth Center teems with area youth.

Bodyboarders and surfers flock here for the waves and a number of downhill bike companies finish tours here after descending 6,500 feet down the mountainside. There are restrooms, a beach shower, and an ever-changing cast of entertaining and colorful characters.

Kuau Cove

The scenic backdrop for Mama's Fish House, where most visitors take an obligatory sunset photo, is this public beach. This small cove has a smattering of sand and an intriguing system of tidepools great for exploring with small children. The beach shrinks at high tide, so low tide is the best for poring over the rocks to take a peek at all the slippery critters. There are a few parking spots near Mama's Fish House; the spaces with blue cones are designated as beach parking.

Tavares Bay (aka Blue Tile Roof)

Barely visible from Hana Highway, the access for the sandy cove at **Tavares Bay** can be found by turning at the house with the blue tile roof. Located 0.6 miles past the stoplight in Pa'ia, this beach gets windy in the afternoon and offers marginal, shallow swimming. Tavares can get popular on the weekends, but the crowds during the weekdays are usually thin. The only facilities are a couple of port-a-potties in the dirt parking lot. On occasion the parking lot can turn into a raucous local tailgate party.

Ho'okipa Beach Park

The global epicenter of the windsurfing world, **Ho'okipa** also offers a thin, sandy beach better for tanning than any form of swimming. A fringing reef creates a small pond nice for small children. A wide range of international visitors can usually be found sunning here. Mornings are usually calm at Ho'okipa. When the surf isn't too high, local spearfishers dive for *tako* (octopus) and you'll see numerous sea turtles coming up to breathe. There are two lifeguard towers as well as showers. A heavy local crowd usually dominates the pavilion area. The best place for visitors is on the stretch of sand on the left side of the beach. The parking can be tight.

HANA TOWN
Pa'iloa Beach (Black Sand Beach)

The black sand beach at Wai'anapanapa State Park is the most popular in Hana. Just a few miles before the sleepy center of Hana (and just past the turnoff for Hana Airport), this is a place where dense foliage and black lava rock come face-to-face with crashing blue surf. The water along the shoreline is often rough, particularly in the afternoon. The result of this tumultuous wave erosion is a beach formed of crushed black lava rock. The color of the sand here is as black as the sky that envelops the town of Hana each night. To reach the shoreline you need to walk down a paved path from the parking lot of the state park. When you reach the bottom, you'll notice some sea caves you can explore at low tide. Since the sand is formed from lava rock, it isn't the most comfortable; bring a blanket or a towel if you plan on hanging out for a while. Once back at the parking lot, don't leave without checking out the freshwater caves. You can also walk the trail winding along the shoreline.

Hana Bay

Hana Bay is a laid-back crescent of gray sand smack in the middle of Hana town. Tucked in the lee of Ka'uiki Head—a large promontory where Queen Ka'ahumanu was born—Hana Bay is where the town's boat ramp is located and the outrigger canoe club holds practice. This is a working-class, community bay—it's also where many confused visitors end up when they "can't find Hana." Compared to neighboring Hamoa Beach, Hana Bay is more utilitarian: a nice area for a picnic and stretching your legs after the long drive. Swimming is calm but not spectacular.

HANA TO KIPAHULU

Visitors lament that there aren't any nice beaches in Hana. Waterfalls, yes, but beaches, no. This is a common misperception among those who made the mistake of turning around in the town of Hana, thinking they had reached the final destination. A few miles past the town of Hana are two of the most stunning beaches you'll find

MAUI

© HEATHER ELLISON

Koki Beach

in East Maui, including one that consistently ranks as one of the top 10 in the United States.

Koki Beach

To reach Hana's two famous beaches, travel 1.5 miles past the center of town (Hana Ballpark) and then make a left on Haneo'o Road. Going downhill, the first beach you'll come to is **Koki Beach,** a favorite hangout of local surfers. Koki gets windy during the afternoon. On the left side of the beach, you can scramble over some rocks to reach some hidden sections of sand. Access to these smaller beaches is only possible at low tide, so most visitors stay on the main section of beach. The dark-red sand is a product of a cinder cone known as Ka Iwi O Pele ("the bones of Pele"). According to legend, this is where Pele, the volcano goddess, met her mortal end. Her bones were stacked high on the shoreline before her spirit traveled southeast to the Big Island.

◖ Hamoa Beach

Continue along Haneo'o Road, paralleling the ocean, the snowcapped peak of Mauna Kea on the Big Island occasionally visible in the distance. At low tide you can also see the remnants of the ancient Haneo'o Fishpond, although access to the fishpond rests on private land. As the road rounds back to the right, you'll finally catch glimpses of a beach that Mark Twain considered one of the most beautiful in the world.

Before you experience **Hamoa Beach** for yourself, however, you need to find a parking spot. Parking is tight; park only on the right side of the road so that traffic flows smoothly on the left. You might have to drive past the beach before you can find a space. Access to the beach is down the stone stairway. The park area at the bottom of the stairs is property of the Travaasa Hana hotel but the sandy beach is public property.

This is the best spot in Hana for a relaxing day at the beach. On the calmest of days it's possible to snorkel along the rocky coastline, though most visitors will prefer to bodysurf the consistent, playful shorebreak. This can also be one of the best surf breaks in the area.

Surfing

Surfing in East Maui is reserved for only intermediate and advanced surfers. While places such as Hoʻokipa Beach Park and Hamoa Bay can see surf at any time of the year, this stretch of coast roars to life October-April with massive North Pacific swells. This is some of the largest, heaviest surf on the planet. Most visitors are better off as spectators than participants. Even watching from the shoreline, you can still feel the rush of waves large enough to rumble the ground beneath you.

Paʻia
SURF SPOTS
Although it's rarely surfed, a break in front of the lifeguard tower at **Baldwin Beach** offers fun longboarding before the afternoon wind picks up. If the surf is too large at places such as Hoʻokipa or Paʻia Bay, there is a reform on the shallow reef here that can offer a long ride if you know where to sit. The downside to surfing here is that on your way back in it can be a challenge to wrangle your longboard through the shorebreak. On the opposite side of the beach, down toward **Baby Beach,** there are also a couple of breaks better for shortboarding, although the rides are noticeably shorter and the entry and exit can be challenging.

If you're renting a board in Paʻia, the closest beach break to town is **Paʻia Bay**. While the inside section is popular with bodyboarders, there is a second peak a little farther out that is better for surfing. Mornings are best before the wind blows the wave to pieces. Since the wave can be fast and steep, it's best for intermediate surfers.

Moving east from town toward Hana, the left break at **Tavares** is popular with north shore locals, although since the wave can only handle a small crowd you need to be a competent surfer. The parking lot for Tavares is found by making a left at the house with the blue tile roof 0.6 mile outside of town and following the beach access sign to the end of the road.

Paddling out from the beach can be shallow at low tide.

The epicenter for surf on the island's north shore will forever be **Hoʻokipa Beach Park,** three miles past the town of Paʻia. This legendary, windswept cove is a year-round playground for everyone from up-and-coming surf stars to world-champion windsurfers. For surfers, Hoʻokipa is broken up into four sections: Pavilions (Pavils), Middles, The Point, and Lanes. If you are standing on the beach, Pavilions is the break that's the farthest to the right; a spot that can pick up wrapping windswell even during the summer. Since it's the most consistent, it can also be the most localized, so beginners should only paddle out on the smallest of days. In the center of the beach, Middles is a big left that breaks in deep water and can get board-shatteringly heavy during the winter. The wave can accommodate a larger crowd than Pavils, although you should still be an intermediate to paddle out. On the left side of the beach is The Point, a heavy A-frame that's popular with windsurfers. Finally, Lanes is a left-hand wave that breaks in the cove to the west of Hoʻokipa, but is frequently accessed by paddling around from the point. Since it's such a long paddle, not as many surfers venture out there. If you're an advanced surfer and want to escape the crowds, this can be a fun wave if you put in the effort. If you get stuck inside, however, the entry to shore can be over sharp, urchin-covered rocks.

SURFBOARD RENTALS
The surfboard rental scene is remarkably casual. Both **HI Tech Maui** (58 Baldwin Ave., 808/579-9297, www.surfmaui.com, 9am-6pm daily) and **Sailboards Maui** (22 Baldwin Ave., 808/579-8432, www.sailboardsmaui.com, 9:30am-7pm Mon.-Fri., 9:30am-6pm Sun.) offer board rental for $20/day. Both shops have a full range of longboards, shortboards, and fun boards. They are an affordable option

for playing in the waves of Pa'ia Bay or a multiday safari to Hana.

SURF SCHOOLS

Given the advanced surf conditions of the island's North Shore, there aren't nearly as many surf schools in East Maui as there are on parts of the island such as Lahaina or Kihei. There are a couple of highly personalized instruction services where you can learn from the island's top surfers.

One of the best surf schools on the island is **Rivers to the Sea** (855/6284-7873, www.riverstothesea.com), a first-class operation run by local Maui surfer Tide Rivers. Two of the island's top surfers, Tide and his brother Kiva have gained a reputation for giving surf lessons to celebrities who pass through the area. All lessons are customized to the client's ability level, but before venturing out on to the North Shore, take a lesson on the user-friendly waves of the south shore to get a firm grasp of the basics. Tide will meet beginners at a predetermined spot outside of Lahaina and guarantee to have you up and standing before the end of the 1.5-hour lesson. All instructors were born and raised in Hawaii. Lesson rates are $160 for a private lesson, $220 for two people, and $85/person for private groups of three or more. Photo packages are available.

Professional longboard surfer **Zack Howard** (808/214-7766, www.zackhowardsurf.com) also offers the opportunity to surf on the North Shore. While most of his lessons are conducted at locations on the south shore on the road to Lahaina, advanced surfers can paddle out on the North Shore if the conditions are right. Lesson rates are $160 for a private lesson, $220 for two people, and $90/person for private groups of three or more.

Hana
SURF SPOTS

Although there are a number of secret spots scattered around the coastline, the two main Hana surf breaks frequented by visitors are **Koki Beach** and **Hamoa Beach,** both on Haneo'o Road 1.5 miles past the town of Hana.

Because of its easterly location, Hana gets waves any time of the year. Since the waves are often the result of easterly windswell, conditions can be rougher than elsewhere on the island. The steepness of the wave here is better suited for shortboards than for longboards. Koki is where many of Hana's *keiki* (children) first learn how to pop up and ride.

Around the corner at Hamoa, the protected bay offers a respite from the trade winds. Whereas Koki breaks fairly close to shore, the wave at Hamoa breaks farther out over a combination of sand, reef, and rocks. On moderate days, this is a good place for riding a longboard or a stand-up board since the wave isn't as steep, but the largest waves are reserved for locals and experts. There are no lifeguards at either beach in Hana.

WINDSURFING

Despite the fact that the trade winds blow almost every afternoon for the majority of the summer, most windsurfers flock to the island's North Shore in winter. Summer windsurfing is reserved for spots such as Kanaha Beach Park in Central Maui where wind takes precedent over waves. Here on the North Shore the world's best all flock in droves to **Ho'okipa Beach Park** for the chance to combine the trade winds with waves regularly reaching over 20 feet in height. Don't expect to see any windsurfers during your morning drive to Hana, however, as there is a local law that prohibits windsurfing before 11am. Seeing as the trades don't usually start blowing until noon, however, rarely is this ever a problem for those who want to get out on the water.

Windsurfing Spots

Sprecklesville is a local sailing spot that offers conditions less crowded than Kanaha or Ho'okipa. It's an advanced location, so if you're still new to the sport, it's best to stick to the area around Kanaha. If you're a competent sailor, however, the launching point at Sprecklesville can be reached by turning on Stable Road 1.4 miles past the intersection of Hana and Haleakala Highways. On Stable Road there are two main launching points known as Euro Beach and Camp One. Euro Beach (named for the number of European windsurfers who frequent the spot) is the closest to Hana Highway, and Camp One is the spot toward the end of Stable Road. Both have short access roads off Stable Road that lead down to small parking areas by the beach. There isn't any kitesurfing allowed here because the beaches are directly beneath the flight path of departing aircraft, so don't be startled when a jet engine roars over your head while you're rigging up on the sand.

If you're an avid windsurfer, you already know without reading this book that **Ho'okipa Beach Park** is the mecca for the world's best windsurfers. The best place for watching these front-flipping professionals is from the western tip of the beach (the side closest to Pa'ia), since this is the section most frequented by the windsurfing crowd. Since Ho'okipa is a multiuse area for a variety of water sports, there is a rule that states if there are more than 10 surfers in the water at The Point then there isn't any windsurfing allowed. Conveniently,

however, good windsurfing conditions make for bad surfing conditions, so on windy days most surfers will just move down to the surf break known as Pavilions slightly more protected from the wind. Parking can be tough at Ho'okipa, so if you're only coming here to watch the windsurfers, it's best to park up along the highway and leave the spots closer to shore for those who need to move their gear.

Windsurfing Rentals

Although most of the windsurfing rental shops are in Kahului, **Simmer Style** (137 Hana Hwy., 808/579-8484, www.simmerhawaii. com, 10am-7pm daily) is the closest shop to Ho'okipa and is the best spot on the North Shore for windsurfing rentals and supplies.

KITESURFING

Since kitesurfing isn't allowed along the length of Sprecklesville, and since Ho'okipa is dominated by windsurfers and surfers, there are only a handful of places along the island's North Shore amenable for the sport. What few spots

© KYLE ELLISON

windsurfers at Ho'okipa Beach Park

are available, however, are only accessible to advanced riders. If you're still relatively new to kitesurfing, it's best to stick to Kite Beach and Kanaha Beach Park in Central Maui. If you're determined to kite along this stretch of coastline, however, most kiters will launch out of the **Kuau Cove** section of shoreline between Mama's Fish House and The Point at Ho'okipa. Parking can be found either in the beach access stalls within the Mama's Fish House parking lot or at pullouts along the highway by Ho'okipa Beach Park. Entry from the shore, however, means tiptoeing your way across an urchin-covered reef. For the best representation of the island's allowed kitesurfing zones, check out the maps at www.mauikiteboardingassociation.com.

Hiking and Biking

HIKING
Road to Hana
◖ TWIN FALLS

At mile marker 2 (11.4 miles past Pa'ia), **Twin Falls** is one of the easiest and shortest waterfall hikes you'll find in East Maui. It's also the first series of waterfalls you'll encounter on the Road to Hana. Since much of the area weaves through private homes (respect the *Kapu,* or "Keep Out" signs on driveways), most of the "trail" is a gravel road that is wide and easy for strolling. Although there are a few spots where the footing can be tricky, this is the perfect choice for anyone looking for a "tame" walk into the jungle.

An outdoor playground peppered with waterfalls, the only downside about Twin Falls is that it's far from being a secret. During the midmorning hours as visitors make their way toward Hana, there can be well over 50 cars parked along the side of the road, and it's safe to say that you won't have the waterfalls to yourself. If you would prefer to visit without the crowds, you can either stop on your drive *back* from Hana, visit *really* early before everyone else has arrived, or make a separate trip out here in the late afternoon. Regardless of when you visit, bring mosquito repellent.

Although there are myriad waterfalls at Twin Falls, the two main ones are most accessible for visitors. For exploration into the hinterlands of the rainforest, Hike Maui offers an informative guided tour. For casual visitors, however, the 1.3-mile trail begins in the gravel parking lot and makes its way through a small gate in a lush and forested orchard area. There are port-a-potties on the right side of the trail, and visitors are encouraged to leave a donation for their maintenance and upkeep. After five minutes of walking along the gravel road, you'll hear some waterfalls off to your left. While these are nice for a quick photo, the main waterfalls are still farther down the trail. After 10 minutes of walking, you'll come to a stream crossing that can flood during periods of high rain. If the water appears to be rushing violently, it's best to turn around. Five minutes past the stream crossing, you'll come to a three-way fork in the road. Go straight. After five more minutes you'll come to another fork, where the trail to your left has a wooden plank crossing over a small stream. Go straight, and after two minutes of clambering around an irrigation flume, you'll reach a waterfall that has a small pool for swimming. While this waterfall is nice enough, there's a second waterfall known as Caveman that is far more dramatic, although it can be a little tougher to reach.

To get to Caveman, turn around and go back to the fork in the trail where there was the wooden plank. Cross over the wooden plank, ascend a small hill, take the fork to the left, and then a take a right 50 yards later. You'll now find yourself walking downhill, and a few minutes later you'll reach a concrete irrigation structure with steps leading up and over it. From here you'll begin to see the waterfall in the distance, although to reach the base of the falls you must wade across a stream that is usually about knee-deep. If the

© HEATHER ELLISON

Cool off during a hike to Twin Falls.

stream is manageable, a short scramble past it will bring you to a cavernous waterfall begging you to take your photo behind it. Since the water isn't clear enough to see the bottom, don't even think about jumping off the top. Adjacent to the pool at Caveman you'll notice a thin trail which switchbacks its way up the hill. Following this trail will bring you to more pools and waterfalls, although since it's easy to get lost back here it's best to have a guide if you plan on venturing any farther. On your way out from Caveman, after you climb up and over the irrigation structure and ascend the hill, by following the trail to the right when it forks you'll end up at the three-way fork in the trail you originally encountered on your walk in, ultimately having done a full loop. From here it's a short walk back to the parking lot and the rest of East Maui's treasures.

◖ NA'ILI'ILI HAELE (BAMBOO FOREST)

The waterfalls of **Na'ili'ili haele** are one of the highlights of the Road to Hana, but it's important to understand that this hike is not for everyone. Dangers include traversing steep, slippery slopes as well as crossing streams prone to flash floods.

At the 6.5 mile marker, you'll first know that you're approaching the trailhead when you make an enormous hairpin turn flanked on the right by a narrow rock wall. The road becomes narrow here, and parking can be difficult during the busiest times of day. As long as your car doesn't obstruct the road, you can park on the right side against the bamboo, although the passenger will need to climb out of the driver's seat. If all these spots are taken, there are more pullouts within the next quarter mile. The first place where many visitors go wrong is in finding the correct trailhead, which is marked by a lone metal pole springing up from a break in a wire fence. On the other side of the fence, the trail will be narrow at first and wind its way downhill. After two minutes of walking you'll reach an intersection where you'll turn left and be confronted with a steep scramble down a hill. This area can become slick, so use your hands to aid against a slip or a fall. Once

Na'ili'ili haele

few minutes into this bamboo trail you'll encounter a clearing off toward your left. After a few more minutes, you'll come to a second clearing. When you come to a third clearing on your left, you should hear the rush of a waterfall. Turn left to cross the stream again here; this will bring you to the first waterfall where there's a small pool.

Many visitors make it this far and decide that this is enough, because beyond this point the trail gets exponentially more challenging and treacherous. Should you want to continue, however, trace the edge of the pool to the far side of the streambed and you'll notice a thin rope dangling over a slippery rock face. This is where the trail continues; shimmy your way up the slick rock area using the rope to rejoin the trail. Once you've successfully navigated that obstacle, the trail will flatten out and pass through more bamboo before arriving at another pool, which is larger and less crowded than the first. Slip off your shoes and slide in for a dip.

at the bottom of the hill, you'll encounter a stream crossing with a wooden plank stretching over a gap. Once on the other side of the stream, you'll continue straight through a tunnel of bamboo before the path wraps around to the left and you rejoin the main trail. Make a right and follow the trail for another two minutes until you come to a major stream crossing.

The stream crossing is the second point (after the trailhead) where most visitors get turned around. Since the trail runs cold at the stream, it can be confusing where to go from here. When you look across to the other side of the stream, you'll notice a downed tree on the opposite bank and slightly to the left. Follow the tree trunk to its base, and here you'll notice where the continuation of the trail is on the other side of the stream. This is where you're aiming for during your stream crossing. Once on the other side, the trail will parallel the water as you move upstream. This section has some of the densest bamboo on the whole trail, and even when the sun is high in the sky, the thick grove can nearly block out the sun. A

WAIKAMOI RIDGE TRAIL

The **Waikamoi Ridge Trail** (mile marker 9.5) provides a calming respite to get out and stretch your legs on a 30-minute loop trail that takes you just far away enough from the road that the only sound you can hear is the call of native birds and the creak of bamboo as it sways in the wind above you. The trail itself gains 200 feet in elevation and consists of two parts: the loop trail and the spur trail to the upper picnic area. Hike in a counterclockwise direction since this is the best-maintained section of trail. The second half of the loop heading back downhill toward the parking lot isn't as well maintained and is a lot muddier than the platform steps found on the way up.

If you choose to take the spur trail to the upper picnic area, you'll be rewarded with an open clearing few visitors take the time to explore. The trail to the upper picnic area will take about 10 minutes. It is covered in *lau hala* leaves and slippery roots. At the end of the trail is a simple picnic area where a covered pavilion provides a relaxing place for a snack and a rest.

Pack mosquito repellent if you plan on stopping to eat here.

Hana Town
KING'S HIGHWAY COASTAL TRAIL

One of the few hiking options in East Maui that doesn't involve a waterfall, this three-mile trail that runs between Wai'anapanapa State Park and the northern tip of Hana Bay is one of the few navigable remnants of the ancient King's Highway, which once circled the island. Today, only scarce remnants of this ancient trail are evident, but the most prominent section lies right here on the coastline leading south from Wai'anapanapa. Parking for the trailhead is in the main lot of the state park. Along the course of this three-mile trail you'll weave around azure bays flanked by black sand, pass beneath dense groves of dry *lau hala* trees, and gaze upon lava rock arches carved from the coastline by the often tumultuous sea.

Wear hiking boots, as the jagged *a'a* lava can rip rubber slippers to pieces. Carry plenty of water as there are no facilities along the trail. As you get closer to Hana Bay, the trail becomes a little more treacherous, and most visitors start from the Wai'anapanapa trailhead and hike about halfway before turning back. To take the literal road less traveled, continue to the north of Wai'anapanapa and pass a series of smaller black sand coves before eventually emerging near the Hana Airport. Expect to devote at least three hours to this trail if hiking round-trip from the trailhead.

For a quick and easy hike which still offers a rewarding view, the trail leading from the Travaasa Hana parking lot up to **Fagan's Cross** will take most hikers about 20 minutes and has a steep enough grade to offer a good leg workout. Keep a keen lookout for fresh guavas growing on the trees, in addition to the fresh cow pies left by the free range cattle.

A two-mile long **walking trail** leads from the trail to Fagan's Cross south toward the beach at Hamoa. The track is little more than flattened grass running through the pasturelands, although you'll have the coastal views all to yourself.

Kipahulu and Beyond
PIPIWAI TRAIL

Hands down, **Pipiwai Trail** is the best in Maui. In the Kipahulu section of Haleakala National Park, the **Pipiwai Trail** is comprised of the upper portion of 'Ohe'o Gulch in the area known as Seven Sacred Pools. While most visitors to 'Ohe'o only pay a cursory visit to take photos, the Pipiwai Trail which runs *mauka* (mountain-side) of the highway is the undisputed highlight of the Kipahulu section of the park. The four-mile trail is just long enough to be adventurous and just short enough to be accessible, and the trail is at a moderate enough grade that most hikers should be able to reach the end. Speaking of the end, the last half mile of this trail winds its way through bamboo which is so thick it blocks out the sun, and just when you think the scenery couldn't get any more tropical, the trail emerges at the base of 400-foot Waimoku Falls. This two-hour expedition more than justifies the winding drive out here. Or, for the best way to experience the trail, camp overnight at the Kipahulu campground and hit the path before the throngs of day-tripping tourists arrive.

To find the trailhead for the Pipiwai Trail, drive 30-40 minutes past the town of Hana. At mile marker 41.7 you'll reach the entrance to the Kipahulu section of Haleakala National Park, and parking for the trailhead is within the park boundaries. You'll have to pay the park entry fee ($10/car) to hike, but since you should spend additional time exploring the pools down by the ocean, it's no different than if you were visiting the park.

Find the trailhead by walking back out to the road and going 100 yards toward Hana. Here you'll see the signs for the trailhead on your left. From the time the trail departs the road it steeply climbs its way up a rocky slope until you are greeted with a sign offering trail distances and words of caution. Much of the Pipiwai Trail parallels 'Ohe'o Gulch, and you can hear the rush of the water as you make your way uphill toward the falls. However, it's never safe to access the pools or waterfalls located in the river. There may be days when you *can* get

MAUI

© MARK DRIESSEN

The climax of the Pipiwai Trail is 400-foot Waimoku Falls.

to the river by scrambling down a sketchy hillside or undefined trail, but a number of visitors have been swept to their death in flash floods. The National Park Service advises against any attempt to access the stream.

After 10 minutes on the trail you'll reach the lookout for Makahiku Falls, a 200-foot plunge that can be anything from a trickle during drier months of the year to a torrent of violent water during the throes of a flash flood. After Makahiku Falls the trail will begin gaining in elevation for another five minutes before emerging in the shade of one of the most beautiful banyan trees you'll ever see. The section between "the tree" and the first bridge is one of decisions. Multiple spur trails lead to waterfall overlooks, offering views of the canyons and pools.

Ten minutes past the tree you'll reach the first of two bridges that zigzag their way across the stream. This is a great place to snap pictures of the waterfalls and your first taste of the bamboo forest. You'll notice after crossing the second bridge that when the trail turns

into stairs that climb steeply toward the bamboo, there's an opening in the railing on the left side where a path leads down to a rocky streambed. This is the Palikea Stream, and if you rock hop up the riverbed for about 15 minutes, you'll emerge at a waterfall that is less dramatic—but also less-visited—than neighboring Waimoku Falls. The waterfall here trickles its way down the towering canyon walls, and the pool at the bottom can occasionally be frequented by those who prefer to bathe *au naturel*.

Back on the main trail, by continuing up the stairs you'll find a boardwalk through the densest bamboo on the island. As you emerge from the creaking cavern, five more minutes of rock hopping brings you to the piéce de résistance, which of course is 400-foot Waimoku Falls. Welcome to one of the most beautiful corners of the island.

ALELELE FALLS

Most visitors never take the time to make the short hike back to 60-foot **Alelele Falls,** where there is a refreshing pool for swimming. Located on the fabled "back road" about three miles past the pools of 'Ohe'o, the trailhead is at Alelele Bridge at mile marker 38.8; park in one of the few parking spots available on the Kaupo side of the bridge. If you have the tiniest shred of energy left in you for a 10-minute hike through the jungle, the reward is a waterfall of just the right height which offers just the right amount of seclusion. Although parking for the trailhead is on the Kaupo side of the bridge, the trailhead itself is back on the Kipahulu side at the spot where the bridge begins. Following this well-defined trail you'll crisscross the stream a couple of times and pass by ancient lava rock walls before emerging at the base of the pristine falls.

BIKING

The town of Pa'ia is the elbow joint for two of the most popular rides of the island: the frigid ride down Haleakala and the weaving journey out toward Hana. With East Maui's prominent location as a hub for island cycling, it should come as no surprise there are also a few bike shops sprinkled around town.

Pa'ia

Far and away one of the most comprehensive cycling experiences on Maui is found at **Maui Cyclery** (99 Hana Hwy., 808/579-9009, www.gocyclingmaui.com, 8am-6pm Mon.-Fri., 8am-4pm Sat., 8am-noon Sun.), a small but thorough shop in the heart of Pa'ia. In addition to offering rentals, parts, services, and sales, the staff at Maui Cyclery offer a "fantasy camp for cyclists." This is the only place on the island that offers a tour for visitors who are avid about cycling. Rentals range from $30/day for a single day and go up from there for elite performance bikes. Group rides begin at $140 for a four-hour riding experience.

Ha'iku

Over in the Ha'iku Cannery, **Haleakala Bike Company** (810 Ha'iku Rd., #120, 808/575-9575 or 888/922-2452, www.bikemaui.com, 8:30am-5pm Mon.-Sat., 9am-4pm Sun.) mainly specializes in tour groups making the ride down Haleakala Volcano. In addition to the volcano run, you can also rent your own bike from $35/day, and as long as you arrange your own transportation to the top, you'll be able to ride from the summit of the volcano.

Adventure Sports

ZIPLINING
Ha'iku

Even though most of the adventure sports along Maui's North Shore take place in the water, **North Shore Zipline Company** (2065 Kauhikoa Rd., 808/269-0671, www.nszipline.com, closed Sun.) provides a course of seven ziplines that weave their way through the trees of a rural Ha'iku location that at one time served as an island military base. The course here is family-friendly and caters mainly to first-time zippers. Children as young as five are welcome to participate as long as they're accompanied by a paying adult. Don't think that you won't still get a rush, however, as you can hit speeds of up to 45 mph on the last line

of the course, and the viewing platforms provide a unique vantage point for peering out over the rural section of mountainside.

SOARING AND HANG GLIDING
Hana

Those who feel that helicopters tours are *way* too cliché will enjoy two adventures that push them outside their comfort zone to see the beauty of Hana from the air.

    Skyview Soaring (Hana Airport, 808/244-7070, www.skyviewsoaring.com, $165 and up) is a self-powered glider where your pilot, Hans, will take you as high as 10,000 feet before killing the engines and gliding all the way back to your starting point at the airport. This

MAUI

isn't for the faint of heart, although the views afforded of Haleakala Crater and the eastern flank of mountainside far surpass any you could ever get from driving along the highway. Bring your camera as you glide silently past towering waterfalls and above the shoreline of Waiʻanapanapa State Park. Flights last for either 30 minutes or an hour, and if you decide to go for the full hour, you'll be able to soar all the way to the rim of Haleakala Crater and reach speeds of 50-100 mph on the ride down.

Despite the similarities, **Hang Gliding Maui** (808/572-6557, www.hanggglidingmaui.com) offers a completely different experience. The flight is an instructional lesson which can go toward earning a certification in sport flying. You won't travel nearly as high as you would with soaring, although this ultra-light "trike" places you in an exposed outdoor seating arrangement open to the winds. Consequently, you feel as if you're one step closer to flying. The time in the air is a one-on-one instructional period with your pilot, Armin, so this isn't an experience you can share as a couple. You can also purchase still photos or video of your experience from a camera fixed to the wing. Rates for the hang gliding experience range from $170 for a 30-minute lesson to $280 for a full hour.

Shopping

PAʻIA
Once known only for hippies, surf culture, and sugarcane, Paʻia now features some of the island's trendiest boutiques. The bikini shops, beachwear boutiques, and craft galleries populating this one-stoplight town keep serious shoppers occupied for hours.

Art Galleries
One of the only art galleries in town is **Turnbull Fine Art** (137 Hana Hwy., 808/579-9385, www.turnbullfineart.com, 11am-7pm Mon.-Sat.) on the Hana side of the intersection. This store is an extension of the rural showroom on the twisting road to Kahakuloa. Art aficionados will appreciate the creative style of these longtime local artists.

Surf Shops
If you're in need of any surf, skate, or even snowboard wear, you'll find that **HI Tech Maui** (58 Baldwin Ave., 808/579-9297, www.surfmaui.com, 9am-6pm daily), **Sailboards Maui** (22 Baldwin Ave., 808/579-8432, www.sailboardsmaui.com, 9:30am-7pm Mon.-Fri., 9:30am-6pm Sun.), **Hana Highway Surf** (149 Hana Hwy., 808/579-8999, www.hanahwy-surf.com, 10am-7pm daily), and **Honolua Surf**

Company (115 Hana Hwy., 808/579-9593, 9am-9pm Mon.-Sat., 9am-7:30pm Sun.) all offer apparel for looking the part in one of the happiest surf towns in the United States.

Clothing and Swimwear
The only genre of shopping which rivals surf gear in Paʻia is women's clothing boutiques and bikini stores. Along Baldwin Avenue, **Alice in Hulaland** (19 Baldwin Ave., 808/579-9922, www.aliceinhulaland.com) offers a snarky range of clothing and accessories, and **Mahina** (23 Baldwin Ave., 808/579-9132, www.shopmahina.com, 9:30am-8pm Mon.-Sat., 10am-6pm Sun.) offers trendy women's clothing which can also be found in its sister stores all around the island. On the finer end of apparel are **Nuage Bleu** (76 Hana Hwy., 808/579-9792, www.nuagebleu.com, 9:30am-6pm daily) and **Tamara Catz** (83 Hana Hwy., 808/579-9184, www.tamaracatz.com, 10am-6pm daily), which sit along Hana Highway toward the entrance to town. These are two of the more popular clothing boutiques among elegant and fashionable locals.

When it comes to bikinis, sun-seekers will love bouncing around between **Pakaloha** (151 Hana Hwy., 808/579-8882, www.

pakalohamaui.com, 10:30am-6pm daily), **Maui Girl** (12 Baldwin Ave., 808/579-9266, www.maui-girl.com, 9am-6pm daily), and **Letarte** (24 Baldwin Ave., 808/579-6022, www.letarteswimwear.com, 10am-6pm daily), the latter two advertising that their bikinis were featured in the 2013 *Sports Illustrated* magazine shoot.

Jewelry

While Pa'ia doesn't boast nearly the same number of jewelry stores as Lahaina, **Studio 22K** (161 Hana Hwy., 808/579-8167, www.studio22k.com, 10am-6pm Tues.-Sat.) on the far Hana side of town is a small studio that specializes in handmade 22 karat gold items with metal malleable enough to morph into all sorts of twisting shapes and designs.

If sterling silver is more of what you're looking for, **Oceania Maui** (120 Hana Hwy., 808/579-6063, www.oceaniamaui.com, 10am-6:30am daily) operates a gallery between Charley's restaurant and the Da Kine surf shop that has a wide range of over 400 sterling silver jewelry designs.

If you would prefer to make your own jewelry, **Aloha Bead Company** (43 Hana Hwy., 808/579-9709, www.alohabead.com, 10:30am-5:30pm Mon.-Sat., 11am-5pm Sun.), right next door to Pa'ia Bay Coffee, has a huge selection of beads and glass for creating unique island-inspired accessories.

Furnishings

Although you probably aren't looking for much furniture while on vacation, **Indigo** (149 Hana Hwy., 808/579-9199, www.indigopaia.com, 10am-6pm daily) is still an eclectic and fascinating store that also has large displays of photography, rugs, and jewelry from the owner's travels all over the globe. There are heavy Asian and African influences in a lot of the pieces.

ROAD TO HANA
Gifts and Souvenirs

The best place to do any real shopping along the Road to Hana is at **Nahiku Ti Gallery** (mile marker 28.7, 808/248-8800, 10am-5pm daily), a small gallery within the Nahiku Marketplace.

This curious "strip mall in the jungle" is already strange enough in that it offers legitimate food options in the middle of nowhere. The curiosity is only amplified by the fact that there's an actual art and souvenir gallery that rivals any you might find in the tourist enclaves of Ka'anapali or Wailea. While nowhere near as large as the south shore shopping venues, the Nahiku Ti Gallery still has a varied selection of jewelry, crafts, paintings, pottery, and a surprising collection of art you wouldn't expect to find in this part of the island.

HANA TOWN
Art Galleries

By far the most comprehensive gallery in all of Hana, the **Hana Coast Gallery** (5031 Hana Hwy., 808/248-8636, www.hanacoast.com, 9am-5pm daily) could be the nicest art gallery on the island. A freestanding building within the Travaasa Hana hotel, the Hana Coast Gallery features fine works by Hawaiian artists and is a must-stop for anyone who appreciates fine art. Everything from oil paintings to ceramics and wooden sculptures is on display in this sophisticated space, and the depth of knowledge of the staff on the intricacies of individual pieces provides an educational component to this fine art experience.

Gifts and Souvenirs

Within the same complex as the post office and the Hana Ranch Restaurant is the small **Hana Treasures** (5031 Hana Hwy., 808/248-7372, 10am-5pm Mon.-Fri., 10am-3pm Sat.-Sun.) souvenir store which sells everything from clothing and trinkets to "Thank God for Hana" bumper stickers.

For Hawaiian-themed souvenirs and resort wear, visit **Noe Noe** inside the Travaasa Hana hotel (3501 Hana Hwy., 808/359-2401, 9am-7pm daily). It has a selection of island-infused apparel to help you look fashionable down at Hamoa Beach. For a full-range of Hawaiian beauty products, continue on a short walk down to the spa.

Although the selection is more utilitarian than artistic, you can also pick up some basic gifts and souvenirs at the **Hasegawa General Store** (5165 Hana Hwy., 808/248-7079, www.hanamaui.com, 7am-7pm Mon.-Sat., 8am-6pm Sun.) in the center of town. Here you'll find everything from tank tops and hats to Hana-themed stickers and merchandise.

HANA TO KIPAHULU
Art Galleries
Along the road between Hana and Kipahulu on the ocean side of the highway, **Karen Davidson Fine Art** (mile marker 46.3, 808/248-4877, www.karendavidson.net) focuses on the unique art of handcrafted paper. Many of the works are either oil paintings on handmade paper or an array of paper collages. There's a Hawaiian/Polynesian theme coursing through much of the artwork unique and relevant to Hana. The studio itself is a work of art in that it opens out to the Hana coastline. If you are more interested in fine art than tumbling waterfalls, call ahead to arrange a visit.

Ark Ceramics studio and gallery (808/344-3885, www.arkceramics.net, 11am-4pm) is nestled eight miles past Hana in a section known locally as Koali. You'll need to call ahead and arrange an appointment, but if you're a tea-lover, you'll be amazed at artist Arrabella Ark's pottery prowess in creating teapots in the traditional *raku* form.

Entertainment

LIVE MUSIC
Pa'ia
The de facto late-night watering hole for all of the North Shore continues to be **Charley's** (142 Hana Hwy., 808/579-8085, www.charleysmaui.com, open until 2am), where there's live music on most nights of the week. Charley's is the only place in Pa'ia where you can dance. There can also occasionally be live music in the courtyard of **Café des Amis** (42 Baldwin Ave., 808/579-6323, www.cdamaui.com, open until 8:30pm), which is an intimate venue for taking in some tunes.

Hana
The most happening show in town is at the **Travaasa Hana** hotel (5031 Hana Hwy., 808/359-2401, www.travaasa.com/hana) every Sunday, Monday, and Thursday evening in the dining room. Thursday is usually the most eventful, when local people will put on their finest wear and head out on the town for a drink and entertainment. You never know the local talent that might roll through the dining hall. Many famous Hawaiian artists have Hana roots either in that they were raised here or have family who live here. It also isn't uncommon to have a local person jump out of a chair mid-meal and dance hula to a favorite song before sitting back down to finish the meal. More so than at any other establishment on the island, the evening entertainment is rich with community and a feeling of aloha, and an evening experiencing the live entertainment at the Travaasa can be more of a cultural experience than any resort luau or show.

Live music can also be found at the **Hana Ranch Restaurant** (5031 Hana Hwy., 808/270-5280, 7:30pm-9:30pm Tues.) one night a week. A scheduled band will usually provide the entertainment for the first hour, followed by a second hour of open-mic night. When it comes to open-mic night in Hana, you'd be surprised how much talent a small community can foster when you eliminate the so-called conveniences of the modern world. Ukulele, hula, music, and song are ways of life when living in Hana, and the artistic talent which courses through this community is inspiring.

Food

PA'IA
Seafood
 Mama's Fish House (799 Poho Pl., 808/579-9764, www.mamasfishhouse.com, 11am-2:30pm and 4:15pm-9pm daily, $20-40 lunch, $28-55 dinner) has become synonymous with Maui dining. Many in its cult-like following claim that if you haven't been to Mama's, you've never been to Maui. The oceanfront location is unbeatable, the romantic ambience is better than anywhere on the island, and the fish is so fresh that the menu not only tells you where your fish was caught that morning, it tells you who caught it. Prepare for a meal where the beauty of Polynesia is evident in every bite. Call well in advance for reservations (timing your meal for sunset is best). To get there, travel a mile past the town of Pa'ia as if headed to Hana; just as the road meets up with the ocean again, you'll see the Mama's Fish House sign and the entry to Kuau Cove.

While your hotel concierge will recommend Mama's, the local surfer will point you to **Pa'ia Fish Market** (100 Baldwin Ave., 808/579-8030, www.paiafishmarket.com, 11am-9:30pm daily, $10), on the corner of the only stoplight in town. Lines stretch out the door for the popular ono and mahi burgers. My personal favorite is the ahi burger. Pair your fish with a draft Hefeweizen, locally canned Bikini Blonde lager, or maybe even a glass of wine.

Mexican
On the *other* corner of Pa'ia's only stoplight, separated by the bustling crosswalk, **Milagros** (3 Baldwin Ave., 808/579-8755, www.milagrosfoodcompany.com, 11am-10pm daily, $10-18) is known for Mexican fare with a funky island twist, enormous portions, and the best happy hour in town. The black bean nachos, ahi burrito, and blackened ahi tacos are all local favorites. Get a seat at the outdoor patio, which has some of the best people-watching in Pa'ia.

Italian
As the name of **Flatbread Pizza Co.** (89 Hana Hwy., 808/579-8989, www.flatbreadcompany.com, 11am-10pm daily, $16-22) implies, you won't find any Chicago-style deep dish here. All of the pizzas use organic, locally sourced ingredients and are fired in an open kiawe (mesquite) wood oven. Try the Mopsy (free-range kalua pork, organic mango barbecue sauce, organic red onions, Maui pineapple, and goat cheese from Surfing Goat Dairy), or Coevolution (kalamata olives, organic and local rosemary, red onions, goat cheese from Surfing Goat Dairy, sweet red peppers, and organic herbs), both made with organic dough. A lively bar scene fills up nightly; get there early or expect a wait. Tuesday nights, the restaurant hosts benefits for the local community.

American
Charley's (142 Hana Hwy., 808/579-8085, www.charleysmaui.com, 7am-10pm daily, $8-14) is as integral a part of town as a dawn patrol at Ho'okipa or a bodysurfing session at Baldwin Beach. Known as "Willie's Place" because Willie Nelson frequently dines here, Charley's breeds a colorful cast of characters. You may find yourself dining next to a famous celebrity on an incognito North Shore vacation. The run-down exterior of the wooden saloon exudes a gritty, no-nonsense vibe. On the inside, it's a jovial, comfortable sports bar and bistro that offers healthy menu options with locally sourced ingredients. Top off an early morning surf session with macadamia nut pancakes. Classic burgers such as a "bacon and blue" are filling and won't break your budget.

Natural Foods
Natural foods enclave **Mana Foods** (49 Baldwin Ave., 808/579-8078, www.manafoodsmaui.com, 8am-8:30pm daily) is the epicenter of the island's health-conscious community, with a selection of organic and

MAUI

natural offerings. There's a hot bar as well as a deli section where you can build your own health-conscious picnic lunch for the Road to Hana.

Coffee Shops

Start your day off at **(** **Anthony's Coffee Company** (90 Hana Hwy., 808/579-8340, www.anthonyscoffee.com, 5:30am-6pm daily). This legendary Pa'ia mainstay is known as the refueling center for some of the North Shore's biggest names. You just might catch sight of a passing celebrity as you slurp up the last of your eggs Benedict or acai smoothie. A full espresso bar adds a jolt into your morning. Twenty different varieties of freshly roasted beans (including those from Kona, Moloka'i, and Ka'anapali) are on sale. As the sign says, it offers the "last Wi-Fi before Hana."

If you would rather enjoy a casual coffee in a garden setting, **Pa'ia Bay Coffee** (43 Hana Hwy., 808/579-3111, www.paiabaycoffee.com, 6:30am-6pm Mon.-Sat., 7am-6pm Sun.) is steps away from the bay on the ocean side of the highway. Enjoy a small selection of sandwiches, croissants, salads, and bagels in the shaded grove along with free Wi-Fi.

ROAD TO HANA

Seemingly every store in Pa'ia (and even some as far away as Ka'anapali) offers "Road to Hana picnic lunches" as a means of staving off starvation, even though the longest stretch without any food options is a little under seven miles. There are plenty of places to pull over and enjoy an outdoor meal, but don't settle on a picnic lunch out of desperation. A better plan is a hearty breakfast in Pa'ia followed by occasional stops at the roadside food trucks and fruit stands to get some local flare along with your snacks. Once you reach the Nahiku Marketplace (39 miles past Pa'ia and six miles before Hana) you're presented with more options, ranging from coffee shops to barbecue to freshly made Thai. So when setting out for Hana, the question shouldn't be whether you're going to starve, but rather, *which* place to stop to eat! Go slow, "talk story" with those serving

your food, and sample the local flavors of the East Maui jungle.

Fruit Stands

The first fruit stand on the road is **Huelo Lookout** (7600 Hana Hwy., 808/280-4791, www.huelolookout.coconutprotectors.com, open daily), just past mile marker 4. Enjoy your fresh fruit, smoothies, and coconut candies at the coastal lookout a few steps behind the stand. They also sell local arts and crafts.

Market

The accurately named **Halfway to Hana** (www.halfwaytohanamaui.com, 8:30am-4pm daily, $2-6, cash only) is located at the 17.3 mile marker between the Ke'anae Overlook and the turnoff for Wailua. It's basically a hot dog, sandwich, and shave ice stand with an ATM around the corner, making it the closest thing to a store around Ke'anae. Ask about the freshly baked banana bread.

HANA

In the last few years, Hana has seen a huge proliferation of food options. However, too many visitors continue to drive to Hana Bay thinking it's the end of the road, and don't take the time to look around. Spend the day in Hana and you'll be rewarded with a tasty cornucopia.

American

A longtime staple of the town's restaurant scene, the **Hana Ranch Restaurant** (5031 Hana Hwy., 808/270-5280, 11am-8:30pm daily, $8-10) is located on the mountain side of the road in the "center of town." There are shoyu chicken plate lunches, fish and chicken sandwiches, and soothing bowls of saimin noodles to calm your upset stomach. The takeout window is open from 11am-4pm; the inside seating area stays open for dinner.

Hawaiian Regional

If you're craving a meal in a resort setting, the **(** **Ka'uiki** (5031 Hana Hwy., 808/359-2401, 7:30am-9pm, $20-40) restaurant and **Paniolo Lounge** (11:30am-9pm daily) inside the

Travaasa Hana hotel are the best (and only) options in Hana. This is hands-down the town's best breakfast option (think French-pressed coffee and eggs Benedict). The lunch options of fish tacos, grilled vegetable pitas, and ahi nicoise salad provide a solid dose of civilization. Dinner means risottos, fish, steak, and chicken dishes that coddle your taste buds. The entrée menu uses locally sourced ingredients. A full-service bar and wine list add some libations to a romantic meal in paradise. Prices are higher than a food cart on the road, but you're getting a relaxing respite in one of the nicest hotels in the state.

Fruit Stands

Only a few miles before the town of Hana, the legendary **(Hana Farms Banana Bread Stand** (mile marker 31.2, 8am-7pm daily) features six different types of banana bread, as well as a full range of fruits, coffee, sauces, and flavorings. There will be more fruit stands as you wrap your way between Hana and Kipahulu, but none of them are like this. Do yourself a favor and stop for a coffee, banana bread (get a loaf with chocolate chips), and advice on your Hana adventure.

Farmers Market

One of the best Hana lunch options, and one of the few actually open on Sunday, is **Hana Fresh Market** (4590 Hana Hwy., 10am-4pm Mon., 10am-2pm weekends, $8), in the parking lot of the Hana Health Clinic between the town of Hana and the turnoff for Wai'anapanapa. Not only do the proceeds support the Hana Health Clinic, but many of the vegetables and fresh produce are grown in a greenhouse on the property. There is also an ample selection of filling lunch options such as ham apple brie paninis, Italian sausage pasta, and lemon caper mahimahi. Wash it all down with a fruit smoothie or freshly brewed coffee.

Italian

Right next door to the Hana Farms fruit stand, **(The Clay Oven** (4pm-8pm Fri.-Sat, $14-17) is the best thing to happen to the Hana dinner

© HEATHER ELLISON

MAUI

Don't be surprised if your pizza box is made from banana leaves.

scene in a long time. Don't be fooled by the appearance of this outdoor pizza kitchen in the jungle or the "pizza box" of fresh banana leaves. You'll be surprised to find a full menu of seven different pizza options ranging from classic margherita to creative potato and pesto. The pizzas are filling enough for two. Large groups can enjoy sitting in "the fireside lounge," a tent behind the open-air kitchen. It's at mile marker 31.2 (a few miles past Wai'anapanapa if heading back toward Kahului).

Thai

(Thai Food by Pranee (5050 Uakea Rd., 10:30am-4pm Mon.-Fri., 10:30am-6pm Sat.-Sun., $10-12) has diversified the town's culinary scene for the better. Located on Uakea Road, smack in the center of town between Hana Ballpark and Hana Bay, this open-air restaurant gets packed for lunch. The filling portions of pad thai and green curry are worth the wait. The cooks aren't messing around: The curry is served with sweat-inducing spice. Ask them to pour a ladle of coconut milk over the fiery dish. Parking can be tough. If you park along Uakea Road, be sure to face the correct direction to avoid a ticket.

KIPAHULU AND BEYOND

If you plan on driving "the back road" all the way to the other side of the island, don't expect many food options. In nearly 35 miles of roadway between Hasegawa General Store and Kanaio, there are exactly three—one of which is only open on Sunday nights. The other two are known to close without warning. If you're planning on venturing from Hana to 'Ohe'o (Seven Pools) and then continuing around the back side of the island, stock up on water and snacks at Hasegawa General Store or a fruit stand, lest you get marooned with a rumbling stomach and parched lips.

Vegetarian

Spunky **Café Attitude** (6:30pm-10pm Sun.) only operates on Sunday nights and is closer to a community potluck than an actual restaurant. Organic farmers gather on Sunday evenings and take turns preparing a weekly meal, which is open to all who care to attend. Guests are suggested to trade a donation ($15) for a large plate of freshly prepared vegetarian cuisine. There are usually exotic teas, homemade kombucha, and all-natural popsicles available by small donation as well. More important than the food is the open-mic jam session, which takes place on the small stage. Sit around the communal fire pit and listen to local artists perform everything from acoustic guitar and harmonica to lyrical spoken word. A strong sense of aloha permeates the rural setting: As the banner hanging from the dining area says, "Be grateful, or get out." To find Café Attitude, travel past the Laulima Farm stand in the direction of Kaupo and keep an eye out on the *makai* (ocean side) of the road for a driveway with two pillars of a sun and a moon. Follow the steep driveway down into a grassy parking area and listen for the sound of laughter and bongos.

Market

Six miles past Kipahulu at mile marker 34.6 is the historic **Kaupo Store** (808/248-8054, 10am-5pm Mon.-Sat.), a welcome stop for those in need of a cold drink, a bag of chips, or an ice-cream bar pulled out of the old-fashioned freezer. You have to go another 20 miles to find a real restaurant.

Getting There and Around

CAR
Rental Car

The only rental car operator is East Maui is **Manaloha Rent a Car** (375 W. Kuiaha Rd., 808/283-8779, www.manaloharentacar. net, 9am-5pm daily) in Ha'iku. Since it's in a rural location, they'll offer to pick you up at the airport for free (with a minimum one-week rental). The rates that you'll find here are some of the best on the island. If you're flying into Hana Airport, you'll need to arrange for a pickup at the airport (although wherever you are staying will almost assuredly have it arranged for you).

Gas

There are three gas stations within walking distance of each other in **Pa'ia;** be sure you have close to a full tank if you're going to be taking the long, winding journey out to Hana. None of the stations offer a public restroom (the closest ones are at Pa'ia Bay).

Tucked away on a back road that visitors only end up on if they're lost, the only gas station in **Ha'iku** can be found at **Hanzawa's** (1833 Kaupakalua Rd., 808/298-0407, 6am-8pm Mon.-Sat., 7am-7pm Sun.) store about halfway between Hana Highway and the town of Makawao.

In all of **Hana** there is only one gas station: the **Chevron** (808/270-5299, 7am-8:30pm Mon.-Sat., 7am-6pm Sun.) on the highway next to the horse stables. It has a few auto supplies, snacks, and a telephone, although for a public restroom you're better off going down to the Hana ball field. Gas in Hana is expensive, roughly $0.50 per gallon higher than the already high prices elsewhere on the island. Fill up before leaving town because the nearest gas station west is in Pa'ia; going south around the bottom, the closest is in Keokea

in Upcountry, and it isn't open in the evening hours.

GUIDED TOURS

Despite how much fun it is to craft your own Hana adventure, a surprising number of visitors decide to visit Hana as part of a private tour.

Temptation Tours (808/877-8888, www.temptationtours.com, $219 and up) offers small group tours in "limo vans" and has a number of different tour options for visiting Hana. One of the tours spends time exploring the recesses

MAUI

Understanding "The Back Road"

The back road from Hana is truly unlike any other stretch of road on the island. It feels as if you've journeyed to the edge of the earth. Panoramic views stretch out to the blue horizon and the back of Haleakala opens up before you in a rugged swath of mountainside plunging from summit to sea. Waterfalls tumble directly into the ocean and the noises of the modern world are given over to the sound of the wind.

At the beginning of the drive, the terrain changes from a lush paradise laden with waterfalls to windswept grasslands. Past Kaupo Store, the road straightens out. The last half of the drive, between Manawainui and Kanaio, is one of the nicest stretches of pavement on the island. There's a good chance you'll like this section of road better than even the more famous front section.

The biggest misconception about the Road to Hana is that the "back road" around the Kaupo section of the island is only accessible with four-wheel drive. You'll be told that driving this section of road violates your rental car policy. Neither of these commonly held opinions is accurate. Driving the full loop around the entire east end of the island is by far the best way to experience Hana.

On virtually all days of the year the back road (which is technically Highway 31) is passable in any form of vehicle, including a regular rental car. The road is unpaved, well-graded

dirt for five miles. At some points it is only one-lane wide and has precipitous drop-offs, but at no point is four-wheel drive essential. The only time you would need four-wheel drive would be during a torrential rainstorm—and in that situation, you should just stay off the road altogether. Your rental car company won't penalize you just because you drove out here, but if something goes wrong, you're liable for any damage, injury, or inconvenience. Luckily, island locals are some of the friendliest people you'll meet. If anything were to go wrong, you won't have any trouble flagging someone down for help.

Preparation is key to enjoying a drive around the back side. Make sure that you have plenty of gas. If you have half a tank or less when leaving Hana, you're cutting it too close and should stop for gas. Driving this road at night can be dangerous—and is pointless since you miss the expansive views. Keep an eye out for free range cattle on the road. Other than Kaupo Store, there isn't anywhere to get food or water, so be sure that you have enough water and snacks—it's a long way back to civilization. If you're not a confident driver, the narrow sections and steep drop-offs mean this isn't the road for you. The back road can be closed due to a landslide or overflowing streams. Call 808/986-1200, ext. 2, for the latest information.

of Ka'eleku Caverns, while there is also a Hana picnic tour similar in itinerary to the other options but with much nicer vans. The top choice, however, is to drive the Road to Hana and then hop aboard a helicopter at the Hana Airport for a ride back to Kahului. During the flight you'll zip by towering waterfalls you would never see from the road, and also buzz over the multi-hued cinder cones of Haleakala Crater. Prices for this Hana Sky Trek option are understandably higher at about $345/person.

Valley Isle Excursions (808/661-8687, www.tourmaui.com, $132/adult, $94/child), **Roberts Hawaii** (800/831-5541, www.robertshawaii.com, $124/adult, $74/child), and **Mahalo Tours** (877/262-4256, www.mahalotoursandtrans.com) also offer tours in larger vans that make all of the usual stops, and you'll wrap all the way around the back of the island and make a stop at the Tedeschi Winery in Ulupalakua.

For smaller, private, customized tours, **Awapuhi Adventures** (808/269-6031, www.awapuhiadventures.com) and **Open Eye Tours** (808/572-3483, www.openeyetours.com) provide personalized experiences which—if you are going to choose a guide trip for Hana—are the best, albeit most expensive ways to go.

BUS

The **Maui Bus** provides regular service between Pa'ia, Ha'iku, the Kahului Airport, and Queen Ka'ahumanu Center in Kahului (where you can connect with buses to anywhere else on the island). The rate is $2/boarding or $4 for a day pass, and pickup begins in Pa'ia at 5:53am if headed toward Ha'iku and 6:29am if headed toward Kahului. The route also makes stops at the Ha'iku Marketplace and Ha'iku Community Center, with the final bus going from Ha'iku to Kahului departing the community center at 7:47pm.

FLIGHTS
Hana

At the small airport in Hana, you can swap the nausea of a three-hour drive for the convenience of a 20-minute flight. Of course, you'll miss out on all the sights along the Road to Hana, but if your focus is on getting to Hana and relaxing at the resort, then **Mokulele** (866/260-7070, www.mokuleleairlines.com, 7am-7pm daily) operates flights twice daily between Kahului Airport and the landing strip in Hana. Often the Travaasa Hana hotel will run specials in which you can bundle airfare with a stay of three nights or more, and occasionally the airfare will actually be free. If you fly to Hana, however, remember that there aren't any rental cars here, so you'll need to have your airport transport arranged before you get on the flight.

LANA'I

It's hard to find an outdoor playground more stunning than Lana'i, home to a mere 3,300 residents and crisscrossed by just over 30 miles of paved roads. The late 1980s saw this island's cash crop transition from the world's largest pineapple plantation to cash-heavy tourists. With the construction of two luxurious resorts Lana'i was instantly transformed into one of

© KYLE ELLISON

HIGHLIGHTS

LOOK FOR ◖ TO FIND RECOMMENDED SIGHTS, ACTIVITIES, DINING, AND LODGING.

coastline has been the demise of dozens of ships, including the WWII Liberty ship that provides a dramatic backdrop for this windswept beach (page 432).

◖ **Scuba Diving Cathedrals:** The beauty of these caverns, regarded as two of the top dives in all of Hawaii, is so striking that they have even been the site of underwater weddings (page 435).

◖ **Surfing at Lopa:** A refreshingly remote stretch of sand which is protected from the wind, Lopa's waves are suited to beginners (page 437).

◖ **Munro Trail:** This 12.8-mile hiking trail winds its way to the island's 3,370-foot summit (page 438).

◖ **Lana'i Culture and Heritage Center:** Everything from wooden spears used in ancient battles to old photographs of Lana'i's plantation days adorn this authentic cultural resource (page 442).

◖ **Keahiakawelo (Garden of the Gods):** It's an otherworldly landscape of tortured earth dotted with red boulders which appear to have fallen from the sky (page 444).

◖ **Keomoku Village:** Little more than a collection of old homes and a haunting abandoned church, this stretch of shoreline exhibits what life on Lana'i must have been like a century ago (page 445).

◖ **Hulopo'e Beach Park:** This crescent of white sand has the island's best snorkeling when the ocean is calm and its best surf on a southern swell (page 431).

◖ **Kaiolohia (Shipwreck Beach):** The fringing reef ringing the island's northwest

the Hawaiian Islands' most exclusive getaways.

There's far more to Lana'i than sitting in a lawn chair and being spritzed by an Evian bottle. Typical visitors come to enjoy the snorkeling at Hulopo'e Beach Park, the plantation-era charm of Lana'i City, and tackling the greens at one of the island's two championship golf courses. Choose to explore a little deeper,

however, and you will find yourself enjoying morning hikes on pine-shrouded mountain trails, off-roading through otherworldly moonscapes, or surfing empty waves along a beach you will have all to yourself.

Lana'i is an island of unparalleled luxury and oceanfront massages, but it's also an island of four-wheel-drive trucks with deer

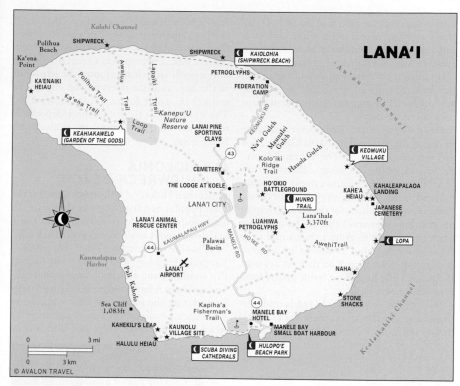

LANA'I

skulls mounted to the bumper, aging Filipino plantation workers "talking-story" in Dole Park, and historic petroglyphs scattered across rock faces which predate any of the island's multiple phases. It's a tight-knit community where everyone knows everyone else's business and townsfolk greet each other with first names and a smile. It truly is like nowhere else—and the people who live here want to keep it that way.

Beaches

Unless you have a four-wheel drive or high-clearance vehicle, Lana'i only has one accessible beach. That beach has been voted one of the best in the country; it's also the only beach with any sort of facilities. If, however, you happen to procure a Jeep or a local's truck, there are a number of undeveloped beaches where you could run around naked and there would be no one there to care.

◖ HULOPO'E BEACH PARK

Hulopo'e Beach Park is the undisputed hangout for island locals. It was crowned number one beach in America in 1997. Within walking distance from the Manele small boat harbor, Hulopo'e is the only beach on the island with restrooms and showers, and despite being the island's most popular beach, it's a far cry from crowded. The right side of the beach is used by guests of the Four Seasons Manele Bay Hotel who have access to the white umbrellas and lounge chairs. Similarly, Monday-Friday, guests of Trilogy Excursions' snorkel tour from Maui inhabit the left-hand side of the beach, thereby leaving the middle section of the beach as the place for visitors to relax in the shade or bake out in the sun.

Hulopoʻe Bay is a marine reserve and home to one of the few reefs in Maui County that isn't in a state of decline. The reef extends over the left side of the bay, where colorful parrotfish the size of your forearm can easily be spotted (and heard) nibbling on the vibrant corals. Hulopoʻe is also famous for the Hawaiian spinner dolphins that enter the bay on a regular basis. In an effort to protect the natural sleep cycles of the dolphins, swimmers are asked to not aggressively encroach on them in any way. If dolphins just happen to swim toward you, consider yourself lucky.

In addition to the sugary sands and perfectly placed palm trees, there are also two nature trails on each side of the beach. The Kapihaʻa Trail departs from the right side of the bay, whereas the trail to the Puʻu Pehe Overlook and Shark's Bay winds its way from the left side. There is also a fantastic system of tidepools stretching around the left point of the bay, and one is even deep enough to snorkel in, great for teaching young kids. The easiest way to get to the tidepools is to use the stairway found on the trail to Shark's Bay.

◖ KAIOLOHIA (SHIPWRECK BEACH)

Other than Hulopoʻe, **Shipwreck Beach** is the most popular beach among island visitors. To get to Shipwreck, drive past the Lodge at Koele and drop down Lanaʻi's windswept "back side" by following the switchbacking—but paved—Keomuku Highway. The views as you descend this winding road stretch all the way to neighboring Maui. A favorite pastime of island teenagers during the plantation days would be to flash their headlights at family members on Maui at a prearranged time, and then wait in

Hulopoʻe Beach

© HEATHER ELLISON

eager anticipation for their cousins to flash them back (Did I mention Lana'i can be *slow?*). Once you reach the bottom of the paved highway, a sign points left toward Shipwreck Beach. Follow the sandy road (four-wheel drive recommended) for 1.5 miles before it dead-ends in a parking area. When you pass the shacks constructed out of driftwood and fishing floats, you'll know that you've arrived.

Traditionally this area was known as Kaiolohia. The current moniker only stuck due to the World War II Liberty ship which was intentionally grounded on the fringing reef. Though numerous vessels have met their demise on this shallow stretch of coral, this concrete oil tanker has rotted slower than most. Stoic in its haunted appearance, the ship remains firmly lodged in the reef as a warning to passing vessels of the dangers.

Because of the persistent northeasterly trade winds, Kaiolohia rarely offers anything in the way of snorkeling or swimming. Your time here is better spent combing the beach for the flotsam and jetsam which finds its way to shore, and Japanese glass balls used as fishing floats are the ultimate beachcomber's reward. To reach the Liberty ship it's about a mile walk along the sandy coastline, although numerous rocks interrupt the thin strip of sand to give the appearance of multiple beaches. From here it's technically possible to walk all the way to Polihua Beach, although unless you have a ride arranged at the other side it's a 16-mile round-trip venture in an area with no services or shade.

Walking as far as the ship gives you ample time to explore, although make a side trip to visit the **petroglyphs** on your way back to the car. About a quarter of a mile after the road ends, you'll encounter the concrete base of what was once an old lighthouse, and if you're uncertain of whether or not you're at the right place, check the concrete base where names were inscribed in 1929. From the base of the lighthouse turn directly inland and rock-hop for 300 yards before you'll see a large rock with the words "do not deface" written on it. A white arrow points to a trail behind the rock which

© KYLE ELLISON

the shipwreck at Kaiolohia Beach

leads to petroglyphs of dogs, humans, and a drawing known as "The Birdman."

KAHALEPALAOA

When you reach the bottom of Keomuku Highway (where the pavement ends), taking a right at the fork in the road will lead you on a rugged coastal track that ranks as one of the best drives on the island. Four-wheel drive is recommended as the deep sand patches can often drift onto the road, and depending upon the recent rain activity, the road can become rutted and rough. Nevertheless, some of Lana'i's nicest beaches lie down this road, and anyone with a Jeep or SUV should be able to navigate the road just fine.

While there are a number of small pull-outs along the side of the road leading to narrow, windswept sand patches, the first beach of any real size is **Kahalepalaoa,** 7.5 miles from where the pavement ended. This Hawaiian name translates to "House of the Whale Ivory" (whale bones are rumored to have once washed ashore here). In more recent times this spot was also the site of a now-defunct, Club Med-style day resort named Club Lana'i. Though the booze-fueled excursion from Maui no longer operates, the coconut grove which once housed the venue marks the start of a long, white sand beach that's perfect for casual strolling.

LOPA

A little over a mile past Kahalepalaoa lies **Lopa,** a protected stretch of sand which is the nicest on Lana'i's back side. Although the beach here isn't all that different from Kahalepalaoa, the fact that Lopa faces south means it's more protected from the northeasterly trades, a geographic benefit which makes reading a book in a beach chair infinitely more enjoyable. Lopa is a popular camping spot for locals and a couple of picnic tables have been placed beneath the thorn-riddled kiawe grove lining the beach. Although the swimming and snorkeling are nothing compared to Hulopo'e Beach Park, Lopa is the perfect place for longboard surfing or paddling along the shore in a kayak (if you brought your own). The chances of encountering anyone else on Lopa are higher on the weekends when locals come to camp and fish, but as at many of Lana'i's beaches, if there happens to be anyone else there it's justified in calling it crowded.

Snorkeling and Diving

SNORKELING

When it comes to snorkeling, **Hulopo'e Beach Park** easily trumps any other place on the island for the health of the reef, clarity of water, and variety of fish. Thanks to its protected status as a marine preserve, the reef here is in better shape than other places on the island, and snorkelers will revel in the large schools of *manini* (convict tang) and vibrant *uhu* (parrotfish) which flit around the shallow reef. The best snorkeling within the bay is on the left side of the beach. Since Hulopo'e faces south it can be prone to large surf and shorebreak April-October. The shorebreak can make entry and exit into the water a little challenging, and the visibility won't be as good as it is on days which are as calm as a swimming pool.

Nevertheless, even a mediocre day at Hulopo'e is better than a good day at many other places. The reef here never gets deeper than 25 feet. Occasionally the Hawaiian spinner dolphins will venture into this bay, although they usually hang out over the sand on the right closer to the hotel.

Not far from Hulopo'e but equally as gorgeous is the vibrant reef at **Manele Bay.** Don't confuse this with snorkeling in Manele Harbor, because that would be disgusting. Instead, the reef at Manele Bay is on the opposite side of the breakwall set between the harbor and the cliffs. Entry from shore can be tricky since you have to come off the rocks, but if you follow the driveway of the harbor all the way to the far end, there is a little opening in the rocks where it's possible to make a graceful entry. Schools of tropical reef fish gather in abundance here, and the same school of spinner dolphins can sometimes hang out in this area as well. Although Manele Bay is a good quarter mile from Hulopo'e Beach, it's still part of the marine preserve, so the same rules apply: Don't stand on the coral, don't feed the fish, and you're best off just not touching anything at all.

There isn't anywhere on Lana'i to rent snorkeling equipment for the day, so your best bet is to have your own before you get on the ferry or plane. The snorkeling equipment at Hulopo'e Beach is privately reserved for Trilogy's day guests who come over from Maui, and the gear at the Four Seasons beach kiosk is exclusively for hotel guests.

If you want to explore the island's remoter reefs, which are only accessible by boat, **Trilogy Excursions** (1 Manele Harbor Dr., 808/874-5649, www.scubalanai.com) provides the best (and only) snorkel charter service operating out of Lana'i. Aboard their 51-foot sloop rigged sailing catamaran *Trilogy III,* Trilogy offers a 3.5-hour snorkeling and sailing excursion which usually heads around the southwestern coastline of the island to the towering sea cliffs of Kaunolu. There can occasionally be other boats from Maui back here, but more often than not this trip provides the opportunity to snorkel the waters of the historic fishing village with only a handful of other passengers. Given that Kaunolu (also known as Shark Fin Cove due to the dorsal fin-shaped rock in the middle of the bay) is exposed to the deeper waters offshore, sightings of pelagic species such as spinner dolphins, bottlenose dolphins, eagle rays, manta rays, and whale sharks have been known to occur on an intermittent basis. The captain and crew aboard Trilogy's catamaran were born and raised on Lana'i, and if you snorkel close to

one of the crew members, there's a good chance they can find you an elusive *tako* (octopus). If there's wind to sail on the way back to Manele, the crew will hoist the sails. The views afforded of the coastal cliffs make this the best way for exploring the southwestern coastline.

During whale season, Trilogy also offers two-hour long **mammal searches,** which depart from Manele Harbor on a jet-propelled inflatable raft for a high-paced marine safari focused on finding humpback whales, green sea turtles, the occasional Hawaiian monk seal, and various species of resident dolphins. The high-speed cruise of the coastline alone is worth the trip, and the crew on this trip are some of the friendliest and most knowledgeable in the industry.

◖ SCUBA DIVING

Those familiar with Hawaii diving will know that Lana'i has some of the best diving in the state. While there are no fewer than 14 named dive sites along the southwestern coastline, the two which make Lana'i famous are **First and Second Cathedrals.** At First Cathedral, just offshore from Manele Harbor, the cavern entrance sits at 58 feet. Inside, beams of sunlight filter down through the ceiling, looking exactly like light passing through a stained glass window. There have even been a few underwater weddings here. The best way to exit the cathedral is via a hole in the wall known locally as The Shotgun, where divers place their hands on the sides of the cathedral and allow the current to wash through a narrow opening. In addition to the main cathedral, there are a number of other swim-throughs and arches where you can catch a glimpse of spiny lobsters, frogfish, colorful parrotfish, and if you're lucky, a pod of spinner dolphins passing overhead.

Down the coast at Second Cathedral, the underwater dome is about the same size but intersected by so many openings it looks like Swiss cheese. Divers can pass in and out of the cathedral from a variety of different entry points. The highlight of the dive is a rare black coral tree that dangles from the cathedral

© KYLE ELLISON

scuba diving Second Cathedral

ceiling. Large schools of *ta'ape* (blue striped snapper) congregate on the back side of the cathedral, and you can swim through a school that numbers in the hundreds. Visibility at both of these sites regularly stretches 80-120 feet, and the water can often be so clear that you see most of the dive site just standing on the pontoon of the dive boat.

While a few dive boats from Maui make regular morning trips to Lana'i, the only scuba outfit operating out of Lana'i is **Trilogy Excursions** (1 Manele Harbor Dr., 808/874-5649, www.scubalanai.com), which offers two-tank dives for certified divers Monday-Friday off its inflatable jet boat raft, *Manele Kai.* Trilogy also offers introductory beach dives off Hulopo'e Beach for divers who aren't yet certified or are working on their certification courses. Another option is **snuba** diving off Hulopo'e Beach, a hybrid between snorkeling and scuba diving. The only gear that the diver has to wear is a weight belt (to sink) and a light shoulder harness (which attaches to the scuba regulator). With this basic gear, divers are able to breathe and stay underwater for just over 20 minutes. Snuba is available to divers ages 8 and up.

Surfing

SURF SPOTS
Hulopo'e Beach Park

Given that **Hulopo'e Beach** is the island's most popular beach, it should come as little surprise that it's also the island's most popular surf spot. Since Hulopo'e faces south, it's exposed to southerly swells, which means that the months of April-October are going to be the best for finding surf. This left point break can be challenging, however, and it's not a spot for beginners. The wave breaks over a shallow coral reef and the takeoff can be steep, although when Hulopo'e is firing it can be one of the best summer waves in Maui County. The long lefthander will hold its size 2-12 feet, and you have to be careful of the inside section, which can carry you straight into the shorebreak. If the angle of the swell isn't quite right, you can occasionally find a better wave by walking the nature path for 200 yards to the next bay over. A short scramble down the rocks will bring you to a hidden, sandy cove, although the wave here is more of a beach break, which pales in comparison to the quality of Hulopo'e. To reach Hulopo'e Beach Park drive a quarter mile past the small boat harbor on Manele Road until the pavement ends in a parking lot.

◖ Lopa

Lopa is the island's preeminent beginner wave. But just because it's user-friendly doesn't mean that it can't be a great wave. A beach break with multiple peaks, the waves at Lopa aren't usually as steep and are better suited for longboards and noseriding. This is where the island's lone surf school takes its students, although on most days—due to the difficult, four-wheel-drive access—you will have Lopa all to yourself other than a handful of fishers or campers. To reach Lopa take Keomuku Highway over to the back of the island to the end of the paved road, then take a right and proceed for nine miles.

Stone Shacks

Bring your hiking boots for this spot, because the only way to surf **Stone Shacks** is to walk a half-mile-long, kiawe riddled trail to a remote and rocky beach. The name refers to two rudimentary stone structures constructed on the shoreline as a place where campers can stay out of the wind. The walk is worth it, however, as Stone Shacks offers one of the best right- and left-hand waves anywhere on the island. The surf can be bigger here than at nearby Lopa, and it can pick up more of a southerly angle, while Hulopo'e faces southwest. To reach Stone Shacks take Keomuku Highway over the back side of the island to the end of the paved road, then take a right and proceed for 11 miles until the dirt road ends at Naha. Then park the car and start walking. Hazards include locals, sharks, and making your way out through the rocky entry.

RENTAL OPERATORS

Having grown up on Lana'i but perfected his surfing skills on the North Shore of O'ahu, owner Nick Palumbo now runs **Lana'i Surf Safari** (808/565-9283, www.lanaisurfsafari. com), your one-stop outfit for all things surf-related on Lana'i. Rentals are arranged off Hulopo'e Beach and include longboards ($58 for 24 hours), shortboards ($58 for 24 hours), bodyboards ($30 for 24 hours), and stand-up paddleboards ($150 full day/$75 half day).

While renting a board and surfing the wave at Hulopo'e are great for the intermediate surfer, for those who are looking to take actual surf lessons and explore the back of the island there's no better option than booking a half-day surf safari (9am-2pm, $200) to pristine and isolated Lopa Beach. Tours include pickup and drop-off from the harbor or your hotel as well as all gear, instruction, drinking water, and transport to Lana'i's rugged back side. Unlike the surf schools of Waikiki or

Lahaina, where you can find yourself fighting to catch a wave amid 50 other students, guests here on Lana'i are treated to a private session on a beach, which is almost guaranteed to have nobody else on it. Even if you aren't staying on the island, day trips from Maui can be arranged.

Hiking and Biking

HIKING
◖ Munro Trail

Munro Trail doesn't look like anywhere else on Lana'i—or anywhere else in Hawaii. Anyone who ventures out on this 12.8-mile dirt road might swear they are in the Pacific Northwest instead of the tropics, yet wandering around the stands of Cook pines is one of Lana'i's most iconic adventures. There are few better ways to spend a morning on Lana'i than by rising early, throwing on a light jacket, and heading into the uplands where the smell of eucalyptus wafts through an understory of ironwoods and pines. For clear skies and dry conditions, it's best to hike Munro Trail in the morning hours before enveloping clouds blow in on the trades.

© KYLE ELLISON

the forested uplands of the Munro Trail

To reach Munro Trail travel past the Lodge at Koele on Keomuku Highway until you reach a sign for Cemetery Road, where you will make a right just before the first mile marker. On Cemetery Road the pavement turns to dirt and then branches off to the left, bringing you to the start of the trail. Technically Munro Trail is a single-lane, dirt road navigable by anyone with four-wheel drive. The Dollar Jeep rental company doesn't allow its Jeeps to go on the steep and potentially muddy track, and even those who have rented a Hummer have occasionally gotten stuck. The other option is to park your car at the trailhead and make the 5.5-mile hike to the summit (one-way), choosing to stop at lookouts along the way.

The first such lookout if starting from Cemetery Road is the **Koloiki Ridge** about 2.5 miles into the trail. A small red and white sign on the left side of the trail points the way to the ridge, and after a brief quarter-mile jaunt you are rewarded with grandiose views peering back into Maunalei Gulch and out to the islands of Maui and Moloka'i. This lookout is also accessible as part of the **Koloiki Ridge Trail** hike which departs from behind the Lodge at Koele.

Back on the main trail you'll continue for a couple miles beneath a shroud of forest until you pass some communication towers. Just past the towers is **Ho'okio Gulch,** a place of historical significance which forever transformed the island of Lana'i. In 1778 Kahekili, ruler of Lana'i and Maui, was besieged by Kalaniopu'u, a powerful chief from the Big Island whose army featured a fearless young warrior by the name of Kamehameha. In the battle at Ho'okio, Kahekili and his warriors attempted to defend the island from the invading warriors by slinging stones down from the hilltop and hiding in crevasses carved into the cliff face. Ultimately, however, Kahekili and his men would emerge defeated, and the ensuing occupation of Lana'i by Kalaniopu'u and his army drove the resource-strapped island into a famine, which decimated much of the native population. It's said that the spirits of those who perished in the battle still reside in the cool forests and keep watch over the eroded gulches and canyons.

Finally, after you've climbed an uphill section of trail, 5.5 miles from the end of Cemetery Road you'll find the 3,370-foot summit of Lana'ihale, or The Hale as it's known to locals. This is the only point in all of Hawaii where it's possible to see five other islands on the clearest of days, and during winter even the snowcapped peaks of Mauna Kea and Mauna Loa on the Big Island can be clearly seen over 100 miles to the southeast. Should you decide to continue the length of the trail you'll descend for seven miles down the southern side of the ridge, past turnoffs for the Awehi and Naha trails, and eventually emerge in the remains of old pineapple fields at Highway 440 (Manele Road). Though properly exploring Munro Trail takes the better part of a day, it's one in which you're able to step out of the tropical "norm" and breath the fresh air of one of Hawaii's most scenic and storied places.

Pu'u Pehe Overlook

This oft-photographed sea stack is an iconic symbol of the island of Lana'i and is easily one of the most scenic sites on the island. Though it's not possible to climb onto Pu'u Pehe itself, the **Pu'u Pehe Overlook Trail** offers hikers a sweeping panorama of the rock and the surrounding coastal area. To reach the overlook, take the dirt road on the south end of Hulopo'e Beach Park (the side opposite the resort) and follow it for 100 yards until it reaches a set of stairs leading down to the tidepools. From here the road becomes a trail that wraps its way left across the headland before reaching a hidden, sandy cove popular with bodyboarders and topless sunbathers. To get down to this sandy cove known as Shark's Bay requires a scramble through a chute in the rocky cliff that is "at

your own risk." To reach the overlook, safely follow the edge of the cliff until it reaches a promontory about 100 feet above the shimmering reef below. Aside from the sweeping vista, it's also possible from here to get a good view of the *heiau* that stands atop Pu'u Pehe, an archaeological site which is a mystery given the near-impossible access to the top of the rock.

Kapiha'a Fisherman's Trail

The **Kapiha'a Fisherman's Trail** begins on the side of Hulopo'e Beach right in front of the Four Seasons Hotel and meanders past the mega-mansions set out on the point. Well-marked by a natural stone walkway, this 1.5-mile trail hugs the rocky coastline as it weaves its way through the ancient village of Kapiha'a. Though little remains of the village today, various historical markers point out the location of *heiau* still visible in the area. Even though this trail catches the coastal breezes off the surrounding water, there is laughably little shade. Given the rugged nature of the path, wear closed-toe shoes. After the trail reaches a dramatic terminus atop sea cliffs on the back nine of the golf course, an easier return route is to follow the cart path back to the golf clubhouse.

Koloiki Ridge Trail

An offshoot of the Munro Trail, the **Koloiki Ridge Trail** is a five-mile out-and-back hike that begins directly behind the Four Seasons Koele Resort. On a nice day this is the perfect way to spend 2-3 hours. Walking the trail is like taking a historical tour through Lana'i's past.

To reach the start of the trail, head to the main entrance of the Four Seasons Koele Resort and then follow the service road toward the golf clubhouse. Once you reach the main clubhouse, another paved service road running behind the fairway ultimately leads to the trailhead. Along the way, you'll encounter white and red signs placed on the trail as part of an interpretive map available at the hotel's concierge desk. A number of these are scattered along the initial paved section of trail.

Once the dirt trail begins, you'll find

Lana'i by Horseback

Lana'i is as steeped in its ranching heritage as anywhere else in Hawaii. Many forget this island was one huge sheep and cattle ranch where *paniolos* on horseback roamed the terrain. Though cattle no longer roam free on the island's barren slopes, the island's ranching heritage lives on at the **Stables at Koele** (1 Keomuku Hwy., 808/563-9385, www.lanai-grandadventures.com), where local guides who are the "real deal" offer guided trail rides through the Lana'i City hinterlands. Keep an eye out for axis deer or mouflon sheep as you ride at your own pace on excursions geared to your skill level. The knowledgeable guides fortify the excursion with tales of the island's history and inside local info.

yourself walking beneath a canopy of ironwood trees and Cook pines which predate the luxurious hotels. Planted in 1912 by the botanist George Munro, the pines were used as a means of securing water by way of trapping moisture from the passing clouds, and even today they still play a major role in providing water for the island's residents.

Making a right at the red and white sign marked "10" places you directly on the Munro Trail. About a half mile down Munro Trail at sign number 17, an arrow points the way down to the dramatic Koloiki Ridge. Once out from beneath the canopy of trees you'll notice that the ridge is flanked on both sides by gulches dramatically carved by the elements and time. From this (often windy) vantage point at the end of the trail, the islands of Moloka'i and Maui spring up on the horizon above the deep blue Pailolo Channel. When facing the islands, the gulch on your left is Naio Gulch, a dry and rock-strewn canyon where you can occasionally catch a glimpse of the island's elusive mouflon sheep. On the right side of the ridge is Maunalei Gulch, a deep cleft in the island, which at one point was home to the island's only free-flowing stream. If you look closely

on the valley floor, you can still notice an old service road leading up to a pump house. Water from Maunalei once serviced the island's sugar plantation.

Awehi Trail

Technically the **Awehi Trail**—like the Munro Trail—is a road and not a hike. You wouldn't want to try and drive this in a rental though, given that the road is steep, eroded, and a long way from help. The cool canopy of pine trees on the Munro Trail is swapped on the Awehi for thorny kiawe trees offering no shade. Nevertheless, the rewards for hiking the Awehi Trail are sweeping views stretching toward the island of Kaho'olawe and the ability to walk from the eucalyptus and pine tree laden summit to an empty white sand beach. Over the course of three miles, the Awehi Trail switchbacks its way down the barren slope of Lana'i's southeastern flank, eventually reaching a terminus on the shoreline not far from Lopa Beach. Unless you have arranged for a car to pick you up at the bottom, however, it's going to be a long and dusty climb back up. The start of the Awehi Trail is a dirt track on the left side of the Munro Trail 1.2 miles south of the summit. You can either park your car at a pullout off Munro Trail, or drive on the Awehi Trail until it gets too sketchy to navigate safely. Good luck.

Naha Trail

Not too different from the Awehi Trail, the **Naha Trail** branches off the Munro Trail and switchbacks down the back of the mountain to the remote southeastern shoreline. It's three miles long, dusty, thorny, and has a terminus not far from Naha Beach. The start of the Naha Trail is two miles south of the summit on Munro Trail. Bring plenty of water and a sturdy pair of shoes capable of handling the vicious kiawe thorns.

Hiking Groups

If you would prefer to hike with a guide, contact **Hike Lana'i@** (808/258-2471, www.hikelanai.com). Guided hikes are offered to the shoreline of Kaunolu, the shoreline of

Kaiolohia, and the ridges and uplands that branch out from the Munro Trail. Most hikes are a little over two hours. The hike along the shoreline at Kaiolohia is the easiest. Depending on the hike, prices vary between $90 for children (ages 10-12), to $125 for adults.

BIKING

Companies have rented out bikes to island visitors in the past, but currently the only way to procure a bike is to either know someone locally or bring one over on the ferry from Maui. Seeing as there are only 30 miles of paved road on the entire island (compared to over 400 which are unpaved), Lana'i is an island more suited to mountain biking than road cycling. Although there isn't any single-track, the hunting roads and old pineapple roads crisscrossing the island are a mountain biker's dream terrain. Intermediate riders can pedal the seven miles of dirt road leading out to the Garden of the Gods, or more advanced riders can make the 3,300-foot descent from the summit of Lana'ihale, down the Munro Trail, hook up with the Awehi Trail, and end at a deserted white sand beach. Logistics are always an issue with Lana'i mountain biking, however, and unless you're into a leg-burning ascent after your downhill ride, a one-way transport will need to be arranged. If riding on the Awehi Trail, Naha Trail, or anywhere on the island's "back side," tire-puncturing kiawe thorns can be a pesky issue, so pack a pump and an extra tube.

Golf

If you find yourself walking around Maui's Lahaina Harbor around 6:30am you'll notice a curious sight: A bunch of nicely dressed people walking around with golf clubs in the middle of a dingy harbor basin. No, they aren't planning on using their seven-iron as a gaff while sportfishing; they're taking the 6:45am ferry to Lana'i for the day to tackle one of the island's two championship golf courses. Although the courses are obviously open to guests of the Lana'i resorts, they're also open to golfers from the general public—many of whom choose to commute from Maui for the day.

At the 7,039-yard, Jack Nicklaus-designed **Challenge at Manele** (1 Manele Bay Rd., 808/565-2000, $210 resort guests, $225 day guest), the course lives up to its name by forcing golfers to tee-off across natural ravines which use the Pacific Ocean as a water hazard. There are five different tees which you can choose from, although pack a few extra balls in your bag, as playing from out of bounds on this course would involve a wet suit and some scuba gear.

Whereas the Challenge at Manele can take your breath away with its panoramic vistas, the **Experience at Koele** (1 Keomuku Hwy., 808/565-4000, $125 resort guest, $185 day guest) course might literally take your breath away with its 2,000-foot elevation. Set among ironwood trees and Cook pines, this 7,014-yard, Greg Norman-designed masterpiece weaves its way through Lana'i's cool and forested uplands, and the signature 17th hole drops 250 feet from tee to green in the heart of a wooded ravine. On a morning when low-hanging clouds usher in a mist, this is truly a course where your competitive spirit is dampened by relaxation.

While the two courses mentioned above have been the recipients of international fame, there's actually a *third* course on the island of Lana'i, which comes with a price tag much easier to stomach. More of the no-shirt, no-shoes, beer-a-hole type of course, the nine-hole **Cavendish Golf Course** is better suited for recreational golfers who either want a quick practice round or haven't quite figured out how to break 100. Best of all, the course is free. Constructed in 1947 as a recreational option for island pineapple workers, the Cavendish still operates as a place for island locals to practice their game

LANA'I

© KYLE ELLISON

the oceanfront greens of the Challenge at Manele

and casually unwind. Although the fairways and tee boxes can be speckled with crabgrass and patches of dirt, the greens are still properly maintained. As there are no carts or cart paths, you also get a good workout walking the course's moderate elevation changes. To reach the first tee box for the Cavendish course, make a right as if going to the Koele golf clubhouse off Keomuku Highway. Just after the turn you will notice an open field on the right side of the road with a small flag fluttering in the distance. Welcome to the Cavendish, although you're going to have to supply your own clubs, balls, tees, and beer.

Sights

◖ LANA'I CULTURE AND HERITAGE CENTER

There's no better place to learn about the history of Lana'i than at the **Lana'i Culture and Heritage Center** (730 Lana'i Ave., 808/565-7177, www.lanaichc.org, 8:30am-3:30pm Mon.-Fri., 9am-1pm Sat.). Started in 2007 in a building adjacent to the Hotel Lana'i, the exceptionally informative little museum features displays pertaining to the days of ancient Hawaii all the way up through the end of the Dole plantation. Black-and-white photos

from Lana'i's ranching days are joined by stone adzes, poi pounders, and a 10-foot-long *'ihe po-lolu* wooden spear used as a weapon similar to a jousting lance. More than just a collection of historical photos and artifacts, the center also highlights how the culture of the people of Lana'i has been influenced by the coming and going of historical events.

KANEPU'U PRESERVE

Six miles down Polihua Road just before reaching the Garden of the Gods, **Kanepu'u**

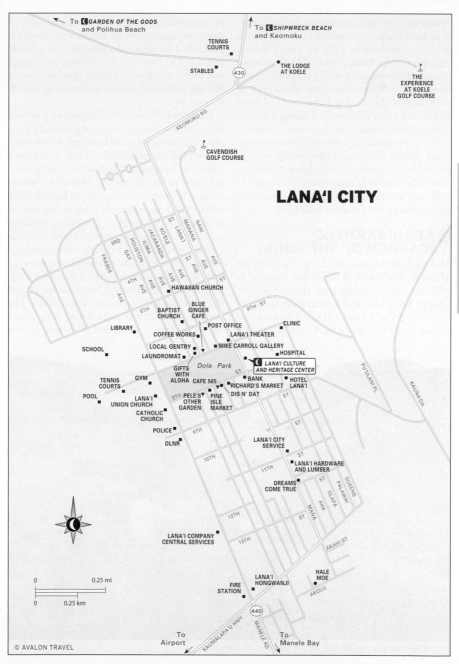

LANA'I CITY

To **C** *GARDEN OF THE GODS*
and Polihua Beach

To **C** *SHIPWRECK BEACH*
and Keomoku

TENNIS COURTS

STABLES

THE LODGE AT KOELE

THE EXPERIENCE AT KOELE GOLF COURSE

KEOMUKU RD

CAVENDISH GOLF COURSE

3RD ST

HOUSTON AVE

FRASER AVE

GAY AVE

ILIMA AVE

JACARANDA AVE

KOELE AVE

LANA'I AVE

MAHANA ST

NANI ST

4TH AVE

HAWAIIAN CHURCH

5TH AVE

6TH ST

BLUE GINGER CAFE

BAPTIST CHURCH

LIBRARY

COFFEE WORKS

POST OFFICE

LANA'I THEATER

CLINIC

SCHOOL

LOCAL GENTRY

MIKE CARROLL GALLERY

LAUNDROMAT

HOSPITAL

Dole Park

C LANA'I CULTURE AND HERITAGE CENTER

GIFTS WITH ALOHA

CAFE 565

BANK

TENNIS COURTS

GYM

8TH ST

RICHARD'S MARKET

HOTEL LANA'I

POOL

LANA'I UNION CHURCH

PELE'S OTHER GARDEN

DIS N' DAT

PINE ISLE MARKET

CATHOLIC CHURCH

POLICE

9TH ST

DLNR

LANA'I CITY SERVICE

10TH ST

11TH ST

LANA'I HARDWARE AND LUMBER

DREAMS COME TRUE

OLAPA ST

PALAWAI ST

QUEENS ST

MANA ST

AHA ST

12TH ST

AKAHI ST

LANA'I COMPANY CENTRAL SERVICES

13TH ST

HALE MOE

AKOLU

FIRE STATION

LANA'I HONGWANJI

MANELE RD

PU'UIANI PL

KAUNA'OA

430

440

0   0.25 mi

0   0.25 km

To Airport

KAUMALAPA'U HWY

To Manele Bay

LANA'I

© AVALON TRAVEL

Preserve is the only remaining dryland forest of its kind found anywhere in Hawaii. Thanks to a fence erected in 1918 by Lana'i Ranch manager George Munro, this 590-acre preserve is home to 48 species of native Hawaiian plants which used to cover most of the island prior to the arrival of the invasive kiawe tree and root-destroying goats and sheep. Managed by the Nature Conservancy, the preserve features a short, self-guided trail where visitors can get a rare chance to see native hardwoods such as *lama* (Hawaiian ebony) and *olopua* (Hawaiian olive). The trail only takes about 15 minutes to walk, and it makes for a nice stopping point before exploring the Garden of the Gods.

◖ KEAHIAKAWELO (GARDEN OF THE GODS)

Although we've successfully put a rover on Mars, Keahiakawelo is the closest most of us will ever get to walking on the red planet. Despite being only seven miles from the pine-lined streets of Lana'i City, the moonscape known as the Garden of the Gods may as well be a universe away. Thousands of years of erosion have created ravines and rock spires which are bathed in deep reds, purples, and sulfuric yellows. The best time to visit this dry, dusty, and often windswept area is at sunset, when the rich palette of color is enhanced by the afternoon light.

Keahiakawelo is almost completely devoid of vegetation, but the strangest part of the panorama is the expanse of boulders which tumble over the barren hillside. While it's anyone's guess just how exactly this otherworldly scenery came to be, the ancient Hawaiians have a number of theories. According to legend, these rocks were dropped here by gods as they tended to their heavenly gardens, providing the basis for the site's English name, "Garden of the Gods," by which it is regularly known today.

Regardless of name or legend or erosion or lore, Keahiakawelo remains a must-see location for Lana'i visitors if for no other reason than the consuming sense of seclusion. The road out here can be rutted and rough, and four-wheel drive is needed if visiting after a

© MARK DRIESSEN

the otherworldly landscape of the Garden of the Gods

heavy rain. To reach the site take a left just after The Lodge at Koele and travel seven miles on Polihua Road, veering right at the fork after the Koele Stables.

KA'ENA IKI HEIAU

On the dusty stretch of road between the Keahiakawelo and Polihua Beach, a side road branches off to the left and leads to the island's westernmost promontory, Ka'ena Point. The deep waters off Ka'ena make this a favorite among island fishers. The main reason for venturing down Ka'ena Trail, however, is to get a look at the largest remaining *heiau* on the island of Lana'i. This large stone platform was constructed in the 17th century. While it doesn't take much time to explore the area around the *heiau,* this makes a nice side trip.

◖ KEOMOKU VILLAGE

Technically there isn't much to *see* in the abandoned village of Keomoku, but rather, you drive through this coastal ghost town as a means of *feeling* Lana'i's recent past. It also makes a great stop if you are heading out to the beaches at Lopa or Naha.

Before the arrival of Europeans, it's believed there were thousands of native Hawaiians living along Lana'i's eastern shoreline. *Heiau* were constructed as places of worship, and petroglyphs such as those found at Kaiolohia depict basic scenes from this ancient way of life. By the time Frederick Hayselden chose Keomoku as the site for his Maunalei Sugar Company in 1899, however, the island's population had dwindled to fewer than 200. Water was routed from Maunalei Valley, a locomotive was installed to move cargo, and Keomoku bustled like any other Hawaiian plantation town. The problem, however, is that the water around it soon turned brackish and the supply at Maunalei quickly dried up. In what is known as one of the state's shortest sugar ventures, the Maunalei Sugar Company closed in 1901 after only two years in operation. Native Hawaiians living in the area attribute the company's demise to the fact that the stones from ancient *heiau* were used in constructing the

LANA'I

© HEATHER ELLISON

the abandoned village of Keomoku

plantation. This, it would seem, did not sit well with Hawaiian deities. In 1951, the last resident of Keomoku—Daniel Kaopuiki—begrudgingly moved his family into the uplands, and Keomoku, once the pulse of the island of Lana'i, was officially abandoned.

Keomoku remains almost abandoned to this day. Driving the sandy four-wheel-drive road through the former plantation town is like taking a tour through Lana'i's ancient history. Simple beachfront fishing shacks dot the sandy road, their yards ringed with fishing nets and the memories of years passed. The number one attraction in Keomoku is **Ka Lanakila Church,** 5.5 miles from where the pavement ends on Kemoku Highway. The hauntingly beautiful wooden structure was constructed in 1903 to house a Hawaiian-speaking congregation. Abandoned for years, the church is currently in the process of being restored, and special sermons are still conducted in Hawaiian intermittently throughout the year. A small shrine 1.5 miles past the church honors the Japanese field laborers who died on Lana'i in the few short years of the sugar plantation's existence, and a half mile beyond the shrine is the abandoned pier at Kahalepalaoa, which offers good fishing and sweeping views of neighboring Maui.

LUAHIWA PETROGLYPHS

The good thing about the **Luahiwa Petroglyphs** is they are only 10 minutes from Lana'i City and accessible with two-wheel drive. The bad part is they have been permanently scarred by modern graffiti, and they no longer resemble the rock art they originally must have been. The petroglyphs at Kaunolu and Kaiolohia are in better shape but require a two-hour round-trip drive from Lana'i City. There are also a greater number of petroglyphs at Luahiwa—nearly 1,000 drawings—and bouncing from one rock to the other will reveal a different tale emblazoned on the out of place boulder formations. While 95 percent of the drawings are believed to from pre-Western times, some etchings such as those featuring horses suggest that the petroglyphs offered a multigenerational canvas for recording Lana'i's varied history.

© KYLE ELLISON

etchings in the rocks at Luahiwa

To reach the Luahiwa Petroglyphs head south on Manele Road from Lana'i City as if you're driving down toward Hulopo'e Beach Park. After 1.5 miles turn left at a small building on the left side of the road. If you notice a locked gate, then proceed to the dirt road that immediately parallels it on your left-hand side. Head down this road for 0.7 miles until you reach a Y-junction, at which point you will go left again. After 0.3 miles you will make an extreme right-hand turn (almost doubling back the way you came) up onto a higher road. If you're unsure if this is the correct turn, look for a rock just after the intersection that has the name "Luahiwa Petroglyphs" emblazed on it facing the opposite direction. Proceed for 0.4 miles on the upper road until you reach another rock that says "Luahiwa," and park in the small dirt pullout. The petroglyphs are on the large boulders at the base of the hill, and a thirty-second scramble through the bush will bring you face-to-face with the ancient rock carvings.

Shopping

Lana'i officially takes the cake for being the only Hawaiian Island where you could potentially visit every store on the island without having to repark the car. With the exception of the small stores within the Four Seasons resorts, every single venue on the island is within walking distance of the parking area around Dole Park.

CLOTHING AND SOUVENIRS

The nicest gas station on the island (also the *only* gas station), the **Lana'i Plantation Store** (1036 Lana'i Ave., 808/565-7227, 6:30am-10pm daily) offers a great selection of island souvenirs and clothing items to go along with the usual snacks and beverage options. Plus, it's open later than nearly every other store on the island, so if you're in need of anything from a T-shirt to a six-pack, this is the place to go.

Just down the street, the aptly named **Dis N' Dat Shop** (418 8th St., 808/565-9170, 10am-5:30pm Mon.-Sat.) sells everything from hand-painted ceramic ornaments to women's jewelry to the wind chimes which dangle from the ceiling (duck!). The Balinese woodwork gives an exotic feel to the interior. To find the store, just look for the old yellow car on the lawn.

Tucked away just one block back from Dole Park is **Lana'i Beach Walk** (850 Fraser Ave., 808/565-9249, 10am-6pm Mon.-Sat.), a clean and modern boutique selling women's clothing. There are a number of Lana'i-centric clothing options, and the selection is so trendy

you'd expect to find the store in Pa'ia instead of Lana'i City.

Facing the park, **The Local Gentry** (363 7th St., 808/565-9130, 10am-6pm Mon.-Fri., 10am-5pm Sat., 9am-1pm Sun.) offers a larger men's selection as well as a full range of women's clothing and Olu Kai shoes.

ART AND JEWELRY

The most prominent gallery on the island is the **Mike Carroll Gallery** (443 7th St., 808/565-7122, www.mikecarrollgallery.com, 10am-5:30pm Mon.-Sat., 9am-2pm Sun.) set right between Canoe's restaurant and the Lana'i City theater. There's a good chance that you'll find Mike painting right there in the store, and many of his pieces focus on the simple yet captivating beauty of Lana'i. He is an in-demand artist who is constantly crafting original works. The gallery will occasionally feature visiting artists who come to relax and hone their craft in this charming, plantation-style studio.

For a look at local artwork, visit the **Lana'i Art Center** (339 7th St., 808/565-7503, www.lanaiart.org, variable hours) to see just how much talent exists on an island of only 3,300 people. Fine photography and handmade jewelry accompany paintings and woodworking. A portion of all proceeds from this nonprofit go toward funding local art programs for Lana'i's youth. This gallery is a worthwhile stop either after the Saturday Farmer's Market or while walking off a Blue Ginger cheeseburger.

LANA'I

Food

FARMERS MARKET

Even though it's no longer a sprawling pineapple plantation, the red dirt of Lana'i still manages to produce some locally grown crops. The **Lana'i City Farmer's Market** (Dole Park and behind Richard's Supermarket, 6am-11am Sat.) is the best place for grabbing fresh items such as corn, papaya, and pineapple. It's a great weekend activity for putting your finger on the pulse of the island's only town.

LOCAL STYLE

While the outside decor might not look like much, at **Blue Ginger** (409 7th St., 808/565-6363, www.bluegingercafelanai. com, 6am-8pm Thurs.-Mon., 6am-2pm Tues.-Wed., $6-11) the swinging screen door and funky, plantation-style appearance are all part of the hole-in-the-wall charm. Breakfast is categorized by heaping loco moco plates comprised of fried eggs, hamburger meat, rice, and gravy, and the homemade hamburger patties are the lunchtime draw which have kept patrons funneling in from Dole Park since the restaurant's founding in 1991. A true local hideout. Cash only.

When you've had your fill of plate lunches, infuse your diet with some fresh fish at the **Lana'i Ohana Poke Market** (834 Gay St., 808/559-6265, 10am-3pm Mon.-Fri., $7-17, cash only), which in classic Lana'i fashion is either open until 3 o'clock or until they run out of fish. While the *poke* alone can be expensive, your best bet for a cheap and filling lunch is a poke bowl: one-third pound of fish served with two scoops of either white or brown rice. Simple outdoor picnic tables provide the seating for this hole-in-the-wall takeout stand.

AMERICAN

Pele's Other Garden (811 Houston St., 808/565-9628, www.pelesothergarden. com, lunch 11am-3pm Mon.-Fri., dinner 4:30pm-8pm Mon.-Sat. $7-19) is the de facto hangout of anyone hankering for a good sandwich or a cold draft beer. The bistro also whips up healthy and affordable food options, ranging from avocado and feta wraps to chicken parmesan. The place is so popular that it accepts online reservations for dinner Wednesday nights, when the live band starts playing (7pm-10pm), which is the closest Lana'i City gets to nightlife.

HAWAIIAN REGIONAL

Despite its location in what is often regarded as Lana'i's "third hotel," the **Lana'i City Grille** (828 Lana'i Ave., 808/565-7211, www.hotellanai.com/grille, 5pm-9pm Wed.-Sun., $15-38) takes the cake for the island's finest restaurant. Under the direction of award-winning chef Bev Gannon (of Hali'imaile General Store fame), Lana'i City Grille puts out a fine dinner menu that is usually reserved for birthdays, anniversaries, proposals—or a special vacation. The fare here is going to be more expensive than at the hole-in-the-wall plate lunch stands, of course, but when the waiter serves you a plate of pan-roasted venison loin with a mushroom risotto, cost gets thrown to the wind, and you become wrapped up in culinary splendor. It's paired with the island's most comprehensive wine list. Reservations are highly recommended, particularly on Friday evenings when the live jazz band provides the best entertainment anywhere in town.

COFFEE SHOPS

Even sleepy Lana'i City needs some help waking up in the morning, and **Coffee Works** (604 Ilima Ave., 808/565-6962, 7am-3pm Mon.-Sat.) is the island's only full-time java establishment catering to the under-caffeinated. Breakfast bagels and lunch sandwiches accompany the usual range of coffee offerings, and the outdoor porch is a great place for watching the mellow town slowly spring to life.

THE FOUR SEASONS LODGE AT KOELE

Of the two main restaurants, **The Terrace** (7am-2pm and 6pm-9:30pm daily, $18-23) is more relaxed and informal. This American bistro looks out over the reflecting pool and well-manicured croquet lawn. Order an ahi tuna wrap or combat the evening chill with a bowl of venison chili.

Adjacent to The Terrace, the **Dining Room** (6pm-9:30pm daily, $59) is an immaculate and sophisticated venue offering a grandiose experience. The multicourse offerings, with entrées like beef tenderloin and *keahole* lobster, don't disappoint. Reservations are recommended. Ditch the tank top and rubber slippers for a nice shirt and pair of slacks.

RESTAURANTS AT FOUR SEASONS MANELE BAY HOTEL

If you've only made it as far as the pool by lunch and have no real intentions of leaving, order some food poolside from **Kailani** (11am-4pm and 6pm-9:30pm daily, $18-29), where you can get a Mediterranean seafood salad or rock shrimp and bay scallop ceviche. Having at least a drink or appetizer alongside one of the world's most scenic swimming pools is worth the price. Or, if you spent the morning hitting the golf course and are looking to replenish at the 19th hole, **The Challenge at Manele Clubhouse** (11am-3pm daily, $21) has the most reasonable lunch options with burgers, club sandwiches, and local beer.

Splurge and reserve a table at **Nobu Lana'i** (6pm-9:30pm daily, $30), the island's most highly anticipated restaurant in recent memory. As at other fine Nobu locations around the globe, the selections of yellowtail sashimi with jalapeño, lobster ceviche, rock shrimp tempura with butter ponzu sauce, and sushi are some of the freshest and most creative seafood offerings you'll find on the island. Expect to spend at least $50 per person.

Getting There and Around

GETTING THERE
Plane

Flying into Lana'i requires a jump from neighboring Honolulu or Maui. **Island Air** (800/652-6541, www.islandair.com) operates turboprop planes with four flights between Honolulu (HNL) and Lana'i (LNY) on weekdays and five flights on weekends. Island Air also flies to Lana'i from Maui, but you're going to have to make a stopover in Honolulu. **Mokulele Airlines** (866/260-7070, www.mokuleleairlines.com) also offers nonstop service between Honolulu and Lana'i, with two direct flights per day, and one direct flight every afternoon from Kahului to Lana'i.

Ferry

If you are traveling from Maui, the easiest and most practical way to get to Lana'i is by taking the **Expeditions Ferry** (808/661-3756 or 800/695-2624, www.go-lanai.com, $30/adult, $20/child one-way), which runs five times daily between Lahaina and Manele harbors. Travel time between the two islands is usually about an hour, and during whale season (December-April), you can frequently spot humpback whales from the outdoor seating of the upper deck. Expeditions can also arrange golf, Jeep, and activity packages at a slight discount if you are planning a Lana'i day trip from Maui. Although you can buy tickets at the harbor kiosk in Lahaina the morning of your journey, make reservations ahead of time, particularly for the early morning trip. Don't be late. This is one ferry that doesn't wait around.

GETTING AROUND
Shuttle

Moving from point A to point B on Lana'i works a little differently than on the other

Lahaina-Lana'i Ferry Schedule

DEPART LAHAINA HARBOR (MAUI)

- 6:45am
- 9:15am
- 12:45pm
- 3:15pm
- 5:45pm

DEPART MANELE HARBOR (LANA'I)

- 8am
- 10:30am
- 2pm
- 4:30pm
- 6:45pm

Hawaiian Islands, and Lana'i has some options you won't find elsewhere in the state. In lieu of renting a car, guests at the Four Seasons can pay a one-time fee of $47.50 per adult ($23.75 per child) for all-inclusive access to the resort's shuttle for the duration of their stay. Resort shuttles run every 30 minutes to destinations such as the harbor, airport, Lana'i City, and between the two resorts. The shuttle also makes a stop at Hotel Lana'i, although the one-time shuttle fee for Hotel Lana'i guests is only $35.

Visitors to the island who aren't staying at the Four Seasons are still welcome to use the resort shuttle at a cost of $10 per person/trip. If you have made reservations for a Jeep from **Dollar Lana'i Rent a Car,** a company shuttle will meet you at the harbor and provide complimentary transportation to the shop in Lana'i City (20 minutes) for the driver, although all other passengers will be charged $10/person. If you are traveling with a group of four, depending upon your budget, it's probably a better bet to have three of your party walk five minutes to Hulopo'e Beach from Manele Harbor while the driver goes "up-city" to procure the Jeep and then comes back down to scoop up the rest of the group.

Rentals

The longest running and most reputable Jeep rental company on the island, **Dollar Lana'i Rent a Car** (1036 Lana'i Ave., 808/565-7227 or 800/JEEP-808, www.dollarlanai.com, 7am-7pm daily) provides minivans ($129/day),

four-wheel-drive Jeeps ($139/day 2dr, $169/day 4dr), and Hummers ($189/day). The company requests that the vehicles be returned by 3:30pm, so if you come over from Maui on the early morning ferry, you will arrive at the harbor by 7:45am, be at the rental car counter by 8:15am, and on your way with your Jeep by no later than 8:45am, thereby giving you more than six hours to explore the island. The rental company provides you with a map of the island

© KYLE ELLISON

Jeeps are best for exploring the backroads of Lana'i.

and clearly lays out which roads are off limits. If you end up requiring a tow from someplace "out of bounds," it's going to cost you $500.

Lana'i Jeep Rental (808/280-7092, www.lanaijeeprental.net) has two Jeep Wranglers ($120/day 2dr, $135/day 4dr) for rent to island visitors. Rather than you taking a shuttle up to Lana'i City, John will come and meet you at the harbor or the airport and hand over the keys after some basic formalities, so you can get going on your Lana'i adventure that much quicker. There are no official rules on where you can and cannot go, although he'd prefer you defer to common sense.

808 Hummers (808/286-9308, www.808hummers.com, 8am-8pm, $199/day) has a fleet of the famous off-road vehicles which are perfectly suited for Lana'i's rugged terrain. The company will arrange to pick you up.

Hawaii Western Adventures (1 Keomuku Hwy., 808/563-9385, www.lanaigrandadventures.com) operates guided UTV tours from its scenic Koele headquarters where you can either navigate your own vehicle or enjoy a leisurely, guide-driven expedition in vehicles which can hold up to six people. Choose from either a 1-hour scenic ride through the uplands ($75), or a 1.5-hour ($100) or 3-hour ($200) foray onto the Munro Trail.

Gas

There is only one station on the entire island: The **Lana'i City Service** station (1036 Lana'i Ave., 808/565-7227, 6:30am-10pm daily) supplies fuel for all 3,300 residents. Don't worry about the price; you're better off just not looking (often $1-1.50 more per gallon than on Maui). Then again, with only 30 miles of paved roads here, it isn't uncommon for a tank of gas to last a month or more.

LANA'I

MOLOKA'I

The island of Moloka'i is shrouded in mystery and misconceptions. While the Kalaupapa Peninsula was once the site of a leper colony, a visit to Kalaupapa is now one of the island's most revered historical and cultural experiences. And while there are no resorts on Moloka'i, there are plenty of bed-and-breakfasts, condominiums, and easygoing inns that serve as a relaxing

HIGHLIGHTS

LOOK FOR ◖ TO FIND RECOMMENDED SIGHTS, ACTIVITIES, DINING, AND LODGING.

© AVALON TRAVEL

◖ **Papohaku Beach:** A day with six people is considered crowded on Papohaku Beach. The solitude is trumped only by the sunsets (page 455).

◖ **Mo'omomi:** Wild and secluded, Mo'omomi feels is Moloka'i's lost coast. The sand dunes and empty beaches are meant to be shared with only the wind (page 457).

◖ **Moloka'i Forest Reserve:** This is one of the few places in the state with an ecosystem virtually identical to the one the Polynesians first found over 1,500 years ago. Nearly 98 percent of the plant species are indigenous to Moloka'i (page 465).

◖ **Kalaupapa Peninsula:** The Kalaupapa Peninsula fuses some of Moloka'i's darkest moments with its most dramatic surroundings. The former leper colony is now home to the most scenic mule ride on the planet (page 467).

◖ **Halawa Valley:** Families living in Halawa Valley have inhabited these same plots of land for centuries. A guided hike through the valley is as close to old Hawaii as you can get (page 470).

base for exploring the island's valleys, waterfalls, and beaches.

Regarded as the birthplace of hula, Moloka'i is a time capsule of Hawaiian history and culture. Visiting the island is an enlightening journey into a culture straddling the divide between modernity and tradition. It's one of the few places in Hawaii where it's still possible to hear people speaking the Hawaiian language—possibly while stopped in the middle of

the road, "talking story" in a "Moloka'i traffic jam." That may be the only cause of traffic on the island: its 7,500 residents still don't have to worry about stoplights.

From the east end of the island, the high-rise resorts of Ka'anapali can be seen glittering at night, a floating sea of lights. From the empty beaches of the island's west end, the lights of Honolulu shine brightly behind Diamond Head crater. In the middle, between the two,

MOLOKA'I

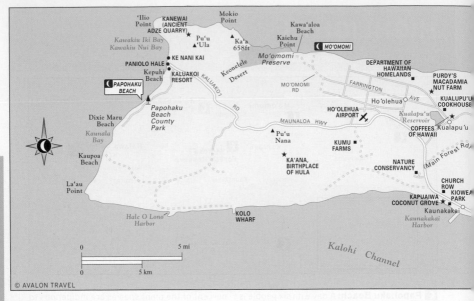

© AVALON TRAVEL

Moloka'i hides beneath a blanket of stars, already asleep while its neighbors stay awake late into the night.

Moloka'i has a slow pace of life, but by no means is it boring. On the contrary, this island is a tropical playground where the volume of adventure opportunities can keep outdoor lovers busy for days. Imagine surfing perfect waves, scuba diving the longest fringing reef in the Hawaiian Islands, or hiking through rainforests inhabited by 219 species of plants found nowhere else on the planet. If all of the adventure is too much for you, relax on a westward-facing beach, watching the sun sink into the horizon.

Beaches

Empty and remote, only a few Moloka'i beaches are good for snorkeling or casual swimming. North- and west-facing beaches are prone to rough surf and hazardous shorebreak in winter, while south shore beaches are ringed by the long fringing reef. If having an entire beach to yourself and listening to nothing but the crashing surf seems like your kind of afternoon, then pack a beach chair and a good book to tune out the rest of the world. No beachside tiki bars, no pesky activity agents—just you, the sand, and the vast blue Pacific stretched out before you.

WEST MOLOKA'I

The west end of the island has the best beaches on all of Moloka'i, which are usually spared the relentless northeasterly trade winds that frequently crank on the eastern half of the island. Summer is best for swimming. During winter, swells turn the coastline into a dangerous stretch of high surf and rip currents. Regardless, the dry, empty shorelines are always good for sunbathing and the sunsets from this western-facing vantage point are among the best in the state.

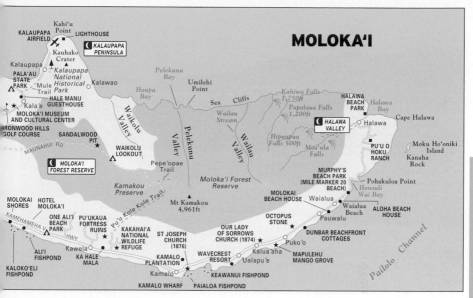

Papohaku Beach

At over two miles long and nearly 100 yards wide, **Papohaku Beach** is where most visitors who drive out to the west end of the island will end up. Despite being the most heavily visited beach on the island, Papohaku rarely sees more than six or seven people at a time. Though smatterings of private homes adorn the southern portion of the beach, the majority of Papohaku is still undeveloped shoreline with empty sand made for strolling. Swimming is a terrible idea here as the rip currents and undertow can be overwhelming during any part of the year. Your time at Papohaku is better spent taking a morning jog or watching the sun set over the distant lights of Honolulu. To get here, follow Highway 460 toward the town of Maunaloa until you take a right on to Kaluakoi Road. Follow Kaluakoi down to sea level and until it wraps around to the left. The beach park will have multiple entrances on the right side of the road. Camping is possible at Papohaku if you obtain a permit from the County Parks Department (808/553-3204).

The only time of year when this beach is truly hopping is during the annual **Moloka'i Ka Hula Piko** festival each May, which celebrates the area as the birthplace of hula.

Kepuhi Beach

Kepuhi Beach fronts the Kaluakoi Villas and the abandoned structures which once formed the Sheraton resort. It's an ideal beach for swimming during the summer. To reach Kepuhi Beach, follow the signs for Kaluakoi Villas off Kaluakoi Road. Public beach parking is available within the complex.

Dixie Maru (Kapukahehu)

Named after a fishing boat that sank near the bay, **Dixie's** is as far south as the road will take you. From Papohaku Beach Park, follow Kaluakoi Road until it reaches Pohakuloa, turn *makai* (toward the sea), and follow it to the end of the cul-de-sac. The narrow alleyway that looks like a driveway is the beach access, and there's a small parking area about 100 yards down. In the kiawe trees behind the

MOLOKA'I

© KYLE ELLISON

Papohaku Beach

beach you'll notice a hidden trail that leads back through the scrub brush and eventually over a fence. Follow this trail for 10 minutes and it will bring you to a sandy cove frequented by surfers and nudists, but more often than not you'll be the only person there.

Kawakiu

Heading north from Kepuhi the coastline becomes wild, scraggy, and utterly deserted. The far northern tip of the island—'Ilio Point—at one point served as a target area for the military, although now all that remains are empty bullet casings and the howl of the northeasterly trades. Between Kepuhi and 'Ilio, however, a number of hidden, sandy coves tucked out of the wind provide perfect swimming and splendid isolation. You would never even know that **Kawakiu Beach** was here unless someone told you. It's that remote. To reach Kawakiu follow the signs to the Paniolo Hale condominium complex from Kaluakoi Road by making a right on Kaka'ako and then turning left down Lio Place, where you will follow the pavement

to the end. From here you'll notice a rudimentary sign pointing the way toward the beach. When the dirt road ends in a parking lot, it's only a short walk to the shore. While the beach you come to first is nice enough, it's nothing compared to Kawakiu. Keep heading north along the shoreline and scramble over some rocks until you cross a stretch of sand known as **Make Horse Beach** (Dead Horse Beach). You'll notice a dirt road running along the top of the bluff, which will lead you all the way to Kawakiu. Or, if the tide is low and the surf calm, meander your way along the shoreline. The protected cove is idyllic in summer, tumultuous in winter, and almost always empty. If you prefer to bathe in the buff, then this is the place. Bring lots of water, as well as proper footwear capable of withstanding sharp lava rocks and kiawe thorns.

Hale O Lono

Hale O Lono is not a place that many visitors go. Not because it isn't beautiful, but because it's incredibly remote. With the closing of

Moloka'i Ranch, the dirt roads once plied by ranch guests now are sporadically used by fishers, canoe racers, or no one at all. Known for its sunsets and solitude, **Hawela Beach** on the east side of the old harbor entrance is the most accessible and most protected. Rough conditions can persist at any time of the year, but on days with light winds and flat surf, the swimming and sunbathing at Hawela can be on par with anywhere else on the island. To find Hale O Lono, follow Highway 460 until its terminus in the town of Maunaloa. From here Mokio Street will lead to a sloping, rutted, seven-mile dirt road running down to the shoreline. Two-wheel drive vehicles with high clearance can make this if it hasn't been raining. A 4WD is recommended in the event that it has.

◀ Mo'omomi

Although **Mo'omomi** is technically on the northern coast of the island, it fits in with the "Wild West" conditions found on the western half. With numerous beaches and windswept dunes, **Mo'omomi** holds incredible cultural significance for native Hawaiians, particularly those living in the Hawaiian Homesteads of nearby Ho'olehua. Mo'omomi is a controversial spot to visit because it's on private property administered by Hawaiian Home Lands, although access has fluctuated from freedom of exploration to talk of erecting a locked gate. While enforcement is rare and the area is usually deserted, anyone wanting to visit should first get permission by contacting **The Department of Hawaiian Home Lands** (600 Maunaloa Hwy., 808/560-6104) to enquire about any current restrictions.

Untouched save for the marine debris, which washes onto the shores, Mo'omomi is a place for fishing, lobster diving, and soul-searching. The western portions of Mo'omomi are part of The Nature Conservancy, and visitors are asked to stay out of the sensitive ecosystem in the dunes. All hikers are advised to stick to established trails or follow the shoreline. To reach the Mo'omomi pavilion, follow Farrington Avenue until the road becomes dirt and veer to the right at the fork in the road. Walking

MOLOKA'I

© KYLE ELLISON

the windswept beaches of Mo'omomi

along the shoreline takes you to a series of underwhelming beaches, but once you hook back up with the dirt road, the beauty of windswept **Kawaʻaloa Beach** opens up before you in what is potentially one of the most scenic stretches of coastline on the island. Though it's possible to hike the shoreline for miles, there are zero facilities, no places to procure water, and it all looks the same. Swimming at Kawaʻaloa can be rough during almost all parts of the year. The chief benefits are scenery and isolation.

EAST MOLOKA'I

The eastern beaches are the most popular among locals despite being heavily exposed to the northeasterly winds. Morning hours are best. Like scenes out of a South Pacific postcard, white sand coves ringed by lazy palms are dotted by fishing boats of varying colors and styles. More than anywhere else on the island, a sense of calm envelops this shore. The swimming and snorkeling are best at high tide, the beachcombing and sunbathing better at low tide, and everything is better before the afternoon wind.

Pukoʻo Beach

Just east of the Manaʻe Goods & Grindz, a small beach access sign points down a dirt driveway to the tucked away **Pukoʻo Beach.** Despite being only 50 yards long, this sliver of a beach is protected from the wind and offers calm swimming most times of the year. The water isn't as murky as spots closer to town. This is a good spot for eating a plate lunch beneath the shade of a tropical palm or taking a quick dip to cool off.

Waialua Beach

Waialua Beach is a narrow ribbon of sand 18.5 miles east of Kaunakakai with some the island's best swimming, snorkeling, and small waves for learning to surf. As at other beaches in the area, the wind gains in strength throughout the

day, and at high tide the sand almost disappears completely. This is a great spot for taking a dip. Watch out for coral heads exposed during low tide.

Murphy's Beach

Known as "Twenty Mile Beach" to locals, **Murphy's Beach** is by the 20-mile marker of Highway 450 and the last stretch of sand before the road narrows to one lane. While the swimming here isn't as nice as at Waialua, the beach is a little larger, making it a good option for laying a blanket down. In the afternoon hours you might see kitesurfers running laps down the coast. From this vantage point the views of West Maui provide a scenic backdrop for the most popular beach on the island's east end.

Sandy Beach

Although parking can be an issue, **Sandy Beach** is a simple cove tucked into a bend in the road on the drive to Halawa. The beach is protected from the trade winds and, most of the time, from the surf. Although the beach is small, there's just enough room to lay a towel down. You might also share space with kids wading in the shallows or locals selling bananas out of the back of a truck.

Halawa Bay

After weaving your way 10 miles over the rocky coastline and down through the lush eastern valleys, the two beaches which form **Halawa Bay** appear like the gold at the end of a rainbow. At the terminus of Highway 450, Kamaʻalaea Bay is the more protected beach on the far side of the stream. This is the best option for swimming and escaping the wind. Kawili Beach at the bottom of the cliff is more exposed to the currents and trade winds. The sand here is darker than the white sand of Waialua, and it's a surreal feeling to hang out on the shores of a place considered to be one of the oldest settlements in the state of Hawaii.

Snorkeling and Diving

Don't tell anybody, but Moloka'i has some of the best snorkeling and diving in all of Hawaii. The only reason you haven't heard about it is because—with the exception of a few protected areas—the majority of Moloka'i's dive and snorkel spots are best accessed from a dive boat or charter. Dixie Maru Beach on the west shore and Waialua Beach on the east shore (accessible for snorkeling only at high tide) are the only two bays where you could snorkel from the shoreline without getting caught in a rip current or scraping your stomach on the shallow reef. Moloka'i is still home to the longest fringing reef in Hawaii, and dive outfitters have no less than 20 spots along the outer edge of the reef. Moku Ho'oniki on the eastern tip of the island is home to a population of scalloped hammerhead sharks, a vibrant coral reef, and occasionally some larger species with the ability to get your heart racing.

MOKU HO'ONIKI

While it's for advanced divers only, Moku Ho'oniki is the crown jewel in most charter boat offerings. The water is too deep here for any sort of mooring system, so often divers will have to flop backward off the drifting boat for a Navy SEAL-style entry into the rough waters of the Pailolo Channel. At the rock's most popular dive site—Fish Rain—divers usually descend to 100 feet or more along a sloping reef where myriad species of tropical fish appear to rain down from above.

Once at your bottom depth, your heart rate really picks up as you head out into the open blue in search of scalloped hammerheads. Other sightings have included whale sharks, tiger sharks, mahimahi, and even humpback whales during the winter season. Dive charters visit the rock from both Maui and Moloka'i.

CHARTERS AND TOURS

With an office right on the corner of Kaunakakai's main thoroughfare, **Moloka'i Fish and Dive** (61 Ala Malama Ave., 808/553-5926, www.molokaifishanddive.com, 7:30am-6pm Mon.-Sat., 8am-2pm Sun.) operates its own charter boat departing out of Kaunakakai wharf and offers three-hour snorkeling trips for $79. Scuba diving trips visit either the south shore's fringing reef for $145 or locations farther afield (such as Moku Ho'oniki) for $295. This shop is the premier (and only) PADI operation on the island and can accommodate whatever snorkel or dive excursion you're hoping to sort out. Prices and times can vary, so it's best to contact the dive shop directly about current rates and availability.

Operating the 40-foot catamaran *Manu Ele'ele,* **Moloka'i Ocean Tours** (808/553-3290, www.molokaioceantours.com) can accommodate up to six passengers and offers snorkeling excursions out of Kaunakakai. This boat mostly travels the 30 miles of fringing reef along the south shore in front of Kaunakakai. Prices vary depending on the number of people on the boat, from $240/person for two people to $90/person for six people.

For a private sea tour of the northern sea cliffs—something which is only possible when the conditions allow—local adventure guide Walter Naki runs **Moloka'i Action Adventures** (808/558-8184) and is one of the few people you will find who can take you to remote valleys and the dramatic coastline of the world's tallest sea cliffs. Because conditions are variable, inquire directly about rates and availability, although if all aligns correctly it's guaranteed to be the most memorable day of your vacation.

MOLOKA'I

Surfing

To say that the surf spots on Moloka'i are empty would be a lie, but a crowded day by Moloka'i standards would be considered almost empty in Maui. If there are more than three people, maybe four, just go somewhere else. With a little walking (or a high clearance vehicle), it's still possible to find spots where there's a good chance you'll have the waves all to yourself. Since finding surf spots like this is such a rarity in Hawaii, however, it's not surprising that Moloka'i locals can be protective of their surf breaks, so following basic surf etiquette here can go a long way.

WEST MOLOKA'I

Remote and empty, West Moloka'i is the best in winter for mixing big surf with fiery sunsets. The same swells that send waves to the North Shore of O'ahu come crashing into western Moloka'i, the differences being that there aren't 200 people vying for the same wave and traffic on the highway consists of a deer crossing the road. While the quality isn't the same as at Sunset Beach, the surf in western Moloka'i can still get heavy, and only experts and advanced surfers should paddle out on the bigger days.

The most well-known (and consequently, most crowded) spot on this end of the island is **Sheraton's** at Kepuhi Beach, named after the now-defunct resort which fronts the beach. The access at Sheraton's is sandy and easy, although you have to be careful of a few shallow boulders while paddling out. The wave is on the left side of the beach, and on its better days can be an A-frame that holds its shape in faces exceeding 10-15 feet. Sheraton's is a decent spot for intermediate surfers if it's small, and is an experts-only venue if really pumping.

If Sheraton's is too big, drive south to **Dixie Maru's** where a right point break wraps into the bay at sizes often half that of Sheraton's. If Dixie's is crowded (i.e., more than three people), or you're up for a little adventure, a goat

trail leading from the center of the beach back through the kiawe trees brings you to a sandy cove where another right point break bends into the often empty beach. The takeoff can be a little sketchy as you have to sit just off the rocks, but it's a fun wave to get a few turns in when Sheraton's is a cauldron of white water.

Even though the beaches around **Hale O Lono** harbor face south, they're still able to pick up swells during all parts of the year, which can often be heavy during the winter. The wind can be fierce in the afternoon, and the murky conditions conjure images of toothy predators. Plus, there's a 95 percent chance you'll be the only one surfing there. If everything comes together though, and the wind is down, the waves are up, and the water is clear, the beaches off Hale O Lono can offer some of the most adventurous surf on Moloka'i. Just follow the dirt road from Maunaloa town and take it straight downhill until you reach the shoreline seven miles later.

KAUNAKAKAI

Since Kaunakakai faces directly south, the best time of year for scoring waves in town is May through September. Despite the fact that the area surrounding Kaunakakai boasts miles of shoreline, the majority of it is blocked by the fringing reef, which makes paddling out virtually impossible. Nevertheless, locals still flock to **Kaunakakai Wharf** during the big swells of summer. Anyone surfing here can expect a long paddle since you need to head out past the reef to get to the waves, but the long paddle is rewarded by Moloka'i's best summer wave. Expect a very local crowd.

EAST MOLOKA'I

Technically, East Moloka'i is the most consistent place to find surf year-round. It might not be *good* surf, but when there's nothing else to ride, this is where you head. Winter months pick up wrapping north swell, and if a northeast swell comes barreling down the Pailolo Channel, then this is the place to be. During summer this same stretch of rural coastline is able to pick up windswell generated by the trades, but on the flip side this means that it's often blown out and completely unrideable. Morning hours are always best, and although there are ample waves along this coastline, accessing them isn't always the easiest.

For beginner surfers, the easiest waves can be found at **Waialua Beach,** where gentle rollers provide enough of a push to practice getting up on two feet. While the waves can be fun, it can be shallow at low tide.

Just past Murphy's Beach (mile marker 20) where the road turns to a single lane sits one of Moloka'i's most well-known surf spots, **Rock Point.** This local favorite can be a tricky place to surf for a number of reasons: finding the spot in the first place, figuring out where to park, getting it when the wind isn't up, and trying to figure out how to paddle into a wave which breaks in knee-deep water.

Rental Shops

Your best bet is to bring boards over from Maui on the ferry, but if you're in need of a rental board on the island, there are a couple of outfitters to help you out. **Moloka'i Fish and Dive** (61 Ala Malama Ave., 808/553-5926, www. molokaifishanddive.com, 7:30am-6pm Mon.-Sat., 8am-2pm Sun.) is the only retail store in downtown Kaunakakai openly renting out surfboards. Although the selection isn't huge, for $25/day they can get you a board and provide tips on the best places to check out.

While they don't have an actual shop and are only accessible by phone or online, the staff at **Moloka'i Outdoors** (808/553-4477, www. molokai-outdoors.com) can similarly get you in the water and give you inside info on where—and when—to embark on your Moloka'i surf excursion. Rates are usually a few dollars cheaper than at Moloka'i Fish and Dive, and they currently are the only company that also rents out other water sports equipment such as stand-up paddleboards or windsurfing boards.

MOLOKA'I

Hiking and Biking

Even for Maui locals, the hiking trails of Moloka'i are shrouded in mystery. Often the trails require either four-wheel drive access or permission from private landowners, although there are still a number that are accessible to the public. You're rewarded for your effort with sweeping views of the entire island.

HIKING
Topside
Bathed in the scent of eucalyptus and pine, the "topside" of central Moloka'i is where you truly feel as if you're in the mountains. With trails ranging in elevation from 1,500 to 4,000 feet, the air is cooler up here, and once you enter the Kamakou Preserve, the weather turns wetter and the surroundings lush. Songs of the native *i'iwi* birds ring from the treetops while mists hang in the silence of deeply carved valleys.

KALAUPAPA OVERLOOK
The easiest walk is the 1,500-foot paved walkway leading to the **Kalaupapa Overlook** starting at the end of the road in Pala'au State Park. Take Highway 470 past the mule barn for the Kalaupapa trail rides and continue until it dead-ends in a parking lot. Here you'll find some basic restrooms but no potable water. Be prepared for high winds that can blow your hat off, and get your camera ready for a view of the Kalaupapa Peninsula which is the best you're going to find short of actually hiking down there.

KALAUPAPA TRAIL
The **Kalaupapa Trail** is the most popular hike on Moloka'i. Descending over 1,700 vertical feet over the course of 3.2 miles and 26 switchbacking turns, this trail was hand-carved into the mountain in 1886 by Portuguese

immigrant Manuel Farinha as a way to establish a land connection with the residents living topside. The trail today remains in good shape, although you do need to be physically fit and keep a keen eye out for the "presents" left on the trail by mules. Since this is part of the National Historic Park, reservations are required to tour the peninsula, and those who try to sneak into Kalaupapa could end up facing possible prosecution. Those wanting to hike the trail instead of riding a mule can contact **Damien Tours** (808/567-6171), which, for the cost of $50/person, will meet hikers at the bottom of the trail at 10am and provide a four-hour guided tour of the Kalaupapa Peninsula. To reach the trailhead, drive 200 yards past the mule barn on Highway 470 and park on the right side of the road.

PEPE'OPAE BOG

Constantly shrouded in cloud cover and dripping in every color of green imaginable, if ever there were a place to visualize Hawaii before the arrival of humans, then that spot is the

Pepe'opae Bog. Ninety-eight percent of the plant species here are indigenous to the island of Moloka'i, and 219 of the species in this preserve are found nowhere else on earth. Following Highway 460 from Kaunakakai, make a right before the bridge at the Homelani Cemetery sign and follow the dirt road for 10 miles all the way to the parking area at Waikolu Overlook. Even making it this far in a two-wheel-drive vehicle requires high clearance and the best road conditions. Trying to go any further will just get you stuck. Those with four-wheel drive can knock 2.6 miles one-way off the journey by continuing to the trailhead, but even this is precarious at best and the driver needs to know what they're doing behind the wheel.

Look for the signs for Pepe'opae Bog and follow them. Once the trail begins, it's imperative you stay on the metal boardwalk. If you accidentally step off, you can expect to sink shin-deep into the soggy moss and mud. The boardwalk runs for 1.5 miles through some of the most pristine rainforest left in the state. Hikers who make it to the end are rewarded

view of the Pelekunu Valley

© KYLE ELLISON

with a view into **Pelekunu Valley** which plunges 4,000 feet through the uninhabited, untouched wilderness below. Hikers are free to attempt the climb on their own, or the **Nature Conservancy** (808/553-5236, hike_molokai@tnc.org) leads hikes into Pepeʻopae once per month, March-October. Make advance reservations.

PUʻU KOLEKOLE

On the same 4WD road leading to the Pepeʻopae trailhead, hikers who take the fork to the right will instead reach the start of the **Puʻu Kolekole trail.** This two-mile trail leads you to the 3,951-foot summit of Puʻu Kolekole. From here the view overlooks the southern shoreline and fringing reef to offer the best view of southern Molokaʻi.

West Molokaʻi

Given the lack of mountains in western Molokaʻi, most of the hikes on this side of the island follow the coastline.

KAWAKIU

A nice walk from the condo complexes of Kaluakoi is to follow either the coastline or a dusty dirt road to the secluded beauty of **Kawakiu Nui Beach.** From Maunaloa Highway (Hwy. 460) take the Kalukaoi Road exit and follow it to the bottom of the hill before making a right on Kakaʻako Road. Finally, a left on Lio Place brings you to the Paniolo Hale parking lot, where you can follow the signs for the beach, crossing over the fairway of the old golf course before you reach the shoreline. Make a right, and 45 minutes of walking along the coastline will bring you to Kawakiu. Or, if the tide or surf is too high to walk along the coastline, turn inland past Make Horse Beach. After a few minutes you'll meet up with a dirt road which leads north and deposits you at Kawakiu. About 100 yards before the road drops onto the

sand at Kawakiu, there's an ancient Hawaiian *heiau* out on the rocky point.

East Molokaʻi

Deeply carved down from the 4,961-foot summit of Kamakou, the valleys of eastern Molokaʻi beckon to be explored. Despite being beautiful, forested and laden with waterfalls, many of the valleys are cut off from public use. Liability concerns have forced landowners to restrict access to many valley trails, although some are still available by taking part in a guided tour.

Halawa Valley

At Halawa, the trail can only be accessed by going through a local company and paying to hire a local guide. Bookings to hike into Halawa Valley can be made through either **Molokaʻi Outdoors** (808/553-4477, www.molokai-outdoors.com) or **Molokaʻi Fish and Dive** (61 Ala Malama Ave., 808/553-5926, www.molokaifishanddive.com).

BIKING

All of the best mountain biking in Molokaʻi is found on the roads of the Molokaʻi Forest Reserve. Road cyclists can enjoy miles of open road with minimal traffic. The ride east from Kaunakakai to Halawa Valley is comparable to Maui's ride to Kahakuloa.

In downtown Kaunakakai, **Molokaʻi Bicycle** (80 Mohala St., 808/553 5740 or 808/553-3931, www.mauimolokaibicycle.com, 3pm-6pm Wed., 9am-2pm Sat.) can cater to every bike need, whether it's rentals, parts, or just advice on good rides. The company can arrange free pickups and drop-offs from a number of Molokaʻi hotels, with a $20-25 surcharge for the airport and hotels which are farther afield, such as Wavecrest or Kaluakoi. Rentals begin at $32/day, $20/day thereafter, or $120 for the week.

Other Recreation

BIRD-WATCHING

Although many of Hawaii's original bird species have gone the way of the dodo, there are still a number of rare and critically endangered native bird species which cling to existence high in the Moloka'i forests or down on the protected seashore. Anyone interested in volunteering in one of Moloka'i's wetlands or learning more about the island's endangered bird species is encouraged to contact **Nene O Moloka'i** (808/553-5992), a nonprofit organization dedicated to protecting Moloka'i's endangered waterfowl.

The last known sightings of the Moloka'i thrush (*oloma'o*) and Moloka'i creeper (*kakawahie*) were both in the **Kamakou Preserve,** a rugged and wet mountain area that requires four-wheel drive to access. In this protected area home to 219 endemic species of plants, the trademark calls of honeycreepers (*i'iwi*), *'apapane, 'amakihi,* and the Hawaiian owl (*pueo*) can still be heard resonating through the lush green treetops. The Nature Conservancy leads trips into the preserve once per month March through October. Find out more by calling 808/553-5236.

Although not open to the public, the **Kakahai'a National Wildlife Refuge** 5.5 miles east of Kaunakakai can be visited by arranging a tour through the Maui County National Wildlife Refuge office at 808/875-1582. This 45-acre protected area five miles east of Kaunakakai is home to endangered Hawaiian stilts (*a'eo*) as well as endangered Hawaiian coots (*'alae ke'oke'o*).

During the fall and winter months it is common to see Pacific golden plover (*kolea*) scuttling their way across the shorelines and grassy areas of the island. These birds migrate all the way to the Arctic Circle during summer before returning to Hawaii for the long, cold winter. Once the *kolea* are seen in the islands, locals know that the humpback whales aren't far behind.

FISHING

To say that fish play a large role in Moloka'i's culture would be a big understatement. The southern coast of the island is ringed with dozens of fishponds, and seemingly every third house you pass has long bunches of fishing nets drying in the yard. The Penguin Banks between Moloka'i and O'ahu are considered to be some of the most fertile fishing grounds in the state, although even if you stay near shore the chances of hauling in a fresh catch are still good. The earlier you depart, the better your chances for success.

Charters

The best place in Kaunakakai for buying fishing accessories, **Moloka'i Fish and Dive** (61 Ala Malama Ave., 808/553-5926, www.molokaifishanddive.com, 7:30am-6pm Mon.-Sat., 8am-2pm Sun.) also operates its own charter service offering both half-day ($500) as well as full-day trips ($650) aboard the 38-foot Delta cruiser *The Coral Queen.*

Not only is owner and captain Mike Holmes of **Fun Hogs Fishing** (808/567-6789 or 808/336-0047, www.molokaifishing.com) an accomplished waterman and avid canoe racer, but he also runs one of the best operations for deep-sea fishing available for visitors. Aboard the 27-foot *AHI,* Holmes can take guests trolling for blue water game fish such as mahimahi, ono, ahi, and marlin. Four-hour charters run $450, while a full-day, eight-hour charter can be booked for $600. Fun Hogs can also arrange seasonal whale-watching trips for $70/adult, private snorkeling charters, or any other sort of outing provided there are six passengers or fewer.

Based out of Kaunakakai, Captain Joe Reich of **Alyce C. Sportfishing** (808/558-8377, www.alycecsportfishing.com) similarly offers half-day, three-quarter-day, and full-day charters aboard his 31-foot cruiser. A knowledgeable fisher who will go wherever the fish are biting,

Captain Joe's goal is to send you home with as much fresh fish as you can possibly make use of.

GOLF

Now that the fairways of the Kaluakoi Golf Course have reverted back to dirt, the lone remaining course on the island is the 9-hole

Ironwood Hills Golf Club (Kalae Hwy., 808/567-6000, www.molokaigolfcourse.com, $36) in the cool eucalyptus groves of Kala'e off Highway 470. Set at a 1,200-foot elevation and not far from Pala'au State Park, this course is easy on the pocketbook and the only option for breaking out the clubs while in town. Clubs and carts are available for rent.

Sights

People who claim that there isn't a lot to *do* on Moloka'i have most likely never even scoured the island to see what's out there. Although Moloka'i is a place you go to decompress, there are still a healthy number of visitor sites relating to the island's history, culture, and agricultural heritage.

KAUNAKAKAI
Moloka'i Plumeria Farm

Just west of town on Highway 460 as the road starts heading uphill sits the **Moloka'i Plumeria Farm** (808/553-3391, www.molokaiplumerias.

com, 9am-12pm Mon.-Sat., free) where you can tour the 10-acre property and even make your own lei.

TOPSIDE
Moloka'i Forest Reserve

As you head west from Kaunakakai, slowly gaining in elevation, the turnoff for the **Moloka'i Forest Reserve** is just before mile marker 4. Turn right before the bridge, and after a few hundred yards you'll pass the Homelani Cemetery. Here, red-dirt Maunahui

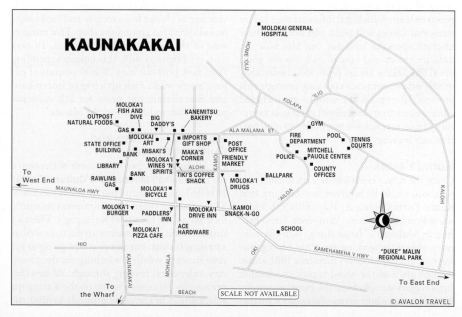

KAUNAKAKAI

MOLOKAI GENERAL HOSPITAL

HOME 'OLU

'ILIO

KOLAPA

MOLOKA'I FISH AND DIVE

OUTPOST NATURAL FOODS

BIG DADDY'S

KANEMITSU BAKERY

ALA MALAMA ST.

GYM

GAS

MOLOKAI ART

STATE OFFICE BUILDING

IMPORTS GIFT SHOP

MISAKI'S

MAKA'S CORNER

POST OFFICE

FIRE DEPARTMENT

POOL

TENNIS COURTS

BANK

MOLOKA'I WINES 'N SPIRITS

FRIENDLY MARKET

POLICE

MITCHELL PAUOLE CENTER

LIBRARY

ALOHI

KAMOI

BANK

TIKI'S COFFEE SHACK

MOLOKA'I DRUGS

BALLPARK

COUNTY OFFICES

RAWLINS GAS

MAUNALOA HWY.

To West End

MOLOKA'I BICYCLE

'AILOA

MOLOKA'I BURGER

PADDLERS' INN

MOLOKA'I DRIVE INN

KAMOI SNACK-N-GO

KALOHI

MOLOKA'I PIZZA CAFE

ACE HARDWARE

HIO

SCHOOL

KAUNAKAKAI

MOHALA

OKI

KAMEHAMEHA V HWY.

"DUKE" MALIN REGIONAL PARK

To the Wharf

BEACH

SCALE NOT AVAILABLE

To East End

© AVALON TRAVEL

Road winds its way into the mountains. Your car-rental agency will tell you that this road is impassable except in a four-wheel drive, and it's right—if it's raining or has rained recently. The road is rough even when it's dry; anyone without a high-clearance truck or jeep shouldn't even consider it. If you have the proper vehicle, however, follow the rutted road up into the hills and you'll soon be in a deep forest of 'ohi'a, pine, eucalyptus, and giant ferns which have thrived since their planting in the early 1900s. The cool, pleasant air mixes with rich earthy smells of the forest, and at 5.5 miles you enter the Moloka'i Forest Reserve.

Purdy's Na Hua O Ka 'Aina Farm (Macadamia Nut Farm)

One of the most popular visitor stops on the island is **Purdy's Na Hua O Ka 'Aina Farm** (808/567-6601, www.molokai.com/eatnuts, 9:30am-3:30pm Tues.-Fri., 10am-2pm Sat., free) behind the public high school on Lihi Pali Avenue near the homesteads of Ho'olehua. This is the only macadamia nut farm on the island. If there was ever anything you wanted to know about a macadamia nut, then you're going to learn it here. An informal tour led by the jovial owner will teach you not only how to crack open the hard nut, but also how the nuts are grown and how to pick out the good ones. Plus, there are no pesticides, herbicides, or any other chemicals coursing through this grove of 50 trees. While samples are included with the free tour, a small gift shop sells everything from macadamia nut honey to mac nut-themed clothing.

Kumu Farms

Given the recent explosion of farm to table cuisine, you could be forgiven for thinking that **Kumu Farms** (Hua Ai Rd., 808/351-3326, www.kumufarms.com, 9am-4pm Tues.-Fri., free) is Moloka'i's "latest thing." On the contrary, this fully working farm has been growing crops in the Moloka'i dirt since 1981 and is the best place on the island to pick up a haul of fresh veggies straight from the *kumu*, or source. Not only can visitors peruse the outdoor market

© KYLE ELLISON

treats at Purdy's Macadamia Nut Farm

for certified organic and non-GMO produce, but you can also glean some expert culinary advice free of charge from recipes and cookbooks found sprinkled around the shop. Five minutes west of the airport on Hua Ai Road, an easy turn off Highway 460, this rapidly expanding farm now puts out over 20,000 pounds of papaya every week. Pick up a bag of frozen basil and macadamia nut pesto for a homemade pasta dinner unlike any in the islands.

Moloka'i Museum and Cultural Center

Off Highway 470, two miles north of Kualapu'u sits the **Moloka'i Museum and Cultural Center** (808/567-6436, 10am-2pm Mon-Sat., $5 adult, $1 student), a simple museum predominantly focused on the history of Kalaupapa. There's a small exhibit on Hawaiian artifacts as well as a basic gift shop, but where you're going to get your money's worth is watching the documentary videos and reading through old newspaper articles pertaining to life on the Kalaupapa Peninsula. On the same grounds behind the

fresh produce at Kumu Farms

museum sits the **R.W. Meyer Sugar Mill,** constructed in 1878 during the island's short-lived sugar era.

Pala'au State Park

Above the residential town of Kala'e and past the mule barn, Highway 470 eventually dead-ends in the parking lot of **Pala'au State Park.** The park offers decent camping, and there are public restrooms available at the parking lot, although there is no potable water and very basic facilities. The air up here is noticeably cooler than down on the shoreline, and by the midmorning hours the northeasterly trade winds are usually blowing when you head out toward Kalaupapa Overlook. To reach the lookout, follow the paved path at the edge of the parking lot until it reaches a terminus at a low rock wall perched at the edge of a cliff. From this vantage point you can take in unobstructed views of the town of Kalaupapa, the former leper settlement that still houses a handful of patients. Unless you have booked a mule ride or plan to hike in to meet a tour

group, this is the closest to Kalaupapa that you can get, so drink in the view and take a moment to reflect on what life on the peninsula must have been like.

Back at the parking lot an unpaved trail leads 200 yards through a cool canopy of trees before emerging at a sacred spot by the name of **Ke Ule O Nanahoa,** also known as "Phallic Rock" for obvious reasons. According to legend, Nanahoa, the male god of fertility, once lived nearby in the forests surrounding Pala'au. One day when Nanahoa sat to admire a beautiful young girl who was looking at her reflection in a pool, Kawahua, Nanahoa's wife, became so jealous that she attacked the young girl by yanking on her hair. Nanahoa became outraged in turn and struck his wife, who rolled over a nearby cliff before finally turning to stone. Nanahoa also turned to stone in the shape of an erect penis, and there he sits today still pointing toward the sky.

KALAUPAPA PENINSULA

There was once a time when Kalaupapa wasn't shrouded in the stigma of leprosy. During the days of ancient Hawaii this northern peninsula was occupied by original settlers who lived in much the same way as those elsewhere in the state. All of that changed, however, when the first confirmed case of Hansen's disease was reported in Honolulu in 1848. Although those living in Kalaupapa at the time didn't know it, this remote peninsula on Moloka'i's northern shore would become an outpost of desperation and a place where the human spirit was tested on a daily basis.

Now registered as a National Historic Park, Kalaupapa is one of the most powerful day trips you can take in the islands. There are three ways in to Kalaupapa (hike, mule ride, or fly). All require the services of **Damien Tours** (808/567-6171, 10am Mon.-Sat.) as your guides around what remains of the settlement. The cost of $50 is for those who choose to hike in on their own, and the fee is incorporated into the prices of the mule ride and air tours. All participants will spend a couple of hours learning the history of the

MOLOKA'I

MOLOKA'I

© RITU JETHANI/123RF.COM

the Kalaupapa Peninsula

isolated peninsula, and lunch is enjoyed at Kalawao—the first landing site of the original lepers at the base of Hawaii's tallest sea cliffs. Visitors will also get the chance to visit **St. Philomena Church,** the house of worship from which Father Damien displayed his overwhelming courage in the face of insurmountable odds. From this humble Kalaupapa house of worship, you'll learn the story of how this Belgian-born priest improved the living conditions of patients and dedicated his life to their salvation and betterment.

Those wanting to ride in on a mule can contact **Moloka'i Mule Ride** (808/567-6088, www.muleride.com, 8am-3pm Mon.-Sat., must be over 16 years old and under 250 lbs., $199) for a switchbacking tour down the sea cliffs that ranks as one of the best adventures on the island.

Pacific Wings (808/567-6381 or 888/575-4546 toll free, www.pacificwings.com) and **Mokulele Airlines** (808/567-6381 Moloka'i or 866/260-7070 toll free, www.mokuleleairlines.com) offer flights connecting Honolulu

and Kahului with topside in Ho'olehua, where you can catch a connecting flight with **Makani Kai Air Charters** (808/834-1111 or 877/255-8532, www.makanikaiair.com). If you are traveling from Honolulu, Makani Air offers flights directly to Kalaupapa. Space is limited on flights to Kalaupapa and prices and schedules change regularly, so inquire directly about current availability and rates. When booking a tour from an outer island, air tickets are often included as a package tour bundle. Unfortunately, it isn't possible to visit Kalaupapa as part of a day trip on the Lahaina to Moloka'i ferry.

Finally, hikers can drive 200 yards past the mule barn on Highway 470 past the town of Kala'e and park on the right side of the road next to a locked metal gate. While you can arrange a permit in advance with Damien Tours for $50 (or potentially even pay cash at the bottom when you meet the tour guide at 10am), you can also play it safe and arrange a permit with Moloka'i Mule Ride, which will also include a light lunch for $69.

WEST MOLOKA'I

Ever since a group of wealthy Honolulu businesspeople purchased 70,000 acres of land in 1897, the western half of Moloka'i has been known as Moloka'i Ranch. Never completely steady, the ranch tried its hand at a number of different ventures for the next 111 years until finally succumbing in 2008 to public pressure over proposed development. The closing of the ranch's hospitality operations did away with 120 jobs, and in the years since, the area has yet to recover. During its tenure, the ranchland supported sugarcane, pineapples, sweet potatoes, wheat, cattle, safari tours, a luxury lodge, an 18-hole golf course, a movie theater, and rustic accommodations on Kaupoa Beach colloquially known as "tentalows." With ranch operations mostly on hold (sustainable energy and cattle ranching make up most of the current business), the small, residential town of **Maunaloa** is all that remains.

EAST MOLOKA'I

Since the arrival of the original Polynesians, the fertile valleys and shorelines of eastern Moloka'i have supported the majority of the island's population. The mountains provide freshwater for farming and pigs and deer to put on the dinner table. The lowlands and river valleys provide fertile ground for planting crops such as taro. The fishponds lining the shoreline provide a bounty from the sea, which has been sustainably managed for more than 1,000 years. Many of the residents of eastern Moloka'i still maintain this subsistence-based lifestyle: the people serve as the stewards of the land and it, in turn, provides the people with the nourishment to live.

Given that eastern Moloka'i has historically been the population center, there are also a number of visitor sites that are worth your time. Many of the historical sites in this area have limited access due to their being situated on private land. Out of respect for the landowners, places such as 'Ili'iliopae (the largest *heiau* on the island) are not included here so as not to be disturbed.

Nevertheless, a day trip to the sites along the eastern end of the island can still be one of the best ways to spend a day on Moloka'i, as the views stretching back toward Maui are only amplified by the "main highway" which at some points nearly crumbles into the sea. Life in eastern Moloka'i is relaxed, friendly, and refreshingly isolated, ticking along at its own slow place.

Ali'i Fishpond

Driving east from Kaunakakai, one of the first sites you will come to is **Ali'i Fishpond**, at mile marker 3 just before One Ali'i Beach Park. This 35-acre fishpond was originally constructed with rocks that had been hand-carried 10 miles over the adjacent mountain. Having fallen into disrepair, the Ali'i Fishpond has been painstakingly brought back to life by *Ka Honua Momona,* a nonprofit organization dedicated to sustainable land practices on the island of Moloka'i. If you pull in to the parking lot and staff members are working on the property, they will be more than happy to show you around. Workers are usually here in the morning hours before the wind picks up, although if no one is around, it's best to admire the fishpond from afar.

View from the Heights

Even though the road parallels the southern coastline, from the vantage point of sea level it's difficult to find a good view. For a panoramic photo of the island's fringing reef, one of the best views is a few minutes east of One Ali'i Beach Park by driving to the top of Kawela Plantation, located on the *mauka,* or mountain side of the road. After turning into the Kawela Plantation I development, make your way down a plumeria-lined street until taking your first left and following it up until it dead-ends in a cul-de-sac. From this vantage point you can make out a large swath of the coastline, and this is your best coastal photo-op until you reach mile marker 20 where the road gets narrow and curvy.

St. Joseph's Church

Driving along Highway 450, past One Ali'i

MOLOKA'I

MOLOKAʻI

Beach Park, you will reach **St. Joseph's Church** right around mile marker 10. Although Father Damien is famous for having reached out to the patients of Kalaupapa, he would also frequently make the arduous trek over the mountains down to the southern coastline where, in 1876, he constructed St. Joseph's Church as a place of Christian worship. There is a statue of Damien standing outside this small, recently restored building. Given the lack of modern development, it isn't hard to imagine what the area would have looked like when the first nails of the church were pounded in 135 years ago. For a quick peek inside, check the doors; they are often unlocked. In an effort to convert Hawaiians to Christianity, it's believed that Father Damien purposely chose this spot in Kamalo to provide an alternative to the Puili *heiau,* which lies just inland.

Puʻu O Hoku Ranch

Past the beaches of Waialua and Murphy's, the road gets narrow and nearly runs into the sea. It is true country living this far out on the island, and often you'll encounter groups of locals just hanging out, cruising, and taking life easy. Be sure you have more than a quarter tank of gas if you plan to venture farther, as there are no facilities as you continue heading east.

Once Highway 450 starts gaining in elevation, the sweeping pasturelands of **Puʻu O Hoku Ranch** (808/558-8109, www.puuohoku.com) begin coming into view. At this point you have driven so far north and east that it's possible to see the northern coastline of Maui. This 14,000-acre working ranch and farm dominates the eastern flank of the island. There's a basic store at the ranch headquarters that sells local, organically grown produce and herbs such as kale, chard, eggplant, cherry tomatoes, and sweet apple bananas tiny enough to fit in the palm of your hand. The ranch is also one of the only places which grows and sells *ʻawa,* a traditional Polynesian herb known for its medicinal and painkilling properties. The ranch also has a number of accommodation options for couples looking to get away from it all or large groups in search of a team-building retreat.

◖ Halawa Valley

At the end of Highway 450, after utopian plantation homes, single-lane turns, the bluffs of the ranchlands, and heavily forested valleys, the road reaches a left hairpin turn where a cleft in the mountainside opens up like an amphitheater before you. This is **Halawa Valley.** At the lookout, try to snap a shot of Moaʻula Falls toward the back of the valley, because this is the best view of it that you're going to have unless you're part of a guided hike.

This is believed by many to be the original landing site of Polynesians inhabiting Molokaʻi (circa AD 650). There are some who say that visiting Halawa is like visiting another country, and in a lot of ways, they're right. This truly is the "old Hawaii" out here, a place where mythology, lore, nature, and people all commune in a way not found back in "modern society." The handful of residents who still inhabit this valley live a subsistence-based lifestyle which in many ways parallels that of their original ancestors. Electricity is scarce, and taro *loʻi* (fields) weave their way up the verdant valley floor.

© MARK DRIESSEN

Halawa Valley

Father Damien

HAWAII STATE ARCHIVES/PUBLIC DOMAIN/WIKIMEDIA COMMONS

MOLOKA'I

Father Damien with the Kalawao Girls Choir

By accident or miracle, Catholic priest Joseph de Veuster, Father Damien, came from Belgium to Hawaii. His brother, also a priest, was originally slated for the trip, but he became ill and Father Damien took his place. Damien spent several years on the Big Island of Hawaii, building churches and learning the language and ways of the people, before traveling to Kalaupapa in 1873.

What he saw touched his heart. Damien saw the lepers at Kalaupapa as children of God who deserved life and comfort. When they hid under a bush at his approach, he picked them up and stood them on their feet. He carried water to the sick and dying, bathed their wounds, and built them shelters with his own hands. When clothes or food or materials ran short, he walked topside to beg for more. Other church groups were against him and the government gave him little aid, but he persevered. Working long days alone, he collapsed exhausted at night.

Father Damien modified St. Philomena Church, originally built in Honolulu in 1872, and shipped it to Moloka'i in segments. He invited his charges inside, but those grossly afflicted could not control their mouths, so spittle would drip to the floor. They were ashamed to soil the church, so Damien cut squares in the floor through which they could spit onto the ground. Slowly, the authorities began to take notice. Damien eventually contracted leprosy himself, but he died in 1889 at age 49 knowing his people would be cared for. In 1936, Damien's native Belgium asked that his remains be returned. His body was exhumed and sent home, but a memorial still stands where he was once interred at Kalaupapa. After lengthy squabbles with the Belgian government, Father Damien's right hand was returned to Kalaupapa in 1995 and has been interred as a religious relic. He was beatified by Pope John Paul II in 1994 and canonized by Pope Benedict XVI in 2009.

The two beaches in Halawa Bay are suitable for swimming. The cove accessed by walking across the streambed offers more protection and a soft, sandy bottom. Other than snapping photos and walking barefoot down the beach, the main visitor attraction in Halawa Valley is taking part in a guided hike to Moa'ula Falls. Permits are stringently required for hiking, and conversing with the local guides is the best (and only) way to feel the *mana,* or strength of this valley.

Shopping

If your idea of a vacation well-spent is a day at the mall, jump off the ferry and start swimming back to Maui. Most shops on Moloka'i are utilitarian general stores, although there are some shops with worthy souvenirs.

KAUNAKAKAI

The good news about shopping in Kaunakakai is that you don't have to go far. All of the stores are on the same street, which means you can park your car on Ala Malama Avenue and use it as a base for scouring every shop in town.

As the name implies, **Imports Gift Shop** (82 Ala Malama Ave., 808/553-5734, 8am-6pm Mon.-Sat., 8am-1pm Sun.) offers a small selection of imported gifts and locally made items in addition to clothing, souvenirs, and snacks.

Kalele Bookstore and Divine Expressions (64 Ala Malama Ave., 808/553-5112, www.molokaispirit.com, 10am-5pm Mon.-Fri., 9am-2pm Sat.) offers not only books, but also locally crafted artwork, jewelry, wooden bowls, and even just advice on touring Moloka'i. It's an eclectic and worthwhile stop if you are killing time while in town.

Moloka'i Art from the Heart (64 Ala Malama Ave., 808/553-8018, www.molokaigallery.com, 10am-5pm Mon.-Fri., 9am-2:30pm Sat.) is a consignment boutique where over 136 local artists are able to showcase and sell their products. You can find anything in here from sarongs to CDs to original paintings. It's a great stop for supporting the local community.

Across the street, **Moloka'i Fish and Dive** (61 Ala Malama Ave., 808/553-5926, www.molokaifishanddive.com, 7:30am-6pm Mon.-Sat.,

8am-2pm Sun.) provides any basic gear you might need for the beach, as well as clothing, gear rentals, maps, or anything that has to do with a day in the sun.

Toward the wharf, upstairs from the American Savings Bank is **A Light from Heaven** (40 Ala Malama Ave., 808/553-3332, 9am-2pm Mon.-Sat.), a store specializing in any gear related to camping, hunting, fishing, or the outdoors.

On the more practical side, **Moloka'i Drugs** (28 Kamoi St., 808/553-5790, 8:45am-5:45pm Mon.-Fri., 8:45am-2pm Sat.) in the Kamoi Professional Center has you covered for any medicinal or prescription needs while on the island.

TOPSIDE

When it comes to shopping up on the topside of the island, there are only two options. Across the street from the Kualapu'u Cookhouse in the Kualapu'u Business Center is **Moloka'i Furniture and Denise's Gifts** (100 Kalae Hwy., 808/567-6083, 10am-4pm Mon.-Fri., 9am-2pm Sat.) which sells, as you might expect, fine wooden furniture as well as jewelry, women's clothing, and locally made crafts.

Adjoining the Coffees of Hawaii Espresso Bar across the street, the **Blue Monkey** (1630 Farrington Ave., 808/567-6776, 10am-4pm Mon.-Sat., 1pm-5pm Sun.) gift shop sells a fun-loving mix of everything from ukuleles to photography to handmade jewelry or hats.

WEST MOLOKA'I

With the 2008 closing of Moloka'i Ranch, a lot of Maunaloa businesses just up and closed with them. Given the commercial exodus from the western half of the island, the options for shopping are limited.

A Maunaloa staple which has been around since 1980, the **Big Wind Kite Factory** (120 Maunaloa Hwy., 808/552-2364, www.bigwindkites.com, 8:30am-5pm Mon.-Sat., 10am-2pm Sun.) is an eclectic hodgepodge of everything from handmade kites to woodwork from Bali. Plus, it's the only store left in this town, so by process of elimination it's well worth a look. The owner Jonathan is only too happy to give free factory tours of where the kites are made, help you fly a kite in the park, or even make a free kite for any children you may be toting along with you. The store also sports the largest collection of book titles found anywhere on the island. It's possible to visit this place four times over and still find something

new. Just look for the rainbow stairs in what little is left of downtown Maunaloa.

EAST MOLOKA'I

The pickings out here can be remarkably slim. If you need any basic item, general store **Mana'e Goods & Grindz** (mile marker 16 on Hwy. 450, 808/558-8498, 6:30am-4pm Mon.-Fri., 7:30am-4:30pm Sat.-Sun.) is your only option. Farther up the road toward Halawa Valley, you need to be in dire need to warrant shopping at the **Pu'u O Hoku Ranch Store.** Not that it's bad by any means, just that the selection can be random and thin. It's a good place to buy locally grown vegetables or free range beef cultivated right on the ranch. The store does have a few basic clothing items and some cold drinks if the midday heat is causing you to work up a sweat.

Entertainment

You know where most of the local people go to get their fix of nightlife? Las Vegas. After that it's Honolulu, then Maui. Most of the entertainment on Moloka'i is of the live music variety, and that usually means that it's going to be traditional island music played in a *kanikapila* style (island jam session, get-together, talk story,). Witnessing a live jam session can be captivating and a true island experience.

DAYTIME ENTERTAINMENT

While there can often be impromptu ukulele sessions which pop up during the weekdays on the porch outside of the **Coffees of Hawaii Espresso Bar** (1630 Farrington Ave., 6am-5pm Mon.-Fri., 8am-8pm Sat., 8am-5pm Sun.), Sunday afternoons are when things on this laid-back wooden deck get hopping. Hawaiian and contemporary music is played live 3pm-5pm, so this is the de facto social gathering for a late Sunday afternoon.

The **Kualapu'u Cookhouse** (102 Farrington

Ave., 808/567-9655, 7am-8pm Mon.-Sat., 9am-8pm Sun.) also has live music on Thursday afternoons at 5pm to accompany the weekly dinner specials.

EVENING SHOWS

The longest running and most iconic show on the island is the performance of Na Kupuna 4pm-6pm on Friday afternoons at **Hotel Moloka'i** (1300 Kamehameha V Hwy., 808/660-3397, www.hotelmolokai.com). *Kupuna* is a Hawaiian word meaning elder, and children are taught that *kupuna* are to be revered and treated with respect—something easy to do when it comes to the musical capabilities of the island's most well-known band. Sit out on the well-manicured grounds of the hotel and enjoy a mai tai or a Longboard Lager while listening to these guys play. They offer more than simply music; the personal anecdotes, humorous stories, and island-style banter that accompany the songs all combine to make a Na Kupuna performance the best evening on Moloka'i.

BARS

Even on sleepy Molokaʻi there is still "ladies night." Once the late afternoon ukulele performances are through and you feel like a few more beers, **Paddler's Inn** (10 Mohala St., 808/553-3300, 11:30am-11pm Mon.-Sun) is the closest thing that you're going to get to a sports bar or a dance hall on all of Molokaʻi. On the side of the highway in downtown Kaunakakai, you'll find this place with a couple of pool tables occupying the interior while a full-service bar sits in the outside lanai. There are live bands some nights of the week, top 40 music on others.

Other than Paddler's, the only other option in town is the bar at **Hotel Molokaʻi** (1300 Kamehameha V Hwy., 808/660-3397, www.hotelmolokai.com). While a kitchen fire closed the restaurant for 2013 and the bar currently closes early, once the restaurant reopens in 2014, the bar will be moved to the ocean side of the resort and potentially stay open until 2am. Inquire with the hotel about the current status.

Food

Kaunakakai has a varied selection of food. The same can't be said once you get outside town: there are only three restaurants outside the main drag.

KAUNAKAKAI
Local Style

As a restaurant, ⟨ **Kanemitsu Bakery** (79 Ala Malama Ave., 808/553-5855, 5:30am-6:30pm Tues.-Sun., $5-9) is no better or worse than anywhere else in town. Breakfast consists of fried eggs, spam, and rice, and lunch includes standard plate lunch fare such as chicken katsu or hamburger steak. All plate lunches are of course served with the staple sides of two-scoop rice and macaroni salad in an aging interior. The best part of this hole-in-the-wall eatery isn't the food that's served during the day, however, it's what comes hot out of the oven late at night. Like some sort of crazed drug fiend, once you've had a taste of Kanemitsu's famous "hot bread" you, too, will find yourself walking down the dark alleyway at 9 or 10pm to the back door of the shuttered restaurant. Here, assembled in the dark, a crowd of local people vie nightly for their fix of Kanemitsu's addictive hot bread, so much so that the dingy alleyway is simply known as "Hot Bread Lane." Taking a trip down Hot Bread Lane is one of the most authentic local experiences on the island.

On the corner of the Highway 450, **Molokaʻi Drive Inn** (857 Ala Malama Ave., 808/553-5655, 6am-10pm daily, $5-9) serves up budget, local-style meals for breakfast, lunch, and dinner. Lunch items such as chicken sandwiches, plate lunches, or any other of your moderately unhealthy but oh-so tasty local food options are also available.

American

After the kitchen fire that broke out at the Hula Shores Restaurant at Hotel Molokaʻi, ⟨ **Paddler's Inn** (10 Mohala St., 808/553-3300, 11:30am-9pm daily, $10-18) for the foreseeable future is about the only place you can go for dinner and also shoulder up to the bar. Strip steaks, rib plates, and salmon or mahimahi filets round out the entrée menu, and the Mexican Mondays are as close as you're going to get to Mexican food anywhere on Molokaʻi. This place has nightly music on the patio, pool tables inside, and good vibes all around.

Even sleepy Kaunakakai has to have its token burger joint, and the patties at **Molokaʻi Burger** (20 Kamehameha V Hwy., 808/553-3533, 7am-9pm daily, $5) don't disappoint. Little more than a drive-through shed right next door to Molokaʻi Pizza Café, this place has budget burgers big enough to properly fill you up. For a local treat, skip the bun and spring for a loco

MOLOKA'I

© KYLE ELLISON

Grab a plate lunch for a taste of local flavor.

moco, a hamburger patty served with two eggs, white rice, and gravy.

Natural Foods

If you're in need of a little health in your diet after all of the plate lunches and spam musubis, **Outpost Natural Foods** (70 Makaena Pl., 808/553-3377, 9am-6pm Sun.-Fri.) offers a basic selection of fresh produce, energy bars, bulk grains, healthy lunch options, or a cold drink. This is also a great place to pick up some all-natural ginger candies for what is usually a stomach-churning ferry ride back to Maui.

Pizza

The undisputed place where Moloka'i heads for a slice is **Moloka'i Pizza Café** (15 Kaunakakai Pl., 808/553-3288, 10am-10pm Mon.-Thurs., 10am-11pm Fri.-Sat., 11am-10pm Sun., $10-16), in the last building before you start heading down the road to the ferry dock. Pizzas are served either whole or by the slice ($2.50). There's also a decent selection of pasta dishes.

Filipino

Big Daddy's (67 Ala Malama Ave., 808/553-5841, 8am-6pm daily, under $9) along the main strip of Ala Malama serves a variety of inexpensive Filipino food and Hawaiian fare, in addition to the eggs and omelets for breakfast and local-style plate lunches. Next door is Big Daddy's Market for a limited selection of groceries, some prepared foods, and a few true Filipino delicacies such as *balut*.

Coffee Shop

Anyone visiting **Tiki's Coffee Shack** (35 Mohala St., 808/553-3488, 6:30am-6pm Mon.-Fri., 8am-2pm Sat., 9am-noon Sun., $6-10) will find a casual blend of metropolitan sophistication with the laid-back island flavor of Moloka'i. Relax in the downtown parlor with free Wi-Fi while sipping on coffee grown just up the road in Kualapu'u. Gourmet sandwiches and paninis are popular lunch items with as many ingredients as possible sourced here on island.

MOLOKA'I

Markets

Given the lackluster evening activities on the island, there's a joke among locals that if you're looking for a place to hang out at night just go down to the **Friendly Market** (Ala Malama Ave., 8:30am-8:30pm Mon.-Fri. 8:30am-6:30pm Sat.), because everyone is going to be there anyway. It's stays open later than most places on the island.

If for some reason the Friendly Market doesn't have what you need, then **Misaki's Groceries and Dry Goods** (Ala Malama Ave., 8:30am-8:30pm Mon.-Sat., 9am-noon Sun.) a few doors down should be able to fill the gap.

FARMERS MARKET

If you're in town on Saturday morning, visit the **farmers market** held 7am-noon on the sidewalk in front of the bank buildings for local produce and craft items. This seems as much of a social event as a shopping exercise for locally grown food.

TOPSIDE
Local Style

The biggest culinary staple on the topside of the island, **(Kualapu'u Cookhouse** (1700 Farrington Ave., 808/567-9655, 7am-2pm Mon., 7am-8pm Tues.-Sat., 9am-2pm Sun., $8-11) is a plate-lunch institution where the going is easy and life moves nice and slow. Order inside at the drab counter, but go ahead and sit outside on the open-air lanai. When your food is ready, that's when you're going to get it. No sooner. No later. No worries. Try the chicken katsu or hamburger steak. Live Hawaiian music on Thursday evenings at 5pm fills out the area's lone entertainment, and on Thursdays it isn't uncommon to have a prime rib special suddenly spring on to the menu.

Coffee Shop

Although the Coffees of Hawaii plantation used to have a bustling operation that included tours of the plantation and the coffee making process, all that remains now is the **Coffees of Hawaii Espresso Bar** (1630 Farrington Ave., 6am-5pm Mon.-Fri., 8am-8pm Sat., 8am-5pm Sun.) and the self-guided informative tour on the outdoor deck. By process of elimination this is the happening spot to grab a coffee, mocha, guava pretzel, baked item, ice cream, or any other sort of snack you could possibly be craving. The coffee here is grown right across the street, and the sprawling front porch has been known to host impromptu ukulele jam sessions among the affable island locals.

WEST MOLOKA'I
Maunaloa General Store

The good news when it comes to finding food in western Moloka'i is that you don't have to think hard about where you want to go. To be fair, even the **Maunaloa General Store** (200 Maunaloa Hwy., 808/552-2346, 9am-6pm Mon.-Sat., 9am-12pm Sun.) is a stretch in that it's just a supermarket. With the Moloka'i Ranch having shuttered its operations, there's nothing on this side of the island which could be considered an actual restaurant, but if you want to put together a picnic for the beach, then the general store will more than suffice.

EAST MOLOKA'I

The only restaurant on the east end, the **(Mana'e Goods & Grindz** (mile marker 16 on Hwy. 450, 808/558-8498, 6:30am-4pm Mon.-Fri., 7:30am-4:30pm Sat.-Sun., $6-9) takeout window which accompanies the general store serves up everything from chicken katsu plates to freshly made fruit smoothies. If the banana pancakes happen to be on the menu, don't even hesitate. Just order them.

Getting There and Around

GETTING THERE

Plane

When flying to Moloka'i there are two things you shouldn't expect: a big plane and a smooth ride. Most airlines employ either 9- or 37-seat aircraft vulnerable to the brisk trade winds, although what the flights lack in size they make up for in scenery. Often flights from Maui will treat visitors to views of Moloka'i's dramatic northern sea cliffs as well as aerial views of the Kalaupapa Peninsula. Sit on the left side of the aircraft for the best chance of waterfall photography and coastal views.

Mokulele Airlines (808/567-6381 Moloka'i or 866/260-7070 toll free, www.mokuleleairlines.com) offers direct flights to Honolulu and Kahului, although any other city will require a connecting flight. **Pacific Wings** (808/567-6381 or 888/575-4546 toll free, www.pacificwings.com) offers direct flights from Honolulu and Kahului to Ho'olehua and can also provide connecting service to cities farther afield. In addition to providing direct service to Kahului and Honolulu, **Island Air** (808/567-6840 Moloka'i or 800/652-6541 toll free, www.islandair.com) is the only commercial airline also offering direct service between Ho'olehua and the island of Lana'i. Island Air employs the largest airplanes and is less likely to be fully booked.

For private flightseeing and helicopter flights, **Makani Kai Air Charters** (808/834-5813 or 877/255-8532, www.makanikaiair.com) operates between Moloka'i, Lana'i, and O'ahu, and also has service between Kalaupapa and Ho'olehua. **Kukui Air** (808/558-8407, www.kukuiair.com) focuses exclusively on Moloka'i and runs hour-long scenic flights departing out of Ho'olehua Airport.

Moloka'i Airport

The airport at Ho'olehua is a small, open-air facility where you still walk out on the runway to board your plane. It's a throwback to what the larger airports of Kahului and Kona once were. Here in Ho'olehua many airlines still opt for calling roll by first-name rather than handing out tickets. There is one small gift shop and a small coffee shop selling snacks and locally grown coffee, though I wouldn't plan on showing up three hours before my flight and having many things to do. There is an Alamo rental car counter at the terminal, taxis patrol outside, and tour companies all offer pickup for those arriving with a previously scheduled reservation.

FERRY

Compared to flights from Kahului, the **Moloka'i Ferry** (877/500-6284, www.molokaiferry.com) is slightly less expensive, but takes longer. Due to a recent approval of a fuel surcharge, one-way fares are now $64 for adults and $32 for children. Usually discounts can be found when buying tickets in batches of six.

The ferry is a more economical option when traveling with children and allows you to bring on more luggage. Running twice daily between Kahului and Kaunakakai Harbors, the boat most often used is the *Moloka'i Princess*, a 100-foot-long, two-story vessel capable of navigating the brutally rough Pailolo Channel, a name that directly translates to "crazy fisherman" in reference to those who voluntarily head out into the channel. The ride takes 1.25 hours and may be rough, but it's safe and it will get you there. Ferries depart from Kaunakakai Monday-Saturday at 5:15am and 4pm, with Lahaina departures running Monday-Saturday at 7:15am and 6pm. A Sunday crossing departs Moloka'i for Lahaina at 4pm and departs Lahaina for Moloka'i at 6pm.

Rental cars can be combined with a round-trip ferry ticket through the **Moloka'i Ferry** (877/500-6284, www.molokaiferry.com) Cruise and Car Package with a shuttle transporting you from the Kaunakakai Wharf to your rental vehicle. Rates run $245 for a driver 25 years of age or older, and $145 for each

MOLOKA'I

additional adult. Children are $55 from 4-12 and under 4 is free.

Moloka'i Outdoors (808/553-4477, www.molokai-outdoors.com) also offers an Ali'i Tour package which includes a round-trip ferry ticket from Maui and a six-hour guided tour in an air-conditioned van once on the island. Rates for adults are $190 and $127 for children.

GETTING AROUND
Car Rental
The only rental car agency with a booth in the airport is **Alamo** (808/567-6381 or 888/826-6893 toll free, www.alamo.com, 6am-8pm daily), which also has the largest fleet of cars on the island. For those staying a minimum of three days, **Moloka'i Outdoors** (808/553-4477, www.molokai-outdoors.com) rents SUVs, cars, and vans, and can provide cheaper rates for extended stays. If you've taken the ferry, check the Cruise and Car Package deal offered by the **Moloka'i Ferry** (877/500-6284, www.molokai-ferry.com).

Gas
There are only two gas stations on the island—right next to each other in Kaunakakai. Be sure you have at least half a tank of fuel before heading out on an adventurous day trip to Halawa or Papohaku. **Rawlins Chevron** (Hwy. 450 and Kaunakakai Pl., 6:30am-8:30pm Mon.-Thurs., 6:30am-9pm Fri.-Sat., 6:30am-6pm Sun.) has longer hours and more supplies, though it still will cost you at least $0.75 more per gallon than back on Maui.

Taxi
Best known as a conduit between the airport, ferry, and wherever it is you're staying, **Hele Mai Taxi** (808/336-0937 or 808/646-9060, www.molokaitaxi.com) also offers private tours of the island and will get you wherever you need to go 24 hours a day, seven days a week. Also available is **Mid-Nite Taxi** (808/658-1410 or 808/553-5652), although the service can be a little spottier at times.

Shuttle Bus
The closest thing to public transportation on all of Moloka'i, the **MEO public shuttle bus** operates three routes throughout the island at times just frequent enough to make it convenient. Service in Kaunakakai originates in front of Misaki's Market on Ala Malama Street and runs six times daily to Maunaloa and eight times daily to Puko'o in East Moloka'i. Along the routes the driver will usually let you stop off wherever you please. Though the service is technically free, donations to keep the shuttle going are graciously accepted. Exact schedules can be found by visiting http://meoinc.charityfinders.org.

Tours
Moloka'i Outdoors (808/553-4477, www.molokai-outdoors.com) offers an Island Tour package which scours the island from Halawa Lookout all the way to Papohaku Beach. Operating three times per week, these tours cover the island in an air-conditioned van and usually carry a small group of only 4-8 people. Rates for the island tour run $150 for adults and $78 for children.

WHERE TO STAY ON MAUI, LANA'I, AND MOLOKA'I

West Maui

KAPALUA, NAPILI, AND HONOKOWAI
Over $150

The largest, most well-known resort on the northwestern side of the island is the lavish **Ritz-Carlton Kapalua** (1 Ritz-Carlton Dr., 808/669-6200 www.ritzcarlton.com, $400), an exquisitely manicured luxury resort set back from D.T. Fleming Beach. The resort offers what you've come to expect of a Ritz-Carlton, and there are also a number of cultural and environmental programs such as the acclaimed Ambassadors of the Environment. While it can often be windy and wet here, many of the showers pass quickly, although it is still wetter than downtown Lahaina. Rates begin around $400 and work their way up from there.

Condominiums

Occupying much of the point between Napili and Kapalua Bays, the **☾ Napili Kai Beach Resort** (5900 Lower Honoapi'ilani Rd., 808/669-6271, www.napilikai.com, $270-500) is a West Side classic that offers individually owned condos in a family-friendly resort setting. Since the rooms are pricey, this is a great option for families whose goal is to largely stay in one place and do little more than play on

Where to Stay in West Maui

Name	Type	Price
'Aina Nalu Resort	condo	$285-400
Camp Olowalu	camping	$15
Garden Gate B&B	B&B	$119-169
Ho'oilo House	B&B	$329
Hyatt Regency	resort	$375-900
🌙 Ka'anapali Beach Hotel	hotel	$165-325
Kahana Falls	condo	$99-250
Lahaina Shores Beach Resort	condo	$225-300
Makai Inn	inn	$110-190
Maui Eldorado	condo	$199-369
Maui Kai	condo	$200-400
🌙 Napili Kai Beach Resort	condo	$270-500
Napili Village	condo	$99-149
Pioneer Inn	hotel	$159-200
🌙 Plantation Inn	B&B	$158-265
🌙 Puamana	condo	$200-600
Ritz-Carlton Kapalua Resort	resort	$400-999
Royal Lahaina	hotel	$189-550
Sheraton Maui	resort	$400-700

the beach. There is a miniature putting course, multiple swimming pools, and a weekly mai tai party. The Sea House restaurant has one of the best breakfasts and happy hours on the island. Many of the units have been recently renovated and are the nicest they've ever been.

If the price of the Napili Kai is too steep, yet you still want to be on Napili Bay, the **Napili Village** (5425 Lower Honoapi'ilani, 808/669-6228, www.napilivillage.com, $149) offers condos within walking distance that are the best value in Napili. Rates can be as low as $99/night during slower seasons of the year (but are regularly $149), and these studios and one-bedroom apartments include air-conditioning, maid service, and full kitchens for those who want to cook their own meals. The rooms aren't as luxurious as some of the other options on the beach, but it's hard to argue with the price for being steps from Napili Bay.

In Kahana, **Kahana Falls** (4260 Lower Honoapi'ilani Rd., 808/669-1050, www.the-sandsofkahana.com, $99-250) is one of the largest complexes in the area and features a large fitness center, spacious rooms, and hot tubs with sandy bottoms. It's only a five-minute drive to Napili or Kapalua Bay, and the small beach at Pohaku Beach Park is walking distance away.

In Honokowai, the **Maui Kai** (106 Ka'anapali Shores Pl., 808/667-3500, www.mauikai.com, $200-400) is at the edge of Honokowai and Ka'anapali, so it's possible to take a long morning stroll down the beach to the center of the Ka'anapali strip. All units have full kitchens, free parking, free Wi-Fi, gas barbecues, and the convenience of being just steps from the beach. This is a good place for families who want to base themselves near Ka'anapali but save a few dollars from the steep resort prices.

Features	Why Stay Here?	Best Fit For
pool, kitchen	location	couples
restrooms, oceanfront	location, affordable	budget travelers
gardens, breakfast	location, quiet	couples, solo travelers
pool, breakfast	quiet, view	couples, honeymooners
waterslides, oceanfront	location, pools	families
free hula show	location	families, couples
fitness center, hot tub	amenities	families, couples
pool, oceanfront	location	couples
oceanfront, gardens	location, affordable	budget travelers
kitchens, golf	location	families, couples
kitchens, oceanfront	location	families, couples
pool, oceanfront	full amenities	families, couples
oceanfront	location, price	families, couples
garden, pool	location	couples, budget travelers
pool, breakfast	location, quiet	couples, honeymooners
pool, oceanfront	location, quiet	families, couples
golf, spa	full-service resort	luxury-lovers, honeymooners
oceanfront, tennis	location	couples
pool, oceanfront	full-service resort	families, honeymooners

KA'ANAPALI
Over $150

All hotels in the Ka'anapali resort fit in the luxury category.

As their slogan says, **◖ Ka'anapali Beach Hotel** (2525 Ka'anapali Pkwy., 808/661-0011, www.kbhmaui.com, $165-325) is truly Maui's most Hawaiian hotel. A genuine feeling of aloha permeates this laid-back resort, and while nowhere near as lavish as its fellow Ka'anapali neighbors, KBH occupies prime oceanfront real estate a two-minute stroll from Pu'u Keka'a (Black Rock). The open lawn is the perfect place to relax in the shade of an *ulu* tree, and while there is no hot tub, there is a swimming pool next to the popular tiki bar which is a welcoming place for families. On the lawn, there is an outrigger sailing canoe crafted by the employees of the resort, and free hula shows are held each night on the hotel's outdoor stage. Guests are made to feel like *ohana,* and the rates are much more affordable than larger resorts along the strip.

Right in front of Pu'u Keka'a is the 510-room **Sheraton Maui Resort** (2605 Ka'anapali Pkwy., 808/661-0031, www.sheraton-maui.com, $400-700), the original Ka'anapali resort which celebrated its 50th anniversary in 2013. This luxurious beach resort is tucked into the sacred cliff face, and despite being the "oldest" hotel on the strip (though renovated numerous times), the Sheraton doesn't skimp on any of the modern amenities. There is a large oceanfront pool, tennis courts, spacious rooms, and a spa. A few of the rooms are set on top of the legendary Ka'anapali promontory.

On the far southern end of the Ka'anapali strip is the **Hyatt Regency** (200 Nohea Kai Dr., 808/661-1234, www.maui.hyatt.com,

© KYLE ELLISON

Napili Kai Beach Resort

$375), listed here for having the best pool system in all of Ka'anapali. This is a favorite of families who want to spend the day by the pool and the best place along the strip to grab a drink from a bar tucked behind a waterfall or ride down a twisting waterslide. This southern end of the beach is also sheltered from the afternoon trade winds, although the sand immediately in front of the resort has been steadily eroding for years. Rates begin around $375 and work their way up depending on view and size.

The **Royal Lahaina** (2780 Keka'a Dr., 808/661-3611 www.royallahaina.com, $189-over 500), on the northern side of Pu'u Keka'a offers rooms for tighter budgets. Rates can begin as low as $189 for a standard room. In addition to the oceanfront tower there are a number of individual cottages scattered around the property, where the Ka'anapali golf course runs right through the resort. A little more laid-back than some of the glitzier resorts, this is one of Ka'anapali's best oceanfront values.

Condominiums

While there are a handful of condos in Ka'anapali, one of the best values is the **Maui Eldorado** (2661 Keka'a Dr., 808/661-0021, www.outrigger.com, $199-369), managed by Outrigger Resorts. The condos are only a three-minute walk to the beach but don't have the prices of an oceanfront resort. Plus, you can cook your own meals. The golf course cuts right through the property, there are a number of small swimming pools, and discounts are fairly common.

LAHAINA

While there are no large resorts in Lahaina, the town's accommodations range from historic inns and modern condos to a handful of budget options.

$100-150

The **Pioneer Inn** (658 Wharf St., 808/661-3636, www.pioneerinnmaui.com, $159-175, suites $165-200) is the oldest hotel on Maui still accommodating guests, and it was the only hotel in West Maui until 1963. Now a Best Western hotel, the P.I. is across the street from Lahaina Harbor and right in the center of the action. Food, drinks, and live music are served downstairs at the popular local bar.

On the northern end of the town, one of Lahaina's most basic but affordable oceanfront accommodations is the **Makai Inn** (1415 Front St., 808/870-9004, www.makaiinn.net, $110-190), an old concrete apartment building which was turned into vacation rentals. The garden setting is surprisingly pleasing, oceanfront rooms have their own private lanai, and you're right on the water for watching for the sunset either from your balcony or the inn's open courtyard. Rates are affordable considering you're on the oceanfront, and this laid-back Hawaiian setting is a practical option for basing yourself near Lahaina.

Bed-and-Breakfasts
Couples looking for a romantic retreat will love the **(Plantation Inn** (174 Lahainaluna Rd., 808/667-9225, www.theplantationinn. com, $158-265), a hidden little pocket of calm in otherwise frantic Lahaina. On Lahainaluna Road just a one-minute walk from Front Street, this 19-room getaway has a swimming pool, free parking, free Wi-Fi, and daily maid service, and manages to retain its 19th-centuy charm. Breakfast is served daily until 9:30am and features French-inspired cuisine from chef Gerard Reversade, whose acclaimed restaurant on the same property gives hotel guests a discount.

The **Garden Gate Bed and Breakfast** (67 Kaniau Rd., 808/661-8800, www.gardengatebb.com, $119-169) set between Lahaina and Ka'anapali in a quiet, residential area. All of the rooms are comfortable and well worth the price considering the cost of lodging in Lahaina. Breakfast is often served on the lanai, although not on Sunday.

Condominiums
Right on the water by 505 Front Street, the **Lahaina Shores Beach Resort** (475 Front St., 808/661-4835 or 800/642-6284, www.

lahainashores.com, $225-300) is a six-story condo with individually owned units which has just undergone a major renovation. This is a convenient base for those who want to take a surf lesson, stroll down the beach, access Lahaina Harbor, or be walking distance from town. Rates vary considerably, but most studios and once bedrooms will be $300 and under.

Smack in the center of town a block off Front Street is the 188-room **'Aina Nalu Resort** (660 Waine'e St., 800/367-5226, fax 808/661-3733, www.outriggercondominiums.com, $285-400), a modern condo complex in a garden atmosphere that has the benefit of being right in town. Rooms are spacious and recently renovated, and a swimming pool provides a respite from the heat.

While the above two options are perfectly acceptable, the best condo complex in Lahaina is **(Puamana**, a 28-acre private community on the southern edge of town. There is a sandy beach in front of the complex good for swimming, and a luxurious pool sits out on a point surrounded by the ocean. There are tennis courts and a beautiful old clubhouse. It's just a 10-minute stroll into downtown Lahaina. Oceanfront rentals are much nicer than those along the highway, and reservations are available through various West Side rental agents such as www.puamanavacations.com.

SOUTH OF LAHAINA
Bed-and-Breakfasts
Set in the residential community of Launiupoko above the beach park by the same name, the **Ho'oilo House** (138 Awaiku St., 808/667-6669, www.hooilohouse.com, $329) is one of the most luxurious B&Bs on the island's West Side. The views from this vantage point are out toward Lana'i and offer panoramic sunset views on a nightly basis. Everything about this house, from its Thai-inspired architecture to its furnishings and outdoor garden area, says comfort and relaxation. Six suites are decorated in unique style, a continental breakfast is served daily, and guests can make use of the swimming pool and lounge area with a view over the water. There is a three-night minimum, and only two adults per room.

Central Maui

If the vision you've always had of your Maui vacation was a luxurious resort on a world-famous beach, you'll be disappointed if you stay in Central Maui. Most of the options here are of the budget variety, and while the Old Wailuku Inn has some privacy and charm, all other options are utilitarian, cheap, and frequented by travelers who simply need a shower and four walls. If your main reason for being in Maui is to explore the island, you'll be happy to stay in Central Maui so you can save your dollars for activities and adventure.

WAILUKU
Hostels

The most affordable places to stay in Wailuku are the two hostels in the funkier, older part of town. While they are by no means a beach resort, they are practical, centrally located, and provide an affordable base for exploring the island. All hostel guests must display a valid passport and ticket off the island as a prerequisite for booking a bed.

If you're on a budget, the (**Banana Bungalow** (310 N. Market St., 808/244-5090, www.mauihostel.com, $32-98) offers free adventures around the island. While it's expected that you tip the guides, tours to Hana, Haleakala, 'Iao Valley, Pa'ia, or Little Beach just for the cost of a tip are a nice perk. The rooms are clean and basic (there are private as well as shared dorm rooms) and the garden surroundings are relaxing, but the hostel is in an unattractive part of the island and can often be a party scene (although "quiet hours" go into effect at 10pm). Rates range from $32/night for a dorm bed to $75/night for a private single, $84 for a double, and $98 for a triple. Linens are included, towels aren't, and surfers are always welcome.

Closer to the center of Wailuku is **Northshore Hostel** (2080 W. Vineyard St., 808/986-8095, www.northshorehostel.com, $29-89), which is great if you're looking to be centrally located, save some cash, and get some sleep. The rooms are clean, there is free breakfast, free Wi-Fi, free airport transfers, free shuttles to Kanaha Beach, and linens are included. There aren't any private bathrooms, but the rates are reasonable at only $29/night for a dorm bed and $69-89 for a private room. While Vineyard Street is a funky and slow-going part

Where to Stay in Central Maui

Name	Type	Price
(Banana Bungalow	Hostel	$32-98
Courtyard Marriott	Hotel	$200-250
Maui Beach Hotel	Hotel	$89-150
Maui Seaside Hotel	Hotel	$105-129
Northshore Hostel	Hostel	$29-89
(Old Wailuku Inn at Ulupono	B&B	$165-190

of town, you can't argue with the price for a clean, safe, and welcoming place.

Bed-and-Breakfasts

The nicest place to stay in Wailuku is the **Old Wailuku Inn at Ulupono** (2199 Kahoʻokele St., 808/244-5897, www.maui-inn.com, $165-190), built in 1924 and listed on the Hawaii Register of Historic Places. The 10 rooms are filled with period furniture that evokes the feeling of grandma's house. Although it sounds like a slogan, this truly is Maui's most Hawaiian bed-and-breakfast. Free Wi-Fi is available, and each room has a private bath. A filling gourmet breakfast is served at 8am. There is a two-night minimum stay and most rooms are set up for double occupancy.

KAHULUI
Under $100

You would figure a hotel with the name **Maui Beach Hotel** (170 Kaʻahumanu Ave., 808/954-7421, www.mauibeachhotel.net, $89) would be the epitome of paradise. It's a hotel, on Maui, on the beach. What else could you need? The reality, however, is that the beach is on the inside of Kahului Harbor and you're in an industrial part of town. At $89 for a standard room, however, the price is right, and there is free Internet, a free airport shuttle, and a $5 parking fee.

$100-150

In the same area is the 200-room **Maui Seaside Hotel** (100 W. Kaʻahumanu Ave., 808/877-3311, www.mauiseasidehotel.com, $105-129), which is of the same older ilk as its neighbor. There is a swimming pool in the central courtyard, access to the beach, and continental breakfast. While more motel-like than its neighbor, the Maui Seaside is clean and well cared for. This is a utilitarian yet affordable option for basing yourself in the center of the island.

Over $150

The **Courtyard Marriott** (532 Keolani Pl., 808/871-1800, $200) is the newest and nicest hotel in Kahului. Granted, it's just an airport hotel, but if that's what you're looking for, then this is your best option. Rates that hover around $200/night are expensive for a view of Costco. Nevertheless, the hotel is modern, new, and conveniently located near the North Shore as well as the airport. There is also a large swimming pool, a fitness room, and a trendy bistro, although there is a $10 parking fee if traveling with your own car.

Features	Why Stay Here?	Best Fit For
free tours	affordable	budget travelers
modern fitness room, swimming pool	location	business travelers
airport shuttle	affordable	budget travelers
swimming pool	affordable	budget travelers
quiet	affordable	budget travelers
breakfast, quiet	historic	couples

South Maui

South Maui is the island's sunniest area and one of its most popular tourist zones. Ma'alaea and Kihei are dominated by condos with few hotels or cottages. Wailea offers the island's most luxurious resorts, although there are still some moderately priced condos. In the deep south, Makena has one of the island's most affordable resorts as well as some oceanfront condos.

MA'ALAEA

The only accommodations in Ma'alaea are condos, all of which are found along Hauoli Street.

The benefits of staying in Ma'alaea inlcude the central location, walking distance to Ma'alaea Harbor, the ability to cook your own meals, and some of the most affordable ocean views on the island. **Maalaea Bay Rentals** (808/244-5627, 808/244-7012, or 800/367-6084, www.maalaeabay.com) has an office at the Hono Kai Resort (280 Hauoli St., Ma'alaea) and handles more than 140 units in a majority of the condos along this road. All units are fully furnished with complete kitchens, TVs, telephones, and a lanai, and each property has a pool and laundry

Where to Stay in South Maui

Name	Type	Price
Aston Maui Hill	condo	$165-400
Aston Maui Lu	hotel	$119-232
Days Inn	hotel	$83-250
€€ Fairmont Kea Lani	resort	$550-1,200
Four Seasons Resort	resort	$600-1,500
Grand Wailea	resort	$564-1,200
Hale Pau Hana	condo	$240-350
Hotel Wailea	hotel	$359-500
Maalaea Bay Rentals	condo	$100-300
€€ Makena Beach and Golf Resort	resort	$210-600
Makena Surf	condo	$600-800
Mana Kai Maui	condo	$240-500
€€ Maui Coast Hotel	hotel	$169-275
Maui Sunseeker	LGBT resort	$120-190
Maui Vista	condo	$189-280
Menehune Shores	condo	$150-310
Nona Lani Cottages	cottages	$150
Sugar Beach Resort	condo	$150-425
Wailea Beach Marriott	resort	$340-550
Wailea Beach Villas	condo	$700-1,500
€€ Wailea Ekolu Village	condo	260-$350

facilities. Rates range from $150-300 mid-December-mid-April, but summer and fall rates can be as low as $100. Many of the condos have a three-night minimum, or longer during the Christmas holidays. For monthly stays, rates are reduced by 10 percent.

KIHEI
Under $150

Set in an old coconut grove, the **Aston Maui Lu** (575 S. Kihei Rd., 808/879-5881, www.astonmauilu.com, $119-232), is an older 28-acre property at the north end of Kihei. The Maui Lu is not designed as an ordinary hotel—it looks more like condo units—but none of the rooms have a kitchen. All include TV, air-conditioning, refrigerator, and daily maid service, while other amenities include an activities desk, tennis courts, a Maui-shaped swimming pool, two small beaches, and free Wi-Fi in the lobby. Room prices vary according to season. Special rates as low as $99 are sometimes available, and you can find discounts for longer stays.

The most affordable hotel option in South Kihei is the **Days Inn** (2980 S. Kihei Rd., 808/879-7744, www.daysinn.com, $83-200), which sits on the north end of Keawakapu Beach. Rooms are small, there is air-conditioning and a small refrigerator, and while it might be basic, it's tough to argue with the price, considering the location. There is free Wi-Fi,

Features	Why Stay Here?	Best Fit For
pool, kitchen	location, amenities	couples, families
pool, quiet	affordable	budget travelers
oceanfront, barbecue	affordable, location	budget travelers
pool, oceanfront	romantic, luxury	families, couples, honeymooners
pools, spa, oceanfront	romantic, luxury	couples, honeymooners, luxury-lovers
waterslides, spa, oceanfront	romantic, luxury, pools	families, couples, honeymooners
oceanfront, kitchen	location, amenities	couples, families
pool, spa, amenities	boutique, romantic	couples, luxury-lovers
pool, kitchen, laundry	location, ocean view	families, extended stay
pool, activities, oceanfront	location, great value	couples, families, honeymooners
oceanfront, kitchen	location, luxury	families, couples
kitchen, oceanfront	location, water sports	couples, families
pool, fitness center, shuttle	full amenities	couples, business travel
kitchenette, hot tub	quiet, location	couples
pool, tennis, kitchen	location, practical	couples, families
pool, lanai, oceanfront	affordable	couples
gardens, kitchenette	quiet, affordable, location	couples
pool, spa, kitchen	oceanfront	couples, families
pool, spa, luau	oceanfront, watersports	families, couples
pool, oceanfront	romantic, luxury	luxury-lovers
kitchen, amenities	location, affordable	couples, families

free parking, and outdoor grills. As expected, oceanfront suites can stretch upward to $250.

Over $150

On the northern edge of South Kihei is the ▐ **Maui Coast Hotel** (2259 S. Kihei Rd., 808/874-6284, www.mauicoasthotel.com, $169), a 265-room high-rise hotel a three-minute walk from the beach. You'll find tennis courts, a fitness room, and a swimming pool. Rooms have free Wi-Fi and air-conditioning. There is free parking, as well as a free resort shuttle for transport around the South Kihei and Wailea area. Rates begin at around $169, although there are frequently a number of specials including AAA discounts and weekly rates. There is also a $17.50 resort fee.

Condominiums

One of the several condos at the far north end of Kihei is **Sugar Beach Resort** (145 N. Kihei Rd. 808/879-2778, www.crhmaui.com, $150-425), an oceanfront building with individually owned units as well as a swimming pool, spa, and sundries shop. Rates often vary depending upon the rental agency and time of year.

Across from the south end of Mai Poina 'Oe Ia'u Beach Park is the **Maui Sunseeker** (551 S. Kihei Rd., 808/879-1261, www.mauisunseeker.com, $120-190) resort, a gay-friendly, adult-only property featuring 16 rooms in a small and quiet setting. A sundeck with a hot tub is on the roof, there are kitchenettes in the rooms, and laundry facilities are available on-site.

Menehune Shores (760 S. Kihei Rd., 808/879-3428, www.menehunereservations.com, $200-310) is a huge, family-oriented, and moderately priced high-rise condo on the beach overlooking an ancient fishpond. All units have an ocean view, and although the ocean swimming is poor, there is a swimming pool. Rates range from $150-275 during slower season and $200-310 in the high season. There is a three-night minimum and discounts for longer stays. This is an affordable setting just slightly removed from town.

Sandwiched between the Cove and Kamaole I, **Maui Vista** (2191 S. Kihei Rd., 808/879-7966, www.mauivistacondo.com, $210-230) is a 10-acre condo complex on the *mauka* side of South Kihei Road. There are three swimming pools, six tennis courts, and barbecue grills, and most rooms have kitchens and air-conditioning. Units are individually owned, so rates vary, but expect studios which are $189, one-bedroom suites $210-230, and two-bedroom suites $280.

Right on the sands of Kamaole II, the **Hale Pau Hana** (2480 S. Kihei Rd., 808/879-2715, www.hphresort.com, $240-350) is one of the best options for condos right on the water. There is free parking, free Internet, grilling facilities, a full kitchen, a swimming pool, and a private lanai in each room. Rates vary by season. This is a good location in a happening part of town.

Within walking distance of Kamaole III, Kihei Boat Ramp, and Keawakapu Beach is the **Aston Maui Hill** (2881 S. Kihei Rd., 808/879-6321, www.astonmauihill.com, $165-400), an upbeat condo with a Spanish motif. This quality condo resort sits high on a hill and is a nice alternative to expensive Wailea. There is a tennis court, swimming pool, putting green, and Wi-Fi, and each room comes equipped with a kitchen.

Closer to the water, the eight-story **Mana Kai Maui** (2960 S. Kihei Rd., 808/879-1561, www.manakaimaui.com, $240-500), offers the nicest resort accommodations in South Kihei. This 50-unit complex is on the north end of Keawakapu Beach and offers snorkeling and water activities right out the front door. The Five Palms restaurant is one of Kihei's best, or there are full kitchens for those who would rather cook. Expect rates of $240 for a standard hotel room to $500 for suites with private balconies.

Cottages

Cottages provide an affordable charm not found at large condos or hotels. On the north end of Kihei, **Nona Lani Cottages** (455 S. Kihei Rd., 808/879-2497 www.nonalanicottages.com, $150) has eight cottages in a garden setting across the street from the beach.

The property has a refreshing throwback to the simpler times of yesteryear. There is an Internet surcharge.

WAILEA
Over $150
Wailea hotels are expensive, fancy, and meant to provide indulgence. The northernmost of the Wailea resorts is **The Wailea Beach Marriott** (3700 Wailea Alanui Dr., 808/879-1922, www. marriott.com, $340), a 497-room oceanfront resort that is the oldest in Wailea (although it's been extensively restored). Families will enjoy the large system of pools, and the snorkeling and sand of Ulua Beach is only a few steps away. Parking is $25/day, Internet is $15/day, and rates begin around $340 during the slower seasons of the year.

Not far from the Marriott are the ultra-luxurious **Wailea Beach Villas** (3800 Wailea Alanui Dr., 808/891-4500, www.drhmaui. com, $850), directly fronting the beach and steps from the Shops at Wailea. Grab a private cabana overlooking the shoreline, relax in the oceanfront infinity pool, and bask in the aura of extravagant luxury at Wailea's nicest accommodations. Parking is free of charge, although as you can imagine, these rooms don't come cheap.

Directly in front of Wailea Beach are two of Wailea's largest resorts, the sprawling, pink **Grand Wailea** (3850 Wailea Alanui Dr., 808/875-1234, www.grandwailea.com, $565) and the ultra-luxurious **Four Seasons Resort** (3900 Wailea Alanui Dr., 808/874-8000, www. fourseasons.com, $600). While both resorts offer the highest quality, the Grand Wailea is famous for its pool system. Families will enjoy navigating the waterslides, rope swings, and the water elevator. Next door, at the Four Seasons, the pool scene is much more reserved, but the cream villas looking out over the water redefine island luxury. Rooms are expensive and amenities lavish.

Around the southern end of Wailea Point are the twirling white spires of the **☾ Fairmont Kea Lani** (4100 Wailea Alanui, 808/875-4100, www.fairmont.com, $550). Located on the sands of Polo Beach, the property has undergone extensive renovations and appears nicer now than ever before. Each room is arranged like a one-bedroom suite, and the resort is involved in a number of ecoconscious initiatives to help protect the island environment. The resort has more of an exclusive feel since it's set off on its own.

If you'd rather have a boutique hotel experience instead of an oceanfront mega-resort, the **Hotel Wailea** (555 Kaukahi St., 808/874-0500, www.hotelwailea.com, $359) is tucked away up on a hill with views looking over the coastline. There is a spa, swimming pool, and fine dining on property. This is Wailea's most intimate option for luxury boutique hotels.

Condominiums
Those who want to be walking distance from the beaches of Wailea without the hefty price tag can look into some of the affordably priced condos on the northern edge of the resort. The **☾ Wailea Ekolu Village** (808/891-6200, www. drhmaui.com) offers one- and two-bedroom condos with free parking, free Internet, kitchens, and rates that start around $260.

MAKENA
Over $150
A gleaming, wing-shaped building where every room has at least a partial ocean view, the **☾ Makena Beach and Golf Resort** (5400 Makena Alanui, 808/874-1111 www.makenaresortmaui.com, $210-275) offers South Maui's best resort value. Recent renovations have spruced up everything from the rooms to the exterior, and activities to dining. The resort offers free bicycles and a shuttle to Wailea. Parking is free, Internet is free, there is no resort fee, and all of the activities of Maluaka Beach are right out the front door. There are six tennis courts, a relaxing swimming pool, and the golf course will reopen in the beginning of 2014 after a massive series of improvements. What's best, rates at Makena are far more affordable than at neighboring Wailea, with rooms as low as $210-275 during slower times of the year.

Condominiums

While there aren't too many condos in Makena, the luxurious **Makena Surf** (808/879-6284, www.makenasurfresort.com) is directly on the beach and looks straight out at Molokini Crater. These units are individually owned and rented, although rates usually hover in the $600 range. This is the perfect spot to escape the crowds and have a sliver of South Maui nearly all to yourself.

Upcountry

Upcountry is completely free of resorts and different than most Maui experiences. Peace and tranquility replace mai tais and swimming pools, and the cool mountain area is a refreshing change from the sun-baked shorelines below. Most accommodations are 20 minutes from the beach, although most are also conveniently located within an hour of Haleakala Volcano. Rustic, cool, and blissfully laid-back, Upcountry is where visitors come to relax.

MAKAWAO
Over $150

(Lumeria (1813 Baldwin Ave., 855/579-8877, www.lumeriamaui.com, $300) is a holistic retreat center set between Makawao and Pa'ia. Housed within a brilliantly restored plantation building and home to its own organic garden, Lumeria focuses on providing an educational vacation experience that centers on rejuvenation and wellness. All of the 24 rooms are decorated differently, and Asian accents punctuate the courtyard. Lumeria is popular with yoga retreats, and there are regularly-scheduled classes and workshops.

Bed-and-Breakfasts

Built in 1924 and used by a Portuguese family

Where to Stay in Upcountry

Name	Type	Price
(Aloha Cottage	cottage	$199-299
Banyan Bed and Breakfast	B&B	$165-190
Haleakala National Park	camping and cabins	$10-75
(Hale Ho'okipa Inn	B&B	$138-158
(Kula Lodge	Inn	$125-195
Kula Sandalwoods	cottage	$149-159
(Lumeria	hotel	$300
Peace of Maui	inn	$85-95
Polipoli Springs State Recreation Area	camping	$18
Puluke Farms B&B	B&B	$95
(Star Lookout	vacation rental	$200
Upcountry Bed and Breakfast	B&B	$150

to raise 13 children, the five-bedroom plantation house **⟨** **Hale Ho'okipa Inn** (32 Pakani Pl., 808/572-6698, www.maui-bed-and-breakfast. com, $138-173) has been turned into a lovely B&B within walking distance from Makawao town. While improvements are constantly made, this still has the feel of an old-fashioned country home, and the accommodating owners provide local tips and insight into everyday Maui life. Organic fruits are served from the garden, rates for the one-bedroom rooms are $138-158, and the two-bedroom suite is $173.

Half a mile down the hill from Makawao town, the **Banyan Bed and Breakfast** (3265 Baldwin Ave., 808/572-9021, www.bed-breakfast-maui.com, $165-190) is an old plantation bungalow with adjoining cottages that provides laid-back accommodations in a country setting. The complex is shaded by a monkeypod and banyan, where swings hang from the wide boughs to complete the rural feel. All cottages and suites have kitchens or kitchenettes, breakfast is included, and Makawao town is a short walk away.

Down near the intersection of Hali'imaile Road and Baldwin Avenue is the **Peace of Maui** (1290 Hali'imaile Rd., 808/572-5045, www. peaceofmaui.com, $85-95 main lodge, $185 cottage) guesthouse, which is centrally located between Makawao and Pa'ia. Peace of Maui overlooks the pineapple fields, and while the rooms aren't extravagant, they are clean and affordably priced. Rooms in the main lodge share a kitchen and bathrooms. For your own bathroom, rent the two-bedroom cottage, which also provides access to the property Jacuzzi.

In the forest above Makawao town, you will find **⟨** **Aloha Cottage** (808/573-8555, www. alohacottage.com, $199-299) down a quiet country lane off rural Olinda Road. As quiet as quiet can be, its only neighbors are the horses in the pastures beyond the distant fence. This intimate venue sits on a five-acre estate and offers panoramic views from the deck of the octagonal structure. Slink into the two-person hot tub on the cool Olinda nights, and wake each morning to the chirp of the birds as they sing from the surrounding forest. Rates vary

Features	Why Stay Here?	Best Fit For
hot tub, kitchen, lanai	quiet, peaceful, romantic	couples
kitchen, breakfast	quiet, location	couples
pit toilets, kitchen	quiet, adventurous, backcountry	couples, groups, families, budget travelers
breakfast, garden	quiet, historic	couples
fireplace, lanai	location, romantic, quiet	couples, hikers
lanai, views	quiet, location, retreat	couples
yoga classes, garden courtyard	meditative retreat	solo travelers, couples, groups
kitchen	affordable	budget travelers
none	quiet, wilderness	budget travelers, adventure travelers
kitchenette, breakfast	quiet, affordable	budget travelers, couples
kitchen, views	location, quiet, romantic	couples
fireplace, views, breakfast	quiet, peaceful	couples

depending on length of stay, and there is $100 cleaning fee added to the total cost.

KULA
$100-150

The **(Kula Lodge** (15200 Haleakala Hwy., 808/878-1535, www.kulalodge.com, $125-195) is Upcountry's most popular accommodation option. On Route 377 at a 3,200-foot elevation, the air is crisp and cool up here and much more comfortable than down on the coastline. There are five detached chalets that all feature private lanais, two of which have wood-burning fireplaces. The rustic yet comfortable setting makes the perfect base for visiting Haleakala Crater.

Just up the road, the **Kula Sandalwoods** (15427 Haleakala Hwy., 808/878-3523, www.kulasandalwoods.com, $149-159) is another Kula classic that is far more laid-back than its popular neighbor. These stand-alone cottages sit up on a hillside and offer sweeping views of the island's central valley. While there is complimentary Wi-Fi as well as morning coffee, the cottages are otherwise free of appliances. This is a place to just kick back and relax. The summit of Haleakala is only a 45-minute drive from this 3,300-foot location.

Bed-and-Breakfasts

In Lower Kula on the drive out toward Keokea, **Upcountry Bed and Breakfast** (4925 Lower Kula Rd., 808/878-8083, www.upcountry-bandb.com, $150) has rooms in a relaxing Upcountry setting. The owner is a wealth of information on everything island-related, and locally grown Upcountry fruit is served with each morning's breakfast. There is also free Wi-Fi, fireplaces in winter, and sweeping sunset views.

Above Highway 377 is **Puluke Farms B&B** (26 Wahelani Rd., 808/878-3263, puluke@maui.net, $95). Attached to the main house, this one-room hideaway has great views over the isthmus. The studio has a kitchenette and full bath, and continental breakfast is included with the stay. Sunset and early-morning hours are best appreciated on the deck. Since the house is at 3,500 feet, winter nights can be refreshingly cool.

KEOKEA AND ULUPALAKUA

Those looking for rural tranquility in a cool Upcountry setting need look no farther than the **(Star Lookout** (622 Thompson Rd., 907/346-8028, www.starlookout.com, $200). On Thompson Road just minutes from Grandma's Coffee House, this single cottage provides a ranch-style retreat with views over the Keokea pastureland down to the shoreline of South Maui. A two night minimum is required. Perhaps Upcountry's best-kept secret.

East Maui

PA'IA
Under $150

A short walk above Pa'ia, the **Rainbow Surf Hostel** (221 Baldwin Ave., 808/579-9057, www.mauirainbowsurfhostel.com, $30-100) offers dorm rooms for $30 or private rooms for $80-100. There is a communal kitchen and free Wi-Fi, but those who can spend a few dollars more should seek out better options.

Over $150

Smack in the center of town, the **(Pa'ia Inn** (93 Hana Hwy., 808/579-6000, www.paiainn.com, $189-999) is a trendy, chic, boutique hotel just steps from the beaches of Pa'ia. All the decor within this relaxing compound has a dark wood, Balinese, tropical tone, and each individually designed room offers a luxurious and private getaway in the center of Pa'ia bustle. Sip a coffee in the outdoor courtyard or take a morning stroll along Pa'ia Bay. Rates for standard rooms begin at $189 and go all the way up to $999 for the swanky, oceanfront, "I wish I lived here" beach house, and this is a pleasing and welcoming lodging option in Maui's happiest town.

Also in the center of town is the **Nalu Kai Lodge** (18 Nalu Pl., 808/385-4344, www.nalukailodge.com, $125-175) offering simple and comfortable accommodations just steps from Pa'ia Bay. There is a second-story deck with ocean views, as well as outdoor showers and a tiki bar. While you can't beat the location and the price, the area can sometimes be prone to road noise.

Right on Kuau Cove, **The Inn at Mama's Fish House** (799 Poho Pl., 808/579-9764, www.mamasfishhouse.com, $175-575) provides the warmth of Polynesia that the famous restaurant is known for, and this is one the island's best boutique hotels. The suites, studios, and cottages feature amenities such as full kitchens, maid service, and 15 percent off at the restaurant. The real perk, however, is the location; there is nothing like watching the sunset from beneath a rustling palm as you get the benefit of staying in this secluded cove that most visitors can only enjoy for the length of a meal.

Bed-and-Breakfasts

Between Pa'ia and Ho'okipa Beach Park, the **Kuau Inn** (676 Hana Hwy., 808/579-6046, www.kuauinn.com, $125-145) is a four-room house that offers clean B&B accommodations just minutes from the shoreline. Breakfast and Wi-Fi are both included. There is a full kitchen, covered lanai, and communal living room area. There is a minimum three-night stay.

ROAD TO HANA

Down at the end of a road near Twin Falls is the **Tea House Cottage** (808/572-5610, www.mauiteahouse.com, $150 d, $130 s). This B&B is "off the grid," generating its own power by photovoltaic cells and collecting its own water. It's quiet, with no distractions, and from here you have broad views of the ocean. The room rates are $150 and $130, with a two-night minimum, and breakfast is provided on the first day. A tunnel through the trees leads you to the house, and walkways run throughout the

property, one to a small stupa built in 1976 by a Tibetan monk. The private Tiara Cottage, also on the property, can be rented by the week for $500. Breezy and light, it has a full kitchen and a bathroom and shower in an adjacent building.

In the community of Huelo you'll find the **Huelo Point Lookout** (808/573-0914, www.mauivacationcottages.com, $215-405), a collection of five vacation rentals in a lush and heavenly section of the island not for the resort-loving crowd. These five separate vacation rentals provide sweeping views of the Huelo coastline and are truly a place to escape from it all. While there is no white sand beach outside your front door, there is a blanket of stars every night, and outdoor hot tubs from which to enjoy them. Discounts are given for weekly stays.

HANA

There are two completely different ways of experiencing Hana: trying to see it all in one day or making the smart move to spend a night and enjoy the beauty at a relaxed pace. Choosing to spend a night in Hana—even if it means paying for two hotels in one night by not checking out of the other one—is the best $200 you'll spend on vacation.

Under $100

Basic, practical, and perfect for those on a steep budget, **Joe's Rentals** (4870 Uakea Rd., 808/248-7033, www.joesrentals.com, $50-60) is close to the entrance to Hana Bay and walking distance from the center of town. This home has been split into eight guest rooms, and rates are $50 for a shared bathroom or $60 for a room with a private bath. You'll find kitchen access, a communal TV room, and daily towel change, but if a little dirt and the occasional bug bother you, then you might want to look somewhere else. Cash or travelers checks only, and if no one is in the office, just ring for assistance.

Over $150

There are places to stay during your time in Hana, and then there is the **Travaasa Hana**

MAUI

Where to Stay in East Maui

Name	Type	Price
Ala 'aina Ocean Vista	B&B	$198-218
(Bamboo Inn	B&B	$195-265
Ekena	vacation rental	$245-400
Guest Houses at Malanai	vacation rental	$245-290
Haleakala National Park-Kipahulu	camping	$10
Hana Bay Hale	vacation rental	$145-245
Hana Kai Maui Resort	condo	$200-300
Hana Lani Treehouses	treehouse	$135-210
(Huelo Point Lookout	vacation rental	$215-405
Joe's Rentals	Inn	$50-60
Kuau Inn	B&B	$125-145
(Pa'ia Inn	inn	$189-999
Nalu Kai Lodge	inn	$125-175
Rainbow Surf Hostel	hostel	$30-100
Tea House Cottage	B&B	$130-150
The Inn at Mama's Fish House	inn	$175-575
(Travaasa Hana	resort	$400-700

(5031 Hana Hwy., www.travaasa.com/hana, $400-650). This luxurious compound in the center of town was the island's first resort hotel when it opened in 1946, and since that time the boutique hotel has continued as the island's best resort. In addition to the standard amenities of tennis courts, a swimming pool, a fitness center, and spa, the Travaasa makes a conscious effort to help guests forge a meaningful connection with the Hawaiian culture of Hana. Resort experiences include throw net fishing, coconut husking, lei making, hula dancing, and ukulele classes, and adventure activities such as horseback riding and gliding can be booked through the resort's concierge. Wellness and culture permeate the resort, and for a real splurge, base yourself in one of the Sea Ranch cottages with its own private lanai and romantic two-person hot tub. Rates for standard rooms begin at $400, with Sea Ranch cottages ranging from $450-650.

Vacation Rentals

Set high above the west end of town, the luxurious **Ekena** (808/248-7047, www.ekenamaui.com, $245-400) vacation rental offers arguably one of the best views in Hana. This large pole house has an upper and lower unit which are each spacious enough to easily be shared by two couples. Both floors have large living rooms, fully equipped kitchens with all modern conveniences, two master bedrooms, and spacious bathrooms. There are private hiking trails departing from the property, and the on-site caretakers can provide all the info on Hana you could possibly need. The Jasmine level with one bedroom goes for $245 per night; with two bedrooms for $320. The Sea Breeze level is $350 for a couple and $400 for four people. There's a three-night minimum; no kids younger than 14.

The **Hana Lani Treehouses** (808/248-7241, www.hanalani.maui.net, $135-210) are exactly

Features	Why Stay Here?	Best Fit For
gardens, hot tub, barbecue	quiet, peaceful	couples
oceanview lanai, breakfast	location, romantic	couples
kitchen, amenities, ocean view	location, quiet	couples
kitchen, gardens	location, amenities	couples, families
pit toilets, barbecue	location, affordable	budget travelers
kitchens	location, amenities	couples, families, groups
kitchen, lanai, oceanfront	location, quiet	couples
gardens, cooking facilities	quiet, unique	couples
hot tub, ocean view	location, quiet, peaceful	couples
kitchen	location, affordable	budget travelers
kitchens, lanai	location, affordable	couples, budget travelers
oceanfront, gardens	location, boutique	couples
oceanfront, tiki bar	location, affordable	couples
kitchen	affordable, location	budget travelers
off the grid, gardens	location, quiet, peaceful	couples
kitchens, oceanfront	location, romantic	couples, honeymooners
spa, pool, activities	location, luxury, amenities	couples, honeymooners

what they sound like: real treehouses inside a real jungle. Imagine sleeping beneath the stars in a screened-in bungalow set up in the trees, the path to your jungle chalet lit only by tiki torches. This "camping with a roof" is available in a number of forms, from the three-level "treetop" house to the more traditional bed-and-breakfast cottage that has its own electricity. There is also a five-person tree pavilion with views looking out at the ocean. Flowers abound everywhere you look. Rates are $135 for the treetops house, $145 for the tree pavilion, and $210 for the entire cottage. Two-night minimum usually required, but one-night stays will also be accepted for an additional $20 cleaning fee.

Closer to town, the funky, ultra-relaxing **(Bamboo Inn** (www.bambooinn.com) offers three oceanfront accommodations that look out over the water toward Waikoloa Beach. A thatched roof hut serves as the centerpiece for the property. The owner, John, is a wealth of information on Hana history and culture, and this is a modern, soothing place to base yourself in Hana town and fall asleep to the crash of the waves. The one-story Honu and 'Iwa suites are $195 and $210/night, and each features its own private lanai gazing out over the calming bay. The two-story Naia suite is $265 with another private lanai. Wi-Fi is available in the courtyard and breakfast is included.

The **Hana Bay Hale** (808/248-4999, www. hanabayhale.com, $145-245) looks out over Hana Bay and features three separate suites. The Kauiki and Waikoloa one-bedroom units are $145/night plus a $25 cleaning fee for one-night stays, and the two-bedroom Hana Bay suite is $245/night plus a $35 cleaning fee for one-night stays. One-bedroom units have kitchenettes whereas the two-bedroom suite has a full kitchen, and the units can all be combined into a single large house for anyone traveling in a large group.

On the southern end of town between Hana and Kipahulu are the **Guest Houses at Malanai** (808/248-8706, www.hanaguesthouses.com, $245-295). This lush property features the one-bedroom Hale Ulu Ulu guesthouse and the larger, two-bedroom Hale Manu, both of which rent for the same rate depending upon length of stay. These two separate houses are located a 15-minute stroll from Hamoa Beach and Waioka Pool, and the owners can provide basic accessories you might need for the beach as well as insight on the area.

Condominiums

The **Hana Kai Maui Resort** (1533 Uakea Rd., 808/248-8426, www.hanakaimaui.com, $200-300) is the only condo rental in town. All units are well maintained and offer a lot for the money. Because there are only 18 rental units, you know this is an intimate place. The condo is set right on the water looking out over Hana Bay, each unit has a private lanai, and you fall asleep every night to the gentle lap of the waves. Rates vary depending on size and location of the unit but often run between $200-300.

KIPAHULU
Over $150

One of the best parts of staying in Kipahulu is the relaxing nature of the remote community and the ability to wake up in the morning and have the Pools of 'Ohe'o walking distance away. One of the most peaceful accommodations in this area is the **Ala'aina Ocean Vista** (808/248-7824, www.hanabedandbreakfast.com, $198-218), a tropical bed-and-breakfast on four lush acres that is the exact opposite of

© KYLE ELLISON

Be sure to book ahead for Hana Kai Maui Resort.

the Ka'anapali resort experience. Here you are bathed in a forest of mango trees that gaze over the blue Kipahulu coastline. Birds chirp in the nearby treetops, there is a barbecue area for those who want to cook their own dinner, and a large assortment of various fruit trees sustain the daily breakfast. The bamboo forest of the Pipiwai Trail is only a short walk away, and this is a romantic getaway set out in the country for those who just want to unwind. Rates vary depending on length of stay, but there is no cleaning fee.

MAUI

Lana'i

While Lana'i is home to two of the most luxurious resorts in the state, there are a handful of more affordable options for those on more of a budget.

$100-150

Small and historic **(Hotel Lana'i** (828 Lana'i Ave., 808/565-7211 or 877/665-2624, fax 808/565-6450, www.hotellanai.com, $119-219) sits in the center of tranquil Lana'i City. This was the island's first hotel, built in 1923 for visiting guests of the ruling Dole Pineapple Company. While you won't find the same amenities as at the more expensive and posh resorts, the 10 rooms of this plantation-style building retain a historic feel without sacrificing comfort. The best rooms are those with their own private lanai, and there is also a cottage removed from the main building. Wi-Fi and breakfast are both complimentary, rates range from $119 for a standard room to $219 for the cottage, and shuttle service down to the beach is available for a fee of $36, which is good for the duration of your stay.

OVER $150

Lavish, luxurious, and delightfully over the top, the Four Seasons resorts on the island of Lana'i are two of Hawaii's best. New owner Larry Ellison devoted millions of dollars to major renovations when he took over from David Murdock, and the Asian decor that once dominated the hotels has been replaced by Hawaiian designs. The resorts look better now than they ever have, and if it was even possible to make these resorts nicer, it's recently been accomplished. While both hotels are the pinnacle of luxury, each, however, offers a completely different experience although the amenities are

© KYLE ELLISON

Hotel Lana'i

MAUI

Where to Stay on Lana'i

Name	Type	Price
Apo's House	vacation rental	$195
Dreams Come True	vacation rental	$129
€ Four Seasons Manele Bay	Resort	$450-1,500
Four Seasons Lodge at Koele	Resort	$350-1,200
Hale Moe	vacation rental	$85'95
€ Hotel Lana'i	hotel	$119-229
Hulopo'e Beach Park	camping	$30 + $15/person
Lana'i City Vacation Rental	vacation rental	$250

interchangeable. Which resort you choose to stay in depends on the vacation you're looking for.

Offering an iconic beach resort experience, the € **Four Seasons Manele Bay** (1 Manele Dr., 808/565-2000, www.fourseasons.com/manelebay, $450-up) is set stunningly above the cobalt waters of protected Hulopo'e Bay. The immaculate pool area sparkles in the sun and half of Hulopo'e Beach is reserved for hotel guests. You feel like a celebrity when staying here. Expect rates to begin around $450 during slower times of the year.

Above Lana'i City on the edge of open pastureland, the **Four Seasons Lodge at Koele** (808/565-4000, www.fourseasons.com/koele, $350-up) is a mist-shrouded mountain lodge where you're struck with the urge to trade the freedom of a bathing suit for the comforting warmth of a robe. While staying at Koele, play a round of croquet on the private course or stroll through the manicured gardens. Hunker down with a newspaper in the Grand Hall and pair it with a nice warm drink. Take a horseback ride through the surrounding countryside, or try your hand at skeet shooting. Marvelously dignified and impossibly romantic, rates at the Lodge are more affordable than Manele and begin as low as $350 during slower times of the year.

At the time of publication, a third resort was under construction on the east-facing Kahalepalaoa shoreline, with the vision being of private beach bungalows at the site of the abandoned Club Lana'i. The status of the resort remains to be seen, although it could potentially provide a luxurious accommodation option for the island's eastern shoreline.

BED-AND-BREAKFASTS

The **Dreams Come True** (808/565-6961 www.dreamscometruelanai.com, $129) guesthouse has four rooms available for rent. While the house itself dates to 1925, it was largely renovated in 2000, with hardwood floors and Italian marble in the bathrooms. The local owners have a wealth of island knowledge. Breakfast is included, as is free Internet.

Hale Moe (502 Akolu St., 808/565-9520, $85-95) is a modern, clean, and comfy island house on the south side of town that rents three rooms, each with a bathroom, or the entire house. Food for breakfast is available each morning, and guests can use the kitchen for other meals. Two rooms go for $85 and the third is $95; the whole house can be rented for $300.

VACATION RENTALS

To experience Lana'i from a more local perspective (i.e., not be spritzed by Evian bottles),

Features	Why Stay Here?	Best Fit For
kitchen	affordable, location	couples, families
kitchen	affordable, location	couples, budget travelers
pool, golf, oceanfront	luxury, romantic	couples, honeymooners, luxury-lovers
croquet, gardens, golf	luxury, romantic	couples, honeymooners, luxury-lovers
kitchen, breakfast	affordable, quiet	budget travelers, couples
lanai, breakfast	romantic, location, historic	couples
restrooms, water, oceanfront	location, affordable	budget travelers, groups, families
kitchen, amenities	location, quiet	couples, groups, families

consider one of the smaller, more affordable rental options scattered throughout Lana'i City.

Located in town is **Apo's House** (www.lanaicityrental.com, $195), a three-bedroom, two-bath house. The house is fully furnished, and there is a full kitchen. While it might be set in an older plantation home, you have the convenience of walking into Lana'i City and the feeling that you're part of the local community.

The **Lana'i City Vacation Rental** (www.lanaiforvacation.com, $250), a three-bedroom house in the center of Lana'i City, rents for $250 per night with a three-night minimum. The plantation home is set in a tropical, relaxing surrounding, can accommodate groups of 9-11 people, and can arrange any holistic retreat options you're hoping to find on the island.

Moloka'i

Moloka'i is gloriously free of resorts, and no buildings on the island are taller than a palm tree. Accommodations provide calming sanctuaries where you can relax and hear yourself think. Since most Moloka'i condos are managed through vacation rental agencies, contact **Moloka'i Vacation Properties** (808/553-8334, www.molokai-vacation-rental.net) or **Friendly Isle Realty** (808/553-3666, www.molokairealty.com) about their large selection of vacation rentals across the island.

WEST MOLOKA'I

While Kaluakoi was once the home of an oceanfront resort with an 18-hole golf course, the resort was shuttered with the closing of

the Moloka'i Ranch. The benefits of staying in West Moloka'i are the comfortable, modern accommodations, the fact that you're within walking distance of the island's best beaches, and the fiery sunsets that take place each evening.

One of the largest complexes in West Moloka'i is the **Ke Nani Kai** (50 Kepuhi Pl., 800/490-9042, www.kenanikai.com, $100-200), an expansive complex that has a swimming pool, one- and two-bedroom units, and affordable rates.

Closer to the beach, the **Paniolo Hale** offers similar accommodation just steps from the shoreline. Units here rent for $110-225 per night with a two- to three-night minimum,

Where to Stay on Moloka'i

Name	Type	Price
◖ Aloha Beach House	vacation rental	$250
Dunbar Beachfront Cottages	vacation rental	$175
Halawa Valley	camping	free in summer, inquire ahead
Hale Manu Guesthouse	vacation rental	$55-80
◖ Hotel Moloka'i	hotel	$175-250
Ka Hale Mana	B&B	$80-
Kaluakoi Villas	condo	$150-190
Ke Nani Kai	condo	100-200
Moloka'i Beach House	vacation rental	$250
Moloka'i Shores	condo	$190-250
One Ali'i Beach Park	camping	$5
Pala'au State Park	camping	$18
Paniolo Hale	condo	110-225
Papohaku Beach Park	camping	$5
◖ Pu'u O Hoku Ranch	cottages	$200-300
Waikolu	camping	$18
Wavecrest Resort	condo	$100-200

although some units have longer minimum stays.

Some of the units at the old Kaluakoi Hotel complex, collectively called the **Kaluakoi Villas** (1121 Kaluakoi Rd., Maunaloa, HI 96770, 808/552-2721 or 800/367-5004, www.castleresorts.com, $150-190), are managed by Castle Resorts and Hotels. Each studio, suite, and cottage has been tastefully decorated and includes a color TV and a kitchen or kitchenette.

CENTRAL MOLOKA'I
Under $100
In the cool uplands of Kala'e, **Hale Manu Guesthouse** (808/567-9136, www.halemalu-molokai.com, $55-80) is a small, relaxed, one-bedroom accommodation with two guest rooms and a small cottage. Guest rooms share a bathroom, and all rooms have access to a full kitchen in the main house. Refreshingly basic and in a non-touristy part of the island, guest rooms are $55/night, with an $80 rate for the cottage. Discounts are available for longer stays, no credit cards accepted. The guesthouse is centrally located near the Kualapu'u Coffee Farms and Kalaupapa Peninsula.

Over $150
Kaunakakai has the island's widest accommodation options and offers the closest thing to an island "resort."

The ◖ **Hotel Moloka'i** (877/553-5347, www.hotelmolokai.com, $175-250) is set right on the water and offers A-frame accommodations in a resort-type setting. It offers a swimming pool and activities desk, free Wi-Fi, and live entertainment on select evenings. All rooms have a refrigerator and microwave.

Features	Why Stay Here?	Best Fit For
oceanfront, kitchen	location, romantic	couples, groups, families
oceanfront, kitchen	location, quiet	couples
toilets	oceanfront, affordable	budget travelers
kitchen	location, affordable	budget travelers, solo travelers, couples
kitchenette, pool, breakfast	modern, activities desk	couples, families
gardens, kitchen	quiet, affordable	budget travelers, couples, solo travelers
kitchen	close to beach, location	couples
pool, kitchen	close to beach, location	couples, families
oceanfront, kitchen	location, full amenities	couples, groups, families
pool, barbecue, kitchen, oceanfront	location	families, couples
restrooms, water, oceanfront	last resort	budget travelers
restrooms, pavilion	affordable, location	budget travelers
	oceanfront, kitchen	location, quiet
toilets, water	oceanfront, quiet	budget travelers
kitchen, views	quiet, retreat	couples, honeymooners, families
toilets, picnic tables	quiet, nearby hiking	budget travelers, adventure travelers
pool, tennis, amenities	oceanfront, modern	couples, families

The rooms have been refurbished numerous times. Breakfast is complimentary. This is a convenient, comfortable, and relaxing option for those who are more comfortable in a semi-resort setting. Rates vary depending on room size and season.

The **Moloka'i Shores** is a condominium complex with a large number of individually owned units as well as others managed by Castle Resorts (808/553-5944). Set on a tiny sliver of a beach, the three-story complex has a large open courtyard area with barbecue facilities and a swimming pool. The trade winds here are pronounced in the afternoon, and the swimming out front is marginal at best, but this is another convenient and comfortable option for basing yourself toward the center of the island. Rates range from $190-250 for one- and two-bedroom units.

EAST MOLOKA'I

Along this eastern section of the island are the bulk of its vacation rentals, cottages, and B&Bs. Afternoons are punctuated by brisk trade winds and the setting is more tropical than arid West Moloka'i.

Bed-and-Breakfasts

Ka Hale Mala (808/553-9009, www.molokai-bnb.com, $80-90) is less than five miles east of Kaunakakai on Kamakana Place. This quiet vacation rental is the ground floor of a family house, set amid a tropical garden. Here you have a large living room, full kitchen and bath, separate bedroom, and a laundry room, plus use of snorkel gear. Rates are $80 without breakfast or $90 with. No credit cards. Good place, convenient location. For more information, contact hosts Cheryl or Chuck Corbiell.

MAUI

Condominiums

The largest condo on the east end of the island is the **Wavecrest Resort** (808/558-8101), at mile marker 13 and with individually owned units. While every unit is different, general amenities include a swimming pool, tennis court, laundry facilities, and a nicely manicured, five-acre setting. One- and two-bedroom units have full kitchens and look across the Pailolo Channel toward Maui, and rates vary between $100-200. There is a front desk that is open 7:30am-1:30pm Monday-Friday. Contact island rental agents for individual units.

Vacation Rentals

The **(Aloha Beach House** (808/828-1100 or 888/828-1008, www.molokaivacation.com) is a great little two-bedroom cottage right on the beach in Puko'o. This house is just down the road from a sundries store, so you can pick up supplies there. This beach house has a full kitchen and washer and dryer. With a view like the one looking across toward Maui, there's a good chance you'll never want to leave. Perhaps best of all, a swimmable beach is just out the front door. Rates are $250 a night with a three-night minimum, plus a $175 cleaning fee.

The neat and trim **Dunbar Beachfront Cottages** (808/558-8153, www.molokai-beachfront-cottages.com) are 2 two-bedroom cottages set right on a secluded section of beach. Each has a full kitchen, living room, laundry, and deck, and the beach is right in front of you. These are quiet places, perfect for a relaxing holiday, but you still have television and free Wi-Fi. Cottages can sleep up to four people comfortably, and rates run $175 a night, with a three-night minimum and $75 cleaning fee. No credit cards.

Some distance farther is the **Molokai Beach House** (808/599-3838, www.molokaibeachhouse.com), a three-bedroom, two-bath, oceanfront home with all the conveniences. A large yard with a picnic table spreads out before you on the ocean side, and inside this island-style house is a big living room, full kitchen, and laundry room. The house sleeps up to six and runs $250 per night or $1,600 per week, with a $125 cleaning fee and three-night minimum.

At the far eastern end of the island high on the eastern hillside sits 14,000-acre **(Pu'u O Hoku Ranch** (808/558-8109, www.puuohoku.com). The three cottages and one lodge are some of the best and most remote on the island. If you're looking for a place to get away from everything, this is it. This is a real, working ranch, and it's also minutes away from the shores of Halawa Bay. This is a great place to tap into Hawaii's history and culture, but those who prefer large beach resorts should probably just stay away. Wi-Fi is available at a few spots, but most accommodations are "unplugged." Check in at the ranch office along the highway at mile marker 25, where there is a small sundries store that sells basic food and gift items.

The two-bedroom Sunrise Cottage is $225/night, has a full kitchen, covered lanai, and can accommodate up to four people. The larger, four-bedroom Grove Cottage is $300/night for four people and $30/night for each additional guest, and can comfortably accommodate up to eight people. From this cottage there are ocean views looking out toward Maui with amazing whale-watching in winter. Five miles closer to Kaunakakai along the main highway, the one-bedroom Sugar Mill cottage is $200/night, sleeps four people, has a full kitchen, and is walking distance from one of the island's nicest beaches. For groups of 14 or more, the all-inclusive lodge includes three meals a day and spacious accommodations for $165/person/night. All cottages have a minimum two-night stay and a $100 cleaning fee; the lodge has a four-night minimum.

BIG ISLAND OF HAWAI'I

© MARTY WAKAT/123RF.COM

The Big Island of Hawai'i is the newest island, geologically speaking, in the chain of islands that make up the state of Hawaii. While lava formed the island's physical structure, it is the sugar plantation industry, established in the mid-1800s, that is credited for creating the Big Island's culture, through bringing numerous immigrants to work the island's land. Much of the island's modern-day customs, from language (Hawaiian pidgin, or *da' kine*) to food (like the *loco moco* or Spam *musubi*) to clothing (the classic aloha shirt), reflect this merging of Chinese, Filipino, Japanese, Polynesian, Portuguese, and Mainland American cultures.

Many visitors are beckoned by the Big Island's warm weather and well-known spectacular landscape—including pristine Hapuna Beach, picture-perfect Waipi'o Valley, and the lava flow rush into the ocean in Pahoa. The island provides an array of activities for outdoor lovers, from "fluming the ditch" (kayaking through an old plantation-era ditch in Kohala) to surfing the popular Honoli'i Beach Park; from night snorkeling with the manta rays in Keauhou Bay to stargazing at the Mauna Kea Observatory. And you're never more than 10-20 minutes away from a gorgeous beach.

The Big Island doesn't offer just one kind of experience. When the weather gets too hot seaside, drive upcountry to Waimea, the cool interior part of the island, where a fireside meal will be waiting for you. Or spend an early Sunday morning at one of the island's numerous farmers markets adorned with tropical fruits, *malasadas* (Portuguese doughnuts), and food carts with mouthwatering *huli huli* chicken and smoked fish.

When your visit is over, say *"a hui hou"* (until we meet again). You'll want to come back.

Planning Your Trip

WHERE TO GO
Kona
Kona is dry, sunny, and brilliant—most visitors' introduction to the island. When watered, the rich soil blossoms, as in the small artists' enclave of Holualoa and South Kona, renowned for its diminutive **coffee plantations.** As the center of this region, **Kailua-Kona** boasts an array of art and designer shops, economical accommodations, great restaurants, and historical and cultural sites like **Moku'aikaua Church,** a legacy of the first missionaries to arrive in the islands, and **Hulihe'e Palace,** vacation home of the Hawaiian royalty. **Kealakekua Bay** is one of the best snorkel sites in the islands. Nearby is **Pu'uhonua O Honaunau National Historical Park,** the location of a traditional Hawaiian safe refuge.

Kohala
North of Kailua-Kona, otherworldly black lava bleeds north into Kohala. Up the coast is **Hapuna Beach,** one of the best on the island. Expansive resorts make this the island's

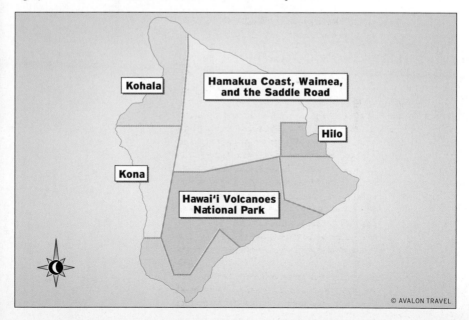

© AVALON TRAVEL

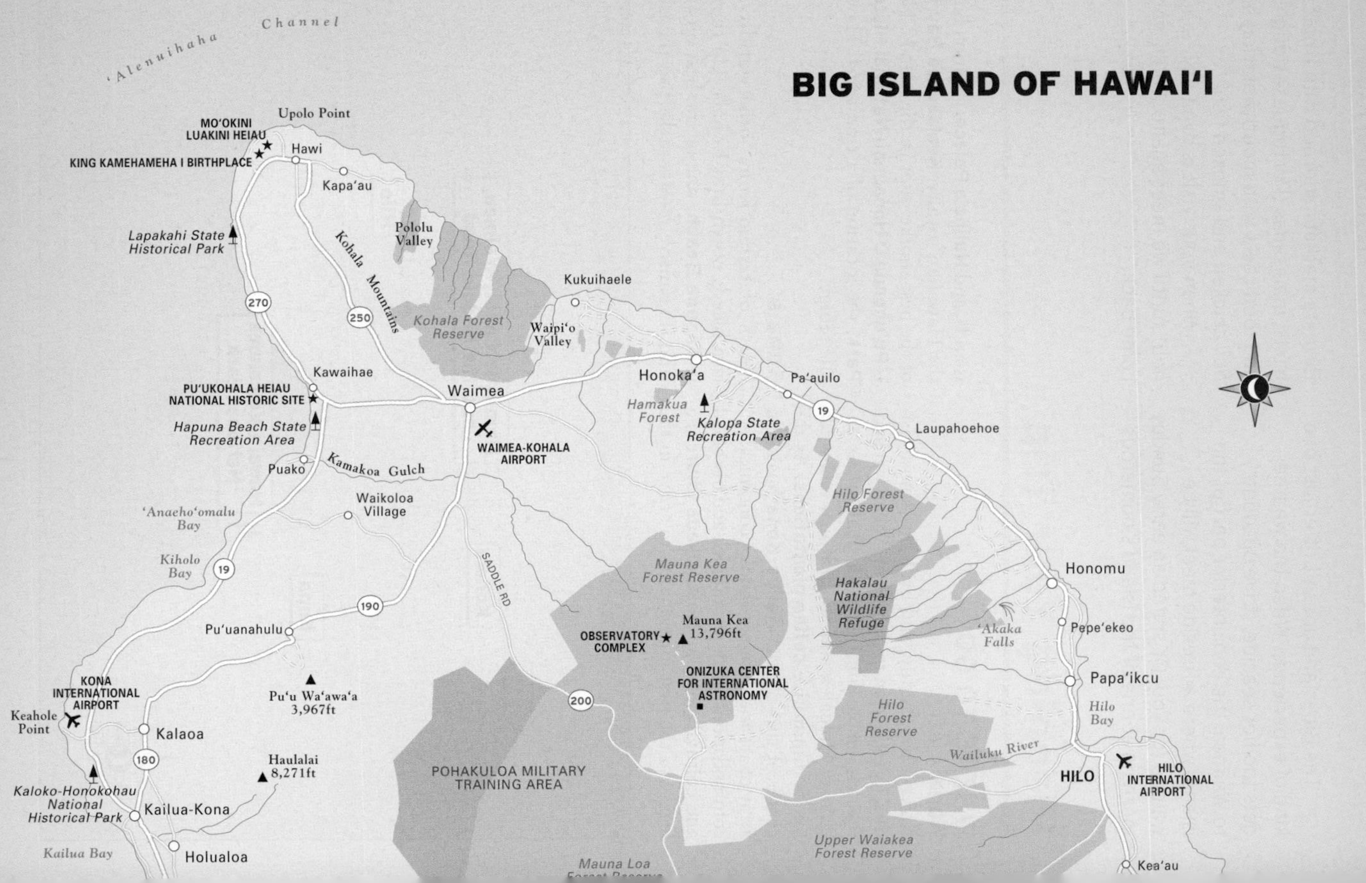

BIG ISLAND OF HAWAI'I

Alenuihaha Channel

Upolo Point

MO'OKINI
LUAKINI HEIAU ★
KING KAMEHAMEHA I BIRTHPLACE

Hawi
Kapa'au

Lapakahi State
Historical Park †

Kohala Mountains

Kohala Forest
Reserve

Pololu Valley

250

Kawaihae

PU'UKOHALA HEIAU
NATIONAL HISTORIC SITE ★
Hapuna Beach State
Recreation Area

Puako

270

'Anaeho'omalu
Bay

Kiholo
Bay

Keahole Point ▲
KONA
INTERNATIONAL
AIRPORT ✈

Kaloko-Honokohau
National
Historical Park

Kailua Bay

Kailua-Kona

Holualoa

180

Kalaoa

Pu'uanahulu

19

Haualai
8,271ft ▲

Pu'u Wa'awa'a
3,967ft ▲

190

Waikoloa
Village

Kanakua Gulch

Waimea ✈
WAIMEA-KOHALA
AIRPORT

SADDLE RD

200

Kohala Forest
Reserve

Wai'pi'o
Valley

Kukuihaele

Honoka'a

Hamakua
Forest

Kalopa State
Recreation Area †

Pa'auilo

19

Laupahoehoe

Mauna Kea
Forest Reserve

Mauna Kea
13,796ft ▲

OBSERVATORY
COMPLEX ★

ONIZUKA CENTER
FOR INTERNATIONAL
ASTRONOMY ■

POHAKULOA MILITARY
TRAINING AREA

Mauna Loa
Forest Reserve

Hilo Forest
Reserve

Hakalau
National
Wildlife
Refuge

'Akaka
Falls

Hilo
Forest
Reserve

Upper Waiakea
Forest Reserve

Honomu

Pepe'ekeo

Papa'ikou

Hilo
Bay

Wailuku River

HILO ●
HILO
INTERNATIONAL
AIRPORT ✈

Kea'au

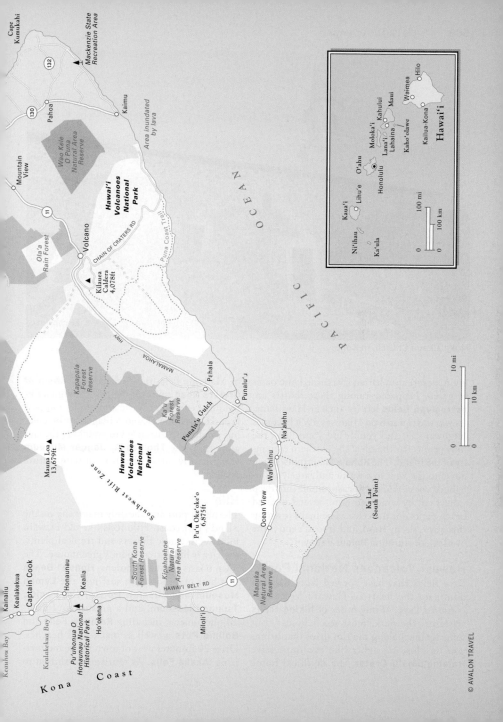

Moku'aikaua Church, in Kona

luxury resort area, barren lava turned into oases of green. Peppered among these resorts are **petroglyph fields** left by ancient Hawaiians. As you travel north on Highway 19, it becomes Highway 270 and you'll find yourself in the hilly peninsular thumb at the northern extremity of the island. The **Kohala Mountains** sweep down to the west to a warm and largely uninhabited coast, and to the east tumble into deep valleys cut by wind and rain. Several isolated beach parks dot the coast. The main town up this way is sleepy **Hawi,** and at road's end is the overlook of stunning **Pololu Valley.**

Hawai'i Volcanoes National Park

Lava fields that have spewed from **Kilauea** dominate the heart of Hawai'i Volcanoes National Park. While miles of **hiking trails** crisscross the park, most see it by car (but some by bike) along the rim drive that brings you up close to sights like the impressive **Halema'uma'u Crater,** the mythical home of Madame Pele, the fire goddess. **Chain of Craters Road** spills off the *pali* through a forbidding yet vibrant wasteland of old and new lava. Nights in Volcano Village can be cold, but you'll be so distracted by watching the lava glow from the **Thomas A. Jaggar Museum** you'll hardly notice the drop in temperature at all.

Hilo

The oldest port and the only major city on the island's east coast, Hilo feels like old Hawaii. Filled with exotic flowers and tropical plants, the city is like a tremendous greenhouse. The town boasts Japanese gardens, **Honoli'i Beach** (the best place to watch surfing), the **Lyman Museum and Mission House,** the **Pacific Tsunami Museum,** and a profusion of natural phenomena, including **Rainbow Falls** and **Boiling Pots** as well as black-sand beaches. Drive 20 minutes west of town to the mesmerizing **'Akaka Falls.** As tourism has shifted to the Kona side, Hilo is a place where deals can be found.

Hamakua Coast, Waimea, and the Saddle Road

Hamakua refers to the northeast coast above Hilo, where streams, wind, and pounding surf have chiseled the lava into cliffs and precipitous valleys. The road north from one-street Honoka'a dead-ends at the lookout at **Waipi'o Valley,** the most spectacular and enchanted valley on the island. Upcountry is **Waimea,** the heart of Hawaiian cowboy country and home to the **Hawaii Regional Cuisine** movement. From Waimea one can traverse the island via the **Saddle Road** separating the mountains of Mauna Loa and Mauna Kea. At the top of **Mauna Kea,** at 13,796 feet, **observatories** peer into the heavens through the clearest air on earth. A hiking trail for the hale and hearty heads to the top of **Mauna Loa.**

PLANNING YOUR TIME ON THE BIG ISLAND

The sheer size of the Big Island means that logging some miles on the rental car is inevitable. While the Hawaii Belt Road that circles the island ensures that navigating from region to region is straightforward, the key is planning your route to minimize spending unnecessary time behind the wheel.

For a limited stay on the Big Island, selecting one main destination, windward or leeward, and making small half-day excursions also makes sense. The Kona side holds most of the resorts and accommodations, including those along the Kohala Coast. Stay there to maximize beach, snorkeling, and diving opportunities. If you're staying along the Kohala Coast, it's a quick trip to Waimea or Waipio Valley. Staying in Hilo makes day trips to Volcanoes National Park, which is 29 miles away, about a 45-minute drive. Accommodations near Volcanoes National Park are another option, affording the opportunity to spend several days exploring the natural wonder.

If you're starting out in Kona and planning on making the drive to Hilo, taking the northern portion of the beltway will save some time. The stretch is 93 miles and takes about two hours. The southern portion of the beltway from Kona to Hilo is 125 miles and takes about three hours. For a historical stop on your way from Kona to Hilo, take the time to venture off the belt road and head north to explore North Kohala's cultural treasure, Lapakahi State Historical Park. Back on the belt road, Waimea town offers a chance to learn about Hawai'i's paniolo days and also is a great place to get out of the car and get a bite to eat. Once you reach Honoka'a on the windward side, you can backtrack for breathtaking views of Waipi'o Valley. Shoot down the Hamakua Coast and you're in Hilo. For those looking to get away from it all and take in the volcanic origins of Hawai'i, take the Saddle Road to Hilo, which is a bold 55-mile cut across the Big Island through a broad high valley separating the two great mountains, **Mauna Loa** and **Mauna Kea.**

GETTING TO THE BIG ISLAND

The Big Island has two major airports that service the leeward and windward sides of the island. The **Kona International Airport** (code: KOA, 73-200 Kupipi St., 808/327-9520, hawaii.gov/koa) serves international, overseas and interisland flights. It is the primary airport on the island, located on the west side of Hawai'i Island, seven miles from Kailua. The **Hilo International Airport** (code: ITO, 2450 Kekuanaoa St., 808/961-9300, hawaii.gov/ito), on the east side of the island, serves interisland carriers.

In addition to the national and international carriers that have routes to the Big Island, **Hawaiian Airlines** (800/367-5320, hawaiianairlines.com) is Hawaii's leading commercial carrier with the largest selection of flights between the main Hawaiian Islands. **Mokulele Airlines** (866/260-7070, mokuleleairlines.com) utilizes a prop caravan service to ferry passengers to and from Kahului, Maui and Kona.

KONA

Kona can feel like the hottest place on the island, not just due to the warm temperatures, but because there is always something going on, from frequent festivals celebrating everything from coffee and chocolate to beer and fishing, to serious nightlife, which locals will tell you means anything open later than 9pm. It's no wonder that most visitors spend the majority of their time on the Kona side, as it is called. Although Kona

HIGHLIGHTS

LOOK FOR ◖ TO FIND RECOMMENDED SIGHTS, ACTIVITIES, DINING, AND LODGING.

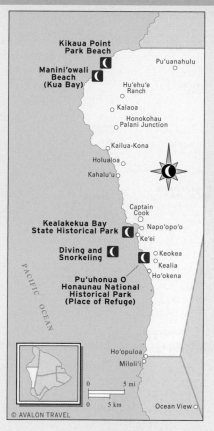

◖ **Kikaua Point Park Beach:** Bring a picnic to this uncrowded beach—the water remains calm here, making it a perfect spot for kids (page 519).

◖ **Manini'owali Beach (Kua Bay):** This small white-sand beach offers close parking and clear waters that are excellent for body boarding and snorkeling (page 519).

◖ **Kealakekua Bay State Historical Park:** Tourists flock here for novice-friendly kayaking and stellar snorkeling. Depending on the season, it's common to see dolphins (page 521).

◖ **Diving and Snorkeling:** Because the reef is so close to the shoreline, nearly the entire coast presents ideal snorkeling conditions. The best spots are Kealakekua Bay and Pawai Bay during the day and Keauhou Bay at night for the manta ray sightings (page 524).

◖ **Pu'uhonua O Honaunau National Historical Park (Place of Refuge):** Get a glimpse of ancient Hawaii at this safe haven for defeated chiefs and *kapu*-breakers. It's especially magical at sunrise (page 534).

BIG ISLAND OF HAWAI'I

is talked about as if it were a city, it is actually a large district. From national historical parks to some of the best white-sand beaches on the island to nearly every ocean activity possible, Kona is a microcosm of what the larger island has to offer.

In March 2011 Kona was affected by a tsunami resulting from a large earthquake in Japan. Damage to some oceanfront areas was significant, with beaches completely changing overnight, and in some cases buildings were destroyed from the force of the wave. The reviews of beaches in this guide were conducted both before and after the tsunami hit, but as rebuilding continues it is possible that some locations will differ in appearance from what is written here.

ORIENTATION
North of the Airport: North Kona
This is what you were imagining when you

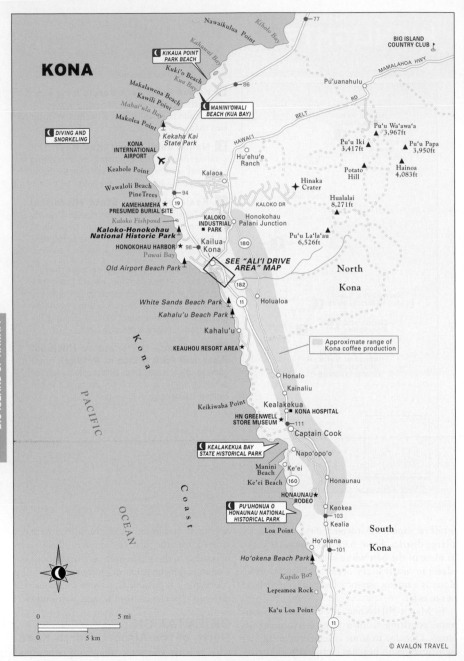

KONA

BIG ISLAND OF HAWAI'I

Nawaikulua Point

Kīhole Bay

77

BIG ISLAND
COUNTRY CLUB

KIKAUA POINT
PARK BEACH

Kahuwai Bay

MAMALAHOA HWY

Kuki'o Beach

86

Pu'uanahulu

Kua Bay

RD

Makalawena Beach

MANINI'OWALI
BEACH (KUA BAY)

Kawili Point

BELT

Mahai'ula Bay

Pu'u Wa'awa'a
3,967ft

Makolea Point

Pu'u Iki
3,417ft

Pu'u Papa
3,950ft

DIVING AND
SNORKELING

Kekaha Kai
State Park

HAWAI'I

KONA
INTERNATIONAL
AIRPORT

Hu'ehu'e
Ranch

Hinaka
Crater

Potato
Hill

Hainoa
4,083ft

Keahole Point

Kalaoa

Wawaloli Beach
PineTrees

94

KALOKO DR

Hualalai
8,271ft

KAMEHAMEHA
PRESUMED BURIAL SITE

19

Kaloko Fishpond

KALOKO
INDUSTRIAL
PARK

Honokohau
Palani Junction

Kaloko-Honokohau
National Historic Park

Pu'u La'la'au
6,526ft

HONOKOHAU HARBOR

98

Kailua-
Kona

180

Pawai Bay

SEE "ALI'I DRIVE
AREA" MAP

North

Old Airport Beach Park

182

Kona

White Sands Beach Park

11

Holualoa

Kahalu'u Beach Park

Kahalu'u

KEAUHOU RESORT AREA

Approximate range of
Kona coffee production

Honalo

Kainaliu

Keikiwaha Point

Kealakekua

KONA HOSPITAL

HN GREENWELL
STORE MUSEUM

111

Captain Cook

KEALAKEKUA BAY
STATE HISTORICAL PARK

Napo'opo'o

Manini
Beach

Ke'ei

Ke'ei Beach

160

Honaunau

HONAUNAU
RODEO

PU'UHONUA O
HONAUNAU NATIONAL
HISTORICAL PARK

Keokea

103

Kealia

Loa Point

South

Ho'okena

101

Kona

Ho'okena Beach Park

Kapilo Bay

Lepeamoa Rock

Ka'u Loa Point

11

PACIFIC

Kona

Coast

OCEAN

0   5 mi
0   5 km

© AVALON TRAVEL

booked your trip to Hawaii: turquoise waters beside long stretches of white-sand beaches. Amazingly, there are several good options for these types of beaches within 20 minutes of Kona International Airport—and they are all public places! What might surprise you the most is that parts of this area look like they were hit by a bomb: It is completely desolate. The landscape is made up of lava fields, and in recent years, the black rocks have become dotted with white stones that spell out names of favorite teams and loved ones. Don't be thrown off by the lack of infrastructure in the area. The ocean and beaches lurking behind the lava fields are some of the most magical the island has to offer for those looking for white-sand beaches and astonishing underwater life.

South of the Airport

The small area south of the international airport looks a lot like anywhere else in suburban America. It's most significant as a landmark; many refer to Costco, which can be seen like a beacon of light up above Hina Lani Street, and Target in the Kona Commons shopping center, when giving directions. You'll likely use this area to get from one place to another and for its resource-laden shops, but don't miss out on Pine Trees, one of the best surfing spots on the island.

Ali'i Drive: Kailua and Keauhou

The heart of Kona, Ali'i Drive is the north-south thoroughfare stretching from the Keauhou resort area (the south end) through downtown Kailua and ending in the north near where Highway 11 becomes Highway 19 (and the counting of the mile markers starts all over again—actually, it starts backward). Starting at the south end of Ali'i Drive are a few larger resorts, like the Sheraton Keauhou Bay Resort and Spa and Outrigger Keauhou Beach Resort. There are really only two big resort areas on the Big Island, and Keauhou is one of them (the other is the Kohala "Gold" Coast). Since Keauhou is designed as a resort area, it is constructed so that a visitor never really has to leave its proximity. The beach access here from the

hotels and Keauhou Bay is rocky and the water can get rough. Most visitors use their hotel's or condo's pools and save a dip in the water for an evening excursion to view the manta rays that hang out in the bay.

As you drive north you'll pass by a slew of vacation rentals and crowded urban beaches. The downtown area, which is Kailua, is a combination of New Orleans and Key West. This is the area where the cruise ships dock (usually on Wednesdays), and you'll see passengers running ashore to shop. At night there is street life on Ali'i, so if you're looking to go out on the town, this is where you go. Especially on the weekends there is music blasting from the bars overhead, local kids cruising and parking in their rigged-up trucks, and tourists strolling from shop to shop. There are many stores in the downtown Ali'i section—but it's a lot of the same T-shirt shops, jewelry stores, and tour agents hocking luau and kayak adventures.

Captain Cook Area: South Kona

Captain Cook is an actual town, named for the explorer James Cook, who in 1778 was the first European to have contact with the

A Road by Any Other Name

Highway 11 and Highway 19 are the main routes in the Kona region. Highway 11 has several names: Kuakini Highway, Hawai'i Belt Road, Queen Ka'ahumanu Highway, Mamalahoa Highway. These names are sometimes used in addresses, but sometimes businesses simply use Highway 11. Highway 19 on some maps and in some addresses is also called Hawai'i Belt Road, Queen Ka'ahumanu Highway, and Mamalahoa Highway when it runs through Waimea. Remember that in Kailua town, Highway 11 and Highway 19 merge, and thus, it is important to note which highway you are on when looking for the mile marker (i.e., there is a mile marker 100 on Highway 11 and another on Highway 19). Using the mile markers is a great way to gauge how far you must travel.

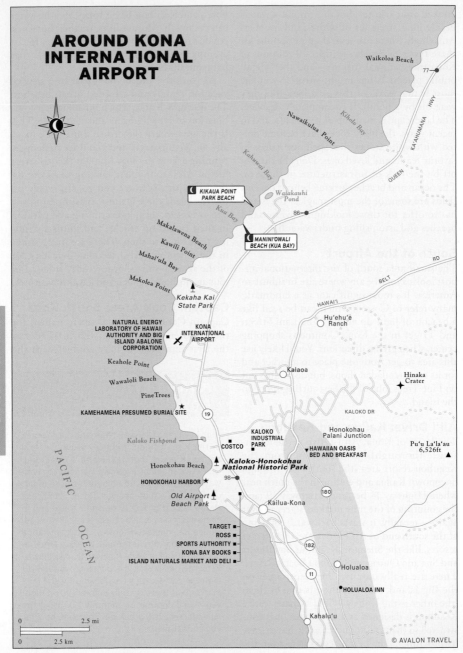

AROUND KONA INTERNATIONAL AIRPORT

Waikoloa Beach

77

KA'AHUMANA HWY

QUEEN

Nawaikulua Point

Kiholo Bay

Kahuwai Bay

Waiakauhi Pond

86

KIKAUA POINT PARK BEACH

Kua Bay

MANINI'OWALI BEACH (KUA BAY)

Makalawena Beach

Kawili Point

Mahai'ula Bay

Makolea Point

Kekaha Kai State Park

BELT RD

HAWAI'I

Hu'ehu'e Ranch

NATURAL ENERGY LABORATORY OF HAWAII AUTHORITY AND BIG ISLAND ABALONE CORPORATION

KONA INTERNATIONAL AIRPORT

Keahole Point

Wawaloli Beach

PineTrees

KAMEHAMEHA PRESUMED BURIAL SITE

Kalaoa

Hinaka Crater

KALOKO DR

19

KALOKO INDUSTRIAL PARK

Honokohau Palani Junction

Pu'u La'la'au 6,526ft

Kaloko Fishpond

COSTCO

HAWAIIAN OASIS BED AND BREAKFAST

Honokohau Beach

Kaloko-Honokohau National Historic Park

HONOKOHAU HARBOR

98

Old Airport Beach Park

Kailua-Kona

180

PACIFIC OCEAN

TARGET
ROSS
SPORTS AUTHORITY
KONA BAY BOOKS
ISLAND NATURALS MARKET AND DELI

182

11

Holualoa

HOLUALOA INN

Kahalu'u

0   2.5 mi

0   2.5 km

© AVALON TRAVEL

BIG ISLAND OF HAWAI'I

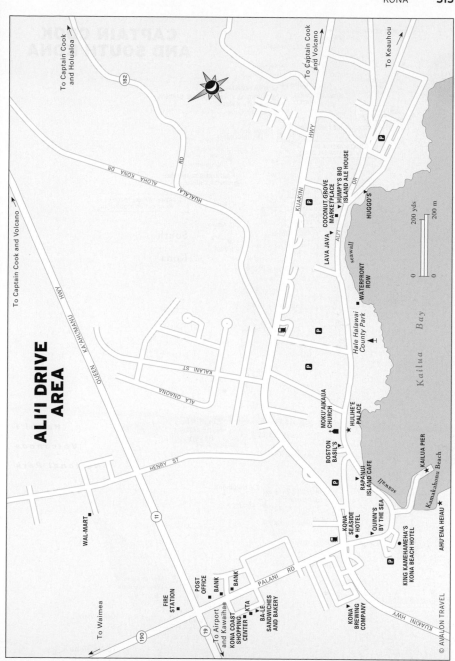

BIG ISLAND OF HAWAI'I

ALI'I DRIVE AREA

To Waimea

To Airport and Kawaihae

To Captain Cook and Volcano

To Captain Cook and Holualoa

To Captain Cook and Volcano

To Keauhou

QUEEN KA'AHUMANU HWY

HUALALAI RD

ALOHA KONA DR

KUAKINI HWY

KUAKINI

ALI'I DR

Kailua Bay

Kailua Bay

WAL-MART

FIRE STATION

POST OFFICE

BANK

BANK

KTA

BA-LE SANDWICHES AND BAKERY

KONA COAST SHOPPING CENTER

PALANI RD

HENRY ST

KALANI ST

ALA ONAONA

BOSTON BASIL'S

LAVA JAVA

COCONUT GROVE MARKETPLACE

HUMPY'S BIG ISLAND ALE HOUSE

HUGGO'S

WATERFRONT ROW

seawall

Hale Halawai County Park

MOKU'AIKAUA CHURCH

HULIHE'E PALACE

RAPANUI ISLAND CAFE

KONA SEASIDE HOTEL

QUINN'S BY THE SEA

seawall

KAILUA PIER

Kamakahonu Beach

KING KAMEHAMEHA'S KONA BEACH HOTEL

AHU'ENA HEIAU

KONA BREWING COMPANY

KUAKINI HWY

0   200 yds
0   200 m

© AVALON TRAVEL

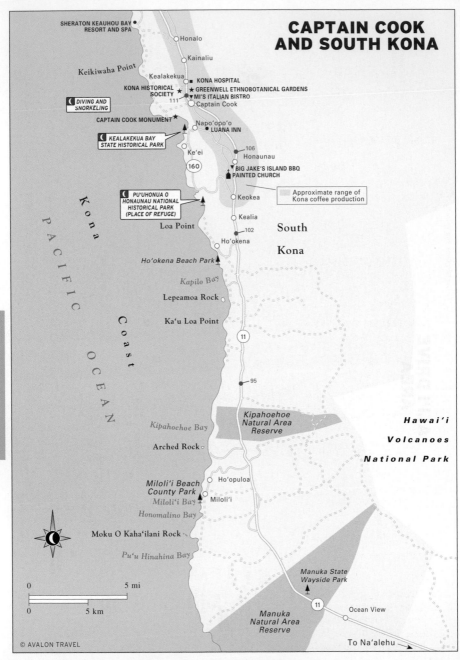

CAPTAIN COOK AND SOUTH KONA

SHERATON KEAUHOU BAY RESORT AND SPA

Honalo

Kainaliu

Keikiwaha Point

Kealakekua
KONA HOSPITAL
GREENWELL ETHNOBOTANICAL GARDENS
KONA HISTORICAL SOCIETY
MI'S ITALIAN BISTRO
111
Captain Cook

DIVING AND SNORKELING

CAPTAIN COOK MONUMENT

Napo'opo'o
LUANA INN

KEALAKEKUA BAY STATE HISTORICAL PARK

Ke'ei

160

106
Honaunau

BIG JAKE'S ISLAND BBQ
PAINTED CHURCH

PU'UHONUA O HONAUNAU NATIONAL HISTORICAL PARK (PLACE OF REFUGE)

Keokea

Kealia

Approximate range of Kona coffee production

Loa Point

102

Ho'okena

South Kona

Ho'okena Beach Park

Kapilo Bay

Lepeamoa Rock

Ka'u Loa Point

11

Kona Coast

PACIFIC OCEAN

95

Kipahoehoe Bay

Kipahoehoe Natural Area Reserve

Arched Rock

Hawai'i Volcanoes National Park

Ho'opuloa

Miloli'i Beach County Park

Miloli'i Bay

Miloli'i

Honomalino Bay

Moku O Kaha'ilani Rock

Pu'u Hinahina Bay

Manuka State Wayside Park

11

Ocean View

Manuka Natural Area Reserve

To Na'alehu

0   5 mi

0   5 km

BIG ISLAND OF HAWAI'I

© AVALON TRAVEL

Your Best Day in Kona

© MARK WASSER

BIG ISLAND OF HAWAI'I

Pu'uhonua O Honaunau National Historical Park

- Visit **Pu'uhonua O Honaunau National Historical Park** in the early morning when you'll have the place to yourself.

- Join a guided **kayaking** tour of **Kealakekua Bay,** where you'll be side-by-side with the dolphins and experience some of the best **snorkeling** on the island.

- After a busy morning, relax at the white-sand **Manini'owali Beach/Kua Bay** in Kekaha Kai State Park (or any number of gorgeous white-sand beaches north of the Kona airport).

- In the late afternoon, cool off by heading up the mountain to gallery-filled **Holualoa,** also home of the fabulous **Holuakoa Gardens and Café,** where a dinner reservation is a must.

- Finish this long day bar-hopping or dancing on **Ali'i Drive.**

RAINY DAY ALTERNATIVE

It doesn't often happen in Kona, but every once in a while you'll catch yourself in less-than-perfect weather. If so, visit the **Natural Energy Laboratory of Hawaii Authority (NELHA)** for an indoor talk on natural energy technology and efforts in Hawaii and a tour and tasting at an abalone farm.

Hawaiian Islands. An obelisk of Cook adorns Kealakekua Bay where he was killed (rumor say that the small area surrounding the obelisk is considered British territory). There are several other little towns in the area, like Kainaliu and Kealakekua (all off Highway 11), but the area generally is referred to as "Captain Cook" or South Kona.

A visit to the Kona area would not be complete without spending as much time as possible in this area, where kayak trips and snorkeling adventures are plentiful and the beaches are easily accessible. If you are water-logged and looking for some drive time, head to the main road for antiquing or to try one of several excellent restaurants in the area.

PLANNING YOUR TIME

There is probably more to do in the Kona district than any other place on the Big Island, but the good news is that even though the district is split into smaller sections, nothing is actually that far from anything else. If there is no traffic, you can make it from the airport to the town of Captain Cook in about 40 minutes.

It's best to treat the Kona region like a mini road trip starting either north or south. **Kealakekua Bay** to the south should not be missed. The water here is perfection for nearly every water activity, and there are abundant tours to choose from to assist you in exploring the grandeur that exists underwater. If you feel like staying dry for a bit, there are several nearby historical sites well worth exploring.

In many cases, the bulk of your day will occur before lunchtime, as early morning is when you'll venture out on kayaking, snorkeling, dolphin-swimming, and deep-sea fishing tours. The warm afternoons are a perfect time to relax, with little effort, on a nearby beach, such as **Kikaua Point Park Beach** or **Manini'owali Beach** in north Kona. If it's just too hot out, head north up the hill to **Holualoa,** where the weather is cooler than down below and the street is lined with art galleries. The late afternoon presents the best time to hike to one of the beaches, like **Makalawena,** that does require some walking—usually over an open lava field.

Kona is one of few places on the island with nightlife. Many first-time visitors arrange to see a luau at one of the hotels or take a stroll on Ali'i Drive to people-watch. On the weekends or holidays, the open-air Ali'i Drive bars can become quite bustling when the cover bands come out to play.

Beaches

Many of the best Kona beaches require some work to get to them. Keep in mind that it's often the destination, not the journey. The majority of routes to the beaches can be accomplished in a good pair of sandals, but the walk, which is usually over uneven lava, can be difficult for some. There are equal amounts of beaches that don't require any walking beyond from the parking lot to the sand, so don't fret if you opt out of the beaches that require more effort to get to them.

NORTH OF THE AIRPORT: NORTH KONA
Kiholo Bay

If you stop at the scenic point near mile marker 82 you get a great panoramic of **Kiholo Bay** (Hwy. 19 near mile marker 81 and also between mile markers 82 and 83, gate open 7am-7pm),

and chances are you'll want to get closer to it to see what looks like completely untouched paradise: a deserted beach with turquoise water and what appears to be an island off the bay. If you start your journey at the south end of the beach, you'll find a cold freshwater lava tube bath called the **Queen's Bath** (Keanalele Waterhole). It is a sacred site, so please be respectful. A sign there asks people to take care to respect the water by not using it for bathing. As you continue on the shoreline you'll see fancy homes with private property signs. If you continue walking north on the shoreline, you'll see turtles nesting nearby. Feel free to jump in and take a dip with them. This also is a good place for snorkeling when the water is clear. The beach ends and then you need to walk over the lava rock around the bend to a wonderful little shaded cove. From here you can swim out to that "island," which is actually attached to the landmass on its north side. Be careful of the many turtles you are likely to see in this area.

To drive to the south end of the bay, look for the stick with the yellow reflector on it on the *makai* side of the road between mile markers 82 and 83. If you're driving north on Highway 19 and you passed the blue scenic point sign, you went too far. The road you turn onto is gravel, but a rental car can make it to the end, where there are portable bathrooms. If you decide to walk all the way from Highway 19 to the beach, the makeshift parking lot is right before mile marker 81. Usually there are other cars parked on the side of the road. The trail, which will take you about 20 sweaty minutes to walk, starts to the left of the parking lot and veers left as you're walking. The benefit in walking and not driving down is that the walk will get you much closer to the bay. If you drive, you end up on the south side of the bay and need to walk around it for about 15 minutes.

Kuki'o Beach (Four Seasons Resort Beach)

The wonderful thing about Hawaii is that the entire shoreline is public—so even when the beach is at a five-star hotel, as it is in this case with **Kuki'o Beach** (Hwy. 19 between mile markers 86 and 87), the public must have access to it. The beach usually offers calm water for swimming and has a pleasant, unshaded, small white-sand area off a paved path that makes for an excellent oceanfront jogging trail. The path is part of the historical *ala loa* (long path) route that ancestors would use for a nightly procession. Given that the beach actually is maintained by the Four Seasons Resort and since they don't want "the public" sneaking off into the hotel to use facilities, they have provided bathrooms, showers, and drinking water for the public here, and they are nice (I mean, it is the Four Seasons). There is no lifeguard on duty. This bay is a fisheries management area, which means that you can fish here but a board alerts you to how many fish you can catch of each type.

To get to Kuki'o Beach, you are required to stop at the Four Seasons Resort gate and alert the guard that you are going to the public access beach. Note: The resort is open to the public, so you can also say you are visiting it and go take a peek if you want. Follow the signs to the "public access" and park in the lot where the road ends.

Kikaua Point Park Beach

Kikaua Point Park Beach (Kuki'o Nui Dr., off Hwy. 19 between mile markers 87 and 88) is perfect in so many ways. Perhaps due to the fact that entry is limited (passes are handed out at the security gate), it's never as crowded as you'd expect it to be. The water is glorious. Even when there are waves at other places on the same shoreline, it remains calm here, making it a perfect spot for kids, although there is not a lifeguard on duty. Bring a picnic—locals tend to bring pizza from Costco—and head to the grassy area shaded by the coconut trees. Bathroom, shower, and drinking water are available and they are lovely facilities due to the fact that they are maintained privately.

To get to Kikaua Point Park Beach, turn *makai* onto Kuki'o Nui Drive and proceed to the security booth. The guards only hand out 28 passes per day, but the turnover is pretty high, so if you wait around long enough, and people do, you'll likely end up with a pass. Another option is to park at the Kuki'o Beach parking lot near the Four Seasons Resort and walk south to Kikaua—it's only a 10-minute walk. Don't get tricked in the parking lot with the Beach Access sign pointing to the left—this is only the tide pool area. Take the paved path straight back, about a five-minute walk, to the sandy portion. When you're done with the best beach day ever, don't forget to return your access card to the security guard so that someone else can enjoy the beach.

Manini'owali Beach (Kua Bay)

Before about 15 years ago there wasn't a road to get to **Manini'owali Beach** (Hwy. 19 between mile markers 88 and 89, daily 9am-7pm) in the Kua Bay section of Kekaha Kai State Park. One had to really want to get there by hiking

BIG ISLAND OF HAWAI'I

© MARK WASSER

Makalawena Beach

or finding a four-wheel-drive way. And even with all those barriers, people still went—so you know it has to be good. It's a small white-sand beach with turquoise water that is excellent for body boarding and snorkeling. There is not much shade, but if you're aching for sun this is a perfect place to spend the day absorbing some rays. Nowadays, the state has made it easier to get here. A lovely paved road reaches a parking lot and full facilities. It's getting so crowded that now there is a security guard at the entrance to the beach itself (he doesn't seem to do much besides protect the beauty of the place). To get there from Highway 19, look for the Kehaha Kai Park sign and turn *makai* across from West Hawaii Veterans Cemetery.

Makalawena Beach

In the state beach section of Kekaha Kai State Park, **Makalawena** (Hwy. 19 between mile markers 90 and 91, daily 9am-7:30pm) is a favorite beach of many locals, probably because it's an authentic Big Island experience given that it requires a little bit of hiking to

get there. If you make the 30-minute trek to the beach, you'll be rewarded by the isolated white sand and turquoise water. Given the walk, Makalawena is often fairly deserted (it has no facilities). The beach itself is made up of three crescent-shaped white-sand areas that are backed by trees (although there isn't much shade). Body boarding and snorkeling are possible.

Before you get excited about coming here, you should know that while you can do it in a standard rental car, it's a slow-going 20-minute drive and then there is a 30-minute walk over a lava field. From Highway 19, look for the Kekaha Kai Park sign and turn *makai*. The initial road starts off paved but then quickly becomes uneven lava.

To get to Makalawena, walk from the parking lot through the first beach, **Mahai'ula,** where the bathrooms are located, and then through the lava field. When you start coming to sand again, you're close. You might want to wear good shoes on the walk, as the lava field can be tricky to navigate.

SOUTH OF THE AIRPORT
Pine Trees

Although famous with surfers and the site of many competitions, **Pine Trees** (Hwy. 19 near mile marker 95, access road gate open daily 7am-7pm) is not a good swimming beach, nor are there any pine trees. There are a few one-towel coves along the rocky shoreline where you can gain access to the water, but mostly it's a place from which to observe the action. To get to Pine Trees, turn *makai* where you see the sign for the Natural Energy Laboratory of Hawaii Authority (NELHA). You can also follow the road toward the NELHA facility a short way to **Wawaloli Beach,** a small public beach of sand and crushed coral, fronted by plenty of rock near the south end of the airport runway. There are a few restrooms and some picnic tables.

Old Airport Beach Park and Pawai Bay

We should thank whatever politician decided to take this old abandoned airport and turn it into **Old Airport Beach Park** (Hwy. 19 between mile markers 99 and 100). There are nicely kept picnic areas that get busy, and the facilities are placed between the parking lot and sandy area, which doesn't make for an ideal beach. The runway is now utilized as a jogging area, but if you're looking for some beach jogging, head north on the sand toward Pawai Bay. Since you are near a reef here, the little bay with sand is the best place to get in the water for some excellent snorkeling. Locals will tell you that you can camp here, but I don't recommend it.

ALI'I DRIVE: KAILUA AND KEAUHOU
Kahalu'u Beach Park

With a large covered picnic pavilion, barbecue pits, a guy sitting around playing ukulele on a bench, and locals drinking from the backs of their trucks in the parking lot, **Kahalu'u Beach Park** (Ali'i Dr. near the Outrigger Keauhou Beach Resort between mile markers 3.5 and 4, daily 6am-11pm) has all the makings of a quintessential urban beach park. Although

there is a small sandy beach area and a lifeguard on duty, it's not so much a place to lay out. But it is a good spot for snorkeling and ideal for kids since the water is shallow and calm. Bathroom and shower facilities are available.

White Sands Beach (La'aloa Beach Park)

Even though **White Sands Beach** (Ali'i Dr. between mile markers 3.5 and 4, daily 7am-11pm, gate closes at 8pm) is also right off the road, it still retains a peaceful feel to it. Officially known as La'aloa (Very Sacred) Beach Park and nicknamed Disappearing Sands Beach, it is popular for body boarding, surfing, and sunning (there is little shade here). Grab your towel and head out early because this beach gets crowded on weekends. Bathroom and shower facilities are available and there is a lifeguard on duty.

Parking can be tricky. Locals park on the *makai* side of the road (where it says No Parking) or in a small lot across the street.

CAPTAIN COOK AREA: SOUTH KONA
C Kealakekua Bay State Historical Park

Tourists flock to **Kealakekua Bay State Historical Park** (Beach Rd. off Hwy. 160, daylight hours) to kayak, go on kayak tours to the monument, or to simply snorkel. The park is exactly at the intersection where Beach Road intersects with Napo'opo'o Road. There is a parking lot with a boat launch right at the intersection, and a few yards away is the historical park with bathrooms, showers, picnic areas, drinking water, and an ample parking area.

Given the proximity to the reef, the snorkeling here is excellent, and depending on the season, it's common to see dolphins swimming up next to you. The kayaking here is some of the easiest ocean kayaking, so it's suitable for novices.

After some recent controversy, it is now required that you obtain a permit (go to www. hawaiistateparks.org/parks/hawaii and click on Kealakekua Bay State Historical Park) to land

BIG ISLAND OF HAWAI'I

© MARK WASSER

Kealakekua Bay is a great place for novice snorkelers to get their start.

at the monument across the bay. You don't need a permit if you're just going to paddle around and not land. The controversy has ensued, however, because there is no regulation of the permits and many of them are taken by the tour operating companies. If you make it across the bay and "permit" yourself to get out, a trail heads uphill from the statue.

Manini Beach

Manini Beach (off Hwy. 160) is a prime snorkeling and kayaking area with great views of the Captain Cook Monument in the distance, but it was greatly affected by the tsunami in March 2011, which forced two beachfront homes into the ocean. Currently, the beach area is slowly being restored, and locals think it will be an even nicer beach now that it will be less rocky. Instead there will be more sand and a larger open area. There are very few places to park here so it may be hard to find a spot, but the good news is that the water never gets too crowded. From Highway 160, also called Pu'uhonua Road, turn *makai* onto Kahauloa

Road and then right onto Manini Beach Road—follow it around for 0.2 mile until you see cars parked and a bay.

Ke'ei Bay Beach

A real local place, **Ke'ei Bay Beach** (off Hwy. 160) has a lovely beach, and it can get surprisingly busy given how you have to be in the know to get here. There is white sand and the water is calm for swimming or snorkeling. Since you're staring at prime real estate you'll likely be surprised by the small, somewhat underdeveloped homes surrounding the area. The land is owned by Kamehameha Schools trust, and long-term leases are given for less than market value to native Hawaiians.

From Highway 160, also called Pu'uhonua Road, turn onto an unmarked dirt on the *makai* side between Ke'ei transfer station and Keawaiki Road, which it is gated. Four-wheel drives are best for this road to the beach, but you can reach it in a standard car with some careful slow driving. Drive toward the ocean (or you can walk about 15 minutes) until you can't drive anymore. Park in the semi-designated lot in front of the houses.

Ho'okena Beach Park

The road down to **Ho'okena Beach Park** (Hwy. 11 near mile marker 101) is worth the trip; it has excellent views of the coastline and the surrounding area, and if you are an advanced biker you might want to try this route for a challenge. There is an actual sandy beach here, and it makes for a nice place to bring a towel and sit the day away. There is even some shade.

The water here is not too rough, so it's a nice place to swim, snorkel, or kayak (rentals are available at the beach or by calling 808/328-8430, $20 for a single kayak for two hours or $25 for a tandem). If you get there early you might see a spinner dolphin, as this area is one of their habitats. Facilities such as showers, bathrooms, barbecues, and a large covered picnic area are available. Camping is allowed is designated areas, and permits can be obtained starting at 9am at the beach from the attendant or online (http://hookena.org/camping.html). There is also a separate area to park if you're camping here, to the left of the main parking lot. The area is popular with locals and can get crowded and rowdy at night, so it might not be the best place if you're camping with kids or looking for a peaceful evening.

From Highway 11 it is a two-mile paved windy road to the entrance. Where the road splits when you are almost at the ocean, fork to the left—don't go straight—where there is usually a sign for kayak rentals, and head on the one-lane road into the parking lot. You will see the sign for Ho'okena on the ocean side of the road.

EXCURSIONS TO KA'U

While Ka'u often serves simply as the stretch that gets visitors between Kona and Volcanoes National Park, hidden away off the main highway are magnificent secluded beaches of all colors (from green to black to white sand) and sizes. Some of these beaches require a greater sense of adventure and more than just the average rental car. An all-wheel-drive or four-wheel-drive will serve you well. Ka'u is often the hottest part of the island, thus beaches are best experienced early in the morning while the day is still cool.

Punalu'u Black Sand Beach

If you want to see some turtles lazily basking in the sun, I can almost guarantee that you will see one at **Punalu'u Black Sand Beach** (Hwy. 11 between mile markers 56 and 57). It is the most easily accessible and nicest beach in the area, so it can get pretty busy on weekends. Park on either the right side of the beach near the picnic stands and bathroom area or on the left side closer to the beach itself. Closer to the left-side parking area is a lovely, peaceful pond filled with lily pads and ducks. Camping is allowed here, and on holiday weekends local families take full advantage of it and it can get packed.

South Point

South Point is exactly what you think it is—the most southern landmass of the island and the United States of America. It lies at a latitude 500 miles farther south than Miami and 1,000 miles below Los Angeles. Known in Hawaiian as Ka Lae, it was probably the first landfall made by the Polynesian explorers on the islands. Most people drive down **South Point Road** (off Hwy. 11 between mile markers 69 and 70) so that they can say they've been there and then to do one of the most thrilling activities possible on the Big Island—jump off Ka Lae and enjoy the 50-foot fall into the ocean. Luckily, there is a rope ladder available to get you back to the top. On your way down South Point Road to Ka Lae, look at the Kamoa Wind Farm—where windmills go to die—and the mostly functioning Pakini Nui Wind Farm towering overhead.

The sign to South Point Road will be obvious off Highway 11. Follow it south for 12 miles for some of the best photo opportunities on the Big Island. The drive down South Point is now paved and easy for any car, although it is narrow, so watch for oncoming cars and pull off to the side if necessary. The road splits somewhat—stay to the right. Where the road ends you'll surely see many other cars parked and you should also park here.

Cashing in on its proximity to South Point, the closest town, **Na'alehu,** is best known as the place that has all the "southernmost" restaurants, bars, and bakeries. It is a mecca of southernism, and in addition to that fun fact it has some of the better culinary delights in the area. Check out the overhanging monkeypod trees forming a magnificent living tunnel in front of some of the former plantation managers' homes as you pass through on Highway 11.

Water Sports

CANOEING AND KAYAKING

Kealakekua Bay is the perfect place to canoe or kayak given the calm water, the abundance of nearby dolphins, and the lure of boating toward the Captain Cook Monument; however, there are a lot of politics around this activity. You are required to obtain a permit (go to www.hawaiistateparks.org/parks/hawaii and click on Kealakekua Bay State Historical Park) to land your boat at the monument. Only a few permits are given each day, and it seems that the big tour operators have pre-reserved them, leaving the small operators without permits.

If you drive down to the bay you'll see many locals renting boats out by the hour. As the day goes on it's easy to haggle down the price (usually $20-30 per boat). The large tour operators do not like these "rental agencies," as they aren't insured and do not take care to *malama 'aina* (take care of the environment). But they have cheap boats that are at the bay and don't require any additional transport besides putting them in the water. All the larger companies rent single and double kayaks by the day (prices vary but are all around the same range of $40), which are newer, better boats than the ones you'd pick up at the bay, and the companies will assist you in putting the kayak on your car.

The larger companies offer the same tour of the bay, which includes four-hour morning or afternoon combination trips of kayaking, snorkeling, looking for dolphins, and paddling to the Captain Cook Monument. The differences between the tours are the quality of the boats and expertise of the tour guides.

The preferred company for the Kealakekua kayak tour, because of its quality of tours and equipment, is **Kona Boys** (79-7539 Mamalahoa Hwy./Hwy. 11, 808/328-1234, www.konaboys.com, $125 per person). Kona Boys also offers kayak tours to Pawai Bay (near the Old Airport Beach Park with the fantastic snorkeling). In addition, a trip in an old-style canoe leaves from the Kailua dock (1 hour, $50); someone boats you around the bay while giving you the history of the coastline.

Other choices for kayak tours include the capable **Aloha Kayak Company** (Hwy. 11 between mile markers 113 and 114, 808/322-2868, www.alohakayak.com, $109 adults, $59 children).

For a different kind of kayak adventure (and one that might be a little less crowded), try **Ocean Safaris** (on Keauhou Bay, 808/326-4699, www.oceansafariskayaks.com, Mon.-Sat., 3.5-hour morning tour, $64). This tour starts in Keauhou Bay and journeys to a sea cave in Kuamoo Bay. You'll snorkel on the way in an effort to view dolphins and turtles.

◖ DIVING AND SNORKELING

Nearly every kayak trip or boating trip includes snorkeling, but if you're simply looking to rent gear on your own, there are several longstanding shops in the area. Nearly the entire coast presents ideal snorkeling conditions given how close the reef is to the shoreline; however, some areas are harder to access due to the rocky coast. Beginners can easily start at Two Step or Pu'uhonua O Honaunau National Historical Park. The best spots are Kealakekua Bay and

© KEVIN PANIZZA/123RF.COM

diving off the Kona coast

Pawai Bay during the day and Keauhou Bay at night for the manta ray sightings.

Big Island Divers (74-5467 Kaiwi St., 808/329-6068, www.bigislanddivers.com) offers a similar deal to other providers in the area. A two-tank guided tour ($130 per person or $80 for snorkeling includes lunch) is offered most days (8am-1:30pm), and most nights they offer manta ray night dives and snorkeling trips ($100-135 per person diving or $80-90 snorkeling) with several different combinations of options, from one tank to two tanks and depending on the length of trip. The best thing about this company is that it offers discounts for the more you dive—so if you think you'll go out at least twice, Big Island Divers is a good deal for you.

Body Glove Cruises (75-5629 Kuakini Hwy., check in at Kailua Pier, 800/551-8911, www.bodyglovehawaii.com) is one of the larger companies with a big boat. The 4.5-hour deluxe snorkel and dolphin-viewing tour ($120 adults, $78 children 6-17) is a full-service excursion with breakfast, lunch, snacks, cash bar,

snorkel gear, and instruction. However, given the immense amount of time that you're eating and drinking, the water time is only about half the time that you're on the boat. The same goes for the non-deluxe shorter three-hour excursion ($78 adults, $58 children 6-17); only half the time is in the water and the other half is spent snacking and drinking.

Captain Zodiac (Honokohau Harbor, 808/329-3199, www.captainzodiac.com) offers a four-hour snorkel and dolphin-watching tour, but does it from a Zodiac boat and leaves from the harbor near Kailua, although the tour travels to Kealakekua Bay ($104 per adult, $84 per child with online discount). This is an extremely professional and dedicated company that truly values customer service. Also, Zodiacs are a good option if you don't want to paddle around yourself but still want to be close to the dolphin and snorkeling action.

Fair Wind (78-7130 Kaleiopapa St., Keauhou Bay, 808/322-2788, www.fair-wind.com, snorkel and dive tour $165 plus tax per person, manta ray diving $89 per person, discount if booked online) is your first-class deluxe option for snorkeling and diving tours. Fair Wind offers a five-hour morning snorkel and dive that includes breakfast and lunch. The boat, the *Hula Kai,* is comfortable, and staff is undoubtedly there to meet your every need. The manta ray night snorkel 6:30-8:30pm includes all gear and a snack. Other places offer manta ray night tours, but Fair Wind's service sets them apart. A manta ray expert on board films the entire experience for purchase after the trip.

A longtime favorite of locals, **Jack's Diving Locker** (75-5813 Ali'i Dr., 808/329-7585, www.jacksdivinglocker.com) offers two-tank morning dives (8:30am, $125 per person plus gear rental or $55 for snorkeling; all prices include lunch) and manta ray night trips ($145 per person plus gear rental and $95 per person for snorkeling, not offered Sun. or Tues.). A four-day open-water PADI certification course ($550, minimum two students) is also available.

Kona Honu Divers (74-5583 Luhia St., 808/324-4668, konahonudivers.com) is another outfitter with a good reputation for service and luxury, and this one really specializes in diving (not just snorkeling). They offer a few different types of tours, from a manta ray night dive ($95 for one tank and $130 for two tanks) to manta ray night snorkeling ($80 per person) to two-tank daytime dives for beginners to advanced divers ($130-170 per person). On Wednesday they have a black-water night dive that occurs after the manta ray dive for those who really want to experience the ocean by night ($150 just for the dive or $230 plus tax with the manta ray dive).

Kona Boys (79-7539 Mamalahoa Hwy./ Hwy. 11, 808/328-1234, www.konaboys.com) rents snorkeling gear and offers discounts if you rent for several days.

Sandwich Isle Divers (75-5729 Ali'i Dr., 808/329-9188, www.sandwichisledivers.com, daily 8am-6pm) is a reputable company that offers a slew of services, from rentals to charters (two tanks, two locations runs $120-165 per person depending on level of instruction and equipment needed). In addition to their daily dives and manta ray night dives, they also offer a four-day open-water PADI certification course ($550).

SURFING AND STAND-UP PADDLE-BOARDING

Surfing is not as significant a sport on the Big Island as on the other islands. Proportionally for the size of the island, there are fewer good surfing spots on this island, and many of the traditional surfing sites are just not easy to access. Whether this is due to the lack of the underwater environment necessary to create

Watching Manta Rays

Many say that Kona is the number one place in the world to see manta rays, partly because they have become conditioned over time to feed at night in Keauhou Bay, eating the plankton attracted to the light at the Sheraton hotel. Snorkeling companies offer nighttime excursions into the bay so that you can snorkel with the manta rays.

Manta rays are completely harmless. Although their wingspan averages 5-8 feet, they have no teeth or stinger—but given their large size, seeing a manta ray close up can be both terrifying and exhilarating. If you are apt to get seasick, this might not be the best trip for you. Even though the tour boats don't travel far, at night the water can be rough. Once one person gets sick, it seems like several more people follow.

While you won't be up close and personal with the manta rays, an alternative is simply to watch them from the Sheraton Keauhou Resort and Spa. The aptly named **Manta Ray Bar and Grill** (5:30-11pm with a good happy hour 5:30-6:30am) has a viewing area and offers complimentary manta talks every day but Sunday at sunset.

the right kind of waves or for some other reason, conditions seem to be lacking for great surf that the other islands have in abundance. However, a few local sites on the Kona side do draw the faithful. Perhaps the most popular is the break along the reef at **Kahalu'u Bay** in front of the beach park. Two alternative spots are **Banyans** near White Sands Beach (a.k.a. Disappearing Sands Beach) and **Pine Trees,** north of town near the airport. Any of the shops that sell or rent boards can give you current information about surfing conditions and sites.

Stand-up paddle-boarding is the newest and hottest sport around. In many cases, paddle boarders can be found where the surfers are. However, you'll also see paddle boarders out with boogie boarders since smaller waves are much more practical for the stand-up paddle board and essential for novices. If you are just beginning, try a lesson or rent a board and test it out on some flat, still water. Most places that rent surfboards also rent stand-up paddle boards.

If you need a rental, oftentimes there will be beachfront peddlers hocking boards at hourly rates (you can bargain). Many of the tour outfitters, such as the ones located near the Kailua Pier, rent boards out by the day or week. **Kona Boys** (79-7539 Mamalahoa Hwy./Hwy. 11, 808/328-1234, www.konaboys.com) is one of few providers in Kona that offers stand-up paddle-board instruction ($75 per person for 1.5-hour group class, minimum two people, or $175 for private instruction). They also rent stand-up paddle boards ($25 per hour or $67 per day). If you're looking for surf instruction, contact **Ocean Eco Tours** (Honokohau Harbor off Hwy. 19, 808/324-7873, www.oceanecotours.com, 8:30am or 11:30am check in, group lessons $95, private $150 for 2 hours), which holds the first permit to operate in Kaloko-Honokohau Park boundaries.

DOLPHIN SWIMS AND WHALE-WATCHING

Many of the kayaking and snorkeling trips offer dolphin options (both viewing and swimming with dolphins), since Kealakekua Bay has it all and the majority of boat trips will state that whale viewing is available during the winter season. Listed here are outfitters and excursions that are fully dedicated to dolphin and/or whale swims and watches. If you want to swim with the dolphins it's best to join an organized trip so that you have some instruction and assistance with this undertaking.

Dan McSweeney loves whales and wants you to love them too. At **Dan McSweeney's Whale Watching Learning Adventures** (Honokohau Harbor off Hwy. 19, 888/942-5376, http://ilovewhales.com, Dec.-Mar. only, $90 adults, $80 children), he personally conducts each tour and guarantees that you will see whales. If you're interested in learning about whales, this tour is for you. There is no open bar on the boat. Morning and afternoon departures are available and the tour lasts three hours.

One Love One Spirit (808/987-0359, www.oneloveonespirit.com/boat.html, 4-hour tour $185 plus tax per person)—the name gives

dolphin jumping at Kealakekua Bay

© MARK WASSER

it away (doesn't it?). Phillipa, the company owner, runs morning tours, mini-retreats, and week-long retreats training visitors how to connect with the dolphins. This company is all about communing with spinner dolphins in the most respectful manner possible—but this is a good thing. There is some touchy-feely stuff that goes along with the swimming, but you'll really "get" dolphins when you're done.

Sunlight on Water (Honokohau Harbor off Hwy. 19, 808/896-2480, sunlightonwater.com) offers whale-watching tours (afternoons daily during winter, $75 per person), a three-hour tour to swim with spinner dolphins (mornings daily, $110 per person if booked online, includes snorkel gear) and manta ray swims (nightly, $71 per person if booked online). The good deal here is that they will offer you a discount if you book more than one trip with them. They are highly recommended for the dolphin swim since that is their real passion, but other companies might be better for whale-watching and manta ray trips.

SPORTFISHING

The fishing around the Big Island's Kona Coast ranges from excellent to outstanding! It's legendary for marlin fishing, but there are other fish in the sea. The best time of year for big blues is July-September; August is the optimum month. Rough seas can keep boats in for a few days during December and early January, but by February all are generally out. A large fleet of charter boats with skilled captains and tested crews is ready to take you out. Most of the island's 80 charter boats are berthed at Honokohau Harbor off Hwy. 19, about midway between downtown Kailua and Kona airport. When the big fish are brought in, they're weighed in at the fuel dock, usually around 11:30am and 3:30pm. Honokohau Harbor has far eclipsed Kailua pier, which is now tamed and primarily for swimmers, triathletes, and body boarders.

There is some correlation between the amount you pay for your charter or tour and the experience you have. What you want to check for when booking a tour is if there is a minimum requirement of passengers if you are signing up for a shared boat. But not all boats even have the shared option and instead require you to charter the entire boat. Also, for larger companies that have multiple boats and captains, you might want to check what boat/captain you'll be joining and what their success rate is out at sea. If you visit **Honokohau Harbor** (on Kealakehe Pkwy. off Hwy. 19 between mile markers 97 and 98) and walk around the dock, you'll surely find someone eager to get you onto their boat early the next morning. Here are some places to get started for booking your fishing excursion.

Kona Billfish Charter (808/329-2840) has a few different boats, including the *Wild Hooker* boat with Captain Randy Parker. Randy is the son of George Parker, who is well known in Kona as the father of sportfishing. Other boats are: *The Silky* (808/938-0706, silkysportfishing@msn.com), *Hapa Laka* (808/322-2229, www.hapalakafishingcharters.com), and *Sea Wife II* (808/329-1806, seawifecharters.com, shared charter $95 per person for 4 hours). **Bite Me** (808/936-3442, www.bitemesportfishing.com) is a well-known corporate option with many boats and captains, and *The Camelot* (www.camelotsportfishing.com), which touts itself as family run, is an excellent option. They only offer shared boat options if others call for the same day (it rarely happens), but their charters are reasonably priced, their boat is in good shape, and the family that operates the boat is experienced with a good track record.

BOAT TOURS

Boat tours are more popular during the winter season when whale-watching is at its prime; nevertheless, during off-season an evening (or day) on the water can still be a fun experience, and don't fret—the dolphins are available year-round.

Kailua Bay Charter (Kailua Harbor in front of Courtyard King Kamehameha's Kona Beach Hotel, 808/324-1749, www.konaglassbottomboat.com, daily 10:30am, 11:30am, and 12:30pm, $40 adults, $20 children under

12) offers the unique experience of an hour-long glass bottom boat cruise. It's sort of like snorkeling but on a boat—you get to see wonderful marine life without getting wet. It's a nice way to see coral and tropical fish—and an especially easy way to show young children what lies beneath the ocean—but for the hour-long excursion your money and time might be better used elsewhere, since at times it can be difficult to actually see anything from above the glass.

What is most notable about **Body Glove Cruises** (75-5629 Kuakini Hwy., check in at Kailua Pier, 800/551-8911, www.bodyglove-hawaii.com) is that they can accommodate wheelchairs on their boat. Body Glove will also accommodate gluten-free and vegan dietary restrictions with 48 hours notice. They offer two types of dining cruises with different vibes. The first tour is the historical dinner cruise ($94 adults, $58 children), which includes a full dinner, one complimentary cocktail, live entertainment, and the highlight—a tour with instruction of historical sites on the coast. The sunset cocktail cruise is the same price as the historical dinner cruise but only serves heavy appetizers, although you won't mind since there is a full open bar and live entertainment. Both tours offer whale-watching opportunities during winter.

Hiking and Biking

HIKING

If serious hiking is what you're looking for, you'll want to visit other regions of the islands. Instead, the Kona area offers a lot of moderate trails that are almost always the means to getting to some awesome beach.

For instance, you can hike to **Captain Cook Monument** via the inland trail. It's not the most exciting hike ever, but the destination is the goal. The trail starts on Napo'opo'o Road just 500 feet below where it drops off Highway 11 (between mile markers 110 and 111). Look for a group of three coconut trees right near a telephone pole. The trailhead will be obvious, as it is worn there. It will take you 60-90 minutes to descend and much longer to return to the top. While on the trail, if you see any side paths, just always keep to the left.

If you are looking for something more organized, try **Hawaii Forest and Trails** (74-5035B Queen Ka'ahumanu Hwy./Hwy. 19, 808/331-8505, www.hawaii-forest.com). Although their headquarters is in the heart of Kona, their tours are outside this region, mainly to Kohala and Volcano. It is a wonderful company with an excellent environmental ethic—the tours are highly recommended.

BIKING

Home to the famous Ironman World Championship, Kona takes biking seriously. On any given day you'll easily see many serious bikers riding along Highway 19, sometimes faster than the cars. Some areas have semi-designated bike lanes. Highway 19 is an ideal ride: smooth and flat and uninterrupted for many miles. Check out PATH (www.pathhawaii.org) to learn more about efforts in Hawaii to develop bike lanes.

Since Kona is a bike town, there are many shops that build custom bikes for elite athletes. If you're just looking for a rental, visit **Cycle Station** (73-5619 Kauhola St., 808/327-0087, www.cyclestationhawaii.com or www.konabik-erentals.com, Mon.-Fri. 10am-6pm, Sat. 10am-5pm, Sun. 10am-4pm, $20-75 a day). The website has an extensive list of what bikes are available, ranging from hybrid to luxury bikes. Another option with online booking options is **Bike Works** (74-5583 Luhia St., 808/326-2453, http://bikeworkskona.com, Mon.-Sat. 9am-6pm, Sun. 10am-4pm, $40-60).

If you're aching for a guided or group riding tour, consider **Orchid Isle Bicycling** (808/327-0087, www.cyclekona.com, $125-145 per person), which offers four different trips. Some

BIG ISLAND OF HAWAI'I

trips are for beginners while others are for more experienced riders, like the ride up the Kohala Mountain Range. Orchid Isle also offers week-long bicycling tours that include accommodations ($3,000) for those who want to cycle around the entire island.

Golf

Sometimes it seems that half of available land on the Big Island is dedicated to golf courses (that's not a real statistic, it just seems that way). With perfect weather for the sport, the Kona side does a good job creating courses to meet the demand of visitors. The majority of resorts have their own courses (or courses that they partner with to offer discounts). However, some truly public courses do exist and usually offer lower prices than those at the resorts. If the greens fees seem a little much for you, wait until midafternoon when the fees tend to drop substantially.

The **Kona Country Club** (78-7000 Ali'i Dr., 808/322-2595, www.konagolf.com) is a lovely golf course near the end of Ali'i Drive in Keauhou that has 18-hole ocean and mountain courses with grand views over this eminently rocky coast. Greens fees run $145 for the mountain course and $165 for the ocean course, with senior and "twilight" discounts available. The pro shop is open daily, and the adjacent Vista Restaurant at the clubhouse serves breakfast and lunch (daily 8am-3pm, lounge open till 6:30pm).

A little farther afield but still close enough to Kailua to make a good play date are Big Island Country Club and Makalei Hawaii Country Club—both are along Mamalahoa Highway heading toward Waimea. The **Big Island Country Club** (Hwy. 190 at mile marker 20, 808/325-5044, www.bigislandcountryclub.net) is a rolling, challenging course with wonderful vistas over the Kohala Coast. Greens fees run $69 for morning play and $55 in the afternoon (*kama'aina* discount available). Carved from ranchland up on the steep hillside closer to Kailua is the equally challenging **Makalei Hawaii Country Club** (72-3890 Hawai'i Belt Rd., 808/325-6625, www.makalei.com), where play costs $85 before 11am, $65 11am-1pm, or $55 after that. A nice *kama'aina* discount is available.

Sights

SOUTH OF THE AIRPORT
Kaloko-Honokohau National Historical Park

Looking to learn more about the lives of ancient Hawaiians? Well, look no further. Kaloko-Honokohau National Historical Park (Hwy. 19 between mile markers 97 and 98, 808/326-9057, www.nps.gov/kaho, 8:30am-4pm) houses fishponds that highlight the engineering skills of ancient Hawaiians. These fishponds are home to birds migrating for the winter as well as endangered Hawaiian stilts and coots. Take a walk around the fishponds to **Honokohau Beach,** where on any given day you'll see plenty of sea turtles lounging in the sand. If you're lucky you might also see a monk seal. Continue on the beach and visit the *heiau* (temple) that sits on the south end of the beach and then follow the well-marked trail back over the lava field to the visitors center near the restrooms and parking lot.

The park is serious about locking the gate at 4pm. Another option for accessing the park is through the **Honokohau Harbor** (on Kealakehe Pkwy. off Hwy. 19 between mile markers 97 and 98), where there is a parking lot and restroom area. Although this is a national historical park, quite a few people use it solely as a beach

Kaloka-Honokohau National Historical Park

spot. It's a nice enough beach, usually not that crowded and with calm waters, but it is at the small boat harbor and next to the airport, making the water a bit murky.

ALI'I DRIVE: KAILUA AND KEAUHOU
Historical Kailua

In reality, Kailua proper extends farther than Ali'i Drive, but commonly Kailua refers to the historical area, which is the north end of Ali'i Drive with the shops. For instance, Ali'i Drive is the location for the Hulihe'e Palace—the last royal palace in the United States of America and where King Kamehameha spent his last days. If historical Kailua is truly what you are seeking, contact the **Kona Historical Society** (808/938-8825, khs@konahistorical.org). The society's 90-minute tours are given only to groups of 10 or more, but likely you'll be able to get your hands on an extensive pamphlet that outlines the historical relevance of the area.

Also, **Body Glove Cruises** offers historical sunset dinner cruises (808/326-7122 or 800/551-8911, www.bodyglovehawaii.com, Tues., Thurs., Sat., adults $94, youth 6-17 $58, under 6 free) that will take you to some of the coastal historical sights, and part of the proceeds from this two-hour sunset cruise go to support the Kona Historical Society. Price includes dinner, dessert, and complimentary cocktail. You'll cruise around the bay in this "you'll do it all tour" that combines food, entertainment, a historical spiel, and the promise of seeing dolphins and/or whales depending on the season. It's sort of a luau on the water but a good way to check lots of "must do" activities off your list at once.

AHU'ENA HEIAU

Directly seaward of Courtyard King Kamehameha's Kona Beach Hotel (75-5660 Palani Rd.), at the north end of "downtown" Kailua, is the restored **Ahu'ena Heiau.** Built on an artificial island in Kamakahonu (Eye of the Turtle) Beach, it's in an important historical area. Kamehameha I, the great conqueror, came here to spend the last years of his life, settling down to a peaceful existence after many years of war and strife. The king, like all Hawaiians, reaffirmed his love of the 'aina and tended his own royal taro patch on the slopes of Mount

Hualalai. After he died, his bones were prepared according to ancient ritual on a stone platform within the temple, then taken to a secret burial place, which is believed to be just north of town somewhere near Wawahiwaʻa Point—but no one knows for sure. It was Kamehameha who initiated the first rebuilding of Ahuʻena Heiau, a temple of peace and prosperity dedicated to Lono, god of fertility.

The tallest structure on the temple grounds is the ʻanuʻu (oracle tower), where the chief priest, in deep trance, received messages from the gods. Throughout the grounds are superbly carved kia akua (temple image posts) in the distinctive Kona style, considered some of the finest of all Polynesian art forms. The spiritual focus of the heiau was humanity's higher nature, and the tallest figure, crowned with an image of the golden plover, was that of Koleamoku, a god of healing. Another interesting structure is a small thatched hut of sugarcane leaves, Hale Nana Mahina, which means "house from which to watch the farmland." Kamehameha would come here to meditate while a guard kept watch from a nearby shelter. The commanding view from the doorway affords a sweeping panorama from the sea to the king's plantations on the slopes of Mount Hualalai. Though the temple grounds, reconstructed under the auspices of the Bishop Museum, are impressive, they are only one-third their original size. The heiau itself is closed to visitors, but you can get a good look at it from the shore.

KAILUA PIER

While in the heart of downtown, make sure to visit **Kailua Pier,** which is directly in front of Ahuʻena Heiau. Tour boats and the occasional fishing boat use this facility, so there is some activity on and off all day. Shuttle boats also use this pier to ferry passengers from cruise ships to town for land excursions. While it varies throughout the year, more of these large ships make Kailua a port of call during the late spring and fall months than during the rest of the year, and interisland cruise ships make regular stops here throughout the week. When periodic canoe races and the swimming portion of the Ironman Triathlon competition are held in the bay, the pier is crowded with plenty of onlookers.

MOKUʻAIKAUA CHURCH

Kailua is one of those towns that would love to contemplate its own navel if it could only find it. It doesn't really have a center, but if you had to pick one, it would be the 112-foot steeple of **Mokuʻaikaua Church** (75-5713 Aliʻi Dr., www.mokuaikaua.org, daily dawn-dusk). This highest structure in town has been a landmark for travelers and seafarers ever since the church was completed in January 1837. Established in 1820, the church claims to be the oldest house of Christian worship in Hawaii. The site was given by King Liholiho to the first Congregationalist missionaries, who arrived on the brig Thaddeus in the spring of that year. Much thought was given to the orientation of the structure, designed so the prevailing winds blow through the entire length of the church to keep it cool and comfortable. The walls of the church are fashioned from massive, rough-hewn lava stone, mortared with plaster made from crushed and burned coral that was bound with kukui nut oil. The huge cornerstones are believed to have been salvaged from a heiau built in the 15th century by King Umi that had occupied this spot. The masonry is crude but effective—still sound after more than 170 years.

Inside, the church is extremely soothing, expressing a feeling of strength and simplicity. The pews, railings, pulpit, and trim are all fashioned from koa, a rich brown, lustrous wood that begs to be stroked. Although the church is still used as a house of worship, it also has the air of a museum, housing paintings of historical personages instrumental in Hawaii's Christian past. The crowning touch is an excellent model of the brig Thaddeus, painstakingly built by the men of the Pacific Fleet Command in 1934 and presented to the church in 1975.

HULIHEʻE PALACE

Go from the spiritual to the temporal by walking across the street from Mokuʻaikaua Church and entering **Hulihe'e Palace** (75-5718 Ali'i Dr., 808/329-1877, www.huliheepalace.com, Mon.-Sat. 9am-4pm and Sun. 10am-4pm, except major holidays. You can look around on your own or ask the staff for a tour, which usually lasts 45 minutes. Admission is $6 adults, $4 seniors, $1 students. This two-story Victorian structure commissioned by Hawaii's second royal governor, John Kuakini, dates from 1838. A favorite summer getaway for all the Hawaiian monarchs who followed, especially King Kalakaua, it was used as such until 1914. At first glance, the outside is un-impressive, but the more you look the more you realize how simple and grand it is. The architectural lines are those of an English country manor, and indeed Great Britain was held in high esteem by the Hawaiian royalty. Inside, the palace is bright and airy. Most of the massive furniture is made from koa. Many pieces were constructed by foreigners, includ-ing Wilhelm Fisher, a German. The most magnificent pieces include a huge formal din-ing table, 70 inches in diameter, fashioned from one solid koa log. Upstairs is a tremen-dous four-poster bed that belonged to Queen Kapi'olani, and two magnificent cabinets built by a Chinese convict serving a life sentence for smuggling opium. King Kalakaua heard of his talents and commissioned him to build the cabinets. They proved to be so wonderfully crafted that after they were completed the king pardoned the craftsman.

Prince Kuhio, who inherited the palace from his uncle, King Kalakaua, was the first Hawaiian delegate to Congress. He decided to auction off all the furniture and artifacts to raise money, supposedly for the benefit of the Hawaiian people. Providentially, the night be-fore the auction each piece was painstakingly numbered by the royal ladies of the palace, and the name of the person bidding for the piece was dutifully recorded. In the years that fol-lowed, the **Daughters of Hawai'i,** who now operate the palace as a museum, tracked down the owners and convinced many to return the items for display. Most of the pieces are pri-vately owned, and because each is unique, the owners wish no duplicates to be made. It is for this reason, coupled with the fact that flashbulbs can fade the wood, that a strict *no photography* policy is enforced. The palace was opened as a museum in 1928. In 1973, Hulihe'e Palace was added to the National Register of Historic Sites.

Historical artifacts are displayed in a down-stairs room. Delicate and priceless heirlooms on display include a tiger-claw necklace that belonged to Kapi'olani. You'll also see a portrait gallery of Hawaiian monarchs. Personal and mundane items are on exhibit as well—there's an old report card showing a 68 in philosophy for King Kalakaua—and lining the stairs is a collection of spears reputedly belonging to the great Kamehameha himself.

CAPTAIN COOK AREA: SOUTH KONA
H.N. Greenwell Store Museum

It's *Little House on the Prairie* meets Hawaii. Constructed in the 1870s to make sup-plies available to the Euro-American immi-grant community, the **H.N. Greenwell Store Museum** (Hwy. 11 between mile markers 111 and 112, 808/323-3222, www.konahistorical. org, Mon.-Thurs. 10am-2pm, $7 adults, $3 children 5-12) is the oldest surviving store in Kona and one of the oldest buildings in the area. A great experience for kids or history buffs, the volunteer-led tour of the building filled with historical pictures and relics of the area takes about a half hour and occurs on de-mand. Foodies will want to visit around 10am on Thursdays, when you can assist in baking Portuguese bread in the stone oven located be-hind the building. If you're just passing by on a Thursday, stop and pick up a loaf—but they are usually sold out by 2pm.

Amy B.H. Greenwell Ethnobotanical Garden

Ethnobotany is the study of how plants are used by different cultures. **Amy B.H. Greenwell Ethnobotanical Garden** (Hwy. 11 at mile marker 110, 808/323-3318, www.bishopmu-seum.org/greenwell, Mon.-Fri. 8:30am-5pm,

Coffee Farm Tours

coffee beans on the vine in Kona

The upland Kona district is a splendid area for raising coffee, and Kona coffee has long been accepted as gourmet quality and is sold in the better restaurants throughout Hawaii and in fine coffee shops around the world. It's a dark, full-bodied coffee with a rich aroma.

There are a lot of options for tours of working coffee farms, and many include quick coffee tastings followed by a brief nudge for you to buy their product. One of the better, non-pushy tours is at **Greenwell Farms** (81-6581 Mamalahoa Hwy./Hwy. 11, Kealakekua, between mile markers 111 and 112, 808/323-2275, www.greenwellfarms.com, daily 8:30am-5pm, last tour at 4:30pm). They offer a free 20-minute walking tour through their coffee farm, discussing the roasting and processing of coffee and ending with some coffee sampling.

$5 suggested donation), a 15-acre garden dedicated to the pursuit of ethnobotany, showcases over 275 rare species of native plants grown in Kona before Western contact. The placards labeling the plants throughout the garden offer detailed descriptions of how the plant arrived to the island (many plants although native to Hawaii were brought by Polynesians) and how Hawaiians traditionally used them. One can spend anywhere from 30 minutes to an hour walking around the loop learning this interesting botanical history. One-hour guided tours are offered Monday and Wednesday at 1pm and on the second Saturday of the month at 10am ($5).

☾ Pu'uhonua O Honaunau National Historical Park (Place of Refuge)

If you are going to do one historical activity while on the Big Island, do **Pu'uhonua O Honaunau National Historical Park** (off Hwy. 11 on Hwy. 160, 808/328-2326, www.nps.gov/puho). The gate is open daily 7am-7pm, while visitors center hours are daily 8:45am-5:30pm. Admission is $5 per car, $3 to walk in, free with a national park pass, or included in the $25 pass for three national parks on the Big Island. To get there from Highway 11, between mile markers 103 and 104 turn onto Highway 160 and travel down the hill a few miles to the entrance on the *makai* side.

This is where you see the true old Hawaii, circa the 1600s. A park ranger explains that there is a calming feeling here because it is a religious site dedicated to the god Lono, who was a god of life. No killing or wars occurred at Pu'uhonua O Honaunau—it was, as it is sometimes called, a place of refuge or the Camp David for Hawaiian chiefs. During times of war, women and children would seek safety on the grounds, and if defeated chiefs or those accused of sins could make it to the shore by swimming across the bay, then they would be absolved of their sins and given a second chance. In fact there were 30 such places like Pu'uhonua O Honaunau across the islands, but

© MARK WASSER

Pu'uhonua O Honaunau National Historical Park

are original, but many are replicas. Kids tend to be particularly impressed by the imposing structures and sculptures of ancient times. The best time to visit the park is early morning—even before the gate opens. There is a wonderful sense of peace that overtakes the area around and just after sunrise. Tours with the knowledgeable staff are free and offered daily at 10:30am and 2:30pm, and are highly recommended. Otherwise, pamphlets are provided for your self-guided tours, which would take a half hour if you just walked straight through, or you can do a self-guided audio cell phone tour by calling 808/217-9279.

The majority of tourists head straight to **Two Step** (turn *makai* off Hwy. 160 where you see the Pu'uhonua O Honaunau park sign, and instead of driving straight into the gate turn right onto the road directly before the gate), called such because of the lava shelf that requires you to take two steps down into the water. It's an incredibly popular area because it does have great snorkeling and it's shallow so it's popular with non-experts and kids. There are no facilities, so it is recommended that you park in Pu'uhonua O Honaunau's lot, where there are bathrooms and walk to the two minutes to the right back to Two Step.

this site is the only one that remains. It's sort of a bonus that it's actually at the beach.

Some of the structures in place at the park

BIG ISLAND OF HAWAI'I

Shopping

ALI'I DRIVE: KAILUA AND KEAUHOU
Ali'i Drive

The shops that line Ali'i Drive are tchotchke central. There are many gift shops—the kinds with the "My grandmother went to Hawaii and all I got was..." T-shirts and assorted items like snorkel equipment and sunscreen needed for a day at the beach. There are also local non-chain jewelry stores selling the island specialty of black pearls. The quality of goods at these shops tends to be low, so buyer beware.

Keauhou

If you need to escape the heat during the day,

there is the **Keauhou Shopping Center** (78-6831 Ali'i Dr.). A good independent bookstore, **Kona Stories** (808/324-0350, www.konastories.com, Mon.-Sat. 10am-6pm, Sun. 11am-4pm) has a significant stock of new books (and some are discounted).

CAPTAIN COOK AREA: SOUTH KONA
Kainaliu

It's only about a city block long, but Kainaliu (Mamalahoa Hwy./Hwy. 11 between mile markers 113 and 114) makes for a pleasant stroll. There are also several good restaurants if you get hungry while you're shopping.

Yoganics (79-7401 Mamalahoa Hwy. Ste. C, 808/322-0714, www.yoganicshawaii.com, Mon.-Sat. 10am-5pm) is an eco boutique to go to if you forgot your organic or hemp yoga pants at home. Aside from the somewhat pricey exercise and yoga wear, there is jewelry and locally made bath products. Check the website or call for the schedule of yoga classes, which are offered in-store nearly every day.

Next door to Yoganics is **Kiernan Music** (808/322-4939, www.kiernanmusic.com, Tues.-Sat. 11am-6pm), the best place to buy that ukulele you promise you'll learn to play. The instruments are beautifully crafted, some are vintage, and they also do custom made. If you don't have enough room to put one in your suitcase, no worries, they'll ship your uke home for you for a reasonable price.

Antique Row

In Kealakekua (South Kona) between mile markers 111 and 112, you'll come upon a slew of antiques shops that are definitely worth a browsing. They tend to be a mix of Hawaiiana, old bottles, and beautiful furniture made of koa wood. All the shops are within walking distance from one another, so park your car and take a stroll.

Entertainment and Events

ENTERTAINMENT
Luau

There are two main luau in the Kona area: at **Courtyard King Kamehameha's Kona Beach Hotel** (in Kailua-Kona) and at the **Sheraton Keauhou Bay Resort and Spa** (in Keauhou).

They are both produced by the same company, Island Breeze (http://ibphawaii.com/luaus); tickets can be purchased through the website. You'll likely pick which luau to attend purely on what day of the week you want to go because they aren't offered every day of the week at each hotel.

Is It Worth Going to a Luau?

Answer: How much do you like watching musicals or theater? A luau might not be what you think it is. Gone are the days of roasting a pig as onlookers watch in awe. Attending a luau is like going to dinner theater. It's a good opportunity to try a lot of local foods at once, but nearly all the buffets are only mediocre. If the food is what you're most interested in, it would be better to go to a restaurant (like Jackie Rey's in Kona) instead of spending $100 (the average price for most luau). Drinkers may get their money's worth—nearly all the luau include an open bar.

If you really enjoy a good Broadway show, then you might enjoy a luau, and kids seem to love them. The productions vary, but **Island Breeze** (http://ibphawaii.com/luaus), the company that puts on luau at the Courtyard

King Kamehameha's Kona Beach Hotel (in Kailua-Kona), the Sheraton Keauhou Bay Resort and Spa (in Keauhou), and The Fairmont Orchid (in Kohala) offers the best show. For a traditional luau with lots of hula, try the King Kamehameha version. For a more Cirque de Soleil experience (with more modern dance and less hula), head to The Fairmont Orchid, which does offer a more pricey experience—but the food is better here than at other luau. Lastly, all luau offer preferred seating options, meaning that you pay about $20 per person extra to sit closer but you are still eating the same food as everyone else (although you get to visit the buffet line first). Unless you have some extra money to spend, preferred seating isn't really worth the splurge.

Live Music and Theater

Live music pops up on weekend nights at numerous bars and restaurants on Aliʻi Drive. You don't have to go too far to find it. The majority of hotels also offer live music in their cocktail lounges—but nothing too notable.

If you're looking for something a little different from the standard cover band, stop by **Boston Basil's** (75-5707 Aliʻi Dr., Kailua, 808/326-7836, www.bostonbasils.com, daily 11am-9:30pm) upstairs, which books fairly good bands from jazz to bluegrass.

Food

ALIʻI DRIVE: KAILUA AND KEAUHOU

While there are many restaurants on Aliʻi Drive, most of them cater to tourists and offer poor service. So beware: While a crowded restaurant is a usually a sign of high quality, that's no indication on Aliʻi Drive!

◖ Rapanui Island Café (75-5695 Aliʻi Dr., Kailua, 808/329-0511, Tues.-Fri. 11am-2pm, Mon.-Sat. 5pm-9pm, $12-20) offers cuisine from New Zealand and with it a lesson on what is cuisine of New Zealand. The restaurant's location is a bit odd—across from a hair salon in a strip of shops—but one can still hear the ocean breeze just across the street. Most dishes involve meat and/or fish skewers served over house-made coconut rice and well-flavored sauces. The lunch specials are a real bargain, and locals run to order the lamb burger (it has a hint of mint in it) when it is available. Overall, the portions are generous, but save room for dessert: peanut butter rolled in chocolate and coconut with a hint of wasabi inside. You'll want to order one per person.

With a great oceanfront view (the majority of seating is outside), **Lava Java** (75-5799 Aliʻi Dr. next to the Coconut Grove shopping area, Kailua, 808/327-2161, www.islandlavajava.com, daily breakfast 6:30-9:30am, lunch 9:30am-5pm, dinner 5pm-9pm, coffee anytime, $12-20) keeps busy. In fact, sometimes it's even hard to get a table at 7am for breakfast. The service can be slow at times, but the food is consistently good and the portions are large. If you're in a rush for breakfast you can grab a pastry to go. The non-breakfast cuisine is mostly pizzas, salads, and burgers, but vegetarian options are available and the sandwiches are highly recommended.

The original restaurant is in Anchorage, and this **Humpy's Big Island Ale House** (75-5815 Aliʻi Dr., Kailua, 808/324-2337, www.humpys.com/kona, bar daily 8am-2am, kitchen daily 8am-midnight, happy hour daily 3pm-6pm, $12-28) is their second location. Humpy's is where to go to watch sports, to drink, and to eat breakfast. At night, this place gets packed upstairs, where sometimes there is a live band. Downstairs is a bit calmer and cooler, and you can enjoy drinks on the patio facing the ocean. Lunch and dinner are good enough—they have the usual bar food. Try the luau feast with all the kinds of foods you'd find at a luau. The real winner here is breakfast. The blackened halibut Benedict is fantastic. Those with smaller appetites can order a side, which also comes with potatoes.

Right on the oceanfront, **Huggo's** (75-5828 Kahakai Rd., entrance on Aliʻi Dr., Kailua, 808/329-1493, www.huggos.com, dinner Sun.-Thurs. 5:30-9pm, Fri.-Sat. 5:30-10pm, brunch Sun. 10am-1pm, $22-37) is a great spot if you're looking for a romantic dinner (try getting there for the sunset). The food isn't trendy—there aren't many complex flavors. Instead, it's simple dishes plated to look elegant. But perhaps sticking with what they know has allowed Huggo's to survive in the same location for the last 40 years (while other restaurants on the strip come and go). The fish, especially the fresh catch of the day ($36) cooked in different ways, is recommended given the restaurant's close relationship with local fishers. Here is also a good opportunity to try a local delicacy, *ulu* (breadfruit) in a familiar way—they make them into french fries. Note: Huggo's has parking in a small lot right in front of the restaurant.

With at least a dozen variations of fish, seasonings, sauces, and the make-your-own option, **Da Poke Shack** (76-6246 Ali'i Dr., Kailua, 808/333-7380, daily 10am-6pm) is a *poke* dream come true. If you're not sure what to get, the friendly staff will let you sample as many kinds as you need to convince you that *poke* is for you. There isn't really anywhere to sit here, but it's not that kind of place. Grab a to-go container and bring it with you to the beach.

In the Keauhou Shopping Center, **Bianelli's Gourmet Pizza and Pasta** (808/322-0377, http://bianellis.com, Mon.-Sat. 11am-9pm, happy hour 4pm-6pm, $15 for large pizza) is notable for its signature pink sauce (a white wine mushroom sauce mixed with marinara pasta sauce), and gluten-free as well as vegan pizza options. If you happen to be in the area and hungry weekdays 4:30-6:30pm, try **Kenichi Pacific** (808/322-6400, www.kenichihawaii.com) for an excellent happy hour of half-price sushi and drink specials. On Saturdays stop by the **Keauhou Farmers Market** (8am-noon) near the movie theater and Longs Drugs.

Near Ali'i Drive

The portions are huge and inexpensive, and for a restaurant close to Ali'i Drive, that alone makes **Quinn's Almost By The Sea** (75-5655A Palani Rd., Kailua, 808/329-3822, daily 11am-11pm, $11-24) notable. Whereas many other restaurants in the area cater to tourists, Quinn's keeps it local and casual. As the restaurant's name indicates, there aren't any views here, just an outdoor covered area bordering a parking lot and an inside bar scene with several beers on tap and reasonably priced cocktails. The fish and chips are fresh and one of the more popular dishes—but also try the short ribs. A few vegetarian options also are available.

A craft beer lover's fantasy, **Kona Brewing Company** (75-5629 Kuakini Hwy., 808/334-2739, http://konabrewingco.com, Sun.-Thurs. 11am-10pm, Fri.-Sat. 11am-11pm, happy hour Mon.-Fri. 3pm-6pm, brewery tours daily at 10:30am and 3pm, $9-18) offers not only supreme beer on tap, but also pretty good food. The "brew your own" pizza allows you to pick your toppings and sauces, and there are fish and salad options (the salads should be avoided as they sound much better on the menu than they appear in person). The restaurant can get crowded on the weekends, so call ahead or expect to wait for a bit. If you're going to be in town awhile, pick up a growler (full growler $22, refill $13.50) and save some money on beer.

This is old school Kona at its finest: A great family restaurant, **Jackie Rey's Ohana Grill** (75-5995 Kuakini Hwy., Kailua, 808/327-0209, www.jackiereys.com, lunch Mon.-Fri. 11am-2pm, appetizers Mon.-Fri. 2pm-5pm, happy hour Mon.-Fri. 3pm-5pm, dinner daily 5pm-9pm, lunch $12-14, dinner $16-28) has a well-deserved excellent reputation. The restaurant itself has a casual atmosphere with butcher paper lining the tables (and crayons for coloring), but the food is consistently good and the service usually attentive. Most dishes are either fish or meat served in a way that makes them local style—either by including fruit salsas or macadamia nuts or local sweet potatoes. A

Parking on Ali'i Drive

Parking is no fun on Ali'i Drive. But luckily, it's probably the only place on Hawai'i where you can't find parking. There are very few spaces on the actual street itself and only a handful of free public lots, as well the option to pay for parking. If you are spending a night on the town, try the Coconut Grove parking lot via Kuakini Highway (it's the one with Outback Steakhouse). Usually parking is plentiful there and you can avoid the slow nighttime traffic of Ali'i Drive.

good gluten-free option is the *mochiko*-crusted fish (*mochiko* is sweet rice flour). There is a children's menu available as well as a full wine list. If you like cocktails try the Ling Mui martini (*li hing mui,* a salted dried plum, is a specialty flavoring in Hawaii).

Markets

One of the larger locations of **Island Naturals Market and Deli** (74-5487 Kaiwi St., Kailua, 808/326-1122, www.islandnaturals.com, Mon.-Sat. 7:30am-8pm, Sun. 9am-7pm), a local chain natural foods grocery store, is in Kailua. It has a coffee and smoothie bar as well as an excellent hot bar with many gluten-free and vegan options. Beer and wine (non-organic and organic varieties) are available and on sale for 20 percent off every Friday.

Although the hours are posted, it always seems that the **Kailua Village Market-Kona Farmers Market** (in the parking lot next to the Kona Public Library, at Hualalai Rd. and Ali'i Dr., across from Waterfront Row, Kailua, www.konafarmersmarket.com, Wed.-Sat. 9am-noon) stays open later and that the crafts vendors are there at all times. Beware; not all the produce and food items sold at the market are in fact locally grown.

CAPTAIN COOK AREA: SOUTH KONA

The best barbecue on the island, **(Big Jake's Island BBQ** (Hwy. 11 near mile marker 106, *mauka* side, Honaunau, 808/328-1227, daily 11am-6pm, $7-12) will make you feel like you're in Memphis. The portions are huge, mouthwatering, and slow-cooked on local keawe wood. The plates all come with rice, coleslaw, and beans. For Hawaiian fusion, try their barbecue bowls of pulled chicken or pork over rice. There is only outdoor picnic style seating, so it's not the best place if it's raining outside. BYOB is encouraged and you can grab a beer from the store next door while you wait. Call ahead because hours are variable due to catering.

Directly across from Big Jake's BBQ, **Coffees n' Epicurea** (Hwy. 11 near mile marker 106, *makai* side, Honaunau, 808/328-0322, www.coffeeepicurea.com, daily 6:30am-6pm) is a proper coffee shop with a few tables and outdoor seating. They brew ice coffee (it takes nearly 24 hours to do this in a really neat-looking device) and bake their own European-style pastries, such as croissants, scones, and danishes. They run out of pastries early and some days coffee too. It's a nice place to stop and grab something to go early in the morning on your way out of town.

The killer view of Kealakekua Bay from the balcony of **The Coffee Shack** (Hwy. 11 between mile markers 108 and 109, *makai* side, Captain Cook, 808/328-9555, www.coffeeshack.com, daily 7:30am-3pm, breakfast mains $11, lunch $10-13) send tourists flocking here. It can get quite crowded, especially on the weekend. The food is good, but not impressive. There are egg dishes and sandwiches, but you are paying for the view. You can get the same food cheaper other places, but then you'd miss the view.

(Mi's Italian Bistro (81-6372 Mamalahoa Hwy. between mile markers 110 and 111, *mauka* side, Kealakekua, 808/323-3880, www.misitalianbistro.com, Tues.-Sun. 4:30-8:30pm, reservations recommended, $19-32) is up there as one of the better restaurants on the island. Even though the strip mall location doesn't seem ideal, the restaurant itself feels quaint and romantic. Service is attentive. The chef ensures that you order the perfect dish and pair it with the right wine. For appetizers, try the marinated beets with candied macadamia nuts. The mains are good-size portions. Try a dish with local veal or beef, but save room for their award-winning tiramisu or flourless chocolate torte.

A hole-in-the-wall serving up pizza and *malasadas* (Portuguese doughnuts) that contend with those of the island's best bakers, **Patz Pies** (81-6596 Mamalahoa Hwy./Hwy. 11 between mile markers 111 and 112, Captain Cook, 808/323-8100, $3 per slice) is a new foodie favorite. The pizza is thin-crust style and served with top-notch vegetables and meats. Salads are also available. Although you may be full, don't forget to pick up a hot *malasada* to go (otherwise how will you be able to fairly judge who makes the best *malasadas* on the island?).

Their slogan is "our only additive is aloha," and that pretty much tells all you need to know about **The Nasturtium Café** (Hwy. 11 between mile markers 112 and 113, *mauka* side, Kealakekua, 808/322-5083, Mon. 9am-3pm, Tues.-Fri. 9am-7:30pm, breakfast $8, lunch/dinner $11-15). The restaurant is small with only six tables, but the menu has a lot to offer and is perfect for vegetarians, vegans, and gluten-free individuals. Breakfast includes wraps with tofu or turkey sausage, whole grain pancakes, and an assortment of egg dishes. Lunch offers a soup of the day with a tasty homemade spelt biscuit and salad combo or sandwiches with flavorful sauces and locally made cheeses. The dinner menu is rotating and there is a $10 BYOB fee—or try the *mamaki* lemongrass herbal tea, a homeopathic treat.

A good foodie choice is **Annie's Island Fresh Burgers** (79-7460 Mamalahoa Hwy./Hwy. 11 between mile markers 112 and 113, 808/324-6000, www.anniesislandfreshburgers.com, Kealakekua, daily 11am-6pm, $11). The meat is local, the salads have local organic lettuce and local vine-ripe tomatoes, and there are vegan options in addition to the numerous local beef hamburgers with all kinds of toppings and savory sauces. The French fries are a must. Beer on draft is available.

Donkey Balls and Surfin Ass Coffee Company (79-7411 Mamalahou Hwy. between mile markers 113 and 114, *mauka* side, Kainaliu, 808/322-1475, www.alohahawaiianstore.com, daily 8am-6pm) are not the same donkey balls as the stores you see throughout Kailua. These donkey balls are better. Donkey balls are dark/white/milk chocolate covered coffee beans, and they are addictive! Buy a few bags to take with you as a snack or to bring home. There are samples available and the staff is friendly. The coffee drinks are fantastic and huge, so order small.

The exterior of **Roadhouse Café** (79-7399 Mamalahoa Hwy. between mile markers 113 and 114, *mauka* side, Kainaliu, 808/322-0616, Mon.-Fri. 11am-4pm, $6.25) is inviting with its old diner look. The inside of the diner is less inviting. The food is not local style. The flavorful sandwiches and specials that change daily are cheap and all baking is done on premises. Some days vegan options are available. The pastries are displayed beautifully in a case and are equally as good to taste. So-so gluten-free cookies and a flourless ganache chocolate cake are available.

An institution in town, **Teshima Restaurant** (79-7251 Mamalahoa Hwy./Hwy. 11 between mile markers 113 and 114, *mauka* side, Kainaliu, 808/322-9140, daily 6:30am-1:45pm and 5pm-9pm, $8-17 for fresh catch, cash only) has been serving it up the same for years and it works well. It's a casual Japanese-style diner run for generations by the Teshima family, who opened it as a general store in 1929 and then a restaurant in 1940. Get a bento box, to go or to stay. It comes with meat, egg roll, fried fish, and additional sides. Meals from fish to teriyaki beef come with a lot of extras, ensuring that you'll leave completely satisfied.

Getting There and Around

AIR

The **Kona International Airport** (code KOA) is just north of Kailua-Kona on Highway 19. The drive from the airport to Kailua is only about 20 minutes. The airport is small and outdoors. However, although it is tiny, it can get crowded due to the sheer number of travelers moving through it. So do arrive early as the check-in and security lines can get quite long. If you are dropping someone off or coming to the airport to pick someone up, it's free to park in the lot if you are there less than 20 minutes.

Hawaiian Airlines (www.hawaiianair. com) offers interisland flights that tend to board minutes before their scheduled departure times. There are many daily direct flights to Honolulu and a few to Maui; however, to get to the other islands, it is often necessary to travel through Honolulu. From Kona, it is possible to fly directly to the Mainland on airlines such as Alaska Airlines, American Airlines, Delta Airlines, United Airlines, and US Airways.

SHUTTLE

If you're not renting a car, many of the resorts will arrange a pickup for you (for a fee). If you would like to schedule your own shared ride service, try **SpeediShuttle** (808/329-5433, www.speedishuttle.com, beginning at $12 per person for minimum 2 people. It is a shared ride although they charge more if you're not traveling with two people. For a private taxi you can expect to pay $25 to Kailua and upward of $60 to the Kohala resorts.

BUS

Via **Hele-On Bus** (www.heleonbus.org, 808/961-8744, $1 per ride, $1 each for luggage, large backpacks, bikes) it is possible, with a little planning, to make it from the Kona side to the Hilo side and from Kona north to Kohala as far as Hawi. Check the website for bus stop locations.

BIG ISLAND OF HAWAI'I

KOHALA

The Kohala district, also known as the Gold Coast, is the peninsular thumb in the northwestern portion of the Big Island. At its tip is Upolu Point, only 30 miles from Maui across the 'Alenuihaha Channel. Kohala was the first section of the Big Island to rise from beneath the sea. The long-extinct volcanoes of the Kohala Mountains running down its spine have been reduced by time and the elements from lofty, ragged peaks

HIGHLIGHTS

LOOK FOR ◖ TO FIND RECOMMENDED SIGHTS, ACTIVITIES, DINING, AND LODGING.

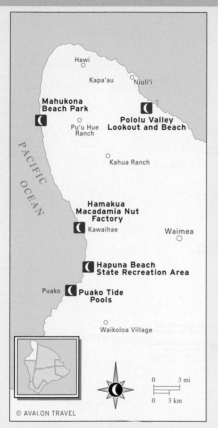

© AVALON TRAVEL

◖ **Puako Tide Pools:** Teeming with sea life, this watery wonderland offers some of the best snorkeling and diving on the island (page 551).

◖ **Hapuna Beach State Recreation Area:** With pristine white sands and turquoise waters perfect for snorkeling, body boarding, and swimming, this is one of the best beaches on the island (page 551).

◖ **Mahukona Beach Park:** Here you'll find an underwater treasure of ruins from the plantation days—a good opportunity for beginning snorkelers (page 552).

◖ **Hamakua Macadamia Nut Factory:** Nibble on macadamia nuts of every variety imaginable while you watch the workings of the factory (page 558).

◖ **Pololu Valley Lookout and Beach:** The view of the coastline is spectacular. It's worth driving to the road's end and simply staring for a few minutes, or taking a steep hike down to the secluded beach (page 560).

BIG ISLAND OF HAWAI'I

to rounded domes of 5,000 feet or so. Kohala is divided into North and South Kohala. North Kohala, an area of dry coastal slopes, former sugar lands, a string of sleepy towns, and deeply incised lush valleys, forms the northernmost tip of the island. South Kohala boasts *the* most beautiful swimming beaches on the Big Island, along with world-class hotels and resorts.

South Kohala is a region of contrast. It's dry, hot, tortured by wind, and scored by countless old lava flows. The predominant land color here is black, and this is counterpointed by scrubby bushes and scraggly trees, a seemingly semi-arid wasteland. This was an area that the ancient Hawaiians seemed to have traveled through to get somewhere else, yet Hawaiians did live here—along the coast—and numerous archaeological sites dot the coastal plain. Still, South Kohala is stunning with its palm-fringed white-sand pockets of beach, luxury

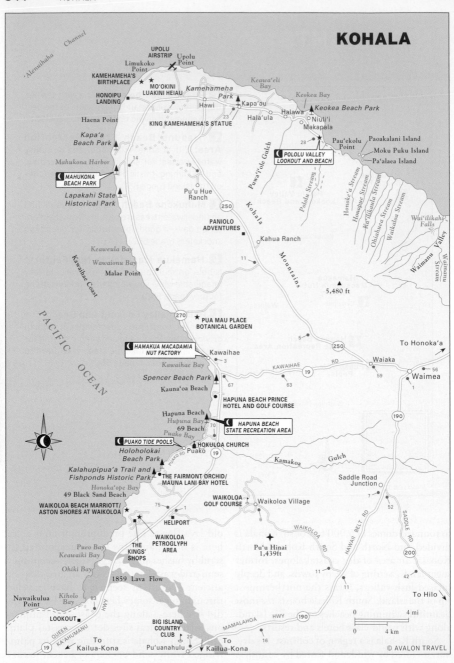

KOHALA

BIG ISLAND OF HAWAI'I

'Alenuihaha Channel

UPOLU AIRSTRIP
Upolu Point
Limukoko Point
KAMEHAMEHA'S BIRTHPLACE
MO'OKINI LUAKINI HEIAU
Kamehameha Park
HONOIPU LANDING
Hawi
Kapa'au
Hala'ula
Haena Point
KING KAMEHAMEHA'S STATUE

Keawa'eli Bay
Keokea Bay
Keokea Beach Park
Halawa
Niuli'i
Makapala
Pau'ekolu Point
Paoakalani Island
Moku Puku Island
Pa'alaea Island

Kapa'a Beach Park

Mahukona Harbor

MAHUKONA BEACH PARK

Lapakahi State Historical Park

Pu'u Hue Ranch

PANIOLO ADVENTURES

Kahua Ranch

Pawa'i'ole Gulch
Pololu Gulch

POLOLU VALLEY LOOKOUT AND BEACH

Pololu Stream
Honoke'a Stream
Honopue Stream
Ka'iilikahala Stream
Ohiahiaea Stream
Waikahua Stream
Wai'ilikahi Falls

Keaweula Bay
Wawaionu Bay
Malae Point

Kohala Mountains

5,480 ft

Waimanu Stream
Waimanu Valley
Awini Stream

Kawaihae Coast

PACIFIC OCEAN

PUA MAU PLACE BOTANICAL GARDEN

HAMAKUA MACADAMIA NUT FACTORY

Kawaihae

Kawaihae Bay
Spencer Beach Park
Kauna'oa Beach

KAWAIHAE RD

To Honoka'a

Waiaka

Waimea

HAPUNA BEACH PRINCE HOTEL AND GOLF COURSE

Hapuna Beach
Hupuna Bay
69 Beach
Puako Bay

HAPUNA BEACH STATE RECREATION AREA

PUAKO TIDE POOLS
Holoholokai Beach Park
HOKULOA CHURCH
Puako

Kamakoa Gulch

Kalahupipua'a Trail and Fishponds Historic Park
THE FAIRMONT ORCHID/ MAUNA LANI BAY HOTEL

Honoka'ope Bay
49 Black Sand Beach

WAIKOLOA BEACH MARRIOTT/ ASTON SHORES AT WAIKOLOA

WAIKOLOA GOLF COURSE
Waikoloa Village

Saddle Road Junction

HELIPORT
THE KINGS' SHOPS
WAIKOLOA PETROGLYPH AREA

Pueo Bay
Keawaiki Bay
Ohiki Bay

Pu'u Hinai
1,439ft

WAIKOLOA

HAWAII BELT RD

SADDLE RD

To Hilo

1859 Lava Flow

Nawaikulua Point
Kiholo Bay

LOOKOUT

BIG ISLAND COUNTRY CLUB

MAMALAHOA HWY

QUEEN KA'AHUMANU HWY

To Kailua-Kona
Pu'uanahulu
To Kailua-Kona

0   4 mi
0   4 km

© AVALON TRAVEL

resorts, green landscaped golf courses, colorful planted flowers, and deep blue inviting water. You come here to settle into a sedate resort community, to be pampered and pleased by the finer things that await at luxury resorts that are destinations in and of themselves. Of the many scattered villages that once dotted this coast, only two remain: Puako, now a sleepy beach hideaway, and Kawaihae, one of the principal commercial deepwater ports on the island. In Kawaihae, at the base of the North Kohala peninsula, Highway 19 turns east and coastal Route 270, known as the Akoni Pule Highway, heads north along the coast.

North Kohala was the home of Kamehameha the Great. From this fiefdom he launched his conquest of all the islands. The shores of North Kohala are rife with historical significance, and with beach parks where few ever go. Among North Kohala's cultural treasures is Lapakahi State Historical Park, a must-stop offering a walk-through village and "touchable" exhibits that allow you to become actively involved in Hawaii's traditional past. Northward is Kamehameha's birthplace and within walking distance is Moʻokini Luakini, one of the oldest *heiau* in Hawaii and still actively ministered by the current generation of a long line of *kahuna*.

Hawi, the main town in North Kohala, was a sugar settlement whose economy turned sour when the last of the seven sugar mills in the area stopped operations in the mid-1970s. Hawi is making a big comeback, along with this entire northern shore, which has seen an influx of small boutiques and art shops. The main coastal road winds in and out of numerous small gulches, crosses some one-lane bridges, and ends at Pololu Valley lookout, where you can overlook one of the premier taro-growing valleys of old Hawaii. A walk down the steep *pali* into this valley is the Hawaii you imagined from movies and reruns of *Lost*.

ORIENTATION
South Kohala: Resort Area
Distinctive for its abundance of large resorts and rental properties, white-sand beaches lined with coconut trees, and its proximity to the airport, the Waikoloa and Mauna Lani areas are geared to meet the needs of tourists. This small area holds enough beaches and restaurants to keep you occupied for days. With the three shopping centers within the resorts, you really never have to leave the premises.

This coast's fabulous beaches are known not only for swimming and surfing, but for tide-pooling and awe-inspiring sunsets as well. There are little-disturbed and rarely visited archaeological sites, expressive petroglyph fields, and the best preserved portion of the Ala Kahakai National Historic Trail. Note: The Waikoloa Beach Resort area *(makai)* is drastically different than the Waikoloa Village area *(mauka)*. Waikoloa Village is where many of the workers from the resorts live. You won't find your hotel or beaches there!

Kawaihae
Kawaihae is just a pass-through port town with a gas station and some restaurants worthy of a stop. Some dive outfitters are based out of the harbor, but they often take their clients to the waters of South Kohala or Kona, although the nearby waters are just as nice and less crowded.

Hawi to the End of the Road
Located on the northwest tip of the island, these communities are nearly perfect small towns offering walkable main streets filled with excellent restaurants, art galleries, and coffee shops. The beaches here are rocky but offer breathtaking views of the coast and, if you're lucky, of Maui too. Unlike the southern part of the Kohala district, northern Kohala doesn't look like a lava-filled landscape from outer space. Instead, although it is quite dry in this region, there are gorgeous large trees providing shade from the sun. Spend the day strolling the streets of Hawi, explore the backroads of Kohala on an ATV or kayak, watch the sunset at Pololu Valley, and then finish your day with dinner at Sushi Rock or Bamboo Restaurant or live music at Luke's Place in Hawi.

Your Best Day in Kohala

- Start your day on the **Ala Kahakai National Historic Trail.** Pick a point on the trail and go for a short walk, leaving plenty of time to stop at any number of beaches (especially the secret ones).

- Stop to sample all sorts of flavors of macadamia nuts and brittle at the **Hamakua Macadamia Nut Factory** on your way north to Hawi.

- Visit the galleries and shops in **Hawi** and eat lunch at one of the excellent restaurants in town.

- Try an adventure like **ziplining** or **"fluming the ditch"** (kayaking down an old irrigation ditch from the plantation days).

- Drive to the lookout at **Polulu Valley** to watch the sunset and witness one of the best views on the island.

- Finish your day with dinner and dancing at the **Blue Dragon Coastal Cuisine & Musiquarium** in Kawaihae.

RAINY DAY ALTERNATIVE

Most people come to Kohala and never leave the beach, so there aren't many daytime indoor activities in the area. Thus, if it's raining in Kohala, take a peek to the south to Kona and then look *mauka* toward Waimea and see if you can spot any clouds in either direction—head to where there are no clouds. If it's simply raining everywhere on the island, your best bet is to drive the 15 minutes to nearby Waimea or Kona to spend some time inside one of the museums or movie theaters.

PLANNING YOUR TIME

The only reason to plan your time in Kohala is so that you remember to leave that perfect beach you've been lounging on for days. The afternoons in Kohala can cloud over, so plan your day accordingly. If you are spending an entire week in Kohala, as many do, take the time to explore the assorted beaches, such as the well-regarded Hapuna Beach State Recreation Area or a resort beach, which you are free to visit because all beaches must have public access points even for nonguests. Experienced divers and snorkelers should head to the Puako tide pools for a multitude of sea life or to Mahukona Beach Park to discover an unofficial underwater museum of debris left from the plantation and railroad days.

There are some great trails best visited early morning or late afternoon—the short Kalahupipua'a Trail near the Mauna Lani Bay Hotel, the Malama Trail to view ancient petroglyphs, or the Ala Kahakai National Historic Trail, which spans most of the length of the Kohala region. If you need more breaks from the beach, hop in the car and take an extremely scenic drive up the coast (from Highway 19 to Highway 270), watching for whales peeking out from the ocean (only in the winter) on your way to the Pololu Valley for sunset. Even though the distance is short, you can take your time with this drive, stopping at the Hamakua Macadamia Nut Factory on the way and then wandering through the shops in Hawi. Or, use the afternoon for several short jaunts to the north for some of the best lunch places on the island or for ziplining and kayaking the ditches of plantation days or even for traveling to Waimea, which is only about 20 minutes away from the Kohala Coast and has cooler weather.

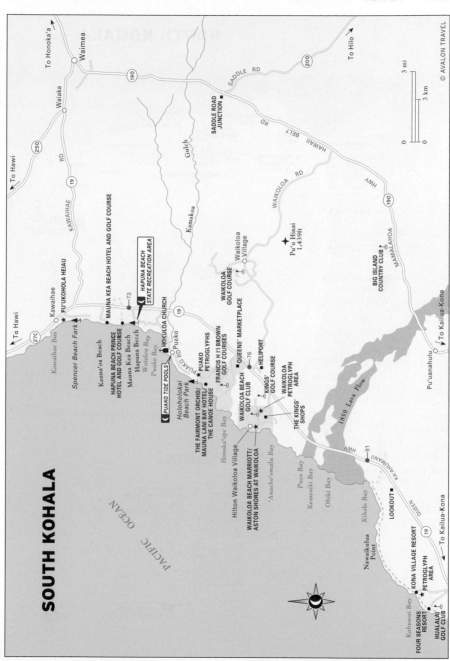

SOUTH KOHALA

BIG ISLAND OF HAWAI'I

© AVALON TRAVEL

PACIFIC OCEAN

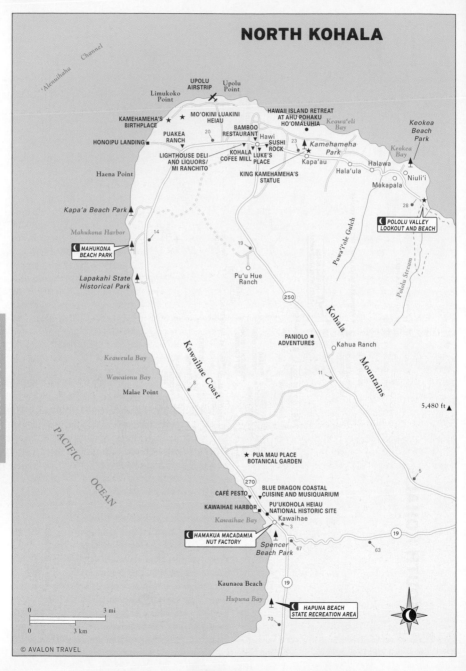

NORTH KOHALA

'Alenuihaha Channel

Limukoko Point

UPOLU AIRSTRIP

Upolu Point

KAMEHAMEHA'S BIRTHPLACE

MO'OKINI LUAKINI HEIAU

HAWAII ISLAND RETREAT AT AHU POHAKU HO'OMALUHIA

Keawa'eli Bay

Keokea Beach Park

PUAKEA RANCH

BAMBOO RESTAURANT

Hawi

SUSHI ROCK

Kamehameha Park

Keokea Bay

HONOIPU LANDING

LIGHTHOUSE DELI AND LIQUORS/ MI RANCHITO

KOHALA COFEE MILL

20

LUKE'S PLACE

Kapa'au

Hala'ula

Halawa

Niuli'i

KING KAMEHAMEHA'S STATUE

23

Mākapala

Haena Point

Kapa'a Beach Park

28

Mahukona Harbor

14

POLOLU VALLEY LOOKOUT AND BEACH

MAHUKONA BEACH PARK

19

Pololu Stream

Lapakahi State Historical Park

Pu'u Hue Ranch

Puaka'ole Gulch

250

Kohala

Keaweula Bay

PANIOLO ADVENTURES

Kahua Ranch

Mountains

Wawaionu Bay

Malae Point

8

Kawaihae Coast

11

5,480 ft

PUA MAU PLACE BOTANICAL GARDEN

PACIFIC

270

BLUE DRAGON COASTAL CUISINE AND MUSIQUARIUM

5

OCEAN

CAFÉ PESTO

KAWAIHAE HARBOR

PU'UKOHOLA HEIAU NATIONAL HISTORIC SITE

Kawaihae Bay

Kawaihae

3

19

HAMAKUA MACADAMIA NUT FACTORY

Spencer Beach Park

67

63

Kaunaoa Beach

19

Hupuna Bay

HAPUNA BEACH STATE RECREATION AREA

70

0   3 mi

0   3 km

© AVALON TRAVEL

Beaches

SOUTH KOHALA: RESORT AREA
Anaeho'omalu Bay (A Bay)

Once a long narrow strip of inviting salt-and-pepper sand, **Anaeho'omalu Bay,** or **A Bay** (Hwy. 19 at mile marker 76, daily 6am-7pm), the beach that fronts hotels such as the Waikoloa Beach Marriott Resort and Hilton Waikoloa Village, was split into two parts by the March 2011 tsunami. Now the only option to walk the beach is via the walkway behind the sandy area where some ancient fishponds are located. Enter through Waikoloa Beach Resort area and park behind Queens' MarketPlace. Although the beach is used by the resort hotels, it is accessible for nonguests via a huge parking lot (where the Hele-On buses wait). All the standard water sports are possible here, and rentals for equipment are available from a kiosk in front of the Marriott. Also in front of the Marriott are lounge chairs that are open to the public. The public restrooms and showers are near the parking lot.

Holoholokai Beach Park and Malama Trail

A shaded park with a grassy area, **Holoholokai Beach Park** (Holoholokai Beach Park Rd., daily 6:30am-6:30pm) makes a nice place to picnic or to fish away the afternoon. There are better places to access to the ocean, but you might want to jump in after walking the Malama Trail to view the **Puako Petroglyphs,** approximately 3,000 individual rock carvings considered some of the finest and oldest in Hawaii. The trail is 1.4 miles round-trip (about a 45-minute walk), but avoid going midday when the unshaded trail can be extremely hot. Bathrooms and drinking fountains are available in the parking

© ANNE FARAHI

the Puako Petroglyphs in Holoholokai Beach Park

BIG ISLAND OF HAWAI'I

lot. To get there, from Highway 19 (between mile markers 73 and 74) turn onto Mauna Lani Drive, turn right at the first turn on the roundabout to North Kaniku Drive, and then turn right onto Holoholokai Beach Park Road.

Kalahupipua'a Trail and Fishponds Historic Park

The short, paved **Kalahupipua'a Trail** (Mauna Lani Bay Hotel, daily 6:30am-6:30pm), which can be connected with the larger shoreline trail system, the **Ala Kahakai National Historic Trail,** passes through ancient fishponds (still stocked with fish) and the Eva Parker Woods Cottage Museum, originally constructed in the 1920s as part of a larger oceanfront estate. To get there, from Highway 19 (between mile markers 73 and 74) turn onto Mauna Lani Drive and gain access through the Mauna Lani Bay Hotel, or for public access follow Mauna Lani Drive and turn left on Pauoa Road; look for the public access lot on the right side.

If you continue to walk south on the Kalahupipua'a Trail for a few more minutes, you'll end up at **Makaiwa Bay,** a white-sand beach that is a great spot for snorkeling, especially for beginners (the signage is so good here that there is a diagram indicating where to go snorkeling in the water based on your level of expertise). Behind the beach is the Mauna Lani Beach Club (the parking lot is not open to the public before 4:30pm, but you can walk there via the trail), housing the upscale restaurant **Napua** (1292 S. Kaniku Dr., 808/885-5022, daily 11am-4pm and 5pm-9pm, lunch $12-16, dinner $28-36). If you walk through the beach and up the stairs at the end of the beach, you'll be on **Ala Kahakai National Historic Trail,** passing by some amazing-looking homes, and you can continue on this scenic path to 49 Black Sand Beach.

49 Black Sand Beach

A little known quiet beach with little shade and calm water, **49 Black Sand Beach** (Mauna Lani Resort) makes for a nice place to get away. The parking lot, including shower and

ancient fishponds located on the Kalahupipua'a Trail

bathroom facilities, is only a minute away from the beach, making this spot a good place to go if you don't want the hassle of parking and trekking far out to a beach.

To get there from Highway 19, between mile markers 73 and 74 turn onto Mauna Lani Drive; continue around the roundabout and turn right onto North Kaniku Drive, then left on Honokaope Place. Check in with the security guard to get a beach pass.

69 Beach (Waialea Bay)

The name of the beach is mostly what gets curious onlookers to visit it, but they are usually happy they made the trip. The **69 Beach on Waialea Bay** (Hwy. 19 between mile markers 70 and 71, daily 7am-8pm) is pleasant: a long, narrow stretch of white sand, lots of shade, and excellent snorkeling. Restroom and shower facilities are available as are several picnic areas. This isn't the best beach in the area, but you won't be disappointed if you spend an afternoon here.

To get to 69 Beach from Highway 19, between mile markers 70 and 71 turn *makai* onto Puako Beach Drive and take the first right onto old Puako Road and then the first left after that; follow the road into the parking area.

◖ Puako Tide Pools

One of the most developed fringing reefs on the island, the **Puako tide pools** (Puako Beach Dr., off Hwy. 19 between mile markers 70 and 71) are an underwater wonderland offering some of the best snorkeling and diving on the island. Once you are in the water, look for submerged lava tubes and garden eels hiding under the sandy ocean bottom. There are no facilities or rental companies located here, so bring in what you need, including equipment and snacks.

Access is available at several different points along the shorefront, but the easiest point may be right before the road dead-ends; from Highway 19 between mile markers 70 and 71 turn *makai* onto Puako Beach Drive and follow the road through the village—even though there is a Dead End sign—head toward the

dead end and turn *makai* into the dirt parking area.

◖ Hapuna Beach State Recreation Area

Locals allege that the **Hapuna Beach State Recreation Area** (Hwy. 19 near mile marker 69, daily 7am-8pm) is one of the top 20 beaches in the world, and that assertion might be true. Even on weekdays the large parking lot fills up early as locals and tourists alike rush to this white-sand beach to get a top spot (especially since there is little shade). The turquoise waters are perfect for snorkeling, body boarding, and swimming. There is a lifeguard on duty, and the picnic areas, some of which are shaded, have great views of all the action on the beach. If you forgot your snorkel gear, towels, boogie boards, or chairs, you can rent from the **Hapuna Beach Grill** (on the grassy area near the parking lot, 808/882-4447, grill daily 11am-3pm, $8, rentals daily 10am-4pm, cash only). The grill offers burgers, fries, ice cream, and fruit smoothies that are better than your usual beach shack foods.

Kauna'oa Beach

Since all beaches in Hawaii are public, it's just knowing how to access them that is the trick. The Mauna Kea Beach Hotel's beach, **Kauna'oa Beach** (Hwy. 19 near mile marker 68), is another example where you merely have to ask a security guard for a pass to park in the public lot at the hotel. Technically, there are even different bathroom and shower facilities for the public users versus the hotel guests, but since it's the same beach, there is a lot of intermingling, including public use of lounge chairs reserved for guests. Once you're in, you'll want to stay for the entire day. The water is perfect for swimming and there is a long stretch of white sand as well as a grassy area ideal for a picnic or just lounging with a book.

To get to Kauna'oa Beach, from Highway 19 turn *makai* onto Mauna Kea Beach Drive near mile marker 68 and ask the guard if you can have a parking permit for the public beach.

Spencer Beach Park

A top family beach and one of the best camping spots on the Big Island (you need a permit), **Spencer Beach Park** (Hwy. 270 between mile markers 2 and 3, 6am-11pm) gets crowded on weekends and holidays. Enter through the entrance to Puʻukohola Heiau National Historic Site. There are picnic pavilions with barbecues, lots of shade, a sandy beach with calm waters, restroom and shower facilities, and just a general congenial atmosphere. It's more popular among locals than tourists, probably given the fact that nearby Hapuna Beach provides a more idyllic beach setting.

HAWI TO THE END OF THE ROAD
◖ Mahukona Beach Park

There is no sand at this beach; instead, **Mahukona Beach Park** (Hwy. 270 between mile markers 14 and 15) is a modern-day ruin. It was a shipping port during the plantation days, and you can still see the decrepit structure of the Hawaii Railroad Company (from 1930) standing in the parking lot. History or archaeology buffs will want to take a quick detour just to see the ruins that are above ground. Snorkelers can delight in an underground adventure not so much for the fish, but for plantation and shipping artifacts scattered under the water. To enter the water, look for the ladder at the old dock. There are no facilities in this section of the beach park; instead, at the fork in the road veer left to the campground area, where there are portable bathrooms. It's not a great campsite, but the picnic area is nice and sheltered.

Mahukona Beach Park

© BREE KESSLER

BIG ISLAND OF HAWAIʻI

Water Sports

The Waikoloa resort area and Anaeho'omalu Bay (A Bay) are not as much of an apex of ocean activities as other areas in the region. Each resort tends to offer ocean and beach equipment rental to its guests, and most also offer quick instruction for snorkeling and stand-up paddling. Fees for activities and rentals tend to be higher when purchased through hotels. You'd be better off to go directly to the source to get a better price.

DIVING AND SNORKELING

Given that there is a harbor in Kawaihae, it seems like a natural location for diving and snorkeling tours; however, there isn't much activity here as most tourists prefer Kona. There really is no reason to avoid diving and snorkeling here; in fact, the benefits are that it is less crowded than the Kona Coast and the water is just as full of remarkable marine life.

Those with experience snorkeling or diving should explore the Puako tide pools, one of the most developed fringing reefs on the island. One can spend the entire day surveying sea life. There aren't rental agencies here so it is imperative to rent before you come. Alternatively, Mahukona Beach Park with its shallow water presents a good opportunity for beginners to get their feet wet and discover some nearby underwater treasure (or garbage, depending how you look at it).

If you want to join a tour, **Kohala Divers** (Hwy. 270 in Kawaihae Shopping Center, 808/882-7774, www.kohaladivers.com) has a great reputation for good service and quality equipment. Since this part of the coast is much less trafficked, the dive sites are usually less worn and you won't have to worry about bumping into many divers down below. Kohala Divers offers a PADI open-water certification course ($600). Experienced divers can book a trip such as the popular two-tank morning charter ($130 per person), a two-tank night dive ($140), or a shorter one-tank dive ($100).

Both diving and snorkeling equipment is available to rent.

The other option is **Mauna Lani Sea Adventures** (66-1400 Mauna Lani Dr., 808/885-7883, www.hawaiiseaadventures.com), but it doesn't specialize in scuba diving. For certified divers, two-tank dives with gear ($160 plus tax) are offered twice daily, and one-tank dives ($115 plus tax) with a minimum of two divers are offered three times daily. PADI-certified courses are available and more information is available upon request.

BODY-BOARDING, SURFING, AND STAND-UP PADDLE-BOARDING

The Kohala Coast is a good place to try out your bodyboarding and stand-up paddling skills since the waves here tend not to be too big or rough. Conversely, these conditions are not ideal for surfing. Experienced surfers tend to try the beach at Pololu Valley, but you have to really want to surf there since a visit requires carrying your board down (and more importantly up) this steep trail.

Ocean Sports (Queens' MarketPlace and beach shack on Anaeho'omalu Bay, 808/886-6666) offers rentals for all your ocean needs. The individual ($50) or family plan ($140 for up to four people) includes unlimited use of equipment for a day, a great deal considering a stand-up paddle board is $50 for an hour. You must return at the end of each hour with your equipment and can only take it out again if no one else is waiting. If you need some help getting started, they offer beach boys (who are like lifeguards) to aid you in short classes. Snorkeling is $30 for 45 minutes ($10 for an extra person), and stand-up paddling is $40 for 30 minutes of instruction.

BOAT TOURS

During winter Kawaihae Harbor is a prime location for whale-watching. Leaving from here will save you some time on the road, as this harbor is closer to the majority of resorts and also tends to be less crowded than Honokohau. Boat trips range from snorkeling and/or diving adventures to whale- and dolphin-watching rides (remember that whales are only around in the winter) to sunset open-bar cruises.

Extending their monopoly on the water, **Ocean Sports** (Whale Center in Kawaihae Harbor, 61-3657 Akoni Pule Hwy./Hwy. 270, 808/886-6666, www.hawaiioceansports.com) touts a champagne sunset cruise on a sailing catamaran. It is a good deal ($115 adults, $58 children, *kama'aina* rates available) for those who like to combine drinking with cruising.

The open bar (including a sunset champagne toast) comes with lots of appetizers, and for only an extra $25 you can renew your vows on board! The Moku Nui Cocktail Sail (Sun., Tues., Thurs. only, $99 adults, $50 children) is similar to the champagne cruise, but with less food and no champagne. The champagne cruise might be worth the extra $16 if you don't have dinner plans afterward. In summer (April-November), Ocean Sports offers a 3.5-hour morning dolphin snorkel trip (Sun., Tues., Thurs., $138 adults, $69 children) complete with lunch and an open bar (that they assure is only available after the snorkeling is complete).

Hiking and Biking

HIKING

Guided hikes aren't a big business in Kohala as there aren't too many established trails here, but the Kohala Mountains do offer some splendid scenery if you decide to explore on your own or join **Hawaii Forest and Trail** (808/331-8505, www.hawaii-forest.com, adults $159 plus tax, children $129 plus tax). This top-rated tour company offers an all-day hiking experience along the Kohala Ditch trail to Kapoloa Waterfall at the back of the Pololu Valley and another hiking trek to other waterfalls in the area. It also takes guests on its six-wheel Pinzgauer vehicle into rugged former sugarcane lands for views of waterfalls and the coast. The hiking portion is pretty minimal (only 1.5 miles), making this tour accessible to anyone comfortable walking that distance over uneven terrain.

BIKING

Highway 19 extending north of the airport provides a nice, flat stretch of road. It's an ideal place to ride fast, and you'll see many serious bikers doing just that. Otherwise, renting a bike simply to ride around the resort area can make for a nice afternoon. Riders wishing to follow the Kona **Ironman route** will want to continue from Highway 19 to Highway 270 north to Hawi to experience the steep climb. Beware: As you travel north on Highway 270 there is not much of a shoulder for bike riding.

For do-it-yourself rentals in the area, **Bikeworks Beach and Sport** (Queens' MarketPlace, 808/836-5000, www.bikeworkshawaii.com) has a nice selection of ultra-deluxe road bikes ($60 per day), deluxe bikes ($50), and cruisers ($25).

Alternatively, **Orchid Isle Bicycling** (808/327-0087, www.cyclekona.com, $125 plus tax) has a two- to three-hour 21-mile tour that starts at the summit of the Kohala mountain range and then continues downhill through Hawi, ending at the ocean. The tour includes equipment rental and snacks.

Adventure Sports

DITCH FLOATS AND ATV TOURS

There is little in the way of organized recreation along the north coast, but what there is can be exciting. Perhaps the most unusual activity is a kayak ride down a section of the Kohala Ditch. Completed in 1906 and considered a feat of engineering, this 22-mile-long irrigation system, with its 57 tunnels, supplied the Kohala sugar mills with a steady supply of water until the last plantation ceased business in 1975.

The ditch was damaged in 2006 during a big earthquake but after a long delay is finally repaired. **Kohala Ditch Adventures** (Hwy. 270 between mile markers 24 and 25, Kapa'au, 808/889-6000, www.kohaladitchadventures. com, $129 per person, $65 for children 5-12), the company that facilitates this journey down two miles of the ditch, recently reopened and is eager for guests to return to "flume the ditch." The specially designed five-person inflatable kayaks drift down the flume, into and out of 10 tunnels and over gullies. Prepare to get wet. The journey ends with an ATV ride through a macadamia nut orchard.

ATV Outfitters (Hwy. 270 between mile markers 24 and 25, 808/889-6000, www.at-voutfittershawaii.com, adults $129-149, children

The King's Trail

A conglomeration of several trails, the **Ala Kahakai National Historic Trail** system stretching over half the island was formalized in 1847 as a way to increase access for missionaries and transportation of goods. But even before the trails became a more formalized system in the 1800s, these trails were the method ancient Hawaiians used to travel the island since they linked together the kingdom of Hawaii's major districts. Thus, the trails present sites of significant events in Hawaiian history, from the arrival of the Polynesians to the islands to the arrival (and subsequent killing) of Captain Cook in Hawaii. Historically, the trail began in the northern part of Kohala (at Upolu Point) and extended into south Puna (at Waha'ula Heiau). Much of this route is not visible anymore due to modern-day construction and/or lava covering it up.

Nowadays, the trail is most visible and walkable between Kawaihae and Pu'uhonua O Honaunau (south of Captain Cook). The National Park Service is working on improving the usability of these trails even more, but for now, there is about a 15-mile section that one can easily

follow. If you start at Spencer Beach Park, you can follow the trail south along the coast. Or another well-marked section starts at the Mauna Kea Beach Hotel, where you can travel south toward Hapuna Beach or north to a secret beach that can only be accessed by the trail. Since the trail is a combination of a historical shore trail and the *ala loa* (king's trail or long trail), you will see different signage depending on where you are (many of the signs read Ala Kahakai, though) and in some places it seems like there are two parallel trails. One of the nicest sections of the trail starts near the Mauna Lani Bay Hotel and Bungalows and takes you through ancient fishponds to some beautiful beaches, and then passes by million-dollar homes. The trail can be easily accessed in sections for a stroll of an hour or two, or you can try a larger portion of the trail from Spencer Beach Park to Hapuna Beach (about three miles one-way) if you are looking for a half-day or a whole-day activity. This route will take you through two desolate hidden beaches (Mau'umae Beach and a beach literally called "secret beach") that make for excellent stops on your journey.

5-11 $80-130) offers an equally extreme way to experience the Kohala backcountry—and the tours aren't limited to just the ditches. There are three options of varying duration, each available twice daily: a historical tour (one hour), waterfall tour (two hours), and waterfall and rainforest tour (three hours). Each will take you to out-of-the-way places along the coast and up into the rainforest on former Kohala sugar plantation land on rugged four-wheel motorcycles. You'll ride over backroads and fields, through lush gullies to waterfalls, come to the edge of ocean cliffs, or dip down to a pebble beach. These fully equipped machines let you get to places that you wouldn't be able to reach otherwise. Safe and reliable, the four-wheelers are easy to operate even for those who have had no experience on a motorcycle. Helmets, gloves, and goggles are supplied and instruction is given. Wear long pants and closed-toe shoes. Mention the website for a discount; reservations are recommended as the tours do get filled up quickly.

ZIPLINING

The ziplining business (also known as the business of suspending oneself on a line in the tree's canopy) is flourishing on the Big Island, with three new courses opening just in 2011. **Big Island Eco Adventures** (55-510 Hawi Rd., 808/889-5111, www.bigislandecoadventures. com, $169 per person plus tax) has a good reputation for not only their professionalism but also for having a more advanced course than other outfitters on the island. If you're keen on doing a zipline course, this is your best bet. In addition to the four-hour zipline course, which consists of eight actual lines, guests are taken offroading on the way to and from the course while guides provide excellent information about the history of the area and the surrounding natural environment. There are seven tours daily beginning at 8am. If you're on a tight schedule, book ahead of time because tours fill up; although you'll still probably be able to book a time, the options might be limited.

HELICOPTER TOURS

The majority of helicopter tours leave from the heliport just south of the Waikoloa resort area or from a heliport next to the Hilo airport. Companies tend to focus on tours to see lava at Hawai'i Volcanoes National Park, and the longer or deluxe tours will circle the island to get a glimpse of Waipi'o Valley and waterfalls in Kohala. These tours inevitably are expensive, but if you have the funds do it, people always say that it was their favorite part of the trip.

Sunshine Helicopters (808/882-1233 or 800/622-3144, www.sunshinehelicopters. com), one of the larger companies with service on each island, runs a 40-minute Kohala Mountain and Hamakua Valley tour ($170 per person with online discount) and a two-hour Volcano Deluxe tour that circles the island ($510 per person with online discount or $485 for the early-bird tour).

Another large operation with a spotless safety record, **Blue Hawaiian Helicopters** (808/886-1768 in Waikoloa, 800/786-2583, www.bluehawaiian.com) operates tours from both the Kona and Hilo sides with two helicopter options—the A-Star and the Eco-star. The difference between the helicopters is that the Eco-star is "the first touring helicopter of the 21st century," meaning that its seats are more comfortable, it is quieter, and it has larger windows for a less obstructed view than the A-Star. Most importantly, it costs more. From the Kona side, there are three tour options: a 90-minute Kohala Coast Adventure ($213 for A-Star, $259 for Eco-Star), the standard trip to see the waterfalls of the region; the two-hour Big Island Spectacular ($396, $495), an all-encompassing trip that circumvents the island to witness all its highlights; and the two-hour Big Island-Maui trip ($440, $495), a quick jaunt over to Maui to view Haleakala Crater and then a glimpse of the Kohala waterfalls on the way back. This particular tour has a six-person minimum.

Golf

The resorts in South Kohala offer half a dozen of the best golf courses in the state, and they are all within a few miles of each other.

Like rivers of green, the Waikoloa Scottish-links **Kings' Golf Course** (600 Waikoloa Beach Dr., 808/886-7888, http://waikoloa-beachgolf.com), designed by Tom Weiskopf and Jay Morrish, and the **Beach Golf Course** (808/886-6060), a Robert Trent Jones Jr. creation, wind their way around the hotels and condos of Waikoloa Beach Resort. Both have plenty of water and lava rock hazards, and each has its own clubhouse. Lessons, a golf clinic, and a half-day golf school can be arranged through both courses. Prices are reasonable, ranging $85-165. Off-property guests pay about $30 more per round than Waikoloa Beach Resort guests. Discounts are available after 3pm and for nine-hole rounds. Family golf days, where children under 17 play for a discounted rate, are a great deal.

Surrounding the Mauna Lani Bay Hotel are the marvelous **Francis H. I'i Brown North Course** and **Francis H. I'i Brown South Course,** whose artistically laid out fairways, greens, and sand traps make it a modern landscape sculpture. The 18-hole courses are carved from lava, with striking ocean views in every direction. Call the pro shop (808/885-6655) for information, tee times, clinics, and lessons. Discounts are available for booking online (www.maunalani.com/g_rates.htm). Guests pay $165, and non-resort guests can expect to pay at least $215 for a round.

The Mauna Kea's classic, trend-setting **Mauna Kea Golf Course** (808/882-5400, www.princeresortshawaii.com/mauna-kea-golf-course/) was designed by the master, Robert Trent Jones Sr., and has been voted among America's 100 greatest courses and one of Hawaii's finest. Deceptive off the tee, it's demanding at the green. It lies near the ocean and has been joined by the more spread-out **Hapuna Golf Course** (808/880-3000, www.princeresortshawaii.com/hapuna-golf.php), designed by Arnold Palmer and Ed Seay, which has been cut into the lava up above the hotels and highway. Both 18-hole courses give even the master players a challenge. Rates for the Mauna Kea course range $155-225 for resort guests depending on the time of day (discounts given for twilight play) and $250 for nonguests. The Hapuna course ranges $75-125, and *kama'aina* discounts are also available.

Sights

KAWAIHAE
Pu'ukohola Heiau National Historic Site

While Pu'uhonua O Honaunau is the "city of refuge," **Pu'ukohola Heiau National Historic Site** (Hwy. 270 between mile markers 2 and 3, 808/882-7218, www.nps.gov/puhe, gate hours 7:45am-4pm, park open 24 hours, free), which means "the temple on the hill of the whale," was a place of war. Present day, it is one of the best-preserved and most significant temple sites in Hawaii. A walk around the park will take you about 30-45 minutes. Call 808/206-7056 for a self-guided cell phone audio tour or ask a ranger in the visitor center for a tour ($2 suggested donation) if one is available. You can also call ahead to reserve a tour, and I encourage you to do just that as the rangers are a true wealth of information about all things Hawaii. If you're bringing kids, ask the ranger for the Junior Ranger activity book, which comes with a free pin.

Visit in the early morning for the best chance of seeing black tip reef sharks. Also keep a

© BONITA CHESHIER/123RF.COM

a lei hangs on a tiki at Pu'ukohola Heiau National Historic Site

BIG ISLAND OF HAWAI'I

lookout for birds, as the park ranger guarantees you will see at least 10 different kinds during your visit.

【 Hamakua Macadamia Nut Factory

The **Hamakua Macadamia Nut Factory** (Maluokalani St., off Hwy. 270 between mile markers 4 and 5, 808/882-1690, www.hawnnut.com, 9am-5:30pm) might become your happy place (unless you have a nut allergy—then please don't go here). Imagine a room full of macadamia nuts of every variety imaginable, all available to sample for free. Candy corn, brittles, and coffee can be sampled as well. If you're planning on purchasing some nuts to take home, the prices are comparable to the local grocery stores. Or if you really love mac nuts, buy one of the four-pound bags—a good deal for about $32 depending on the variety. You can also watch the interior workings of the factory or try to crack a macadamia nut yourself.

Pua Mau Place Botanical Garden

This 12-acre garden doesn't get much traffic, but it's quite a sight for plant enthusiasts. The one-hour self-guided tour through **Pua Mau Place Botanical Garden** (Ala Kahua Dr. off Hwy. 270 near mile marker 6, 808/882-0888, www.puamau.org, daily 9am-4pm, $8) takes you though the landscaped garden, an unlikely location here in arid Kohala. The focus here is on flowering plants, ones that thrive and flourish in a windy and arid environment. While many plants have been established, some of the showiest are the hibiscus, plumeria, and date palm. With so much sunshine and so little rain, this is a harsh environment, and only certain types of plants survive. A greater challenge for the plants is that no pesticides are sprayed and brackish water is used for irrigation. Only the hardy make it, and those that do seem to love it. Heavy mulch guides you along the well-signed paths; plant numbers correspond to a book you take on your self-guided tour. Whimsy is added by the giant bronze sculptures of insects that dot the garden here and there, the aviary, and the Magic Circle, a circle of stones reminiscent of megalithic stone monuments like Stonehenge. The garden is open for private functions such as weddings.

HAWI TO THE END OF THE ROAD
Lapakahi State Historical Park

Want to experience Hawaii as early settlers did 600 years ago? A visit to **Lapakahi State Historical Park** (Hwy. 270 between mile markers 13 and 14, daily 8am-4pm, gate closes 3:30pm), a reconstructed historical village, is a good place for kids and history buffs. The self-guided tour is one of the better ones on the island because the pamphlet available at the small visitors center in the parking lot is user-friendly, and the trail is well marked and maintained. The trail, made up of two 0.5-mile loops, takes about 45 minutes. As you walk clockwise around the numbered stations, you pass canoe sheds and a fish shrine dedicated to Ku'ula, to whom the fishermen always dedicated a portion of their catch. A salt-making

© HAWAII'S BIG ISLAND VISITOR BUREAU (BIVB)

Lapakahi State Historical Park

area demonstrates how the Hawaiians evaporated seawater by moving it into progressively smaller "pans" carved in the rock. There are numerous home sites along the wood-chip trail. Particularly interesting to children are exhibits of games like *konane* (Hawaiian checkers) and *'ulu maika* (a form of bowling using stones) that the children are encouraged to try. Throughout the area, numerous trees, flowers, and shrubs are identified, and as an extra treat, migrating whales come close to shore December-April.

Upolu Airport Road Scenic Drive to Kohala Historical Sites State Monument

At mile marker 20, turn off Highway 270 down a one-lane road to Upolu airstrip. You'll know you're on Upolu Airport Road when you see the wind farm on your right. You really need a Jeep to do the scenic drive. Follow the road until it reaches a dead end at the runway. Turn left onto a *very* rough dirt road, which may not be passable. This entire area is one of the most rugged and isolated on the Big Island,

with wide windswept fields, steep sea cliffs, and pounding surf. Pull off at any likely spot along the road and keep your eyes peeled for signs of cavorting humpback whales, which frequent this coast November-May. After bumping down the road for about two miles (count on at least 45 minutes if you walk), turn and walk five minutes uphill to gain access to **Mo'okini Luakini Heiau.**

In 1962, Mo'okini Heiau was declared a national historic landmark. Legend says that the first temple at Mo'okini was built as early as AD 480. This incredible date indicates that Mo'okini must have been built immediately upon the arrival of the first Polynesian explorers, who many scholars maintain arrived in large numbers a full two centuries later. Regardless of its age, the integrity of the remaining structure is remarkable and shows great skill in construction.

When you visit the *heiau* (temple), pick up a brochure from a box at the entrance; if none are available, a signboard nearby gives general information. The entire *heiau* is surrounded by a stone wall erected for its protection in 1981. In one corner of the enclosure is a traditional Hawaiian structure used in some of the temple ceremonies. On occasion, this building is blown down by the strong winds that lash this coast. Notice the integration of the stone platform. This thatched structure is perfectly suited to provide comfort against the elements. Look through the door at a timeless panorama of the sea and surf. Notice that the leeward stones of the *heiau* wall are covered in lichens, giving them a greenish cast and testifying to their age. A large, flat stone outside the wall was used to prepare victims for the sacrificial altar. The only entrance to the *heiau* itself is in the wall roughly facing southwest. Inside is an enclosure used by the person responsible for finding and catching the human sacrifices that were offered at the temple.

This was once a closed temple for the *ali'i* only, but the *kapu* was lifted in 1977 so that others may visit and learn. Be respectful, as this temple is still in use, and stay on the designated paths, which are cordoned off by woven rope. Along the short wall closest to the sea is a "scalloped" altar where recent offerings of flowers are often seen. Inside the *heiau* are remnants of enclosures used by the *ali'i* and space set aside for temple priests. The floor of the temple is carpeted with well-placed stones and tiny green plants that give a natural mosaic effect.

A few minutes' walk south of the *heiau* along this coastal dirt track is **Kamehameha's birthplace,** called **Kamehameha 'Akahi 'Aina Hanau.** Rather unpretentious for being of such huge significance, the entrance to the area is at the back side, away from the sea. Inside the low stone wall, which always seems to radiate heat, are some large boulders believed to be the actual "birthing stones" where the high chiefess Kekuiapoiwa, wife of the warrior *ali'i* Keoua Kupuapaikalananinui, gave birth to Kamehameha sometime around 1758. There is much debate about the actual year and place of Kamehameha's birth, and some place it elsewhere in 1753, but it was to the Mo'okini Heiau nearby that he was taken for his birth rituals, and it was there that he performed his

religious rituals until he completed Pu'u Kohola Heiau down the coast at Kawaihae around 1791. This male child, born as his father prepared a battle fleet to invade Maui, would grow to be the greatest of the Hawaiian chiefs—a brave, powerful, but lonely man, isolated like the flat plateau upon which he drew his first breath. The temple's ritual drums and haunting chants dedicated to Ku were the infant's first lullabies. He would grow to accept Ku as his god, and together they would subjugate all of Hawaii. In this expansive North Kohala area, Kamehameha was confronted with unencumbered vistas and sweeping views of neighboring islands, unlike most Hawaiians, whose outlooks were held in check by the narrow, confining, but secure walls of steep-sided valleys. Only this man with this background could rise to become "The Lonely One," high chief of a unified kingdom.

Together, Mo'okini Heiau, King Kamehameha's birthplace, and several other nearby historical sites make up the seven-acre **Kohala Historical Sites State Monument.** In 2005, Kamehameha Schools bought a large tract of land surrounding Kamehameha's birthplace and Mo'okini Luakini Heiau in order to protect the environs from residential and commercial development that might disturb the sacred nature of these cultural sites.

Note: You'll have to return to Highway 270 the way you came because the road is closed off on the south end (but there is a small dirt turnaround there).

Pololu Valley Lookout and Beach

If you are looking for the *Lost* experience on the Big Island, the **Pololu Valley lookout and beach** (Hwy. 270 where the road ends) is it. Park your car in the lot at the end of the highway; grab your bathing suit, tent, some food and water; and hike the one-mile trail to the beach (about 30 minutes down and 45 minutes up for a novice hiker). If you're not interested in the hike, the view itself is worth driving to the road's end and simply staring for a few minutes. If you do walk down, the beach at the bottom

© MARK WASSER

the Pololu Valley lookout

has wonderful blackish sand, but the shoreline can be rocky and the waves hit hard depending on the day.

It's about 12 miles from Pololu Valley to Waipi'o Valley, with five deep-cut valleys in between, including the majestic Waimanu, the largest. It's not possible to drive to Waipi'o here, but a super hiker could likely make it between the two.

Locals swear that you don't need a permit to stay here, and it's not patrolled at night—but don't worry, no safety issues have ever been reported. Pitch your tent on top of one of the small green hills and it's likely that you will have the place to yourself, or you won't notice if anyone else is there. There are no facilities, so make sure to bring enough food and water for your visit. Enjoy a nighttime dip in the ocean, but take care because the tide can be rough!

Shopping and Entertainment

SHOPPING
South Kohala: Resort Area

The two main shopping areas in Waikoloa, **Kings' Shops** and **Queens' MarketPlace,** are across the street from one another on Waikoloa Beach Drive. The Kings' Shops are high-end stores like Louis Vuitton, Coach, Tiffany's, and the tiniest Macy's that you will ever see. Across the street, the Queens' MarketPlace offers typical mall selections, such as Lids, Claire's, and Quiksilver, as well as a food court (daily 7:30am-9:30pm).

Hawi to the End of the Road

Hawi and the adjoining Kapa'au epitomize the notion of "cute towns" with a small main street (it's actually Hwy. 270) lined with shops, galleries, and restaurants. It's definitely worth making a short detour here, parallel parking your car and strolling from store to store. The entire walk will take you less than two hours. Yes, there is some Hawaiiana here, but this area has an artist colony feel to it, lending to goods that are higher quality than the standard kitsch you'll find in Kona or Hilo.

ENTERTAINMENT

All the resort hotels in the area have bars with live music performances on the weekends and sometimes also weekday evenings. The Waikoloa Beach area hosts daily events at the Queens' MarketPlace, Kings' Shops, Hilton Waikoloa Village, and Waikoloa Beach Resort. Many of the events are free and can be found on the website (www.waikoloabeachresort.com). Many of the events are ideal for children—such as Hawaiian storytelling. One notable event is the weekly free concert with Big Island slack-key guitarist John Keawe. I highly urge you to attend that show. He plays other places on the island during the week, but you usually have to pay to see him.

For something a little more local, go to **Sansei Seafood Restaurant and Sushi Bar** (201 Waikoloa Beach Dr. in Queens' MarketPlace, 808/886-6286, www.dkrestaurants.com) for weekend karaoke coupled with cheap sushi and drink deals.

North of the resort area in Kawaihae, the **Blue Dragon Coastal Cuisine & Musiquarium** (Hwy. 270 between mile markers 3 and 4, 808/882-7771, www.bluedragonhawaii.com) has the best of both worlds: live music and dancing. It's one of few places on the island where people get dressed up for a night out. No, it's not a club, it's more like an old-timers' big band dance hall—classy and romantic with excellent cocktails.

In Hawi, both **Bamboo Restaurant** (Hwy. 270, Hawi, 808/889-5555, www.bamboorestaurant.info) and **Luke's Place** (55-514 Hawi Rd., 808/889-1155, www.lukeskohala.com) have live music on the weekends. Bamboo's variety is quieter, while Luke's is a louder bar scene.

The larger resorts all hold **luau** on alternating days during the week (see calendar online at www.waikoloabeachresort.com). They mostly feel like factory luau—getting people in and out and fed quickly. While it is more convenient to simply attend a luau at your hotel, you might want to venture out for a more Cirque de Soleil experience at **The Fairmont Orchid** (www.fairmont.com/orchid). This luau is more expensive than its counterparts, but the food is better than at other luau.

Food

SOUTH KOHALA: RESORT AREA

All the resorts in the area have at least one restaurant located on the premises. These restaurants, for the most part, are fine but not notable and tend to be more expensive than off-premises restaurants. If you don't want to travel too far away from your hotel or condo, but still want to eat out, there are some worthwhile options nearby.

This would be a number one spot on the Mainland, but given the immense amount of great sushi on the Big Island, **(Sansei Seafood Restaurant and Sushi Bar** (201 Waikoloa Beach Dr., Queens' MarketPlace, 808/886-6286, www.dkrestaurants.com, dinner Sun.-Thurs. 5:30-10pm, Fri. and Sat. 5:30pm-1am, rolls $4-18, appetizers $3-14, entrées $18-48) is simply good. What is of note here is their amazing specials and the fact that it is open much later than almost any other restaurant around. The daily early-bird special offers 25 percent off sushi, appetizers, and entrées 5pm-6pm, and locals get 50 percent off Sunday and Monday for early-bird dining. Friday and Saturday there is late night karaoke (free for 21 and over, 10pm-1am) with drink specials and 50 percent off sushi and appetizers.

A fine restaurant by Peter Merriman, one of the well-known chefs of Hawaii Regional Cuisine, **Merriman's Market Café** (250 Waikoloa Beach Dr., Kings' Shops, 808/886-1700, daily 11:30am-9pm, happy hour 3-5:30pm, bar open till 9:30pm, $11-28) utilizes local ingredients to create standard dishes of fish, burgers, and salads. It isn't the same experience as Merriman's more upscale Waimea location, but is still a worthy choice, especially given the children's menu and vegetarian and gluten-free options.

If you're seeking something on the lighter side, **Juice 101** (68-1330 Mauna Lani Dr., The Shops at Mauna Lani, 808/887-2244, www. juicebar101.com, daily 7am-9pm) is just what you're looking for. As their name implies, they have fresh juice squeezed from fruits and greens as well as smoothies. Try the kale smoothie and acai bowl to energize you for the day. If that's not your thing, enjoy the breakfast bagels and a cup of coffee. Lunch is available, and kid-friendly too, with options such as grilled cheese. It's more a takeout place than a dine-in joint, but they do have free wireless Internet.

Among the usual humdrum of resort restaurants, **(The Canoe House** (68-1400 Mauna Lani Dr., Mauna Lani Bay Hotel, 808/885-6622, www.maunalani.com/d_ch_overview. htm, $40) stands out. The menu is thoughtful, using local ingredients (as much as possible) to create beautiful, well-thought-out dishes, and the wine list is extensive. I recommend any of the fresh fish or the rack of lamb. And the view! Right on the ocean, this restaurant makes for an ideal romantic evening. Best of all, the chef is more than willing to accommodate food allergies.

KAWAIHAE

There is a surprisingly large number of restaurants in this small town, which attracts the overflow of resort visitors seeking food outside the bounds of their hotel. Thus prices are somewhat higher than what you'd expect. Since there is a harbor right in town many restaurants offer fresh seafood.

One of the most fun eating experiences on the Big Island, the **(Blue Dragon Coastal Cuisine & Musiquarium** (Hwy. 270 between mile markers 3 and 4, 808/882-7771, www. bluedragonhawaii.com, Thurs.-Sun. 5:30-11pm, $30) is always crowded with locals and visitors alike dancing away the evening while breaking for bites of the coastal cuisine. The menu offers good choices of local fish and produce, and the online menu notes which items are gluten free, vegetarian, and/or vegan. The food is tasty and definitely highlights what the island has to offer—like the Hamakua mushroom dishes—but the food can be over-priced and service can be slow when the place gets really bumping. Sometimes, however, you can find a coupon for the restaurant on the website or in the *Big Island Weekly* newspaper. What you're really paying for is the live entertainment, and it's worth it. Reservations are a must; however, sometimes you can get a seat at the small bar. Kids are welcome, but I would recommend bringing them early as the restaurant feels more like a club as it gets later.

The other choice close by is **Café Pesto** (Kawaihae Center, 808/882-1071, www.cafepesto.com, daily 11am-9pm, pizzas average $9, dinner mains $18-35), which feels entirely like your hometown Italian restaurant meets Hawaii. The menu is a little all over the place, from pizza and calzones to fish and Thai-style food. I'd stick with the Italian side of the menu. Vegetarian and gluten-free options are available. Reservations are recommended.

HAWI TO THE END OF THE ROAD

Hawi is the spot were ex-New Yorkers or ex-restaurateurs come to open restaurants, and you will reap the benefits of their decision. Nearly every restaurant in the area offers something better than the next. In fact, one of your biggest hardships in Hawaii will be finding time to eat everywhere in town.

Best known for their *liliko'i* (passion fruit) infused drinks, **Bamboo Restaurant** (Hwy. 270, Hawi, 808/889-5555, www.bamboorestaurant.info, Tues.-Sat. 11:30am-2pm and 6pm-8pm, Sun. brunch 11:30am-2:30pm, happy hour Mon.-Fri. 4pm-6pm, $20) is a Hawi mainstream offering classic dishes like chicken, fish, and vegetarian options such as polenta with a hint of Hawaiiana—meaning that the standard dishes are seasoned with teriyaki sauce, coconut milk, and passion fruit sauces galore. The food is good enough, but the restaurant is located in an early 1900s building that provides a wonderful ambiance for a hot afternoon, and the overall experience is worthwhile. There is live music on Friday and Saturday nights.

A few doors down from Bamboo Restaurant, **Lighthouse Deli** (55-3419 Akoni Pule Hwy./Hwy. 270, Hawi, www.lighthousedelihi.com, 808/889-5757, Mon.-Sat. 10am-6pm, Sun. 9am-4pm, happy hour Mon.-Fri. 4pm-6pm, $12) is the Jewish deli you've been looking for in Hawaii. Classic deli sandwiches are served on locally made bread. They have wine and beer on draft, not to mention they own the **Lighthouse Liquors** store (808/889-0505, Sun.-Tues. noon-8pm, Wed.-Sat. 11am-10pm) next door, which has an extensive wine and beer selection, and you're welcome to pick something up there to pair with your meal as well. The Sunday brunch is a big hit in town, and likewise you'll want to come early to get a taste of their Benedict. Limited seating is available inside, but the additional sidewalk seating makes for a wonderful people-watching spot.

Next door to Lighthouse Deli, one of few authentic Mexican restaurants on the island, **Mi Ranchito** (55-3419 Akoni Pule Hwy./Hwy. 270, Hawi, daily 11am-8pm, $9-16), is a true taquería and one of the best choices if you're looking for something a little less pricey than the majority of Hawi restaurants. The price is right and the portions are huge. Vegetarian and gluten-free options available. You won't see it from the street; it is in the interior of the building where Lighthouse Liquors is located.

If you're looking for a quick to-go treat while strolling the streets, stop in to **Kohala Coffee Mill** (55-3412 Akoni Pule Hwy./Hwy. 270, Hawi, 808/889-5577, Mon.-Fri. 6am-6pm, Sat.-Sun. 7am-6pm, $7-10) for an ice cream cone or a cookie or take a seat outdoors and listen to a live music performance that tends to pop up on any given day. This is a laid-back coffee shop with beverages like hot coffee and ice-cold chai as well as breakfast bagel sandwiches. Salads and hamburgers are available for lunch.

Originally opened in 1950, **Luke's Place** (55-514 Hawi Rd., Hawi, 808/889-1155, www.lukeskohala.com, 11:30am-9pm, happy hour 3pm-6pm, $12) serves up bar food that is better than the usual fare at reasonable prices for large portions. The burgers, which are made from Big Island beef, are flavorsome and have the usual fixings. A good vegetarian option is the veggie wrap. Many people eat here for convenience before or after their zipline trip, but there is better food in town if you're not in a rush or not on a budget. There is a nighttime scene here, so it is worth stopping by after dinner for drinks and live music. Drinks are 20 percent off all day Thursday for "Thirsty Thursdays," and the bar stays open until *pau* (when everyone is finished).

A real treat for those who love sushi and even those who do not, the rolls at 【 **Sushi Rock** (55-3435 Akoni Pule Hwy./Hwy. 270 in Hawi Town, 808/889-5900, www.sushirockrestaurant.net, daily noon-3pm and 5:30-8pm, rolls $17) truly are a fusion of traditional sushi combinations and local ingredients, such as purple sweet potatoes with ahi and goat cheese. Don't forget to ask for the local wasabi grown in Volcano. It really tastes different than the green wasabi you're used to getting at sushi restaurants. Rolls can be ordered individually or by platter, such as the Ali'i, which includes 32 premium rolls. Feel free to ask the chef to pick your rolls if you can't decide for yourself. The platters are a good deal—the larger the better if you're with friends.

Getting There and Around

CAR

If you're heading back to the airport from the Kohala Coast, the **last gas station** you'll pass before you get to the airport is the **Shell station** in the **Kings' Shops** in the Waikoloa resort area. The problem is that it's still about 20 miles from the airport, but if you top your tank off you should be okay. There isn't a close gas station south of the airport either. The closest station is probably at Costco in Kailua and isn't open early in the morning or late at night. If you're heading north from Waikoloa, your next gas station is about 15 miles away in Kawaihae.

BUS

It is possible, with some good planning, to make it from the Kona side to the Hilo side and from Kona to Kohala on the **Hele-On Bus** (www.heleonbus.org, 808/961-8744, $1 per ride, $1 each for luggage, large backpacks, bikes).

The North Kohala to South Kohala route bus is a commuter route for those who work at the resorts. It only runs once daily Monday-Saturday, leaving from Kapa'au at 6:30am, making stops south of Highway 270 (such as in Hawi and Kawaihae) and then on Highway 19 at all the resorts, ending at at the Hilton Waikoloa Village. The bus returns north from the Hilton Waikoloa Village at 4:15pm, arriving in Kapa'au at 5:35pm.

A second option gets you farther south to Kona and east to Waimea, but unfortunately only runs Monday-Friday. The bus leaves from Kapa'au at 6:45am and travels south on Highway 270 to the junction of Highway 19, where it goes east to Waimea, arriving at the Parker Ranch Shopping Center. From the Parker Ranch Shopping Center, it is possible to connect on a different bus to the Hamakua Coast and Hilo.

BIG ISLAND OF HAWAI'I

HAWAI'I VOLCANOES NATIONAL PARK

The indomitable power of Hawai'i Volcanoes National Park is apparent to all who come here. Mark Twain, enchanted by his sojourn through Volcanoes in the 1860s, quipped, "The smell of sulphur is strong, but not unpleasant to a sinner." Wherever you stop to gaze, realize that you are standing on a thin skin of cooled lava in an unstable earthquake zone atop one of the world's most active volcanoes.

© MARK WASSER

HIGHLIGHTS

LOOK FOR 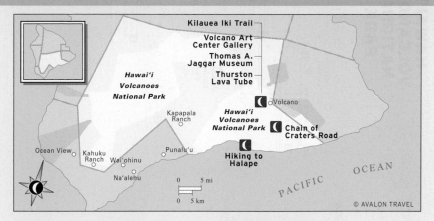 TO FIND RECOMMENDED SIGHTS, ACTIVITIES, DINING, AND LODGING.

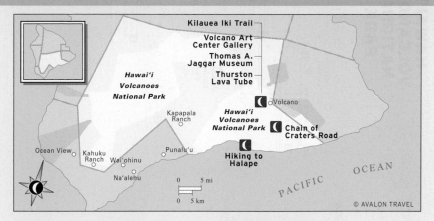

◖ Volcano Art Center Gallery: This is one of the finest art galleries in the entire state, boasting the best the islands have to offer (page 574).

◖ Thomas A. Jaggar Museum: This state-of-the-art museum offers a fantastic multimedia display of the amazing geology and volcanology of the area. At night you can watch the lava glow from the viewing area (page 575).

◖ Thurston Lava Tube: Ferns and moss hang from the entrance of this remarkable natural tunnel. It's as if the very air is tinged with green (page 577).

◖ Chain of Craters Road: Every bend of this road offers a panoramic vista. The grandeur and power of the forces that have been creating the earth from the beginning of time are right before your eyes (page 577).

◖ Kilauea Iki Trail: This trail takes you from the top of the crater with its lush tropical vegetation to the crater floor, which still breathes volcanic steam (page 585).

◖ Hiking to Halape: Your reward for the strenuous hike is a white sugary beach and sheltered lagoon—by far the most remote and pristine beach on the island (page 586).

Established in 1916 as the 13th U.S. national park, Hawai'i Volcanoes National Park now covers 333,000 acres. Based on its scientific and scenic value, the park was named an International Biosphere Reserve by UNESCO in 1980 and given World Heritage Site status in 1987 by the same organization, giving it greater national and international prestige. This is one of the top visitor attractions in the state.

With a multitude of ways to access the park—by foot, by car, by bike, and by helicopter—Hawai'i Volcanoes National Park truly does offer

something for everyone. Even non-nature lovers are impressed by the environmental oddities offered there, such as the vastly different landscapes situated next to each other. Within moments one can pass through a tropical rainforest to what appears like a moon landscape. Even if this doesn't impress, it will be hard to tear yourself away from the lava flow or glow. It's surreal.

In conjunction with a visit to the park, you'll surely pass through Volcano Village, known for the cadre of artists and scientists that live there. With wineries, farmers markets, restaurants,

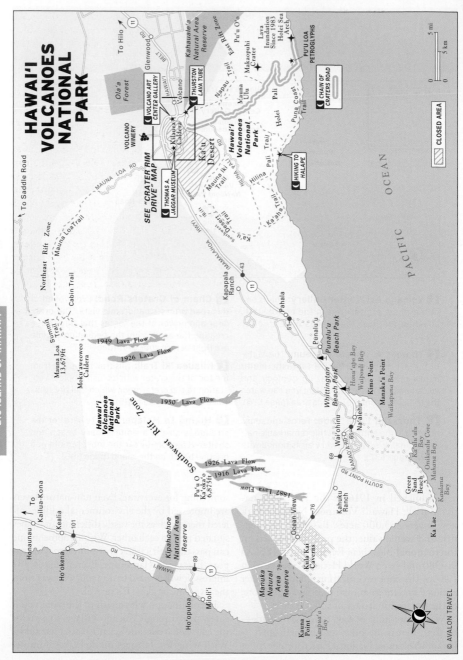

HAWAI'I VOLCANOES NATIONAL PARK

© AVALON TRAVEL

and galleries, it can feel like the Sonoma of Hawaii and not just somewhere to pass through on the way to somewhere else.

ORIENTATION
Hawai'i Volcanoes National Park

Practically speaking, you'll find the main entrance to the park off of Highway 11 near mile marker 28; however, the park itself extends far to the north and the south of the main entrance. The upper end of the park is the summit of stupendous Mauna Loa, the most massive mountain on earth. Mauna Loa Road branches off Highway 11 and ends at a foot trail for the hale and hearty who trek to the 13,679-foot summit. The park's heart is Kilauea Caldera, almost three miles across, 400 feet deep, and encircled by 11 miles of Crater Rim Drive. At the park visitors center you can give yourself a crash course in geology while picking up park maps, information, and backcountry camping permits. Nearby is Volcano House, Hawaii's oldest hotel, which has hosted a steady stream of adventurers, luminaries, royalty, and heads

of state ever since it opened its doors in the 1860s. Just a short drive away is a pocket of indigenous forest, providing the perfect setting for a bird sanctuary. In a separate detached section of the park is 'Ola'a Forest, a pristine wilderness area of unspoiled flora and fauna.

Crater Rim Drive circles Kilauea Caldera past steam vents, sulphur springs, and tortured fault lines that always seem on the verge of gaping wide and swallowing. On the way you can peer into the mouth of Halema'uma'u Crater, home of the fire goddess, Pele, and you'll pass Hawaiian Volcano Observatory, which has been monitoring geologic activity since the turn of the 20th century. Adjacent to the observatory is the Thomas A. Jaggar Museum, an excellent facility where you can educate yourself on the past and present volcanology of the park. An easy walk is Devastation Trail, a paved path across a desolate cinder field where gray, lifeless trunks of a suffocated forest lean like old gravestones. Within minutes is Thurston Lava Tube, a magnificent natural tunnel overflowing with vibrant fern grottoes at the entrance and exit.

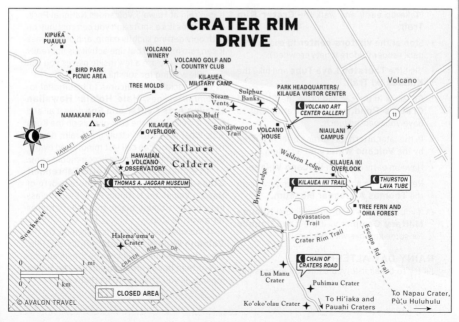

The southwestern section of the park is dominated by the Ka'u Desert, not a plain of sand but a semi-arid slope of lava flow, cinder, scrub bushes, and heat that's been defiled by the windblown debris and gases of Kilauea Volcano and fractured by the sinking coastline. It is a desolate region, an area crossed by a few trails that are a challenge even to the sturdy and experienced hiker. Most visitors, however, head down the Chain of Craters Road, down the *pali* to the coast, where the road ends abruptly at a hardened flow of lava and from where visitors can glean information about current volcanic activities from the small ranger station and try to glimpse the current volcanic activity in the distance.

Volcano Village

Driving north on Highway 11, you will pass by the park's entrance before reaching the main part of Volcano town (if you are driving from Hilo, you pass the town first). Although there are residential communities on both sides of the road, the *mauka* side is where the center of Volcano town is. Nearly every restaurant and shop is on the short Old Volcano Road—the inner road that parallels Highway 11 through town. The golf course area, where the Volcano Winery is also housed, is on Highway 11 between mile markers 30 and 31 just south of the park.

PLANNING YOUR TIME

It's best to decide ahead of time how much time you want to spend at the park and whether you're visiting by car, by foot, or by bike. Regardless of your plan, your first stop should be the visitors center to check with a park ranger about any new closures in the park, new safety advisories, or a special program going on

---

Your Best Day in the Volcano Area

- Wake up early and walk the **Crater Rim Trail.**
- Stop at the **visitors center** to chat with a park ranger (before it gets crowded).
- Visit the **Thurston Lava Tube** and hike the **Kilauea Iki Trail.**
- Get back in the car and drive the **Chain of Craters Road,** stopping at a lookout to have your packed lunch.
- In the later afternoon, after a brief rest, stop by the **Volcano Winery** for a tasting.
- Have an early dinner in **Volcano Village.**
- Return to the park to watch the glow from the **Thomas A. Jaggar Museum.**
- If you're not too tired, go bowling at **Kilauea Military Camp** or visit the **Lava Lounge** for some karaoke with the locals.

RAINY DAY ALTERNATIVE

I'll try to break it to you as gently as possible:

It can rain at Hawai'i Volcanoes National Park. Sometimes it's a spritz and you can continue on with only getting slightly damp, and other times it can rain hard and outside activity is not really possible. There are a few inside places you can go while waiting for sunshine.

From facials to pedicures to traditional *lomilomi* massages, **Hale Ho'ola: Hawaiian Healing Arts Center and Spa** does it all and does it well at half the cost of spas on the Kona side. What makes this a truly great rainy day activity is that you can call last minute and owner Suzanne Woolley will try to accommodate you.

Art enthusiasts will love **2400 Fahrenheit Glass Blowing,** just a few minutes north of Hawai'i Volcanoes National Park. Even if glass blowing isn't taking place, this gallery makes for a worthy stop.

If the weather still hasn't cleared up, try the **Volcano Winery** for a tasting or drive to Hilo. Often the weather in Hilo can be drastically different than in Volcano (you can see the clouds moving as you drive north on Highway 11).

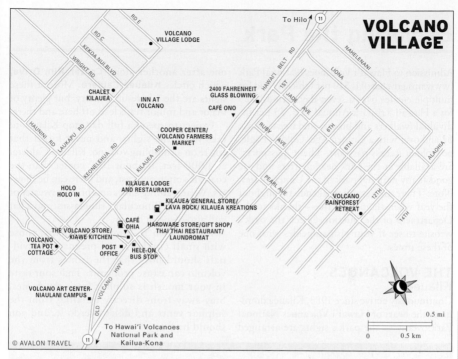

that day. Start early. The park looks entirely different in the early morning—the colors are different and it is much quieter before the busloads of tourists start to arrive. Lastly, pack a lunch. The food options in the park are nearly nonexistent. Better to bring a great sandwich with you so that you don't have to return to town midday to get fed.

It is possible to see the park's "greatest hits" in one long day if you drive from sight to sight on Crater Rim and then Chain of Craters Road. You'll even have time to get out and walk around, have a leisurely dinner, and then come back to catch the glow at night. There are a handful of fairly easy hikes that only take 2-3 hours. If you're planning on doing one or more of those hikes (such as Kilauea Iki), you might want to give yourself an extra day in the park. Two days at Hawai'i Volcanoes National Park will allow you to see all the major sights

and accomplish at least two beginner- to medium-level hikes. At least three days in the park will be necessary to get into the backcountry and then maybe more importantly, to get back out.

In this age of Internet, you can see the park without physically being there. If want to check out conditions before you head into the park (i.e., is it worth driving to the park at night), there are several useful websites you can use to check on **lava status** (http://volcano.wr.usgs. gov/kilaueastatus.php for the viewing area in Puna, http://volcanoes.usgs.gov/hvo/cams/ HMcam (for the Thomas A. Jaggar Museum viewing area) and **trail closures** (www.nps. gov/havo/closed_areas.htm0).

The National Park Service also offers the free *Your Guide to Hawai'i Volcanoes National Park* app for iPhone users for download from iTunes (www.nps.gov/havo/planyourvisit/hike.htm).

Exploring the Park

Admission to Hawai'i Volcanoes National Park (www.nps.gov/havo) is $10 per vehicle (good for multiple entries over a seven-day period), $25 for a Hawaii Tri-park Annual Pass, $5 per individual (walkers and bikers), and free to those 62 and over with a Golden Age, Golden Eagle, or Golden Access passport. These "passports" are available at the park headquarters and are good at any national park in the United States. Note: There are several weekends throughout the year when the park is free—thanks to the Department of the Interior. Check the park's website to see if your visit coincides with one of these times.

THE VOLCANOES
Kilauea

Continuously active since 1983, Kilauea dominates the heart of Hawai'i Volcanoes National Park. Many of the park's sights are arranged one after another along **Crater Rim Drive,** which circles **Kilauea Caldera.** Most of these sights are the "drive-up" variety, but plenty of major and minor trails lead off here and there.

Expect to spend a full day atop Kilauea to take in all the sights, and never forget that you're on a rumbling volcano. Kilauea Caldera, at 4,000 feet, is about 10°F cooler than the coast. It's often overcast, and there can be showers. Wear walking shoes and bring a sweater or windbreaker. Binoculars, sunglasses, and a hat will also come in handy.

People with respiratory ailments, those with small children, and pregnant individuals should note that the fumes from the volcano can cause problems. That sour taste in your mouth is sulphur from the fumes. Stay away from directly inhaling from the sulphur vents and don't overdo it, and you should be fine.

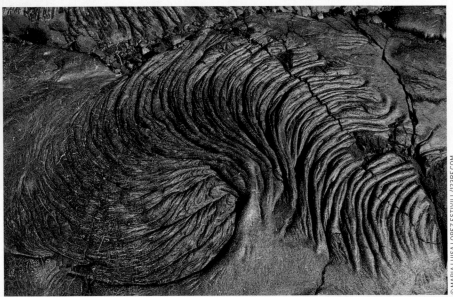

Pahoehoe lava is smooth and looks like pancake batter.

Mauna Loa

It's a little discombobulating at times—you're sweating in the hot lava fields of the park and in the background you see the snowcapped Mauna Loa. The largest mass of mountain to make up the Big Island at 13,680 feet, this magnificent mountain is a mere 116 feet shorter than its neighbor Mauna Kea, which is the tallest peak in the Pacific, and by some accounts, tallest in the world.

But still, Mauna Loa holds its own impressive statistics. It is the most massive mountain on earth, containing some 19,000 cubic miles of solid, iron-hard lava, and it's estimated that this titan weighs more than California's entire Sierra Nevada mountain range! In fact, Mauna Loa (Long Mountain), at 60 miles long and 30 miles wide, occupies the entire southern half of the Big Island. Unlike Mauna Kea, Mauna Loa has had some recent volcanic activity, spilling lava in 1949, 1950, 1975, and 1980. The top of this mountain is within the Hawai'i Volcanoes National Park boundary.

The summit of Mauna Loa, with its mighty **Moku'aweoweo Caldera,** is all within park boundaries. Mauna Loa's oval Moku'aweoweo Caldera is more than three miles long and 1.5 miles wide and has vertical walls towering 600 feet. At each end is a smaller round pit crater. From November to May, if there is snow, steam rises from the caldera. This mountaintop bastion is the least visited part of the park since this land is remote and still largely inaccessible.

Plans for future use of this area include opening up several hundred miles of trails and Jeep tracks to hiking and perhaps other activities as well as creating additional campsites and cabins; these uses will undoubtedly take years to facilitate. For now, it is possible to drive or bike the 10-mile Mauna Loa Road to the trailhead at over 6,600 feet, hike nearly 20 miles to the summit, and stay overnight at some true backcountry cabins before you head back down.

VISITORS CENTER AREA
Kilauea Visitor Center

As they say in the *Sound of Music,* "Let's start at the very beginning, the very best place to start," i.e., the park's **Kilauea Visitor Center** (808/985-6000, daily 7:45am-5pm) and headquarters. It's the first building you pass on the right after you enter through the gate. By midmorning it's jammed, so try to be an early bird. The center is well run by the National Park Service, which offers a free film about geology and volcanism, with tremendous highlights of past eruptions and plenty of detail on Hawaiian culture and natural history. It runs every hour on the hour starting at 9am. Free ranger-led tours of the nearby area are also given on a regular basis, and their start times and meeting places are posted near the center's front doors. Also posted are After Dark in the Park educational interpretive program activities, held two or three times a month on Tuesdays at 7pm. If you are visiting with kids, ask the rangers about the free **Junior Ranger Program.** They'll give each child a park-related activity book, pin, and patch.

The museum section of the visitors center looks like it was constructed at least 20 years ago before museums got technological updates, but it still offers relevant information about the geology of the area, with plenty of exhibits on flora and fauna. If you are interested in these topics, a quick stop here will greatly enrich your visit. A walk around the museum will only take about a half hour. If you're looking for more volcano-specific information, you'll find that at the Thomas A. Jaggar Museum a few minutes up the road.

The small gift shop in the visitors center has park posters, postcards, T-shirts, sweatshirts, and raincoats as well as lots of books and maps to help navigate you through the park and kid-friendly volcano-related toys, too.

In addition to all the fun stuff at the visitors center, there is serious business that takes place. For safety's sake, anyone hiking to the backcountry *must* register with the rangers at the visitors center, especially for sites that have occupancy limits. There is no charge for camping, and rangers can give you up-to-the-minute information on trails, backcountry shelters, and

BIG ISLAND OF HAWAI'I

cabins. Trails routinely close due to lava flows, tremors, and rock slides. The rangers cannot help you if they don't know where you are, so it is imperative to let them know where you're going.

Many day trails leading into the caldera from the rim road are easy walks that need no special preparation. Before you head down the road, ask for a trail guide from the rangers at the visitors center, fill up your water bottle, and use the public bathroom.

Volcano House

Even if your plans don't include an overnight stop, go into **Volcano House,** across the road from the visitors center, for a look. A stop at the lounge provides refreshments and a tremendous view of the crater. Volcano House still has the feel of a country inn. This particular building dates from the 1940s, but the site has remained the same since a grass hut was perched on the rim of the crater by a sugar planter in 1846. He charged $1 a night for lodging. A steady stream of notable visitors has come ever since: almost all of Hawaii's kings and queens dating from the middle of the 19th century, as well as royalty from Europe. Mark Twain was a guest, followed by Franklin Roosevelt. More recently, a contingent of astronauts lodged here and used the crater floor to prepare for walking on the moon. Since 1986 the hotel has once again been under local management as a concessionaire to the National Park Service.

◖ Volcano Art Center Gallery

Across the parking lot at the visitors center is the **Volcano Art Center Gallery** (808/967-7565, daily 9am-5pm except Christmas), which lives in the original 1877 Volcano House. A new show featuring one of the many superlative island artists is presented monthly, and there are always ongoing demonstrations and special events. Artworks on display are in a variety of media, including canvas, paper, wood, glass, metal, ceramic, fiber, and photographs. There is also a profusion of less expensive but distinctive items like posters, cards, and earthy basketry made from natural fibers collected locally. One of the functions of the art center is to provide interpretation for the national park. All of the 300 or so artists who exhibit here do works that in some way relate to Hawaii's environment and culture. Volcano Art Center is one of the finest art galleries in the entire state, boasting works from the best the islands have to offer. Definitely make this a stop.

As a community-oriented organization, the Volcano Art Center sponsors classes and workshops in arts, crafts, and yoga, the Kilauea Volcano Wilderness Runs, and a season of performing arts, which includes musical concerts, hula, dance performances, and stage plays. Some involve local performers, while others headline visiting artists. Performances, classes, and workshops take place at the Kilauea Theater at the military camp, at the hula platform within the park, or in Volcano at the Niaulani campus building. Tickets for performances are sold individually at local outlets or you can buy a season ticket. For current information and pricing, call the Volcano Art Center office (808/967-8222, www.volcanoartcenter.org) or check out its website for what's happening.

CRATER RIM DRIVE

The 11-mile road that circles the Kilauea Caldera and passes by nearly all the main sights in the park is **Crater Rim Drive.** For the past few years a part of the road has been closed due to elevated levels of sulphur dioxide gas. You can still drive on the road, but you can't always complete the entire circle. However, don't let this deter you. A large part of the road is still open, and there are so many intriguing nooks and crannies to stop at along Crater Rim Drive that you'll have to force yourself to be picky if you intend to cover the park in one day.

Along this road you will travel from a tropical zone into desert, then through a volcanic zone before returning to lush rainforest. The change is often immediate and differences dramatic. Since you can't circle the caldera, the following sights are listed in two sections: those to the right of the visitors center and those to the left of the visitors center. The sights to the left of the visitors center can also be reached by turning left immediately after you pass through the entrance gate of the park.

To the Right of the Visitors Center

SULPHUR BANKS

You can easily walk to **Sulphur Banks** from the visitors center along a 10-minute paved trail. Your nose will tell you when you're close. Alternatively, walk the 0.6-mile trail from the Steam Vents parking lot. A boardwalk fronts a major portion of this site. As you approach these fumaroles, the earth surrounding them turns a deep reddish-brown, covered over in yellowish-green sulphur. It's an amazing sight, especially in the morning when the entire area seems to look pink. The rising steam is caused by surface water leaking into the cracks, where it becomes heated and rises as vapor. Kilauea releases hundreds of tons of sulphur gases every day. This gaseous activity stunts the growth of vegetation. And when atmospheric conditions create a low ceiling, the gases sometimes cause the eyes and nose to water.

STEAM VENTS

Within a half mile you'll come to **Steam Vents,** which are also fumaroles, but without sulphur. In the parking lot there are some vents covered with grates, and if you walk just two minutes from the parking lot toward the caldera on the gravel trail, you'll see how the entire field steams. It is like being in a sauna or getting a wonderful free facial. There are no strong fumes to contend with here, just other tourists. If you walk back toward the caldera, you'll see a gravel trail that follows the caldera around. This is the **Crater Rim Trail,** and you can walk it from here to many of the sights, including the Thomas A. Jaggar Museum—an easy 20-minute walk (one-way) through the woods from here.

KILAUEA MILITARY CAMP

If you continue in the same direction on the road, you'll pass the **Kilauea Military Camp.** It's where military families come to vacation. Although it looks like it's not open to the public, many parts of it actually are open to non-military personnel, including the post office, the Lava Lounge bar, the cafeteria, the bowling alley, and the Kilauea theater, used for community events.

KILAUEA OVERLOOK

Some distance beyond the Kilauea Military Camp is **Kilauea Overlook,** as good a spot as any to get a look into the caldera, and there are picnic tables near the parking lot. Here too is **Uwekahuna (Wailing Priest) Bluff,** where the *kahuna* made offerings of appeasement to the goddess Pele. A Hawaiian prayer commemorates their religious rites. Unless you're stopping for lunch or making your own offering, it's perhaps better to continue on to the observatory and museum, where you not only have the view outside but get a scientific explanation of what's happening around you.

◖ THOMAS A. JAGGAR MUSEUM

The **Hawaiian Volcano Observatory** (http://hvo.wr.usgs.gov) has been keeping tabs on the volcanic activity in the area since the turn of the 20th century. The actual observatory is filled with delicate seismic equipment and is closed to the public, but a lookout nearby gives you a spectacular view into the eye of **Halema'uma'u Crater** (House of Ferns), Pele's home. From here, steam rises and, even more phenomenally spectacular, a lake of molten lava forms. The lava has been rising and falling over the last few years, and when it does rise, it puts on one of the best nighttime shows you'll ever see. You can check the webcam (http://volcanoes.usgs.gov/hvo/cams/hmcam) located within the crater to see what it is doing and decide if it's worth heading back there at night to watch its performance.

This is a major stop for all passing tourists and tour buses. Information plaques in the

© MARK WASSER

Smoke billows out from the Halema'uma'u Crater.

immediate area tell of the history and volcanology of the park. One points out a spot from which to observe the perfect shield volcano form of Mauna Loa—most times too cloudy to see. Another reminds you that you're in the middle of the Pacific, an incredible detail you tend to forget when atop these mountains.

Next door to the observatory, the state-of-the-art **Thomas A. Jaggar Museum** (808/985-6049, daily 8:30am-8:30pm, admission free) offers a fantastic multimedia display of the amazing geology and volcanology of the area, complete with a miniseries of spectacular photos on movable walls, topographical maps, inspired paintings, and video presentations. The expert staff constantly upgrades the displays to keep the public informed on the newest eruptions. The 30-45 minutes it takes to explore the teaching museum will enhance your understanding of the volcanic area immeasurably. There is also a gift shop here, much like the one at the visitors center, which carries sweatshirts

and raincoats that visitors are, at times, desperate to get their hands on. Drinking water and bathrooms are available here. From the Jaggar Museum the rest of the Crater Rim Road is closed; thus, it's necessary to turn around and go back the way you came.

Left of the Visitors Center
KILAUEA IKI OVERLOOK

The first parking lot you'll pass on the right is the gateway to **Kilauea Iki** (Little Kilauea). In 1959, lava spewed 1,900 feet into the air from a half-mile crack in the crater wall (there is an amazing picture showcasing this occurrence on a board in the parking lot). It was the highest fountain ever measured in Hawaii. Within a few weeks, 17 separate lava flow episodes occurred, creating a lake of lava. In the distance is the cinder cone, **Pu'u Pua'i** (Gushing Hill), where the lava flowed from its brownish-red base in 1959. The cone didn't exist before then. Present day, if you look down from the overlook into the crater floor you'll see something that

© MARK WASSER

Kiluea Iki

resembles a desolate desert landscape that is still steaming in spots. Unbelievably, you can fairly easily walk across this on the Kilauea Iki trail. Surrounding the crater is a rainforest filled with native birds and plants.

THURSTON LAVA TUBE

Just up the road from the overlook is the remarkable **Thurston Lava Tube,** otherwise called Nahuku, which resembles a Salvadar Dali painting. As you approach, the expected signboard gives you the lowdown on the geology and flora and fauna of the area. The paved trail starts as a steep incline, which quickly enters a fern forest. All about you are fern trees, vibrantly green, with native birds flitting here and there. As you approach the lava tube, it seems almost manmade, like a perfectly formed tunnel leading into a mine. Ferns and moss hang from the entrance, and if you stand just inside the entrance looking out, it's as if the very air is tinged with green. The tunnel is fairly large and shouldn't be a problem for those who suffer from mild claustrophobia. The walk through takes about 10 minutes, undulating through the narrow passage. At the other end, the fantasy world of ferns and moss reappears, and the trail leads back, past public restrooms, to the parking lot. The entire tunnel is lit and paved; however, for some extra fun take a flashlight to visit the unlit portion. As you walk up the stairway to exit the tube, you'll see on your left an open gate that looks into the darkness: This small unlit section *is* open to the public at their own risk. If you're good on your feet, take a quick look.

CHAIN OF CRATERS ROAD

The 36-mile round-trip **Chain of Craters Road** that once linked the park with Kalapana village on the coast in the Puna district was severed by an enormous lava flow in 1995 and can now only be driven to where the flow crosses the road beyond the Holei Sea Arch. It's pretty amazing when you get to the end of the road, though, where lava literally covers the pavement

Don't Take the Lava Home!

Legend has it that taking lava rock from Hawaii will bring you bad luck. Pele, the goddess of fire, does not like when her rocks leave Hawaii. Every year the park receives lava rocks returned to them by mail with notes of explanation handwritten by the recipients of bad luck. I am not saying either way whether or not I think this legend holds true, but I can say, it's best not to take the rock.

If you so happen to take something and want to send it back, you can send it to Hawai'i Volcanoes National Park. They have a pile of them. If you want your rock to return with a ceremony of forgiveness, with just a $15 donation you can send your rock to Rainbow Moon (Attn: Lava Rock Return, P.O. Box 699, Volcano, HI 96785). Your rock will be returned to its source wrapped in a ti leaf. In addition, Rainbow Moon will happily send you an email to confirm that your rock was returned appropriately.

and you can see now-defunct street signs in the distance.

Remember that the volcanic activity in this area is unpredictable, and that the road can be closed at a moment's notice. As you head down the road, every bend—and they are uncountable—offers a panoramic vista. There are numerous pull-offs; plaques provide geological information about past eruptions and lava flows. The grandeur, power, and immensity of the forces that have been creating the earth from the beginning of time are right before your eyes. Although the road starts off in the 'ohi'a forest, it opens to broader views and soon cuts diagonally across the *pali* to reach the littoral plain. Much of this section of the road was buried under lava flows from 1969 to 1974.

When the road almost reaches the coast, look for a roadside marker that indicates the Puna Coast Trail. Just across the road is the Pu'u Loa Petroglyph Field trailhead. The lower part of the road is spectacular. Here, blacker-than-black sea cliffs, covered by a thin layer of green, abruptly stop at the sea. The surf rolls in, sending up spumes of seawater. In the distance, steam billows into the air where the lava flows into the sea. At road's end you will find a barricade and an information hut staffed by park rangers throughout the afternoon and into the evening. Read the information and heed the warnings. The drive from atop the volcano to the end of the road takes about 45 minutes and drops 3,700 feet in elevation.

While hiking to the lava flow is not encouraged, park staff do not stop you from venturing out. They warn you of the dangers and the reality ahead. Many visitors do make the hike, but there is no trail. The way is over new and rough lava that tears at the bottom of your shoes. Many hike during the day, but if you go in the evening when the spectacle is more apparent, a flashlight with several extra batteries is absolutely necessary. To hike there and back could take three to four hours. If you decide to hike, bring plenty of water. There is no shade or water along the way, and the wind often blows along this coast. Do not hike to or near the edge of the water, as sections of lava could break off without warning. Depending upon how the lava is flowing, it may or may not be worth the effort. When the lava is flowing, it is often possible to see the reddish glow at night from the end of the road, but you probably won't see much that's distinguishable unless you use high-power binoculars. When the lava is putting on a good show, there could be several hundred cars parked along the road, stretching back for over a mile, so expect a bit of a walk before you even get to the ranger station to start the hike over the lava. For a much closer walk, park at the lava-viewing area near Kalapana in Puna.

Craters

As you head down Chain of Craters Road you immediately pass a number of the depressions

© WHITETAG/123RF.COM

Chain of Craters Road

for which the road is named. First on the right side is **Lua Manu Crater,** a deep depression now lined with green vegetation. Farther is **Puhimau Crater.** Walk the few steps to the viewing stand at the crater edge for a look. Many people come here to hear the echo of their voices as they talk or sing into this pit. Next comes **Ko'oko'olau Crater,** then **Hi'iaka Crater** and **Pauahi Crater.** Just beyond is a turnoff to the east, which follows a short section of the old road. This road ends at the lava flow, and from here a trail runs as far as **Napau Crater.**

The first mile or more of the Napau Trail takes you over lava from 1974, through forest *kipuka,* past lava tree molds, and up the treed slopes of **Pu'u Huluhulu.** A *kipuka* is a piece of land that is surrounded by lava but has not been inundated by it, leaving the original vegetation and land contour intact. From this cone you have a view down on Mauna Ulu, from which the 1969-1974 lava flow disgorged, and east toward **Pu'u O'o** and the currently active volcanic vents, some seven miles distant. Due to the current volcanic activity farther along the rift zone, you will need a permit to day hike beyond Pu'u Huluhulu; the trail itself may be closed depending upon where the volcanic activity is taking place. However, the trail does continue over the shoulder of **Makaopuhi Crater** to the primitive campsite at Napau Crater, passing more cones and pit craters, lava flows, and sections of rainforest.

Roadside Sights

For several miles, Chain of Craters Road traverses lava that was laid down about 40 years ago; remnants of the old road can still be seen in spots. There are long stretches of smooth *pahoehoe* lava interspersed with flows of the rough *'a'a.* Here and there, green pokes through a crack in the rock, bringing new life to this stark landscape. Everywhere you look, you can see the wild "action" of these lava flows, stopped in all their magnificent forms. At one vantage point on the way is **Kealakomo,** a picnic overlook where you have unobstructed views of the coast. Stop and enjoy the sight before

Ohelo berry bushes are some of the first plants to grow back after a landscape has been devastated by lava.

proceeding. Several other lookouts and pull-offs have been created along the road to call attention to one sight or another. Soon the road heads over the edge of the *pali* and diagonally down to the flats, passing sections of the old road not covered by lava. Stop and look back and realize that most of the old road has been covered by dozens of feet of lava, the darkest of the dark.

The last section of road runs close to the edge of the sea, where cliffs rise up from the pounding surf. Near the end of the road is the **Holei Sea Arch,** a spot where the wave action has undercut the rock to leave a bridge of stone. Enjoy the scene, but don't lean too far out trying to get that perfect picture!

Puʻu Loa Petroglyphs

The walk out to **Puʻu Loa Petroglyphs** is delightful, highly educational, and takes less than one hour. As you walk along the trail (1.5 miles round-trip), note the *ahu,* traditional trail markers that are piles of stone shaped like little Christmas trees. Most of the lava field leading to the petroglyphs is undulating *pahoehoe* and looks like a frozen sea. You can climb bumps of lava, 8-10 feet high, to scout the immediate territory. Mountainside, the *pali* is quite visible and you can pick out the most recent lava flows—the blackest and least vegetated. As you approach the site, the lava changes dramatically and looks like long strands of braided rope.

The petroglyphs are in an area about the size of a soccer field. A wooden walkway encircles most of them and helps to ensure their protection. A common motif of the petroglyphs is a circle with a hole in the middle, like a doughnut; you'll also see designs of men with triangular heads. Some rocks are entirely covered with designs, while others have only a symbolic scratch or two. These carvings are impressive more for their sheer number than the multiplicity of design. If you stand on the walkway and trek off at the two o'clock position, you'll see a small hill. Go over and down it, and you will discover even better petroglyphs, including a

© MARK WASSER

the Holei Sea Arch, near the end of the Chain of Craters Road

© BONITA CHESHIER/123RF.COM

sailing canoe about two feet high. At the back end of the walkway a sign proclaims that Pu'u Loa meant Long Hill, which the Hawaiians turned into the metaphor "Long Life." For countless generations, fathers would come here to place pieces of their infants' umbilical cords into small holes as offerings to the gods to grant long life to their children. Concentric circles surrounded the holes that held the umbilical cords. The entire area, an obvious power spot, screams in utter silence, and the still-strong mana is easily felt.

The Big Island has the largest concentration of petroglyphs in the state, and this site holds its greatest number. One estimate puts the number at 28,000!

OTHER PARK ROADS
Hilina Pali Road

About two miles down the Chain of Craters Road, **Hilina Pali Road** shoots off to the southwest (to the left) over a narrow, roughly paved road all the way to the end at Hilina Pali

Lookout—about nine miles. Soon after you leave the Chain of Craters Road, the vegetation turns drier and you enter the semi-arid Ka'u Desert. The road picks its way around and over old volcanic flows, and you can see the vegetation struggling to maintain a foothold. On the way you pass the **Mauna Iki trailhead,** Kulanaokuaiki Campground, and former Kipuka Nene Campground—closed to help the *nene* recover their threatened population. You should see geese here, but leave them alone and don't feed them.

The road ends right on the edge of the rift, with expansive views over the benched coastline, from the area of current volcanic flow all the way to South Point. From here, one trail heads down the hill to the coast while another pushes on along the top of the cliff and farther into the dry landscape. At the *pali* lookout is a pavilion and restrooms, but no drinking water. This is not a pleasure ride, as the road is rough, but it is passable. For most it probably isn't worth the time, but for those looking for isolation and a special vantage point, this could be it. If you drive just slightly past the turnoff for Hilina Pali Road, you'll arrive at **Devil's Throat,** a pit crater formed in 1912. It's not directly off the road, so you'll have to park your car at the small gravel area by the side of the road, cross the street, and walk back about 50 feet to catch a glimpse.

Mauna Loa Road

About 2.5 miles south of the park entrance on the Highway 11, **Mauna Loa Road** turns off to the north. This road will lead you to the Tree Molds and a bird sanctuary, as well as to the trailhead for the Mauna Loa summit trail. As an added incentive, a minute down this road leaves 99 percent of the tourists behind.

Tree Molds is an ordinary name for an extraordinary area. Turn right off Mauna Loa Road soon after leaving the Belt Road and follow the signs for five minutes. This road runs into the tree molds area and loops back onto itself. At the loop, a signboard explains what occurred here. In a moment, you realize that you're standing atop a lava flow, and that the

BIG ISLAND OF HAWAI'I

scattered potholes were entombed tree trunks, most likely the remains of a once-giant koa forest. The lava stayed put while the tree trunks burned away, leaving the 15- to 18-foot-deep holes. Realizing what happened here and how it happened is an eye-opener.

Kipuka Puaulu is a sanctuary for birds and nature lovers who want to leave the crowds behind, just under three miles from Highway 11 up Mauna Loa Road. The sanctuary is an island atop an island. A *kipuka* is a piece of land that is surrounded by lava but has not been inundated by it, leaving the original vegetation and land contour intact. A few hundred yards away, small scrub vegetation struggles, but in the sanctuary, the trees form a towering canopy a hundred feet tall. The first sign takes you to an ideal picnic area called Bird Park, with cooking grills; the second, 100 yards beyond, takes you to **Kipuka Puaulu Loop Trail.** As you enter the trail, a bulletin board describes the birds and plants, some of the last remaining indigenous fauna and flora in Hawaii. Please follow all rules. The dirt trail is self-guided, and pamphlets describing the stations along the way may be dispensed from a box near the start of the path. The loop is only one mile long, but to really assimilate the area, especially if you plan to do any bird-watching, expect to spend an hour minimum. It doesn't take long to realize that you are privileged to see some of the world's rarest plants, such as a small, nondescript bush called *'a'ali'i.* In the branches of the towering *'ohi'a* trees you might see an *'elepaio* or an *'apapane,* two birds native to Hawaii. Common finches and Japanese white eyes are imported birds that are here to stay. There's an example of a lava tube, a huge koa tree, and an explanation of how ash from eruptions provided soil and nutrients for the forest. Blue morning glories have taken over entire hillsides. Once considered a pest and aggressively eradicated, they have recently been given a reprieve and are now considered good ground cover—perhaps even indigenous. When you do come across a native Hawaiian plant, it seems somehow older, almost prehistoric. If a precontact Hawaiian could come back today, he or she would recognize only a few plants and trees seen here in this preserve. As you leave, listen for the melodies coming from the treetops and hope the day never comes when no birds sing. To hear the birds at their best, come in early morning or late afternoon.

Mauna Loa Road continues westward and gains elevation for approximately 10 miles. It passes through thick forests of lichen-covered koa trees, cuts across **Kipuka Ki,** and traverses the narrow **Ke'amoku Flow.** At the end of the pavement, at 6,662 feet, you will find a parking area and lookout. If the weather is cooperating, you'll be able to see much of the mountainside; if not, your field of vision will be restricted. A trail leads from here to the summit of Mauna Loa. It takes two long and difficult days to hike. Under no circumstances should it be attempted by novice hikers or those unprepared for cold alpine conditions. At times, this road may be closed due to extreme fire conditions.

Ka'u Desert Footprints

An entry to the **Ka'u Desert Trail** starts about eight miles south of the park entrance along Highway 11, between mile markers 37 and 38. There isn't a parking lot here; just park your car on the side of the road on the gravel. There are usually one or two other cars there. You don't have to pay to walk on this trail since the trailhead isn't through the park entrance. It is just good old free fun.

It's a short 20-minute hike from this trailhead to the **Ka'u Desert Footprints.** The 1.6-mile round-trip trek across the small section of desert is fascinating, and the history of the footprints makes the experience more evocative. Because of deterioration, the footprints are faint and difficult to see.

The predominant foliage is *'ohi'a,* which contrasts with the bleak desert surroundings. You pass a wasteland of *'a'a* and *pahoehoe* lava flows to arrive at the footprints. A metal fence in a sturdy pavilion surrounds the prints, which look as though they're cast in cement. Actually they're formed from pisolites: particles of ash stuck together with moisture, which formed mud that hardened like plaster. The story of these footprints is far more exciting than the prints themselves, which are eroded and not very visible.

In 1790, Kamehameha was waging war with Keoua over control of the Big Island. One of Keoua's warrior parties of approximately 80 people attempted to cross the desert while Kilauea was erupting. Toxic gases descended upon them, and the warriors and their families were enveloped and suffocated. They literally died in their tracks. (Although romanticism would have it otherwise, the preserved footprints were probably made by a party of people who came well after the eruption or perhaps at some time during a previous eruption.) This unfortunate occurrence was regarded by the Hawaiians as a direct message from the gods proclaiming their support for Kamehameha.

Hiking and Biking

HIKING

There are over 150 miles of hiking trails within the park. One long trail heads up the flank of Mauna Loa to its top; a spiderweb of trails loops around and across Kilauea Caldera and into the adjoining craters; and from a point along the Chain of Craters Road, another trail heads east toward the source of the most recent volcanic activity. But by far the greatest number of trails, and those with the greatest total distance, are those that cut through the Ka'u Desert and along the barren and isolated coast. Many have shelters, and trails that require overnight stays provide cabins or primitive campsites.

Because of the possibility of an eruption or earthquake, it is *imperative* to check in at park headquarters, where you can pick up current trail information and excellent maps. In fact, a hiking permit is required for most trails

BIG ISLAND OF IHAWAI'I

© MARK WASSER

Hawai'i Volcanoes National Park offers some of the best hiking on the island.

outside the Crater Rim Drive area and that stretch along the coast beyond the end of Chain of Craters Drive. Pick up your free permit no more than one day in advance. Much of the park is hot and dry, so carry plenty of drinking water. Wear a hat, sunscreen, and sunglasses, but don't forget rain gear because it often rains in the green areas of the park. Stay on trails and stay away from steep edges, cracks, new lava flows, and any area where lava is flowing into the sea.

If you will be hiking along the trails in the Kilauea Caldera, the free park maps are sufficient to navigate your way. To aid with hikes elsewhere, it's best to purchase and use larger and more detailed topographical maps. One that is readily available and of high quality is the *Hawai'i Volcanoes National Park* map by Trails Illustrated, and it is available at the gift shop at the visitors center.

Self-Guided Easy Hikes

If you find yourself only having one day to venture through Hawai'i Volcanoes National Park, there are several short hikes that will offer you a glimpse of what it's like to live next to an active volcano.

VOLCANO ART CENTER'S NIAULANI CAMPUS TRAIL

Just outside the park in Volcano Village is a four-acre rare old-growth tropical rainforest growing in volcanic ash from the 18th century. Some of the trees at the Volcano Art Center (19-4074 Old Volcano Rd., Volcano, 808/967-8222) are at least 200 years old and more than 65 feet tall. The **Niaulani Campus Trail,** which is filled with placards explaining the area and art, is only a 0.7-mile-long loop and is flat. Bird lovers will delight in this opportunity to see native birds. The tour is easy to complete on your own, but a one-hour guided tour is available every Monday (including holidays) at 9:30am (free). If you get there early, you can participate in an hour-long **yoga** class on Monday at 7:30am or stop by to unwind on Tuesday at 5:30pm after a day of hiking.

CRATER RIM TRAIL

Although a large part of Crater Rim Drive is currently closed due to the sulphur dioxide (vog) from Halema'uma'u, it is possible to hike along the **Crater Rim Trail.** If you park at the Thomas A. Jaggar Museum and hike along the Crater Rim toward the visitors center, you will be offered unparalleled views of the vast Kilauea Caldera. Along the way you pass through desert-like conditions with sparse vegetation to lush native tropical forests. You will also encounter the **Steam Vents,** where the water heated from the volcanic heat rises up from cracks in the earth. The hike along the Crater Rim Trail to/from the Thomas A. Jaggar Museum to the visitors center is approximately 2.5 miles and can take anywhere from 45 minutes to an hour. Parts of it are shaded while other parts are in an open field. The trailhead for this Crater Rim hike is left of the museum and parking lot and also across the street from the visitors center (next to Volcano House). Parts of the trail have been paved and provide a good place for road or mountain biking.

SULPHUR BANKS TRAIL

From the visitors center parking lot you can get a good glimpse of some interesting volcanic geology. The **Sulphur Banks Trail** is a short and easy hike that offers intriguing sights. Bright yellow mineral deposits of sulphur line the trail as volcanic gases spew from the earth. This trail may remind some people of the volcanic vents in Yellowstone, and it just reminds one of the geologic variety found here on the Big Island. Interpretive signs offer explanations of the volcanic activities so it's easy to understand what you're seeing. To get to this trail, walk to the left of the visitors center past the Volcano Art Center. A paved trail will lead you through a grassy field with a *heiau* (temple) and down a hill. If you see signs warning you that you may encounter volcanic gases, you're going the right way. It's 0.5 mile one way from the visitors center to the Sulphur Banks. If you want to make it into a longer hike, you can cross the road and connect to the Crater Rim trail by the Steam

Vents and hike all the way to the Thomas A. Jaggar Museum.

EARTHQUAKE TRAIL
If from the visitors center you head left (behind the Volcano House facing the caldera) on Crater Rim Trail, you'll walk one mile roundtrip toward **Waldron Ledge** on the **Earthquake Trail,** so named due to the damage this area received during the 1983 6.6 magnitude earthquake. Waldron Ledge is known to be one of the best views in the park, and the trail, which is paved and wheelchair- and stroller-accessible as well as bike-friendly, presents an easy walk.

DEVASTATION TRAIL
Farther up Crater Rim Drive, most visitors hike along the one-mile roundtrip **Devastation Trail,** which could aptly be renamed Regeneration Trail. The mile it covers is fascinating; it's one of the most-photographed areas in the park. It leads across a field devastated by a tremendous eruption from **Kilauea Iki.** The area was once an *'ohi'a* forest that was denuded of limbs and leaves, then choked by black pumice and ash. The vegetation has regenerated since then, and the recuperative power of the flora is part of an ongoing study. Notice that many of the trees have sprouted aerial roots trailing down from the branches: This is total adaptation to the situation, as these roots don't normally appear. As you move farther along the trail, tufts of grass and bushes peek out of the pumice and then the surroundings become totally barren.

Self-Guided Moderate Hikes
If you're willing and able to complete more moderate hikes and want to experience the volcano with your own two feet, then attempt one or both of these hikes. Both hikes can easily be completed in one day.

☾ KILAUEA IKI TRAIL
The **Kilauea Iki Trail** takes you from the top of the crater and lush tropical rainforest of native vegetation and native birds to the bottom of the crater floor, which is devoid of vegetation but

Pay attention to warning signs when hiking around the park.

still breathes volcanic steam. This is a moderate four-mile loop because you descend and ascend 400 feet to and from the crater floor. It takes on average three hours to complete.

The trail for this hike is clearly marked. The parking lot for Kilauea Iki is the first one on the right on the Chain of Craters Road. It's usually packed. From the parking lot go right and follow the Kilauea Iki sign, which will keep you to the left. As you hike along the rim look to the left and down at the various railed off lookouts. Below you is where you'll be as you descend the trail into the crater floor. Essentially you are passing along the rim and then descending across the barren landscape and back up through the trees.

Upon ascending the trail out of the crater floor, you will pass by the **Thurston Lava Tube** parking lot. This is a worthy addition to the hike to see a lava tube, but it is also one of the most popular stops with tour buses so it can get crowded. Note: Your car was not stolen; you are in the Thurston Lava Tube parking lot, not the lot you parked in. Keep walking through the parking lot to the next parking lot where you left your car.

The best time to do this hike is first thing in the morning for several reasons. It's cooler in the morning and more of a pleasant hike in the floor of the crater. When it's cooler it's also easier to spot all the steam vents, which are an active reminder that the crater could erupt again at any time. Finally, the birds are also much more active in the morning. Look for them along the crater rim as they search for insects to keep their bellies filled. Pick up a trail guide for this particular trail at the visitors center or download it from the park's website for further descriptions of the sights you'll pass on your way.

PU'U HULUHULU TRAIL

Another notable hike that can be completed in just two or three hours is the 2.5-mile roundtrip **Pu'u Huluhulu Trail** to Mauna Ulu. This hike is for those who like adventure, since the trail isn't marked well. Follow the signs along the Chain of Craters Road. Turn left where the road splits and there will be a sign for Mauna Ulu. Follow the road and the signs until it ends. The trailhead will be to the left of the parking lot. This moderate hike will take you to the summit of a steaming volcanic crater that can also provide you with 360-degree panoramic views of the park, and on a clear day, if you're lucky, you even see the ocean. The trail crosses lava flows from the 1970s so you will still see young plants sprouting out from cracks in the lava. Follow the trail to Pu'u Huluhulu (Hairy Hill), a crater that has an island of vegetation *(kipuka)* that didn't burn during the 1970s flows. It's a short hike to the top of the *pu'u* (hill), which gives you a good view of Mauna Ulu, the big mountain right in front of you. You can't hike past Pu'u Huluhulu without a permit, but you can follow the old flows up toward the top of Mauna Ulu. There aren't official trail markers to the top but it's easy to pick your own way up the young lava and return the way you came back to the trail. From the top of Mauna Ulu you can peer into the crater, which is hundreds of feet deep, and imagine what it must have been like when lava was spewing from it up to 1,700 feet into the air. A trail guide is available at the visitors center or online on the park's website.

Self-Guided Advanced Hikes

For experienced hikers who want to do some overnight camping and hiking, the park has several options for backcountry wilderness trips.

◖ HIKING TO HALAPE

A large section of the park has trails that run along the coast and has several beaches that offer premier camping. By far one of the most remote and pristine beaches on the island is **Halape.** Getting here is something you have to earn, though.

The absolute closest you can get is the **Hilina Pali Trailhead,** from where it is an eight-mile descent to the beach across hot, dry, rugged terrain. The first two miles are straight down the *pali* (cliff) with multiple switchbacks to get you safely to the bottom. Halape is the sandiest beach along the coast, but there are also other beautiful places to access the ocean that aren't quite as sandy. One stunning option: After descending the switchbacks to the bottom of Hilina Pali, take the trail to the right toward Ka'aha. This is a nice bay that offers lots of room to explore all the way to the *pali* that extends to the ocean. Some nice tide pools here offer unique snorkeling and swimming. If you keep to the left, the trail will lead you to Halape after six extremely hot miles that include some more steep ascents and descents—but your reward is a white sugary beach and a sheltered lagoon that offer you sand and protection from the raw ocean that crashes just past the lagoon. This spot is popular, so you're likely see other campers, but you'll never see the crowd you would in the more accessible sections of the park. Bathroom facilities are available here. There is water available at the backcountry sites, but it must be treated before drinking since it is just from a cistern of collected rainwater. Before you go, make sure to ask a ranger if there is water available since at times there is a drought.

The park requires backcountry permits to camp in these sections. They are available for free at the visitors center. There is a limit to the number of people they allow at any given time, so plan accordingly and know to get your permits ahead of time before you begin your trek.

If you have the option for someone to pick you up, the best route with the most variety is to hike down from Hilina Pali, spend a night or two at Halape, then enjoy a nice flat hike out by heading toward Keahou and Apua, both of which have shelter and water. This route is technically longer distance wise, but it is not as steep as the route you came on.

HIKING TO MAUNA LOA'S SUMMIT

The most extreme hike of them all, Mauna Loa offers a unique experience to climb to the summit of the island's largest volcano. This trip will take you to high altitudes of almost 14,000 feet, so be prepared for altitude sickness and changes of weather. Winter conditions can occur any time of the year here. In 2011 it snowed here in

May! Yes, it snows in Hawaii. There are cabins available to stay in along the way that are free but require a permit from the Kilauea Visitor Center; you can only get them the day before your hike. The Pu'u 'Ula'ula (Red Hill) cabin contains 8 bunks, and the Mauna Loa summit cabin has 12 bunks. Visitors are allowed a three-night maximum stay per site. Pit toilets are available at the cabins as well as drinking water (although check with park rangers about the water level). Don't forget to treat the water. No water is available on the trails themselves.

There are two trail options for your hike: via the Mauna Loa Road trailhead (an hour drive from the Kilauea Visitor Center) or the Mauna Loa Observatory trailhead (a two-hour drive via Saddle Road), which is not in the park. The **Mauna Loa Road trail** ascends 6,600 feet over 18 miles. Depending on your hiking speed, it will take 4-6 hours to hike the 7.5 miles from the trailhead to the Pu'u 'Ula'ula cabin. Then, it's 8-12 additional hours to hike the 11.5 miles from the Pu'u 'Ula'ula cabin to the Mauna Loa summit cabin.

The **Mauna Loa Observatory Trail** climbs 1,975 feet over 3.8 miles up the volcano's north slope until it reaches the rim of the Moku'aweoweo Caldera (the summit). From here, the Mauna Loa summit cabin is 2.1 miles. In all, it takes about 4-6 hours to hike from the Observatory trailhead to the Mauna Loa summit cabin. However, the hike back from the Mauna Loa summit cabin to the Mauna Loa Observatory trailhead is much quicker—only about three hours.

In summary, you have a few options for this hike. If you have friends on the ground (or means to hire a taxi), you can start from the Mauna Loa Road trailhead and finish at the Mauna Loa Observatory trailhead (for a quicker exit). But again, you'll need someone to pick you up or arrange to leave a car at the trailhead. Otherwise, most hikers choose to hike from the Mauna Loa Observatory to the Mauna Loa summit cabin and return to the observatory for a challenging but manageable hike. A great resource for this hike is available here: www.kinquest.com/misc/travel/

trailguide.php. The guide on this site provides a mile-by-mile description of what you'll see.

Note: Mauna Loa is at a high altitude, so it is *imperative* to wait at least 24 hours between scuba diving and ascending Mauna Loa in order to avoid getting the bends.

Guided Hikes

When picking a guided hike of the park, the most important factors to consider are: How many people will be on the tour? If the minimum isn't met, will the tour get canceled? How much hiking and walking will you actually be doing? Will the hiking be for beginners or more advanced walkers?

Ranger-led hikes are a great way to explore the park for free with certifiably experienced guides. The **Exploring the Summit hike** is offered daily at 10:30am and 1:30pm. This 45-minute walk over a paved trail meets in front of the Kilauea Visitor Center and takes guests around the rim while the ranger lectures on Hawaiian history and geology. Check the bulletin board outside the visitors center for daily postings of additional hikes. Often, there is at least one additional hike (on some specific topic) each day.

If you're one of the lucky few, you'll grab a spot on the highly desired ranger-led Wednesday **Pua Po'o Lava Tube Tour.** The tour, which explores a lava tube that is otherwise not open to the public, must be reserved one week in advance by calling the visitors center (808/985-6000) at 7:45am the Wednesday before you want to attend. There are only 12 spots available and they go quickly! Really, some park employees haven't even made it on the tour yet. You can reserve spots for four people with each reservation, and children must be older than 10. If you do make it on the tour, it meets at 12:30pm and lasts about five hours. You have to be in fairly good physical shape to attend as you descend a 15-foot ladder into a lava tube, scramble along it, and then walk over uneven surfaces. A truly one-of-a-kind experience.

Several private tour guides happily take groups around the park on hikes. Dr. Hugh Montgomery, the owner and president of **Hawaiian Walkways** (800/457-7759, www.hawaiianwalkways.com) receives excellent reviews for his Kilauea Volcano Discovery Tour ($119 children, $169 adults plus tax) as well as his private tours, which are actually a pretty good deal if your group has more than four people. Hugh is truly an expert on Hawaiian flora and fauna and offers a lot of personal attention to his small groups, making his tours a great choice for hikers at any level.

Volcano Discovery (808/640-4165, http://hawaii.volcanodiscovery.com, $150-250) is another tour company that persistently receives good feedback, especially for beginning hikers and/or families traveling with children. Tours are somewhat customizable, meaning participants can work with the guides to pick which hikes they'd like to complete. There are some set tours that you can reserve if you're looking to join something already scheduled. The dates and prices for these tours are listed on the website. A four-hour tour for 3-6 people will run you $150 per person and a six-hour tour for 3-6 people will set you back $175 per person, and so on up to a 12-hour tour. Tour guides are known as trained geologists and provide first-rate narration.

Similarly, Warren Costa, a.k.a. **Native Guide Hawaii** (808/982-7575, www.nativeguidehawaii.com, $300 for one person or $150 parties of two or more, cash only!), will personally pick you up (and return you safely) after guiding you through the park on a hike that includes narration on Hawaiian culture, legends, and geology of the park. Warren is concerned with not only teaching about the environment about the park, but also raising awareness about how the environment relates to Hawaiian culture. Tours have a maximum of six guests, and children are welcome.

BIKING

Biking is permitted in the park on paved roads, paved sections of the Crater Rim Trail, and on some dirt trails. The park has created an excellent *Where to Bicycle* brochure available on the website: www.nps.gov/havo/planyourvisit/bike.htm.

The suggested bike rides include a moderate 11-mile loop to circle the rim, a moderate 18-mile round-trip ride on Hilina Pali Road, a challenging 40-mile roundtrip Summit to Sea ride following the Mauna Ulu eruption, and a challenging 27-mile round-trip ride up (climbing 2,600 feet!) and down Mauna Loa Road. The guide includes several short offshoots from the Mauna Loa Road for those who want to do some mountain biking.

If you don't have a bike with you or are not an experienced rider, or you're simply looking for a different way to see the park, I highly recommend taking a guided bike tour of the park with **Bike Volcano** (808/934-9199, www.bikevolcano.com, children/van riders $95, adults $99 per person). What makes this a great way to see the park is that it takes some cars off the road and the ride is all downhill and truly easy for anyone (including youngsters and those of us who are out of shape). There are snacks at several stops on the four-hour tour. Experienced riders may be bored or frustrated by the slow pace. The ride stops at all the major sights along the Crater Rim, where the tour guide, who is trained in geology and Hawaiian culture, gives informative talks about the park. In addition to this tour of the park, other options include a sunset ride to view the lava flow ($119-129) and the basic park tour with a winery visit/tasting as an add-on ($119-129). Bike Volcano offers several pickup points for riders (including from Hilo), or riders may meet at the Kilauea Visitor Center.

Another company that does a similar basic bike tour of the park, but picks up from both Hilo and the Kona side, is **Nui Pohaku** (808/937-0644, www.nuipohaku.com, $135-239). The bike tour guides between companies tend to know each other, so the actual tour and information given on the tour aren't that different. The main difference is that Nui Pohaku uses older bikes than the other companies. In addition to the basic park ride, Nui Pohaku offers combo tours that include a nighttime guided hike to the lava flow in Puna.

Tours

BUS TOURS

If you have rented a car, there isn't much of a reason to take a tour bus around the park unless you really want to be able to ask questions of someone semi-knowledgeable while you're sightseeing. Otherwise, this guide as well as the brochures available at the park visitors center should provide you with enough information for your journey.

Guided tour bus trips to the park tend to be best and most utilized by day trippers to the park—either those flying in from another island for the day or those traveling from the Kona side who don't want to worry about driving back to Kona late at night. These guided tours are also great for visitors who might need translation into languages besides English.

The most ubiquitous tour company of them all, **Roberts Hawaii** (866/898-2519, www. robertshawaii.com, $290) offers pickup from Hilo and then a full-day journey to the park with stops at the Mauna Loa Macadamia Nut Factory (in Hilo) and the major sights in the park. Roberts has been doing this tour for a long time and has the schedule down pat. They know what they're doing, but you likely won't get much personal attention or willingness to alter their schedule at all.

A new player in town, **Kapoho Kine Adventures** (25 Waianuenue Ave., Hilo, 808/964-1000, www.kapohokine.com) is working hard to build its business and create exciting tours for its participants. They offer a range of incredibly full day tours to the park with possible pickup from the Kona side, traveling over the Saddle Road, then a second (or third) pickup from Hilo before heading to the park. In the later afternoon, if there is lava flowing, guests travel to Kaimu Beach in Puna for a gourmet dinner, possible farm tour, and to view the lava. The entire tour, from pickup to drop-off, is 16 hours long! The tour is $159 for children and $179 for adults (plus tax) with Kona pickup, less if you meet in Hilo or at the park. If a 16-hour tour sounds like no fun while you're on vacation, they also offer a shorter Evening Volcano Adventure tour with later pickup that visits solely the lava flow viewing area in Puna ($139 children, $159 adults plus tax).

The crème de la crème, for those leaving from the Kona side, is **Hawaii Forest and Trails** (808/331-8505 www.hawaii-forest.com, $149 children, $179 adults plus tax), with an eco-friendly ethic, extremely in-the-know tour guides, and flexibility with their small groups. This 12-hour roundtrip adventure (includes continental breakfast and lunch) is mainly a tour of the main park sights but makes stops along the Ka'u Coast for some sightseeing as well. Although you'll mostly stay on the bus during this tour, there are several less-than-a-mile walks—ideal for those who do want to do some walking in the park.

A Twilight trip is also available and offers something a little different from the usual twilight excursion. Tour goers, leaving later in the afternoon, travel to the park via the Saddle Road, making stops at **Mauna Kea State Park** and near Hilo to explore the **Kaumana Cave** before arriving to the park around sunset to witness the lava flow from Puna or the glow from near the Thomas A. Jaggar Museum.

HELICOPTER TOURS

A dramatic way to experience the awesome power of the volcano is to take a helicopter tour. The choppers are perfectly suited for the maneuverability necessary to get an intimate bird's-eye view. The pilots will fly you over the areas offering the most activity, often dipping low over lava pools, skimming still-glowing flows, and circling the towering steam clouds rising from where lava meets the sea. When activity is really happening, tours are jammed, and prices, like lava fountains, go sky-high.

Remember, however, that these tours are increasingly resented by hikers and anyone else trying to have a quiet experience, and that new regulations might limit flights over the lava area.

Also, these tours are not without danger, as helicopters have crashed near lava flows during commercial sightseeing flights. Nonetheless, if you are interested, contact one of the helicopter companies located in Hilo or Kona. Alternatively, fixed-wing plane tour companies also offer flights over the volcano area from both Hilo and Kona.

Sunshine Helicopters (808/882-1233 or 800/622-3144, www.sunshinehelicopters.com), leaving from Hapuna on the Kona side, offers a two-hour Volcano Deluxe tour that circles the island ($510 per person with online discount or $485 for the early-bird tour).

Another large operation with a spotless safety record, **Blue Hawaiian Helicopters** (808/886-1768 in Waikoloa, 800/786-2583, www.bluehawaiian.com) operates tours from both the Kona and Hilo sides with two helicopter options—the A-Star and the Eco-star. The difference between the helicopters is that the Eco-star is "the first touring helicopter of the 21st century," meaning that its seats are more comfortable, it is quieter, and it has larger windows for a less obstructed view than the A-Star. Most importantly, it costs more. From the Kona side, there is a two-hour Big Island Spectacular ($396/$495), an all-encompassing trip that circles the island to witness all its highlights, including a quick flyover of the park. From the Hilo side, the one-hour Circle of Fire plus Waterfalls tour ($196/$241) will take you over the waterfalls near Hilo on your way to Hawai'i Volcanoes National Park.

BOAT TOURS

If you need still another way to catch a glimpse of the lava flow, and you're not apt to get seasick, a boat ride is another possibility—with a strong caveat, if the lava happens to be flowing into the ocean at the time. Before you book your tour, check with the park to make sure that the lava is going in that direction since it doesn't always flow into the ocean. There are many stories about boat tour companies taking passengers aboard to see the lava flow that doesn't exist. At the time of writing, the lava was not flowing into the ocean.

The company with the best reputation, **Lava Ocean Adventures** (808/966-4200, www.lavaocean.com, $133 for adults, $107 for children under 12) provides a two-hour cruise along the Puna Coast en route to view the lava flowing into the ocean. On your way you'll see black-sand beaches and sea life galore (turtles and whales are a possibility December-May). Fishers can add an hour to the tour ($160/$140) and try their hand at catching *ono* and ahi. When the lava isn't always flowing, this company still takes riders out on the ocean and gives talks about the history and geology of the coast.

Entertainment and Events

ENTERTAINMENT

After a long day at the park, you might be too tired to do anything, but there are several opportunities for "nightlife" in Volcano.

The **Lava Lounge** at Kilauea Military Camp in the park can offer you not only cheap drinks but karaoke every Thursday night, live music sometimes on the weekends, and big parties for holidays like Halloween and St. Patrick's Day. If you want an activity to go along with your drinking, the **Bowling Alley** across the street from the Lava Lounge has five old-school lanes and rents shoes. You don't have to drink while you bowl, and actually if you want alcohol you need to purchase it at the Lava Lounge and bring it to the bowling alley.

The **Volcano Art Center** (808/967-8222, volcanoartcenter.org) organizes monthly poetry slams (usually on a Friday night toward the end of the month), frequent music concerts (not just Hawaiian music), and demonstrations of Hawaiian culture such as hula. Check the website for additional information.

The **After Dark in the Park** program (Kilauea Visitor Center, Tues. 7pm, park entrance fee applies plus recommended $2 donation) presents talks by top experts in the fields of volcanology, geology, and Hawaiian culture. Check the schedule (www.nps.gov/havo/planyourvisit/events_adip.htm) for more information. Note: It's not always a lecture; sometimes there are slack-key guitarists or choral groups performing. In addition, some months additional programs are added on Wednesday nights. Check the bulletin board just outside the Kilauea Visitor Center for additional information of what's happening in the park.

EVENTS

The **Volcano Art Center Rain Forest Runs** (808/967-8240, www.volcanoartcenter.org, $30-75 entry fee) event is an annual tradition in Volcano usually held in mid-August. For almost 25 years this run through the park was the largest trail run in the state of Hawaii. In 2010 it was decided that it wasn't appropriate to hold the race in the national park (for safety and probably also bureaucratic reasons) and it was moved to Volcano Village. Participants can choose from a 5K walk/run, 10K, or a half marathon. All three runs are out and back courses through the village at 4,000 feet elevation. Even though the run is no longer in the park, it still offers dramatic views of Mauna Loa in the distance and beautiful scenery.

Since 1986, around Thanksgiving each year the Volcano Village Hui artists have hosted the annual **Art Studio Tours** and sale (www.volcanovillageartistshui.com). Visitors can pick up a map at the Volcano Art Center—Niaulani Campus (19-4074 Old Volcano Rd., Volcano, 808/967-8222) that lists the participating sites. The village really comes alive as art walkers travel from gallery to gallery meeting with artists from several different mediums: fiber arts, pottery, glass art, block prints, etc. Since the sale takes place at the artists' studios or homes, the art for sale is often at bargain prices.

Want to See Some Lava Flow?

© MARK WASSER

Lava rushes into the ocean near the Kalapana viewing area.

That's why you came to Hawai'i Volcanoes National Park–to see lava, right? Unfortunately, you can't see it all the time. Months, even years, will go by when it's visible every night, and then (for instance, in March 2011, timed with the tsunami and a series of small earthquakes that shook the Big Island) it disappears. So even if some assertive tour guide tells you that he or she will take you there, call the **Kalapana lava viewing hotline** (808/967-8862) first to see if there is actual lava flowing, or check online (http://volcanoes.usgs.gov/hvo/activity/kilaueastatus.php).

The **viewing area on Highway 130** (follow the signs and veer right when the road splits; it's right before it reaches Hwy. 137) opens mid-afternoon, but there is really no reason to get there before sunset since you can't see anything until it's dark. Aim for arriving around sunset. From the parking area to the viewing area, depending on conditions, is usually about a 15-minute walk–it used to be longer when they'd let you get closer to the flow. Bring a flashlight and some warm clothes, as it can get chilly at night.

Another way to see lava is by boat. Arguably, it is not the most enjoyable way to see the lava–the water can be rough at night and it is not the most economical option. But it is a way to get close to it and take some great photos. Only a handful of companies organize these tours, and they all offer sunrise and sunset choices: **Lava Boat Tours** (808/934-7977, www.lavaboat.com, $165 per person), **Lava Ocean** (808/966-4200, www.lavaocean.com, $175 per person), and the small tour operator **Lava Roy's Ocean Adventure Tours** (808/883-1122, http://volcanooceanadventures.com, $150 per person). Before you book a trip, check with the **lava-viewing hotline** (808/967-8862) to make sure there's lava to see.

Food

VOLCANO VILLAGE

I wish the dining experience in Volcano—with its captive audience of tourists who are starving after a long day touring the park—were so much better than it actually is. There are a few options, but they tend toward mediocre and overpriced, so keep your expectations low. If you're not too hungry, are in the area for a few days, or are simply in the mood for a drive, it might be worth heading to Hilo (only 40 minutes away) to seek better options. The options in Volcano are listed from south to north on Old Volcano Road. They are all within minutes of one another.

Often crowded, **Kiawe Kitchen** (19-4005 Huanani Rd.—but find it on Old Volcano Rd., 808/967-7711, breakfast Mon.-Fri. 7:30-10am, lunch daily 11am-2:30pm, dinner daily 5:30-8:30pm, $18-25) offers above-average (if overpriced) food, but service is a consistent issue and they are often out of main dishes. It's a good place to get a starter and a cocktail, or better yet, order one of the wood-fired thin-crust pizzas to go.

In the back side of the same complex, the food is much more reasonably priced at **Café Ohia** (corner of Old Volcano Rd. and Huanani Rd., daily 6am-7pm, $7). There never seem to be enough people working here for as crowded as it gets. But the crowds are here for a reason: homemade breads, pastries, and lunch specials. For $7 you have your choice of deli sandwich with Hawaiian-style sides. The portions are large. If you're not too hungry, try the Portuguese bean soup. It's a non-vegetarian hearty stew that will warm you up during the sometimes chilly Volcano days. There is no indoor seating, so either take your sandwiches to go into the park or enjoy them outside on picnic tables. Since the wait can get long, the staff encourages patrons to head next door to the grocery store and grab a beer to enjoy outside.

The most romantic and rustic option in town is the long-standing **Kilauea Lodge** (19-3948 Old Volcano Rd., 808/967-7366, www.kilauealodge.com, daily 7:30am-2pm and 5pm-9pm, lunch $11, dinner $30). The food is expensive, but the setting seems to match. The large fireplace sets the mood for this truly lodge-like setting with game animals adorning the ceiling and featured on the menu. Vegetarian choices are limited here. The meat dishes are prepared well and come with satisfying sides like mashed potatoes, but overall, the meat dishes are better in the restaurants of Waimea. Foodies and those who like to drink might try their *li hing mui* (salted dried plum) rimmed cocktails, like *liliko'i* (passion fruit) margaritas. Eating isn't a requirement for drinking here. If you solely want drinks, you can simply walk in, cozy up on the couch in front of the fireplace, and order away. Reservations are a must for dinner, and if you want to surprise your dinner guest, call ahead to ask for your name on the menu.

Some locals say that **Thai Thai** (19-4084 Old Volcano Rd., 808/967-7969, www.lavalodge.com/thaithairestaurant.htm, daily except Wed. noon-9pm, $11-28) is their favorite Thai food place on the island. The food is all spicy and authentic, with traditional dishes such as soups, rice noodles, and curries. Beer, wine, and plenty of gluten-free and vegetarian options are offered, and a children's menu is available. The restaurant is attached to a gift shop with tourist items and toiletries. Call ahead; sometimes they don't follow their posted hours.

Farther down the road, **Lava Rock** (19-3972 Old Volcano Rd., 808/967-8526, Mon. 7:30am-5pm, Tues.-Sat. 7:30am-9pm, Sun. 7:30am-4:30pm, $12) serves burgers (made with local beef), sandwiches, local-style plate lunches, and Volcano-grown garden salads all at a reasonable price—such an anomaly for Volcano! The interior looks like a diner, with those leather booths that stick to you and waitresses who are simultaneously nice and assertive. Sit outside in the garden area if it's not raining. The food is on the high end of diner food—more of it is homemade than not. Even though there is the salad option, the bulk of items on the menu are fried and breaded. Not a haven for health-conscious eaters. Although locals don't really utilize this space as a coffee shop, it does have a variety of coffee drinks and wireless Internet.

Right before the road comes to a dead end, you'll find Ira Ono's place (that's what the locals call it): **Café Ono** (19-3834 Old Volcano Rd., 808/967-7261, www.volcanogardenarts.com, gallery Tues.-Sun. 10am-4pm, café 11am-3pm, $11). It's the kind of place that you either love or hate. The menu lists only three or four mains, drinks, and one or two desserts each day. But the food tastes like something you could have made but you probably would have seasoned better. The service is quick enough here. The setting is lovely, with a few tables in the back of the art gallery and more outdoors among the trees.

Markets

The small **Volcano Store** (Old Volcano Rd., daily 5am-7pm) is pretty much the equivalent of a bodega. From fresh *musubi* to chips, some frozen foods, books, local jams, wine, and some of the nicest flower bouquets around, it somehow has everything you might need in a small space, including an ATM inside. What it does not have is a great selection of food for camping. Prices are a little bit more expensive than the larger stores in Hilo or Kona.

Down the street, the **Kilauea General Store** (19-3872 Old Volcano Rd., 808/967-7555, Mon.-Sat. 7am-7:30pm, Sun. 7am-7pm) has fewer goods than the Volcano Store, but still has wine, an ATM, and dry goods like bread and jam (actually, their jam is made in-house) as well as DVDs to rent. There is also an in-house sub shop open at lunchtime, but with fresh coffee on hand all day long.

The Sunday morning **Volcano Farmers Market** (19-4030 Wright Rd. at the Cooper Center, http://thecoopercenter.org/FarmersMarketVolcano.html, Sun. 6:30-10am) is attended by what seems like every single resident of Volcano Village. It serves as an important community event. It entails the usual farmers markets accoutrements like produce and plants, but it also has jams, chocolate brittle, and prepared foods. Come early for breakfast (really early!—most vendors are sold out by 8am) and stay to chitchat with the locals.

HAWAI'I VOLCANOES NATIONAL PARK AND SOUTH

Outside of Volcano Village there are a few noteworthy dining options. Just two miles south of the park, in the Volcano Golf Course subdivision, is the **Pele's Backyard** restaurant in the **Volcano Golf and Country Club** (Pi'i Mauna Dr., 808/967-8228, Mon.-Thurs. 10am-7pm, Fri. 8am-5pm, Sat. 8am-7pm, Sun. 8am-5pm, $10)—which is not really a country club in any shape or form. This unpretentious place happens to have the best mahimahi eggs Benedict this side of the island. Brunch is only served on the weekend, and sometimes they run out of the hollandaise sauce. There are other options, like crepes and eggs. All good and all reasonably priced. Lunch and dinner are also available but are just as mediocre as the bulk of Volcano's joints: local dishes like mahimahi, chicken *katsu,* and *loco moco* as well as clubhouse food like burgers and chicken wings. Service is extremely friendly, but the kitchen can be slow if many people come in at the same time. Full bar available.

Inside the park there essentially are no eating options (at least not until Volcano House reopens) except at the Kilauea Military Camp (808/438-6707) eateries **Lava Lounge** (Mon.-Sat. 4pm until no one is there, Sun. open at 2pm in football season) and **Crater Rim Café** (Mon.-Fri. 6:30am-1pm, Sat.-Sun. 6:30-11am, daily 5pm-8pm). Both are entirely open to the public and the best way to mingle with park employees—especially at the Lava Lounge, where after a few drinks, park employees are thrilled to speak with anyone who doesn't work at the park. The café serves breakfast, lunch, and dinner (à la carte and buffet options) and often has special events or themed meals for holidays. The Lava Lounge only offers a few options, entirely of the bar food variety, like chicken wings and garlic fries. But yes, they do have a full bar and lots of beer on draft.

Getting There and Around

While it's not possible to travel inside the park on public transportation, you can get to and from the park on it with **Hele-On Bus** (www.heleonbus.org, 808/961-8744, $1 per ride, $1 each for luggage, large backpacks, bikes). The bus travels twice in the morning and once in the evening, starting at the Kilauea Visitor Center, passing through Volcano Village, and then traveling north on Highway 11 to Hilo.

The bus leaves from Hilo once in the morning and twice in the afternoon. The trip takes a little over an hour depending on how many people are getting on and off (sometimes it can be a lot). It is possible from Hilo to make connections to the Kona side, Waimea, and the Hamakua Coast. Or, once a day the bus continues on to Ka'u, where it also is possible to make connections to the Kona side.

HILO

Hilo is hip. It has the potential to be the new Brooklyn or the new Portland or maybe a Berkeley or Ann Arbor. It has dive bars, walkable streets, historical buildings, cheap rents, two universities, and, most importantly, it's an underrated foodie mecca—all elements that could quickly lead to gentrification. But alas, Hilo has resisted change and happily retains itself as a relic of old Hawaii.

HIGHLIGHTS

LOOK FOR ◖ TO FIND RECOMMENDED SIGHTS, ACTIVITIES, DINING, AND LODGING.

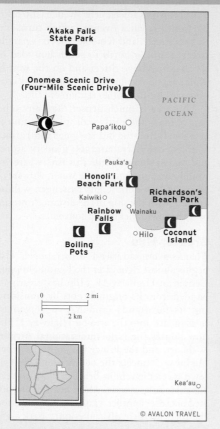

© AVALON TRAVEL

◖ **Richardson's Beach Park:** Head to this black-sand beach for terrific snorkeling, swimming, or just snoozing in the shade (page 605).

◖ **Honoli'i Beach Park:** This beach is one of the finest surfing spots on this side of the island. Even if you're not a surfer, it's worth coming here to watch the local talent hit the big waves (page 605).

◖ **Coconut Island:** A favorite picnic spot for decades, Coconut Island offers the best panorama of the city, bay, and Mauna Kea beyond (page 609).

◖ **Rainbow Falls and Boiling Pots:** The 80-foot Rainbow Falls is true to its name, its mists throwing flocks of rainbows into the air. At the potholed riverbed of Boiling Pots, river water cascades from one bubbling whirlpool tub into the next (page 612).

◖ **Onomea Scenic Drive (Four-Mile Scenic Drive):** Along the short four-mile route you'll see jungle that covers the road like a living green tunnel, the Hawaii Tropical Botanical Garden, and one fine view after another (page 613).

◖ **'Akaka Falls State Park:** In addition to the falls, this park offers a pristine valley and an accessible foray into the island's beautiful interior (page 614).

BIG ISLAND OF HAWAI'I

At around 40,000 people, Hilo has the second-largest population in the state after Honolulu. It is the county seat, has a bustling commercial harbor, and has a long tradition in agriculture and industry. Hilo is a classic tropical town, the kind described in books like Gabriel García Márquez's *Love in the Time of Cholera*. Many of the downtown buildings date back to the early 1900s, when the plantation industry was booming and the railroad took workers

and managers from the country to the big city of Hilo. Sidewalks in older sections of town are covered with awnings because of the rains, which adds a turn-of-the-20th-century gentility. You can walk the central area comfortably in an afternoon, but the town does sprawl some due to the modern phenomena of large shopping malls and residential subdivisions in the outlying areas.

Hilo really is both spiritually and physically the yin to the yang of Kailua-Kona. There, everything runs fast to a new and modern tune. In Hilo the old beat, the old music, and that feeling of a tropical place where rhythms are slow and sensual still exist. Hilo nights are alive with sounds of the tropics, namely coqui frogs, and the heady smells of fruits and flowering trees wafting on the breeze. Hilo days epitomize tropical weather, with predictable afternoon showers during the winter and spring months. In spite of, and because of, the rain, Hilo is gorgeous. Hilo's weather makes it a natural greenhouse; botanical gardens and flower farms surround Hilo like a giant lei. Black-sand beaches are close by waiting for you to come cool off. To counterpoint this tropical explosion, Mauna Kea's winter snows backdrop the town. Hilo is one of the oldest permanently settled towns in Hawaii, and the largest on the windward coast of the island. Don't make the mistake of underestimating Hilo, or of counting it out because of its rainy reputation.

Leaving Hilo, it takes only moments to leave the urban behind and you're back in the tropics with no Target in sight. 'Akaka Falls is less than a half hour from downtown Hilo, but there is a lot to see on the way right off the highway, including an incredible four-mile scenic drive that will wind you through a rainforest that smells overwhelmingly like papayas.

Back on the highway moving west, you'll arrive in Honomu (Silent Bay). During its heyday, Honomu was a bustling center of the sugar industry, boasting saloons, a hotel/bordello, and a church or two for repentance. It was even known as "Little Chicago." Now Honomu mainly serves as a stop as you head elsewhere, but you should definitely take the time to linger. Honomu is 10 miles north of Hilo and about a half mile or so inland on Highway 220, which leads to 'Akaka Falls. On entering, you'll find a string of false-front buildings doing a great but unofficial rendition of a living history museum. The town has recently awoken from a long nap and is now bustling—if that's possible in a two-block town—with a gaggle of art galleries, craft shops, and small cafés. It takes only minutes to walk the main street, but those minutes can give you a glimpse of history that will take you back 100 years.

ORIENTATION
Downtown Hilo and the Bayfront
You'll know you are nearing downtown when you start seeing parking spaces that require parallel parking. The central downtown area is made up of Kamehameha Avenue (also called Bayfront), Kilauea Avenue (which turns into Keawe Street), and Kinoole Streets—parallel streets running north to south bounded on the east by Mamo Street and on the west by Waianuenue Avenue before one has to cross over a bridge to another section of Hilo.

This area is much denser than any other part of town and easily walkable. Within this area you'll find the bus station, Hilo Farmers Market, cafés, restaurants, grocery stores, and tourist shops. While this isn't where you would come to jump in the water, this area is where you'll see cruise ship passengers walking around (with the ship in the distance towering over the town) picking up souvenirs.

Greater Hilo
Thanks to our old friend "urban sprawl," Hilo begins almost right after the Kea'au Shopping Center on Highway 11. Hilo has greatly expanded from its original roots by transforming its farmlands (and native Hawaiians settlements) into the area on Highway 11 that now houses the Hilo International Airport, Walmart, and the Prince Kuhio Mall. Where Highway 11 meets the ocean, you'll find the town's secret jewels: its beaches. Travel east on Kalaniana'ole Avenue, where beaches are situated one after another, easily recognizable from the road by their official county park signs. Although these beaches are easily accessible, you'll be entering into a coastal wonderland that couldn't feel farther from the suburban enclave just up the road.

North Hilo to 'Akaka Falls
Pass over the "Singing Bridge" leaving downtown Hilo and soon after you're in the North Hilo district traveling on Highway 19 toward the Hamakua Coast. This route, one of the prettiest on the island with its ocean views, passes by several old plantation towns that are

historic downtown Hilo

still residential communities that do not offer anything of interest to tourists. Just seven miles out of Hilo, you'll pass the sign for Four-Mile Scenic Drive. You should turn onto it immediately; it's the old route that parallels the highway. Back on the highway as you drive north, you'll arrive at the town of Honomu, the gateway to 'Akaka Falls. From here it's still necessary to climb *mauka* on Highway 220 (about 20 minutes) until you reach the entrance to this must-see sight.

PLANNING YOUR TIME

While many visitors to the Big Island stay only on the Kona side, those who know the island well and appreciate its diversity split their time between the Kona and Hilo sides. Hilo, being the largest city and main hub on the east side, is the logical place to use as a base. The city is bite-size, but you'll need a rental car to visit most of the sights around town. Hilo itself has plenty to keep a traveler busy for a number of days. First, spend time exploring the natural beauty of the city and close-by botanical

gardens, its bay and beaches, and the pretty waterfalls only a few minutes from downtown. Both Rainbow Falls and the potholed riverbed of Boiling Pots are photogenic, and perhaps best when there's plenty of rain to make them perform at their best. Take an hour or two to walk under the giant banyan trees that canopy Banyan Drive, stroll through the relaxing Lili'uokalani Gardens, and walk the bridge to Coconut Island for a perfect view of the bay and waterfront with snowcapped Mauna Kea as a backdrop. While you are out that way, continue on down Kalaniana'ole Avenue for a morning or afternoon in the water at one of the small beaches along the Keaukaha strip.

Hilo is an old town. Reserve a morning or afternoon for a walking tour of town, viewing its well-kept historical buildings, and then spend a few hours at both the Pacific Tsunami Museum, where you will learn about the brutal waters that destroyed much of Hilo's bayfront, and the Lyman Museum and Mission House, where the life of early missionaries to Hawaii comes alive. A bit

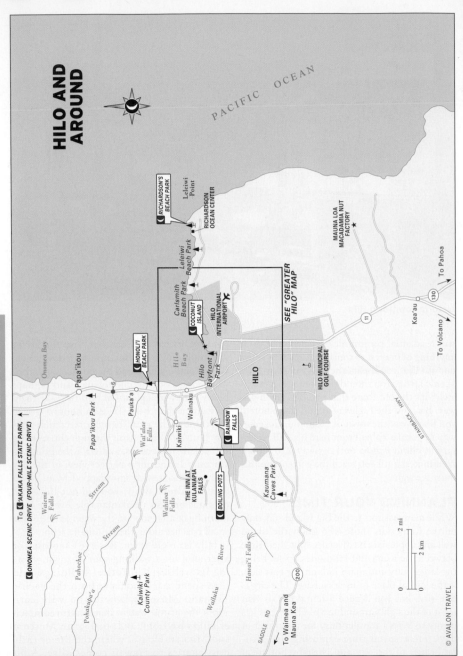

BIG ISLAND OF HAWAI'I

HILO AND AROUND

PACIFIC OCEAN

RICHARDSON'S BEACH PARK

Leleiwi Point

RICHARDSON OCEAN CENTER

MAUNA LOA MACADAMIA NUT FACTORY

Leleiwi Beach Park

To Pahoa

Onomea Bay

Carlsmith Beach Park

COCONUT ISLAND

HILO INTERNATIONAL AIRPORT

SEE "GREATER HILO" MAP

Papa'ikou

HONOLI'I BEACH PARK

Kea'au

Hilo Bay

Hilo Bayfront Park

HILO

To Volcano

Papa'ikou Park

Pauka'a

Wainaku

HILO MUNICIPAL GOLF COURSE

Wai'ale Falls

Kaiwiki

RAINBOW FALLS

Waiemi Falls

Waihilau Falls

THE INN AT KULANIAPIA FALLS

BOILING POTS

Kaumana Caves Park

Pahoehoe

Kaiwiki County Park

Wailuku River

Hawai'i Falls

To Waimea and Mauna Kea

SADDLE RD

To ONOMEA SCENIC DRIVE (FOUR-MILE SCENIC DRIVE)

To ʻAKAKA FALLS STATE PARK, ONOMEA SCENIC DRIVE (FOUR-MILE SCENIC DRIVE)

0 2 mi

0 2 km

© AVALON TRAVEL

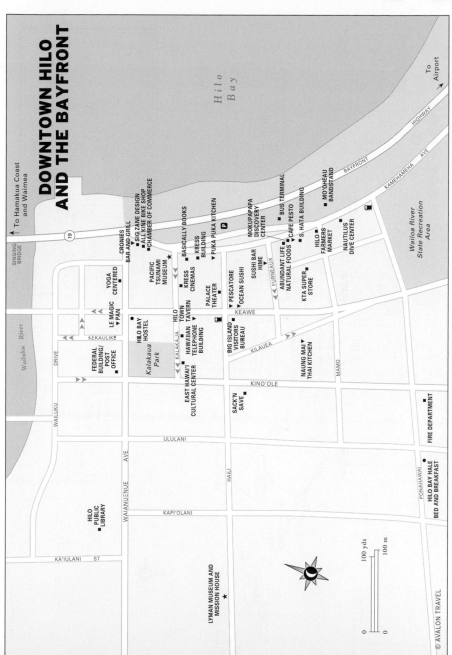

DOWNTOWN HILO AND THE BAYFRONT

To Hamakua Coast and Waimea

Wailuku River

SINGING BRIDGE

Hilo Bay

To Airport

BAYFRONT HIGHWAY

KAMEHAMEHA AVE

Wailoa River State Recreation Area

CRONIES BAR AND GRILL
SIG ZANE DESIGN
ALL KINE BIKE SHOP
CHAMBER OF COMMERCE

YOGA CENTERED
LE MAGIC PAN

PACIFIC TSUNAMI MUSEUM

BASICALLY BOOKS

KRESS BUILDING

PUKA PUKA KITCHEN

KRESS CINEMAS

HILO BAY HOSTEL

HILO TOWN TAVERN

HAWAIIAN TELEPHONE BUILDING

PALACE THEATER

PESCATORE
OCEAN SUSHI

SUSHI BAR HIME

MOKUPAPAPA DISCOVERY CENTER

CAFE PESTO
S. HATA BUILDING

BUS TERMINAL

MO'OHEAU BANDSTAND

ABUNDANT LIFE NATURAL FOODS

HILO FARMERS MARKET

NAUTILUS DIVE CENTER

KTA SUPER STORE

FURNEAUX

BIG ISLAND VISITORS BUREAU

KEAWE

KILAUEA

MAMO

NAUNG MAI THAI KITCHEN

KINO'OLE

EAST HAWAI'I CULTURAL CENTER

Kalakaua Park

KALAKAUA

KEKAULIKE

FEDERAL BUILDING/ POST OFFICE

DRIVE

WAILUKU

SACK'N SAVE

ULULANI

WAIANUENUE AVE

HAILI

KAPI'OLANI

HILO PUBLIC LIBRARY

KA'IULANI ST

PONAHAWAI

FIRE DEPARTMENT

HILO BAY HALE BED AND BREAKFAST

LYMAN MUSEUM AND MISSION HOUSE

100 yds

100 m

0

0

© AVALON TRAVEL

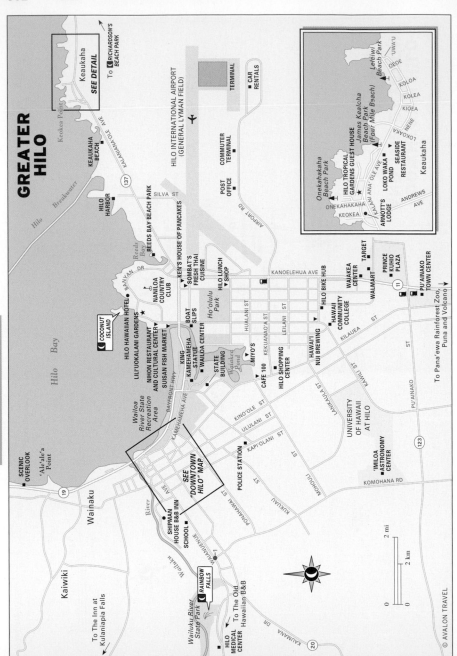

BIG ISLAND OF HAWAI'I

GREATER HILO

SEE DETAIL

To RICHARDSON'S BEACH PARK

Keaukaha

Keokea Point

Hilo Breakwater

KEAUKAHA BEACH

KALANIANA'OLE AVE

HILO HARBOR

REEDS BAY BEACH PARK

Reeds Bay

SILVA ST

HILO INTERNATIONAL AIRPORT (GENERAL LYMAN FIELD)

TERMINAL

CAR RENTALS

COMMUTER TERMINAL

POST OFFICE

AIRPORT RD

Hilo Bay

Hilo Bay

BANYAN DR

NANILOA COUNTRY CLUB

COCONUT ISLAND

HILO HAWAIIAN HOTEL

LILI'UOKALANI GARDENS

SUISAN FISH MARKET

NIHON RESTAURANT AND CULTURAL CENTER

BOAT SLIPS

WAILOA CENTER

KAMEHAMEHA STATUE

KING KAMEHAMEHA AVE

STATE BUILDING

MIYO'S

CAFE 100

Wailoa Pond

Ho'olulu Park

KANOELEHUA AVE

KEN'S HOUSE OF PANCAKES

SOMBAT'S FRESH THAI CUISINE

HILO LUNCH SHOP

HILO BIKE HUB

HUALANI ST

LEILANI ST

KEKUANAO'A ST

WAIAKEA CENTER

TARGET

WALMART

PRINCE KUHIO PLAZA

PU'AINAKO TOWN CENTER

HAWAII COMMUNITY COLLEGE

HAWAI'I NUI BREWING

HILO SHOPPING CENTER

KILAUEA

PU'AINAKO

To Pana'ewa Rainforest Zoo, Puna and Volcano

Waiakea Pond

BAYFRONT HWY

KAMEHAMEHA AVE

Wailoa River State Recreation Area

Wailuku River

SCENIC OVERLOOK

'Ale'ale'a Point

Waiaku

Kaiwiki

KINO'OLE ST

ULULANI ST

KAPI'OLANI ST

POLICE STATION

PONAHAWAI ST

SEE "DOWNTOWN HILO" MAP

UNIVERSITY OF HAWAII AT HILO

'IMILOA ASTRONOMY CENTER

LANIKAULA ST

KAMILI ST

PU'AINAKO

KOMOHANA RD

MOHOULI

KUKUAU ST

KO'OKAU

SHIPMAN HOUSE B&B INN

SCHOOL

WAIANUENUE AVE

WAINAKU

To The Inn at Kulaniapia Falls

Wailuku River State Park

RAINBOW FALLS

To The Old Hawaiian B&B

HILO MEDICAL CENTER

KAUMANA DR

2 mi

2 km

0

0

© AVALON TRAVEL

GREATER HILO Detail (inset)

Onekahakaha Beach Park

ONEKAHAKAHA

KEOKEA

HILO TROPICAL GARDENS GUEST HOUSE

ARNOTT'S LODGE

LOKO WAKA POND

KALANI ANA'OLE AVE

James Kealoha Beach Park (Four Mile Beach)

SEASIDE RESTAURANT

ANDREWS AVE

Keaukaha

LOKOAKA

NENE

KIOEA

KOLEA

KOLOA

OEOE

'UWA'U

Leleiwi Beach Park

Your Best Day in Hilo

- Wake up early and come to **Honoli'i Beach Park** to surf or to watch the surfers.

- Afterward, stop at the **Hilo Lunch Shop** to taste a piece of a local culinary tradition.

- If it's a Wednesday or Saturday, head to the **Hilo Farmers Market** to see the wide range of fruits that grow on the island.

- Take a **walking tour of downtown Hilo** to see the architecture of early-20th-century Hawaii.

- Stop in the **Pacific Tsunami Museum** or the **Lyman Museum.**

- In the afternoon, relax at one of the many black-sand beaches just 10 minutes from downtown, such as **Richardson's Beach Park.**

- Have dinner at one of Hilo's undervalued foodie joints: **Puka Puka Kitchen, Sushi Bar Himi,** or **Sombat's Fresh Thai Cuisine.**

- For a low-key night, catch an art film or a performance at the **Palace Theater.**

- For a high-energy night, meander over to **Kim's Karaoke Lounge** for drinks, pupu, and, of course, karaoke.

- Late at night go where the locals go to end the evening: **Ken's House of Pancakes.**

RAINY DAY ALTERNATIVE

Hilo is a great place to spend a rainy day, given the large number of museums and movie theaters. Here are a few other ideas, and they are mostly free and kid-friendly.

If you want to feel like you're outside even when you're not, the **Kapoho Kine Adventures** office has a small climbing wall inside—and it's free!

Hawaiiana Live at the Palace Theater (Wed. only) showcases Hawaiian history and culture through storytelling, music, film, and hula. If you haven't gone to a luau, this is a great way to see some traditional Hawaiian culture.

Right on the bayfront, it's easy to totally miss the **Mokupapapa Discovery Center for Hawaii's Coral Reefs.** This small museum is great for spending a few minutes perusing its information about reefs and fish of the Northwestern Hawaiian Islands.

out of town is the Pana'ewa Rainforest Zoo, also good for a couple of hours to view tropical animals in a natural environment, and the opportunity to see some of the thick and luxuriant forest cover that surrounds the city. For exploration from Hilo, it's an hour's drive down to the steamy Puna Coast, about the same up to the stark lava lands of Hawai'i Volcanoes National Park or along the wet and wonderful Hamakua Coast to time-lost Waipi'o Valley, but a bit longer for a trek to the top of the Mauna Kea to see the astronomical observatories and experience a sunset from the heights.

Beaches

If you define a beach as a long expanse of white sand covered by a thousand sunbathers and their beach umbrellas, then Hilo doesn't have any. If a beach, to you, can be a smaller, more intimate affair where a good number of tourists and families can spend the day on pockets of sand between fingers of black lava, then Hilo has a few. Hilo's beaches are small and rocky—perfect for keeping crowds away. The best beaches all lie to the east of the city along Kalaniana'ole Avenue, an area known as the Keaukaha Strip, which runs six miles from downtown Hilo to its dead end at Leleiwi Point. Not all beaches are clearly marked, but even those are easily identified by the cars parked along the road.

DOWNTOWN HILO AND THE BAYFRONT
Hilo Bayfront Park
A thousand yards of gray-black sand that narrows considerably as it runs west from the Wailoa River toward downtown, at one time **Hilo Bayfront Park** (along Kamehameha Ave.) went all the way to the Wailuku River and was renowned throughout the islands for its beauty, but commercialism of the waterfront ruined it. By 1960, so much sewage and industrial waste had been pumped into the bay that it was considered a public menace, and then the great tsunami came. Reclamation projects created the Wailoa River State Recreation Area at the east end, and shorefront land became a buffer zone against future inundation. Few swimmers come to the beach because the water is cloudy and chilly, but the sharks don't seem to mind! The bay is a perfect spot for canoe races, and many local teams come here to train. Notice the judging towers and canoe sheds of local outrigger canoe clubs. Toward the west end, near the mouth of the Wailuku River, surfers catch long rides during winter, entertaining spectators. There is public parking along the eastern half near the canoe clubs or at the Wailoa river mouth where the fishing boats dock.

GREATER HILO
Although these beaches are outside of the downtown area, they are really only a few minutes from downtown, and all the beaches are within minutes of one another. With only one exception, all the beaches are either black-sand beaches or have no sand and just a grassy area fronting the beach.

Reeds Bay Beach Park
Technically part of Hilo Bay, **Reeds Bay Beach Park** (at the end of Banyan Dr.) is a largely undeveloped area on the east side of the Waiakea Peninsula. The water here is notoriously cold because of a constantly flowing freshwater spring, hence the name Ice Pond, at its innermost end. Mostly it's frequented by fishers and locals having a good time on weekends and holidays, and some sailors park their private boats here. Restrooms, water, and shower facilities are available.

Keaukaha Beach at Carlsmith Beach Park
Keaukaha Beach at Carlsmith Beach Park, located on Puhi Bay, is the first in a series of beaches as you head east on Kalaniana'ole Avenue. Look for Baker Avenue and pull off to the left into a rough parking area. This is a favorite spot with local people, who swim at Cold Water Pond, a spring-fed inlet at the head of the bay. A sewage treatment plant fronts the western side of Puhi Bay. Much nicer areas for swimming and snorkeling await you just up Kalaniana'ole Avenue, but this beach does have a restroom, shower, pavilion, and weekend lifeguard.

Onekahakaha Beach Park
Farther up the road, **Onekahakaha Beach Park** has it all: safe swimming, small white-sand

NORTH HILO TO 'AKAKA FALLS

(map labels) Kolekole Beach Park · 'AKAKA FALLS STATE PARK · Honomu · PACIFIC OCEAN · Honomu Park · 12 · Pepe'ekeo · ONOMEA SCENIC ROUTE · 19 · Kawainui Stream · ONOMEA SCENIC DRIVE (FOUR-MILE SCENIC DRIVE) · WHAT'S SHAKIN' · HAWAII TROPICAL BOTANICAL GARDEN · Waiemi Falls · Onomea Bay · Papa'ikou · Pahoehoe Stream · Papa'ikou County Park · Pe'epe'e Falls · 6 · Pauka'a · HONOLI'I BEACH PARK · Wai'alae Falls · Wahiloa Falls · Kaiwiki · Wainaku · Hilo Bay · THE INN AT KULANIAPIA FALLS · RAINBOW FALLS · BOILING POTS · HILO · © AVALON TRAVEL · COASTAL ROUTE · 0   2 mi · 0   2 km

beach, lifeguards, and amenities. Turn left onto Onekahakaha Road and park in the lot of Hilo's favorite family beach. Swim in the large, sandy-bottomed pool protected by a manmade breakwater. Outside the breakwater the currents can be fierce, and drownings have been recorded. Good thing there is a lifeguard on duty during the weekends. Walk east along the shore to find an undeveloped area of the park with many small tidal pools. Beware of sea urchins.

James Kealoha Beach Park (Four Mile Beach)

James Kealoha Beach Park, also known locally as **Four Mile Beach,** is next; people swim, snorkel, and fish here; during winter it's a favorite surfing spot. Stay to the left side of the beach since it's more protected than the right side, which can get rough with strong currents during times of high surf.

Just offshore is an island known as Scout Island because local Boy Scouts often camp there. This entire area was known for its fishponds, and inland, just across Kalaniana'ole Avenue, is the 60-acre Loko Waka Pond. This site of ancient Hawaiian aquaculture is now a commercial operation that raises mullet, trout, catfish, perch, tilapia, and others. There is a restroom here but no other amenities.

Leleiwi Beach Park

A favorite local spot for scuba divers due to its plentiful sea life, **Leleiwi Beach Park** lies along a lovely residential area carved into the rugged coastline. This park, unlike the majority of them, has a full-time lifeguard, and it is a good thing they have one, since the shore here is open to the ocean, and currents may be strong.

Richardson's Beach Park

Adjacent is Richardson Ocean Park, known locally as Richardson's Beach Park. A seawall skirts the shore, and a tiny cove with a black-sand beach is the first in a series. This is a terrific area for snorkeling, with plenty of marine life, including *honu* (green sea turtles). Walk east to a natural lava breakwater. Behind it are pools filled and flushed by the surging tide. The water breaks over the top of the lava and rushes into the pools, making natural whirlpool tubs. This is one of the most picturesque swimming areas on the island and is often crowded with families since it offers a lot of shade and a full-time lifeguard on duty. Full amenities are available.

NORTH HILO TO 'AKAKA FALLS

Honoli'i Beach Park

Traveling north a few miles out of Hilo brings you to **Honoli'i Beach Park** (Hwy. 19 between mile markers 4 and 5). Turn right onto Nahala Street, then left onto Kahoa, and follow it around until you see cars parked along the road. The water is down a steep series of steps, and while the black-sand beach is not much appreciated for swimming, it is known as one of the finest surfing spots on this side of the island. If you're not a seasoned surfer, no worries, there is a "kiddie" area as well as two lifeguards if any issues should arise. I highly recommend just coming for a quick viewing session to see the local talent try their hand at big waves. Restroom facilities and showers are available.

Kolekole Beach Park

Kolekole Beach Park (Hwy. 19 near mile marker 14) is popular with local people, who use its pavilions for all manner of special occasions, usually on weekends. A pebble beach fronts a treacherous ocean. The entire valley was inundated with more than 30 feet of water during the great 1946 tsunami. The stream running through Kolekole comes from 'Akaka Falls, four miles inland. Take care while wading across it—the current can be strong and push swimmers out to sea. Local kids tend to take advantage of the ocean's pull to try their hand at body-boarding. Amenities include portable bathrooms, grills, electricity, picnic tables, pavilions, and a camping area (county permit required); no drinking water is available.

To get to Kolekole Beach Park, look for the tall bridge a few minutes north of Honomu, where a sign points to a small road that snakes its way down the valley to the beach park below. Slow down and keep a sharp eye out, as the turnoff is right at the south end of the bridge and easy to miss.

EXCURSION TO PUNA

The pace of life on the Big Island is slow, but somehow, it moves even slower in the southern Puna district, where free spirits spend Sunday afternoon soaking in warm tide pools hidden in the forest. This region south of Hilo is also notable for a string of beaches that are truly off the beaten path. You can also visit natural areas where the sea tortured the hot lava into caves, tubes, arches, and even a natural hot bath. You can camp, swim, surf, or just play in the water to your heart's delight, but realize that there are few places to stop for food, gas, or supplies.

Secret Black Sand Beach

Chances are that you'll be alone or only a few other people will be at the **secret black-sand beach** on Highway 137. If you set your odometer as you pass **MacKenzie State Recreation Area,** the secret black beach is exactly two miles west of the recreation area's entrance. You'll pass under a canopy of trees and the path to the beach is on the ocean or *makai* side of the road where the road curves and it looks like there is room for a car to park—if you're lucky there might be one parked there, which will alert you where to stop. The other marker to look for is two trees that look like they have fallen horizontally. Pass through the horizontal trees or go around them to the right—if you look closely you'll see that there is a trail worn from previous users. Head back through the forest toward the ocean and after two minutes you'll have arrived to the black-sand beach.

As you exit the forest onto the sand, you'll be pleasantly thrilled to have arrived on a deserted beach where you can bask in the sun all day long. But there is more! To the right it looks like there is a natural wall. Climb up it and on the other side are small tide pools and an even more secret black-sand beach.

Water Sports

Although all water sports are possible in Hilo, it's more difficult to rent equipment on this side of the island, probably because fewer tourists come to Hilo to engage in water sports.

CANOEING AND KAYAKING
The Hilo Bay is home to many outrigger canoe clubs. In fact, it's a pretty big club sport on this side of the island. If you glance out onto the Hilo Bay almost any day you'll see numerous canoes and kayaks rowing by. Most canoes on the bay are owned by clubs and they do not rent out their canoes. It may be possible to find a canoe rental if you hang out near the launch area on Bayfront and ask around. Finding a kayak is easier at **Aquatic Perceptions** (111 Banyan Dr., 808/935-9997), which rents kayaks ($15-35 for a single, $20-45 for a tandem) out by the hour or by the day.

DIVING AND SNORKELING
Nearly all the beach parks on on Kalaniana'ole Avenue offer worthy snorkeling and diving, but the best spots are at Leleiwi Beach Park and Richardson's Beach Park. Because everyone knows those are the best spots, they can become crowded. However, if you swim out just a little bit you'll leave the crowds behind and it will just be you and the turtles.

Nautilus Dive Center (382 Kamehameha Ave., 808/935-6939, www.nautilusdivehilo.

com, Mon. 9am-noon, Tues.-Sat. 9am-5pm) offers introductory diving courses ($85 per person), three- to five-day scuba certification ($480 per person), and more advanced courses. Rentals are $35 per day and discounts are available for longer rental periods. If you're looking for a guide, they do that too. For $85 you can arrange a charter tour that includes a two-tank dive.

SURFING AND STAND-UP PADDLE-BOARDING
There are some top surfing and stand-up paddle-boarding destinations on this side of the island. The most popular is Honoli'i Beach Park, where surfers and boarders don't have to worry about getting in the way of swimmers. Hilo Bay also lacks swimmers, but the water is usually cold and murky. North of Hilo in Hakalau it is possible to surf near the bridge, where waves can reach up to 16 feet. At the beach parks on Kalaniana'ole Avenue, such as Richardson's, it's also possible to surf if the weather is right, but these beaches all are prime stand-up paddle-boarding haunts when the water is calm.

The hardest part of your surfing/boarding attempt might not be getting up, it might be finding a board if you just want to rent one. Your best bet for renting is **Orchidland Surfboards** (262 Kamehameha Ave., 808/935-1533, www.orchidlandsurf.com).

Sights

Before the shift of tourism to the drier Kona side of the island, Hilo was the Big Island's major visitor destination. This old town and steamy tropical port still holds many attractions, from missionary homes to forest waterfalls, and landscaped tropical gardens to diminutive beaches with great snorkeling options.

DOWNTOWN HILO AND THE BAYFRONT
Lyman Museum and Mission House
A few short blocks above downtown Hilo, the **Lyman Museum and Mission House** (276 Haili St., 808/935-5021, www.lymanmuseum. org, Mon.-Sat. 10am-4:30pm, $10 adults, $8

What Happens on the Island Stays on the Island

What happens on the island stays on the island. Although this phrase now is most known for its reference to mischievous acts, in Hawaii, locals know that it means that whatever material goods arrive to the islands—cars, furniture, books—tend to stay on the islands. It's not so easy to move heavy or big items across the ocean, and this trend is more than apparent in the myriad of excellent thrift shops located throughout the islands. So, when you live on an island, you must constantly consider where things go when they get left behind and where you might be able to find a discarded treasure.

Hawaiian garbage is actually shipped to the Mainland since there is no place to leave it here. This past year, the state ran into a quandary when the shipping of 20,000 tons of garbage became delayed and began to send a foul odor throughout O'ahu. Some environmental activists argue that the best way to reduce our waste—our environmental imprint—is not only to recycle but, more importantly, to reuse. Thus, on Hawaii, this reusing principle is even more salient given the difficulties of getting rid of waste coupled with the available resources, like used goods left behind by people leaving Hawaii.

On the Big Island, Bill Jackson has created a creative and economical way to reuse. At his **All Kine Bike Shop** (144 Kamehameha Ave., Hilo, 808/345-3417, www.bicyclehawaii.com, Mon.-Fri. 10am-5pm, Sat. 9am-5pm) on the Hilo bayfront, he buys used bikes and salvages some from dumps and then rebuilds them into "new" custom-made bikes. Jackson explains that bikes are the perfect item to recycle "because they are simple." The parts are interchangeable since they all have frames and wheels and are easy to repair.

The shop's storage area is overflowing with over 200 bikes and thousands of parts in crates waiting to be stripped down and remade into wholly new machines. "If someone needs something, I probably have it," Jackson happily says as a man walks in and asks if he carries parts for BMX bikes. His clientele are mainly "people who love to ride and people who have to ride." With gas prices rising, Jackson foresees that his sales will go up as people try to save money on gas by biking. "Biking itself isn't unique to Hawaii," Jackson explains, "but Hawaii by bike is something unique."

seniors, $3 children, $21 family, $5 students) showcases the oldest wood building on the Big Island, originally built in 1839 for David and Sarah Lyman, some of the first Christian missionaries on the island. The museum is a Smithsonian affiliate with a bit of everything, from fine art to mineral and gem collections to exhibits on habitats of Hawaii. The first-floor Earth Heritage Gallery holds a mineral and rock collection that's rated one of the best in the entire country, and by far the best in Polynesia. The museum also holds a substantial collection of archival documents and images relating to Hawaii's history.

Next door is the Lyman Mission House, which opened as a museum in 1931. The furniture is authentic "Sandwich Isles" circa 1850.

Some of the most interesting exhibits are of small personal items like a music box that still plays and a collection of New England autumn leaves that Mrs. Lyman had sent over to show her children what that season was like. Upstairs are bedrooms that were occupied by the Lyman children. Mrs. Lyman kept a diary and faithfully recorded eruptions, earthquakes, and tsunamis. Scientists still refer to it for some of the earliest recorded data on these natural disturbances. The master bedroom has a large bed with pineapples carved into the bedposts, crafted by a ship's carpenter who lived with the family for about eight months. The bedroom mirror is an original, in which many Hawaiians received their first surprised look at themselves. Guided tours of the Lyman Mission House are included with museum admission and are given twice a day (11am and 2pm) by experienced and knowledgeable docents who relate many intriguing stories about the house and its occupants.

Pacific Tsunami Museum

Hilo suffered a devastating tsunami in 1946 and another in 1960. Both times, most of the waterfront area of the city was destroyed, but the 1930 Bishop National Bank building survived, owing to its structural integrity. Appropriately, the **Pacific Tsunami Museum** (130 Kamehameha Ave., 808/935-0926, www.tsunami.org, Mon.-Sat. 9am-4:15pm, $8 adults, $7 seniors, and $4 students) is now housed in this fine art deco structure and dedicated to those who lost their lives in the devastating waves that raked the city. The museum has numerous permanent displays, an audiovisual room, computer linkups to scientific sites, and periodic temporary exhibitions. The most moving displays of this museum are the photographs of the last two terrible tsunamis that struck the city and the stories told by the survivors of those events. Stop in for a look. It's worth the time.

Mokupapapa Discovery Center for Hawaii's Coral Reefs

A small museum right on the bayfront, the **Mokupapapa Discovery Center for Hawaii's Coral Reefs** (280 Kamehameha Ave., Suite 109, 808/933-8195, www.papahanaumokuakea. gov, Tues.-Sat. 9am-4pm, free) has a few interactive features and is filled with information about reefs and fish of the Northwestern Hawaiian Islands.

Around Banyan Drive

If your Hilo hotel isn't situated along Banyan Drive, go there. This bucolic horseshoe-shaped road skirts the edge of Waiakea Peninsula, which sticks out into Hilo Bay. Lining the drive is an almost uninterrupted series of banyan trees forming a giant canopy. Skirting its edge are the Lili'uokalani Gardens, a concentration of hotels, and Reed's Bay.

This peninsula was once a populated residential area, an offshoot of central Hilo. Like much of the city, it was destroyed during the tsunami of 1960. Park your car at one end and take a stroll through this park-like atmosphere. Or arrive early and join other Hilo residents for a morning jog around the loop.

The four dozen banyans that line this boulevard (the first planted in 1933, the last in 1972) were planted by notable Americans and foreigners, including Babe Ruth, President Franklin D. Roosevelt, King George V, Hawaiian volcanologist Dr. Thomas Jaggar, Hawaiian princess Kawananakoa, pilot Amelia Earhart, Cecil B. DeMille, and then-senator Richard Nixon. A placard in front of most trees gives particulars. Time has taken its toll here, however, and as grand as this drive once was, it is now a bit overgrown and unkempt in spots, with much of the area needing a little sprucing up.

LILI'UOKALANI GARDENS

The **Lili'uokalani Gardens** are formal Japanese-style gardens located along the west end of Banyan Drive. Meditatively quiet, they offer a beautiful view of the bay. Along the footpaths are pagodas, torii gates, stone lanterns, and half-moon bridges spanning a series of ponds and streams. Along one side sits a formal Japanese tea house, where women come to be instructed in the art of the tea ceremony. Few people visit this 30-acre garden, and if it weren't for the striking fingers of black lava and the coconut trees, you could easily be in Japan.

COCONUT ISLAND

Coconut Island (Moku Ola) is reached by footbridge from a spit of land just outside Lili'uokalani Gardens. It was at one time a *pu'uhonua* (place of refuge) opposite a human sacrificial *heiau* on the peninsula side. Coconut Island has restrooms, a pavilion, and picnic tables shaded by tall coconut trees and ironwoods. It's been a favorite picnic spot for decades; kids often come to jump into the water from stone abutments here, and older folks come for a leisurely dip in the cool water. The only decent place to swim in Hilo Bay, it also

© MARK WASSER

The annual Merrie Monarch Festival celebrates Hawaiian culture.

offers the best panorama of the city, bay, and Mauna Kea beyond.

Wailoa River State Recreation Area

To the east of downtown is **Waiakea Pond,** a brackish lagoon where people often fish, although that might not be such a great idea given the rumored levels of pollution. The **Wailoa River State Recreation Area,** which encompasses the lagoon, is a 132-acre preserve set along both sides of this spring-fed pond. City residents use this big broad area for picnics, pleasure walks, informal get-togethers, fishing, and launching boats. On the eastern side are picnic pavilions and barbecue grills. Arching footbridges cross the river connecting the halves.

Stop at the **Wailoa Center** on the western side for tourist information and cultural displays (Mon.-Tues. and Thurs.-Fri. 8:30am-4:30pm, Wed. noon-4:30pm). The walls in the upstairs gallery of this 10-sided building are used to display works of local artists and cultural/historic exhibits, changed on a regular basis. On the lower level hang astonishing pictures of the 1946 and 1960 tsunamis that washed through the city. The Wailoa Center sits in a broad swath of greenery, an open, idyllic park-like area that used to be a cramped bustling neighborhood known as Shinmachi. It, like much of the city, was almost totally destroyed during the tsunami of 1960. Nearby stands the **Tsunami Memorial** to the residents of this neighborhood who lost their lives in that natural disaster.

Also close by is the county **Vietnam War Memorial,** dedicated to those who died fighting that war, and a **statue of King Kamehameha,** a new version of that which graces the town of Kapa'au at the northern tip of the island.

East of Waiakea Pond and across Manono Street you'll see **Ho'olulu Park,** with the Civic Center Auditorium and numerous athletic stadiums. This is the town's center for organized athletic events, large cultural festivals, the yearly **Merrie Monarch Festival** (www.merriemonarch.com), and the annual county fair.

GREATER HILO
Mauna Loa Macadamia Nut Factory

Mauna Loa Macadamia Nut Factory (16-701 Macadamia Road, 808/966-8618, www.maunaloa.com, Mon.-Sat. 8:30am-5pm) is several miles south of Hilo off Highway 11, nearly to Kea'au. Head down Macadamia Road for about three miles, through the 2,500-acre plantation, until you come to the visitors center. Inside is an informative free video explaining the development and processing of macadamia nuts in Hawaii. Walkways outside the windows of the processing center and chocolate shop let you view the process of turning these delicious nuts into tantalizing gift items, but this is best viewed from August through January when most of the processing is done. Then return to the snack shop for macadamia nut goodies like ice cream and cookies, and to the gift shop for samples and an intriguing assortment of packaged macadamia nut items. While you're here, step out back and take a self-guided tour of the small garden, where many introduced trees and plants are identified.

Pana'ewa Rainforest Zoo

Not many travelers can visit a zoo in such a unique setting, where the animals virtually live in paradise. The 150 animals at the 12-acre zoo are endemic and introduced species that would naturally live in such an environment. While small and local, the zoo is a delight and the only natural tropical rainforest zoo in the United States of America. The road to the **Pana'ewa Rainforest Zoo** (800 Stainback Hwy., 808/959-9233, www.hilozoo.com, daily 9am-4pm, closed Christmas and New Year's Day) is a trip in itself, getting you back into the country. On a typical weekday, you'll have the place much to yourself. The zoo, operated by the county Department of Parks and Recreation, does feedings every Saturday around 1:30pm, and the tiger is fed every day at 3:35pm, so you may want to be around for these events. Admission is free, although donations to the nonprofit Friends of the Pana'ewa

Zoo, which runs the gift shop at the entrance, are appreciated.

Here you have the feeling that the animals are not "fenced in" so much as you are "fenced out." The collection of about 75 species includes ordinary and exotic animals from around the world. You'll see pygmy hippos from Africa, a rare white Bengal tiger named Namaste, a miniature horse and steer, Asian forest tortoises, water buffalo, monkeys, and a wide assortment of birds like pheasants and peacocks. The zoo hosts many endangered animals indigenous to Hawaii, like the *nene,* Laysan duck, Hawaiian coot, *pueo,* Hawaiian gallinule, and even a feral pig in his own stone mini-condo. There are some great iguanas and mongooses, lemurs, and an aviary section with exotic birds like yellow-fronted parrots and blue and gold macaws. The zoo makes a perfect side trip for families and will certainly delight the little ones.

To get to the zoo from Hilo, take Highway 11 (Hawai'i Belt Road) south toward Volcano. About 2.5 miles past Prince Kuhio Shopping Plaza look for the Zoo sign on a lava rock wall, just after the sign Kulani 19. Turn right on Mamaki.

'Imiloa Astronomy Center

Located on the upper campus of University of Hawai'i at Hilo, the **'Imiloa Astronomy Center** (600 Imiloa Pl., 808/969-9700, www.imiloahawaii.org, Tues.-Sun. 9am-5pm, adults $17.50, children 4-12 $9.50, senior, military, and *kama'aina* discounts available) opened in 2006 dedicated to the integration of science and indigenous culture. The word *'imiloa* means "exploring new knowledge," and the center educates visitors by separating its exhibits into "origins" and "explorations." Although in another place, the combination of studying astronomy and voyages may not make as much sense, here in Hawaii the two matters are linked given that the ancient Polynesians used the stars to wayfind from Polynesia to Hawaii and back.

In addition to the exhibits, a planetarium hosts daily kids' programs as well as Friday

© GEOFFREY WHITEWAY

Rainbow Falls

night laser light shows. Special events and workshops frequently occur at the center. Check the website for more information and for the Hawaiian word of the day. Say it at the register and get a $2 discount for each individual who speaks the word.

◖ Rainbow Falls and Boiling Pots

A few miles out of town as you head west on Waianuenue Avenue, two natural spectacles within Wailuku River State Park are definitely worth a look. A short way past Hilo High School a sign directs you to **Rainbow Falls,** a most spectacular yet easily visited natural wonder. You'll look down on a circular pool in the river below that's almost 100 feet in diameter; cascading into it is a lovely waterfall. The 80-foot falls deserve their name because as they hit the water below, their mists throw flocks of rainbows into the air. Underneath the falls is a huge cavern, held by legend to be the abode of Hina, mother of the god Maui. Most people are content to look from the vantage point near the parking lot, but if you walk to the left, you

can take a stone stairway to a private viewing area directly over the falls (be careful; it can be slippery). Here the river, strewn with volcanic boulders, pours over the edge. Follow the path for a minute or so along the bank to a gigantic banyan tree and a different vantage point. The falls may be best seen in the morning when the sunlight streams in from the front.

Follow Waianuenue Avenue for two more miles past Hilo Medical Center to the heights above town. A sign to turn right onto Pe'epe'e Falls Street points to **Boiling Pots.** Few people visit here. Follow the path from the parking lot past the toilets to an overlook. Indented into the riverbed below is a series of irregularly shaped depressions that look as though a peg-legged giant left his peg prints in the hot lava. Seven or eight resemble naturally bubbling whirlpool tubs as river water cascades from one into the next. This phenomenon is best after a heavy rain. Turn your head upriver to see **Pe'epe'e,** a gorgeous, five-spouted waterfall. Although signs warn you not to descend to the river—it's risky during heavy rains—locals hike down to the river rocks below to sunbathe and swim in pools that do not have rushing water. Be careful as it can get slippery; flash floods can and have occurred here.

Kaumana Cave

In 1881, Mauna Loa's tremendous eruption discharged a huge flow of lava. The river of lava crusted over, forming a tube through which molten lava continued to flow. Once the eruption ceased, the lava inside siphoned out, leaving the tube now called **Kaumana Cave** (Rte. 200). Follow a steep staircase down into a gray hole draped with green ferns and brightened by wildflowers. Smell the scent of the tropical vegetation. You can walk only a few yards into the cave before you'll need a strong flashlight and sturdy shoes. It's a thrill to turn around and look at the entrance, where blazing sunlight shoots through the ferns and wildflowers.

To get to Kaumana Cave from downtown Hilo, turn left on Waianuenue Avenue. Just past mile marker 1 stay to the left onto Kaumana Drive (Saddle Road). Kaumana Cave is on the right just past mile marker 4.

NORTH HILO TO 'AKAKA FALLS

C Onomea Scenic Drive (Four-Mile Scenic Drive)

Highway 19 heading from Hilo to Honoka'a has magnificent inland and coastal views one after another. Most people find the **Onomea Scenic Drive** when coming north from Hilo. Only five minutes from the city, you'll come to Papa'ikou town. Just past mile marker 7 and across the road from the Papa'ikou School, a road posted as the scenic drive dips down toward the coast. Take it. (If you are coming from the Kona side you'll see a sign between mile markers 10 and 11). Almost immediately, signs warn you to slow your speed because of the narrow winding road and one-lane bridges, letting you know what kind of area you're coming into. Start down this meandering lane past some modest homes and into the jungle that covers the road like a living green tunnel. Prepare for tiny bridges crossing tiny valleys. Stop, and you

can almost hear the jungle growing. Along this short four-mile route are sections of an ancient coastal trail and the site of a former fishing village. Drive defensively, but take a look as you pass one fine view after another. This road runs past the Hawaii Tropical Botanical Garden and a couple of places for quick eats before heading up to higher ground to rejoin Highway 19 at Pepe'ekeo.

If you're coming from Hilo, just a few minutes (or 1.5 miles) along the Onomea Scenic Drive is the **Hawaii Tropical Botanical Garden** (27-717 Old Mamalahoa Hwy., 808/964-5233, www.hawaiigarden.com, daily 9am-5pm, last entry 4pm, adults $15, children 6-16 $16). Remember that the entrance fee not only allows you to walk through the best-tamed tropical rainforest on the Big Island but helps preserve this wonderful area in perpetuity. Tours are offered Saturday at noon for an additional $5 per adult.

The gardens were established in 1978 when Dan and Pauline Lutkenhouse purchased the 25-acre valley and have been open for viewing since 1984. Mr. Lutkenhouse, a retired San Francisco businessman, personally performed the work that transformed it into one of the most exotic spots in all of Hawaii. The locality was amazingly beautiful but inaccessible because it was so rugged. Through personal investment and six painstaking years of toil aided by only two helpers, he hand-cleared the land, built trails and bridges, developed an irrigation system, acquired more than 2,000 different species of trees and plants, and established one mile of scenic trails and a water lily lake stocked with *koi* and tropical fish. Onomea was a favorite spot with the Hawaiians, who came to fish and camp for the night.

These inviting gardens, a "living museum" as they call it, will attract lovers of plants and flowers, and those looking to take really great photographs. The loop through the garden is about a mile long, and the self-guided tour takes about 90 minutes. As you walk, listen for the songs of the native birds that love this ancient spot. The walk is not difficult, but there are steps down to the gardens that are not wheelchair accessible. Golf carts ($5) are available to help those who need it down the boardwalk, and then non-motorized wheelchairs are allowed in the garden itself.

◖ 'Akaka Falls State Park

Everybody's idea of a pristine Hawaiian valley is viewable at **'Akaka Falls State Park** (on Hwy. 220, gate open 7am-7pm, $5 per car or $1 per pedestrian, no charge for Hawaii residents), one of the most easily accessible forays into Hawai'i's beautiful interior. Take the Honomu turnoff from Highway 19 onto Highway 220 to get here. From the parking lot, walk counterclockwise along a paved "circle route" that takes you 0.4 mile in about a half hour. The footpath does require some physical exertion. Along the way, you're surrounded by heliconia, ti, ginger, orchids, azaleas, ferns, and bamboo groves as you cross bubbling streams on wooden footbridges. Many varieties of plants that would be in window pots anywhere else are giants here, almost trees. An overlook provides views of **Kahuna Falls** spilling into a lush green valley below. The trail becomes an enchanted tunnel through hanging orchids and bougainvillea. In a few moments you arrive at **'Akaka Falls.** The mountain cooperates with the perfect setting, forming a semicircle from which the falls

© MARK WASSER

'Akaka Falls

tumble 442 feet in one sheer drop, the tallest single-tier waterfall in the state. After heavy rains, expect a mad torrent of power; during dry periods marvel at liquid-silver threads forming mist and rainbows.

Shopping

DOWNTOWN HILO AND THE BAYFRONT

The bayfront area is most definitely set up to encourage shopping. Unfortunately, it doesn't always inspire shops to stay open late or to stay open at all. Don't be surprised if by 5pm downtown Hilo feels like a ghost town. Likewise, while there are a few stores that have kept their doors open for over 20 years, many more close every year. So don't be surprised if your favorite store is nowhere to be found.

The majority of shops on the bayfront cater to cruise ship passengers. It's difficult to distinguish from one shop to another and the same

Hawaiiana tchotchke (made in China) that they offer. Nevertheless, one store that stands apart is **Basically Books** (160 Kamehameha Ave., 808/961-0144, www.basicallybooks.com, Mon.-Sat. 9am-5pm, 11am-4pm). This isn't where you get recently published bestsellers; instead, it has a good selection of Hawaiiana, out-of-print books, and an unbeatable selection of maps and charts. You can get anywhere you want to go with these nautical charts, road maps, and topographical maps, including sectionals for serious hikers. The store also features a good selection of travel books and national flags, as well as children's books and toys with Hawaii themes. The owners also publish books about Hawaii under their Petroglyph Press name.

Another longstanding store, **Sig Zane Design** (122 Kamehameha Ave., 808/935-7077, www.sigzane.com, Mon.-Fri. 9:30am-5pm, Sat. 9am-4pm), sells distinctive island wearables in Hawaiian/tropical designs. This store is the real deal. Sig Zane designs the fabrics, and Sig's wife, Nalani, who helps in the shop, is a *kumu hula* who learned the intricate dance steps from her mother, Edith Kanakaole, a legendary dancer who has been memorialized with a local tennis stadium that bears her name. You can get shirts, dresses, and pareu, as well as affordable T-shirts, *hapi* coats, and even futon covers. The shelves also hold leather bags, greeting cards, and accessories.

GREATER HILO

The majority of shopping for everyday living happens within the same four corners off of Highway 11. More importantly, this area serves as a main wayfinding point for giving directions to all other points around town (including the airport, which is nearby).

Prince Kuhio Plaza (111 E. Puainako St., 808/959-3555, www.princekuhioplaza.com, Mon.-Thurs. 10am-8pm, Fri.-Sat. 10am-9pm, Sun. 10am-6pm) is the closest thing the Big Island has to a Mainland-looking indoor mall. It's filled with mall stores like Radio Shack, Spencer's Gifts, Macy's, and Sears. And yes, there is a food court filled with your standard pretzel shop, hot dogs on a stick, and a Maui Taco. Since no mall would be complete without a cineplex, you'll find a Hollywood theater affiliate here too.

NORTH HILO TO 'AKAKA FALLS

The 'Akaka Falls road passes through the town of Honomu. In addition to the multitude of sarong shops dotting the main street (it's like the sarong capital of the world here), the non-sarong shops along the main street are worth a stop.

Glass from the Past (28-1672-A Old Mamalahoa Hwy., 808/963-6449) has been in Honomu for 25 years, and its merchandise has been in the area for nearly a hundred years. As the store's name indicates, it carries antique glass. What's so interesting about this glass is that it is from the different area plantations—all of which had their own soda works and dairy. Each piece of glass tells a story about Hawai'i's past. Even if you're not going to make a purchase, stop in and talk story with the shop owner, who scrounges the area to find his products. It's like a modern-day archaeological dig.

A few doors down, **Mr. Ed's Homemade Jams and Bakery** (808/963-5000, Mon.-Sat. 6am-6pm, Sun. 9am-4pm) stocks every imaginable type of jam made from local ingredients like jaboticaba, jackfruit, starfruit, and purple sweet potato. The baked goods get bad reviews, but come in and taste one of the hundreds of jams. Low-sugar as well as no-sugar options are available; they also ship jars to the Mainland if you don't want to check your luggage.

Entertainment

ENTERTAINMENT
Nightlife

People in Hilo tend not to stay out late. Maybe it's because we like to get up early and surf or maybe it's because bars open and then quickly shut down due to noise complaints from neighbors. So for the most part, bars have stopped opening around town.

Nevertheless, driving around Hilo you'll surely see a lot of intriguing bars. Many of them are geared toward specific groups of locals. So there is one that serves Japanese clientele, and one that serves a Korean clientele, and one for Filipino clientele, etc. If you're not from the island or with a local, you might feel a little out of place at some of these establishments, but that doesn't mean you shouldn't check them out.

A bar definitely worth experiencing is **Kim's Karaoke Lounge** (760 Piilani St., 808/935-7552, open late), the favorite bar of nearly every Hilo resident. Why is it so loved? After the purchase of two cheap drinks, the waitresses start bringing unlimited pupu and there is a lot of drunken karaoke. While I did receive more attentive service when I was there with a more "local" crowd, don't let this anecdotal evidence deter you from coming if you don't look local. Kim's is probably the furthest thing from a tourist bar.

Another place with pupu included with alcohol purchase is **Bamboo Garden** (718 Kinoole St., 808/935-8952). Less popular than Kim's, this place doesn't always have a crowd. This would be the place to come if you're not looking for a scene and want to ease yourself into the world of Hilo bars.

Hilo Burger Joint (776 Kilauea, 808/935-8880, http://hiloburgerjoint.com, daily 11am-11pm, happy hour daily 4pm-6pm, $11) is your quintessential college town bar. In addition to 20 varieties of Big Island beef burgers, there's a full bar with lots of beers on draft. Service can be slow at times. There's live music on the weekends.

That sports bar you've been searching for to watch your team on the big-ish screen is **Cronies Bar and Grill** (11 Waianuenue Ave., 808/935-5158, www.cronieshawaii.com, Mon.-Thurs. 11am-9pm, Fri. 11am-10pm, Sat. 11am-9pm, Sun. 11am-8pm, $10-15). On the weekends, it's jammed with sports lovers rooting for their favorite teams. Cronies is tempting for its prime location right on Bayfront.

The **Hilo Town Tavern** (168 Keawe St., 808/935-2171, Mon.-Fri. 2pm-2am, Sat. 10am-2am, Sun. 10am-midnight, happy hour Mon.-Fri. 4pm-6pm, pizzas $8) fills a much-needed hole in downtown Hilo, where it seems like everything else closes down by 5pm. You might find yourself meandering inside after hearing live music as you walk by. The bands are all local and the music styles vary, but for no cover, why not come for a listen and a drink? The back part of the bar has a pool table and more chairs.

The Arts

Hawaiiana Live at the Palace Theater (38 Haili St., 808/934-7010, www.hilopalace.com, Wed. 11-11:45am, $5 adult, free for kids under 12) showcases Hawaiian history and culture through storytelling, music, film, and hula. You'll wish that it wasn't only on Wednesdays and only 45 minutes long. It's not much different than the luau you might have already attended at the resorts, but if you haven't gone, it's a great way to see some of traditional Hawaiian culture. If you're into art deco buildings, you'll enjoy the renovated Palace Theater with its proscenium stage and wonderful old murals. Movies are shown Friday-Tuesday.

East Hawaii Cultural Center (141 Kalakaua St., 808/961-5711, www.ehcc.org, 10am-4pm Mon.-Sat.) is a nonprofit organization that supports local arts and hosts varying festivals, performances, and workshops throughout the year, here and at other locations on the island. It also hosts Shakespeare in the Park performances by a local repertory group that stages, directs, designs, and enacts Shakespearean plays under the large banyan tree in Kalakaua Park during the month of July. If you're in Hilo at this time, it shouldn't be missed.

Monthly juried and non-juried art exhibits are shown on the main floor gallery; a venue for various performing artists is upstairs. The bulletin board is always filled with announcements of happenings in the local art scene. Stop in as there is always something of interest on the walls, and because this organization is worthy of support. The Big Island Dance Council, Hawaii Concert Society, Hilo Community Players, and Bunka No Izumi are all member groups.

Food

DOWNTOWN HILO AND THE BAYFRONT

Establishments are listed from east to west on each respective street beginning farther from the bay and ending on Bayfront (also known as Kamehameha Avenue).

Saimin, a noodle soup that developed during Hawaii's plantation days, is just one of many dishes served at **Nori's Saimin and Snacks** (688 Kinoole St., 808/935-9133, Mon. 10:30am-3pm, Tues.-Sat. 10:30am-3pm and 4pm-midnight, Sun. 10:30am-10pm, $7). Even though this Korean-style noodle house is featured in a Hawaiian Airlines ad, it doesn't get a lot of tourists. The daily specials greatly range from fried chicken to pigs' feet soup to meatloaf, making it a little difficult to get a handle on Nori's culinary identity. But what is for certain is that the portions are large and inexpensive and there is Hello Kitty paraphernalia surrounding the Formica booths. If you want to taste a bunch of local dishes in one sitting, try the Big Plate with ahi tempura, fried noodles, kalbi ribs, teri beef, chicken sticks, *musubi,* and macaroni salad. I have seen a good eater attempt to eat this himself and he needed some help. It is a legitimately big plate.

Local Brewing

Hilo has its own microbrewery, **Hawai'i Nui Brewing** (275 E. Kawili St., 808/934-8211, www.hawaiinuibrewing.com, Mon.-Sat. 8:30am-5:30pm). A small operation—about 1,200 barrels a year—and in business since 1996, this microbrewery (formerly known as the Mehana Brewery) crafts five varieties of light beer with no preservatives, brewed especially for the tropical climate. Stop at the small tasting room/logo shop for a sample or gift any day except Sunday. If it's not too busy, someone may show you around.

Try their self-designated "famous" chocolate *mochi* cookies and cakes. I am skeptical of their fame, but you can't go wrong with a chocolate-*mochi* mix.

A gourmet anomaly, **Short N Sweet Bakery and Café** (374 Kinoole St., 808/935-4446, www.shortnsweet.biz, Mon.-Fri. 8am-4:30pm, Sat.-Sun. 8am-3pm, $9) earned itself the designation of "America's most beautiful cakes" by *Brides* magazine in 2010. This is a well-deserved honor. Don't be mistaken, though; Short N Sweet is more than a bakery. Their lunch menu of panini and salads is a welcome break from local cuisine, and their Sunday brunch menu is gaining in popularity thanks to their homemade smoked salmon bagels and quiches. Weekdays are stocked full of deals. Ask about the early-bird special (8-10am) and discounts during the afternoon happy hour (2:30-4:30pm). Vegetarian and wheat-free options are available, along with wireless Internet.

Just Cruisin' Coffee (835 Kilauea Ave., 808/934-7444, daily 5:30am-8pm, $6) has wireless Internet, drive-thru windows, and outdoor seating. But where Just Cruisin' Coffee excels is with their delectable chicken macadamia nut salad with pesto sandwich, hot breakfast sandwiches, cold brewed coffee, smoothies, and coffee milk shakes.

Named after a famous all-Japanese fighting battalion, the C **Cafe 100** (969 Kilauea Ave., 808/935-8683, http://cafe100.com, Mon.-Thurs. 6:30am-8:30pm, Fri. 6:30am-9pm, Sat. 6:30am-7:30pm, $7) is a Hilo institution. The Miyashiro family has been serving food at its indoor-outdoor restaurant here since the late 1950s. Cafe 100 has turned the *loco moco* (a hamburger and egg atop rice smothered in gravy) into an art form. Offerings include the regular *loco moco,* teriyaki *loco,* Spam *loco,* hot dog *loco, oyako loco,* and, for the health conscious, the mahimahi *loco.* If your waistline, the surgeon general, and your arteries permit, this is *the* place to have one. Breakfast choices include everything from bacon and eggs to coffee and doughnuts, while lunches feature beef stew, salmon mixed plate, and fried chicken, or an assortment of sandwiches from teriyaki beef to good old BLT. Make your selection and sit at one of the picnic tables under the veranda to watch the people of Hilo go by.

The "Best Thai Food" of the Big Island showdown continues at **Naung Mai Thai Kitchen** (86 Kilauea Ave., 808/934-7540, www.hilothai.com, daily 11am-9pm, $12), where the great lunch specials, pineapple curry, and vegan tapioca pudding give the other "best" Thai restaurants a run for their money. The space is intimate.

Next door to Naung Mai is the newly opened **Pho Viet** (80 Kilauea Ave., 808/935-1080, Mon.-Sat. 11am-9pm, $8), serving the traditional Vietnamese soup called *pho* (pronounced "fuh"): beef noodle or chicken noodle soup served with sprouts and lime on the side. The *pho* is *pho*-nomenal. Vegetarian options are available and the soups are gluten-free-friendly.

At the end of Keawe Street in a beautiful historical building you'll find **Le Magic Pan** (64 Keawe St., 808/935-7777, daily 11am-2pm and 5pm-9pm, $10-15), and it's worth stopping by. Both dessert crepes with Nutella and bananas, and savory crepes, like shrimp with pesto, are available. The meals are surprisingly filling, and with live music filling the air of this stylish long-standing building, Le Magic Pan makes for a good date night option.

Front and center on Bayfront, with a black-and-white checkerboard floor, linen on the tables, an open-air kitchen, a high ceiling with ceiling fans, and the calming effect of ferns and flowers, is **Café Pesto** (308 Kamehameha Ave., 808/969-6640, www.cafepesto.com, Sun.-Thurs. 11am-9pm, Fri.-Sat. 11am-10pm, reservations recommended, lunch $14, dinner $20), in the historic S. Hata Building. One of Hilo's fine established restaurants, it offers affordable gourmet food in an open, airy, and unpretentious setting that looks out across the avenue to the bay. Pizzas from the ʻohiʻa wood-fired oven can be anything from a simple cheese pie for $8.50 to a large Greek or chili-grilled shrimp pizza for $18; you can also create your own. Lunchtime features sandwiches, calzones, and pasta. For dinner, try an appetizer like Asian Pacific crab cakes or sesame-crusted Hamakua goat cheese. Heartier appetites will be satisfied with the main dinner choices, mostly $15-28, which might be mango-glazed chicken, island seafood risotto, or a combination beef tenderloin and tiger prawns with garlic mashed potatoes. Follow this with a warm coconut tart or *lilikoʻi* cheesecake. Café Pesto also has a brass-railed bar where you can order caffe latte or a fine glass of wine to top off your meal. A kids' menu is available.

It has it all: well priced food with flavors your palate may not be familiar with in a cute (very local) setting. It's imperative to get to ◖ **Puka Puka Kitchen** (270 Kamehameha Ave., 808/933-2121, lunch Mon.-Sat. 11am-2:30pm and dinner Fri.-Sat. 5:30-8:30pm, $12) early, otherwise the best dishes are gone. However, if you get there late (after 2pm) the bento boxes are half price and quite a deal. The food is Middle Eastern meets Indian food meets Hawaii with Japanese writing on the menu. The sautéed lamb plate is delicious, with tender pieces of meat (locally sourced) served with a green salad and rice. Order the house garlic rice to create the perfect plate of flavors. Other choices are the ahi plate, curry dishes, and the pita sandwiches—all hearty options. I would not get the barbecued chicken or the falafel as they do their other plates better. There are several vegetarian options on the menu and they accommodate special diets.

Even with only 10 seats in the restaurant, one rarely has to wait a few minutes to try the freshest and best-styled sushi in town at gem-in-the-wall ◖ **Sushi Bar Himi** (14 Furneaux Ln., 808/961-6356, daily 11:30am-2:30pm and 5pm-8pm). The menu, which also adorns the wall on colorful scraps of paper, is a mixture of the usual with the unimaginable. It includes maki rolls in pink soy wrappers, mushrooms stuffed with crab and smothered with warm hollandaise sauce, and daily specials with creative names highlighting local fish like mahimahi and topped with a dash of tahini sauce.

If you are short on time, don't worry. Each plate arrives within minutes after ordering but always appears as if extra care was taken to plate it perfectly, giving Bar Himi's food a one-of-a-kind taste.

Kava is one of those local specialties that tourists who are keen on experiencing all Hawaii has to offer should try, and **Bayfront Coffee, Kava, and Tea Co.** (116 Kamehameha Ave., 808/935-1155, http://bayfrontkava.com, Mon.-Thurs. 9am-10pm, Fri.-Sat. 10am-10pm, $5) is the place to do it. However, besides offering kava, the "coffee" or "tea" or "café" part of the name is a bit misleading. To be clear, they do have coffee and tea, but nothing fancy—you can order a cup of coffee or a cup of tea. There are only a few tables inside and a couple of seats outside. Café workers are excited to introduce non-drinkers to kava. Be warned, though: kava is an acquired taste, and until you acquire it, it tastes much like dirt. In addition to drinks, there is a limited menu of bagels and sandwiches. On the weekend the café gets buzzing with live music and a regular crowd of onlookers.

Two Ladies Kitchen (274 Kilauea Ave., 808/961-4766, Wed.-Sat. 10am-5pm) brings *mochi* to a whole new level, crafting it from sweet rice flour according to their secret family recipe. Each piece looks like a work of art. You can sense the sheer excitement when the sign comes up that reads "we still have strawberry *mochi* today." The strawberries are real, which leads to a second sign that reads "you can't bring them to the Mainland," due to the agricultural inspection. You'll wish you could, though.

Locals all have their favorite shave ice place, but with 18 different flavors, **Wilson's by the Bay** (224 Kamehameha Ave., Hilo, 808/969-9191, $3) on the bayfront is a standard crowd pleaser. Try Hawaiian-inspired essences like guava, *liliko'i*, and *li hing mui*.

GREATER HILO

If you're aching for the huevos rancheros from your last vacation to Oaxaca, drive quickly to ◖ **Emma's** (Shipman Industrial Park, 16-203 Wiliama Pl., Kea'au, 808/966-6300, Mon.-Fri. 8am-2pm, $7). The flavors are spot on at this hidden gem situated in a hole in the wall. Upgrade to the "plate" portion, which includes rice and beans, but don't forget to save room for the homemade churros. There are daily lunch specials, and most locals talk endlessly about Friday's fish tacos. And did I mention the corn tortillas? They are made right here in Hilo and you're likely to see the *abuelita* (the grandmother) sitting in the dining room shucking corn during your visit. Most dishes can be made vegetarian, and corn tortillas can easily be substituted for gluten-free eaters.

The menu at the **Hilo Bay Café** (315 Makaala St., Hilo, 808/935-4939, www.hilobaycafe.com, Mon.-Sat. 11am-9:30pm, Sun. 5-9:30pm, lunch $15, dinner $22) seems like it was written by a food writer. It has dishes such as vegetarian flax sweet potato burger and roasted free-range chicken breast stuffed with cilantro-cumin mascarpone. The names of the dishes certainly make it hard to pick just one. The menu changes with the season and the meat, fish, and produce are from local farmers. The food here tastes good and they make excellent cocktails that are classics with a Hawaii twist. Service is attentive. A children's menu is available.

The ◖ **Hilo Lunch Shop** (421 Kalanikoa St., Hilo, 808/935-8273, Tues.-Sat. 5:30am-1pm, $3) is a one-stop shop for local flavors. The friendly staff is happy to explain each dish even when the customer line is long. The restaurant is set up in *okazuya* style. There is a long buffet and as you walk down it you point to what you want and a nice server boxes it for you. Most items are around $1 per piece or under and the selections include nori chicken, tempura, cone sushi, fishcakes, and salads. You can mix and match as you like and still not pay over $10 for a lot of food. There is limited seating inside but most people take their food to go. Come early! They often are sold out before noon.

Another restaurant that reflects Hilo's Japanese Hawaiian culinary tradition, this is the restaurant to go to for a romantic evening: **Miyo's** (400 Hualani St., Hilo, 808/935-2273,

Mon.-Sat. 11am-2pm and 5:30am-8:30pm, reservations recommended, $13) is set up like a Japanese tea house and overlooks a pond. The overall atmosphere makes eaters feel like they are no longer in Hawaii. The menu is short: combination plates of sashimi or tempura served with chicken or beef. Miso butterfish is one of the best dishes and there is always a fish special. The restaurant is BYOB and has live music on weekends.

With no exaggeration, **《 Sombat's Fresh Thai Cuisine** (88 Kanoelehua, Hilo, 808/969-9336, www.sombats.com, Mon.-Fri. 10:30am-1:30pm and 5-8:30pm, Sat. 5-8:30pm, lunch $7, dinner $14) is probably some of the best Thai food you'll have outside of Thailand. Sombat, the owner and chef, grows the herbs in her garden in order to get her dishes flavored just right. Eaters can often see her in the restaurant chatting with guests and checking to make sure everything is up to par. The lunch special is an outstanding deal with portions almost large enough to feed two people. Usually you choose between a curry and a noodle dish. Come early, as the special often sells out by 12:30pm and then only the à la carte options are available. Try the coco soup with ahi. It's large enough that it can feed two or more people. Keep in mind that hot in Hawaii is very, very hot on the Mainland. So you might want to order a level down.

Pancakes are only about one-tenth of the massive menu at **《 Ken's House of Pancakes** (1730 Kamehameha Ave., Hilo, 808/935-8711, www.kenshouseofpancakes. com, 24 hours), an institution in Hilo, so don't let the pancake part throw you off. Year after year Ken's wins awards for "Best Diner on the Island," and the accolade is well deserved. There are so many good things about Ken's it's hard to know where to start. To begin with, it's one of few places in Hawai'i

that is open 24 hours. Check the menu for nightly specials: Sunday is all-you-can-eat spaghetti night. Breakfast is available anytime, but you'll be torn between a three-egg omelet with Portuguese sausage or the short ribs. Or, go big and order the Sumo Loco: six scoops of rice, five ounces of Spam, gravy, and three eggs. If that seems like overdoing it, order off the kids' menu or from the "lighter stuff." Save room, if you are capable, for the homemade pies.

NORTH HILO TO 'AKAKA FALLS

The options in this area are beyond few and far between so plan accordingly.

Halfway through the Onomea Scenic Drive you'll come across the glorious oasis of **《 What's Shakin'** (27-999 Old Mamaloahoa Hwy., Pepe'ekeo, 808/964-3080, daily 10am-5pm, smoothies $7, lunch $10). It might sound like a lot, $7 for a smoothie—but I can almost guarantee that it will be the best smoothie you'll ever have and they are filling enough to split between two people. The fruit is all grown on the farm that houses this stand, and you can taste the freshness in every sip. The food, usually a daily special as well as their standard menu of nachos, salmon burgers, and burritos, is equally delicious with huge portions and several vegetarian options. Note: If you are coming from the Kona direction, you'll pass a different smoothie stand as you turn right onto the scenic drive—What's Shakin' is just two minutes up the road from there.

Farmers Market

On Wednesday and Saturday mornings, stop by the corner of Kamehameha Avenue and Mamo Street for the **Hilo Farmers Market,** perhaps the best farmers market on the island. This is a lively affair, great for local color, where

© BONITA CHESHIER/123RF.COM

the colorful offerings at the Hilo Farmers Market

you can get healthy, locally grown produce and bouquets of colorful flowers at bargain prices. It's not all locally grown; ask where it comes from if that's important to you. Across the street at The Market Place and also a few steps up the road under the big tents are more vendors selling flowers, arts and crafts, and other gift items.

Getting There and Around

AIR

The **Hilo International Airport** (code ITO) is right in town—so much so that you can see the Hawaiian Airlines logo overhead on the planes that are about to land (it's like the beginning montage of *Hawaii Five-0*). The airport is currently only an international airport in theory. Most international flights have to connect through one of the other Hawaiian airports (like Honolulu) before arriving to Hilo.

After many years of no direct flights to the Mainland, in June 2011, United Airlines began direct service between Hilo and Los Angeles and San Francisco. These flights are only a few times a week. Otherwise, the airport is mostly used by interisland flights serviced by **Hawaiian Airlines** (www.hawaiianair.com). To get to the other islands, it is often necessary to travel through Honolulu. Hawaiian Airlines offers one direct flight to Maui daily.

BUS

Hilo's **Mooheau Bus Terminal** (between Kamehameha Ave. and Bayfront Hwy.) is the only proper bus terminal on the island—it's so official that there is actually a **tourist information kiosk** located inside. From the bus terminal it is possible to get anywhere on the island by utilizing the **Hele-On Bus** (www. heleonbus.org, 808/961-8744, $1 per ride,

$1 each for luggage, large backpacks, bikes). Buses make almost hourly trips to Waimea via the Hamakua Coast as well as to Puna. For Volcano, Ka'u, Kona, and Kohala, a little bit more planning is necessary as there are only 3-4 daily direct buses to these regions. Check the website for exact times.

There are four separate intra-Hilo routes; however, some of these routes overlap. All the buses pass through the downtown terminal, and by selecting the correct route (check the website or ask at the terminal) it is possible to travel to the in-town beaches, shopping areas, and the University of Hawai'i at Hilo. During peak times you can catch a bus nearly every 20 minutes or so. By the evening it's more like every 40 minutes or every hour. If you're not going too far, it usually is quicker to walk to your destination than wait for the bus.

TAXI

There are nearly two dozen taxi companies in town. For service 24 hours a day try **Ace One Taxi** (808/935-8303) and **Hot Lava Taxi** (808/557-0879). Hot Lava Taxi services the Hilo airport, along with **Percy's Taxi** (808/969-7060) and **Bobby Taxi** (808/937-6008). You can get most anywhere in town or to/from the airport for under $13. If you're interested in a shared ride taxi, you must purchase pre-paid vouchers. Call 808/961-8744 for additional information on where to purchase the coupon books. For shared rides, it's one coupon per person for traveling 1-4 miles and two coupons per person for traveling 4.1-9 miles. Farther afield, you might expect about $50 to Pahoa, $75 to Volcano, and $100 to Honoka'a.

HAMAKUA COAST, WAIMEA, AND THE SADDLE ROAD

When residents of the Big Island talk about the Big Island, they separate the island into two regions: "Hilo side" and "Kona side"—entirely leaving Hamakua and Waimea off the map. In an effort to increase visitors to the region, there is a movement afoot to start thinking about the Big Island in north (Hamakua and Waimea) and south (Ka'u) terms. Whatever way you divvy

up the island, you'll be surprised by how, yet again, this northern slice of the island appears and feels so drastically different from other regions of the island.

The Hamakua stretch of the island has recently been named the "Hilo-Hamakua Heritage Coast" in an effort to draw attention to its historical and cultural significance, and that is what visitors should focus on, since there is not much beach to be had on this coast, as rough cliffs create difficult access to the ocean. Along the 50-mile stretch of Highway 19 from Hilo to Honoka'a, the Big Island grew its sugarcane for 100 years or more. Water was needed for sugar—a ton to produce a pound—and this coast has plenty. Present-day Hamakua is becoming known for its fertile growing land that is ideal for kava, mushrooms, vanilla, and macadamia nuts. Restaurants around the region source their ingredients from Hamakua, so indulge in some culinary delights on your drive around the coast.

With a population of around 2,200, Honoka'a (Rolling Bay) is the major town on the Hamakua Coast. In the past, it was a center for cattle, sugar, and macadamia nut industries. Now it's mainly a tourist town. The main street, Mamane Street, is filled with old false-front wooden buildings built in the 1920s and 1930s by Chinese and Japanese workers who left the sugar plantations to go into business for themselves. From Honoka'a, Highway 19 slips down the long Hamakua Coast to Hilo and Highway 240 heads north for nine miles to the edge of Waipi'o Valley, which you should not miss.

Waipi'o Valley (Curving Water) is the kind of place that is hard to believe unless you see it for yourself. It's vibrantly green, always watered by Waipi'o Stream and lesser streams that spout as waterfalls from the *pali* at the rear and to the side of the valley. The green is offset by a wide band of black-sand beach. From the overlook at the top of Waipi'o, you can make out the overgrown outlines of garden terraces, taro patches, and fishponds in what was Hawaii's largest cultivated valley.

Waimea, also known as Kamuela, is technically in the South Kohala district, but because of its inland topography of high mountain pasture on the broad slope of Mauna Kea, it is vastly different than the long Kohala coastal district. It also has a unique culture inspired by the range-riding *paniolo* (cowboys) of the expansive Parker Ranch. But a visit here isn't one-dimensional. In town are homey accommodations, inspired country dining, and varied shopping opportunities. The town supports arts and crafts in fine galleries and has the island's premier performance venue. There's an abundance of fresh air and wide-open spaces, the latter not so easily found in the islands.

There is old lava along both sides of the road as you approach the broad tableland of the Saddle Road. Much of the lava here is from the mid-1800s, but some is from a more recent 1935 flow. Everyone with a sense of adventure loves this bold cut across the Big Island through a broad high valley separating the two great mountains, Mauna Loa and Mauna Kea. Heading up to the observatories at the top of Mauna Kea, the tallest peak in the Pacific, affords some truly stellar stargazing, while massive Mauna Loa offers one of the most extreme hikes on the island.

This chapter is organized as if you are driving east to west on Highway 19 from Hilo along the Hamakua Coast toward Waimea. If you are coming from the Kona side, follow this chapter in reverse.

ORIENTATION
Hamakua Coast

Officially, the Hamakua Coast begins soon after the four-mile Onomea Scenic Drive out of Hilo and curls around to Waimea, but in reality the entire coastline should be named an official scenic drive. Even people who hate driving love this drive. This is the kind of road that asks for a convertible with a great soundtrack playing from the stereo.

The Hamakua Coast is a good application of appreciating the journey and not necessarily the end point. The entire drive, without stopping, takes only 45 minutes. But you can extend your drive by taking one of the many side roads that

HIGHLIGHTS

LOOK FOR ◖ TO FIND RECOMMENDED SIGHTS, ACTIVITIES, DINING, AND LODGING.

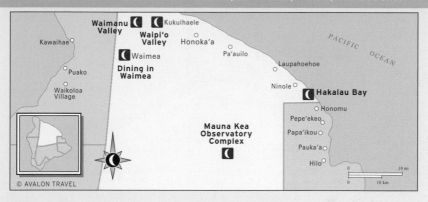

◖ **Waimanu Valley:** The hike down to Waipi'o and over the *pali* to the wild, verdant Waimanu Valley is one of the top treks in Hawaii (page 633).

◖ **Hakalau Bay:** Photographers and history buffs will be eager to visit the plantation-era ruins of Hakalau Mill, destroyed in the tsunami of 1946 (page 639).

◖ **Waipi'o Valley:** Once a burial ground of Hawaiian royalty, this verdant valley is postcard perfect, with one of the best (if not the very best) views on all of the Big Island (page 641).

◖ **Mauna Kea Observatory Complex:** View the heavens from the top of Mauna Kea, where astronomers expect an average of 325 crystal-clear nights per year (page 646).

◖ **Dining in Waimea:** The birthplace of the Hawaii Regional Cuisine movement offers inspired dining in the heart of cowboy country (page 652).

jettison off the main highway. Unfortunately, the majority of these roads end up paralleling the highway and don't go far—mainly through the old housing areas from the plantation days.

If you are inclined to make stops along the way, there are several scenic points that allow you to soak in the magnificent ocean views down below. If you're looking for some longer excursions close to the road, stop at the Laupahoehoe Train Museum to peruse artifacts showcasing the history of the region or visit some actual plantation artifacts at Hakalau Bay. If you really want to get out of the car and into the trees, hike one of the short trails of Kalopa Native Forest State Park, which is filled with native trees and birds, or try ziplining through the canopy of the World Botanical Gardens in Hakalau.

Honoka'a and Waipi'o Valley

Located on Highway 19 just 45 minutes west of Hilo and 20 minutes north of Waimea, Honoka'a is sort of a Hawaiian-style bedroom community. Follow the green sign pointing *makai* from Highway 19 to Mamane Street, the main street passing through the center of town that leads toward Highway 240 and Waipi'o Valley and the meeting points for the majority of organized Waipi'o trips. Mamane Street has a number of shops specializing in locally produced handicrafts, local-style restaurants, clothing and gift shops, and general

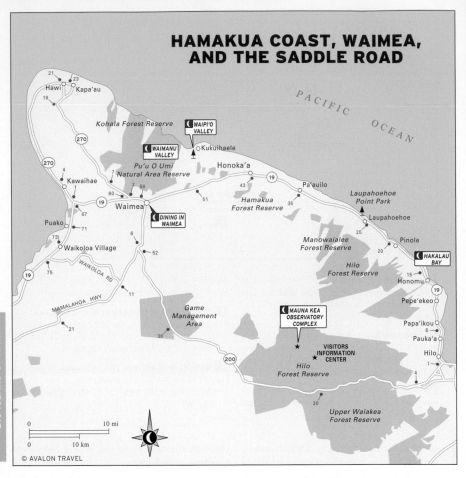

HAMAKUA COAST, WAIMEA, AND THE SADDLE ROAD

PACIFIC OCEAN

Hawi
Kapaʻau
Kohala Forest Reserve
WAIPIʻO VALLEY
WAIMANU VALLEY
Kukuihaele
Puʻu O Umi Natural Area Reserve
Honokaʻa
Kawaihae
Waimea
DINING IN WAIMEA
Paʻauilo
Laupahoehoe Point Park
Hamakua Forest Reserve
Laupahoehoe
Puako
Manowaialee Forest Reserve
Pinole
Waikoloa Village
HAKALAU BAY
WAIKOLOA RD
Hilo Forest Reserve
Homomu
MAMALAHOA HWY
Pepeʻekeo
Game Management Area
MAUNA KEA OBSERVATORY COMPLEX
Papaʻikou
Paukaʻa
VISITORS INFORMATION CENTER
Hilo
Hilo Forest Reserve
Upper Waiakea Forest Reserve

0   10 mi
0   10 km

© AVALON TRAVEL

merchandise stores next to antiques shops. The town also holds a small health center, a post office, two banks, a movie theater, public library, and a nine-hole golf course.

Highway 240 ends a minute outside of Kukuihaele at an overlook, and 900 feet below is Waipiʻo (Curving Water), the island's largest and most southerly valley of the many that carve into the Kohala Mountains. A sacred land for ancient Hawaiians, the valley is a mile across and six miles from the ocean to its back end.

You can spend an hour in the sleepy Honokaʻa town checking out the quaint handicraft boutiques and then stop back again at the end of the day after a visit to Waipiʻo Valley to watch a game at Hamakua Sports Bar—the only sports bar on the Hamakua Coast. And believe me, you'll be ready to relax after traveling by four-wheel-drive, horse, all-terrain vehicle, or your own two legs down the nearly vertical road to Waipiʻo Valley.

Waimea

Parker Ranch, founded early in the 19th century by John Palmer Parker, dominates the heart and soul of the region. Waimea revolves

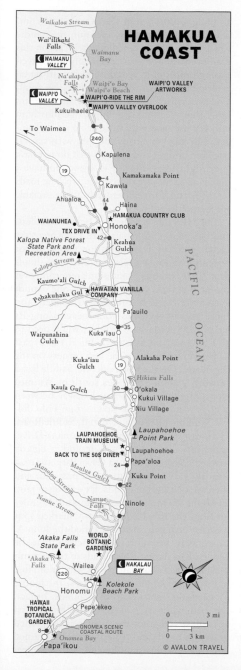

HAMAKUA COAST

Waikaloa Stream
Wai'ilikahi Falls
WAIMANU VALLEY
Waimanu Bay
Na'alapa Falls
Waipi'o Bay
Waipi'o Beach
WAIPI'O VALLEY ARTWORKS
WAIPI'O VALLEY
WAIPI'O-RIDE THE RIM
WAIPI'O VALLEY OVERLOOK
Kukuihaele
To Waimea
240
Kapulena
19
Kamakamaka Point
Kawela
Ahualoa
44 Haina
HAMAKUA COUNTRY CLUB
WAIANUHEA
TEX DRIVE IN
Honoka'a
Kalopa Native Forest State Park and Recreation Area
42 Keahua Gulch
Kalopa Stream
Kaumo'ali Gulch
Pohakuhaku Gul
HAWAIIAN VANILLA COMPANY
Pa'auilo
Waipunahina Gulch
Kuka'iau
35
Kuka'iau Gulch
19 Alakaha Point
Hikiau Falls
Kaula Gulch
30 O'okala
Kukui Village
Niu Village
LAUPAHOEHOE TRAIN MUSEUM
Laupahoehoe Point Park
BACK TO THE 50S DINER
Laupahoehoe
Papa'aloa
24
Kuku Point
Manoloa Stream
Maulua Gulch
22
Nanue Stream
Nanue Falls
Ninole
'Akaka Falls State Park
WORLD BOTANIC GARDENS
'Akaka Falls
Wailea
220
HAKALAU BAY
14
Kolekole Beach Park
Honomu
HAWAII TROPICAL BOTANICAL GARDEN
Pepe'ekeo
8
ONOMEA SCENIC COASTAL ROUTE
Onomea Bay
Papa'ikou

PACIFIC OCEAN

0   3 mi
0   3 km

© AVALON TRAVEL

around ranch life and livestock, with herds of rodeos and "Wild West shows" scheduled throughout the year.

Waimea is also known as **Kamuela,** the Hawaiianized version of Samuel, after one of John Parker's grandsons. Kamuela is used as the post office address, so as not to confuse this town of Waimea with towns of the same name on the islands of O'ahu and Kaua'i.

In the last 30 years, Waimea has experienced real and substantial growth. In 1980 it had no traffic lights and was home to about 2,000 people. Now the population has grown more than threefold, there are three lights along the main highway, and there are occasional traffic jams. Waimea is modernizing and gentrifying, and its cowboy backwoods character is rapidly changing.

The town, at elevation 2,670 feet, is split almost directly down the center—the east side is the wet side, and the west is the dry side. Houses on the east side are easy to find and reasonable to rent, while houses on the dry side are expensive and usually unavailable. You can literally walk from verdant green fields and tall trees to semi-arid landscape in a matter of minutes. This imaginary line also demarcates the local social order: upper-class ranch managers (dry), and working-class *paniolo* (wet).

Waimea is at the crossroads of nearly all the island's roads: Highway 19 from Hilo (via the Hamakua Coast) and Highway 190 from Kailua-Kona. Highway 19 continues west through town, reaching the coast at Kawaihae, where it turns south and cuts along the Kohala Coast, passing by all the resorts on the way to Kailua-Kona. The upper road, Highway 190, connects Waimea to Kailua-Kona and the route looks much more like Marlboro Country than the land of aloha, with grazing cattle amid fields of cactus. On Highway 190 seven miles south of Waimea you'll find the turnoff to the Saddle Road (Highway 200), the road leading up to the Mauna Kea Observatory. This is the only road that travels through the middle of the island, and it's currently in the process of being paved and expanded.

BIG ISLAND OF HAWAI'I

Mauna Kea and the Saddle Road

Slicing across the midriff of the island in a gentle arch from Hilo to the Mamalahoa Highway near Waimea is Highway 200, the Saddle Road. Access to both Mauna Loa and Mauna Kea is possible from the Saddle Road.

Along this stretch of some 55 miles you pass rolling pastureland, broad swaths of lava flows, arid desert-like fields that look a bit like Nevada, a *nene* sanctuary, trailheads for several hiking trails, mist-shrouded rainforests, an explorable cave, and spur roads leading to the tops of Mauna Kea and Mauna Loa. Here as well is the largest military training reserve in the state, with its live firing range, and the Bradshaw Army Airfield. What you won't see is much traffic or many people. It's a great adventure for anyone traveling between Hilo and Kona. Keep your eyes peeled for convoys of tanks and armored personnel carriers as they sometimes sally forth from the Pohakuloa Training Area, and also watch out for those who make this a high-speed shortcut from one side of the island to the other.

The Saddle Road was constructed in 1942 and left as gravel until about 30 years ago. While the road up both sides is at a good incline, the saddle itself is reasonably flat and

Gulches and Traffic Delays

Driving the extremely scenic Highway 19 through the Hamakua Gulch, you'll see several signs for "gulches." A gulch is a deep ravine formed by erosion, sometimes with a stream running through it, and is usually larger than a gully. These gulches are also newly notable because they are the sites of huge traffic delays in the area. The county recently received funds to better secure the cliffs from the problem of rocks coming loose from them and falling onto cars. As construction crews work their way down the coast to place netting onto the cliffs, traffic is reduced to one lane Monday-Friday 10am-3pm. Plan for some extra time if you are in a rush.

at about 6,000-6,500 feet. Car-rental companies cringe when you mention the Saddle Road. Most still do not allow their cars on this road even though it is reasonably well paved through most of its length. Check your rental agreement, as it'll be very specific on this point. They're terrified you'll rattle their cars to death. Only short sections are rough, due mostly to military use, and with little or no solid shoulder. The road is curvy, though, with several one-lane bridges and sections that do not have good sight lines. Plus, it is known to have a higher accident rate than other two-lane roads on the island. Drive defensively at a reasonable speed and do not pass.

The Hilo side is wider, has better shoulders, and has seen more repair than the Kona side. Department of Transportation plans call for widening and new pavement, adequate shoulders, better drainage, and some rerouting over the next several years. However, one cannot escape the fact that this road *is* isolated, and there are no facilities whatsoever along its length. If you do have trouble, you'll need to go a long way for assistance, but if you bypass it, you'll miss some of the best scenery on the Big Island. On the Kona side, the Saddle Road turnoff is about six miles south of Waimea along Highway 190, about halfway between Waimea and Waikoloa Road. From Hilo, follow Waianuenue Avenue inland. Saddle Road, Highway 200, also signed as Kaumana Drive, splits left after about a mile and is clearly marked. Passing Kaumana Caves Park, the road steadily gains elevation as you pass into and then out of a layer of clouds. Expect fog or rain.

About 28 miles out of Hilo and 25 miles up from the Kona side, a clearly marked spur road to the north, officially called the John A. Burns Way, but most often referred to as the Mauna Kea Access Road, leads to the summit of Mauna Kea. You can expect wind, rain, fog, hail, snow, and altitude sickness. Intrigued? Proceed—it's not as bad as it sounds. In fact, the road, while steep, is well paved for the first six miles, and from there the road is graded gravel, banked, and usually well maintained but sometimes like a washboard, with the upper

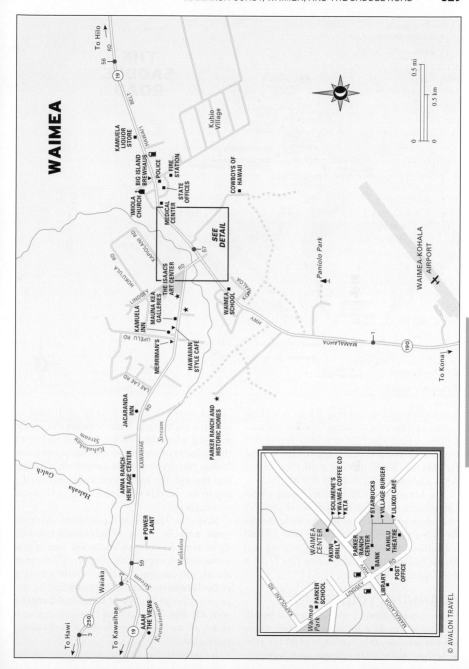

WAIMEA

To Hilo

56 RD.

19

BELT

HAWAI'I

Kubio Village

0.5 mi
0.5 km

KAMUELA LIQUOR STORE

BIG ISLAND BREWHAUS
POLICE
FIRE STATION

'IMIOLA CHURCH
STATE OFFICES

MEDICAL CENTER

COWBOYS OF HAWAII

SEE DETAIL

THE ISAACS ART CENTER

57

Paniolo Park

WAIMEA-KOHALA AIRPORT

MAUNA KEA GALLERIES

KAPI'OLANI RD.

HOKU'ULA RD.

LINDSEY

KAMUELA INN

MERRIMAN'S

HAWAIIAN STYLE CAFÉ

'OPELU RD.

WAIMEA SCHOOL

KOHALA

MAMALAHOA HWY

To Kona

190

JACARANDA INN

LAE LAE RD.

KAWAIHAE RD.

Stream

PARKER RANCH AND HISTORIC HOMES

ANNA RANCH HERITAGE CENTER

Kohākohau Stream

Haleaha Gulch

POWER PLANT

Waikoloa

59

Keanuiomanō

Stream

2

Waiaka

19

250

3

To Hawi

To Kawaihae

AAAH THE VIEWS

BIG ISLAND OF HAWAI'I

SEE DETAIL

KAPI'OLANI RD.

LINDSEY

WAIMEA PARK

PARKER SCHOOL

WAIMEA CENTER

PAKINI GRILL

SOLIMENE'S
WAIMEA COFFEE CO
KTA

STARBUCKS
VILLAGE BURGER
LILIKOI CAFÉ

PARKER RANCH CENTER

BANK

KAHILU THEATRE

LIBRARY

POST OFFICE

RD.

MAMALAHOA

© AVALON TRAVEL

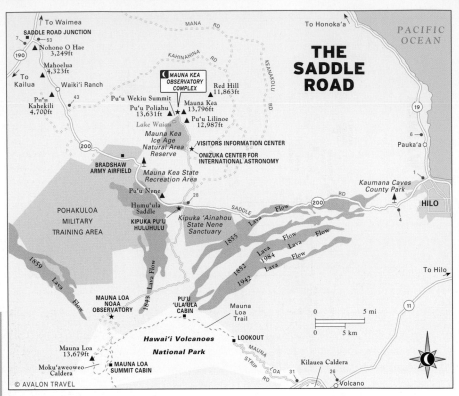

four miles paved so that dust is kept to a minimum to protect the sensitive "eyes" of the telescopes. A four-wheel-drive vehicle is required beyond the visitors center, and if there's snow, the road may not be passable at all. (For current road conditions, call 808/935-6268.)

The Mauna Loa Observatory Road, a one-lane paved road with long stretches of potholes and rough patches, turns south off the Saddle Road between mile markers 27 and 28 and leads about 17 miles in a big zig and zag and gentle incline up to the Mauna Loa NOAA Atmospheric Observatory.

PLANNING YOUR TIME

If you came to Hawai'i not to sit on the beach, but instead to do a lot of sightseeing where it's not too hot, this region is ideal for you. Whether you're starting your trip from the east or west side of the island, you'll want to plan around being in **Waipi'o Valley** during the morning when the weather is better and when the majority of organized trips are set to leave. Unless you're going to do an overnight hiking trip through the valley, you really only need a day to see the valley and trek down it in whatever capacity.

Since the Hamakua Coast drive, without stops, actually is only 45 minutes, it can easily be completed in an afternoon even if you make several stops along the way. If you plan ahead, you can book reservations for a tasting at the **Hawaiian Vanilla Company** and/or trapezing through the **World Botanical Gardens** with **Zip Isle.** No planning is required to stop at any of the scenic overlooks of parks along the highway.

It's unfortunate that there isn't more to see

in Waimea because there is so much good food that you'll want to stay all day. I recommend visiting Waimea as a way to cool off from the hot afternoons of the Kohala Coast or to pick up provisions on your way to Mauna Kea. Stroll through the stores at **Parker Square** or schedule a private tour with arts and crafts projects for the kids at **Anna Ranch Heritage Center** before heading to dinner.

Regardless of how much time you want to spend at the top of **Mauna Kea,** it's important to account for how much time it will take to get there. First there is traveling on the Saddle Road to the observatory access road, which can take about an hour from Waimea, depending on weather. Then, the drive up to the visitors center takes an additional half hour

and an additional 40 minutes to the summit after you've spent time at the visitors center to acclimate to the altitude. If you're driving in the dark, these travel times can be much longer.

The point is, a trip to Mauna Kea is hardly a quick jaunt and especially is not quick if you're traveling on a group tour. Those planning on traveling to the summit to catch the sunset should leave a few hours ahead of time and even earlier if you might hike around the area first. After sunset, most visitors to Mauna Kea reconvene at the visitors center for an hour or two of star and planet gazing. Don't expect to head down before 8pm—it will be hard to walk away from the most awe-inspiring sky you might ever see.

Beaches

It seems as if this region should be a prime beach spot, but it isn't. Although the Hamakua district has some of the most spectacular ocean views of the entire Big Island, there is little access to the water from the soaring cliffs. Waimea is completely landlocked; however, it feels like the beach is so close because you can see it from town!

HONOKA'A AND WAIPI'O VALLEY
Waipi'o Beach
Stretching over a mile, **Waipi'o Beach** (access via Waipi'o Valley Rd.) is the longest black-sand beach on the island. A tall and somewhat tangled stand of trees and bushes fronts this beach, capping the dune. If you hiked the one-hour vertical road to get here you'll likely want to jump in immediately, but be careful: The surf here can be dangerous, and there are many riptides. If there is strong wave action, swimming is not advised. It is, however, a good place for surfing and fishing. There are two sections of the beach, and in order to get to the long expanse of beach

Waipi'o Beach

Your Best Day in the Hamakua Coast, Waimea, and the Saddle Road

© BREE KESSLER

the plantation ruins at Hakalau Bay

- Wake up early to catch the **view of Mauna Kea** from Waimea before the clouds come rolling in.

- Get breakfast at **Hawaiian Style Café** in Waimea.

- Head to **Waipi'o Valley** to join a group tour or venture down into the valley on your own.

- In the afternoon, take a drive east on Highway 19, stopping at **Hakalau Bay** to see some plantation ruins.

- Either head back the way you came or travel through Hilo and back over the **Saddle Road,** grabbing food and drinks for a picnic. Aim to arrive at the **Onizuka Center for International Astronomy** visitors information center on **Mauna Kea** just at sunset.

- Settle in for some **stargazing** that will astound you.

RAINY DAY ALTERNATIVE

At some point during the day, rain or a mist is expected in Waimea –so don't let that throw you off. If it's really raining hard, you have a few options. The good news is, from Waimea you can see if it's raining down below in Kohala. If it's not, travel down the hill 20 minutes to soak up the sun.

If you want to stay in Waimea, visit the **Anna Ranch Heritage Center.** You can spend at least an hour or two touring on your own or with a guide. If you pay for the tour, for a few extra dollars you can get an "enhanced tour" that includes arts and crafts.

If you're on the Hamakua Coast, visit the **Laupahoehoe Train Museum** or the **Hawaiian Vanilla Company**.

across the mouth of the stream, you have to wade across it. It's best to try closer to where it enters the ocean as there are fewer slippery boulders there. To compound matters, waves sometimes wash water up the mouth of the stream. If possible, go at low tide. Note there are no changing areas here. Portable bathrooms are located behind the beach near the parking area.

To get to the beach, you have to get down the gripping Waipiʻo Valley Road first. Whether you walk or drive down, when you get to the bottom turn at the first right instead of continuing straight into the valley and into private property. You'll find the next portion of your walk or drive to be muddy and filled with potholes. This road takes you directly to the beach. If you drove, park your car in the area under the trees, where there will likely be other cars. If you walked, it's often possible to hitch a ride back up with someone driving from the beach.

Hiking

This region is hike central, with many different kinds of hikes, from easy to difficult, with every type of scenery imaginable. Don't trespass on private land. Local residents don't want hikers wandering through their backyards on the way to find some hidden view. There are plenty of on-the-beaten track and underutilized legal hikes in this area that will challenge you for days.

KALOPA NATIVE FOREST STATE PARK AND RECREATION AREA

This spacious natural area is five miles southeast of Honokaʻa, 12 miles north of Laupahoehoe, three miles inland on a well-marked secondary road, and 2,000 feet in elevation. Little used by tourists or residents, **Kalopa Native Forest State Park and Recreation Area** (Kalopa Rd., off Hwy. 19 between mile markers 39 and 40, gate open daily 7am-8pm) is a great place to get away from the coast and up into the hills. Hiking is terrific throughout the park and adjoining forest reserve on a series of nature trails—but the trails are not marked clearly and are difficult to follow. Most of the forest here is endemic, with few alien species. Some of what you will see are ʻohiʻa, koa, the hapuʻu tree fern, and kopiko and pilo, both species of the coffee tree family. Near the entrance and camping area is an **arboretum** of Hawaiian and Polynesian plants. Beyond the arboretum is a 0.75-mile nature loop trail through an ʻohiʻa forest, and a three-mile loop trail takes you along the gulch trail and back to camp via an old road. Next to the area where you park your car there is a board with pamphlets outlining the trails. Unfortunately, the actual trails bear no resemblance to the map; however, someone with some time and know-how might have a great time exploring. Birdlife here may not be as varied as high up the mountainside, but still you can catch sight of ʻelepaio, aukuʻu (a night heron), the white-eye, cardinal, and the Hawaiian hoary bat. The park is best used for day-use picnicking, tent camping, and large furnished cabins (state permit required) that can house up to eight people. For reservations, contact the state park office (75 Aupuni St. #204, Hilo, HI 96721, 808/974-6200).

To get to Kalopa Native Forest State Park, turn *mauka* on Kalopa Road and follow the signs up to the park—it will take about 15 minutes. There is more than one way from the highway to the park, so don't worry if you end up turning *mauka* on a different road.

◖ WAIMANU VALLEY

The hike down to Waipiʻo and over the *pali* to **Waimanu Valley** is considered by many one of the top three treks in Hawaii. You must be fully prepared for camping and in excellent condition to attempt this hike. Also, water from the streams and falls is not good for drinking due to irrigation and cattle grazing topside; hikers should bring purification tablets or boil or filter it to be safe. To get to Waimanu Valley, a

© MARK WASSER

the Waimanu Valley

switchback trail, locally called the Z trail but otherwise known as the **Muliwai Trail,** leads up the 1,200-foot *pali,* starting about 100 yards inland from the west end of Waipi'o Beach. Although not long, this is by far the most difficult section of the trail. Waimanu was bought by the State of Hawaii some years ago, and it is responsible for trail maintenance.

The trail ahead is decent, although it can be muddy, but you go in and out of more than a dozen gulches before reaching Waimanu. In the third gulch, which is quite deep, a narrow cascading waterfall tumbles into a small pool right at trailside, just right for a quick dip or to dangle your feet. Another small pool is found in the fifth gulch. After the ninth gulch is a trail shelter. Finally, below is Waimanu Valley, half the size of Waipi'o but more verdant, and even wilder because it has been uninhabited for a longer time. Cross Waimanu Stream in the shallows where it meets the sea. The trail then continues along the beach and back into the valley about 1.5 miles, along the base of the far side, to Wai'ilikahi Falls, some 300 feet high. For drinking water

(remember to treat it), walk along the west side of the *pali* until you find a likely waterfall. The Muliwai Trail to the Waimanu Valley floor is about 15 miles round-trip from the trailhead at the bottom of the *pali* in Waipi'o Valley, or 18 miles round-trip from Waipi'o Lookout.

Regardless of how long it takes you to complete this hike, it's quite the badge of honor. Some have been known to finish it in 24 hours and others take a few leisurely days at normal hiking speed. To stay overnight in Waimanu Valley, you must have a camping permit available through the Division of Forestry and Wildlife (http://camping.ehawaii.gov); permits are for up to six people ($12 residents, $18 non-Hawaii residents). Before you go, check the news release section of the Division of Forestry and Wildlife website (http://hawaii.gov/dlnr) to make sure that the trail is not closed due to hazardous conditions such as rain and/or mud.

MAUNA KEA

Hiking on **Mauna Kea** means high altitude hiking. Although the height of the mountain

(13,796 feet) is not necessarily a problem, the elevation gain in a short hour or two of getting to the top is. It takes time for the body to acclimatize, and when you drive up from the ocean you rob yourself of the chance to acclimatize easily. What you may expect to experience normally are slight dizziness, a shortness of breath due to reduced oxygen levels, and reduced ability to think clearly and react quickly. Some people are more prone to elevation problems, so if you experience more severe symptoms, get to a lower elevation immediately! These symptoms include prolonged or severe headache, loss of appetite, cramped muscles, prolonged malaise or weakness, dizziness, reduced muscle control and balance, and heart palpitations. Use your head, know your limits, and don't push yourself. Carry plenty of water (more than you would at a lower elevation) and food. Wear a brimmed hat, sunglasses, sunscreen, and lip balm, a long-sleeved shirt and long pants, and sturdy hiking boots or shoes. Carry a jacket, sweater, and gloves, as it can be cold and windy at and near the top. Don't alter the natural environment and stay on established trails.

There are a few good trails on the mountain. About six miles above the Onizuka Center for International Astronomy Visitors Information Center, a dirt track heads off the access road to the west and downhill to a parking lot. From the parking area, it's about one mile farther west, over the saddle between two small cones, to Lake Waiau and its placid waters. This should take less than 30 minutes. On the way, you cross the Mauna Kea Humu'ula Trail, which starts at the third parking lot near the T intersection above and heads down the mountain to the visitors center. Taking the Humu'ula Trail to Lake Waiau should also take about 30 minutes. Continuing on down the Humu'ula Trail a couple of miles brings you past an ancient adze quarry site. Perhaps the most convenient hike is that to the true summit of the mountain. Start from the roadway across from the University of Hawai'i's 2.2-meter telescope, cross over the guardrail, and follow the rough path down into the saddle and steeply up the hill, a distance of less than half a mile.

THE SADDLE ROAD

Besides having the access road to Mauna Kea, the Saddle Road is a great place to explore by foot—especially on your way to Mauna Kea or on your way to/from the Hilo side and the Kona side.

Pu'u O'o Trail

Just after mile marker 24 on the way up from Hilo is the trailhead for **Pu'u O'o Trail.** From the small parking lot along the road, this trail heads to the south about four miles where it meets Powerline Road, a rough four-wheel-drive track, and returns to the Saddle Road. This area is good for bird-watching, and you might have a chance to see the rare 'akiapola'au or 'apapane, and even wild turkeys. This area is frequently shrouded in clouds or fog, and it could rain on you. You may want to walk only partway in and return on the same trail, rather than making the circle.

Kipuka Pu'u Huluhulu

Bird-watchers or nature enthusiasts should turn into the **Kipuka Pu'u Huluhulu** parking lot across the road from the Mauna Kea Access Road turnoff. A *kipuka* is an area that has been surrounded by a lava flow, but never inundated, that preserves an older and established ecosystem. The most recent lava around Pu'u Huluhulu is from 1935. At the parking lot you'll find a hunters' check-in station. From there, a hiking trail leads into this fenced, 38-acre nature preserve. One loop trail runs through the trees around the summit of the hill, and there is a trail that runs down the east side of the hill to a smaller loop and the two exits on Mauna Loa Observatory Road, on its eastern edge. Pu'u Huluhulu means Shaggy Hill, and this diminutive hill is covered in a wide variety of trees and bushes, which include *mamane, naio, 'iliahi* (sandalwood), koa, and 'ohi'a. Some of the birds most often seen are the greenish-yellow 'amakihi, the red 'i'iwi and 'apapane, and the dull brown and smoky-gray 'oma'o. In addition, you may be lucky enough to spot a rare 'io, Hawaiian hawk, or the more numerous *pueo,* a short-eared owl. The entire loop will take you 45 minutes or less, so even if you are not particularly drawn to the birds or the trees, this is a good place to get out of the car, stretch your legs, and get acclimatized to the elevation before you head up to Mauna Kea.

MAUNA LOA

The Saddle Road is the other choice, besides near Hawai'i Volcanoes National Park, for accessing **Mauna Loa** and its trails. The **Mauna Loa Observatory Road** turns south off the Saddle Road and zigs and zags up to the **Mauna Loa NOAA Atmospheric Observatory** at 11,140 feet, which you can see high on the hillside above as you progress along this road. According to the signboard below this small complex, measurements are gathered here for carbon dioxide, carbon monoxide, methane, CFCs, ozone, solar radiation, atmospheric dust, stratospheric aerosols, and temperatures, among other items. Even a two-wheel-drive vehicle could handle this road without problems, but driving it would abrogate your rental car

contract. Use a four-wheel-drive rental vehicle that is approved for this road. Although it could be done faster, give yourself an hour to take in the surroundings, check out the distant sights, and reach the end of the road. Use your vehicle lights, particularly if there are low clouds, and straddle the reflective white line that runs down the center of this single-lane road all the way up to the observatory, pulling over only to let vehicles from the other direction get by. The atmospheric observatory is not open to the public, but you can park in a small parking lot below it at the end of the pavement.

About two miles in from the turnoff is a rock formation at the side of the road that, at a certain angle, looks remarkably like Charles deGaulle, former president of France—and you don't have to use your imagination much at all. As you continue, you get a fine, distant look at the observatories on top of Mauna Kea across the saddle, Pu'u Huluhulu below at the turnoff, and the military reservation beyond to the west. About four miles in, at a turn in the road, there is a gravel road that

© MARK WASSER

The Mauna Loa hike offers rough lava, unpredictable weather, and unparalleled views.

heads over the horizon to the west, an abandoned attempt at a highway shortcut to Kailua-Kona. About eight miles up, at a point where there are a number of telephone and television transmitter towers, the road makes a big zag and heads almost in a straight-line shot, following power poles to the observatory. Notice the different colors of lava that the road crosses and the amount of vegetation on each type. The older brown lava has some grasses and small bushes growing from it, while the newer black lava is almost totally barren. There are large areas of red lava as well, and some of that has been used as road base and paving material. You will see several collapsed lava tubes near the road as you make your way up. Still farther on, areas of ropy *pahoehoe* lava stick up through newer *'a'a* lava. Around mile 15, new pavement has been laid so your ride gets smoother even as the road goes through a series of roller coaster waves as you approach the end of the road. Beyond the end of the pavement, an extremely rough Jeep track continues—best used as a hiking trail. This track zigzags up the mountainside, eventually ending near the crater rim after about seven miles. The **Mauna Loa Observatory Trail** leaves the gravel Jeep track several hundred yards beyond the end of the pavement and heads almost straight up the mountainside, crossing the Jeep trail several times. The Observatory Trail climbs 1,975 feet over 3.8 miles up the volcano's north slope until it reaches the rim of the Moku'aweoweo Caldera summit. From this point, the Mauna Loa summit cabin is 2.1 miles. It takes about 4-6 hours all together to hike from the Observatory trailhead to the Mauna Loa summit cabin. The hike back from the Mauna Loa summit cabin to the Mauna Loa Observatory trailhead is only about three hours, since you're going downhill.

A helpful resource for this hike can be found at www.kinquest.com/misc/travel/trailguide.php. This site provides a guide with a mile-by-mile description of what you'll see while you hike.

The Mauna Loa summit cabin is available to stay in for free but requires a permit from the Kilauea Visitor Center in Hawai'i Volcanoes National Park; you can only get them the day before your hike. The Mauna Loa summit cabin has 12 bunks. Visitors are allowed a three-night maximum stay. Pit toilets are available at the cabin as well as drinking water. Don't forget to treat the water. There's no water available on the trail.

Mauna Loa is at a very high altitude, so wait at least 24 hours between scuba diving and ascending Mauna Loa in order to avoid getting the bends.

Other Recreation

HORSEBACK RIDING

All the available outfitters more or less have the same restrictions for riders: usually no children under 7 (the exact age might vary), and riders above 250 pounds must notify the tour operator prior to the ride of their exact weight. It is also important to be honest with the tour operator about the your ability level, since some operators do not allow beginners on certain tours and others do not want advanced riders.

Views of the Kona and Kohala Coasts are abundant on **Paniolo Adventures** (mile 13.2 Kohala Mountain Rd./Rte. 250, 808/889-5354, www.panioloadventures.com, tours range $69-159 depending on length). Paniolo Adventures has a good reputation for being professional, knowing what they are doing, and enjoying their work. With six different rides ranging from picnic adventures to sunset trots, you'll likely find a ride that suits your skill level and your schedule.

If you're aching to see the actual Parker Ranch this is your chance. **Cowboys of Hawaii** (Pukalani Road Stables behind Parker Ranch Shopping Center, 808/885-5006, www.cowboysofhawaii.com, $79) offers two-hour rides

© MARK WASSER

Go riding at one of Waimea's many ranches.

through parts of ranch, where you'll learn more about the history of the Parker dynasty and how the ranch still functions today. Beginners are welcome.

Dehana Ranch (47-4841 Old Mamalahoa Hwy./Hwy. 19, 808/885-0057, www.dahanaranch.com, daily, $70-130) offers a menu of choices (from 1.5-hour to 2.5-hour rides) and is excellent at meeting the needs of riders. Most rides are through the ranch with lovely faraway views of Waipi'o and Mauna Kea. If you are looking for a longer cowboy experience, they offer a weekend package ($1,195 plus tax) that includes a one-bedroom cottage at their ranch, riding lessons, and participating in a cattle drive!

ZIPLINING

Zipline rides, also known as canopy tours, are booming on the Big Island, with each company competing with the next for the best course. Not all the courses are "certified" or have insurance, and accidents, although rare, have occurred with those who are not.

Inquire about the company's credentials before you go.

The only course that is certified in this area is **Zip Isle** (Hwy. 19 at mile marker 16, *mauka* side, Hakalau, 808/963-5427, www.zip-isle.com, daily 9am-5:30pm, $147, *kama'aina* discounts available), located in the World Botanical Gardens, the state's largest botanical garden. If you have gone ziplining in Costa Rica, this course isn't for you. The thrills are minimal, but the staff is friendly and knowledgeable, making this an ideal course for first-timers and children (minimum weight requirement of 70 pounds although they are lenient on this). Also, the course was constructed in partnership with certified engineers in order to guarantee the utmost safety for zipliners. There are six tours daily and it's a good idea to reserve a week in advance.

GOLF

Golfing on the Big Island can be an adventure in itself due to the hilly and rocky terrain. For instance, carts aren't even allowed on the 15-acre

Paniolo: Hawaiian Cowboys

In 1793 on a visit to the Big Island, Captain George Vancouver gave cattle as a gift to King Kamehameha I, the first on the island. In 1830 King Kamehameha III invited three *vaqueros* from Mexico to Hawaii to teach locals cowboy skills. The story goes that when the Hawaiians asked the new visitors who they were, the Mexican cowboys responded *"Español"* (Spanish). The Hawaiians then pronounced the word es-pañol as *paniolo* and thus were born Hawaiian cowboys known as *paniolo.*

To learn more about the unique history of cowboys in Hawaii visit the **Paniolo Heritage Center** (at Pukalani Stables on Pukalani Rd., Waimea, behind Parker Ranch Shopping Center, 808/854-1541, Tues. and Thurs. 10am-2pm, $5 suggested donation). It's run by the **Paniolo Preservation Society** (www.paniolopreservation.org).

course at the **Hamakua Country Club** (Hwy. 19 between mile markers 42 and 43, 808/775-7244, $15-20) because of how steep it is. The course is small and you play the nine holes twice. Designed in the 1920s by Frank Anderson, the course works on the honor system, with a box for dropping off payment next to the course. The course is usually only open to nonmembers during the weekdays, but call ahead to check.

The Scottish links style course at the **Waimea Country Club** (Hwy. 19 between mile markers 51 and 52, 808/885-3517, www.waimeagolf.com, daily first tee time 7:45am, last tee time 2:45pm, $25-60) is a great alternative to the Kona and Kohala Coast courses due to the lower fees here and the cool temperatures with lush greenery carved from rangeland located at over 2,000 feet in elevation. If you're in the mood for some additional exercise, walk and save nearly half the price for the round of golf. A snack bar with light snacks and drinks is open daily 7:30am-5pm.

Sights

HAMAKUA COAST
◀ Hakalau Bay
There are residents of the Big Island who have never been to see the abandoned plantation remnants in Hakalau Bay, a short detour off the highway. To get here from Highway 19, between mile markers 15 and 16 turn *makai* near the footbridge and follow the street around under the bridge and down toward the ocean and the park. Local kids come here to swim in the stream under the highway bridge (look up and you'll see that this bridge was once a train track and was turned upside down to be used as a road). Even if you're not interested in swimming in the murky water that flows into the ocean, photographers and history buffs will be eager to visit the ruins of Hakalau Mill, destroyed in the tsunami of 1946, which are scattered around the parking lot.

World Botanical Gardens
Touted as the state's largest botanical garden with over 5,000 different species, the **World Botanical Gardens** (Hwy. 19 at mile marker 16, *mauka* side, 808/963-5427, www.wbgi.com, daily 9am-5:30pm, self-guided tours adults $13, teens $6, children 5-12 $3, guided tours adults $33, teens $23, children $13) is really the backdrop of the Zip Isle zipline that makes use of the botanical gardens. The entry fee to the gardens is included with the price of the zipline, and during the zip course itself you'll end up walking around a large portion of the gardens. When you are doing zipping, you

© MARK WASSER

Laupahoehoe Point Park

can walk down to the river on a short trail or drive up to catch a glimpse of their waterfall. If you are planning to just come for the botanical gardens portion, your better bet might be to visit the Hawaii Tropical Botanical Garden in Onomea Bay down the road.

Laupahoehoe Train Museum

Although small in size, the **Laupahoehoe Train Museum** (36-2377 Mamalahoa Hwy./ Hwy. 19 near mile marker 25, 808/962-6300, www.thetrainmuseum.com, Mon.-Fri. 9am-4:30pm, Sat.-Sun. 10am-2pm, adults $4, seniors $3, children $2, families $16) is big on the history of the Hamakua region. Interwoven with the history of the coastal train route, a 34-mile stretch with 21 stops that was destroyed in 1946 by a tsunami, the museum offers abundant archival photos detailing what life on the Big Island looked like in the early 1900s. Next to the museum is a reconstructed train car and tracks. You only need about a half hour here, but it's worth stopping in if you have the time

(it's a nice break when paired with lunch or dessert at the Back to the 50s Diner next door).

Laupahoehoe Point Park

This wave-lashed peninsula is a popular place for weekend family outings. A plaque at water's edge commemorates the tragic loss of 20 schoolchildren and their teacher, who were taken by the great tsunami of 1946. Afterward, the village was moved to the high ground overlooking the point. **Laupahoehoe Point Park** (Laupahoehoe Point Rd. off of Hwy. 19 between mile markers 27 and 28) now occupies the low peninsula; it has nice shaded picnic tables, showers, electricity, and a county camping area. The park can get busy on the weekends with local families cooking out and bringing their ukuleles around to play some tunes. The sea is too rough to swim in, except perhaps by the boat launch ramp, but many anglers come here, along with some daring surfers. The road down to the park is narrow and winding and runs past several rebuilt homes and a restored

Jodo Mission. It will take about 10 minutes to drive down to the park from the highway.

◖ WAIPI'O VALLEY

Waipi'o, which means curved or arched waters, is known to Hawaiians as the Sacred Valley of the Kings. Locals know it as one of the best views on all of the Big Island—the valley really is postcard perfect, with a river running through deep green hills.

The valley itself has been inhabited by Hawaiians for over 1,200 years and is the site of many ancient temples and burial sites. Traditionally, the valley also held importance as a fertile ground for growing taro that is made into poi, a staple of the Hawaiian diet. Today, **Waipi'o Valley** (where Hwy. 240 ends) is home to waterfalls (the two most recognizable ones are Hi'ilawe and Hakalaoa), ancient fishponds close to the front of the valley, and, closer to the shore, sand dunes intermixed with old burial grounds.

Every foodstuff known to the Hawaiians once flourished here; even Waipi'o pigs were said to be bigger than pigs anywhere else. In times of famine, the produce from Waipi'o could sustain the populace of the entire island. On the valley floor and alongside the streams you'll still find avocados, bananas, coconuts, passion fruit, mountain apples, guavas, breadfruit, tapioca, lemons, limes, coffee, grapefruit, and pumpkins. The old fishponds and streams are alive with prawns, wild pigs roam the interior, as do wild horses, and there are abundant fish in the sea. Carrying on the traditions of farmers of old, some farmers in the valley still raise taro, and this has once again become one of the largest taro-producing regions on the island and one of the principal production centers in the state.

Getting There

You can travel down into the valley in nearly every imaginable way: by horse, by ATV, by foot, by car, etc. It really depends on how much time you have to spend there, how much money you want to spend, and your physical ability. For those who just want to

© STEFFEN FOERSTER/123RF.COM

Waipi'o Valley

BIG ISLAND OF HAWAI'I

catch a glimpse and a photo of the valley's glory from above without much effort, there is a lovely, easily accessible scenic overlook in front of the parking area (with restroom facilities).

Spend some time considering which method of visiting Waipi'o meets your needs, depending on how much time you have, how much money, and your physical prowess. The other important factor to consider is whether or not you want to actually go into the valley or simply go around the rim from above. The majority of organized tours meet at stores in Kukuihaele, a small town just a few miles east of Waipi'o. As you drive west on Highway 240 from Honoka'a, when the road forks go toward the right (the sign will point to the right for Kukuihaele), follow the road and you will see the tour storefronts on the *makai* side of the road.

ATV (ALL-TERRAIN VEHICLE)

As you can probably guess, **Ride the Rim** (check in at Waipi'o Valley Artworks, 48-5416 Kukuihaele Rd., Kukuihaele, 808/775-1450, www.ridetherim.com, morning and afternoon tours, $160 per person) offers a three-hour tour around the rim (not the valley) through eucalyptus trees, stopping to swim at a secluded waterfall. Riders must be over 16 years old and weigh between 100 and 350 pounds; however, those who can't drive can ride in an open-air buggy driven by a tour guide. This is a good way for families to tour together even if not everyone wants to get down and dirty with an ATV.

Similarly, **Waipi'o On Horseback** (Hwy. 240 at mile marker 7, *mauka* side, 808/775-9888 www.waipioonhorseback.com, daily 9:30am, 1:30pm, and 4:30pm during summer, $100 plus tax, discount if booked with horseback riding) takes you on a 2.5-hour trip through a working ranch and beside the old Hamakua Ditch, the irrigation system built over 100 years ago during plantation days. There are views of the valley, but you're not actually in the valley itself. Reservations must be made 24 hours in advance.

WAGON

Perhaps the most unexpected way to experience the valley is by mule-drawn wagon. This narrated cultural and historical tour organized by **Waipi'o Valley Wagon Tours** (meet at Last Chance Store, Kukuihaele, 808/775-9518, www.waipiovalleywagontours.com, three tours Mon.-Sat., adults $55, senior $50, children 4-12 $25) allows you to get down into the valley without exhausting yourself. The tour is only 1.5 hours and that is a bit short given the amount of time it takes to actually get down into the valley. It's a good option for people short on time or families who want to travel together.

HIKING

It is possible to walk into the valley on your own. More complicated, however, is to walk the rim, as it is private property and tour companies lease rights to pass through it. Most people only take the journey into the valley as a means to the end—the end being the beach at the end of the road. To begin the vertical trek down into the valley park your car in the lot at the end of Highway 240 or, inevitably, on the street. The road walkers take down to the bottom and onward to the beach is the same paved road the cars use. Bring *plenty* of water and sunscreen for the walk—and a snack (I recommend picking up *malasadas* at Tex's in Honoka'a before you go—you'll thank me for this tip). You'll be sweaty and thirsty by the time you get to the bottom. And don't underestimate the downhill part of the journey—for many it's actually more challenging than the uphill part since it's quite hard on the knees. Give yourself about 45 minutes to get down and an hour to get back to the top. There are no public restrooms in the valley and just the portable potties at the beach, so use the nicer facilities at the Waipi'o Overlook before you head down.

HORSEBACK

Waipi'o Ridge Stables (check in at Waipi'o Valley Artworks, 48-5416 Kukuihaele Rd., Kukuihaele, 808/775-1007, www.

waipioridgestables.com, morning and afternoon 2.5-hour ride $85, five-hour morning ride $165) can accommodate beginners, but it may be nerve-wracking since no training is provided. The horses are on auto-pilot, so there isn't much for you to do but enjoy the views. The important thing to note is that the ride is not through the valley, but through a eucalyptus forest to a great lookout spot. The ride is still nice and relaxing, but it doesn't offer the nonstop outstanding views that a ride through the valley might have. Also, while the wranglers are incredibly friendly and want to make you feel comfortable, they offer minimum background information about the area while you ride.

But if touring the valley is what you want, then your best option is **Na'alapa Stables** (check in at Waipi'o Valley Artworks, 48-5416 Kukuihaele Rd., www.naalapastables.com, Mon.-Sat. 9am and 12:30pm, $68-89). Known for their quality service and excellent guides who share stories of Hawaiian history and culture, this tour books up quickly, so make sure to plan ahead. Riders meet at Waipi'o Valley Artworks and then are transported down into the valley in the ranch's four-wheel vehicle. The road down to the valley is steep, so this trip might not be for the faint of heart. The entire tour is 2.5 hours, but actual horse time is not that long given the amount of time it takes to travel up and down into the valley.

Similarly, **Waipi'o On Horseback** (Hwy. 240 at mile marker 7, *mauka* side, 808/775-9888, www.waipioonhorseback.com, daily 9:30am and 1:30pm, $85 plus tax, discount if booked with ATV tour) is another valley trip that will get you there and near to the waterfalls. The ride through the valley is similar to those of other companies, but the guides do not seem as knowledgeable or as engaged with riders as guides at other companies.

FOUR-WHEEL-DRIVE OR SHUTTLE

The road leading down to Waipi'o is outrageously steep and narrow, averaging a 25 percent gradient! If you attempt it in a regular car,

it'll eat you up and spit out your bones. More than 20 fatalities have occurred since people started driving it, and it has only been paved since the early 1970s. You'll definitely need four-wheel-drive to make it; vehicles headed downhill yield to those coming up.

Not everyone can walk down to the valley on their own or has time or funds to join a tour. But residents of the area have asked me to nicely request that you do not drive down unless it is completely and utterly necessary. Residents have been organizing the last few years to cut off the tourist traffic to the valley as the cars not only create a preventable traffic mess on the road but also inflict environmental havoc on the landscape.

If you do want to be shuttled down to the bottom, the **Waipi'o Valley Shuttle** (808/775-7121, www.waipiovalleytour.com, $45 adults, $20 children under 11, reservations recommended) makes a 90-minute descent and tour of Waipi'o Valley in air-conditioned, four-wheel-drive vans that leave from Waipi'o Valley Artworks in Kukuihaele, at 9am, 11am, 1pm, and 3pm Monday-Saturday. Along the way, you'll be regaled by legends and stories and shown the most prominent sights in the valley by drivers who live in the area. This is the easiest way into the valley, and the guys know what they're doing, as they've been at it since 1970. Sometimes drivers of this shuttle will give hikers a ride down to the valley floor or up the road to the overlook parking lot for a few bucks, if there's room in the vehicle.

WAIMEA
Parker Ranch and Historic Homes
Due to the downturn in the economy, the ubiquitous Parker Ranch organization has reorganized, leading to changes for visitors wanting a glimpse of Parker Ranch life. The ranch's **historic homes** (67-1435 Mamalahoa Hwy./Hawai'i Belt Rd., 808/885-7311, www.parkerranch.com), dating from the 19th century, are no longer open to the public on a regular basis, but the surrounding gardens are still open for visitors to walk around. At least one of the homes is expected to be open for tours in the

Waipi'o: Then and Now

When Captain Cook came to Hawaii, 4,000 natives lived in Waipi'o; a century later only 600 remained. At the turn of the 20th century many Chinese and Japanese moved to Waipi'o and began raising rice and taro. There were schools, stores, a post office, churches, and a strong community spirit. Waipi'o was painstakingly tended. The undergrowth was kept trimmed and you could see clearly from the back of the valley all the way to the sea. In the 1940s, many people were lured away by a changing lifestyle and a desire for modernity. The tsunami in 1946 swept away most of the homes that remained; the majority of the residents pulled up stakes and moved away. For 25 years the valley was abandoned. The Peace Corps considered it a perfect place to build a compound to train volunteers headed for Southeast Asia. This too was later abandoned. Then in the late 1960s and early 1970s a few "back to nature" hippies started trickling in. Most only played Tarzan and Jane for a while and moved on.

Waipi'o is still unpredictable. In a three-week period from late March to early April of 1989, 47 inches of rain drenched the valley. Roads were turned to quagmires, houses washed away, and more people left. Part of the problem is the imported trees in Waipi'o. Until the 1940s, the valley was a manicured garden, but now it's heavily forested. All of the trees you will see are new; the oldest are mangroves and coconuts. The trees are both a boon and a blight. They give shade and fruit, but when there are floods, they fall into the river, creating logjams that increase the flooding dramatically. Waipi'o takes care of itself best when humans do not interfere. Taro farmers, too, have had problems because the irrigation system for their crops was washed away in the last flood.

Nowadays, those who live in the valley learned to accept life in Waipi'o and genuinely love the valley. A few families with real commitment have stayed on and continue to revitalize Waipi'o. The valley now supports perhaps 40 residents. More people live topside but come down to Waipi'o to tend their gardens.

In the summer of 1992, the Bishop Museum requested an environmental impact survey on Waipi'o Valley because the frequency of visitors to the valley had increased tremendously. Old-time residents complained not only about the overuse of the valley but about the loss of their secluded lifestyle. As a result of the impact study, commercial tours are not allowed to go to the beach area on the far side of the stream, which is now open to foot traffic only.

The socio-ethnic battle for the valley continues. Some long-term residents, mostly but not exclusively of Hawaiian descent, have largely withdrawn the spirit of aloha from visitors. Their dissatisfaction is not wholly without basis: Some who have come to the valley have been disrespectful, trespassing on private property, threatening to sue landowners for injuries they themselves caused, or finding themselves stuck in a river that no one in their right mind would try to cross. Many wonderful, open, and loving people still live in the valley. Be respectful and stay on public property. If the sign says *Kapu* (which means "forbidden") or Keep Out, believe it. It is everyone's right to walk along the beach, the switchback that goes to Waimanu, waterways. These are traditional free lands in Hawaii open to all people, and they remain so. With proper behavior from visitors, Waipi'o's aloha will return.

future; call ahead or check the website to see if tours have become available.

If you are really eager to see part of the ranch, you can visit parts of it via a two-hour horseback riding tour organized through **Cowboys of Hawaii** (808/887-1046 or 808/885-5006, www.cowboysofhawaii.com, Mon.-Sat., twice a day, 8:15am and 12:15pm, $79).

The Isaacs Art Center

One of the preeminent galleries on the island is **The Isaacs Art Center** (65-1268 Kawaihae

Rd., 808/885-5864, www.isaacsartcenter.org, Tues.-Sat. 10am-5pm). This art store/museum, part of Hawai'i Preparatory Academy, is worth a stop in. In the next two years they will be expanding into two distinct spaces, but for now the museum and the store are intermixed, and the pieces dating from 19th- and 20th-century Hawaii and Asia are some of the finest (and priciest) on the island. Even if you don't have the means to afford fine art, the center's staff is happy to talk about each piece and give you a little lesson on Hawaiian art.

Anna Ranch Heritage Center

Dedicated to Anna Leialoha Lindsey Perry-Fiske, the "first lady of ranching" in Hawaii, the living history museum at **Anna Ranch Heritage Center** (65-1480 Kawaihae Rd., Hwy. 19 near mile marker 58, 808/885-4426, www.annaranch.org, Tues.-Sat. 10am-4pm, guided tours 10am and 1pm by appointment $10-20, self-guided garden tour free) is a great entrée into what Hawaiian ranch life was like in the early 20th century. The property consists of the original house, a restored blacksmith area, and placards explaining the surrounding views of Waimea. Anna's house is nicely staged with lots of original artifacts, including parts of Anna's extensive hat and clothing collections. Fashion lovers will truly appreciate the collection. If you walk around the house yourself, you might only need about 30 minutes. The guided tour, on the other hand, can run nearly two hours. If you don't think you'll make it to one of the scheduled tours, call ahead to schedule a tour at a convenient time. Also, if you call ahead it is possible to schedule an enhanced tour that includes activities for the kids: a lesson in lassoing, leather crafting, and a blacksmith demonstration.

MAUNA KEA
Onizuka Center for International Astronomy

The entire mountaintop complex, plus almost all of the land area above 12,000 feet, is managed by the University of Hawai'i. Visitors are welcome to tour the observatory complex and stop by the visitors information center at the **Onizuka Center for International Astronomy** (808/961-2180, www.ifa.hawaii.edu/info/vis, daily 9am-10pm) at the 9,300-foot level. Named in honor of astronaut Ellison Onizuka, born and raised on the Big Island, who died in the *Challenger* space shuttle tragedy in 1986, this center is a must-stop for stargazers. Inside are displays of astronomical and cultural subjects, informational handouts, computer links to the observatories on the hill above, and evening videos and slide shows, as well as a small bookstore and gift shop. At times, 11- and 16-inch telescopes are set up outside during the day to view the sun and sunspots; every evening they are there to view the stars and other celestial objects. The visitors center is about one hour from Hilo and Waimea and about two hours from Kailua-Kona. A stop here will allow visitors a chance to acclimate to the thin, high-mountain air—another must. A stay of one hour here is recommended before you head up to the 13,796-foot summit. The visitors center provides the last public restrooms before the summit and is a good place to stock up on water, also unavailable higher up.

Free stargazing is offered nightly 6-10pm, and there's a summit tour every Saturday and Sunday (weather permitting) at 1pm. These programs are free of charge. For either activity, dress warmly. Evening temperatures will be 40-50°F in summer and might be below freezing in winter, and winds of 20 miles per hour are not atypical. For the summit tour, you must provide your own four-wheel-drive transportation from the visitors center to the summit.

Going Up the Mountain

If you plan on continuing up to the summit, you must provide your own transportation and it must be a four-wheel-drive vehicle. People with cardiopulmonary or respiratory problems or with physical infirmities or weakness and women who are pregnant are discouraged from attempting the trip. In addition, those who have been scuba diving should not attempt a trip to the top until at least 24 hours have elapsed. As the observatories are used primarily

telescopes on the summit of Mauna Kea

© MARK WASSER

at night, it is requested that visitors to the top come during daylight hours and leave by a half hour after sunset to minimize the use of headlights and reduce the dust from the road, both factors that might disrupt optimum viewing. It's suggested that on your way down you use flashing warning lights that let you see a good distance ahead of you while keeping bright white lights unused. However, as one security person has stated, safety is their primary concern for drivers, so if you feel you must use your headlights to get yourself down without an accident, by all means do so. Some rental companies have changed their rules regarding taking cars up to the summit and it is not allowed. Others have not wavered. Cars can have a difficult time handling the climb up, so decide for yourself if it is worth making the trip on your own. It is possible to hitch a ride from the visitors center to the summit with a nice passerby, but plan ahead to make sure that you also have a ride back! It would be a long cold walk down in the dark.

Alternatively, make arrangements for a guided tour to the top. These tours usually run seven to eight hours and run $175-200 per person. Tour operators supply the vehicle, guide, food, snacks, and plenty of warm clothing for your trip. They also supply telescopes for your private viewing of the stars near the visitors center after seeing the sunset from the top. From the Kona side, try **Mauna Kea Summit Adventures** (808/322-2366 or 888/322-2366, www.maunakea.com) or **Hawaii Forest and Trail** (808/331-5805 or 800/464-1993, www.hawaii-forest.com). In Hilo, contact **Arnott's Hiking Adventures** (808/969-7097, www.arnottslodge.com, discounts available for hotel guests). Take extra layers of warm clothing and your camera.

◖ MAUNA KEA OBSERVATORY COMPLEX

Atop the mountain is a mushroom grove of astronomical observatories, as incongruously striking as a futuristic earth colony on a remote planet of a distant galaxy. The crystal-clear air and lack of dust and light pollution

Mauna Kea: From Silversword to Snow

a rare silversword plant on Mauna Kea

As you climb Mauna Kea (White Mountain), you pass through the clouds to a barren world devoid of vegetation. The earth is a red, rolling series of volcanic cones. You get an incredible vista of Mauna Loa peeking through the clouds and what seems like the entire island lying at your feet. In the distance the lights of Maui flicker.

Off to your right is **Pu'u Kahinahina,** a small hill whose name means Hill of the Silversword. It's one of the few places on the Big Island where you'll see this rare plant. The mountaintop was at one time federal land, and funds were made available to eradicate feral goats, one of the worst destroyers of the silversword and many other native Hawaiian plants.

Lake Waiau (Swirling Water) lies at 13,020 feet, making it the third-highest lake in the United States. For some reason, ladybugs love this area. This lake is less than two acres in size and quite shallow. Oddly, in an area that has little precipitation and very dry air, this lake never dries up or drains away, fed by a bed of melting permafrost below the surface.

Here and there around the summit are small caves, remnants of ancient quarries where Hawaiians came to dig a special kind of fired rock that is the hardest in all Hawaii. They hauled roughed-out tools down to the lowlands, where they refined them into excellent implements that became coveted trade items. These adze quarries, Lake Waiau, and a large triangular section of the glaciated southern slope of the mountain have been designated **Mauna Kea Ice Age Natural Area Reserve.**

A natural phenomenon is the strange thermal properties manifested by the cinder cones that dot the top of the mountain. Only 10 feet or so under their surface is permafrost that dates back 10,000 years to the Pleistocene epoch. If you drill into the cones for 10-20 feet and put a pipe in, during daylight hours air will be sucked into the pipe. At night, warm air comes out of the pipe with sufficient force to keep a hat levitating.

Mauna Kea was the only spot in the tropical Pacific thought to be glaciated until recent investigation provided evidence that suggests that Haleakala on Maui was also capped by a glacier when it was higher and much older. The entire summit of Mauna Kea was covered in 500 feet of ice. Toward the summit, you may notice piles of rock—these are terminal moraines of these ancient glaciers—or other flat surfaces that are grooved as if scratched by huge fingernails. The snows atop Mauna Kea are unpredictable. Some years it is merely a dusting, while in other years, such as 1982, there was enough snow to ski from late November to late July.

© TOMOKO JONES/123RF.COM

BIG ISLAND OF HAWAI'I

one of the observatories on Mauna Kea

make the **Mauna Kea Observatory Complex** *the* best in the world. At close to 14,000 feet, it is above 40 percent of the earth's atmosphere and 98 percent of its water vapor. Temperatures hover around 40-50°F during the day, and there's only 9-11 inches of precipitation annually, mostly in the form of snow. The astronomers have come to expect an average of 325 crystal-clear nights per year, perfect for observation. The state of Hawaii leases plots at the top of the mountain, upon which various institutions from all over the world have constructed telescopes. Those institutions in turn give the University of Hawai'i up to 15 percent of their viewing time. The university sells the excess viewing time, which supports the entire astronomy program and makes a little money on the side. Those who work at the top must come down every four days because the thin air makes them forgetful and susceptible to making calculation errors. Scientists from around the world book months in advance for a squint through one of these phenomenal telescopes, and institutions from several countries maintain permanent outposts there.

The second telescope that you see on your left is the United Kingdom's **James Clerk Maxwell Telescope** (JCMT), a radio telescope with a primary reflecting surface more than 15 meters in diameter. This unit was operational in 1987. It was dedicated by Britain's Prince Philip, who rode all the way to the summit in a Rolls Royce. The 3.6-meter **Canada-France-Hawaii Telescope** (CFHT), finished in 1979 for $33 million, was the first to spot Halley's Comet in 1983.

A newer eye to the heavens atop Mauna Kea is the double **W. M. Keck Observatory.** Keck I was operational in 1992 and Keck II in 1996. The Keck Foundation, a philanthropic organization from Los Angeles, funded the telescopes to the tune of over $140 million; they are among the world's most high-tech, powerful, and expensive. Operated by the California Association for Research in Astronomy (CARA), a joint project of the University of California and Cal Tech, the telescopes have an aperture of 400 inches and employ entirely new and unique types of technology. The primary reflectors are fashioned from a mosaic of 36 hexagonal mirrors, each only three inches thick and six feet in diameter. These "small" mirrors have been carefully joined together to form one incredibly huge, actively controlled light reflector surface. Each of the mirror segments is capable of being individually positioned to an accuracy of a millionth of an inch; each is computer-controlled to bring the heavenly objects into perfect focus. These titanic eyeballs have already spotted both the most distant known galaxy and the most distant known object in the universe, 12 and 13 billion light years from earth, respectively. The light received from these objects today was emitted not long after the "Big Bang" that created the universe theoretically occurred. In a real sense, scientists are looking back toward the beginning of time!

In addition to these are the following: The **NASA Infrared Telescope Facility** (IRTF), online since 1979, does only infrared viewing with its three-meter mirror. Also with only infrared capabilities, the **United Kingdom Infrared Telescope** (UKIRT), in operation since 1979 as well, searches the sky with its 3.8-meter lens. Directly below it is the **University of Hawai'i 0.6-meter Telescope.** Built in 1968, it was the first on the mountaintop and has the smallest reflective mirror. Completed in 1970, the **University of Hawai'i 2.2-meter Telescope** was a huge improvement over its predecessor but is now the second smallest telescope at the top. The **Caltech Submillimeter Observatory** (CSO) has been looking into the sky since 1987 with its 10.4-meter radio telescope. **Subaru** (Japan National Large Telescope) is a monolithic 8.3-meter mirror capable of both optical and infrared viewing. It is the most recently completed telescope on the mountain, fully operational since 2000. The **Gemini Northern 8.1-meter Telescope,** also with both optical and infrared viewing, is run by a consortium from the United States, United Kingdom, Canada, Chile, Argentina, and Brazil. Its southern twin is located on a mountaintop in Chile, and together they have been viewing the heavens since 1999. Situated to the side and below the rest is the **Submillimeter Array,** a series of eight six-meter-wide antennae. About two miles distant from the top is the **Very Long Baseline Array,** a 25-meter-wide, centimeter wavelength radio dish that is one in a series of similar antennae that dot the 5,000-mile stretch between Hawaii and the Virgin Islands.

Currently, while the state is considering expansion of the complex to include additional telescopes and support facilities, a number of groups, including The Hawaiian-Environmental Alliance, are calling upon the state to proceed in a culturally and environmentally friendly manner or to not proceed at all. This is a highly contested issue on the island.

VISITING THE TELESCOPES

At present, only the **Subaru Telescope** (www. naoj.org) allows visitors on organized tours, and you *must* reserve at least one week ahead of time. These free, 40-minute tours are given at 10:30am, 11:30am, and 1:30pm only on weekdays that they are offered. Tours are run in English and Japanese, with the first and last tours of the day usually in English. The tour schedule is posted two months in advance on the telescope website. Transportation to the telescope is the visitor's responsibility. This tour is a brief introduction to the telescope itself and the work being performed. There is no opportunity to actually view anything through the telescope. All safety precautions pertaining to visiting the summit also apply to visiting this telescope for the tour.

While the Keck telescopes do not offer tours, the visitors gallery at the telescope base is open weekdays 10am-4:30pm for a 12-minute video, information about the work being done, and a "partial view of the Keck I telescope and dome." Two public restrooms are also available to visitors. The same information and video are available in the lobby at the Keck headquarters in Waimea.

ALONG THE SADDLE ROAD
Pohakuloa

The broad, relatively flat saddle between Mauna Kea and Mauna Loa is an area known as **Pohakuloa** (Long Stone). At an elevation of roughly 6,500 feet, this plain alternates between lava flow, grassland, and semi-arid desert pockmarked with cinder cones. About seven miles west of the Mauna Kea Access Road, at a sharp bend in the road, you'll find a cluster of cabins that belong to the Mauna Kea State Recreation Area. This is a decent place to stop for a picnic and potty break. No camping is allowed, but housekeeping cabins that sleep up to six can be rented (permits are required). Nearby is a game management area, so expect hunting and shooting of wild pigs, sheep, and birds in season. A few minutes west is the Pohakuloa Training Area, where maneuvers and bomb practice can sometimes disturb the peace in this high mountain area. If the military is on maneuvers while you're passing through, be attentive to vehicles on or crossing the road.

Shopping

HONOKA'A AND WAIPI'O VALLEY

Honoka'a isn't a shopping destination, but the town is so cute that you'll probably want to get out and walk around to make the most of it. It looks like there are quite a few shops on the main street, Mamane Street; however, many of them seem to never be open. What shops tend to be left standing are congregated on the eastern and *makai* side of Mamane Street. There are a few antiques and collectible stores that include Hawaiiana items like old aloha shorts, airline posters from the 1960s, and glass bottles from the old plantation bottle works. Also, a few souvenir shops have Hawaiian prints, quilts, and local cookbooks.

WAIMEA

There are three main shopping areas in Waimea, each a little bit different from the next. The Parker Ranch Center and Waimea Center are strip malls, although the Parker Ranch Center is the more upscale of the two. Parker Square also houses shops in an open air setting, but in a more historical-looking building with several galleries worth browsing through.

Parker Ranch Center

The long-established **Parker Ranch Center** (67-1185 Mamalahoa Hwy./Hwy. 19, www. parkerranchcenterads.com) was totally rebuilt in 2002, completely changing the face of the center of town. With more of a country look, the mall now has more store space than it originally held and many new upscale vendors. Anchoring the center is the Foodland grocery store with a Starbucks next door. There is a food court in the center of the complex and many fast-food joints. The **Parker Ranch Store** (808/885-5669), in its prominent spot up front, focuses on its country cowboy heritage; the shop sells boots, cowboy hats, shirts, skirts, and buckles and bows, and many handcrafted items are made on the premises. Filling in some of the shops surrounding the Parker Ranch Store are midrange clothing stores selling items like jeans and surf wear. If you need to get a few extra layers of clothing before heading up to Mauna Kea, this shopping area is a good place to stop to grab a sweatshirt and/or socks with cowboys on them.

Waimea Center

Across the street from the Parker Ranch Center and behind McDonald's is the **Waimea Center.** Most Waimea Center stores are open 9am-5pm weekdays and 10am-5pm Saturday. Among its shops you will find a **KTA Super Store,** with everything from groceries to pharmaceuticals; a number of eateries, including **Solimene's** with coffees, teas, and Italian fare; as well as a few lower end gift shops.

Parker Square

Located along Hwy. 19, heading west from town center, **Parker Square** has a collection of fine boutiques and shops, as well as the Waimea Coffee Company shop. Here, like an old trunk filled with family heirlooms, the **Gallery of Great Things** (808/885-7706, www.galleryofgreatthingshawaii.com) really is loaded with great things. Inside you'll find novelty items like a carousel horse, silk dresses, straw hats, koa paddles, Japanese woodblock prints, and less expensive items like shell earrings and koa hair sticks. The Gallery of Great Things represents about 200 local artists on a revolving basis, and the owner, Maria Brick, travels throughout the Pacific and Asia collecting art, some contemporary, some primitive. With its museum-quality items, the Gallery of Great Things is definitely worth a careful browse.

Also in the complex is the **Waimea General Store** (808/885-4479, Mon.-Sat. 9am-5:30pm, Sun. 10am-4pm), which sells mostly high-end sundries with plenty of stationery, kitchen items, children's games, stuffed toys, books on Hawaiiana, and gadgets—overall, lots of neat and nifty gifts. At the end of the complex is the similarly themed **Bentley's Home and Garden Collection** (808/885-5565), stacked filled with kitchenware, Hawaii-themed cookbooks, and locally made soaps.

Entertainment

This region, luckily, attracts musicians, dancers, and performers (and some fairly big names) to its venues big and small. In Honoka'a, the **Honoka'a People's Theater** (43 Mamane St., 808/775-0000, http://honokaapeople.com) doubles as an art movie theater (tickets $6 adults, $4 seniors, $3 children) and a live music venue. Built in the 1930s by the Tanimoto family who built several of the other historical theaters on the Big Island, it was and remains the largest theater on the island, with seating capacity of 525 people. In its heyday, it must have been a sight, as plantation workers would pack the building to watch the newest Hollywood films. With the closing of the plantation industry, the theater went into disrepair and closed for a few years. When the theater reopened in the late 1990s, it once again truly became a centerpiece of the community—used by community groups in need of space. Check the schedule online for event listings. A few times a month there are live performances with local musicians as well as semi-popular Mainland groups traveling through the area.

Also in Honoka'a, even if it sounds counterintuitive, check out the **Hamakua Sports Bar** (45-3490 Mamane St., 808/775-1444) on Friday and/or Saturday night at 7pm for live music. They also have karaoke and open mic events at varying times during the week.

For some live music and dancing to accompany dinner, the **Back to the 50s Diner** (Hwy. 19, *mauka* side, Laupahoehoe, 808/962-0808) has cowboy and swing music on Friday and Saturday nights. It gets jam-packed with locals looking for a night out, so get there early to save your spot.

In Waimea, theatergoers will be impressed by the newish (from 1981) structure built by Richard Smart, heir to the Parker ranch, that now houses his private collection of Broadway memorabilia. The **Kahilu Theatre** (67-1186 Lindsey Rd., Parker Ranch Shopping Center, www.kahilutheatre.org, 808/885-6868) attracts first-rate local and Mainland performers, like the Martha Graham dance company, internationally known jazz musicians, and master ukulele players. Best of all, tickets are reasonably priced and at times even free for the community events. In addition to the usual season schedule, the theater also hosts community performances, such as the Hawaii youth symphony and sometimes the **Waimea Community Theater** (65-1224 Lindsey Rd., Parker School Theater, 808/885-5818, www.waimeacommunitytheatre.org), which has been performing plays and musicals on the Big Island since 1964.

For less formal entertainment, your best bet in Waimea is the **Big Island Brewhaus** (Hwy. 19 between mile markers 56 and 57 at intersection of Kamamiu St., 808/887-1717, http://bigislandbrewhaus.com) at their Tuesday and Thursday open mic nights or Friday night for live music—usually a local rock band. The crowd is usually on the younger side and the venue is small, so expect to feel a little claustrophobic.

For a more mature crowd in a larger space, the **Pakini Grill** (65-1144 Mamalahoa Hwy./Hwy. 19, 808/885-3333) on Thursday, Friday, and Saturday nights has local bands playing anything from slack key to bluegrass. This is more of a *paniolo* crowd, but they are welcoming here and you won't feel out of place here if you are from out of town.

Food

HAMAKUA COAST

The food choices on the coast are far and few between. The only real choice is the **Back to the 50s Diner** (Hwy. 19, *mauka* side, Laupahoehoe, 808/962-0808, Wed.-Thurs. 8am-7pm, Fri. 8am-8pm, Sun. 8am-3pm, $12), awesome for both its food quality and its kitsch. It really feels like the 1950s in there, the result of a community effort donating personal paraphernalia from the era. On Friday and Saturday nights there is live music, cowboy and swing. The menu is extensive and reasonably priced with burgers and local favorites like chicken and pork prepared Hawaiian style. Vegetarian and gluten-free options are possible. Try their salad or anything they offer with Hamakua mushrooms. You'll be thinking about them for days later.

HONOKA'A AND WAIPI'O VALLEY

Don't have your heart set on eating somewhere specific in Honoka'a. Although hours are posted for restaurants, they frequently change. Waimea is only about 15 minutes away and offers many top-notch dining options, so it might be worth the extra few minutes in the car rather than eating in Honoka'a.

It's hard not to stop daily at **(Tex Drive In** (Hwy. 19 at the corner of Pakalana St., 808/775-0598, daily 6am-8pm, dinners $9), a Big Island institution—and rightfully so. The long-established Hamakua restaurant is known for its fresh *malasadas:* sugared Portuguese pastries filled with passion fruit cream, chocolate, or strawberry. Best of all, you can watch the production process showcased behind plate glass windows inside. Get there before 7pm before they sell out. Tex has a fast-food look, a drive-up window, walk-up counter, and inside and outside tables, as well as a cavernous dining room in the back. Besides the *malasadas*, they serve *ono kine* local food, specializing in *kalua* pork, teriyaki chicken and beef, hamburgers, and fresh fish.

In Honoka'a town, you'll find **Cafe Il Mondo** (Mamane St. at the corner of Lehua St., 808/775-7711, www.cafeilmondo.com, Mon.-Sat. 11am-8pm, $12 small pizzas and calzones, cash only), an Italian pizzeria and coffee bar that's the best Honoka'a has to offer. But that doesn't say much. This is a cheery place with Italian music on the sound system and Hawaiian prints on the walls. Here you feel the spirit of Italy. While handmade pizzas with toppings, mostly $12-13, are the main focus, you can also get tasty calzones, pasta dishes, sandwiches, and salads for under $10, as well as ice cream and gourmet coffee. Medium and large pizzas aren't served in-house and are only available to go. When having dinner, it's okay to bring your own bottle of wine.

Peek in for a quick to-go treat at the **Hamakua Fudge Shop** (45-3611 Mamane St. #105, 808/775-1430, www.hamakuafudge.com, Mon.-Sat. 10:30am-4pm) to bring with you on your Waipi'o adventure, or stay in for some ice cream in their small attached café. There are over 25 flavors, all made in-house. "Made with real butter and cream" is their motto, and it sure tastes like it.

The only sports bar in the Hamakua region, the **Hamakua Sports Bar** (45-3490 Mamane St., 808/775-1444, Sun.-Thurs. 3-10pm, Fri.-Sat. 3pm-midnight) looks more like an old cowboy bar. What makes it a sports bar is the large TV playing sporting events. As of now, the owners serve up the standard cheap beers on draft as well as some from the Kona Brewing Company, but they hope one day soon to serve their own homebrew. Don't come here hungry, as they only have bar appetizers available.

(WAIMEA

It's almost guaranteed that eating in Waimea will lead you to exclaim, "that was the best steak of my life!" The beef doesn't get more local than this and has the reputation of being grass fed with ocean views. Waimea also is home to several longstanding upscale restaurants. Entries are listed from north to south and then east to west on Highway 19.

You'd think there would be more barbecue in Waimea given its country feel, but **Huli Sue's** (64-957 Mamalaho Hwy./Hwy. 19 across from mile marker 56, 808/885-6286, www.hulisues. com, Mon.-Sat. 11:30am-8pm, $10-29) is the only game in town. The restaurant is charming with its picnic tables, serving ware, and furniture resembling something from a down-home barbecue joint of North Carolina. The sampler plate is more than enough for two people and comes with brisket, local ribeye, pork, and chicken. The platter comes with sides like slaw, fries, corn pudding, and bok choy. There are also burgers, hot dogs, and fish tacos on the menu, but I'd stick to the barbecue options. You can guarantee that the beef came from down the road, and the various sauces have good flavor.

Nearly across the street is the restaurant formally known as Tako Taco, now called **Big Island Brewhaus** (Hwy. 19 between mile markers 56 and 57 at intersection of Kamamiu St., 808/887-1717, http://bigislandbrewhaus. com, Mon.-Sat. 11am-8:30pm, Sun. noon-8:30pm, $10). It's the highest brewery in Hawaii at 2,812 feet. The restaurant is decorated from the point of view of someone who wanted it to look straight out of Mexico—it's sort of Mexican kitsch meets Hawaii. The food isn't so *authentico* Mexican, but it's priced right and overall hits the spot. There are the standard dishes like burritos, tortilla soup, enchiladas, and tacos. Vegans and gluten-free eaters rejoice with the substantial options available. What isn't so splendid here is the service. In fact, at times it's so terrible it can be downright frustrating. Arguably, now that they have their homebrews on tap, it makes the wait more bearable—but oftentimes it doesn't make any sense why you have to wait 45 minutes for a taco. Don't come hungry or in a rush. Tuesdays and Thursdays are open mic night and Friday there is live music.

Pakini Grill (65-1144 Mamalahoa Hwy./ Hwy. 19, 808/885-3333, Mon., Tues., Thurs. 11am-10pm, Wed., Fri., Sat. 11am-midnight, Sun. 11am-9pm, drinks happy hour daily 3pm-6pm, food happy hour Sun., Wed., Fri. 3pm-6pm, $10-20) is a local-style restaurant, with good values and quick service. The happy hour offers excellent appetizer choices, such as smoked pork and a and marinated *tinono* pork. On Thursday, Friday, and Saturday, there is live entertainment, ranging from slack-key guitar to bluegrass. On Sunday, this is the place to watch sporting events at the bar. A kids' menu is available.

The cool temperatures in Waimea afford lots of coffee shops in the area. For a local coffee shop, you'll find **Solimene's** (65-1158 Mamalahoa Hwy./Hwy. 19, 808/887-1313, Mon.-Sat. 11am-3pm and 5pm-9pm, Sun. 7am-noon, $15). A café and restaurant duo, Solimene's is another unassuming restaurant located in a strip mall. The café serves excellent coffee and tea in dozens of varieties, and the Italian restaurant next door offers 20 different combinations of pizzas, pastas, fresh salads with mozzarella, vegetarian options, and daily specials. Sunday mornings are a jam-packed treat with made-to-order omelets and waffles topped off with a mimosa and bloody mary station.

There is some hard competition in the area, yet **Lilikoi Café** (67-1185 Mamalahoa Hwy./ Hwy. 19, Parker Ranch Shopping Center, 808/887-1400, Mon.-Sat. 7:30am-4pm, breakfast $7, lunch $9) still fares well. The atmosphere along with the menu is simple: sandwiches, fresh salads that come as a combo with a choice of deli meat, and crepes for vegetarians. The breakfast choices of granola, burritos, and crepes are ideal for those looking to eat a wholesome and nourishing meal that doesn't include Spam, as many breakfast options do on the island.

Also in the Parker Ranch Shopping Center is literally one of the best burgers you will ever have (and so agrees *USA Today,* in its list of 50 burgers you must have before you die). **Village Burger** (67-1185 Mamalahoa Hwy./19, Parker

Ranch Center Food Court, 808/885-7319, www.villageburgerwaimea.com, Mon.-Sat. 10am-8pm, Sun. 10:30am-6pm, $8-12) is a true farm-to-table establishment with nearly every ingredient sourced from a nearby farm. The veal burger is spectacular and can be served on a beautiful bed of lettuce for those who don't want the bun. The taro burger is an excellent vegan option—a well-thought-out conglomeration of garden vegetables. Try the *mamake* ice tea: a blend of a local leaf, mint, and tarragon. The restaurant is located in the food court with no ambiance and little seating. So grab it go—although you'll probably finish your burger by the time you walk to your car.

On weekends be prepared to wait as visitors line up around the corner patiently anticipating the scrumptious breakfast at **C Hawaiian Style Café** (65-1290 Kawaihae Rd./Hwy. 19 between mile markers 57 and 58, 808/885-4295, Mon.-Sat. 7am-1:30pm, Sun. 7am-noon, breakfast $8, plate lunch $9-17). It's not healthy food, it's comfort food served by a friendly staff. Be prepared to make new friends as the semi-communal counter area invokes conversation with fellow eaters. Try the *kalua* hash with eggs. It's the kind of food that's so good that you just keep eating it, even though you're full. Other local favorites are on the menu, like several varieties of *loco moco*.

Waimea Coffee Company (65-1279 Kawaihae Rd./Hwy. 19, 808/885-8915, www.waimeacoffeecompany.com, Mon.-Fri. 6:30am-5:30pm, Sat. 8am-4pm, Sun. 9am-3pm, lunch $8) has a college town coffee shop atmosphere: the kind of place where you can grab a coffee, bagels and lox, soup or sandwich, and enjoy a book outside in the brisk Waimea air.

As one of the original homes of Hawaii Regional Cuisine, **Merriman's** (65-1227 Opelo Rd., 808/885-6822, http://merriman-shawaii.com, Mon.-Fri. 11:30am-1:30pm, daily 5:30-9pm, reservation recommended, lunch $11-15, dinner $25-38) has a lot of street cred—and that's without adding the fact that its owner, Peter Merriman, is a James Beard Finalist. In theory, it's fairly amazing that Merriman's started doing local foods decades before it was trendy, but in practice the restaurant is perhaps a bit overrated now that everyone is going local. The dining experience is superb, with well-trained waitstaff and white linen tablecloths. It's a good place to go if you are looking for fine dining. The menu changes, but offers the usual Hawaiian dishes of mahimahi or ahi, spicy soups, and local vegetables. Perhaps go for lunch instead of dinner. The lunch menu is similar to the dinner menu, but less expensive.

Getting There and Around

BUS

All roads lead through Waimea—or at least many of them do since it's a bus hub for the **Hele-On Bus** (www.heleonbus.org, 808/961-8744, $1 per ride, $1 each for luggage, large backpacks, bikes) traveling between the east and west sides of the island.

The Hilo to Honoka'a route has eight daily trips, with five additional buses during weekdays, and makes all intermediate stops, taking about an hour. In Hilo you can get the bus at the Mooheau Bus Terminal on Bayfront (and twice daily it makes additional stops throughout Hilo). In Honoka'a, buses begin pickup at Blane's Drive-in on Mamane Street, the main street in town.

With seven daily trips and three additional weekday buses, it couldn't be any easier to travel the two hours (sometimes less) between Waimea and Hilo. Buses pick up/drop off passengers at the back of the Parker Ranch Center and make all intermediate stops on the Hamakua Coast ending at the Mooheau Bus Terminal on Bayfront (and twice daily it makes additional stops throughout Hilo).

The buses traveling from Kona to Hilo

make two daily morning stops and one afternoon stop at the back parking lot of the Parker Ranch Center. Those traveling on to Hilo take the Hamakua Coast route, making all intermediate stops and arriving about two hours later to Hilo. Buses traveling to Kona take the lower road, passing by all the Kohala resorts and traveling as far as Captain Cook and Honaunau in the afternoon. The entire route takes about two hours.

SHUTTLE

The **Waimea Shuttle** makes hourly trips 6:30am-4:30pm around Waimea from the west side to east side of Highway 19. When the bus was free, locals utilized this service for quick shopping trips, but it likely won't be too crowded now that you must pay $1 just to go a few minutes. For more information, check www.heleonbus.org.

WHERE TO STAY ON THE BIG ISLAND

Kona

The majority of Kona's accommodations lie along the six miles of Ali'i Drive from Kailua-Kona to Keauhou. Most hotels and condos fall in the moderate to expensive range. A few inexpensive hotels are scattered here and there along Ali'i Drive. If you're looking to branch out from Ali'i Drive, the town of Holualoa is an excellent alternative located only 20 minutes away from Kailua on the mountain above.

HOSTELS
Under $50
The least expensive place to stay in the area is **Pineapple Park** (81-6363 Mamalahoa Hwy., Kealakekua 808/323-2224 or 877/800-3800, www.pineapple-park.com, $25-85). This clean and commodious hostel accommodation is in a converted plantation-era house along the main highway. The dorm rooms are located in the converted walk-out basement, which also has a TV lounge and free WiFi access. Private rooms are also available, both with shared bath and private bath. Discounts are available for longer stays. All guests share baths, have use of laundry facilities and a large kitchen, and can rent kayaks and snorkel gear on-site for minimal fees. If you don't have a car, you'll need to be a real whiz on the bus to get around since

the hostel isn't that close to town (although it's right off the highway). Guests are friendly with one another (inspired by the hostel—not hostile—atmosphere), but rumor has it that management can be rude.

BED-AND-BREAKFASTS AND INNS
$100-150
As a working coffee farm, **Mango Sunset** (73-4261 Mamalahoa Hwy./Hwy. 190, Kailua-Kona, 808/325-0909, www.mangosunset.com, $100-120) is definitely not for everyone. It's up the road from the airport, so it's convenient for an early-morning or late-night flight, and has excellent views of Kona below. Hans, the owner and grower, can provide an extensive history of the coffee industry. It has the feel of a hostel: The rooms are simple (all but one have private bathrooms) and without TV (there is a shared one in a small common area). The rooms are wheelchair-accessible. Laundry is available for $5 a load and WiFi is free. Hot breakfast utilizes mainly ingredients from the farm. The walls are paper thin, so it's not a great place for someone who is a light sleeper.

Navigating the nearly vertical road up to **Lilikoi Inn** (75-5339C, Mamalahoa Hwy., Holualoa, 808/333-5539, www.lilikoiinn. com, $110-135) quickly alerts you that you're not arriving to a run-of-the-mill place. The house is surrounded by lush greenery (papaya and banana trees as well as some coffee), and the views from the lanai are spectacular. You can see nearly all of Kailua as well as the ocean below—the view as you eat breakfast on the lanai. Owners Shai and Trina are friendly and talkative, so it feels like you're staying at your friend's house with a private entrance. The two upstairs rooms are smaller and less expensive. The downstairs rooms with queen-size sleigh beds—the Green Papaya and Plumeria rooms—are separated by a lounge area in the middle and can be rented out as one large space to accommodate a family. Food is where the Lilikoi Inn excels; Shai is a trained chef who once owned a restaurant in the San Francisco Bay Area and creates gourmet dishes using local

ingredients. A separate kitchen is available for guest use. Additional amenities include cable television, a DVD player, WiFi, and a hot tub that will make you feel like you're in the rainforest. It's cooler in Holualoa than in Kailua. A separate kitchen is available for guest use.

Once considered one of the best on the island, **Areca Palms Estate Bed and Breakfast** (Hwy. 11, Captain Cook, 808/323-2276, www. konabedandbreakfast.com, $115-145), near Kealakekua Bay, is a bit old school: The clientele tends to be on the older side, and they have no online reservation or availability system. All reservations are by phone or email. Innkeepers Janice and Steve Glass work hard to stay competitive against the newer options. The house is always perfumed by freshly cut flowers, and Hawaiian music plays in the background to set the mood. Rooms are on the small side and decorated with Hawaiiana such as floral design quilts. Cable and WiFi are available in each room. The outdoor hot tub deck is set in a broad manicured lawn surrounded by tropical flowers. Rates include a sumptuous breakfast feast; a two-night minimum stay is required.

$150-250
Owners Kona Dave and Wendi once worked with rock stars; now they want all their guests to feel like rock stars. Their love, attention, and utter dedication to ensuring that guests at **Honu Kai** (74-1529 Hao Kuni St., Kailua-Kona, 808/329-8676, www.honukai.com, $160-195) have the best (and most Zen-like) experience at their home and on the Big Island makes this property attractive. Before guests even get here, Wendi emails them a questionnaire so that she can begin preparing for their arrival. Guest rooms are pleasant with Hawaiian decor, large beds, and a small bathroom. One of the rooms has wheelchair accessibility. Amenities include access to a private beach at the Mauna Lani in Kohala, free use of beach gear, laundry facilities, a cooking area, cable television, and WiFi. A two-night minimum is required and no children are allowed. Wendi and Kona Dave are in the know (e.g., they can call ahead get a restaurant reservation even when one might

not be available). The location is in a residential neighborhood just 10 minutes north of Ali'i Drive and 20 minutes from the airport—ideal for those who want to be close to the action but not right in it.

A perfect place for honeymooners and large families alike, beautiful (**Hawaiian Oasis Bed and Breakfast** (74-4958 Kiwi St., Kailua-Kona, 808/937-6453, www.hawaiianoasis.com, $195-305 per room or $1,000 for entire house)

Where to Stay in Kona

Name	Type	Price
Areca Palms Estate Bed and Breakfast	B&B	$115-145
Aston Kona by the Sea	condo	$180-300
Casa de Emdeko	condo	$100-135
Courtyard King Kamehameha's Kona Beach Hotel	hotel	$140
Dragonfly Ranch	B&B	$100-250
Four Seasons Resort, Hualalai at Historic Ka'upulehu	resort	$220-600
Hale Kona Kai	condo	$150-195
(Hawaiian Oasis Bed and Breakfast	B&B	$195-305
(Holualoa Inn	B&B	$295-405
Holua Resort at Mauna Loa Village	condo	$150-250
Honu Kai	B&B	$160-195
Hotel Manago	hotel	$36-78
Kona Bali Kai	condo	$100-300
Kona Seaside Hotel	hotel	$69-125
Lilikoi Inn	B&B	$110-135
(Luana Inn	B&B	$155-205
Mango Sunset	B&B	$100-120
Outrigger Keauhou Beach Resort	resort	$170-450
Pineapple Park	hostel	$25-85
(Sheraton Keauhou Bay Resort and Spa	resort	$125-450
Silver Oaks Ranch	vacation rental	$125-200

has Hawaii-meets-India decor that makes it feel dreamy and exotic—especially the Aloha Room and the Waterfall Suite. This is the kind of house—with the view—that you wish you owned. It has it all: poolside outdoor kitchen, hot tub, and tennis courts. Guests have the entire house to themselves, as it is solely a guest residence. In fact, oftentimes the house is rented as a single unit for large families or parties. Amenities include free laundry, common

Features	Why Stay Here?	Best Fit For
immaculate rooms	near Kealakekua Bay	first-timers to Hawaii, an older crowd
sofa beds, kitchen, laundry, pool, hot tub, barbecue	location	families, couples
pools, barbecue, beach equipment	affordable	families, couples
pool, luau	downtown location	families
unique decor, wholesome breakfast	close to snorkeling	new age free thinkers
pools, spa, day-care	truly exclusive, quality service	luxury lovers, families
kitchen, sofa bed, lanai, pool, barbecue, Wi-Fi	downtown location	couples, families
pool, tennis courts, outdoor kitchen	downtown location	couples, large families
pool, kitchen, breakfast	views, service, quiet	honeymooners, luxury lovers
kitchen, pool, hot tub, activities desk	uncrowded, easy parking, helpful staff	couples, families
laundry, kitchen, beach gear	concierge service, downtown location	first-timers, couples
restaurant	old Hawaii feel	budget travelers
pool, restaurant	frequent upgrade	budget travelers, large groups
pool	downtown location	budget travelers
huge breakfast	great views of Kailua	couples, families
pool, delicious breakfast	views, sweet hosts	couples
free coffee tour	experiencing a working coffee farm	foodies and history buffs
pool, tennis courts, activities desk, fitness center	one of the few true resorts in Kona, low season deals	families
kayak rental, free Wi-Fi	hostel scene	budget travelers
pool, tennis courts, spa, business center	watching manta rays from the bar	families
kitchen, laundry	privacy, service	families, couples

TV, and WiFi. The bottom rooms are wheel-chair accessible. When the house isn't rented as an entire estate, hot breakfast is is served on the balcony. Currently, the host of the property is Jenifer, who has years of experience as a concierge to the stars at the big resorts. In addition to the great stories she has to tell, she is eager to assist guests in booking excursions and recommending restaurants. Rumor is that the property is for sale, so make sure Jenifer is your host before you book!

The view of Kealakekua Bay from the ☾ **Luana Inn** (82-5856 Napo'opo'o Rd., Captain Cook, 808/328-2612, www.luanainn.com, $155-205) is priceless, but it's available at an extremely reasonable price. Ken and Erin have fully dedicated their time to this business—so much so that they have made their own booklet of restaurant reviews. The rooms overlooking the pool/hot tub are identically furnished to look like an IKEA showroom and include a kitchenette with sink, microwave, mini-fridge, and coffeemaker. WiFi and TVs with DVD players are also available. The rooms are large with king-size beds; however, the bathrooms are shower only with no tub. The large, nutritious, breakfast is served in the adjoining main house (again, with the view), and communal hangout space is downstairs. Located on the back of this large property is the Ohana Cottage, which houses a full kitchen and room for four—but no ocean view. A short-stay fee is charged for stays under three nights. The location is fantastic, only a few minutes' drive down to the bay for snorkeling and kayaking or to Pu'uhonua O Honaunau National Historical Park for some sightseeing.

Rainbow streamers and a Buddha in a butterfly banner greet you at **Dragonfly Ranch** (near Pu'uhonua O Honaunau, Captain Cook, 808/328-2159 or 800/487-2159, www.dragonflyranch.com, $100-250), an open, airy place, where the outside and inside boundaries begin to blur. Free-spirited adventurers will feel comfortable here; others may not Maybe that's why owner Barbara Moore has posted on her website a piece called "A Marriott We Are Not." The hosts are friendly and inviting, with an alternative, counterculture, new age leaning. The Dragonfly offers "tropical fantasy lodging" set among thick vegetation on the way down to Pu'uhonua O Honaunau. Intriguing rooms range from the Honeymoon Suite (featuring a king-size bed in a screened outdoor room), the airy Lomi Lomi suite, and the more private Writer's Studio to the smaller Dragonfly and Dolphin rooms. All include a small refrigerator and basic cooking apparatus, indoor bathroom, private outdoor shower, cable TV, stereo, and small library. There is a three-night minimum, with discounts for longer stays. Breakfast is a dream come true for those who love chia seeds, gluten-free bread, or organic yogurt with flax. Occasionally, alternative healing arts and wellness workshops are given.

Over $250

It's the perfect place for a honeymoon or those looking to rekindle romance. The ☾ **Holualoa Inn** (76-5932 Mamalahoa Hwy., Holualoa, 808/324-1121, www.holualoainn.com, $295-405) was the retirement home of Thurston Twigg-Smith, CEO of the *Honolulu Advertiser* and member of an old *kama'aina* family. In 1987 it was converted into a bed-and-breakfast. The home is a marvel of taste and charm—light, airy, and open. Top to bottom, it is the natural burnished red of cedar and eucalyptus. The front lanai is pure relaxation, and stained glass puncturing the walls here and there creates swirls of rainbow light. A pool table holds king's court in the commodious games room, as doors open to a casual yet elegant sitting room where breakfast is served. A back staircase leads to a gazebo. From here, Kailua-Kona glows with the mistiness of an Impressionist painting, and 50 acres are dotted with coffee trees and cattle. Just below is the inn's swimming pool and off to the side is the hot tub. The six island-theme rooms, each with private bathroom and superb views of the coast, all differ in size and decor. The Coffee Cherry Room has a private hot tub. Other rooms offer private sitting areas and sofa beds that can accommodate a third person. The communal sitting area and kitchen area are available for guest use.

the Holualoa Inn

Unlike traditional B&Bs, this place has a staff including a professional chef, who has worked at some of the best restaurants on the island. There is a two-night minimum and discounts for stays longer than seven days. Breakfast is included. No preteen children, please.

HOTELS AND RESORTS
$50-100

Stay at **Kona Seaside Hotel** (75-5646 Palani Rd., Kailua-Kona, 808/329-2455 or 800/560-5558, http://seasidehotelshawaii.com, $69-125) if you will only be in your room to sleep and want to be close to the action on Ali'i Drive. The rooms are small and the decor evokes Hawaii in the early 1980s, but rooms stay cool with excellent air-conditioning and ceiling fans. Cable TV is available, but no WiFi. Spend some time on the sundeck, which looks out to the ocean across the street, and take a dip in the pool (but not at night—the pool closes at dusk). AAA and *kama'aina* discounts bring the rate down; some online rates also come with a free or discounted breakfast. There is an extra charge for parking per night, but a nearby public lot is free.

Run by the same family (since 1917!), **Hotel Manago** (Hwy. 11 between mile markers 109 and 110, Captain Cook, 808/323-2642, www.managohotel.com, $33-75 single, $36-78 double, each additional person $3) isn't trying to be anything but what it is— a simple place with a local feel offering basic services. It's so "old school" hotel it has a smoking section. Rates increase by floor (so lower floors are cheaper than higher floors). The rooms are small and can be musty. Rooms with private bathrooms or communal baths are available, and discounts are offered for weekly stays. The hotel's restaurant is a local favorite of locals for its huge combo lunches. It's right on the main highway about 45 minutes from the Kona airport.

$100-150

Despite the addition of "Courtyard" to its name, **Courtyard King Kamehameha's Kona Beach Hotel** (75-5660 Palani Rd., Kailua-Kona, 808/329-2911, www.konabeachhotel.

com, $140-250), still holds the same reputation it's had for decades. Following the March 2011 tsunami, the King Kam received a major revamping to bring its outdated rooms into the 21st century. The 452-room hotel is ideally located next to all the action of Ali'i Drive. It's the place during any of the large festivals in the area, many of which take place at the hotel. The King Kam also offers one of the best luau on the island. You don't need to be a guest to attend the luau, but staying over makes it easier to crawl back to your room after the open bar and massive buffet. WiFi is available (sometimes at a cost), and parking is extra (although a public free lot is close by). Online specials can bring the price down and may include parking and breakfast with the room rate. There is a nice oceanfront pool. Kids like the beach because it's shallow, but the ocean access at Kailua pier is not that nice. Because it's right in the middle of things, it can get loud.

$150-250

There's a wonderful old Hawaii feeling at the **Outrigger Keauhou Beach Resort** (78-6740 Ali'i Dr., Kailua-Kona, 808/322-3441 or 800/688-7444, www.keauhoubeachresort-hawaii.com, $170-450), built on a historic site that includes the remains of three *heiau,* a reconstruction of King Kamehameha III's summer cottage, two freshwater springs, and several fishponds. Kahalu'u Bay Beach Park is adjacent with its white-sand beach and famous surf break, and the entire area is known for fantastic tide pools. Rates are lower during value season, and many special discounts (like free breakfast buffet) are available all year. Each of the 309 rooms has air-conditioning, TV, phone, private lanai, and small refrigerator. The open-air Kama'aina Terrace restaurant is open for breakfast and dinner; the Kalanikai Bar and Grill near the water serves wraps, sandwiches, and other light fare for lunch; and the Verandah Lounge offers drinks throughout the day and free music every evening. The resort also has a swimming pool, activities desk, and a fitness center. Daily activities include Hawaiian dance, music, arts and crafts, as well as a torch lighting ceremony. A free cultural tour of the historical sites on the grounds is offered daily.

Sitting on the black lava seashore south of Keauhou Bay, the 521-room **Sheraton Keauhou Bay Resort and Spa** (78-128 Ehukai St., Kailua-Kona, 808/930-4900 or 888/488-3535, www.sheratonkeauhou.com, $125-450) has risen like a phoenix from the old Kona Surf Hotel. The grounds have been extensively landscaped to add color and some formality to this otherwise black and forbidding coastline. Rooms and public areas are comfortable with good views. Three separate multistory buildings face the water; one faces inland for mountain views. They surround a large courtyard swimming pool with a long and twisting water slide. There are actually two pools—one overlooks the ocean—but there isn't direct access to the beach. Amenities include a children's program, a business center, fitness center, tennis courts, basketball court, the full-service Ho'ola Spa, and a luau and Polynesian show held twice a week. Dine at the Restaurant Kai, the casual poolside Manta Ray Bar and Grill, the stylish Crystal Blue Lounge, or the ground-level Cafe Hahalua. The resort shines a light on the water each evening hoping to attract manta rays; best viewing is May-October.

Over $250

Known worldwide for luxury, the 243-room **Four Seasons Resort, Hualalai at Historic Ka'upulehu** (100 Ka'upulehu Dr., 888/340-5662, www.fourseasons.com/hualalai, $220-600) is split into 36 low-rise bungalows in four crescent groups that front a half-mile beach. Located in among old lava flows from the Hualalai volcano, 32 of these units have ocean views, while four are located along the 18th green of the accompanying Hualalai Golf Club. There is no skimping on space, furnishings, or amenities. Authentic Hawaiian art pieces from the late 1700s to the present are displayed throughout the hotel. Just downstairs from the lobby, the Cultural Center with its 1,200-gallon reef aquarium offers insight into the surrounding water and the lives of ancient Hawaiians. In addition to the natural lagoons, the resort has both freshwater and saltwater swimming pools set just back from the beach. There's supervised day care for kids (5-12) and an activity center with indoor games for teens (and their parents). The full-service Sports Club and Spa offers a a 25-meter lap pool, exercise machines, massage and spa therapies, and sand volleyball and basketball courts. Each room looks out onto a private garden, lanai, or patio. The resort also has three on-site restaurants and two bars.

CONDOS AND VACATION RENTALS
$100-150

A Castle Resorts and Hotels property, **Kona Bali Kai** (76-6246 Ali'i Dr., Kailua-Kona, 808/329-9381 or 800/367-5004, www.castleresorts.com, $100-300) is a decent, comfortable place with an indoor swimming pool, activities desk, concierge, and *poke* shop on property. The 154 condos—split between three-floor buildings on the *mauka* and *makai* sides of Ali'i Drive—include studio, one-bedroom, two-bedroom, and three-bedroom units that all contain fully equipped kitchens and cable TV. The *makai* building has an elevator; however, not all rooms are large enough for wheelchairs to navigate. All apartments are individually owned so the decor differs, but most have muted colors and an old tropical feel. Rates depend on the unit size and its view (ocean, partial ocean, or mountain). There are often online specials and you have a good chance of getting upgraded for no additional charge when you check in. This is a great place to crash with a bunch of people and still be close to the action.

The condos at **Casa de Emdeko** (75-6082 Ali'i Dr., Kailua-Kona, www.casadeemdeko.org) are individually owned by people off-island, so the quality really varies. You can rent worry-free the one-bedroom condos numbered 125 ($135 double, $10 each additional guest) and 327 (starting at $100 a night). If you are interested in the other condos in the complex, ask for photos to ensure that they are updated. At these prices, it's worth doing the research. Rooms have king-size beds and pull-out sofa beds in the living areas. All are stocked with beach equipment. The complex has two pools and a sandy beach and barbecue area where guests mingle. Book directly from the owners, who have numbers and emails listed on the website. Some condos require a three-night minimum stay (10 nights during Ironman and the Christmas season). This place is unbelievably cheap for the area close to downtown Kailua.

$150-250

The one- and two-bedroom suites at **Aston Kona by the Sea** (75-6106 Ali'i Dr., Kailua-Kona, 808/327-2300, www.astonhotels.com, $180-300) have all the amenities of a home away from home: kitchen, washer/dryer, swimming pool/hot tub, barbecue area, cable TV, WiFi in the lobby, and activities desk. A range of rooms are available; you pay extra for the ocean view, as well as an "amenity fee" for Internet, DVD rentals, and in-room coffee. Even the one-bedrooms come with a pull-out sofa, so they are big enough to sleep up to four people. Some of the rooms are a bit outdated, so ask for photos ahead of time or at least ask to see a few rooms before you unpack. It's a good budget option and close to downtown Kailua (although not in walking distance). Book early; these condos sell out fast during high season.

If your dream vacation is accessing WiFi from the pool, check out the one-bedroom condos at **Hale Kona Kai** (75-5870 Kahakai Rd., Kailua-Kona, 800/421-3696, www.halekonakai-hkk.com, $150-195). Almost all are oceanfront, and all come with a small kitchen, cable TV, sofa beds, and lanai—some with better ocean views than others. Shared extras include a nicely sized pool (right on the ocean) and a barbecue area. They are also really proud of their two parking lots. Each unit is individually owned, so the decor and datedness of furniture (as well as TVs and kitchen appliances) vary. Look at the pictures on the website before you decide which one to rent. Many condos require a three-night minimum. The location sets you close to downtown—close enough to walk—and the price is right, but if you think you'll spend a lot of time in the room, I'd rent elsewhere.

Sometimes the best way to experience the ocean is from way above it. If this sounds about right to you, come stay at **Silver Oaks Ranch** (808/325-2000, www.silveroaksranch. com, $125-200), which is close to the hustle and bustle of Kona, but just far enough away to get some space. This is a farm, with tons of animals around, and two types of rentals: the Ranch House Cottages, with a large bedroom, kitchen, TV, washer/dryer, and WiFi, and the Garden Cottage, which has the same amenities except it only has a kitchenette. While this rental sounds pretty standard, it is the hosts—and the added touches that they bring—that set it apart. They offer you a laptop computer, stock the fridge, provide beach equipment, and offer advice about things to do in the area. It's

the best of both worlds—the privacy of a vacation rental with the concierge service of a hotel. A five-night minimum stay is required.

The **Holua Resort at Mauna Loa Village** (78-7190 Kaleiopapa St., Keauhou, 808/324-1550, www.shellhospitality.com, $150-250) is best suited for couples and families. Each cluster of eight condo units has its own small pool and hot tub, so the pool is never too crowded and you can always get a lounge chair. One- and two-bedroom condos are available, with pull-out sofas, kitchen, large cable TVs, and bright carpets. There's lots of covered parking. There helpful activities desk that can can set you up with tennis lessons and tee times. Keauhou shopping is nearby for quick trips to the grocery store. Many guests are involved with Shell hospitality's time share program, but you don't have to be to stay here.

Kohala

Kohala is where you'll find the big chain resorts, the ones with a few hundred rooms and lots of staff. However, Kohala also is where you'll find updated vacation rentals (a great deal for large families staying together) and a few new players: boutique-like rentals and retreat centers. So don't just think about the Waikoloa and Mauna Launi resort areas; also consider places near Hawi on the northwest tip of the island. No matter where you stay in Kohala, this district is how you imagined your Hawaii getaway: first-rate beaches near first-rate restaurants.

HOTELS AND RESORTS
$150-250
On a perfect spot fronting palm-fringed 'Anaeho'omalu Bay, **Waikoloa Beach Marriott Resort and Spa** (69-275 Waikoloa Beach Dr., Waikoloa, 808/886-6789, www.marriotthawaii.com, $150-350) looks out over ponds that once stocked fish for passing *ali'i*. The hotel lobby is a spacious open-air affair that lets the trade winds blow across its cool sandstone floor.

Six floors of rooms extend out in wings on both sides, flanking the landscaped courtyard with swimming pool and water slide. Greeting you as you enter the lobby is a marvelous old koa outrigger canoe set in front of a three-part mural by renowned Hawaiian artist Herb Kane of a royal canoe and Western frigate meeting off the Kona Coast. All 555 hotel rooms and suites are tastefully decorated in light, soothing colors, with king-size beds, rattan furnishings, custom quilts, and island prints of a mid-20th century art deco style. Each room has air-conditioning, color TV, high-speed Internet access (with a fee), *yakuta* robes, in-room safe, small refrigerator, marble vanities, and a private lanai. Online discounts can drop the prices at low season; however, many guests seem to be using their Marriott points. Hotel services and amenities include an activities desk for all on-site and off-property excursions and several retail shops and boutiques. You can take part in daily Hawaiian cultural programs, use the business center, or have your kids properly cared for at the Waikoloa Keiki Club children's program.

The hotel is just a few minutes' stroll past the royal fishponds to the beach or to a nearby ancient but now restored *heiau*. The pool area is wonderful and the hot tubs are great at night. You're are seconds from a great beach that offers all kinds of water activities (with paddle board, snorkeling, and surfing rentals). The nearby shopping area is just a three-minute walk, with access to restaurants, shops, and groceries. The service at the hotel is probably not the best of the resorts in the area.

At the **Hilton Waikoloa Village** (425 Waikoloa Beach Dr., Waikoloa, 808/886-1234 or 800/445-8667, www.hiltonwaikoloavillage.com, $200-315), the idea was to create a reality so beautiful and naturally harmonious that it offers a glimpse of paradise. The three main towers, each enclosing a miniature botanical garden, are spread over the grounds almost a mile apart and are linked by pink flagstone walkways, canals navigated by hotel launches, and a quiet, space-age tram. The museum promenade displays choice artwork from Hawaii, Oceania, and Asia. The beach fronting the property offers excellent snorkeling, while two gigantic pools and a series of lagoons are perfect for water activities and sunbathing. You can swim in a private lagoon accompanied by reef fish, help feed the dolphins, dine at any one of the nine first-rate restaurants, and take in the extravagant dinner show of the twice-weekly Legends of the Pacific luau. The grandeur and expansiveness can seem a bit overblown. Forget intimacy—you don't come here to get away, you come here to participate. With 1,240 rooms on a 62-acre property, it's so big that entering the lobby can be like walking into Grand Central Station, and navigating certain walkways, particularly at dinnertime, is like pushing through throngs at a fair. There can be kids everywhere (great for kids, not great for adults who want quiet), boats, and a train going around. Cable TV is available, but in-room WiFi and parking have an additional fee. Check out the website for discounts, packages, and special offers like free breakfast, free luau, or golfing discounts.

Over $250

The vision of Jeanne Sunderland, the 50-acre 【 **Hawaii Island Retreat at Ahu Pohaku Ho'omaluhia** (250 Maluhia Rd., Kapa'au, 808/889-6336, www.hawaiiislandretreat.com, $195-500) is dedicated to "elegant earth-friendly living." Jeanne was the founder of the Spa Without Walls at the former Ritz Carlton at Mauna Lani and is well known in the community as a healing arts therapist. The nine-bedroom house looks like a mansion in the Mediterranean. The center courtyard is open with beautiful landscaping, and all rooms have private balconies that overlook either the ocean, valley, or garden. Explore the gardens and cliffs, do yoga, relax at the modern pool (there's no good beach access here for swimming), or enjoy the many spa treatments. In addition to the main house, there is a second option called "Hawaiian Hales," yurts located down the hill from the house. Each *hale* has accommodation for two (queen-size bed or twin beds) and private toilet. The shower is nearby in the spa locker room, which is equivalent to what you'd find at a five-star hotel. There's a two-night minimum stay with a $50 charge for additional persons occupying a room. Large discounts are given for stays of three nights or more, or opt for an all-inclusive package that includes three meals a day and spa treatments.

Ever since Laurance Rockefeller became interested in the lucrative possibilities of a luxury hideaway for the rich and famous, 【 **Mauna Kea Beach Hotel** (62-100 Mauna Kea Beach Dr., Kohala Coast, 808/882-7222 or 800/882-6060, www.maunakeabeachhotel.com, $325-950) has set the standard of excellence in Kohala's coast. This beautiful coastal land was leased from the Parker Ranch and the hotel opened in 1965. Over the years, the Mauna Kea has aged a bit and suffered stiff competition from newer resorts nearby. But class is always class, and the landmark Mauna Kea again receives high accolades as a fine resort hotel. The Mauna Kea fronts beautiful Kauna'oa Beach, one of the best on the island. Million-dollar condos also grace the resort grounds. The hotel itself is an

BIG ISLAND OF HAWAI'I

Where to Stay in Kohala

Name	Type	Price
€ Aston Shores at Waikoloa	condo	$175-300
The Fairmont Orchid	hotel	$225-500
Hale Hoʻokipa	vacation rental	$145
Hapuna Beach Prince Hotel	resort	$300-650
€ Hawaii Island Retreat at Ahu Pohaku Hoʻomaluhia	boutique hotel	$195-500
Hilton Waikoloa Village	resort	$200-315
€ Mauna Kea Beach Hotel	hotel	$325-950
€ Mauna Lani Bay Hotel and Bungalows	hotel	$350-1,500
Mauna Lani Terrace	condo	$350-575
Outrigger Fairway Villas	condo	$190-285
€ Puakea Ranch	vacation rental	$235-650
Waikoloa Beach Marriott Resort and Spa	resort	$150-350

eight-story terraced complex of simple, clean-cut design. The grounds and lobbies showcase more than 1,000 museum-quality art pieces from throughout the Pacific and more than a half million plants add greenery and beauty to the surroundings.

The award-winning Mauna Kea Golf Course surrounds the grounds, and on a bluff overlooking the water, tennis courts vie for use. Swimmers can use the beach or the round courtyard swimming pool. A host of daily activities are scheduled, including a twice-weekly stargazing program and horseback riding at the Parker Ranch up in Waimea. The 310 beautifully appointed rooms feature an extra-large lanai and specially made wicker furniture. From there, rates rise for beachfront units and deluxe ocean-view rooms. The rooms are, like the rest of the hotel, the epitome of understated elegance. The Mauna Kea has four restaurants and several lounges. A resort shuttle operates between here and the Hapuna Beach Prince Hotel, where Mauna Kea guests have signing privileges. The only downside is that the restaurant choices are mediocre and expensive. The good news is that excellent dining options in Waimea are only 15-20 minutes away.

The aptly named **Hapuna Beach Prince Hotel** (62-100 Kaunaʻoa Dr., Kohala Coast, 808/880-1111, www.hapunabeachprincehotel.com, $300-650) is about one mile down the coast from its sister resort, the Mauna Kea Beach Hotel. These two hotels are separate entities but function as one resort. Long and lean, this AAA Four-Diamond Prince hotel steps down the hillside toward the beach in

Features	Why Stay Here?	Best Fit For
kitchen, laundry, pool, private lanai, beach gear	nice condo	families, long-term stays
pool, hot tub, water sport rentals, luau, fitness center, golf, tennis courts, spa	the best luau on the island	honeymooners, families, luxury lovers
kitchen, laundry, beach gear	location, local feel	families, large groups
golf, pool, spa, fitness center	beach location, golf	golfers, beach-lovers
lounge, ocean views, infinity pool, spa, yoga	luxury, personalized spa experience	honeymooners, weddings or reunions
pool, penguins and dolphins, restaurants, luau	a true mega resort experience	families, luxury lovers
pool, hot tub, beach access, restaurant, tennis, golf	beach, trail, and golf	honeymooners, couples
pool, hot tub, beach, restaurant, golf	beach access	honeymooners, luxury lovers
pool, hot tub, kitchen, laundry,	affordable access to beach and golf	golfers, couples, extended stay
tennis, pool, kitchen, private lanai, beach gear	affordable, location	families, extended stay
pool, kitchen, horseback riding, children's play room	beautiful decor, relaxation	couples, families
restaurants, pool, hot tub, luau	beach and location	families, Marriott members

eight levels. A formal portico fronts the main entryway, through which you have a splendid view of palm trees and the ocean. Lines are simple and decoration subtle, letting surrounding nature become part of the whole. A free periodic shuttle connects the Hapuna Beach to the Mauna Kea, and all services available at one are open to guests of the other.

Bedrooms are spacious, allowing for king-size beds, and the bathrooms have marble floors. Each of the 350 large and well-appointed rooms has an entertainment center, comfy chairs, and a lanai. Although rooms are air-conditioned, they all have louvered doors, allowing you to keep out the sun while letting breezes flow through. In addition to regular rooms and suites, there is an 8,000-square-foot estate on the property that rents for $7,000 a night. Four restaurants serve a variety of food for all meals during the day, and the lounges stay open for evening drinks.

Recreation options include the links-style Hapuna Golf Course, a fitness center, and spa. Set in the garden below the lobby, the swimming pool is great recreation during the day and reflects the stars at night. Speaking of the stars, four nights a week, the hotel hosts a stargazing program for hotel guests (reservations required, $25), and numerous other activities are scheduled through the week. A few shops whet the appetite of those needing sundries or resort wear. At the Prince Keiki Club at the Hapuna, children 5-12 years old can fill their time with fun activities and educational projects. If you love golf, stay here. Otherwise, stay at the Mauna Kea—it has a nicer beach and a more Zen feel to it than the Hapuna Prince.

As soon as you turn off Highway 19, the entrance road, trimmed in purple bougainvillea, sets the mood for the AAA Five-Diamond award-winning ◖**Mauna Lani Bay Hotel and Bungalows** (68-1400 Mauna Lani Dr., Kohala Coast, 808/885-6622 or 800/367-2323, www.maunalani.com, $350-1500), a 350-room hotel that opened in 1983. A short stroll beyond the central courtyard leads you past the swimming pool and through a virtual botanical garden to a perfect white-sand beach. From here, any number of water sports activities can be arranged. Away from the shore you find a sports and fitness club with tennis courts, a lap pool, and the full-service Mauna Lani Spa. A cave complex and petroglyph field lies right in the middle of the resort complex. Surrounding the hotel is the marvelous Francis I'i Brown Golf Course, whose artistically laid-out fairways, greens, and sand traps make it a modern landscape sculpture.

Rooms are oversized; the majority come with an ocean view, and each includes a private lanai, cable TV, in-room safe, and all the comforts of home. The exclusive 4,000-square-foot, two-bedroom bungalows rent for an average of $4,000 a night, but each comes complete with a personal chef, butler, and swimming pool. In addition, one-, two-, and three-bedroom home-like villas go for $650-2,115, three-night minimum required. Weekly rates are available on the villas and bungalows, and there are always many different specials and packages. Guest privileges include complimentary use of snorkeling equipment, Hawaiian cultural classes and activities, hula lessons, and complimentary morning coffee. Five restaurants and lounges cater to the culinary needs of resort guests, from quick and casual to classic island fare. The hotel offers the Kids' Club of Mauna Lani for children ages 5-12. Once a month Hawaiian musicians, dancers, and storytellers gather to share their cultural talents at Twilight at Kalahuipua'a at the Eva Parker Woods cottage. Some additional excellent beaches are just down the road. For an added bonus, the on-site

restaurant, **The Canoe House** offers five-star cuisine and service with excellent sunset views. It's great for couples.

In a tortured field of coal-black lava made more dramatic by pockets of jade-green lawn rises **The Fairmont Orchid** (1 N. Kaniku Dr., Kohala Coast, 808/885-2000 or 800/845-9905, www.fairmont.com/orchid, $225-500). A rolling drive lined with *haku* lei of flowering shrubs entwined with stately palms leads to the open-air porte cochere. Nature, powerful yet soothing, surrounds the hotel in a magnificent free-form pool and trimmed tropical gardens; every set of stairs boasts a velvety smooth koa banister carved with the pineapple motif, the Hawaiian symbol of hospitality. The Fairmont Orchid is an elegant place to relax in luxury and warm aloha. Located in two six-story wings off the main reception hall, the 539 hotel rooms, each with private lanai and sensational view, are a mixture of kings, doubles, and suites. Done in neutral tones, the stylish and refined rooms feature handcrafted quilts, twice-daily room attendance, an entertainment center, and spacious marble bathrooms.

In addition to several restaurants and lounges, the hotel offers first-rate guest services, amenities, and activities that include a small shopping mall, tennis courts, a fitness center, and full-service spa. The pool area is enormous and lovely, with hot tubs and a sun deck, but there is only a small area for beach access. The luau at the hotel is one of the better ones in the area, but not traditional. It's like Lady Gaga designed it, and thus even if it's not standard, it's really fun to watch. In addition, the food is excellent—probably the best *lu'au* food around.

CONDOS AND VACATION RENTALS $100-150

Surrounded by fruit trees that you can pick from, **Hale Ho'okipa** (in Kapa'au on the road to Keokea Beach Park, reserve through www.vrbo.com/87130, $145) has a large wrap-around lanai with barbecue and great ocean and mountain views. This three-bedroom, 2.5-bath rental sleeps six and is tastefully decorated with island furniture. The kitchen is packed with everything you need to make gourmet meals. Snorkel gear and beach gear/toys are available in the garage. A three-night minimum is required and there's a $125 cleaning fee for stays of less than a week. This is a location where tourists often don't think to rent a house, but it's a great place to spend a few days—not too far from the nearby beaches and the valley as well as a few minutes drive from nearby Hawi, with its galleries and exceptional restaurants.

$150-250

The attractive three-story **Outrigger Fairway Villas** (69-200 Pohakulana Pl., Waikoloa, 808/886-0036 or 800/688-7444, www.outrigger.com, $190-285) is opposite the Kings' Shops. Deluxe two- and three-bedroom units have all top-of-the-line amenities as well as a private pool, exercise center, and guest service center. The two-bedroom with two-bath is reasonably priced for the area and could likely fit 4-6 people; many of the units have convertible sofas. The units themselves are decorated with the standard Hawaii condo furniture (pictures of shells and pink couches). It's close to the Waikoloa action and walking distance to the beach.

The condos at ◖ **Aston Shores at Waikoloa** (69-1035 Keana Pl., Waikoloa, 808/886-5001, www.astonhotels.com, $175-300) feel newer than many of the others in the area, with more modern decor. Guests choose from one- and two-bedroom suites or two-bedroom villas. The modern units have well-stocked kitchens, washer/dryers, private lanai, cable TV and Internet, as well as daily maid service. The gated community also offers a swimming pool, hot tub, free tennis courts, fitness center, and outdoor barbecues. The two-bedroom deluxe suite is large enough to sleep 4-6 people utilizing the pull-out couch. Call ahead and request photos of the unit to make sure that you are getting one that you like. If you prefer a pool close by and want to cook some meals, this is the best choice for you.

Over $250

You'll want to stay here forever. There is nothing else, on the Big Island at least, like ◖ **Puakea Ranch** (Hwy. 270 near Hawi, http://puakearanch.com, $235-650). The four guest bungalows originally date from the early 1900s, when they were the homes of plantation workers, cowboys, and their families working the surrounding 2,000 acres. Christie Cash, the owner, personally transformed each one into a space that looks like it could be in a magazine. Every single detail is gorgeous, from the linens to the couches to four post beds to the state-of-the-art kitchen. My favorite is Yoshi's House, a two-bedroom house with two bathrooms—one a separate structure with an antique copper tub for two. The house sleeps six and has its own private pool and is often used for events from weddings to dinner parties. Guests can help themselves to fresh eggs in the morning and fresh herbs and produce from the garden. A three- to five-night minimum stay is required during high season, and a departure cleaning fee of $200 is applied to every room reservation.

Located just behind the Mauna Lani Bay Hotel and Bungalows is the **Mauna Lani Terrace** (69-1399 Mauna Lani Dr., Kohala Coast, 800/822-4252, www.southkohala.com, $350-575), spread out across a small pond. Average one- and two-bedroom condos (superior and deluxe) are available with rates varying depending on size and length of stay (discounts for over a week). All units have a kitchen, washer/dryer, twice weekly maid service, cable and WiFi, as well as a lanai overlooking the pond and further out the ocean. There is a pool on-site, a hot tub, and a fitness center. The draw here is access to the beach at the Mauna Lani resort and some of the amenities in the area (such as a parking pass to the beach club down the road).

Hawai'i Volcanoes National Park and Volcano Village

There are a great number of accommodations in and around Volcano Village. While most are near the heart of the village, several are located in the fern forests south of the highway and a few are located around the golf course about two miles west of town. Most are bed-and-breakfasts, some are vacation homes where you take care of your own meals, and there is one hostel. These places run from budget and homey to luxurious and elegant, but most are moderate in price and amenities. Some of these establishments also act as agents for other rental homes in the area, so your choices are many. The weather in Volcano is substantially colder than the rest of the island, so don't look for rooms with air-conditioning; instead make sure they have warm blankets. Check if bed-and-breakfasts actually serve hot breakfast. It is difficult for establishments in Volcano to become certified kitchens (it has to do with the fact there is no county water here), so the majority of B&Bs don't really serve breakfast but simply provide muffins.

HOSTELS
Under $50

An inexpensive option is **Holo Holo In** (19-4036 Kalani Honua Rd., Volcano, 808/967-7950 www.volcanohostel.com, private rooms $56-71, dorms $22). The owners are committed to cleanliness; due to their cleaning schedule, there is daily lockout 11am-4:30pm. This means that you can't access the place at all during this time. This might not be ideal for everyone, but could work for those who plan on hiking all day and really just need somewhere to crash afterward with a hot shower and free WiFi. Dorm beds are available, as are private rooms both with private or shared bath. Communal spaces include a comfortable lounge area with books, computer, television, and couches as well as a shared kitchen and

Where to Stay in Volcano Village

Name	Type	Price
Chalet Kilauea Inn at Volcano	hotel	$125-400
Holo Holo In	hostel	$22-56
◖ Kilauea Lodge	hotel	$170-185
Tutu's Place	vacation rental	$200
Volcano House	hotel	$100-230
Volcano Places	vacation rental	$110-205
◖ Volcano Rainforest Retreat	vacation rental	$110-260
◖ Volcano Teapot Cottage	vacation rentaAl	$195
◖ Volcano Village Lodge	inn	$215-315

BIG ISLAND OF HAWAI'I

laundry facilities. Most guests are hikers (of all ages), lending a nice sense of camaraderie. The "In" is located in Volcano Village close to the park; it's a 30-minute walk. It's a great place to stay before or after a big backcountry trip.

BED-AND-BREAKFASTS AND INNS
Over $250

Volcano Village Lodge (19-4183 Road E, Volcano, 808/985-9500 http://emmaspencer-living.com/volcano-village-lodge, $215-315) feels like it's in the middle of a secluded rainforest. The five rooms of this luxury getaway are spread out across the property. There is something ethereal about them: All are romantically decorated with large beds, sitting areas, and views of the surrounding trees. Your arrival is greeted by a bottle of wine, as well as supplies to make your own breakfast (store-bought items like yogurt, cereal, and some boiled eggs). WiFi is available and there is a TV (no cable) in each room, as well as a library stacked with DVDs and books in the common area. A hot tub is also available. The staff at the lodge can arrange an in-room couples massage. There's a two-night minimum for stays. The staff are dedicated to making sure guests have a memorable stay.

HOTELS AND RESORTS
$150-250

The premier restaurant and lodge atop Volcano, **Kilauea Lodge** (19-3948 Old Volcano Rd., Volcano, 808/967-7366, www.kilauealodge.com, $170-185), owned and operated by Lorna and Albert Jeyte, is also one of the best on the island. The solid stone and timber structure was built in 1938 as a YMCA camp and functioned as such until 1962, when it became a "mom and pop operation." It faded into the ferns until Lorna and Albert revitalized it in the late 1980s. The lodge is a classic, with a vaulted, open-beamed ceiling, and a cozy "international fireplace" embedded with stones and plaques from all over the world. Rooms are located in three adjacent buildings; all include a complete breakfast in the restaurant. There is a hot tub in the rear garden. Each room in Hale Maluna, the original guesthouse, has a bathroom with vaulted 18-foot ceilings and a skylight, a working fireplace, queen-size or twin beds, and swivel rocking chair. A separate one-bedroom cottage, set in the ferns to

Features	Why Stay Here?	Best Fit For
hot tub, lounge	rainforest atmosphere	couples
hot showers	affordable	budget travelers, campers
restaurant, breakfast included, hot tub	park access, location	couples
fireplace, kitchen	park access, location	families, couples
restaurant	park access, location	park visitors
kitchen	cabin feel, friendly management	couples
kitchen, Japanese *ofuro* tubs	cozy rainforest setting	families, couples
fireplace, hot tub, kitchen	fairy-tale setting	couples
hot tub	romance	honeymooners

the side, features a gas fireplace, a queen-size bed, private bath, and small living room with queen-size pull-out sofa. One downstairs room is wheelchair-accessible. Each room has WiFi and cable TV. Since this is one of few restaurants in the area, both visitors and locals come here in the evenings to eat and socialize.

Peeking from the *hapu'u* fern forest in a manicured glen is **Chalet Kilauea Inn at Volcano** (19-4178 Wright Rd., Volcano, 808/967-7786 or 800/937-7786, www.volcano-hawaii.com, $125-400). Downstairs there's an outdoor lounge area, and a black-and-white checkerboard dining room where wrought-iron tables sit before a huge picture window. A three-course candlelight breakfast is served here every morning ($6-12). On the second level is the guest living room, where you can play chess, listen to a large collection of CDs, or gaze from the wraparound windows at a treetop view of the surrounding forest. Beyond the koi pond in the garden, a freestanding gazebo houses an eight-person hot tub available 24 hours a day. The main house, called The Inn at Volcano, is known for elegance and luxury. It holds four suites and two theme rooms. The adjacent Hapu'u Suite has a fireplace in the cozy living room, but perhaps its best feature is the master bathroom, which looks out onto the back garden. The best room at the inn is the Treehouse Suite, which has two floors with a huge bed and tub for two. The other rooms at the inn are smaller and noise seems to travel easily between them. Rooms all have WiFi and cable TV (and some even have cable TV in the bathroom).

Chalet Kilauea also has many other accommodations in Volcano Village. **Lokahi Lodge** has four rooms that run $125-185, or rent the entire property for a group of up to 14 people. For those on a tighter budget, the **Volcano Hale** rents rooms for $65-90 and still has plenty of common space. The entire house can be rented and can sleep 13. In addition, several vacation homes dotted here and there about town in the secluded privacy of the forest are available for $375-775. Whatever your needs and price range, Chalet Kilauea will have something for you.

Ever dreamed of sleeping with a goddess? Cuddle up with Pele at **Volcano House** (inside Hawai'i Volcanoes National Park, www.hawaiivolcanohouse.com, $100-230), the only hotel located on the rim of Kilauea caldera. Its history began in 1846, when a sugar planter perched a grass hut on the rim of the crater and charged $1 a night for lodging. A steady stream of notable visitors has come ever since: almost all of Hawaii's kings and queens dating from the middle of the 19th century, as well as royalty from Europe. Mark Twain was a guest, followed by Franklin Roosevelt. Most recently, a contingent of astronauts lodged here and used the crater floor to prepare for walking on the moon. In 1866 a larger grass hut replaced the first, and in 1877 a wooden hotel was built. It is now the Volcano Art Center and has been moved just across the road. In 1885, an expansion added 14 rooms and the dining room, and 35 more rooms were constructed in the mid-1920s. Today, the hotel is managed by the National Park Service. This particular building dates from the 1940s. A renovation completed in 2012 made the hotel more secure in case of earthquake and updated its decor and facilities. It may not be the nicest place to stay in Volcano, but it's worth it for the view. You can see the glow of the crater from your window—how cool is that?

CONDOS AND VACATION RENTALS $150-250

Just up the road from the Kilauea Lodge is a cute little two-bedroom cottage, **Tutu's Place** (808/967-7366, www.kilauealodge.com, $200). Built in 1929 by Uncle Billy of hotel chain fame for "Tutu" (Grandma), it was bought several decades later by the Warner family, who were active in Hawaiian politics. They lived in the cottage for many years until it was bought in 1995 by Lorna Larson-Jeyte, the owner of the Kilauea Lodge, who used to visit as a child. Although it's been completely refurbished, people in the know say that the cottage is still imbued with the spirit of Ruth Warner. This two-bedroom house, done in rattan and koa, has a fireplace in the living room, a full kitchen, and a wonderful little bathroom. For a small place, it has a surprisingly roomy feel. WiFi and cable TV are available. The rate is based on double occupancy; it's $20 for each additional person. Full breakfast at the lodge is included. It's great for anyone who wants privacy along with the availability of the staff at the lodge.

The three cottages of **《 Volcano Rainforest Retreat** (11-3832 12th St., Volcano, 808/985-8696, www.volcanoretreat.com, $110-260) are embraced within the arms of ferns, 'ohi'a, and bamboo. It's like staying in a private rainforest. Constructed in an open style of cedar and redwood, these handcrafted buildings are warm and welcoming, rich in color and detail, and have plenty of windows that look out onto the encircling forest. Hale Kipa (Guest Cottage) has a cozy living room with full kitchen and sleeping loft, perfect for a couple or small family. The six-sided Hale Ho'ano (Sanctuary House), the smallest and with the most obvious Japanese influence, has the benefit of an outdoor *ofuro* tub and shower. The octagonal Hale Nahele (Forest House) is one large room with an attached full bath, efficiency kitchen and sitting area, and covered lanai—just right for a cozy couple. Each has a small heater for chilly nights. The newest addition is the cedar-shingle Bamboo Guest House, an exquisite one-bedroom vacation rental with a full kitchen and dining area, sitting room under clerestory windows, and a relaxing bath with outdoor *ofuro* tub. All units are stocked with breakfast foods and have WiFi. The rooms are close to town and the park. Rates are discounted for three nights or longer; expect an extra charge for stays of just one night.

For a one-stop vacation rental shop, check out **Volcano Places** (808/967-7990, www.volcanoplaces.com, $110-205). Ranging from studios to two bedrooms, these four rentals have a cabin in the woods feel. Nothing luxurious here, just comfortable places to stay—as if you were going for a visit a family member's home. Kathryn, the owner, receives rave reviews for her friendliness and spotless accommodations. The top-rated Nohea is a one-bedroom cottage with high ceilings that can fit a couple (or squeeze in three adults), with a nicely sized kitchen, living area, WiFi, and cable TV. It backs up to a state forest that you can enjoy from your private lanai—just the place you want to return after a long day at the park. Discounts are available for stays longer than three days. Rates are for double occupancy; it's $15 for each additional guest.

How good is **《 Volcano Teapot Cottage** (19-4041 Kilauea Rd., Volcano, 808/967-7112, www.volcanoteapot.com, $195)? It will probably be booked by the time you finish reading this sentence. Why so much demand? The service is great and the place is really charming—like something from a fairy tale. Bill and Antoinette Bullough pay attention to details and pay attention to their guests. Originally built in the early 1900s by a Hilo businessman, the cottage is two bedrooms and one bath filled with antiques and a gas fireplace. Even though the cottage has two bedrooms, the owners prefer to host only two people (you'll have to negotiate for a third). Mixed with the historical elements are WiFi, a TV with DVD player, and a hot tub situated in the lush landscape behind the house. Breakfast items are stocked daily in the kitchen. It has all everything you want, including easy access to the park. A two-night minimum stay is required.

BIG ISLAND OF HAWAI'I

Hilo

Lots of visitors come to Hilo for the day but don't want to stay here. "Too much rain!" they say. Well, it depends what time of year it is—and what time of day. You can expect rain in the afternoons November-March; although, due to global climate change, even that has been more erratic, with some years completely dry. Hilo doesn't have large resorts like the Kona side; instead, it has bed-and-breakfasts with eager innkeepers, asking for less than you'd pay on the Kona side. Hilo can make a good base to explore the island: It's only 45 minutes to Volcano and about an hour to Mauna Kea, and it's at the beginning of the drive on the Hamakua Coast. And yes, it has beaches, too. They aren't as large and white-sanded as on the Kona side, but they offer good access for swimming, snorkeling, and surfing.

HOSTELS
Under $50

Out near the beaches east of town, **Arnott's Lodge** (98 Apapane Rd., 808/969-7097, www.arnottslodge.com, $25-130) is a good option for budget travelers. Arnott's has six two-person lockable rooms, as well as have a few open-air bunks, all with shared bath. A room with private bath sleeps three, and a two-bedroom suite sleeps up to five. There's also tenting space ($10 per person) on the lawn. Free WiFi is available throughout. No check-in is available after 10pm. Arnott's also runs wonderful, inexpensive touring excursions.

Located downtown in a huge, historical building that dates to 1912, **Hilo Bay Hostel** (101 Waianuenue Ave., 808/933-2771, www.hawaiihostel.net, $70 private, $25 dorm) is similar to what you'd find in Quito or Bogota.

Where to Stay in Hilo

Name	Type	Price
Arnott's Lodge	hostel	$25-130
[Hilo Bay Hale	B&B	$119-159
Hilo Bay Hostel	hostel	$25-70
Hilo Hawaiian Hotel	hotel	$105-300
[Hilo Tropical Gardens Guest House	hostel	$25-65
[The Inn at Kulaniapia Falls	B&B	$139-225
The Old Hawaiian Bed and Breakfast	B&B	$80-110
Orchid Tree Bed and Breakfast	B&B	$149 plus
[Shipman House Bed and Breakfast Inn	B&B	$219-249

There is a shared kitchen (with lots of people around cooking) and free WiFi. It's close to the bus station and downtown shops. Stay at one of these places if you're traveling solo—otherwise, it's not that much more expensive for two people to stay at a nearby bed-and-breakfast while splitting the cost.

The best of the hostels is [C] **Hilo Tropical Gardens Guest House** (1477 Kalaniana'ole Ave., 808/217-2650, www.hilogardens.com, camping $15, dorms $25, private $55-65 double), a stone's throw from the beaches off Kalaniana'ole Avenue. The atmosphere is relaxed, with lots of backpackers hanging around playing games and watching TV. Features include a barbecue area, a communal kitchen, and a convenience store. Most important, the Hilo Tropical Café ice cream shop, owned by the same family as the guest house, is in front. The backyard has an amazing tropical garden, where there are camping sites. I'd camp here: It's peaceful, quiet, and has a nearby bathroom, shower, WiFi, and TV!

BED-AND-BREAKFASTS AND INNS $50-100

Overlooking the Wailuku River near the Boiling Pots, **The Old Hawaiian Bed and Breakfast** (1492 Wailuku Dr., Hilo, 808/961-2816, www.thebigislandvacation.com, $80-110) is one of the best values on the Big Island. Stewart and Lory have transformed the back of their house into a three-bedroom bed-and-breakfast. The rooms, all with private entryways and private baths, overlook the large manicured lawn and the river. They share a covered lanai with microwave and refrigerator. Rates are based on double occupancy; there's a $10 charge per night for an extra person. One-night stays have an additional $15 charge. Master chef Lory cooks amazing breakfasts; the gluten-free pastries are so good! The breakfast alone would run about $30 at a local café. Overall, this place is a fantastic deal.

Features	Why Stay Here?	Best Fit For
kitchen	beach location, organizes outings	backpackers
private lanai	urban experience	couples and singles, queer-friendly
historic building, kitchen	affordable dorm experience	budget travelers
pool, restaurant	location	conference attendees, short-term guests
barbecue, kitchen, convenience store	best of the backpacker options	backpackers
hot tub, massage, waterfall, breakfast	a waterfall in your backyard	honeymooners
fridge and microwave, shared lanai, huge breakfast	best value B&B	budget travelers
pool, hot tub, shared lanai	pool near the ocean	surfers, families, couples
historic, great breakfast	one of the most well-known families and houses in Hawaii	couples, history buffs

$100-150

Matthew and Danny, the innkeeper and owner of ☾ **Hilo Bay Hale** (301 Ponahawai St., 808/745-5049, www.hilobayhale.com, $119-159), have transformed a traditional plantation-style house into a hipster's Hawaiian dream—a slice of Brooklyn in Hilo. The rooms are perfectly decorated with just the right amount of reappropriated antiques and artifacts to create the ambiance of 1950s Hawaii. The house has four rooms. My favorite is named in homage to author James Michener, with queen-size bed, private lanai overlooking a koi pond, blue tiled bathroom with an amazing tub, and a non-functioning record player (for ambience). The breakfast, served on a lanai off the kitchen, offers large portions of quiches, cereal, yogurt, and bacon. Located just a few minutes' walk up the hill from the farmers market and the downtown shops, this is where you'd want to live if you lived in Hilo.

$150-250

On both the State and National Registers of Historic Places, ☾ **Shipman House Bed and Breakfast Inn** (131 Ka'iulani St., 808/934-8002, www.hilo-hawaii.com, $219-249) is the grandest B&B in all Hawaii. This Victorian house was once the home of the Shipman family, prominent Big Island landowners, and is now presided over by Barbara, a Shipman descendant. Does she have stories to tell! She's happy to talk story about recipes, hula, and all things Hawaiian. History buffs will enjoy the outstanding antiques that fill the house. It's like staying at your fancy grandmother's house. The main house offers three guest rooms with antique beds, private baths, and stately views through enormous windows. Others will lodge in the Cottage, originally built for the express purpose of accommodating visitors, with two spacious bedrooms, each with queen-size bed, window seats, and private bath. Both rooms have private entrances, ceiling fans, and a small refrigerator. This is strictly a no-smoking establishment and a "no TV zone," and children are not encouraged. The library is open to guests, along with use of the 1912 Steinway piano

Shipman House Bed and Breakfast Inn

©MATT KRANE

The Inn at Kulaniapia Falls

detached space to the left of the house, is light, airy, and perfect for couples. Both rooms have cable TV and WiFi. Breakfast, served on the lanai, includes waffles or pancakes and an arrangement of fruits.

Just a 10-minute drive from town (on a road that can be hard to navigate), **(The Inn at Kulaniapia Falls** (1 Kulaniapia Dr., Hilo, 866/935-6789, www.waterfall.net, $139-225) consists of three properties spread across the backdrop of a waterfall. Yes, they own a waterfall! It's close to Hilo but really feels away from it all. The owners traveled to the Far East to purchase items to furnish the house and the result is a Japanese-style aesthetic. Rooms are small with large flat-screen TVs (with cable) and WiFi. Each of the two main houses has its own respective breakfast area and staff to prepare food. A private pagoda sleeps up to six ($25 for each additional guest). The fridge in the pagoda is stocked for guests to make their own food. Try to get a room that faces the waterfall; the rushing water will soothe you to sleep.

HOTELS AND RESORTS $150-250

The classic **Hilo Hawaiian Hotel** (71 Banyan Dr., 808/935-9361 or 800/367-5004, www.castleresorts.com, $105-300) occupies the most beautiful grounds in Hilo. From the vantage of the hotel's colonnaded veranda, you overlook formal gardens, Coconut Island, and Hilo Bay. Designed as a huge arc, the hotel's architecture blends well with its surroundings and expresses the theme set by the bay: a long, sweeping crescent. The hotel still has a 1970s feel, but for down-home quality with a touch of class in Hilo, you can't do better than the Hilo Hawaiian. It's neat, clean, well maintained, and has all necessary amenities. There's a swimming pool and all rooms have air-conditioning, phone, and cable TV. There are restaurants on the property, but you'd do better to walk the five minutes to Ken's House of Pancakes for a better meal. Substantial online discounts are available, especially during low season.

whose keys were once tickled by Lili'uokalani. One evening a week, a hula class is held on the lanai. Breakfast is an expanded continental with homemade cereals, assorted local fruits, juices, Kona coffee, yogurt, and breads.

Located just minutes from Honoli'i beach, the best surfing beach this side of the island, is a small neighborhood scattered with vacation rentals and bed-and-breakfasts. **Orchid Tree Bed and Breakfast** (6 Makakai Pl., 808/961-9678, www.orchidtree.net, $149 plus tax dd, $15 for each additional guest) has an outstanding reputation as a really chill place with consistently good service. Steve, the owner and innkeeper, is a laid-back surfer who wants his guests to relax and have a great time. That's not too hard here! The house looks small from the front, but has a small swimming pool (hard to find at B&Bs on the Hilo side), covered hot tub, and a great outdoor lanai. The Hula Suite is a converted section of the main house that sleeps four ($149 for double occupancy). The second suite, in a

Hamakua Coast, Waimea, and the Saddle Road

You want views, I'll give you some views. The accommodations on the Hamakua Coast and Waimea offer some of the best scenes around: You get your ocean and your mountain at the same time. The best places to stay in this area tend to be the bed-and-breakfasts—each offering something unique. Due to the difference in the extra amenities, rates tend to vary, but are lower than in Kona or nearby Kohala. On the Hamakua Coast, you'll have to drive a bit to get some dinner. In Waimea, you'll be minutes away from the island's best cuisine.

BED-AND-BREAKFASTS AND INNS
$150-250

Literally the most spectacular view on the island can be found outside your room at ❰ **Waipi'o Rim** (48-5561 Honoka'a-Waipi'o Rd., Waipi'o Valley, 808/775-1727, www.waipiorim.com, $200 dd). This B&B, owned by Nancy and Steve Roberson, overlooks Waipi'o Valley in all its splendor. Only one room is available, in a building separate from the Robersons' main house; it has awkwardly placed furniture including a queen bed, eating area, couch, and a TV that is placed on top of an armoire. WiFi is available as is cable TV and access to Netflix. But all of that is secondary given the backdrop. Waking up to Waipi'o Valley is really a once-in-a-lifetime event. Nancy and Steve are passionate about the area and offer a lot of attention, including a wine and pupu welcome and scrumptious breakfasts each morning, made from local produce. Ask Steve about the trails surrounding the house, which tour operators use for the horseback riding and ATV trips. You can just walk them on your own with Steve's directions. After four consecutive nights, your fifth night is free. The biggest downside is that it's a little out of the way: about 15 minutes or so to Honoka'a, 30 minutes to Waimea, and about an hour to Hilo.

Aaah the Views (66-1773 Alaneo St., 808/885-3455, www.aaahtheviews.com, $115-195)! Really, the views! They're worth a stay at this bed-and-breakfast. Opt for one of the rooms with views of Mauna Kea (the Dream Room or Stream Room, which has a shared bath), or if you're traveling with a group, rent the two upper rooms (Stream Room and Sunset Room) as the Treetop Suite. Each room in the suite has a small loft with a bed in it. Hypothetically, 3-4 people could fit in each room and a large family really could utilize the entire suite for themselves (any guests beyond

Where to Stay on the Hamakua Coast, in Waimea, and on the Saddle Road

Name	Type	Price
Aaah the Views	B&B	$115-195
Hotel Honoka'a Club	hotel	$20-130
The Jacaranda Inn	inn	$120-200
❰ Waianuhea	B&B	$210-400
❰ Waipi'o Rim	B&B	$200

two are an extra $20 each). You'll also be charged extra for just the one night. There are all the usual amenities (TV/DVD and WiFi), but no hot tub or swimming pool (although their property borders a river for the adventurous types). Breakfast is served early (at 7:30am). The rooms themselves are small, clean, and average—you'll be so distracted by the views (I'll say it again) from the windows or balcony that you won't care about the size or the decor. The location is excellent, just a few minutes west of Waimea and only 10-15 minutes drive to the Kohala Coast. It makes a great base to explore a large part of the island.

Built in 1897 as the Parker Ranch manager's house, this plantation estate has gone through several metamorphoses and has now become **The Jacaranda Inn** (65-1444 Kawaihae Rd., 808/885-8813, www.jacarandainn.com, $120-200 for rooms, $250-450 for the cottage). Set amidst towering trees, the main house retains the original Victorian flavor, with rich koa wood and numerous antiques. Enter the huge living room with its imposing fireplace, and then move to the dining rooms, library, billiard room, bar, or terrace. Separate oversized suites have also been constructed to the rear. While decorated according to different themes and colors, they all have a similar romantic feel, with names like White Lily, Iris, Orchid, and Passion Flower. A three-bedroom, three-bath cottage sleeps up to six, with a three-night minimum. When you drive past this inn from the road, you'll want to stay here—its exterior is welcoming, and it sits perched over a view of the valley. Breakfast is no longer included in the price of accommodation.

Over $250

The staff is so attentive at boutique hotel **(Waianuhea** (near Honoka'a, 808/775-1118, www.waianuhea.com, $210-400) that it might be hard to stay anywhere else afterward. Located along a windy dirt road, it's not the easiest place to reach, but make sure you arrive in time for the late afternoon wine and pupu hour. There are a lot of open spaces where guests can interact or just spend time alone. Inside the house, the Malamalama Suite has a sleigh bed, sofa sleeper, and large bathroom with tub. Outside the main house, the Kaulana Akea Suite has a bedroom with a king bed, a living room with a queen sleeper sofa, and a gas-burning stove. It's ideal for a group. A private patio area fenced by lava rock features a two-person spa. A gourmet, mainly organic and local breakfast prepared by an exceptional chef is included. Thought has gone into everything: a huge DVD library, lots of magazines to borrow, goat milk soaps in the bathrooms, cell phones in each room, and three- or five-course dinner available to order, served over candlelight. It's a great choice for honeymooners or those who want something plush and intimate. The only down side is that it takes about 10 minutes or so to get back to the main road, and the closest town is Honoka'a. Waimea is another 20 minutes away.

BIG ISLAND OF HAWAI'I

Features	Why Stay Here?	Best Fit For
breakfast	sunset views, location	budget travelers
continental breakfast	location	budget travelers
fireplaces	location	couples
hot tub, breakfast, wine and pupu hour	first-class staff, free extras	couples
wine and pupu hour	best views, friendly hosts	couples

HOTELS AND RESORTS
$50-100

Centrally located along Route 240 in downtown Honoka'a, **Hotel Honoka'a Club** (45-3480 Mamane St., Honoka'a, 808/775-0678, www.hotelhonokaa.com, $20-130) is a good budget option if you want to stay near Waipi'o Valley. Built in 1908 as the plantation manager's club, it's still infused with the grace and charm of the old days. What it lacks in elegance it makes up for in cleanliness and friendliness.

The hotel, the only one right in town, is old and well used but clean and comfortable. From the back rooms, you get a view over the tin roofs of residential Honoka'a and the ocean. Choose a two-room suite, an ocean-view room with TV, private bath, and queen-size bed, or an economy room with a private bath. Rates include a simple continental breakfast and WiFi. Hostel rooms, located in the basement, share bath and kitchen facilities. It's not a fancy place, but it's sweet and likable.

KAUA'I

Kaua'i seduces people from all walks of life. Hawaii's oldest island is a place where everyone—locals and traveling nomads, celebrities and hippies, adventure seekers and lovers of luxe—all coexist peacefully. Yes, all of the islands have sun, sand, and surf, but none with the unique spirit of aloha found here. It's as rampant as the island's wild chickens.

Approximately 90 percent of the island's land is uninhabited, thanks to Mount Wai'ale'ale (the world's wettest place) and the vast Waimea Canyon. So visitors can experience undisturbed white-sand beaches, lush jungles, and extraordinary wildlife. Kaua'i isn't all trails, sand, and vegetation. The island has changed with the times, welcoming an influx of residents and modern-day development, including a limited number of luxury hotels, spas, and golfing greens. Epicurean restaurants are scattered throughout the island, and it boasts enough shopping to necessitate extra baggage fees on the flight home. Surfing, zip-lining, hiking, and four-wheel-driving opportunities will exhaust any adventure addict's adrenaline supply. And history buffs can explore the island's rich culture through its ancient archaeological sites, plantation architecture, and various museums.

Kaua'i isn't only a collection of stops and must-see sights, but a

romance between visitor and island. Explore the Na Pali Coast, catch your first wave in Hanalei Bay, or watch the sunset over a forbidden island. Get pampered at an oceanside spa, hit par on the greens, or work on an organic farm. Your experiences on the Garden Isle may change you; the memories of your time on Pele's first-born will stay with you forever.

Planning Your Trip

WHERE TO GO
East Side
The east side, also referred to as the Coconut Coast, is by far the busiest side of the island. Stretching from Lihu'e to Kapa'a, it holds a vast mix of historical sites, outdoor activities, and modern comforts like restaurants, shopping, and hotels. **Lihu'e** is the island's main town, with Kaua'i's largest airport; it's also a good place to explore the island's rich history at the **Kilohana Plantation** and the **Kaua'i Museum.** Although Lihu'e serves as the go-to spot for locals seeking to fulfill daily needs such as work and shopping, those in search of activities can surf at **Kalapaki Beach** or stand-up paddle on the **Hule'ia River.** From **Wailua** to **Kapa'a** you'll find the famous **Wailua Falls** and **Wailua River** cultural sites, such as the **Fern Grotto.** Inland behind Kapa'a are miles of great hiking trails with amazing views, including the lovely walk to **Ho'opi'i Falls.**

North Shore
The magical north shore is a true tropical paradise. Its vibrant green cliffs back some of the island's most spectacular white-sand beaches with great snorkeling and world-class waves. The north side begins with **Kilauea,** a former sugar town that is home to the **Kilauea Lighthouse** and a small shopping center. The more upscale **Princeville** features a modern hotel and a large community of homes resting above beautiful beaches nestled below the cliffs. Down in **Hanalei Valley** you'll come to quaint **Hanalei** town, where you will find charming shops, lovely eateries, and freshwater rivers running into the ocean. At the end of the road here is the **Na Pali Coast,** where miles of raw hiking trails lead adventurers to secluded beaches, waterfalls, and valleys.

South Shore
The south shore offers something for everyone: luxurious indulgences for those looking for ultimate relaxation, beaches perfect for family outings, and great snorkeling opportunities. Along the dry, sunny coast, **Po'ipu** is lined with white-sand beaches that offer snorkeling, swimming, and surfing, with several large resorts and golf courses nearby. **Po'ipu Beach** and the **Maha'ulepu Beaches** provide exquisite beach time. On the opposite end of Po'ipu are some must-see sights, including **Spouting Horn** and the **National Tropical Botanical Garden.** Inland from here is the quaint and historical town of **Koloa,** with eateries, shopping, and a more local feel. Here you'll drive through lush green pastures and dense jungle. It's a mix of locals and visitors living amid modern comforts and historical influences. Slightly inland and west is **Kalaheo,** a quaint, historical town where you'll also find **Kukui O Lono Park,** a great place for history buffs and golf lovers alike.

West Side
Out on the west side, you'll find empty land, roads, and beaches, and the very small historical town of **Waimea.** With its laid-back vibe, dusty red dirt, lack of rain, and small historical buildings, it almost resembles the Wild West. The landscape is extremely different than the rest of the island, but it is not to be missed.

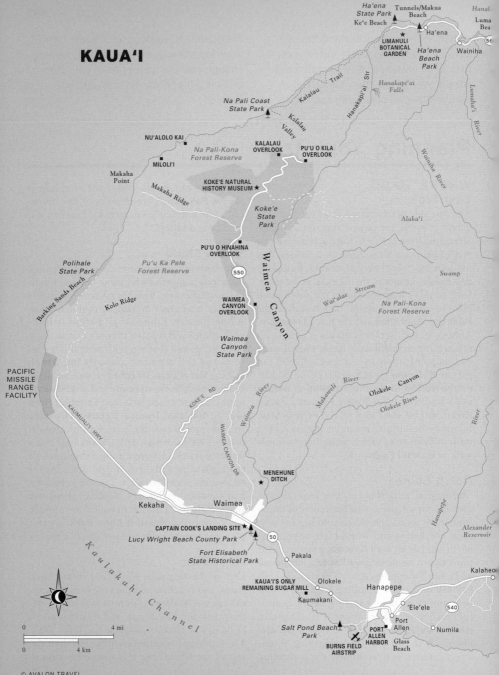

KAUA'I

Hanal

Luma
Bea

Ha'ena
State Park   Tunnels/Makua
Ke'e Beach   Beach   Ha'ena

56

★ LIMAHULI   Ha'ena
BOTANICAL   Beach
GARDEN   Park

Wainiha

Lumaha'i River

Na Pali Coast
State Park

Kalalau
Trail

Kalalau
Valley

Hanakapi'ai Str

Hanakapi'ai
Falls

Wainiha River

NU'ALOLO KAI

Na Pali-Kona
Forest Reserve

MILOLI'I

KALALAU   PU'U O KILA
OVERLOOK   OVERLOOK

Makaha
Point

Makaha Ridge

KOKE'E NATURAL
HISTORY MUSEUM ★

Alaka'i

Koke'e
State
Park

Polihale
State Park

Pu'u Ka Pele
Forest Reserve

PU'U O HINAHINA
OVERLOOK

Swamp

550

Waimea Canyon

Barking Sands Beach

Kolo Ridge

WAIMEA
CANYON
OVERLOOK

Wai'alae Stream

Na Pali-Kona
Forest Reserve

PACIFIC
MISSILE
RANGE
FACILITY

Waimea
Canyon
State Park

KOKE'E RD

Makaweli River

Olokele Canyon

KAUMUALI'I HWY

WAIMEA CANYON DR

Waimea River

Olokele River

River

MENEHUNE
DITCH ★

Kekaha   Waimea

Alexander
Reservoir

CAPTAIN COOK'S LANDING SITE ★
Lucy Wright Beach County Park

50

Pakala

Hanapepe

Kalaheo

Fort Elisabeth
State Historical Park

KAUA'I'S ONLY
REMAINING SUGAR MILL

Olokele

'Ele'ele   540

Kaumakani

Port Allen

Port
Allen

Numila

Salt Pond Beach
Park

PORT
ALLEN
HARBOR

Glass
Beach

Kaulakahi Channel

BURNS FIELD
AIRSTRIP

N

0   4 mi

0   4 km

© AVALON TRAVEL

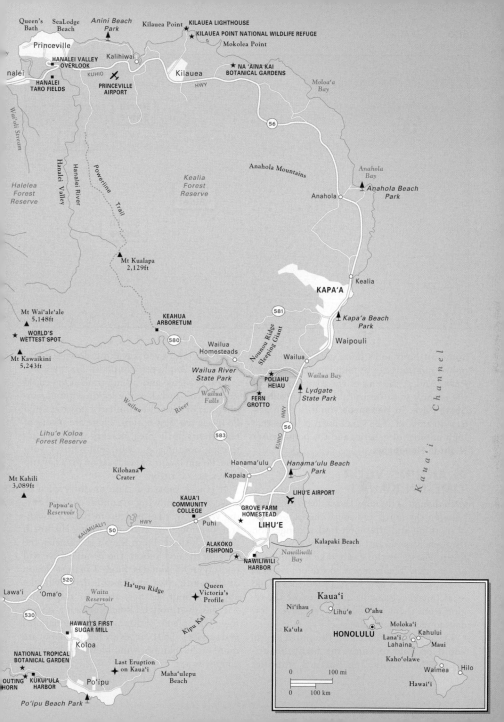

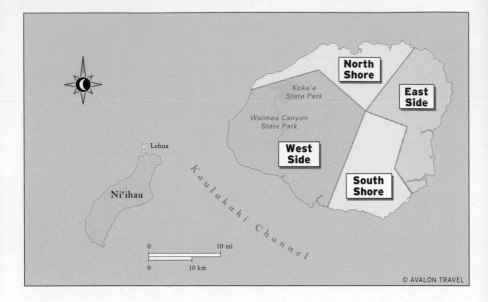

Some of the island's most spectacular viewpoints and trails can be found in **Koke'e State Park.** And at the end of the road lies one of the island's most beautiful beaches, **Polihale State Park.** In **Hanapepe** you'll find an artist's dreamland. The small town is home to a high number of galleries and the popular **Art Night in Hanapepe.**

PLANNING YOUR TIME ON KAUA'I

Even though as the crow flies it doesn't seem far between the north and south shores, because of morning and afternoon traffic, congestion through Kapa'a, and moderately slow speed limits, the drive can easily take a chunk out of your day. The best way to explore Kaua'i's diverse regions is to drive to a particular island locale, make a home base, and explore the region from there, especially if you have a few days to relax in each place.

Once you're situated on the north shore, you'll be able to enjoy the many beautiful beaches, snorkeling, surfing, stand-up paddling, and even kayaking down a river. There are ample restaurants in Hanalei, botanical gardens, and hiking trails. One could easily spend a week in the region without running out of activities. Similarly, posting up in Po'ipu is the best option. There are plenty of restaurants in the area, beaches and ocean activities, botanical gardens, and natural wonders. Po'ipu is also a great location for a day trip to Waimea Canyon.

If you're short on time or don't wish to worry about moving accommodations during your stay, then post up in Kapa'a, a central location in relation to visiting the north and south shore. From Kapa'a to Hanalei, the heart of the north shore, the 29-mile drive will take about 45 minutes. From Kapa'a to Po'ipu on the south coast, the 23-mile drive will take about an hour, as there are more traffic signals passing through Lihue. Kapa'a is a vibrant town with plenty of dining, accommodations, and services. The beaches are beautiful, but are more often than not wind blown with rough, choppy water.

© IRIANA SHIYAN /123RF.COM

GETTING TO KAUA'I

Lihue Airport (3901 Mokulele Loop, 808/274-3800, hawaii.gov/lih) is the primary airport on the island handling domestic, overseas, and interisland commercial flights, including commuter and air taxis. It is a small airport on the southeast coast of Kaua'i, about 1.5 miles east of Lihue town.

If you're island hopping, **Hawaiian Airlines** (800/367-5320, hawaiianairlines.com) is Hawaii's leading commercial carrier with the largest selection of flights between the main Hawaiian Islands. **Mokulele Airlines** (866/260-7070, mokuleleairlines.com) utilizes a prop caravan service to ferry passengers to and from Moloka'i and Lana'i. With their small prop planes they also service the smaller airports in Hana and Kapalua, Maui. **Island Air** (800/652-6541, islandair.com) has a fleet of turboprop planes that service routes from Kaua'i, Maui, Moloka'i, and Lana'i to O'ahu. All interisland flights to and from Kaua'i are routed through the **Honolulu International Airport** (300 Rodgers Blvd., 808/836-6411, http://hawaii.gov/hnl).

EAST SIDE

Kaua'i's east side stretches from Lihu'e to Anahola and is a bustling area (by Kaua'i standards) lined with beaches, dotted with homes and businesses, yet still adorned with cultural sites and natural wonders. Sacred archaeological sites, dramatic waterfalls, rivers, and hikes with stunning views provide a backdrop to Kaua'i's central areas. There are many outdoor possibilities

HIGHLIGHTS

LOOK FOR **⟨** TO FIND RECOMMENDED SIGHTS, ACTIVITIES, DINING, AND LODGING.

© AVALON TRAVEL

⟨ Donkey Beach: This long, remote white-sand beach is perfect for sunbathing and beachcombing (page 696).

⟨ Surf at Kalapaki Beach: The crescent moon-shaped beach is ideal for surfing and body-boarding. Watch the action or catch a wave yourself (page 698).

⟨ Kayak the Wailua River: A waterfall, lush jungle, and calm waters make kayaking on the Wailua River an adventure (page 699).

⟨ Nounou Mountain East Trail: This strenuous trail offers both solitude and spectacular views—from Mount Wai'ale'ale to far down along the coast (page 702).

⟨ Ho'opi'i Falls: This gorgeous nature walk leads through a tunnel of trees before its climax at two waterfalls (page 703).

⟨ Kaua'i Museum: Learn about the history and culture of Kaua'i and its people (page 711).

⟨ Kilohana Plantation: Take a trip back in time by exploring this expansive and elegant estate. Ride the sugar train, shop, and enjoy a meal at the upscale restaurant (page 714).

⟨ Wailua Falls: The famous 80-foot waterfall is easily accessible by car (page 715).

⟨ Lydgate Beach Park: Bring your snorkeling gear to view the fish in the calm protected pools, which are perfect for a swim (page 693).

to be explored here: Have an adventurous day on ATVs and ziplines in rarely explored territory behind Lihu'e, paddle up Wailua River past cultural sites to a waterfall, hike along one of many long jungle hikes with views, or surf, swim, and sunbathe on the white-sand beaches.

Lihu'e is home to Kaua'i's most concentrated population of both people and buildings. Kaua'i's most developed district prospered as a plantation town until 1996, when the sugar mill shut down, putting an end to an era that defined the island. The area is busy, but still extremely laid-back, and is the island's central place for shopping and

running errands, with a large selection of high-end dining. The main city on the island is home to big shopping centers, state and county buildings, and Kaua'i Community College, as well as important sites to visit like the Kaua'i Museum, Kilohana Plantation, and Alakoko Fishpond, which encompass the area's history. And of course, like the rest of the island, Lihu'e has its fair share of outdoor locations to satisfy watersport lovers, beach bums, and jungle explorers.

Farther north is the Coconut Coast, where Kapa'a and Wailua are decorated with coconut trees planted by a copra plantation entrepreneur

KAUA'I

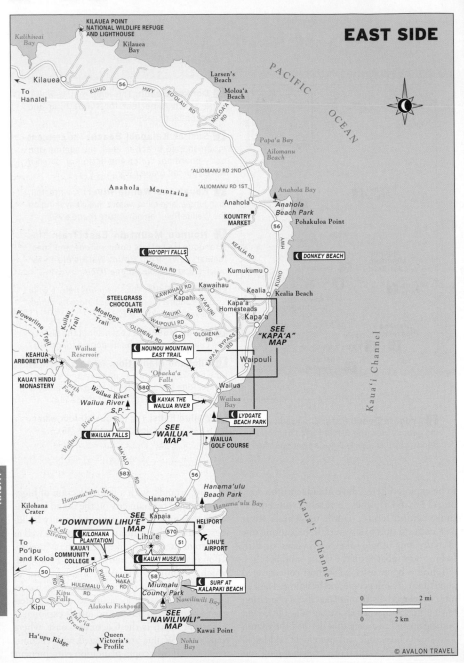

EAST SIDE

Kalihiwai Bay

★ KILAUEA POINT NATIONAL WILDLIFE REFUGE AND LIGHTHOUSE

Kilauea Bay

Kilauea

To Hanalei

KUHIO HWY 56

KO'OLAU RD

MOLOA'A RD

Larsen's Beach

Moloa'a Beach

PACIFIC OCEAN

Papa'a Bay

Ailomanu Beach

Anahola Mountains

'ALIOMANU RD 2ND

'ALIOMANU RD 1ST

Anahola Bay

Anahola

KOUNTRY MARKET

Anahola Beach Park

Pohakuloa Point

56

KEALIA RD

Kealia Beach

☾ DONKEY BEACH

☾ HO'OPI'I FALLS

KAHUNA RD

Kumukumu

Kealia

KAWAIHAU RD

Kawaihau

Kapahi

KA'APUNI RD

Kapa'a Homesteads

HAUIKI RD

Kapa'a

STEELGRASS CHOCOLATE FARM

WAIPOULI RD

'OLOHENA RD

581

'OLOHENA RD

SEE "KAPA'A" MAP

Powerline Trail

Kuilau Trail

Moalepe Trail

KEAHUA ARBORETUM ★

KAUA'I HINDU MONASTERY

Wailua Reservoir

North Fork

☾ NOUNOU MOUNTAIN EAST TRAIL

KAPA'A BYPASS RD

Waipouli

'Opaeka'a Falls

580

Wailua

Wailua River

Wailua River S.P.

☾ KAYAK THE WAILUA RIVER

Wailua Bay

☾ LYDGATE BEACH PARK

☾ WAILUA FALLS

MA'ALO RD

SEE "WAILUA" MAP

WAILUA GOLF COURSE

Wailua River

Kaua'i Channel

583

56

Hanama'ulu Stream

Hanama'ulu

Hanama'ulu Beach Park

Kilohana Crater ✦

Kapaia

Hanama'ulu Bay

Kaua'i Channel

To Po'ipu and Koloa

Pu'ali Stream

SEE "DOWNTOWN LIHU'E" MAP

☾ KILOHANA PLANTATION

KAUA'I COMMUNITY COLLEGE

570

Lihu'e

51

HELIPORT

☾ KAUA'I MUSEUM

LIHU'E AIRPORT

50

Puhi

HALE-HAKA RD

58

HULEMALU RD

KIPU RD

Puhi

Miumalu County Park

☾ SURF AT KALAPAKI BEACH

Nawiliwili Bay

Kipu Falls

Kipu

Alakoko Fishpond

Hale'ia Stream

SEE "NAWILIWILI" MAP

Kawai Point

Ha'upu Ridge

Queen Victoria's Profile ✦

Nohiu Bay

0   2 mi

0   2 km

© AVALON TRAVEL

KAUA'I

who had dreams of making it big on a plantation. The palms still tower today, moving their slender fronds in the trade winds as gracefully as hula dancers. Locals call the area home, and many independent shops, restaurants, and activity outfitters are scattered around this area. Wailua means "two waters," a name that makes sense considering it lies along the ocean and inland harbors freshwater rivers and waterfalls. Perhaps Wailua's most intriguing element is the Wailua River, where *ali'i* gathered traditionally for sacred events and left archaeological remains to tell the story. That is why the *ali'i* referred to it as Wailua Nui Ho'ano (Great Sacred Wailua). The extra-tall royal palms symbolize a place of royalty in Hawaiian culture. Many *heiau* were built in the area, and their sparse remains still can be seen along the banks of the river. The road leading along the Wailua River was called the King's Highway, and only those invited were allowed to approach the royal settlement. The mountains behind Wailua are lush and green and home to the mountain range Sleeping Giant, with hiking trails boasting views that can't be beat.

Just down the road is Kapa'a, a quaint town with an eclectic mix of local style and hip, offbeat culture. Meaning, "to hold," as in to hold a canoe on course, Kapa'a historically served as a place for the canoes to stop and prepare for making the journey to O'ahu. Running along the coast, Kapa'a offers bohemian boutiques, elegant and healthy eateries, and a historical feel that enhances the Kaua'i experience. In downtown Kapa'a, small eateries and cafés offer a range of cuisines from local style to vegetarian to fresh fruit stands. Beaches line the area, and surfing, body-boarding, and a bike path create a beach town atmosphere. Behind the town on the northern end is Ho'opi'i Falls, where you'll find a wonderful hike along a river and to a waterfall.

Heading north from Kapa'a, you'll pass through Anahola. Although some like to consider this part of the northern side because of the increased greenery and lush feeling, locals stay true to Anahola remaining part of the eastern side. Out here, the white-sand beaches lining the coast are usually less crowded than the east-side beaches behind them or the northern beaches ahead.

Beaches

The east side's coast is dotted with numerous white-sand beaches, and each location's environment is very different. Sunbathe or surf in Lihu'e, snorkel and barbecue in Wailua, and catch some more waves or enjoy a beach-side bike ride in Kapa'a. They're all pretty, but most are some of Kaua'i's more popular and crowded beaches. If you're staying in Lihu'e and don't want to go far, they will more than satisfy, but I recommend traveling north or south for Kaua'i's most spectacular beaches.

LIHU'E
Niumalu Beach Park
Just west of the Nawiliwili Small Boat Harbor, **Niumalu** is a county park resting along the bank of the Hule'ia River, where scenes from *Raiders of the Lost Ark* were filmed. Popular with locals, it has with pavilions, showers, and toilets. The beach park is used mostly for launching kayaks to explore the river, for barbecues, and for family functions. If you're in the area and looking for a quick picnic stop this will do, but other beaches are much nicer. To get here, turn off of Nawiliwili Road onto Niumalu Road. Follow it to the end.

Kalapaki Beach
Although **Kalapaki Beach** fronts the Kaua'i Marriott Resort, access to the beach is open to anyone. The sand is white, but down by the stream it's a little darker from dirt and sediment. Because it's so popular and fronts the hotel, it lacks the feeling of seclusion that many Kaua'i beaches offer. The nice thing about Kalapaki Beach is that the waves break pretty

Your Best Day on the East Side

To experience the best of the best on the east side, begin early and be ready for a busy day. Because Kaua'i's most spectacular beaches are found on other parts of island, a day on the east side should be spent with activities rather than lounging on the sand. Begin in Kapa'a and work your way toward Lihu'e because some of the Kapa'a and Wailua sights are best in the morning. If you begin your day early with breakfast around 8am, you should be finished and ready for dinner around 7:30pm.

- Welcome the day with breakfast at **Kountry Kitchen** or the **Country Moon Rising Bakery** in Kapa'a.
- When your belly is full, either walk along the river to **Ho'opi'i Falls** or kayak the **Wailua River.** If you choose the hike, just head up the road, but if you'd rather paddle up the Wailua River, book a reservation in advance. Check with your outfitter to see if they provide lunch; you can grab lunch in Kapa'a afterward if they don't.

- After your morning nature experience, head back to Kapa'a for lunch at **Mermaids Cafe.**
- After lunch, head south to **Lydgate Beach Park** for some spectacular snorkeling and cooling off in the calm pools. Spend some time viewing the underwater world and relaxing in the sun. Don't forget your snorkel equipment here.
- Don't miss **Wailua Falls,** usually a quick stop by car.
- Head over to Lihu'e for a visit to the **Kilohana Plantation.** Browse the shops and plantation grounds, or take a ride on the historical train.
- For dinner there are two great options in Lihu'e. For a spectacular dinner of local food, try **Gaylord's.** To enjoy a classic Hawaiian restaurant in a semi-formal atmosphere, head to **Duke's.**

far out, so they've usually turned into gentle surges of water before they get to shore. It is a very good spot for swimming, bodysurfing, and occasionally snorkeling. Far out in the bay, stand-up paddlers, surfers, and body boarders take advantage of the breaking waves. The popular eatery Duke's fronts the beach here, and is another reason why it's a well-known spot.

To get here, take Rice Street down toward the ocean and stick to your right as it becomes Route 51. Access is via the hotel on your left if you park in the visitors area. Or, if you keep going, on the north end of Nawiliwili Park before the Anchor Cove Shopping Center there's a small parking lot. Look for the narrow footbridge going over Nawiliwili Stream to the hotel property and the beach.

Ninini Beach

Located to the harbor side of Ninini Point and the lighthouse, **Ninini Beach** is a narrow, sandy

beach fronting the low cliff. It's calm most of the year, but during large surf or windy days the beach can be a little rougher. This is a small and less-visited beach that is very good for sunbathing and a secluded beach day. Snorkeling can be good on the left side by the rocks, but it's a little dangerous. To get here, take Pali Kai Road past The Marriott, walk along the edge of the Kaua'i Lagoons Golf Club, and keep to your right until you see the steep trail to the beach below. If you take the fork on your left you'll find its sister beach, also known as Ninini, which is another less-visited area for sunbathing and swimming.

WAILUA
Wailua Beach

Wailua Beach reaches from the mouth of the Wailua River to the first rocky point heading north. On this point are the nearly nonexistent remains of a sacred *heiau,* one of many

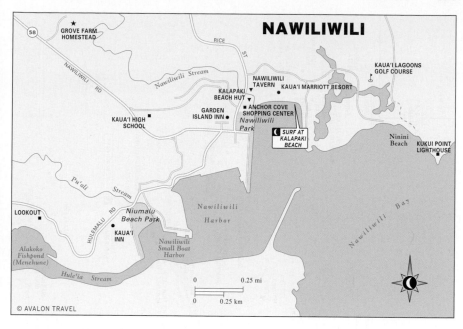

NAWILIWILI

in the area. Surfers sometimes catch waves here, but the ocean is unprotected and often gets windy and dominated by strong currents. So, it's not the most ideal spot for swimming. However, when this beach is calm it is a local favorite for a beach stroll and sunbathing. The river mouth adds an element of action, but when the river is flowing heavily it can be unsafe to go in the water. It's not one of Kaua'i's most spectacular beaches, but it's centrally located and rests in an area that was important to Hawaiians in the past. Petroglyphs can be seen carved into rocks at the mouth of the river when the tide is very low. It's at the mouth of the Wailua River, and you can pull up roadside off of Route 56.

Lydgate Beach Park

On the south side of the Wailua River and behind the Aston Hotel lies **Lydgate Beach Park.** Two protected pools that create calm places to swim and snorkel are the highlight of Lydgate. The pools are protected by lava rock barriers that create perfect places to swim and snorkel

regardless of surf conditions. It's safe for young children and anyone else who prefers to relax in the water worry-free. There is a lifeguard here, as well as sheltered picnic tables, grills, and restrooms and showers, but camping is not allowed.

The **Kamalani Playground** is also here and is any child's dream. The castle-like playground is about as huge and elaborate as a playground could ever get. Towers, slides, swings, interactive parts such as a huge xylophone, and a lot more are here to entertain children for a long time. A large pavilion is perfect for lunch or a birthday party.

A newly created section of the beach park has a number of bike paths and walkways as well as more restrooms, picnic benches, and another children's playground. To get to the second section drive down the paved road at the northern end of the Wailua Municipal Golf Course until it branches toward the sea. Turn onto Leho Drive and there are two access roads that head to the ocean. You can find parking along the way to the beach.

KAUA'I

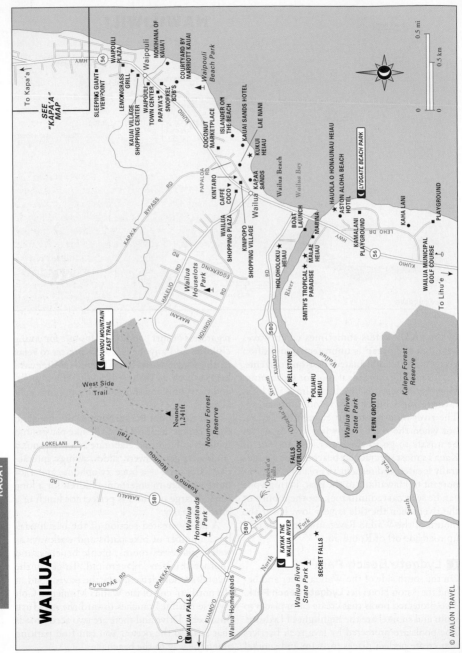

WAILUA

KAUA'I

To Kapa'a

SEE "KAPA'A" MAP

0.5 mi
0.5 km

SLEEPING GIANT VIEWPOINT
WAIPOULI PLAZA
LEMONGRASS GRILL
KAUAI VILLAGE SHOPPING CENTER
WAIPOULI TOWN CENTER
PAPAYA'S
SNOFKEL/BOB'S
Waipouli
MOKIHANA OF KAUA'I
COURTYARD BY MARRIOTT KAUAI
Waipouli Beach Park

COCONUT MARKETPLACE
ISLANDER ON THE BEACH
KAUAI SANDS HOTEL
LAE NANI
KUKUI HEIAU
LYDGATE BEACH PARK

KINTARO
CAFFÉ COCO
Wailua
KAPA'A SANDS
Wailua Beach
Wailua Bay
HAUOLA O HONAUNAU HEIAU
ASTON ALOHA BEACH HOTEL
KAHA LANI
PLAYGROUND

WAILUA SHOPPING PLAZA
KINIPOPO SHOPPING VILLAGE
BOAT LAUNCH
MARINA
KAMALANI PLAYGROUND

PAPALOA RD
KUHIO
KUHIO

Wailua Houselots Park

HOLOHOLOKU HEIAU
MALAE HEIAU

LEHO DR

WAILUA MUNICIPAL GOLF COURSE
KUHIO
56

To Lihu'e

KAPA'A BYPASS RD
KAPA'A RD
HALEILIO RD
EGGERKING RD
MAKANI
NOUNOU RD

NOUNOU MOUNTAIN EAST TRAIL

West Side Trail

Nounou 1,241ft

Nounou Forest Reserve

Nounou Trail
Kuamo'o

SMITH'S TROPICAL PARADISE

580

Wailua River

Kuamo'o RD

BELLSTONE

POLIAHU HEIAU

Kalepa Forest Reserve

Wailua River State Park

FERN GROTTO

'Opaeka'a Stream

LOKELANI PL

RD

581

Wailua Homesteads Park

KAMALU RD

'Opaeka'a Falls

FALLS OVERLOOK

580

KAYAK THE WAILUA RIVER

Wailua River State Park

North Fork

South Fork

SECRET FALLS

PU'UOPAE RD

OPAEKA'A RD

KUAMO'O RD

To
WAILUA FALLS

© AVALON TRAVEL

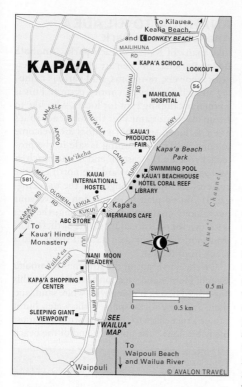

KAPA'A

To Kilauea,
Kealia Beach,
and **DONKEY BEACH**

MAILIHUNA RD

KAPA'A SCHOOL

LOOKOUT

KANAELE RD
APOPO RD
HAUA'ALA RD
KAWAIHAU RD
KUHIO HWY 56

MAHELONA HOSPITAL

Mo'ikeha
CANAL

KAUA'I PRODUCTS FAIR

Kapa'a Beach Park

MALU
581
OLOHENA RD
LEHUA ST
KAUAI INTERNATIONAL HOSTEL

SWIMMING POOL
KAUA'I BEACHHOUSE
HOTEL CORAL REEF
LIBRARY

KAPA'A BYPASS
KUKUI
Kapa'a
MERMAIDS CAFE

Kaua'i Channel

ABC STORE

To Kaua'i Hindu Monastery

Waika'ea Canal

NANI MOON MEADERY

KAPA'A SHOPPING CENTER
KUHIO HWY

0   0.5 mi
0   0.5 km

SLEEPING GIANT VIEWPOINT

SEE "WAILUA" MAP

To Waipouli Beach and Wailua River

Waipouli

© AVALON TRAVEL

KAPA'A
Waipouli Beach

Just north of Lydgate Beach Park is **Waipouli Beach.** Although it's not ideal for swimming because of strong currents and a sharp reef, the paved trail here is a great place for a long oceanside jog. The beach is narrow and is an easily accessible and central spot that begins at the Coconut Marketplace. It runs a good distance in front of a number of hotels, such as the Kaua'i Sands Hotel, Islander on the Beach, Lae Nani, and Kapa'a Sands Resort.

Waipouli Beach Park (Baby Beach)

While on Kaua'i you'll probably hear the name Fuji Beach or Baby Beach. Both refer to **Waipouli Beach Park,** lying north of Waipouli Beach. Perfect for children and a popular spot

for local families, it's a wonderful location to spend the day in the water rather than on the beach watching big waves. A large part of the ocean is protected by a long, natural stone breakwater, and unless the waves are huge, this spot is normally swimmable. Turn onto Pahihi or Makana Street and Moanakai runs parallel to the ocean. Although it's known as a great spot for children, always check out the ocean conditions first.

Kapa'a Beach Park

A little north of Baby Beach is another local favorite, **Kapa'a Beach,** composed of white sand and scattered rocks. The beach runs north from Waikaea for almost a mile between mile markers 8 and 9 until it ends near a community swimming pool and the Kapa'a library. Various roads lead to the beach from the highway and all are obvious; there is nothing obstructing the view from highway to coast. The beach park comprises just over 15 acres, with a pavilion, picnic tables, showers, toilets, and grills at the southern end. Several patches of sand break up the somewhat rocky beach, enabling swimming if the waves are mellow. It's a nice place for a meal or a bike ride along the coast, but otherwise it's best to move on to a sandier beach for swimming.

Kealia Beach

Shortly after Kapa'a Beach Park is **Kealia Beach,** a popular spot for locals and visitors alike. The half-mile-long beach has restrooms, lifeguards, and pavilions with picnic tables. The east end of the beach is usually the emptiest and is often covered with debris from the mouth of the Kapa'a Stream. Parking usually isn't a problem here as numerous parking spots back the beach. This is a popular place for surfing and body-boarding with locals, and is good for swimming when the waves are small. This is definitely one of the more crowded beaches on Kaua'i, but it makes for an easy swim while in the area. The waves here are known to be pounding, so it's best to stay near shore. The beach begins about a half mile before mile marker 10.

◖ Donkey Beach

A short distance down the road from Kealia Beach is **Donkey Beach.** This is a beautiful, remote white-sand beach where the swimming is less than ideal but the atmosphere is wonderful. It is a hidden treasure thanks to the 10-minute walk down to the beach. Swimming can be rough, but sunbathing is nice here thanks to the ample space and the good chance you'll be alone. The ocean here is choppy with a strong current on a regular basis and has no lifeguards. The occasional monk seal is spotted here, so if you see one stay a good distance away. This is a beach known to be a favorite for those who like nude sunbathing, but most likely you'll find the beach empty or see a few people enjoying it with their suits on.

To get here, turn right about a half mile past mile marker 11 at the brown sign with hikers on it. Parking is up top near the restrooms, and the easily noticeable trailhead is on the east end of the parking lot.

ANAHOLA TO KILAUEA
Anahola Beach Park

Like many of Kaua'i's beach parks, **Anahola Beach Park** has an open area for picnic tables, grills, showers, restrooms, and various camping spots if you have a county permit. This is a popular camping spot for locals, who like to set up elaborate camps for the weekend, so it's not a secluded spot, but visitors are welcome to enjoy it. The swimming is safe in the protected cove on the eastern end of the beach as well as in the river. Toward the north end the currents are usually stronger and the waves bigger. If you do plan to camp, don't leave your possessions unattended for too long; the area is known for occasional incidents of theft. The ironwood trees provide a natural shade and a break from the sun.

On the north side of the stream is **Aliomanu Beach.** Homes and vacation rentals border this less-visited beach. It's long with white sand, and there are some rocky spots in the water, but it can be a nice place to come and stroll and most likely be alone. The northern end of the beach

Donkey Beach

© JADE ECKARDT

KAUA'I

is nicer, so take a stroll down and explore. To get here, turn right onto the second Aliomanu Road, just a bit after mile marker 15, and keep to your right to access the eastern beach or take the first left and then right to access the northern beach.

Papa'a Bay

Papa'a Bay is another beautiful white-sand beach. The best thing about this beach is that you'll most likely be alone. It's great for a stroll or sunbathing, but swimming can be a bit rough. To get here, turn right onto the second Aliomanu Road, just a bit after mile marker 15. Take the first left, then a right, and then follow the trail on the left. Park up here and walk about five minutes down through some bushes and over large rocks for a few minutes.

Water Sports

SNORKELING AND DIVING

The east side of Kaua'i has one spectacular snorkeling spot and several worth taking out the mask just to see what you find. It's always a good idea to have some basic gear other than a mask and snorkel, like protective gloves, foot coverage, fins, and of course an underwater camera. On the east side it's easy to run to a shop to grab any last-minute items because shops and beaches are all close together.

Wailua

LYDGATE BEACH PARK

Lydgate Beach Park is a snorkeler's dreamland, with two wonderfully protected pools in the ocean that, thanks to a rock barrier, are an easy and relaxing place to snorkel and swim. The fish go crazy in this spot and never fail to present an explosion of vibrant tropical colors underwater. The ponds are almost always swimmable and calm, unless the surf is abnormally huge. Don't forget a camera here. There will usually be quite a few other snorkelers and beach goers, so it's not the place for seclusion, but the snorkeling is awesome.

OUTFITTERS AND RENTALS

At **Boss Frog's** (4-746 Kuhio Hwy., 808/823-0220, www.bossfrog.com, 8am-5pm daily) divers and snorkelers can find pretty much anything they could need to explore Kaua'i's underwater world. Snorkel rentals include everything from the basics to full professional snorkel sets. The average snorkel set that will get you through an enjoyable session rents for $8 per day. The shop offers all other beach needs, such as board rentals and other beach gear. Service is friendly and open here and the workers are happy to guide you to the best spots.

Another tried and true place for snorkel rentals is **Snorkel Bob's** (4-734 Kuhio Hwy., 808/823-9433, www.snorkelbob.com, 8am-5pm daily), where you can rent all the snorkel gear you could need. They offer complete sets, including a mask, snorkel, and net gear bag with grade A surgical quality silicone for ultimate comfort and water seal. The adult package goes for $35 a week or $22 per week for children. The budget crunch package offers a basic mask, snorkel and fins, and dive bag for $9 a week. A unique rental package is what they call The 4 Eyes RX Ensemble to compensate for nearsightedness while snorkeling. This includes a mask with a prescription lens for $44 per week for adults and $32 for kids. They also offer rentals for single snorkels ($7-12 per week), various fins ($8-12 per week), wetsuits ($20 per week), snorkel vests, life jackets, and flotation belts ($20 a week), and boogie boards for $26 a week. A fish identity card is a fun thing to pick up so you can tell friends later on what you saw.

Seasport Divers (4-976 Kuhio Hwy., 808/823-9222, www.seasportdivers.com, 9am-5pm daily) has been in business since 1987 and is locally owned and operated. The Kapa'a location only rents gear and takes reservations

Surfers love the waves at Kalapaki Beach.

© JADE ECKARDT

for tours. They offer complete snorkel gear sets for *kama'aina* rates of $6 a day or $19 a week and visitor rates of $8 a day or $25 a week. A unique treat with these guys is the Ni'ihau or "Forbidden Island dive," where you explore the waters around Ni'ihau and Lehua Island. Thanks to the lack of visitors and fishing on the island, Ni'ihau's waters are alive and thriving. Two- to three-tank dives off a boat are offered from $185 for just snorkeling or $310 for certified divers.

SURFING AND STAND-UP PADDLING

Surfing on the east side is usually at two main surf breaks. If you want to try surfing on the Coconut Coast and are a beginner, it's a good idea to get a surf lesson rather than renting a board and going for it alone. Experienced surfers will have fun at these breaks and should be comfortable in somewhat crowded waves with some currents. Surfers can rent gear at several shops or bring their own board. Stand-up paddling can be done at most surf spots if the paddler is experienced.

Lihu'e
◖ KALAPAKI BEACH
A great place for beginner surfing, stand-up paddling, and body-boarding, Kalapaki Beach is a local favorite. A rocky point lines the northern side of the bay, and a left-hand breaking wave diminishes as it gets closer to the beach. Mornings usually provide the best conditions, with light wind. Wind usually picks up in Hawaii midmorning and mellows out in late afternoon or early evening. Head down Rice Street and look for the small road behind the Anchor Cove Shopping Center. There's a small dirt parking lot by the river and Duke's Canoe Club.

OUTFITTERS
For lessons at the popular Kalapaki Beach try **Kalapaki Beach Boys** (808/821-1000, lilikoi@ trykauai.com, $80 pp), which offers 90-minute

KAUA'I

classes at the beach with no more than four people in a class. Classes begin with about 30 minutes on land with the instructor giving tips and sharing information, and the rest of the class in the water. Classes include land demo, boards, rash guards to protect against sun and rash, and booties for foot protection. Lessons are daily and usually at 10am, noon, and 2pm.

To explore a river on a board, try the stand-up paddle tour offered by **Outfitters Kauai** (2827A Po'ipu Rd., 808/742-9667, www.outfitterskauai.com, $122). The tour takes you on an adventure up the Hule'ia River. You will paddle downwind on the calm river, hike to waterfalls, and even get some water zipline action. The two-mile paddle lasts about a half day.

Kapa'a
KEALIA BEACH
Kealia Beach is very popular, and is often crowded with locals for surfing and bodyboarding. The waves can get very pounding here, and the conditions can make for a strong current and windy surf session. For the experienced surfer it's a fun wave. The waves break both right- and left-handed. For beginners, it's possible for mellow conditions but with the usual crowd it can be a bit tough. If you're a surfing novice and you feel the conditions are good for you, try to sit on the very inside of the waves where they're smallest. The farther out you go, the bigger the waves and the better the talent. You can't miss Kealia in full view from Route 56, near mile marker 10 at the northern end of Kapa'a.

OUTFITTERS
Kaua'i Water Ski & Surf Co. (4-356 Kuhio Hwy., Kinipopo Shopping Village, 808/822-3574, www.kauaiwaterskiandsurf.com, 8am-6pm Mon.-Sat. and 9am-4pm Sun.) offers surf gear rentals and private surf lessons. Surfboards 6-10 feet long are for rent. Body boards and stand-up paddle boards are also available for rent.

They also provide private surf lessons one on one with an instructor, or you and a friend with an instructor. Both lessons last two hours, and if you still have energy afterward they allow you to play around with your board for a few extra hours at no charge. They do lessons in Wailua Bay but say that if you feel that the conditions aren't right for you they are happy to move to another location that you are more comfortable with. Lessons are available any time and day, but you must call and book in advance. The surf shop offers all the surf gear you need for the water or just for style. Men and women's swimwear, clothing, accessories, and other surf-themed products are available in the shop.

KAYAKING
Kayaking is popular on east-side rivers. Avid kayakers will find exciting adventures to embark on, and those new to the sport will have plenty to choose from, too.

Lihu'e
OUTFITTERS
Visit **Aloha Canoes and Kayaks** (Kalapaki Marketplace, Ste. 106, 808/246-6804, 7:30am-6pm Mon.-Fri.) to rent gear to paddle up the Hule'ia River through the rainforest. Guided trips will take you up the river and help you navigate your way through the terrain.

Kapa'a
◖ WAILUA RIVER
The Wailua River is Kaua'i's most popular spot for kayaking. The vast river holds a lot of gorgeous sights. Up the river you'll find **Fern Grotto,** a natural amphitheater where ferns hang in abundance; **Secret Falls** with its swimmable pool; and gorgeous views inland and on the banks. **Uluwehi Falls,** also known as Secret Falls, lies on the north side and is reachable after a paddle and a hike. It's about five miles round-trip and roughly three hours without stopping to explore the river. The most common way to navigate the river is with guided kayak tours. Only a few companies rent kayaks for independent paddling up the river. The Hollywood film *Outbreak* was filmed on north side of the river.

KAUA'I

the Wailua River

OUTFITTERS

Ali'i Kayaks (174 Wailua Rd., 808/241-7700, www.aliikayaks.com, 7:30am-7:30pm Mon.-Sat., $40) offers a Wailua River kayak tour. The tour is led by a local guide who shares Hawaiian history and legends as you kayak along. The tour heads up the river's north fork and takes a short hike through the rainforest, ending at Secret Falls. Offered every day except for Sunday, the trip's check-in time is either 8:30 or 10:30am, and reservations are required. They provide kayak equipment, a dry bag, and walking sticks. The tour lasts approximately 4.5 hours and includes four miles of kayaking and 1.5 miles of moderate hiking.

Another reliable option is **Kayak Kaua'i** (5-5070 Kuhio Hwy., 808/826-9844, www.kayakkauai.com, 7am-8pm daily, $85 plus tax adults, $60 children under 12). They offer a one-day guided paddle up the Wailua River and hike to Secret Falls. The five-hour tour is fitting for families and allows you to swim in the freshwater stream or pool of the falls. Offered daily except Sunday, this tour has a

12-person capacity. Several tours are offered daily beginning with 7:45 and 8:45am check-ins, then 12:15 and 12:30pm. They provide kayaks with foot pedals and rudders, dry bags, life vests, juices and water, and a deli sandwich lunch with snacks and a vegetarian option.

Kayak Kaua'i is one of the few selected by the state to be an exclusive outfitter for lone kayaking up the Wailua River. They rent kayaks to those who wish to go unguided. The Wailua River Rental package includes double kayaks with a permit, life preservers, car racks, paddles, back rests, a map, and bow line. Dry bags, coolers, and walking sticks can also be rented separately. Kayakers need to bring lunch and other necessary supplies on this trip. The kayaks are dispatched between 8:30 and 11:30am and can be returned after sunset or before 8am the next day to the Kapa'a shop. No singles are available and price is $27 per person.

Kayak Wailua (4564 Haleilio Rd., 808/822-3388, www.kayakwailua.com, Mon.-Sat., $48) offers guided tours up the Wailua River. They offer dry bags and coolers to bring your

KAUA'I

own refreshments and food. They even offer adult sized triple kayaks for a family or group of friends. A trip up the river and a hike and swimming usually lasts about 4.5 hours. Tours depart at 9 and 10am and noon and 1pm.

Wailua Kayak Adventures (6575 Kuamoʻo Rd., 808/822-5795, www.kauaiwailuakayak. com, Mon.-Sat.) offers four tours a day. The roughly 4.5-hour tour provides paddlers with a two-mile round-trip paddle and a hike to Secret Falls for a swim. They offer cruise ship shuttle services for $80 per van load. Price is $47.87 with tax per person.

A favorite with many is **Outfitters Kauai** (2827A Poʻipu Rd., 808/742-9667, www.out-fitterskauai.com), which offers a guided Wailua River tour to Secret Falls. A lunch is included with a choice of a turkey watercress wrap or Mediterranean veggie wrap. Lunch comes with pasta salad and a cookie. Cold drinks are available throughout the day. Prices are $102 per adult and $82 for children 5-14 years old. The company asks that participants are comfortable kayaking for 60-90 minutes and walking two miles of rugged trail.

One of the original kayak companies on the Wailua River, **Wailua Kayak and Canoe** (169 Wailua Rd., 808/821-1188, www.wailuakay-akandcanoe.net) offers both four-hour guided kayak tours as well as five-hour kayak rentals (single $45, double $75). The four-hour water-fall guided tour includes a class one easy paddle and a short hike to Secret Falls for $49. The company does not provide lunch.

WATERSKIING, WAKEBOARDING, AND OTHER POWER SPORTS
Wailua

The only company to offer these kinds of boarding opportunities is **Kauaʻi Water Ski and Surf Co.** (4-356 Kuhio Hwy., Kinipopo Shopping Village, 808/822-3574, www.kau-aiwaterskiandsurf.com, 9am-5pm Mon.-Fri. and 9am-noon Sat.). For a unique experience on the gorgeous Wailua River, hop on some water skis for an experience you'll never forget. The company also offers wakeboarding on the

river, kneeboarding, and hydrofoil, where your board rises above the water while supported by a hydrofoil wing that remains under the water. The company offers the experience for beginners as well as experienced boarders who want to work on their technique while in Kauaʻi. The boat fits five extra passengers, who can come along for free and watch while you board around the river.

FISHING
Lihuʻe

Departing from Lihuʻe's Nawiliwili Harbor, **Kai Bear Sportfishing Charters** (808/652-4556, www.kaibear.imoutdoorshosting.com, reservations required) offers a variety of shared and exclusive private charters for a range of interests and budgets. Charters go out on one of their two boats, the 38-foot *Kai Bear* or the 42-foot *Grander*. The boats offer at least one custom-made Blue Water Rod and Penn International Gold two-speed reel. Beverages are included. Four-hour charters range $130-945. Six-hour charters range $130-1,395. Eight-hour charters range $1,400-1,795, and for a to-be-determined price you keep all the fish, a unique offer considering the catch usually belongs to the captain. Bottled water and soft drinks are provided, and guests are allowed to bring their own food and alcoholic beverages but no glass containers.

Lahela Sportfishing (Slip 109, Nawiliwili Small Boat Harbor, 808/635-4020, www.la-hela-adventures.com, reservations required) leaves out of Nawiliwili Harbor and takes guests out on the 34-foot *Lahela*. The boat is the only fishing boat certified by the Kauaʻi Coast Guard in operation on the island and takes up to 14 passengers. Private fishing charters range from $575 for four hours to $1,725 for 12 hours. Deluxe shared charters are priced at $219 with spectators at half price. Economy shared charters require a minimum of four anglers at $135. Guests must be at least seven years old.

Kapaʻa
C-Lure Charters (Nawiliwili Harbor,

808/822-5963, www.clurekauai.com) takes anglers out on the Mele Kai, a custom-built 41-foot Noosa cat equipped with Shimano tackle, depth sounders, and a GPS. It seats six people in the shade and has a fighting chair. Guests must bring their own food and alcoholic beverages, but C-Lure provides fishing tackle, bait, soft drinks, and water. They cannot take more than six people but can arrange for additional boats to caravan if you want to bring more people. Charters range from half-day to whole-day trips and custom charters. Prices range from $100 for non-fishing spectators to $1,050 for a full day up to six anglers.

Going out with **Hawaiian Style Fishing** (1651 Hoomaha Pl., 808/635-7335, www.hawaiianstylefishing.com) means you go out to sea on a 25-foot Radon. They do sport and bottom fishing and say they're prepared for any fish. You're invited to bring along your lucky lure or pole and the captain will most likely give it a try. Four-hour shared charters run from $130 per person, while private are $600. Eight-hour private charters are $900.

Hiking and Biking

HIKING

Miles of trails weave through the east side's interior behind Wailua and Kapa'a. Much hiking here winds through lush green forest, while some goes through dry and shadeless areas. A great thing about hiking in this area is that vistas are abundant, offering sweeping views from the island's center and all along the coast.

Wailua

The Nounou Mountain Trails comprise three trails. They are all inland in the mountains above Wailua and zigzag over Nounou Ridge, the Sleeping Giant.

◖ NOUNOU MOUNTAIN EAST TRAIL

Many feel the nearly four-mile round-trip **Nounou Mountain East Trail** is the prettiest of the three and can easily take up most of the day if you take your time enjoying views and lunch. The trail is rather tough but can be done by a fit family and sees a nearly 1,000-foot elevation gain while hiking.

The east side of the trail begins off of Haleilio Road. The trailhead leads to a series of well-defined switchbacks. It continues with an incline through lush forest providing some shade. As you walk along, look for flowers and guavas and passion fruit, and feel free to enjoy some. At the half-mile mark there is a fork; *be sure not to go to the left here.* It's dangerous, as

are most side trails on this hike. At the 1.5-mile marker the west trail intersects, but stick to the east trail. Farther along at the main fork in the trail, take the left path, which leads to a picnic table, shelter, and bench. Take in the views because they're wonderful here. At the table, where you hopefully enjoyed a meal, a trail goes south up to the giant's head and face. The view is truly amazing!

However, as gorgeous as this part of the trail is, it's what locals would call gnarly. It goes across the giant's throat, up the head, and is dangerous, narrow, and steep. But for the truly adventurous folks, the view is one of the biggest rewards you could ever get. So, the picnic table is a good idea for the end of this trail unless you are fearless. If you proceed, you'll walk along the spine of the mountain with deadly drops of hundreds of feet on each side. From the face, you'll be treated to an amazing all-around view. To get here, drive 1.2 miles up Haleilio Road. Parking is by the 38th pole on the right, which has a sign indicating it is pole 38.

KUAMO'O-NOUNOU TRAIL

The **Kuamo'o-Nounou Trail** is about two miles one way and is tough, but suitable for a fit family. The trail begins with a wooden bridge over the Opaeka'a Stream. From here you veer left gradually at an incline. It takes about one hour each way and sees about an 800-foot elevation gain or loss depending on which way you're going. This trail is steeper than the east trail. The end of the trail intersects the west side trail. About three-quarters of a mile from the trailhead is a shelter on a perch with great views of Kaua'i's highest point, Kawaikini, Wailua Homesteads, and views to the northwest. At the 1.8-mile point it begins the decline to the west trail. You can usually see waterfalls if it's been raining. To get here, head up Kuamo'o Road, after Opaeka'a Falls. There is a pasture on the near corner of Maile Street on the right side and a home on the far corner. You'll see the Nounou Trail sign.

NOUNOU MOUNTAIN WEST TRAIL

The **Nounou Mountain West Trail** is 1.5 miles and one hour each way. A little shorter and less steep than the east-side trail, the west trail has more shade, provided by tall pines, and meets up with the Kuamo'o Nounou Trail after about a half mile in. The trail ascends faster than the others, making it quite a workout. Keep going and you'll meet up with the east-side trail and then have access to the incredibly dangerous trail to the summit and giant's head.

Kapa'a

⟨ HO'OPI'I FALLS

This low-impact hike is more of a forest walk and brings explorers to **Ho'opi'i Falls** on the Kapa'a Stream, accessed by a lovely walk along it. It's hard to say how long the walk is—it just keeps following the stream—but the good news is that you can walk five minutes down the dirt hill just to meet the stream under a magical canopy and enjoy time there (while braving mosquitos). Or, you can continue to walk for a half hour or so. As you head down the trail look for *liliko'i* (passion fruit) on the ground; they fall from very high up on the jungle canopy. You'll probably run into the occasional resident going for a jog or walking a dog. Along the trail are thimbleberry bushes that have bright red berries similar to raspberries. Give one a try. When you come down to the river, hang a right slightly up from the river and continue on the well-worn, narrow trail. You'll see multiple

offshoot trails going down to the river. They're a bit steep, and the red dirt can be slippery. When you can hear the falls, this is most likely the right side trail down to the top of the falls. Here you can sit, spend some time, eat, or just hang out near the falls and along the river. To get to the bottom of the falls you'd have to continue downstream, then head back up in the water. When you're done, backtrack up the side trail and continue on.

Eventually you'll have to go down to the river and walk along the edge. Stay near the water's edge to stay off of private land. Right before the second waterfall the trail goes over the river to the top of the falls, and this is the end of the trail. Don't forget your camera on this hike, and make sure you have enough time to leisurely explore. If you want to really enjoy it, bring mosquito repellent.

To get here, turn onto Kawaihau Road from Kuhio Highway. Head inland for about 12 minutes and then take a right onto Kapahi Road. Look for the yellow metal post on your left at the trailhead. Right past here is a dirt pull-off spot that fits about three cars. Drive slowly; this is a very local and mellow neighborhood.

POWERLINE TRAIL

The 13-mile, strenuous **Powerline Trail** will take you from the east side to the north over the course of the day. If you choose to complete the whole thing, you'd need a pickup on the north side, or you could take the bus back to the east side. The problem with trekking the whole path, though, is that you'd have to get a taxi or ride a couple miles back up to the trailhead, so I'm recommending to just go as far as you like and turn around back to the beginning. The rough road was built for the installment of power transmission lines between Lihu'e and Hanalei, although some believe the trail was originally a connection between the two areas for Hawaiians.

Starting at the Kapa'a trailhead, you'll encounter a rather steep incline for a little while, and from there it's pretty level traveling with an eventual descent into Hanalei. Not too far

© JADE ECKARDT

Start the day with a long riverside walk to Ho'opi'i Falls.

from the beginning you'll see **Kapakaiki Falls** on your right, and soon after is **Kapakanui Falls.** These falls aren't close enough to access but make a nice sight. The part of the island the trail weaves through is densely lush and green and creates a feeling of strolling through a magical forest. But the road itself is bare, dry, and hot. This means that although the surrounding foliage is thick, the trail itself provides no shade. Bring water. Roughly halfway down you begin to see the ocean, and glorious views are offered along the way. Random roads jut off the main road, but I don't recommend following any. Footing off the main road can be unstable, and the biggest thrills are found by sticking to the road. After completing the incline from the trailhead you'll be treated to great views of **Mount Wai'ale'ale.**

Others you may see on this trail are mountain bikers, dirt bikers, and hunters and their dogs in season. Still, you'll most likely have the trail to yourself. To get here, head up Kuamo'o Road and pass the Wailua Reservoir till the pavement ends and then go about a mile to the

Keahua Arboretum. At the arboretum, cross the stream and walk up the steep road; you'll see a four-wheel-drive track heading uphill to your right. This is the start of the trail.

KUILAU AND MOALEPE TRAILS
The 4.5-mile **Kuilau Trail** begins about 200 yards before the entrance to the Keahua Arboretum and takes about 2-3 hours round-trip. There are a few parking spots at the trail-head marker on the right side of Kuamo'o Road. This somewhat mellow trail leads to a picnic area with tables and shelter after about a mile. Not long after this, the prize of this trail is the mountain views, which are some of the best you can find. Views to Mount Wai'ale'ale and the crater, and down to Kilohana and Ha'upu Ridge, are in sight. From here, keep following the trail circling around the hill until you come to a small wooden footbridge. Here, about two miles from where you began your nature stroll, the Kuilau Trail meets the **Moalepe Trail.** After crossing the bridge, the Kuilau Trail weaves through a tunnel of trees to an open flat spot

and then turns east. The Moalepe Trail begins at the end of Olohena Road. This trail is popular with local horseback riders and offers awesome views before joining back with the Kuilau Trail almost three miles from Olohena Road.

SWIMMING POOL TRAIL

For a cool pool and Mount Wai'ale'ale views, take this hike. The best thing about this adventure is the two pools of water you are treated to, depending on how far you go. This trail heads into the center of the island and leads to a stream-gauging station and dammed section of the river. The locked gate at the beginning of the trail is where scenes of the entrance gate were filmed for *Jurassic Park*. Walk around the gate and head up the road for roughly 45 minutes up an incline and you will be at the gauging station and the dammed part of the river. Here, you are very close to the center of the island. This is a great place to just relax, meditate, or enjoy a picnic lunch. From here you can see the crater, and if it's been rainy, as the center of Kaua'i usually is, you may see many waterfalls cascading down the green cliffs.

From here it's about an hour and a half via either a walk through a tunnel in the hill that requires most people to hunch over or a trek over the hill to the falls and the refreshing pool at the bottom. A flashlight is a good idea for the tunnel, and of course the water level has a lot to do with safety. Soon after, you'll see the chilly and refreshing pool, and if you swim through it and stick to the right for just a few minutes you'll come to the falls, with another small and refreshing bubbling pool. Only go in if the water flow isn't too treacherous—it's a highly enjoyable experience.

To get here, head to the Keahua Arboretum off of Kuamo'o Road and follow the gravel road running across the stream at the arboretum. Stick to the main road for about four miles. The road is marked as being for four-wheel-drives, but it is usually fine for two-wheel-drives unless it is very muddy. At the fork in the road keep to the left, then there's another fork with a gate. If the gate is open, keep driving. If it's closed, park here and you'll just have

to walk longer. The second gate is the *Jurassic Park* gate. Go around the gate and begin your adventure.

HIKING TOURS AND GEAR

For all the hiking gear you could need, stop by **Da Life** (3500 Rice St., on Kalapaki Beach, 808/246-6333, www.livedalife.com, 9am-5pm Mon.-Fri. and 10am-4pm Sat. and Sun.). The shop offers a thorough array of outdoor gear. Name brands fill the store, providing all the hiking gear you could need. Stop by for anything you may need, especially before any serious hikes.

For a private guided tour contact **Kaua'i Hiking Adventures** (808/634-1018, www.kauaihikingadventures.com, full-day tours $285, half-day tours $185). According to the company, the tours are suitable for all fitness and ability levels. Each tour is customized to the hiker's personal preference, ability, and weather conditions. The guide shares knowledge of Hawaii's plants, history, and culture while hiking. Prices include you and up to three of your friends. The guide is a National Outdoor Leadership School Certified Outdoor Skills and Ethics Trainer and has explored Kaua'i extensively.

BIKING

Much of Kaua'i has narrow, winding roads without shoulders. Therefore, it can be quite unsafe for biking around. But if you really enjoy cruising on two wheels, you're in luck because the east side is home to the **Ke Ala Hele Makalae bike path.** The name translates to "the path that goes by the coast," and true to its name, the bike path stretches along part of the east coast while staying almost entirely level. Multiple beaches, swimming, and picnic spots are located along the path. The path begins at the Lihi Boat Landing to the south and winds north to Kealia Beach.

Lihu'e

Long-time bike doctor **Bicycle John** (3142 Kuhio Hwy., 808/245-7579, 10am-6pm Mon.-Fri. and 10am-3pm Sat.) offers a thorough

KAUA'I

© JADE ECKARDT

the coastal Ke Ala Hele Makalae bike path

selection of road and mountain bikes to rent and own. Also available is a selection of other biking gear including bikes, helmets, lights, repair services, and more. Bicycle John himself is known to be straight-to-the-point kind of guy, no bells (except for bikes) or whistles, but he knows what he's doing.

Kapa'a

At **Coconut Coasters Beach Bike Rentals** (4-1586 Kuhio Hwy., 808/822-7368, www. coconutcoasters.com, 9am-6pm Tues.-Sat., 9am-4pm Sun.-Mon.), you will find a variety of bikes: classic and three-speed cruisers ($22 half day, $25 full day, $95 weekly) for adults and children, tandem bikes (half day $36, full day $45, weekly $190), mountain bikes (half day $25, full day $30, weekly $120), trainers

that attach to adult bikes for 6-9 year olds, and covered trailers for toddlers that connect to the back of the bike. The classic beach cruiser is slightly less expensive, but I would recommend the three-speed; it makes it a lot easier to go uphill. Rates for kids' mountain bikes and cruisers vary. Reservations are required for rentals.

Kauai Cycle (934 Kuhio Hwy., Kapa'a, 808/821-2115, www.kauaicycle.com, 9am-6pm Mon.-Fri. and 9am-4pm Sat.) offers cruisers, road bikes, and mountain bikes for rent. It also provides maps, trail information, clothing, accessories, and guidebooks. Rentals include a helmet and a lock and start at $20 per day. Multiday rates are also available, as well as car racks. It also has a full certified repair shop in case your own bike needs help.

Adventure Sports

LIHU'E
Ziplining and Tubing

You flew to Kaua'i on a plane, so why not fly through the air on a harness? **Kaua'i Backcountry Adventures** (3-4131 Kuhio Hwy., 808/245-2506, www.kauaibackcountry.com) offers ziplining and tubing on 17,000 acres of old sugar plantation land. You have the choice of seven different courses for your zipline experience. Zipline sessions begin at 8 and 10am, noon, and 2pm daily for $99.

Tubing begins at 9 and 10am and 1 and 2pm daily for $102. The ride takes you down the plantation's old irrigation system. Float through open canals and several tunnels dug in the late 1800s.

Another option is **Outfitters Kauai** (2827A Po'ipu Rd., 808/742-9667, www.outfitterskauai.com), which offers ziplining in the Kipu area on the southern border of Lihu'e. The Zipline Trek Nui Loa offers an 1,800-foot tandem zipline over the Ha'upu Mountains, valleys, waterfalls, and huge trees. You fly for about a quarter mile, enjoying over 90 seconds of air time. This tour includes a picnic lunch of a turkey or veggie wrap, pasta salad, a cookie, and cold water. It costs $152 for adults and $132 for children 14 and under. Another zipline trek is the Kipu Zipline Safari, which includes kayaking two miles up a river, exploring swimming holes and waterfalls, views of features that appeared in the films *Jurassic Park* and *Raiders of the Lost Ark,* and ziplining through jungle terrain. This tour includes snacks, a picnic lunch, and cold drinks. It costs $182 for adults and $142 for those 14 and under.

ATVing

Muddy family fun can be had when driving an all-terrain vehicle (ATV) with **Kipu Ranch Adventures** (Kipu Rd., 808/246-9288, www.kiputours.com, 6:30am-6pm daily). Guided ATV tours take adventurous drivers into 3,000 acres of Kaua'i's uninhabited interior. Driving yourself into otherwise inaccessible parts of the island offers awesome views, mud puddles to plow through, and exciting terrain in Kipu Ranch just outside of Lihu'e. The land is former plantation property turned working cattle ranch and offers adventure driving through its pastures and up to Kilohana Crater. Drivers must be 16 or older, but there are other vehicles available for younger guests. Long pants and shoes are a must. After getting muddy and dusty drivers can cool off in a stream. Three different tours are offered and range $75-160 depending on guests' ages and the tour chosen.

Aloha Kaua'i Tours (1702 Haleukana St., 800/452-1113, www.alohakauaitours.com) offers a range of tours into the interior of the island. The rainforest hike is actually a combo of four-wheel-driving and hiking. The tour goes inland from Wailua into the heart of the island. After a bumpy ride, the tour walks from the gate where scenes from Jurassic Park were shot. Guests walk for about three miles to freshwater pools while learning about Hawaiian culture and history. The guides provide umbrellas, ponchos, and walking sticks, as well as backpacks, snacks, and beverages. Groups are required to be a minimum of four and maximum of 12. Adults cost $80 and children 5-12 are $62.50. They also offer a Kaua'i backroads four-wheel-drive tour over the 22,000-acre Grove Farm Plantation, offering a scenic route of the interior. The half-day tour departs at 8am and 1pm from Kilohana Plantation. The tour covers 33 miles of mostly private roads from the top of 1,250-foot Kilohana Crater, along the rugged coastline of Maha'ulepu, and through a cane tunnel. Prices are $80 for adults and $62.50 for children under 12. Tours run seven days a week.

Helicopter Tours

Blue Hawaiian Helicopters (3501 Rice St., Ste. 107A, 808/245-5800 or 800/745-5800, www.bluehawaiian.com, 7am-5pm daily) offers a tour

KAUA'I

© MALGORZATA SLUSARCZYK/123RF.COM

A Blue Hawaiian helicopter comes in for a landing.

they call the Kaua'i ECO adventure. The company's new American Eurocopter ECO-Star offers more interior room to take you over the Hanapepe Valley, then on to Manawaiopuna, otherwise known as Jurassic Park Falls. Then it's on to the Olokele and Waimea Canyons, then over the Na Pali Coast, Bali Hai Cliffs, and Hanalei Bay. If weather permits, you get to explore the crater of Mount Wai'ale'ale by air for a finale. Regular price is $240 with special online prices.

Near the airport is **Jack Harter Helicopters** (4231 Ahukini Rd., 808/245-3774, www.helicopters-kauai.com, 8am-6pm daily), which offers two tours. The 60- to 65-minute tour hits all of Kaua'i's major scenic areas in their AStar and Hughes 500 helicopters. Price totals $259 including fuel surcharge. A longer tour of 90-95 minutes flies at slower speeds and explores deeper into Kaua'i's valleys and canyons. In this tour, the helicopter takes more turns than in the other, providing more photo opportunities. The only tour on the island of this length, it takes place only on the

Astars. Regular price is $384 including fuel surcharge.

With **Safari Helicopters** (3225 Akahi St., 808/246-0136, www.safarihelicopters.net, 7:30am-5:30pm daily) you have the opportunity to tour a waterfall owned by the owner of Ni'ihau. The Deluxe Waterfall Safari is a 60-minute trip to Wai'ale'ale Crater, Waimea Canyon, and the Na Pali Coast. Regular price is $254 per person with special web fares. For the Kaua'i Refuge Eco Tour they offer a 90-minute trip over the same sites as the other tour as well as a stopover at the Kaua'i Botanical Refuge overlooking Olokele Canyon. The price is $279 per person or a special web price of $268.

Sunshine Helicopters (Kahului Heliport #107, 866/501-7738, www.sunshinehelicopters.com/kauai/tours/kauai.html, 6am-8pm daily, $244 or online price of $194) offers a tour called the Ultimate Kaua'i Adventure, which leaves out of Lihu'e before 8:30am. The tour flies over Waimea Canyon, Mount Wai'ale'ale and the nearby Alaka'i Swamp, and Wailua Falls. Views of the Na Pali Coast are also offered. The flight is about 45-55 minutes.

Island Helicopters (Ahukini Rd. across from the Lihu'e Airport helipads, 808/245-8588 or 800/829-5999, www.islandhelicopters. com, 7am-6pm daily) flies over the sought-after Manawaiopuna Falls, otherwise known as Jurassic Falls. The Kaua'i Grand Circle Tour provides views of Waimea Canyon, the Na Pali Coast, and the north shore. The tour lasts 50-60 minutes but doesn't include a landing at the falls. The Jurassic Falls Tour lasts about 75-85 minutes and includes all views from the Grand Circle Tour as well as a stop at the 400-foot falls.

Golf

LIHU'E
Kaua'i Lagoons Golf Club
The Kaua'i Marriott Resort's new and improved **Kaua'i Lagoons Golf Club** (3351 Ho'olaule'a Way, 808/241-6000, www.marriottgolf.com) reopened in 2011 after being refurbished and renamed. This golf course has won many awards and was recently rated one of the top 50 golf resorts by *Golf World Magazine*'s Readers' Choice Award. In 2009 *Golfweek* rated it #5 for America's Best Courses You Can Play in Hawaii. The course, which sits atop a bluff over the ocean, can be experienced two ways. The Kiele Moana Nine features all new putting surfaces and bunkers, boasting the longest stretch of continuous ocean holes of any course in Hawaii. These nine holes have been paired with the original front nine holes, the Kiele Mauka Nine, to create 18 holes of Jack Nicklaus-inspired golf.

Children under 15 years old play for free after 3pm when accompanied by a full-paying adult. One child is allowed to play for free per round for each full-paying adult. Also, free instruction is available for children under 15 when accompanied by an adult who is paying for a lesson at the same time with the same instructor. Proper golf attire is required for all ages at Kauai Lagoons Golf Club. Golfers must be at least six years old to play. Single ride golf is available here but you must contact the golf shop in advance for reservations and availability.

To accommodate a range of golfers, the 18-hole course offers gold tees with a 7,120 yardage, blue with a 6,675 yardage, white with a 6,252 yardage, and red with a 5,377 yardage. Tee times can be made up to 30 days in advance. Golf shoes are available, and rentals include a shared golf cart, two bottles of water, a cooler, and a warm-up bucket of range balls. Eighteen-hole prices range $75-120 depending on the time of day, $75-175 for visitors. Nine-hole fees range $65-75 depending on time of day, and $95-100 for visitors. Guests at select hotels can receive discounted rates. Juniors pay $60 before 3pm for 18 holes and $20-35 for nine holes. The clubhouse at Kaua'i Lagoons has an upscale ambience on a lake, providing a convenient spot to enjoy a drink and recap your game while overlooking the lagoon.

Puakea Golf Course and Pro Shop
A favorite with local and visiting golfers, **Puakea Golf Course** (4150 Nuhou St., 808/245-8756, www.puakeagolf.com) was ranked by *Golfweek* magazine as 15th in Hawaii, and in 2009 it ranked 14th in *Golf* magazine's Reader's Choice Awards. Just several minutes from the Lihue Airport, the course travels up, down, and around deep ravines. Beautiful Ha'upu Mountain views are in sight on about three-quarters of the course, and ocean views are in sight for the rest of it. Shopping center "views" are also there, but the course is fun enough to keep your eyes off of them. Golfers love that each hole is sharply different from the rest, inspiring a new challenge at each hole. Robin Nelson was the golf course

architect, and golfers report repeated satisfaction with the course.

Avid golfers say the course ranks about medium on the difficulty scale. The course begins on the easier side and increases in difficulty as you move along. It lies behind the Kukui Grove Shopping Center in Lihu'e and offers golf club rentals for those who don't want to haul clubs on the plane.

The **Pro Shop** (866/773-5554) offers a wide spectrum of golf accessories and clothing. Anything you might need to complete your gear selection can be found here. The laid-back restaurant serves up food that will satisfy after a day on the greens.

Golf Gear

The **Pro-Am Golf Shop** (4303 Rice St. #B9, Lihu'e, 808/632-0609) offers a variety of name-brand gear for a day on any of Kaua'i's courses.

For a unique golf shirt or quality useable souvenir, check out **Garden Island Golf Co.** (3411 Hinahina St., Lihu'e, 808/822-7135, www.gardenislandgolf.com). The locally owned and operated shop offers quality golf wear. The idea for the company originated with former pro surfer Cody Graham and former pro body boarder Chris Burkart. The apparel is marked with their petroglyph-like logo of a golfer.

WAILUA
Wailua Municipal Course

Just a few miles north of the Lihue Airport, the **Wailua Municipal Golf Course** (3-5350 Kuhio Hwy., 808/241-6666, www.kauai.gov/golf) offers 18 holes, a golf shop, locker rooms with showers, a driving range, putting and chipping greens, and a practice bunker. For two players, tee times can be booked up to seven days in advance, while single golfers go out on a stand-by basis. The course offers blue tees at a 6,991 yardage, white tees at a 6,585 yardage, and red tees at 5,974 yardage. The course lines the ocean, and the ocean breeze enhances the experience. Visitor weekday price is $48, and weekends and holidays are $60. *Kama'aina* rates are $15 weekdays, weekends and holidays $20. Twilight prices are offered in the morning and afternoon for half the daily rate. Junior and senior rates are also offered. A motorized cart available for $18. Don't be shocked that it's directly across from the Kaua'i Correctional Facility.

Spas

LIHU'E

Get pampered at the **Alexander Day Spa and Salon** (Kaua'i Marriott Resort, 3610 Rice St., Suite 9A, 808/246-4918, www.alexanderspa.com, 8am-7pm) and you will truly get lost in a luxurious experience. Massages in the spa or beachside cabana range $70-175, and in your room they cost $150-200. Various modalities are offered, including couples, sports, deep tissue, Hawaiian *lomilomi,* aroma massage, and more. Body treatment combos of masks, scrubs, massage, and more range $70-185 and all involve island-themed scents and ingredients. Facials with delicious scents like green tea, ginger, and fruit range $70-180. Packages combine a facial, massage, mani-pedi, and more for $160-310. Full bridal services are offered.

KAPA'A

Relax and get centered at **The Yoga House** (4-885 Kuhio Hwy., 808/823-9642, www.theyogahousekauai.com), which offers a wide array of classes and styles. In the Hot Power and Yoga Blast classes, yogis will strengthen the body and relax the mind during a 75-minute heated session. During Hot Flow yoga, participants will spend 75 minutes combining postures, breathing, and vinyasa. Yin yoga addresses the health and suppleness of the joints, fascia, ligaments, and bones. Slow Flow Vinyasa encourages a balanced practice of challenging sun poses along with relaxing moon poses. Times and rates vary widely, so it's a good idea to call or visit the website.

The name says it all for **Kaua'i Yoga on the Beach** 808/635-6050, www.kauaiyogaonthebeach.com), where beach yoga is offered at 6am on various east-side beaches. Classes are $15 per person, and private lessons are offered for $50. Bring a beach towel, a yoga mat, and water. Mats can also be rented for $2.

Spa by the Sea at Waipouli Beach Resort (4-820 Kuhio Hwy., 808/823-1488, www.spabytheseakauai.com) has a thorough array of options to indulge in. The experienced therapists offer a variety of massage techniques, from traditional Hawaiian *lomilomi* and hot stone to therapeutic deep tissue. Couples and beach massages are also available and massages range $125-330. The spa uses the high-quality skin-care line Epicurean and offers organic skin-care treatments, including volcanic clay and custom facials from $20 for an exfoliant to $1,140 for an anti-aging series. It also offers Hawaiian sea salt body scrubs, volcanic wraps, and many more decadent choices. Ayurvedic, body, and foot treatments range $20-290.

Sights

LIHU'E
【 Kaua'i Museum

The **Kaua'i Museum** (4428 Rice St., 808/245-6931, www.kauaimuseum.org, 10am-5pm Mon.-Sat., $10 adults, $8 *kama'aina* and seniors 65 and up, $6 students 13-17, $2 children 6-12, and under 5 free) is a real treat. This two-building complex is in downtown Lihu'e, and although it's a good place to visit anytime, exploring it at the start of your trip leaves you with a background that enhances the rest of the visit. The island art exhibits change on a regular basis; however, the museum focuses on displaying ethnic heritage such as koa furniture, feather lei, and more. Permanent exhibits include the Story of Kaua'i, which takes up two floors in the Rice Building. The exhibit constructs the island's past, highlighting the geological aspects of the island and settlement by the Hawaiian people. Island chiefs, Captain Cook, traders, and whalers are highlighted. The exhibit even features a life-size camp house to walk through, shedding light on the many different people who came to the island.

The **William Hyde Rice Building** was built in 1960 to house the museum, and the Albert Spencer Wilcox building was built in 1924. Although small on the scale of national museums, the Kaua'i museum exudes a strong presence with arches, a cement front, and broad steps. The building has a lava rock exterior, sloped roof, barrel-vaulted ceilings, original antique light fixtures, and a mezzanine with a balcony overlooking the first floor. The building is on the National Historic Register. The museum shop sells books, cards, Hawaiian prints, a magnificent selection of Hawaiian craft items, and a fine selection of detailed U.S. geological survey maps of the entire island.

In the **Juliet Rice Wichman Heritage Gallery,** exquisite finds are on display. Beautiful and rare N'ihau shell lei and items that belonged to Kaua'i *ali'i* and monarchs are out for viewing. Furniture and other household items are on display. In the Oriental Art Gallery exhibit, housewares from Asia are on display. Asian china, sculptures, and art that had been in homes on the island are shared with viewers here.

There are also temporary exhibits. These include exhibits on the Kekaha train robbery, various art exhibits, textiles, and an aviation history of Kaua'i.

It's a good idea to dedicate at least a couple of hours for a thorough visit to the museum. The entrance fee is valid for several days and includes docent tours, so ask for a pass if you'd like to return. Free family admission is offered the first Saturday of every month.

KAUA'I

KAUA'I

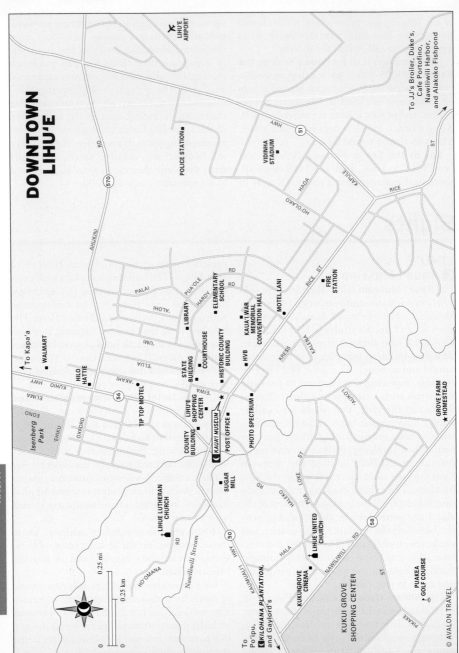

DOWNTOWN
LIHU'E

LIHU'E AIRPORT

To JJ's Broiler, Duke's,
Cafe Portofino,
Nawiliwili Harbor,
and Alakoko Fishpond

AHUKINI

RD

570

POLICE STATION

HWY

51

VIDINHA
STADIUM

HAOA

KAPULE

HO'OLAKO

RICE

To Kapa'a

WALMART

ELIMA

EONO

KUHIO   HWY

EHIKU

OXFORD

HILO
HATTIE

TIP TOP MOTEL

56

'AKAHI

'ELUA

'IWI

'ALOHI

PALAI

Isenberg
Park

PUA'OLE

RD

HARDY

RD

LIBRARY

ELEMENTARY
SCHOOL

RD

MOTEL LANI

RICE ST

FIRE
STATION

STATE
BUILDING

COURTHOUSE

HISTORIC COUNTY
BUILDING

KAUA'I WAR
MEMORIAL
CONVENTION HALL

HVB

KRESS

KALENA

COUNTY
BUILDING

LIHUE
SHOPPING
CENTER

'EIWA

KAUA'I MUSEUM

POST OFFICE

PHOTO SPECTRUM

SUGAR
MILL

HALEKO   RD

PUA   LOKE   ST

'AUKI'I

GROVE FARM
HOMESTEAD

Nawiliwili Stream

HO OMANA   RD

LIHUE LUTHERAN
CHURCH

KAUMUALI'I   HWY

50

HALA   RD

LIHUE UNITED
CHURCH

NAWILIWILI   RD

58

To
Po'ipu,
KILOHANA PLANTATION,
and Gaylord's

KUKUIGROVE
CINEMA

KUKUI GROVE
SHOPPING CENTER

ST

PUAKEA
GOLF COURSE

PIIKEA   ST

© AVALON TRAVEL

0   0.25 mi

0   0.25 km

Alakoko Fish Pond

© JADE ECKARDT

Alakoko Fishpond

The **Alakoko Fishpond** is commonly known as Menehune Fishpond. Overlooking the Hule'ia River and the Ha'upu ridge on the far side, the pond tells the story of Hawaiian history and myths. This fishpond has been used to raise mullet and other commercial fish. But unlike most other fishponds, which are built along the edge of the ocean, this pond was constructed along the riverbank and is said to have been built by the *menehune* in just one night.

Legend says that these little people built the rock wall surrounding this pond for a royal prince and princess and made only one demand: that no one watch while they were working. It's said that throughout the night the *menehune* passed the stones needed from hand to hand in a 25-mile-long line. Meanwhile, the prince and princess grew curious and watched from nearby. The *menehune* saw them and turned the royal pair into two pillars of stone that you can see on the mountain overlooking the pond. The small workers stopped their work and left holes in the wall. To get here, follow Hulemalu Road until you see the overlook. It's a beautiful sight.

Grove Farm Homestead

The **Grove Farm Homestead** (4050 Nawiliwili Rd., 808/245-3202, www.grovefarm.net, tours Mon., Wed., and Thurs. 10am and 1pm, $20 donation for adults or $10 for children 5-12) is a former sugar plantation that was started in 1864 by George Wilcox, the son of Congregational missionary teachers who worked for the original owner of the bordering land. Wilcox bought 500 acres for $12,000 through a lease-to-purchase arrangement. The property had been chopped out of a large grove of kukui trees—hence the name Grove Farm. Bringing water down from the mountains, Wilcox formed one of the most profitable sugar plantations in Hawaii. He purchased more land as the years went by, and now the property encompasses 22,000 acres (one of the five largest landholdings on the island).

The homestead was a working plantation until the mid 1930s when Wilcox died. His

KAUA'I

nieces went on to care for the property, and in 1971 Mabel Wilcox created a nonprofit organization to preserve Grove Farm Homestead as a historical living farm. Reservations for tours are preferred, but the staff will most likely accommodate unexpected visitors. They ask that visitors call at least 24 hours in advance to book a tour. Reservations are also accepted by snail mail up to three months in advance by writing to Grove Farm Homestead (P.O. Box 1631, Lihu'e, HI 96766). Exact directions will be given on the phone. Wear comfortable shoes that can be slipped off because, as in most homes in Hawaii, shoes are not worn indoors here. Tours are sometimes canceled on rainy days.

(Kilohana Plantation

For an elegant trip back in time, visit the **Kilohana Plantation** (3-2087 Kaumuali'i Hwy., 808/245-5608, www.kilohanakauai. com, shops open 9:30am-9:30pm Mon.-Sat. and 9:30am-5pm Sun.), a sprawling estate with manicured lawns, fruit, flowers, a train, and the former mansion of Gaylord Wilcox. At the time that Gaylord Wilcox moved the business offices of Grove Farm from the homestead site, he had the 16,000-square-foot Kilohana plantation house built in 1936. After decades of family use, the building was renovated in 1986 and turned into shops that sell arts and crafts. Exploring the antique mansion's rooms, still decorated with original furnishings, jewelry, and other elegant artifacts, serves as a tangible experience of history.

Kilohana Plantation has several restaurants, as well as Lu'au Kilohana every Tuesday and Thursday evening. A horse-drawn carriage operates 11am-6pm daily. Just show up and stand in line near the front entrance to take a ride. The 20-minute carriage ride is $12 for adults and $6 for children; call 808/246-9529 for reservations.

The **Kauai Plantation Railway** (www. kauaiplantationrailway.com) is a popular attraction here also. With a whistle to get the excitement going, the 1939 Whitcomb diesel engine, named Ike, pulls mahogany coaches

© JADE ECKARDT

the historic Kilohana Plantation

modeled after King Kamehameha's personal car. The first stop is at a housing of wild pigs, goats, sheep, horses, and other farm animals. You can even feed the animals with the bread supplied by the conductor. Go on the tour that includes riding the train, hiking in the surrounding rainforest into a valley with streams, and having a picnic with a dessert of fresh fruits right off the tree.

WAILUA
Fern Grotto

The Wailua River's **Fern Grotto,** a natural rock amphitheater where a dense forest of ferns hangs from the grotto, is a popular place to visit. An upriver tour run by **Smith's Kauai** (Kuamo'o Rd., 808/821-6895, www.smiths-kauai.com, boats depart at 9:30 and 11am and 2 and 3:30pm daily, $20 adults, $10 children 3-12) is the way to access it. A two-mile, 90-minute round-trip river journey takes you to the grotto. On the trip you'll also be treated to a hula dance and Hawaiian music.

It's a pretty sight, but some say the grotto

KAUA'I

isn't as romantic as it used to be. This is due to Hurricane 'Iniki taking a toll on the overlying canopy and ferns in 1992 and a lack of water seepage from the close of the sugar plantation. Although it has regrown, it isn't quite as wonderful as it once was. In efforts to reestablish the ambience, improvements have been made to bring back the irrigation to the ferns. Many couples come here to get married.

Kamokila Hawaiian Village

For a cultural experience, explore **Kamokila Hawaiian Village** (on Kuamo'o Rd. along the Wailua River, 808/823-0559, www.villagekauai.com, 9am-5pm daily, $5 adults, $3 children 5-12). Kamokila (the name means "stronghold") is Kaua'i's only re-created Hawaiian village. It has been formed on the site of an ancient royal village, the first of seven ancient villages in this valley. Resting on four acres, the location was once home to the last reigning king of Kaua'i, King Kaumuali'i. Village sites include the canoe house, the *Outbreak* movie set, a birth house, taro patches,

wood-carving house, village lagoon, petroglyphs, medicinal plants, and a lot more.

When fruit is in season visitors are welcome to help themselves to it, and several huts have been reconstructed with traditional methods. In the courtyard traditional Hawaiian games are featured, such as spear throwing and Hawaiian bowling. Kamokila has been resurrected to give visitors a glimpse of what island life was for ancient Hawaiians. It opened in 1981 and was almost destroyed by Hurricane 'Iwa in 1982, only to be damaged again in 1992 by Hurricane 'Iniki. The village also offers outrigger canoe rides, hiking and swimming, access to Secret Falls, weddings, and a luau.

(Wailua Falls

One of Kaua'i's most beautiful and easy-to-view waterfalls, the 80-foot **Wailua Falls** were featured on the opening credits of the television show *Fantasy Island*. Legend says the Hawaiian *ali'i* would dive off the falls to prove their physical prowess, and commoners were not allowed to participate. The ride up Ma'alo Road to the

© JADE ECKARDT

Wailua Falls

© JADE ECKARDT

Opaeka'a Falls

falls is gorgeous itself, as the road is surrounded by wide open pasture. The falls are about four miles up at the end of the road, so you can't miss them. The falls can be viewed from a lookout spot where there is a parking lot, which is a perfect place for a photo op. There is usually a line of onlookers here and hat makers selling their shade-providing palm hats. The lookout spot is the only place to view the falls unless you take one of the two trails down to the falls, but they are slippery and can be dangerous.

Smith's Tropical Paradise

Smith's Tropical Paradise (5971 Kuhio Hwy. 808/821-6895, www.smithskauai.com, 8:30am-4:30pm daily, $6 adults, $3 ages 3-12) is a 30-acre botanical and cultural garden along the Wailua River. On the property many plants are labeled, including an array of fruit and common island foliage as well as other plants that are rare and hard to find. There are two main buildings here; one is home to a luau and the other is a lagoon theater used for music shows. A path over one mile long leads you around the property. A Japanese garden is nice to roam around.

Opaeka'a Falls

Two miles up Kuamo'o Road are the roughly 150-foot **Opaeka'a Falls.** The scenic lookout is on the right after the first mile marker and has a large parking lot and restrooms. The majestic falls are easy to see and make for a good photo opportunity. Along Kuamo'o Road on the way to the falls, look out for the Poliahu Heiau.

Kuamo'o Heiau

Along the Wailua River off of Route 580 are seven sacred *heiau* from the pre-contact period that are easily accessible. At the river mouth are several ancient petroglyphs that can be seen at low tide—if they're not covered by sand or sediment. The first *heiau* is called **Hauola O Honaunau** and was where *kapu* (rule) breakers came to make up for their indiscretions by having a priest redeem them. This is located on the south side of the river mouth. Near the marina entrance is **Malae Heiau,** which is said by some to have been constructed by the *menehune*. It's on the road into Smith's Tropical Paradise and is believed to be the biggest *heiau* on Kaua'i. There really isn't much to see here; it's the cultural significance that counts. On the outcrop of land at the end of Wailua Beach is the **Kukui Heiau.** There is only a tiny part of the structure left, but it once measured 230 by 70 feet. It's not really worth the walk over, but knowing of it enhances the sacredness of the area. Traditionally it was used as a makeshift lighthouse, a fire beacon to lead canoes to shore. It's located on what is now property belonging to a condominium.

Holoholoku Heiau is up Kuamo'o Road right after the state park boat-launch area along the river on your left. Some say this place was used for human sacrifice, and some say for animal sacrifice. There is a big flat stone near the front of the area that was the altar. Very close is **Pohako Ho'o Hanau,** the royal birthstones where the royal women came to give birth. The mother rested her back on one of the two stones and placed her feet on the other while giving birth.

Along the river and just before Opaeka'a Falls is **Poliahu Heiau.** This was once a very sacred site and is said to have been built by the *menehune* and used by King Kaumuali'i, Kaua'i's last king. Although its exact function is not known and the structures inside are long gone, the size of it leads archaeologists to believe that it was a *luakini heiau* (human sacrifice). A rock wall in the shape of a rectangle is all that's left, which is more than most other *heiau.* Please don't walk on the wall. Enjoy, and use your imagination to think of what may have gone on in that very spot generations ago. There is a great lookout here over Wailua River and a good photo opportunity. Farther up the road, turn down a dirt road after the first mile marker, head to the end of the road, and walk down the path past the guard rail till you see a few large stones. One is known as the **Bellstone.** When it is struck a certain way the stone produces a metallic sound, which historically announced the birth of a royal child.

KAPA'A
Kaua'i Hindu Monastery
A very intriguing place to visit is the **Kaua'i Hindu Monastery** (Kaholalele St., 888/735-1619, www.himalayanacademy.com, 9am-noon daily). Located up the Wailua River, the monastery is built completely from hand-carved stones from India. Each stone takes seven years to carve and there are 4,000 of them. Free guided tours are offered once a week, but it is open for visitation daily. The holidays vary with the Hindu calendar. Wear long plants and shirts that cover the shoulders; no mini skirts for women or going shirtless for men. On-site are the Kadaval Hindu Temple building, Ganesha Shrine, and Bangalore Gallery. Call for specific guided tour dates and to reserve a parking space.

Nounou, the Sleeping Giant
Legend says that a long time ago, a giant lived in Kawaihau behind Kapa'a town. He was very friendly and helped the people of the area. He had a hard time staying awake for more than a hundred years at a time, and when he would sleep, he would use a small hill as a pillow. The people called him Kanaka Nunui Moe, the sleeping giant. After a chief requested that the people bring rocks and trees from Koke'e and Waimea to build a *heiau* for him, the giant helped, bringing all the material down. To show appreciation, the people provided the giant with a wonderful meal of poi, pig, and fish. He filled his belly and was so full he laid down to rest for the last time.

At Kipuni Place is the **Sleeping Giant Viewpoint** pull-off. From this angle you can see the mountain, and with some imagination you can see why they call it Sleeping Giant. You can see the vague outline of legs and an incline going up to a chest and head. Wonderful trails go up both the front and the back of this hill, bringing you up to a picnic spot on the chest; from there a narrow trail leads over the throat to the chin and forehead, but these hikes are very dangerous.

Nani Moon Meadery

Nani Moon Meadery (Yasuda Center, 4-939 D Kuhio Hwy., 808/823-0486, www.nanimoon-mead.com, noon-5pm Tues.-Sat.) offers an opportunity to enjoy the tastes of the islands at the state's only producer of honey wine. Made with local ingredients, the tasty honey wine is produced, bottled, and sold on-site at the tasting room. Try the Cacao Moon mead, made with macadamia nut blossom honey and Kaua'i cacao.

Steelgrass Chocolate Farm

Steelgrass Chocolate Farm (808/821-1857, www.steelgrass.org, 9am-noon Mon., Wed., and Fri., $60 adults, under 12 free) offers a tour entitled Chocolate from Branch to Bar. The eight-acre farm specializes in vanilla, bamboo, and cacao, the chocolate tree. Smelling and tasting are part of a three-hour tour that explores the gardens and the orchard. Hawaii is the only state with an environment hospitable to cacao.

Shopping

LIHU'E

Shopping in Lihu'e is best explored in the main shopping centers. This is because much of the town serves daily functional needs, so quaint independent boutiques aren't as common here as on other parts of the island. Yet Lihu'e is the best spot for mall shopping and to find the best hiking and beach gear.

Shopping Centers
KUKUI GROVE SHOPPING CENTER

In Lihu'e's largest shopping center, you will find an array of stores. Department stores such as **Macy's** and **Sears,** as well as **Kmart,** offer their standard products. **Jeans Warehouse** offers low-priced clothing for trendy teens and young women. **Deja Vu Surf Hawaii** provides extensive surf gear and clothing, and **San Lorenzo Bikinis** offers top-quality bikinis very popular in the island as well as clothing and accessories. For footwear stop into **Footlocker** or **Payless Shoe Source.** If you're looking for electronics there is a **Radio Shack.** Several jewelry stores can be found here, along with a **GameStop** for the kids and a few salons. The center is located at 3-2600 Kaumualii Highway and you can't miss it. There are some basic eateries. The shopping center is open 9:30am-7pm Monday-Thursday and on Saturday. Friday it opens at the same time but closes at 9pm, and on Sundays it's open 10am-6pm

KILOHANA PLANTATION

Historic **Kilohana Plantation** (3-2087 Kaumuali'i Hwy., 808/245-5608, 10:30am-9:30pm Mon.-Sat., 10:30am-3pm Sun.) holds a nice selection of shops with art, knickknacks, hand-made items, clothing, and other island-style products. The shops can be found on both levels of the house and include **Grande's Gems and Gallery,** offering jewelry with Tahitian black pearls, opals, tanzanite, and other unique items. At **Sea Reflections** you can find unique objects from the sea as well as Hawaiian shells. The **Artisans Room** on the lower level of the house is decorated with work from local artists. Originals, prints, and sculptures can all be found here. A fun shop is **The Country Store,** where distinctive gifts, collectibles, and local crafts like quilts and things made with local woods are found. A popular shop is **Clayworks at Kilohana,** a working ceramics gallery. Browse work by local artists or take a workshop and clay-making class yourself. **The Hawaiian Collection Room** has an array of intriguing island finds, like Ni'ihau shell lei, Hawaiian collectibles, and local jewelry and gifts.

KAPA'A AND WAILUA
Galleries

Aloha Images (1467 Kuhio Hwy., 877/821-1382, www.alohaimages.com, 10am-6:30pm Mon.-Sat., 11am-3pm Sun.) has prided itself on being a "candy store for art lovers" for 15

years. It's a good slogan, as the shop is loaded with affordable local art. Hundreds of original works line the walls, along with giclees, prints, and other things for the home. Featured artists paint in the gallery daily.

Noticeable by the mural of a ship on the northern wall of the gallery, **Ship Store Galleries** (4-484 Kuhio Hwy., 800/877-1948 or 808/821-1249, www.shipstoregalleries.net, 8:30am-5pm Mon.-Fri., 10am-5pm Sat. and Sun.) is decorated with ocean-themed art, such as paintings of ships, canoe paddlers, and beautiful landscape and ocean paintings.

Inside **Kela's-A Glass Gallery** (4-1354 Kuhio Hwy., 888/255-3527 or 808/822-4527, 10am-7pm Mon.-Sat., noon-5pm Sun.) is a dreamy, glistening underwater world of pretty things. With over 150 glass artists' work on display, Kaua'i's natural beauty is represented in jewelry to wear and things to decorate the home with. Staff is friendly and happy to help you find that perfect gift. It can be pretty pricey in here, but it's at least worth window shopping.

Earth and Sea Gallery (4504 Kukui St., Ste. 3, 808/821-2831, 10am-8:30pm daily) is stocked with locally made products from over 30 artists. The boutique has something to offer for everyone, with shell jewelry, children's clothing and toys, artwork, bath and body products, and more. The staff is always friendly and outgoing and the products are unique.

Clothing and Accessories

At **Island Hemp and Cotton** (4-1373 Kuhio Hwy., 808/821-0225, www.islandhemp.com, 10am-8pm Mon.-Sat., 11am-5pm Sun.) you can find a wide selection of clothing made from, you guessed it, hemp. The airy shop is in the center of downtown Kapa'a, and here you can find dresses, boxers, surf shorts, shoelaces, smoking pants, and even some really nice aloha shirts.

A lovely shopping stop is **Bamboo Works** (4-1388 Kuhio Hwy. #C-109, www.bambooworks.com, 808/821-8688, 10am-6pm Mon.-Sat., 11am-4pm Sun.). The shop offers women's clothing, accessories, and home decor made from bamboo with a down-to-earth elegance. The bamboo clothing is amazingly soft with a classy look. The owners also offer prefabricated buildings and other supplies made from the sustainable wood.

Women will love the clothing at **The Root** (4-1435 Kuhio Hwy., Ste. 101, 808/823-1277, 9:30am-7pm Mon.-Sat., noon-5pm Sun.), where quality clothing is available in a combination of relaxed and classy. The skirts, dresses, and shirts are comfortable yet stylish and perfect for island wear or anywhere else. Clothing is a little on the pricey side, but it's a nice break from cookie-cutter clothing.

Sweet Bikinis (4-871 Kuhio Hwy. #B, 808/821-0780, 10am-6pm daily) offers a selection of swimwear in a seemingly infinite array of colors and styles. Separates, tankinis, Brazilian cut bottoms, and accessories like beach wraps and jewelry can also be found. They're cute, they're fun, and there are some for sunbathing or for being active. The staff is usually knowledgable about which fabric holds up well for surfing and about sizing.

With all of the hikes and beaches on the island, a stop at **Work It Out** (4-1312 Kuhio Hwy., 808/822-2292, www.workitoutkauai. com, 10am-6pm Mon.-Sat.) may be necessary. The store is loaded with stylish apparel for hiking, biking, jogging, yoga, martial arts, and paddling. A running and walking group meets at the shop on Wednesdays at 6pm and runs the path, a three- to seven-mile jaunt before returning to the shop for refreshments. The staff is always happy to share input on Kaua'i activities.

Shopping Centers

Located on the ocean side of the highway, **Coconut Marketplace** (4-484 Kuhio Hwy., www.coconutmarketplace.com, 9am-9pm Mon.-Sat. and 10am-6pm Sun.) is home to many shops and eateries. From high-end souvenirs and locally made ones to classy resort wear and amazing jewelry, you'll find it all here. Apparel can be found at **Crazy Shirts,** which has an abundance of souvenir clothing; **By the Sea,** which offers jewelry and resort clothing; and **Nakoa Surf Co.,** which has loads of surf-related stuff. Other highlights include **Paradise Music,** a great source for Hawaiian music; **Island Rush/Mystical Dreams,** offering fine gifts, souvenirs, clothing, and more; as well as **Elephant Walk Gift Gallery & Boutique,** where you find unique art, home decor, jewelry, accessories, and clothing. The **Coconut Marketplace Farmers Open Market** takes place every Tuesday from 9am to noon and is worth a look with locally made gifts and locally grown food.

Surf Shops

At the **Deja Vu Surf** outlet (4-1419 Kuhio Hwy., 808/822-4401, www.dejavusurf.com, 9:30am-6pm daily) in Kapa'a an extensive selection of surf gear is provided: clothing, swimwear, boards for rent and sale, and everything else for catching waves or relaxing on the beach.

The locally owned and operated **Tamba Surf** (4-1543 Kuhio Hwy., 808/823-6942, www.tambasurfcompany.com) is a popular shop and brand with locals. They carry their own brand of clothing, as well as name-brand clothing, accessories, gear, and boards. Boards for rent and sale are offered.

Gifts and Souvenirs

Densely stocked with souvenirs and beach gear, the **ABC Store** (4-831 Kuhio Hwy., 808/822-2115, www.abcstores.com, 8am-9:30pm daily) is a tourist trap, but it's fun. The store is loaded with all kinds of not-one-of-a-kind souvenirs, shirts, and snacks. Drinks and alcoholic beverages are also for sale, along with underwater cameras, limited snorkel and beach accessories, and beach supplies.

Shell lovers must make a stop at **Shell World Kaua'i** (4-1621 Kuhio Hwy., 808/821-9070, www.shell.com, 8am-8pm daily) or the **Shell Factory** (4-901 Kuhio Hwy., 808/822-2354, www.shellskauai.com, 9am-5pm Mon.-Sat. and 10am-5pm Sun.). Both are adorned with beautiful tropical shells, although most are not from Hawaii. Still, they are perfect, fully intact, and exhibit some of nature's most intricate work.

Jewelry

Imperial Jewelers (4-831 Kuhio Hwy., 808/822-0094, 10am-6pm Mon.-Sat.) sells Hawaiian hand-crafted heirloom jewelry. Pendants, bracelets, rings, and earrings are available in the local style of carved 14-karat gold with a name in black if you like. The carvings come in an array of Hawaiian designs like whales, sea turtles, flowers, and more. A highlight is the plumeria lei flowers collection, where elegant small plumerias are connected in a permanent lei.

Jim Saylor Jewelers (1318 Kuhio Hwy., 808/822-3591, 9:30am-5:30pm Mon.-Sat.) is another nice jewelry store selling unique designs. The designer uses precious stones, black pearls, and diamonds in his unique settings and styles. He's been designing on Kaua'i for over two decades.

A very fun stop is **Kauai Crafters** (4-1176 Kuhio Hwy., 808/346-7700, www.kauaicrafters.com, 9am-6pm daily). The small shop is jam-packed full of local crafts with a strong shell theme. They sell *kahelelani* jewelry, koa and mammoth ivory fishhook necklaces, coconut faces, and a lot more. It's a fun store to check out, everything is gorgeous, and there are some affordable items.

Outdoor Markets

The **Kaua'i Products Fair** (4-1613 Kuhio Hwy., 808/246-0988, www.thekauaiproductsfair.com, 9am-5pm Mon.-Sun.) is an outdoor market with a wide variety of souvenirs, clothing, jewelry, and more sold in tents and on tables. Mostly everything here has an island theme and style, although many of the products aren't from Hawaii. It's a fun place to shop and is a great souvenir stop. Vegetables and fruits are also available here.

A "no import" market, **Kealia Kountry Market** (4100-4199 Kealia Rd., 808/635-5091, www.kealiakountrysundaymarket.com, 11am-4pm Sun.) brings local vendors together, offering shoppers locally grown and made products. Live music usually takes place, and local crafts, produce, and ready-to-eat food are available.

Locals come to shop and socialize; it's definitely worth a stop while on Kaua'i.

On the way north out of Kapa'a is the **Anahola Marketplace** (4523 Ioane Rd., 808/820-8029, www.ahha96703.org, 9am-5pm Wed.-Sun.), another place for residents to sell fruit and veggies, locally made crafts, and other things. It's worth a stop to or from the north shore.

Entertainment

LIHU'E
Polynesian Dance, Luau, and Theater

Lu'au Kalamaku takes place at Kilohana Plantation (3-2087 Kaumuali'i Hwy., 808/245-5608, www.kilohanakauai.com) and entertains with hula, poi, food, music, and a full-scale theater experience. Lu'au Kalamaku is Kaua'i's only theatrical luau. Hula dancers, fire poi ball twirlers, traditional Polynesian fire knife dancers, and a vivid story line all combine for an exciting evening and view of Hawaiian culture. Your main course is cooked in the plantation's *imu,* an underground oven, and is unearthed while you are there. Then it's time for live Tahitian music, Hawaiian games, and hula dancing.

The evening begins outside in the estate's garden for fun and games before entering the theater. A storyteller tells of the settling of the island by voyagers from Tahiti. The evening is enchanting, fun, and educational.

WAILUA
Luau and Theater

A riverside luau takes place at **Smith's Tropical Paradise** (5971 Kuhio Hwy., 808/821-6895, www.smithskauai.com, 5pm Mon.-Fri. Jun.-Aug.; 5pm Mon. and Wed.-Fri. Feb.-May and Sept.-Oct.; 4:45pm Mon., Wed., and Fri. Nov.-Jan.; $88 adults, $30 7-13, $19 3-6).

The location is home to a garden luau where your belly will be full as you enjoy music and hula. Dinner includes *kalua* pig cooked in an *imu,* teriyaki beef, mahimahi, chicken adobo, poi, and more. Hula is presented later on, and guests may go on stage to try out some moves. Tahitian drum dances and a Samoan fire knife dance are also treats.

Guests are welcomed at 5pm with an *imu* ceremony, cocktails, and music, followed by the luau feast and ending with the rhythm of an aloha show. Those who choose to eat dinner elsewhere can purchase show-only tickets.

In the 1950s, the film *South Pacific* was filmed on Kaua'i, and paying homage to it is **South Pacific Dinner and Theater** (4331 Kaua'i Beach Dr. at the Kaua'i Beach Resort, 808/346-6500, www.southpacifickauai.com, 5:30pm Wed., $85 adults, $30 6-12, under 5 free, premier seating $105). Based on the original Broadway show, the production has been brought to Kaua'i by the Hawaii Association of Performing Arts and producer Alain Dussaud. In its eighth year of production, the show tells the love story set on the island during World War II.

An all-you-can-eat buffet is included with the show and offers salad, pasta salad, teriyaki chicken, vegetables, desserts, coffee, and more. Tickets include the show, a buffet dinner, gratuity, and parking. A no-host cash bar is offered.

Food

Kaua'i's east side is home to many great restaurants and eateries. This is where you'll find the majority of the island's high-end and elegant restaurants, but there's also a great array of hole-in-the-wall local eateries.

LIHU'E
American

The **Kaua'i Bakery** (4-356 B Kuhio Hwy., 808/821-0060, 6am-2pm Sun.-Tues., 6am-2pm and 5pm-8pm Wed.-Sat.) serves tasty pastries to start the day. They don't have the broadest selection, but what they do have is very good. The pumpkin crunch pie is wonderful when in season, and the pastries and cakes are great daily. A local favorite. Service is quick and to the point.

Eat, drink, and be merry at the **Nawiliwili Tavern** (3488 Paena Loop, 808/245-1781, www.nawiliwilitavern.com, 2pm-2am daily). The tavern is a very casual place to throw back a few drinks, watch some sports, and grab WiFi at Nawiliwili Bay.

A Lihu'e staple is **(JJ's Broiler** (3416 Rice St., 808/246-4422, 11am-11pm daily) on Kalapaki Bay. A chart house feel with sailboats hanging from the ceiling, it is a classic Lihu'e stop. Meats and local fish are offered on their extensive menu. The bilevel restaurant overlooks Kalapaki Bay, which enhances the experience greatly. The bottom level is more casual, offering a full bar and a veranda. Upstairs is a bit more formal and romantic. Their claim to fame is the Slavonic Steak, a thin broiled tenderloin dipped in butter, wine, and garlic sauce. Portions are large, the food is good, and it rarely disappoints.

The tried and true **Kalapaki Beach Hut** (3474 Rice St., 808/246-6330) serves up breakfast and lunch with burgers that have proved to be a local favorite and never a letdown. The restaurant offers views of the harbor and for breakfast has the standard fare plus local dishes like *loco moco*. Lunch includes fish and chips and sandwiches along with buffalo, turkey, fish, veggie, and beef burgers. A good reliable choice for a relaxed meal.

Hawaiian Regional

(Gaylord's (3-2087 Kaumualii Hwy., 808/245-9593, www.gaylordskauai.com, 11am-2:30pm and 5:30-9:30pm Mon.-Sat., 9am-2:30pm Sun. for brunch, $21-32) is a farm-to-table restaurant at the Kilohana Plantation. Using local ingredients, the classy restaurant features American comfort food and Asian-fusion cuisine options. They use produce grown in the fields at Kilohana, and their meat and fish comes from Kaua'i ranchers and fishers. Some of the main dishes include potato-crusted mahi mahi, sesame seed-seared ahi tuna, chipotle barbecued pork chop, and grilled ribeye steak. Lunch mains include salads, sandwiches, fish and chips, steak frites, and vegetarian quiches.

A classic eatery in the islands, **(Duke's** (3610 Rice St., 808/246-9599, www.duke-skauai.com, 11am-11pm, $11-30) is a must-stop on the to-eat-at list in Hawaii. Named after the legendary Hawaiian surfer Duke Kahanamoku, the restaurant is split into two levels, where railing-side seats with unobstructed ocean views are the best. The downstairs Barefoot Bar is steps from the sand and serves up sandwiches, burgers, fish tacos, Hawaiian plates, and more. The Dining Room serves dinner daily and offers fresh fish and seafood, steaks and prime rib, and a salad bar. Lanai seating is the best and music is offered several nights of the week.

On Kalapaki Beach is **Kukui's** (Kaua'i Marriott Resort, 808/246-5166, www.kukuis. kauaimarriott.com, 6:30-11am and 5-10pm Mon.-Sat., 6:30-10am and 5-10pm), offering Pacific Rim food for breakfast and dinner. The poolside seating adds to the romantic and elegant experience. Sunday brunch is also offered. Service is always on point here.

Italian

The open air and views over Kalapaki Bay from **(Cafe Portofino** (3481 Ho'olaule'a Way, 808/245-2121, www.cafeportofino. com) offer one of the most ideal backdrops, especially to enjoy always-great Italian food. The food is good and the wine selection is well done. The owner is a genuine Italian, which reflects in the quality of the food. Seafood, pasta, veal, filet mignon, and other meat dishes are available, along with enough meat-free options for vegetarians. Homemade gelato and fruit sorbets are also served. This is romantic fine dining.

A local favorite, **Kaua'i Pasta** (4-939B Kuhio Hwy., 808/822-7447, www.kauaipasta. com, 11am-9pm daily, $12-22) offers a not-over-done sleek atmosphere. Tasty appetizers, wonderful and unique salads, paninis, and an array of main dishes with several suitable for vegetarians are combined with a few Pacific-inspired apps on the lounge menu. There are locations in Lihu'e and Kapa'a. The atmosphere is modern yet warm.

Mexican

Another stop in Nawiliwili is **Mariachie** (3501 Rice St., 808/246-1570, 8am-9pm Mon. and 8am-10pm Wed.-Sun.), where basic Mexican food is served up. The menu is quite extensive and offers many common Mexican options. Nothing is bad, but nothing is really amazing either. This is a decent stop while exploring Nawiliwili Bay.

Thai, Japanese, and Filipino

A homestyle place is **Mama Lucy's Kitchen** (4495 Puhi Rd., 808/245-4935, 6am-6pm Mon.-Fri., 6am-4pm Sat.), where you can get authentic Filipino food served with a smile. The desserts and treats are good too. The environment is nothing fancy.

Shaved Ice

Shakas Shave Ice (3474 Rice St., 808/652-1793) serves up standard shave ice beachside at Kalapaki Bay. Portions are good sized and I recommend trying local flavors.

WAILUA AND KAPA'A

American

The quaint and simple **(Kountry Kitchen** (1485 Kuhio Hwy., 808/822-3511, 6am-1:30pm daily, $7-11) is a perfect place to grab a classic breakfast of eggs, omelets, pancakes, French toast, coffee, and more. The place is a favorite with locals and visitors, and you may have to wait a few minutes on a weekend morning. True to its name, a country theme sets a homey feeling for the decor. Portions are large and service is friendly and on top of it.

Killah Steaks (across from the Waipouli Town Center, 808/631-1935, 11am-5pm Tues.-Thurs. and Sun., 11am-5:30pm Fri.-Sat., $6-10) is a local favorite. Customers leave stuffed and satisfied every time. The roadside restaurant in a wagon serves up steaks at decent prices to go or to enjoy at a picnic table. Two local guys own and operate the portable restaurant, and serve up "killah" affordable steaks. There is no menu here, just two options: the salt and pepper steak or a mushroom onion steak with gravy. Both options come with a side salad and rice. Sometimes they sell out and close early.

At **Olympic Cafe** (1354 Kuhio Hwy., 808/822-5825, 6am-9pm daily), the open-air side of the café overlooks the sidewalk in downtown Kapa'a. Usual breakfast fare like eggs and pancakes is offered for breakfast. Lunch is wraps, burgers, salads, and sandwiches. Dinner offerings include pasta, fish, burgers, Mexican dishes, steaks, and more. The restaurant is known for its large portions. You won't leave here hungry.

Chicken in a Barrel (4-1586 Kuhio Hwy., 808/823-0780, 10am-8pm Mon.-Sat., $5-15) is famous for its smoked foods and classic barbecue. Service is great, with the occasional slow meal. For lunch or dinner it makes a perfect stop while cruising Kapa'a. The chicken is known to be tender and moist. Indoor and outdoor seating are available. Try the sampler or the chicken burrito in the casual atmosphere.

Coffee and Bakeries

Country Moon Rising Bakery (4-1345 Kuhio Hwy., 808/822-0345, www.roxysquare.com/

countrymoonrising.htm, 8am-8pm Sun.-Thurs., 8am-5pm Fri.-Sat.) is a sweet place to get fresh baked breads and pastries. The bakery uses only organic flour in its hand-formed breads and bagels. Hawaiian sweet breads to take home include macadamia nut ginger and cinnamon raisin; they are so good! Stop by for a tasty pastry.

Sweet describes **Sweet Marie's Hawaii Bakery** (4-788 Kuhio Hwy., 808/823-0227, www.sweetmarieskauai.com, 7am-2pm Tues.-Sat.), a quaint and cute bakery. The small bakery is in with today's health trends of serving up gluten-free baked goods, desserts, and wedding cakes, as well as gluten-free catering. Freshly baked pastries, muffins, and cookies are a delightful treat. Try the amazing *liliko'i* (passion fruit) burst. You can even take home some gluten-free muffin mixes and pizza dough. Great for breakfast or dessert.

The artsy and funky **(Small Town Coffee** (4-1495 Kuhio Hwy., 808/821-1604) serves up an array of tasty quality coffee to get your day started. The staff is friendly, usually young, hip, and tattooed. The decor is simple and offers seats and free WiFi. The coffee is always good and never burnt, and various breakfast bagels and pastries are available for a quick eat.

Hawaiian Regional

A sea of seafood is available at **Wahooo Bar and Grill** (4-733 Kuhio Hwy., 808/822-7833, www.wahooogrill.com, 11am-9:30pm daily, $13-50), bordering a coconut grove on the Coconut Coast. They have a wide array of all the seafood you could ask for, from local fish to wonderful lobster tail. For those not in the mood for seafood there is a cheeseburger for the lowest priced meal, as well as beef dishes and ribs. There's not really much for vegetarians here except for a grilled cheese and dessert. And for dessert, try the baked papaya, a unique twist on a fruit usually reserved for breakfast.

Escape reality at **(Oasis** (4-820 Kuhio Hwy., in Waipouli Beach Resort, 808/822-9332, 5:30-9pm daily, $10-17), which offers oceanfront dining in an environment that is truly an oasis from the outside world. Service is always on point, and the eatery focuses on local cuisine, using 90 percent ingredients from Kaua'i, from veggies to fish. A perfect location for a romantic dinner or celebratory meal. The eatery opens to a white-sand beach.

(Caffe Coco (4-369 Kuhio Hwy., 808/822-7990, 11am-2pm Tues.-Fri., 5pm-9pm Fri.-Sat.) is a garden bistro emanating a relaxed island ambience. Made-to-order gourmet food with a Pacific theme and many vegetarian dishes are offered here. Outdoor seating can be enjoyed in the gravel courtyard surrounded by numerous fruit trees, tiki torches, delicate lighting, and umbrellas. Indoor seating is offered and there is also an indoor gallery. Order at the counter and don't forget to use the house's "jungle juice" if the mosquitos get bothersome. A full espresso bar and good desserts are also offered. Live music happens every evening, and it's bring your own drinks.

Named after the plant that decorates the island, the **Naupaka Terrace** (4331 Kaua'i Beach Dr., 808/245-1955, 6:30-11am and 6pm-9pm daily, breakfast $9, dinner $25-40) offers breakfast and dinner overlooking Kaua'i's shore. The open-air restaurant is a plantation-style building that offers steak and seafood dishes, an abundant salad bar, and other entrées suitable for vegetarians. The tranquil and elegant environment offers views of waterfalls, ponds, and the ocean. A prime rib and seafood buffet is offered every Friday and Saturday night.

Health Foods

Rainbow Living Foods (4-1384 103A Kuhio Hwy., 10am-7pm Mon.-Fri., 10am-5pm Sat.) offers healthy and gourmet meals like Russian caviar, kale salad (a personal favorite), and delicious juices and desserts. Service is friendly and warm and they even offer catering. Check the daily specials and enjoy the healthy meals.

The Coconut Cup Juice Bar & Cafe (4-1516 Kuhio Hwy., 808/823-8630, www.coconutcupjuicebar.com, 9am-5pm daily, $6-9) is the best stop for a healthy meal on your way to the beach. They serve up sandwiches, bagels, wraps, acai bowls, smoothies, and more. A real treat here is their natural shave ice, a nice break from the common artificial and sugary shave ice. Enjoy your meal on the go or at the picnic tables.

A true hole in the wall, **(Mermaids Cafe** (1384 Kuhio Hwy., 808/821-2026, www.mermaidskauai.com, 11am-9pm daily, $9-12) is nestled between shops in downtown Kapa'a. The food is delicious and on the healthy side, although not completely vegetarian. The order-at-the-window café serves wraps, burritos, sandwiches, and stir-fry, all with unique twists and most with tofu, chicken, and fresh fish options. Check for daily specials. Try the ahi nori wrap. Good drinks include spearmint and lemongrass iced tea and hibiscus lemonade. There's limited sidewalk seating and a small bar tucked around the side.

Ice Cream

Tropical and traditional ice creams and sorbets at **Lappert's** (484 Kuhio Hwy., 808/822-0744, www.lappertshawaii.com, 10am-9pm Sun.-Sat.) are the perfect cool accent to a warm Hawaiian day. Originating on Kaua'i, the shop now has outlets statewide and has about 16 percent butterfat in its regular flavors and around 8 percent in its fruit flavors, making for some pretty creamy ice cream. There's a wide array of delicious flavors, so I recommend sampling a few before making a decision.

Japanese

(Kintaro (4-370 Kuhio Hwy., 808/822-3341, 5:30-9:30pm Mon.-Sat., $11-21) has great sushi, a full bar, a lovely atmosphere, and a great teppanyaki area (where they prep the food in front of you). The fish is local and always fresh, the service is outstanding, and it's nice enough to get dressed up but still fun and not yuppy. Make reservations for the teppanyaki. Lobster, filet mignon, and other seafood are available for those not in the mood for Japanese food.

Pizza

Brick Oven (4-361 Kuhio Hwy., 808/823-8561) is a local favorite. It's very child friendly with the option for the kiddos to have a free ball of dough to play with. Wheat or white crust is offered, as well as the option to have garlic butter brushed on the dough. Thursday night is all-you-can-eat buffet night. Service is friendly but sometimes on the slow side. It's a good place for a group or family dinner or a very casual date.

JJ's Pizza (4-1345 Kuhio Hwy., 808/822-5743, www.jjspizzakauai.com, noon-9pm Mon.-Sat., $11-40) makes its pizza dough daily. The pizza is really good, but at JJ's the service can really be on "island time." They offer various sized pies with up to seven toppings. Calzones are also available.

Getting There and Around

CAR

The most convenient way to get to and around the east side is by car. Highway 56 heads west straight out of Lihu'e and runs all the way to the end of the road, turning into Route 560 by Hanalei. Rental cars are the best bet here and are available at the airport. Gas prices go up the farther north you go, so it's a good idea to fill up in Lihu'e.

BUS

The **Kaua'i Bus** (808/241-6410, www.kauai. gov/Transportation, 5:27am-10:40pm Mon.-Fri. and 6:21am-5:50pm Sat., Sun., and holidays) runs island-wide with numerous stops from Lihu'e to Anahola. The bus is a green, convenient, and affordable way to get around and even goes to the airport. Fares are $1 for children and seniors, and $2 for adults.

Monthly passes are also available. Bus schedules for the east side are available on the website.

TAXI AND LIMOUSINE

Pono Taxi (808/635-3478, www.ponotaxi.com) in Lihu'e offers taxi, airport shuttle, and tour services island-wide. They provide spacious and clean minivans. **Island Taxi** (808/639-7829) is based out of Lihu'e and provides airport rides as well as rides island-wide. Service is prompt and friendly. Lihu'e's **Ace Kaua'i Taxi Services** (808/639-4310) will take you wherever you need to go. Hawaii taxi rates are $3 per mile and 0.40 cents a minute. Prices are per minivan, not per person.

SCOOTER

Hop onto a moped to zip around the east side and save on gas at **Island Scooter Rental** (at Coconut Coasters in Kapa'a, 401586 Kuhio Hwy., 808/822-7368, www.mobilemopeds.com, 9am-5pm daily). If you rent by the week the company offers free airport pickup, and they offer four-hour tours for $100. Call for prices and reservations.

NORTH SHORE OF KAUA'I

Kaua'i's north shore is a true paradise with lush green land, deep blue ocean, bright sunlight, and nourishing rain sustaining the area's fertile soil. The road through the north shore weaves through taro fields, quaint towns, valleys and jungle, and beaches, ending at the start of the Na Pali Coast.

HIGHLIGHTS

LOOK FOR **⟨** TO FIND RECOMMENDED SIGHTS, ACTIVITIES, DINING, AND LODGING.

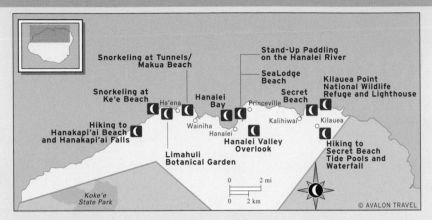

⟨ Secret Beach: Located at the end of a short downhill hike, Secret Beach offers a view of the Kilauea Point Lighthouse, a refreshing waterfall, and fine white sand (page 733).

⟨ SeaLodge Beach: This beautiful, secluded spot is perfect for sunbathing, swimming, and snorkeling when the sea is calm (page 735).

⟨ Hanalei Bay: Nearly two miles of fine white sand make up this heavenly crescent-moon-shaped beach (page 737).

⟨ Snorkeling at Tunnels/Makua Beach: When the ocean is calm, Tunnels Beach offers the best snorkeling sites on the island (page 741).

⟨ Snorkeling at Ke'e Beach: Marking the beginning of the Na Pali Coast, Ke'e offers a semi-protected natural swimming pool and spectacular snorkeling (page 741).

⟨ Stand-Up Paddling on the Hanalei River: Rent a board and hit the long and winding Hanalei River for some exercise and sun (page 743).

⟨ Hiking to Secret Beach Tide Pools and Waterfall: Scramble over rocks and hike to a beautiful area full of clear tide pools and a lovely ocean-side waterfall (page 745).

⟨ Hiking to Hanakapi'ai Beach and Hanakapi'ai Falls: The two-mile hike to Hanakapi'ai Beach offers splendid views; it's another two miles up to the magnificent falls and an icy cold pool (page 748).

⟨ Kilauea Point National Wildlife Refuge and Lighthouse: Enjoy great views of the north shore's coastline (page 753).

⟨ Hanalei Valley Overlook: Take in amazing views of a wildlife preserve and acres of farmland (page 753).

⟨ Limahuli Botanical Garden: Take a botanical stroll through history along terraced taro fields used by ancient Hawaiians (page 756).

Kilauea is the first main town you'll encounter on Kaua'i's north side. The dense jungle, winding rivers, and long beaches of Kilauea exist in an area without defined borders, ranging from slightly before the town to somewhere between Anini and Princeville. Kilauea town is small and sweet, built on the sugar industry, which left the area in the 1970s. Hidden from view on the highway, the town is toward the coast after you turn right near mile marker 23 and a Shell gas station. The quaint town offers a surprising array of eateries and shops that serve as bustling gathering places for visitors and locals alike. Near town is the area's claim to fame, the historic Kilauea Lighthouse, as well as marvelous white-sand beaches, secret tide pools, waterfalls, and sandy havens.

Farther north lies Princeville on a high bluff. It is 9,000 acres of planned luxury homes, condos, and a hotel with a view of Hanalei Bay that can't be beat. Its modern name stays true to the area's traditional uses, as it was used by the *ali'i* (Hawaiian royalty) and was also home to various sacred *heiau*. The pandanus tree grew here in abundance, providing Hawaiians with a valuable leaf called hala that was used for weaving. Because the first Europeans to the area realized the value of the location, the Russian Fur Trading Company built Fort Alexander here, one of the three forts built under King Kaumuali'i of Kaua'i. The only remains are the faint outlines of walls on the lawn in front of the St. Regis Princeville Resort, a prime spot to watch the sunset. Princeville is a destination within itself, providing accommodations, shops, eateries, a grocery store, postal services, a library, a playground, top quality golf courses, a luxury hotel, and just about anything a visitor could need or want. The area also holds beautiful beaches and a wonderful natural saltwater swimming pool, all nestled at the bottom of the cliffs.

Descending into Hanalei Valley, visitors enter into another element, one which dreams and tropical fantasies are made of. Hanalei town is backed by prominent green cliffs lined with waterfalls whose numbers are relative to how much rain has fallen on the area. Where the cliffs meet the land, acres of bright and dark green taro *lo'i* (irrigated terraces) glisten in the sun. There is a great photo opportunity of the terraces from the Hanalei Overlook. The essence of old Hawaii holds strong in Hanalei, with historic buildings, a mix of homes from small plantation cabins to luxury homes owned by celebrities, and a raw landscape. Hawaiians native to the area still live here, while celebrities, hippies, surf-happy travelers, and the upper class have all made homes in the jungle and along the beach.

From Hanalei to the start of the Na Pali Coast at the end of the road, the coast is made up of some of the state's most spectacular beaches. Rivers trace the land from the mountains to the ocean, and fertile dirt lends a hand in helping tropical jungle flourish. The Kalalau Trail, leading miles along the wild and gorgeous Na Pali Coast, leads to waterfalls, secluded beaches, and camping far off the beaten path.

Kaua'i's green and lush windward north side also provides the other vacation luxuries you may be looking for, with local boutiques and galleries, top-of-the-line gourmet food, and world-class surfing. Your journey to the north shore can include a range of experiences. Take a muddy hike to a waterfall or sit poolside overlooking the bay, eat a gourmet meal or enjoy lunch at a local lunch wagon, or snorkel a beautiful bay after a morning on the greens. Kaua'i's north side isn't just a destination, it's a feeling, an essence, a spirit, and it shouldn't be missed.

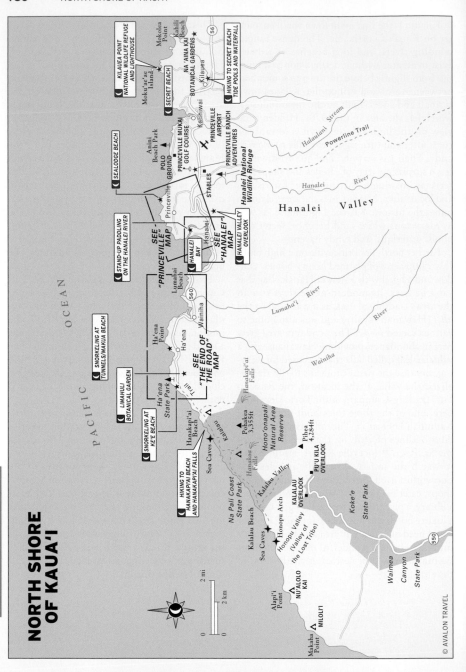

NORTH SHORE OF KAUA'I

KAUA'I

PACIFIC   OCEAN

Hanalei   Valley

Halaulani   Stream

Powerline Trail

Hanalei   River

Lumaha'i   River

Wainiha   River

Waimea Canyon State Park

Koke'e State Park

Na Pali Coast State Park

Hono'onapali Natural Area Reserve

Kalalau Valley

Honopu Valley (Valley of the Lost Tribe)

Hanakoa Falls

Hanakapi'ai Falls

- KILAUEA POINT NATIONAL WILDLIFE REFUGE AND LIGHTHOUSE
- SECRET BEACH
- HIKING TO SECRET BEACH TIDE POOLS AND WATERFALL
- SEALODGE BEACH
- STAND-UP PADDLING ON THE HANALEI RIVER
- SNORKELING AT TUNNELS/MAKUA BEACH
- LIMAHULI BOTANICAL GARDEN
- SNORKELING AT KE'E BEACH
- HIKING TO HANAKAPI'AI BEACH AND HANAKAPI'AI FALLS

NA 'AINA KAI BOTANICAL GARDENS

Mokolea Point
Kahili Beach
Moku'ae'ae Island
Kilauea

Kalihiwai

Anini Beach Park
POLO GROUND
PRINCEVILLE MUKAI GOLF COURSE
PRINCEVILLE AIRPORT
PRINCEVILLE RANCH ADVENTURES
STABLES
Hanalei National Wildlife Refuge

Princeville
"PRINCEVILLE" MAP

HANALEI BAY
Hanalei
SEE "HANALEI" MAP
HANALEI VALLEY OVERLOOK

Lumahai Beach
Wainiha

Ha'ena Point
Ha'ena
Ha'ena State Park
Trail
SEE "THE END OF THE ROAD" MAP

Sea Caves
Hanakapi'ai Beach
Kalalau Trail
Pohakea 3,355ft
Pihea 4,284ft
PU'U KILA OVERLOOK
KALALAU OVERLOOK

Honopu Arch
Kalalau Beach
Sea Caves
Alapi'i Point
NU'ALOLO KAI
MILOLI'I
Makaha Point

56
560
550

N

0   2 mi
0   2 km

© AVALON TRAVEL

Your Best Day on Kaua'i's North Shore

The best day on the north shore is all about good food, beach-hopping, colorful sunsets, snorkeling, and catching a few waves. It can all be experienced in one day if you begin early (around 9am).

- Begin your day on the north side with views of the **Kilauea Point National Wildlife Refuge.** Gaze down into the clear blue water of the cove, where birds nest and whales make wintertime visits. It's a classic photo opportunity with the lighthouse standing proudly above the cove.

- Now head back up to **Kilauea Bakery & Pau Hana Pizza** for a quick but quality breakfast of sweet and savory pastries, coffee, and other treats. If you'd like you can drop into some other shops here.

- Then it's off to Princeville for a short hike down to **Queen's Bath** or **SeaLodge Beach** (or both if you'd like). Queen's Bath is only recommended in summer, while SeaLodge requires more time.

- After working up an appetite hiking, stop at the **Hanalei Valley Overlook** for a photo and then head down to Hanalei for a healthy local lunch at the **Hanalei Taro and Juice Co.** This is a great place to try some healthy Hawaiian dishes.

- Now to experience what the north side is all about—surf. There are two options here:

You can rent a surfboard at **Hanalei Surf Company** or **Backdoor Surf** for a self-guided surf lesson, or if you're more comfortable with a surf school, visit the **Titus Kinimaka Hawaiian School of Surfing** in Hanalei and book a lesson. Another option is renting a stand-up paddle board and hitting the **Hanalei River** or **Hanalei Bay** if the waves are flat.

- For lunch, stop at **Red Hot Mama's** in Wainiha for some unique burritos and local fish. Enjoy them on a nearby beach.

- If it's summer and the waves are small, **Tunnels Beach** is the next stop for excellent snorkeling, so don't forget your snorkel gear.

- From here, drive to the **Maniniholo Dry Cave** across from Ha'ena and take a quick peek. It's fun to take photos here.

- Then it's a stop for photos and dipping your feet in the cold water at **Waikapala'e Wet Cave.** Some people like to swim here, but the cave is rather dark and eerie.

- To end the day, head down to **Ke'e Beach** to snorkel and enjoy the sunset.

- On the way back, stop in Hanalei at **Postcards Cafe** or **Bar Acuda Tapas and Wine** for dinner. Enjoy live music at **Bouchons Hanalei** or **Tahiti Nui.**

Beaches

The north shore holds Kaua'i's most exotic beaches. They instill a feeling of bliss in their visitors. Each one is covered in a thick blanket of white sand lining clear blue water, and many boast perfect waves for surfers. All are great for tanning and picnicking, many are wonderful for snorkeling, and a lot are ideal for surfing. The north shore picks up Hawaii's big swells in the winter, so make sure to be careful during winter's big waves.

KILAUEA
Moloa'a Beach

Moloa'a means "matted roots" in Hawaiian, and the relevance of the name is apparent at the river mouth, where tree roots are exposed to the

KAUA'I

© JADE ECKARDT

Moloa'a Beach

elements. **Moloa'a Beach** is a beautiful white sand break in the shape of the crescent moon. At this lesser-visited beach, black rocks jut out through the water to the far left and right of the large bay. Oceanfront houses back the east half of the beach, but it still provides an undisturbed haven from the more crowded beaches. While several of the beaches out here have calm rivers good for swimming for children, the river mouth here is usually a little rough, and the water in it appears to be a bit more murky than others. The south side of the beach is nicer than the north, providing shade and safer swimming and body-boarding than the other end of the beach. As at all beaches out here, swimming should only be attempted when the waves are very calm, and at Moloa'a the ocean can be a bit rough and windy. Moloa'a is a perfect place to watch a colorful sunset, which will most likely be enjoyed alone. To get here, turn onto the rough Ko'olau Road between mile markers 16 and 17. Then turn onto Moloa'a Road and follow it to the end to Moloa'a Bay. Parking is very limited here, but signs alert visitors of

where it's okay to park. It's worth it to bring a snorkel here.

Larsen's Beach

Named after the former manager of Kilauea Plantation, L. David Larsen, **Larsen's Beach** offers seclusion and enough space to stroll and see what you can find. Larsen's is another place where the crowds are usually nonexistent, and many times you will be alone or a good distance from other visitors. The very dangerous Pakala Channel is right before the point on the north end and features an extremely strong current that visitors absolutely must stay out of. When I consulted friends while writing this book, the Pakala Channel was one of two places people warned of. If the waves are flat and conditions are very mellow, snorkeling can be marvelous here—again, only when staying out of the channel. To get here, turn down the second Ko'olau Road headed north, right before mile marker 20, and a little over one mile down take the left Beach Access road to the end. After the

© JADE ECKARDT

Secret Beach tide pools

cattle gate is a trail and it's about a 10-minute walk to the bottom.

◖ Secret Beach

Secret Beach is a wonderful treasure at the end of a dirt road and short trail. The long beach is backed by steep, tall cliffs that provide a small waterfall perfect for rinsing off about halfway down the beach. Secret Beach is full of surprises. Depending on the season, wave size, rain, currents, and tides, you may find swimming ponds in the sand, exposed rock creating tide pools, or rocks to cross over about halfway down. In winter, waves pound the shore, resulting in strong currents. In summer, when the waves are small, swimming is possible. The walk down takes about 10 minutes and is a steep trail on roots and dirt. The way back up can be pretty tough because of the incline.

Secret has always been the unofficial nude beach on the north shore, but nowadays there are flyers posted by the police department stating that it's illegal to go naked here. However, this hasn't entirely stopped dedicated nudists.

It's also known as Kauapea Beach, and the Kilauea Lighthouse is visible on the point at the east end. There are awesome, even more secret tide pools and another waterfall farther west past the beach. To get here, turn onto the first Kalihiwai Road heading north and take the first right onto a dirt road. Head to the end of the road; parking is behind large homes.

Kahili/Quarry Beach

A long, fine white-sand beach backed by an ironwood forest, **Kahili Beach** is also known as **Quarry Beach.** A popular spot with locals for surfing and boogie-boarding, Kahili Beach is gorgeous but doesn't provide the calmest swimming. The ironwood forest growing out of the red dirt backing the beach makes for a fun place to experiment with photography. There are two sides to the beach, with a ridge of rock dividing them, and the east side serves as an unofficial campsite. It's not a wide section of rock though, and crossing over it is simple when the waves aren't huge. A river meets the ocean on the west end of the beach, and along

KAUA'I

the river can be a good calm place for swimming. During weekdays, there's a good chance Quarry Beach will be empty, but it's popular with locals on weekends.

Local fishers come here to catch a fish they use for bait called 'o'io. The fish is too bony to fry and eat, but the fishers get the meat off the bones by cutting off the tail, rolling a soda bottle over the body, and then squeezing the meat out of the cut. It's then made into fish balls by mixing it with water, hot pepper, and bread crumbs.

To get to Kahili Beach, head north and turn right on Wailapa Road between mile markers 21 and 22. Turn left at the yellow post and cement blocks marking the top of the road and go about a half mile down to the beach.

Waiakalua Beach

The great thing about **Waiakalua Beach** is that it's usually empty and secluded. The beach offers shade, which enables visitors to spend several hours here without overheating and needing to leave. Soft white sand, a fringing reef, and a spring at the north end add character to this beach. As usual, ocean conditions dictate whether it's swimmable here. When it's very mellow, snorkeling can be okay, but be careful. To get here, turn onto North Waiakalua Road and turn left on the dirt road just before you reach the end. Park at the end and walk the trail on the left. Waiakalua Beach is on the left after about a 10-minute mini hike down the steep path. To the right after the large rocks is **Pila'a Beach,** which is reachable after about 15-30 minutes of walking.

KALIHIWAI
Kalihiwai Beach

Kalihiwai is another beautiful bay nestled between two rocky points with a river at the west that usually offers a perfect place for a refreshing and calm swim. The sand is white and very fine, and the right-hand breaking wave is excellent for surfing, but it's much too advanced for beginner surfers. There are no amenities here, but there is sufficient parking under the ironwood trees. Swimming in the river is great

for children, but make sure to stick by them. The edge of the water varies from a gradual slope to a steep drop. Coming from the east side, turn down the first Kalihiwai Road to get here. The road ends at the river, where the other side is visible. The road used to connect but was destroyed in a 1946 tsunami, so to reach the other side take the second Kalihiwai Road and take the right at the fork. It leads to the other side of the beach, where locals sometimes come to fish or paddle across the river to the beach.

Anini Beach Park

The seemingly endless white sand of Anini Beach stretches for approximately two miles. Much to the delight of beach goers who like to laze about in the water, a barrier reef creates great swimming for children and others who appreciate calm waters. The swimmable water here is a highlight. There's really no safer swimming on the north side than at Anini, and the water is surprisingly shallow very far out. Along the drive down, various pull-off stops dot the road. They are all near small patches of beach where it's likely you'll be alone.

Anini Beach Park, about halfway down the road, is a popular beach with a camping area, restrooms, showers, picnic tables, and barbecue pits. The beach park is almost always very crowded, so if you're looking for less of a crowd try any of the spots on the way down. Past the park, beach access continues until the end, where a stream meets the ocean. The occasional tide pool may be spotted along the way down depending on the tide, and feel free to pull over anywhere and take a dip or enjoy the beach. Near the end of the road is a swing hanging from a false kamani tree, a perfect opportunity for an ocean-side swing. To get here, take the second Kalihiwai Road headed north. Keep to the left at the fork in the road (going right leads to the north side of Kalihiwai Beach) and keep driving.

Wyllie Beach

After the stream at the end of Anini is **Wyllie Beach,** named after the road that accesses it

© JADE ECKARDT

SeaLodge Beach

from Princeville. If you want to check it out, park at the end of Anini and walk across the stream. It's the narrow strip of sand before the point and is lined with false kamani trees. The water is still really calm here.

PRINCEVILLE
◖ SeaLodge Beach

Seclusion, white sand, shade, and a pristine cove of crystal clear water compose **SeaLodge Beach,** offering everything a beach lover could want. Accessed by a shaded hike through the trees and then a short walk along the rocky coast, the beach provides good snorkeling when the ocean is calm. There's no lifeguard or amenities here, so it's important to be careful in the water. Located near the SeaLodge condos at the end of Kamehameha Road in Princeville, parking is in the unmarked stalls toward the top of the parking lot. The trailhead is in front of building A and marked with a sign. Here is an amazing panoramic view worth taking a minute to indulge in and snapping a few photos.

Take the dirt trail down past the small stream on the way to the ocean. Once you reach the ocean keep to your left, where you can walk along the black rocks or on the narrow trail a little up on the dirt. After a minute or so you will see SeaLodge Beach, nestled in its own cove and backed by a vertical cliff. The back of the beach is lined with trees that provide enough shade that you can spend a few hours at the beach. It's quite an amazing beach and worth the effort. The trail isn't super strenuous, but it is rather steep and tiresome on the way up.

Queen's Bath

Queen's Bath is a tide pool on the edge of a cliff looming above the ocean. Nature has created an extremely unique and picturesque combination that is at its best when the waves are small, but big enough to wash freshwater into the pool. This spot is dangerous. There's a plaque at the base of the trail with a safety warning stating that as of 2011, 28 people have died here, which speaks for itself. On

KAUA'I

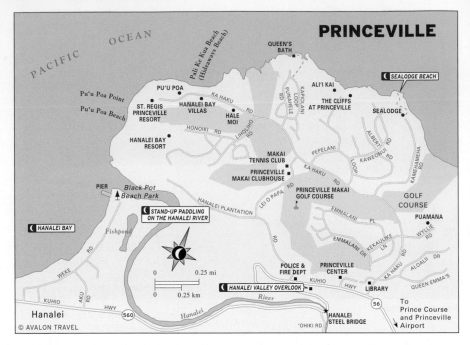

very calm days, the pool is crystal clear and swimmable, but on any rough day in winter it's risky. There's a five-minute walk from the bottom of the trail to the pool that puts visitors at the edge of the cliff, and the pool itself isn't far from the edge and waves either. The hike down is intriguing in itself and offers several sights along the way, including a river, a couple of waterfalls, and a pool that usually has a few fish resting in it.

To get here, turn right on Punahele Road and take the second right onto Kapiolani Loop. The parking lot is on the left-hand corner bordered by a green cement wall. The trailhead is easy to find, marked with both a warning sign and another one giving notice of the shearwater breeding grounds. About 10-15 minutes down the dirt trail it veers to the left at a waterfall pouring right into the ocean. Go left past the warning signs and almost right on the edge of the cliff is the pond. During winter (September through April), the pool is pretty much unusable due to the large surf.

Hideaways Beach

Hideaways is a great beach for snorkeling, as is its sibling beach on the far side of the rocky point on the right. When the surf is small, snorkelers will usually see a gorgeous variety of fish and some green sea turtles. As at many other north shore beaches, false kamani trees provide shade, enabling beach goers to spend some quality time here without turning into lobsters right away. The trail leading down consists of steps for the first half before turning into a dirt path that can be muddy and slippery if it has rained. So although it's not a really strenuous hike, it takes a little agility to get down there and can be slightly tough for kids.

Check ocean conditions before going to this beach. When the waves are big in Hanalei Bay, they will probably be washing far up the beach at Hideaways. To get here, take the trail that starts shortly before the St. Regis Princeville Resort gate house and next to the Pu'u Poa tennis courts. To reach the other side of the beach, either swim to the right from Hideaways (when conditions allow, of course) or walk the paved trail from the Pali Ke Kua condominiums.

Pu'u Poa Beach

Directly below the St. Regis Princeville Resort is the easily accessible and popular **Pu'u Poa Beach.** Swimming and snorkeling are both good here when ocean conditions allow. The white-sand beach reaches toward the mouth of the Hanalei River to the left, and the sandy bottom is enclosed by a narrow reef. When surf is up, experienced and elite surfers catch some of the biggest waves the north side musters up in the winter. For hotel guests, access is by the hotel pool area. There's a small parking area for visitors, by the hotel entrance, where the cement path begins.

HANALEI
◖ Hanalei Bay

Hanalei Bay is a crescent-moon-shaped, nearly two-mile long stretch of unbroken white sand beach consisting of several different spots that make up the heavenly stretch. The bay was used as one of Kaua'i's three main ports until recently and is still visited by large yachts. Constructed in 1912 for rice transportation, the pier on the right side of the beach is now utilized mostly by children, who love to jump off of it, and by fishers, who enjoy lazing on it with a pole.

To the left of the pier is **Queen Reef,** and to the right is **King Reef.** Surfing for both experts and beginners takes place here, along with body-boarding, sailing, swimming, and stand-up paddling. At the end of Weke Road between the pier and river is **Black Pot.** The name refers to the days when a large black pot was always cooking over a fire on the beach here with a big meal for everyone to share. Nearby and *mauka* (on the mountain side) of Weke Road is the headquarters of the Hanalei Canoe Club. You will see the sign when driving in, along with the sign for a shave ice wagon.

West of that is **Hanalei Pavilion** by the pier, recognizable of course by the large pavilion on the side of the road. Farther west and roughly in the center of the bay is **Pine Trees,** a popular

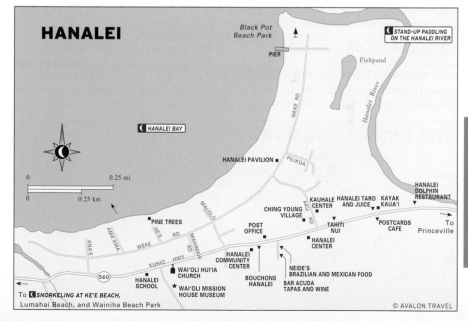

surf spot for local children and families. Access to Pine Trees is at the end of He'e, Ama'ama, and Ana'e Roads. It's a good place to watch locals surf or take surfing lessons yourself. More access is available nearing the west end of the bay before the bridge. Hanalei Pavilion and Pine Trees both have lifeguards, and all of these spots are county-maintained and have showers, restrooms, picnic tables, and grills. When in Hanalei, turn off of Highway 560 onto Aku Road right before Ching Young Village. Turn right on Weke Street, and near the end you'll see the beach where the pier is. Turn left onto Weke and then right onto He'e, Ama'ama, or Ana'e Road to reach Pine Trees.

Waikoko Beach

Located at the west end of Hanalei Bay is **Waikoko Beach** and surf break. Another white-sand beach with black rocks dotting the area in the water and on the beach, it can be a less-crowded place to hang out, perhaps because the number of visitors here is limited by the roadside parking. To get here, look for the small parking area on the side of the road after the bridge and mile marker 4. If a spot is available, look for the short trail through the trees.

TO THE END OF THE ROAD
Lumahai Beach

After Waikoko Beach is the first access to **Lumahai Beach.** Lumahai is slightly over a mile long, running between mile markers 5

and 6, and has two accesses. The locals call the north end by the river "local" Lumahai and the east end "tourist" Lumahai. Don't be put off by nicknames, as tourist Lumahai has a nice trail down and this end of the beach is prettier. Heading north, about a mile after the last bridge at the end of Hanalei Bay is a curve in the road with several parking spots alongside. This is before mile marker 5. Look for the trailhead, located where the trees open up to the ocean the most. Past the first access is an HVB warrior sign at a roadside lookout where you can view the beach. It will probably entice you to go down.

To access the north end of the beach, head about a mile past the first access. If you pass mile marker 6 and the bridge, you've gone too far. The best thing about this end of Lumahai is the river. The river is a great place for children to swim and play in the sand, but only upriver from the mouth. Local parents and children spend a lot of time here, and it's a good place to bring beach toys and floats. It's best to stay out of the open ocean here. Lumahai is one of the most dangerous beaches to swim on the north side, and there isn't a lifeguard, so be careful.

Wainiha Beach

Beachfront homes sit on **Wainiha Beach,** most notable by the Wainiha General Store and other small shops. A river runs into the ocean here, and the bay is almost always windy and choppy with a strong current. Access to the

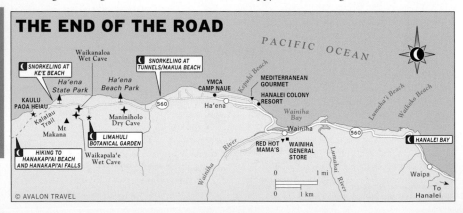

THE END OF THE ROAD

debris-covered beach is through trees at the far end of the bay, and it's usually so deep and muddy that only a four-wheel-drive could make it in.

Kepuhi Beach

After mile marker 7, ironwood trees line the beach; parking spots under them provide access to the start of **Kepuhi Beach**. The long white-sand beach can also be accessed at the Hanalei Beach Resort, where parking is free. This long beach isn't good for swimming, especially considering how nice all the other beaches are out here. It is a nice place to eat the food you might get at the Na Pali Art Gallery & Coffee Shop or for a romantic stroll before dinner at Mediterranean Gourmet.

Tunnels/Makua Beach

Named after its surf break, **Tunnels** offers some of the best snorkeling on the island. Reef fish can usually be found enjoying the waters not far from shore, and the sea caves to the left entertain bigger fish. There is a drop-off farther out that is intriguing, but this area is for experienced snorkelers and divers only, and should only be explored when the waves are small. The surf spot out here is a pretty intense wave, sending heavy white wash inside when the waves are breaking. This part of the beach is less crowded than Ha'ena Beach Park on the north end of Tunnels thanks to the limited parking. The beach is beautiful and long and makes a perfect place for a walk or run. Access borders homes located on two narrow side roads past mile marker 8. The first is just short of a half mile past the marker, and the second is slightly farther and most recognizable by the bent metal post with red paint. It is across from the 149th telephone pole, although at press time the 9 was missing so it looks like pole 14.

Ha'ena Beach Park

A picturesque beach with a backdrop of lush green mountains highlighted by perfect surfing waves and a river, **Ha'ena Beach Park** is a must. Before the sand is a grassy lawn for tent camping, along with restrooms, showers, and picnic tables. A river bordering the east end of the park area runs over the road as you drive in. Swimming is good here only when the waves are small, but the river makes a good spot for the kids when it's running onto the beach. The reef has great snorkeling, again only when the waves are small in the summer. If the main parking lot is filled up, which it often is, there is a bit more parking at the west end right past the showers. Ha'ena is ideal for camping because of its location, scenery, and surrounding sights. Past the rocks on the west end the beach keeps going, and it's a great long solitary stroll if you're up for it, passing the area formerly known as Taylor Camp and eventually two *heiau*. Ha'ena Beach Park is located off of Kuhio Highway after mile marker 8 and just before mile marker 9, across from the dry cave.

Ke'e Beach

The pot of gold at the end of the road is **Ke'e Beach** and its natural large swimming pool. The snorkeling here is truly wonderful, and between the snorkeling popularity and the fact that the base of the Kalalau Trail is here, Ke'e and its parking lot are almost always crowded. You may have to wait in the car for a few minutes for a spot to open up or drive a minute back up the road to the parking lot on the ocean side of the road. It's beautiful, provides amazing photo opportunities, and has full amenities and a lifeguard. Venturing east down the beach will lead you to the spot where Taylor Camp stood, which makes for a nice beach stroll. To get here, drive to the very end of Highway 560; the road turns into a parking area at the base of the Na Pali Coast.

NA PALI COAST
Kalalau Trail Beaches

Those dedicated to a serious hike can continue about two miles from Ke'e Beach is **Hanakapi'ai Beach.** There's a freshwater stream and it's a favorite campsite for hikers who make the trek out there. Brave surfers venture out here to catch some waves, but the ones who do this are serious risk takers.

Four strenuous miles after Hanakapi'ai is

Hanakoa Beach, a good place to camp. The biggest thrill here are the falls that are another half-mile inland. In this area you'll also see wide terraces and wild coffee trees.

Five miles down the coast from Hanakoa is **Kalalau Beach.** It's important to note that this is a serious hike, requiring proper prepping and serious dedication. Kalalau Beach is about a half mile long with a small waterfall often used by campers for a shower and portable toilets. Many people who camp here like to pitch tents in the caves for wind and rain protection.

Past Kalalau is **Honopu Beach,** and the only legal way to get there is to swim from Kalalau. No surfboards, boats, or other crafts are allowed on shore, but you could paddle in a ways, anchor in the water, and swim up to the beach. Honopu Beach is actually composed of two picturesque, undisturbed beaches separated by an impressive arch. These are perhaps the most magical beaches on the island. You'll find a wonderful waterfall here and a stream to rinse off the salt water. Vertical cliff walls that are more than 1,000 feet high back these beaches.

Water Sports

SNORKELING AND DIVING

Good snorkeling is frequent on the north shore. Several beaches offer the option to break out your snorkeling gear. Because of the reefs and currents, gear in addition to a mask and snorkel is a good idea. Reef shoes, swim fins, and gloves for holding onto rocks are useful, but remember not to grab or step on coral. When snorkeling, always remember to only go out when the waves are small, and it's safest with a partner. Dive fins are always a must, not only as minor (although unofficial) foot protection, but also as an enormous help with speed and when fighting even a minor current.

A water camera is always a good idea, and even the disposable ones available at most supermarkets take pretty good photos. Snorkel gear rentals are available at the **Hanalei Surf Company** (808/826-9000, www.hanaleisurf. com, 8:30am-9pm daily), **Pedal-n-Paddle** (in Ching Young Village, 808/826-9069, www. pedalnpaddle.com, 9am-6pm daily), and the **Snorkel Depot** (5-5075 Kuhio Hwy., 808/826-9983). The last chance for snorkel rentals is the **Wainiha General Store.**

Kilauea
ANINI BEACH
The calm water and the long fringing reef make for great snorkeling at Anini Beach. The water

stays shallow shockingly far out and maintains a depth of around just four feet. From the beach park down, some of the safest snorkeling on the north side can be experienced. Snorkelers who head far enough out will see the ledge dropping into the deep sea. To get here, take the second Kalihiwai Road headed north. Keep to the left at the fork in the road (going right leads to the north side of Kalihiwai Beach) and keep driving.

Princeville
HIDEAWAYS BEACH
Hideaways is the best snorkeling in Princeville as long as the waves are small. Snorkelers will be treated to a colorful array of tropical fish. Green sea turtles are known to cruise through the water at a leisurely pace. To get here, take the trail shortly before the St. Regis Princeville Resort gate house and next to the Pu'u Poa tennis courts. To reach the other side of the beach, either swim to the right from Hideaways (when conditions allow, of course) or walk the paved trail from the Pali Ke Kua condominiums.

SEALODGE BEACH
Hike down to SeaLodge Beach for a secluded, lively underwater world. There's a reef right off the beach here in a cove, which means some pretty fish like to linger around. There's no

lifeguard here, so don't go out too far. If you haven't rented gear yet, you can buy some at the Princeville Foodland.

To get here, drive to the SeaLodge condos at the end of Kamehameha Road in Princeville; parking is in the unmarked stalls toward the top of the parking lot. The trailhead is in front of building A and marked with a sign. Take the dirt trail down past the small stream on the way to the ocean. Once you reach the ocean, keep to your left, where you can walk along the black rocks or on the narrow trail a little up on the dirt. After a minute or so you will see SeaLodge Beach.

Hanalei
WAIKOKO BEACH

If you're going to check out Waikoko Beach anyway, you can hop in with a snorkel and mask since you're there. The reef draws fish in and it's worth a glance, but it's not the best snorkeling on the north side. This area is rocky and waves break here, so it's a good place for snorkeling gloves and foot protection. It's at the north end of Hanalei Bay; to get here, look for the small parking area on the side of the road after the bridge and mile marker 4. If a spot is available, look for the short trail through the trees.

To the End of the Road
◖ TUNNELS/MAKUA BEACH

You'll see a rainbow of fish at Tunnels. Reef fish spend their time not far from shore, and the sea caves to the left are a favorite hangout for bigger fish, along with the outside drop-off. The outer area is for experienced snorkelers and divers only, and should be done only when the waves are small. Sea turtles, the occasional reef shark, caves, and fish can be seen. Access borders homes located on two narrow side roads past mile marker 8. The first is just short of a half mile past the marker, and the second is slightly farther and most recognizable by the bent metal post with red paint. It is across from the 149th telephone pole, although at press time the 9 was missing so it looks like pole 14.

◖ KE'E BEACH

Another location known for spectacular snorkeling, Ke'e offers good views inside the natural pond, where there is usually a crowd of snorkelers. Outside in the open ocean the views get even better but snorkeling here should only be attempted when the waves are flat in summer. Advanced snorkelers find that heading a bit to the left and snorkeling along the reef offers the best views. To get here, drive to the very end of Highway 560; the end of the road turns into a parking area at the base of the Na Pali Coast.

Na Pali Coast

The best and safest way to snorkel along the Na Pali Coast is definitely with a boat tour company. A couple leave from the north side and head down the coast, but many leave from the west side. The underwater world along the coast is nothing short of amazing. Sea turtles, a spectrum of fish, the occasional reef shark, underwater caves, and more are all out there.

Na Pali Catamaran (5-5190 Kuhio Hwy., 808/826-6853, www.napalicatamaran.com) has been launching out of Hanalei Bay for almost 40 years. People are loaded onto an outrigger canoe that takes them to a 34-foot catamaran that takes 16 passengers maximum. They offer snorkeling cruises, which they conveniently provide the gear for. A deli-style meal is provided; visitors have the option of a meat or veggie sandwich. Snack, drinks, and water are also provided. All tours depend on ocean conditions. Adults pay $160, children 5-11 years old $130. The office is right next to the Hanalei Post Office.

Also leaving from Hanalei Bay is **Captain Sundown** (P.O. Box 607, Hanalei, 808/826-5585, www.captainsundown.com). A six-hour Na Pali snorkel sail ($199) takes you down the coast and stops at a sea-turtle cleaning station where trigger fish clean the turtles. Trampoline nets allow great views below to dolphins and other sea life. Captain Sundown also offers a three-hour Na Pali sunset sail ($144) down the coast. Snacks, soft drinks, and bottled water are provided.

Na Pali snorkeling tours leaving from the

west side are much higher in number, and some include **Holo Holo Charters** (4353 Waialo Rd. Suite 5A, Port Allen, 808/335-0815 or 800/848-6130, www.holoholokauaiboattours. com), which offers a Na Pali snorkel sail ($99-139). The well-established company's cats, one motorized and one sailing, run out of Port Allen Harbor. The company has a reputation for treating guests well.

Catamaran Kahanu (4353 Waialo Rd., Port Allen, 808/645-6176 or 888/213-7711, www. catamarankahanu.com) is a Hawaiian-owned tour company offering Na Pali Coast snorkeling combined with a glimpse into Hawaiian culture. Passengers are treated to craft demonstrations such as basket, hat, and rose weavings, which guests take home as mementos. Rates are $80-122 with special children's rates. They also leave from the west side.

Hanalei Activity Center (kiosk near Big Save, 808/826-1898) will book you on various tours and other activities and can be visited at Ching Young Village.

SURFING AND STAND-UP PADDLING

The coast from Kilauea to the Na Pali Coast has been blessed with perfect surf breaks. The area has also produced a number of professional surfers, including Bruce Irons and his late brother Andy, Bethany Hamilton, and others. If you haven't brought a board (which is a good idea for truly experienced avid surfers who just *need* their favorite board), you can rent your own and head out yourself, or take surf lessons. Surf lessons are a good idea if you're a novice to the sport. Besides the goal to eventually carve down the line there are some basic tips to learn, like how to wax your board and put on a leash (I've seen a lone novice surfer with no leash at a very crowded spot), and how to paddle for a wave and stand up.

If you'd like to learn to stand-up paddle (SUP) or are already a fan of it there are several beaches and rivers ideal for the sport. SUPs are a good thing to rent on Kaua'i; only the most serious paddlers would want to travel with a stand-up paddle board. They're huge.

If you're spending time on the north side, board rentals are available from **Hanalei Surf Company** (in Hanalei Center, 808/826-9000, www.hanaleisurf.com, 8:30am-9pm daily) and **Backdoor Surf** (Ching Young Village, 808/826-1900, www.hanaleisurf. com, 8:30am-9:30pm). For lessons, **Hawaiian Surfing Adventures** (5134 Kuhio Hwy., 808/482-6749, www.hawaiiansurfingadventures.com, 8am-5pm daily) and the **Titus Kinimaka Hawaiian School of Surfing** (in the Quicksilver shop, 5-5088 Kuhio Hwy., 808/652-1116, www.hawaiianschoolofsurfing. com) will take you out and most likely get you on a wave. **Hanalei Activity Center** (Ching Young Village, 808/826-1898) also arranges surf lessons.

Kilauea
KALIHIWAI BEACH AND QUARRY BEACH

When the conditions and swell direction are right, Kalihiwai Beach is home to a sometimes-perfect right-hander peeling off of a rocky point. Locals surf and stand-up paddle here, and when the surf spot is breaking, the shore break is usually intense too. The river is an ideal place for stand-up paddling, and paddlers can head up and down the river as well as across from the beach to the end of the second Kalihiwai Road. Quarry Beach offers another good wave for experienced surfers, and is mostly utilized by locals. There are no lifeguards at either beach.

To get to Kalihiwai when coming from the east side, turn down the first Kalihiwai Road. The road ends at the river, where the other side is visible. To reach the other side take the second Kalihiwai Road and go right at the fork. It leads to the other side of the beach, where locals sometimes come to fish or paddle across the river to the beach. To get to Quarry Beach when headed north, turn right on Wailapa Road between mile markers 21 and 22. Turn left at the yellow post and cement blocks marking the top of the road and head about a half mile down to the beach.

Bethany Hamilton: Soul Surfer

At the age of 13, Bethany Hamilton, now a professional surfer, was attacked by a 14-foot tiger shark while surfing Tunnels on the north shore. It was Halloween 2003, and the shark took her left arm. After losing over 60 percent of her blood she made it through several surgeries without infection and returned to the water just one month after the attack. In January 2004, Bethany entered a surf contest and placed fifth in the open women's division (all ages) of that contest and continued to compete with no prosthetic arm. Just over a year after the attack she took first place in the explorer women's division of the 2005 NSSA National Championships and won her first national title. She's now been surfing professionally since 2007 and competes in professional contests all over the world. Her autobiography, *Soul Surfer*, was released in October 2004, and a movie of the same title was released in major theaters in early 2011. You may see Bethany on Kaua'i catching waves.

Hanalei

HANALEI BAY

All of Hanalei Bay is ideal for stand-up paddling, either on waves for experienced paddlers or around the bay when the waves are small. The outside break is known as **The Bay** and breaks when the waves are huge during the winter. This break is for experts only but is awesome to watch from the beach. Hanalei Bay has several surf breaks within the long stretch. When in Hanalei, turn off of Highway 560 onto Aku Road right before Ching Young Village. Turn right on Weke Street and near the end you'll see the beach.

PINE TREES

Roughly in the center of Hanalei Bay is Pine Trees, a perfect break for kids and beginners. Both right- and left-hand breaking waves are here and offer fun for all levels of surfers. Rent a board in Hanalei and catch a wave, if the waves are small. The fairly shallow waters and sandy bottom make it a good spot for beginners. On any given day the lineup will probably be packed with kids, so it can be a good idea to paddle out before the nearby elementary school is out for the day (around 2pm). When in Hanalei, turn off of Highway 560 onto Aku Road right before Ching Young Village. Turn left onto Weke and then right onto He'e, Ama'ama, or Ana'e Road to reach Pine Trees.

◖ HANALEI RIVER

The Hanalei River is a favorite for stand-up paddlers. While crossing the Hanalei Bridge into town you'll probably see paddlers enjoying a leisurely paddle on the river. Morning is a nice time before it gets too hot, and it's a great way to start the day. You'll first notice the river as you come into Hanalei and drive over the one-lane bridge. **Kayak Kaua'i** (5-5070 Kuhio Hwy., 808/826-9844, www.kayakkauai.com) offers SUP lessons and rentals from their dock up the Hanalei River. It's about a 20- to 30-minute paddle down the river to the ocean. Lessons cost $85 and rentals are $45 per day or $225 per week. Both include leash and, if requested, a car rack.

WAIKOKO BEACH

At the north end of Hanalei Bay is Waikoko Beach, and it's a left-hand-breaking rocky reef break. Although it's not one of the *most* dangerous spots, it's a good idea to leave it alone unless you're an experienced surfer. The break requires walking out on very shallow and very sharp reef, and hopping off at the end of the wave into a shallow reef. To get here, look for the small parking area on the side of the road after the bridge and mile marker 4. If a spot is available, look for the short trail through the trees.

The Legacy of Andy Irons

Three-time world surfing champion Andy Irons was born and raised in Hanalei. Irons grew up traveling the world surfing, becoming a local and national sports figure revered as one of the world's best surfers. Irons always called Kaua'i home, and his parents and his brother, professional surfer Bruce Irons, still live there. Sadly, Irons died on November 2, 2010, leaving his wife and unborn son behind. He was only 32 years old. An autopsy concluded that the cause of death was a sudden cardiac arrest due to a severe blockage of a main artery of the heart. A contributing but secondary factor might have been drugs.

Irons's death broke the hearts of surfers worldwide but especially affected the people of his home town. While driving the winding route from Hanalei to the end of the road, you'll likely see roadside surfboards and signs proclaiming "We love you, Andy" and other affectionate sayings.

On November 14, 2010, thousands gathered at Pine Trees in Hanalei Bay, where the Irons brothers grew up surfing, to pay tribute to the icon. On December 8, Irons's widow, Lyndie, gave birth to their son, Andrew Axel Irons, and the family continues to call Kaua'i home. The Irons Brothers Pine Trees Classic children's surfing competition is held each year in March or April.

To the End of the Road
TUNNELS/MAKUA BEACH

Right before Ha'ena Beach Park, Tunnels Beach has an epic right-hand-breaking wave. Tunnels is definitely for expert surfers only, but if that's you, this is a great wave. The beach is beautiful here too, and if the waves are good it can be fun to watch people surf. This is where local surfer Bethany Hamilton lost her arm to a shark at the age of 13. If the big waves don't keep you on the beach, that might. The movie *Soul Surfer* was released in 2011, documenting the Kaua'i native's loss and her comeback.

A little west down the beach from Tunnels is the surf break known as **Cannons.** This wave is reserved for experts, due to the intensity of the barreling, left-hand-breaking wave as well as the shallow reef in front of it. This can be another fun spot to watch people surf when the waves are good.

Access borders homes located on two narrow side roads past mile marker 8. The first is just short of a half mile past the marker, and the second is slightly farther and most recognizable by the bent metal post with red paint. It is across from the 149th telephone pole, although at press time the 9 was missing so it looks like pole 14.

KAYAKING
Hanalei

Kayak Kaua'i (5-5070 Kuhio Hwy., 808/826-9844, www.kayakkauai.com) offers a leisurely adventure on the Hanalei River with kayak rentals and guided tours where kayakers have the option of a single kayak for $29 or a double for $54.

A tour of Hanalei River and Hanalei Bay is also offered by **Kayak Hanalei** (5-5190 Kuhio Hwy., in Ching Young Village, 808/826-1881, www.kayakhanalei.com) from March through October. Suitable for all ages, the tour explores the bay and river and takes paddlers snorkeling. A complete sandwich lunch is provided, with vegetarian as an option, and is enjoyed on the beach. The price for children is $96, adults $107.

Na Pali Coast

Kayaks can be rented for a trip down the Na Pali Coast ending at Polihale, but only in summer when seas are calm. **Outfitters Kauai** (2827A Po'ipu Rd., Po'ipu, 808/742-9667 or 999/742-9887, www.outfitterskauai.com, $230) runs a 16-mile sea kayak adventure along the coast. The trip features an exploration of sea caves; opportunities to see waterfalls, dolphins, and sea turtles; and respites on deserted beaches that feel far from civilization. The tour offers tandem, open-cockpit, or sit-on-top self-bailing kayaks with foot pedal controls, and the tour is only available from mid-May until mid-September on Tuesdays and Thursdays.

Kayak Kaua'i (5-5070 Kuhio Hwy., 808/826-9844, www.kayakkauai.com) also offers sea kayaking along the Na Pali Coast. It's a serious adventure only for the very fit and hardy and can only be done in the summer. The kayaking adventure requires 5-6 hours of paddling and runs about $200.

Na Pali Kayak (5-5070 Kuhio Hwy., 808/826-6900, www.napalikayak.com) takes adventurous day trippers, honeymooners, and campers on various trips along the Na Pali Coast. Adventures include guided day kayaking trips, camping along the coast, a honeymoon private charter for two, and private guided tours. Fees vary from $200 to $3,000 for a group charter, so call for the most up-to-date rates and details.

FISHING
Na Pali Coast
Na Pali Sportfishing (808/635-9424, www. napalisportfishing.com) will take you down the coast, but they leave out of Kikiaola Harbor on the west side. They leave at 6am—they say that's when serious anglers fish. That time can be hard to make if you're on the north shore; later trips are also available. They take people out to a 35-foot Baja cruiser with a fly bridge and outriggers for a maximum of six people. Boaters must bring their own food and snacks, but the company provides soft drinks, fishing tackle, and zipper-lock bags so guests can take fish home. Half days shared run $135 an angler, full days are $220, and a full-day fishing charter runs $1,050. Check for other rates and tours. Restrictions include no pregnant women, no recent back surgeries or injuries, and no children under four years old.

WHALE-WATCHING
During the months of December through March or April, humpback whales *(kohola)* spend time in the islands singing and giving birth. After bulking up on weight in Alaska through the summer, the whales don't eat while they're here and may lose up to about one-third of their weight. During these months keep an eye out any time you look at the ocean. They breech, they spout; it's one of the best sights to be seen.

From November through March, **Bali Hai Tours** (808/634-2317, www.balihaitours.com) heads north from Kapa'a, taking people out to see the whales. Although the boat can handle 12 people, they take no more than six people out on their 20-foot Zodiac with a two-stroke 100 hp Mercury motor. The company provides snorkel gear, floater noodles and boogie boards, dry bags, and snacks. Prices are $155 for adults and $90 for children.

Hiking, Biking, and Bird-Watching

HIKING
The north shore is home to some of the most outstanding hikes on the island. From short walks to secluded beaches, to hikes to hidden waterfalls, to the 19-mile trek along the Na Pali Coast, the north shore is a hiker's dream land. The value of a mile-long beach walk shouldn't go underestimated; it can be one of the most peaceful and memorable experiences to be had on Kaua'i.

Kilauea
◖ SECRET BEACH TIDE POOLS AND WATERFALL
Tide pools and an oceanside waterfall are the beautiful rewards at the end of this hike (about a half-hour long). It's important to note that this hike should only be done during summer when the ocean is completely flat. It's actually a combination of two hikes, one down to Secret Beach and another to the falls and tide pools.

KAUA'I

At the northern end of the beach at the bottom of the access trail, head over the rocks. After the small sandy area is a pretty spot where the water juts into the cliffs, and you'll need to pass behind this. There's a roughly 10-foot-tall vertical cliff to climb that presents two options: climb up over the cliff and stick to the rocks, or climb up on the end that's over the water.

After passing this, stick to the trail high on the wall that backs the small cove. After going around that, it's pretty level and self explanatory. When you reach the area where the tide pools start, there will be quite a few. They are nice in size and shape, and home to different sea life. They are a little murky, but it's worth it to take a peek in them. At the end, right before another finger of water juts into the cliffs, you'll see the wonderful deep and smooth boulder-bottomed pools. Once you're here it looks like this could be the end, but it's not. There are several pools here and they're five- to six-feet deep at the deepest. The beautiful pools that are clean and clear, and the rock bottom is smooth. The pool closest to the edge of the cliff needs to be avoided when the waves are anything but flat.

Where the cliff meets the finger, there is another small vertical cliff, about six- to eight-feet high. For an even better reward, climb it and head a very short distance inland to see the waterfall coming out of a small lush green crevice, pouring into more tide pools. This is far from Kaua'i's tallest waterfall, but the combination of an oceanside waterfall with salt tide pools is a unique sight to see and enjoy. The falls pour down onto a fairly flat rock area, and there is a small cave in back of the water perfect for sitting in as long as the falls aren't pouring too heavily. The rock leading to the falls is extremely slippery, so taking your time is important, or walking above the falls and coming back down and around works too. In front of this are several salt tide pools that the freshwater runs into. This hike is dangerous when the waves are big; it should only be attempted in summer. Even when the waves are small, be aware of the ocean. There's another, easier way to get here. If you take the first Kalihiwai Road

and pass the road to Secret Beach, stop at the yellow fire hydrant. Take the trail here about 10 minutes down to the top of the waterfall. This isn't nearly as exciting as the hike from Secret Beach, but it's shorter and safer.

To get here, turn onto the first Kalihiwai Road heading north and take the first right onto a dirt road. Head to the end of the road, where parking is behind large homes.

Princeville
POWERLINE TRAIL

It's takes a powered-up person to attack the entire day-long journey along the roughly 13-mile **Powerline Trail.** Completing it is only recommended for those who have a ride waiting on the other side, where the trail ends at the Keahua Arboretum in Wailua. The sights range from a few views into Hanalei Valley to an abundance of mountain views, the north and south shores, the center of the island, and the Hanalei region. The trail is hot and dry and lacking in shade. It's best for hikers to go as far they like but to return to the Princeville trailhead. Around two hours from the start of the trail, the pass is a good place to turn around and head back. To get to the northern trailhead, turn at the Princeville Ranch Stables about a half mile east of Princeville. Head uphill for about two miles until the pavement ends. Go a little farther to the parking area near the green water tank. This is a serious trail for mountain bikers, but it's strenuous. Don't attempt to go four-wheeling here.

Hanalei
'OKOLEHAO TRAIL

Intense **'Okolehao Trail** is good preparation for the Kalalau Trail. 'Okolehao refers to the Hawaiian version of moonshine, made from the ti root planted up here. It's said the literal translation is "iron bottom" for the iron pots used to ferment it. The hike provides a serious workout that will mostly likely be experienced in solitude. The trail gains about 1,200 feet and will have hikers huffing and puffing in no time. Yet the 'Okolehao Trail offers a light at the end of the steep metaphorical tunnel, with truly amazing views of the island that begin about half a mile up. From the end of the trail the Kilauea Lighthouse, Hanalei River, Waiʻaleʻale, Hanalei Bay, and the area by Keʻe and as far as Anahola can be seen. When hiking after a rain, be very careful, as the trail gets slippery. To get to the trailhead, turn left right after the one-lane bridge into Hanalei onto Ohiki Road. A little over a half mile down the road there's a parking lot on the left. A small bridge marks the trailhead on the opposite side of the road.

MOKOLEA TIDE POOLS

The reward for this fairly easy, quarter- to half-mile hike (depending on how far you can drive in) is a dip in the cool, refreshing **Mokolea Tide Pools.** The hike is really a slow walk over lava rock along shore line. Take your time and be mindful of your footing. You'll notice very weathered metal remnants of sugar mill gear. There are two ways to get here. One is through Quarry Beach Road in Kilauea village, via a partial four-wheel-drive road that leaves only about a quarter-mile hike. The other is from the Quarry Beach access off of Wailapa Road via a two-wheel-drive road and then a half-mile walk from the river.

Na Pali Coast

The heavenly and harsh **Na Pali Coast** is where all of nature's wonder joins together, a world that will both amaze and test those who choose to explore it. Other than the ocean, this is the only access to the rugged coastline where sea cliffs, five lush valleys, waterfalls, and camping wait on the 15-mile stretch from Keʻe to Polihale. The cliffs rise up to 4,000 feet in certain areas, and sea level is found only at the four main beaches along the way. The largest and most magnificent valley here is the Kalalau Valley, where ancient Hawaiians lived and archaeological evidence still remains. Other valleys also hold evidence of inhabited sites, as Hawaiians lived in various locations along the way. Rain falls here in excess, creating an abundance of waterfalls and streams.

The Na Pali Coast State Park comprises 6,175 acres of raw land. The remaining cliffs, coastline, and valleys are either state forests or natural area reserves.

There is a ranger stationed at Kalalau Valley who oversees the park and who will ask campers for permits. There is a trailhead by Keʻe Beach that you can't miss, and at Kalalau Valley there's a sign-in box. Day-use permits are required to go beyond Hanakapiʻai (where there are composting toilets), about two miles in, and a camping permit is necessary to stay overnight at Hanakapiʻai, Hanakoa, or Kalalau. Camping is permitted for up to five nights total, but two consecutive nights are not allowed at Hanakapiʻai or Hanakoa. More than the basics are needed to camp out here: a waterproof tent, mosquito repellent, first-aid kit, biodegradable soap, food, sleeping bag, and whatever else you think you may need and don't mind carrying on your back mile after mile. Water bladders as opposed to water bottles are a good idea, because they're lighter and run a constant line of water to the mouth. Tree cutting is not allowed, and there isn't much natural firewood, so bring a stove if you want to cook. Drinking out of the streams is not advised; doing so can cause serious stomach illness, so boil the water or bring purification tablets. Don't litter; take out whatever you carried in. Reachable only by boat or kayak, the Nuʻalolo Kai can be visited for the day only, and Miloliʻi can be camped at for a maximum of three nights and has very basic campsites. The most accurate idea of what to expect is from hikers who have recently made the journey, because the trail changes with the weather.

THE KALALAU TRAIL

What may be the best way to experience the coast is the 11-mile **Kalalau Trail,** which begins right at Keʻe Beach. Mother nature dictates what condition the trail is in, so hikers may find a somewhat dry and firm trail or a narrow trail so steep, wet, and crumbling that they must scoot along on a cliff's edge while leaning into the earth and digging their hands deep into the dirt to hang on. Upon reaching Kalalau Beach, hikers may be welcomed to the beach by nude campers, as some people take

KAUAI

advantage of the remote location and leave swimwear in their packs.

The path was originally created as a land route between Kalalau Valley and Ha'ena. It was rebuilt in 1930 for horses and cows to pass over. To experience the trail is to experience what old Hawaii must have been like, when people lived off the land and close to nature. It usually takes a full day to get to Kalalau Beach, and it's really the best hike in the whole state. The trail is well worn from decades of use, so you're not likely to get off track and lost. Yet roots weave through it, and it gets extremely muddy and slippery when there's been rain, a frequent occurrence out here. Small streams fill up to flooding rivers after a heavy rain but they drain out rather quickly, so instead of crossing a dangerous stream it's usually best to wait it out. Mountain climbing out here is a risky and dangerous idea because the dirt crumbles and falls easily. The trail is filled with continuous amazing views. From the impressively tall mountains to the coastal views and lush foliage, this is not a trail to forget the camera on.

The currents along the coast are dangerous too, so stay out of the water from around September through April, when the surf mellows out for the summer. In summer, the sand is usually returned to Hanakapi'ai, the most commonly visited part of the hike, after being swept away by the winter's large surf. Hanakapi'ai, like Queen's Bath, has a list of the names and ages of people who have died at this beach due to the pounding surf often washing over bare rock.

◖ HANAKAPI'AI BEACH AND HANAKAPI'AI FALLS

It's about two miles and a 1.5- to 2-hour hike from Ke'e to Hanakapi'ai Beach. The first mile goes uphill to about 800 feet, with the last mile going down and ending at the beach. Depending on the season, you may get lucky and see some brave and slightly crazy surfers out here. During low tide only during the summer, caves on the beach are good for camping, but on the far side of the stream up from the beach is the best place.

From the west side of the stream at Hanakapi'ai Beach, the Hanakapi'ai Trail starts, leading two miles inland up into the valley to the wonderful Hanakapi'ai Falls, passing old taro fields and crumbling rock walls. You will cross the stream several times on the way up, so if the stream looks full and rushing, just turn around and head back. It can be dangerous during high water. If the stream is low, keep going. The hike to the 300-foot-high falls is rewarding and worth it. There is a wonderful ice-cold swimmable pool at the bottom, but don't swim directly under the falls. From Hanakapi'ai Camp near the beach, the hike should take around 2-3 hours, and it's about 5-6 hours from Ke'e Beach.

HANAKAPI'AI BEACH TO HANAKOA

It's a strenuous 4.5-mile, three-hour trek from Hanakapi'ai Beach to Hanakoa. The trail climbs steadily and doesn't go back down to sea level until Kalalau Beach nine miles later. You are taken about 600 feet out of Hanakapi'ai Valley through a series of switchbacks, and although the trail is heavily utilized, it can be very rough in certain spots. You will walk through the hanging valleys of Ho'olulu and Waiahuakua, both parts of the Hono'onapali Nature Area Preserve and loaded with native flora, before arriving at Hanakoa. In the past Hanakoa was a major food-growing area for Hawaiians, and many of its terraces are still intact. Wild coffee plants can be seen here. Hanakoa is a bit rainy, but it's on and off and the sun usually dominates throughout the day. Numerous swimmable pools are born from the stream here. To get to Hanakoa Falls from here, you'll need to take a worthwhile half mile detour inland. Cross the Hanakoa Stream and hang a left at the trail near the shelter. Walk for about 150 feet or so and take a left at the fork and continue for 15 to 20 minutes.

HANAKOA TO KALALAU BEACH

From Hanakoa to Kalalau Beach the trek is less than five miles, but it's a tough one and takes around three hours. It's important to start this one early in the morning to get as much time as possible in before the heat sinks in. The trail gets drier and more open as you approach Kalalau, but the views along the way make it all worth it. Out here the mana of the island is strong. Try to clear your head of thoughts and concerns of the outside world and soak in the invigorating beauty and peace of the valley. Around mile marker 7 is land that until the late 1970s was part of the Makaweli cattle ranch. After Pohakuao Valley is Kalalau Valley, spanning two miles wide and three deep. Freshwater pools dot the area and look inviting after the long hot hike. The area was cultivated until the 1920s, and fruit trees are abundant in the area. Camping is only allowed in the trees along the beach, or in the caves west of the waterfall, not along the stream, its mouth, or in the valley. The falls have a wonderful, refreshing pool. On the far side of the stream is a *heiau* on top of a little hill. If you follow the trail here inland for around two miles you'll find Big Pool, which is really two pools connected by a natural water slide.

HONOPU, NU'ALOLO KAI, AND MILOLI'I

If you somehow have it in you to keep going, other destinations include Honopu, Nu'alolo Kai, and Miloli'i. Honopu is less than a half mile west of Kalalau Valley, and is known as "Valley of the Lost Tribe" due to a legend that says the small Mu people lived out here. The beach is separated by a big rock arch that has been used in at least two movies. You can get to Nu'alolo Kai by staying on the Kalalau Trail, and it is right after Awa'awapuhi Valley, about nine miles down the coast. It has a lovely beach and dunes right up against a tall cliff. There's a pair of reefs here that provide good snorkeling opportunities when the water is calm. A community of Hawaiians lived out here until 1919, and their archaeological remnants still exist as stone walls and *heiau* platforms. Taro was cultivated out here in the adjoining Nu'alolo 'Aina Valley, and fishing was good too. The reef out here was utilized as a rest stop by canoeists, who would anchor out here while going between Hanalei and Waimea. Another mile west is Miloli'i, another ancient site that

was inhabited by Hawaiians. Here there is a very basic camping area with restrooms and a simple shelter, and down the beach is another *heiau*. Miloli'i only gets about 20 inches of rain a year, a big contrast from the rest of the wet Na Pali Coast.

BIKING

Hanalei and Princeville are the best areas on the north side for biking. After Hanalei there are numerous one-lane bridges and a narrow winding road to Ke'e that could push bikers into the traffic. Princeville is the safest and most convenient place for a leisurely ride, although the steady incline heading up can be rough. To rent a beach cruiser, stop at **Pedal-N-Paddle** (Ching Young Village, 808/826-9069, www.pedalnpaddle.com, 9am-6pm daily) for hybrid road bike and cruiser rentals for $12 daily or $50 for the week. Biking accessories are also available, along with watersport supplies.

BIRD-WATCHING

Birds can be seen all over the island, but there are few official places to go birding on the north side. Binoculars and patience are good accessories to bring. No matter how you may be exploring the island, there's a good chance various birds will be seen throughout the day, and of course, there are always the unavoidable Kaua'i chickens running wild in parking lots, hotel lawns, and shopping centers.

Kilauea

At the **Kilauea Point National Wildlife Refuge** (end of Kilauea Rd., 808/828-1413, 10am-4pm daily, http://pacificislands.fws.gov/wnwr/kkilaueanwr.html), 31 acres protect numerous birds. Red-footed boobies, shearwaters, great frigate birds, brown boobies, red- and white-tailed tropic birds, and Laysan albatrosses, as well as green sea turtles and humpback whales, occupy the refuge. There's an informational plaque at the top, and if you look down into the trees right in front of this area, birds can often be seen resting in their nests.

Princeville

Shearwaters nest at **Queen's Bath** (go right on Punahele Road and take the second right onto Kapiolani Loop) and can be seen along the trail and cliffs. Residents are not allowed to bring dogs here due to a high number of dog-related deaths.

Hanalei

At the 917-acre **Hanalei National Wildlife Refuge** in Hanalei Valley, endangered native water birds such as the Hawaiian coot, black-necked stilt, koloa duck, and gallinule can be spotted, as well as several migrant species that have reclaimed their ancient nesting grounds. The area is decorated with taro plants; the root supplies about half of Hawaii's poi. Although visitors are allowed in Hanalei Valley, no one is permitted in the designated wildlife area other than for fishing or hiking along the river. After crossing the first one-lane bridge into Hanalei, turn left onto Ohiki Road.

Adventure Sports

ZIPLINING
Princeville

For the thrill of flying through the air, **Princeville Ranch Adventures** (5-4280 Kuhio Hwy., 808/826-7669 or 888/955-7669, www.adventureskauai.com, by appt.) has three different ziplines combined with a horseback ride. The lines travel through valleys with mountain and ocean views and will get your adrenaline pumping. You can't miss the ranch entrance on the north side of Kuhio Highway before Princeville.

HELICOPTER TOURS
Princeville

For a bird's-eye view of Kaua'i, catch a ride with

See Princeville by horseback.

© ANA PHELPS/123RF.COM

KAUA'I

Heli USA (808/826-6591 or 866/936-1234, www.heliusahawaii.com, $267). Although the carrier currently departs from Lihu'e, the Na Pali Coast tour offers a unique view of the cliffs, beaches, and valleys without having to hike for miles and miles. Flying A-Star machines, the company offers several different routes and free hotel pickup.

Departing out of the small Princeville airport is **Sunshine Helicopters** (Princeville Airport, 866/501-7738, www.sunshinehelicopters.com). A 40- to 50-minute flight will take you over the Na Pali Coast, Waimea Canyon, and many places utilized in Hollywood films. Open seating is priced at $289, and first class is $364.

HORSEBACK RIDING
Princeville
The **Princeville Ranch Stables** (808/826-6777, www.princevilleranch.com, by appt.) offers horseback rides and other adventures through a 250-acre working cattle ranch. It's about a half mile east of Princeville Center on the *mauka* (mountain) side of the road.

Hanalei Activity Center (Ching Young Village, 808/826-1898) offers horseback rides out of Princeville. Call for rates and times.

Polo matches are open to the public every Sunday at 3pm across from Anini Beach Park. Spectating makes for a unique Hawaiian experience and a great tailgate party.

Golf

KILAUEA
To take in some lighthearted time on the greens, hit the little white ball around **Kaua'i Mini Golf** (5-2723 Kuhio Hwy., Kilauea, 808/828-2118, www.kauaiminigolf.com, 11am-9pm Tues.-Sun., plus Mon. Memorial Day-Labor Day). The miniature golf course can be viewed from the highway in Kilauea and is lacking in clown mouths and other toy-inspired themes. At this course, putters take a trip through Hawaiian history as they move through botanical gardens, each inspired by different a ethnic group found in Hawaii. It's ideal to take the family or for a honeymoon date.

PRINCEVILLE
At the **Princeville Makai Golf Course** (4080 Lei O Papa Rd., 808/826-1912, www.makaigolf.com), the already excellent course recently underwent a multimillion-dollar renovation. Designed by Robert Trent Jones Jr. in 1971, the course was rated one of the top 25 golf courses in America for 2004-2005 by *Golf* magazine and has been ranked by *Golf Digest* as one of Hawaii's top courses. From the central clubhouse there are three nine-hole, par-36 courses. The Makai course combines two of them and weaves around

lakes, native woodlands, and the coastline with views of Bali Hai and Hanalei Bay.

The 18-hole course plays a par 72 with four different sets of tees. The renovations, also done by Jones, feature seashore paspalum turf grass on all tees, fairways, and greens, making a wonderful playing surface for all levels. All bunkers also experienced a bold reshaping. The cliff-top Ocean 7 is regarded as a tough hole, with a shot over a ravine, and the Lake 9 hole sets two lakes in the way of the shot, but the toughest hole is known to be Woods 6, with a long dogleg into the trade winds. The nine-hole Woods Course is revered as a leisurely course for the casual golfer with family and friends. The practice area at the Makai Golf Club has also been improved and includes two new practice tees, a practice fairway bunker, seven target greens with bunkers, a teaching tee, and game practice complex. The club provides rentals for men, women, and juniors. Tee time can be booked at the pros shop, and the snack shop offers decently priced sandwiches, burgers, and snacks. Greens fees are $50 for the Woods Course and $140-210 for the Makai Course, with generous discounts for juniors. Various rates are also offered for golf passes and weekly packages.

KAUA'I

Kama'aina rates are also offered with Hawaii state ID.

The 18-hole **Prince Course** (808/826-5070, www.princeville.com/prince_course.html) opened in 1987 on almost 400 acres of golf heaven. However, the course closed on January 29, 2011 to undergo several months of renovation and reopened in 2012. The renovation was done by the original architect, Robert Trent Jones Jr. and cost five million dollars. Named after Prince Albert, the son of King Kamehameha IV and Queen Emma, the course has both ocean and mountain views. It was ranked the number one golf course in Hawaii and one of America's Top 100 greatest courses by *Golf Digest*.

Spas

KILAUEA

Time at **Pure Kaua'i** (4270 Kilauea Rd. Unit D, 808/828-6570 or 866/457-7873, www.purekauai.com) is not your average spa day. The luxury spa creates Hawaiian getaways as well as honeymoon vacations and romantic retreats. Luxurious accommodations, healthy meals prepared by a private chef, spa activities and services, and various sports such as yoga and surfing are all offered here. Unique services such as astrological consultations, life coaching, and relationship coaching are offered in addition to traditional services like massage ($150-195), facials ($135), manicures ($55), and pedicures ($95).

PRINCEVILLE

To lounge in the lap of luxury, visit the **Halele'a Spa** (808/826-9644) at the St. Regis Princeville Resort, where a consultant will customize a wellness regime to fit each person's needs. The spa combines Hawaiian healing traditions with western techniques to create a truly heavenly experience. Massages are offered with various Hawaiian elements, including hot stones with taro butter, traditional *lomilomi,* sports massage, pregnancy massage, and couples massage. Facials combine healing properties to rehydrate and fight aging, while the clay wrap uses Hawaiian plants to detoxify and relax. Scrubs, baths, waxing, manicures, pedicures, salon treatments, and specialized bridal treatments are also offered.

HANALEI

The **Hanalei Day Spa** (808/826-6621, www.hanaleidayspa.com, 9:30am-6pm Mon.-Sat., walk-ins allowed if there's availability, otherwise by appt.) is nestled near the ocean in the Hanalei Colony Resort. Beachside and in-spa couples massage, Hawaiian *lomilomi* massage, facials, waxing, body wraps and scrubs, and Ayurveda healing treatments are all offered with the sound of the ocean in the background. Retreats, wedding services, and private yoga lessons are also offered.

Sights

KILAUEA
◖ Kilauea Point National Wildlife Refuge and Lighthouse

A picture-perfect view makes the **Kilauea Point National Wildlife Refuge and Lighthouse** (end of Kilauea Rd., 808/828-1413, 10am-4pm daily, http://pacificislands.fws.gov/wnwr/kkilaueanwr.html) a must-see. The beautiful inlet is speckled with white birds—a treat for dedicated bird watchers. Permanent and migrating seabirds spend their time here, including the frigate bird, boasting an eight-foot wingspan, the red-footed booby, the *nene,* wedgetail shearwaters, and red- and white-tailed tropic birds. Sea turtles, dolphins, and Hawaiian monk seals can all be seen from the cliffs. The waters here are also part of the Hawaiian Islands Humpback Whale National Marine Sanctuary, and whales can be seen here during winter and spring.

Stroll on the narrow peninsula to reach the Kilauea Lighthouse, a designated National Historical Landmark and visitors center. Originally boasting the world's largest "clam-shell lens," which could send a beam of light 20 miles out to sea, it was replaced in 1976 with a small high-intensity beacon. The visitors center holds a wealth of information about bird and plant life, the history of the lighthouse, and Hawaiian history.

To get here, turn into Kilauea at the Shell gas station near mile marker 23, then down Kilauea Road. Drive straight to the end to the lighthouse, where entrance is free for 16 and under, and all others cost $5 per person.

Na 'Aina Kai Botanical Gardens

Just past the Quarry Beach access road is **Na 'Aina Kai Botanical Gardens** (808/828-0525, www.naainakai.org, 8am-noon Mon. and Fri., 8am-5pm Tues.-Thurs.), encompassing a whopping 240 acres of tropical hardwoods and fruit trees. Over 100 acres of the property is a tropical hardwood plantation with about two dozen types of trees, including teak, mahogany, zebra wood, rosewood, and cocobolo, along with a lot of tropical fruit trees. The gardens take a creative twist in the central areas, where theme gardens feature various types of plants and around 60 life-like bronze sculptures add life to the experience. Admission may feel a bit pricey, from $25 for a 90-minute walk to $70 for a five-hour walk and tram ride through all areas, but the view from the parking lot is enticing and it's truly an enjoyable treat. The visitors center and gift shop are a fun stop to explore the gifts, books, and plants. To get here, turn down Wailapa Road after mile marker 21 and go to the end.

HANALEI
◖ Hanalei Valley Overlook

The sights over Hanalei Valley tend to inspire a dreamy feeling harking back to the days of old Hawaii. Different photo opportunities present themselves as the soft morning light changes to

© JADE ECKARDT

Kilauea Lighthouse

KAUA'I

Love Flowers

Naupaka shrubs have light green, somewhat waxy leaves and distinctive white flowers; they look like half flowers with petals missing. One species grows along the coast, another in the mountains. Several Hawaiian legends explain their unique appearance.

One legend tells of Pele being so jealous that she turned two lovers into the plant, sending one to the mountains and one to the coast. Legend says that since they were soul mates, the flowers are incomplete, and when they are brought together they form a whole.

A Kaua'i legend tells of the lovers Nanau and Kapaka, who broke a hula *kapu* (taboo) the night before their graduation. It's said they fled across Limahuli Stream and passed Maniniholo Cave while chased by their *kumu* (teacher). When they reached Lumahai Beach, Nanau fled to the cliffs and Kapaka hid in a beach cave called Ho'ohila. As the teacher approached the cliffs, Kapaka tried to block the *kumu* so her lover could escape. The *kumu* was enraged and killed Kapaka, continuing to chase Nanau. Eventually, Nanau was also struck dead, and later that day fishermen at Lumahai discovered a plant they'd never seen before growing where Kapaka had died. The *kumu* noticed the same plant growing where Nanau had died.

Another Pele legend says the goddess was enamored with a young man who was greatly devoted to his lover. No matter what she did, he remained loyal to his lover. Pele was angered and chased the young man into the mountains, throwing molten lava at him. Pele's sisters saw this happen, and to save him they changed him into half of a naupaka flower and sent him to the mountains. Pele went after his young lover and chased her toward the ocean. Again, Pele's sisters stepped in and changed her into the beach naupaka. It is said that if the mountain and the beach naupaka are reunited, the young lovers will be together again.

bright afternoon sun and then to a demure sunset light, all bringing out different colors in the taro patches below. Right after the Princeville turnoff on the left is the Hanalei Valley scenic overlook. This is a view not to be missed. The Hanalei River cuts through the valley until it meets the ocean, and along its banks green radiates from the valley, which reaches back into the 3,500-foot pali for almost nine miles. Waterfalls hang in the valley, either as light curtains or heavy torrential falls when there's lots of rain. There's a saying on Kaua'i's north side: "When you can count 17 waterfalls, it's time to get out of Hanalei." Legend says that Pele sent a thunderbolt to split a boulder in Hanalei so that Hawaiians could run an irrigation ditch through the center to their fields. While Princeville was for *ali'i* (royalty), Hanalei was for the "commoners."

Originally Hanalei produced taro, which is evident far back in the valley, where the outlines of the old fields can still be seen. The bay and fishponds produced fish. When the foreigners arrived they tried and failed at coffee here, then sugar, which didn't last as in other places on the island, and all the while Hanalei was bringing in poi from the Kalalau Valley. The bay was one of the most popular ports for a long time and was also a whaling harbor. Chinese immigrants eventually moved in and re-terraced the valley with rice. Rice was a successful crop until the 1930s, when the valley took a turn back to taro.

Wai'oli Hui'ia Church and Wai'oli Mission House Museum

The **Wai'oli Hui'ia Church** (5-5363 A Kuhio Hwy., 808/826-6253) lies near the west end of town and stands tall with its colorful stained-glass windows illuminated by sunlight. Wai'oli means "joyful water," and it pays to go inside to look at the windows and take in the open-beam ceiling of the quaint church. Built in 1912, the church was part of a mission station that also included a home for the preacher, a school for Hawaiian boys, and accommodations for the teacher.

© JADE ECKARDT

the Hanalei Valley Overlook

Behind and slightly to the right of the church is the **Wai'oli Mission House Museum** (808/245-3202, 9am-3pm Tues., Thurs., and Sat.) which was originally the teacher's house. The lush green parking lot welcomes visitors to the home, which boasts a New England-style interior that was built in 1836 by Reverend William P. Alexander. It was then passed to the Wilcox family, who owned and occupied the house until recently. Wilcox family members founded the Grove Farm in Lihu'e and the nonprofit organization that operates both the Wai'oli Mission House Museum and the Grove Farm Homestead. Inside, you enter the parlor, where Lucy Wilcox taught Hawaiian girls how to sew and paintings of the families are on the walls. Around the house are artifacts including dishes, knickknacks, and a butter churn from the 1800s. It's interesting to note, now that the Hawaiian language has experienced a resurgence, that Abner Wilcox, a missionary, teacher, doctor, public official, and veterinarian, wrote letters to the king urging him to make Hawaiian the first language, with English as the second.

Ho'opulapula Haraguchi Rice Mill

The **Ho'opulapula Haraguchi Rice Mill** (5-5070 A Kuhio Hwy., 808/651-3399, www.haraguchiricemill.org, kiosk hours 11am-3pm Mon.-Fri.) is an agrarian museum nestled in the taro fields of the Hanalei Valley within a national wildlife refuge usually not accessible to the public. Dating back to the 1800s, it's listed on the National Register of Historic Places. It was purchased by the Haraguchi Family in 1924, who have restored the mill three times: after a 1930 fire, after Hurricane 'Iwa in 1982, and following Hurricane 'Iniki in 1992. This mill is the last remaining rice mill in all of Hawaii, although it stopped operating in 1960 when the rice industry ceased to thrive. A nonprofit organization was formed to preserve and share the mill, and tours (donation only) are offered for out-of-state visitors, local schools, and others. The Haraguchi family continues to farm taro on nearby land that used to grow rice. Guided tours and private tours (which can be paid for in monetary or volunteer donations) are available by reservation on Wednesdays

KAUA'I

the Wai'oli Hui'ia Church

only, so you need to call first. Tours share Hawaii's agricultural and cultural history, and visitors can view endangered native water birds and learn about taro cultivation and the uses of taro. A complimentary picnic lunch including taro grown at the farm is offered. When making a reservation, you must choose between a sandwich or Hawaiian plate lunch. The entrance kiosk is one mile after the Hanalei one-lane bridge on the north side of the road.

TO THE END OF THE ROAD
⟨ Limahuli Botanical Garden

At the **Limahuli Botanical Garden** (5-8291 Kuhio Hwy., 808/826-1053, 9:30am-4pm Tues.-Sat.) you'll take a trip back in time to see the native plants that decorated Hawaii before invasive species moved into the islands. Visitors have a choice of self-guided tours ($15 adult, children 12 and under free) and tours with a guide ($30 adult, children 10-12 $15). Guided tours are 2-2.5 hours, and self-guided ones last 1-1.5 hours. Reservations are required for the guided tour only.

Part of the National Tropical Botanical Garden, the gardens lie in front of Mount Makana (*makana* means "gift") on 1,016 acres that help both ancient and modern plants flourish. The original 14 acres were donated by Juliet Rice Wichman in 1976, then expanded to 17, and the final 985-acre parcel in the above valley was donated by Wichman's grandson, Chipper Wichman, in 1994. It's a good idea to wear good shoes, and umbrellas are provided. The visitors center is where the tours begin, and this is where books, crafts, gifts, and other things are on sale. Taro *lo'i* (patches) here are believed to be around 900 years old. The brochure and the tour guide share legends of the valley.

The majority of the preserve lies in the valley and is only available to biologists and botanists for research. To get to the gardens, take a left inland at the HVB warrior sign about a half mile after mile marker 9. The marker points to the gardens, which are in the last valley before Ke'e Beach. Just past this is the Limahuli Stream, which locals use as a rinse-off

KAUA'I

Limahuli Botanical Garden

after you've walked up a short hill to look down into the **Waikapala'e Wet Cave.** Also known as the "Blue Room" because of another hidden cave here that's accessible only through an underwater tunnel that turns a vibrant blue, the cave is a contradiction. It's beautiful and spacious, but since the trees have grown up and block the light, it exudes a slightly eerie feeling. Visitors will find a tranquil place to spend time, and many people swim in the cold water. It's said that the Blue Room is no longer blue due to a change in the water table height and other environmental changes, and I'm not recommending searching for it because it is dangerous! To get here, drive about three minutes past Ha'ena. It's on the left, just past the big parking lot on your right, and is only identifiable by the obviously worn path up the rocky hill, and the pull-off spot across the street. It's about a 1.5-minute walk up, where you can peer into the cave from above or take a short but steep and slippery trek down into it.

Waikanaloa Wet Cave

The **Waikanaloa Wet Cave** is clearly seen from the road a little before Ke'e Beach. The cave is a nice sight and another good photo opportunity. There is no swimming allowed, as the sign indicates. Look at the floor of the pond itself to see some interesting patterns.

Kaulu Paoa Heiau and Kaulu O Laka Heiau

To the right of Ke'e are **Kaulu Paoa Heiau** and **Kaulu O Laka Heiau,** where it's said that the art of hula was born. Legend says the goddess Laka bestowed hula to the Hawaiians here. *Heiau* are the religious sites for Hawaiians, do pay them the proper respect. Do not disturb or touch anything. The views up here are wonderful, especially during sunrise or sunset, when the sky changes to all shades of color. For over 1,000 years the area was used as a valued hula school. It's said that the pupils were asked to swim from here down to Ke'e Beach for a final induction sort of thing. At Ke'e Beach look for the trail weaving inland through the jungle up to the *heiau.*

spot after swimming. There's only one good spot to pull off the road here. On your way to the Limahuli Botanical Garden, stop at the **Lumahai Overlook** for a view of the Lumahai Beach and a great photo op. After the fifth mile marker you'll notice a small pull off area where a Hawaii Visitors Bureau sign points to the ocean.

Maniniholo Dry Cave

Directly across from Ha'ena Beach Park is the wide, low, and deep **Maniniholo Dry Cave.** Take a short stroll inside the cave. There's no water in here, just a dusty dirt bottom, but it can be fun to take photos, especially from the inside facing out. Sometimes walking around in here you may look at all of the footprints on the ground and wonder how long they go undisturbed. Although the cave seems to stay dry there is no archaeological evidence that it was used for permanent habitation.

Waikapala'e Wet Cave

The earth opens up here to crystal-clear water

KAUA'I

Shopping

KILAUEA
Kilauea Plantation Center

The Kilauea Plantation Center on Kilauea Road is home to the **Healthy Hut** (4270 Kilauea Rd., 808/828-6626, www.healthyhut-kauai.com, 8:30am-9pm daily), where you'll find organic produce, fruit, and other natural foods. There are natural home wares and gifts, along with a health and beauty section, vitamins, and natural baby products. A very small wine and beer selection is also available.

Kong Lung Historic Market Square

Also on Kilauea Road is the **Kong Lung Historic Market Square** (2484 Keneke St., 808/828-1822, konglungkauai.com). The shopping center began when the Kilauea Sugar Plantation rented one of its buildings on the current market site to a Chinese businessman named Lung Wah Chee, who opened an all-in-one general store with merchandise, a barber shop, butcher shop, diner, and post office. The original wood-frame building was replaced in the 1940s by the stone building that stands there today. The building is now listed on the National Register of Historic Places for its role in the town's development.

The market square is home to an array of shops and eateries, including the **Lotus Gallery** (808/828-9898, www.jewelofthelotus.com, 10am-6pm daily), selling a spectrum of antique and modern Asian art and elegant jewelry made from pearls, opals, black diamonds, jade, and other stones, as well as Hawaiian *kahelelani* and sunrise-shell jewelry. Much of the jewelry is set in gold and is designed by the owners, who share a history in jewelry design and gemology. The shop is also stocked with carvings, garden art, and various artifacts. The shop pulls you in from the outside with its outdoor waterfall and tranquil pond, and sets a high-end museum mood.

Exploring **Coconut Style** (808/828-6899, www.coconutstyle.com, 9:30am-5:30pm Mon.-Sat., 11am-5:30pm Sun.) leaves no one wondering why the shop was cited by *Architectural Digest* as one of Kaua'i's must-stop shopping spots. Exclusive hand-painted shirts, sarongs, bedding, and other clothing adorn the shop, which holds the title of having the largest collection of each in Hawaii. Each piece is a marriage between Hawaiian and Balinese style.

Island Soap and Candle Works outlets (808/828-1955, www.islandsoap.com, 9am-8pm daily) can be found around the island. The Kilauea location is not only a retail shop, but also a working factory where visitors can watch the soap being made by hand. The shop offers a full line of all-natural products to pamper yourself with while on vacation or at home. The scents of the lotions, sugar scrubs, beeswax candles, balms, and more will make you long for a spa day, which you can do yourself after dropping into the shop.

Kong Lung Trading (808/828-1822, www.konglung.com, 10am-6pm Mon.-Sat., 11am-6pm Sun.) offers a spectrum of quality and Pacific-inspired clothing, gifts, and art and more. It's a great place to window shop, make a purchase to bring home, or absorb decor representing the various cultures in the islands.

PRINCEVILLE
Princeville Center

A variety of shops to fit most needs can be found in the Princeville Center (5-4280 Kuhio Hwy., 808/826-9497, www.princevillecenter.com). **Foodland** (808/826-9880, 6am-11pm daily) offers the usual supermarket foods, as well as a drugstore section, beach and snorkeling supplies, and other basic needs. The large air-conditioned market is usually crowded and also has a pharmacy and a DVD vending machine requiring only a credit or debit card.

Meanwhile, clothing, accessories, and swimwear for the whole family can be found at **Taro Fields** (808/826-6205, www.tarofields.com,

10am-6pm daily). The products reflect the island lifestyle and are a perfect accent for going out on the island or wearing back at home. Service is friendly and helpful, and staff is usually happy offer tips for exploring the island.

Kaua'i-made jewelry is available at **Majestic Gems International Inc.** (808/826-7057, 10am-6pm Mon.-Sat., noon-6pm Sun.). Black Tahitian pearls, gold jewelry, and other stones are available. Staff here is knowledgeable about the various gems for sale.

Visit the **Hawaiian Music Store** (808/826-4223, 9am-9pm daily) to find a soundtrack for your trip. It's actually a kiosk near the Foodland entrance, and listening to the music back at home will always take you back to Kaua'i. The kiosk usually has local music playing on speakers, adding an element of island style to the shopping center.

For a drink, the **Princeville Wine Market** (808/826-0040, 10am-7pm Mon.-Sat., 1pm-7pm Sun.) holds an array of wines, something for each person's palate. Pick up a bottle for a romantic night at your accommodations or a sunset glass on the beach.

At the **Magic Dragon Toy & Art Supply** (808/826-9144, 9am-6pm daily), a compilation of unique and educational toys, games, activities, and kites can be found. Great art supplies are also available.

Kaua'i Shell Kreations (808/652-4338, 10am-7pm daily) sells unique *kahelelani* shell jewelry, among other shells. Various shell creations like shell frames, fresh flower lei, and other accessories are available. Other services are offered here, including a hardware store, postal service, and more.

HANALEI
Kahaule Center

In the **Kahaule Center** (4489 Aku Rd.) on the ocean side of the road, **The Bikini Room** (808/826-9711, www.thebikiniroom.com, 10am-6pm Mon.-Sat., 11am-5pm Sun.) is where unique and quality Brazilian bathing suits can be found. They're stylish, small, and fit for both sunning and surfing, so this is a must-stop when bikini shopping. A sale rack can often be found in front of the shop and the staff is especially helpful with insight on what suits are best for swimming or sunning.

The Root (808/826-2575, 9:30am-7pm Mon.-Sat., noon-6pm Sun.) has an array of fun, funky, simple, sweet, and trendy women's clothing. From dressy to relaxed, it's of high quality and pretty.

Find the famous Tahitian pearls (among others) at **Hanalei Pearls** (4489 Aku Rd., 808/826-0230, www.hanaleipearls.com, 11:30am-6pm). Designed by a long-time Kaua'i resident, the jewelry boasts a sparkling array of pearls, larimar, and other precious stones. Tahitian pearls are a local treasure and highly valued by those raised in the islands.

Hanalei Center

At the historic **Hanalei Center** (5-5121 Kuhio Hwy.) on the *mauka* side of the highway lies an array of shops and eateries making a home in the old school building. **Harvest Market Natural Foods and Cafe** (5-5161 Kuhio Hwy. #F, 808/826-0089, 9am-7pm Mon.-Sat., 9am-6pm Sun.) brings healthy food to Hanalei. The shelves are stocked with organic and natural food, produce, body products, and vitamins. Premade meals are in the refrigerator at the back of the store, and a salad bar offers an array of food.

At the west and back side of the center is **Havaiki Oceanic and Tribal Art** (5-5161 Kuhio Hwy. #G, 808/826-7606, www.havaikiart.com, 10:30am-6:30pm daily), where a visit feels like an exploration through the Pacific. The collection resembles what you may find while visiting a museum, with all of the most prized gifts the area has to offer. Interesting and amazing artifacts, statues, carvings, jewelry, and much more pack this store full, ranging from normally affordable to the outstanding. Every piece tells a story.

Near here is the **Yellowfish Trading Company** (808/826-1227, 10am-8pm daily), an extremely interesting store that feels like a journey through Hawaiian history. The store is loaded with Hawaiiana, collectibles, hula girl lamps, aloha shirts, carvings, swords, candles, jewelry, and so much more.

KAUA'I

At the far east end in the old Hanalei School building is the **Hanalei Surf Company** (808/826-9000, www.hanaleisurf.com, 8:30am-9pm daily), which sells and rents boards and water gear, along with a good stock of clothing and swimwear for the whole family. There are more shops in the center.

Ching Young Village

The bustling **Ching Young Village** (5-5190 Kuhio Hwy., 808/826-7222, www.chingyoungvillage.com) has many shops, including **Divine Planet** (808/826-8970, www.divineplanet.com, 10am-6pm daily) and **Aloha From Hanalei** (same phone and number), which are two connected shops, but different. The former features bamboo women's clothing, beads, Asian-themed collectibles, and pretty and fun paper star lanterns. The latter shop has a unique array of local gems, handmade creamy soaps and lotions made by a local goat dairy, and Hawaiiana. **Robin Savage Gifts & Gourmet** (808/826-7500, www.robinsavagegiftsandgourmet.com, 8:30am-7pm daily) may be the most fun gift shop in Hanalei. Local cards, children's clothing, books, lotions, home and kitchen wares, and gourmet foods fill the shop. The shop is stocked with an abundance of products, and it's almost hard to move, but there are a lot of good finds.

Hula Moon Gifts (808/826-9965, 10am-6pm daily) offers local trinkets, jewelry, shirts, and house decorations. Located on the back strip of shops, the store offers island-inspired products and souvenirs.

On the east end of the shopping center, **Backdoor Surf** (808/826-1900, www.hanaleisurf.com, 8:30am-9:30pm) rents and sells surfboards, and offers a large array of men's, women's, and children's swimwear, surf gear, and clothing.

With an interesting array of souvenirs and housewares, the **Village Variety Store** (808/826-6077, 9am-6:30pm Mon.-Sat., 10am-5pm Sun.) is fun to dig around in. The cashiers are usually no-muss no-fuss.

Colorful and cute describes the clothing in **Kokonut Kids** (5-5190 Kuhio Hwy., 808/826-0353, www.kokonutkidskauai.com, 10am-6pm Mon.-Sat., 10am-5:30pm Sun.), which offers all things local for children. From play clothes to dress clothes, Kokonut Kids can deck out the children for the whole trip.

Speaking of kids, the **Hanalei Toy and Candy Store** (808/826-4400, 10am-6pm daily) offers just that, and has a unique selection of quality toys. It's a good idea not to bring the little ones in here unless you're prepared to buy something.

Big Save (808/826-6652, 7am-9pm daily) is also here for all the basic supermarket needs. In addition to food and liquor, beach gear and school supplies are available, along with ice for the cooler and an ATM.

Hanalei Colony Resort

Na Pali Art Gallery & Coffee Shop (5-7132 Kuhio Hwy., 808/826-1844, www.napaliartgallery.com, 7am-5pm daily) is a wonderful art gallery filled with local art, jewelry, house decorations, tribal carvings, and more. The collection of Ni'ihau and sunrise-shell jewelry at the back of the small shop should not be missed. Paintings, scratchboard art, and local shell puzzles decorate the place. Coffee, smoothies, and bagels are offered too.

Entertainment

The very best entertainment on the north side may very well be the sunset. But for those looking for a little more action, there are a few places in town with live music.

PRINCEVILLE

At the **St. Regis Lobby Bar** (inside the St. Regis Princeville Resort), those looking for a mellow social evening or date night will find a 180-degree view of Hanalei Bay accented by unique art. Live jazz or Hawaiian music will highlight the evening. The bar is open 3:30-10:30pm daily.

HANALEI

Hanalei Gourmet (808/826-2524, www.hanaleigourmet.com, 8am-10:30pm daily) in the Hanalei Center often has live music at night but is more of a bar scene than a nightclub. Call for music schedules.

At **Tahiti Nui** (5-5134 Kuhio Hwy., 808/826-6277, www.thenui.com, dinner and music 6-8:30pm and late music 9:30pm-1am) dinner is offered nightly, but more importantly

it's the only place that could be considered real nighttime entertainment in Hanalei. Karaoke and Hawaiian music are played. Check the website for monthly schedules.

Bouchons Hanalei (808/826-9701, www. bouchonshanalei.com) in Ching Young Village has live music Thursday-Sunday nights. Call for hours and music selection.

TO THE END OF THE ROAD

The oceanfront luau at **Mediterranean Gourmet** (5-7132 Kuhio Hwy., 808/826-9875, www.kauaimedgourmet.com, 6-8:15pm Tues.) offers the opportunity to fill your belly with a buffet dinner of traditional Hawaiian food while taking in hula dancing, fire knife dancing, and local music. Some of the mouthwatering buffet highlights include *lomilomi* salmon, traditional *kalua* pork, *haupia,* coconut cake, and of course, Hanalei poi. Because it's limited to 80 guests, reservations are required, so call to get your spot. The adult charge is $69, which includes a drink, those ages 12-20 pay $59, and for children 11 and under it's $35.

Food

KILAUEA
Quick Bites

◖ Banana Joe's fruit stand (5-2719 Kuhio Hwy., 808/828-1092, www.bananajoekauai.com, 9am-6pm Mon.-Sat., until 5pm Sun.) is a family- and friend-run small yellow shop that sells smoothies, fresh fruit, baked goods, and local honey. The variety of fruit here makes Carmen Miranda's hat look boring. It's a perfect place for a pre-beach snack stop, a gift run, or an after-scenic-route stop.

Thai 2 Go (Kauai Pacific School parking lot, 4480 Ho'okui Rd., 808/652-3699, 11am-8pm Mon.-Sat., $9-10) serves up Thai food quickly out of a lunch wagon. The chefs from Thailand

are health conscious. The food is MSG- and GMO-free, and the chicken they use is hormone- and antibiotic-free. Try the green papaya salad and take your meal on the road or enjoy it at the on-site picnic table.

The roadside **Moloa'a Sunrise Fruit Stand** (right after mile marker 16 on Kuhio Hwy., 808/822-1441, 7:30am-5pm Mon.-Sat., Sun. 10am-5pm) is a tasty and easily accessible place to pick up smoothies, juices, a variety of coffee drinks, and sandwiches. Although it's a roadside stand, it sits on a well-kept piece of property with a grassy lawn and coconut trees. There are seats on the porch or you can take your food to go.

Seafood

"There's a whole lot more than fish in store" is the self-described motto of the **Kilauea Fish Market** (Kilauea Plantation Center, 4270 Kilauea Road # F, 808/828-6244, 11am-8pm Mon.-Sat., $10-30), and it's true. Free-range beef, salads, and plate lunches are also available, along with vegetarian specials. Take the food to eat at home or on the beach, or enjoy it in the outdoor seating area.

Natural Foods

At the **Healthy Hut** (Kilauea Plantation Center, 4270 Kilauea Rd., 808/828-6626, www.healthyhutkauai.com, 8:30am-9pm daily) you will find local produce, wine and beer, health and beauty supplies, and other natural groceries. A very small wine and beer selection is also available. They don't offer any pre-made meals; the only ready-to-eat food is fruit and snacks.

Hawaiian

Lighthouse Bistro (Kong Lung Historic Market Square, 2484 Keneke St., 808/828-0480, www.lighthousebistro.com, noon-2:30pm and 5:30-9pm, happy hour 5:30-6pm daily, lunch $7-10, dinner $15-30) is near the lighthouse, not right by it. This is the closest to fine dining for the immediate area, but it isn't entirely formal; you can dress up for fun or go low-key. Lunch includes garden and fish tacos, garden and beef burgers, fish sandwiches, soups, and salads. Dinner includes ginger-crusted fresh catch, shrimp parmesan, coconut-crusted pork, ribs, and a lot more, including an all-you-can-eat pasta bar. Vegetarians will have plenty of options here. Wine, beer, and cocktails are available.

Deli, Pizza, and Bakery

◖ **Kilauea Bakery & Pau Hana Pizza** (2484 Keneke St., 808/828-2020, www.kilaueabakery.wordpress.com, 6:30am-9pm daily, $15-33) in the Kong Lung Historic Market Square serves up satisfying breakfasts and coffee along with tasty pizzas. Mornings usually bring a line of loyal locals coming in for the sweet and savory breakfast pastries. Pizza starts being served at 10:30am and comes with a heap of toppings.

Kilauea Town Market and Deli (2484 Keneke St, 808/828-1512, www.kilaueatownmarket.com, 8am-8pm daily for already-made food and 10am-2pm for special-order sandwiches, $8-10) serves up sandwiches with options like ahi, Chinese chicken, and teriyaki tofu. Tasty desserts include bread pudding with whiskey sauce and silken chocolate pie. You can also pick up groceries and wine.

Farmers Market

Sunshine Farmers Market at the **Kilauea Neighborhood Center** (4:30pm Thurs.) offers fresh produce and fruits. You can also find an abundance of locally made crafts, some ready-to-eat food, and other locally made food. Bring your own shopping bag.

PRINCEVILLE
American

CJ's Steak & Seafood (5-4282 Kuhio Hwy., 808/826-6211, www.cjssteak.com, lunch 11:30am-2:30pm Mon.-Fri., dinner 6-9:30pm daily, $15-38) is a steakhouse in the Princeville Center with a Pacific twist to most dishes. As at many steakhouses, saddles and other western-themed decorations are found throughout. The open-beam-ceilinged restaurant has seating indoors or on the lanai. Lunch and dinner are both offered with a wide array of pupu. Lunch consists of hot and cold sandwiches, burgers, and salads, ranging $10-12. Dinner offers a salad bar, freshly caught local fish, lobster, and prime rib. A senior and children's menu offers a discount for their meals.

The **Kaua'i Grill** (808/826-9644, www.kauaigrill.com, 5:30-9:30pm Tues., Wed., and Thurs., 5:30-10pm Fri. and Sat., $15-32) inside the St. Regis Princeville Resort offers sweeping views of beautiful Hanalei Bay. The eatery stays true to its surroundings with a nautilus shell spiraling ceiling. Chef Colin Hazama, who was recently recognized by the James Beard Foundation as a finalist in the Rising Star Chef of the Year category, cooks up a tasting menu, unique salads, a vegetarian menu, and lamb, meats, and fish, all with a unique island twist. A kids' menu helps keep the prices down.

Thai

Enjoy authentic Thai food at **Tamarind Thai and Chinese Cuisine** (Princeville Center, 5-4280 Kuhio Hwy., 808/826-9999, www.tamarind-thai.com, noon-8pm Mon., Wed., Thurs., and Fri., 5pm-8pm Sat., and noon-8pm Sun., $9-20). Entrées include soups, curries, fried rice, and vegetable, meat, and seafood dishes, with vegetarian and vegan options. They even deliver.

Supermarket

Foodland (Princeville Center, 5-4280 Kuhio Hwy., 808/826-9880, 6am-11pm daily) sells not only food that needs to be prepared, but deli foods like fried chicken, macaroni and cheese, fries, freshly made sushi, and much more. The made-to-order sandwiches are actually pretty good for about $6, and are perfect for a beach day.

HANALEI
Cafés and Breakfast

The scent alone in **Java Kai** (5-5161 Ste. 210, 808/826-6717, www.javakai.com, 6:30am-6pm daily, $5-10) in the Hanalei Center will make anyone who enters want to try the local coffee. The coffees are good, and food is limited but includes a really good Belgian waffle, papaya and bagels, and a small selection of breakfast dishes including a breakfast burrito. Eat and run or drink your cup of joe on the porch.

Japanese and Fish

◖ Bouchons Hanalei (5-5190 Kuhio Hwy., 808/826-9701, www.bouchonshanalei.com, 11:30am-9:30pm daily, lunch $9-15, dinner $11-30) delivers what they call Pacific American cuisine. The lunch menu, served 11:30am-4pm, features a range of foods from burgers to ribs, to taco salads and chicken dishes. Dinner is served 5:50-9:30pm and includes exquisite sushi, a Pacific-themed menu, ribs, burgers, and other Asian dishes. An array

of drinks and live music on certain nights are also offered. The restaurant is the best of two previous ones fused together by the owner.

Just after entering Hanalei you'll see **◖ Hanalei Dolphin Restaurant** (5-5016 Kuhio Hwy., 808/826-6699, www.hanaleidolphin.com, 11:30am-3pm, 5:30-9pm daily, $10-35), consisting of the restaurant, a fish market, and sushi lounge. The restaurant serves an array of Pacific Rim salads, burgers, and seafood in all of its glory. Your meals will be enjoyed on the lanai at riverside tables or in the open-air restaurant. You can go casual here, but it's also nice enough to dress up. The sushi lounge (5:30-9pm daily) has a wonderful array of sushi and a good sake selection. The **Hanalei Fish Market** (10am-7pm daily) offers a wide selection of fresh fish. Here you'll find a good variety of seafood, specialty cheeses, organic produce, beef, and desserts.

Hawaiian

The family-run **◖ Hanalei Taro and Juice Co.** (5-5070 Kuhio Hwy., 808/826-1059, www.hanaleitaro.com, 11am-3pm Mon.-Sat., $4-10) serves up a modern take on traditional Hawaiian food. Established in 2000, the company is part of the Haraguchi family farm (of the rice mill) and creates the meals with local foods and taro. They put a new twist on Hawaiian food, as with the taro smoothie and taro veggie burgers, while staying traditional with *kalua* pig, *laulau*, poi, *lomilomi* salmon, and a whole lot more. *So ono, brah.*

◖ Postcards Cafe (808/826-1191, www.postcardscafe.com, 6pm-9pm daily, $19-31) is a vegetarian's (or seafood lover's) dream, with a spectacular menu of gourmet vegetarian and seafood cuisine. No meat, poultry, or refined sugar is used here, which makes the abundance of organic ingredients and local produce stand out. Many dishes are vegan or can be made vegan.

Health Food

Harvest Market Natural Foods and Cafe (Hanalei Center, 5-5161 Kuhio Hwy., 808/826-0089, 9am-7pm) brings healthy food

KAUA'I

to Hanalei. The shelves are stocked with organic and natural food, produce, and body products. Pre-made meals are in the refrigerator at the back of the store, and a salad bar offers an array of food. Coffee and pastries are available in the morning and the deli takes orders off their menu. It's slightly on the pricey side, but it's healthy.

To the left of Ching Young Village is the **Aloha Juice Bar** (808/826-6990), where you can find veggie and fruit juices along with acai bowls and chocolate-dipped bananas.

American
Hanalei Gourmet Cafe, Bar, and Delicatessen in Hanalei Center (5-5161 Kuhio Hwy., 808/826-2524, www.hanaleigourmet.com, 8am-10:30pm daily, lunch $7-13, dinner $10-27) offers a variety of restaurants in one. It's in the old school building, so a historical element is added to the atmosphere. Happy hour is 3:30-5:30pm daily, early-bird specials are offered 5:30-6:30pm, and selected sports are available on cable TV. A really unique thing about this place is that they offer picnic services. They will help you pack your food and wine into insulated backpacks or coolers so you can hike the Na Pali Coast or paddle up a river. The meal selection is varied, from appetizers of seafood, nachos, and the tasty artichoke dip to the dinners of pork loin, poultry, steak, and pastas, many with a Pacific twist. Salads are available in abundance, as well as sandwiches and burgers. This place has plenty of vegetarian options.

Brazilian and Mexican
◖ Neide's Brazilian and Mexican Food (Hanalei Center, 808/826-1851, www.neidesalsaandsamba.com, 11:30am-2:30pm and 5:30-9pm daily, $10-20) serves up some really good margaritas, as well as unique dishes. The head chef from Brazil has a unique take on South American food, like adding cabbage and carrots to the dishes, but it's good and interesting. The service is very laid-back, and there is outdoor and indoor seating. It can be a good place to bring kids because the porch seating

lies on a yard-like area with a picnic table and garden, so children can roll around while you enjoy a really tasty, strong, and slightly pricey margarita. Vegetarians will not leave here with an empty belly.

Tropical Taco (5-5088 Kuhio Hwy., 808/827-8226, www.tropicaltaco.com, 8am-8pm daily, $5-11) is in the green Halele'a Building on the ocean side of the highway, the green being similar to the green lunch wagon the owner ran the business out of for 20 years. The tacos, burritos, and tostadas are good, simple, and can be grabbed on the run or enjoyed sitting at the location. Vegetarians will find a sufficient meal here.

Tapas
◖ Bar Acuda Tapas and Wine (808/826-7081, www.restaurantbaracuda.com, bar 5:30-10:30pm daily, dinner 6-9:30pm daily, $6-16) in the Hanalei Center may be home to the most modern decor in Hanalei. They serve tapas, which are defined on the menu as a variety of small savory dishes typically shared communally among friends. To never have a boring month, the menu here changes by the week and the season; offerings include local honeycomb with goat cheese, short ribs, local fish, salads, desserts, and a great wine menu.

Farmers Market
The **Waipa Ranch Farmers Market** (5-5785A Kuhio Hwy., 808/826-9969), which takes place on Tuesdays 2pm-4pm, is loaded with local produce, fruit, jewelry, and other crafts. It's a good idea to get here at the start, as the good stuff sells out fast.

TO THE END OF THE ROAD
Mexican
◖ Red Hot Mama's (808/826-7266, 11am-5pm daily but sometimes closes on Sun., $8-11) is a hole in the wall and thankfully one of the last stops before having no food options at the beach. I say thankfully because I'm thankful every time I eat there. The food always comes in a hefty serving, and fresh local fish is almost always an optional addition. Vegetarians can

always find a substantial meal here. The owner has enough postings around the eatery to let you know *not* to linger right in front and keep asking if your meal is done. Browse the neighboring shops or hang in the grass to the left and she will come out and call you.

Mediterranean

€ Mediterranean Gourmet (5-7132 Kuhio Hwy., 808/826-9875, www.kauaimedgourmet.com, 11am-3pm and 4:30-8:30pm Mon., 11am-3pm and 6pm-8pm Tues., 11am-3pm and 4-8:30pm Wed.-Sat., $17-65) has been voted by *Honolulu* magazine as the best new restaurant on Kaua'i in 2007 and best restaurant on Kaua'i in 2008, 2009, 2010, and 2011.

If that doesn't speak for itself, then the oceanfront location paired with the menu will amaze you. Lebanon native and chef Imad Beydoun and his wife Yarrow feature Greek, French, Spanish, Italian, and Lebanese-influenced dishes for lunch or dinner. Dinner reservations are recommended, and music is provided each night. On Tuesday nights, a luau is offered at 6pm, Wednesday is jazz and half-price wine night, Thursday is belly dancing, and Friday and Saturday offer more guitar. Try the homemade sangria or a mojito. Lunch includes wraps, vegetarian dishes, fish, and more. For dinner, there are vegetarian, lamb, beef, fish, chicken, and vegetarian dishes, along with their famous rack of lamb for two.

Getting There and Around

CAR

The most convenient way to get to and around the north shore is by car. Highway 56 heads west straight out of Lihu'e and runs all the way to the end of the road, turning into Route 560 by Hanalei. Rental cars are the best bet here and are available at the airport. Gas prices go up the farther north you go, so it's a good idea to fill up in Lihu'e. The last gas station on the north side is in Princeville. So when you're headed to Hanalei from another locale make sure to fill up. It's a bit of a drive from here to the end of the road, not a place you want to run out of gas.

BUS

The **Kaua'i Bus** (808/241-6410, www.kauai.gov/Transportation, 5:27am-10:40pm Mon.-Fri. and 6:21am-5:50pm Sat., Sun., and holidays) runs island-wide with several stops through Kilauea, Princeville and Hanalei. The bus is a green, convenient, and affordable way to get around. The last stop is in Hanalei at the old Hanalei courthouse. Fares are $2 for adults and $1 for children and seniors. Monthly passes are also available.

TAXI AND LIMOUSINE

Pono Taxi (808/634-4744, www.taxihanalei.com) offers taxi, airport shuttle, and tour services in Hanalei to any destination. **North Shore Cab Co.** (808/639-7829, www.northshorecab.com) provides rides to and from the airport and island-wide, and offers sightseeing tours. For a more upscale ride, **Kaua'i North Shore Limousine** (808/828-6189, www.kauainorthshorelimo.com) offers limousine service for a special date, wedding, or corporate travel.

SCOOTER

Hop onto a moped to zip around the north side and save on gas at **Island Scooter Rental** (5-5134 Kuhio Hwy., Kilauea, 866/225-7352, www.mobilemopeds.com, 9am-5pm daily). If you rent by the week the company offers free airport pickup, and they even offer four-hour tours for $100. Call for prices and reservations.

KAUA'I

SOUTH SHORE

The south shore, which includes the Koloa, Kalaheo, and Po'ipu areas, boasts lush green pastures above warm sunny coastlines, oceanfront accommodations bordered by the birthplace of Hawaiian royalty, and thick tropical inland jungles. A blend of vacationers and locals, raw land and modern luxuries, the south shore is the island's main resort destination, with sunny

HIGHLIGHTS

LOOK FOR ◖ TO FIND RECOMMENDED SIGHTS, ACTIVITIES, DINING, AND LODGING.

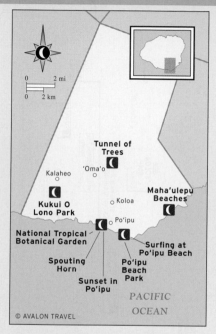

Tunnel of Trees

'Oma'o

Kalaheo

Kukui O Lono Park

Koloa

Maha'ulepu Beaches

National Tropical Botanical Garden

Po'ipu

Surfing at Po'ipu Beach

Spouting Horn

Po'ipu Beach Park

Sunset in Po'ipu

PACIFIC OCEAN

© AVALON TRAVEL

◖ **Maha'ulepu Beaches:** The long dirt road deters many beach-goers, but the expan-

sive beaches offer enough space for everyone (page 770).

◖ **Po'ipu Beach Park:** A joy for everyone, this beach offers protected swimming and manicured grounds for picnicking. The calm ocean makes it a wonderful place for children (page 771).

◖ **Surfing at Po'ipu Beach:** Po'ipu Beach offers ideal conditions for beginners to catch their first wave (page 772).

◖ **Tunnel of Trees:** Eucalyptus trees form a natural tunnel over Maluhia Road, creating a great photo opportunity (page 780).

◖ **Spouting Horn:** Salt water erupts through a hole in the lava sea cliffs at the South Shore's claim to fame (page 782).

◖ **Sunset in Po'ipu:** End a wonderful day on the South Shore with a spectacular sunset (page 782).

◖ **National Tropical Botanical Garden:** The only tropical plant research facility in the United States boasts two gardens with a vast array of tropical plants (page 783).

◖ **Kukui O Lono Park:** Stroll through Japanese gardens and enjoy a picnic with an ocean view (page 784).

skies and a coastline dotted with large hotels and condominiums, while just inland are old plantation homes that still house local residents.

The area holds claim to what may be the most important part of Hawaiian history: the first successful sugar mill in Hawaii. Koloa was home to the mill, therefore spearheading the sugar industry and bringing together many ethnicities to coexist in the island. Seven ethnic groups became the main source of labor on the plantations and others came and went, many leaving descendants that still live in the area. The sugar mill was the central feature of society and life on the south side.

On the south side you see the area's character

change as you drive toward the coast. If you take Maluhia Road down to Koloa, you'll drive through open green pastures and then the gorgeous Tunnel of Trees. Past that and just a bit west, you'll begin your journey inland in a lush green area called Lawa'i Valley, where you'll notice a prominent backdrop of luxuriant jungle reaching inland to the high central part of the island. On the way down Koloa Road notice the rolling green pastures usually dotted with happily grazing sheep and horses. In Koloa, plantation homes, remnants of the mill, and small shops and eateries make up a quaint and historical central area. This is

KAUA'I

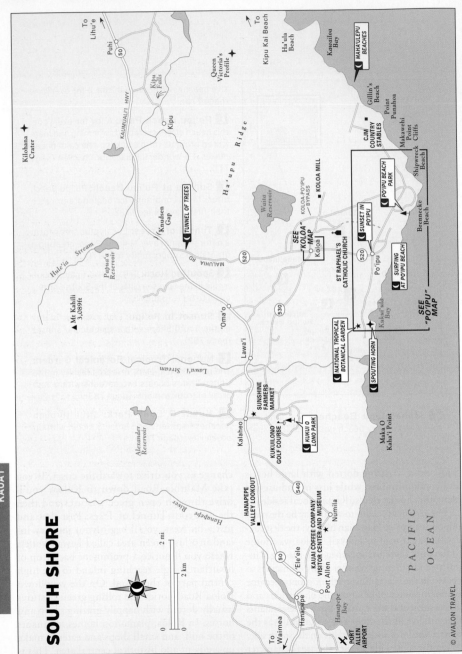

SOUTH SHORE

KAUA'I

To Lihu'e

Puhi

50

KAUMUALII HWY

Kilohana Crater

Kipu Falls

Knudsen Gap

Papua'a Reservoir

Hule'ia Stream

Mt Kahili 3,089ft

'Oma'o

MALUHIA RD

520

530

Lawa'i

Lawa'i Stream

Kalaheo

SUNSHINE FARMERS MARKET

KUKUIOLONO GOLF COURSE

KUKUI O LONO PARK

Alexander Reservoir

Hanapepe River

HANAPEPE VALLEY LOOKOUT

540

Numila

KAUAI COFFEE COMPANY VISITOR CENTER AND MUSEUM

'Ele'ele

50

Hanapepe

Hanapepe Bay

To Waimea

PORT ALLEN AIRPORT

Port Allen

2 mi
2 km

PACIFIC OCEAN

Maka O Kaha'i Point

NATIONAL TROPICAL BOTANICAL GARDEN

SPOUTING HORN

Kukui'ula Bay

ST RAPHAEL'S CATHOLIC CHURCH

Koloa

SEE "KOLOA" MAP

520

Po'ipu

SUNSET IN PO'IPU

SURFING AT PO'IPU BEACH

SEE "PO'IPU" MAP

PO'IPU BEACH PARK

Brennecke Beach

Shipwreck Beach

CJM COUNTRY STABLES

Makawehi Point

Point Punahoa

Gillin's Beach

Kawailoa Bay

MAHA'ULEPU BEACHES

Ha'ula Beach

Kipu Kai Beach

To

Queen Victoria's Profile

Ha'upu Ridge

Waita Reservoir

KOLOA MILL

KOLOA-PO'IPU BYPASS

TUNNEL OF TREES

Kipu

Ha'upu

Ridge

© AVALON TRAVEL

a great place to stroll through the town, sampling food, enjoying the aloha, and mingling with visitors while locals go about their daily business. Most of the shops in the small yet bustling town are actually remodeled old plantation buildings. Parking here is always hard to find, but the town is so small that it's fine to park anywhere and stroll around. Make a point to look inland at different points in the road. The views are gorgeous and the raw green landscape is captivating.

From 1835 to 1880 Koloa was Kaua'i's most densely populated area. Koloa Landing, down in Po'ipu, was one of the top three active whaling ports in the entire state. Sugar was a booming business for the majority of the century; the newest mill, the McBryde Sugar Co. Koloa Mill, shut its doors in 1996, ending the sugar industry for the area. Its remains can still be seen off of Maha'ulepu Road.

The vibrant green foliage gives way to a dry and sunny beach resort area, known as Po'ipu. Down here the road weaves along the ocean, past historical sites, surf breaks, and numerous white-sand beaches. Po'ipu is a vacationer's paradise: gorgeous white-sand beaches, eateries galore, shopping, surf lessons, golf courses, and a few sights to see. Although mainstream development may have made its way into the area in the form of hotels and condominiums, natural sights and raw land still exist here. Locals access the surf breaks and enjoy the beaches as much as any visitor. At the end of the day you'll often see local surfers enjoying the sunset and an after-work beer across from Lawa'i Beach. Down here are some of the most intriguing sights on the island, including Spouting Horn and the National Tropical Botanical Garden. Although there is no shortage of soft white sand down here, the sandy coast also has its share of black boulders dotting the area along

with reefs, drawing in tropical fish and creating perfect waves for surfing and body-boarding. Po'ipu's resort area also offers upscale shopping and eating.

Inland on the south side and on the way to the west is Kalaheo, home to quaint restaurants, small shops, and a population of generations of local residents. Kalaheo doesn't have much going on, but the laid-back feeling is part of its appeal. Here you can find the beautiful Kukui O Lono Park and golf course. If you're headed to the west side you'll take a drive through Kalaheo because Kaumuali'i Highway is the only road that leads there.

Many visitors decide to stay on the south shore because of its sunny coast, resort options, and world-class beaches, but if you don't stay in a hotel here, make sure to schedule at least a one-day visit to this side of the island. Enjoy the popular tourist spots, but don't miss the vacant beauty of the south shore's interior jungles and the secluded coastline.

Beyond the south shore is Kaua'i's leeward coast, locally known as the west side. A geologist's dreamland, the landscape out here contradicts itself with rolling white beaches, vast canyons, deep rivers, and dry desert. The west and driest side of the island is a land without frills, but there are two places worth making a day trip to visit: Hanapepe town, which calls itself "Kaua'i's Biggest Little Town," where art enthusiasts can view local creations and mingle with their crafters, and Waimea town, which claims to be Kaua'i's most historic town. About 15 miles inland from Waimea are Waimea Canyon and Koke'e State Parks, where the "Grand Canyon of the Pacific" claims part of the island. Koke'e State Park, a few miles past Waimea, is full of trails and hikes galore for all levels of hikers. The park is also home to inspiring lookouts over the Na Pali Coast.

KAUAI

Your Best Day on the South Shore

You can easily experience the best of the south shore in one day without missing out on anything. While the best days on other parts of the island require visitors to move quickly through many activities, you can see the best of the south shore in a more relaxed manner. If you start with breakfast around 8am, you should be able to get it all done by sundown.

- Begin your day with breakfast at **Kalaheo Cafe.** Sit down or order takeout; either way you'll have plenty of time for the day.

- While in Kalaheo, head over to **Kukui O Lono Park.** This is a good place to bring a takeout breakfast to enjoy at a picnic table. Otherwise, take a stroll, explore the rock garden, and smell the pink plumerias.

- Now it's off to a few minutes at **Spouting Horn.** Snap a few photos, wait for a couple of big bursts, and it's on to the next stop.

- Enjoy a walk through the **National Tropical Botanical Garden.** Spend about 60-90 minutes here to make sure there's enough time for everything else on the south side.

- Head down the road to **Po'ipu Beach** for surf lessons. Make sure to book the lessons in advance, and have fun trying to catch waves.

- Now you have a choice. For a relaxing time with full amenities, bask in the sun and salt at **Po'ipu Beach Park.** This is an especially good option if you have children. For a more secluded experience, drive to the **Maha'ulepu Beaches.**

- To end the day, enjoy the sunset in Po'ipu. Watch the sunset over boats and Spouting Horn from **Kukui'ula Small Boat Harbor** or from the **Beach House Restaurant.**

- For dinner, stay at the **Beach House Restaurant,** a good place with or without children. **Brick Oven Pizza** is a great family more casual option.

Beaches

Some of Kaua'i's best beaches are found on the south side. They're blanketed in fine white sand and range from popular and crowded to secluded and hardly visited. All of the beaches are in the Po'ipu area, as Koloa, Kalaheo, and Lawa'i are all inland areas. The beaches provide a selection of coveted Hawaii activities, such as snorkeling, surfing, swimming, and sunbathing.

PO'IPU
(Maha'ulepu Beaches
For a little adventure into the outskirts of the south side, take the drive out to the **Maha'ulepu Beaches** at the east end of Po'ipu. You'll travel down a long road through undeveloped land with great views of the green mountains. The road is fit for two-wheel drive cars but is usually pocked with potholes, making the ride quite bumpy. To get here, drive past the Grand Hyatt Kauai until the road turns to dirt. You'll see the CMJ Stables sign as the road turns to dirt and a gate with a sign that states the gates are locked at 6pm. Access is privately owned, and locals are hoping the owners won't close it, so respect the area and take out all that you brought. The long strip of beaches consists of Gillin's Beach, the first you come to; Kawailoa Bay, the second; and the third and most secluded, Ha'ula Beach.

Gillin's Beach is accessed via a short trail through the forest. Parking is out of sight from the beach and behind the forest, so bring any valuable belongings to the beach or leave them at home. The beach is very, very long with fine white sand. Swimming is

© JADE ECKARDT

a monk seal sunning at Maha'ulepu Beach

doable, but be careful and use good judgment. Conditions can be windy with a strong current. Although the beach is very long, it's not the widest from dunes to ocean. As the tide gets higher the sand gets narrower, and you will most likely see sunbathers bordering the dunes. To the right of the beach after Elbert Gillin's house, whom the beach is named after, is the Makauwahi Sinkhole, which is fun to explore. The open sandstone sinkhole has some fun elements to check out and has unearthed archaeological finds.

Swimming is the most protected east of Gillin's at **Kawailoa Bay.** You can keep driving and notice the beach as it becomes roadside, or walk from Gillin's east around the bend. The cove is calmer here than anywhere else on the beach, but the beach isn't quite as nice as the rest. A nice aspect of Kawailoa is that since it's in a semi-protected cove, the whipping winds can be less offensive here.

To get to **Ha'ula Beach** you must walk for a while along the lithified cliffs. The cliffs look wild and prehistoric; they're rough, and you'll want shoes for this. After about 15 minutes of walking while taking in the unique landscape, you'll reach Ha'ula Beach. Swimming out here is almost always dangerous, but on the bright side, secluded beachcombing and sunbathing are plentiful. There is rarely anyone out here and you'll most likely be alone, the main appeal of making the trip.

Farther east and accessible only by boat or over the gnarly ridge is **Kipu Kai Beach.** So unless you want to rent a boat or hike over an extremely uncomfortable ridge, you shouldn't visit this beach.

Shipwreck Beach

Shipwreck Beach fronts the Grand Hyatt Kaua'i Resort and Spa. Named after an old shipwreck that used to rest on the eastern end and is now long gone, the beach is often crowded because of its location. It offers plenty of space with about a half mile of sand, but the ocean here is usually too rough for swimming except for those who are experts in the water. Local surfers and body boarders utilize the east end of the beach for catching waves. Also on the eastern end is Makawehi Point, the high cliff that locals like to launch off of for fun. If you feel like going on a treasure hunt, a hard-to-find interesting thing here is a petroglyph carved into the base of the cliff. The ancient art is nearly always covered by sand, and you must be extremely lucky to be there when the sand is pulled away, exposing the petroglyph. To get here, drive toward the Hyatt on Weliweli Road and turn right on Ainako Road. Park in the small parking lot at the end.

◖ Po'ipu Beach Park

Po'ipu Beach Park (at the end of Kuai Road) is hands down the most ideal beach for families and children on the south side. A protected swimming area, playground, full amenities, and grassy lawn come together to create everything you could need for a full day at the beach. It's often crowded here, with visitors and local families, but it's a testament to how wonderful the beach is. The

KAUA'I

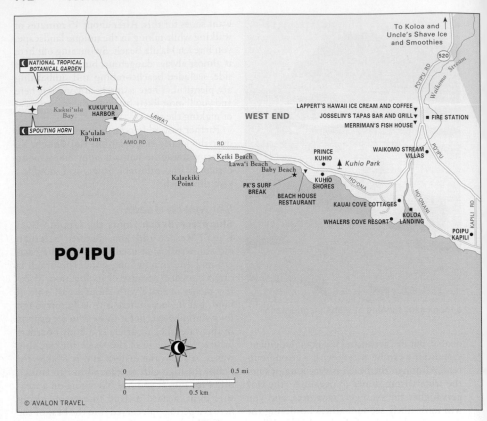

To Koloa and
Uncle's Shave Ice
and Smoothies

NATIONAL TROPICAL
BOTANICAL GARDEN

LAPPERT'S HAWAII ICE CREAM AND COFFEE

Kukui'ula
Bay   KUKUI'ULA
HARBOR

WEST END   JOSSELIN'S TAPAS BAR AND GRILL ▼   ■ FIRE STATION

MERRIMAN'S FISH HOUSE ▼

SPOUTING HORN   Ka'ulala
Point

AMIO RD   RD

Keiki Beach
Lawa'i Beach

PRINCE
KUHIO   WAIKOMO STREAM
VILLAS

Kuhio Park

Kalaekiki
Point   Baby Beach

KUHIO
SHORES

PK'S SURF
BREAK

BEACH HOUSE
RESTAURANT   KAUAI COVE COTTAGES

WHALERS COVE RESORT   KOLOA
LANDING

POIPU
KAPILI

PO'IPU

0   0.5 mi
0   0.5 km

© AVALON TRAVEL

semi-enclosed part of the water to the east is protected by a short rock wall, providing nearly always calm and shallow water within the rock barrier. It's a great swimming pool for children to float and play. The water isn't as protected on the right side of the beach as it is on the left, but if the waves are small it's usually pretty safe. Snorkeling at the west end is pretty good too.

An elaborate playground for children is located at the east side of the park alongside a tree offering shade. Picnic tables dot the grassy lawn, showers and bathrooms are on-site, and lifeguards watch over the area. There is parking available across the street from the beach, but on most days the spots are full. You may have to wait a little while for someone to leave and

open up a spot for you. The beach was mauled by Hurricane 'Iniki but has been restored to all of its glory.

Just east of Po'ipu Beach Park is **Brennecke Beach.** The waves are great for boogie-boarding and bodysurfing only, because fiberglass boards, which is what surfboards are, are not allowed. This is a good place for beginners to rent a boogie board from **Nukumoi Surf** across the street and charge the waves. To get here, turn down Ho'owili Road off of Po'ipu Road. The beach is right at the bottom along Ho'one Road.

Po'ipu Beach

Also known as Sheraton Beach (because it fronts the Sheraton Kaua'i) and Kiahuna

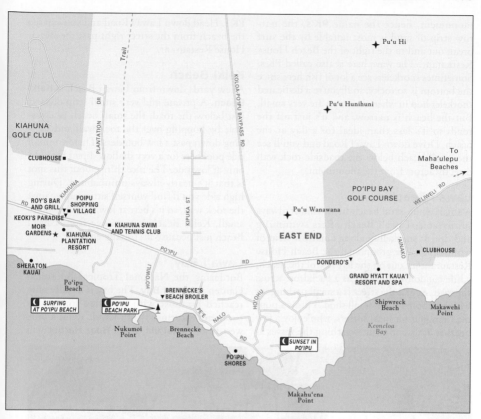

Beach, beautiful **Po'ipu Beach** is popular and generally crowded. The swimming just off-shore is usually pretty mellow thanks to the reef farther out. A good wave for surfing is also created here by the reef, and it's a popular spot with local surfers and surf schools. Surf lessons are taught here frequently, and there's no doubt you'll see surf school students with soft-top longboards. Body-boarding and body surfing are fun in the shore break. It's also a good spot for snorkeling if the ocean is calm, so bring your gear. There are restrooms at the grassy lawn above the sand. Parking here and along the street can be tight, so keep a lookout for several parking areas along the road. The beach is at the end of coastal Ho'onani Road.

Baby Beach

True to its name, **Baby Beach** is perfect for small children and babies. The small beach is nearly always calm, still, and shallow. The water here feels more like a saltwater swimming pool than the open ocean. There is a narrow strip of white sand descending into the water, leading to a rocky bottom. Hawaiian rocks can always be a bit tough on the feet, so bringing water shoes is a good idea. Kids will love jumping around in the water with floats here. To get here, turn off of Lawa'i Road onto Ho'ona Road and look for the beach access sign. The beach is behind the oceanfront homes.

PK's

Located right across from the Prince Kuhio

KAUA'I

monument, hence the name **PK's,** the narrow strip of sand is most notable by the surf break-out and to the right of the Beach House Restaurant. The wave here is also called PK's. Sometimes snorkelers see a lot of fish here since the bottom is so rocky, so if you're a dedicated snorkeler hop in when the waves are very small. But the beach is narrow, and it's just off the road, so it's less than ideal for a day at the beach. Drive down Lawaʻi Road and you'll see the small beach below the roadside rock wall directly across from the monument.

Lawaʻi Beach

A small white-sand beach in an almost always sunny area, Lawaʻi Beach offers swimming and decent snorkeling along a narrow strip of white sand. The grounds of the Beach House Restaurant jut out on the left side of the beach, while condominiums act as a backdrop across the road. Across the street is a small parking lot with restrooms and a small shop. This is a popular hangout for local surfers, who enjoy a few beers at day's end while watching the waves at

PK's. Head down Lawaʻi Road and you can see the beach from the street right past the Beach House Restaurant.

Keiki Beach

A few yards down from Lawaʻi Beach is **Keiki Beach.** A private and very small strip of sand just below the road, the small beach is accessible by hopping over the rock wall and stepping down past a few boulders. There's a small tide pool here for a very shallow dip or for kids, only at low tide. The nice thing about this spot is that it's nearly always uninhabited. During high tide you'll find yourself sitting up against the rock wall, so it's best at low tide. Although small, Keiki Beach is a change from Lawaʻi Beach just because it's usually empty.

Lawaʻi Bay

Bordering the National Tropical Botanical Garden is **Lawaʻi Bay.** The bay is usually only reached by those with a passion for serious ocean adventuring. If you kayak about a mile west from **Kukuiʻula Small Boat Harbor** you

Lawaʻi Beach lies alongside the Beach House Restaurant.

will reach it. Those who make it there are asked to be respectful and not enter the gardens. Needless to say, you'll most likely be alone here if you make the trip. Park your vehicle at Kukui'ula Small Boat Harbor at the end of Lawa'i Road. Hop in the water with your kayak and paddle about a mile west down the coast.

Water Sports

SNORKELING AND DIVING

The south side has decent snorkeling at several spots. One of the highlights here is the large number of green sea turtles that frequent the waters. They are slow and gentle creatures, so please don't bother them. Although they rarely bite, it is painful when they do. They usually cruise along leisurely, but be careful and keep board leashes away from them. They can get very tangled and angry.

Po'ipu
DIVING SPOTS

Hop in the water at **Lawa'i Beach** and you may see some colorful fish. The sea life isn't the most populated but it's definitely worth a shot if you're spending time at the beach. The bottom here is rocky, which means fish are attracted to the area because seaweed and algae grow here for them to eat. Just east of Lawa'i Beach and across from the Prince Kuhio monument is **PK's**. The beach is tiny, and the ocean floor is rocky, which again attracts fish into the area. The beach is rarely visited because it's right off the road, and fish seem to like to hang out here. Maybe they appreciate the lack of disturbance compared to other areas. Down the road, **Po'ipu Beach Park** is a good option for snorkeling. There's usually something to see at either end of the beach and the water is often calm here. Jump in on either end of the beach and you'll most likely see some ocean life.

GEAR

You can rent or buy snorkel gear at **Nukumoi Beach & Surf Shop** (2080 Ho'one Rd., 808/742-8019, www.nukumoisurf.com, 7:45am-7pm Mon.-Sat., 10:30am-6pm Sun.). They provide all kinds of beach gear, including snorkel gear, for about $7 a day to $20 for the week. At **Snorkel Bob's** (3236 Po'ipu Rd., 808/742-2206, www.snorkelbob.com, 8am-5pm daily) you'll find a wide variety of gear for rent. They offer complete sets including a mask, snorkel, and net gear bag with grade A surgical quality silicone for ultimate comfort and water seal. The adult package goes for $35 a week or $22 per week for children. The budget crunch package offers a basic mask, snorkel, fins, and dive bag for $9 a week. A unique rental package is what they call The 4 Eyes RX Ensemble to compensate for nearsightedness while snorkeling. This includes a mask with a prescription lens for $44 per week for adults and $32 for kids.

In Po'ipu, **Fathom Five** (3450 Po'ipu Rd., 808/742-6991, www.fathomfive.com, 7am-5pm daily) offers everything you could need for casual snorkeling or serious diving. They offer rentals for $6 daily and $35 a week. **Boss Frog's** (5022 Lawa'i Rd., 808/742-9111, www.bossfrog.com, 8am-5pm daily) has rental snorkel gear for $8 a day or $30 a week. It's at Lawa'i Beach in the same building as the Beach House Restaurant.

SURFING
Po'ipu
SURFING SPOTS

If you choose to bring your own board or paddle out alone, the break at **Po'ipu Beach** is a good bet. It's rarely super intense or huge here, but of course evaluate the conditions before you paddle out. For a local spot with both left- and right-hand breaking waves, paddle out to **PK's** in front of Lawa'i Beach. The waves here mostly break as lefts, but the deepest section directly in front of the restaurant breaks as a

Live Like Sion

While driving around the south side, you may see signs that say *RIP Sion* or *Live Like Sion*. Just as the loss of professional surfer Andy Irons was mourned by many on the north side of Kaua'i, the south side will forever be mourning the loss of Sion Milosky. Hailing from Kaua'i's south shore, Milosky rose to the top of the Hawaiian surf world in his mid-30s and drowned at big wave spot Mavericks in March 2011. During a contest at Mavericks, Milosky was held down by two huge waves, reportedly 60 feet tall, before he disappeared. His body was eventually found about a mile down the coast.

Those who knew him enjoyed his incredible kindness and say he was a good person, great friend, and most importantly, a family man. He was a father of two and a dedicated husband. In the winter before he died, he paddled into what was believed at the time to be the largest wave ever paddled into (surfers often use Jet Skis to catch huge waves) at a break called Himalayas on the north shore. His family still resides on the south side.

right sometimes. Paddle out from the beach here but keep an eye out for the shallow reef below. The wave is usually dotted with locals, so be mellow and respectful. During the right swell, the heavy and intense right-hand breaking wave called **Acid Drops** is to the west of PK's. It's much coveted by experienced surfers and definitely not for beginners.

LESSONS AND GEAR
Po'ipu is a hot spot for surf lessons, and a Hawaiian vacation wouldn't be complete without at least trying to catch a few waves. Catching a wave is like flying, but on the ocean and in the sun. Give it a shot while you're out here. Several surf schools offer lessons at Po'ipu Beach, or the brave can rent a board and charge the waves alone.

For lessons from a company started by a true surf pioneer, try **Surf Lessons by Margo Oberg** (808/332-6100, www.surfonkauai. com) at Po'ipu Beach. You'll have the option of group lessons ($68), semi-private lessons ($90), or private lessons ($125). The surf school is known for satisfying customers and was recently named in *National Geographic Traveler Magazine* as one of the top 25 things to do on Kaua'i. Lessons begin with a short instruction on land to learn the basics of the sport along with ocean safety. Soft boards and protective booties are provided. Instructors are locals who are previous or current professional surfers.

Also offering lessons at Po'ipu Beach is the **Garden Island Surf School** (808/652-4841, www.gardenislandsurfschool.com). They offer group lessons for $75, private lessons for $150, or $120 for two students. For something different try outrigger canoe surfing, where you'll catch waves in a canoe. They claim a 97 percent success rate.

Kaua'i Surf School (808/651-6032, www. kauaisurfschool.com) offers lessons at Po'ipu Beach as well as week-long surf clinics. For group classes of no more than four they charge $75 per person; a one-hour private lesson costs $100 while a two-hour private lesson is $175; and a two- to three-person semi-private lesson is $240. They provide a beginner surfboard, protective booties, and a rash guard.

Located in Koloa, **Progressive Expressions** (5428 Koloa Rd., 808/742-6041, 9am-9pm Mon.-Sun.) rents surfboards for $25 a day or $110 a week and body boards for $5 a day or $25 a week. **Nukumoi Beach & Surf Shop** (2080 Ho'one Rd., 808/742-8019, www. nukumoisurf.com, 7:45am-7pm Mon.-Sat., 10:30am-6pm Sun.) rents longboards and short boards, both hard and soft top, for $5-20.

Margo Oberg: Living Legend

Before women's surfing became the popular sport it is today, Margo Oberg was in the water paving the way for generations of female surfers behind her. A pioneer for women's surfing, Oberg dominated the sport for over three decades. Growing up in La Jolla, California, Margo Godfrey began surfing at 10 years old and won her first world championship title at 15. In her first surf contest she won the open women's division and a coed children's event, proving she had something special. She kept surfing, and by high school she had made a name for herself, winning the 1968 World Contest and the Western Surfing Association's women's title. Her early accomplishments were taking place when women's surfing was nowhere near as popular as it is today.

She moved to Kaua'i's south side in the early 1970s after marrying Steve Oberg in 1972. For three years Oberg spent time on Kaua'i, taking a break from surfing professionally. In 1975 she got back into the game, winning contests left and right. Throughout her career she won a total of seven world championships.

At home in Kaua'i, Oberg began giving surf lessons in the mid-'70s and after a few years started the Margo Oberg Surfing School. She had a strong business going that supported her life on Kaua'i. No longer competing, Oberg still lives on the south side of Kaua'i, helping out with surf contests and working with her surf school. Today, women's surfing has many more competitors, surfing at a higher talent level than they did 40 years ago. Oberg was truly a pioneer and an influence on many women on the surfing tour today.

KAYAKING
Po'ipu

You can kayak the south shore's coastline with **Outfitters Kauai** (2827A Po'ipu Rd., 808/724-9667, www.outfitterskauai.com) on their kayaking and whale-watching secluded beach adventure, which is available Tuesday-Saturday from mid-September through May. They use tandem, open cockpit or sit-on-top-type self-bailing kayaks with foot-pedal-controlled rudders to explore the coast. You'll paddle to secret beaches and snorkel and body surf at beaches that are only accessible by the water. Because the tours are done in the wintertime, whale sightings are common, as well as dolphin and sea turtle sightings. Price for adults is $152 and children 12-14 are $122.

Adventure Sports

ATVS
Koloa

A fun and wild thing to do is ride ATVs with **Kaua'i ATV** (5330 Koloa Rd., 877/707-7088, www.kauaiatv.com, 7:30am-5pm daily, $125-175). They have a pretty large collection of vehicles and can take family groups or individuals. You'll go rambling through pastureland, mud, or dirt. They have clothing to loan, which means you don't have to get yours dirty. They also offer *'ohana* (family) buggies to ride with your group, and lunch often happens at a waterfall.

ZIPLINING
Lawa'i

Adrenaline junkies can fly through the air with **Just Live** (P.O. Box 166, 808/482-1295, www.justlive.org, 8am-5pm daily). The adventure sport company offers three different zipline eco-tours as well as a ropes course. The Zipline Treetop Tour takes place on

KAUA'I

seven different zipline courses and lets you walk over four canopy bridges for $120. The ziplines run up to 800 feet long and are suspended 60-80 feet in the air. The Wikiwiki Zip Tour utilizes three different ziplines, two of which are over 700 feet long, and three bridge crossings for $79. The Zipline Eco Adventure combines three ziplines, three bridges, rappelling, a monster swing, and rock-wall climbing for $125. Tours include snack and water.

BOAT TOURS
Po'ipu

Several boat tour companies cruise along Po'ipu waters. They also offer **whale-watching** from the months of December through April. **Captain Andy's Sailing Adventures** (4353 Waialo Rd., 808/335-6833, www.napali.com) offers various boat cruises, and each one includes whale-watching during the season. Combine whale-watching with a two-hour sunset sail, which takes you down to the secluded Maha'ulepu Beaches and Kipu Kai. Adults cost $69, children $50, and kids under two are free. The sail includes live Hawaiian music, appetizers, beer, and wine.

Blue Dolphin Charters (4354 Waialo Rd., 808/245-8681, www.kauaiboats.com) also offers whale-watching in season and a two-hour sunset sail. Food and cocktails add to the romance. Rates run $62 for those 12 and up and $53 for ages 2-11.

GUIDED HIKING TOURS
Koloa

Kaua'i Nature Tours (808/742-8305, www.kauainaturetours.com) offers guided hikes in the Maha'ulepu area on the east end of the south side. They also offer hikes in other parts of the island. The guides authored a geology book about Kaua'i, so they share insight into its geological formation and history. On this hike they'll take you around the area to see wildlife and enter a sinkhole where fossil-filled sediment has revealed island history. The 2.5-mile coastal walk begins after a 9am pickup at Po'ipu Beach Park. They provide lunch after a four-hour walk to a private beach cove, and snorkeling and swimming in Kawailoa Bay.

HORSEBACK RIDING
Po'ipu

A down-to-earth and peaceful way to explore the south side is with **CJM Country Stables** (1831 Po'ipu Rd., 808/742-6096, http://cjm-stables.com, 8am-5pm daily for reservations). Located on the east end of Po'ipu, they offer scenic horseback rides through the forest and along the coast. Journeying into the undeveloped Maha'ulepu area, they take you along secluded beaches as well as into the green interior of the land. The Scenic Beach and Valley Ride includes beverages for $103, but you must bring your own lunch. They also offer the Secret Beach Picnic Ride ($130), which includes a good picnic lunch on an otherwise empty beach. Experienced riders can request private rides for $130 an hour.

Golf

PO'IPU
Po'ipu Bay Golf Course

Golf fanatics will be in heaven at the **Po'ipu Bay Golf Course** (2250 Ainako St., 808/742-8711, www.poipubaygolf.com) at the Grand Hyatt Kaua'i Resort and Spa. Designed by ultimate course architect Robert Trent Jones Jr., the high-end course offers fabulous surroundings, mountain and ocean views, and open space on 210 oceanfront acres. The 18-hole course consists of 85 bunkers, five water hazards, and sometimes wild trade winds that are mother nature's way of testing your game. It is always perfectly groomed, and it's obvious here that it was designed, constructed, and maintained with attention to detail.

It's known to be not quite as tough as other courses on the island, but expert golfers as well as beginners will all have fun. A sacred *heiau* is on the grounds, along with ancient stone walls. Modern amenities are offered, like in-cart satellite navigation systems and an on-course beverage court, and daily clinics are offered by pros. The ocean-links-style course has over 30 acres of tropical plants and flowers with wonderful views. The large clubhouse is home to a golf shop open 6:30am-6:30pm daily, locker room facilities, a restaurant, lounge, and club storage.

Tee times can be made up to 30 days in advance. First tee time is at 7am and they get everyone off the course at 6:15pm. The public rate is $240, hotel guests pay $160, after noon the rate drops to $145, and after 2:30pm it's $85. Club rentals are $55 and include Callaway, Titleist, Cobra, and TaylorMade. Carts are mandatory and appropriate attire (such as collared shirts) is required.

Kiahuna Golf Club

The **Kiahuna Golf Club** (2545 Kiahuna Plantation Dr., 808/742-9595, www.kiahunagolf.com) inland in Po'ipu offers 18 holes on a course also designed by Robert Trent Jones Jr. The course features remnants of ancient Hawaiian structures and good mountain views with glimpses of the ocean. The course was recently renovated, and although it's not quite as nice as Po'ipu Bay, it is more affordable and still satisfies. Notable sights on the course include the endangered state bird, the *nene* goose, which you may see wandering around the greens. The Hawaiian stilt and moorhen

may also be seen here. To the left of the 15th fairway are the remnants of a house where a Portuguese immigrant lived during the early 19th century. There aren't any urban legends of a ghost here, but nearby is the crypt where he and his family were laid to rest.

The first tee time is 7am and the last is at 4:30pm, with players required to be off the course by 7pm. To play 18 holes with a cart costs $103, while golfers 17 and under can spend a day on the greens for $47. After 2pm the price drops to $72. They offer a bounce-back rate of $88 for the duration of your stay, cart included. Club rentals are offered for $52 for 18 holes and $32 for 9 holes.

KALAHEO
Kukuilono Golf Course

The nine-hole **Kukuilono Golf Course** (854 Pu'u Rd., 808/332-9151, www.hawaiiweb.com, $7 adults, $3 under 17) is a very affordable place to spend the day on the greens. Donated to the state by Walter McBryde in 1919, the course was only the second built on Kaua'i. McBryde loved the course so much that he was buried by the eighth hole. A Japanese garden, many fragrant plumeria trees, and a Hawaiian rock collection are also on-site, and wonderful views of the ocean are enjoyed while playing. Carts can be rented for $6 a day. The course doesn't book tee times; it's first come, first served, with first play time at 6:30am. For those renting clubs, last tee time is at 3pm, while those who brought their own can tee off at 4:30pm. The surroundings are gorgeous and the course is fun.

Spas

PO'IPU

Pure luxury can be indulged in at **Anara Spa** (1571 Poʻipu Rd., 808/240-6440, www.anara-spa.com, 7am-8pm daily) at the Grand Hyatt Kauaʻi. Services are offered both indoors and outdoors in the enchanting Lokahi Garden, with waterfalls, soaking pools, and open-air bungalows. You can find a full-service salon here, a spa boutique, a garden Vichy shower, a lap pool, steam rooms, saunas, fitness, and more. Hawaiian healing methods are integrated into the treatments as well as tropical scents. Relax in the lap of luxury and receive ultimate pampering here. This is a great vacation from your vacation.

Anara Spa offers massage in a variety of modalities ranging $160-235, including Hawaiian *lomilomi* and maternity. Facials with tropical scents and ingredients range $105-250. Body treatments run $165-320. Luxurious (and pricey) spa packages are also available.

Not far inland from the beach is **Poipu Day Spa** (3176 Poʻipu Rd., 808/742-8502, www.poipudayspa.com, 8am-6pm Mon.-Sat.). Priding themselves on being a go-to spot for holistic health and beauty for visitors and residents, they specialize in massage, facials and waxing, manicures and pedicures, scrubs, wraps, and bridal services. They provide great services for lower prices than many of the big hotel spas. Massages range $50-130 while body treatments with exotic ingredients and scents run $55-185. Facials are priced $65-125. Call or visit the site for many other services, like anti-aging masks, waxing, and other treatments. A highlight here is the hot stone therapy.

Sights

KOLOA

🄲 Tunnel of Trees

Entering Koloa via Maluhia Road takes you through a grove of eucalyptus trees bending over the road and weaving together, forming a natural tunnel. This is known as the **Tunnel of Trees.** The trees were brought in from Australia by the Knudsen family (said to be the largest landowner in the area) to stabilize the road because it was quite muddy at the time. If you can find a safe pull-off spot along the road, this is a wonderful photo opportunity if you can get a traffic-free shot. On very sunny days the tunnel is especially pretty with sparkling sunlight shining through the branches.

Koloa History Center

Get some insight into the history of Koloa via artifacts and photographs of the old days at the quaint **Koloa History Center** (Building 10 in the Waikomo Shops on Koloa Rd., www.

the Tunnel of Trees

© JADE ECKARDT

KAUAʻI

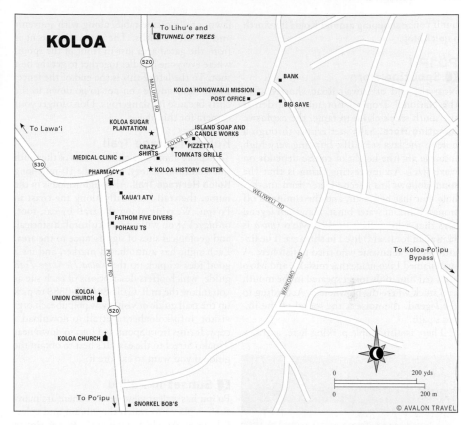

KOLOA

To Lihu'e and
TUNNEL OF TREES

520

MALUHIA RD

To Lawa'i

To Lawa'i

KOLOA SUGAR
PLANTATION ★

MEDICAL CLINIC ■

530

PHARMACY ■

KOLOA HONGWANJI MISSION ■
POST OFFICE ■

BANK ■

BIG SAVE ■

ISLAND SOAP AND
CANDLE WORKS ■

KOLOA RD

CRAZY
SHIRTS ▼

PIZZETTA ▼
TOMKATS GRILLE ■

★ KOLOA HISTORY CENTER

WELIWELI RD

KAUA'I ATV ■

FATHOM FIVE DIVERS ■
POHAKU TS ■

PO'IPU RD

WAIKOMO RD

To Koloa-Po'ipu
Bypass

KOLOA ▲
UNION CHURCH ▲

520

KOLOA CHURCH ▲

0   200 yds
0   200 m

To Po'ipu ↓

■ SNORKEL BOB'S

© AVALON TRAVEL

oldkoloa.com, 9am-9pm daily). Focused on the plantation era, since the area was home to Hawaii's first successful sugar mill, the center is very small. Yet the few small displays and photographs that offer background about the area are a good place to start a south side visit for a deeper understanding during the rest of your stay. The visit won't take up much of your time. Near Waikomo Stream, the center is at the former site of an old hotel and provides picnic tables and a small garden to enjoy in a courtyard. Take notice of the old and huge monkey pod tree that shades much of the immediate area.

Koloa Sugar Plantation

All that's left of the foundation of Koloa town is the remnants of the **Koloa Sugar**

Plantation, the first successful attempt at a mill in Hawaii. Koloa was the birthplace of the Hawaiian sugar industry, and just across from the shops at the end of Maluhia Road is what's left of the mill, which was established in 1835. A plaque gives a brief history and explains the significance of the mill and sugar industry. You can see and touch sugar in its original form in the cluster of about 12 different varieties of sugar cane that grow on-site. There isn't really much to see here, but reading the plaque leaves visitors with an understanding of the town. A bronze sculpture shows respect to the seven ethnic groups that worked on Hawaii's plantations: Hawaiians, Chinese, Japanese, Puerto Ricans, Filipinos, Koreans, and Portuguese. It's not a super-exciting place, but if you're shopping around Koloa it's worth a quick stop.

PO'IPU
(Spouting Horn

Near the end of Lawa'i Road shortly after the National Tropical Botanical Garden is the south side's claim to fame, the explosive **Spouting Horn.** Saltwater erupts through a hole in the lava sea cliffs, bursting very high into the air (the height of course depends on wave size). An interesting thing is that the sound follows just a second later from another hole that just blows air, and the timing is off from the initial water burst. Hawaiian legend says that a huge lizard called Mo'o (*mo'o* is Hawaiian for lizard) lived in this area. The lizard would eat anyone who tried to fish here. A man named Liko made that mistake, and Mo'o attacked him, only to get speared in the mouth and stuck where the blowhole is. According to the legend, the noise is the sound of the lizard's pain.

There is also ample parking here, a grassy lawn, and a picnic table, along with souvenir and jewelry booths. The main viewpoint is from the gated area just in front of the spout, where everyone huddles together to get the best shot. To the left of this is the end of the fence, where signs advise you not to go down to the cliffs because it's dangerous. Don't forget your camera for this one.

Koloa Heritage Trail

To explore about five million years of the south side's cultural history, follow the 10-mile-long **Koloa Heritage Trail.** Although Koloa is in the name, the trail is actually along the coast in Po'ipu. Weaving along the trail by car, foot, or bicycle, you will visit 14 cultural, historical, and geological sites of significance to the area. Each sight has a numbered marker, and it's a good idea to pick up the *Koloa Heritage Trail* guide, which offers descriptions of each site as you follow the trail. Call 888/744-0888 to pick up the trail guide or visit www.poipubeach.org/visitor_info/koloaheritagetrail to download a copy. It runs from Spouting Horn to down near Ainako Street to the east. It's best to obtain the guide if you want to explore it.

(Sunset in Po'ipu

Po'ipu has a clear view west, so there are many perfect places to watch the vibrant and colorful sunset. An ideal spot is at the **Beach House Restaurant** (5022 Lawa'i Rd., 808/742-1424, www.the-beach-house.com, 5-10pm daily, $20-40 entrées) on Lawa'i Beach. The open-air restaurant serves dinner, pupu, and drinks overlooking the ocean. The best part of this place is the front lawn on the water, which offers tiki-torch-lit outdoor lounging while watching the sunset over wave riders at PK's. Although many locals and visitors like to spend the evening on the lawn here without eating at the restaurant, the lawn is technically part of the restaurant grounds.

At the very end of Lawa'i Road is **Kukui'ula Small Boat Harbor.** Here you will find a pavilion, a lawn backing a small strip of sand, picnic tables, and a small pier to watch the sunset over Spouting Horn. Swimming here isn't

© JADE ECKARDT

KAUA'I

the Spouting Horn

recommended, but it is a great place to end the day watching the sun set over boats and the coastline.

Prince Kuhio Park and Hoʻai Heiau

Across from the ocean on Lawaʻi Road and across from Hoʻona Road is the birthplace of beloved Prince Kuhio. The well-maintained **Prince Kuhio Park** has a large lawn, a pond, a pavilion, the **Hoʻai Heiau,** and foliage. There isn't really much to see but it's a very pretty outdoor area worth meandering around, and a great place for culture and history buffs. The *heiau* is in great condition.

National Tropical Botanical Garden

Consisting of both the McBryde and Allerton Gardens, the **National Tropical Botanical Garden** (visitors center, 4425 Lawaʻi Rd., 808/742-2623, www.ntbg.org, 8:30am-5pm daily) is the only tropical plant research facility in the United States. In an effort to preserve,

propagate, and dispense knowledge about tropical plants, the nonprofit organization is supported only by private donations. You'll want to remember your camera for this stop, and it's a fun place for photography fans to spend time trying to get good angles and lighting. If you don't have the time or the motivation to explore the gardens, go for a gander around the entrance. Even wandering around the entrance of the gardens is enjoyable. A pond with beautiful pink lilies and numerous varieties of tropical flowers to smell are here.

Over 6,000 tropical plant species flourish at the 259-acre **McBryde Garden.** Here you can explore a seemingly infinite array of plants and flowers ranging from bamboo to orchids. The gardens are divided into sections dedicated to medicinal and nutritional plants, herbs and spices, endangered species, fruits, and much more. Trams take visitors into the McBryde Garden every hour daily beginning at 9:30am until 2:30pm; self-guided tours cost $20 for adults 13 years old and up, $10 for children 6-12, and children 5 and under are free.

© JADE ECKARDT

KAUAʻI

the entrance of the National Tropical Botanical Garden

The People's Prince

Prince Jonah Kuhio Kalanianaole was raised in Koloa. He was a worldly prince who attended the Royal School on O'ahu and studied for four years at St. Matthews College in California. He also attended the royal Agricultural College in England and eventually graduated from a business school there. King David Kalakaua, also Kuhio's uncle, appointed Kuhio to a seat on the royal cabinet. Not long after, in 1893 the Hawaiian Kingdom was overthrown. Kuhio joined with fellow Hawaiians to restore the monarchy and the attempt was unsuccessful. He was sentenced to a year in prison while other activists were executed for treason. After getting out, Kuhio left the islands and traveled in South Africa for a few years with a vow to never return to his homeland as long as it was inhospitable to its native people. When he came back to Hawaii it had been annexed as a territory of the United States.

For his efforts to help his people and work toward conserving the Hawaiian culture, Kuhio was nicknamed Ke Ali'i Maka'ainana, meaning "prince of the people." While part of Congress, he was a leader in the passage of the Hawaiian Homes Commission Act, which provides land for native Hawaiians to live on. Prince Kuhio served as Hawaii's delegate to Congress from the early 20th century until his death in 1922.

He was loved and respected by his people for his efforts in working for the respect and rights of Hawaiians. Kuhio loved his home island and returned home whenever he could.

The 80-acre **Allerton Garden** is named after John Allerton, who started the garden and was a member of a Mainland cattle-raising family that founded the First National Bank of Chicago. The garden dates from the 1870s, when Queen Emma first planted here at one of her summer vacation homes. In 1938 Robert Allerton bought the property, and for the next two decades he and his son John cleared the land. John traveled the Pacific extensively, bringing back exotic plants to Kaua'i. Cutting through the property is the Lawa'i River, and small garden rooms and pools make it quite an enchanting experience. Here guided tours are offered beginning at 9 and 10am and 1 and 2pm from Monday to Saturday. Reservations are necessary even about a week in advance, as they are often booked up, especially during holiday seasons. The price to visit the Allerton Garden is higher than the McBryde. It's $45 for those 13 years old and up and $20 for children 8-12. Children under eight are not allowed on the tour.

Drop by the visitors center across from Spouting Horn to check out the gift shop and displays in the former plantation manager's restored house. In here you can find Hawaiian crafts, Ni'ihau shell lei, and books about Hawaii. Around this center, which was constructed in 1997 after the last center was destroyed in Hurricane 'Iniki, are the demonstration gardens, which are worth exploring on their own. Tours leave from the visitors center. Remember good walking shoes and mosquito repellent, and scan the sky to determine if you want to bring an umbrella. Don't forget your camera.

KALAHEO
(Kukui O Lono Park
Oftentimes public parks are aren't exceptional places to visit, but **Kukui O Lono Park** (Pu'u Rd., 6:30am-6:30pm daily) is quite an enjoyable experience. A unique combination of Japanese gardens, rocks used by Hawaiians for various purposes, abundant plumerias, and a public golf course, the park is beautiful and has a great ocean view. It was given to the people of Kaua'i in 1919 by Walter D. McBryde, a plantation owner, and a plaque

in honor of his memory is on the grounds. After entering through the large stone and metal gate, go straight to find the gardens and memorial, or take the right at the fork in the road to find the golf clubhouse about a half mile up. The views in every direction are wonderful. Be mindful of flying golf balls and carts. Pink plumerias are usually flourishing here, and they smell exceptionally great. The collection of rocks used by Hawaiians for various functions is quite interesting and worth a gander. Near the front it says parking here is reserved for joggers, and if you're a runner this is a great place to get some exercise.

To get here turn onto Papalina Road in Kalaheo. About two miles up turn right at the large gate on the second Puʻu Road.

LAWAʻI

Along the hillside at **Lawaʻi International Center** (3381 Wawae Rd., 808/639-4300, www.lawaicenter.org, donation), 88 Buddhist shrines replicate the 88 temples along the thousand-mile trail and pilgrimage route in Shikoku, Japan. The center was opened in 1904 in a small lush valley that was originally used by Hawaiians as a place of worship before being adopted by Japanese Taoists and Shintoists. The area is lush and green, and dotted with orchids. During the tour you'll learn the history of the property and enjoy tea and local pastries. The tour begins through a small cave and leads to the miniature shrines, where previous visitors have left jewelry, shells, coins, and other offerings. The shrines can be viewed on the second and last Sundays of each month, with tours at 10am, noon, and 2pm,

Shopping

Shopping on the south side is contained to several areas where shops are clustered together. The area is filled with many boutiques, galleries, souvenir shops, and clothing stores. Most daily shopping needs for residents are found in nearby Lihuʻe.

KOLOA
Clothing
For a unique array of clothing check out **Jungle Girl** (5424 Koloa Rd., 808/742-9649, 9am-9pm daily). They also have a collection of accessories and housewares. There are some locally made items as well as creations from around the world. If you're looking for aloha wear drop into **Pohaku Ts** (3430 Poʻipu Rd., 808/742-7500, www.pohaku.com, 10am-6pm daily). They offer cotton aloha shirts that are designed, cut, and sewn on Kauaʻi for men, women, and children. Suits galore decorate the inside of **South Shore Bikinis** (3450 Poʻipu Rd., 808/742-5200, 9am-7pm daily), where they specialize in the tiny-backed Brazilian bikini. They also offer a variety of

other suits along with beachwear for all ages, hats, sandals, and other accessories. A huge spectrum of Kauaʻi and Hawaii souvenir shirts can be found in **Crazy Shirts** (5356 Koloa Road., 808/742-7161, www.crazyshirts.com, 10am-9pm). A chain found throughout the islands, they sell shirts and a few other items for men, women, and children with a heavy Kauaʻi and Hawaii theme.

Gifts, Crafts, and Souvenirs
Island-style souvenirs and gifts can be found at **Hula Moon Gifts** (5426 Koloa Rd., 808/742-9298, 9am-9pm Mon.-Sat. and 10am-9pm Sun.). They sell unique locally made crafts, gifts, and jewelry. At the **Emperor's Emporium** (5330 Koloa Rd. #3, 808/742-8377, 9am-9pm daily) you will find a resort-style store offering jewelry, gifts, and clothing. The scent radiating out of the shop will draw you into **Island Soap and Candle Works** (Koloa Rd., 808/742-1945, www.kauaisoap.com, 9am-9pm daily). The locally run store has shops island-wide where they manufacture natural Hawaiian botanical

products, beeswax candles, and other gifts. While shopping you'll get a behind-the-scenes look into how it's all made.

PO'IPU
Galleries and Home Decor
For a lovely selection of island-style home decor check out **Aspire Furniture** (808/245-9015, www.aspirefurniture.com, 10am-5pm Mon.-Sat.). From artwork to furniture to decorations, the store helps bring the island into the home and also offers interior design services. More island-style merchandise can be found at **Bungalow 9** (808/742-1961, www.bungalow-nine.com, 11am-9pm daily). Here a selection of home accessories, clothing, gifts, and more can be found with a modern beach theme.

Admire the work of local crafters and artists at **Halele'a** (808/742-9525, www.haleleagallery.com). Island artisans and designers have their creations in stock here, from wall art to koa furniture and apparel. A wonderful source for locally made products is **Palm Palm** (808/742-1131, www.palmpalmkauai.com, 10am-9pm daily). It's well stocked with fashionable clothing, bath products, high-end jewelry, and quality accessories, and the owner has been in the jewelry industry for a decade and brings style to the shop.

All of these shops are in the **Kukui'ula Shopping Village** (Ala Kalanikaumaka St., 808/742-9545, www.kukuiulavillage.com), open 10am-9pm daily.

Clothing, Accessories, and Swimwear
In the **Kukui'ula Shopping Village** lies a selection of clothing ranging from mainstream gear to unique island-style apparel. For high-quality aloha wear stop at **Tommy Bahama** (808/742-8808, www.tommybahama.com, 10am-9pm daily). The store offers high-end casual island wear for men and women. Swimwear is available at **Bikini Planet** (808/742-8860,

10am-8pm daily), where you can find a huge selection of Brazilian bikinis and many other styles, along with beach accessories, workout apparel, and some clothing and jewelry.

Sunglass Hut (808/742-9065 www.sunglasshut.com, 10am-9pm daily) offers shades in any style you could want. A combination of clothing and art can be found at **Hawaiian Salt** (808/742-6030, 10am-9pm daily). Clothing here is mostly for visitors, with a lot of gear boasting Kaua'i and Po'ipu local icons. Hats, bath products, and jewelry are also sold here. In **Quiksilver** (808/742-8088, 10am-9pm daily) you will find a huge selection of men's, women's, and children's surf-themed clothing for both in the water and out. Accessories like sunglasses and hats and sandals are also sold here.

Arts, Crafts, and Jewelry
At the intriguing **Red Koi Collection** (808/742-2778, www.redkoicollection.com, 10am-9pm daily) you'll find an array of fine arts, from hand-painted silks to original paintings, koa furniture, and jewelry. The high-end products make it feel like a hip and modern island museum combined with the home decor of a wealthy world traveler. The prices are high, but it's a nice place to window shop.

Amazing Kaua'i outdoor photography decorates **Scott Hanft Photography** (808/742-9515, www.scotthanftoutdoorphotogallery.com, 10am-8pm daily). Here you will find wonderful air, underwater, nature, and landmark shots from around the island. Originals and prints are both available, along with magnets, cards, jewelry, and more.

Beautiful and elegant jewelry is on display at **Ocean Opulent Jewelry** (808/742-9992, www.oceanpoipu.com, 10:30am-9pm daily), where semiprecious stones, freshwater pearls, and other stones are set in gold, silver, and platinum. Unique gifts and accessories are available here.

Entertainment

PO'IPU
Luau
A night at the **Grand Hyatt Kaua'i Lu'au** (1571 Po'ipu Rd., 808/240-6456, www.grandhyatt-kauailuau.com) is well spent. On Thursdays and Sundays 6-8:30pm, guests are treated to a dinner with traditional foods from Hawaii and the Pacific, along with arts, crafts, and bar drinks. Entertainment includes Polynesian dancing, hula, and fire knife dancing.

Bars and Live Music
The Grand Hyatt Kaua'i is also home to several lounges and bars, including **Stevenson's Library.** Here you can find live jazz nightly 8pm-11pm and enjoy it while sipping cocktails. Live music happens at the **Seaview Terrace** 6pm-8pm daily. An evening here begins with a torch-lighting ceremony, and performances may include a Hawaiian soloist, Hawaiian duet, or a children's hula show.

Surrounded by flaming tiki torches and the Moir Gardens of the Kiahuan Plantation Resort, the **Plantation Gardens Bar and Restaurant** (2253 Poipu Rd., 808/742-2121, www.pgrestaurant.com, 5pm-9:30pm daily) mixes classic elegance with tropical nights. The restaurant and full bar feature a unique and delicious Pacific Rim menu with a Hawaiian flair. You can sit outside on the lanai and enjoy specially cocktails, tropical drinks, wine, and beer.

At **Lavas** (inside Sheraton Kaua'I, 2440 Ho'onani Rd., 808/742-1661 or 800/782-9488, www.sheraton-kauai.com) you can enjoy views of the sunset along with unique, handcrafted tropical drinks. Happy hour happens daily from 3pm-5pm and again from 9pm-11pm.

KALAHEO
Live Music
There really isn't much going on in Kalaheo at night, but **Kalaheo Steak & Ribs** (4444 Papalina Rd., 808/332-4444, www.kalaheosteakandribs.com) has live music every Friday and Saturday at 7pm. Add appetizers and drinks at the saloon and you have a night out.

Food

KOLOA
Italian
Head over to **((** **Pizzetta** (5408 Koloa Rd., 808/742-8881, www.pizzettarestaurant.com, 11am-9pm Mon.-Fri., 11am-10pm Sat. and Sun., $11-25) for great pizza and other wonderful Italian dishes, such as calzones and chicken parmigiana. A custom beer, named Rooster Brew in honor of the Kaua'i's free-range chickens, nicely complements the dishes. The atmosphere is laid-back and casual. Nestled in a historic clapboard building, the restaurant is in central Koloa town. Vegetarians will have a sufficient array of options here.

Local Cuisine
Koloa Fish Market (5482 Koloa Rd., 808/742-6199, 10am-6pm Mon.-Fri., till 5pm on Sat., $8-11) offers fish, of course, as well as plate lunches and other local dishes like *laulau* and *poke*. The selection is rather limited, but it's really popular with locals. It's order at the counter and take out—but what could be better than a plate lunch on the beach?

Ice Cream and Shave Ice
Koloa Mill Ice Cream and Coffee (5424 Koloa Rd., 808/742-6544, www.koloamill.com, 7am-9pm daily) serves up items to satisfy the sweet

tooth and provide a caffeine fix. They pride themselves on serving only Hawaiian-made foods, such as Kauaʻi coffee and Maui-made ice cream with local flavors.

Farmers Market

Sunshine Farmers Market in the **Koloa Ball Park** (noon Mon.) offers fresh produce and fruits. You can also find an abundance of locally made crafts, some ready-to-eat food, and other locally made food. Bring your own shopping bag.

POʻIPU
American

A wonderful atmosphere can be found at **(Keoki's Paradise** (2360 Kiahuna Plantation Dr., 808/742-7534, www.keokisparadise.com, 11am-10:30pm daily, $15), where ponds, a small waterfall, greenery, and a large beautiful tree make a very relaxing vibe. Here you'll find a mix of visitors and locals enjoying a drink at the bar. Service is friendly and good, and the food is pretty good but not spectacular. They have nachos, steaks, burgers, and seafood in large portions. It's in the Poipu Shopping Village with outdoor and open-air yet covered seating.

Open-air eatery **Brennecke's Beach Broiler** (2100 Hoʻone Rd., 808/742-7588, www.brenneckes.com, lunch and dinner daily, $10-30) is right across from Poʻipu Beach, offering great views along with lunch and dinner. The food can't match the views, but it's not bad. They're famous for their *kiawe*-broiled meat and chicken. A children's menu is offered for lunch and dinner.

Hawaiian Regional

Two farm-to-table restaurants are **Merriman's Downstairs Cafe** (808/742-2856, www.merrimanshawaii.com, opens at 11am daily for lunch and dinner, $12-22) in Kukuiʻula Shopping Village and **(Merriman's Fish House** (808/742-8385, opens at 5:30pm daily for dinner, $25-35), where good food and sustainability are combined to produce high-quality Hawaiian regional cuisine. Both eateries utilize locally grown or caught ingredients, constituting 90 percent of the food they use. The downstairs café offers casual dining while the upstairs fish house offers mountain and ocean views with a full bar. They purchase produce daily.

The open-air **(Beach House Restaurant** (5022 Lawaʻi Rd., 808/742-1424, www.the-beach-house.com, 5-10pm daily, $20-40 entrées) has a prime oceanfront location on Lawaʻi Beach. The front lawn is dotted with tiki torches, making it a perfect spot for watching the sunset (although you can't bring drinks out there). Opening later in the day just for dinner, the Beach House serves seafood, steaks, and even a roasted duck dish. They also have a great wine list. Make reservations; it can get crowded.

Always a good choice is **(Roy's Bar and Grill** (808/742-5000, www.roysrestaurant.com, 5:30am-9:30pm daily, $25-35) in the Poipu Shopping Village. The elegant yet island-style restaurant serves seafood, steaks, and pastas cooked perfectly consistently. Menu specials change nightly, with fresh local fish, produce, meats, and game made into creative dishes. Vegetarians are treated to a special meat-free menu with appetizers, main courses, and specials. Service is always great and you can bring your own wine if they don't carry that particular kind. Roy's doesn't require exceptionally formal attire, but don't roll in straight off the beach.

Italian

At the elegant **(Dondero's** (1571 Poʻipu Rd., 808/240-6456, 6-10pm Mon.-Sat., $18-42) you will be treated to a wonderful meal with a romantic and high-end atmosphere. You can sit outdoors under the stars, overlooking the ocean, or enjoy your meal inside with Italian decor of murals and tiles similar to a villa in Italy. They have a great wine list to complement their fresh local fish, veal, pastas, and decadent desserts. Vegetarians can find plenty to eat here. It's in the Grand Hyatt Kauaʻi, and dressing up is required, meaning covered shoes and collared shirts for men.

Spanish

Okay, so the food here isn't entirely Spanish, but the style of eating tapas is. 【 **Josselin's Tapas Bar and Grill** (808/742-7117, www.josselins.com, 5-10pm daily, $8-32) in Kukui'ula Shopping Village inspires sharing with friends and family by serving up tapas, a variety of small dishes served to share. The chef has won numerous awards with his Pacific-inspired eateries, often named the best of the best. From fresh fish tapas to tapas made in the wood-burning oven, Chef Josselin has it covered. The truly exotic array includes tapas, scallops, oxtail, vegetarian tapas, duck, fish, and so much more. They also serve lovely *liliko'i* and pomegranate sangrias along with other signature drinks.

Ice Cream and Shave Ice

For a local treat head to 【 **Uncle's Shave Ice and Smoothies** (Kukui'ula Shopping Village, 808/742-2364, www.uncleskauai.com, 11am-9pm daily), where you can expect just what the name says. Shave ice and fruit smoothies are made to cool a hot Hawaiian day. They offer 25 shave ice flavors, with extras like cream caps (really good), fruit, and ice cream. They also sell other snacks like caramel apple bites and popcorn. Sugar-free syrups sweetened naturally with stevia are a progressive option here.

Quick Bites

Shrimp is a constant throughout Hawaii, and the south side's **Savage Shrimp** (Kukui'ula Village, 808/212-2197, www.savageshrimp.com, 11am-9pm daily, $12) serves up shrimp plates, fish tacos, shrimp tacos, fish and chips, and fried shrimp (am I sounding like Bubba Gump?). A favorite with beach-going locals, it used to be in a lunch wagon and now has a permanent home.

Spacious and elegant, **Living Foods Market and Cafe** (Kukui'ula Shopping Village, 808/742-2323, www.livingfoodskauai.com, 8am-8pm daily) prides itself in being a gourmet food store, but also offers normal snacks like candy bars. Pick up homemade breads and dips, made-to-order pizzas, and sandwiches, or packaged foods. Outside tables are provided.

KALAHEO
American

The always-good 【 **Kalaheo Cafe** (2-2560 Kaumuali'i Hwy., 808/332-5858, www.kalaheo.com, 6:30am-2:30pm Mon.-Sat., 6:30am-2pm Sun., and dinner at 5pm Tues.-Sat., $13) is the south side's answer to the cute, local, friendly café where you can relax reading the paper or have Sunday brunch with 10 friends. To speed along the large influx of customers, you order at the counter and then choose a table, but there's no rush to get out of the spacious hardwood floor café, which is adorned with local art and music. Coffee is served in varied forms, along with eggs, breakfast burritos, waffles, pastries, and sides. Salads and off-the-grill specialty sandwiches are available for lunch, along with bottled beer. Vegetarians can find a decent array of meat-free options. Service is good, and the only downfall is that they charge extra for additional plates.

The name says it all, almost, at **Kalaheo Steaks and Ribs** (4444 Papalina Road., 808/332-4444, www.kalaheosteakandribs.com, Tues.-Sun. 4-10pm, dinner 5-9:30pm, $17-36). For three decades the restaurant has been serving ribs, steaks, fresh fish, pastas, appetizers, and salads. As one would expect, there isn't much for vegetarians here, but there is a nice array of salads and one vegetarian entrée of veggie stir-fry with soba noodles, so meat-free diners can enjoy a night here. A full bar, the Saloon, adds to the fun. The atmosphere also fits the name here—ia knotty pine interior with the usual steakhouse theme. At the Saloon, happy hour is held 4pm-6pm daily with a menu of appetizers.

Italian

An island highlight, not just south side, is 【 **Pomodoro Ristorante** (2-2514 Kaumuali'i Hwy., 808/332-5945, 5:30-9:30pm daily), a small gem hidden in Kalaheo, and yes, it's run by real Italians. Known for serving the best Italian food on the island, the owners have created a delightful environment as well as an upscale fee. A full bar is offered, and the ravioli is amazing, as are most dishes. The husband and wife owners are very friendly. If you have children don't be deterred by the quiet and small eatery; the wife has expressed how much she loves kids. Pomodoro is on the second floor of a small shopping center with a very nice atmosphere including Italian music and dim lighting. Since it doesn't take very long to get around Kaua'i, Pomodoro is worth making the trip to even when you're on another side of the island.

A local favorite is **(Brick Oven Pizza** (2-2555 Kaumuali'i Hwy., 808/332-8561, 11am-10pm Tues.-Sun., 4-10pm Mon.), and it's a good place for a family night or a casual date. A very kid-friendly spot, it offers free dough for kids to play with during dinner. They offer a pretty big selection of pizza, beer, and wine, and you can get your crust in white or wheat dough as well as basted with garlic butter. The decor has a countryside feel, and the walls are covered in license plates from around the country that almost all say something Hawaii-related on them. All-you-can-eat buffets on Monday and Thursday nights are fun.

Hawaiian Local

Ohana Cafe (2-2436 Kaumuali'i Hwy., 808/332-7602, $8-13, 11am-2:30pm and 5pm-9pm) serves up a combo of American food like burgers and fries, along with local food like saimin, oxtail soup, teriyaki meats, and big and sweet desserts. The atmosphere is simple, service is friendly, and the prices are good. Not gourmet, but good, simple, local food with no frills.

Farmers Market

Sunshine Farmers Market in the **Kalaheo Neighborhood Center** (3pm Tues.) offers fresh produce and fruits. You can also find an abundance of locally made crafts, some ready-to-eat food, and other locally made food. Bring your own shopping bag.

Getting There and Around

CAR

The most convenient way to get around the south side is by car. Highway 50 heads west straight out of Lihu'e and runs through Kalaheo all the way to the end of the road far past the south side. To get down to Koloa and Po'ipu you can turn down Maluhia Road and drive through the pretty tree tunnel, or turn down Koloa Road and drive through lush Lawa'i. Rental cars are the best bet here and are available at the airport. Gas prices go up the farther west you go, so it's a good idea to fill up in Lihu'e; a tankful will most likely last the day.

BUS

The **Kaua'i Bus** (808/241-6410, www.kauai.gov/Transportation, 5:27am-10:40pm Mon.-Fri. and 6:21am-5:50pm Sat., Sun., and holidays) runs island-wide with many stops in Kalaheo, Koloa, and Po'ipu. Check the website for bus stops and times. The bus is a green, convenient, and affordable way to get around. Fares are $2 for adults, $1 for children and seniors. Monthly passes are also available.

TAXI

No matter which company you choose, Hawaii's standard taxi rates apply of $3 per mile and 40 cents per minute, per van. **South Shore Taxi** (808/742-1525) offers island-wide tours along with services for individual and large groups. **Pono Taxi** (808/634-4744, www.ponotaxi.com) will take you on a south-side sightseeing tour as well as usual taxi runs.

KAUA'I

WEST SIDE

Locally known as the west side, Kaua'i's leeward coast is Hawaii's take on the wild west. A geologist's dreamland, the landscape out here contradicts itself with rolling white beaches, vast canyons, deep rivers, and dry desert land. The west and driest side of the island is a land without frills, but it offers something unique for art buffs, history fans, nature lovers, and

HIGHLIGHTS

LOOK FOR ◖ TO FIND RECOMMENDED SIGHTS, ACTIVITIES, DINING, AND LODGING.

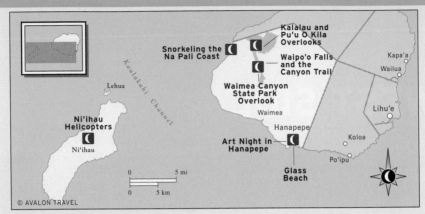

© AVALON TRAVEL

◖ **Glass Beach:** A colorful layer of beach glass adds sparkle to the dark sand (page 795).

◖ **Snorkeling the Na Pali Coast:** Hop on a boat in Port Allen for an unforgettable snorkeling trip (page 797).

◖ **Waipo'o Falls and the Canyon Trail:** Hikers who endure the trek will be rewarded with an 800-foot double waterfall (page 803).

◖ **Ni'ihau Helicopters:** Virtually the only way to explore Ni'ihau's beaches is through a helicopter tour (page 805).

◖ **Waimea Canyon State Park Overlook:** The views down into this vast, deep canyon are not to be missed (page 807).

◖ **Kalalau and Pu'u O Kila Overlooks:** The best views in the Pacific include looming vertical mountains reaching down to the sea (page 808).

◖ **Art Night in Hanapepe:** Sixteen galleries open their doors wide every Friday night (page 809).

beach bums alike. Art enthusiasts can view local creations and mingle with their crafters. Those hot for history can take a historical walking tour, browse an antiques shop, and visit landmarks that mark the change that led Hawaii to its current state. The outdoors types can camp in the mountains or at the beach, hike, bird-watch, and bicycle. Beach bums can surf, swim, stand-up paddle, and snorkel.

From Hanapepe to the west end of the Na Pali Coast the sun is almost always shining, and the red dirt tints everything from vehicles to buildings. The large number of historic buildings, plantation-style homes, and agricultural areas make the region seem like it is frozen in time. Most buildings have a story to tell, and towns are small, low-key, and quiet. From the longtime artist residents in Hanapepe who relocated to the area to paint Kaua'i's beauty to the west-side born-and-raised Hawaiians in Waimea, locals are friendly and warm.

Hanapepe town and the still-active Port Allen near Kalaheo welcome visitors to the west. Hanapepe, which means "crushed bay," calls itself "Kaua'i's Biggest Little Town." It originally thrived as a central place for taro and rice cultivation and later evolved into a bustling town during World War II. Thousands of GIs

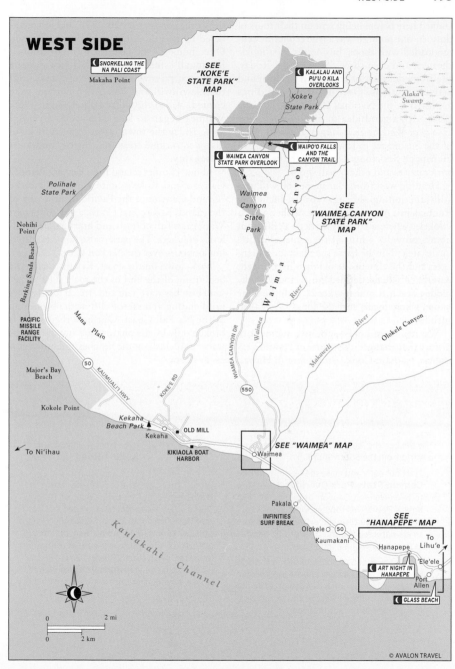

WEST SIDE

SNORKELING THE NA PALI COAST

Makaha Point

SEE "KOKE'E STATE PARK" MAP

KALALAU AND PU'U O KILA OVERLOOKS

Koke'e State Park

Alaka'i Swamp

WAIPO'O FALLS AND THE CANYON TRAIL

WAIMEA CANYON STATE PARK OVERLOOK

Polihale State Park

Waimea Canyon State Park

SEE "WAIMEA CANYON STATE PARK" MAP

Nohihi Point

Waimea   Canyon   River

Barking Sands Beach

PACIFIC MISSILE RANGE FACILITY

Mana Plain

KOKE'E RD

WAIMEA CANYON DR

Olokele Canyon

Makaweli   River

Major's Bay Beach

KAUMUALI'I HWY   50

550

Kokole Point

Kekaha Beach Park

OLD MILL

Kekaha

KIKIAOLA BOAT HARBOR

SEE "WAIMEA" MAP

To Ni'ihau

Waimea

Pakala

INFINITIES SURF BREAK

SEE "HANAPEPE" MAP

Olokele

50

To Lihu'e

Kaumakani

Hanapepe

Ele'ele

Kaulakahi   Channel

ART NIGHT IN HANAPEPE

Port Allen

GLASS BEACH

N

0   2 mi

0   2 km

KAUA'I

© AVALON TRAVEL

trained here before being sent on their tours of duty. At one point, it was a true economic center, loaded with shops, businesses, two movie theaters, and even three skating rinks. Today, the riverside town offers country charm and artisan creations. Over 40 of the buildings are listed in the National Register of Historic Places. It's a good idea to pick up a *Historic Hanapepe Walking Tour Map,* available at many of the businesses in town. The newer part of Hanapepe lies along Route 50 and is dotted with eateries and other small shops.

Heading west from Hanapepe you will pass still-functioning old sugar towns, including Kaumakani. About a half mile farther west is Olokele, where a strip of modern oceanfront homes provides a hint of the upper-class life in the area. This is where the plantation managers and the elite of the old days lived. Right past that is Pakala, defined mostly today by the hidden beach at mile marker 21 with the same name, where locals surf the long wave called Infinities.

Waimea town holds claim to a moment in history that changed the course of Hawaii's existence. Captain Cook first set foot in Hawaii in Waimea on January 20, 1778, and is remembered by two monuments in the small town. Once home to the last great king of Kaua'i, Kaumuali'i, for many years Waimea was one of the central towns and ports of Kaua'i until the Nawiliwili and Port Allen harbors were created. When the sugar mill closed in 1969, Waimea began to lose its place as a central area. Today the town offers opportunities to discover antique treasures, history and local personality.

About 15 miles inland from here are Waimea Canyon and Koke'e State Parks, where the "Grand Canyon of the Pacific" claims part of the island. Koke'e State Park, a few miles past Waimea, is full of trails and hikes galore for all levels of hikers. The park is also home to inspiring lookouts over the Na Pali Coast.

Back down on the coast, Kekaha marks the beginning of the end of the road. The white-sand beaches start here and stretch for 15 miles until ending at a sacred cliff at the beginning of the Na Pali Coast. Out here the silence is broken only by the picturesque and dangerous waves that crash on the beaches and lull campers to sleep.

Your Best Day on the West Side

The best of the west can be experienced as a day trip from the South Shore.

- Start out early and make the trek to **Waimea Canyon State Park Overlook.** Make sure to take Waimea Canyon Drive rather than Koke'e Road. This road provides clear views of Ni'ihau, multiple valley lookouts, and a small waterfall flowing over bright red dirt at the 1,500-foot elevation sign.

- There are about 45 miles of hiking trails in **Koke'e State Park,** just past the Waimea Canyon overlook, with a range of difficulty levels. Most of the hikes begin along Koke'e Drive or the dirt roads that veer off of it.

- On the way back down from Waimea Canyon State Park, take **Koke'e Road** just to see the other views.

- Stroll through the riverside town of **Hanapepe,** just 10 miles west of Po'ipu, which offers country charm and artisan creations that can be experienced while on a walking tour of the historic buildings, over 40 of which are listed in the National Register of Historic Places. Explore the local arts scene in historical Old Hanapepe, where art galleries have a monopoly on the main strip.

Beaches

Kaua'i's west coast may be on the dry side, but the beaches out here are rampant. They range from sufficient to spectacular, narrow to wide, black to white, remote to popular, and, depending on mother nature's mood, swimmable to unsafe. The Pacific is easily accessible from many areas. Check a few beaches out and find your favorite to spend some time on. As on all beaches on the island, don't leave valuables in the car. Stay out of the water if the waves are big. If in doubt, don't go out.

HANAPEPE
【 Glass Beach

The saying "one person's trash is another's treasure" fits **Glass Beach.** On this small black- and gray-sand beach, sand exists in its most pure and processed forms: Colored beach glass blankets the sand, making a colorful landscape that sparkles in the right light. Although near a former dump site, in front of a backdrop of large gas tanks in an industrial area, the small beach is actually quite nice and easily accessible. The water is a bit darker than at some other beaches because of the underlying reef, and it's not really

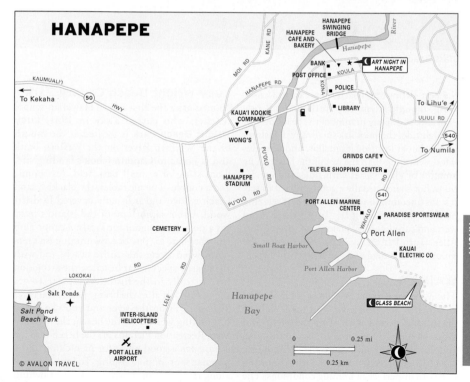

© JADE ECKARDT

Glass Beach

the best swimming beach. You can still enjoy a dip, though, if you hop in the natural tide pool almost directly in front of the beach access. At high tide, the pool has small waves rushing into it, but at low tide it's mellow and provides safer swimming than the rest of the beach. The amount of glass varies with tides and conditions, but there's usually a good amount to see. It's not uncommon to see a monk seal relaxing here for the day; let it be. To get there, head west and turn left on Waialo Road toward Port Allen. Turn left on Aka Ulu then right at the fork in the dirt road and you will see the beach.

WAIMEA

The Waimea district lies along a black-sand beach. It is long, narrow, and made of fine black sand mixed with river sediment and green olivine. Rivers are common in this area and during heavy rain cause the surrounding ocean to get dark with the red dirt, resulting in less-than-perfect swimming conditions. The beaches are still worth checking out, and are great for a picnic or walk.

Lucy Wright Beach County Park
Named after the first native Hawaiian school teacher, who passed away in 1931, **Lucy Wright Beach Park** is located at the mouth of the Waimea River on the western bank and is home to Captain Cook's landing site. Consisting of a small ball field, restrooms, and a couple of picnic tables, the blackish sand beach is nice and is usually covered in driftwood, but it is not one of the island's best. It's a popular hangout for locals; a canoe club launches here for practice. Swimming isn't recommended along this entire beach, and with the nearby spectacular beaches, the attraction here is really in the historical aspect. To get there, turn left after the bridge just as you enter Waimea. It's on the river and you can't miss it. Looking west down the beach, the Waimea State Recreation Pier juts off the beach into the ocean. It's a good place for picnicking and a popular spot for pole fishing. To access it walk along the beach or down a back street behind the Waimea Library.

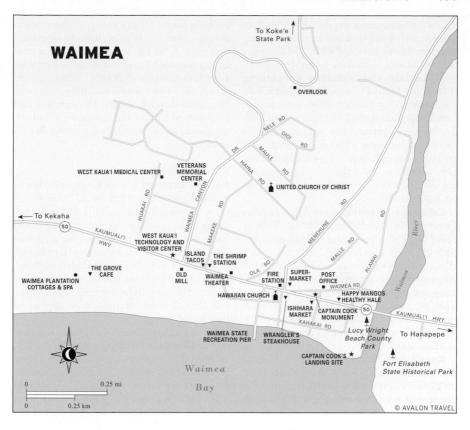

WAIMEA

To Koke'e
State Park

OVERLOOK

WEST KAUA'I MEDICAL CENTER

VETERANS
MEMORIAL
CENTER

UNITED CHURCH OF CHRIST

← To Kekaha

KAUMUALI'I HWY

WEST KAUA'I
TECHNOLOGY AND
VISITOR CENTER

ISLAND
TACOS

THE SHRIMP
STATION

THE GROVE
CAFE

WAIMEA PLANTATION
COTTAGES & SPA

OLD
MILL

WAIMEA
THEATER

FIRE
STATION

SUPER-
MARKET

POST
OFFICE

WAIMEA RD

HAWAIIAN CHURCH

ISHIHARA
MARKET

CAPTAIN COOK
MONUMENT

HAPPY MANGOS
HEALTHY HALE

KAHAKAI RD

KAUMUALI'I HWY

WAIMEA STATE
RECREATION PIER

WRANGLER'S
STEAKHOUSE

Lucy Wright
Beach County
Park

To Hanapepe

CAPTAIN COOK'S
LANDING SITE

Fort Elisabeth
State Historical Park

Waimea
Bay

0   0.25 mi

0   0.25 km

© AVALON TRAVEL

Water Sports

SNORKELING AND DIVING

Beach snorkeling on the west side isn't the best on Kaua'i. However, numerous boat tour companies that leave from the west side offering guided trips along the Na Pali Coast for spectacular snorkeling. Fish, sea turtles, and reef life can be seen while snorkeling, and dolphins and whales in the winter and early spring months can be seen from the boat. Port Allen and Kikiaola Boat Harbor are the main mooring and departure points for Na Pali cruises.

Na Pali Coast
BOAT TOURS FROM PORT ALLEN

Holo Holo Charters (Port Allen Marina Center, 4353 Waialo Rd., Ste. 5A, 808/335-0815 or 800/848-6130, www.holoholokauai-boattours.com) offers the only tour available to the island of Ni'ihau ($179) and a 3.5-hour Na Pali sunset tour as well as Na Pali snorkel sail ($99-139). The company uses two catamarans, one 65 feet long and another with a shaded cabin and large bar area, to get ocean goers to their destination from the Port Allen Harbor. They provide a deli-style buffet for lunch along with soft drinks, beer, and wine. The company has a reputation of treating guests well.

At **Captain Andy's Sailing Adventures** (Port Allen Marina Center, 4353 Waialo Rd., 808/335-6833 or 800/535-0830, www.napali.com/kauai_sailing, $69-159 with special children's rates), Captain Andy will take you on a number of cruises on a 55-foot catamaran that are either snorkeling or dining focused. They offer a barbecue sail, prime rib sail, a snorkeling sail, and a sunset or dinner cruise along the Na Pali Coast.

Catamaran Kahanu (Port Allen Marina Center, 4353 Waialo Rd., 808/645-6176 or 888/213-7711, www.catamarankahanu.com, $80-122 with special children's rates) is a Hawaiian-owned, 22-year-old tour company offering whale-watching, Na Pali Coast swimming and snorkeling, and sunset dinner tours. They give visitors a glimpse into Hawaiian culture with craft demonstrations such as basket, hat, and rose weavings, which guests take home as mementos.

Kaua'i Sea Tours (Port Allen Marina Center, 4353 Waialo Rd. #2B, 808/826-1854, 800/733-7997, www.kauaiseatours.com) offers power sailing catamaran tours and ocean raft tours out of Port Allen. A snorkel tour is offered as well as a sunset dinner cruise.

To explore the outskirts of forbidden Ni'ihau, try **Bubbles Below Kauai** (Port Allen Marina Center, 4353 Waialo Rd., 808/332-7333 or 866/524-6268, www.bubblesbelowkauai.com, $80-310) for unique diving experiences in the waters of Ni'ihau, Lehua Island, and the Na Pali Coast, including a night crustacean dive and a twilight dive. They offer private boats and instruction as well.

Blue Dolphin Charters (Port Allen Marina Center, 877/511-1311, www.kauaiboats.com, $63-175 with special children's and Internet booking prices) offers a variety of tours. Scuba diving is available on all of them, no experience necessary. A Na Pali snorkel tour with a snorkeling stop on Ni'ihau is available, along with a Na Pali sunset and dinner cruise, a Po'ipu sunset sail, and a whale-watching tour from December through March. The company uses a 63-foot or 65-foot catamaran with freshwater showers and provides all gear needed for snorkeling.

BOAT TOURS FROM WAIMEA

Na Pali Explorer (9643 Kaumuali'i Hwy., Waimea, 808/338-9999 or 877/335-9909, www.napaliexplorer.com, $105-149 with children's rates) is in Waimea right next to Island Tacos and offers various tours on a 26-foot RIB, 48-foot RIB, or 46-foot inflatable hull RIB. Their expeditions include dolphins, whales, shore landings, snorkeling, a visit to an ancient fishing village, sea cave explorations, and Na Pali views. Available tours depend on the time of year.

Kaua'i native Liko Ho'okano is the captain at **Liko Kaua'i Cruises** (4516 Alawai Rd., Waimea, 888/732-5456, www.liko-kauai.com, $140 for adults and $95 for children), where a five-hour Na Pali snorkeling and sights tour is available year-round. Dolphin-watching is included, and whale-watching is part of the tour during the season. A deli lunch and soft drinks are included aboard the 49-foot powered catamaran.

Na Pali Riders (intersection of Hwy. 50 and Hwy. 550, Waimea, 808/742-6331, www.napaliriders.com, $130 for adults, $100 for children) uses Zodiac rafts for a tour combining snorkeling, dolphin- and whale-watching, and sea cave exploration. Departing from the Kikiaola Harbor in Waimea, the five-hour tour covers all 17 miles of the Na Pali Coast. They reach the north shore's Ke'e Beach before turning around and heading back west.

Ni'ihau: The Forbidden Island

Known as Hawaii's "Forbidden Island," Ni'ihau is in reality privately owned, passed down through generations by the Robinson family. It was run as a cattle and sheep ranch until 1999, and is home to approximately 120 pure-blooded Hawaiians who are allowed to come and go as they wish. Some commute daily from Ni'ihau to Kaua'i. Outsiders can only come on shore by Invitation from the owners, a resident, or via a tour with **Ni'ihau Helicopters.** The small island boasts the state's largest and second largest lakes, several perfect surf breaks, and famous shells.

The island can be seen from the shores of Kaua'i's west side from Waimea to Polihale. Measuring just 18 miles long by 6 miles wide, Ni'ihau has a total area of 70 square miles. The surrounding waters are popular with divers who spear fish and the 17-mile Kaulakahi Channel separating the island from Kaua'i is a popular hangout for whales. The highest point on the island, Pani'au (1,281 feet) lies on the east-central coast.

Because Ni'ihau is so low and lies in lee of Kaua'i, it gets only about 30 inches of rain each year. The low rainfall results in a lack of flowers on the island; this is why Ni'ihau Hawaiians made leis using shells. Because of the lack of rain and poor soil, Ni'ihau was never as populated as the other islands. The islanders traded with Kaua'i frequently for poi and other necessities, bartering with the abundant fish around Ni'ihau and mats made from *makaloa.*

Kaua'i and Ni'ihau became part of the Kingdom of Hawaii under Kamehameha the Great. Ni'ihau was passed down to his successors, and in 1864 Kamehameha V sold the island for

$10,000 to the Sinclair family. It's said that the king offered them a swampy beach area on O'ahu, but the Scottish family didn't want it. It turns out the swampy beach was Waikiki, which means they could have had a much better investment. Through marriage Ni'ihau became property of the Robinson family. It's not really known exactly why the Robinsons choose to let Hawaiians live on the island and even pay them to care for their sheep and cattle. One of the current owners, Keith Robinson, is an environmentalist who wants to preserve land and culture.

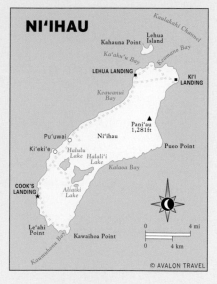

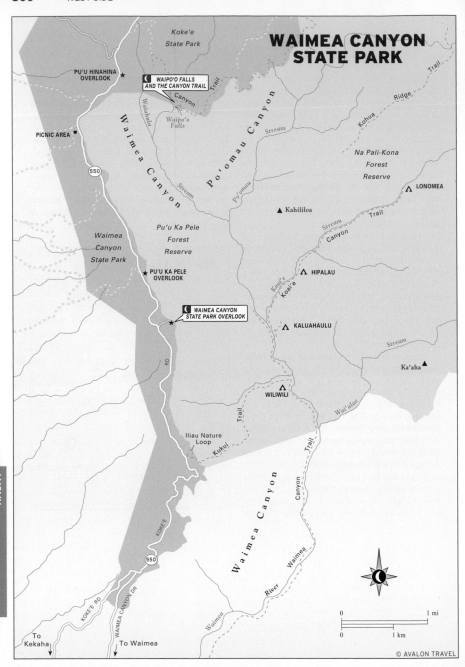

WAIMEA CANYON STATE PARK

Kokeʻe State Park

PUʻU HINAHINA OVERLOOK

WAIPOʻO FALLS AND THE CANYON TRAIL

Trail

Canyon

Waihala

Waipoʻo Falls

Poʻomau Canyon

Stream

Kohua

Ridge

Trail

PICNIC AREA

Waimea Canyon

550

Stream

Poʻomau

Na Pali-Kona Forest Reserve

LONOMEA

Kahililoa

Stream

Canyon Trail

Waimea Canyon State Park

Puʻu Ka Pele Forest Reserve

PUʻU KA PELE OVERLOOK

HIPALAU

Koaiʻe

Koaiʻe

KALUAHAULU

Stream

WAIMEA CANYON STATE PARK OVERLOOK

Kaʻaha

RD

WILIWILI

Waiʻalae

Iliau Nature Loop

Trail

Kukui

Trail

Canyon Trail

Waimea Canyon

Canyon

KOKEE

550

Waimea

River

Waimea

KOKEʻE RD

WAIMEA CANYON DR

To Kekaha

To Waimea

0   1 mi

0   1 km

© AVALON TRAVEL

Hiking and Biking

HIKING
Waimea Canyon State Park

Waimea Canyon State Park is home to the beautiful and vast canyon, but it's also decorated with numerous trails weaving through the forest, ranging from serious hikes to short walks. Once you've gazed at the views on the drive up it's worth it to take a walk or a long hike through the area.

ILIAU NATURE LOOP

A perfect family walk, the **Iliau Nature Loop** begins off of Koke'e Road and also marks the beginning of the Kukui Trail. Pull all the way off of the road between mile markers 8 and 9 to access the easy, quarter-mile-long trail, which takes about 15 minutes to complete. Views of Waimea Canyon and Wai'alae Falls open up about midway along the loop. The self-guided trail sits at about 3,000 feet elevation and is home to its namesake, the *iliau* plant. The *iliau* is a relative of the silversword, which grows high on Haleakala on Maui, and the greensword, which grows on the Big Island. This rare plant grows only on the dry mountain slopes of western Kaua'i. White-tailed tropicbirds and the brown-and-white *pueo* (Hawaiian owl) are known to fly through the area.

KUKUI TRAIL

The **Kukui Trail** leads down into Waimea Canyon and is home to the Iliau Nature Loop, therefore starting at the same location between mile markers 8 and 9. This 2.5-mile trail takes about 60-90 minutes to complete just the walk in. It is strenuous, descending over 2,000 feet very quickly, which of course you have to climb up on the way out. Thanks to the steep grade, it takes longer and a lot more effort and energy on the way back up. Don't forget to bring plenty of water if you're planning on hiking all the way down and up. Water bladders are a good idea for this one; they weigh less than bottles and you can drink from the tube as you hike. There are gorgeous views of the canyon along the way, so don't forget your camera, even though it may be tempting to leave extra weight behind. The Wiliwili Campground marks the end of the Kukui Trail. You can set up camp for the night with a permit and continue on other trails or head back out the same day.

KOAI'E CANYON TRAIL

From the end of the Kukui Trail, the serious hiker can head up the Waimea River for about a half mile, where you'll have to cross the river to find the trailhead for the three-mile-long **Koai'e Canyon Trail.** This trail has about a 720-foot loss and gain in elevation. If the river water is high and rushing, do not cross it. Flash flooding is always a concern here. The trailhead is near the Kaluahaulu Campground on the east side of the river. The trail leads you to the south side of Koai'e Canyon, where there are many pools of freshwater, which are usually lower in summer than in winter. The canyon was once used for farming, as you might guess while walking the fertile and lush trail. There are two more campsites here. It is strongly advised to avoid this trail during rainy weather.

WAIMEA CANYON TRAIL

If you head south from the Kukui Trail, you can connect with the 11.5-mile, strenuous, and usually hot and dry **Waimea Canyon Trail.** This lengthy trail parallels the Waimea River through the canyon. It can also be reached by hiking eight miles inland from Waimea town. This trail is popular with serious hikers who enjoy a challenge, but many regard the trail as lacking in sights and views, and don't find many interesting qualities along the hike. The hike is well worn and passes back and forth over the river, which usually has plenty of water, but it needs to be boiled or treated before drinking.

Koke'e State Park

There are about 45 miles of trails in **Koke'e**

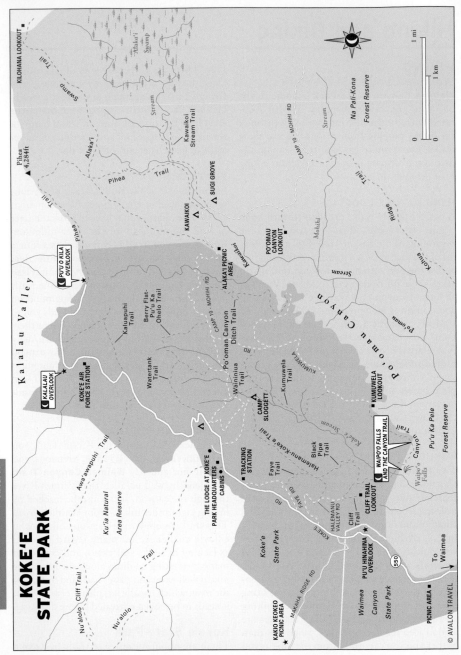

KAUA'I

KOKE'E STATE PARK

KILOHANA LOOKOUT ■

Alaka'i Swamp

Swamp Trail

Pihea ▲ 4,284ft

Pihea Trail

Kawaikoi Stream Trail

Alaka'i Trail

Kawaikoi Stream

Trail

△ KAWAIKOI

△ SUGI GROVE

CAMP 10 - MOHIHI RD

Na Pali-Kona Forest Reserve

Kawaikoi

ALAKA'I PICNIC AREA ■

PO'OMAU CANYON LOOKOUT ■

Mohihi

Mohihi Stream

Kohua Ridge

PU'U O KILA OVERLOOK

Kaluapuhi Trail

Berry Flat-Pu'u Ka Ohelo Trail

CAMP 10 - MOHIHI RD

Po'oman Canyon Ditch Trail

Kalalau Valley

KALALAU OVERLOOK ★

KOKE'E AIR FORCE STATION ■

Watertank Trail

Wainiinua Trail

RD

Kumuwela Trail

KUMUWELA

Po'omau Canyon

Po'omau Stream

KUMUWELA LOOKOUT ■

△ CAMP SLOGGETT

Kohe'e Stream

Pu'u Ka Pele Forest Reserve

△

Awa'awapuhi Trail

Ku'ia Natural Area Reserve

THE LODGE AT KOKE'E PARK HEADQUARTERS CABINS ■

TRACKING STATION ■

Halemanu-Koke'e Trail

Faye Trail

Black Pipe Trail

WAIPO'O FALLS AND THE CANYON TRAIL

Canyon Trail

Waipo'o Falls

Nu'alolo Cliff Trail

FAYE RD

CLIFF TRAIL LOOKOUT ★

Cliff Trail

Nu'alolo Trail

Trail

KOKE'E RD

HALEMANU VALLEY RD

Koke'e State Park

Waimea Canyon State Park

PU'U HINAHINA OVERLOOK ★

550

To Waimea →

KAKIO KEOKEO PICNIC AREA ★

MAKAHA RIDGE RD

PICNIC AREA ■

© AVALON TRAVEL

1 mi

1 km

0

0

State Park with a range of difficulty levels. Most of the hikes begin along Koke'e Drive or the dirt roads that veer off of it. The trails generally fall into five categories: Na Pali Coast overlook trails, Alaka'i Swamp trails, forest trails, canyon overlook trails, and even a few bird-watching trails. Bring good hiking shoes, lots of water, sunblock, food, and even swimwear, depending on which trail you take.

Trail maps and information are provided by the staff at the **Koke'e Natural History Museum** (3600 Waimea Canyon Dr. after mile marker 15, 808/335-9975, www.kokee.org, 10am-4pm daily). A basic trail map put out by the state, called *Trails of Koke'e,* can be picked up at **Na Pali Explorer** (9643 Kaumuali'i Hwy., 808/338-9999 or 877/335-9909, www. napaliexplorer.com) in Waimea, but much more thorough trail maps are Hawaii Nature Guide's *Koke'e Trails* map and *Northwestern Kaua'i Recreational Map* by Earthwalk Press.

THE CLIFF TRAIL

For an easy family trail take a 10-minute walk on the **Cliff Trail.** Located off of Halemanu Road, it's a leisurely stroll of only a tenth of a mile and leads to a wonderful viewpoint of Waimea Canyon. From the lookout you may see some wild goats hanging out on the canyon walls. This trail also accesses the Canyon Trail.

◖ WAIPO'O FALLS AND THE CANYON TRAIL

The semi-strenuous 1.8-mile **Canyon Trail** branches off Cliff Trail and leads to the upper section of the 800-foot **Waipo'o Falls** before going up and along the edge of the canyon. It takes about three hours and could be done by a family, if the family is up for a challenge. Wonderful views of the canyon are offered on this popular trail, and the reward of swimming in freshwater pools makes it a choice hike. The trail goes down into a gulch and then weaves along the cliff to the Koke'e Stream and the falls. It follows the eastern rim of the canyon. Parking is at the Pu'u Hinahina Lookout between mile markers 13 and 14. The trailhead is at the back of the parking lot. The trail ends

at the Kumuwela Lookout, where you can head back on the Canyon Trail or walk back on Kumuwela Road.

FAYE TRAIL

At the end of Halemanu Road is the 0.1-mile **Faye Trail,** which crosses a wooded valley and accesses other trails in the Halemanu area. The trail brings you to an undrivable section of Faye Road, which leads left and back up to the highway not far from the Halemanu Road turnoff. Take a right at Faye Road to end up on the highway below the state park cabins.

NATURE TRAIL

A good trail for children is the 0.1-mile **Nature Trail.** Starting behind the Koke'e Natural History Museum it parallels the meadow. It's an easy and enjoyable walk through forest and offers good examples of native vegetation. Before beginning the trail pick up a free copy of a plant guide at the museum. This trail takes about 15 minutes to complete.

KUMUWELA TRAIL

Off of Mohihi Road is the one-mile **Kumuwela Trail.** This trail is somewhat strenuous but could be done by a tough family. It takes about one hour on the way in and offers lush native vegetation and fragrant flowers. It's a good birding trail, and you can connect to the Canyon Trail at Kumuwela Road at the end of the trail.

PU'U KA OHELO BERRY FLAT TRAIL

Near park headquarters is pole #320, which marks the beginning of Camp 10-Mohihi Road. This is generally a four-wheel-drive road, but occasionally two-wheel-drive cars can make it if the weather has been really dry. Numerous trails start here and head into the forest, along ridges with canyon views and across minor streams. The roughly 1.6-mile loop called the **Pu'u Ka Ohelo Berry Flat Trail** is a semi-tough trail that can be done with a family up for a challenge. The trail has a beautiful forest of sugi pine, California redwoods, Australian eucalyptus, and the valuable native koa as well

KAUA'I

as the *'ohi'a* tree. The small, red, strawberry guava with a thick flesh and edible seeds grows here, and this is a popular spot for locals to harvest the fruit. Picking season is midsummer, so it's important to check with park headquarters before snacking on the fruit while hiking. To access this trail, begin at the Pu'u Ka Ohelo trailhead, near some cabins about a quarter mile up a road off Camp 10-Mohihi Road, and hike clockwise, which will take you downhill.

PO'OMAU CANYON DITCH TRAIL

The beautiful **Po'omau Canyon Ditch Trail** is less than a half mile past the Berry Flat Trail. Developed to maintain the Koke'e irrigation ditch, this trail is less than four miles long round-trip. It's pretty strenuous and it deserves plenty of time to be completed. This trail leads you to wonderful views of the Po'omau Stream, lush green forests, and a great view of two waterfalls below you from a peninsula of land that extends out into the canyon. If you bring a picnic lunch you will find a grassy overlook to sit on and enjoy the views. Take Waineke Road across from the Koke'e Museum to Mohihi Road. You will need to park well before the trailhead on Mohihi Road, a little over 1.5 miles from Highway 550. Walk about three-quarters of a mile to an unmarked trailhead on your right.

PIHEA TRAIL AND
ALAKA'I SWAMP TRAIL

Beginning at the end of Waimea Canyon Drive at the Pu'u O Kila Overlook is the **Pihea Trail,** about 3.7 miles in length. It leads to the **Alaka'i Swamp Trail,** about 3.5 miles long. The Pihea Peak, accessed by a very steep trail, is about 1.3 miles after the lookout. This trail runs along the back edge of the Kalalau Valley, and you will be treated to wonderful views into the valley and out to the ocean. About 1.6 miles in, a wooden boardwalk has been constructed to help keep hikers from getting extremely submerged in mud. When you hit the Alaka'i Trail, take a left, and it's about two miles to the end. A majestic, gorgeous, and unique trail, the Alaka'i Swamp Trail heads down toward

the Kawaikoi Stream and then up a ridge across boggy forestland to the Kilohana Overlook, the trail's ultimate destination. When you can catch a very clear day, which can be tough, the views of the Wainiha and Hanalei Valleys are awesome.

The approximately five-million-year-old swamp is about 4,500 feet above sea level, and is one of the most distinctive experiences on the island. The surroundings up here feel like another world. Mossy trees, birds, and fog create an environment different from anywhere else. It's a great birding trail but the views are iffy with the lingering mist and clouds of the area. The entire trail totals about eight miles, so it's important to bring snacks, water, and energy.

AWA'AWAPUHI/NU'ALOLO LOOP

For a nearly day-long hike with spectacular views, explore the **Awa'awapuhi/Nu'alolo Loop.** This trail is home to some of the most fantastic views on the island, and it's a must-do hike if you are up for a strenuous and long hike. It's nearly 10 miles, about 11 if you walk the paved road back to your car at the end. But, the views on this trail are picturesque and sublime. Most hikers do the full loop, beginning on the **Nu'aloalo Trail** then turning right (north) about 3.2 miles in onto the **Nu'alolo Cliff Trail,** which connects with the **Awa'awapuhi Trail.** At the end take a left for amazing views, ending on a narrow ridge. A highlight is the thin finger of cliff where you can look down at the sea and a vibrant valley 2,500 feet below. From here you hike uphill back to the road while gaining 1,500 feet in elevation. Along the hike bright red wild berries called thimbleberries (resembling raspberries) can be snacked on, along with the sweet and sour *liliko'i,* or passion fruit. The damage Hurricane 'Iniki did to the area is still evident in the upland forest here.

There are no views until the end of the trails. Because they are on the western slopes of Koke'e, it gets extremely sunny out here in the afternoon, so it's a good idea to begin around 9am. It's a tough hike. Take your time, bring plenty of water and food, and expect to spend half to a full day on the hike. Lastly, the museum parking lot is probably safer for your car than the trailhead, and down the road after you emerge from the Awa'awapuhi trailhead back to the museum is easier than hiking up the road to your car.

BIRD-WATCHING TRAILS

For bird-watching in Koke'e, try the 3.5-mile **Alaka'i Swamp Trail.** The 1.6-mile **Kaluapuhi Trail** is also a good bet for birds, as well as the 3.7-mile **Pihea Trail.** For a shorter birding trail, take a stroll on the **Halemanu-Koke'e Trail,** which is slightly over a mile, or the one-mile-long **Kumuwela Trail.**

BIKING

Sunrise and sunset group bike tours are offered for an 11-mile downhill ride, but of course you can always take the ride on your own. Starting in the cool mountain air along the rim of Waimea Canyon at around 3,600 feet, the ride skirts the rim and then heads down the roller coaster foothills to the coast at Kekaha. All of the tours are done in groups and participants are given a helmet and jacket to wear. Cruiser bikes with comfortable seats are available for the half-day tour. Refreshments and information on Hawaiian culture are offered. Sunglasses, sunscreen, and sometimes pants are a necessity. A sag wagon follows for bikers who need a rest and to alert traffic from behind. If you'd like to spend about five hours on a bike tour, contact **Outfitters Kauai** (2827 Po'ipu Rd., Po'ipu, 808/742-9667 or 999/742-9887, www.outfitterskauai.com).

For serious mountain bikers only, the **Waimea Canyon Trail** is a good adventure. This lengthy eight-mile trail leads back down to the town of Waimea via an old 4WD track and crosses through a game management area. A special permit, required to walk through the area, is available at the trailhead. You can connect to the Waimea Canyon Trail by going south from the Kukui Trail.

Adventure Sports

West-side tours explore Kaua'i's coffee industry, history, and nature. Get a glimpse of history through town walking tours, gain insight into the tropical flora and fauna in Koke'e, explore the beaches of Ni'ihau, and see Kaua'i from a bird's-eye view. Unique to the west side is the opportunity for hang gliding and skydiving, offered nowhere else on the island. The adventure sports add some real action to an otherwise mellow locale.

HANG GLIDING AND SKYDIVING

If you like to live on the edge, go hang gliding with **Birds in Paradise** (Port Allen Airport, 3666 Kuiloko Rd., 808/332-0790 or 888/359-3656, www.birdsinparadise.com). Founder and instructor Gerry Charlebois has helped over 100,000 people get their kicks high up in the air. There are three different aircraft available, and safety features include a backup rocket parachute that will bring the entire craft safely to the ground. If you would like to fly up to 100 miles per hour in the air, prices run from $165 for a mini introductory lesson to $360 for an advanced lesson. Photo packages start at $50.

For skydiving excursions, **Skydive Kauai** (Port Allen Airport, Kuiloko Rd., 808/335-5859, www.skydivekauai.com, $229) will take you to free fall out of a plane to 4,500 feet, where the chute opens and you glide back to the airfield. The ride only takes people 18 and older and under 200 pounds. They offer videos of you flying through the air on DVD for $70.

HELICOPTER TOURS
◖ Ni'ihau Helicopters

Unless you're invited by an islander, the only way to visit the beaches of Ni'ihau is via a

KAUA'I

tour with **Ni'ihau Helicopters** (877/441-3500, www.niihau.us, 8am-2pm Mon.-Sat., $385 including lunch and refreshments), which will take you there for a half day on the beach to snorkel and sunbathe. A safari hunting excursion is also offered ($500-1,750). Owned and operated by the owners of Ni'ihau, the company offers free-chase hunting for boars, sheep, and oryx. Five people are required for both tours, and you reach the island in a twin-engine Agusta 109A helicopter that was originally set up to provide medical services for Ni'ihau residents.

Inter-Island Helicopters
Departing from the Port Allen Airport, **Inter-Island Helicopters** (3441 Kuiloko Rd. Hanapepe, 808/335-5009 or 800/656-5009, www.interislandhelicopters.com) offers views of Ni'ihau and the west side of Kaua'i from its fast Hughes 500 four-seater. Because there is no back middle seat, everyone gets a great view.

A waterfall adventure is offered, along with an island tour that flies straight into the Waimea Canyon, over Koke'e State Park, and along the Na Pali Coast.

Island Helicopters
Movie and waterfall buffs will enjoy a trip to Manawaiopuna Falls, which was used in Steven Spielberg's 1993 blockbuster *Jurassic Park* and is located on land that is said to belong to the Robinsons, the same family that owns Ni'ihau. The nearly 400-foot-tall falls are hidden in a valley near Hanapepe and have been restricted to the public for years. Around five years ago the owner and pilot at **Island Helicopters** (Ahukini Rd., Lihu'e, 808/245-8588 or 800/829-5999, www.islandhelicopters.com) began pursuing permits from the state and county to land at the falls. He was successful and now flies people out there five days a week for a 25-minute landing at the falls as part of a 85-minute circle island tour for $269.

Sights

Sights from Hanapepe to the end of the road share two common themes: history and natural wonders. They're all easily accessible and camera-worthy.

HANAPEPE
Hanapepe Valley and Lookout
As you come around the bend from Kalaheo and first lay eyes on the Port Allen area, a Hawaii Visitors Bureau sign points out an overlook pull-off spot for the **Hanapepe Valley.** It offers a peek down into the valley and it's easily accessible. Pull over, open your door, and you are there. The vast and beautiful valley is a reminder of the geological activity that shaped the Hawaiian Islands and is home to some overgrowth and small taro fields. It's good for a quick look since it's so easy, but the valley is tiny in comparison to Waimea Canyon.

Hanapepe Swinging Bridge
Extended over the Hanapepe River, this wooden plank footbridge runs between the historic town and the inland side of the river. With enough bounce and shake to inspire a little excitement as well as a lovely view down the river, the Hanapepe Swinging Bridge is fun to take a walk on. It's easily accessible from the town and free. Originally built to run a water line across the river and into town, the bridge ends nearly in someone's back yard. Once off the bridge take a left to walk the levee back to the old vehicular bridge and come back into town along Hanapepe Road. A stroll across the bridge fits in easily with any gander through town.

WAIMEA
Fort Elisabeth
State Historical Park
Just before the Waimea River and right past

mile marker 22 is **Fort Elisabeth State Historical Park.** The shape of this Russian fort somewhat resembles an eight-pointed star, and it dates from 1817, when according to traditional history, a German doctor named Georg Anton Schaeffer constructed it in the name of Czar Nicholas of Russia and named it after the czar's daughter.

However, in 2002 University of Hawai'i at Hilo anthropologist Peter R. Mills studied the fort and drew the conclusion that "Hawaiians had been left out of their own history." Mills used hundreds of firsthand accounts along with field research to show that the fort was originally built and used by Hawaiians as a *heiau,* a Hawaiian sacred site. He shows that after the Russians' departure, Hawaiians continued to use the fort, but they did so in ways that reflected an ongoing transformation of cultural values as a result of contact with outsiders and the development of multiethnic communities in Waimea and other port settlements throughout the Hawaiian chain. For more information, read Mills' book *Hawai'i's Russian Adventure.*

History goes on to say that Schaeffer, an agent for the Russian-American Company, built two other forts on the island, one on the bluff at Princeville and another farther down in Hanalei Bay. It's said that Czar Nicholas never quite warmed up to Schaeffer's work and withdrew official support. Eventually Schaeffer was banned from Kaua'i, sent to Honolulu, and then forced to leave the islands altogether. No longer maintained and cared for, the fort fell apart and was dismantled in 1864 when 38 guns were removed. The walls were once 30 feet thick and are now rubble left to wither away from the elements. Brochures are usually available at the entrance, and plaques on the board tell the history.

Captain Cook Monuments

The **Captain Cook monuments** pay tribute to James Cook, the explorer who is credited with "discovering" the Hawaiian Islands (for the western world, that is; let's remember the Hawaiians were already there). A life-size statue of the man himself is located on the strip of grass that is Hagaard Park, between Waimea Road and Highway 150. Benches are nearby if you'd like to have a seat and enjoy a snack. The other monument is a plaque attached to a boulder at Lucy Wright Beach Park.

◖ Waimea Canyon State Park Overlook

The drive up to **Waimea Canyon State Park Overlook** offers a series of majestic sights. Make sure to take Waimea Canyon Drive rather than Koke'e Road (which the street sign in Waimea recommends). This road provides clear views of Ni'ihau, multiple valley lookouts, and a small waterfall flowing over bright red dirt at the 1,500-foot elevation sign. Depending on the time of day, the lookout offers different views of the 10-mile-long, 3,000-foot-deep canyon. Its colors change as the sun moves across the sky, so different photo opportunities present themselves.

To get there, take Waimea Canyon Drive and stick to the right at the fork in the road at the Koke'e State Park sign. At the top there is a lookout with wheelchair accessibility, bathrooms, and often a snack and gift tent. On the way back down, take Koke'e Road just to see the other views. At the bottom are several gift shops and a general store.

Koke'e Natural History Museum

The **Koke'e Natural History Museum** (3600 Waimea Canyon Dr. after mile marker 15, 808/335-9975, www.kokee.org, 10am-4pm daily, suggested donation of $1) offers several displays. The museum calls the outdoors the real plant displays, but inside is an exhibit called Treasury of Trees, Resources of a Traditional Lifestyle. The exhibit is on forest trees and their traditional Hawaiian uses. It's interesting to get an idea of how the Hawaiians utilized their natural surroundings. Game animals that were introduced to the island are also on display, including a wild boar, a stag, goats, game birds, and trout. A weather exhibit focuses on the devastating Hurricane 'Iniki. Perhaps the most interesting display is a collection of land and sea shells from Ni'ihau and

© JADE ECKARDT

Waimea Canyon

Kaua'i. A large whale vertebrae and a sea turtle shell are quite intriguing. The museum staff can help you choose which of the 19 trails and hikes in the park are right for you, which is very helpful. Detailed hiking maps are also available.

◖ Kalalau and Pu'u O Kila Overlooks

Many regard these two overlooks as the best views on Kaua'i, and even the best in the Pacific. At mile marker 18, the Kalalau Overlook opens to an expansive view over **Kalalau Valley,** the biggest one on the Na Pali Coast. The valley was inhabited until the beginning of the 1900s, and since then, occasionally hippies looking to live off of fruit in the jungle stay a while.

About a mile down the road is the even better **Pu'u O Kila,** which offers a window into Kalalau Valley, from the Alaka'i Swamp to Mount Wai'ale'ale. If you get there on a cloudy day there's a chance the views won't be visible at all. Check the weather and go when it looks best; earlier in the day is usually better. To get here, go past the Koke'e Lodge and onto a road that turns into potholes and broken up pavement.

KAUA'I

Shopping

High-end fashion and big box stores are absent on the west side. Small boutiques, local crafts, jewelry, and seemingly infinite art are abundant. The west side offers some unique souvenirs, from Ni'ihau jewelry to local art.

HANAPEPE

Art galleries featuring photography, paintings, drawings, sculptures, glass, and more line the streets of Hanapepe. The town is always worth a stroll through to window shop or take something home.

Art Galleries

Kaua'i Fine Arts (3905 Hanapepe Rd., 808/335-3778, www.brunias.com, 9am-5pm daily) calls a small white building on the eastern end of Old Hanapepe home. The shop has the feel of an antiques store, as much of its stock is previously used items. Prints of local artists, shell jewelry, maps, books, antique maps, carvings, and other art objects make up the shop's unique collection. Staff is friendly and happy to let visitors browse for a while.

Colorful and unique jewelry, home decor, and handbags can be found in **Kaua'i Finds** (3890 Hanapepe Rd., 808/332-5056, www.kauaifinds.com). Dichroic glass, a glass containing multiple micro-layers of metal oxides giving the glass dichroic optical properties, is used to reflect the various colors found throughout the island in jewelry. Each piece of glass is unique and contains several colors but has one main color per piece.

Giorgio's Fine Art Gallery (3871 Hanapepe Rd., 808/335-3949, www.giorgiosart.com, 11am-5pm daily) is an extravaganza of color reflecting the beauty of the islands in landscape, floral, and abstract paintings. Using a method called plein air, Giorgio creates palette knife oil paintings, often on location around Kaua'i.

The friendly staff is happy to chat about the art and the island.

If you look to your left as you enter **Banana Patch Studios** (3865 Hanapepe Rd., 808/335-5944, www.bananapatchstudio.com, 10am-4:30pm Mon., Tues., Wed., Thurs., and Sat., 10am-9:30pm Fri.) you will see art being made through a large window looking right into the studio. This is a great place for souvenirs such as ceramic tiles saying "please remove shoes," and "aloha." Owner Joanna Carolan creates the tiles, an array of jewelry, and nature-inspired paintings. Island-style trinkets and home decor from other crafters are also in stock.

Traditional watercolors and out-of-this-world island photography capturing nature's spectacular moments can be found in the **Arius Hopman Gallery** (3840C Hanapepe Rd., 808/335-0227, www.hopmanart.com, 10:30am-2pm Mon.-Fri., 6pm-9pm Fri.), where the artwork can be printed up to 12 feet long. Both the paintings and photos reflect Kaua'i's beauty, life, and energy. Hopman's artistic ability is in his blood; his mother was a world-renowned artist who was commissioned to sculpt Mahatma Gandhi twice. The native of India moved to Hawaii in 1985 and lives in Hanapepe.

◖ Art Night in Hanapepe

Around 16 art galleries open their doors for a night of art celebration each Friday 6pm-9pm on Hanapepe Road. **Art Night** is an opportunity to socialize with locals and other visitors, explore the town, and meet artists. A gallery manager recently said that any shops in the historic town that don't sell art (there aren't many) will tell you the celebratory night is called "Festival Night." Don't be fooled, he said—it's all about the art. The night can be enjoyed casually if you're coming straight from the beach

KAUAI

Ni'ihau Shells

Diamonds and platinum may be a sign of luxury in the U.S. Mainland, but in Hawaii it's Ni'ihau shell jewelry. The rare and highly valued shells (*kahelelani, laiki, momi,* and *kamoa*), are found on the beaches of Ni'ihau and crafted by the island's residents into various styles of lei, earrings, and bracelets, equaling one of Polynesia's most precious art forms. Captain Cook returned from Hawaii with a Ni'ihau shell lei that now resides in the British Museum. The jewelry is mostly sold on Kaua'i, while some of it makes it to shops on other islands. A large amount is sold in stores on the west side and made by the shop's owner or relatives on Ni'ihau. It's not uncommon to encounter a clerk at one of Waimea's shops and ask where she got her jewelry, only to hear that her niece or nephew made it. Here's an opportunity to purchase the jewelry directly from its crafter, as many of these people are happy to give you a phone number to contact the person who made it.

The shells wash up on the beaches mostly October-March, when winter swells bring waves big enough to wash them ashore. This is when islanders rush to gather the shells and either make the jewelry on the island or send the shells to family on Kaua'i to craft. The tiny shells are sorted by size and color, and only the best are kept; around 80 percent are thrown away. Many of the pink *kahelelani* that are found are a dull flesh color, worn rough, or are broken. The shell colors include bright pink, deep red, white, yellow, blue, and, rarely, gold. Holes are delicately drilled into the small shells, and they are then strung in a traditional fashion to make various types of jewelry. Most common are the necklaces and lei. Roughly twice as many shells than go into a lei are needed because around half are expected to break during the process. The lei are usually a combination of many strands, either hanging below each other or spiraling around each other.

The making of the jewelry, along with the entire process, is an intricate task and can take up to six months to complete. The Ni'ihau women usually do the work, and whole families are involved in collecting, but I recently had a Waimea Big Save cashier tell me that her nephew made the beautiful earrings she was wearing and that he sells them, too. Ni'ihau shell lei are the only shell necklace in the world that can be insured. Shells are used for Ni'ihau lei because the dry island doesn't have a sufficient environment to grow the abundance of flowers the other islands have.

To see a museum-type collection of Ni'ihau shell work, visit the Hawaiian Trading Company in Lawa'i, visible from Highway 50. For a rare and valuable souvenir, Ni'ihau jewelry is the perfect thing. The best book on Ni'ihau jewelry is *Ni'ihau Shell Leis,* by Linda Paik Moriarty, published by the University of Hawai'i Press.

but it can also be an opportunity to dress up for a night out on the small, historical town.

Crafts and Books

There's something warm and cozy about independently owned bookstores, and **Talk Story Bookstore** (3785 Hanapepe Rd., 808/335-6469, www.talkstorybookstore.com, 10am-5pm Mon.-Thurs., 10am-9:30pm Fri.) doesn't disappoint. The family-run business is Kaua'i's only new and used bookstore and is located in the historic Old Yoshiura Store. Over 40,000 used, rare, and collectible books are available, along with Hawaiian gifts, crafts, records, and Hawaiian slack-key and ukulele lesson courses. Any books you may be done with can be traded in for store credit. The shop stays open late on Art Night, offering live entertainment.

Crafts and jewelry decorate **JJ Ohana** (3805-B Hanapepe Rd., 808/335-0366, www.jjohana.com, 8am-6pm Mon.-Thurs., 8am-9pm Fri., 8am-5pm Sat.). The highlight here is the Ni'ihau shell jewelry made by the owner, whom you may find overseeing the shop when you visit. She makes beautiful earrings, necklaces, and bracelets that are some of the most valuable Kaua'i souvenirs.

WAIMEA
Gourmet Treats and Beauty Products

Known as one of the tastiest tropical flavors and used across the culinary board from desserts to entrées, the *liliko'i,* or passion fruit, is used in all of its glory at **Aunty Liliko'i** (9633 Kaumuali'i Hwy., 808/338-1296, www.auntyilikoi.com, 10am-6pm daily). The sweet and sour fruit is the highlight in jams, jellies, mustards, dressings, syrups, and even skin-care products. Drop by the quaint shop in Waimea to pick up a snack.

Antiques

Antiques from around the islands can be found at **Collectibles and Fine Junque** (9821 Kaumuali'i Hwy., 808/338-9855). An array of Hawaiiana, books, trinkets, jewelry, and so much more fills the small shop to the brim. The staff is usually happy to "talk story" with shoppers, and even just browsing here can be fun. The small building that houses the shop is an antique itself. Those looking for it may question if the run-down building is being utilized, but the historic look adds to the shop's spirit.

Food

Good food isn't hard to find out west. There are a number of *ono* (delicious) places to eat, from snacks and desserts to local brews and dinner. For such small towns there's a wide array of cuisines and a decent number of vegetarian dishes scattered through the eateries.

HANAPEPE
American

The roadside **Grinds Cafe** (4469 Waialo Rd., 808/335-6027, www.grindscafe.net, 5:30am-9pm daily, breakfast $6-10, dinner $18-20) serves their entire menu all day long. They offer pizzas, sandwiches, pasta, salads, and more. Indoor and patio seating is available to enjoy a meal along with a glass of beer or wine, or passersby can take some food to go for the beach or a boat trip from nearby Port Allen. Here you will find a mix of locals picking up a cup of coffee and visitors passing through the area. *Grinds* is local slang for food.

Local Food

If you're looking for a true local experience, have a meal at **Da Imu Hut** (1-3529 Kaumuali'i Hwy. Suite A, 808/335-0300) and try plate lunch local food. Their signature dishes include the Hawaiian plate lunch and the Imu Hut teri-fried chicken. *Ono, brah.*

Mostly Vegetarian

The **(Hanapepe Cafe and Bakery** (3830 Hanapepe Rd., 808/335-5011, 7am-3pm Mon.-Thurs., 5-8:30pm Fri., $15-35) never fails to satisfy with their mostly vegetarian menu, which is backed up with local fish dishes and what the owner calls "the occasional turkey club sandwich." Pastries are made on site. Many different forms of sweet goodness are available; try at least two. The old plantation building is adorned with Hawaiian crafts, creating a homey atmosphere. Service always comes with a smile. The bakery opens once a week for dinner on Fridays.

Thai

(Toi's Thai Kitchen (in the 'Ele'ele Shopping Center, 808/335-3111, 10:30am-2pm and 5:30-9pm Tues.-Sat.) is a local favorite and staple. The atmosphere is relaxed and lacking in ambience, but the food is tasty and portions are good. Service can be a bit on the slow side, but it's always friendly. They offer a substantial menu that will satisfy traditional diets as well

KAUA'I

as vegetarians with their seafood, meat, and tofu options. Lunch dishes come with a green papaya salad that I highly recommend, and the option of brown, sticky, or jasmine rice.

Treats and Desserts

Chocolate, especially local, is enough of a reason to stop at the **Kaua'i Chocolate Company** (4341 Waialo Rd., 808/335-0448, www.kauaichocolate.us, 8am-6pm Mon.-Fri., 11am-5pm Sat., noon-3pm Sun.). Serving up truffles, macadamia nuts, and ice cream, the shop will either fill your belly on the spot or your suitcase for gifts at home. The small shop is like a mini version of Willie Wonka's factory, and it's nearly impossible to leave without a treat.

Wong's (13543 Kaumaualii Hwy., 808/335-5066, 9:30am-9pm Tues.-Sun.) claims to serve up Kaua'is best *liliko'i* (passion fruit) pie. Wong's is a Chinese restaurant, but I'm citing them for the pie. The light *liliko'i* chiffon pie is delicious, and it actually tastes like real *liliko'i*. Stop in and enjoy a piece for under $3, or take a whole pie to go.

The **Kaua'i Kookie Company** (1-3529 Kaumuali'i Hwy., 808/335-5003, www.kauaikookie.com, 8am-4pm Mon.-Fri., 11am-4pm Sat.-Sun.) is another local treat that makes a great snack or gift. At the Hanapepe factory outlet they sell their macadamia shortbread, Kona coffee, guava macadamia, and coconut krispies cookies and more. The cookies are also distributed around the island and can be purchased by mail order.

Farmers Market

A year-round, open-air market, the **Hanapepe Farmers Market** provides local produce and crafts. Located behind the Hanapepe fire station in **Hanapepe Park,** the market happens every Thursday 3pm-5pm. Try to remember to bring your own reusable shopping bag or a preused plastic bag from another store.

WAIMEA

American

The decor stays true to the name at **《 Wrangler's Steakhouse** (9852 Kaumuali'i Hwy., 808/338-1218, for lunch 11am-4pm Mon.-Fri., for dinner 4pm-9pm Mon.-Sat., $17-28), where the restaurant is decorated with cowboy trinkets and gear. Indoor and outdoor seating are offered, and I've learned that with little ones who have a hard time sitting still, the outdoor seating in the back is a good idea. Wrangler's is known for their great steaks, and they offer a salad and soup bar with each meal. A full bar is stocked with a variety of liquors, wines, and beers to please any palate. The menu offers a hefty assortment of red meats, poultry, and seafood, but surprisingly, vegetarians can enjoy a sufficient and tasty meat-free meal. Service is friendly and there is also a small *paniolo* (Hawaiian cowboy) museum as well as shell jewelry for sale.

To peel, or not to peel, that is the question at **《 The Shrimp Station** (9652 Kaumuali'i Hwy., 808/338-1242, $11-12), where shrimp is served up in a number of ways. At this very laid-back eatery, seating is on picnic tables under a tent right on the side of the main road. The menu includes shrimp entrées, drinks, desserts, and ice cream. *Kama'aina* discounts are available and service is friendly but to the point. It's across from Island Tacos.

Breakfast

Obsessions (9875 Waimea Rd., 808/338-1110, 6am-2pm Wed.-Sun.) is a homestyle breakfast café with absolutely no frills. Eggs, sausage, pancakes, coffee and other usual breakfast dishes are served. The food is decent, simple, and perfectly satisfying. The atmosphere is very homey, with artwork and letters from the town's schoolchildren on the wall. Food is served on disposable plates.

Hawaiian Regional

《 The Grove Cafe (9400 Kaumualii Hwy., 808/338-1625, 11am-10pm daily, $11-25) serves good food with a local twist and beer brewed in the islands. The plantation-style building has high ceilings, hardwood floors, and fans that enhance the breezy environment. Sit down for a meal on the lanai or enjoy the indoor bar. The menu includes local seafood dishes, steak, spicy ahi roles, and various vegetarian options. Local bands play for dinner guests most nights a week.

Italian

In the same building as Wrangler's is **Pacific Pizza and Deli** (808/338-1020, 11am-9pm Mon.-Sat.). They serve really good pizza, calzones, deli sandwiches, drinks, and ice cream. The small shop puts a twist on traditional pizza with options such as Thai, Filipino, Portuguese, and Mexican tastes, reflecting the flavors of each country. Smoothies, coffee, and ice tea are offered to refresh you in the westside heat.

Local Treats

Finely shaved ice and 60 flavors can be found at **(Jo-Jo's Clubhouse** (9734 Kaumuali'i Hwy. across from mile marker 23). What's commonly known as a snow cone in the Mainland is called shave ice in Hawaii. The line can be long, but it's a testimony to their great shave ice. Try some local flavor combos like lychee and coconut or *liliko'i* and *melona*.

An easy and healthy breakfast or snack in the hotel room or while camping can be found at **Kaua'i Granola** (9633 Kaumuali'i Hwy., 808/338-0121, www.kauaigranola.com, 10am-5pm Mon.-Sat., 10am-3pm Sun.). Unique flavors like pina colada, Hawaiian zest, and guava crunch are available and sold along with Waimea-made chocolate-dipped coconut macaroons, dried fruit, cookies, and pastries. Nestled in a small shop next to Island Tacos, it's another option to bring home a taste of paradise.

Mexican

(Island Tacos (9643 Kaumualii Hwy., 808/338.9895, www.islandfishtaco.com, 11am-5pm Mon.-Sun., $12) in Waimea is a simple order-at-the-counter taco stand with seating, reminiscent of roadside taco stands in Mexico. The large menu offers local fish, pork, chicken, and even a wide variety of satisfying vegetarian and vegan options. Portions here are large, with unique toppings like a wasabi-spiked aioli sauce and the option of fat-free dishes. Perfect for a quick stop on a drive through Waimea or to satisfy a craving after camping at Polihale, this place is really good. As locals would say, 'nuff said.

Mostly Vegetarian

Organic, vegetarian, vegan, and natural breakfasts, lunches, smoothies, and desserts can be found at the new family-run **(Happy Mangos Healthy Hale** (Alawai Rd., 808/338-0055, www.happymangos.com, store 6:30am-5pm, café till 4pm Mon.-Fri., 7am-3pm, café till 2pm Sat., $8). The local owners serve freshly made food along with natural and organic groceries and produce. Located in a small plantation-style building across from Lucy Wright Beach Park, the health food store is the only natural and organic choice in Waimea. They serve non-vegetarian sandwiches too.

KOKE'E STATE PARK
Local Food

Stop at the **Koke'e Lodge** (808/335-6061, www.thelodgeatkokee.net, 9am-2:30pm, $7-10) for breakfast or lunch. The soups accent the cool weather nicely, and their banana bread and Koke'e corn bread are good for a treat. The menu also includes local dishes like *kalua* pork and a few vegetarian options, as well as wine, beer, and cocktails are also on the menu. The next eatery along the road is about 15 miles away.

KAUA'I

Getting There and Around

CAR

The most convenient way to get around the west side is by car. Highway 50 heads west straight out of Lihu'e and runs all the way to the end of the road to Polihale. Rental cars are the best bet here and are available at the airport. Gas prices go up the farther west you go, so it's a good idea to fill up in Lihu'e.

BUS

The **Kaua'i Bus** (808/241-6410, www.kauai. gov/Transportation, 5:27am-10:40pm Mon.-Fri. and 6:21am-5:50pm Sat., Sun., and holidays) runs island-wide as far west as Kekaha, and is a green, convenient, and affordable way to get around. But with Kekaha as the last stop, and no routes up to the parks, taking the bus out west means you are far away from the biggest draws of the west side—the far west beaches and the state parks. It does stop at the Kaua'i Coffee Company Visitor Center and in Hanapepe, allowing for a visit to the art galleries. Fares are $1 for children and seniors, and $2 for the general public. Monthly passes are also available.

KAUA'I

WHERE TO STAY ON KAUA'I

East Side

WAILUA
Under $100

Easy on the wallet is the **Rosewood Kaua'i Bunk House** (872 Kamalu Rd., 808/822-5216, www.rosewoodkauai.com, $50-60), where you can choose from three studios with kitchenettes and private entrances with shared bathroom and outdoor shower. Very cute and clean with hardwood floors and bright white walls. There's a $25 cleaning fee.

Located in a private home in Wailua is the **Whispering Ferns Studio Apartment** (808/822-5216, www.rosewoodkauai.com/whispering_ferns, $95). With a three-night minimum and $50 cleaning fee, it offers 350 square feet of space with its own entrance. A nice treat is that the owners provide daily breakfast and a welcome basket. You'll have wireless Internet and a kitchenette. The apartment has an elegant island decor.

A good deal is **The Garden Room** (808/822-5216, www.rosewoodkauai.com/garden, $75), an affordable studio apartment in a private home in Wailua. It's just three miles from the ocean, and you'll find a welcome basket upon arrival. The studio is very clean with a well-kept interior and lovely manicured grounds with a fishpond. Beach gear is available here,

Where to Stay on Kaua'i's East Side

Name	Type	Price
Aloha Hale Orchid	studio	$55
(Aston Aloha Beach Hotel	hotel	$201-315
Courtyard by Marriott	hotel	$200-309
Dilly Dally House	B&B	$115-185
Fern Grotto Inn	cottages	$99-149
Garden Island Inn	small inn	$135-160
The Garden Room	apartment	$75
Green Coconut Studio	private home	$110
Hale Lani B&B	B&B	$125-195
Hotel Coral Reef	hotel	$110-175
Inn Paradise	B&B	$85-120
Kaha Lani	condos	$235-375
Kapa'a Sands Hotel	condos	$90-185
Kaua'i Beach House	hostel	$30-70
Kaua'i Country Inn	B&B	$129-179
Kaua'i Inn	small inn	$85-139
Kauai International Hostel	hostel	$25-65
(Kaua'i Marriott Resort	large resort	$250-575
Kaua'i Palms Hotel	budget hotel	$75
(Kaua'i Sands Hotel	budget hotel	$59-80
(Lae Nani	condos	$204-355
Lani Keha	rooms	$55-250
(Motel Lani	hotel	$64
No Ka Oi Studio	studio	$79-99
Opaeka'a Falls Hale	vacation rental	$110-130
Orchid Tree Inn	studios	$85-110
Rosewood Kaua'i Bunk House	rooms	$50-60
Sleeping Giant Cottage	private home	$95
Traditional Room	apartment	$95
Wailua Bayview	condos	$163-175
Whispering Ferns Studio Apartment	apartment	$95

along with Internet access and a private entrance. There's a $50 cleaning fee.

A privately owned apartment dubbed the **Traditional Room** (808/822-5216, www.rosewoodkauai.com/traditional, $95) is located in the hills of Wailua and is an immaculately maintained unit with a private bathroom.

You'll wake up to breakfast each morning here. It sleeps two with a three-night minimum and $35 cleaning fee. It's a gorgeous room with an elegant island style.

On three acres on the Sleeping Giant mountain is **Lani Keha** (848 Kamalu Rd., 808/822-1605, www.lanikeha.com, $55-65), which

Features	Why Stay Here?	Best Fit For
mini-fridge	on orchid farm, affordable	budget travelers
pool	affordable, good location	families, couples
pool, business center	friendly service	families, couples
pool, breakfast	amenities	couples, no children allowed
kitchens	privacy	anyone
kitchenettes, beach gear	affordable, central location	couples
welcome basket	affordable	couples
overlooks the ocean	affordable	couples
breakfast, hot tub	all-around nice	couples
pool	oceanfront	couples
laundry, beach gear	friendly, homey	couples
tennis court, pool	oceanfront	couples, families
pool, barbecue	oceanfront, affordable	couples, families
kitchen area	near the water	budget travelers
Beatles museum	breakfast	couples
pool	free breakfast	budget travelers
common kitchen area	affordable	thrifty and young people
full resort amenities, child care	full-service resort	families, couples
free muffins and coffee	affordable	budget travelers
pool	oceanfront, affordable	budget travelers
pool, tennis court	oceanfront	couples, families
communal kitchen	affordable	budget travelers
showers	affordable	budget travelers
beach gear, barbecue	affordable	budget travelers, couples
pool	really nice	couples
full kitchen	location	budget seekers
kitchenettes	affordable	budget travelers
beach gear, grill	nice, private	couples
breakfast	affordable	couples
pool	affordable	couples
breakfast	welcome basket	budget travelers, couples

offers very casual accommodations perfect for the traveler who is looking to meet others. They offer three rooms with a communal kitchen and living room. You can rent the whole house for $250 with a two-night minimum. No frills but nice, simple, and clean.

The lovely **Sleeping Giant Cottage** (5979 Heamoi Pl., 505/401-4403, www.wanek.com/sleepinggiant, $95) is a one-bedroom simple cottage with three lanai nestled in a lush yard. It's about a 10-minute drive down to the ocean, and they require a three-night minimum. They offer specials for weekly and monthly stays with a one-time $50 cleaning fee. It has a homey simple island style with full bathroom and kitchen, cable TV, washer and dryer, some beach gear, gas grill, king-size bed, and a queen-size sleeper sofa.

At the ◖ **Kaua'i Sands Hotel** (420 Papaloa Rd., 808/822-4941 or 800/560-5533, www. kauaisandshotel.com, $59-80) you'll find a perfect blend of simple island style and great affordability in 200 rooms on six oceanfront acres. Reminiscent of a 1970s hotel in the simple style and color mix, the hotel is quite nice, although simple with no frills. Each room has a small refrigerator, TV, air-conditioning, and either one king-size or two double beds. Service is always friendly, and out by the usually uncrowded pool, the lawn opens up to the ocean.

$100-200

Inn Paradise (6381 Makana Rd., 808/822-2542, www.innparadise.com, $85-120) has three suites. The King Kaumualii Suite can house up to four people and is a two-bedroom one-bath unit. With a full kitchen it runs for $120 a night for a three-night minimum. The Queen Kapule Suite is a one-bedroom that can hold up to four people. It has a small kitchen and a three-night minimum stay is required. A cute studio that accommodates two people perfectly, the Prince Kuhio Suite is decorated in island-style décor. There's a three-night minimum. Personalized welcome baskets, beach gear, and a Jacuzzi are all offered.

Opaeka'a Falls Hale (120 Liahu St., 800/262-9912, www.bestbnb.com/OpaekkaUpper.html, $110-130) has two units. The upper is called the Royal Palm and the Queen Emma is on the lower level. The Royal Palm sleeps two people. Both require a $50 cleaning fee and a five-night minimum. There's a beautiful pool on-site and it's a short drive from the ocean. Both have a full kitchen, lanai, and washer and dryer.

The **Fern Grotto Inn** (4561 Kuamo'o Rd., 808/821-9836, www.ferngrottoinn.com, $99-149) consists of three cottages and a house. All are remodeled simple plantation-style homes with shared laundry and either full or limited kitchens. The friendly owners live on-site and it's near the Wailua River. All of the accommodations are decorated with a clean island style. There's a $60 cleaning fee.

Four clean cottages make up the **Hale Lani B&B** (283 Aina Lani Pl., 808/823-6434, www. halelani.com, $125-195). Kanoa's Cottage has a private hot tub. Melia's Suite is a two-bedroom with kitchenette and private hot tub. Nani's Retreat is a studio with kitchenette. All have private entrances, personalized gift baskets, and home-cooked meals left outside your door in a cooler if you choose. Three-night minimums are required. If it works out they offer a half-day rate of $45 if you have a late return flight home.

A great deal is **Kapa'a Sands** (380 Papaloa Rd., 808/822-4901 or 800/222-4901, www. kapaasands.com, $90-185) along the ocean with under 30 units. It's just off the beach with a nice lawn between the units and the ocean, and you'll find a pool, barbecue area, and free Internet access. Oceanfront and ocean-view studios and two-bedroom units are available with lanai and maid service. A three- or seven-night minimum stay is required.

A steal of a deal is at **Wailua Bayview** (320 Papaloa Rd., 800/367-5242, www.wailuabay. com, $163-175), where fewer than 50 units are located just off the beach. Condominium amenities include pool, free Internet access, and a barbecue area. A four-night minimum stay is required.

At the **Courtyard by Marriott** (650 Aleka Loop, 808/822-3455, www.courtyardkauai. com, $100-200) in Kapa'a you'll find very nice accommodations. The rooms have a clean-cut, island feel, with lovely furniture made from coconut wood and really comfortable beds. They have a business area with free Internet access and a computer and printer for guests. It was renovated in 2011. The property is along the ocean, and rooms have ocean or mountain views. Rates vary by season, but this is a very affordable hotel. A pool, spa, tennis courts, fitness center, and lounge decorate the centrally located hotel. Check for *kama'aina* rates here; they make a big difference.

Over $200

Backing the wonderful Lydgate Beach Park is the ◖ **Aston Aloha Beach Hotel** (3-5920 Kuhio Hwy., 808/823-6000 or 888/823-5111, www.abrkauai.com, $200-315). The location is great for anyone who loves swimming in the calm ocean, especially families. Consisting of 216 rooms, the hotel boasts two pools, a tennis court, a jet spa, an on-site restaurant, fitness room, high speed Internet, and coin-operated laundry. Rooms have sliding doors but no balcony, and offer small refrigerators. Two-room cottages are also available. One wing has bathtubs while the other has showers.

Between the Wailua golf course and Lydgate Beach Park, location is just one of the appeals of **Kaha Lani** (4460 Nehe Rd., 808/822-9331, www.castleresorts.com, $235-500). The complex is luxury on the ocean, but with ample space between the units and the water. There is a pool, a lighted tennis court, and all units have full kitchens and a lanai. Prices vary slightly between seasons.

A real treat is the condominium ◖ **Lae Nani** (410 Papaloa Rd., 808/822-4938, $204-355). All nicely decorated units have full kitchens, a lanai, TVs, and one and a half baths. Guests are also treated to a pool, poolside grill, and tennis court. Bookings can be made through different companies. A minimum stay of two nights is required.

KAPA'A
Under $100

Proof of a round-trip ticket or continuing voyage is required to stay at the **Kauai International Hostel** (4532 Lehua St., 808/823-6142, www.kauaiinternationalhostel.com, $25-65), where bunk beds are available for $25 a night. Private rooms that share a bathroom with the dorm, deluxe rooms, and the suite are a bit more. Check-in is from 11am to 10pm. Kitchen and main house common areas are open from 8am to 10pm, and it's lights out at 11pm. Key and linens are issued without a deposit and expected to be returned at checkout. Bring your own bath supplies and towels; kitchen utensils and use of the communal

kitchen are provided. There is an in-office safe for valuables, and the hostel is pretty well kept and clean. A coin-operated washer and dryer are on-site.

Another hostel is the **Kaua'i Beach House** (4-1552 Kuhio Hwy., 808/822-3424, www.kauaibeachhouse.net, $30-70). Most rooms look out across a lawn and out onto the water. There is a separate mini kitchen area that is for guest use. Females and couples have priority for beds that have complete privacy and curtains in a dorm. There are shared bathrooms and a gathering place on the second-level lanai.

The **Aloha Hale Orchid** (5087-A Kawaihau Rd., 808/822-4148, www.yamadanursery.com, $55) offers simple and clean accommodations for a low price with a three-night minimum. It's a very simple and affordable studio with a queen-size bed, shower and tub, fan, TV, and mini refrigerator. It's located on a functioning orchid nursery.

Meaning "the best" in Hawaiian, the **No Ka Oi Studio** (4691 Pelehu Rd., 808/651-1055, www.vrbo.com/125884, $79-99) has a two-night minimum and a $75 cleaning fee. It's a studio that can fit two to three people. It is comfortable with a kitchenette, videos and books, barbecue, great ocean views, and beach gear for guest use.

The **Orchid Tree Inn** (4639 Lahua St., 808/822-5469, www.vrbo.com/118213, $85-110) is made up of two very small but simple and functional units right in Kapa'a that sleep 4-6 with the addition of convertible beds. The good thing about this place is its central location, allowing for guests to catch the bus around and save money there. A full kitchen is offered, along with washer and dryer. Rates vary with an average $100 cleaning fee. Weekly or monthly rates are available.

$100-200

Hotel Coral Reef (1516 Kuhio Hwy., 808/822-4481 or 800/843-4659, www.hotelcoralreefresort.com, $110-175) was one of the first hotels in Kapa'a, and it has recently undergone renovations that have brought a modern island style to the rooms. The hotel is rather small with around 20 rooms and a pool. It sits right on the ocean. All rooms have air-conditioning, microwaves, in-room refrigerators, and flat-screen TVs, and guests receive a continental breakfast. Mountain-bike rentals and barbecue facilities are also offered. Oceanfront suites start at $245. Check the website for pretty good "eSpecials"; they also offer *kama'aina* and senior citizen discounts.

On a bluff overlooking the ocean is the **Green Coconut Studio** (4698 Pelehu Rd., 808/647-0553, www.greencoconutstudio.com, $110). Decorated with a bright clean island style and bamboo furniture, the studio also has a lanai with great views. Rates are based on double occupancy, with an additional $20 for a third person. Weekly and monthly rates are available. There's a $100 fee for stays under three nights.

Located inland in the lush interior, the **Dilly Dally House** (6395 Waipouli Rd., 808/631-9186, www.lolohale.com, $115-185) is an impressive collection of units in a nice house with a large pool with tables by it. Five rooms are offered with a welcome basket and wonderful breakfast of local themed dishes, such as taro or macadamia nut pancakes. The grounds are immaculate, very classy plantation style. A two-night minimum stay is required, and no children are allowed. Rooms are all very high end with elegant island-style decor. Amenities include Hawaiian toiletries, beach gear, wireless Internet, and a grill.

The **Kauai Country Inn** (6440 Olohena Rd., 808/821-0207, www.kauaicountryinn.com, $129-179) has a unique twist—the only private Beatles museum in the United States! A simple continental breakfast is supplied every morning, and all units have private entrances and bathrooms, and a full kitchen or kitchenette. Wireless Internet is available in each of the four gorgeous suites.

LIHU'E
Under $100
The **◖ Motel Lani** (4240 Rice St., 808/245-2965, $64), consisting of only eight rooms, provides usually clean and very simple rooms

with shower only, and no TV or phone. They only take cash—no credit cards—and it's very affordable. This is the type of place to stay if you are planning on being outdoors all the time and looking for a cheap place to store your stuff. This is a very good option for leaving stuff while hiking for days along the Kalalau Trail, since you don't want to risk it getting stolen out of your car at the trail parking lot. They don't have a website; just call.

The **Kaua'i Palms Hotel** (2931 Kalena St., 808/246-0908, www.kauaipalmshotel.com, $75) offers very simple and affordable rooms without many amenities (no phones). There are full kitchens in the higher priced rooms. Another good option for the outdoors type since the hotel itself doesn't offer the lap of luxury. There's free wireless Internet throughout the property and a coin-operated laundry, and it's a good place to stash your stuff and explore the island. They offer complimentary muffins and coffee in the lobby in the mornings. Amenities include refrigerators and TVs, and some rooms have air-conditioning, so check when booking.

Located on the south end of Lihu'e past Nawiliwili Bay, the **Kaua'i Inn** (2430 Hulemanu Rd., 800/808-2330, www.kauai-inn.com, $85-139) is another rather simple place. Rooms include a small refrigerator, microwave, and air-conditioning. There's a shallow swimming pool, and ground floor rooms have lanai. A little bonus here is a free continental breakfast each morning. Mountain views are seen from the property. Rooms have a king, queen, or two double beds.

$100-200
You'll feel the aloha at the **Garden Island Inn** (3445 Wilcox Rd., 800/648-0154, www.gardenislandinn.com, $135-160), where you'll find more simple rooms at a decent price. Flat-screen TVs, kitchenettes, air-conditioning, and complimentary use of a variety of beach gear are what you'll find here. Rooms have a modest tropical decor, and discounts are offered for three nights or more.

Over $200

The **[** **Kaua'i Marriott Resort** (3610 Rice St., 808/245-5050, www.marriott.com, $220-429) overlooks beautiful Kalapaki Bay and is fronted by the large beach, with two more smaller ones nearby. The immaculate resort makes a home on hundreds of acres over the bay with nearly 600 rooms on-site. The high-end Kaua'i Lagoons Golf Course is here too, offering world-class golf on 18 holes. The hotel offers a complimentary airport shuttle. You'll find a spa, fitness center, and six restaurants right there, including the option for private cabana dining. The hotel is within walking distance to some shopping and other eateries. All rooms offer high-speed Internet access, a mini refrigerator, and a safe. There is a huge, centrally located swimming pool where you can easily spend the entire day lounging and sunning. Guests have the option of one king or two double beds in the rooms, many with balconies. They offer child care on-site, freeing up parents to relax, golf, or enjoy a romantic dinner. Features include a business center, tennis courts, and wedding services, and the hotel has a smoke-free policy.

North Shore

KILAUEA

Large hotels and condominiums are absent in the lush jungle area of Kilauea. Accommodations here are limited to vacation rentals and small cottages, which is a good thing in hopes of maintaining the country feel. Staying in Kilauea is convenient, and enables guests to be very close to everything the north shore has to offer but be within a quick driving distance to the other sides of the island.

Under $100

Enjoy the scent of citrus at **Green Acres Cottages** (5-0421 Kuhio Hwy., 808/651-6173 or 866/484-6347, www.greenacrescottages.com, $75-90), where three free-standing studios (no shared walls) are nestled among 300 citrus trees. Each studio has a queen-size bed with a kitchenette, wireless Internet, cable TV, and barbecue supplies, as well as access to beach gear and a shared hot tub. You'll find complimentary danishes, coffee, and teas inside and can help yourself to picking fruit on site. Two of the cottages (16 by 20 feet) sleep two, while the third cottage (around 500 square feet) sleeps up to four.

$100-200

Self-proclaimed ecotourism destination **North Country Farms** (808/828-1513, www.northcountryfarms.com, $150) offers two cottages on a four-acre farm. A stay on the farm enables guests to stroll the land and pick fruit to eat and flowers to enjoy. Both cottages are cute, clean, and decently priced for the north shore.

On six and a half lush acres lies the **[** **Manu Mele Cottage** (808/828-6797 or 808/651-9460, www.kauaibirdsongcottage.com, $160). The picturesque cottage is perfect for two and decorated with hardwood Asian furniture. The free-standing structure has a private outdoor shower and tub as well as its own driveway. They charge a $100 cleaning fee and have a three-night minimum, with discounts for seven nights or longer. This is a very cute cottage, with an elegant Asian island decor.

Cozy up near the fireplace at the **Bamboo Cottage** (808/828-0812, www.surfsideprop.com, $175), a one-bedroom located upstairs of the owner's home. Private facilities are offered, and it's a short walk to the beaches, with ponds and a waterfall in the lush yard. The home has a full kitchen, TV, and wireless Internet access, and the bathroom has a spa tub. There's a three-night minimum and a weekly rate of $1,100. The Bamboo Cottage also offers guests the use of beach gear.

KAUA'I

Where to Stay on Kaua'i's North Shore

Name	Type	Price
◖ Ali'i Kai	condos	$100-175
Bamboo Cottage	apartment	$175
Bed, Breakfast and Beach in Hanalei	B&B	$120-170
The Cliffs at Princeville	condos	$290-380
Emmalani Court	condos	$125-150
Green Acres Cottages	B&B	$75-90
◖ Hanalei Bay Resort	condos	$100-550
Hanalei Bay Villas	stand-alone homes	$150-175
◖ Hanalei Colony Resort	condos	$204-352
Hanalei Inn	motel	$139-149
Hideaway Bay	cottage	$295
Kaua'i Coco Cabana	private home	$125
◖ Manu Mele Cottage	private home	$160
Mauna Kai	condos	$100-150
North Country Farms	cottages	$150
Ohana Hanalei	studio	$115
Plumeria Moon Cottage	cottage	$295
Plumeria Vacation Rental	private home	$230
Puamana	condos	$100-150
The River Estate	private homes	$275-300
◖ SeaLodge	condos	$110-150
St. Regis Princeville Resort	luxury resort	$375-1,625
Westin Princeville Ocean Resort Villas	villas	$250-800
YMCA Camp Naue	cabins, tents	$15

Over $200

The secluded homes **Plumeria Moon Cottage** and **Hideaway Bay** (4180 Waiakalua St., 888/858-6562, www.kauaivacationhideaway. com, $295) are perfect for visitors looking to be alone for a romantic getaway. Located on a three-acre farm, each cottage has its own hot tub, and a unique feature is free long-distance calls to the Mainland and inter-island. Hideaway Bay is a two-bedroom vacation rental with everything a visitor could need. There is a spa tub in the bathroom, and lovely ocean views can be taken in from the home. It's decorated with an Asian Pacific elegant yet relaxed decor. Plumeria Moon Cottage has a deck for sunning with great ocean views and a hot tub. The home has full amenities, including a washer and dryer and a barbecue on the deck.

The **Plumeria Vacation Rental** (808/828-0812, www.surfsideprop.com, $230) is just 300 yards from Anini Beach, which usually has peaceful, calm waters. The home has a master suite, a loft bedroom, and a den with more sleepers. A lanai wrapping around three sides of the home offers a place for enjoying the sunsets and a screened-in area for dining. There are two bathrooms along with a private outdoor shower.

Features	Why Stay Here?	Best Fit For
pool, tennis	location	couples, families
spa tub, kitchen	privacy	couples
breakfast	location	couples
pool, tennis	views, location	couples, families
pool, barbecue	affordable	couples
studios	location, affordable	budget travelers
pool, tennis courts	location, decent price	families, couples
mountain views	location	families, couples
pool	oceanfront location	honeymooners, couples
barbecue, TV, hammock	simple, location	couples
hot tub	privacy	couples
beach gear, outdoor shower	location	couples
outdoor shower	privacy	couples
pool	affordable	families, couples
orchard	location	nature lovers
private outdoor shower	location	couples
hot tub, beach gear	privacy	couples
near beach	privacy	couples, families
pool	affordable	budget travelers, families
hot tub	location	couples, families
pool, barbecue	location, price	couples, families
pools, beach, restaurants, spa	luxurious stay	lovers of luxury
pools	resort amenities	luxury-seeking families and couples
oceanfront	affordable, simple	thrifty, younger travelers

The home offers use of beach gear and bicycles, and sleeps up to five people.

PRINCEVILLE

Princeville offers luxury hotel rooms and thousands of condominiums. One might assume that with so many condos in one area, finding a place to stay would be easy. But since there isn't one main booking agency, one condominium complex can have several booking agents, all with different contact info and rates. With each condo privately owned, it's up to the owner to find someone to manage it. Many of the condos have become time shares. The Internet is the best resource for exploring the condo options. Expect a minimum-night requirement and a cleaning fee. Prices are lower in the off-season.

$100-200

For unbeatable views, try **SeaLodge** (3700 Kamehameha Rd., 866/922-5642, $110-150), which offers nearly 100 condo units along the cliffs of Princeville. The location is a real treat: near SeaLodge Beach, a wonderful hidden cove. It's accessible by a roughly 15-minute easy hike down a dirt path and along the coast. Features include a pool, places to barbecue, coin-operated laundry and washer and dryer in many units, Internet access, and full kitchens. One- and two-bedroom units are available, and prices are pretty good.

Mauna Kai (search for Mauna Kai phone numbers on www.vrbo.com, $100-150) isn't on the cliffs and doesn't have an ocean view but offers a pool and is within walking distance of the Princeville Center and Anini Beach.

Puamana (search for Puamana phone numbers on www.vrbo.com, $100-150) has a pool but no views, and offers one-, two- and three-bedroom units. There are 26 units and a clubhouse in the collection of condos, and a few are right on the golf course.

With great ocean views, the ☾ **Ali'i Kai** (3830 Edward Rd., 877/344-0692, www.aliikairesort.com, $100-175) offers proximity to Hideaways Beach and Queen's Bath. All units are two-bedroom, two-bath, with full kitchen, washer and dryer, lanai, and living room. On-site facilities include a barbecue area, tennis courts, and a pool. Rates vary between units and booking agencies.

At the bottom of Princeville are the **Hanalei Bay Villas** (5451 Ka Haku Rd., 800/222-5541, search for Hanalei Bay Villas on www.vrbo.com, $150-175). Lovely mountain views can be taken in from these two-story villas offering two- and three-bedroom options in stand-alone homes. The rental company offers the seventh night for free with weekly rentals. Location is the appeal here, with a short drive to the lovely beaches of the north shore, and Hanalei town nearby.

At the affordable **Emmalani Court** (5200 Ka Haku Rd., 808/826-7498 or 808/826-9675, www.kauai-vacations-ahh.com, $125-150) you'll find a pool, hot tub, and barbecue area. Again the units are individually owned, so decor will vary. Rates change slightly with season. Discounts are offered for week-long and month-long rentals.

Over $200

☾ **Hanalei Bay Resort** (5380 Honoiki Rd., 808/826-9775 or 800/826-7782, www.hanaleibayresort.net, $200-550) offers privately owned condo units as vacation rentals on over 20 acres at the bottom of Princeville. Accommodations range in size from one bedroom plus loft to three bedroom plus loft, adding up to nearly 300 rooms. There are eight tennis courts on-site with a full-time tennis pro, as well as a swimming pool with a small waterfall. The suites have the added convenience of kitchens. The resort is located behind the St. Regis Princeville Resort, and guests have access to the white-sand Pu'u Poa Beach. Just about any type of beach gear can be rented on-site, including chairs. Rates vary greatly, and most have a three-night minimum.

The high end **The Cliffs at Princeville** (3811 Edward Rd., 808/826-6219 or 800/367-8024, $290-380) offers one-bedroom units with two bathrooms, fully equipped kitchens, large living rooms, and two lanai. You'll be treated to on-site tennis, swimming pool, hot tub, putting green, volleyball court, recreation room, laundry room, and barbecue pavilion near the ocean.

Quite an elaborate collection of units is the **Westin Princeville Ocean Resort Villas** (3838 Wyllie Rd., 808/827-8700, www.westinprinceville.com, $250-800). The grounds feature many amenities, including a main pool, a kids' pool, hot tub, a kids' club, fitness center, plunge pool, and more. Entertainment is offered by the pool nightly, barbecue areas are offered for your enjoyment, and they even have daily activities offered like hula. Rates for the one-bedrooms and studios vary greatly depending on seasons and specials.

True to its name, the **St. Regis Princeville Resort** (5520 Ka Haku Rd., 808/826-9644, www.stregisprinceville.com, $425-1,100) will have you feeling like royalty during your stay at the north shore's premier resort. Resting above Hanalei Bay, which is in full view from the ocean-view rooms while others look out to a garden or the lush green mountains, Princeville can provide enough awe, comfort, and intriguing moments for the whole vacation. While staying at Princeville, guests can venture off the hotel property to experience activities like surfing, hiking, and exploring nearby historical Hanalei town. Or they can remain in Princeville, indulging in ocean-side spa treatments, staying cool in the pool while the kids play in the adjacent children's pool, sunning on the white-sand beaches in front of the hotel, or playing a round of golf while the children are looked after by the on-site Keiki Aloha program. Other hotel features include day and night child care, three restaurants and bars, spa lounge, pool and beach, ballrooms and boardrooms, and valet parking. Princeville is a destination within itself.

The mountain- and garden-view rooms offer approximately 540 square feet of modern Hawaiian decor. Each room has a queen- or king-sized bed, marble bathroom, oversized tub, double vanity, and unique transparent glass electronically controlled for views or privacy. These rooms are located on floors two through seven and nine. Rooms with the same views and features are also available with a terrace on floors one, four, nine, and ten.

Ocean-view rooms offer beautiful Pacific and garden views. Features are similar to the other rooms but include a sitting room. Located on floors two through seven and nine, these rooms offer an oversized tub and shower combination. The ocean-view rooms with terrace are the beginning of the high-end rooms. Located on the ground floor at pool level, with wonderful views of the ocean and gardens, you'll have either two queen beds or a king bed covered with 300-thread-count linens. The rooms have a sitting area with a loveseat and coffee table. Each of these rooms offers an entertainment console that contains a 42-inch HD flat-screen TV, and business travelers will be happy to find an elaborate work space with a large desk and high-speed Internet access. Privacy is enhanced with a glass partition between the bathroom and sleeping area that can be electronically controlled, and plush bathrobes and slippers wait here for guests.

The premium ocean-view rooms have many of the same features and decor as the garden-view rooms, along with spectacular views of Hanalei Bay. In front of the large window looking out on the ocean is a seating area perfect for taking in the breathtaking views and relaxing.

These rooms are located on floors four through eleven.

The top-tier suites are nothing short of amazing. The Prince Junior Suite has a foyer, bedroom, entertainment system, sitting and dining area, and bath suite all serviced by a 24-hour butler. The suites climb through four more levels of luxury to the St. Regis Ocean View Suite, the Bali Hai Signature Suite, the Presidential Suite, and finally to the Royal Suite, all with butler service. The Royal Suite is more like a high-end apartment, with a large walk-in shower for two, a royal spa with a whirlpool bathtub, an entertaining room, master bedroom, kitchen, wet bar, and more.

HANALEI TO THE END OF THE ROAD
$100-200
Hanalei Inn (5-5468 Kuhio Hwy., 808/826-9333 or 877/445-2824, www.hanaleiinn.com, $139-149) offers five quaint and cute rooms just a block from beautiful Hanalei Bay. The rooms are simple, without frills, and provide queen-size beds, homey local style decor, air-conditioning, TV, and a covered lanai to take in the mountain views. Rooms without a kitchen are priced at $139 and with a kitchen go for $149. The kitchen is a nice touch for those who are looking to save money by grocery shopping and cooking at home. The great thing about the Hanalei Inn is that it's right out in Hanalei, just minutes from snorkeling, hiking, and all of the spectacular north shore beaches at the end of the road. In the yard you'll find a barbecue pit, hammocks, and a picnic bench to enjoy the outdoors. There are no phones in the rooms here, only a pay phone outside, but since most people travel with cell phones that doesn't seem to be a problem. This is a good choice for those who intend to stay on the north shore while in Kaua'i, and they offer a small discount for booking four nights or longer. They also have no minimum-night requirement, which is quite nice. There isn't much going on in the rooms, but being outdoors on the north shore is heaven.

Located just a short walk from both the

beach and Hanalei town, **Ohana Hanalei** (Pilikoa Rd., 808/826-4116, www.hanalei-kauai.com, $115) is centrally located, but in a quiet neighborhood near the ocean. A studio that is under the friendly owner's house, it rents for $115 a night with a three-night minimum and a $35 cleaning fee. Weekly rates are available with a $55 cleaning fee. Nearly 500 square feet with a king-size bed, the place has both indoor bathroom and private outdoor shower. It's a good deal and great location.

Good location and a tasty breakfast are the highlights at **Bed, Breakfast and Beach in Hanalei** (5095 Pilikoa Rd., 808/826-6111, www.bestvacationinparadise.com, $120-170). The home is a very short distance from Hanalei Beach but doesn't offer ocean views. Only one or two people are allowed to stay in the three rooms available. The three-story house with a large lanai makes for a good place to stay if you don't mind meeting others. Breakfast is served daily 8:30-9am, including local fruits, banana pancakes, lemon coconut coffee cake, and more. Beach gear is available for use. On the second floor, the Country Cedar room has a queen bed while the Pua Lani room has a king bed; both have private baths and a two-night minimum. The third-floor Bali Hai suite is 700 square feet with a king-size bed, large private bath, and a three-night minimum. It's not super private but nice, clean, and friendly.

The location can't be beat at the **Kaua'i Coco Cabana** (4766 Ananalu Rd., 866/369-8968, www.kauaivacation.com/coco_cabana.htm, $125), a one-bedroom, one-and-a-half-bath home on a lush two acres in a wonderful area in Wainiha toward the end of the road. The home sleeps one to two people and is placed along the Wainiha River, which you can swim in. This is a great spot for those who want to enjoy the peace and solitude of the beaches near the end of the road. It's a fully equipped home with a $125 cleaning fee. The home is not suitable for children but is a great place for honeymooners, with a private outdoor shower, hammock, and beach gear.

Over $200

Nearing the end of the road and all of the north shore's wonderful beaches is the **(Hanalei Colony Resort** (5-7130 Kuhio Hwy., 808/826-6235 or 800/628-3004, www.hcr.com, $204-352 low season, $220-352 high season). The hotel stakes claim to one of the best locations to stay. Here you will find 48 condominium units on five oceanfront acres with ocean or mountain views. Each condo features the same size and floor plan with a full kitchen, dining and living room area, two bedrooms with sliding louvre doors (one has twin beds), and one and a half or two bathrooms. Each unit has a lanai to enjoy the ocean breeze, large picture windows, and is decorated with a relaxed and classy island theme. You are very close to the ocean here no matter what room you're in, but the premium ocean rooms house you just a few yards from the sand. To enhance the experience of Kaua'i's raw nature, units do not have televisions, stereos, or phones, although pay phones are located outside. Cell phones work out here but may be a little unreliable. High-speed wireless is available. There is a pool outside, a long beach to walk on out front, and many other beaches in the immediate area. Rates change a bit throughout the year. The resort is beautiful, the location couldn't be more convenient for enjoying the north shore, and everything is peaceful. Every seventh night is free.

Two glorious homes make up **The River Estate** (Ala Eke Rd., 800/390-8444, www.riverestate.com, $275-300), composed of two high-end and immaculate homes on lush green land along a stream. The two-bedroom, two-bathroom Guest House is perfect for honeymooners. Additional guests are allowed for $15 a night. The River House is a three-bedroom, two-bath home with a hot tub on a screened-in lanai. Both are gorgeous, perfectly kept, unique, and fun with a great location. Located in Wainiha, the land itself is green, vibrant, and a tropical experience of its own. Everything you could need can be found here.

South Shore

The south shore is known as Kaua'i's resort area. Large resorts can be found along the coast, along with condominiums and vacation rentals. The relaxed small town of Kalaheo has modest and affordable accommodations that are ideal to stay in while visiting the south or west side of the island. Koloa is a nice, green, lush area with a few cottages to stay in to avoid the bustle of large resorts in nearby Po'ipu. Po'ipu is great to stay in if you're looking to be a beach bum during your stay on the south side.

KALAHEO
Under $100

Affordable studios can be found with **Sea Kaua'i** (3913 Ulualii St., 808/332-9744, www.seakauai.com, $75-95). The modestly decorated and clean Ti Room is a roomy studio with living area, kitchenette, lanai, and king-size bed. It's perfect for those looking for a place to stay while exploring what nature has to offer on the south or west side. The Ti Room is right next to the Seaview Suite, and they can be rented together for friends or family. It's simply decorated with clean, spacious interior, a large full kitchen, two-person shower, and a king bed with two convertible twin beds. There's a three-night minimum.

In quiet, laid-back Kalaheo town, the **Kalaheo Inn** (4444 Papalina Rd., 808/332-6023, www.kalaheoinn.com, $87-187) offers 15 private suites in a lush garden setting. Rooms are simple with a quaint island theme. Options include studios, one-bedrooms with a kitchenette, and two-bedrooms all with kitchenette and some with lanais. There's also three-bedroom, two-bathroom house with a full kitchen. You'll be a short drive from the beaches of Po'ipu and not too far from the west side. Seventh-night-free specials are available for certain months, and other discounts depend on the length of your stay. It's an affordable place to stay on the south side if you're looking for simple accommodations without frills.

$100-200

A mix of island style and elegance, **Kauai Garden Cottages** (5350 Pu'ulima Rd., 808/332-0877, www.kauaigardencottages.com, $100-135) is on two acres with a small stream. The two suites are in an elevated home with separate access. The Torch Ginger Suite measures about 500 square feet and is a one-bedroom with lovely green views from lanai. The Orchid Suite is over 400 square feet and has one bedroom. Both suites have wireless, full bathrooms, and kitchenettes. Each room opens onto a large shared open lanai with valley and tree-top views, and some beach gear is available for guest use. Different rates are available if renting both rooms or for over two weeks.

The island-decorated **Hale O Nanakai B&B** (3726 Nanakai Pl., 808/652-8071, www.nanakai.com, $75-170) offers a mix of Hawaiian style and luxury. The Kahili Suite rents for $125-135 a night with a $53 cleaning fee. The suite boasts nice teak furniture and a private entrance. Named after the goddess of hula, Laka's Garden is an 800-square-foot 'ohana (family) unit with two bedrooms. It has a screened-in lanai, is wheelchair accessible, and offers a welcome basket. It comes with a three-night minimum and $65 cleaning fee. The more affordable rooms are Hina's Bed Chamber and the Maile Room. Both are single bedrooms with a $35 cleaning fee. Daily breakfast is included. All rates go down if multiple rooms are booked.

The **Bamboo Jungle House** (3829 Waha Rd., 888/332-5115, www.kauai-bedandbreakfast.com, $130-150) appeals to couples and honeymooners. No children are allowed. Choose from three rooms: the Waterfall Room, Jungle Room (both three-night minimums), and the Bamboo Garden Room (five-night minimum). Breakfast is provided daily, and there is a swimming pool and hot tub. There's a $35 cleaning fee. The owners consider the inn a "green" inn.

KAUAI

Where to Stay on Kaua'i's South Shore

Name	Type	Price
Bamboo Jungle House	B&B	$130-150
Boulay Inn	apartment	$85
Classic Vacation Cottages	vacation rentals	$80-150
Grand Hyatt Kaua'i Resort and Spa	spa	$290-910
Hale Kua	B&B	$120 and up
Hale O Nanakai B&B	B&B	$75-170
Hale Pohaku	private homes	$195-595
Hideaway Cove Villas	high-end villas	$175-635
☾ Kalaheo Inn	inn	$87-187
Kaua'i Banyan Inn	private suites	$120-225
Kaua'i Cove Cottages	cottages	$99-185
Kaua'i Garden Cottages	private home suites	$100-135
☾ Kiahuna Plantation Resort	cottages	$179-620
Kuhio Shores	condo	$150-300
Marjorie's Kaua'i Inn	B&B	$130-195
Nihi Kai Villas	condos	$145-625
Poipu Kapili	condos	$250-650
Poipu Shores	condo	$250-650
☾ Prince Kuhio	condo	$64-145
Sea Kaua'i	rooms in home	$75-95
Sheraton Kaua'i	resort	$209-785
Turtle Cove Cottage	private home	$1,350 weekly
Waikomo Stream Villas	condos	$115-270
☾ Whalers Cove	condo	$400-700

There's a variety of options with **Classic Vacation Cottages** (2687 Onu Pl., 808/332-9201, www.classiccottages.com, $80-150) which offers nine different accommodations—a combination of cottages, vacation rentals, and studios. Each place has either a kitchen or kitchenette and lanai and sleeps 1-7 people total. All have TV, free use of beach towels, chairs, and mats, snorkel gear, tennis gear, golf clubs, bikes, barbecues, coolers, boogie boards, hot tub, and unlimited free use of the tennis courts at the Kiahuna Swim and Tennis Club in Po'ipu.

KOLOA
Under $100

A very short drive from historic Koloa town, the **Boulay Inn** (4175 Omao Rd., 808/742-1120, www.boulayinn.com, $85) is a one-bedroom, private, 500-square-foot unit. It is at the owner's home but is on top of the garage, so it has a private entrance and no shared walls

Features	Why Stay Here?	Best Fit For
pool, hot tub	romance	couples
beach gear, private room	affordable	budget travelers
beach gear, hot tub	lots of options	anyone
two pools, golf course, restaurants, spa	location, live in luxury	families, couples
kitchenettes, beach gear	private units	couples, families
breakfast, welcome basket	affordable, location	anyone
pool	privacy, good for gatherings	anyone
Jacuzzi tubs, kitchens, beach gear	it's really nice	those in search of luxury
kitchenettes	affordable, location	couples, families
kitchenettes	location	no children under 10
kitchens	honeymoon cottages	couples
lanai	privacy	couples
gardens, restaurant	lovely grounds	couples
oceanfront	location	couples, families
pool, hot tub	nice and affordable	couples
heated pool, oceanfront, hot tub, tennis	full amenities	anyone
pool, oceanfront	it's really nice	couples, families
pool	location	families, couples, honeymooners
pool, barbecue	affordable, location	families, budget travelers
kitchenette	location, affordable	anyone
two pools, spa, shopping	full-service resort	families, couples
lanai, full home	close to beach	families, couples
pool, hot tub, kiddie pool, tennis	amenities	anyone
pool, hot tub, oceanfront	great place	couples

KAUA'I

with the owners. Free beach gear use is available. There is a three-night minimum and a $50 cleaning fee. Weekly and monthly rates are also available.

$100-200

Five options are available at **Hale Kua** (800/440-4353 or 808/332-8570, www.hale-kua.com, $120-175). The Vacation Cottage sleeps four and is a full house. The Coral Tree has three bedrooms and sleeps six. The Gardenia Unit sleeps four and overlooks a citrus farm. The Banana Patch has a wraparound lanai and sleeps four with a separate bedroom. The Taro Patch sleeps four and has a separate bedroom and a wraparound lanai. All have kitchenettes and access to beach gear and barbecue facilities.

Overlooking lush Lawa'i Valley is **Marjorie's Kaua'i Inn** (P.O. Box 866, 808/332-8838 or 800/717-8838, www.marjorieskauauiinn.com, $130-195), where all rooms include breakfast.

The Sunset View Room fits two people and has a lovely view, mini kitchen, and queen bed with pull-out couch. The largest room at Marjorie's is the Valley View Room. The Trade Wind Room has a mini kitchen. On the grounds of the inn you'll find a pool, hot tub, Bali-style hut bar, surfboard, bikes, and use of a kayak and snorkel gear.

Located on one acre in Lawa'i, the **Kaua'i Banyan Inn** (3528-B Mana Hema Pl., 888/786-3855, www.kauaibanyan.com, $130-225) offers six self-contained private suites. All are clean, with an elegant Hawaiian-style decor. All have kitchenettes and wireless Internet access. No children under 10 years old are allowed.

PO'IPU
Under $100

Bordering Prince Kuhio Park, **(Prince Kuhio** (5061 Lawa'i Rd., 800/367-5025 or 808/245-8841, $64-145) offers studios and one-bedroom units close to beaches with a five-night minimum stay. The grounds are nice, and there's a pool and barbecue area. It's a great location to enjoy sunsets.

$100-300

Decorated like luxury island jungle escapes, **Kaua'i Cove Cottages** (2672 Pu'uholu Rd., 808/742-2562 or 800/624-9945, www.kauaicove.com, $99-185) are the ideal honeymoon accommodations. The Plumeria cottage has woven bamboo on the walls, full kitchen, canopy bed, and a tasteful tropical decor. The Wild Orchid has an island decor, nice tiled bathroom, and kitchen. The Hibiscus is a studio with a canopy bed, kitchen, and porch with barbecue. There's a $50-85 cleaning fee.

Waikomo Stream Villas (2721 Po'ipu Rd., 808/742-2000 or 800/742-1412, www.parrishkauai.com, $130-270) is a small place of 60 condo units with a pool and hot tub. It's not on the ocean but a short walk, drive, or bike ride from it and is directly across from a shopping center. One- and two-bedroom units with one or two bathrooms are available with covered lanai. Units range in size from 1,000 to 1,500 feet and include free parking. There are several barbecue areas, a three-foot-deep kiddie pool, and tennis courts. A nice accent is toiletries from the local Malie Organics line. The majority of units are managed by Parrish Kauai.

The **Nihi Kai Villas** (1870 Ho'one Rd., 808/742-2000 or 800/742-1412, www.parrishkauai.com/kauai-condos/nihi-kai-villas, $145-625) are steps away from the ocean, just a bit over 300 yards to Brennecke's Beach and Po'ipu Beach Park. You'll be treated to a large heated oceanfront pool and hot tub, along with tennis courts, paddleball court, and barbecue area. Units are individually owned, so interior decoration varies, but Parrish Kauai manages the majority. Units range from 1,000 to 1,800 square feet with oceanfront, ocean-view, or garden-view options, including one-bedroom, two-bedroom, and three-bedroom ($300-625) units. Expect wonderful local body products from Malie Organics.

On the water is **Kuhio Shores** (5050 Lawa'i Rd., 800/543-9180 or 808/742-7555, www.kuhioshores.net, $150-300). One-bedroom and two-bedroom condos are available, and many beaches and a surf break are nearby. There isn't a pool, but it is near the beach.

On a half acre near Po'ipu Beach village, **Hale Pohaku** (2225-2231 Pane Rd., 808/212-9749 or 866/742-6462, www.vacationrental-kauai.com, $195) consists of four separate homes that share a private swimming pool. Two are fully restored two-bedroom, one-bath historical Kaua'i plantation cottages. The Jungle, Orchid Cottage, and Beach Rose each rent for $195 a night with a two-night minimum. For large groups the five-bedroom, three-bathroom Manager's Home rents for $475-595 a night. The managers are happy to accommodate weddings and business meetings.

The lovely **(Kiahuna Plantation Resort** (2253 Poipu Rd., 866/733-0587, www.outriggerkiahunaplantationcondo.com, $179-620) is operated by Hawaii's own Outrigger, although some units are managed by Castle Resorts and Hotels. The grounds have history connecting to the sugar industry, which is the foundation of the area. Before the grounds opened to the public in 1972, they were the estate and gardens of Mr. and Mrs. Hector Moir, a manager of the Koloa Sugar Company. What is now the reception building was once the owner's private home, and the dining area of the Plantation Garden Restaurant is located in the home's living room and other rooms. In the yard is the Moir Garden, where cactuses and tropical flowers flourish. Lying on 35 acres, the gardens have had more foliage added to them and now have over 3,000 types of tropical flowers, trees, and plants. Just over 300 units make up the resort. Because each unit is individually owned, they are all decorated differently. They have queen or full-sized beds. Each unit has its own lanai with patio furniture, one bedroom or two, bathroom, living room, and dining area. All are a very short walk from the beach. Concierge service can book anything on the island, and there's daily maid service. Room rates vary between seasons.

The exquisite units at **Hideaway Cove Villas** (2307 and 2315 Nalo Rd., 866/849-2426, www.hideawaycove.com, $205-635) are high-end, extremely nice places to stay. Cleaning fees range $115-345, depending on the size of the unit. Features include kitchens with granite countertops, entertainment centers, Jacuzzi tub in the bathrooms, high-speed wireless throughout the property, covered lanai, barbecues, beach chairs and towels, and coolers.

Along the ocean is the **Sheraton Kaua'i** (2440 Ho'onani Rd., 808/742-1661 or 800/782-9488, www.sheraton-kauai.com, $209 and up), wonderfully placed on Po'ipu Beach. A total of 394 rooms make a home on the property, boasting a casually upscale island-style decor. Each has a private lanai. The hotel was one of the last to reopen after the devastating effects of Hurricane 'Iniki. The resort is elegantly decorated but not over the top, and is also home to retail shops and a fitness center. There are two freshwater pools. The Beach Pool lies near Po'ipu Beach and has a hot tub, while the Garden Pool is slightly inland and surrounded by exotic koi ponds and a waterfall. Both pools have a children's pool. Two restaurants, child care, a spa, and beach rentals and gear are available on-site. Prices vary greatly between the high and low seasons.

Over $300

At **Poipu Kapili** (2221 Kapili Rd., 888/699-0354, www.poipukapili.com, $250-500) you'll find one- and two-bedroom condos and suites. A very, very nice place, it's high class, well maintained, and luxurious. The oceanfront property has a large pool. Well-equipped kitchens are offered in each, along with free wireless Internet, cable, and queen or king beds. You can walk to the beach from here. All rates depend on views and season.

Poipu Shores (1775 Pe'e Rd., 808/742-7700 or 800/367-5004, www.castle-poipu-shores. com, $250-650) offers condo units with a swimming pool and is very close to the ocean. Units are individually owned, so upkeep varies, but they're well kept. One- and two-bedroom units are available. There's a penthouse available for around $500 a night.

Po'ipu's **Grand Hyatt Kaua'i Resort and Spa** (1571 Po'ipu Rd., 808/742-1234 or 800/633-7313, www.grandhyattkauai.com, $290-910, suites $1,570-5,100) has been recently renovated and boasts a grand, elegant, magnificent, luxurious air from nearly every element. The four-level hotel is home to 602 rooms, but it isn't any taller than the palm trees waving in the wind outside. The hotel holds four restaurants, lounges, and bars that offer excellent food and nightly entertainment. Resort shops are also within the hotel walls, enticing those in need of a break from the beach. Both fresh- and saltwater pools lie in the oceanside grounds, complete with slides, waterfalls, and whirlpools. Rooms are entered through heavy hardwood doors and boast minibars, an entertainment center, robes, and lanai sitting area with Hawaiian quilts and other island themes. You can even kayak the hotel's lagoons. Bathrooms are constructed of elegant marble and you will find iPod docks and stereos in the room. On-site child care is available, along with golf and a luxury spa. There are many types of rooms available, from garden views to the presidential suite, but a unique one is the

KAUA'I

hypo-allergenic room for allergy sufferers. All rooms come with the option of two beds or one king. Prices vary greatly depending on season and room type.

At [C] **Whalers Cove** (2640 Puuholo Rd., 800/225-2683, www.whalerscoveresort.com, $400-700) you'll find condos right on the ocean. On-site treats include a heated pool, hot tub, and barbecue area. The individually owned one- and two-bedroom units have free wireless Internet, jacuzzi tubs, and are all well kept.

Just 80 feet from the ocean is **Turtle** **Cove Cottage** (831/479-3885, www.vrbo. com/292422, $1,350 a week, six-night minimum), a plantation-style cottage that was built in 1992, with ocean views from the kitchen, living room, and deck. The neighborhood is peaceful and close to Po'ipu's lovely beaches, including Lawa'i Beach for snorkeling, Baby Beach for children, and PK's for surfing. You'll find queen beds here along with a full kitchen, barbecue grill, wireless Internet, linens, and washer and dryer. The home is wheelchair accessible. There is a $150 cleaning fee and a $500 deposit.

West Side

Accommodations on the west side are somewhat limited, as the area is perhaps the least-busy locale on the island. The west side does offer some of the best places to camp though, both along the ocean and up in the mountains.

HANAPEPE
$100-200

A very unique and "green" place to stay is **Coco's Kaua'i Bed and Breakfast** (P.O. Box 169, Makaweli, 96769, 808/338-0722, www. cocoskauai.com, $110-130). Owned by the Robinson family, the owners of Ni'ihau, the bed-and-breakfast offers single or double occupancy on the 12-acre estate. There are two rooms. A private nearly 600-square-foot guest room has a king-size bed, couch, kitchenette, a living room area, and a connecting private full bath. Another bedroom is across the hall, perfect for two people, and futons can be put on the floor for children. Wireless Internet and use of beach gear are included, along with laundry and barbecue facilities. The place is off the electrical grid and uses hydroelectric power, compact fluorescent light bulbs, and plant-based cleaners, and makes sure to recycle.

WAIMEA
$100-200

Sprawling on 30 acres of oceanfront land

Where to Stay on Kaua'i's West Side

Name	Type	Price
Coco's Kaua'i Bed and Breakfast	B&B	$110-130
Halepule Suites	B&B	$110-120
The Lodge at Koke'e	cabins	$65
[C] Waimea Plantation Cottages & Spa	hotel	$176-892
West Inn Kaua'i	small hotel	$199-349

adorned with coconut trees, ▮ **Waimea Plantation Cottages & Spa** (9400 Kaumuali'i Hwy., 808/338-1625, www.waimeaplantation. com, $176-892) is a combination of contrasting elements and styles. A collection of quite a few original sugar plantation cottages from the 1900s, the homes exude a unique blend of history and elegance, island style, and luxurious comforts. The homes still have their original layout, style, and wood but have been refurbished and are very clean. Set along a black-sand beach and swimming pool where hammocks stretch from one original plantation coconut tree to another, cottages range in size from one to five bedrooms, providing guests with the space and privacy of their own home and fully equipped kitchen, with the comforts and ease of being guests. Live in the lap of luxury lounging at the pool, napping in a oceanside hammock, indulging at the spa, and exploring the hotel's museum. Or you can go low-key and local style here with a backyard barbecue in a yard with an old mango tree, watch the sunset over Ni'ihau from your porch while sipping a locally brewed beer from the on-site Waimea Brewery, or make dinner in a classic plantation kitchen in your own home. Cottages range from a one-bedroom to a five-bedroom home.

Nestled in the small town of Waimea, **Halepule Suites** (4469 Halepule Rd., 808/338-1814, www.innatwaimea.com, $110-120) offers four quaint suites near the ocean. The home-turned-inn was once the residence of the pastor of the Waimea Japanese Christian Church and was renovated in 2001 as a four-suite inn. A lanai allows guests to take in the breeze, and it's a very short walk to the ocean, although the beach here isn't ideal for swimming. The Banana Suite holds one king bed, a Jacuzzi tub, and a living room and rents for $120 a night. The ocean-view Bamboo Suite ($110) has one queen bed, a living room, and a normal shower. In the Hibiscus Suite, you'll find one queen bed, a mountain view, a shower, and a living room. The Taro Room has a king bed, living room, and renovated bathroom. All rates are for two or more nights. All rooms have Internet access, coffeemaker, and small refrigerator. The Hibiscus Suite and Taro Room have TVs.

Over $200

The **West Inn Kaua'i** (9690 Kaumuali'i Hwy., 808/338-1107, www.thewestinn.com, $199-249) is directly across from the historic Waimea Theater. It has a two-night minimum (it will take guests for one-night reservations but only on short notice the day before). Rooms are available with a king bed or two double beds ranges. One- and two-bedroom suites have a seven-night minimum.

KOKE'E
Under $100

In the cool mountain air is ▮ **The Lodge at**

KAUAI

Features	Why Stay Here?	Best Fit For
breakfast, off grid	unique, nice	green travelers
lanai	near beach; friendly service	couples
wood-burning stoves, cooking utensils	affordable, in nature	outdoors types or budget traveler
pool, oceanfront	lovely, unique	families, couples
kitchenettes	location	anyone

Koke'e (3600 Koke'e Rd., 808/335-6061, www.thelodgeatkokee.net, $64), offering cabins up in Koke'e State Park. The wooden cabins are nice and clean with wood-burning stoves and mattresses and often remind visitors of Mainland mountain cabins. Hot showers, cooking utensils, bedding, and wood for the stoves are provided. There is a five-night maximum stay and two-night minimum stay if one night is a Friday or Saturday, which can be perfect for hiking and enjoying overlooks the park. The cabins provide all you need for a simple frills-free weekend in the forest. Call between 9am and 3:30pm to make a reservation.

BACKGROUND
AND
ESSENTIALS

BACKGROUND

The Land

Ancient Hawaiians worshipped Madame Pele, the fire goddess whose name translates equally well as Volcano, Fire Pit, or Eruption of Lava. When she was angry, she complained by spitting fire, which cooled and formed land. And so the Hawaiian islands were born.

The islands' volcanic origins have a basis in science as well as myth. From a stationary hotspot in the earth's mantle, the islands of Hawaii are created as molten lava rises though weak points in the earth's crust. On the Big Island, Mauna Kea, the world's tallest mountain, reaches to 13,796 feet above sea level, or 31,000 feet tall when measured from the ocean floor, almost 3,000 feet taller than Mount Everest. And it's still growing. Once islands move past the hot spot on the Pacific Plate, volcanic activity ceases, and they begin a slow process of erosion, moving northwest across the vast Pacific Ocean. Over thousands of years, the mountains erode to shoals and atolls (barrier reefs just below the ocean surface), returning to their underwater origins. The Lo'ihi Seamount, located southeast of the Big Island, is likely to be the next Hawaiian island. Emerging from the flank of Mauna Loa, its summits are about 50 miles apart. Lo'ihi is roughly 3,000 feet below sea level and isn't expected to become a

© HEATHER ELLISON

full-fledged island for at least 10,000 years or longer, depending on volcanic activity.

Lava comes in two distinct types, for which the Hawaiian names have become universal geological terms: 'a'a and pahoehoe. They're easily distinguished by appearance, but chemically they're the same. 'A'a is extremely sharp, rough, and spiny. Conversely, pahoehoe is billowy, ropelike lava that can mold into fantastic shapes. Examples of both are visible across the islands.

GEOGRAPHY

About 2,400 miles from the nearest continental shore, Hawaii is most isolated group of islands on the planet. There are eight main Hawaiian Islands: Ni'ihau (the Forbidden Island), Kaua'i (the Garden Isle), O'ahu (the Gathering Place), Moloka'i (the Friendly Isle), Lana'i (the Pineapple Isle), Kaho'olawe (the Target Isle), Maui (the Valley Isle) and Hawai'i (better known as the Big Island). The Hawaiian archipelago consists of 132 islands, islets, and atolls, stretching roughly 1,500 miles from northernmost Kure Atoll to the still-growing Big Island of Hawai'i at the southeastern end of the chain. The eight main islands have a total area of 10,931 square miles. The Big Island is the largest island, accounting for about 63 percent of the state's total landmass; the other islands could fit within it two times over. Next largest is Maui, followed by O'ahu, Kaua'i, Moloka'i, and Lana'i. There are approximately 750 miles of coastline in the state. The main Hawaiian Islands are located in the Tropic of Cancer.

Hawaii's landscape is extremely diverse, offering everything from dry arid desert to snow-capped mountains. There are rivers, streams and waterfalls, vertical cliffs, extinct tuff cone volcanoes, tranquil bays and high-elevation plateaus. Because of their dramatic rise out of ocean depths, the islands include examples of 11 of the world's 13 climate zones.

The Leewards

Like tiny gems of a necklace, the Northwest Hawaiian Islands stretch across the vast Pacific. Popularly called the Leewards, most were discovered in the 19th century. The Leewards are the oldest islands of the Hawaiian chain, believed to have emerged from the sea 25-30 million years ago. Slowly they floated west-northwest past the suboceanic hot spot as the other islands were built. Measured from **Nihoa Island,** about 100 miles off the northwestern tip of Kaua'i, they span just under 1,100 miles to **Kure Atoll.** There are islets, shoals, and half-submerged reefs in this chain: Kure, Midway, Pearl, and Hermes Atolls and Lisianski, Maro Reef, Gardner Pinnacles, French Frigate Shoals, Necker, and Nihoa. Most have been eroded flat by the sea and wind, but a few tough volcanic cores endure. Together they make up a landmass of approximately 3,500 acres, the largest being the three Midway islands, taken together at 1,580 acres, and the smallest is **Gardner Pinnacles** at six acres.

Politically, the Leewards are administered by the City and County of Honolulu, except for Midway, which is under federal jurisdiction. None, except Midway, are permanently inhabited, but there are some lonely wildlife field stations on Kure and the French Frigate Shoals. All, except for Midway Atoll, are part of the **Hawaiian Islands National Wildlife Refuge,** established at the turn of the 20th century by Theodore Roosevelt. In 1996, following the closure of the Naval Air Base on Midway Island, Midway Atoll was turned over to the Department of the Interior and is now administered as the **Midway Atoll National Wildlife Refuge.** In June 2006, this 140,000-square-mile string of 10 islands and atolls and their surrounding waters, roughly 1,400 miles long and 100 mile wide, were officially designated a **Marine National Monument** (www.hawaiireef.noaa.gov), effectively creating the nation's largest wilderness preserve and the world's largest marine preserve.

CLIMATE
Temperature

Hawaii has comfortable weather year-round. Near the coast, the average daytime high temperature in winter is about 82°F, with the average daytime high in summer raising the thermometer only a few degrees to 87.5°F. Nighttime temperatures drop about 10 degrees. Elevation, however, does reduce temperatures: about three degrees for every 1,000 feet you climb.

Temperatures are both constant and moderate because of the trade winds, prevailing northeast breezes that blow at about 10-20 miles per hour. You can count on the trades to be blowing on an average of 300 days per year, hardly missing a day during summer and occurring half the time in winter. Although usually calm in the morning, they pick up during the heat of the afternoon, then weaken at night.

The Tropic of Cancer runs through the center of Hawaii, yet the latitude's usually oppressively hot and muggy weather is most often absent in the islands. Honolulu, on the same latitude as sweaty Hong Kong and Havana, has an acceptable 60-75 percent daily humidity factor.

Winds blowing from the south and southwest are known as kona winds. *Kona* means leeward in Hawaiian. Kona winds bring hot, humid air and unstable weather. If they persist for more than a couple of days, they also bring vog, a thick haze caused by the Kilauea Volcano on the Big Island. Kona winds are most common October-April.

Rainfall

Precipitation is the biggest differentiating factor in Hawaii's climate. Rainfall is most often localized and comes in waves of passing showers. Precipitation also occurs mostly at and below the 3,000-foot level with the mountains acting as rain magnets. As the trade winds push warm, moist air up against the mountains, the air rises, cools, and drops a payload of rain to the ground. The heaviest rainfall occurs on the windward side of the islands and over mountain ranges, and dry conditions prevail on the leeward sides and south shores. For example, the Honolulu International Airport and Waikiki average only 20-25 inches of rain per year, while the Nu'uanu Reservoir in the mountains above Honolulu gets a whopping 120-130 inches yearly.

Localized weather means that weather patterns are very specific. If it's raining where you are, simply relocate to another part of the island or just wait a few minutes for the precipitation to pass. You can usually depend on south shore beaches and the leeward side to be sunny and bright. Ocean temperatures run 75-80°F year-round.

Severe Weather

Tsunami is the Japanese word for tidal wave. Hawaii's location in the middle of the Pacific Ocean puts it in the path of tsunamis as they travel from their point of origin and spread across the Pacific. A Hawaiian tsunami is actually a seismic sea wave that has been generated by an earthquake or landslide that could easily have originated thousands of miles away in Japan, South America, or Alaska. Not actual waves that break like the ones seen along the reefs, tsunamis show up as a series of three to five tidal surges that affect coastal waters and shorelines over several hours, with about 30 minutes between each surge. Tsunamis can range from simply a larger than usual fluctuation in sea level over the duration of the event to a devastating tidal surge that can floor and damage shoreline property, especially the harbors, and cause loss of life. For visitors staying in shoreline hotels with six or more stories, the safest place to be during a tsunami event is on the third floor or higher. Otherwise, shoreline areas should be evacuated.

Hurricanes are also a threat in Hawaii. They are rare, but destructive. Most hurricanes originate far to the southeast off the Pacific coast of Mexico and Latin America; some, particularly later in the season, start in the midst of the Pacific Ocean near the equator south of Hawaii. Hurricane season is considered June through November. Most hurricanes pass harmlessly south of Hawaii, but some, swept

Hurricanes

A **tropical depression** is a low-pressure system or cyclone with winds below 39 mph. A **tropical storm** is a cyclone with winds 39-73 mph. A **hurricane** is a cyclone with winds over 74 mph. These winds are often accompanied by torrential rains, destructive waves, high water, and storm surges.

The National Weather Service issues a **Hurricane Watch** if hurricane conditions are expected in the area within 36 hours. A **Hurricane Warning** is issued when a hurricane is expected to strike within 24 hours. The state of Hawaii has an elaborate warning system against natural disasters using sirens high atop poles along many beaches and coastal areas to alert the public of potential or imminent natural disasters, like tsunamis and hurricanes. Over the decades, hurricanes have caused a great deal of property damage, but, thankfully, the loss of life has been minimal.

MAJOR HURRICANES SINCE 1950

- Hurricane Hiki: Occurred in August 1950, on Kaua'i. Resulted in one death.

- Hurricane Nina: Occurred in December 1957, on Kaua'i. No reported damages.

- Hurricane Dot: Occurred in August 1959, on Kaua'i. Resulted in damages of $5.5 million.

- Hurricane Fico: Occurred in July 1978, on the Big Island. No direct damage, since it didn't make landfall.

- Hurricane Iwa: Occurred in November 1982, on Kaua'i and O'ahu. Resulted in one death and $234 million of damage.

- Hurricane Estelle: Occurred in July 1986, on Maui and the Big Island. Resulted in $2 million of damage.

- Hurricane 'Iniki: Occurred in September 1992, on Kaua'i and O'ahu. Resulted in eight deaths and caused $1.9 billion of damage.

along by kona winds, do strike the islands. The most recent and destructive was Hurricane 'Iniki, which battered the islands in 1992, killing eight people and causing an estimated $2 billion in damage. It had its greatest effect on Ni'ihau, the Po'ipu Beach area of Kaua'i, and the leeward coast of O'ahu.

Kona storms are another matter. These subtropical low-pressure storms develop west of the Hawaiian Islands, and as they move east, they draw winds up from the south. Common only in winter, they can cause considerable damage to crops and real estate. There is no real pattern to kona storms. Some years they come every few weeks, whereas in other years they don't appear at all.

Flora and Fauna

The Hawaiian Islands, about 2,500 miles from any continental landfall, were originally devoid of plant or animal life. Over time, as plants, animals, and insects found their way to the islands, they slowly evolved into highly specialized organisms occupying the gamut of each island's microclimates. In Hawaii, it is not uncommon for a particular plant species only to be found in a single valley across the entire island chain.

The unique plants and animals found only in Hawaii are known as endemic, those species naturally occurring in Hawaii but found elsewhere in the world are known as native, and those brought to the islands by people are called introduced species. Introduced species that are fast growing, rapidly increase in number, and easily spread over a region are referred to as invasive species. Invasive species and loss of habitat have been detrimental to the survival of Hawaii's highly specialized native and endemic flora and fauna. Hawaii is also known as the endangered species capital of the world, with most of its endemic plants and animals listed as rare and endangered, with many species having already gone extinct. The majority of the remaining pockets of native Hawaiian flora in Hawai'i have been relegated to inaccessible valleys and steep mountain cliffs.

INTRODUCED PLANTS

Before settlement, Hawaii had no fruits, vegetables, coconut palms, edible land animals, conifers, mangroves, or banyans. The early Polynesians brought in 27 varieties of plants that they needed for food and other purposes, like banana, sweet potato, breadfruit, sugarcane, and taro. They also carried along gourds to use as containers, 'awa to make a basic intoxicant, and the ti plant to use for offerings or to string into hula skirts. About 90 percent of plants on the Hawaiian Islands today were introduced after Captain Cook first set foot here. Non-Hawaiian settlers over the years have brought mangoes, papayas, passion fruit, pineapples, and the other tropical fruits and vegetables associated with the islands. Also, most of the flowers, including protea, plumeria, anthuriums, orchids, heliconia, ginger, and most hibiscus, have come from every continent on earth. Tropical America, Asia, Java, India, and China have contributed their most beautiful and delicate blooms.

TREES

Koa and **'ohi'a** are two endemic Hawaiian trees still seen quite often in the state. Both have been greatly reduced by the foraging of introduced cattle and goats, and through logging and forest fires. The *koa* (*Acacia koa*) is Hawaii's finest native tree. It can grow to more than 70 feet high and has a strong, straight trunk, which can measure more than 10 feet in circumference. The Hawaiians used *koa* as the main log for their dugout canoes, and elaborate ceremonies were performed when a log was cut and dragged to a canoe shed. *Koa* wood was also preferred for paddles, spears, and even surfboards. Today it is still considered an excellent furniture wood. To protect fine specimens found in reserves, *koa* is now being grown on plantations for future harvesting for commercial purposes.

The *'ohi'a* (*Metrosideros polymorpha*) is a survivor and a pioneer plant, one of the first types of plants to colonize lava flows. It is the most abundant of all the native Hawaiian trees. Coming in a variety of shapes and sizes, it grows as miniature trees in wet bogs or as 100-foot giants on cool slopes at higher elevations. The *'ohi'a* produces a tuft-like flower—usually red, but occasionally orange, yellow, or white, the latter being very rare and elusive—that resembles a bottlebrush. The flower was considered sacred to Pele; it was said that she would cause a rainstorm if 'ohi'a blossoms were picked without the proper prayers. The flowers were fashioned into lei that resembled feather

The All-Purpose Kukui Tree

Reaching heights of 80 feet, the *kukui* (candlenut) tree was a veritable department store to the Hawaiians, who made use of almost every part of this utilitarian giant. Its nuts, bark, or flowers were ground into potions and salves to be taken as a general tonic, applied to ulcers and cuts as an effective antibiotic, or administered internally as a cure for constipation or asthma attacks. The bark was mixed with water, and the resulting juice was used as a dye in tattooing, tapa-cloth making, and canoe painting, and as a preservative for fishnets. The oily nuts were burned in stone holders as a light source, and they were ground and eaten as a condiment called *'inamona*. Polished nuts took on a beautiful sheen and were strung as lei. Finally, the wood was hollowed into canoes and used as fishnet floats.

boas. The strong, hard wood was used to make canoes, poi bowls, and especially for temple images. *'Ohi'a* logs were also used as railroad ties and shipped to the mainland from the Big Island. It's believed that the "golden spike" linking rail lines between the U.S. East and West Coasts was driven into an *'ohi'a* log from the Big Island when the two railroads came together in Ogden, Utah.

MARINE LIFE

Although decades of overfishing have taken their toll on the marine life along island reefs, entire populations of reef dwellers are bouncing back in specific locations thanks to managed Marine Protected Areas. These managed zones are designed to promote reef health and bolster populations of reef-dwelling species. In turn, these healthy areas allow populations of fish to grow rapidly and reproduce in exponentially larger numbers, spilling over into unprotected waters and benefiting species higher up the food chain. Hawaii has over 200 species of native fish.

Whales and **dolphins** are also common in Hawaiian waters. The most famous whale, and commonly seen, is the **North Pacific humpback,** but others include the sperm, killer, false killer, pilot, Cuvier's, Blainsville, and pygmy killer. There are technically no porpoises, but dolphins include the common, bottlenose, white-sided, broad- and slender-beaked, and rough-toothed. Small and sleek spinner dolphins are the ones you'll often see near the shore. The **mahimahi,** a favorite food fish found on many menus, is commonly referred to as dolphin fish but is unrelated and is a true fish, not a cetacean.

The **Hawaiian monk seal** is one of only two mammals native to Hawaii (the Hawaiian hoary bat is the other). These curious seals are critically endangered and protected by law. Monk seals frequently relax on the beach and have a nap in the sun. If you see a monk seal, give it ample space and do not disturb or touch the seal in any way. **Green sea turtles** at rest are also common along island shorelines. They share the endangered designation and should be given the same respect.

BIRDS

Due to the lack of native mammals and reptiles in pre-contact Hawaii, native birds flourished, becoming widespread and highly specialized. Not to mention, they were able to feast on over 10,000 species of native insects. However, one of the great tragedies of natural history is the continuing demise of Hawaiian birdlife. Perhaps only 15 original species of birds remain of the more than 70 native families that thrived before the coming of humans. Since the arrival of Captain Cook in 1778, 23 species have become extinct, with 31 more in danger. And what's not known is how many species were wiped out before white explorers arrived. Experts believe that the Hawaiians annihilated about 40 species, including seven species of geese, a rare one-legged owl, ibis, lovebirds, sea eagles, and honeycreepers—all gone before Captain Cook showed up. Hawaii's endangered birds account for 40 percent of the birds officially listed as endangered or threatened by the U.S.

Fish and Wildlife Service. Most of the remaining indigenous Hawaiian birds can be found on any island below the 3,000-foot level.

Hawaii shoreline cliffs, dunes and islets are home to thriving colonies of marine birds. Look for several birds from the tern family, including the **white, gray,** and **sooty tern.** Along with the terns are **shearwaters** and the enormous **Laysan albatross,** with its seven-foot wingspan. **Tropicbirds,** with their lovely streamer-like tails, are often seen along the windward coasts.

If you're lucky, you can also catch a glimpse of the *pueo* (Hawaiian owl) in mountainous areas. Deep in the forests you can sometimes see elusive birds like the *'elepaio, 'amakihi,* and the fiery red *'i'iwi*. The *'amakihi* and *'i'iwi* are endemic birds not endangered at the moment. The *'amakihi* is one of the most common native birds; yellowish-green, it frequents the high branches of the *'ohi'a, koa,* and sandalwood trees looking for insects, nectar, or fruit. It is less specialized than most other Hawaiian birds, the main reason for its continued existence. The *'i'iwi,* a bright red bird with a salmon-colored, hooked bill, is found in the forests above 2,000 feet. The most common native bird, the *'apapane* is abundant and easiest to see. It's a chubby, red-bodied bird about five inches long with a black bill, legs, wingtips, and tail feathers.

Exotic, introduced birds are the most common in the beach parks and in urban areas. **Black myna birds** with their sassy yellow eyes are common mimics around town. **Sparrows,** introduced to Hawaii through O'ahu in the 1870s, are everywhere. **Munia,** first introduced as caged birds from Southeast Asia, have escaped and can be found almost anywhere around the island of O'ahu.

INTRODUCED ANIMALS

Almost all of the mammals in Hawaii are introduced, and many have had severe and detrimental consequences for Hawaii's natural environment and native species. **Rats, mice,** and **mongooses** thrive and are responsible for disease and the decline of ground nesting bird populations. Feral ungulates like **pigs** and **goats** destroy native forests as they root up and eat vegetation, creating fetid pools of water where mosquitoes thrive, contributing to the decline of forest bird populations through disease. In years past, grazing **cattle** were responsible for the deforestation of watersheds that led to landslides. **Geckos, anoles,** and **chameleons** are a few of the introduced reptiles that are common.

History

HAWAII'S SETTLERS

The great "deliberate migrations" from the southern Pacific islands seem to have taken place AD 500-800, though the exact date is highly contested by experts. The first planned migrations were from the violent cannibalistic islands called the Marquesas, 11 islands in extreme eastern Polynesia. The islands themselves are harsh and inhospitable, breeding toughness into the people that enabled them to withstand the hardships of long, unsure ocean voyages and years of resettlement. They were masters at building great double-hulled canoes with the two hulls fastened together to form a catamaran, and a hut in the center provided shelter in bad weather. The average voyaging canoe was 60-80 feet long and could comfortably hold an extended family of about 30 people. These small family bands carried all the staples they would need in the new lands.

For five centuries the Marquesans settled here and lived peacefully on the new land. The tribes coexisted in relative harmony, especially because there was no competition for land. Cannibalism died out. There was much coming and going between Hawaii and Polynesia as new people came to the settlement over the course of hundreds of years. Then, it appears that in the 12th century a deliberate exodus of warlike Tahitians arrived and subjugated the islanders. This incursion had a terrific significance on the Hawaiian religious and social system. The warlike god Ku and the rigid *kapu* system were introduced, through which the new rulers became dominant. Voyages between Tahiti and Hawaii continued for about 100 years, and Tahitian customs, legends, and language became the Hawaiian way of life. Then suddenly, for no recorded or apparent reason, the voyages discontinued and Hawaii returned to total isolation.

CAPTAIN COOK

The islands remained forgotten for almost 500 years until the indomitable English seafarer, Captain James Cook, sighted O'ahu on January 18, 1778, and stepped ashore at Waimea on Kaua'i two days later. At that time Hawaii's isolation was so complete that even the Polynesians had forgotten about it. The Englishmen had arrived aboard the 100-foot flagship HMS *Resolution* and its 90-foot companion HMS *Discovery*. The first trade was some brass medals for a mackerel. Cook provisioned his ships by exchanging chisels for hogs, while common sailors gleefully traded nails for sex. Landing parties were sent inland to fill casks with freshwater. After a brief stop on Ni'ihau, the ships sailed away, but both groups were indelibly impressed with the memory of each other.

Almost a year later, when winter weather forced Cook to return from the coast of Alaska, the *Discovery* and *Resolution* found safe anchorage at Kealakekua Bay on the kona coast of the Big Island on January 16, 1779. By the coincidence of his second arrival with religious festivities, the Hawaiians mistook Cook to be the return of the god Lono. After an uproarious welcome and generous hospitality for over a month, it became obvious that the newcomers were beginning to overstay their welcome. During the interim a sailor named William Watman died, convincing the Hawaiians that the *haole* were indeed mortals, not gods. Inadvertently, many *kapu* were broken by the

English, and once-friendly relations became strained. Finally, the ships sailed away on February 4, 1779.

After plying terrible seas for only a week, *Resolution*'s foremast was badly damaged. Cook sailed back into Kealakekua Bay, dragging the mast ashore on February 13. The natives, now totally hostile, hurled rocks at the sailors. Confrontations increased when some Hawaiians stole a small boat and Cook's men set after them, capturing the fleeing canoe, which held an *ali'i* named Palea. The Englishmen treated him roughly, so the Hawaiians furiously attacked the mariners, who abandoned the small boat.

Next, the Hawaiians stole a small cutter from the *Discovery* that had been moored to a buoy and partially sunk to protect it from the sun. For the first time, Captain Cook became furious. He ordered Captain Clerk of the *Discovery* to sail to the southeast end of the bay and stop any canoe trying to leave Kealakekua. Cook then made a fatal error in judgment. He decided to take nine armed mariners ashore in an attempt to convince the venerable King Kalani'opu'u to accompany him back aboard ship, where he would hold him for ransom in exchange for the cutter. The old king agreed, but his wife prevailed upon him not to trust the *haole*. Kalani'opu'u sat down on the beach to think while the tension steadily grew.

Meanwhile, a group of mariners fired on a canoe trying to leave the bay, and a lesser chief, No'okemai, was killed. The crowd around Cook and his men reached an estimated 20,000, and warriors outraged by the killing of the chief armed themselves with clubs and protective straw-mat armor. One bold warrior advanced on Cook and struck him with his *pahoa* (dagger). In retaliation Cook drew a tiny pistol lightly loaded with shot and fired at the warrior. His bullets spent themselves on the straw armor and fell harmlessly to the ground. The Hawaiians went wild. Lieutenant Molesworth Phillips, in charge of the nine mariners, began a withering fire; Cook killed two natives.

Overpowered by sheer numbers, the sailors headed for boats standing offshore, while

Lieutenant Phillips lay wounded. It is believed that Captain Cook stood helplessly in knee-deep water instead of making for the boats because he could not swim. Hopelessly surrounded, he was knocked on the head, then countless warriors passed a knife around and hacked and mutilated his lifeless body. A sad Lieutenant King lamented in his diary, "Thus fell our great and excellent commander."

UNIFICATION OF THE HAWAIIAN ISLANDS

In the 1780s the islands were roughly divided into three kingdoms: Kalani'opu'u ruled Hawai'i and the Hana district of Maui; wily and ruthless warrior-king Kahekili ruled Maui, Kaho'olawe, Lana'i, and later O'ahu; and Kaeo, Kahekili's brother, ruled Kaua'i. War ravaged the land until a remarkable chief, Kamehameha, rose and subjugated all the islands under one rule. Kamehameha initiated a dynasty that would last for about 100 years, until the independent monarchy of Hawaii forever ceased to be.

Hawaii under Kamehameha was ready to enter its "golden age." The social order was medieval, with the *ali'i* as knights, owing their military allegiance to the king, and the serf-like *maka'ainana* paying tribute and working the lands. The priesthood of *kahuna* filled the posts of advisors, sorcerers, navigators, doctors, and historians. This was Polynesian Hawaii at its apex. But like the uniquely Hawaiian silversword plant, the old culture blossomed, and as soon as it did, it began to wither. Ever since, all that was purely Hawaiian has been supplanted by the relentless foreign influences that began bearing down upon it.

MISSIONARIES AND WHALERS

Kamehameha was as gentle in victory as he was ferocious in battle. Under his rule, which lasted until his death on May 8, 1819, Hawaii enjoyed a peace unlike any the warring islands had ever known. However, the year 1819 was of the utmost significance in Hawaiian history. With the death of Kamehameha came the overthrow of the ancient *kapu* system, the arrival of the first whalers in Lahaina, and the departure of Calvinist missionaries from New England determined to convert the heathen islanders. Great changes began to rattle the old order to its foundations. With the *kapu* system and all of the ancient gods abandoned (except for the fire goddess Pele of Kilauea), a great void opened the souls of the Hawaiians. In the coming decades Hawaii, also coveted by Russia, France, and England, was finally consumed by America. The islands had the first American school, printing press, and newspaper west of the Mississippi. Lahaina, in its heyday, became the world's greatest whaling port, accommodating more than 500 ships of all types during its peak years.

In 1823, the first mission was established in Lahaina, Maui, under the pastorate of Reverend Richards and his wife. Within a few years, many of the notable *ali'i* had been, at least in appearance, converted to Christianity. By 1828 the cornerstones for Waine'e Church, the first stone church on the island, were laid just behind the palace of Kamehameha III.

THE GREAT MAHELE

In 1840, after moving the royal court to Honolulu, the new center of commerce in the islands, Kamehameha III ended his autocratic rule and instituted a constitutional monarchy. This brought about the Hawaiian Bill of Rights, but the most far-reaching change was the transition to private ownership of land, known as The Great Mahele. Formerly, all land belonged to the ruling chief, who gave wedge-shaped parcels called *ahupua'a* to lesser chiefs to be worked for him. The commoners did all the real labor, their produce heavily taxed by the *ali'i*. The fortunes of war, the death of a chief, or the mere whim of a superior could force a commoner off the land.

The Hawaiians, however, could not think in terms of owning land. No one could *possess* land, one could only *use* land, and its ownership was a foreign concept. As a result, naive Hawaiians gave up their lands for a song to unscrupulous traders, and land ownership issues remain a basic and unrectified problem to this day. In 1847 Kamehameha III and his advisors separated the lands of Hawaii into three groupings: crown land (belonging to the king), government land (belonging to the chiefs), and the people's land (the largest parcels). In 1848, 245 *ali'i* entered their land claims in the *Mahele Book,* assuring them ownership. In 1850 the commoners were given title in fee simple to the lands they cultivated and lived on as tenants, not including house lots in towns. Commoners without land could buy small *kuleana* (farms) from the government at 50 cents per acre. In 1850, foreigners were also allowed to purchase land in fee simple, and the ownership of Hawaii from that day forward slipped steadily from the hands of its indigenous people.

THE END OF A KINGDOM

Like the Hawaiian people themselves, the Kamehameha dynasty in the mid-1800s was dying from within. King Kamehameha IV (Alexander Liholiho) ruled 1854-1863; his only child died in 1862. He was succeeded by his older brother Kamehameha V (Lot Kamehameha), who ruled until 1872. With his passing the Kamehameha line ended. William Lunalilo, elected king in 1873 by popular vote, was of royal lineage, but not of the Kamehameha bloodline. He died after only a year in office, and being a bachelor, he left no heirs. He was succeeded by David Kalakaua, known far and wide as the "Merrie Monarch," who made a world tour and was well received wherever he went. He built 'Iolani Palace in Honolulu and was personally in favor of closer ties with the United States, helping to push through the Reciprocity Act. Kalakaua died in 1891 and was replaced by his sister, Lydia Lili'uokalani, last of the Hawaiian monarchs.

REVOLUTION AND ANNEXATION

When Lili'uokalani took office in 1891, the native population was at a low of 40,000, and she felt that the United States had too much influence over her homeland. She was known to personally favor the English over the Americans. She attempted to replace the liberal constitution of 1887 (adopted by her pro-American brother) with an autocratic mandate in which she would have had much more political and economic control of the islands.

When the McKinley Tariff of 1890 brought a decline in sugar profits, she made no attempt to improve the situation. Thus, the planters saw her as a political obstacle to their economic growth; most of Hawaii's American planters and merchants were in favor of a rebellion. A central spokesperson and firebrand was Lorrin Thurston, a Honolulu publisher who, with a core of about 30 men, challenged the Hawaiian monarchy. Although Lili'uokalani rallied some support and had a small military potential in her personal guard, the coup was relatively bloodless—it took only one casualty. Naturally, the conspirators could not have succeeded without some solid assurances from a secret contingent in the U.S. Congress as well as outgoing President Benjamin Harrison, who favored Hawaii's annexation. Marines from the *Boston* went ashore to "protect American lives," and on January 17, 1893, the Hawaiian monarchy came to an end.

Sanford B. Dole, who became president of the Hawaiian Republic, headed the provisional government. Lili'uokalani surrendered not to the conspirators, but to U.S. Ambassador John Stevens. She believed that the U.S. government, which had assured her of Hawaiian independence, would be outraged by the overthrow and would come to her aid. Incoming President Grover Cleveland *was* outraged, and Hawaii wasn't immediately annexed as expected.

In January 1895, a small, ill-fated counter-revolution headed by Lili'uokalani failed, and she was placed under house arrest in 'Iolani Palace. Officials of the Republic insisted that she use her married name (Mrs. John Dominis) to sign the documents forcing her to abdicate her throne. She was also forced to swear allegiance to the new Republic. Lili'uokalani went on to write *Hawaii's Story* and the lyric ballad "Aloha O'e." She never forgave the conspirators and remained queen in the minds of Hawaiians until her death in 1917.

On July 7, 1898, President McKinley signed the annexation agreement, arguing that the U.S. military must have Hawaii in order to be a viable force in the Pacific.

PEARL HARBOR ATTACK

On the morning of December 7, 1941, the Japanese carrier *Akagi,* flying the battle flag of Admiral Togo of Russo-Japanese War fame, received and broadcast over its public address system island music from Honolulu station KGMB. Deep in the bowels of the ship a radio operator listened for a much different message, coming thousands of miles from the Japanese mainland. When the ironically poetic message "east wind rain" was received, the attack was launched. At the end of the day, 2,325 U.S. soldiers and 57 civilians were dead; 188 planes were destroyed; 18 major warships were sunk or heavily damaged; and the United States was engaged in World War II. Japanese casualties were ludicrously light. The ignited conflict would rage for four years until Japan, through the atomic bombing of Nagasaki and Hiroshima, was brought into total submission. By the end of hostilities, Hawaii would never again be considered separate from America.

STATEHOOD

Several economic and political motivations explain why the ruling elite of Hawaii desired statehood, but put simply, the vast majority of people who lived there, especially after World War II, considered themselves Americans. The first serious mention of making the Hawaiian Islands a state was in the 1850s under President Franklin Pierce, but the idea wasn't taken seriously until the monarchy was overthrown in the 1890s. For the next 50 years statehood proposals were made repeatedly to Congress, but there was stiff opposition, especially from the southern states. With Hawaii a territory, an import quota system beneficial to mainland producers could be enacted on produce, especially sugar. Also, there was prejudice against creating a state in a place where the majority of the populace was not white.

During World War II, Hawaii was placed under martial law, but no serious attempt to confine the Japanese population was made, as it was in California. There were simply too many Japanese, and many went on to gain the respect of the American people through their outstanding fighting record during the war. Hawaii's own 100th Battalion became the famous 442nd Regimental Combat Team, which gained notoriety by saving the Lost Texas Battalion during the Battle of the Bulge and went on to be *the* most decorated battalion in all of World War II. When these GIs returned home, *no one* was going to tell them that they were not loyal Americans. Many of these Americans of Japanese Ancestry (AJAs) took advantage of the GI Bill and received higher education. They were from the common people, not the elite, and they rallied grassroots support for statehood. When the vote finally occurred, approximately 132,900 voted in favor of statehood with only 7,800 votes against. Congress passed the Hawaii State Bill on March 12, 1959, and on August 21, 1959, President Eisenhower announced that Hawaii was officially the 50th state.

People and Culture

POPULATION

Of the nearly 1.4 million people that reside in Hawaii, 963,607 live on Oʻahu, with slightly less than half of these living in the Honolulu metropolitan area. Statewide, city dwellers outnumber those living in the country by nine to one. Oʻahu's population accounts for 70 percent of the state's population, yet the island comprises only 9 percent of the state's land total. Sections of Waikiki can have a combined population of permanent residents and visitors as high as 90,000 per square mile, making cities like Tokyo, Hong Kong, and New York seem roomy by comparison. The next most populous islands are the Big Island, at more than 185,000 residents, and Maui with nearly 150,000 residents. Kauaʻi has just over 68,000 people. Molokai has just over. 7,000, while Lanaʻi is home to just over 3,000.

PEOPLE

Nowhere else on Earth can you find such a kaleidoscopic mixture of people as in Hawaii. More than 50 ethnic groups are represented throughout the islands, making Hawaii the most racially integrated state in the country. Ethnic breakdowns for the state include 25.3 percent Hawaiian/part Hawaiian, 20.5 percent Caucasian, 18.4 percent Japanese, 10 percent Filipino, 8.9 percent Hispanic/Latino, and 4.2 percent Chinese.

Niʻihau, a privately owned island, is home to about 160 pure-blooded Hawaiians, representing the largest concentration of Hawaiians, per capita, in the islands. The Robinson family, which owns the island, restricts visitors to invited guests only. The second largest concentration is on Molokaʻi, where 2,700 Hawaiians, living mostly on a 40-acre *kuleana* of Hawaiian Home Lands, make up 40 percent of that island's population. The majority of mixed-blood Hawaiians, 240,000 or so, live on Oʻahu, where they are particularly strong in the hotel and entertainment fields.

Native Hawaiians

When Captain Cook first sighted Hawaii in 1778, there were an estimated 300,000 natives living in relative harmony with their ecological surroundings; within 100 years a scant 50,000 Hawaiians remained. Today, although more than 240,000 people claim varying degrees of Hawaiian blood, experts say that fewer than 1,000 are pure Hawaiian.

Ancient Hawaiian society was divided into rankings by a strict caste system determined by birth, and from which there was no chance of escaping. The highest rank was the *aliʻi,* the chiefs and royalty. The impeccable genealogies of the *aliʻi* were traced back to the gods themselves, and the chants (*moʻo aliʻi*) were memorized and sung by a rank of a *aliʻi* called *kuʻauhau.* Ranking passed from both father and mother, and custom dictated that the first mating of an *aliʻi* be with a person of equal status.

A *kahuna* was a highly skilled person whose advice was sought before any major project was undertaken, such as building a house, hollowing a canoe log, or even offering a prayer. The *moʻo kahuna* were the priests of Ku and Lono, and they were in charge of praying and following rituals. They were very powerful *aliʻi* and kept strict secrets and laws concerning their various functions.

Besides this priesthood of *kahuna,* there were other *kahuna* who were not *aliʻi,* but commoners. The two most important were the healers (*kahuna lapaʻau*) and the sorcerers (*kahuna ʻanaʻana*) who could pray a person to death. The *kahuna lapaʻau* had a marvelous pharmacopoeia of herbs and spices that could cure over 250 diseases common to the Hawaiians.

The common people were called the *makaʻainana,* "the people of land"—the farmers, craftspeople, and fishers. The land they lived on was controlled by the *aliʻi,* but they were not bound to it. If the local *aliʻi* was cruel or unfair, the *makaʻainana* had the right to leave and reside on another's lands. The *maka'ainana* mostly loved their local *ali'i*, much like a child loves a parent, and the feeling was reciprocated. *Maka'ainana* who lived close to the *ali'i* and could be counted on as warriors in times of trouble were called *kanaka no lua kaua* (a man for the heat of battle). They were treated with greater favor than those who lived in the backcountry, *kanaka no hi'i kua*, whose lesser standing opened them up to discrimination and cruelty. All *maka'ainana* formed extended families called *'ohana* who usually lived on the same section of land, called *ahupua'a*. Those farmers who lived inland would barter their produce with the fishers who lived on the shore, and thus all shared equally in the bounty of land and sea.

A special group called *kauwa* was an untouchable caste confined to living on reservations. Their origins were obviously Polynesian, but they appeared to be descendants of castaways who had survived and became perhaps the aboriginals of Hawaii before the main migrations. It was *kapu* for anyone to go onto *kauwa* lands; doing so meant instant death. If a human sacrifice was needed, the *kahuna* would simply summon a *kauwa* who had no recourse but to mutely comply. To this day, to call someone *kauwa,* which now supposedly only means servant, is still considered a fight-provoking insult.

Although there were horrible wars, most people lived quiet and ordered lives based on the strict caste society and the *kapu* system of rigidly observed cultural taboos and laws. Famine was known, but only on a regional level, and the population was kept in check by birth control, crude abortions, and the distasteful practice of infanticide, especially of baby girls. The Hawaiians were absolutely loving and nurturing parents under most circumstances and would even take in *hanai* (an adopted child or oldster), a lovely practice that lingers to this day.

A strict division of labor existed among men and women. Men were the only ones permitted to have anything to do with taro. This crop was so sacred that there were a greater number of *kapu* concerning taro than concerning a man himself. Men pounded poi and served it to the women. Men were also the fishers and the builders of houses, canoes, irrigation ditches, and walls. Women tended to other gardens and shoreline fishing and were responsible for making tapa cloth. The entire family lived in the common house called the *hale noa.*

Certain things were *kapu* between the sexes. Primarily, women could not enter the *mua* (men's eating house), nor could they eat with men. Certain foods, such as pork, coconut, red fish, and bananas were forbidden to women, and it was *kapu* for a man to have intercourse before going fishing, engaging in battle, or attending a religious ceremony. Young boys lived with the women until they underwent a circumcision rite called *pule ipu.* After this was performed, they were required to keep the *kapu* of men. A true Hawaiian settlement required a minimum of five huts: the men's eating hut, women's menstruation hut, women's eating hut, communal sleeping hut, and prayer hut. Without these five separate structures, Hawaiian society could not happen because the *i'a kapu* (forbidden eating between men and women) rules could not be observed.

Ali'i could also declare a *kapu* and often did so. Certain lands or fishing areas were temporarily made *kapu* so that they could be revitalized. Even today, it is *kapu* for anyone to remove all the *'opihi* (a type of limpet) from a rock. The greatest *kapu, kapu moe,* was afforded to the highest-ranking *ali'i:* anyone coming into their presence had to prostrate themselves. Lesser-ranking *ali'i* were afforded the *kapu noho:* lessers had to sit or kneel in their presence. Commoners could not let their shadows fall on an *ali'i,* nor enter the house of an *ali'i* except through a special door. Breaking a *kapu* meant immediate death.

RELIGION

The Polynesian Hawaiians worshipped nature. They saw its forces manifested in a multiplicity of forms to which they ascribed godlike powers, and they based daily life on this animistic philosophy. Handpicked and specially trained storytellers chanted the exploits of the gods. These ancient tales, kept alive in a special oral tradition called *mo'olelo,* were recited only by day. Entranced listeners encircled the chanter; in respect for the gods and in fear of their wrath, they were forbidden to move once the tale was begun.

Any object, animate or inanimate, could be a god. All could be infused with *mana,* especially a dead body or a respected ancestor. *'Ohana* had personal family gods called *'aumakua* on whom they called in times of danger or strife. There were children of gods called *kupua* who were thought to live among humans and were distinguished either for their beauty and strength or for their ugliness and terror. It was told that processions of dead *ali'i,* called "Marchers of the Night," wandered through the land of the living, and unless you were properly protected, it could mean death if they looked upon you. There were simple ghosts known as *akua lapu* who merely frightened people. Forests, waterfalls, trees, springs, and a thousand forms of nature were the manifestations of *akua li'i,* "little spirits" who could be invoked at any time for help or protection. It made no difference who or what you were in old Hawaii; the gods were ever present, and they took a direct and active role in your life.

Behind all of these beliefs was an innate sense of natural balance and order. It could be interpreted as positive-negative, yin-yang, life-death, or light-dark, the main idea being that everything had its opposite. The time of darkness when only the gods lived was *po.* When the great gods descended to the earth and created light, this was *ao,* and humanity was born. All of these *mo'olelo* are part of *The Kumulipo,* the great chant that records the Hawaiian version of creation. From the time the gods descended and touched the earth at Ku Moku on Lana'i, the genealogies were kept. Unlike in the Bible, these included the noble families of female as well as male *ali'i.*

Ancient Hawaiians performed religious ceremonies at *heiau,* temples. The basic *heiau* was a masterfully built and fitted rectangular stone wall that varied in size from about as big as a basketball court to as big as a football field. Once the restraining outer walls were built, the interior was backfilled with smaller stones, and the top dressing was expertly laid and then rolled, perhaps with a log, to form a pavement-like surface. All that remains of Hawaii's many *heiau* are the stone platforms or walls. The buildings on them, constructed in perishable wood, leaves, and grass, have long since disappeared.

The Hawaiian people worshipped gods who took the form of idols fashioned from wood, feathers, or stone. The eyes were made from shells, and until these were inlaid, the idol was dormant. The hair used was often human hair, and the arms and legs were usually flexed. The mouth was either gaping or formed a wide figure-eight lying on its side, and more likely than not was lined with glistening dog teeth. Small figures made of woven basketry were expertly covered with feathers. Red and yellow feathers were favorites, taken from specific birds by men whose only work was to roam the forests in search of them.

In the 1820s, missionaries brought Congregational Christianity and the "true path" to heaven to Hawaii, setting out to convert the pagan Hawaiians and "civilize" them. Catholics, Mormons, Adventists, Episcopalians, Unitarians, Christian Scientists, Lutherans, Baptists, Jehovah's Witnesses, the Salvation Army, and every other major and minor denomination of Christianity that followed in their wake brought their own brand of enlightenment. Chinese and Japanese immigrants established major sects of Buddhism, Confucianism, Taoism, and Shintoism. Today, Allah is praised, the Torah is chanted in Jewish synagogues, and nirvana is available at a variety of Hindu temples, even the Church of Scientology is selling books and salvation.

LANGUAGE

In Hawaii, English is the primary language spoken, yet the beat and melody of the local dialect is noticeably different. Hawaii has its own unmistakable linguistic regionalism. The many ethnic people who make up Hawaii have enriched the English spoken with words, expressions, and subtle shades of meaning that are commonly used and understood throughout the islands. The greatest influence on the English spoken here comes from the Hawaiian language, and words such as *aloha, hula, luau,* and *lei* are familiarly used and understood by all.

Pidgin

Other migrant peoples, especially the Chinese, Japanese, and Portuguese, influenced the local dialect to such an extent that the simplified plantation lingo they spoke has become known as "pidgin." English is the official language of the state, business, and education, but pidgin is the language of the people. Hawaiian words make up most of pidgin's non-English vocabulary, but it includes a good smattering of Chinese, Japanese, and Samoan as well. The distinctive rising inflection is provided by the melodious Mediterranean lilt of the Portuguese. Pidgin is not a stagnant language. It's kept alive by new slang words introduced by younger generations of speakers. *Maka'ainana* of all socioethnic backgrounds can at least understand pidgin. Most islanders are proud of it, but some consider it a low-class jargon.

Hawaiian

The Hawaiian language sways like a palm tree in a gentle wind. Its words are as melodious as a love song. With its many Polynesian root words easily traced to Indonesian and Malay, Hawaiian is obviously from this same stock. The Hawaiian spoken today is very different from old Hawaiian. Its greatest metamorphosis occurred when the missionaries began to write it down in the 1820s. Still, it nearly vanished. There has been a movement to reestablish the Hawaiian language over the last couple of decades. Not only are courses offered at the University of Hawai'i, but there is also a successful elementary school immersion program in the state, some books are being printed in it, and more and more musicians are performing in Hawaiian.

Hawaiian is, by and large, no longer spoken as a language except on Ni'ihau and in Hawaiian-language immersion classes and family settings; the closest tourists will come to it is in place-names, street names, and words that have become part of common usage, such as *aloha* and *mahalo.* There are sermons in Hawaiian at some local churches. Kawaiaha'o Church in downtown Honolulu is the most famous of these, but each island has its own.

Thanks to the missionaries, the Hawaiian language is rendered phonetically using only 12 letters. They are the five vowels, a-e-i-o-u, sounded as they are in Spanish, and seven consonants, h-k-l-m-n-p-w, sounded exactly as they are in English. Sometimes "w" is pronounced as "v," but this only occurs in the middle of a word and always follows a vowel. A consonant is always followed by a vowel, forming two-letter syllables, but vowels are often found in pairs or even triplets. A slight oddity about Hawaiian is the glottal stop called *'okina.* This is an abrupt break in sound in the middle of a word, such as "oh-oh" in English, and is denoted with a reverse apostrophe ('). A good example is the one in *ali'i* or, even better, the O'ahu town of Ha'iku, which actually means Abrupt Break.

Pronunciation Key

For those unfamiliar with the sounds of Spanish or other Romance languages, the vowels are sounded as follows:

A—pronounced as in "ah" (that feels good!). For example, *tapa* is "tah-pah."

E—short "e" is "eh," as in "pen" or "dent" (thus *hale* is "hah-leh"). Long "e" sounds like "ay" as in "sway" or "day." For example, the Hawaiian goose (*nene*) is a "nay-nay," not a "nee-nee."

I—pronounced "ee" as in "see" or "we" (thus *pali* is pronounced "pah-lee").

O—pronounced as in "no" or "oh," such as "oh-noh" (*ono*).

U—pronounced "oo" as in "do" or "stew." For example, "kah-poo" (*kapu*).

Diphthongs and Stresses

Eight vowel pairs are known as "diphthongs" (ae-ai-ao-au-ei-eu-oi-ou). These are the sounds made by gliding from one vowel to another within a syllable. The stress is placed on the first vowel. In English, examples would be **soil** and **bail.** Common examples in Hawaiian are *lei* and *heiau.*

The best way to learn which syllables are stressed in Hawaiian is by listening closely. It becomes obvious after a while. There are also some vowel sounds that are held longer than others; these can occur at the beginning of a word, such as the first "a" in *"'aina,"* or in the middle of a word, like the first "a" in *lanai.* Again, it's a matter of tuning your ear and paying attention. When written, these stressed vowels, called *kahako,* are noted with a macron, or short line, over them. Such stressed vowels are not indicated in this book.

Many Hawaiian words are commonly used in English, appear in English dictionaries, and therefore would ordinarily be subject to the rules of English grammar. The Hawaiian language, however, does not pluralize nouns by adding an "s"; the singular and plural are differentiated in context. The following are some examples of plural Hawaiian nouns treated this way in this book: *haole* (not *haoles*), *kahuna,* lei, and luau.

No one is going to give you a hard time if you mispronounce a word. It's good, however, to pay close attention to the pronunciation of street and place-names because many Hawaiian words sound alike; a misplaced vowel here or there could be the difference between getting where you want to go and getting lost.

FOOD

Thanks to Hawaii's plantation past, immigrants from around the world also brought their cuisine to the islands, and many of the dishes remain local favorites to this day. You'll find Chinese dim sum and bao, char siu stuffed steamed buns called manapua, Korean kimchi, Vietnamese pho, Puerto Rican pasteles, Portuguese malasadas, tonkatsu from Japan, and SPAM, biscuits, and gravy from World War II Americans in ethnic eateries and on menus across the state.

While local Hawaiian food is rooted in Polynesian techniques and flavors, it is also an amalgam of the cuisine from the immigrants who became an integral part of Hawaiian culture. Plate lunches, found mainly at drive-in restaurants (island-style fast food) are served with two scoops of rice, macaroni salad, and a protein including chicken katsu, kalbi, or kalua pork. This affordable and filling meal incorporates Japanese, Korean, American, and Hawaiian cooking. Loco moco is another favorite plate for lunch as well as breakfast: two fried eggs, a hamburger patty over rice smothered in gravy—talk about East meets West.

The food served at luau is very similar to what you'll find at a Hawaiian food restaurant, and there are several staple dishes no matter where you go. Kalua pig is a favorite, a smoky-flavored pulled pork tossed with cabbage. Traditionally, it is cooked in an *imu,* an underground earthen oven. Chicken long rice has bits of thigh meat cooked with ginger, green onions, and long rice noodles in a chicken broth. Lau lau is fish, pork, or chicken wrapped in taro leaves and steamed in *ti* leaves, lomi salmon is raw cubed salmon tossed with tomatoes, onion, and chile peppers, and squid luau is young taro leaves and squid cooked in coconut milk, the end product a tasty dish resembling creamed spinach. *Poke* (pronounced like okay with a p), is a raw fish salad made with ahi tuna, soy sauce (called shoyu in Hawaii), and sesame oil. There are all different kinds of *poke*, some have onions and seaweed, some are spicy, some are mayonnaise based, and sometimes the fish is replaced with *tako* (octopus). No Hawaiian luau is complete without poi, a staple starch made from pounded taro root, and haupia, a coconut milk-based dessert usually served as a congealed pudding.

THE ARTS
Music
Ancient Hawaiians passed along stories through chants, in which the emphasis was placed on historical accuracy, not melody. The missionaries were the first to introduce the Hawaiians to melody through Christian hymns, and soon singing became both an

The Luau

The luau is an island institution. Local families have big luau for a baby's first birthday, anniversaries, graduations, and family reunions. Commercial operators have packaged the luau as nightly dinner and entertainment so visitors can get a glimpse of the tradition and traditional Hawaiian fare—kalua pig, lau lau, chicken long rice, lomi salmon, white rice, and poi. For a fixed price, you can gorge yourself on a tremendous variety of island foods, sample a few island drinks, and have an evening of entertainment as well. Luau run from about 5pm to 8:30pm. On your luau day, eat a light breakfast and skip lunch.

All commercial luau have pretty much the same format, though the types of food and entertainment differ somewhat. The tourist variety of luau is a lot of food, a lot of fun, but definitely a show. To have fun at a luau you have to get into the swing of things, like the Polynesian Revue. Local performers dance and lead the tourist's hula—the fast version with swaying hips and dramatic lighting—a few wandering troubadours sing Hawaiian standards, and a muscular, sweaty man will swing flaming torches. Some offer an *imu* ceremony where the pig is taken from the covered oven, as well as traditional games, arts, and crafts. Food is usually served buffet-style, although a few do it family-style. Most tourist luau have American and Asian dishes for those less adventurous souls.

To cook the pig, the luau master starts the *imu* on the morning of the gathering. He lays the hot stones and banana stalks to create an underground oven, which must maintain a perfect 400°F. In one glance, the luau master can gauge the weight and fat content of a succulent porker and decide just how long it should be cooked. The water in the leaves covering the pig steams and roasts the meat so that it falls off the bone. Local wisdom has it that "All you can't eat in the *imu* are the hot stones."

---

individual and group pastime. Early in the 1800s, Spanish vaqueros from California were imported to teach the Hawaiians how to be cowboys. With them came guitars and moody ballads. Immigrants who came along a little later in the 19th century, especially from Portugal, helped create Hawaiian-style music. Their biggest influence was a small, four-stringed instrument called a *braga* or *cavaquinho,* the prototype of the homegrown Hawaiian instrument that became known as the ukulele. Jumping flea, the translation of ukulele, is an appropriate name devised by the Hawaiians when they saw how nimble the fingers were as they jumped over the strings. Over many decades, Hawaiian music has evolved through techniques like slack key tuning, the twang and easy slide of the steel guitar, and the smooth falsetto singing that accompanies the relaxed melodies. Today, popular Hawaiian music has fused with the beat of reggae, creating a style of music locally known as jawaiian.

Hula

The hula is more than an ethnic dance; it is the soul of Hawaii expressed in motion. It began as a form of worship during religious ceremonies and was danced only by highly trained men. It gradually evolved into a form of entertainment, but in no regard was it sexual. It was history portrayed in the performing arts. In the beginning an androgynous deity named Laka descended to earth and taught men how to dance the hula. In time the male aspect of Laka departed for the heavens, but the female aspect remained. The female Laka set up her own special hula *heiau* at Ha'ena on the Na Pali coast of Kaua'i, where it still exists. As time went on women were allowed to learn the hula. Scholars surmise that men became too busy wresting a living from the land to maintain the art form.

Men did retain one type of hula for themselves called *lua.* This was a form of martial art employed in hand-to-hand combat that evolved into a ritualized warfare dance called *hula ku'i.*

During the 19th century, the hula almost vanished because the missionaries considered it vile and heathen. King Kalakaua saved it during the late 1800s, when he formed his own troupe and encouraged the dancers to learn the old hula. Many of the original dances had been forgotten, but some were retained and are performed to this day.

Today, hula *halau* (schools) are active on every island, teaching hula and keeping the old ways and culture alive. Hula combines the chanting of the *mele* (story) and is accompanied by traditional instruments like the *ipu* (gourd). Performers spend years perfecting their techniques telling stories through dance. They show off their accomplishments during the fierce competition of the Merrie Monarch Festival in Hilo every April. The winning *halau* is praised and recognized throughout the islands.

Almost every major resort offering entertainment or a luau also offers a hula revue. Most times, young island beauties accompanied by proficient local musicians put on a floor show for the tourists. It's entertaining, but it's not traditional hula.

Weaving and Carving

Hawaiians became the best basket makers and mat weavers in all of Polynesia. *Ulana* (woven mats) were made from *lau hala* (pandanus) leaves. Once split, the spine was removed and the leaves stored in large rolls. When needed they were soaked, pounded, and then fashioned into various floor coverings and sleeping mats. Intricate geometrical patterns were woven in, and the edges were rolled and well fashioned. A wide variety of basketry was made from the aerial root *'ie'ie,* and the shapes varied according to use. Some baskets were tall and narrow, some were cones, others were flat like trays, and many were woven around gourds and calabashes.

Wood was a primary material used by Hawaiian artisans. They almost exclusively used *koa* because of its density, strength, and natural luster. It was turned into canoes, woodware, calabashes, and furniture for the *ali'i.*

Temple idols were another major product of woodcarving. A variety of stone artifacts were also turned out, including poi pounders, fish sinkers, and small idols.

The most respected artisans in old Hawaii were the canoe makers. With little more than a stone adze and a pump drill, they built canoes that could carry 200 people and last for generations—sleek, well-proportioned, and infinitely seaworthy. The main hull was usually a gigantic *koa* log, and the gunwale planks were minutely drilled and sewn to the sides with sennit rope. Apprenticeships lasted for years, and a young man knew that he had graduated when one day he was nonchalantly asked to sit down and eat with the master builders. Small family-sized canoes with outriggers were used for fishing and perhaps carried a spear rack; large ocean-going double-hulled canoes were used for migration and warfare. On these, the giant logs had been adzed to about two inches thick. A mainsail woven from pandanus was mounted on a central platform, and the boat was steered by two long paddles. The hull was dyed with plant juices and charcoal, and the entire village helped launch the canoe in a ceremony called "drinking the sea."

Lei Making and Featherwork

Any flower or blossom can be strung into lei, but the most common are orchids or the lovely-smelling plumeria. Lei are all beautiful, but special lei are highly prized by those who know what to look for. Of the different stringing styles, the most common is *kui*—stringing the flower through the middle or side. Most "airport-quality" lei are of this type. The *humuhumu* style, reserved for making flat lei, is made by sewing flowers and ferns to a *ti,* banana, or sometimes *hala* leaf. A *humuhumu* lei makes an excellent hatband. *Wili* is the winding together of greenery, ferns, and flowers into short, bouquet-type lengths. The most traditional form is *hili,* which requires no stringing at all but involves braiding fragrant ferns and leaves such as *maile.* If flowers are interwoven, the *hili* becomes the *haku* style, the most difficult and most beautiful type of lei.

Every major island is symbolized by its own lei made from a distinctive flower, shell, or fern. Each island has its own official color as well, although it doesn't necessarily correspond to the color of the island's lei. O'ahu, "The Gathering Place," is symbolized by yellow, the color of the tropical sun. Its flower is the delicate *'ilima,* which ranges in color from pastel yellow to a burnt orange. The blooms are about as large as a silver dollar, and lei made from *'ilima* were at one time reserved only for the *ali'i,* designating them as a royal flower.

The highly refined art of featherwork was practiced only on the islands of Tahiti, New Zealand, and Hawaii, but the fashioning of feather helmets and idols was unique to Hawaii. Favorite colors were red and yellow, which came only in a very limited supply from a small number of birds such as the *'o'o, 'i'iwi, mamo,* and *'apapane.* Professional bird hunters in old Hawaii paid their taxes to *ali'i* in prized feathers. The feathers were fastened to a woven net of *olona* cord and made into helmets, idols, and beautiful flowing capes and cloaks. These resplendent garments were made and worn only by men, especially during battle, when a fine cloak became a great trophy of war. Featherwork was also employed in the making of *kahili* and lei, which were highly prized by the noble *ali'i* women.

Tapa Cloth

Tapa, cloth made from tree bark, was common throughout Polynesia and was a woman's art. A few trees such as the *wauke* and *mamaki* produced the best cloth, but a variety of other types of bark could be utilized. First the raw bark was pounded into a felt-like pulp and beaten together to form strips (the beaters had distinctive patterns that helped make the cloth supple). The cloth was then decorated by stamping (a form of block printing) and dyed with natural colors from plants and sea animals in shades of gray, purple, pink, and red. They were even painted with natural brushes made from pandanus fruit, with an overall gray color made from charcoal. The tapa cloth was sewn together to make bed coverings, and fragrant flowers and herbs were either sewn or pounded in to produce a permanent fragrance. Tapa cloth is still available today, but the Hawaiian methods have been lost, and most tapa comes from other areas of Polynesia.

ESSENTIALS

Getting There and Around

AIR

With its isolated location in the middle of the Pacific Ocean, the only way to get to Hawaii is via airplane. Most commercial flights to Hawaii are routed to the **Honolulu International Airport** (code: HNL, 300 Rodgers Blvd., 808/836-6411, http://hawaii.gov/hnl); however, some carriers provide direct service to neighbor islands. The Honolulu airport has three terminals: the **Overseas Terminal** accommodates international and mainland flights, the **Interisland Terminal** handles Hawaiian Airlines flights, and the **Commuter Terminal** handles the small interisland carriers.

There is a free intra-airport shuttle service for getting around the airport. Ground transportation is available just outside the baggage claim areas on the lower level, along the center median. The airport is 10 miles from Waikiki and six miles from downtown Honolulu.

The Big Island has two major airports. The **Kona International Airport** (code: KOA, 73-200 Kupipi St., 808/327-9520, hawaii.gov/koa) serves international, overseas and interisland flights. It is the island's primary airport, located on the west side of the island, seven miles from Kailua. The **Hilo International Airport** (code: ITO, Kekuanaoa St., 808/961-9300,

hawaii.gov/ito), on the east side of the island just two miles east of Hilo, serves interisland carriers.

In Maui County, the **Kahului Airport** (code: OGG, 1 Kahului Airport Rd., 808/872-3830, hawaii.gov/ogg) is the primary airport on Maui, a hub for overseas and interisland flights. Two smaller airports are serviced by only commuter airlines: **Hana Airport** (code: HNM, 808/248-4861, hawaii.gov/hnm) on the northeast coast and the **Kapalua Airport** (code: JHM, 808/665-6108, hawaii.gov/jhm) on the west side, a quick drive from Ka'anapali and Lahaina.

The **Moloka'i Airport** (code: MKK, 808/567-9660, hawaii.gov/mkk), located about seven miles northwest of Kaunakakai, is serviced by interisland and commuter planes, while the tiny **Kalaupapa** Airport (code: LUP, 808/838-8701, hawaii.gov/lup) is serviced by commuter planes for residents and visitors touring the Kalaupapa National Historic Park. A permit from the **Hawaii Department of Health** (808/567-6924, health.hawaii.gov) is necessary prior to making air reservations. **Lana'i Airport** (code: LNY, 808/565-7942, hawaii.gov/lny), located three miles southwest of Lanai City, is serviced by interisland and commuter planes.

On Kaua'i, the **Lihue Airport** (code: LIH, 3901 Mokulele Loop, 808/274-3800, hawaii.gov/lih) is the primary airport on the island, handling domestic, overseas, and interisland commercial flights, including commuter and air taxis. It's located on the southeast coast, about 1.5 miles east of Lihue town.

Air is the only commercial way to island hop, except for ferries between Maui and Moloka'i and Lana'i. **Hawaiian Airlines** (800/367-5320, hawaiianairlines.com) is Hawaii's leading commercial carrier, with the largest selection of flights between the main Islands. **Mokulele Airlines** (866/260-7070, mokuleleairlines.com) utilizes a prop caravan service to ferry passengers to and from Moloka'i and Lana'i. Their small prop planes also service the smaller airports in Hana and Kapalua, Maui. **Island Air** (800/652-6541, islandair.com) has a fleet of turboprop planes that service routes from Kaua'i, Maui, Moloka'i, and Lana'i to O'ahu.

Everyone visiting Hawaii must fill out a *Plants and Animals Declaration Form* and present it upon arrival in the state. Anyone carrying any of the prohibited items, including fruits, vegetables, plants, seeds, and soil, as well as live insects, seafood, snakes, and amphibians, must go through an inspection at the airport. For additional information on just what is prohibited, contact any U.S. Customs Office or check with an embassy or consulate.

Before you leave Hawaii for the mainland, all of your bags are subject to **agricultural inspection** before you enter the ticketing line to check luggage and get your boarding pass. There are no restrictions on beach sand from below the high-water line, coconuts, cooked foods, dried flower arrangements, fresh flower lei, pineapples, certified pest-free plants and cuttings, and seashells. However, papaya must be treated before departure. Other restricted items are berries, fresh gardenias, jade vines, live insects and snails, cotton, plants in soil, soil itself, and sugarcane. Raw sugarcane is acceptabl if it is cut between the nodes, has the outer covering peeled off, is split into fourths, and is commercially prepackaged. For any questions about plants that you want to take to the mainland, call the **Agricultural Quarantine Inspection office** (808/861-8490) in Honolulu.

Shuttle Service

Several shuttle services offer transportation to most hotels and resorts, including **Roberts Hawaii Express Shuttle** (808/539-9400 or 800/831-5541, www.robertshawaii.com) **SpeediShuttle** (877/242-5777, www.speedishuttle.com), and **Executive Airport Shuttle** (808/669-2300 or 800/833-2303).

FERRY

Travelers on Maui have the option of taking a ferry to Moloka'i and Lana'i. **Discover Moloka'i** (658 Front St. #101, 808/667-9266, 877/500-6284, www.molokaiferry.com) provides interisland ferry service from Maui to Moloka'i twice daily with two boats, the *Maui*

Car Rental Agencies

- **Avis** (800/321-3712, www.avis.com)
- **Budget** (800/527-0700, www.budget.com)
- **Dollar** (800/800-4000, www.dollar.com)
- **Enterprise** (800/736-8222, www.enterprise.com)
- **Hertz** (800/654-3011, www.hertz.com)
- **National** (800/227-7368, www.nationalcar.com)
- **A-1** (808/833-7575, http://a1rentacarhawaii.com)
- **Advantage** (808/834-0461, www.advantage.com)
- **Alamo** (800/327-9633, www.alamo.com)
- **Thrifty** (800/367-5238, www.thrifty.com)
- **GreenCar Hawaii** (877/664-2748, www.greencarhawaii.com)

Princess and the *Molokai Princess*. One-way rates for adults are $68.53, children are $34.27, and infants three years and under are free. Rates include taxes and fuel surcharge. The ferries depart from Lahaina Harbor on Maui and Kaunakakai Harbor on Moloka'i. The company also offers ferry and car rental packages. One-way travel time aboard the high-speed ferry is about 90 minutes. For travel from Maui to Lana'i, **Expeditions** (658 Front St., 808/661-3756, 800/695-2624, www.go-lanai.com) operates the Maui-Lana'i Ferry. Ferries depart five times daily from Lahaina Harbor and Manele Bay, Lana'i. One-way rates for adults are $30 and $20 for children. Expeditions also offer golf, hotel, and tour packages.

CAR

The easiest way to get around each island is by car. If you haven't booked a rental car online prior to your arrival, the registration counters are located in the baggage claim area, or just outside. All car rental shuttles stop in the designated area of the airports just outside the baggage claim areas.

In Hawaii, there are several local courtesies to follow on the road. Drivers don't honk their horns except to say hello or in an emergency. It's considered rude to honk to hurry someone along. Hawaiian drivers reflect the climate: They're relaxed and polite. Often on small roads, they'll brake to let you turn left when they're coming at you. They may assume you'll do the same, so be ready, after a perfunctory turn signal from another driver, for him or her to turn across your lane. The more rural the area, the more likely this is to happen. On all roadways, it is customary to let a signaling motorist change lanes in front of you. If you need to change lanes and someone lets you in, always give a thank-you wave. When merging, people allow every other car into the lane.

Hawaii has a **seat belt law** as well as a **ban on cell phones** while driving. Speed limits change periodically along the highways, particularly when they pass through small towns. Police routinely check the speed of traffic with radar equipment, often hiding in a blind spot to radar and ticket speeding motorists.

BUS

On O'ahu, **TheBus** (808/848-4500, www.thebus.org) provides island-wide transportation, including from the airport. If you're planning on riding the bus from the airport to your hotel, keep in mind that your bags have to be able to fit under the seat or on your lap without protruding into the aisle. There are several bus stops on the second level of the airport on the center median. Route Nos. 19, 20, and 31 access the airport, and Route No. 19 eastbound will take you to Waikiki. Fares are $2.50 for adults, $1.25 children ages 6-17, children 5 and under are free if they sit on an adult's lap. The Visitors Pass, a four consecutive day pass, is $25 with unlimited use. Call 808/848-5555 for route information.

The **Maui Bus** (808/270-7511, www.co.maui.hi.us/bus) system has eight routes for an inexpensive way to get around to the major towns. Fares are $2 per boarding or $4 for a day pass, and monthly passes are also available. Although the bus does run to the airport, riders are not allowed to board with luggage that can't fit under their seat. For a full listing of island bus schedules refer to the timetables on the website.

The **Kaua'i Bus** (808/241-6410, www.kauai. gov/Transportation, 5:27am-10:40pm Mon.-Fri. and 6:21am-5:50pm Sat., Sun., and holidays) runs island-wide, with stops from Hanalei to the west side. The bus is a green, convenient, and affordable way to get around. The last stop in Hanalei is the old Hanalei courthouse, so the bus doesn't go out to the end of the road, and on the west side it runs to Kekaha, not out to Polihale. Fares are $2 for adults, $1 for children and seniors. Monthly passes are also available.

On the Big Island, the **Hele-On Bus** (www. heleonbus.org) operates daily routes all around the island. The main bus terminal is in downtown Hilo at Mo'oheau Park, just at the corner of Kamehameha Avenue and Mamo Street. There are a number of intra-Hilo routes with additional intercity routes to points around the periphery of the island, but these all operate on a very limited schedule, sometimes only once a day.

TAXI

On **O'ahu,** taxi service is available at the Honolulu International Airport. From the terminal to Waikiki costs about $35-40 during non-rush hour periods with a maximum of four passengers. The fare is by meter only, and there is a charge of 35 cents per bag. To get around the island by taxi, it's best to call and make arrangements directly from a company, as it is technically illegal for taxi drivers to cruise around looking for a fare. Call **Charley's Taxi** (808/233-3333 or 877/531-1333, http://charleystaxi.com), **City Taxi** (808/524-2121, www.

citytaxihonolulu.com), and **The Cab** (808/422-2222, www.thecabhawaii.com). For earth-conscious travelers, try **Eco Cab** (808/979-1010, www.ecocabhawaii.com). If you need some special attention like a limousine service, try **Cloud 9 Limousines** (808/524-7999, www. cloudninelimos.com). It is one of about 50 limo services on the island.

More than two-dozen taxi companies operate island-wide service on **Maui.** From Kahului Airport, the fare to Lahaina should be roughly $65, $80 to Ka'anapali, $100 to Kapalua, and $55 to Wailea. Expect $5-10 in and around Kahului, and about $14 to the hostels in Wailuku. Those in need of a taxi can call **Surf Taxi** (807/870-9974, www.surftaxi-maui.com), **West Maui Taxi** (808/661-1122, www.westmauitaxi.com), **Kihei Taxi** (808/298-1877, www.kiheitaxi.com), or **Aloha Maui Taxi** (808/661-5432, www.alohamauitaxi.com).

On the **Big Island,** both the Hilo and Kona airports always have taxis waiting for fares, which are regulated. From Hilo's airport to downtown costs about $15, to the Banyan Drive hotels about $10. From the Kona airport to hotels and condos along Ali'i Drive in Kailua fares run $25-40, north to Waikoloa Beach Resort they run about $50, and fares are approximately $70 as far north as the Mauna Kea Beach Hotel.

On **Kaua'i,** most taxi services run island-wide. Taxi rates are $3 per mile and $0.40 a minute. Prices are per minivan not per person. **Pono Taxi** (808/635-3478, www.ponotaxi.com) offers taxi, airport shuttle, and tour services. **North Shore Cab Co.** (808/639-7829, www. northshorecab.com) provides island-wide rides and sightseeing tours. For a more upscale ride, try **Kaua'i North Shore Limousine** (808/828-6189, www.kauainorthshorelimo.com). **Island Taxi** (808/639-7829) is based out of Lihu'e. **Ace Kaua'i Taxi Services** (808/639-4310) will take you wherever you need to go.

Visas and Officialdom

Entering Hawaii is like entering anywhere else in the United States. Foreign nationals must have a current passport and most must have a proper visa, an ongoing or return air ticket, and sufficient funds for the proposed stay in Hawaii. A visa application can be made at any U.S. embassy or consular office outside the United States and must include a properly filled out application form, two photos, and a nonrefundable fee. Canadians do not need a visa but must have a passport. Visitors from many countries do not need a visa to enter the United States for 90 days or less. This list is amended periodically, so be sure to check in your country of origin to determine whether you need a visa for U.S. entry.

Everyone visiting Hawaii must fill out a Plants and Animals Declaration Form and present it to an airline flight attendant or the appropriate official upon arrival in the state. Anyone carrying any of the listed items must have those items inspected by an agricultural inspection agent at the airport. These items include but are not limited to fruits, vegetables, plants, seeds, and soil, as well as live insects, seafood, snakes, and amphibians. For additional information on just what is prohibited, contact any U.S. Customs Office or check with an embassy or consulate in foreign countries.

Hawaii has a very rigid pet quarantine policy designed to keep rabies and other diseases from reaching the state. All domestic pets are subject to 120 days' quarantine (a 30-day quarantine or a newer five-day-or-less quarantine is allowed by meeting certain pre-arrival and post-arrival requirements), and this includes substantial fees for boarding. Basically, it is not feasible to take your pet with you on your Hawaiian vacation. For complete information, contact the Department of Agriculture, Animal Quarantine Division (99-951 Halawa Valley St., Aiea, HI 96701, 808/483-7151) in Honolulu.

Tips for Travelers

WHAT TO TAKE

While Hawaii might be isolated in the middle of the Pacific Ocean, it still has all the products, services, and conveniences of the modern world. Pack light, putting boardshorts or a bikini at the top of your list. Even if you're planning on a fancy night out or two, guys can get away with an aloha shirt and slacks, while the ladies can wear a nice sundress. If you don't have any flip-flops, you can always pick them up when you arrive.

For **sports enthusiasts,** bringing the necessary equipment is a matter of preference. Expert and professional surfers bring their own boards to the islands, but most visitors just rely on the rental options throughout the islands. The airlines charge high fees for checking surfboards.

If you golf and don't want to lug your clubs around the airport, all the courses rent clubs. Hikers should bring their own boots, which will most likely get muddy. For convenience, tennis players should bring their own rackets. **Sunscreen** is a must and **mosquito repellent** quite a good idea, just put them in your checked baggage. A hat will protect your dome from the sun, and binoculars are key if you plan on whale- or bird watching. Don't forget your camera.

TRAVELING WITH CHILDREN

If you're traveling with young children, consider leaving all the gear at home to make your luggage lighter and less cumbersome. Car rental companies rent car seats for a small fee, and you can rent all kinds of other products for your stay on Oʻahu, like a crib, pack-n-play, stroller, and high chair, even beach gear. **Paradise Baby** (808/561-1061, www.paradise-babyco.com) rents luxury baby equipment with free island-wide delivery and pickup. **Baby Aboard** (808/393-7612, www.babyaboard.com) serves the entire island, and **Baby's Away** (808/640-6734 or 800/496-6386, https://baby-saway.com) rents equipment for Honolulu and Waikiki area visitors. On Kauaʻi, contact **Ready Rentals** (800/599-8008, www.ready-rentals.com) to rent various baby supplies. Cribs, tents, strollers, high chairs, and more are available to rent during your stay. One of the best sites on Maui for kids (other than the beach) is the **Maui Ocean Center,** which is full of hands-on activities and educational experiences. On the other hand, if you want to bring the little ones on vacation, but want to sneak away for a romantic dinner, the best service on the island for a short-term sitter is **The Nanny Connection** (808/875-4777, www.thenanny-connection.com), where professional sitting staff will meet you at your hotel and take care of your loved one in your absence.

TRAVELERS WITH DISABILITIES

For a smooth trip, travelers with disabilities should make as many arrangements ahead of time as possible. Tell the transportation companies and hotels you'll be dealing with the nature of your restrictions in advance so they can make arrangements to accommodate you. Bring your medical records and notify medical establishments of your arrival if you'll need their services. Travel with a friend or make arrangements for an aide on arrival. Bring your own wheelchair if possible and let airlines know if it is battery-powered. Boarding interisland carriers sometimes requires steps. They'll board wheelchairs early on special lifts, but they must know you're coming. Most hotels and restaurants accommodate persons with disabilities, but always call ahead just to make sure.

The state Commission on Persons with Disabilities was designed with the express purpose of aiding disabled people. It is a source of invaluable information and distributes self-help booklets, which are published jointly by the Disability and Communication Access Board and the Hawaii Centers for Independent Living. Any person with disabilities heading to Hawaii should write first or visit the office of the **Hawaii Centers for Independent Living** (414 Kuwili St., #102, Honolulu, HI 96817, 808/522-5400, www.hcil.org). Additional information is available on the **Disability and Communication Access Board** (www.hawaii.gov/health/dcab/home) **Access Aloha Travel** (414 Kuwili St., #101, Honolulu, 808/545-1143 or 800/480-1143, www.accessalohatravel.com) rents wheelchair lift-equipped vans on Oʻahu for $200 per day or $723 per week; monthly rentals are also possible. This is a full-service travel agency and a good source of information on traveling with disabilities. Valid out-of-state **handicapped parking placards** may be used throughout the state of Hawaii.

Pet Quarantine

Hawaii has a very rigid pet quarantine policy designed to keep rabies and other mainland diseases from reaching the state. All domestic pets are subject to **120 days quarantine** (a 30-day quarantine and five-day-or-less quarantine are allowed by meeting certain pre-arrival and post-arrival requirements). The process is expensive and time-consuming, and there are additional airline fees as well. Unless you are contemplating a move to Hawaii, it is not feasible to bring pets. Exceptions to the quarantine are made for animals originating in other rabies-free locales like Guam, Australia, New Zealand, and the British Isles. For complete information, contact the Department of Agriculture, Animal Quarantine Division (99-951 Halawa Valley St., ʻAiea, HI 96701, 808/483-7151, http://hawaii.gov/hdoa/ai/aqs) in Honolulu.

LGBT TRAVELERS

The overall mind-set in Hawaii has long been acceptance of the LGBT community. In 2011, the state legalized civil unions for same-sex couples. O'ahu has gay and lesbian bars, nightclubs, accommodations, and beaches. **Hula's Bar & Lei Stand** in Waikiki is a well-known hangout, as is **Queen's Beach** and the surrounding area of Kapi'olani Park on O'ahu, just a short walk from Hula's.

The **Travel Alternative Group** (www.tagapproved.com), a resource for accommodations and attractions, has approved **Aqua Hotels & Resorts** (www.aquagaytravel.com), which offers discounts on reservations for LGBT travelers, and **Aston Hotels & Resorts** (www.AstonHotels.com). Another resource for finding accommodations and tours is the **International Gay and Lesbian Travel Association** (954/630-1637, www.iglta.org). They have tapped **Hotel Renew** (www.hotelrenew.com), **Discover Hawaii Tours** (808/690-9050, www.discoverhawaiitours.com) as gay and lesbian friendly. A few bed-and-breakfast establishments particularly cater to these groups; look for them on **Purple Roofs** (www.purpleroofs.com), a website dedicated to LGBT travel.

Health and Safety

With the perfect weather, a multitude of fresh-air activities, soothing negative ionization from the sea, and a relaxed and carefree lifestyle, everyone seems to feel better in the islands. There are no cases of malaria, cholera, or yellow fever. Because of a strict quarantine law, rabies is also nonexistent. There is no need for vaccinations when traveling to Hawaii, the water is safe and the air quality is the best in the country. The most common health risks come from heatstroke, sunburn, intoxication, dehydration, and drowning. If you cut yourself on the reef, make sure to clean the wound periodically and treat it with an antibiotic ointment to avoid infection, as cuts tend to heal slower in the tropical climate.

SUN

The warming, yet harmful rays of the sun come through more easily in Hawaii because of the sun's angle, and you don't feel them as much because there's always a cool breeze. The worst part of the day to be in direct sun is 11am-3pm. O'ahu lies about 21.5 degrees north latitude, not even close to the equator, but it's still more than 1,000 miles south of sunny southern California beaches. Use sunscreen on your face and exposed skin every day, even if you're not at the beach. Hats, sunglasses, beach umbrellas, plenty of water, and a dose of common sense will keep you active outdoors without a sunburn souvenir. And just because it's cloudy doesn't mean you can skip the sunscreen.

Whether out on the beach, hiking in the mountains, or just strolling around town, be very aware of dehydration. The sun and wind tend to sap your energy and your store of liquid. Carry bottled water with you at all times. Make sure to drink even more water than normal to account for the stress on your body under the strong Hawaiian sun.

MOSQUITOES AND COCKROACHES

Mosquitoes were unknown in the Hawaiian Islands until their larvae stowed away in the water barrels of the *Wellington* in 1826 and were introduced at Lahaina. They bred in the tropical climate and rapidly spread to all the islands. They are a particular nuisance in the rainforests, watersheds, and periodically damp areas like the windward coast and mountains. Be prepared, and bring a natural repellent like citronella oil, available in most health stores on the islands, or a commercial product available in grocery and drugstores. Campers will be happy to have mosquito coils to burn at night as well.

Cockroaches are common in Hawaii, and there are several different kinds you'll come across. There are the small roaches that live in leaf litter and the larger flying roaches that seek out light at night. One comforting thought is that in Hawaii they aren't a sign of filth or dirty housekeeping. They love the climate like everyone else, and it's a real problem keeping them under control. Just do your best to handle it, they won't hurt you.

LEPTOSPIROSIS

Present in streams, ponds, and muddy soil, leptospirosis is a freshwater-borne bacteria deposited by the urine of infected animals. From 2 to 20 days after the bacteria enter the body, there will be a sudden onset of fever accompanied by chills, sweats, headache, and sometimes vomiting and diarrhea. Preventive measures include staying out of freshwater sources and mud where cattle and other animals wade and drink, not swimming in freshwater if you have an open cut, and not drinking stream water. Although not always the case, leptospirosis may be fatal if left untreated.

OCEAN SAFETY

More people drown in Hawaii than anywhere else in the world. In addition, powerful shorebreaks are also the cause of severe injuries like broken backs and necks. But don't let these statistics deter you from enjoying the ocean. Instead, educate yourself on the day and area's ocean conditions and enjoy the water responsibly. Ask lifeguards or beach attendants about conditions and follow their advice. Common sense, good judgment, and respect for the ocean go a long way. And never turn your back on the ocean while enjoying the shoreline. Rogue waves can wash over reef, rock, and beach and pull you out into the water. Obey all warning signs posted on the beach, and if you're swimming, surfing, or snorkeling, return to shore before you get tired. If you engage in an ocean activity by yourself, make sure you tell others in your party your planned whereabouts in the event of an emergency. If you find yourself on the beach psyching yourself up to get in the water, it's probably better to heed the warning, "If in doubt, stay out."

Sharks, Urchins, and Coral

Sharks live in all the oceans of the world. Most mind their own business and stay away from shore. Hawaiian sharks are well fed—on fish—and don't usually bother with unsavory humans. If you encounter a shark, don't panic! Never thrash around because this will trigger their attack instinct.

Portuguese man-of-wars and other jellyfish put out long, floating tentacles that sting if they touch you. Jellyfish are blown into shore by winds on the 8th, 9th, and 10th days after the full moon. Don't wash the sting off with freshwater because this will only aggravate it. Locals will use hot saltwater to take away the sting, as well as alcohol (the drinking or rubbing kind), aftershave lotion, or meat tenderizer (MSG), but lifeguards use common household vinegar. After rinsing, soak with a wet towel. An antihistamine may also bring relief. Expect to start to feel better in about a half hour.

Coral can give you a nasty cut, and it's known for causing infections because it's a living organism. Wash the cut immediately and apply an antiseptic. Keep it clean and covered, and watch for infection. With coral cuts, it's best to have a professional look at it to clean it out. Most infection comes from tiny bits of coral that are left deep in the cut. Never stand on or grab coral. It damages the fragile life form and can send you to the hospital.

Poisonous sea urchins, like the lacquer-black *wana,* are found in shallow tidepools and reefs and will hurt you if you step on them. Their spines will break off, enter your foot, and severely burn. There are cures. Soaking a couple of times in vinegar for half an hour or so should stop the burning. If vinegar is not available, the local cure-all is urine.

Leave the fish, turtles, and seals alone. Fish should never be encouraged to feed from humans. Green sea turtles and seals are endangered species, and stiff fines can be levied on those who knowingly disturb them. Have a great time looking and taking pictures, but give them respect and space.

EMERGENCIES AND MEDICAL SERVICES

For **police, fire, or ambulance**, dial **911**. For **nonemergency police** assistance and information, call 808/529-3111. In case of a natural disaster such as hurricanes or tsunamis on Oʻahu, call the **Civil Defense** at 808/523-4121 or 808/733-4300. The **Coast Guard Search and Rescue** can be reached at 800/552-6458. The **Sex Abuse Treatment Center Hotline** is available at 808/524-7273 for cases involving sexual assault or rape crisis.

On Oʻahu, full-service hospitals include **The Queen's Medical Center** (1301 Punchbowl St., Honolulu, 808/538-9011, www.queensmedical-center.net), **St. Francis Medical Center** (2230 Liliha St., Honolulu, 808/547-6011, www. stfrancishawaii.org), and **Straub Clinic and Hospital** (888 S. King St., Honolulu, 808/522-4000, www.straubhealth.org) in Honolulu; **Castle Medical Center** (640 Ulukahiki St., 808/263-5500, http://castlemed.org) in Kailua; **Wahiawa General Hospital** (128 Lehua St., 808/621-8411, www.wahiawageneral.org) in Wahiawa; and **Kahuku Medical Center** (56-117 Pualalea St., 808/293-9221, www.hhsc. org/oahu/kahuku/index.html) in Kahuku on the North Shore.

On Maui, between downtown Kahului and downtown Wailuku, **Maui Memorial Medical Center** (221 Mahalani St., 808/244-9056) is the only full-service hospital on the island. Several clinics are dotted around the island, including the following in Kihei: **Urgent Care**

Maui/Kihei Physicians (1325 S. Kihei Rd., Ste. 103, 808/879-7781), **Kihei-Wailea Medical Center** (808/874-8100) in the Piʻilani Village Shopping Center, and **Kihei Clinic** (2349 S. Kihei Rd., 808/879-1440). **Kaiser Permanente** has clinics in Lahaina (910 Waineʻe, 808/662-6800), Wailuku (80 Mahalani St., 808/243-6800), and Kihei (1279 S. Kihei Rd., 808/891-6800). In West Maui, the **West Maui Healthcare Center** (808/667-9721) maintains an office at the Whalers Village shopping mall, and in Hana, the **Hana Community Health Center** (808/248-8294) is along the highway just as you enter town.

In Lihuʻe, on Kauaʻi, stands the island's main medical center, **Wilcox Memorial Hospital** (3-3420 Kuhio Hwy., Ste. B, 808/245-1100 or 808/245-1010 for emergencies). The smaller **West Kauaʻi Medical Center** (4643 Waimea Canyon Dr., 808/338-9431) is open for emergency care and surgical needs. Both facilities are open 24 hours. Associated with Wilcox Memorial Hospital and located at the same address is the **Kauaʻi Medical Clinic** (3-3420 Kuhio Hwy., Ste. B, 808/245-1500). It has an urgent-care walk-in clinic (8am-5pm Mon.-Fri. and 8am-noon Sat.). There are other branches in ʻEle ʻEle (808/335-0499), Kapaʻa (808/822-3431), and Koloa (808/742-1621).

On the Big Island, hospitals include the **Kona Community Hospital** (79-1019 Haukapila St., 808/322-9311), **North Hawaii Community Hospital** (77-311 Sunset Dr., 808/329-7314), and **Straub Clinic & Hospital** (75-Nani Kailua Dr. #6B, 808/329-9744). The largest facility on the Hilo side is the **Hilo Medical Center** (1190 Waianuenue Ave., 808/932-3000).

Information and Services

TOURIST INFORMATION

The **Hawaii Visitors and Convention Bureau** (HVCB, 2270 Kalakaua Ave., Ste. 801, 808/524-0722 or 800/464-2924, www.gohawaii.com) is the state of Hawaii's official tourism agency and website. The great thing about the HVCB is that everything they offer is free. The staff is extremely knowledgeable, and the office is packed with excellent brochures on virtually every facet of living in, visiting, or simply enjoying Hawaii. The website features travel tips, quick facts, regional information, and service providers to help inform your vacation.

There is plenty of free tourist literature available at all major hotels, shopping malls, the airport, and stands along Waikiki's streets. They all contain up-to-the-minute information on what's happening and a treasure trove of free or reduced-price coupons for various attractions and services. Always featured are events, shopping tips, dining and entertainment, and sightseeing. The main ones are *This Week Oahu,* the best and most complete; *Spotlight Oahu Gold,* with good sections on dining and sightseeing; and the smaller *Activities and Attractions Oahu.* Heavy on sightseeing attractions and activities, *101 Things To Do: Oahu* also has maps, advertising, and some coupons. *Oahu Drive Guide,* handed out by all the major rental car agencies, has some excellent tips and orientation maps. It is especially useful to get you started from the airport. The major shopping malls also publish their own magazines.

There are two Big Island HVB offices: **Big Island Hawaii Visitors Bureau, Hilo Branch** (250 Keawe St., Hilo, 808/961-5797 or 800/648-2441, www.bigisland.org) and **Big Island Hawaii Visitors Bureau, Kona Branch** (250 Waikoloa Beach Dr., Suite B-15, Waikoloa, 808/886-1655). There is a **Kaua'i Visitors Bureau** (4334 Rice St., Lihu'e, 800/262-1400, www.gohawaii.com/kauai). The best information on Maui is dispensed by the **Maui Visitors Bureau** (1727 Wili Pa Loop, Wailuku, HI 96793, 808/244-3530 or 800/525-6284, www.visitmaui.com). Two other helpful organizations are the **Moloka'i Visitors Association** (P.O. Box 960, Kaunakakai, HI 96748, 800/553-0404 interisland, 808/553-3876 or 800/800-6367 mainland and Canada, www.molokai-hawaii.com) and **Destination Lana'i** (P.O. Box 700, Lana'i City, HI 96763, 808/565-7600 or 800/947-4774, fax 808/565-9316, www.visitlanai.net). Additional online information pertaining to Maui County can be found at the official **County of Maui website** (www.co.maui.hi.us).

Maps

Aside from the simple maps in the ubiquitous free tourist literature, the Hawaii Visitors and Conventions Bureau and other organizations put out folding pocket maps of the island that are available free at the airport and tourist brochure racks around the island. Various street maps can be found at bookstores around the islands. Other useful and detailed maps of the islands are the Rand McNally *O'ahu, Honolulu* map and the AAA *Honolulu Hawaii* map.

The **Waikiki Business Improvement District** (www.waikikibid.org) publishes a free detailed map of Waikiki with an entertainment calendar, important phone numbers, and a TheBus quick reference guide to major attractions. You can pick up a map at the police substation at Kuhio Beach Park or from one of the friendly aloha ambassadors that walk Waikiki's main drags solely to help visitors. They wear fluorescent yellow shirts, blue hats, and blue shorts.

Weather, Marine Report, and Time of Day

For recorded information on O'ahu island weather, call 808/973-4381; for marine conditions phone 808/973-4382; and for the surf report, call 808/973-4383. For surf information on the Internet, check www.surfnewsnetwork.

com or call 808/596-SURF. For time of day, call 808/643-8463. On the Big Island, for recorded information on **local island weather,** call 808/961-5582; for the **marine report,** call 808/935-9883; and for **volcano activity,** call 808/985-6000. For a recorded weather report on Kaua'i call 808/245-6001. For the surf conditions call 808/245-3564.

MONEY
Currency
Hawaii uses U.S. currency. U.S. coinage in use is $0.01 (penny), $0.05 (nickel), $0.10 (dime), $0.25 (quarter), $0.50 (half dollar), and $1 (uncommon); paper currency is $1, $2 (uncommon), $5, $10, $20, $50, and $100. Bills larger than $100 are not in general circulation. Since 1996, new designs have been issued for the $100, $50, $20, $10, and $5 bills. Both the old and new bills are accepted as valid currency.

Banks
Full-service bank hours are Monday through Thursday 8:30am-4pm and Friday 8:30am-6pm. A few banks offer limited Saturday service, and weekday hours will be a bit longer at counters in grocery stores and other outlets. Virtually all branch banks have automated teller machines (ATMs) for 24-hour service, and these can be found at some shopping centers and other venues around the islands. ATMs work only when the Hawaiian bank you use is on an affiliate network with your home bank. Of most value to travelers, banks sell and cash traveler's checks, give cash advances on credit cards, and exchange and sell foreign currency (sometimes with a fee). Major banks in Hawaii are American Savings Bank, Bank of Hawaii, Central Pacific Bank, and First Hawaiian Bank; each has numerous branch offices throughout the islands.

Traveler's Checks
Traveler's checks are accepted throughout Hawaii at hotels, restaurants, rental car agencies, and in most stores and shops. However, to be readily acceptable they should be in U.S. currency. Some larger hotels that frequently have Japanese and Canadian guests will accept their currency. Banks accept foreign-currency traveler's checks, but it'll mean an extra trip and inconvenience. It's best to get most of your traveler's checks in $20 or $50 denominations; anything larger will be hard to cash in shops and boutiques, although not in hotels.

Credit Cards
More and more business is transacted in Hawaii using credit cards. Almost every form of accommodation, shop, restaurant, and amusement accepts them. For renting a car, they're a must. With credit card insurance readily available, they're as safe as traveler's checks and even more convenient. Write down the numbers of your cards in case they're stolen, and keep the numbers separate from the wallet. Don't rely on credit cards completely because some establishments—some bed-and-breakfasts and small local eateries, for example—only accept cash.

Taxes
Hawaii does not have a state sales tax, but it does have a general excise tax of 4.712 percent, which will be added to sales transactions and services. In addition, there is an accommodations tax of 9.25 percent, so approximately 14 percent will be added to your hotel bill when you check out.

RESOURCES

Glossary

HAWAIIAN

There was once a point in time when it was illegal to speak Hawaiian. The language was reserved to the home, children were punished for speaking it in school, and a census performed in 1983 determined there were only 50 island youths who could speak their native tongue. It wasn't until 1978 that the language began a monumental comeback as part of a greater movement known as the Hawaiian Renaissance, and today, Hawaiian is fluently spoken by approximately 8,000 people, not counting the tens of thousands of locals who pepper their daily speech with intermittent Hawaiian words.

While English is the official language of tourism and daily life, the following list provides a basic vocabulary of words you are likely to hear. You might even discover some Hawaiian words that are so perfectly expressive they'll become regular parts of your vocabulary.

'a'a: rough clinker lava; 'A'a has become the correct geological term to describe this type of lava found anywhere in the world.

'ae: yes

ahupua'a: pie-shaped land divisions running from mountain to sea that were governed by *konohiki*, local *ali'i* who owed their allegiance to a reigning chief

aikane: friend; pal; buddy

'aina: land; the binding spirit to all Hawaiians. Love of the land is paramount in traditional Hawaiian beliefs.

akamai: smart; clever; wise

akua: a god, or divine

ali'i: a Hawaiian chief or noble

aloha: the most common greeting in the islands; can mean both hello and good-bye, welcome and farewell. It can also mean romantic love, affection, or best wishes.

anuenue: rainbow

'a'ole: no

'aumakua: a personal or family god, often an ancestral spirit

auwe: alas; ouch! When a great chief or loved one died, it was a traditional wail of mourning.

halakahiki: pineapple

halau: school, as in hula school

hale: house or building; often combined with other words to name a specific place, such as Haleakala (House of the Sun).

hana: work; combined with *pau* means end of work or quitting time

hanai: literally "to feed." Part of the true aloha spirit. A *hanai* is a permanent guest, or an adopted family member, usually an old person or a child. This is an enduring cultural phenomenon in Hawaii, in which a child from one family (perhaps that of a brother or sister, and quite often one's grandchild) is raised as one's own without formal adoption.

haole: a word that at one time meant foreigner, but which now means a white person or Caucasian

hapa: half, as in a mixed-blooded person being referred to as *hapa haole*

hapai: pregnant; used by all ethnic groups when a *keiki* is on the way *haupia:* a coconut custard dessert often served at a luau

he'enalu: surfing

heiau: A platform made of skillfully fitted rocks, upon which temporary structures were built as temples and offerings made to the gods.

hono: bay, as in Honolulu (Sheltered Bay)

honu: green sea turtle; endangered

ho'olaule'a: any happy event, but especially a family outing or picnic

huhu: angry; irritated

hui: a group; meeting; society. Often used to refer to Chinese businesspeople or family members who pool their money to get businesses started.

hukilau: traditional shoreline fish-gathering in which everyone lends a hand to *huki* (pull) the huge net.

hula: a native Hawaiian dance in which the rhythm of the islands is captured by swaying hips and stories told by lyrically moving hands. A *halau* is a group or school of hula.

huli huli: barbecue, as in *huli huli* chicken

imu: underground oven filled with hot rocks and used for baking. The main cooking method featured at a luau, used to steam-bake pork and other succulent dishes. The tending of the *imu* was traditionally for men only.

ipo: sweetheart; lover; girlfriend or boyfriend

kahuna: priest; sorcerer; doctor; skillful person. In old Hawaii *kahuna* had tremendous power, which they used for both good and evil. The *kahuna ana'ana* was a feared individual who practiced black magic and could pray a person to death, while the *kahuna lapa'au* was a medical practitioner bringing aid and comfort to the people.

kai: the sea. Many businesses and hotels employ *kai* as part of their name.

kalua: means roasted underground in an *imu*. A favorite island food is *kalua* pork.

kama'aina: a child of the land; an old-timer; a longtime island resident of any ethnic background; a resident of Hawaii or native son or daughter. Hotels and airlines often offer discounts called *"kama'aina* rates" to anyone who can prove island residency.

kanaka: man or commoner; later used to distinguish a Hawaiian from other races.

kane: means man, but is actually used to signify a relationship such as husband or boyfriend. Written on a lavatory door it means "men's room."

kapu: forbidden; taboo; keep out; do not touch

kaukau: slang word meaning food or chow; grub. Some of the best food in Hawaii comes from the *kaukau* wagons, trucks that sell plate lunches and other morsels.

keiki: child or children; used by all ethnic groups. "Have you hugged your *keiki* today?"

kiawe: an algaroba tree from South America commonly found in Hawaii along the shore. It grows a nasty long thorn that can easily puncture a tire. Legend has it that the trees were introduced to the islands by a misguided missionary who hoped the thorns would coerce natives into wearing shoes. Actually, they are good for fuel, as fodder for hogs and cattle, and for reforestation, none of which you'll appreciate if you step on one of the thorns or flatten a tire on your rental car!

kokua: help. As in "Your *kokua* is needed to keep Hawaii free from litter."

kolohe: rascal

kona wind: a muggy subtropical wind that blows from the south and hits the leeward side of the islands. It usually brings sticky hot weather and one of the few times when air-conditioning will be appreciated.

ko'olau: windward side of the island

kukui: a candlenut tree whose pods are polished and then strung together to make a beautiful lei. Traditionally the oil-rich nuts were strung on the rib of a coconut leaf and used as a candle.

kuleana: home site; the old homestead; small farms. Especially used to describe the small spreads on Hawaiian Home Lands on Moloka'i.

Kumulipo: ancient Hawaiian genealogical chant that records the pantheon of gods, creation, and the beginning of humankind

kupuna: a grandparent or old-timer; usually means someone who has gained wisdom. The statewide school system now invites *kupuna* to talk to the children about the old ways and methods.

Understanding the Okina

You will often notice what appears to be a backward apostrophe inserted in the middle of Hawaiian words such as Lana'i and Ka'anapali. This marking is known as the *okina,* and rather than letting it confuse you even further, use the *okina* to help in determining the proper pronunciation.

To a professional linguist the *okina* denotes a glottal stop, which in layman's terms essentially means that you pronounce both of the vowels it's sandwiched between. To use the above examples, when pronouncing the name of island of Lana'i you would verbalize both the "a" as well as the "i," for a phonetic pronunciation of "Lah-NA-ee." The *incorrect* pronunciation is to blend the final two words together and say "Lah-Nai," which in the Hawaiian language means "a porch," and is spelled *lanai.*

Similarly, the major resort area of Ka'anapali is correctly pronounced by verbalizing both the first as well as the second "a," which phonetically looks like "Kah-ah-naw-PAW-lee." The *incorrect* way to pronounce the word is to slur the two vowels together by saying "KAW-nah-paw-lee," or even worse, the dreaded "Ka-NAH-poli."

The *okina* serves as an instructional guide as to which vowels to pronounce individually and which to blend together. The town of Lahaina—which you notice does not have an *okina*—is correctly pronounced as "Law-HIGH-nah," whereas if it were to be spelled with an *okina* such as Laha'ina, it would then be pronounced as "Law-HUH-ee-na."

Make sense?

la: the sun. Often combined with other words to be more descriptive, such as Lahaina (Merciless Sun) or Haleakala (House of the Sun).

lanai: veranda or porch. You'll pay more for a hotel room if it has a lanai with an ocean view.

lani: sky or the heavens

lau hala: traditional Hawaiian weaving of mats, hats, etc., from the prepared fronds of the pandanus (screw pine)

lei: a traditional garland of flowers or vines. One of Hawaii's most beautiful customs. Given at any auspicious occasion, but especially when arriving or leaving Hawaii.

lele: the stone altar at a *heiau*

limu: edible seaweed of various types. Gathered from the shoreline, it makes an excellent salad. It's used to garnish many island dishes and is a favorite at luau.

lolo: crazy, as in *lolo buggah* (stupid or crazy guy)

lomi lomi: traditional Hawaiian massage; also, raw salmon made into a vinegared salad with chopped onion and spices

lua: the toilet; the head; the bathroom

luakini: a human-sacrifice temple. Introduced to Hawaii in the 13th century at Waha'ula Heiau on the Big Island.

luau: a Hawaiian feast featuring poi, *imu-* baked pork, and other traditional foods. Good ones provide some of the best gastronomic delights in the world.

luna: foreman or overseer in the plantation fields. They were often mounted on horseback and were renowned for either their fairness or their cruelty. Representing the middle class, they served as a buffer between plantation workers and white plantation owners.

mahalo: thank you. *Mahalo nui* means "big thanks" or "thank you very much."

mahele: division. The Great Mahele of 1848 changed Hawaii forever when the traditional common lands were broken up into privately owned plots.

mahimahi: a favorite eating fish. Often called a dolphin, but a mahimahi is a true fish, not a cetacean.

mahu: a homosexual; often used derisively

maile: a fragrant vine used in traditional lei. It looks ordinary but smells delightful.

maka'ainana: a commoner; a person "belonging"

to the *'aina* (land), who supported the *ali'i* by fishing and farming and as a warrior

makai: toward the sea; used by most islanders when giving directions

make: dead; deceased

malihini: what you are if you have just arrived: a newcomer; a tenderfoot; a recent arrival

malo: the native Hawaiian loincloth. Never worn anymore except at festivals or pageants.

mana: power from the spirit world; innate energy of all things animate or inanimate; the grace of god. Mana could be passed on from one person to another, or even stolen. Great care was taken to protect the *ali'i* from having their *mana* defiled. Commoners were required to lie flat on the ground and cover their faces whenever a great *ali'i* approached. *Kahuna* were often employed in the regaining or transference of *mana*.

manini: small; stingy; tight

mauka: toward the mountains; used by most islanders when giving directions

mauna: mountain. Often combined with other words to be more descriptive, such as Mauna Kea (White Mountain)

mele: a song or chant in the Hawaiian oral tradition that records the history and genealogies of the *ali'i*

Menehune: the legendary "little people" of Hawaii. Like leprechauns, they are said to shun humans and possess magical powers.

moa: chicken; fowl

moana: the ocean; the sea.

moe: sleep

mo'olelo: ancient tales kept alive by the oral tradition and recited only by day

nani: beautiful

nui: big; great; large; as in *mahalo nui* (thank you very much)

'ohana: a family; the fundamental social division; extended family. Now often used to denote a social organization with grassroots overtones.

oli: chant not done to a musical accompaniment

'ono: delicious; delightful; the best.

'opihi: a shellfish or limpet that clings to rocks and is gathered as one of the islands' favorite *pupu*. Custom dictates that you never remove all of the *'opihi* from a rock; some are always left to grow for future generations.

'opu: belly; stomach

pahoehoe: smooth, ropy lava that looks like burnt pancake batter. It is now the correct geological term used to describe this type of lava found anywhere in the world.

pakalolo: "crazy smoke"; grass; smoke; dope; marijuana

pake: a Chinese person. Can be derisive, depending on the tone in which it is used. It is a bastardization of the Chinese word meaning "uncle."

pali: a cliff; precipice. Hawaii's geology makes them quite common. The most famous are the *pali* of O'ahu where a major battle was fought.

paniolo: a Hawaiian cowboy. Derived from the Spanish *español*. The first cowboys brought to Hawaii during the early 19th century were Mexicans from California.

pau: finished; done; completed. Often combined into *pau hana*, which means end of work or quitting time.

pilau: stink; bad smell; stench

pilikia: trouble of any kind, big or small; bad times

poi: a glutinous paste made from the pounded corm of taro, which ferments slightly and has a light sour taste. Purplish in color, it's a staple at luau, where it is called "one-, two-, or three-finger" poi, depending upon its thickness.

pono: righteous or excellent

pua: flower

puka: a hole of any size. *Puka* is used by all island residents, whether talking about a pinhole in a rubber boat or a tunnel through a mountain.

pupu: an appetizer; a snack; hors d'oeuvres; can be anything from cheese and crackers to sushi. Often, bars or nightclubs offer them free.

pupule: crazy; nuts; out of your mind

pu'u: hill, as in Pu'u 'Ula'ula (Red Hill)

tapa: a traditional paper cloth made from beaten bark. Intricate designs were stamped in using beaters, and natural dyes added color. The tradition was lost for many years but is now making a comeback, and provides some of the most beautiful folk art in the islands. Also called Kapa.

taro: the staple of old Hawaii. A plant with a distinctive broad leaf that produces a starchy root. It was brought by the first Polynesians and was grown on magnificently irrigated plantations. According to the oral tradition, the life-giving properties of taro hold mystical significance for Hawaiians, since it was created by the gods at about the same time as humans.

ti: a broad-leafed plant that was used for many purposes, from plates to hula skirts. Especially used to wrap religious offerings presented at the *heiau.*

tutu: grandmother; granny; older woman. Used by all as a term of respect and endearment.

ukulele: *uku* means "flea" and *lele* means "jumping," so "jumping flea." The way the Hawaiians perceived the quick finger movements used on the banjo-like Portuguese folk instrument called a *cavaquinho.*

wahine: young woman; female; girl; wife. Used by all ethnic groups. When written on a lavatory door it means "women's room."

wai: freshwater; drinking water

wela: hot.

wiki: quickly; fast; in a hurry. Often seen as *wiki wiki* (very fast), as in "Wiki Wiki Messenger Service."

Useful Phrases

Aloha ahiahi: Good afternoon
Aloha au ia 'oe: I love you
Aloha kakahiaka: Good morning
Aloha nui loa: Much love
E komo mai: Welcome
Ha'uoli la hanau: Happy Birthday
Ha'uoli makahiki hou: Happy New Year
Mahalo nui loa: Thank you very much
Mele Kalikimaka: Merry Christmas

PIDGIN

More so than Hawaiian, pidgin is the language of choice that you will notice being spoken around the islands. A creole which borrows words from English, Hawaiian, and a host of other languages, it has a lilt, cadence, and grammar entirely unto itself. Born out of the sugar plantation camps, pidgin was developed as a melding of languages of workers in the field.

Today, pidgin is likely to be heard spoken among most island locals, and even those *kama'aina* who can speak perfect English can turn their pidgin on and off just like flipping a switch. To most visitors, however, pidgin can be completely undecipherable, mainly because of the sentence structure and introduction of foreign words. For example, the past tense in pidgin is created by placing the word "wen" (as in "went") in front of the present tense of a verb. Examples would be "wen go" (went), "wen eat" (ate), "wen drive" (drove), etc.

A full example of a pidgin sentence might go something like: "Braddah wen drive da odda side and was shaking his *okole* the whole time cuz he needed fo' use da lua," which translates as "Braddah (general subject) drove to the other side (of the island) and was shaking his butt (*okole*) the whole time because he needed to use the bathroom (*lua*)."

In other instances, grammar instructors would be astonished at the blatant disregard for the tenses of the English language, as seen in the common phrase "Try wait brah, I stay coming" ("Hold on, I'm on my way"), or the assertion that "he get choke mangoes already that guy" ("his mango tree is already full").

For those who were raised without the language it can take years to fully understand pidgin, although for the *keiki* who were raised here it comes as naturally as a native tongue. While you probably won't become fluent any time soon, here are some basic phrases for helping you get by.

an' den: and then? big deal; so what's next?
auntie: respected elderly woman
bumbye: Later; after a while.
blalah: brother, but actually only refers to a large, heavy-set, good-natured Hawaiian man
brah: all the bros in Hawaii are brahs; brother; pal. Used to call someone's attention. One of the most common words even among people who are not acquainted. After a fill-up at a gas station, a person would say "Tanks, brah."
chicken skin: goose bumps

choke: lots of something

cockaroach: steal; rip off.

da kine: a catchall word of many meanings that epitomizes the essence of pidgin. Da kine is a euphemism for pidgin and is substituted whenever the speaker is at a loss for a word or just wants to generalize.

geev um: give it to them; give them hell; go for it. Can be used as an encouragement. If a surfer is riding a great wave, the people on the beach might yell, "Geev um, brah!"

grinds: food

hana hou: again. Especially after a concert the audience shouts "hana hou" (one more!).

hele on: let's get going

howzit?: as in "howzit, brah?" What's happening? How's it going? The most common greeting, used in place of the more formal "How do you do?"

lesgo: let's go! do it!

li'dis an' li'dat: like this or that

lolo: stupid, crazy

mo' bettah: A better way of doing something.

pakalolo: "crazy smoke"; marijuana; grass; reefer

pau: a Hawaiian word meaning finished; done; over and done with. Pau hana means end of work or quitting time. Once used by plantation workers, now used by everyone.

seestah: sister, female

shaka: hand wave where only the thumb and baby finger stick out, meaning "thank you, all right!"

shoots: Whatever, sure, in agreement. Example: "What, you like go Makena today?" "Shoots!"

rubbah sleepah: rubber slippers, sandals, flip-flops. Referring to slippers as sandals is only something that "mainlanders" would do.

stink eye: Basically frowning at someone; using facial expression to show displeasure. Hard looks. What you'll get if you give local people a hard time.

talk story: spinning yarns; shooting the breeze; throwing the bull; a rap session. If you're lucky enough to be around to hear *kupuna* (elders) "talk story," you can hear some fantastic tales in the tradition of old Hawaii.

tanks, brah: thanks, thank you

to da max: all the way

wea stay?: literally, "where stay?," as in to ask a location. Examples are "wea the car stay?," "wea you stay?," or the gloriously grammatical "wea you stay going" (where are you going).

We go: Let's go! Usually used in conjunction with "shoots," as in "shoots we go!"

Index

waterfalls: 'Akaka Falls State Park 614; Central Maui flightseeing 299; Halawa Valley 31, 470; Hanakapi'ai Falls 30; Hanalei Valley Overlook 754; Ho'opi'i Falls 703; Kaua'i 20; Lyon Arboretum Trails 29; Makamaka'ole Valley 295; Manoa Falls 88; Maunawili Falls 29, 162; Na'ili'ili haele 396; Na Pali Coast 744; Opaeka'a Falls 716; Pools of 'Ohe'o 396, 405; Powerline Trail 704; Rainbow Falls and Boiling Pots 612; Road to Hana 18, 414-417, 418; Secret Beach 733; Secret Beach Tide Pools and Waterfall 728, 745; Upper Puohokamoa Falls 400; Wailua Falls 689, 715; Wailua River 699; Waipi'o Valley 23; Waipo'o Falls and the Canyon Trail 792, 803
water safety: 862
waterskiing: 701
Wawaloli Beach: 521
weather: 13, 838
weather reports: 864
weaving: 853
West Bowl: 124
West Maui: 223-284; accommodations 479-483; beaches 228-233; entertainment and events 271-276; food 276-282; highlights 224; maps 225-227; planning tips 217; recreation 228-263; shopping 269-271; sights 263-269; transportation 283-284
West Moloka'i: accommodations 499-500; beaches 454-458; hiking 463; shopping 472; sights 469; surfing 460
West Side of Kaua'i: 791-814; accommodations 832-834; best itinerary 794; food 811-813; highlights 792; map 793; planning tips 683; recreation 795-806; shopping 809-811; sights 806-808; transportation 814
Whalers Village: 269, 272
Whalers Village Museum: 265
whales: 841

whale watching: general discussion 254; Kohala 554; Kona 527; Lana'i 435; Makapu'u Point Lighthouse 166; Maui 18; North Shore of Kaua'i 745; O'ahu 20; Southeast and Windward O'ahu 158; South Shore of Kaua'i 778; West Maui 12, 224, 253-255
whaling industry: 265, 844
White Rock: 321
White Sands Beach (La'aloa Beach Park): 521
Wicox family: 713, 714
wildlife: 840
William Hyde Rice Building: 711
Windmills (surf break): 230, 247
windsurfing: Aina Haina 147; Central Maui 291; Ho'okipa Beach Park 409, 412; Kihei 317; Maui 12; schools 293; South Maui 340
wineries: Tedeschi Winery 362, 380; Volcano Winery 570
W. M. Keck Observatory: 648
Wo Hing Museum: 267
Woody's (surf break): 249
World Botanical Gardens: 639
World War II: 192
World War II Valor in the Pacific National Monument: 191
Wyllie Beach: 734

XYZ

yoga: Kapa'a: 710; Surf Yoga Maui: 338; Volcano Art Center: 584
Yoga House: 710
Yokohama Bay: 16, 181, 182, 185
ziplines: Central Maui 298, 305; East Maui: the Road to Hana 419; East Side of Kaua'i 707; Hamakua Coast, Waimea, and the Saddle Road 638; Kohala 546, 556; North Shore of Kaua'i 750; South Shore of Kaua'i 777; Upcountry Maui 375; West Maui 260
zoos: 61, 611

List of Maps

MAP SYMBOLS

═══ Expressway	【 Highlight	✈ Airport	⚓ Golf Course
═══ Primary Road	○ City/Town	✗ Airfield	🅿 Parking Area
═══ Secondary Road	◉ State Capital	▲ Mountain	⬛ Archaeological Site
═══ Unpaved Road	⊛ National Capital	✚ Unique Natural Feature	🕆 Church
─── Trail	★ Point of Interest		Gas Station
⋯⋯ Ferry	• Accommodation	ℱ Waterfall	Dive Site
═══ Railroad	▼ Restaurant/Bar	⬤ Park	Mangrove
Pedestrian Walkway	■ Other Location	⊤ Trailhead	Reef
Stairs	⋀ Campground	Lighthouse	Swamp

CONVERSION TABLES

$$°C = (°F - 32) / 1.8$$
$$°F = (°C \times 1.8) + 32$$

1 inch = 2.54 centimeters (cm)
1 foot = 0.304 meters (m)
1 yard = 0.914 meters
1 mile = 1.6093 kilometers (km)
1 km = 0.6214 miles
1 fathom = 1.8288 m
1 chain = 20.1168 m
1 furlong = 201.168 m
1 acre = 0.4047 hectares
1 sq km = 100 hectares
1 sq mile = 2.59 square km
1 ounce = 28.35 grams
1 pound = 0.4536 kilograms
1 short ton = 0.90718 metric ton
1 short ton = 2,000 pounds
1 long ton = 1.016 metric tons
1 long ton = 2,240 pounds
1 metric ton = 1,000 kilograms
1 quart = 0.94635 liters
1 US gallon = 3.7854 liters
1 Imperial gallon = 4.5459 liters
1 nautical mile = 1.852 km

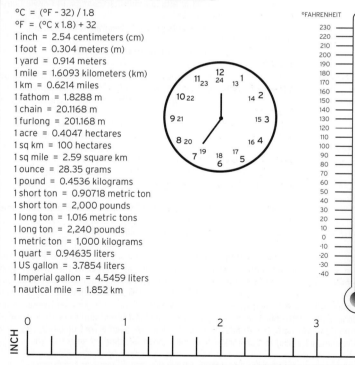

MOON HAWAIIAN ISLANDS

Avalon Travel
a member of the Perseus Books Group
1700 Fourth Street
Berkeley, CA 94710, USA
www.moon.com

Contributors: Kevin Whitton, Jade Eckardt,
Kyle Ellison, Bree Kessler
Editor: Kevin McLain
Series Manager: Kathryn Ettinger
Graphics and Production Coordinator: Elizabeth Jang
Cover Design: Faceout Studios, Charles Brock
Moon Logo: Tim McGrath
Map Editor: Mike Morgenfeld
Cartographer: Stephanie Poulain
Proofreader: Megan Mulholland
Indexer: Rachel Kuhn

ISBN: 978-1-61238-831-1
ISSN: 2372-6792

Printing History
1st Edition – September 2014
5 4 3 2 1

Front cover photo: Kaneohe Bay, Oahu, Hawaii ©
Douglas Peebles/eStock Photo

Title page photo: replica carvings at Pu'uhonua O
Honaunau National Historical Park © Mark Wasser

p. 4 Koko Crater Botanical Garden © Kevin Whitton;
p. 7 Prince Kuhio Beach, Waikiki © Kevin Whitton; p. 8
(top left) © Mark Driessen, (top right) lava at Hawaii
Volcanoes National Park © Mark Wasser, (bottom) a
sea turtle in Makena © Mark Driessen; p. 9 (top) Big
Beach © Jenna Strubhar, (bottom left) church in Puna
© Bree Kessler, (bottom right) Wailua Falls on Kauai
© Jade Eckardt; p. 10 horseback riding at Gunstock

Ranch on O'ahu courtesy Gunstock Ranch; p. 11 (top)
the overlook at Honolua Bay on the northwestern
coast of Maui © Kyle Ellison, (bottom left) pineapple in
the field in East Maui © Heather Ellison (bottom right)
statue of King Kamehameha I in Honolulu © Chee-Onn
Leong/123rf.com; p. 12 © Kevin Whitton; p. 13 © Galyna
Andrushko/123rf.com; p. 14 (top) © Mark Driessen,
(bottom) © gigra/123rf.com; p. 15 courtesy Turtle Bay
Resort; p. 17 © Hawaii Tourism Authority (HTA)/Tor
Johnson; p. 18 © Don Landwehrle/123rf.com; p. 19 (top)
© Steven Heap/123rf.com, (bottom) © Maria Luisa Lopez
Estivill/123rf.com; p. 20 © mark52/123rf.com; p. 21 ©
Matej Hudovernik/123rf.com; p. 22 © Kevin Whitton; p.
23 © Bart Everett/123rf.com; p. 24 (top and bottom) ©
Eddy Galeotti/123rf.com; p. 25 © spectruminfo/123rf.
com; p. 26 © 123rf.com; p. 27 © Globalphoto/123rf.com;
p. 28 © Mark Driessen; p. 29 © Nani Maloof; p. 30 ©
Maria Luisa Lopez Estivill/123rf.com; p. 31 © Mark
Wasser; p. 32 © Visions Of America LLC/123rf.com;
p. 33 © Ritu Jethani/123rf.com; p. 34 © Kyle Ellison

Back cover photo: © Deborah Kolb/123rf.com

Printed in China by RR Donnelley

KEEPING CURRENT

If you have a favorite gem you'd like to see included in the next edition, or see anything
that needs updating, clarification, or correction, please drop us a line. Send your com-
ments via email to feedback@moon.com, or use the address above.